CHI 99 Conference Proceedings

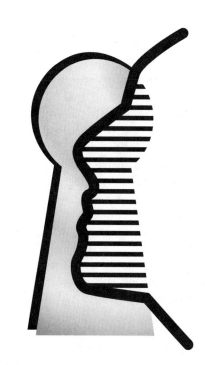

CHI 99

The CHI is the Limit

Human Factors in Computing Systems

EDITORS

Marian G. Williams, Conference and Technical Program Co-Chair

Mark W. Altom, Conference and Technical Program Co-Chair

Kate Ehrlich, Papers Co-Chair

William Newman, Papers Co-Chair

ASSOCIATE EDITOR

Steven Pemberton

CONFERENCE ON HUMAN FACTORS IN COMPUTING SYSTEMS

Sponsored by ACM's Special Interest Group on Computer-Human Interaction (ACM SIGCHI)

Ordering Information
ACM Members
A limited number of copies are available at the ACM member discount. Send order with payment in US dollars to:

ACM Order Department
P.O. Box 11414
New York, NY 10286-1414

Or

ACM European Service Center
108 Cowley Road Oxford
OX41JF

United Kingdom
Tel: +44 1865 382338
Fax: +44 1865 381338
Email: acm_europe@acm.org

Credit Card Orders
From the U.S. and Canada call: +1 800 342 6626
From New York metropolitan area and outside of the U.S. call:
Tel: +1 212 626 0500 or Fax: +1 212 944 1318

Please include your ACM Member Number and the ACM Order Number with your order:
ACM Order Number: 608991
ACM ISBN Number: 0-201-48559-1

Nonmembers
Nonmembers orders placed within the U.S. should be directed to:
Pearson Education Order Department
200 Old Tappan Road
Old Tappan, NJ 07675

Call TOLL FREE:
 +1 800 922 0579
FAX: +1 800 455 6991
PROMPT + PLUS: +1 800 742 5599

Addison-Wesley will pay postage and handling on orders accompanied by a check. Credit card orders may be placed by mail or by calling the Addison-Wesley Order Department at the number above. Follow-up inquiries should be directed to the Customer Service Department at the same number. Please include the Addison-Wesley ISBN number with your order:

A-W ISBN 0-201-48559-1

Nonmember orders from outside the U.S. should be addressed as noted below:

Europe/Middle East/Africa

Pearson Education
Edinburgh Gate
Harlow
Essex CM20 2JE
UNITED KINGDOM

Tel: +44 1279 623 925
Fax: +44 1279 623 627

Asia

Pearson Education
317 Alexandra Road #04-01
IKEA Building
Singapore 159965
Tel: +65 476 4688
Fax: +65 378 0370

Japan

Pearson Education
NISHI-Shinjuku, KF Building
8-14-24 Nishi-Shinjuku, Shinjuku,ku
Tokyo 160-0023
Japan
Tel: +813 3365 9224
Fax: +813 3365 9225

Australia/New Zealand

Pearson Education Australia
Level 2 Unit 4
14 Aquatic Drive
Frenchs Forest NSW 2086
Australia
Tel: +612 9454 2200
Fax: +612 9453 0089

Latin America

Pearson Education
Calle 4, #25 2nd Piso
Fracc. Industrial Alce Blanco
Naucalpan de Juarez
Estado de Mexico 53330
Tel: +525 358 8400
Fax: +525 358 8400

Canada

Pearson Education
26 Prince Andrew Place
P.O. Box 580
Don Mills, Ontario M3C 2T8
Tel: +416 447 5101
Fax: +416 443 0948

Welcome

from the ACM SIGCHI Chair and Executive Vice-Chair

Welcome to CHI 99 and to the SIGCHI community! The CHI conference provides a forum for people to meet, both formally and informally, to share experiences, and to learn. We trust that you will find here the intellectually exciting and personally rewarding forum that brings many people back to this conference year after year.

The CHI conference is sponsored by ACM's Special Interest Group on Computer-Human Interaction (SIGCHI). SIGCHI is comprised of an international group of researchers, practitioners, educators, students, and others who share an interest in one or more of the many facets of human-computer interaction. SIGCHI is committed to the parallel activities of advancing the field of human-computer interaction and exchanging information within the SIGCHI community. This conference also provides an opportunity for you to learn more about SIGCHI activities and to explore taking an active role in those activities. You can do this by stopping by the SIGCHI booth, attending the SIGCHI Business Meeting, or talking with any of the Executive Committee members.

While the CHI conference is the largest and most visible activity of SIGCHI, we also support conferences on computer-supported collaborative work (CSCW), virtual reality software and technology (VRST), user interface software and technology (UIST), design of interactive systems (DIS) and intelligent user interfaces (IUI) and creativity & cognition (C&C). SIGCHI also distributes the quarterly SIGCHI Bulletin to members, as well as others who are interested in human-computer interaction. In addition, SIGCHI supports two of the Transactions on Computer-Human Interaction (TOCHI), and *Interactions*, a magazine focused on practitioners.

The SIGCHI Development Fund supports activities that are proposed by SIGCHI members. If you have ideas for advancing our field and communicating those advances to SIGCHI members we encourage you to review the Call for Proposals, which appears on the SIGCHI web site and frequently in the SIGCHI Bulletin.

On behalf of the Executive Committee and all SIGCHI members, we thank and congratulate the conference committee and all of the volunteers who make this conference possible and who ensure a valuable experience for each of us.

Mike Atwood, SIGCHI Chair

Guy Boy, SIGCHI Executive Vice Chair

CHI 99 is sponsored by the ACM Special Interest Group on Computer-Human Interaction (ACM SIGCHI).

COOPERATING SOCIETIES

ACM/SIGCAPH

ACM/SIGDOC

ACM/SIGGRAPH

ACM/SIGGROUP

ACM/SIGWEB

Austrian Computer Society (OCG)

British HCI Group, B-HCI-G(BCS)

CHISIG New Zealand

Computer Professionals for Social Responsibility (CPSR)

Eurographics

European Association of Cognitive Ergonomics (EACE)

German Society for Informatics (GI), Fachausschuss 2.3

Human Communication Group (HCG) of the IEICE of Japan

Human Factors and Ergonomics Society (HFES)

International Society for Gerontechnology (ISG)

Information Processing Society of Japan, SIGGroupware (IPSJ)

International Artificial Intelligence in Education Society (AIED)

Italian Association for Artificial Intelligence (AIIA)

Swedish Interdisciplinary Interest Group for Human-Computer Interaction (STIMDI)

Swiss Informaticians Society (SI), Fachgruppe Software Ergonomics

Welcome

from the Conference Co-Chairs

For many technologies in many contexts of use, the limiting factor for success is the interaction between the user and the technology. The computer-human interaction (CHI) is, quite literally, the limit.

By taking as its theme, "The CHI Is the Limit," CHI 99 posed the questions:

• What are the limiting factors to the success of interactive systems?

• How can we enable users to overcome those limits?

• What techniques and methodologies do we have for identifying and transcending those limitations?

• And just how far can we push those limits?

The technical contributions to CHI 99 offer a unique opportunity to understand the limitations that far too often prevent people from making optimum use of new technology. CHI 99 presents leading-edge advancements through its program of Demonstrations (both live and on video), Doctoral Consortium, Interviews, Late-Breaking Results, Panels, Papers, Plenary Addresses, Senior CHI Development Consortium, Special Interest Groups, Student Posters, Tutorials, Video Paper, and Workshops.

CHI 99 brings together people from many different disciplines including Computer Science, Gerontechnology, Graphic Design, Human Factors, Medicine, Psychology, and Social Science. We come from diverse work environments that include universities, research labs, small companies, large companies, and the government. We work in a wide range of fields from entertainment to education, from telecommunications to web page design, and from practical applications to the theoretical foundations of CHI. All of this diversity leads to the generation of new ideas, creative research goals and agendas, and opportunities for collaboration that break through the limitations of current technology.

The effects of CHI 99 continue far beyond the end of the conference. Possibly the most important outcome of CHI 99 is the energy that is generated. As you read the contributions to our field in the Conference Proceedings and Extended Abstracts, you cannot help but feel the excitement of the work that we do and the interdisciplinary way we do it. These papers and abstracts are truly ground-breaking contributions to the advancement of our knowledge about human-computer interaction.

Mark W. Altom and Marian G. Williams
CHI 99 Conference Co-Chairs

Sponsor Program

CHI 99 would like to gratefully acknowledge its sponsor program participants. It is the generosity of these organizations that enables the conference to provide technical content and operational services that otherwise might not have been possible.

CHI 99 CHAMPION SPONSORS

CHI 99 CONTRIBUTING SPONSORS

CHI 99 thanks Adobe, Eastman Kodak, KiddieCorp, Menlo Technology Group, Morgan Kaufman, Rent-a-Computer, and User Interface Engineering for their support of CHIKids!

Special Thanks

CHI depends heavily on the efforts of volunteers. The CHI conference would not be possible without the contributions made by the conference committee. We would like to thank the committee members and their organizations, listed below, whose support has made their individual participation possible!

Delft University of Technology

DePaul University

Dray and Associates

EDS

Fraunhofer IAO

The Hiser Group

IBM Research

iContact Consulting

Jacques Hugo Associates

KiddieCorp, Inc.

Lotus Development Corporation

Lucent Technologies

Microsoft Corporation

The MITRE Corporation

Morton Plant Mease Health Care

Nara Institute of Science and Technology

Nielsen Norman Group

Pontifical Catholic University of Rio de Janeiro

Rensselaer Polytechnic Institute

Simon Fraser University

SRA, Inc.

Stanford University

Sun Microsystems

University of Aarhus

University of Illinois

University of Linz

University of Maryland

University of Massachusetts Lowell

University of Paderborn

University of Pennsylvania

University of Vienna

University of Wisconsin - Madison

University of York

Usability/Design/Discovery Adventures

Usable Web

US WEST Advanced Technologies

Virginia Polytechnic Institute

Xerox Research Centre Europe

With changing technology we have made every effort to include special characters in volunteer listings. We apologize in advance for any omission and we will work to correct this for future CHI proceedings.

Management Team

Conference Co-Chairs
Mark W. Altom, *Lucent Technologies*
Marian G. Williams, *University of Massachusetts Lowell*

SIGCHI CMC Liaison
Kevin Schofield, *Microsoft Corporation*

ACM SIGCHI Program director
David S. Riederman, *CAE*

Conference Management
Paul Henning, *Conference & Logistics Consultants, Inc.*

Technical Program

Technical Program Co-Chairs
Mark W. Altom, *Lucent Technologies*
Marian G. Williams, *University of Massachusetts Lowell*

CHIkids
Sue Ann Balogh, *KiddieCorp, Inc.*
Angela Boltman, *University of Maryland*

Demonstrations
Michel Beaudouin-Lafon, *University of Aarhus*
Lisa Neal, *EDS*

Development Consortium
James V. Fozard, *Morton Plant Mease Health Care*
John C. Thomas, *IBM Research*

Doctoral Consortium
Deborah Hix, *Virginia Polytechnic Institute*
Andrew Monk, *University of York*

Interviews
Richard I. Anderson, *Usability/Design/Discovery Adventures*

Late-Breaking Results
Angel R. Puerta, *Stanford University*
Juergen Ziegler, *Fraunhofer IAO*

Mentoring
Robin Jeffries, *Sun Microsystems*
John C. Tang, *Sun Microsystems*

Panels
Stephanie Doane, *University of Illinois*
Susan Dumais, *Microsoft Corporation*

Papers
Kate Ehrlich, *Lotus Development Corporation*
William Newman, *Xerox Research Centre Europe*

Special Interest Groups
Susan Dray, *Dray and Associates*
Garett Dworman, *University of Pennsylvania*

Student Posters
Tom Gross, *University of Linz*
Kori Inkpen, *Simon Fraser University*

Tutorials
Michael Tauber, *University of Paderborn*
Dennis Wixon, *Microsoft Corporation*

Video Papers
Ben B. Bederson, *University of Maryland*

Workshops
Jill Drury, *The MITRE Corporation*
Charles van der Mast, *Delft University of Technology*

Operations

Outreach Liaison
Michael Muller, *Lotus Development Corporation*

Publicity Liaison
Tony Fernandes, *iContact Consulting*

Reviewer Liaison
Keith Instone, *Usable Web*

Sponsorship Liaison
Jakob Nielsen, *Nielsen Norman Group*

Student Volunteers Co-chairs
Julie Jacko, *University of Wisconsin-Madison* Andrew Sears, *DePaul University*

Technology Liaison
Marilyn C. Salzman, *US West Advanced Technologies*

Regional Liaisons

Africa
Jacques Hugo, *Jacques Hugo Associates*

Asian Pacific
Kumiyo Nakakoji, *SRA Inc./Nara Institute of Science and Technology*

Australia
Sarah Bloomer, *The Hiser Group*

Europe
Manfred Tscheligi, *University of Vienna*

North America
G. Bowden Wise, *Rensselaer Polytechnic Institute*

South America
Raquel Oliveira Prates, *Pontificial Catholic University of Rio de Janeiro*

Staff

Conference Administrators/ Conference Logistics
Stacy Riley, *Conference & Logistics Consultants, Inc.*
Mike Yancy, *Conference & Logistics Consultants, Inc.*

Exhibit Promotion
Sharon Rosenblatt, *Stat Marketing, Inc.*

Online Communications
Tom Brinck, *Diamond Bullet Design*

Publications
Jean Tullier, *Tullier Marketing Communications, Inc.*

Publicity
Rosemary Wick Stevens, *Ace Public Relations*

Registration
Carole Mann, *Registration Systems Lab*

Sponsorship
Carol Klyver, *Foundations of Excellence*

Papers Committees

Papers Associate Chairs
Matt Belge, *Vision & Logic*
Sara A. Bly, *Sara Bly Consulting*
Tom Carey, *University of Waterloo*
John M. Carroll, *Virginia Polytechnic Institute and State University*

George Fitzmaurice, *Alias|Wavefront*
Wayne Gray, *George Mason University*
Beverly Harrison, *Xerox PARC*
Michael Harrison, *University of York, England*
James D. Hollan, *UCSD*
Robert J.K. Jacob, *Tufts University*
Bonnie E. John, *Carnegie Mellon University*
Jurgen Koenemann, *GMD German National Research Center for Information Technology*
Paul Luff, *King's College, London*
Marilyn Mantei Tremaine, *Drexel University*
Jim Miller, *Miramontes Computing*
Michael Muller, *Lotus Development Corporation*
Brad A. Myers, *Carnegie Mellon Univ.*
Bonnie Nardi, *AT&T Labs*
Judith S. Olson, *The University of Michigan*
George G. Robertson, *Microsoft Research*
Teresa L. Roberts, *Sun Microsystems, Inc.*
Daniel Russell, *Xerox PARC*
Chris Schmandt, *MIT Media lab*
Loren Terveen, *AT&T Labs - Research*
John C. Thomas, *IBM Research*
Polle Zellweger, *Xerox PARC*

Papers Reviewers

Gregory Abowd, *College of Computing and GVU Center, Georgia Technological Institute*
Mark Ackerman, *University of California at Irvine*
Bengt Ahlstrom, *NOKIA Usability Design*
Motoyuki Akamatsu, *National Institute of Bioscience and Human-Technology*
Ghassan Al-Qaimari, *Royal Melbourne Institute of Technology*
Michael Albers, *Sun Microsystems - Java Software*

Robert (Bob) B. Allen, *University of Maryland*

James Lenton Alty, *Loughborough University of Technology*

Keith Andrews, IICM, *Graz University of Technology*

Mark Apperley, *University of Waikato*

Francine Arble, *Capital One*

Jonathan Arnowitz, *Informaat, BV*

Brent Auernheimer, *California State University, Fresno*

Sandrine Balbo, *CSIRO-MIS*

Michelle Baldonado, *Xerox PARC*

Thomas Baudel, *Ilog*

Michel Beaudouin-Lafon, *University of Aarhus*

Ben Bederson, *University of Maryland, College Park*

Mathilde M. Bekker, *IPO, Center for Research on User-System Interaction*

Victoria Bellotti, *Xerox PARC*

David Benyon, *Napier University*

Nigel Bevan, *National Physical Laboratory*

Jeanette Blomberg, *Xerox PARC*

Sarah Bloomer, *The Hiser Group*

Heinz-Dieter Boecker, *German National Research Center for Information Technology*

Richard A. Bolt, *MIT Media Laboratory*

Kellogg Booth, *University of British Columbia*

Guy A. Boy, *European Institute of Cognitive Sciences and Engineering, (EURISCO)*

Tone Bratteteig, *Dept. of Informatics, Univ. of Oslo*

Paul Brennan, *NORTEL*

Dr Stephen Brewster, *University of Glasgow*

Tom Brinck, *Diamond Bullet Design*

John Brooke, *Redhatch Consulting Ltd.*

Amy Bruckman, *Georgia Institute of Technology*

Hans Brunner, *IBM Global Services*

Margaret Burnett, *Oregon State University*

Mike Byrne, *Carnegie Mellon University*

Licia Calvi, *University of Antwerp (UIA)*

Ellen Campbell, *Inso Inc.*

David A. Carr, *Linkoping University*

Peter Carstensen, *Technical University of Denmark*

Rhona Charron, *ISM-BC Telecom Solutions*

Michael Christel, *Carnegie Mellon University*

Elizabeth Churchill, *FX Palo Alto Laboratory Inc.*

Janette Coble, *Washington Univ. School of Medicine*

Gilbert Cockton, *University of Sunderland*

Andrew Cohen, *Lotus Research*

Maxine Cohen, *Nova Southeastern University*

Penny Collings, *University of Canberra*

Herbert Colston, *University of Wisconsin-Parkside*

Elizabeth Comstock, *PictureTel Corporation*

Matt Conway, *Microsoft*

Joelle Coutaz, *CLIPS (IMAG)*

Colleen Crangle, *Stanford University and CONVERSpeech LLC*

Allen Cypher, *Stagecast Software*

Mary Czerwinski, *Microsoft Corporation*

Mary Carol Day, *M. C. Day Consulting Inc.*

Berardina Nadja De Carolis, *Dipartimento di Informatica - Universita' di Bari*

Elisa del Galdo, *Canon Research Centre Europe Ltd.*

Andreas Dieberger, *Emory University*

Miwako Doi, *Toshiba*

Mike Dooner, *University of Hull*

Allison Druin, *University of Maryland, College Park*

Professor D A Duce, *Rutherford Appleton Laboratory*

Tim Dudley, *Nortel Technology*

Martin Dulberg, *North Carolina State University*

Susan T. Dumais, *Microsoft Research*

Elizabeth Dykstra-Erickson, *Apple Computer, Inc.*

Ernest Edmonds, *Loughborough University*

Alan Edwards, *Unisys*

Michael Eisenberg, *University of Colorado, Boulder*

George Engelbeck, *The Boeing Company*

Tom Erickson, *IBM Research, T.J. Watson Labs*

Steven Feiner, *Columbia University*

Daniel Felix, *ETH Zurich*

Sidney Fels, *University of British Columbia*

Robert S. Fish, *Panasonic Information and Networking Technologies Laboratory*

BJ Fogg, *Stanford University*

Peter W. Foltz, *New Mexico State University*

Paola Forcheri, *CNR-IMA*

Jodi Forlizzi, *E-Lab, LLC*

Ian Franklin, *Employment Service*

George W. Furnas, *University of Michigan*

Susan Fussell, *Carnegie Mellon University*

Deb Galdes

Bjoern Gambaeck, *Swedish Institute of Computer Science, Stockholm*

Nektarios Georgalas, *Data Management Research*

David J Gilmore, *IDEO*

Gene Golovchinsky, *FX Palo Alto Laboratory*

Michael D. Good, *SAP Labs, Inc.*

John Gosbee, *Michigan State University Kalamazoo Center for Medical Studies*

Nicholas Graham, *Queen's University*

Simon Grant, *University of Liverpool*

Saul Greenberg, *University of Calgary*

Marc Green, *Ergo Gero*

Mark Green, *University of Alberta*

Doug Griffith, *ERIM International, Inc.*

Dan Gruen, *Lotus Research*

Steve Guest, *Groupworks*

Ashok Gupta, *Philips Research Labs (U.K.)*

Nils-Erik Gustafsson, *Ericsson Utvecklings AB*

Carl Gutwin, *University of Saskatchewan*

Judy Hammond, *University of Technology, Sydney*

H. Rex Hartson, *Virginia Polytechnic Institue*

Marti Hearst, *University of California at Berkeley*

Frans Heeman, *Elsevier Science*

Austin Henderson, *Rivendel Consulting*

Richard Henneman, *NCR Human Interface Technology Center*

Scott Henninger, *University of Nebraska-Lincoln*

Harry M. Hersh, *Fidelity Investments*

Tom Hewett, *Drexel University*

Stacie Hibino, *Bell Labs/Lucent Technologies*

David R. Hill, *University of Calgary*

William C. Hill, *AT&T Labs - Research*

Ken Hinckley, *Microsoft Research*

Debby Hindus, *Interval Research Corporation*

Stephen Hirtle, *University of Pittsburgh*

Steve Hodges, *Olivetti Research Laboratory*

Hans-Juergen Hoffmann, *Darmstadt University of Technology, Germany*

H. Ulrich Hoppe, *University of Duisburg*

Steve Howard, *Swinburne University of Technology*

Andrew Howes, *Cardiff University*

Roland Hubscher, *Auburn University*

Scott Hudson, *Carnegie Mellon University*

Kori Inkpen, *Simon Fraser University*

Hiroshi Ishii, *MIT Media Laboratory*

Ismail Aras Ismail, *University College London*

Julie Jacko, *University of Wisconsin-Madison*

Maddy D. Janse, *Philips Research Laboratories - USIT*

Robin Jeffries, *Sun Microsystems*

Ljubomir Jerinic, *University of Novi Sad*

Jeff Johnson, *UI Wizards, Inc.*

Peter Johnson, *Queen Mary & Westfield College, University of London*

Anker Helms Jorgensen, *Copenhagen University*

Klaus Kansy, *GMD-FIT*

Clare-Marie Karat, *IBM T.J. Watson Research Center*

John Karat, *IBM T.J. Watson Research Center*

Demetrios Karis, *GTE Laboratories*

Jennifer Kay, *Rowan University*

Judy Kay, *University of Sydney*

Rick Kazman, *CMU*

Paul Kearney, *BT Laboratories*

Reinhard Keil-Slawik, *University of Paderborn*

Wendy A. Kellogg, *IBM T.J. Watson Research Center*

Dr. Kinshuk, *GMD-FIT*

Muneo Kitajima, *National Institute of Bioscience and Human-Technology*

Chris Knowles, *University of Waikato*

Shinichi Konomi, *GMD-IPSI*

Joseph A. Konstan, *University of Minnesota*

Philip Kortum, *Southwestern Bell Technology Resources*

Christopher Koster, *Bellcore*

Masaaki Kurosu, *Shizuoka University*

Gordon Kurtenbach, *Aliasl Wavefront*

Kari Kuutti, *University of Oulu*

Ericca Lahti, *Lotus*

James Landay, *University of California at Berkeley*

Alfred Lee, *Beta Research, Inc.*

Dr. Adrienne Lee, *New Mexico State University*

Mark Lee, *Old Dominion University*

John J. Leggett, *Texas A&M University*

Dr. Ying K Leung, *Swinburne University of Technology*

Laura Leventhal, *Bowling Green State University*

Henry Lieberman, *MIT Media Lab*

Mark Linton, *Vitria Technology*

Zhengjie Liu, *Dalian Maritime University*

Arnold M. Lund, *U S WEST Advanced Technologies*

Christine MacKenzie, *Simon Fraser University*

Allan MacLean, *Xerox Research Centre Europe*

Paul Maglio, *IBM Almaden Research Center*

Scott D. Mainwaring, *Interval Research Corp.*

Catherine R Marshall, *CollabTech, Inc.*

Toshiyuki Masui, *Sony Computer Science Laboratories, Inc.*

Ian McClelland, *Philips Consumer Electronics*

Jean McKendree, *Univ. of Edinburgh*

William W. McMillan, *Eastern Michigan University*

Jon Meads, *Usability Architects, Inc.*

John F. Meech, *National Research Council Canada*

Anne Miller, *PricewaterhouseCoopers (formerly Coopers & Lybrand Consultants)*

David R. Miller, *IBM Global Services*

Dr. Shailey Minocha, *Centre for HCI Design*

Anant Kartik Mithal, *Sun Microsystems Inc.*

Naomi Miyake, *Chukyo University*

Tom Moher, *University of Illinois at Chicago*

Anders Morch, *Oslo College*

Jackie Moyes, *The Hiser Group*

Sougata Mukherjea, *C&C Research Lab, NEC USA*

Judie Mulholland, *Florida State University*

Alice Mulvehill, *BBN Technologies*

Dianne Murray, *Consultant*

Pardo Mustillo, *Media Renaissance Inc.*

Manfred Nagl, *Aachen University of Technology*

Kumiyo Nakakoji, *Nara Institute of Science and Technology; and Software Research Associates, Inc.*

Dr. Yasushi Nakauchi, *National Defense Academy*

Frieder Nake, *University of Bremen*

Jocelyne Nanard, *Univ. Montpellier*

N. Hari Narayanan, *Auburn University*

Christine Neuwirth, *Carnegie Mellon University*

Laurence Nigay, *CLIPS-IMAG*

Alexander Nikov, *Assoc. Prof. Dr.*

Erik Nilsen, *Lewis & Clark College*

Lorraine F. Normore, *OCLC*

David G. Novick, *EURISCO*

Kimberly O'Brien, *Sun Microsystems*

Minoru OKADA, *Nagoya University*

Gary M. Olson, *University of Michigan*

Scott P. Overmyer, *Drexel University*

Nadine Ozkan, *CSIRO - CMIS*

Philippe Palanque, *LIS-FRO-GIS, University Toulouse I*

Fabio Paterno, *CNUCE - C.N.R.*

Gary Perlman, *OCLC Online Computer Library Center*

Kara Pernice Coyne, *Lotus Development Corp.*

Helen Petrie, *University of Hertfordshire*

Richard W. Pew, *BBN Technologies*

Rosalind Picard, *MIT*

Lydia Plowman, *Scottish Council for Research in Education*

Andrea Polli, *University of Illinois Chicago*

Peter G. Polson, *University of Colorado*

Kathy Potosnak, *Interface Concepts*

Gokul Prabhakar, *Member of Technical Staff*

Scott Preece, *Motorola*

Angel Puerta, *Stanford University*

Chris Quintana, *University of Michigan*

Kari-Jouko Raiha, *University of Tampere*

Ramana Rao, *Inxight Software and Xerox PARC*

Mary Elizabeth Raven, *Iris Associates*

Michael J Rees, *Bond University*

Mary Beth Rettger, *The MathWorks, Inc.*

John Rheinfrank, *seespace llc*

John T. Richards, *IBM T.J. Watson Research Center*

Doug Riecken, *Bell Laboratories-Lucent Technologies*

Dr. Frank E. Ritter, *University of Nottingham*

Daniel Robbins, *Microsoft*

Scott Robertson, *US WEST Advanced Technologies*

Dave Roberts, *IBM United Kingdom Limited*

Richard Rubinstein, *Perot Systems*

Daniel Salber, *Georgia Institute of Technology*

Alfredo Sanchez, *Universidad de las Americas-Puebla*

Martina Angela Sasse, *University College London*

Anthony Savidis, *AT-HCI Lab, Institute of Computer Science, FORTH*

Dominique L. Scapin, *INRIA*

Bill Schilit, *FX Palo Alto Laboratory*

Mark Schlager, *SRI INTERNATIONAL*

Egbert Schlungbaum, *University Rostock, Dept. of Computer Science*

Franz Schmalhofer, *DFKI GmbH*

Kurt Schmucker, *Apple Computer*

Kevin Schofield, *Microsoft*

Jean Scholtz, *National Institute of Standards and Technology*

Andrew Sears, *DePaul University*

Dore`e Duncan Seligmann, *Bell Labs*

Abigail J. Sellen, *Xerox Research Centre Europe*

John Seton, *BT Laboratories*

Chris Shaw, *University of Regina*

Donald P. Sheridan, *Auckland University*

Frank M. Shipman III, *Texas A&M University*

Jane Siegel, *Carnegie Mellon University*

Brian Smith, *MIT Media Laboratory*

Phil Smythe, *BT Laboratories*

Michael Smyth, *Napier University*

Benjamin Somberg, *AT&T Labs*

Liz Sonenberg, *The University of Melbourne*

Jared M. Spool, *User Interface Engineering*

Robert St. Amant, *North Carolina State University*

Jan Stage, *Aalborg University*

Constantine Stephanidis, *Institute of Computer Science, Foundation for Research and Technology-Hellas*

Markus Stolze, *IBM Research Division, Zurich Research Lab*

Norbert Streitz, *GMD-IPSI, German National Research Center for Information Technology*

Piyawadee Sukaviriya, *IBM T.J. Watson Research Center*

Joseph W. Sullivan, *FX Palo Alto Laboratory, Inc.*

Tamara Sumner, *The Open University*

Alistair Sutcliffe, *City University, London*

Dan Suthers, *University of Hawaii*

Pedro Szekely, *USC/ISI*

R. Chung-Man Tam, *Carnegie Mellon University*

John C. Tang, *Sun Microsystems, Inc.*

Ross Teague, *Intel Corporation*

Barbee Teasley, *SBC Technology Resources, Inc*

Linda Tetzlaff, *IBM T.J. Watson Research Center*

Bruce Thomas, *University of South Australia*

Richard Thomas, *The University of Western Australia*

Susan Trickett, *George Mason University*

Randall Trigg, *Xerox Palo Alto Research Center*

Manfred Tscheligi, *CURE-Center for Usability Research and Engineering, University of Vienna*

Thea Turner, *Motorola*

Claus Unger, *University of Hagen*

Zita Vale, *University of Porto*

Bradley T. Vander Zanden, *University of Tennessee*

Jean Vanderdonckt, *Université Catholique de Louvain*

Charles van der Mast, *Delft University of Technology*

Gerrit C. van der Veer, *Vrije Universiteit*

Robert A. Virzi, *GTE Laboratories Incorporated*

Willemien Visser, *INRIA*

Annette Wagner, *Sun Microsystems Inc.*

Clive P. Warren, *British Aerospace plc, Sowerby Research Centre*

Benjamin Watson, *University of Alberta*

Joyce Westerink, *Philips Research*

Alan Wexelblat, *MIT Media Lab*

Steve Whittaker, *ATT-Labs Research*

Julie Wilkinson, *Sheffield Hallam University*

Michael Wilson, *Rutherford Appleton Laboratory*

Stephanie Wilson, *City University*

Russel Winder, *King's College London*

Terry Winograd, *Stanford University*

Catherine G. Wolf, *IBM T. J. Watson Research Center*

Peter Wright, *University of York*

Nicole Yankelovich, *Sun Microsystems Laboratories*

Shumin Zhai, *IBM Almaden Research Center*

Juergen E. Ziegler, *Fraunhofer Institute IAO*

Video Paper Review Committee

Matt Conway, *Microsoft Research*

Kara Pernice Coyne, *Lotus Development*

BJ Fogg, *Stanford University*

Peter Gorny, *University of Oldenburg, Germany*

David Hill, *University of Calgary*

Wendy Kellogg, *IBM*

Toshiyuki Masui, *Sony Research*

Jon Meyer, *New York University*

Kristian Simsarian, *Swedish Institute of Computer Science*

Brian Smith, *Massachusetts Institute of Technology*

Charles van der Mast, *Delft University of Technology*

Terry Winograd, *Stanford University*

CHI 99 Is About Overcoming Limitations

The CHI 99 Technical Program represents the leading edge of work in the theory and practice of HCI. The conference theme, "The CHI Is the Limit," which is about understanding and overcoming limitations to the success of interactive systems, runs through the entire program. All contributions to the technical program were selected by peer-review, with the Papers and Late-Breaking Results categories conducting some of the most rigorous review processes in the field.

We could not have asked for more stimulating plenary presentations for CHI 99. The "Sci-Fi@CHI" opening plenary brings together a panel of three distinguished authors of science fiction, Bruce Sterling, Michael Swanwick, and Vernor Vinge, to discuss their visions of the distant future of HCI.

In the mid-conference plenary, "How to Become an Internet Felon in Three Easy Steps: Will Digital Libraries Become Digital Stores?" Barbara Simons, the President of ACM, shows us how new laws concerning intellectual property rights on the Internet can impose far-reaching limitations on our work and on our users. The closing plenary has ACLU attorney Ann Beeson, one of the foremost defenders of free speech on the World Wide Web, discussing "Civil Rights in Cyberspace," with examples from her own litigation against laws that would limit openness and diversity on the Web.

CHI 99 introduces a new presentation format, the interview. Richard Anderson put together a series of conversations with some of the most influential and controversial people in HCI to explore ways to overcome limitations to the success of interactive systems. The interview with Clement Mok and Jakob Nielsen focuses on limitations of graphic design and usability in the creation and use of web sites. The conversation with Bill Buxton and Clifford Nass focuses on inherent limitations that people bring to their interactions with technology. In interviews with Wayne Gray and Bill Gaver, the focus is on limits imposed by our HCI methodologies. And in conversation with Don Norman and Janice Rohn, the focus is on understanding and overcoming organization limits to HCI and the use of user-centered design methods.

The Senior CHI Development Consortium brings together researchers from a variety of backgrounds to create a research agenda for HCI and older users. The goal of the agenda is to understand and remove limitations that keep older users from enjoying the full benefits of the technologies available to them, and thus to enrich their lives by enabling them to remain independent and well-connected to the larger world.

The *CHI 99 Conference Proceedings* is the archival print publication of the conference. It contains the full text of papers presented at the conference. These papers have undergone one of the most rigorous peer-review processes in the field. The *Conference Proceedings* also contains the print portion of the conference's first-ever "video paper," a paper that is presented primarily in the video medium because its content cannot be adequately conveyed in text. The video portion appears in the *CHI 99 Video Proceedings*.

The *CHI 99 Extended Abstracts* contains summaries of technical presentations other than papers. It includes extended abstracts of the:

- Demonstrations (both live and video)
- Doctoral Consortium
- Late-Breaking Results
- Panels
- Plenary Addresses
- Senior CHI Development Consortium
- Special Interest Groups
- Student Posters
- Tutorials
- Workshops

The *CHI 99 Video Proceedings* is the archival video publication of the conference. It contains the video portion of the first-ever video paper. It also contains video figures from the traditional papers, showing ideas that cannot readily be conveyed in print figures.

The *CHI 99 Video Program* contains the video demonstrations, which also have print descriptions in the *CHI 99 Extended Abstracts*. It is distributed on the same physical videotape as the *CHI 99 Video Proceedings*.

A technical program of this quality and depth can be assembled only through the dedication of the area co-chairs, along with the many volunteers who serve on their review committees. On behalf of the entire HCI community, we extend to them enormous appreciation for their hard work and for their insight in selecting a technical program that pushes the limits of human-computer interaction.

Marian G. Williams and Mark W. Altom

CHI 99 Technical Program Co-Chairs

An Empirical Study of How People Establish Interaction: Implications for CSCW Session Management Models

Steinar Kristoffersen
Norwegian Computing Center
Postboks 114 Blindern
N-0314 OSLO, Norway
+45 22 85 26 66
steinar@nr.no

Fredrik Ljungberg
Viktoria Institute
Box 620
405 30 Gothenburg, Sweden
+46 31 773 27 44
fredrik@informatics.gu.se

ABSTRACT

In this paper, we report the results of an empirical study of how people, as part of their daily work activities, go about to establish collaboration. We examine the empirical findings and relate them to existing research on CSCW session management models, i.e., the mechanisms in CSCW systems that define the way in which people can join together in collaboration. Existing models leave a lot to be desired, in particular because they tend to assume that *indexical elements* of interaction management are substitutable by objective representation of artifacts. Based on the empirical findings, we derive three principles to consider in the design of CSCW session management models.

Keywords

Session management, field study, ethnography, design implications

INTRODUCTION

Many people spend large parts of their working day interacting with others. The interaction can take place in physical face-to-face meetings or in an electronic medium. Both these kinds of interaction have increased the last couple of years. One reason for this is extensive adoption of new information technology (IT) [1]. In this paper, we use the term "CSCW systems" to capture all kinds of IT explicitly designed to facilitate cooperation and communication among people.

The need to "ground" the design of CSCW systems in empirical investigations of cooperative work is very much recognized in the literature. So far, the empirical oriented approaches have concentrated primarily on eliciting implications for a particular system, or a class of systems (e.g., coordination) or feature (e.g., awareness widgets). Very little effort has been aimed at understanding cooperation for the purpose of informing the design of *session management models*. A session management model defines the manner in which people can join together in CSCW systems [2]. Thus, all CSCW

systems, although not always explicitly, rely on such a model, which makes it crucial that it is based on the right assumptions of how people collaborate.

The purpose of the study reported in this paper is to begin to explore work in real settings in a systematic way, with a particular objective to inform the design of session management models. Because session management models define how collaborative sessions are initiated, proceeded and terminated, we started the empirical investigation by exploring the first issue: *how people, as part of their daily work activities, go about to establish collaboration*. By "establish interaction" we mean the various activities in which people are involved to make collaboration happen and not happen.

Related work

Because of the importance of session management in CSCW, the topic has received much attention in the literature [3]. One common assumption in this work is the explicit distinction between collaboration and other work activities [e.g., 2]. A collaborative session starts, proceeds, and ends in a sequential and explicit manner.

Moreover, many researchers [e.g., 3] make the distinction between explicit and implicit session management models, where explicit models require participants to take dedicated actions additional to the work itself to initiate a CSCW session. Implicit models do not require this.

Three kinds of implicit session management models are described in the literature. *Artifact based models* assume that people wish to join together in sessions when they use the same artifact, e.g., a document [e.g., 3]. *Activity based models* assume that people wish to join together in sessions when they are involved in the same activity, e.g., using the same system [e.g., 4, 14]. *Place based models* assume that people wish to join together in sessions when they are at the same gathering point in a place based groupware [e.g., 5].

The difficulties associated with setting up sessions automatically based on activity and artifact [4] could be one reason why few systems use these models. Workflow systems, which often use some kind of activity based model, is one exception. Place based models, e.g., collaborative virtual environments [e.g., 6], continuos connections between physical places [e.g., 7], and virtual collaboration rooms [e.g., 5], are based on how people meet each other in the real world.

In contrast to the assumptions of many CSCW session management models are findings in, for instance, ethnomethodological studies of work [e.g., 8]. Hopper [9], for instance, in analyzing how conversations are established among co-located people, suggests a much more blurred distinction between collaboration and other activities:

"Co-present speech routinely grows from non speech pre-beginnings, such as visual recognition displays. It is difficult to pinpoint a moment when such encounters begin." [9, p. 217]

Knowledge of this body of work motivated us to question whether or not current session management models rest upon valid assumptions of collaboration. At the same time, the social science research cited above has not been conducted for the purpose of design, and for that reason, design issues have not been considered in, for example, the analyses of empirical data. The purpose of the study presented in this paper, is to elicit implications for CSCW session management models on the basis of ethnomethodological-oriented investigations of work. This way of working has been documented to be effective [17]. For a recent discussion of the use of ethnomethodology in design, see [11].

The most related research we find in the literature is the study by Whittaker and associates [18]. They studied informal workplace communication for the purpose of design. Although some of the results reported in their paper could inform the design of session management models, this was not the objective of their study, thus they did not plan, conduct or analyze the fieldwork with that in mind.

RESEARCH SITE AND METHOD
Site
Participants in the study were a group of researchers at a pharmaceutical research company in Gothenburg, Sweden. The group employed six people: one group manager, three clinical trial managers, and two secretaries. The main task of the group was to prepare and manage clinical trial projects. Their point of departure is one or several hypotheses about how well a drug recovers a certain indication, documentation of which is demanded by the authorities to certify commercialization of the drug. Many different actors, such as the pre-clinical researchers and the marketing staff suggest hypotheses. These hypotheses and demands from the authorities guide the design of the trial, e.g., sample size and number of treatments. The duration of the trials ranged from one to four years, the number of participating patients from 200 to 10 000, and the number of participating countries from one to ten

Data collection
The empirical study aimed to investigate in detail the day to day work in the clinical research group. In particular, we were interested in *how do people, as part of their daily work activities, go about to establish collaboration?* However, to get an insight in the domain of clinical trial work, with which we were not so familiar, we started the empirical study with interviewing the group members. To investigate the research question we conducted participant observation studies of staff. We spent approximately 80 man-hours doing close participant observations, i.e., following every single move of a particular person [12], and about 240 man-hours doing site observation, i.e., talking to the group members, checking who was doing what, etc. Everybody was aware of the research and its purpose, and field notes were taken continually. The observations were followed by another round of interviewing. This time, the aim was to let people reflect upon some of the notes we made during the observational studies. All together, we conducted 12 interviews, each lasting between 45 and 90 minutes. All interviews were taped.

Data analysis
The analysis of the empirical data aims to "make sense of massive amounts of data, reduce the volume of information, identify significant patterns, and construct a framework for communicating the essence of what the data reveal" [12, p. 371-372]. Having transcribed the interviews and field notes, we started the coding of the empirical data. This meant going through the data carefully, making notes and labeling data that seemed to capture underlying patterns. Gradually, the coding process became a matter of interpretation, i.e., "attach significance to what was found,..." [12, p. 423]. The empirical work was guided by the framework of ethnomethodology, described next.

ETHNOMETHODOLOGY AND INDEXICAL ELEMENTS
The empirical work can be characterized as an ethnomethodologically-oriented investigation [13]. In particular, the notion of "indexical expressions" served as an analytical vehicle.

Indexical expression are utterances whose meaning cannot be established without interpretation that is based on *knowledge* about the *purpose* and *history* of the person using the expression, the *circumstances* of the utterance being made and even the *relationship* between the user and the interpreter. These utterances cannot straightforwardly be repeated or reused outside the context in which they originated, without changing their meaning. Garfinkel [13] comments upon the agreement between many sociologists that indexical expressions are "awkward for formal discourse" and ideally substitutable by objective (i.e., "context-free" or "complete") expressions [13, p. 6]:

"Nevertheless, whenever practical actions are the topic of study the promised distinction and substitutability of objective for indexical expressions remains programmatic in every particular case and in every particular occasion in which the distinction must be demonstrated. In every actual case without exception, conditions will be cited that a competent investigator will be required to recognize, such that in that particular case the terms of the demonstration can be relaxed and nevertheless the demonstration be counted an adequate one."

We believe that this argument about indexical expressions can be used to inspire and inform an analysis of session management beyond utterances. Our thesis is that many session management models (and, thus, CSCW systems) describe and implement *objective elements* of interaction management. Based on a study of practical action we wish to investigate the different roles of indexical elements in how people establish interaction. Moreover, and with particular import to design activities, we aim to resolve the problematic consequences, if any, of using objective elements as mechanisms of establishing interaction.

FINDINGS

In this section we present results from the empirical study. The question investigated was: *How do people, as part of their daily work activities, go about to establish collaboration?*

The role of artifacts in establishing interaction

We found that artifacts played an important role in the process of establishing interaction. Let us consider two examples: the door and the whiteboard.

The door

When people do not want to interact with others, e.g., because they host a meeting, they often shut the door to the office. When doing so, they often try to make it visible for others what they are trying to do, e.g., by explaining for others that they are "shutting the door."

EBS arrives together with another researcher concerned with [and partly responsible for] "the catastrophe project" [a "very badly designed project" which had been discussed among the researchers in the group extensively the last couple of days]. When entering her office, EBS says to the secretary: "I'm shutting the door."

In the situation described above, EBS does not simply "shut the door," but she also explains to the secretary (IG) that this is what she is doing. "Shutting the door" seems to be a social activity that does not only involve the physical operations of shutting the door.

Consider the following situation that took place some minutes later.

PJ arrives. He glances into the secretary's office, which is next to EBS, saying "Her door is shut?" The secretary replies: "Yes, they just arrived,..."PJ while heading towards EBS's office to join them: "This might take some time,..."

[...]

After a while, KK shows up, [also] glancing in to the secretary's office: "I need to discuss my study with EBS, but she's busy now, right?" The secretary replies: "Yes, ... you know,... "the catastrophe," they [EBS and PJ] have a meeting with someone from the UK." KK: "Yeah, ..."

Both PJ and KK thus seemed to have noticed that the door to EBS's office was shut, and both of them appeared to have ideas about the implications of the shut door. For PJ, it meant that a meeting he was going to join has started, i.e., that he was supposed to enter the office (as soon as possible), while for KK it meant that she could not talk to EBS at the moment, i.e., she was not supposed to enter the office. Even though the latter seemed to be the general meaning of "the shut door," PJ (effortlessly) appeared to easily recognize that he was supposed to enter the office.

Thus, "the door" does not seem to regulate the manner in which people join together in cooperation in a fixed, single way. For example, a shut door does not necessarily mean "do not disturb." The meaning of the door seems partly to be derived from interaction between people in the particular situation. Another observation is that even though both PJ and KK seemed to know the (different) implications of "the shut door," both of them wanted their interpretations of the situation confirmed. They did so by addressing "the shut door" in conversations with the secretary.

The whiteboard

A whiteboard was placed on the wall in the corridor outside the offices. It comprised the name of the people in the research group and the days of the week. The idea was to make people aware of each others' schedules.

Similar to how people seemed to make "shutting the door" visible to others, the person updating the whiteboard often seemed to try to make others aware of what she was doing. Consider the following excerpt from the fieldwork.

EBS leaves here office and walks to the whiteboard. "'C-a-n-a-s-t-a U-K'[1] [spelling every single letter while she writes] on

---

[1] The company name is changed for anonymity.

Friday Dec., 12 oh my good...," she says while filling in the schedule. KK [whose office is close to the whiteboard] has apparently recognized EBS, and says: "I thought you liked them,... [laughing, they were responsible for "the catastrophe project"]. EBS replies: "Well, if you like them, then you could join us,... then I update your schedule too!" KK says: "No, no,... I was only joking."

One possible interpretation of the excerpt is that EBS produces an "indexical element" for the group, and in doing so, she manages to establish interaction that seems to give (additional) meaning to the entry.

Below is an example of how the entry made by EBS was used for the purpose of establishing interaction.

[PJ and KK have been discussing how to solve a problem in a trial project.]

PJ says: "OK, let's talk about it over lunch... Wouldn't it be good if EBS could join us?" KK replies: "She has left to,... France I think, I think that was what the schedule [i.e., whiteboard] said this morning. But let's check it out." KK leaves the office to check the whiteboard. KK [from the corridor to PJ in the office]: "Yes, she left 11 o'clock,... for the UK." IG [the secretary] shouts from her office: "She has left,..." KK replies:

"Right,..." walking back to PJ's office. KK to PJ: "Then we have to sort it our ourselves..." PJ replies: "But lets call her. If she left the office 11.00 o'clock, then the plane is taking of,... at 12.30 or so, and then it shouldn't be a problem to reach her now.... I'm giving her a ring and then we go for lunch."

PJ and KK need to talk to EBS. KK recalls that EBS was going away, and, it seems, that the whiteboard contains more information about the visit. To check it out, she walks away to the whiteboard. At the whiteboard, she shouts the whiteboard entry to PJ, who still is in the office. Apparently, the secretary notices the "investigation," confirming that EBS has left already. KK then concludes that EBS cannot join the discussion.

PJ does not agree with that. He explains what it typically means to make a visit to the UK: leaving the office 1,5 hours before the plane takes off, thus being reachable at least one hour after having left the office. Therefore, he concludes, EBS should be reachable until 12 o'clock, thus "give her a ring."

Again, the artifact itself — here the whiteboard — does not seem to regulate the manner in which people join together in cooperation in a fixed, single way. The conclusion made in the situation above relied, among others, on local knowledge such as going to the UK mean going away by plane, going away by plane means leaving the office 1,5 hours before departure, etc.

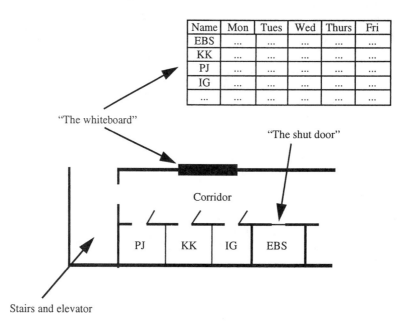

Name	Mon	Tues	Wed	Thurs	Fri
EBS	...	...	...	...	...
KK	...	...	...	...	...
PJ	...	...	...	...	...
IG	...	...	...	...	...
...	...	...	...	...	...

"The whiteboard"

"The shut door"

Corridor

PJ   KK   IG   EBS

Stairs and elevator

Figure 1. The door and the whiteboard.

Establishing interaction "face to face"

Occasionally, one person started to talk to someone already engaged in a conversation. In all cases documented, with no exception, this made the interrupting party excusing herself, e.g.: "Oh... sorry! I didn't recognize you two were talking...". The implication is not that people do not "interrupt" each other, but that they do not usually interrupt each other *in such a way*. We found that interruptions were very common, and that many conversations were "replaced" by new conversations. Consider the following excerpt:

EBS is discussing a future study together with JD, who is a medical advisor for the project. GW arrives to the office. She does not interrupt the discussion, but she places herself in the door. EBS and JD immediately realize that GW arrives, and EBS asks JD: "But we're done, aren't we?" JD replies: "Well, I guess we are. Talk to you later..." and leaves the room. EBS starts a conversation with GW..."

The arrival of GW seems to be noticed by EBS and JD immediately. EBS then says "But we're done, aren't we?". One possible interpretation is that EBS here, at least partly, addresses the possibility for JD *and* GW that GW wants to talk to her. Two main actions follow. First, by saying "Well, I guess we are. Talk to you later...," JD indicates that for him it makes sense to close down the conversation with EBS. Second, by remaining quiet GW does not do anything that contradicts the explanations of EBS and JD, and by being quiet, she seems to confirm the interpretation of the other two parties. Hence, GW manages to interfere with the ongoing conversation in a way that was seemingly effortless and unproblematic for *all* parties involved: the ongoing conversation was "smoothly" finished, and neither EBS nor JD indicated that GW in some way acted inappropriately. However, GW did *not* interfere with the ongoing conversation alone. On the contrary, EBS and JD seemed to play the major roles.

A third party

Another empirical observation was when one person informs others about *another* person's current work activities, and in doing so, provides a context for the potential interaction with that person. Consider the following excerpt:

AS and EBS are engaged in a conversation in EBS' office. PJ arrives, and he starts to talk to EBS. AS does not leave the office. She seems to believe the new interaction will not be long. The conversation between EBS and PJ concerns one of PJ's upcoming studies. When PJ mentions the possibility to involve GW in the discussion "to sort it out once and for all," AS intervenes: "No, she's not available now,... well I mean she is, but no,... that's not a good idea, "the salaries," you know." [EBS and PJ do not contact GW]

In this case, AS informs PJ and EBS that GW, who they consider contacting, is working with "the salaries." This implies, AS explains, that she probably should not be contacted.[2] Inasmuch as PJ and EBS do not contact GW, the reason given by AS seems to be intelligible for everybody involved.

Redirected telephone calls

When people for one reason or another do not want to be accessible for telephone calls, they direct the telephone to the secretary. Sometimes when the secretary receives a redirected phone call, she immediately decided to let it (back) through. We found two main reasons for that: first, because she has been provided with *instructions*, e.g., to let through an awaiting call from a particular person; second, because she *knew by experience* that importance of people, e.g., that a particular professor was very important for the study and that he was virtually impossible to reach, thus that people did not want to fail to talk to him if he happened to call.

When it was not so obvious for the secretary whether to let through the call or not, then she typically started to explain *why*. Consider the following excerpt.

"Canasta[3], IG speaking" [IG, the secretary answers the phone]. IG: "She's at a meeting,... unfortunately, would you like to leave a message for her?"

In this case, the secretary seems to say *what* the receiver is doing as a way of describing *why* she is not available. When this happened, the receiver sometimes explained why she was calling, which in turn often made the secretary offering her to leave a note. This does not usually give rise to problems: "They [the callers] understand," IG told us.

Sometimes the caller managed to be let (back) through. The reason why seemed to be that the circumstances offered by the caller made re-directing the call an adequate move, both for the caller, the secretary, and the receiver. Interviewees argued that the secretary was very skilled when it came to making the right decision in this situation: "She *never* makes a wrong decision," as one of them put it. From this it would follow that in all these cases "the rules" for who to let through are relaxed. Nevertheless, the decisions made by the secretary are "always" appropriate and accountable. This would imply that important factors are open when the interaction starts between the caller and the secretary.

Meetings were sometimes held so close to the secretary that she could "control" exactly how they progressed. This helped her to handle re-routed calls (from meeting

---

[2] "The salaries" referred to the annual negotiation about next year's salaries, which was a frequently discussed issue among staff at the time of the empirical study.

[3] The company name is changed for anonymity.

attendants to her) appropriately. For example, when EBS hosted a long meeting at her office the secretary handed over an incoming telephone call to her during a break, and when the secretary had noticed that a meeting had ended earlier than excepted a call re-routed to her from EBS was re-routed back.

Summing up

Below, we summarize the empirical findings:

- Artifacts are used to regulate interaction. They are given meaning by operation and explanation. The meaning of artifacts is partly open prior to the particular interaction. Therefore, artifacts do not regulate interaction in a fixed, single way. The meaning is "closed" (or, "made less open") through interaction. Particular circumstances can be quoted to temporarily relax the meaning of artifacts used to regulate interaction.

- Establishing interaction usually involves more interaction. Interaction often interrupts, or "replaces" interaction. This is done in an unproblematic, effortless and effective way.

- Knowledge about the receiver, third parties and the previous unfolding of events can play major roles in the interaction to establish interaction. Inasmuch as *rules* are stipulated as regulating the interaction, again, particular circumstances can be quoted to temporarily relax the application of these rules to regulate interaction.

DISCUSSION

The empirical study shed light on important issues in how people, as part of the day to day work, join together in collaboration. In this section, we relate the findings to a typical example of the current way of thinking about session management: *session management based on shared artifact*, as proposed by Edwards [e.g., 3]. Because Edwards' contribution is central and typical for the literature on session management models, we believe it could serve as an appropriate reference model against which to relate the findings.

Many attempts to complement explicit models for session management propose a strategy based on shared artifacts. Edwards [3] presents a model in which activity information, and in particular representations of shared artifact is used to initiate collaborative sessions. Activities are described as tuples of *Users, Tasks* and *Objects*. When activities are detected to subscribe to the same *Object,* a collaborative session is implicitly defined and initiated.

Let us now relate the empirical findings described above to the model suggested by Edwards (the concepts of the model in italics).

The role of the door in establishing interaction

In our case, the door is not in an integral way connected to the *Activity* that takes place, i.e., an informal yet restricted (even confidential) meeting. Indeed, the door, as a regulating artifact, is aimed to inform, to various degrees, also people who are not *Users*. The role it plays is non the less important in indicating who can and who cannot join, therefore Edwards' model breaks down.

Assuming that, in this case, a similarly fine-grained and situated regime applied to a shared object of the activity, there is nothing in Edwards' model that allows the "owner" of the artifact to explicitly inscribe an indexical meaning to it, and different users to be afforded different interpretations. This analysis also applies to the use of the whiteboard described in the fieldwork excerpts.

Establishing interaction "face-to-face"

In these excerpts, there are no *Objects* that are shared in ways that indicate how a collaborative session is to be established, except the "interrupting" persons themselves.

New sessions seem to be able to interrupt without interfering. By this we mean that an awareness of the desire to communicate is itself communicated and acknowledged, before the session actually starts. This can be interpreted as a session in itself, but in many ways this is not an activity, it merely (and subtly, yet significantly) requests communication at a suitable point. The discrete nature of current session management models (including Edwards') prevents support for such activities.

Referring to a third party

In this category, local knowledge is used to modify access to a third party. The object of work ("the salaries") is included in accomplishing session management, but in a prohibitive rather than facilitating manner. This situation (and the "whiteboard" example as well) illustrates the importance of related sessions (logically and physically as well as temporally) in establishing interaction. Aspects of activities that take place elsewhere are brought to bear on the current situation. In Edwards model, as in all other models of which we are aware, sessions are isolated events.

Redirected telephone calls

This excerpt illustrates how people in an effortless and unproblematic way, "quote circumstances" to temporarily relax the meaning of artifacts used to regulate interaction. This observation seems to discourage a very common design proposal, namely the introduction of elaborate and explicit rules to regulate interaction. The model of Edwards involves such assumptions, e.g., collaborative session are defined and initiated when two *Activities* subscribe to the same *Object*.

The role of gatekeepers ("the secretary") is not covered in current models. In our case, "the secretary" was one of utmost importance, not only in administrating and aiding the interpretation of indexical elements, but also in monitoring the ongoing session to detect progress and re-route calls accordingly.

In the discussion above, we related our work to one main contribution on the topic of session management, namely the paper by Edwards [3]. As mentioned previously, this is central and typical for state of the art research on the topic. We maintain the discussion has pointed out general weaknesses in existing research.

CONCLUSIONS

In this section we conclude the paper. We do so by eliciting three principles for session management models derived from the empirical study.

We found that people form *agreements* of artifacts by operation and explanation. Operation is changing the state of the artifact, e.g., by physically shutting the door. Explanation is explaining the operations, e.g., telling others that the door is being shut. Because the agreements concern *the meaning* of the artifacts, we can view artifacts as *agreements of meaning*. If artifacts can "illustrate" agreements of meaning concerning interaction, then they can guide the process of establishing interaction. Therefore, the following principle can be derived:

- **Principle 1**: Artifacts "illustrating" agreements of meaning, obtained through operation and explanation, help people to establish interaction.

Some CSCW systems provide the user with icons that can be operated in various ways. In *Montage*, for instance, the user can configure a door icon to indicate her desired accessibility [15]. A wide open door means you want to interact with people, a shut that you do not, etc.

However, this is not enough, as was clearly shown in the discussion above. There does not seem to exist an objective meaning of the position of a door in regulating interaction. For some people (in a given situation) a closed door means "come in, we have already started," while for other it means "stay out, I'm busy."

Our study documented the importance of *explanation* in forming agreements of the meanings of artifacts. Without explanation it would be difficult to form agreements about meaning, and thus, what to illustrate with the artifact. The importance of explanation has not been considered in the literature so far. This could bee seen as a critique against existing systems and concepts, but also implies a novel observation.

Our study documented that the meaning of session management is partly open prior to the interaction. Even if rules regulating interaction exist, circumstances can be quoted to temporarily relax the meaning illustrated by the artifact. Therefore, interaction seldom has a fixed, identifiable starting point (and, consequently, it "never" ends). Session management models should support a recursive network of interactions that spin-off new opportunities for collaborative work. This should not be interpreted as a normative *formula* for CSCW, inasmuch as there clearly seems to exist, in each particular case, a

convenient "grouping" of interactions that can be seen as belonging together. Designers should *be aware*, however, that a general rule for identifying such events seems hard to establish. The critical principle seems to be:

- **Principle 2**: Establishing interaction always involves interaction. Interaction often interrupts, or "replaces" interaction. This is done in an unproblematic, effortless and effective way.

Since actors of a social setting deals with the seemingly eternal loop in an unproblematic way, there is reason to believe that it could also be support "from the bottom up" by CSCW systems, by allowing sessions to be nested in a situated fashion.

In existing research on CSCW session management models there seems to be an underlying assumption that the notion of "task" or "activities" is important. In addition we found that "non-activity" related knowledge about, for example, the history of events, interaction and information is brought to bear on (the potential of) establishing new interactions. This suggests a third principle:

- **Principle 3**: The participants' knowledge about potential participants, their work and previous interactions plays a major role in the *interaction to establish interaction* as well as the *application of rules that are stipulated to regulate interaction*.

This principle seems to introduce a paradox in our account of how people establish sessions, namely that it is at the same time an integrated aspect of accomplishing work, yet it (sometimes) refers to elements that are *external* to elements of that work. We prefer to see this as a general lesson to be learned from this study, that the *work* that we aim to support is, indeed, far more than just *tasks*.

ACKNOWLEDGMENTS

The research is part of the IMIS project at the Norwegian Computing Centre, Norway. Thanks to the pharmaceutical company. Also thanks to the Swedish Information Technology Research Institute (SITI).

REFERENCES

1. Sproull, L. and Kiesler, S. *Connections. New ways of working in the networked organization*, MIT Press, Cambridge MA, 1993.

2. Patterson, J.F., Hill, R.D., Rohall, S.L., Meeks, W.S. Rendezvous: An architecture for synchronous multi-user applications, in *Proceedings of CSCW'90* (Los Angeles CA, October 1990), ACM Press, 317-328.

3. Edwards, W.K. Session Management for collaborative applications, in *Proceedings of CSCW'94* (Chapel Hill NC, November 1994), ACM Press, 323-330.

4. Isaacs, E., Tang, J., and Morris, T. Piazza: A desktop environment supporting impromptu and planned interactions, in *Proceedings of CSCW'96* (Boston MA, November 1996), ACM Press, 315-324.

5. Roseman, M. and Greenberg, S. TeamRooms: Network places for collaboration, in *Proceedings of CSCW'96* (Boston MA, November 1996), ACM Press, 325-333.

6. Nakanishi, H., Yoshida, C., Nishimura, T. Ishida, T. FreeWalk: Supporting causal meetings in a network, in *Proceedings of CSCW'96* (Boston MA, November 1996), ACM Press, 308-314.

7. Fish, R.S., Kraut, R.E., and Chalfonte, B.L. The VideoWindow system in informal communications, in *Proceedings of CSCW'90* (Los Angeles CA, October 1990), ACM Press, 1-11.

8. Boden, D. *The business of talk. Organizations in action.* Polity Press, Cambridge, 1994.

9. Hopper, R. Hold the phone, in *Talk and social structure*, edited by Boden, D. and Zimmerman, D.H., The University of California Press, Los Angeles CA, 217-231, 1991.

10. Button, G. and Sharrock, W. The production of order and the order of production. The possibilities for distributed organisations, work and technology in the print industry, in *Proceedings of ECSCW'97* (Lancaster UK, September 1997), Kluwer Academic Publishers, 1-16.

11. Button, G. and Dourish, P. Technomethodology: Paradoxes and possibilities, in *Proceedings of*

CHI'96 (Vancouver Canada, April 1996), ACM Press.

12. Patton, M.Q. *Qualitative Evaluation and Research Methods.* Sage, New York, 1990.

13. Garfinkel, H. *Studies in ethnomethodolgy,* Prentice Hall, Englewood Cliffs, 1967.

14. Kristoffersen, S., *Developing collaborative multimedia. The Mediate toolkit*, Ph.D. thesis. Computing Department, Lancaster University, UK, 1997.

15. Tang, J.C. and Rua, M. Montage: Providing Teleproximity for Distributed Groups, in *Proceedings of CHI'94* (Boston MA, April 24-28), ACM Press, 37-43.

16. Buxton, B. Scientific director's report: Living in augmented reality, in *Ontario telepresence project. Final report*, edited by Chattoe, J., Leach, P., and Riesenbach, R. Information Technology Research Centre, Telecommunications Research Institute of Ontario, 19-34, 1995.

17. Bentley, R., Hughes, J. A., Randall, D., Rodden, T., Sawyer, P., Shapiro, D., and Sommerville, I. Ethnographically-informed systems design for air traffic control, In *Proceedings CSCW'92* (Toronto Canada, October-November 1992), ACM Press, 123-129.

18. Whittaker, S., Frohlich, D., and Daly-Jones, O. Informal workplace communication: What is it like and how might we support it?, in *Proceedings of CHI'94* (Boston MA, April 24-28), ACM Press, 131-137.

Chat Circles

Fernanda B. Viegas and Judith S. Donath
MIT Media Lab
20 Ames Street
Cambridge, MA 02139 USA
+1 617 253 9690
{fviegas|judith}@media.mit.edu

ABSTRACT

Although current online chat environments provide new opportunities for communication, they are quite constrained in their ability to convey many important pieces of social information, ranging from the number of participants in a conversation to the subtle nuances of expression that enrich face to face speech. In this paper we present *Chat Circles*, an abstract graphical interface for synchronous conversation. Here, presence and activity are made manifest by changes in color and form, proximity-based filtering intuitively breaks large groups into conversational clusters, and the archives of a conversation are made visible through an integrated history interface. Our goal in this work is to create a richer environment for online discussions.

Keywords

chatroom, conversation, social visualization, turn-taking, graphical history, Internet, World Wide Web

INTRODUCTION

The history of networked computing shows that, given a chance, people will adapt technology for social interaction. E.g., although the ARPANET was developed for remote operation of computers, email and newsgroups have become among its most popular (and arguably, most important) uses [5]. More recently, online service providers have discovered that chat, email and other communicative activities are the key services that people want.

Yet, although interpersonal communication has proved to be an extraordinarily popular and influential use of the computer, the conversational interfaces in use today are still quite primitive, making it difficult to convey many basic social cues. With that in mind, we have developed *Chat Circles,* a chat system that uses abstract graphics to create a richer, more nuanced communicative environment.

CURRENT INTERFACES

There are currently a wide variety of tools that allow for synchronous communication over a computer network. Internet Relay Chat (IRC), for instance, is one of the Internet's most popular applications for interpersonal communication. And, although the World Wide Web's initial protocols were not conducive to live interaction, the advent of Java has made Web-based chatrooms increasingly popular.

When email, newsgroups and chatrooms were first developed, ASCII interfaces were the norm: most systems lacked both the power and the infrastructure for more elaborate graphical interfaces. Today, although faster computers and networks as well as support for visual routines make graphical interfaces quite feasible, text still dominates the arena of on-line conversations [fig 1b]. The reasons for this may be partly tradition – a combination of familiarity and an established application infrastructure – and partly a lack of alternatives – many of the existing graphical systems have significant drawbacks.

Figure 1a. The Palace, a popular avatar-based system.

Figure 1b. Text-based chatroom.

In a text-only communication environment, the text element is overloaded as a multiple signifier. In these environments, the participants type messages which are then displayed sequentially on each person's screen. These messages convey two types of information: one is the content of the message, the other is the presence of the participant. Consequently, if the participant is not actively messaging, he or she is not present on the screen. This ephemeral presence has a strong impact on the style of discourse, for participants often feel compelled to constantly post messages so that they will not be forgotten by the others.

Much important contextual information is difficult to perceive in a text-only chat system. The number of participants is hard to gauge: a session containing 20 users looks nearly the same as a session with two users. It is difficult to distinguish among the participants and form a coherent sense of their individual identities: the users all resemble each other visually, appearing as a user name in text against the background. The interactions among the users are not manifest, for the conversation always appears on the screen as a linear progression of lines of text, regardless of the conversation's dynamics. Finally, the temporal information found in oral conversation, such as turn-taking and the negotiation of conversational synchrony by the participants, is not captured by these sequential lines of text.

There are alternatives to text-based chats. In recent years a number of graphical chat interfaces have been developed; among the most popular systems are: *The Palace* [12], *Comic Chat* [4], and *V-Chat* [13]. These graphical environments make use of avatars to convey social presence and identity. Avatars can be pictures, drawings or icons that users choose to represent themselves. In the case of *The Palace*, for instance, these figures range from simple smiley faces to highly elaborate (often Medieval or sci-fi themed) animated drawings. Graphical chatrooms also make use of background graphics that are designed to transform each room within the system into a unique experience [fig 1a]. On all graphical chat systems, however, text is still used for the actual conversation; users communicate with others via typed text that appears in "speech balloons" that pop up next to the participants' avatars.

The problem of overly ephemeral presence is solved in the graphical chats: one's avatar is continuously displayed on the screen as long as one is logged onto the system[1].This is an effective solution for making presence in these environments more substantial and permanent, making it much easier for users to see how many people are participating in a conversation at any given time, even if users are not actively messaging. Moreover, it becomes much easier for users to follow who is saying what during a conversation because they do not have the overhead of having to read the speakers' names every time something is posted on the screen; one needs only see which avatar "spoke" last.

---

1. One exception is *Comic Chat*, where the system only displays "active" avatars on each one of the comic frames.

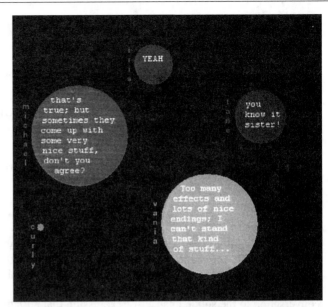

Figure 2. Screen-shot of the conversational interface in *Chat Circles*.

Although the use of avatars solves the problem of presence, it introduces new difficulties. Space needs to be allocated for every user's avatar as well as for their speech bubbles. The screen becomes quickly cluttered, which can hinder communication. More subtly, the avatars can distort expression and intent by providing a small range of (often broadly drawn) expressions that overlays all of a user's communications. Even if an avatar has several expressions, and many do, it is still a far cry from the subtlety of verbal expression, let alone our physical gestures.

The user interface in avatar systems, like text-based chatrooms, is not very supportive of the implicit interactive practices present in face to face conversation. There is no expressive way of conveying turn-taking rhythms nor patterns of replies to specific utterances. Social presence, although permanent, is still given a binary quality in graphical chat systems - either the person is present or not, no subtler reading of presence is allowed.

CHAT CIRCLES

Chat Circles is a graphical interface for synchronous communication that uses abstract shapes to convey identity and activity. Our aim is to use graphics to convey the dynamics of conversation as well as to unveil the patterns of activity that emerge through the interaction among users. We employ simple 2D graphics that change in shape, size and color to communicate the rhythm of conversations.

The interface in *Chat Circles* also features a proximity-based filter that allows users to focus on the conversation in which they are involved without, however, losing track of the activity level in the rest of the system.

Each participant is represented by a colored circle on the screen in which his or her words appear. The circles grow

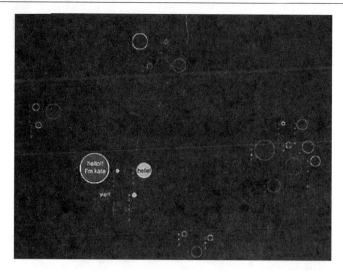 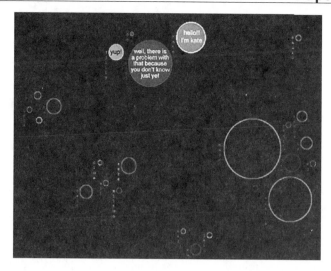

Figure 3. Location becomes meaningful as users move their circles around the screen; clusters of activity are immediately apparent. The local user's own circle appears outlined in white.

and brighten with each message, and they fade and diminish in periods of silence, though they do not disappear completely so long as the participant is connected to the chat.

Identity

Each person who is connected to the chat's server appears as a colored circle [fig 2]. Users choose a color upon logging in and color thus serves as a general indicator of identity. Participants are also identified by name, a small label next to each participant's circle displays their name in the same color as their corresponding circle. The local user's specific circle is differentiated from the other circles through a white outline; this makes it easy for users to locate themselves on the screen at any point in time.

Most people can discriminate among a limited number of non-adjacent colors; once the number of participants rises above that number, color identification will become somewhat ambiguous. However, we believe it will still be useful for two reasons. First, we are much better able to discriminate between adjacent colors. *Chat Circles* is designed so that participants in a particular discussion must be near each other on the screen, so within the group with which one is engaged, the ability to distinguish between say, two shades of blue, will be higher than for the screen as a whole. Second, many participants are likely to remain in the same spot for extended periods of time, and thus location will supplement color as an identifying cue.

Color in *Chat Circles* does not carry any intrinsic meaning. For instance, red does not necessarily mean anger, nor yellow suggest happiness. Indeed, it is one of the challenges in this project to find a palette of colors that will not inadvertently suggest meaningful interpretation: a bright yellow circle might appear to be cheerful, and a dull brown one depressed, regardless of the actual mood of the participant or the content of the speech.

Activity

In *Chat Circles*, activity is conveyed through the changes in size and color of the graphics displayed on the user's screen. The resulting graphical cadence becomes an important articulator of the flow of conversations in the system.

When a user posts a message, his or her circle grows and accommodates the text inside it. Postings are displayed for a few seconds (the exact time varies depending on the length of each posting) after which they gradually fade into the background. In moments of silence, users' circles shrink back to their original size as a colored dot on the screen. This approach mimics real life conversations where, at any given time, the focus is on the words said by the person who spoke last and, progressively, those words dissipate in the midst of the evolving conversation.

Color also plays a key role in communicating one's overall level of activity. Participants' circles appear bright when they post messages and the color progressively fades out in moments of silence. Active users appear as bright circles on the screen and those who have been idle appear as faded dots. As mentioned earlier, one of the benefits of graphical chats is that participants can see the full extent of the audience, unlike in text-based ones, where the listeners are invisible. Yet the appearance of a crowded, avatar-filled room can be misleading if most of those depicted are not contributing (and may, in reality, be far from their computers). By fading the circles of non-active participants, *Chat Circles* can indicate both the overall number of connected users and the actual level of presence and activity. Hence, the rendering of social presence gets tied to the level of activity of each participant.

This approach aims at revealing the level of activity, or lack thereof, of each participant. It differs from text-based environments in that presence is continuous. In the tradition of avatar interfaces, presence in *Chat Circles* is constant but the level of participation is also made clear through the graphics - in contrast with current avatar systems where presence is static. "Lurkers" - users that "listen" to conversations instead of actively contributing - for example, appear as faded dots on the screen.

The use of these dynamic graphics creates a sequence of bright splashes of colors and fading circles in a pulsating rhythm that reflects the turn-taking of regular conversations.

Conversational Groupings

> What attracts people most, in sum, is other people. Many urban spaces are being designed as though the opposite were true...
>
> *- William H. Whyte*

Chats often have numerous rooms where users can engage in conversation with different people. One of the results of such arrangement is that groups of people end up secluded from each other; one can't be in more than one chat room at a time unless one logs in to the system multiple times and creates various personas. We believe that opening up the various isolated rooms adds to the users' social experience of the chatroom at the same time that it allows for an overall view of the activity in the system at all times. For that reason, there are no "rooms within rooms" in our system. Once a user logs in to *Chat Circles*, he or she sees all the other participants in the entire system. Nevertheless, the user needs to be physically close to other participants to be able to "listen" to (i.e. to read) their conversation. Each person in the system has a "hearing range" that allows him or her to engage in conversation only with people who are sufficiently close by. The other users, the ones outside the person's hearing range, maintain their locations and colors but are rendered differently - their circles appear as outlined circles instead of being fully colored and their messages are not displayed [fig 3].

The physical proximity metaphor makes use of the ability we all have of peripherally and selectively sensing activity around us. Whenever one attends a social gathering, such as a party for example, he or she immediately perceives the amount of people present and the level of activity in the environment. Even though the person might not be able to listen to every single conversation in the room, activity as a whole is accessed at all times. The same is true in *Chat Circles* for users are always aware of the number of people logged onto the system as well as the activity level within each cluster of conversation. Users see the physical movement and the fading patterns of other participants in the system therefore getting a greater awareness of the ebb and flow of discussions. The system makes it very easy to spot heated discussions - even when a user is not participating in one - because of the burst of "bubbles" on the screen as opposed to less active conversations where not much visual activity takes place.

In chat systems there are usually numerous conversations occurring at the same time on the screen, a phenomenon that makes following discussion an exercise in winnowing through non-sequiturs. Simply having a graphical interface

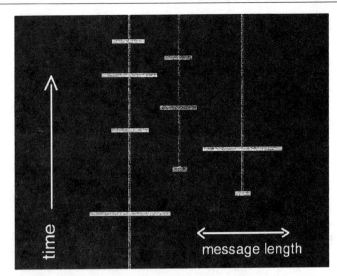

Figure 4. Conversational "threads" represent each one of the users' history during a chat session.

does not solve the problem - people can still respond to statements scattered across the screen without performing any action indicating which remarks they are addressing. We believe that the physical proximity metaphor we are implementing will encourage conversational threads to become spatially localized. This changes the way in which the spatial dimension of the screen has been treated in chat systems so far. By adding a new layer of meaning to the location of users on the screen, we cause their position to filter out information from the outside at the same time that it amplifies the contents of the "readable" material.

By tearing down the virtual walls of current chat systems and by making spatial location meaningful, *Chat Circles* reveals activity clusters and conversation patterns in users' interactions. Users are able to have two different and simultaneous readings of the system: their immediate surroundings - the conversation they are currently involved in - and the overall reading of the state of the entire system. We hope that this kind of multilevel interpretation of the chat space allowed in the *Chat Circles* interface will help provide a more contextualized experience of social presence online.

History

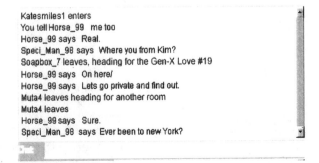

Figure 5. Regular chatroom log.

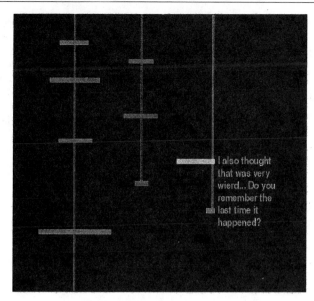

Figure 6. Access to individual postings happens through mouse-over.

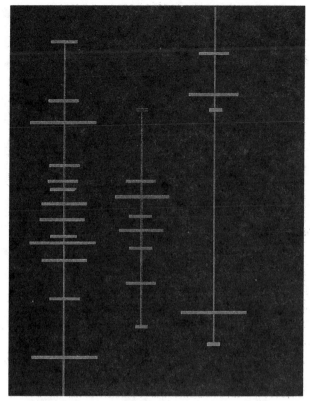

Figure 7. Patterns of activity such as "lurking" become self-evident.

Chatroom conversations tend to be thought of as remarkably ephemeral. Part of this sense of impermanence has to do with the synchronous nature of the interaction itself. In that respect, communication in chatrooms is fundamentally different from the kind of communication that happens, say, in newsgroup discussions. The latter consists mostly of well though out, complete statements written by users prior to their posting. In chatrooms, however, the interaction is not thought out in advance and spontaneity permeates the conversation. Just like in face-to-face conversation, there is no archiving practice in effect; chats happen and then dissipate.

This need not be so. Like other kinds of computer-mediated communication, online chats are intrinsically recordable. The way we choose to record and present the interaction that takes place in chatrooms makes all the difference in terms of readability and social impact. Chat logs read much like unedited transcripts of speech; they do not aid users in understanding the underlying patterns of activity and communication within specific conversations. Once again, all we are given are the black letters on a white background, an arrangement that does not convey any of the most elementary patterns of the social interaction they ought to represent [fig 5].

Following one of the maxims of design, we believe that here too form should follow function. That is why we propose a visualization of the chat archive. Pursuing the same approach we took for the conversational interface, history in *Chat Circles* also springs out of a concern for using graphics to convey identity as well as to reveal social patterns of interaction. The abstract graphics of *Chat Circles* lend themselves to creating a visual archive that is self-documenting in its highlighting of salient events. With that in mind, we have developed Conversation Landscape, an interface to visualize the conversational archive of online chats.

Conversation Landscape can be thought of as a two-dimensional (2D) model of the conversation, with the y axis representing time. Just like in the conversational interface, each user here is represented by a different color (users keep the same colors they had during the conversation for graphical consistency). The temporal sequence results in colored threads on the screen that, when viewed together, reveal the interaction patterns within a conversation. Each participant's thread displays individual postings as horizontal bars crossing the vertical time line [fig 4].

Because we make use of the time axis to display postings, we are able to create a much more faithful rendition of the interaction between users than would be possible through a regular log file. In this archival interface, any horizontal slice of the Conversation Landscape represents a particular moment in the conversation.

Single postings can be accessed on the history threads through a mouse-over effect. When the mouse rolls over one of the horizontal bars, the latter becomes highlighted and the corresponding text appears to the right of that particular bar [fig 6]. This provides a fast and intuitive way of browsing through the specific contents of each posting of the archived conversation.

One of the most innovative aspects of the Conversation Landscape is that, when taken as a whole, the threads instantly reveal the interaction patterns of the conversation. Clusters of activity become self-evident as do periods of silence or pause [fig 7]. With every user's archive displayed

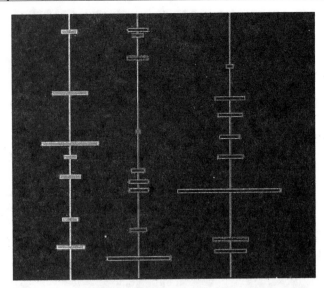

Figure 8. Threads (on the right) showing messages that were posted outside the user's hearing range.

on the screen, it is also very easy to spot inactive users as well as people who tend to dominate conversations. Because threads are spatially displayed according to time, logins and logouts are readily perceived as such. Consequently, the interface allows for a visualization of both group and individual patterns at the same time as it creates, by its mere shape and colors, a snapshot of an entire conversation in one image [fig 9].

Another issue brought forth by the archival interface is that of privacy. Because *Chat Circles* records all the conversations on the screen, it also makes data available about each user's interaction during a chat session. Information such as who the user was interacting with at any given point in a conversation is made public but this might not be desirable at all times.

The visualization of history in Conversation Landscape also takes into account user movement on the screen as well as the "selective" patterns created by the hearing range feature of the conversational interface. Even though all users' threads are continuously displayed on the screen, one's individual interaction history is made clear by the way in which postings get rendered. If a posting occurs within the user's hearing range it appears as a solid horizontal bar, however if a posting occurs outside the user's hearing range, it gets displayed as an outlined horizontal bar. This graphical convention follows the same design principle found in the chatting interface of *Chat Circles* [fig 8].

Because of the ability to move, participants can easily get in or out of each other's hearing range creating interesting patterns of interaction; this can be especially hard to visualize because it calls for the tracking of individual histories within a very fluid system. Our approach to showing these individual interactions follows the same concept found in the conversational interface of nesting the individual data within group data. The 'solid' portions on other users' threads correspond to the time during which these users

were within the hearing range of the particular person whose history we are looking at - the remaining portions of the other users' threads fade into the background. This way we can very quickly understand who was talking to whom at any point of the conversation. These readings of the archive that are based on a single user's point of view present us with unique imprints of both the movement and the hearing range aspects of the system. This is a way to make individual information salient while still in the context of the entire system.

Aesthetics

A simple arrow concentrates more efficiently on pointing than does a realistically drawn Victorian hand with fingernails, sleeve, cuff, and buttons. The arrow is also more nearly a full-time symbol and therefore invites the beholder to treat it as a statement rather than a piece of the practical world

- Rudolf Arnheim

Chat Circles relies on basic, abstract shapes to convey social presence and activity. We are working with circles and other simple geometric elements for several reasons. Our interest in abstract visual representations of conversation has to do with both what they do and do not convey. By rendering the conversation as a visual entity, we hope to give people a better sense of many of the social patterns that are difficult to perceive in a computer-mediated discussion. Our goal is to clarify and highlight what is already there; we wish to avoid introducing spurious and potentially misleading information, as it is all too easy to do with figurative representations. The interface is minimalist in the sense that every aspect of graphical use relates to a function within the system; there is no decorative use of graphics.

Furthermore, the graphical appearance of the interface becomes highly meaningful in the way it affects the tone and feel of social interactions. Users tend to classify different virtual spaces somewhat in the same manner they classify physical ones: depending on the attributes and feel of the environment, different sets of behavior are deployed.

In developing *Chat Circles* we felt the need to break away from the relative rigidity of textual environments for conversations and, in doing so, we were faced with the question of how to create an aesthetically inviting space for users to interact. The use of abstract graphics allowed us to articulate the interface metaphors of hearing range and history without the intrusion of the problem of likeness of representation. Finally, the dynamic quality of the graphics added a more rhythmic and organic feel to the interface.

Current status: implementation and user feedback

Chat Circles is implemented in Java and runs over the World Wide Web on browsers that support Java 1.1. The choice of developing this system as a Java applet complies with our original goal of making the software highly accessible to users. Participants can choose to view their conversation either through the 'chat' mode, where each person is

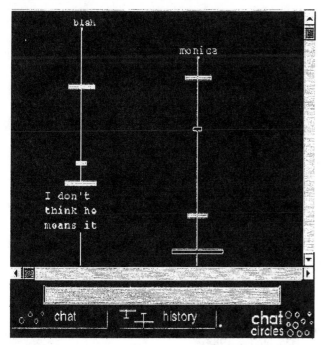

Figure 9. Screenshot of the history mode in a *Chat Circles* session showing six users.

represented by a circle, or through the 'history' mode. Performance in *Chat Circles* is still not as fast as we would like it to be, especially over a slow connection.

Several students used the system in informal tests of a preliminary version of the software. For the most part, the feedback has been positive. The hearing range feature made people curious of what other users were saying and the growing and shrinking circles outside one's hearing range added a pleasant rhythm to the interface. The use of color as an identifier seemed to have worked well and no users had trouble identifying others on the screen - finding oneself on the screen was not a problem either.

The history panel proved to be helpful to users trying to catch up with the recent additions to the conversation they were involved in. Users found it easy to understand which messages had been posted inside and outside their hearing ranges. Nevertheless, one of the observations made by some of the users was that it was difficult to understand how the moving circles relate to the speakers' threads on the history panel. Because the archival threads capture the distinction between messages inside and outside the hearing range but do not show the way in which circles moved on the screen, the relationship between the two modes of the interface is not immediately clear. We hope to make this relationship clearer by experimenting with a 3-dimensional model for the history panel. Users also expressed interest in the history mode as a means to revisit past online interactions.

CONCLUSION & FUTURE WORK

We have presented an overview of *Chat Circles*, an abstract graphical interface for synchronous conversation. One of

the main research questions in this work refers to the development of a graphical interface that creates a richer environment for online discussions. Unlike existing graphical chatroom environments, *Chat Circles* does not make use of avatars. Instead, it provides graphical support of social cues such as turn-taking and activity level that help make online conversation a more transparent medium for social cues present in real interactions.

The next stage in this work is to build up from the fundamental UI so as to provide users with more expressive capabilities.

In the conversational interface, we hope to demarcate different parts of the background in order to allow for distinct modes of conversation. This way, the same screen will support, conversations that are being recorded for archival purposes as well as conversations that won't bear any records at all. We believe that this delimitation of differing sections of the background will happen through the discriminate use of color.

We want to implement a three-dimensional (3D) version of the archival interface so that location as well as time and hearing range can be visualized simultaneously. Depending on the viewpoint used to render this 3D space, one will be able to see different patterns in the conversation. By capturing users' moving locations on the screen, this new version of the Conversation Landscape will generate interesting "weaving" patterns as users rearrange their circles around different parts of the conversational interface. Users will be able to zoom in or out of the 3D model. Zooming in will allow for a closer look at individual postings whereas zooming out will allow for immediate reading of both the length of the conversation as well as the distinct clusters of activity.

We are considering adding a content-based notification system to *Chat Circles*. This feature will operate much in the mode of the "cocktail party effect" - the ability to focus one's listening attention on a single talker among a cacophony of conversations and background noise [2]. Here, a person's attention is automatically geared towards a conversation because of some keyword such as the person's name. Keywords that are of interest to the user will come into focus as they appear on the screen, even if they happen to be located outside the hearing range of the user. This will further enforce the openness of the conversational interface in the sense that people will be able to "overhear" words coming from other locations on the screen.

Our system is nearly at the stage when we will begin formal user testing. As with any attempt to innovate the application of UIs, our approach to the interface design in *Chat Circles* raises several questions about the motivations for and consequences of its use. One of the main questions we hope to tackle is how location patterns will develop in a graphical chatroom environment that does not make use of avatars. Studies on how people move and choose to place themselves in urban spaces [10] show that, there are reasons for the patterns - no matter how awkward they may seem - that develop in any public physical location. Is the same conclusion possible on a location-meaningful online system? It would be interesting to keep track of the spatial distribution of people on the screen over time to understand, for example, if people prefer corner spaces as opposed to the center of the screen and, if so, why that is the case. Another interesting question is whether cultural differences in turn-taking styles will emerge in the archival interface.

ACKNOWLEDGMENTS

Foremost, we would like to thank Rodrigo Leroux, Matthew Lee and Grace Lee for their great work in the deployment of the second version of *Chat Circles*. Our many thanks to Natalia Marmasse - for the help and inspiration - and Karrie Karahalios for the discussions about the project. We also thank the Digital Life and Things That Think consortia of the MIT Media Laboratory for their support of this work.

REFERENCES

1. Arnheim, Rudolf. Visual Thinking. CA: University of California Press, 1969.

2. Arons, Barry. A Review of The Cocktail Party Effect. *Journal of the American Voice I/O Society, Vol. 12, July 1992.*

3. Donath, Judith; Karahalios, Karrie; and Viegas, Fernanda. Visualizing Conversations. In *Proceedings of the 32nd Hawaii International Conference on Systems*, 1998.

4. David Kurlander, Tim Skelly and David Salesin. Comic Chat. In *Proceedings of the SIGGRAPH*, 1996.

5. Reid, Elizabeth. Electropolis: Communication and Community on Internet Relay Chat. Thesis, Dept. of History, University of Melbourne, 1991.

6. Rosenberger, Tara M., and Smith, Brian K. Fugue: A Conversational Interface that Supports Turn-Taking Coordination. In *Proceedings of the 32nd Hawaii International Conference on Systems*, 1998.

7. Saville-Troike, Muriel. The Ethnography of Communication. 2nd Edition. New York, NY:Basil Blackwell, 1982.

8. Suler, John. The Psychology of Avatars and Graphical Space in Multimedia Chat Communities. 1996. http://www1.rider.edu/~Suler/psycyber/psyav.html

9. Turkle, Sherry. Life on the Screen: Identity in the Age of the Internet. New York, NY: Simon & Schuster, 1995.

10. Whyte, William H. City: Rediscovering the Center. NY: Doubleday, 1988.

11. Zebrowitz, Leslie A. Reading Faces: Windows to the Soul? Boulder, CO: Westview Press, 1997.

12. http://www.thepalace.com/

13. Zakon, Robert H'obbes. Hobbes' Internet Timeline v3.3. http://info.isoc.org/guest/zakon/Internet/History/HIT.html

Social, Individual & Technological Issues for Groupware Calendar Systems

Leysia Palen[1]
Department of Computer Science
University of Colorado, Boulder
ECOT 717, Campus Box 430
Boulder, CO 80309-0430 USA
palen@cs.colorado.edu

ABSTRACT

Designing and deploying groupware is difficult. Groupware evaluation and design are often approached from a single perspective, with a technologically-, individually-, or socially-centered focus. A study of Groupware Calendar Systems (GCSs) highlights the need for a synthesis of these multiple perspectives to fully understand the adoption challenges these systems face. First, GCSs often replace existing calendar artifacts, which can impact users' calendaring habits and in turn influence technology adoption decisions. Second, electronic calendars have the potential to easily share contextualized information publicly over the computer network, creating opportunities for peer judgment about time allocation and raising concerns about privacy regulation. However, this situation may also support coordination by allowing others to make useful inferences about one's schedule. Third, the technology and the social environment are in a reciprocal, co-evolutionary relationship: the use context is affected by the constraints and affordances of the technology, and the technology also co-adapts to the environment in important ways. Finally, GCSs, despite being below the horizon of everyday notice, can affect the nature of temporal coordination beyond the expected meeting scheduling practice.

Keywords

Groupware Calendar Systems, ethnography, CSCW, calendars, diaries, time, sociotemporality, meeting scheduling

INTRODUCTION

Groupware offers a challenge to both design and deployment. Intended to support coordination over multiple people, groupware must be useful to single users as well, and have consonance with the norms and practices of its use environment. Unfortunately, groupware applications are frequently masterminded by developers who base a design on their own experience, without testing these designs. Although a *technology-centered* perspective

has fewer up-front costs, it can often yield technology that is not usable nor useful in practice.

The field of human-computer interaction (HCI) arose in reaction to this technology-centered perspective, and has had a positive impact on the quality of individual-user software available today [13]. However, the problem of groupware design continues to elude, even when user-centered design techniques are used [4]. *Individual-centered* approaches have difficulty addressing multiple-user technologies because they cannot be evaluated in a lab.

The field of Computer Supported Cooperative Work (CSCW) has broadened design perspectives still further by addressing the social and organizational contexts of technology use. Examination of work practice, institutional incentive and control structures, the production system of the enterprise, and other aspects of social organization is important because these factors can impact groupware use in unexpected ways. To this end, design may be expanded to include deployment and training issues. However, in an effort to identify and understand these factors, a broad *organization-centered* perspective introduces its own challenges: Turning observations into groupware design implications as well as accounting for technological constraints and individual variance are difficult to do.

Technology-, individual-, or organization-centered perspectives each have their limitations (albeit to varying degrees) when used in isolation to inform groupware design. In an ethnographic study of Groupware Calendar Systems, a synthesis of these perspectives was used to yield a more holistic understanding of groupware technology use to inform design and deployment strategies.

MULTIPLE PERSPECTIVES

Groupware Calendar Systems (GCSs) highlight the need for multiple, convergent perspectives. GCSs appear simple in function, but become complex in execution. Conventional paper calendars support people in idiosyncratic, personally customized ways (Figure 1, arrow 1). GCSs replace conventional calendars, requiring that they be used simultaneously for both personal use *and* social

---

[1] This research was conducted while the author was at the Information & Computer Science Department, University of California, Irvine.

coordination. These dual functions of groupware calendars introduce new challenges and opportunities for interpersonal communication (arrow 2). Additionally, GCSs publicly display the use of "personal" and "company" time, which has implications for both individual users and the function of the system in the business enterprise more broadly. In an effort to make meeting scheduling more efficient, GCSs indirectly affect much more fundamental issues of information sharing and temporal coordination. In this critical position, the social environment and technology co-evolve and co-adapt (arrow 3).

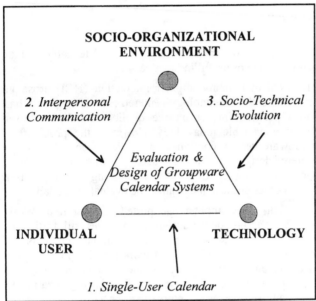

FIGURE 1: **Convergent Perspectives**

GROUPWARE CALENDAR SYSTEMS

What are Groupware Calendar Systems? While specific features vary, GCSs are systems of on-line calendars that can be shared across a network. Individual users keep their own calendar on-line, and allow various degrees of access to other GCS users. Some GCS applications allow for non-person entities to "own" a calendar, such as conference rooms or equipment resources. Collaboration is supported by simple sharing or viewing of other people's calendars, or by sending special meeting invitations through the GCS. The primary site for this research uses a GCS in one of the most open ways possible, where individuals' calendar information is read-accessible to other users by default (an "Open" Model GCS). Other GCSs may reveal only blocks of free and busy times by default (a "Restricted" Model GCS), while still others may reveal no information to other users on the network by default (a "Closed" Model GCS).

GCSs have been available since the late 1970s, making them one of the earliest groupware technologies to emerge. Cited illustratively in discussions of groupware, GCSs are sometimes described in a way that implies simplicity in function, trivialized as generic groupware without the complexities that other collaboration support systems have.

Limitations of Existing Calendar Research

Despite the ubiquity of conventional calendars artifacts and the steady proliferation of electronic calendar systems, relatively little empirical research has been conducted on either conventional paper-based calendars or new electronic calendar technology. Kelley and Chapanis [8] did early empirical work on conventional calendar artifacts to inform the design of the then-emerging electronic, but not networked, calendars. Subsequent studies focused on electronic calendars primarily for individual use [9, 16], although Payne did point out the challenge of the dual nature of networked calendars [16]. Still other studies on electronic calendars emphasize feature design [1,5], although Beard et. al. do address the impacts of particular features on calendar sharing [1].

S.F. Ehrlich [2, 3] was the first to address the social impacts of calendar systems, and insightfully described them as communication devices. Grudin [6] subsequently pointed out important adoption issues around groupware, with meeting scheduling as the focus of these observations. Subsequent work by Grudin and Palen [7] on GCSs identified a set of socio-technical factors that contribute to widespread adoption of groupware, but with less of a focus on the impacts of the calendaring functionality itself. Mosier and Tammaro [12] examined some of the interactions between personal and social use of GCSs in a small, short-term trial. Among other findings, they found that if insufficient use is made of one's calendar by others, maintaining an on-line calendar may not be worthwhile.

THE STUDY

Sun Microsystems has used an internally developed GCS — "Calendar Manager" (CM) — for about a decade, with GCS deployment matching rapid corporate growth from hundreds of employees to over 20,000 today. Although more companies are using GCSs with increased success, Sun is unusual for two reasons. The GCS has been in wide deployment for a long duration (estimates of a 75% deployment rate), and allows for the highest degree of information sharing compared to other commercial GCSs. Specifically, the contents of each user's calendar are readable *by default* by everyone on the internal network. Although employees can customize and change their access settings, over 80% of the users maintain the defaults.

Data were collected through a combination of ethnographic techniques including interviews of multiple members of workgroups selected across the organization (for a total of over 40 subjects). In-office observation was conducted, including some video recording. Subjects' work environments were photographed, and hardcopies of on-line calendars were collected. In cases where subjects also used paper calendars, samples of these were collected as well. Other documents were collected, including orientation training materials, internal web pages on calendar help, and usability "bug" reports. Additionally, a survey was administered to about 3000 employees over an email distribution list, with a 50% response rate. The survey questions were informed by qualitative interview data collected in an early phase of the study. The purpose of the survey was to assess GCS use demographics, and to determine how broadly findings from the interviews applied across the company. In general, qualitative and quantitative data sets were highly consistent.

SINGLE-USER DEMANDS (ARROW 1)

The activities of calendaring and scheduling underpin the use of GCSs. Designers will sometimes try to use metaphors from the physical world to assist in design. In general, this would seem to be a good heuristic for developing useful systems, but can fall short if superficial assumptions are made, which can be easily done for "everyday" artifacts like calendars.

Diversity in Calendar Form & Function

Consider the diverse formats and locations of paper-based calendar artifacts, and the functions afforded as a result. Kelley and Chapanis found that over 150 unique published calendar formats are available through stationers [8]. Daily, monthly, and weekly formats afford different functions and "views" on information. Other formats include appointment calendars, which use a much finer granularity of time, such as 15 minute units. Reference calendars are intended to keep track of days, and have comparably little additional space to record information. Journal-type calendars devote a whole blank page per day, rendering them all-purpose.

Location of calendar artifacts can signal appropriate access by others. The hallway project planner may be intended to communicate important events and deadlines to workgroup colleagues; everyone may be invited and even encouraged to read it, but perhaps social sanctions limit its content and authorship. Desk organizers naturally have more access restrictions; although, again, the social sanctions may deem it appropriate for an officemate to quickly browse the organizer to find the whereabouts of the owner.

"Calendar Work"

The ways in which people interact with calendars extends beyond the activity of meeting scheduling. I call the range of activities for which calendars are employed "calendar work." In brief, calendars support:

Temporal Orientation. Like clocks, calendars orient us in time. Instead of hours, we refer to them to determine the day, month, and year. We also use them to orient to events in time that are relevant to us but may have no relationship to the Gregorian calendar. For example, relative to the current date, one can figure the number of days left until the summer holiday or to prepare for an upcoming meeting.

Scheduling. Scheduling is a complex task of balancing constraints and priorities. Scheduling appointments involve managing competing requirements, priorities, and constraints, meaning that appointments are often juggled and moved around. Scheduling is less an "optimizing" task and more often a "satisficing" task, where, because of the complexity, the appointment is typically made as soon as the requirements are met.

Tracking. Where scheduling is an activity of advanced planning, "tracking" records events that happen in the present, typically for reference later. Contacts, medical conditions, and spending habits are among the examples of things that are tracked.

Reminding. Calendars assist in reminding users of future events. Users may also include non-appointment information to aid memory, such as recurring anniversary-types dates, and "to-do" lists — information that exists only to remind, in fact. Reminding can be opportunistic as well — when scheduling an event, one may be reminded of some other deadline that occurs on that same day. Or, in an example Payne provides, one event — "appointment with director" may remind a person to do some related but unrecorded task like "press suit this evening" [16, p. 92].

Note Recording/Archiving. Calendar artifacts may be used to record notes (like meeting notes, product information, etc.), often with the intention of associating them with a particular point in time for possible retrieval in the future.

Retrieval & Recall. Temporal association of information can assist in retrieval and recall. Some information may be deliberately recorded in calendars for later retrieval, but retrieval may be opportunistic as well. Several subjects said that they will sometimes look through their calendars to locate the spelling of a name or a lost phone number that they previously recorded.

Reconciling Calendar Needs & Design Affordances

Discussions of technology adoption are often restricted to aggregates of users. Although a broad view of the social organization is important, adoption is ultimately accomplished one user at a time. One of the major hurdles in GCS adoption, then, is a reconciliation of individual calendar demands with the affordances of GCSs for calendar support.

For heavy calendar users, this reconciliation is of particular importance. For those whose calendar work habits extend beyond discrete appointment entries, electronic calendars can be poor substitutes. Finding ways to work-around or relocate supplemental information about meetings and business contacts and to-do-lists, for example, are often part of the decision to participate in a GCS. One of the risks for heavy calendar users is *competition between calendar artifacts*. Attracted to the benefits of the GCS but still needing other kinds of calendar support, some people will attempt to employ multiple calendar artifacts. While this approach can be successful, maintenance of multiple artifacts is rarely without some struggle, and often one calendar artifact loses the battle.

For infrequent or erratic calendar users, the requirements for adoption are different. GCSs must make calendar maintenance simple and attractive to users who are not in the habit of keeping paper calendars.

Discretionary Appeal

Electronic calendars have the potential to hold great appeal [7]. Much of calendar work is repetitive: by their very nature, the time-based representations of calendars are cyclic on daily, weekly, monthly and yearly bases. Computer automation suits some tasks superbly: the ability to perform a single one-time entry for weekly staff meetings, anniversary-type dates, pay-days, for example, is attractive. Additionally, automatic reminders (in the form of email, beeps, and dialogue boxes) generated by these entries are repeatedly cited as helpful; in fact, Sun survey subjects cited "reminders" as the most important CM feature.

Recurring appointment settings and automated reminders represent long strides toward making calendaring appeal to low-use users in particular. Some people are infrequent users because they do not have many appointments to attend; these users do not need to check their calendars frequently to enter appointments, which greatly reduces opportunistic reminding of other appointments.

Increased social coordination is another reason to participate in a GCS, even if users must make tradeoffs in personal calendar support.

INTERPERSONAL COMMUNICATION (ARROW 2)

Groupware Calendar Systems create new opportunities for social coordination. They also introduce opportunities for conflict, and challenge notions of personal privacy and control over information and time, especially openly configured GCSs like Calendar Manager

What are the special characteristics of calendar systems that impact interpersonal communication? On first glance, the primary issues appear to be about information disclosure and the mechanics of meeting scheduling. A closer examination of the function of calendars reveals additional coordination challenges and opportunities.

Artifacts of Temporality

Clocks and calendrical systems make time tangible and meaningful by imposing both natural and artificial boundaries on it — minutes, hours, days, weeks, months, years. In this sense, calendrical systems (like the Gregorian calendar) are themselves artifacts. Paper and electronic calendars contain these time system representations, which allow for the manipulation of time: exchanging one meeting hour for another, allotting time for a task, splicing events in between others. It is time-as-artifact that, in part, makes calendars useful.

Peer Judgment & Inference

However, with open calendar systems like Sun's, information about time use becomes public, creating the opportunity for peer judgment about time allocation. Open calendar systems also create the opportunity to use calendars to coordinate with colleagues by allowing them to make inferences about the *quality* of the time allocation. Employees can make inferences about others' workload not only by the numbers of appointments in their calendars, but also by the nature of the appointments. This issue is addressed in more depth later in the paper.

Interpersonal Boundary Management

Unpacking Privacy

Privacy regulation is central to the adoption of an open model GCS. Privacy is a broad term, often serving as a catch-all for more subtle meanings of disclosure and control. With respect to the domain of networked calendars, five primary privacy concerns are at issue. These privacy concerns can be further organized by matters of information- and time-based content.

Privacy Concerns about Information-Based Content:

- *Personal Privacy of Information:* Information considered totally innocuous to some is considered personally private to others (medical appointments are a good example of this).

- *Social Sensitivity of Information:* Information that could have implications for other people, but is not personally private to the calendar owner. A frequently cited example is the internal job interview, where the interviewer may unwittingly include the entry in her calendar making it possible for the interviewee's colleagues to see.

- *Company Security of Information:* Information that is proprietary or reveals undisclosed business strategy (via appointments with other companies, for example).

Privacy Concerns about Time-Based Content:

- *Personal Privacy of Time Allocation:* Concern about judgments made about one's use or allocation of time.

- *Control of Access to Time:* For some, open calendars relinquishes control of their schedules to others; some are more specifically concerned about relinquishing control of access to the self as represented by their schedule.

Managing Privacy

Ways of managing calendar privacy while participating in the open calendar system at Sun involve a combination of techniques utilizing built-in technical mechanisms and strategic uses of information.

Access Settings. Globally across the calendar or locally for each appointment, users can restrict what others see by explicitly using privacy settings. Options include displaying all appointment details, only free/busy times, or nothing at all. Using privacy settings explicitly controls interpersonal boundaries.

Cryptic & Context-Sensitive Entries. This technique allows appointments to be left readable while still protecting one's privacy. Calendar owners both deliberately and inadvertently control access by making entries context-sensitive, such that only restricted audiences understand the meaning. Listing one's daughter's name at 2pm, for example, sufficiently reminds the calendar owner to pick up his child from school, but also signals to immediate group members (who presumably know the child's name) that the appointment probably cannot be moved, and that their colleague intends to return shortly. The entry looks like a business appointment to everyone else.

Omissions. Users may simply omit appointments on their networked calendar that are private, recording them elsewhere or memorizing them. A foolproof way to control sensitive information, the interpersonal boundary unambiguously delimits personal information space.

Scheduling Defensively. Scheduling work time in calendars allows people to participate in the GCS while imparting a feeling of control over time. Time can be protected even further by using a fake appointment to disguise work time, and minimize the possibility of being asked to attend a meeting instead. However, at Sun, this practice is employed judiciously. Expectation by others to cooperate within the groupware system caps excessive blocking out of work time, as does one's own investment in making the calendar accurate enough to act as one's proxy.

Calendar Reciprocity

Reciprocity plays a critical role in GCS use. People are strongly influenced by what others are doing around them: for most of Sun, calendar openness is reinforced every time someone browses another's calendar. Those who have different access settings — either more restrictive or less restrictive — often have immediate colleagues with similar access configurations. Willingness to keep a calendar open is in large part based on the security of knowing that everyone else keeps their calendars open, too. Restricted or closed calendars can challenge norms and expectations, and be perceived as unwillingness to reciprocate the trust others offer. In reaction, calendar openness may give way to closedness. Over time, pockets of users in the same social network develop their own norms. Some employees do not appear to realize that their groups handle calendars differently than the company-wide norm of open calendars, suggesting that some groups have long-entrenched local norms around calendar use.

Meeting Arranging

Many GCSs are touted as applications that can drastically improve the efficiency of meeting scheduling. CM at Sun is used as part of the meeting scheduling negotiation: 88% of survey respondents reported using others' calendars for the purposes of meeting arranging. However, CM is used for more than meeting scheduling: almost 70% of respondents also report reading calendars to locate a colleague. In addition to these survey responses, qualitative data indicates that shared calendars serve a variety of functions.

"Beyond Meeting Arranging"

Many Sun employees cannot imagine using GCSs where only free and busy times are visible, as other GCSs are designed. When given the choice, Sun employees will choose to view calendars so that the content details can be read, instead of viewing only the free/busy times.

With open calendars, a meeting arranger can assess the quality of what appears to be free time in someone's calendar. Examining what immediately precedes and follows a free hour can give some indication of what a colleague might be doing at that time. Does the following meeting require preparation? Is the preceding meeting being held across town, requiring the employee to travel during traffic hours? Does the employee have a big deadline that will preclude any meetings that day? Employees frequently make these kind of determinations about others' schedules, and welcome others to do the same in the hopes of reduced interruption and negotiation overall.

At Sun, the GCS also functions as a distributed information system, around which people organize and synchronize their work.

Information Access

Distributed calendar information is used in several ways, reviewed here in brief:

Locating Someone & Assessing Availability. Some employees will even provide supplemental information, including contact information specifically for others to see.

Meeting Verification. An employee will sometimes browse colleagues' calendars to confirm meeting agreement.

Information Retrieval. Colleagues' calendars can also be used as resources for finding information like the location of meetings that went unrecorded in one's own calendar.

Organizational Learning. Open GCSs act as an opportunistically-created repository for an organization's "memory." A great deal can be inferred about the organization simply by reading calendars.

Synchronization. Employees can synchronize some aspects of their work by perusing calendars. For example, an employee who typically works at home sees upcoming deadlines and meetings that signal when to come to the office. "Schedule inheritance" is when actions or deadlines in one person's schedule are adopted by co-workers and put in their own schedules. The interdependency of schedules is made more explicit with open calendars, and is utilized to support coordination.

SOCIO-TECHNICAL EVOLUTION (ARROW 3)

GCSs are often below the horizon-of-notice for decision makers, and are also taken-for-granted by the users themselves. Because GCSs support an important part of business activity — meetings — and have the potential to support coordination beyond meeting scheduling, their technological constraints can affect use on a large scale. Likewise, the viability of such a technology depends on reasonable consonance with the organizational culture.

Orlikowski's "Duality of Technology" theory describes the process of co-evolution and institutionalization of technology and the behaviors around it. Orlikowski builds upon Gidden's theory of structuration, a social process of "reciprocal interaction of human actors and structural features of organizations" [14, p. 404]. Structural features include rules, procedures, norms — the intangible components of organizations. Employment of structural properties by human agents through the production of work institutionalizes the structures over time, continuing to legitimate their existence and the human agents employing them. For Orlikowski, technology is another structural property of organizations. "Technology is created and changed by human action, yet it is also used by humans to accomplish some action": this describes the duality of technology [14, p. 405].

Development Environment

Decisions about technology's early design and development arise out of one social context, such that the design choices are understood and resonate with the developers-as-users. Calendar Manager, now a commercial application, was developed in-house for Sun's internal use.

The early institutional properties of Sun provided a high degree of freedom for technology development by individual employees: operating under a code of "openness" and the need to develop useful functionality for a new platform, an early calendar program was developed that helped set the direction for calendar sharing.

In such an environment, an open calendar model — where calendars are read accessible — was consistent with the early culture. Company growth did put new demands on its own technology, and also created a need to organize its available technology for commercial release. Calendar Manager was appropriated by the production system of the company for commercial value, while at the same time enmeshing itself in day-to-day business operations.

Impacts of Early Design Choices

Remarkably, the open calendar environment survived and deployment levels were sustained even as the company rapidly grew to over 20,000 people. Although Sun is a high-tech environment that has far fewer technological obstacles to overcome than other industries and institutions, it is no longer the small UNIX shop of a decade ago. Sun today is a large corporation with production functions that require a variety of job positions, with many new employees having no previous UNIX experience.

Today, survey data indicates that 81% of users maintain the defaults for their access settings, leaving their calendars readable for the "world" of Sun. This practice can be explained by two factors: 1) user passivity for customizing default settings — as has long been established in HCI research [10] — and 2) a process of institutionalization of the technology [14]. Consider the very similar results of Microsoft's use of Schedule+ (when studied in 1994): 80% of GCS users maintain their access default settings — except their defaults display only free/busy availability (a "restricted" model GCS)! Interestingly, the GCS in each company can be user-configured to work very much like the other, but are not because the majority of users maintain the defaults.

Social Impacts on Evolving Design

New conditions of the changing environment put restrictions on what the technology could do, which had direct impacts on the technology design. A fourth access setting — the "executable" setting that executed system commands at appointed times as entered in the calendar — was removed. As the company grew and becoming more heterogeneous with respect to job positions, the executable setting was seen as a risk to computer security and — by virtue of the business of Sun — was therefore seen as a risk to *company* security. More recently, a design proposal by engineers to limit the range of privacy access settings in an new incarnation of CM was met with user disapproval, and the full range of controls were reinstituted. Even though most employees do not use the specific controls proposed for removal, retaining the ability to technologically control access was important to them. Also, new features were gradually added. Time zone compatibility became more important as Sun expanded geographically, for example.

Deployment, Institutionalization & Niche-Creation

Catalyzed by distribution of the technology to specific employees — administrative assistants — who found the technology useful in conducting their jobs, awareness of Calendar Manager spread throughout the company laterally and from the bottom-up. Mechanics of structuration appeared in iterative design feature inclusion and exclusion. Structuration also appeared in language, where users would invoke the name of the calendar read feature in everyday language as a directive to others — "Browse me." However, the presence of another scheduling system with its own institutional momentum served to keep the room reservation function beyond the scope of Calendar Manager.

CONVERGENT PERSPECTIVES

I have examined the situated use of a GCS addressing the demands of single-users on calendaring technology (both paper-based and electronic), interpersonal communication and coordination over the medium of calendars, and the co-evolution and institutionalization of the technology and the organizational environment.

A final examination of the situated use of a GCS also requires consideration of the *interaction* between these perspectives. This final convergence of perspectives reveals how institutionally sanctioned "temporal autonomy" affects GCS interpersonal communication; how technological infrastructure helps regulate privacy; and how a combination of conditions result in primarily group-wise interactions over Calendar Manager, despite its highly public configuration.

Institutional Value: Temporal Coordination

Most Sun employees enjoy temporal autonomy, possessing a good deal of control over their work time. The work ethic stresses personal responsibility for quality and completion of work, with comparatively little attention to when the work is actually performed. Although expectations vary between groups, many employees arrive at and depart from work later than conventional business hours, or keep schedules that vary daily. Telecommuting is common, and employees sometimes attend to personal appointments during the work day.

These flexible schedules make requirements for coordination with colleagues different than in workplaces with conventional business hours. With conventional business hours, people can reliably predict when colleagues will be in their offices; greater concurrence of working hours increases opportunities to interact with colleagues. With flexible schedules, the window of time in a day or week that colleagues are co-present may be quite narrow. Calendar Manager plays an important role in supporting temporal coordination by communicating employee availability, enabling people to plan their interactions with others and reduce dependence on chance interactions. In this way, CM substitutes for and elaborates on traditional office in/out boards (and few in/out boards exist at Sun).

These demands for temporal coordination help propel adoption, which is supported by a two-way peer pressure delivery. In return for a great deal of temporal autonomy, employees must be responsible for conveying their availability to their colleagues: this is a source of peer pressure to individual employees to keep a calendar on-line. Likewise, by keeping a calendar on-line, colleagues are expected to refer to employees' calendars to reduce interruptions to calendar owners. Reciprocal peer pressure sustains GCS use.

Technology Constraints Affect Social Interaction

Technological constraints indirectly regulate privacy to further enable the widespread practice of "world" readable calendars at Sun. The technological infrastructure that supports CM limits easy calendar access. An early design decision that suited a much smaller Sun scales up in way that requires users to be quite deliberate about specifying the calendars they browse — calendars cannot be "surfed" like Web pages. Connection to remotes calendars use the convention user@hostname. Another example of structuration, this design decision was influenced by the early socio-technical environment. Although there are reasons to consider this design legacy problematic, I believe that it has instead helped continue to make open calendars viable in the face of rapid corporate growth. In the early days, when Sun was a mere fraction of today's size, hostnames could be almost as easily remembered as usernames. Today's 20,000 employees have at least one workstation each: therefore, for every user name specified, an equally unique machine hostname must be specified to locate the calendar. Even though an on-line company rolodex contains all the necessary information to locate a calendar, doing so requires a few extra steps. Although certainly no obstacle to the persistent, these additional steps have been repeatedly noted by informants as requiring just enough work to reduce rampant browsing.

Group-wise Interactions

In addition to deliberate privacy regulation strategies, socio-technical conditions indirectly control privacy in this highly open calendar environment as well. The technological infrastructure, as noted above, restricts calendar "surfing." Calendar reciprocity means that one's immediate colleagues are more likely to share calendars in the same way. Finally, social anonymity helps control access. Although 20,000 people can read one's calendar, only a few people in the company are actually known to everyone. Employee names are needed to retrieve calendar addresses to in turn read calendars. Privacy breakdowns certainly do occur, but far less than one might expect. Additional treatment of these issues are available in [15].

Despite being "world" readable, Sun's on-line calendars are used for mostly group-wise interactions. In fact, keeping calendars world readable supports group interaction. Open calendars allows group membership boundaries to be fluid, without vigilant maintenance of access lists.

GROUPWARE DESIGN & DEPLOYMENT IMPLICATIONS

Designing for Individual Support

Goodness of Fit with Work Practice. GCSs bring into relief individual user demands even for multiple-user support applications. With expectations for integration into fundamental aspects of work practice, groupware technologies need to pay attention to the functions that physical analogues perform.

Adoption & Discretionary Appeal. Additionally, discretionary appeal is important for adoption by satisfying individual users to sustain them long enough until a

critical mass of users is achieved. Once achieved, groupware benefits commence [7, 11].

However, a potential tradeoff exists between maximizing individual support and privacy regulation in a groupware system. The more GCSs support personal work, the greater the chance that openness might be threatened. Imagine if Calendar Manager — which supports some calendar work very well, and others not at all — was more closely modeled after a paper organizer: would open sharedness be nearly as widespread or successful?

Building "Group"ware

The seemingly small design decisions and features have largest impact on groupware functionality. Access setting defaults — possibly accidents of design — constrain the range of possible behaviors around a GCS. Through a combination of user passivity and institutionalization of the technology, particularly for internally developed applications, defaults settings are rarely changed.

"Heavyweight" groupware features have lower importance, and only become useful after the central norms and practices around the groupware have been established. For example, features supporting meeting invitations that are sent from the GCS to one's inbox can be useful, but the nature of their use is determined only after the degree of information sharing is established. Compared to other companies with other GCSs, Sun users prefer to read the details of each others calendars to make informed invitations to meetings; other companies with other systems more likely send hit-or-miss meeting invitations because colleagues cannot see the details of each others' calendars.

Deployment & Socio-Technical Adaptability

Groupware is not one-size-fits-all; groupware design must be adaptable. An overlooked but important design decision that can affect the fundamental model of collaboration are default settings. Companies acquiring GCSs or other groupware must consider the impact of default settings, and make decisions about their configuration upon initial deployment. Software developers have obligations as well. Mackay notes: "A Software manufacturer should also seriously consider the impact of delivering a poorly-conceived set of default values when the first version of the software is shipped. Unlike many features that can be fixed in subsequent updates, decisions that affect individual patterns of use are likely to have long-term effects" [10]. Furthermore, software developers must make it *possible* for companies to modify deployment default settings to suit conditions. A seemingly trivial requirement, many applications cannot be modified for large-scale deployment.

SUMMARY

Calendar Manager (CM) has grown to be a quiet but important part of day-to-day business operations at Sun. Not a high-profile networked application like others in the Sun environment, CM nevertheless sits in a fundamental substrate of social organization — the "sociotemporal order" [18]. In addition to supporting meeting scheduling, CM supports temporal coordination more generally. Early design decisions configured access setting defaults for maximum sharing of calendar information. Over time, the benefits of an open system became clear: in an environment where employees enjoy temporal autonomy, CM fills a need to communicate one's whereabouts and availability. It is this need that stimulates bilateral peer pressure to adopt and use the openly-configured groupware calendar system.

The role of calendar artifacts in work is integral to understanding CM's place in the sociotemporal order. "Calendaring" is a kind of non-digital technology that depends on the artifactual representation of time for its function. Personally- and socially-significant information are contained and made public in calendars. CM is conceived as a system of individuals' distributed calendars; to use the GCS, users must modify their existing calendaring practice to suit the electronic medium. In addition, users must modify their calendaring practice and calendars to suit a public forum — a potential conundrum for things as idiosyncratic and personal as calendars.

Behavioral and technical mechanisms are employed by individual users to delineate privacy boundaries in an environment where their calendars are open to the "world" of the company network. These, together with features and customs of the social environment (like calendar reciprocity and social anonymity) and affordances of the technological infrastructure, influence how people handle their calendars as personal artifacts in a social space. These conditions conceptually constrain the space in which their calendars are truly accessible. It is in this way that CM, with its read-accessible defaults, is viable on such a large scale.

CM has an institutionalized role in the organization studied, where users depend on its function as a distributed information system in support of coordination. Subtle peer and institutional pressure to keep calendars open in support of these benefits creates an environment protective of liberal interpretations of privacy.

ACKNOWLEDGMENTS
I thank Jonathan Grudin, John King, Mark Ackerman, Tom Moran, Ellen Isaacs, Suzanne Schaefer, Ken Anderson, and Ashley Andeen Mastrorilli for their support and contributions to this work. I thank Don Gentner, John Tang, Harry Vertelney, Mike Albers, Ellen Isaacs and Rick Levenson for their sponsorship and assistance at Sun Microsystems. Kent Sullivan and Marshall McClintock of Microsoft provided invaluable assistance with the Microsoft survey. Roy Fielding, Wayne Lutters, Peyman Oreizy and Jonathan Grudin deserve special thanks for their help with this paper. This work was in part funded by NSF grant #IRI-9612355 and an NSF Graduate Fellowship.

REFERENCES
1. Beard, D., Palanlappan, M., Humm, A., Banks, D., Nair, A. & Shan, Y-P. (1990). A Visual Calendar for Scheduling Group Meetings. *Proceedings of the ACM CSCW'90 Conference*, 279-290.

2. Ehrlich, S.F. (1987a). Social and Psychological Factors Influencing the Design of Office Communication Systems. *Proceedings of the ACM CHI+GI'87 Conference*, 323-329.

3. Ehrlich, S.F. (1987b). Strategies for Encouraging Successful Adoption of Office Communication Systems. *ACM Transactions on Office Information Systems* 5(4), 340-357.

4. Francik, E., Rudman, S.E., Cooper, D. Levine, S. (1991). Putting Innovation to Work: Adoption Strategies for Multimedia Communication Systems. *Communications of the ACM* 34(12), 52 (12 pages).

5. Greif, I. (1984). The User Interface of a Personal Calendar Program. In Y. Vassiliou (Ed.) *Human Factors and Interactive Systems: Proc. of the NYU Symposium on User Interfaces '82*. Ablex, 207-222.

6. Grudin, J. (1988). Why CSCW Applications Fail: Problems in the Design and Evaluation of Organizational Interfaces. *Proceedings of ACM CSCW'88 Conference*, 85-93.

7. Grudin, J. & Palen, L. (1995). Why Groupware Succeeds: Discretion or Mandate? *Proc. of European CSCW (ECSCW'95)*, H. Marmolin, Y. Sundblad, K. Schmidt (eds.), Kluwer Academic Publishers, 263-278.

8. Kelley, J.F. & Chapanis, A. (1982). How Professional Persons Keep Their Calendars: Implications for Computerization. *Journal of Occupational Psychology*, 55, 241-256.

9. Kincaid, C., Dupont, P. & Kaye, A. (1985). Electronic Calendars in the Office: An Assessment of User Needs and Current Technology. *ACM Transactions on Office Information Systems* 3(1), 89-102.

10. Mackay, W.E. (1990). Users and Customizable Software: A Co-Adaptive Phenomenon. *Dissertation, Sloan School of Management*. Cambridge, MA, MIT.

11. Markus, M. L. & Connolly, T. (1990). Why CSCW Applications Fail: Problems in the Adoption of Interdependent Work Tools. *Proceedings of the ACM CSCW'90 Conference*, 371-380.

12. Mosier, J.N. & Tammaro, S.G. (1997). When are Group Scheduling Tools Useful? *CSCW: The Journal of Collaborative Computing*, 6, 53-70.

13. Myers, B. (1998). A Brief History of Human-Computer Interaction Technology. *interactions* 5(2), 44-54.

14. Orlikowski, W. (1992). The Duality of Technology: Rethinking the Concept of Technology in Organizations. *Organization Science* 3(3), 398-427.

15. Palen, L. (1998). Calendars on the New Frontier: Challenges of Groupware Technology. *Dissertation, Info. & Computer Science*, Univ. of California, Irvine.

16. Payne, S.J. (1993). Understanding Calendar Use. *Human Computer Interaction* 8(2), 83-100.

17. Schwartz, B. (1968). The Social Psychology of Privacy. *American Journal of Sociology* 73(6), 741-752.

18. Zerubavel, E. (1981). *Hidden Rhythms: Schedules and Calendars in Social Life*. Univ. of Chicago Press.

The Design and Evaluation of
a High-Performance Soft Keyboard

I. Scott MacKenzie
Dept. Computing and Information Science
University of Guelph
Guelph, ON N1G 2W1 Canada
+1 519 824 4120 x8268
smackenzie@acm.org

Shawn X. Zhang
Dept. Computing and Information Science
University of Guelph
Guelph, ON N1G 2W1 Canada
+1 519 824 4120
shawnz@acm.org

ABSTRACT

The design and evaluation of a high performance soft keyboard for mobile systems are described. Using a model to predict the upper-bound text entry rate for soft keyboards, we designed a keyboard layout with a predicted upper-bound entry rate of 58.2 wpm. This is about 35% faster than the predicted rate for a QWERTY layout. We compared our design ("OPTI") with a QWERTY layout in a longitudinal evaluation using five participants and 20 45-minute sessions of text entry. Average entry rates for OPTI increased from 17.0 wpm initially to 44.3 wpm at session 20. The average rates exceeded those for the QWERTY layout after the 10th session (about 4 hours of practice). A regression equation (R^2 = .997) in the form of the power-law of learning predicts that our upper-bound prediction would be reach at about session 50.

Keywords

Soft keyboards, mobile systems, stylus input, pen input, linguistic models, Fitts' law, digraph probabilities

INTRODUCTION

Besides handwriting recognition, one popular method of text input for pen-based mobile systems is through a soft keyboard. Users enter text by tapping on the image of a keyboard on the system's display. Although the QWERTY layout is entrenched for physical keyboards, soft keyboards are easy to implement and modify. So, a reasonable goal is to search for an alternate, perhaps better, layout than the venerable QWERTY. This paper describes the design and evaluation of one such layout, which we call OPTI in reference to our goal of designing an optimal soft keyboard.

Learning Time and the Elusive Crossover Point

A usability issue is learning time. Users who bring desktop computing experience to mobile computing may fare poorly on a non-QWERTY layout — at least initially. Thus, longitudinal empirical testing is important. We want to establish not only a layout's potential for experts, but also the learning time for typical users to meet and exceed entry rates with a QWERTY layout.

In a general sense, we are comparing the viability of a "new technique" against "current practice". We expect lower performance measures for the new technique initially, but these should eventually "crossover", wherein performance with the new technique exceeds that with current practice. This is illustrated in Figure 1.

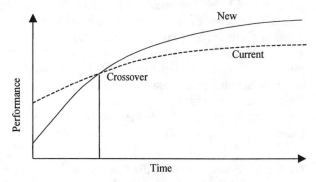

Figure 1. The elusive crossover point

The crossover point may not be achieved, however; and there are a variety of possible explanations. Perhaps the new technique was simply not as good, or perhaps further refinement was needed. It is also possible that the study was terminated before the crossover point could be reached. Two examples are cited below.

McQueen et al. [6] tested six participants in a study on numeric entry with a stylus. Two methods were tested, one using a standard numeric keypad ("current practice") and one using numeric pie menus ("new technique"). In a study involving six participants in 20 20-minute sessions, the crossover point occurred at the 7th session. In another study, Bellman and MacKenzie [1] compared two text-entry techniques for small hand-held devices such as pagers. The technique used five finger-operated buttons to move a cursor and select characters on a small display.

The characters were displayed either in a fixed alphabetic pattern ("current practice") or in a pattern that fluctuated after each entry to minimize the required cursor movement ("new technique"). In a study involving 11 participants in 10 30-minute sessions, a crossover point was not attained. Although a crossover point may have been reached with further practice, a detailed analysis suggested that further refinements to the technique were warranted.

Modeling Text-Entry with Soft Keyboards

Since longitudinal user studies are labor intensive, we developed a prediction model. With pen-based mobile systems, the input channel for text entry is reduced from ten-fingers (as in touch typing) to one finger or pen. This is fortunate because modeling the psychomotor act of stylus tapping is simple compared with touch typing.

Our model has several components, including linguistic data, Fitts' law, a shortest-path model, and a key-repeat-time measure. The model generates a theoretical text entry rate (in words per minute) for any layout of soft keyboard. This allowed us to evaluate alternate designs "on paper" before proceeding to an "empirical" evaluation.

Our linguistic model is for "common English" — the assumed language for text entry. Tables are available giving the 26 letter frequencies and the 26 × 26 letter-pair (digraph) frequencies in common English [5]. Because linguists focus on language, the frequency data do not include spaces — the most common character in text entry tasks. Soukoreff and MacKenzie [7] extended the tables to include space characters. Their data provide 27 letter frequencies and 27 × 27 digraph frequencies. For entering common English, the most common character is space (p = .1863) and the most common digraph is e-space (p = .0457).

We use Fitts' law to predict the time to tap a key given any previous key. We compute the amplitudes (A) for all the 27 × 27 digraph movements in a given keyboard layout, and, for each, compute the movement time (MT) using a Fitts' law model for stylus tapping [3]:

$$MT = \frac{1}{4.9}\log_2\left(\frac{A}{W}+1\right)$$

where W is the width of each key. The mean MT is then computed by summing the 27 × 27 MTs, each weighted by the digraph probability. The mean MT is then converted to text entry speed in words per minute (wpm), assuming five characters per word. The result is an "upper bound" prediction, since it assumes the visual scan time to find a key is zero.

We included two refinements to the model. The first is a "shortest path" model. When a long key (such as key2 in Figure 2) is involved in a key1-key2-key3 sequence, we compute the shortest path among several discrete paths. This is an assumed behavior for experts.

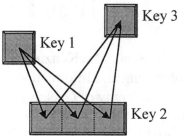

Figure 2. The shortest path model

The second is a key-repeat-time measure. Double letters (e.g., t-t) require no lateral pen movement. They require a repeat tap on the same key. To model this, we conducted a simple experiment. We asked five individuals to make 25 quick taps on the same key on a soft keyboard 10 times. The software captured the entry time between taps. The average key repeat time was 127 ms.

The components of our model were implemented in a spreadsheet; thus, rapid predictions were available for any soft keyboard design. As an example, the QWERTY layout in Figure 3 has a predicted upper-bound entry rate of 43.2 wpm.

Figure 3. A QWERTY soft keyboard layout

DESIGNING A HIGH-PERFORMANCE SOFT KEYBOARD

In addition to the model described above we used the following design rationale:

- The soft keyboard should have no dead space between keys, where no action is assigned.

- The entire keyboard shape should be rectangular to fill in a typical application window.

- There is no limit on how many sizes or shapes can be used. We decided to use only two sizes: square (1 × 1 unit) for alphabet keys and square or rectangular (1 × 2 units) for space keys.

Following substantial trial and error — where each iteration yielded a higher prediction than the previous — we settled on the design in Figure 4, which we call OPTI. The predicted upper-bound text entry rate for OPTI is 58.2 wpm. This is 35% faster than for the QWERTY layout. It is also about 5% faster than our predicted entry rate for a commercial soft keyboard known as *Fitaly*,

Figure 4. The OPTI high-performance soft keyboard

from Textware Solutions (Boston, MA).[1] Many commonly used sequences such as "THE", "WH" "EA", "CK", "LY" or "ING" are tightly located, so the pen travel distance is shorter. The design is nearly symmetrical, making it suitable for either hand. Note that the four space keys are very accessible (about 36% of the digraphs in common English involve the space character).

METHOD

A usability study was undertaken to evaluate the OPTI soft keyboard. Since QWERTY is the most common layout, we included both layouts in the study. Our goal was not just to evaluate the OPTI layout, but to determine its performance relative a QWERTY soft keyboard. We fully expected the QWERTY layout to be better initially — because of users' familiarity with QWERTY — but we wanted to establish the learning trends for both layouts and to determine if and when a crossover point would occur, wherein OPTI would fare better than QWERTY.

Participants

In longitudinal studies, fewer participants are usually engaged but they are tested over a prolonged period of time. In this study, we used five participants. All were university computer science students, four male, one female. All were right handed and used desktop computers on a regular basis. None had regular experience using a pen-based computer. They were recruited from a pool of subjects who participated in other unrelated experiments. Since we are testing a keyboard specifically designed for English, we picked only participants whose first language was English. All were well informed on the time commitment required for the experiment.

Apparatus

The experiment software was developed with Borland C++ 4.0 and ObjectWindows Library (OWL 2.0). The

---

[1] The *Fitaly* keyboard layout fares quite well according to our prediction model. To our knowledge, however, no empirical evaluation of this product has been published. For more information see http://www.twsolutions.com/.

host system was a Packard Bell 486DX-50 PC running Microsoft *Windows for Pen Computing* 1.1. A Wacom *PL-100V* combining an LCD display and digitizing tablet was attached to the system and was the only device used by the participants.

The experiment was conducted in the HCI Lab at the University of Guelph's Dept. of Computing and Information Science. To minimize interference from any other source the lab was completely booked for the experiment. The entire experiment took about four weeks. A special web site was created for information updates and participant scheduling.

Design

The experiment was a 2×20 within-subjects factorial design. The two factors were:

- Keyboard layout {QWERTY, OPTI}
- Session {20 sessions}

Each session lasted about 45 minutes and was divided into two 20-22 minute periods. One of the two layouts was assigned in each half-session period in alternating order from session to session. The order of the conditions was balanced between participants to reduce interactions.

Each half-session contained several blocks of trials. The number of blocks for each half-session period was controlled such that as many blocks as possible were collected within the allotted time. Therefore, in the early sessions, fewer blocks (5 to 6) were administered than in later sessions (9 to 11). A five-minute break was allowed between the two half-sessions.

Each block contained 10 text phrases of about 25 characters each. These 10 phrases were randomly selected from a source file of 70 phrases. Phrases were not repeated within blocks but repeats were allowed from block to block. The phases were chosen to be representative of English and easy to remember (see Figure 5). The sample phrase set was tested for its correlation with common English using the frequency counts in Mayzner and Tresselt's corpus [5]. The result was $r = .9845$ for the single-letter correlation and $r = .9418$ for the digraph correlation.

```
THE INFORMATION SUPER HIGHWAY
THANK YOU FOR YOUR HELP
VIDEO CAMERA WITH ZOOM LENS
THE FOUR SEASONS OF THE YEAR
OUR FAX NUMBER HAS CHANGED
```

Figure 5. Sample phrases used in the experiment (70 phrases in total were used.)

Each participant completed 20 sessions. Sessions were scheduled Mondays through Saturdays, separated by at least two hours but no more than two days. This was to simulate "regular use" of the system while trying to avoid fatigue and accommodating participants' daily schedules.

This was a longitudinal study attempting to practice participants toward expert performance. Data collection included numerous measurements on user input. For each key tapped, the following was collected.

- Given character
- Given character's position (ID on the keyboard)
- User entered character
- User entered character's position. (The four space keys were identified separately.)
- Elapsed time (ms) from previous tap
- Error (1 if the user character was different from the given character; 0 if user character was correct)

Procedure
Each participant was given written instructions explaining the task and the goal of the experiment. They were asked specifically to aim for both entry speed and accuracy. The instructions also stated that if they made more than 10% errors within a phrase (about 3 mistakes) they should slow down on the next phrase to increase accuracy.

As designed, the length of each half-session period was controlled with a timer. Once started the software was self-administered. The entire session was monitored on a separate CRT connected to the system.

Participants were then given the tablet and the stylus. The tablet was tilted off the desk to provide a good viewing angle (about 25°). It was also adjusted to have appropriate contrast and brightness. The overhead lights were turned off to reduce the glare on the tablet's display panel. The height of the desk was 26 inches, a standard height for typing. The desktop could be adjusted by about two inches to allow for different body sizes.

The participants were asked to copy each short phrase by tapping on the soft keyboard. A soft audio feedback "tick" was heard for each character entered. When an error occured a more prominent "click" was heard. The

participants were asked to ignore errors and to carry on with the next correct letter pointed at by the cursor. Typical experiment displays are illustrated in Figure 6 for the OPTI layout and in Figure 7 for the QWERTY layout. The square keys were 1 cm × 1cm.

A plot chart was set up during the experiment to keep the participants motivated. Performance expectations were not explained, however. Instead, participants were constantly reminded to do their best on both layouts.

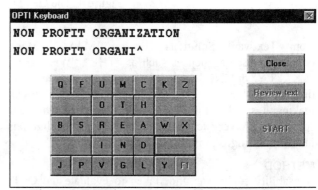

Figure 6. Experiment screen with the OPTI layout

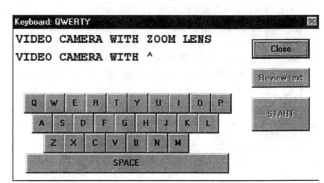

Figure 7. Experiment screen with the QWERTY layout

RESULTS AND DISCUSSION
Text Entry Speed – The Learning Curve
The analysis of variance of text entry speed showed no main effect for keyboard ($F_{1,4} = 0.60$, $p > .05$). There was a significant effect of session ($F_{19,76} = 89.2$, $p < .0001$) and a significant keyboard-by-session interaction ($F_{19,76} = 34.3$, $p < .0001$).

The results above were as expected. That is, the OPTI layout faired poorly initially (17 wpm) in comparison with the QWERTY layout (28 wpm). With practice, however, the OPTI layout eventually out-performed the QWERTY layout (see Figure 8). The crossover occurred

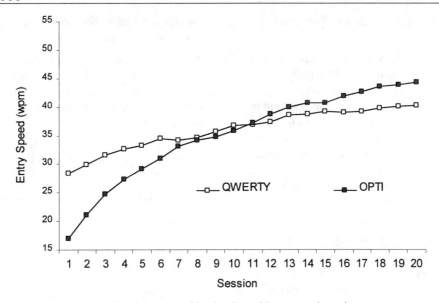

Figure 8. Entry speed by keyboard layout and session

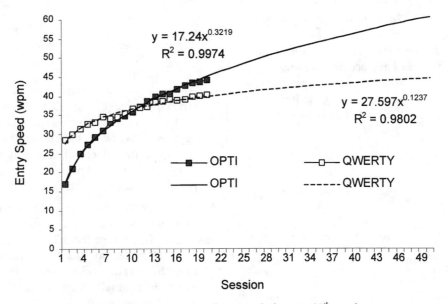

Figure 9. Learning curves and extrapolations to 50th session

at the 10th session. This is just under four hours of practice.

As the experiment progressed performance continued to improve with the OPTI layout, whereas performance showed signs of leveling off with the QWERTY layout. The average text entry rate for the OPTI layout reached nearly 45 wpm by the 20th session and the performance of the QWERTY layout reached about 40 wpm.

For each layout, we derived standard regression models in the form of the power law of learning (e.g., see [2]). The prediction equations and the squared correlation coefficients are illustrated in Figure 9. The high R^2 values

imply that the fitted learning models provide a very good prediction of user behaviour. In both cases over 98% of the variance is accounted for in the models. The somewhat lower R^2 value for the QWERTY layout may be explained as follows. Since our participants were experienced computer users, they were familiar with the QWERTY layout at the start of the study. By no means is the prediction model for the QWERTY layout capturing users' learning behavior from their "initial exposure" to the layout; subjects were "well along" the learning curve. For the OPTI layout, however, users had no prior experience with the layout, and, so, the learning model is more representative of the initial exposure and the learning thereafter.

Although our longitudinal study lasted 20 sessions, the participants had not become "experts" on the OPTI layout by a mere seven hours of use. So, we mathematically extended the learning curves for another 30 sessions to project performance with further practice (see Figure 9). The extrapolation for the QWERTY layout was 44.8 wpm and for the OPTI layout, 60.7 wpm. These two values, representing about 17 hours of practice with each layout, are close to our theoretical upper-bound predictions noted earlier.

Error Rates

An error was recorded when the user-entered character differed from the given character. The error rates ranged from 2.07% for OPTI and 3.21% for QWERTY on the first session to 4.18% for OPTI and 4.84% for QWERTY on the 20th session.

An analysis of variance revealed a significant difference in error rates between the two keyboard designs ($F_{1,4}$ = 12.30, $p < .05$). QWERTY had consistently higher error rates throughout the experiment. There was also a significant increase in error rates over sessions ($F_{19,76}$ = 4.42, $p < .001$). This may have occurred because entry speed increased over sessions, thus participants' input tended to continue into the reaction time following an error. This behaviour has been noted in other text entry studies (e.g., [4]).

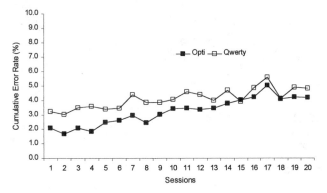

Figure 10. Error rates by layout and session

Use of the Space Keys

Since the space character is so prominent in the text-entry task, it is worth examining participants' behaviour in their use of the four spaces keys in the OPTI layout. For any character-space-character sequence at least one space key would create the shortest path. We call this the "optimal space key". Participants were allowed to use space keys at their discretion; however, the data file distinguished among the four space keys. As learning progressed, a few patterns could emerge, such as a tendency to to use (a) the optimal space key, (b) a randomly-chosen space key, (c)

the closest space key following a character, or (d) a "favorite" space key.

A favorite space is a personal choice, and is not necessarily optimal. It might be the one that stays visible more often than others, for example. Note that for each space entered there was one optimal space key and three non-optimal space keys.[2]

Figure 11 shows a slight increase in participants' use of the optimal space keys, from 38% in session 1 to 47% in session 20.

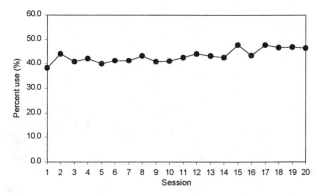

Figure 11. Use of optimal spaces with OPTI over sessions

Although the percentages in Figure 11 are well above random choice (25%), they do not suggest a strong tendency to use the optimal space key. Having four space keys is convenient; but, using the optimal space key requires extra judgement on-the-fly and this is not likely to occur — at least within the confines of the limited practice in the present study.

In re-examining our digraph table, we noted that the ratio of character-only digraphs to digraphs involving spaces is 62:38. This means that 62% of the time, the pen travels from character to character when entering common English. Thus, behavioral improvements or further efforts to optimally accommodate space key usage will have a limited payoff.

CONCLUSIONS

We have described the design and evaluation of a high-performance soft keyboard for mobile systems. Our results indicate that after about four hours of practice users' entry rates will be higher with the OPTI layout than with a QWERTY layout. After about seven hours of practice users achieved a mean entry rate of 44.3 wpm. Our model predicts that entry rates will edge upward, reaching about 58 wpm for expert users.

---

[2]   When the character-space-character pattern is symmetrical there would be two or more space keys that create the same shortest path. In an extreme case with E-Space-E, all the four space keys are equally optimal.

These results are important for designers of pen-based systems supporting text entry. Tapping on a soft keyboard is a viable alternative to handwriting recognition, and the OPTI keyboard layout represents one possible approach to this interesting design problem.

REFERENCES

[1] Bellman, T., and MacKenzie, I. S. A probabilistic character layout strategy for mobile text entry, In *Proceedings of Graphics Interface '98*. Toronto: Canadian Information Processing Society, 1998, pp. 168-176.

[2] Card, S. K., English, W. K., and Burr, B. J. Evaluation of mouse, rate-controlled isometric joystick, step keys, and text keys for text selection on a CRT, *Ergonomics 21* (1978), 601-613.

[3] MacKenzie, I. S., Sellen, A., and Buxton, W. A comparison of input devices in elemental pointing and dragging tasks, In *Proceedings of the CHI '91 Conference on Human Factors in Computing Systems*. New York: ACM, 1991, pp. 161-166.

[4] Matias, E., MacKenzie, I. S., and Buxton, W. One-handed touch typing on a QWERTY keyboard, *Human-Computer Interaction 11* (1996), 1-27.

[5] Maynzer, M. S., and Tresselt, M. E. Table of sigle-letter and digram frequency counts for various word-length and letter-position combinations, *Psychonomic Monograph Supplements 1,2* (1965), 13-32.

[6] McQueen, C., MacKenzie, I. S., and Zhang, S. X. An extended study of numeric entry on pen-based computers, In *Proceedings of Graphics Interface '95*. Toronto: Canadian Information Processing Society, 1995, pp. 215-222.

[7] Soukoreff, W., and MacKenzie, I. S. Theoretical upper and lower bounds on typing speeds using a stylus and keyboard, *Behaviour & Information Technology 14* (1995), 370-379.

Non-Keyboard QWERTY Touch Typing: A Portable Input Interface For The Mobile User

Mikael Goldstein, Robert Book[1], Gunilla Alsiö, Silvia Tessa

Ericsson Radio Systems AB, [1]Now at Logica Svenska AB

Applications Research ERA/T/K

Torshamnsgatan 23, Kista

SE-164 80 Stockholm Sweden

mikael.goldstein@era-t.ericsson.se, bookr@logica.com, erga@swipnet.se, x97-ste@nada.kth.se

ABSTRACT

Using traditional mobile input devices results in decreased effectiveness and efficiency. To improve usability issues a portable Non-Keyboard QWERTY touch-typing paradigm that supports the mobile touch-typing user is presented and investigated. It requires negligible training time. Pressure sensors strapped to the fingertips of gloves detect which finger is depressed. A language model based on lexical and syntactic knowledge transforms the depressed finger stroke sequence into real words and sentences. Different mobile input QWERTY paradigms (miniaturised, floating and Non-Keyboard) have been compared with full-size QWERTY. Among the mobile input paradigms, the Non-Keyboard fared significantly better, both regarding character error rate and subjective ratings.

KEYWORDS

Mobile user, QWERTY, keyboard, touch-typing, text input, stylus input, PDA, portability, Wizard-of-Oz, language model, lexical knowledge, syntactic knowledge.

INTRODUCTION

The physical environment imposes restrictions on the mobile Personal Digital Assistant (PDA) user regarding input as well as feedback. Device size is decreased, compared to a stationary office work place device, in order to enhance portability [13]. A substantial decrease in display size, resulting in increased use of the scroll bar function, and miniaturization of the (character) input facility are regarded as inevitable. Either the "hard" full-size QWERTY keyboard layout is miniaturized, or, is replaced by a "soft" (QWERTY) floating keyboard layout, where stylus taps substitute finger depressions. The result is a performance and productivity decrease. One of the human factor designers' tasks is therefore to improve usability issues of the mobile environment. Such an

environment should match the productivity of the user's conventional office work place as much as possible. By introducing the portable mobile office concept per se, productivity is in fact automatically increased. Tasks that were not possible to accomplish when on the move now lend themselves to accomplishment. Nevertheless, to what extent does the mobile user encounter a performance decrease when performing a task in the mobile environment, as compared to the stationary office? Is there a (significant) *input* performance (productivity) decrease compared to stationary baseline input or not? This research is investigating this crucial issue.

THE CHARACTER INPUT INTERFACE

The typical design of the PDA is a trade-off between portability (size/weight) and usability issues [13]. Several different types of PDAs exist on the market today. The Nokia 9000 Communicator (Figure 1) is a rather heavy (400 grams) cellular phone, incorporating a PDA as well. It has a miniaturized hard keyboard (each letter is mapped on to a hard key) featuring almost full QWERTY layout. The PalmPilot (Figure 1) employs a soft miniaturized floating "full" QWERTY keyboard layout which requires a stylus as input medium, due to the strong miniaturization. This implies one-handed operation, which may decrease character-input speed. However, the benefit is decrease in

Figure 1. Three types of QWERTY keyboard layouts: Full-size, Nokia 9000 miniaturized and PalmPilot miniaturized floating.

size: the PalmPilot is smaller than the Nokia 9000, weight 165 grams, thus supporting portability to a greater extent.

Whereas the full-size QWERTY layout lends itself to touch-typing when inputting text, this skill is difficult to practice when using any of the miniaturized QWERTY layouts. However, since the spatial mapping of the miniaturized QWERTY layouts are almost identical to the full-size QWERTY, valuable knowledge transfer occurs, which is beneficial for the novice user [8]. The width of the keyboard (measured in cm between the Q-P keys) varies between 20 cm (full size QWERTY) and 4,5 cm (PalmPilot miniaturized floating QWERTY) whereas the Q-P distance for the Nokia 9000 keyboard amounts to 13,5 cm.

WORD INPUT SPEED AND CHARACTER ERROR RATE

Word input speed and character error rates are well-known indicators of efficiency and effectiveness in usability studies. Character input speed when touch-typing on a full-size QWERTY keyboard is in the order of 50 words per minute (wpm). Skilled touch typists reach input speed of up to 150 wpm. In order to obtain a higher input speed, chord keyboards (Stenograph or Palantype) are used. Input speed of up to 300 wpm are obtained after three years of practice [7]. Here each character (or word) constitutes a chord involving several simultaneous key depressions. No chords are used when using a QWERTY layout except when generating *capital* letters, the <Shift> key is depressed along with the intended character.

Using the *one-handed* five-finger Chording Glove (no keyboard), users reached an input speed of 16.8 wpm with a character error rate of 17.4% after 11 hours of training [13]. When scanning the literature input speed figures between 10-52 wpm are obtained for various types of "hard" chord keyboards after several hours of training [7].

Word input speed decreases as keyboard size diminishes using fingers as input medium [14]. For novice users input speed was halved (from 20 to 10 wpm) using a miniaturized (Q-P width=8 cm) compared to a full-size QWERTY floating layout (Q-P width=20 cm). Input speed also decreased (by app. 30 per cent) for expert users using the above-mentioned input interfaces. No information is given whether the users had acquired the skill of touch typing or not.

Various types of miniaturized floating keyboard layouts (stylus input), affect word (character) input speed. MacKenzie et al. [8] assessed word input speed of a single short 9-word-long sentence (*the quick brown fox jumped over the lazy dogs*) using stylus as input medium, for novice as well as for experienced users, using different types of miniaturized floating keyboard layouts: QWERTY, ABC, Dvorak, Fitality, Telephone and JustType. Input speed varied between 21-8 wpm. For *novice* users, word input speed of the short sentence was fastest for the familiar QWERTY layout (app. 20 wpm) whereas the less familiar layouts (Fitality, JustTime) fared worst.

A significant productivity decrease, compared to the full-size QWERTY, occurs when downscaling the QWERTY layout. A productivity decrease also occurs for the novice or casual user when the traditional familiar QWERTY spatial layout is abandoned, regardless of if the fingers or a stylus is used as input medium. Less familiar keyboard layouts need ample training time in order to gain efficiency. It is not evident that the typical mobile user will trade a long training time for increased efficiency.

The text material is in some cases based on a very short sentence, generating an extrapolated wpm input speed measure, including errors [8] [14]. This type of task only considers text that you can store in working memory, which is not in accordance with a real-world scenario [16]. What would happen to productivity if text length increases to several hundred words?

Is it possible to design an input paradigm for the mobile user that is devoid of these deficiencies in efficiency, that requires minimal training time to suit the novice user and that supports portability?

KEYBOARD LAYOUT

The Star-Ten-Pound Fuzzy Input Paradigm

The usual typewriter interface uses the QWERTY keyboard layout. When touch-typing with two hands, each hand covers half of the keyboard. The fingers are numbered 1 to 10 starting from the left hand's little finger, 1 to 5 (1 = Little finger <QAZ>, 2 = Ring finger <WSX>, 3 = Middle finger <EDC>, 4 = Index finger <RFVTGB>, 5 = Thumb <Space>). The right hand's fingers 6 to 10 (6 = Thumb <Space>, 7 = Index finger <YHNUJM>, 8 = Middle finger <IK,>, 9 = Ring finger <OL.>, and 10 = Little finger <P;/ ½">) cover the remaining letters [1].

Figure 2. The 10 plus 2 keys Star-Ten-Pound keyboard layout.

In QWERTY touch-typing, between 1-6 letters are mapped to each finger. However, due to the introduction of computational power and a language model, it would be possible to reduce the QWERTY keyboard to a Position and Order Star-Ten-Pound (*10#) keyboard [5] (Figure 2). In other words, the traditional telephone keypad could be reorganized to fit the touch typing metaphor. Each finger depression thus creates a fuzzy input. Capital letters are generated by simultaneous depression of one of the Little fingers (for the <Shift> key) (finger 1 for <*> or 10 for <#>) and the intended character. The analysis is based on a combination of *finger depression order* rather than on spatial position alone. However, *the same touch-typing layout and finger movement patterns* as when using the full-size QWERTY keyboard prevails, enhancing instant positive transfer to occur. The QWERTY touch typing metaphor does not prevail when the keyboard layout is reduced to a miniaturized QWERTY, a telephone keypad or to a chord keyboard since the finger movement patterns are changed to a substantial degree.

Non-Keyboard QWERTY

The reduction of keys may be carried one step further for users that have acquired the skill to touch-type. The Star-Ten-Pound paradigm evolves into the Non-Keyboard paradigm. No keys, and no board at all are in fact necessary for a completely ubiquitous interface that would suit the mobile user. By using the "FingeRing" concept [4] or a type of Motion Processor [11], a "Wearable QWERTY Keyboard" may be accomplished. Thus, the size of the cellular phone/PDA may be drastically diminished in order to maximize portability, thus supporting the mobile user, without inflicting on usability or efficiency when entering information.

The Language Model

The finger stroke input has to be processed into real words by the device. To accomplish this, a language model is needed. The model runs through three levels of analysis: Lexical, Syntactic and Frequency ranking.

Lexical Level Analysis

The depression of a thumb (<Space>) parses the finger stroke sequences into lexical units. Those units are mapped into words [15]. This applies for most languages. The analysis that follows focuses on English, but other languages could follow the same model. Based both on lexical and syntactic knowledge, the language model generates a sentence from the entered input string. On the lexical level, each word input string is first divided into a series of consecutive sliding tri-grams [3]. A tri-gram is a string of three characters. Many different tri-grams can be created, but most of them are ungrammatical. A lexically ungrammatical tri-gram is a string of three letters that is not contained in any English word. For example, "xwx" is ungrammatical, while "exe" (contained in "executable") is grammatical. The word "fun" is a tri-gram itself. The word "placid" consists of six letters, which can be divided into sliding tri-grams (as shown in Table 1). Suppose you want to input the word "placid". The finger strokes sequence will be divided into strings of three characters. A match to the tri-gram dictionary will give 20 grammatical tri-grams. These 20 (English) tri-grams will be accepted for further analysis. Finally, a match to a (English) word dictionary generates the permissible word(s). If only one word remains, it is the right one. When an input string does not generate a unique outcome, the analysis continues on the syntactic level. The grammatical structure of the whole sentence is then analysed and if more than one word is generated, alternatives are suggested.

Table 1. Sliding tri-gram analysis of the fuzzy finger input string <10, 9, 1, 3, 8, 3> generating the intended unique word "**placid**".

Sequence of three finger strokes		Grammatical single tri-grams	Combined sliding tri-grams
Right Little finger	10	poa **pla**	poa **pla**
Right Ring finger	9		
Left Little finger	1		
Right Ring finger	9	oad lae oac	poad plad
Left Little finger	1	lad oze **lac**	poac **plac**
Left Middle finger	3		plae
Left Little finger	1	adi **aci** ack	poadi pladi
Left Middle finger	3		poaci **placi**
Right Middle finger	8		poack plack
Left Middle finger	3	eid **cid** eic cic	poacid pladie
Right Middle finger	8	eke cke ekd	poacie pladid
Left Middle finger	3	ckd ckc	poacic pladic
			pladid placie
			poacke **placid**
			poackd placic
			poackc placke
			poadie plackd
			poadic plackc
Permissible word			**placid**

Syntactic and Frequency Ranking Level Analysis

When at least one ambiguity occurs after the lexical level, a syntactic analysis is needed. Every sentence is analysed as a sequence of phrases. Every word in a phrase corresponds to a word class (Noun, Verb, Determiner, etc.), which is defined as Part Of Speech (POS) [15] and constitutes the basic unit for the syntactic analysis. In the sentence "we can eat apples" some finger stroke sequences are not mapped to unique words at the lexical level. <can> could also be <day>, and <eat> could also be <cab>, <car>, <cat>, <dab> and <ear>. At the lexical level <we> and <apples> are unique, thus not generating any ambiguity according to the Oxford dictionary [8].

The sequences <we day> (Personal Pronoun + Noun) is not allowable, and therefore discarded, while the sequence <we can> is syntactically correct, therefore accepted. The same procedure is used on the rest of the sentence. The outcome consists of two possible sentences <we can eat apples> and <we can dab apples>. They are both syntactically correct, but the second is semantically incorrect. Semantic knowledge is not implemented, instead a frequency approach is chosen, which will depict <we can eat apples> as the first choice. The possibility to choose among all the syntactically correct sentences is valuable. In this particular case, without the syntactic level, 12 possibilities instead of 2 would have been displayed: for instance, <we day car apples> is lexically, but not syntactically, correct.

Simulation on the Lexical Level

Words extracted from four different English texts (486 - 8173 words) and one English dictionary [9] (66500 words) were run through the language model on the lexical level (Table 2). For the two largest vocabularies, per cent ambiguities on the lexical level amounted to 7.5-8.4%. Around 70% of the total number of ambiguities refers to cases containing only a single ambiguity. A syntactic analysis may further diminish the number of ambiguities. The above figures refer to "error-free" input. In reality, spelling errors occur. However, the language model automatically handles within-finger errors. For example, typing a <q> instead of an <a> will not result in an error. In cases where an entered input string does not match a word in the dictionary, a spelling checker could be used. A basic spelling checker will be implemented that handles errors according to their frequency of occurrence: omission, transposition, insertion and substitution [12].

Table 2. Per cent, total number of ambiguities and number of cases generating one ambiguity as a function of vocabulary size using the Star-Ten-Pound reduced QWERTY fuzzy input paradigm.

Vocab-ulary	Size [words]	Ambi-guities [%]	Ambi-guities [Tot.No.]	Cases of 1 ambiguity [No.]
Experi-mental texts	486	3.3	16	16
News-group 1	1565	4.2	65	52
News-group 2	5285	4.4	234	180
Short stories	8173	7.5	613	428
Oxford	66500	8.4	5601	3970

Experimental texts = Vocabulary in the present study
Newsgroup1 = alt.english.usage, (July 1998)
Newgroup2 = alt.british.culture (July 1998)
Short stories = Adventures of Sherlock Holmes (http://yoak.com/sherlock/stories/adventures) (September 1998)
Oxford = A computer usable dictionary file based on The Oxford Advanced Learner's Dictionary of Current English [9].

Simulation on the Syntactic Level

The lexical simulation uses vocabularies as lists of words, avoiding considering word frequency. At the syntactic level, texts are considered instead of dictionaries. The number of lexical ambiguities reaches 40% of the total number of words in the text, using the Oxford dictionary. This figure is reduced to 3.5% after the syntactic and frequency analysis. In only 3.5% of the cases user correction is required, assuming a error free input.

COGNITIVE ASSESSMENT OF THE NON-KEYBOARD INTERFACE

The Non-Keyboard interface has been experimentally tested in a Wizard-of-Oz study. Hypotheses tested are; The productivity will decrease when the proprioceptive, tactile, and visual feedback decreases. The mental workload and muscular tension and thereby the risk for Work related Musculoskeletal Disorder (WMSD) will increase by decreased feedback. Of interest for the study was also the ability to use the interface in a stressful situation (like taking notes at a meeting) and to investigate the effect of document length on error rate. Wickens' Model of Human Information Processing [16] has been used as a theoretical framework.

METHOD

Experimental design

A repeated measurement design has been used with four text input devices. To prevent learning effects, four different texts were used. The Non-Keyboard paradigm was introduced in the form of a pair of touch-typing gloves (Figure 3). Since they were a mock-up, the subjects were

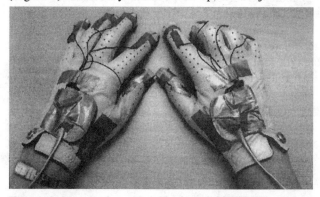

Figure 3. The mock-up Non-Keyboard QWERTY touch-typing gloves.

made to believe that the gloves were connected to the computer and on-line recording of their finger depressions took place when tapping on the table-surface. To make the different conditions as equal as possible no feedback from a screen regarding entered input was displayed in any of the conditions. The presentation order of the input devices was counterbalanced with the four different texts; hence four groups, consisting of five subjects each, received different presentation order. A type from dictation task was chosen for two reasons; 1) to simulate taking notes from a meeting and 2) to avoid additional visual load (compared to text-to-text shadowing) when using the two miniaturized keyboards. Both objective and subjective data were collected. By using a three-minute screening test before the actual experiment took place, it was possible to score the subjects normal touch-typing skill regarding both speed and accuracy.

Subjects

Data gathered from 20 out of 24 subjects were analysed. Four subjects were excluded after the screening test. Six males and 14 females (age=20-51 years) participated in the study. Seventeen were right-handed whereas 3 were left-handed. Thirteen had English as their native language and 7 as their second language. Five subjects were accustomed to audio-typing.

Input devices

Four input devices featuring QWERTY layout were used in the study. A full-size stationary keyboard and three mobile user keyboards: The Nokia 9000 featuring a miniaturized hard keyboard, the PalmPilot with a floating keyboard (stylus input) and the Non-Keyboard QWERTY touch-typing gloves (referred to as the Non-Keyboard) (Figure 1, 3).

Task

A type-from-dictation task (voice-to-text phrase shadowing) [10] was used. To prevent learning effects four different English texts from four thrillers (Barnes 1993, Chandler 1988, Cornwell 1990 and McBain 1958) were used. The different texts were matched regarding number of characters and number of long words (eight or more characters, including <Space>). Using the standardized length for a word (5 characters, including <Space>) the four full texts varied in length between 266-278 words. The texts were recorded using a professional reader at a reading pace of approximately 44 wpm and played back from a CD. Dot and comma <. ,> were replaced by two tones. Each text was preceded by a double tone with the same frequency as for dot, followed by a few seconds pause. At the end of each text, there was a melodious phrase marking the end.

Dependent variables

In the analysis, each text (app. 272 words) was further divided into three parts: A Short Message Service (SMS) document, consisting of the first 32 words (160 characters) a Short document length, consisting of the first 125 words and the original (Long document) length (266-278 words). Character error rate was computed by dividing the number of character errors in the entered text by the number of characters in the original text for the three text lengths. Capital instead of a lower letter or vice versa, extra or omitted characters, extra or omitted spaces, transposed

letters and wrong characters were classified as character errors. Correct word ratio was computed by dividing the number of correctly entered words with the total number contained in the text. In the Non-Keyboard condition, the camera was focused on a mirror image of the subject's hands when entering text. By playing the video frame by frame, this enabled the experimenter to manually copy the subject's finger-movements on a full-size QWERTY connected to a word processor program.

The muscle activity of the forearms (m. extensor carpi radialis), and the shoulders (m. trapezius pars descendence) were measured bilaterally by a four channel wearable EMG equipment (ME3000P, Mega Electronics Ltd) using disposable skin electrodes (M-00-S, Medicotest A/S).

The NASA-RTLX (Raw Task Load Index) workload inventory [6] [2], covering Mental, Physical and Temporal demands as well as Performance, Effort and Frustration level, was used to score the subjective workload after each input device. After the experimental part was completed, the subjects ranked the input devices and were interviewed about their feelings during the Non-Keyboard part.

Procedure

After an introduction and attachment of the skin-electrodes, all subjects began with the three-minute touch-typing screening test using the full-size QWERTY keyboard. All letter keys were covered and no screen was available. The screening text, consisting of 252 words extracted from a novel (McBain 1991), was presented in *written* form and the subjects were instructed to touch-type as fast and correctly as possible. The subjects familiarized themselves with the different sounds used for start, dot, comma and finish before the experimental part started. All subjects sat facing a one-way mirror in a quiet room without windows. Both table and chair were individually adjusted. For the QWERTY and Non-Keyboard input devices, the same table height was used. The Nokia 9000 and the PalmPilot were strapped to the table in order to obtain accurate video recordings. This implies that the non-dominant hand, which is used for holding the PalmPilot, stayed idle. After a two-minute familiarization phase with each of devices (except full-size QWERTY), the subjects entered "the quick brown fox jumped over the lazy dogs" once, at their own pace. The sentence was presented in *written* form. Then the voice-to-text shadowing task started. The subjects were instructed type as correctly as possible and not to correct errors and, if unable to keep up with the reading pace, just to continue. After each task, the EMG-recordings were downloaded to a computer and the subjects filled in the NASA-RTLX workload inventory before they had a ten-minute break and continued with the next input device.

After having entered all different texts, using the different devices, the subjects ranked them. Finally, they were interviewed about their feelings regarding Non-Keyboard touch-typing. They were then debriefed regarding the actual functionality of the gloves.

RESULTS

Objective Experimental Findings

Input Speed, Character Error Rate and Correct Word Ratio
Screening test Input speed, computed as number of Correct wpm (Cwpm) varied between 42-106 Cwpm (M= 64.5). Thus, almost all subjects' touch-typing pace was above the dictation pace (44 wpm). All 20 subjects used only the dominant hand's thumb (finger 5 or 6) for <Space> when using the full-size QWERTY and the Non-Keyboard. This implies that only 9 fingers were used when touch-typing. The outcome of the short 9-word phrase was not analysed in this study.

Since several subjects had a touch-typing pace above the reader's pace, when using the full-size QWERTY and the Non-Keyboard, wpm could not be used to measure input speed. Instead Ratio of Correct Words (RCW) was used (Figure 4). The repeated measurement MANOVA showed

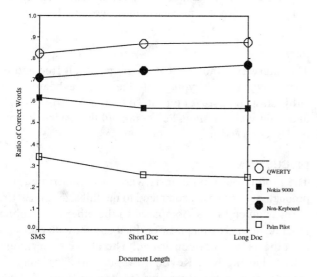

Figure 4. Ratio of correct words for different Input devices as a function of Document length (SMS =32, Short doc. =125 and Long doc. ~ 270 words).

that the main factor Input device was significant (F[3, 57]=84.38, p<.001). The interaction between Input device and Document length was also significant (F [6, 114]=5.0, p<.001). This is due to the fact that the ratio of correct words increases for the QWERTY and the Non-Keyboard, whereas it decreases for the Nokia 9000 and the PalmPilot as a function of Document length. Noteworthy is that the increase in RCW for the full-size QWERTY levels off between Short and Long document while no breaking point can be seen for the Non-Keyboard. Pair-wise comparisons between Input devices showed that all differences were significant (p<.02). Pair-wise comparisons for Document length were non-significant.

The average Character Error Rate (ChER) using full-size

QWERTY amounted to 6.4% whereas the Non-Keyboard generated 12.3%. The Nokia 9000 generated a ChER of 33.5% whereas the PalmPilot amounted to 62%, due mainly to omitted characters. A repeated measurement MANOVA showed that the main factors Input device as well as Document length were significant (F[3, 57]=105.17, p<.001, F[2, 38]=13.99, p<.001). The interaction between Input device and Document length was also significant (F [6, 114]=8.60, p<.001). This is attributable to the Nokia 9000 and the PalmPilot, where ChER increases as a function of document length (Figure 5), whereas it is almost unaffected for the full-size

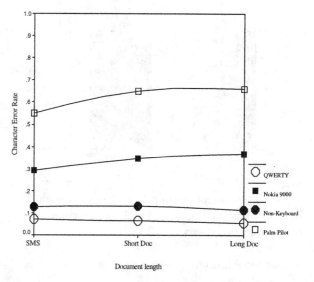

Figure 5. Character error rate for different Input devices as a function of Document length (SMS =32, Short doc. =125 and Long doc. ~ 270 words).

QWERTY and the Non-Keyboard. Pair-wise comparisons between Input devices showed that all differences were significant (p<.02). Pair-wise comparisons between Document length showed that character error rate was significant between SMS and Short document (p<.001) length as well as between SMS and Long document (p<.003).

Muscle Activity

Repeated measurement MANOVAs of the muscle activity recordings (μV, static level) of the left and right forearm (m. extensor carpi radialis) and left and right shoulder (m. trapezius pars descendence) showed that the main factor Input device was significant for both shoulders (Figure 6) and forearms (F[3,57]=8.33, p<.001. F[3,57]=10.43, p<.001). The static level refers to the lower 10% cumulative percentile of the EMG signal that is equal or less than the average μV level. No significant difference was shown between left and right side. Shoulder muscle tension is much higher for the Nokia 9000 than for the full-size QWERTY and the Non-Keyboard. The difference is highly significant (p<.05). The difference between the full-size QWERTY and the Non-Keyboard was not significant, neither for the shoulders nor for the forearms. The PalmPilot EMG recording for the left forearm and shoulder is an artifact since the device was strapped to the table. Normally the device is held by the non-dominant hand. In the experimental setup, the left hand (for 17 out of 20 subjects) was idle (see left vs. right arm EMG recordings).

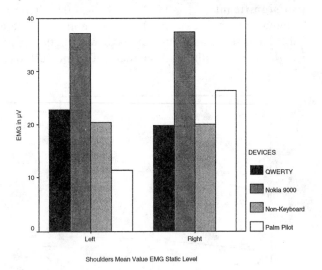

Figure 6. EMG recordings (μV, static level) for left and right shoulder (m. trapezius pars descendence), for the different Input devices.

Subjective Experimental Findings

The NASA-RTLX Workload Inventory

The NASA-RTLX workload inventory ratings [2], for Mental, Physical and Temporal demands as well as Performance, Effort and Frustration level were used when performing a repeated measurement MANOVA. The main factors Input device and Subjective workload were significant (F[3, 57]=36.13 p<.001, (F[5, 95]=8.27, p<.001). The interaction between Subjective workload and Input device was significant (F[15, 285]=2.63, p<.001). The QWERTY and the Non-Keyboard devices are rated equally low regarding Physical demands (Figure 7). Pairwise comparison between Input device showed that the only non-significant difference occurred between the QWERTY and the Non-Keyboard. It is worth to note that Performance level (Factor 4) is rated in the following order: QWERTY, Non-Keyboard, Nokia 9000 and PalmPilot.

Ranking

The subjects were asked to rank the devices according to preference. The QWERTY was rated as 1st choice in 65% of the cases whereas the Non-Keyboard was rated as 1st choice in 30% of the cases. The Nokia 9000 and finally the PalmPilot were rated as 3rd and 4th choice.

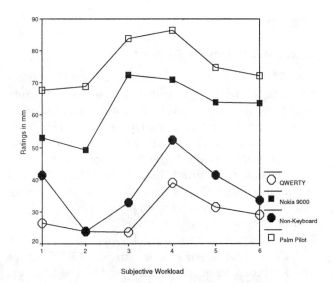

Figure 7. Subjective workload ratings (in mm) of 1. Mental, 2. Physical, 3. Temporal demands and 4. Performance, 5. Effort and 6. Frustration level as a function of Input device for Long document text.

Interview

The interviews showed that 15 subjects felt free and/or relaxed when touch-typing with the Non-Keyboard. Four subjects felt disoriented at first and 3 subjects felt uncertainty all the time. Seven missed the feedback from the keys or a screen.

DISCUSSION

The productivity hypothesis was partly confirmed; the productivity decreased compared to the full size QWERTY, but was much higher compared to the other two mobile input devices. The mental workload and muscular tension hypothesis was not confirmed. The above experiment shows that the Non-Keyboard input paradigm may be regarded as a serious alternative for the mobile user that has acquired the skill of touch-typing, at least from a human factors point of view. Significant differences regarding Character error rate and Ratio of correct words were obtained, compared to the other two mobile devices. Character error rate increases significantly as a function of document length for the Nokia 9000 and the PalmPilot. Performance rating and ranking is in accordance with objective findings. Learning time for the Non-Keyboard is negligible. Input speed is high from the beginning. Previous experiments [8] [14] have employed only a single short sentence that has been used repeatedly when interacting with each device, thus enhancing storage and retrieval from working memory. However, the difficulty of the task (known vs. unknown text) plays an important role when drawing conclusions. Eventually, the mobile user might wish to input a longer text at a fast pace. Here, ample attentional resources have to be spent on the visual tapping/

typing task that interferes with memorizing the audially presented information [10][16]. Presentation speed for the voice-to-text shadowing task was around 44 wpm. In fact, the theoretical upper input speed limit (wpm) for the Non-Keyboard should equal the subject's input speed when using a full-size QWERTY. This is not the case for the miniaturized QWERTY conditions. For initial effective and efficient input of running text, the paradigm works. However, the paradigm was only tested for text containing letters. The dictation text did not contain any special characters, Tabulations or Carriage returns, nor did it contain any digits. Two modes, "Numeric" and "Alpha", will be implemented. In each mode, the user can input either numbers or letters, respectively. Special mnemonics have to be designed and learned in order to switch mode. This will slow initial performance and introduce a short learning phase. Two areas of interest that have not been addressed here are technical solutions for visual feedback and how to accurately register the finger movements when using the Non-Keyboard. In spite of this, the paradigm is worth pursuing.

FUTURE RESEARCH

We are currently working on a finger depression registration device. It uses pressure-sensitive resistors to register finger depressions. The equipment is mounted on gloves similar to the ones depicted in Figure 3. In addition to the language model, the semantic level can be analysed. Adding semantic analysis could reduce ambiguities but is too complex and not cost-effective compared to the benefits.

ACKNOWLEDGMENTS

We would like to thank Kari-Jouko Raiha for very helpful comments on previous versions of this document.

REFERENCES

1. Ben'Ary, R. *Touch typing in ten lessons*, Perigee Books, New York: Berkley Publishing Group, 1989.
2. Beyers, J.C., Bittner, Jr, A. and Hills, S.G. Traditional and raw task load index (TLX) correlations: are paired comparisons necessary? *Advances in Industrial Ergonomics and Safety I*. London: Taylor and Francis, 1989.
3. Eriksson, K. *Approximate Swedish name matching-survey and test of different algorithms,* Report TRITA-NA-E972, Royal Institute of Technology, NADA, Stockholm, 1997. Available at http://www.nada.kth.se/theory/projects/swedish.html
4. Fukumoto, M. and Tonomura, Y. "Body Coupled FingeRing": Wireless Wearable Keyboard, *in Proceedings of CHI'97* (Denver CO, May 1997) ACM Press, 147-154.
5. Goldstein, M., Book, R., Alsiö, G. and Tessa, S. Ubiquitous input for wearable computing: QWERTY keyboard without a board. *In Proceedings of the first workshop on Human Computer Interaction for Mobile Devices* (ed. Chris Johnson) (GIST Technical Report G98-1, Department of Computing Science, University of Glasgow, Scotland) 21-23 May 1998, 18-25.
6. Hart, S.G. and Staveland, L.E. Development of NASA-TLX (Task Load Index): Results of Empirical and Theoretical Research, in P.A. Hancock and N. Meshkati (Eds.) *Human Mental Workload,* (pp. 139-137), (Elsevier Science Publishers B.V., 1988), North-Holland.
7. Lewis, J.R., Potosnak, K.M. and Magyar, R.L. Keys and Keyboards, in M. Helander, T.K. Landauer, and P.V. Prabhu (Eds.), *Handbook of Human-Computer Interaction:* (pp. 1285-1315) Second Edition, North-Holland.
8. MacKenzie, I. S., Soukoreff, R. W. and Zhang, S. (1997), Text entry using soft keyboards, Available at http://www.cis.uoguelph.ca/~mac/BIT3.html
9. Mitton, R., A computer usable dictionary file based on the Oxford Advanced Learner's Dictionary of Current English, Department of Computer Science, BirkBeck College, University of London. Available at ftp://ota.ox.ac.ul/pub/ota/dicts/
10. Norman, D.E. *Memory and Attention-An Introduction to Human Information Processing,* New York: John Wiley & Sons, 1969.
11. Numazaki, S., Morishita, A., Umeki, N., Ishikawa, M. and Doi, M. A Kinetic and 3D Image Input Device, in *Proceedings of CHI '98 Summary* (Los Angeles, April 1998), ACM Press, 239-241.
12. Pollock, J.J, and Zamora, A. Automatic Spelling Correction in Scientific and Scholary Text, *Communications of the AMC, 27, 4* (April 1984), 363.
13. Rosenberg, R. *Computing without Mice and Keyboards: Text and Graphic Input Devices for Mobile Computing,* Doctoral dissertation, (Department of Computer Science, University College, London 1998).
14. Sears, A., Revis, D., Swatski, J., Crittenden, R. and Shneiderman, B. Investigating Touchscreen Typing: The Effect of Keyboard Size on Typing Speed. *Behaviour and Information Technology 12, 1* (1993), 17-22.
15. Suereth, R. *Developing Natural Language Interfaces-Processing human conversations.* New York: McGraw-Hill, 1997.
16. Wickens, C.D. *Engineering Psychology and Human Performance,* Second Edition. New York: Harper-Collins Publishers, 1992.

Implications For a Gesture Design Tool

Allan Christian Long, Jr., James A. Landay, Lawrence A. Rowe

Electrical Engineering and Computer Science Department

University of California at Berkeley

Berkeley, CA 94720-1776 USA

{allanl,landay,larry}@cs.berkeley.edu

+1 510 {643 7106, 643 3043, 642 5615}

http://www.cs.berkeley.edu/~{allanl,landay,larry}

ABSTRACT

Interest in pen-based user interfaces is growing rapidly. One potentially useful feature of pen-based user interfaces is gestures, that is, a mark or stroke that causes a command to execute. Unfortunately, it is difficult to design gestures that are easy 1) for computers to recognize and 2) for humans to learn and remember. To investigate these problems, we built a prototype tool typical fo those used for designing gesture sets. An experiment was then performed to gain insight into the gesture design process and to evaluate this style of tool. The experiment confirmed that gesture design is very difficult and suggested several ways in which current tools can be improved. The most important improvement is to make the tools more active and provide more guidance for designers. This paper describes the gesture design tool, the experiment, and its results.

Keywords

pen-based user interface, PDA, user study, gesture, UI design

INTRODUCTION

This work explores the process of gesture design with the goal of improving gestures for pen-based user interfaces. By observing gesture design in an experimental setting we have discovered certain useful strategies for this task and some pitfalls. Our observations also suggest new directions for future gesture design tools. For example, our results indicate that gesture design tools should be much more active in the design process than they have been heretofore. Only by improving gesture design tools can we fully realize the advantages of pen-based computing.

Pen and paper has been an important, widely used technology for centuries. It is versatile and can easily express text, numbers, tables, diagrams, and equations [12]. Many authors list the benefits pen-based computer interfaces could provide on desktop and portable computing devices [1, 4, 5, 12, 13, 21]. In particular, commands issued with pens (i.e., *gestures*) are desirable because they are faster (because command and operand are specified in one stroke [2]), commonly used, and iconic, which makes them easier to remember than textual commands [13].

Recently, many computer users have adopted pen-based computers. Approximately three million hand-held

computers were sold in 1997 and sales are expected to reach 13 million by 2001 [6]. The use of pen-based input on the desktop is also growing as prices for tablets and integrated display tablets fall. As pen-based devices proliferate, pen-based user interfaces become increasingly important.

Gestures are useful on displays ranging from the very small, where screen space is at a premium, to the very large, where controls can be more than arm's reach away [17]. We performed a survey of PDA users [11] which showed that users think gestures are powerful, efficient, and convenient. Also, users want applications to support more gestures and some want to be able to define their own gestures. However, the survey also revealed that gestures are hard for users to remember and difficult for the computer to recognize.

A disadvantage of gestures is that individual gestures and sets of gestures are difficult to design. We focus on two goals for gesture design:

1. *Gestures should be reliably recognized by the computer.*
2. *Gestures should be easy for people to learn and remember.*

An added complication is that gestures in a set affect the recognition, learnability, and memorability of one another so that individual gestures cannot be designed in isolation.

A great deal of interface research has dealt with WIMP (windows, icons, menu, and pointing) GUIs (graphical user interfaces). There is also a substantial body of work on pen-based interfaces, but many hard problems remain. To a first approximation, pens can be used to replace mice, but what is easy with a mouse is not necessarily easy with a pen, and vice versa. For any given task, the ideal pen-based UI will not be limited to techniques developed for GUIs, but will incorporate pen-specific techniques that take advantage of the unique capabilities of pens.

In our work we have decided to concentrate on gestures in the spirit of copy editing [10, 19] rather than marking menus [20], because we believe that traditional marks are more useful in some circumstances. For example, they can specify operands at the same time as the operation, and they can be iconic.

At first, it might seem that the solution to the gesture set design problem is to invent one gesture set and use it in all applications. We believe standard gestures will be developed for common operations (e.g., cut, copy, paste). However, pens (and gestures) will be used for a wide variety of application areas, and each area will have unique operations that will require specialized gestures. For example, a user will want different gestures for a text markup application than for an architectural CAD application. It is also possible that the best gestures for small devices will be different than the best gestures for large ones. Thus, our solution is to develop tools to support pen-based UI designers in the tasks of inventing gesture sets and augmenting existing sets with new gestures. We want to empower users who do not have experience with recognition technology or in psychology to create good gesture sets.

As a first step, we designed and implemented a prototype tool typical of those used for gesture set design, called *gdt*. We conducted an experiment to evaluate *gdt* and to investigate the process of gesture set design. We found that while *gdt* improved the process of gesture set design, the task is still difficult and there is a great deal more a tool can do to aid the designer.

This paper presents *gdt*, an experiment on gesture design, and the results and implications of that experiment. We begin with an overview of the PDA user survey [11], the recognition algorithm used in *gdt*, and a typical recognizer training program. Next, we describe *gdt*. This is followed by a description of the experiment. Then, we present the experimental results and analysis. The next section discusses implications of the experiment for a gesture design tool. The last section gives some conclusions.

BACKGROUND

This section describes some background information that motivated our design of *gdt* and the experiment. The first subsection summarizes a survey of PDA users. The second briefly describes the recognition algorithm we used in our work. The last subsection describes our experiences with an existing tool for training a gesture recognizer.

PDA User Survey

In the summer of 1997, a survey of ninety-nine PalmPilot and forty-two Apple Newton users was conducted to determine how they viewed gestures and how they used their PDAs (Personal Digital Assistants) [11]. The study found the following:

- Users think gestures are powerful, efficient, and convenient.
- Users want more gestures (i.e., more gesture interfaces to operations).
- Users want to define their own gestures, providing a macro-like capability.
- Users are dissatisfied with the recognition accuracy of gestures. They do not want to sacrifice recognition for the sake of more gestures.

Users want more gestures and the ability to design their own, but designing good gestures is difficult. With current tools, designing gestures that can be recognized by the computer requires knowledge of recognition technology. Similarly, designing gestures that will be easy to learn and remember requires knowledge of psychology. Designers need a tool that encapsulates this knowledge to allow a wider range of people to design good gesture sets.

Gesture Recognition

There are different types of gesture recognition algorithms. Two common ones are neural network- and feature-based. Neural network recognizers generally have a higher recognition rate, but they require hundreds if not thousands of training examples. This requirement virtually prohibits iterative design, so instead we chose to use the Rubine feature-based recognition algorithm [19], which:

- requires only a small number of training examples (15-20) per gesture class.
- is freely available.
- is easy to implement.
- has a reference implementation available (from Amulet [16]).
- other research systems have successfully used [3, 8].

A gesture set consists of gesture classes, each of which is a single type of gesture (such as a circle to perform the select operation). A class is defined by a collection of training examples. The goal of a recognizer is to correctly decide to which class in the set a drawn gesture belongs. A feature-based algorithm does this classification by measuring properties (called *features*) such as initial angle and total length, and computing statistically which class it is most like. Rubine's algorithm computes eleven different features about each gesture. Unfortunately, Rubine's algorithm only works with single stroke gestures. Fortunately, thus far this limitation has not been a handicap for us.

Before the recognizer can classify gestures, the designer must first train it by giving it example gestures for each class. During recognition, the feature values of the unclassified gesture are statistically compared with the feature values of the training examples to determine which class the new gesture is most like. For more details about the algorithm, see [19].

Experiences with *Agate*

The Garnet [15] and Amulet [16] toolkits include an implementation of Rubine's algorithm and a training tool for the recognizer called *Agate* [9]. Before beginning our present work, we used these toolkits and *Agate* to understand how they could be improved.

Although *Agate* is a fine recognizer training tool, it was not intended to be a gesture design tool. *Agate* allows the designer to enter examples to be recognized, so a designer

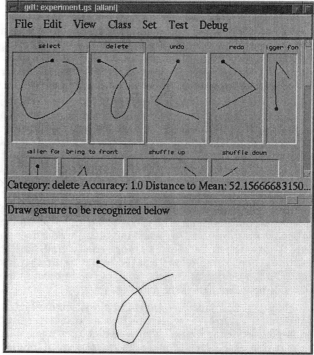

Figure 1: *gdt* main window.

can discover that a recognition problem exists. Unfortunately, *Agate* provides no support for discovering why a recognition problem exists or how to fix it. As a first step toward solving this problem, we decided to build a new tool that would expose some of the information about the recognition process. We believed that by showing designers some of the details underlying the recognition, they could more easily determine why recognition problems exist and how to fix them.

GESTURE DESIGN TOOL

We believe pen-based UI designers need a tool to help them design gestures. We built a prototype gesture design tool (*gdt*) that is loosely based on *Agate*. This section first gives an overview of the differences between *gdt* and *Agate* and then describes the different parts of the *gdt* UI in detail.

The significant improvement of *gdt* over *Agate* are tables intended to help designers discover and fix recognition problems. Other enhancements include: multiple windows for viewing more information at once; cut, copy, and paste of training examples and gesture classes; and the ability to save and reuse individual classes. The remainder of this section describes *gdt* in more detail.

gdt allows designers to enter and edit training examples, train the recognizer, and recognize individual examples. Figure 1 shows the *gdt* main window with a gesture set loaded. Each gesture class is shown as a name and an exemplar gesture (currently, the first training example for the class). In this example, the only fully visible classes are select, delete, undo, redo, and bigger font (in the top part of the window). The user has drawn a gesture to be recognized, which is shown in the white region at the bottom of the window. The recognition result can be seen across the middle of the window. The example shows that the gesture was correctly recognized as delete and gives some additional information about how well it was recognized. From the main window the user can, among other things, see all gesture classes in the set, open a gesture class to examine its training examples, call up data about the gesture set, and enter gestures to be recognized.

gdt allows the designer to examine training examples for a class and enter new ones. Figure 2 shows some training examples for delete. The individual examples can be deleted, cut, copied, and pasted. New examples can be added by drawing them in the white area at the bottom.

Unlike *Agate*, *gdt* also provides tables and a graph to aid the designer in discovering and fixing computer recognition problems. One table, called the distance matrix (shown in Figure 3), highlights gesture classes that the recognizer has difficulty differentiating. Distances are a weighted Euclidean distance (specifically, Mahalonbis distance [7]) in the recognizer's feature space. This table is helpful because gesture classes that are close to each other in feature space are more likely to be confused with one another by the algorithm. The slider on the right side of the window may be used to grey out distances above a threshold so that the user can more easily find similar gestures. For example, one can see in the figure that the most similar classes are smaller font and undo because the distance between them is the smallest.

Another table provided by *gdt* is the classification matrix (shown in Figure 4), which tallies how the training examples are recognized. The row and column names list gesture classes. Each cell contains the percentage of training examples of the class specified by the row name that were

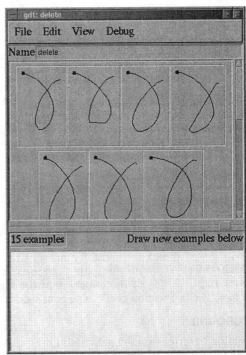

Figure 2: *gdt* class window.

recognized as the class specified by the column name. To make interesting entries stand out, misrecognized entries are colored red (dark shaded in this paper) and diagonal entries that are less than 100% are colored yellow (light shaded in this paper). In this example, six percent of select examples were misrecognized as delete and six percent of smaller font examples were misrecognized as undo. A misrecognized training example is either a poorly entered example or a sign that the gesture class to which it belongs is too similar to another class.

The graph provided by *gdt* is a graphical display of raw feature values for all training examples. We thought that such a display might help designers to determine why classes were similar and how to change them to make them less similar. Unfortunately, it was too complicated and so it was not used in the experiment (described below).

Smallest distance

Class	select	delete	undo	redo	bigger font	s	Threshold
select	0.0	11	13	13	16		
delete	11	0.0	16	11	14		
undo	13	16	0.0	7.4	18		
redo	13	11	.4	0.0	17		
bigger f...	16	14	18	17	0.0		
smaller ...	13	14	6.5	7.4	17		
bring to...	15	17	9.3	12	19		
shuffle ...	13	13	16	13	18		
shuffle ...	15	18	12	14	19		
zoom in	14	10	19	18	12		
zoom out	16	12	18	14	19		
send to ...	11	11	14	11	17		
rotate c...	12	9.9	15	14	9.9		
rotate c...	14	16	15	14	17		
select all	8.2	14	13	13	20		

Figure 3: *gdt* distance matrix. Larger distances are grayed out. The gesture set on which this is based is shown in Figure 1.

Belonging to   Recognized as

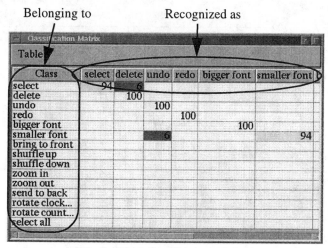

Figure 4: *gdt* classification matrix.

In addition, *gdt* has a test procedure in which it asks the user to draw gestures from the current set. The tool tallies how well the test gestures are recognized. In a single test run, *gdt* displays each class name and exemplar five times in a random order and asks the user to draw it each time. After the test, *gdt* displays the overall recognition rate, or test score, and shows how the entered gestures were recognized in a format identical to the classification matrix (Figure 4). Also, after the test *gdt* allows the user to examine the gestures drawn during the test (this feature was not available during the experiment, which is described below).

gdt Limitations

There is a tension in designing a gesture design tool in the extent to which it should be recognizer-independent versus recognizer-dependent. The benefits of recognizer-independence are obvious: the tool can be run with any recognition technology at design time and a different technology at run-time. On the other hand, by using recognizer-dependent features, the tool may be able to offer better advice, but at the cost of non-portability. In our design of gdt, we included some of both types of features.

The Rubine algorithm is good for prototyping gesture sets, but designers may want to use different recognition technology in a final product. Some features of *gdt* will apply to many types of recognizers, while others are specific to the Rubine algorithm. Recognizer-independent features are: entry and editing of training examples (Figure 2), the classification matrix (Figure 4), and the test mode. Conversely, the distance matrix (Figure 3) and feature graph may not apply to other recognizers. Recognizer-independent features we plan to add to *gdt* are described below in the Discussion section.

gdt was implemented entirely in Java. During the experiment, it was run on a 200MHz Pentium Pro with 64MB RAM using the Visual Café Java run-time environment. Of all the opinions we solicited about the system in the post-experiment questionnaire, system speed was ranked the lowest. We suspect the system did not have enough main memory and so *gdt* often stalled while swapping.[1]

---

1. Interestingly, people who had used PDAs were more forgiving of system sluggishness and unreliability than those who had not.

EXPERIMENT

We ran an experiment to evaluate *gdt* and, more importantly, to gain insight into the process of designing gestures. Prior to the experiment, we formulated the following hypotheses:

- Participants could use *gdt* to improve their gesture sets.
- The tables *gdt* provided would aid designers.
- PDA users and non-PDA users would perform differently.

We recruited two types of participants: technical (mostly computer science undergraduates) and artistic (architects and artists). We paid each participant $25 for participating. We ran ten pilot participants and ten in the experiment proper.

The experiment was performed in a small lab where participants could work without distraction. A video camera recorded participant utterances and facial expressions. The computer screen was videotaped using a scan converter. All computer interaction except for the post-experimental questionnaire was done on a Wacom display tablet using a stylus. The experimenter was present in the room during the experiment, observing the participant and taking notes. The experimenter was allowed to answer questions if the answer was contained in the materials given to the participant.

Experimental Procedure

This section describes the different steps of the experiment. The total time for each participant ranged from 1.5 to 2.5 hours. All participants were required to sign a consent form based on the standard one provided by the Berkeley campus Committee for the Protection of Human Subjects.

Demonstration

Participants were shown a demonstration of *gdt*. They were shown how to enter gestures to be recognized, how to examine gesture classes and training examples, and the distance matrix and classification matrix tables.

Tutorial

Next, participants were given a printed tutorial about *gdt* that gave a simple description of the Rubine algorithm and showed how to perform the tasks necessary to do the experiment. The tutorial also described the distance and classification matrices.

Practice Task

To allow participants to familiarize themselves with *gdt*, we asked them to perform a practice task. This task was their first opportunity to actually use the tool. In this task, they were given a gesture set containing one gesture class and asked to add two new gesture classes of fifteen examples each with specified names and shapes. After adding them, participants were to draw each of the two new gestures five times to be recognized.

Baseline Task

We wanted to compare recognition rates from the experimental task across participants, but recognition rates will vary across participants (e.g., due to being neat or sloppy). To account for this variance, we measured the recognition rate of a standard gesture set for each participant. The gesture set used was the same one used for the experimental task, which had fifteen gesture classes, each of which already had fifteen training examples.

Since users were not familiar with the *gdt* test procedure, we did not want to rely on a single test. We asked participants to perform the test twice with the experimental set.

A drawback of the Rubine algorithm is that a gesture drawn by one person (such as the participant) may not be recognized well if the gesture set was trained by a different person (such as the experimenter). We wanted to know whether participants could improve their recognition rate by adding their own examples to the preexisting gesture set. So, participants then added five examples of their own to each gesture class in the initial experimental set and did another test. The resulting gesture set we term the *baseline gesture set*. We recorded the recognition rate for this third baseline test and used it as the *target recognition rate* for the experimental task.

Experimental Task

The experimental task was to invent gestures for ten new operations and add these gestures to the baseline gesture set. Participants were told to design gestures that were recognizable by the computer and were easy for people to learn and remember. As an incentive, we offered $100 to the creator of the best gesture set, as judged by the experimenters. The participants entered training examples for all the gesture classes and some of them used the tables or did informal testing. After entering all the classes, each participant ran a test in *gdt*. If a participant did not reach the target recognition rate, the experimenter asked the participant to try to improve the recognition rate.

Participants were asked to work until they had either achieved a recognition rate equal to or better than the target rate or until they had spent ninety minutes on the experimental task. Participants were not told that there was a time limit until five minutes before the end, when they were asked to finish up and take the recognition test (again).

Post-experiment Questionnaire

After the experiment, participants were led to a second computer (to avoid negative effects suggested by [18]) where they used a web browser (with a mouse and keyboard) to fill out a questionnaire. The questionnaire asked for three basic types of information: 1. opinions about various aspects of *gdt* and the experiment, 2. PDA usage, and 3. general demographics.

RESULTS AND ANALYSIS

This section describes and analyzes the results of the experiment. First, we will discuss evidence for or against our proposed hypotheses. Then we will discuss general results related to the gesture design process.

Hypotheses

One of the most important questions we wanted to answer was whether participants could use *gdt* to improve their gesture sets. We measured improvement as the difference between the best recognition rate achieved during the experimental task and the recognition rate of the first test done during the experimental task, called the *initial* test. We found that on average participants improved the average recognition rate of their gesture sets by 4.0% (from 91.4% to 95.4%)[1] and that this difference was statistically significant (p < 0.006, 2 tailed t-test). Figure 5 shows

---

1. Recognition rates are the fraction of gestures drawn by the participant during a test run that were correctly recognized by the program.

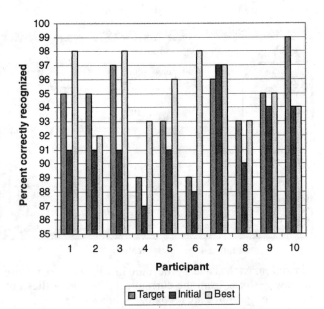

Figure 5: Recognition rates.

participants' performance on the baseline test, initial test, and the best score received during the experimental task.

We were also interested in whether the distance matrix, classification matrix, or test result tables would be helpful in designing gesture sets. Six participants used the classification matrix. Eight used the distance matrix. Seven looked at the test results. For each table, including the test results, we compared the performance of those who used them and those who did not. Surprisingly, usage of none of the three tables had a significant effect.

Among other things, we asked participants on the post-experiment questionnaire to rate their user interface design experience and if and for how long they had used a PDA. As a metric of gesture set goodness, we measured the average pairwise distance between all gesture classes in the final gesture set of each participant (because classes that are farther apart are less likely to be misrecognized). We found that average pairwise distance correlated both with UI design experience and with length of PDA usage (correlation coefficients 0.67 and 0.97). In other words, participants who had designed UIs or used PDAs designed objectively better gesture sets.

Gesture Design Process

This subsection describes qualitative observations made of the participants during the experiment. First we discuss general gesture design strategies. Next we list problems that participants had in the gesture design process.

Overall strategies and observations

No specific strategy was given to participants for how to design good gestures. Most participants followed this general strategy:

1. Think of one or more new gesture classes.
2. Enter training examples for the class.
3. Informally enter examples of the new class(es) to see if they are recognized.
4. Look at the new class(es) statistics in the classification matrix and/or distance matrix.
5. Possibly modify the class(es) just entered.
6. Repeat until all new classes are entered.

Not all participants used all evaluation methods. Specifically, many participants skipped steps 3, 4, and/ or 5, especially before their first test run.

Many participants attempted to use metaphors to help design gestures. For example, two said they were trying to make the gesture for cut scissor-like. Two said they wanted to base the paste gesture on glue somehow. One wanted the copy gesture to be "something where you're drawing a double" and to "mimic what one would do with a real eraser" for the eraser gesture.

Participants noticed that some commands have more direct representations than others. One commented, "I have an easier time with gestures that are geometrical" as opposed to "ones that are more abstract like copy and paste." Another said, "Some of these [operations] have real-world examples," and "Some metaphors are simply visual but other are trying to represent concepts."

Specific problems

Although participants could use *gdt* to improve their gesture sets, it was not an easy task. This section discusses specific problems participants encountered in designing gestures.

1. Finding and fixing recognition problems. Participants had difficulty finding and fixing recognition problems. On the post-experiment questionnaire, using a scale of 1 (difficult) to 9 (easy), finding recognition problems was ranked 5.8 and fixing them was ranked 4.6. The average best recognition rate was 95.4%, which we do not believe is good enough for commercial applications.[1] Much of this was likely due to a lack of understanding of the recognizer, which many participants expressed verbally.

2. Adding new classes. We also found that adding new gesture classes caused a statistically significant drop of 2.4% in the recognition rate of the preexisting gestures ($p < 0.041$, 2 tailed t-test). Most participants did not seem aware that this problem might occur. Many participants thought a low recognition rate was a problem with how they drew the gestures during the test.

3. New similar class. One way new classes were observed to cause a problem is by being too similar to one or more existing classes. Sometimes the participant noticed this problem by informally testing the recognition (i.e., just drawing in the main window and seeing how it was recognized) or with the distance matrix. However, not all participants watched for this problem.

4. Outlier feature values. Another way new classes were seen to cause recognition problems is by having feature values that were significantly different than the values of many old classes. The outlier values caused the values for old classes, which were close together by comparison, to clump together. Unfortunately, these features were important for disambiguating the old classes, and so by adding the new classes the old ones became harder to correctly recognize. Although this is an issue for Rubine's algorithm, it may not be for other recognition algorithms.

5. Drawing gestures backwards. Since several features used in the Rubine recognizer depend on the starting point, it is important for users to be consistent about the placement of the starting point and the initial direction. Unfortunately, some participants drew test gestures backwards (i.e., starting at the end and going to the beginning), either because they had not learned the gesture well enough or

---

1. [1] reports that users found a 98% recognition rate inadequate.

because the start and end points of the gesture were too close together, and it was unclear which direction was the correct one.

6. Radical changes. Participants also varied by what strategy they used to try to solve recognition problems. When they thought two classes were confused with one another, some participants made a small change in one of the two classes. Other participants made a dramatic change to one of the problem classes. One of the success metrics in the experimental task was how much the recognition rate improved from the beginning of the experimental task to the best recognition rate achieved during the experimental task. The improvement in recognition rate of participants who made radical changes was lower than the improvement of those who did not make radical changes (1.4% vs. 6.6%), and this difference was significant ($p < 0.006$, 2 tailed t-test).

7. Over-testing. When faced with a test score lower than the target, some participants elected to take the test again, because they thought they had been sloppy when entering the gesture. They thought if they were neater they would do better. Sometimes this strategy succeeded and other times it did not.

8. Limited test support. Participants in the experiment relied heavily on the test procedure. At present, the tool has only rudimentary support for testing how well a gesture set is recognized. The only test results available were the count of how many gestures of each class were recognized and the overall recognition rate.

9. Multiple gestures for one operation. Several participants wanted to experiment with different gestures for the same operation. For example, a participant wanted to experiment with several gestures for the "pen" operation and so made three classes with three different gestures: pen, pen 2, and pen 3. Unfortunately, the alternative classes affect the recognition of one another, which is undesirable since the final set will contain at most one of them.

We learned a great deal about the gesture design process from this experiment. Based on its results, we think that a tool like *gdt* is valuable, but it falls short of an ideal gesture design tool in many ways. The next section discusses implications of the experiment for building a better gesture design tool.

DISCUSSION

This section discusses results from the experiment and what features a better gesture design tool might have. The first subsection discusses our experimental hypotheses. The second discusses implications of our experiment for building a gesture design tool to better support the task and other features that may lead to a better gesture design tool.

Hypotheses

This subsection discusses why the experimental hypotheses were validated or refuted.

Participants could use *gdt* to improve their gesture sets. The confirmation of this hypothesis did not surprise us, but we were surprised that on average participants were only able to reach a 95.4% recognition rate, although some reached as high a rate as 98% (see Figure 5). We believe that this low performance is because the participants did not understand how the recognizer worked and because the tool was not very sophisticated.

What we did not expect was that none of the tables provided by *gdt* would have a statistically significant effect on the performance of participants. We anticipated that the distance matrix, in particular, would be useful to participants in finding what we expected to be the most common cause of recognition problems: two (or more) gesture classes too close together. We believe that it was not useful because it was too abstract and because users did have a good understanding of how the recognizer works. The tool should not require them to, but instead it should provide higher level feedback. For example, rather than show the user n^2 distance numbers whose units are completely abstract, tell the user, "Class A and class B are too similar."

We also expected that the classification matrix would be useful because we expected some training examples in every set to be misrecognized. In fact, training examples were rarely misrecognized.

Although a fair number of participants consulted the distance matrix and classification matrix, the majority focused much more on the test results and seemed to base many decisions about where recognition problems were on it. We believe this did not improve their performance because the test results are determined not only by the quality of the gesture set, but by the goodness of the test examples themselves. From looking at the test results, participants could not tell what the reason for an unsatisfactory test was.

As expected, we found that performance correlated with participants' self-ranked UI design experience. We believe this is due to experience with the design, prototype, evaluate cycle, which is common to UI and gesture design. Also as expected, PDA usage correlated with performance, which is likely due to familiarity with gestures.

Gesture Design Tool Implications

Both the experiment and our own experiences with gesture design and *gdt* have given us ideas about what capabilities a gesture design tool should have, which are discussed in this subsection. We describe lessons we learned from the experiment and what they imply for future gesture design tools. Next, we discuss design ideas that arose from our own experiences.

Experimental Lessons

The single biggest lesson we drew from the experiment was that users do not understand recognition, so the tool must take an active role in warning them about recognition problems and in guiding them to solutions to those problems. We think that many problems participants encountered in the gesture design process (especially 3-7, described above) could be ameliorated by making the tool more active.

As well as active feedback mechanisms, the experiment also suggested a few other capabilities that would enhance a gesture design tool.

One such capability is better support for testing gesture sets. The testing feature was very popular in the experiment. A gesture design tool should make it easy to create a set of test gestures that are to be recognized against another gesture set. These test gesture sets should be as easy to edit, load, and save as the training gesture sets. This enhancement addresses problem 8.

Another desirable capability is the ability to enable or disable individual gesture classes without deleting and re-entering them. In particular, it would greatly ameliorate problems 8 and 9.

In addition, the experiment suggested the idea of allowing gesture examples and classes to be dragged and dropped between classes and sets, respectively. This capability would solve problem 9 (via drag-and-drop between the main set and a "scratch" set).

We also learned from the experiment that the lack of understanding how the recognizer worked greatly hindered participants both in discovering and in fixing recognition problems. We want designers to be able to make gesture sets without being experts on gesture set design. Unfortunately, this knowledge is required to successfully use current tools.

One capability that would aid designers in understanding the recognition process is to graphically explain the features. For example, superimposing a graphic representation of each feature on top of a gesture would help designers understand what the features are and thus how to change one or more classes to make them less similar. For example, Figure 6 shows a graphic representation of the angle between the first and last points feature. The lighter dotted lines are guidelines and the darker dotted lines are the value of the feature. (They would be drawn in different colors on-screen.)

Additional Capabilities

Besides the results that arose directly out of the experiment, we have ideas from our own experience about features that would be useful in a gesture design tool. We describe those features below.

Another capability we think would be useful is assistance in making a class size- or rotation-independent. If the user indicated that a class should be size-independent, for example, the tool could generate training examples of different sizes by transforming existing examples. This feature could be extended to other types of independence besides size and rotation, such as drawing direction.

A weakness of the Rubine algorithm is that it works best if the values of each feature within each gesture class are normally distributed. That is, for a given class and feature, the distribution of a feature's value across training examples in that class should be approximately normal (ideally, the degenerate case of all values being identical or nearly so). If a feature that is important for disambiguating two classes is

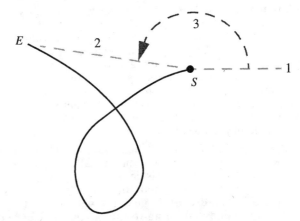

Figure 6: Angle between first and last points visualization. *S* is the start point. *E* is the end point. 1 is a horizontal ray from *S*. 2 connects *S* and *E*. 3 represents the value of the feature, which is the angle between 1 and 2.

not normally distributed in some third class, the recognition of the first two classes might suffer. For example, one might have a gesture set whose classes are disambiguated based on size. If a class is added that is intended to match squares of two very different sizes, then some of its examples will be large and others small, which will make its size feature bimodally distributed. This non-normal distribution may hinder the other classes from being disambiguated based on size.

This problem could be solved by breaking the square class into a "big square" class and a "small square" class. The tool could notice the need for such a split and do it automatically (or after designer confirmation). At application run-time, the recognition system could combine the split classes into one so they would appear to be one class to the application. Such a split may be necessary after automatically generating examples to make a class size- or rotation-independent, as discussed above.

Other recognition systems, especially voice recognition systems, show the n-best recognized results instead of just the best recognized one [14]. This feature would be useful for a gesture design tool as well.

All of the preceding features deal with computer recognition. We also believe that the ability of the user to learn and remember gestures is very important. We are currently researching how to estimate these for gesture sets. Specifically, we are presently analyzing data from an experiment to investigate how people judge gesture similarity. We are also planning an experiment to measure gesture memorability.

CONCLUSIONS

It is difficult to design gesture sets that are well-recognized. There are many pitfalls of which to be wary, and many of them are all but invisible to those unfamiliar with recognition technology. It was very difficult for the participants in our experiment to attain a good recognition rate for their gesture set, and we believe this was due in large part to difficulty in understanding the recognizer.

Pen-based user interfaces are suitable for a wide variety of applications, and those applications will all need different gesture sets. It is important for the usability of pen-based UIs that designers are able to design gesture sets that are easy for the computer to recognize and for humans to learn and remember. To perform this difficult task, designers will require significantly better gesture design tools than are currently available.

The contribution of this work is as a first step in exploring the process of gesture set design. We have shown certain strategies for gesture design to be useful and others to be detrimental. We have provided directions to explore for future gesture design tools.

ACKNOWLEDGMENTS

We would like to thank the GUIR group for pilot testing, the people who participated in the experiment, and Marti Hearst for valuable comments on the final draft of the paper.

REFERENCES

[1] Briggs, R., Dennis, A., Beck, B., and Nunamaker, Jr., J. Whither the pen-based interface? *Journal of Management Information Systems*, 9(3):71–90, 1992-1993.

[2] Buxton, W. There's More to Interaction Than Meets the Eye: Some Issues in Manual Input, pages 319–337. In Norman, D. A. and Draper, S. W., editors, *User Centered System Design: New Perspectives on Human-Computer Interaction*. Lawrence Erlbaum Associates, Hillsdale, N.J, 1986.

[3] Chatty, S. and Lecoanet, P. Pen computing for air traffic control. In *Human Factors in Computing Systems (SIGCHI Proceedings)*, pages 87–94. ACM, Addison-Wesley, Apr 1996.

[4] Frankish, C., Hull, R., and Morgan, P. Recognition accuracy and user acceptance of pen interfaces. In *Human Factors in Computing Systems (SIGCHI Proceedings)*, pages 503–510. ACM, Addison-Wesley, Apr 1995.

[5] Hanne, K.-H. and Bullinger, H.-J. *Multimedia Interface Design*, chapter 8, pages 127–138. ACM Press, 1992.

[6] Hickman, A. Power in your pocket. *PC Magazine Online*, May 1998. http://www.zdnet.com/pcmag/news/trends/t980514a.htm.

[7] Krzanowski, W. J. *Principles of Multivariate Analysis: A Users's Perspective*, volume 3 of *Oxford Statistical Science Series*. Oxford University Press, New York, NY, 1988.

[8] Landay, J. and Myers, B. Interactive sketching for the early stages of user interface design. In *Human Factors in Computing Systems (SIGCHI Proceedings)*, pages 43–50. ACM, Addison-Wesley, Apr 1995.

[9] Landay, J. A. and Myers, B. A. Extending an existing user interface toolkit to support gesture recognition. In Ashlund, S. et al., editors, *Adjunct Proceedings of INTERCHI '93: Human Factors in Computing Systems*, pages 24–29. ACM, Addison Wesley, Apr 1993.

[10] Lipscomb, J. A trainable gesture recognizer. *Pattern Recognition*, 24(9):895–907, Sep 1991.

[11] Long, Jr., A. C., Landay, J. A., and Rowe, L. A. PDA and gesture use in practice: Insights for designers of pen-based user interfaces. Technical Report CSD-97-976, U.C. Berkeley, 1997. Available at http://bmrc.berkeley.edu/papers/1997/142/142.html.

[12] Meyer, A. Pen computing. *SIGCHI Bulletin*, 27(3):46–90, Jul 1995.

[13] Morrel-Samuels, P. Clarifying the distinction between lexical and gestural commands. *International Journal of Man-Machine Studies*, 32:581–590, 1990.

[14] Murray, A., Frankish, C., and Jones, D. *Interactive Speech Technology: Human factors issues in the application of speech input/output to computers*, chapter 15, pages 137–144. Taylor & Francis, 1993.

[15] Myers, B. A. et al. Garnet: Comprehensive support for graphical, highly-interactive user interfaces. *IEEE Computer*, 23(11), Nov 1990.

[16] Myers, B. A. et al. The Amulet environment: New models for effective user interface software development. *IEEE Transactions on Software Engineering*, 23(6):347–365, Jun 1997.

[17] Pier, K. and Landay, J. A. Issues for location-independent interfaces. Technical Report ISTL92-4, Xerox Palo Alto Research Center, Dec 1992.

[18] Reeves, B. and Nass, C. *The media equation: how people treat computers, television, and new media like real people and places*. Center for the Study of Language and Information; Cambridge University Press, Stanford, Calif.: Cambridge [England]; New York, 1996.

[19] Rubine, D. Specifying gestures by example. In *Computer Graphics*, pages 329–337. ACM SIGGRAPH, Addison Wesley, Jul 1991.

[20] Tapia, M. and Kurtenbach, G. Some design refinements and principles on the appearance and behavior of marking menus. In *Proceedings of the ACM Symposium on User Interface and Software Technology (UIST)*, pages 189–195. ACM, Nov 1995.

[21] Wolf, C., Rhyne, J., and Ellozy, H. The paper-like interface. In Salvendy, G. and Smith, M., editors, *Designing and Using Human-Computer Interfaces and Knowledge Based Systems*, volume 12B of *Advances in Human Factors/Ergonomics*, pages 494–501. Elsevier, Sep 1989.

Object Manipulation in Virtual Environments: Relative Size Matters

Yanqing Wang and Christine L. MacKenzie

School of Kinesiology

Simon Fraser University

Burnaby, BC V5A 1S6

Canada

+1 604 291 5794

{wangy, cmackenz}@move.kines.sfu.ca

ABSTRACT

An experiment was conducted to systematically investigate combined effects of controller, cursor and target size on multidimensional object manipulation in a virtual environment. It was found that it was the relative size of controller, cursor and target that significantly affected object transportation and orientation processes. There were significant interactions between controller size and cursor size as well as between cursor size and target size on the total task completion time, transportation time, orientation time and spatial errors. The same size of controller and cursor improved object manipulation speed, and the same size of cursor and target generally facilitated object manipulation accuracy, regardless of their absolute sizes. Implications of these findings for human-computer interaction design are discussed.

KEYWORDS

Size effect, human performance, virtual reality, user interfaces, input device, graphic design, 3D, docking, controls and displays, Fitts' law.

INTRODUCTION

Object manipulation tasks in human-computer interaction (HCI) generally involve three elements: a controller, a cursor and a target. A controller is an input device such as a mouse manipulated by the human hand. A cursor is a graphic object on a display driven by and spatially mapped to the controller's movement. A target is a graphic such as an icon on the display that defines an object manipulation task. In a typical object manipulation scenario, a user controls an input device to move a cursor to a target. Object manipulation is the essential operation for direct manipulation interfaces, e.g., graphic user interfaces. One common spatial property of a controller, a cursor and a target is their sizes which can have significant effects on a user's object manipulation performance. The objectives of this study are to investigate how the size of controllers, cursors and targets affects human performance in object manipulation and to provide further understanding for human-computer interface design.

Previous research

Effects of target size in HCI have been extensively studied in light of Fitts' law and findings have been successfully implemented in human-computer interface design [1] [2] [4]. It is generally concluded that movement time increases with decreases in the target size in a pointing task. Most previous studies on target size used the same input device and a cursor of constant size and were limited to two dimensional pointing tasks (Fitts' tasks). Kabbash and Buxton conducted a study to compare the use of an area cursor with a typical "point" cursor for a two dimensional selection task [3]. In their experiment, the area cursor was a large rectangular area and the point cursor was a small circular dot. Their results showed the area cursor had effects that generally reversed target size effects on task performance. Since the size and shape of the cursor and target changed together for experimental conditions, it was not clear whether their results were due to the compound effect of cursor size and shape or the effect of cursor size alone. The role of the interplay of controller, cursor and target size in object manipulation has not been addressed.

Modern computer systems such as virtual reality usually require multidimensional object manipulation, e.g., graphic object docking and tracking. Relatively few studies on human performance have been conducted in multidimensional environments. Some studies found that it was rather difficult to control all dimensions simultaneously, depending on the specific task and interface systems [7] [8]. In the Virtual Hand Laboratory, Wang et al. reported that users had little difficulties in simultaneous control of object transportation and orientation [6]. They found that object transportation and orientation had a parallel and interdependent structure which was persistent over various visual conditions. Zhai et al. examined human performance on multidimensional object manipulation by comparing two, six degrees of freedom input devices, one attached to the palm, the other manipulated by the finger [9]. They suggested that the size and shape of input devices should be designed to allow better performance through finger manipulation. We are unaware of any study that examined the combined effects of the size of controllers, cursors and targets on object manipulation in virtual environments. This warrants further investigation into the effects of object size on human performance, providing implications for HCI design.

Research hypotheses

An experiment was conducted to systematically investigate the effects of size of controllers, cursors, and targets on object transportation and orientation in a virtual environment. The experiment was designed to test two research hypotheses.

Relative size hypothesis

We first hypothesize that it is the interplay of controller size, cursor size and target size that affects human performance rather than controller size, cursor size, or target size alone. Most previous studies only examined target size while keeping controller size, cursor size, or both constant. Fitts' results in 1954 suggest to us that it is the relative size that matters [1]. We predict that there will be strong interactions among controller size, cursor size and target size.

Same size hypothesis

Specifically, when the sizes of a controller, a cursor and a target are the same, the haptic feedback information on the controller size is consistent with the visual feedback information on the cursor or target size. The consistency between haptic and visual feedback information should facilitate human object manipulation. It is expected that human performance will be better, in terms of the faster completion time and less spatial errors, when the sizes of a controller, a cursor and a target are the same. We call this hypothesis the same size hypothesis.

METHOD

Subjects

Eight university student volunteers were paid $20 for participating in a two-hour experimental session. All subjects were right-handed, and had normal or corrected-to-normal vision. Subjects had experience using a computer. Informed consent was provided before the experiment session.

Experimental apparatus

A virtual environment was set up for this study in The Virtual Hand Laboratory, as shown in Figure 1. A Silicon Graphics Indigo RGB monitor was set upside down on the top of a cart. A mirror was placed parallel to the computer screen and the table surface. A stereoscopic, head-coupled graphical display was presented on the screen and was reflected by the mirror. The image on the mirror was

perceived by the subject as if it was below the mirror, on the table surface. The subject was wearing CrystalEYES Goggles to obtain a stereoscopic view of an image. Three infrared markers (IREDs) were fixed to the side frame of the goggles and their positions were monitored with an OPTOTRAK motion analysis system (Northern Digital, Inc.) with 0.2 mm accuracy to provide a head-coupled view in a 3D space. The subject held a plastic cube on the table surface. Three IREDs were placed on the top of the plastic cube, IRED 1 at the center, IRED 2 and IRED 3 diagonally away from IRED 1. The plastic cube served as the six degrees of freedom (DOF) controller in this system. The cursor was a six DOF wireframe graphic cube driven by the three IREDs on the top of controller cube. The cursor cube was drawn to be superimposed on the bottom center of the controller cube. The target was a wireframe graphic cube that appeared on the table surface to the subject. The stereoscopic, head-coupled, graphic display was updated at 60 Hz with 1 frame lag of OPTOTRAK coordinates. Data from the OPTOTRAK were sampled and recorded at 60 Hz by a Silicon Graphics Indigo Extreme computer workstation. A thin physical L-frame (not shown in the figure) was used to locate the starting position of the plastic cube, at the beginning of each trial. The experiment was conducted in a semi-dark room. The subject saw the target cube and the cursor cube presented on the mirror, but was unable to see the controller cube and the hand. The Virtual Hand Laboratory setup provided a high fidelity system where display space was superimposed on the controller's workspace.

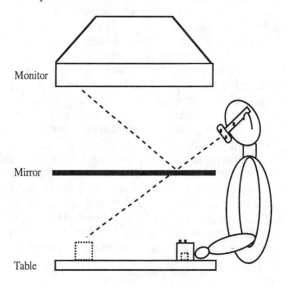

Figure 1. The Virtual Hand Laboratory setup. Shown in schematic are large controller (solid line), small cursor and large target (dashed line).

Experimental design

Independent variables for this experiment were controller size, cursor size, target size, target distance and target angle. Two sizes of the controller, the cursor and the target were used, 20 mm and 50 mm cubes, termed small and large respectively. Trials were blocked on the controller size and the cursor size. Target size was randomized over trials. The target cube was located 100 mm or 200 mm away from the starting position in the midline of the subject's body. The target cube was presented to the subject either 0 or 30 degrees clockwise. Target distance and angle were randomly generated over trials. In each experimental condition, 10 trials were repeated. In summary, we had a balanced experimental design with repeated measures: 2 controller sizes * 2 cursor sizes * 2 target sizes * 2 target distances * 2 target angles.

Seven dependent variables were derived from OPTOTRAK 3-D position data collected from two IREDs on the top of the controller cube. Data from the IRED on the top center of the controller cube were used for object transportation measures, and two IREDs on the top of the controller cube were used to calculate the angular value for object orientation measures. Time measures were: total task completion time (CT), object transportation time (TT), object orientation time (OT). Spatial error measures were: constant distance errors (CED), constant angle errors (CEA), variable distance errors (VED), variable angle errors (VEA).

Experimental procedure

In each experiment session, individual subject eye positions were calibrated relative to the IREDs on the goggles to provide a better stereoscopic, head-coupled view. The table surface and the cursor cube position relative to the controller cube were also calibrated. The subject was comfortably seated at a table, with forearm at approximately the same height as the table surface. The subject held the plastic cube with the right hand, with the thumb and index finger in pad opposition on the center of opposing cube faces which were parallel to the frontal plane of the body. The task was to match the location and angle of the cursor cube to that of the target cube as fast and accurately as possible. When the cursor size was different from the target size, the subject was asked to align the cursor cube and target cube at the bottom center so that the controller cube could finish on the table surface in all experimental conditions. To start a trial, a target cube appeared at one of two distances and two angles (Figure 1). Then, the subject moved the cursor to match the target's location and angle as quickly and accurately as possible. When the subject was satisfied with the match, he/she held the controller still and said "OK" to end that trial. At the beginning of each block of trials, subjects were given 20 trials for practice.

Data analysis

Data were filtered with a 7 Hz low-pass second-order bidirectional Butterworth digital filter to remove digital sampling artifacts, vibrations of the markers, and tremor from the hand movement. Original IRED 3D position data were interpolated and filtered only once, and then were used for the following data manipulation including angular data generation. A computer program determining the start and end of a pointing movement was used for the transportation and orientation processes separately, based on criterion velocities [2]. The start and end of each process were then confirmed by visually inspecting a graph of the velocity profile. A trial was rejected if the program failed to find a start and end or there was disagreement between experimenter's visual inspection and the computer's results.

ANOVAs were performed on the balanced design of 2 controller sizes * 2 cursor sizes * 2 target sizes * 2 target distances with repeated measures on all four factors. Only data with a 30 degree target angle are reported here so that a complete set of object orientation time measures can be presented; trials with zero target angle enabled randomization of the target angle, thus avoiding subject anticipation of the target angle during the experiment.

RESULTS
Time Measures

In general, object manipulation first started with the transportation process alone. After an average of 69 ms, the orientation process joined the transportation process. Both object transportation and orientation processes proceeded simultaneously until the orientation process finished. At the last phase of object manipulation, the transportation process continued alone for an average of 188 ms. In other words, the object transportation process temporally contained the orientation process, consistent with our previous findings [6].

Completion time (CT) and Transportation time (TT)

Average task completion time (CT) over all conditions was 909 ms. CT was dominantly determined by the transportation time (TT). TT took up 97.5% of CT. Results of CT analysis were similar to those of TT data. For brevity, only results on TT data are presented here.

It took 886 ms on average for a subject to complete object translation. There was a significant interaction between the controller size and cursor size ($F(1, 7) = 5.75$, $p < .048$), shown in Figure 2. The average TT was 862 ms when both controller and cursor were small, similar to the average value of 866 when both controller and cursor were large. When the controller was large and the cursor was small, TT increased to 896 ms. A small controller and a large cursor resulted in the greatest average TT of 921 ms. The controller size and cursor size also significantly interacted with the target distance ($F(1, 7) = 19.28$, $p < .003$). It appeared that TT was much slower at the target distance of 200 mm with a small controller and large cursor. However, at both distances, data had a similar pattern as shown in Figure 2. These results demonstrate that it was the relative size between the controller and cursor that significantly affected TT, as predicted in our relative size hypothesis. The same size hypothesis is also supported by the data in that when the controller size and cursor size were the same, the transportation time (TT) was significantly faster.

A significant interaction was also found between the cursor size and the target size ($F(1, 7) = 61.85$, $p < .001$), as shown in Figure 3. However, the nature of the cursor and

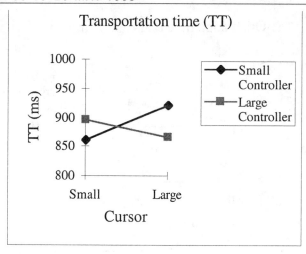

Figure 2. Interaction between controller size and cursor size on transportation time.

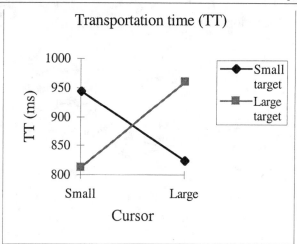

Fig 3. Interaction between cursor size and the target size on transportation time.

target size interaction was very different from the controller and cursor interaction mentioned above. It took a longer transportation time when the cursor and target had the same size than when they were different. When both cursor and target were small, TT was 946 ms, and when both were large, TT was 961 ms. It was much faster when the cursor and the target had different sizes, 825 ms with a large cursor and a small target and 813 ms with a small cursor and a large target. These results seem to be counterintuitive. Actually, the subjects took advantage of the strong visual feedback presented when the cursor and target had the same size to achieve higher accuracy. We will refer to this point when we examine the spatial errors later.

With no surprise, TT significantly increased with the target distance, $F(1, 7) = 131.62$, $p < .001$. The average TT was 786 ms at 100 mm, and 987 ms at 200 mm. No other main effects were found. Neither controller size, cursor size, nor target size alone had significant effects on the transportation time. This clearly demonstrates that human performance in object transportation was influenced by the relative sizes among the controller, cursor and target rather than their absolute size. Note, however, no significant interaction was found between the controller size and the target size.

Orientation time (OT)
The average orientation time (OT) was 630 ms, 71% of the task completion time (CT), much shorter than the 97.5% for transportation time (TT). Overall statistics on OT data were similar to those on TT data, but there were some differences in detail. As shown in Figure 4, there was a significant interaction between the controller size and cursor size ($F(1, 7) = 20.69$, $p < .003$). With both large controller and cursor, the orientation was fastest with a time of 564 ms. However, when both controller and cursor were small, the average OT was 656 ms, greater than the average value of 592 ms where the controller was larger than the cursor. The slowest OT occurred when a large cursor was driven by a small controller (706 ms).

There was a three-way interaction among the cursor size, target size and target distance, $F(1, 7) = 6.20$, $p < .043$, shown in Figure 5A and 5B. At the target distance of 100 mm, OT showed a similar cursor by target pattern as T T (Figure 3). At 100 mm, with the same sized cursor and target, it took longer to complete the object orientation (634 ms for both small and 621 ms for both large) than when the cursor size and the target size were different (Figure 5A). These results may be due to subjects' efforts to obtain a more accurate match by using the strong visual feedback when both cursor and target size were the same. In contrast, at the target distance of 200 mm, when both cursor and target are large, OT (689 ms) was significantly longer than the other three cursor by target conditions (647 - 650 ms), as shown in Figure 5B. It appeared that when the target was small and far away, the visual feedback presented by the cursor and target was not strong enough to make a difference on OT.

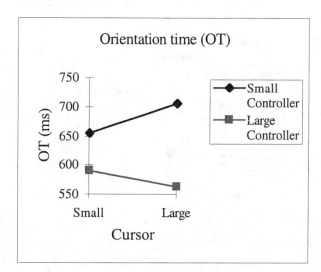

Figure 4. Interaction between controller size and cursor size on orientation time.

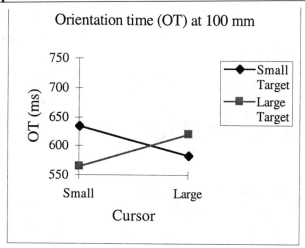

Figure 5A. Interaction between the cursor size and the target size on orientation time at target distance 100 mm

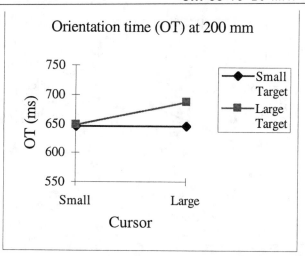

Figure 5B. Interaction between the cursor size and the target size on orientation time at target distance 200 mm.

Target distance had a significant main effect on OT , $F(1, 7)$ = 35.90, $p < .001$. OT increased with the target distance, from 601 ms at 100 mm to 658 ms at 200 mm. Target distance can be considered as an input to the object transportation process, and therefore should have an effect on TT. OT, on the other hand, can be considered as an output of the object orientation process. The main effect of target distance on OT indicated that this input for the transportation process significantly affected the output of orientation process. This result confirms previous findings by Wang et al. that the transportation process and orientation process are interdependent [6]. There were no other main effects on OT. It was the relative size that affected the object orientation process. Similar to TT, again, there was no interaction between controller size and target size on OT.

Spatial error measures

Spatial errors were measured at the end point of a trial. Constant errors were defined as the mean difference between the target distance (angle) and the distance (angle) made on each trial. The constant errors are generally attributed to system features such as the quality of graphics, and individual subject bias [5]. Variable errors were the standard deviation of errors in each experimental condition. It is believed that variable error measures reflect human performance consistency under a certain interface system.

Constant distance errors (CED) and Constant angle errors (CEA)

On average, constant distance error (CED) undershot the target distance by 1.4 mm, significantly different from zero, $F(1, 7) = 13.86$, $p < .007$. CED increased significantly

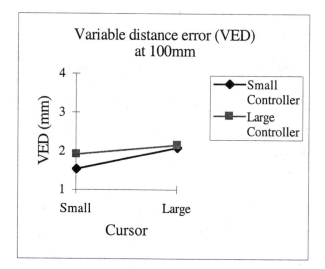

Fig 6A. Interaction between cursor size and controller size on variable distance errors at 100 mm.

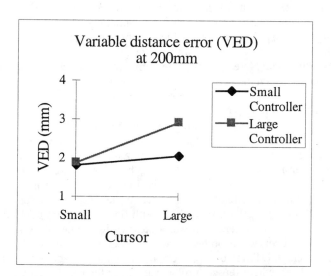

Fig 6B. Interaction between cursor size and controller size on variable distance errors at 200 mm.

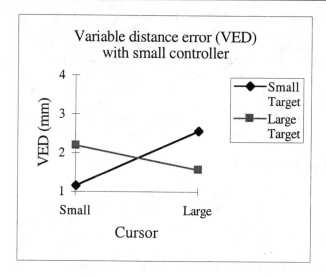

Figure 7A. Interaction between cursor size and target size with small controller on variable distance errors (VED).

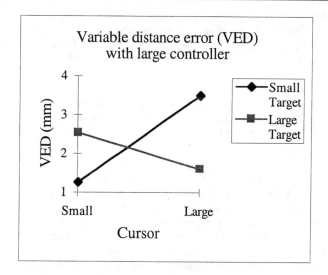

Figure 7B. Interaction between cursor size and target size with large controller on variable distance errors (VED).

with cursor size, from 0.6 mm with a small cursor to 2 mm with a large cursor. The effect of target size was also significant with F(1, 7) = 14.92, p < .006. CED was 2.1 mm with a small target, reduced to 0.6 mm with a large target. No other main effect or interaction was significant. It appeared that the visual display (cursor, target) had significant impact on CED. On average, constant angle error (CEA) was 1.1 degree under-rotated, but this was not significant.

Variable distance errors (VED)
The overall average VED was 2.1 mm. Both controller size (F(1, 7) = 6.30, p < .04) and cursor size (F(1, 7) = 15.11, p < .006) had significant main effects. VED increased from 1.9 mm to 2.2 mm with increases in controller size, and from 1.8 mm to 2.3 mm with increases in cursor size.

An interaction among controller size, cursor size and target distance was found, F(1, 7) = 7.06, p < .033. As shown in Figure 6A, when the controller and cursor were both small, VED was smallest at 100 mm target distance. In contrast, Figure 6B shows, at 200 mm target distance, VED was largest when both controller and cursor size were large. Combined with transportation time results, it appeared that object transportation was fastest and yet most accurate when both controller and cursor were the same small size.

There was a significant interaction between the cursor size and the target size, F(1, 7) = 55.76, p < .001. VED was smaller when the cursor and target had the same size than when they were different. This shows that subjects indeed took advantage of the visual feedback information where the cursor and target sizes were the same to achieve high accuracy. However, there was also a three-way interaction among controller size, cursor size and target size, F(1, 7) = 7.34, p < .03. The interaction of cursor size and target size was more pronounced for the large controller than small controller, as shown in Figure 7A and 7B. It appeared that

VED was particularly large for a large controller, a large cursor and a small target, with a value of 3.5 mm compared to the average VED of 2.1 mm. This was the only time we found a three-way interaction among the controller, cursor and target sizes. No other interactions were found between the controller size and the target size in this study.

Variable angle errors (VEA)
The average VEA was 2.1 degrees across all conditions. There was a significant interaction between cursor size and target size, (F(1, 7) = 8.99, p < .02. As shown in Figure 8, VEA was less with the same sized cursor and target than with the different sized cursor and target. VEA was the smallest when both the cursor and the target were large, 1.9 degrees, compared to 2.2 degrees when both of them were small. When the cursor and target had different sizes, VEA was the same 2.3 degrees no matter which one was larger.

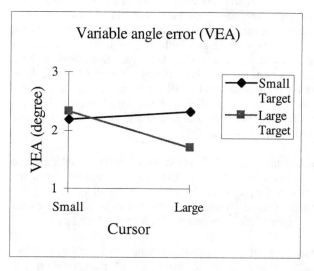

Figure 8. Interaction between cursor size and target size on variable angle errors (VEA).

DISCUSSION

Here we first summarize and discuss the results in light of our research hypotheses. We then relate our findings to theory and applications in HCI design.

Relative size hypothesis.

Results from this study supported the relative size hypothesis. As predicted, interactions among the controller size, cursor size and target size were found on all dependent measures.

In the temporal domain, there were significant interactions between the controller size and cursor size as well as between the cursor size and target size on the total task completion time (CT), transportation time (TT) and orientation time (OT). However, there were no interactions between controller size and target size. At the same time, neither controller size, cursor size, nor target size alone had significant effects on CT, TT or OT. The results did demonstrate that it was the relative size that mattered, rather than the absolute size of controller, cursor or target for temporal measures presented here.

In the spatial domain, the relative size of controller and cursor as well as cursor and target significant affected variable distance errors (VED). A three-way interaction was also found among controller size, cursor size and target size in VED data. It appeared that the interaction between the cursor size and target size was more pronounced with a large controller. This was the only instance in which controller size interacted with target size. For variable angle errors (VEA), the relative size between a cursor and a target showed significant effects. In conclusion, the relative size of controller, cursor, and target were important for spatial errors of object manipulation.

Same size hypothesis

We expected human performance to be better when the controller size, cursor size and target size were the same. We found that transportation times (TT) were faster when the controller and cursor both had either small or large sizes. However, TT was slower when the cursor and target size were the same, either both small or large. In the case of the orientation time (OT), OT was fastest when both controller and cursor were large. However, OT with both the small controller and small cursor was not as fast as that with the large controller and the small cursor. For the interaction between the cursor size and target size, the same size resulted in slower OT.

For spatial errors, VED was smaller when the controller and cursor were both small. VED was also smaller when the cursor and target were the same size, small or large. VEA had the smallest value when the controller size and cursor size or the cursor size and target size were both large.

In general, the above results indicated that the same size of controller and cursor facilitated object transportation and orientation processes in terms of faster TT and OT. On the other hand, the same size of cursor and target helped

accuracy in terms of less VED and VEA. In turn, however, it took extra time of TT and OT to reduce VED and VEA for taking advantage of strong visual feedback presented by the same sized cursor and target. It also was noted that human performance appeared particularly better with the same small sized controller and cursor for object transportation, and with the same large sized controller and cursor for object orientation. These results support our same size hypothesis in the sense of speed-accuracy tradeoff.

Implications in HCI
Theory

It is interesting to note that results of this study do not fit Fitts' law [1]. In general, the task completion time did not increase as the target size decreased; this depended on cursor size. Actually, the target size alone showed no significant effects on either the task completion time, transportation time or orientation time. This demonstrates that multidimensional docking or matching tasks are not Fitts' tasks per se. This further suggests that human information processing for multidimensional object transportation and orientation may be very different from that for pointing.

The interplay of controller, cursor and target sizes affects object manipulation, as illustrated in Figure 9. There is a strong interaction between the controller and cursor, and also between the cursor and target, but not between the controller and target. The matched sizes of controller and cursor facilitate object manipulation speed, while the same sizes of cursor and target improve accuracy. The relative size between the controller and target generally has no significant effects on object manipulation performance.

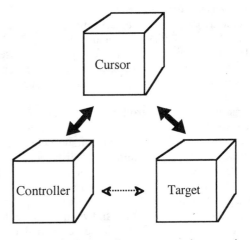

Figure 9. Interplay of controller, cursor and target size.

These findings provide insight into the underlying mechanism of human performance in HCI. Cursor and target are objects in the display domain, while a controller is in the control or hand domain. The cursor is the key which interacts with both controller and target. The intrinsic properties of a cursor such as size and shape are presented in the display domain. At the same time, a cursor can be considered as a visual representation of the controller. The extrinsic properties of a cursor such as location and orientation are determined by the controller in the control domain. In contrast, both intrinsic and extrinsic properties of a target are in the display domain, while both intrinsic and extrinsic properties of a controller are in the control domain. We suggest that it is the nature of domain separation between the intrinsic and extrinsic properties of a cursor that makes it unique: bridging between the controller and the target. Neither controller nor target have properties across another domain besides its own.

There may be different reasons for human performance improvement in speed and accuracy in the same size conditions. The fast object transportation and orientation processes of the same size controller and cursor may be due to the consistency between haptic information of the controller and visual information of the cursor, that is, what subjects feel is consistent with what they see. As discussed previously, the performance improvement in accuracy may be due to processing of visual feedback information when the cursor and target are exactly the same size.

Applications
HCI design should consider the relative size of controller, cursor and target altogether, rather than isolate each element. Particular attention should be paid to cursor properties in relation to the controller and the target. Any moving graphic object driven by an input device can be considered as a cursor. Therefore, the interaction of a controller with a cursor or other graphic is expected to occur in general graphic interaction applications such as animation and gaming. The size effect of a cursor has conventionally been ignored in either input device design or graphic design. As shown in this study, an appropriately sized cursor may significantly improve human performance in HCI.

The relative size of objects should be determined in the context of task requirements. If speed is the main concern, attention should be paid to the controller and cursor size; if accuracy is the main goal, emphasis should be directed to the cursor and target size. Small controller and cursor sizes may benefit object translation tasks, while larger ones may facilitate object rotation tasks. A tradeoff may be achieved by closely examining the size effect to meet the specific task requirements.

The size effect of controller, cursor and target should be taken into account in the experimental design in HCI research. For example, in previous input device comparison studies, the size of different input devices usually was not controlled or not reported in publications. The size of input devices may actually have a compound effect with other factors such as cursor sizes, and even target sizes. Thus, caution is specially needed to interpret results of studies on multidimensional object manipulation in virtual environments.

CONCLUSIONS
We conclude from this study:
1). Relative sizes of controller, cursor, and target matter in object manipulation.

2). Same sizes of controller and cursor improve human performance in object manipulation speed.
3). Same sizes of cursor and target improve human performance in object manipulation accuracy.
4). Relative size effects should be considered in HCI research and design.

ACKNOWLEDGEMENTS
We would like to thank Valerie A. Summers for her help in software design for the Virtual Hand Laboratory.

REFERENCES
1. Fitts, P.M. (1954). The information capacity of the human motor system in controlling the amplitude of movement. Journal of Experimental Psychology, 47, 381-391.

2. Graham, E.D. and MacKenzie, C.L. (1996). Physical versus virtual pointing. Proceedings of the Conference on Human Factors in Computing Systems CHI '96 /ACM, 292-299.

3. Kabbash, P. and Buxton, W. (1995). The "prince" technique: Fitts' law and selection using area cursors. In Proceedings of the Conference on Human Factors in Computing Systems CHI '95/ACM, 273-279.

4. MacKenzie, I.S. (1992). Fitts' Law as a research and design tool in human-computer interaction. Human-Computer Interaction, 7, 91-139.

5. Wang, Y., MacKenzie, C.L. and Summers, V. (1997). Object manipulation in virtual environments: human bias, consistency and individual differences. In Extended Abstracts of the Conference on Human Factors in Computing Systems CHI '97/ACM, 349-350.

6. Wang, Y., MacKenzie, C.L. Summers, V. and Booth, K.S. (1998). The structure of object transportation and orientation in human-computer interaction. Proceedings of the Conference on Human Factors in Computing Systems CHI '98/ACM, 312-319.

7. Ware, C. (1990). Using hand position for virtual object placement. The Visual Computer, 6, 245-253.

8. Zhai, S. and Milgram, P. (1997). Anisotropic human performance in six degree-of-freedom tracking: An evaluation of three-dimensional display and control interfaces. IEEE Transactions on Systems, Man, and Cybernetics-Part A: Systems and Humans, 27, 518-528.

9. Zhai, S. and Milgram, P. and Buxton, W. (1996). The influence of muscle groups on performance of multiple degree-of-freedom input. In Proceedings of the Conference on Human Factors in Computing Systems CHI '96/ACM, 308-315.

Exploring Bimanual Camera Control and Object Manipulation in 3D Graphics Interfaces

Ravin Balakrishnan[1,2] and Gordon Kurtenbach[2]

[1]Dept. of Computer Science
University of Toronto
Toronto, Ontario
Canada M5S 3G4
ravin@dgp.toronto.edu

[2]Alias|wavefront
210 King Street East
Toronto, Ontario
Canada M5A 1J7
{ravin | gordo}@aw.sgi.com

ABSTRACT

We explore the use of the non-dominant hand to control a virtual camera while the dominant hand performs other tasks in a virtual 3D scene. Two experiments and an informal study are presented which evaluate this interaction style by comparing it to the status-quo unimanual interaction. In the first experiment, we find that for a target selection task, performance using the bimanual technique was 20% faster. Experiment 2 compared performance in a more complicated object docking task. Performance advantages are shown, however, only after practice. Free-form 3D painting was explored in the user study. In both experiments and in the user study participants strongly preferred the bimanual technique. The results also indicate that user preferences concerning bimanual interaction may be driven by factors other than simple time-motion performance advantages.

Keywords

Bimanual input, 3D interfaces, camera control, interaction techniques, empirical evaluation

INTRODUCTION

Several user interface researchers over the past decade, having recognized that in the physical world people often use both hands to cooperatively perform many tasks, have explored the possibility of using both hands simultaneously in the computer interface. In an early study, Buxton and Myers [4] showed that in a compound task, a one-handed interface (i.e. the status-quo) was inferior to a two-handed interface which split the compound task into two subtasks that could be performed in parallel by both hands. Kabbash, Buxton, and Sellen [13] came to a similar conclusion, however, they also showed that two hands could be worse than one if an inappropriate interaction technique is employed, particularly when cognitive load is increased.

Building partly on this empirical work, several researchers have demonstrated systems with compelling bimanual interfaces for both 2D [2, 15] and 3D [5, 9, 17, 19, 23] applica-

tions. However, apart from some fundamental work by Hinckley [9, 10, 11], little formal evaluation of bimanual 3D interfaces has been carried out.

In this paper, we describe and evaluate a bimanual interaction technique for desktop 3D graphics applications which not only increases the input control bandwidth but also enhances user perception of the virtual 3D scene. Essentially, we propose using the non-dominant hand to operate the virtual camera controls typically found in 3D graphics applications, thus freeing the dominant hand to perform other manipulative tasks in the 3D scene. Other researchers [5, 9, 19, 23] have demonstrated camera operations using the non-dominant hand but have either done so in concert with the dominant hand (i.e., both hands are used to specify camera parameters) [5, 23] or attempted to directly mimic the real world [9, 17], using higher (>2) degree-of-freedom input devices more suited to virtual reality applications. We focus our attention on mouse and keyboard based *desktop* 3D environments which form the basis of current commercial 3D graphics applications for modeling, design, and animation.

In order to motivate our work, we first briefly review the various depth cues used in 3D displays, followed by a discussion of a current theoretical model of bimanual interaction. We then discuss how one of the most powerful 3D depth cues can be enhanced by following the principles of this bimanual interaction model. Our proposed bimanual interaction technique is then evaluated for a range of typical 3D tasks.

BACKGROUND

Depth Cues in Virtual 3D Scenes

3D graphics applications typically utilize a variety of depth cues to enhance user's perception of the virtual 3D scene. These cues, whose origins can be traced to the human visual perception literature, include *perspective, occlusion* or *interposition, light* and *shadows, relative size, textual gradient, proximity-luminance covariance, relative motion gradient, retinal binocular disparity,* and *motion parallax* (see [8, 22] for a review).

In 3D graphics, *perspective* is one of the most commonly employed cues, as evident in the ubiquitous wireframe "groundplane" present in most 3D applications. Also important are *occlusion* cues which are implemented via hidden line and surface removal techniques. *Lights* and *shadows* are less frequently used in interactive 3D graphics because of the high computational cost involved, although this is changing with ever faster graphics engines. *Stereopsis*, which results from retinal binocular disparity, is a strong depth cue and has been investigated extensively in the virtual reality domain, but is not commonly used in desktop 3D graphics because of the need for expensive and cumbersome viewing apparatus. Also, based on an extensive review of the role of the various depth cues in 3D perception and 3D display design, Wickens et. al. [21, 22] concluded that while stereopsis, motion, and occlusion are all salient cues, *motion* (e.g., the kinetic depth effect [3, 6] generated when the user's view of the scene is continuously varied by manipulating the virtual camera) is particularly important in creating a sense of three-dimensionality since stereopsis may provide no benefit when motion cues are present. Other evidence [3, 6] also demonstrate and emphasize the importance of motion cues.

A Model of Bimanual Interaction

Much recent work in bimanual user interfaces [2, 5, 10, 11, 13, 15, 16] has been guided by the theoretical work of Guiard [7]. In his Kinematic Chain (KC) model of skilled bimanual action, the two hands are thought to be two abstract motors assembled in a serial linkage, thus forming a cooperative kinematic chain. Three general principles emerge from this model:

1. *Dominant-to-Non-Dominant Spatial Reference:* The non-dominant hand sets the frame of reference relative to which the dominant hand performs its motions.

2. *Asymmetric Scales of Motion:* The two hands operate in asymmetric spatial-temporal scales of motion. For instance, when writing on a piece of paper, the motion of the non-dominant hand controlling the position of the paper is of lower temporal and spatial frequency than the writing movements of the dominant hand which nonetheless depends on the non-dominant hand's movement for spatial reference.

3. *Precedence of the Non-Dominant Hand:* Contribution of the non-dominant hand to a cooperative bimanual task starts earlier than the dominant hand. In the handwriting example, the dominant hand starts writing *after* the paper has been oriented and positioned by the non-dominant hand.

This model has been explored and largely validated in the virtual manipulation arena by Hinckley [10, 11]. Leganchuk, Zhai, and Buxton [16] also used this model to help reason about the manual and cognitive benefits they found in an experimental study on bimanual input.

ENHANCING DEPTH PERCEPTION VIA BIMANUAL INTERACTION

In desktop 3D graphics applications, moving the virtual camera enables the user to view different parts of the 3D scene. In addition to the obvious purpose of bringing once occluded objects into the forefront, camera manipulation also serves a less obvious but very important purpose: enhanced depth perception through motion. As discussed earlier, this motion depth cue, called the kinetic depth effect [3, 6], is critical in enabling the user to accurately perceive

the virtual 3D scene. As Kirsh and Maglio have described [14], humans perform actions not only to bring them closer to the physical goals of a task (*pragmatic action*), but also to facilitate perception and cognition (*epistemic action*). Thus, one finds users of unimanual interfaces to 3D graphics applications constantly switching between the epistemic action of camera manipulation for depth perception and pragmatic actions to perform manipulative tasks on objects in the scene. Based on these theories and observations, it is likely that allowing users to perform the pragmatic actions via one input stream (i.e., the mouse in the dominant hand as in the status quo) while the often epistemic actions of camera control are performed via a second input stream (i.e., an input device in the non-dominant hand) will result in both improved time-motion task performance and an enhanced sense of perception (or sense of engagement) of the 3D scene. This style of interaction also squares nicely with Guiard's KC model.

In order to explore the benefits of using the non-dominant hand to operate camera controls in typical 3D tasks, we conducted two formal experiments and one informal user study. In addition to the primary goal of quantitatively and qualitatively evaluating this style of interaction, we also wanted to explore how performance and user preference changed as the complexity of the task increased.

This is the first of a series of planned experiments in this area. At this early stage, we are mainly concerned with how users perform when the operation of camera controls are moved from the dominant hand to the non-dominant hand. While there are several camera control metaphors commonly used in 3D graphics applications, we chose to do all our experiments using one typical metaphor. The issue of which camera control metaphors are better suited to the non-dominant hand, or if several control techniques can be interchangeably used, is left for later investigation. Similarly, numerous different input devices could conceivably be used in either hand. We chose to use a standard two degree-of-freedom mouse in each hand for several reasons. First, the mouse is the status-quo input device for the dominant hand in desktop 3D graphics applications (see [1] for a discussion of why the mouse dominates, despite the availability of higher degree-of-freedom input devices). Second, this is a reasonable configuration for a practical, low cost bimanual interface. Third, using a mouse in both hands means that our experiments measure only the effects of moving camera controls to the non-dominant hand and are not confounded by participants having to learn to use an unfamiliar input device.

EXPERIMENT 1: SELECTION

To begin our evaluation of non-dominant hand camera control, we felt it would be best to start with a simple canonical task, and if the results were promising, we could then move on to more complex tasks. Accordingly, we chose 3D target selection as our first experimental task. Target selection is one of the simplest tasks typically used in studying human performance in computer input control. Other typical tasks like object docking, path following, and pursuit tracking, are considerably more difficult.

Method

Task and Stimuli

Participants were asked to select targets which appeared on the surface of a large cubic object in the 3D scene. As illustrated in Figure 1 (colours in the figure have been changed to accommodate greyscale printing), the scene consisted of the cubic object in the centre of the display and a light grey wireframe grid at the bottom of the display. The purpose of this grid (often called the "groundplane" in 3D graphics parlance) was to provide an additional perspective depth and occlusion cue. The cubic object was an opaque, pink coloured Gouraud shaded cube whose faces were divided into nine equal sized square sections. The target to be selected was a flat, yellow coloured disk which appeared on one of the nine sections of five faces of the cubic object (4 side and 1 top face; the bottom face of the cubic object was not used since one would have to look through the groundplane to view that face). Thus, there are 9x5=45 different locations where the target could appear. Since the cubic object was opaque, not all of its faces are visible in a given view. In order to see the other faces in search of the target, the view of the scene had to be changed by manipulating the virtual camera. To further encourage camera manipulation, "raised walls" were placed on the boundaries around the nine sections of each face of the cubic object. These "raised walls" obscured the sections such that one had to view a section almost "head on" to see if a target was on it, thus necessitating frequent camera movement.

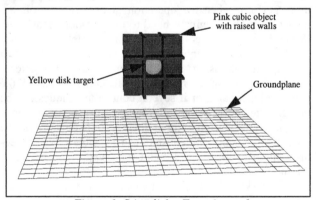

Pink cubic object with raised walls

Yellow disk target

Groundplane

Figure 1. Stimuli for Experiment 1.

The camera control metaphor used is often referred to as "tumbling" the camera, and is analogous to holding and manipulating a turntable (represented by the groundplane in the graphics scene) in one's hand. The turntable can be rotated about its normal axis as well as the horizontal screen axis. Technically, this requires revolving the camera about the centre of the scene by varying the azimuth and elevation angles in the perspective view. This allows objects in the middle of the 3D scene to be viewed from any direction. The viewing distance from the object, as well as the view angle (or focal length of the camera) is kept constant. This camera control metaphor is ideal when the object(s) of interest are located, as in this experiment, in the centre of the 3D scene. It is one of the most frequently used camera controls in mainstream 3D applications, others such as panning (moving the centre of interest), zooming/dolly (moving closer or further away from the centre of interest) are impor-

tant but less frequently used when working on a single object in the scene.

Selection of the target was done by using a mouse to move a 2D selection cursor in the plane of the screen such that the cursor was over the target (in line of sight) and clicking the left mouse button. This "ray casting" method of selecting 3D targets using a 2D cursor is widely employed in 3D graphics applications and has been shown to be superior to selection using 3D cursors [12, 20]. If the target was successfully selected, it disappeared and a new target appeared 500ms later at another location. Errors could not occur since the next target would not appear until the current one had been selected. The participant thus had to manipulate the camera to locate the target, and then select the target using the selection cursor.

The experiment compared task performance using a one-handed (1H) vs. a two-handed (2H) technique. In the 1H technique, participants used their dominant hand to operate a mouse which controlled both the selection cursor and the camera. Clicking on the target selected the target, clicking and dragging anywhere else in the scene moved the camera in the appropriate direction. Thus, participants had to constantly switch between camera control and selection in order to perform the task.

In the 2H technique, participants used their dominant hand to operate a mouse which controlled the selection cursor (as in the 1H technique), while their non-dominant hand operated a second mouse which controlled the camera. In this case, both the camera and the selection cursor could be operated simultaneously. There was no cursor attached to the non-dominant hand mouse. Also, no button presses were required since it was permanently attached to controlling the camera.

Experimental Hypotheses

Our hypotheses were developed from our informal early prototype use of the non-dominant hand for camera control and the formal framework provided by Guiard's KC model. The experimental task using the 2H technique nicely adheres to all three principles of the KC model: 1) moving the camera sets the frame of reference for the selection cursor to select the target; 2) camera control is a coarse grain task, whereas selection is a fine grain task; 3) the camera movement must precede selection. With the 1H technique however, the dominant hand has to perform both camera control and selection - constantly switching between them. Accordingly, we hypothesize that:

H1: The 2H technique will be faster than the 1H technique, primarily because the mode switching time present in the 1H technique is eliminated in the 2H technique. While it is true that in the 2H technique the participant has to switch between using the dominant hand and the non-dominant hand, this switching time should be negligible compared to that of the 1H technique because the non-dominant hand is "ready to go" the moment the dominant hand has completed its task and vice-versa.

H2: Participants will subjectively prefer the 2H technique since it more closely follows their natural real world expectations of holding an object in one hand and manipulating it with the other hand.

Apparatus

The experiment was conducted on a Silicon Graphics Indigo2 Extreme workstation with a 19 inch colour display. Two standard serial/PS2 mice set to the same gain were used as input devices. The workstation ran in single-user mode, disconnected from all network traffic.

Participants

10 right-handed volunteers participated in the experiment.

Design

A within subjects repeated measures design was used. All participants performed the experiment using both techniques (1H and 2H). The presentation order of the two techniques was counterbalanced across the participants. For each technique, participants performed 3 blocks of trials. Each block consisted of 1 trial for each of the 45 possible positions that a target could appear on the cubic object, presented in a constrained pseudorandom order within the block. The constraint imposed was that the target always appeared on a different face of the cubic object from the previous target. This ensured that participants had to manipulate the camera in order to select each target. In target selection experiments, the size of the target is typically manipulated as an experimental factor. However, in pilot testing of our experiment, we found that target size had no effect on the relative performance between the 1H and 2H techniques (i.e., there was no Target Size x Technique interaction). Therefore, we used a single target size in this experiment.

Participants were given eight practise trials to familiarize themselves with the task. They were allowed breaks after each block of 45 trials. The experiment consisted of 2700 total trials, as follows:

10 participants x
2 techniques (1H and 2H) x
3 blocks of trials for each technique x
45 trials per block
= 2700 total trials.

For each subject, the experiment was conducted in one sitting and lasted under half an hour. Subjects were alternately assigned to one of two experimental orders: 1H technique followed by 2H (1H/2H) or 2H first (2H/1H).

A short questionnaire designed to elicit participants' subjective preferences for the two techniques was completed by participants at the end of the experiment.

Results and Discussion

Trial Completion Time

Figure 2 compares participants' mean trial completion time for both techniques over the three blocks of trials. Trial completion time was measured beginning when the target first appeared on the cubic object and ending when the target was selected. Repeated measures analysis of variance with trial completion time as the dependent variable was conducted on the data. As hypothesized (H1), a significant

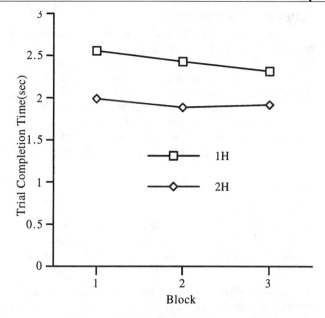

Figure 2. Experiment 1: Mean trial completion time for both techniques over the course of three experimental

main effect was found for the technique used (1H or 2H) ($F_{1,8} = 17.62$, $p < .01$). Overall, the 2H technique was 20% faster than the 1H technique.

The order of presentation (1H/2H or 2H/1H) had no significant effect ($F_{1,8} = 0.12$, $p > .5$). This, coupled with the absence of any Technique x Order interaction ($F_{1,8} = 2.78$, $p > .1$), effectively rules out the possibility of asymmetrical skill transfer – an often overlooked artifact of within-subjects designs [18]. Learning across the three blocks of trials was not significant ($F_{2,16} = 3.50$, $p > .05$). This supports our observations during the experiment that the task was elemental enough that participants had little difficulty performing the task quickly right from the beginning. No other significant interactions were observed.

Subjective Evaluation

At the end of the experiment, participants were asked to rate their preference for each technique on a scale of -2 (very low) to 2 (very high). The results, summarized in Table 1, validate our second hypothesis (H2) and is consistent with the quantitative trial completion time data.

Rating Technique	-2 very low	-1 low	0 ok	1 high	2 very high
1H technique (mean score: -0.4)		6	3		1
2H technique (mean score: 1.6)			1	2	7

Table 1. Subjective preferences in Experiment 1. Each cell contains the number of subjects with that rating.

EXPERIMENT 2: DOCKING

Experiment 1 showed that operating camera controls in the non-dominant hand is beneficial in a 3D selection task. However, the selection task was relatively lightweight in terms of both motor and cognitive effort required of the participant. Few epistemic actions were required to get an understanding of the 3D scene. An obvious question, therefore, is whether similar benefits can be realized in a more demanding task. To answer that question, we ran a second experiment using 3D object docking as the experimental task.

Method

Task and Stimuli

The 3D object docking task required participants to select an object in one corner of the virtual 3D scene and place it inside a target object located at the diagonally opposite corner.

As shown in Figure 3 (colours have been changed to accommodate greyscale printing), the scene consisted of two objects and a groundplane (identical to the one used in experiment 1) in the middle of the virtual scene. The object to be manipulated was a blue coloured sphere. The target was a purple cube with translucent faces. Colours and transparency effects were chosen to ensure that participants were not hindered in their task by insufficient visual cues. The manipulated object was two thirds the size of the target object.

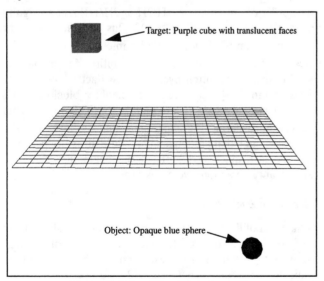

Figure 3. Stimuli for Experiment 2.

As in Experiment 1, we compared task performance using a one-handed (1H) vs. a two-handed (2H) technique. In the 1H technique, participants used their dominant hand to operate a mouse which controlled both the selection cursor and the camera. Clicking and dragging on the object selected and moved the object; clicking and dragging anywhere else in the scene moved the camera in the appropriate direction. When selected, the object could be moved in two dimensions at a time, always parallel to the plane of the screen (i.e., in the screen's x-y plane). In order to move the object along the z-axis in the virtual scene, the camera ide-

ally has to move 90 degrees such that the virtual scene's z-axis became parallel to the screen's x or y axis. This "screen space" or "image plane" style of object movement is commonly employed in 3D graphics applications which use the 2 degree-of-freedom mouse as the primary input device. It works reasonable well, but as discussed in the introduction, requires constant switching between camera control and object manipulation in order to move an object in 3D space.

In the 2H technique, participants selected and manipulated the object with the dominant hand mouse, while the non-dominant hand operated a second mouse which controlled the camera. In this case, both the camera and the object could be manipulated simultaneously. As a result, it becomes possible to move the object into the target in a single movement if the non-dominant hand controlling the camera can coordinate its movements with the dominant hand controlling the object (one way of visualizing this movement is to think of the camera being moved such that the target is being brought closer to the viewer, while the object is also being moved such that it is also being brought closer to the viewer. At some point in the middle, the object and target will meet). Of course, an alternate strategy is to simply move the camera first, followed by the object, and keep alternating between the two until the task is completed. This is similar to the strategy that has to be used in the 1H technique, except that no explicit switching of modes from camera control to object manipulation is required in the 2H technique since each task is assigned to a different hand.

The camera control metaphor was identical to that used in Experiment 1.

When the object was within the target's boundaries, the target turned bright green. Participants released the dominant hand left mouse button while the object was within the target to indicate completion of a trial.

Experimental Hypotheses

Our hypotheses were developed from the results of Experiment 1, and once again the formal framework of Guiard's KC model. If the experimental task using the 2H technique is performed one hand at a time (asymmetric interaction), it adheres to all three principles of the KC model. The results of Experiment 1 indicates that this will outperform the 1H technique. However, if the task is performed by moving both hands simultaneously (symmetric interaction), it may no longer be conceptually perceived as "move camera, then move object"; rather it becomes move camera (or effectively, move the target) and object simultaneously. Although Guiard's KC model does not address the issue of symmetric interaction, we nonetheless expect to see some performance improvement over the 1H technique if this strategy is employed.

Formally, we hypothesize that:

H1: Regardless of the manipulation strategy used, the 2H technique will be faster than the 1H technique, primarily because the mode switching time present in the 1H technique is eliminated in the 2H technique.

H2: Participants will subjectively prefer the 2H technique

since it (a) more closely follows their natural expectations for performing these types of tasks in the real world, and (b) lowers the cost of performing epistemic actions, thus providing a greater sense of "engagement" with the virtual world.

Apparatus

The apparatus was identical to that used in Experiment 1.

Participants

10 right-handed volunteers participated in the experiment. Prior to participating in this experiment, they all participated in Experiment 1. Any skill transfer from Experiment 1 to Experiment 2 should therefore be symmetrical for all subjects and not adversely affect the validity of Experiment 2.

Design

A within subjects repeated measures design was used. All participants performed the experiment using both techniques (1H and 2H). The presentation order of the two techniques was counterbalanced across the participants. For each technique, participants performed 5 blocks of trials. Each block consisted of eight conditions presented at random: we tested participants' ability to move an object from each of the eight corners of the virtual scene's viewing volume to a target located at the diagonally opposite corner. Subjects performed four trials for each of the eight conditions.

Prior to performing the experiment with each technique, participants were shown how to do the task using that technique. For the 2H technique, they were shown how to do the task by simultaneously moving both hands, and also by moving one hand at a time. Participants were given two practice trials for each condition to familiarize themselves with the task. They were allowed breaks after each set of four trials per condition. After completion of a trial, there was a 500ms pause before the next trial began.

The experiment consisted of 3200 total trials, as follows:

10 participants **x**

2 techniques (1H and 2H) **x**

5 blocks of trials for each technique **x**

8 conditions per block **x**

4 trials per condition

= 3200 total trials.

The experiment was conducted in one sitting and lasted under an hour per subject. Subjects were alternately assigned to one of two experimental orders: 1H technique followed by 2H (1H/2H) or 2H first (2H/1H).

A short questionnaire designed to elicit participants' subjective preferences for the two technique was completed by participants at the end of the experiment.

Results and Discussion

Trial Completion Time

Figure 4 compares participants' mean trial completion time for both techniques over the five blocks of trials. Trial completion time was measured beginning when the object and

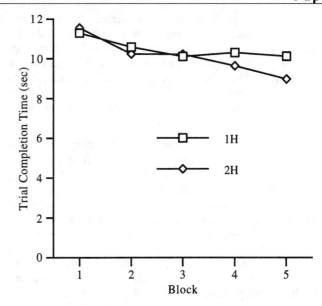

Figure 4. Experiment 2: Mean trial completion time for both techniques over the course of five experimental blocks. Data from all 10 participants.

target first appeared in the scene and ending when the object was successfully placed in the target. Repeated measures analysis of variance with trial completion time as the dependent variable was conducted on the data. Overall, there was no significant difference between the two techniques (1H or 2H) ($F_{1,8} = 0.70$, $p > .1$). This is a somewhat surprising result, especially given the significant performance gains observed in Experiment 1 for the 2H technique. Possible explanations for this result can be found in two observations we made while participants were performing the experiment as well as our own experience with the task.

First, we observed that participants were largely trying to use both hands simultaneously in the 2H technique. When the task is performed in this symmetric manner, it appears to become more difficult than the 1H technique. There are three likely reasons for this: 1) both the target and object have to be monitored continuously, dividing attention and increasing the cognitive load on the participant; 2) four degrees-of-freedom – two controlling the object, two controlling the camera – have to be simultaneously controlled, increasing the load on the participant's motor system; and 3) the geometric transformation that has to be mentally computed in order to bring object and target together is non-trivial, especially for the novice user. The 1H technique, in contrast, time-multiplexes between controlling the camera and controlling the object. This imposes a lighter cognitive and motor load at any one time. From our results, it is clear that the sum of the two subtasks (symmetric strategy in 2H technique) has a greater cost than its parts (1H technique). As noted in the introduction, Kabbash, Buxton, and Sellen [13] also found that increased cognitive load resulted in reduced performance time in some bimanual tasks.

A second observation was that because in the 2H technique there was no explicit switching cost involved in manipulating the camera, participants tended to perform more epistemic actions than in the 1H technique. While this results in participants getting a better perception of the 3D scene, the time cost incurred adds to the overall time taken to perform the pragmatic task of placing the object in the target. In a sense, while the design of the 2H technique was motivated by the desire to facilitate epistemic actions, it appears that in certain situations too much of a good thing can be bad!

Given these observations, the temporal performance result is not surprising. If participants had performed the task asymmetrically (i.e., move camera, then move object) and/ or with fewer epistemic actions, we might have seen a performance gain similar to that obtained in Experiment 1. Moving to a more parallel, symmetric style of interaction, as well as performing more epistemic actions, clearly results in a performance cost in the pragmatic task. However, as expert users of our experimental system, we found that we could perform the task using the 2H technique in a symmetric manner much faster than using the 1H technique.

Now, the question is whether the experimental data supports our personal experience that symmetric 2H performance improves with practice. Further data analysis showed a significant learning effect across the five blocks of trials ($F_{4,32} = 17.52$, $p < .001$). By the time participants reached the last block of trials (block 5), the difference between the two techniques became statistically significant ($F_{1,8} = 5.72$, $p < .05$), thus indicating that as participants get more expert at the task, the cognitive and motor loads discussed earlier are reduced. In terms of magnitude of difference, in block 1 the 2H technique was marginally (2%) slower than the 1H technique, while in block 5 the 2H technique was 11% faster than the 1H technique. No other significant interactions were observed in the data analysis.

Subjective Evaluation

As in Experiment 1, at the end of Experiment 2 participants were asked to rate their preference for each technique on a scale of -2 (very low) to 2 (very high). The results, summarized in Table 2, shows that despite their relatively poor initial temporal performance with the 2H technique, participants strongly preferred it over the 1H technique. This validates our second hypothesis (H2).

Technique ＼ Rating	-2 very low	-1 low	0 ok	1 high	2 very high
1H technique (mean score: -0.5)	1	5	3		1
2H technique (mean score: 1.2)		1		5	4

Table 2. Subjective preferences in Experiment 2. Each cell contains the number of subjects with that rating.

INFORMAL STUDY: PAINTING

In Experiments 1 and 2 we formally studied users' performance using 1H and 2H techniques for 3D selection and docking tasks. Another task that could benefit from non-dominant hand camera manipulation is 3D painting (projective paint or paint on surface) or sculpting. Several commercially available packages (e.g., Amazon's 3Dpaint, Alias|wavefront's Maya) provide 3D painting/sculpting functionality, but generally use the dominant hand for both camera control and painting. We feel that moving the camera controls to the non-dominant hand would provide a greater sense of directness to the task, and also facilitate epistemic actions that enable better visualization of the painting/sculpture being created. Unfortunately, painting or sculpting are tasks where obtaining quantitative performance metrics is difficult. Thus, we informally asked five volunteers who had experience with 3D paint packages to try out a simple 3D painting system we developed. They were asked to paint a "cartoonized" head onto a plain 3D sphere, and to do it with 1H and 2H techniques in turn. In the 1H technique, the dominant hand used a pen on a digitizing tablet to paint on the sphere as well as to control the camera (the "ALT" key on the keyboard was held down to switch into camera control mode – this is the status-quo technique used in commercial packages). In the 2H technique, a mouse in the non-dominant hand controlled the camera while the dominant hand painted using the digitizer pen. The camera control metaphor was identical to that used in Experiments 1 and 2.

The participants were asked to rate their preference for the two techniques. They overwhelmingly preferred the 2H technique (Table 3), despite the fact that they all had prior experience with the 1H status-quo technique. Comments included "I feel like I'm really painting on the sphere", and "wish I had this in Maya".

Technique ＼ Rating	-2 very low	-1 low	0 ok	1 high	2 very high
1H technique (mean score: -1.8)	4	1			
2H technique (mean score: 2)					5

Table 3. Subjective preferences in painting study. Each cell contains the number of subjects with that rating.

CONCLUSIONS

Our experiments and informal study have shown that having the non-dominant hand operate a subset of possible camera controls in 3D graphics interfaces can be beneficial over a range of tasks. The results of Experiment 2, however, caution that when the interaction style deviates from Guiard's KC model and both hands begin to operate in a symmetric manner, temporal benefits may not be immediately apparent. Of particular interest is the strong preference shown by participants for the two-handed technique regardless of their temporal performance in the task. Because subjective preferences cannot be quantified as reliably as, say, time-motion performance, less weight tends to be placed on such data. While there is a possibility that some of this subjective data suffers from the "good participant" effect (where participants will rate highly experimental conditions which they perceive are favoured by the experimenter, even if the favoured conditions are not explicitly revealed to the participants), we believe, however, that the subjective preference data is in some ways more valuable than quantitative data.

The creative people (artists, modelers, animators, designers) who use 3D graphics applications want interfaces that "feel right", and don't necessarily place much importance on speed advantages. If speed is everything, then one could argue that command line interfaces which experts can often operate much faster than GUIs would still dominate the industry. Clearly, GUIs predominate for reasons other than speed efficiency. As discussed in the introduction, there is a large perceptual component to many 3D graphics tasks and frequent epistemic actions are required to gain a good perceptual understanding of the scene. We believe that this translates into the user getting a better or faster understanding or evaluation of the results of their pragmatic actions. Non-dominant hand operation of camera controls, in addition to speed advantages in some tasks, reduces the cost of epistemic actions and provides the user with a greater sense of engagement with the 3D scene – a step in making 3D graphics interfaces "feel right".

ACKNOWLEDGMENTS

We thank George Fitzmaurice, Bill Buxton, and Russell Owen for valuable discussions and assistance during the course of this work. We also thank all the volunteers who participated in our experiments. The support of Alias|wavefront is gratefully acknowledged.

REFERENCES

[1] Balakrishnan, R., Baudel, T., Kurtenbach, G., & Fitzmaurice, G. (1997). The Rockin'Mouse: Integral 3D manipulation on a plane. *Proceedings of the CHI'97 Conference*, 311-318, ACM

[2] Bier, E. A., Stone, M. C., Pier, K., Buxton, W., & DeRose, T.D. (1993). Toolglass and magic lenses: The see-through interface. *Proceedings of the ACM Siggraph Conference*, 73-80, ACM.

[3] Braunstein, M.L. (1976). *Depth perception through motion.* Academic Press.

[4] Buxton, W., & Myers, B. A. (1986). A study in two-handed input. *Proceedings of the CHI'86 Conference*, 321-326, ACM.

[5] Cutler, L.D., Frohlich, B., & Hanrahan, P. (1997). Two-handed direct manipulation on the responsive workbench. *Proceedings of 1997 Symposium on Interactive 3D Graphics*, 107-114, ACM.

[6] Cutting, J.E. (1986). *Perception with an eye for motion.* MIT Press.

[7] Guiard, Y. (1987). Asymmetric division of labour in human skilled bimanual action: The kinematic chain as a model. *Journal of Motor Behaviour, 19,* 486-517.

[8] Haber, R.N., & Hershenson, M. (1973). *The psychology of visual perception.* Holt, Rinehart, and Winston.

[9] Hinckley, K., Pasuch, R., Goble, J.C., & Kassell, N.F. (1994). Passive real-world interface props for neurosurgical visualization. *Proceedings of the CHI'94 Conference,* 452-458, ACM.

[10] Hinckley, K., Pausch, R., Proffitt, D., Patten, J., & Kassell, N. (1997). Cooperative bimanual action. *Proceedings of the CHI'97 Conference,* 27-34, ACM.

[11] Hinckley, K., Pausch, R., & Proffitt, D. (1997). Attention and visual feedback: The bimanual frame of reference. *Proceedings of the 1997 Symposium on Interactive 3D Graphics,* 121-126, ACM.

[12] Johnsgard, T. (1994). Fitts' Law with a virtual reality glove and a mouse: Effects of gain. *Proceedings of Graphics Interface 1994,* 8-15, Canadian Information Processing Society.

[13] Kabbash, P., Buxton, W., & Sellen, A. (1994). Two-handed input in a compound task. *Proceedings of the CHI'94 Conference,* 417-423, ACM.

[14] Kirsh, D. & Maglio, P. (1994). On distinguishing epistemic from pragmatic action. *Cognitive Science, 18(4),* 513-549.

[15] Kurtenbach, G., Fitzmaurice, G., Baudel, T., & Buxton, W. (1997). The design of a GUI paradigm based on tablets, two-hands, and transparency. *Proceedings of the CHI'97,* 35-42, ACM.

[16] Leganchuk, A., Zhai, S., & Buxton, B. (in press). Manual and cognitive benefits of two-handed input: An experimental study. To appear in *ACM Transactions on Computer Human Interaction,* ACM.

[17] Multigen Inc., *SmartScene.* http://www.multigen.com/

[18] Poulton, E.C. (1989). *Bias in quantifying judgements.* Lawrence Erlbaum Associates.

[19] Sachs, E., Roberts, A., & Stoops, D. (1991). 3-draw: A tool for designing 3D shapes. *IEEE Computer Graphics and Applications, 11(6),* 18-26.

[20] Ware, C., & Lowther, K. (1997). Selection using a one-eyed cursor in a fish tank VR environment. *ACM Transactions on Computer Human Interaction,* 309-322, ACM.

[21] Wickens, C.D., Todd, S., & Seidler, K. (1989). Three dimensional displays: Perception, implementation, and applications. *CSERIAC Rep: CSERIAC-SOAR-89-001.* Wright-Patterson Air Force Base, Ohio.

[22] Wickens, C.D. (1992). *Engineering psychology and human performance.* Harper Collins.

[23] Zeleznik, R. C., Forsberg, A. S., & Strauss, P. S. (1997). Two pointer input for 3D interaction. *Proceedings of the 1997 Symposium on Interactive 3D Graphics,* 115-120, ACM.

Towards Usable VR: An Empirical Study of
User Interfaces for Immersive Virtual Environments

Robert W. Lindeman   John L. Sibert   James K. Hahn

Institute for Computer Graphics

The George Washington University

801 22nd Street, NW, Washington, DC, 20052

+1-202-994-7181

[gogo | sibert | hahn]@seas.gwu.edu

ABSTRACT

This paper reports empirical results from a study into the use of 2D widgets in 3D immersive virtual environments. Several researchers have proposed the use of 2D interaction techniques in 3D environments, however little empirical work has been done to test the usability of such approaches. We present the results of two experiments conducted on low-level 2D manipulation tasks within an immersive virtual environment. We empirically show that the addition of passive-haptic feedback for use in precise UI manipulation tasks can significantly increase user performance. Furthermore, users prefer interfaces that provide a physical surface, and that allow them to work with interface widgets in the same visual field of view as the objects they are modifying.

Keywords

3D user interfaces, bimanual interaction, virtual environments, virtual reality, passive-haptic feedback

INTRODUCTION

The introduction of Virtual Environment (VE) systems into mainstream computing has not been as rapid as researchers first projected. Indeed, outside of the entertainment industry, most VE systems in use today remain in research labs and universities. One of the reasons for this is that we do not know enough about the nature of user interaction in VEs to create systems which allow people to do real work [16, 13]. This paper presents empirical results from experiments designed to shed some light on effective user interface (UI) techniques for Immersive Virtual Environments (IVEs). An IVE is a virtual world that a user interacts with using devices that block out all elements of the real world that are not part of the experience. We build on recent work in the application of 2D interfaces to 3D worlds in order to identify those

aspects which promote usability. We focus here on *symbolic* manipulation, as opposed to *direct* manipulation (see [11] for a good overview of direct manipulation techniques).

Current IVE Interaction Techniques

In order to support symbolic interaction in 3-space, some IVE applications have abandoned desktop interface devices for more freeform interface methods. Glove interfaces allow the user to interact with the environment using gestural commands [4, 9, 8, 18] or menus "floating" in space [11, 7, 5, 12, 19, 6]. The latter use either the user's finger or some sort of laser-pointer, combined with a physical button-click, to manipulate widgets. With these types of interfaces, however, it is difficult to perform precise movements, such as dragging a slider to a specified location, or selecting from a pick list. Part of the difficulty in performing these tasks comes from the fact that the user is pointing in free space, without the aid of anything to steady the hands [11].

Feiner et al describe an approach for using 2D windows in 3D worlds [7]. The system they describe is implemented for an augmented reality system, however the idea can be applied to immersive environments as well. Feiner et al identify three different types of windows, differentiated by what the window is fixed to. World-fixed windows (called *surround-fixed* windows in [7]) have an absolute, fixed position in the VE. As the user moves or looks around, the world-fixed windows go out of, or come into, view, as if they were fixed in space. The second type of window is a view-fixed window (*display-fixed* in [7]). These windows move along with the user as they look around within the VE. They remain at a fixed location, relative to the user's viewpoint, and may be suitable for manipulating system-wide attributes, such as the rendering method to use for objects (Phong, Gouraud, wireframe, etc). The third type of window is an object-fixed window (*world-fixed* in [7]). Each object-fixed window is fixed, relative to a specific object in the VE. If the object moves, the window moves along with it. These may be used to display and manipulate object attributes, such as to display the current velocity of an airplane, or to turn on a virtual lamp. We will use the terms world-fixed, view-fixed, and object-fixed for the remainder of this paper in the manner just defined.

Deering uses hybrid 2D/3D menu widgets organized in a disk layout [6]. The disk is parallel to the view plane, and the user selects items with a 3-button, 6-degree of freedom (DOF) wand held in the dominant hand. When invoked, the menu pops up in a fixed position relative to the current position of the tip of the wand. Similarly, Sowizral [15] and Wloka et al [20] use menus that pop-up in the same location relative to a 6-DOF mouse, then use the mouse buttons to cycle through menu entries. Each of these methods, however, provides limited user precision because of a lack of physical support for manipulations.

To counter this, some researchers have introduced the use of "pen-and-tablet" interfaces [1, 2, 11, 3, 10]. These approaches register an object-fixed window with a physical prop held in the non-dominant hand. We call these *hand-held windows*. Users interact with them using either a finger, or a stylus held in the dominant hand. These interfaces combine the power of 2D window interfaces with the necessary freedom provided by 3D interfaces.

There are many advantages to these approaches. First, hand-held windows move along with the user, so they are always within reach. Second, they do not clutter the user's view, unless explicitly moved there by the user. Hand-held windows also take advantage of the proprioceptive sense, because they reside close to the non-dominant hand. Finally, some systems using hand-held windows have incorporated a lightweight, physical surface that the user carries around, increasing precision [2, 3, 17]. Storing the physical surface when not in use can be an issue with these systems, and increased arm fatigue may degrade performance during prolonged use. Most of the previous work in this field has called for detailed study into how these interfaces can most effectively be designed to enhance user performance.

UI Interaction Decomposition

In order to better study UI interaction techniques, we can decompose user interaction into basic motions, using what Shneiderman calls *Widget-Level* decomposition [14]. This approach looks at the widgets that are defined in the system, and bases decomposition on their manipulation. The testbed we have designed provides 2D widgets for testing typical UI tasks, such as drag-and-drop and button presses. We define (at least) two distinct types of actions based on these widgets: *discrete* (or open-loop) actions and *continuous* (closed-loop) actions. Discrete actions involve ballistic selection operations, such as clicking a toolbar icon, double clicking a filename, or positioning an input cursor. Continuous actions include dragging sliders, using drag-and-drop to move a file, or accessing a cascading pull-down menu.

We have designed a number of empirical studies of user performance and preference on tasks which focus on these basic motions. The results of two of these studies are presented here, and can be used to suggest how designers can develop general IVE interfaces that allow users to work efficiently.

Motivation

Recent work in designing interfaces for immersive virtual environments attempts to apply 2D techniques to 3D worlds. However, there is a dearth of empirical study into how best to implement these interfaces; indeed, most designs seem to arise from simple intuition. As has been done for desktop systems, we need to rigorously explore the different characteristics that make up these interfaces, in order to elicit optimal user performance. Our work hopes to define and compare the characteristics that may be used to improve IVE interfaces.

The Haptic Augmented Reality Paddle (or HARP) system is a testbed we have designed to take advantage of bimanual interaction, proprioception, and passive-haptic feedback (Figure 1). This system allows us to compare many characteristics that may be helpful for IVE user interfaces. The HARP system uses a 2D window, called the work surface, for displaying interface widgets. The user selects widgets using the index finger of the dominant hand, as in [1], or a stylus, as in [3]. The work surface can be world fixed [7], or hand held [17, 20]. Finally, the work surface can be registered with a physical surface [2], or not [1]. Unlike others, our system does not provide support for a specific application, but rather serves as a testbed for comparing low-level interaction tasks. Our research attempts to provide some guidelines for designers of IVE interfaces.

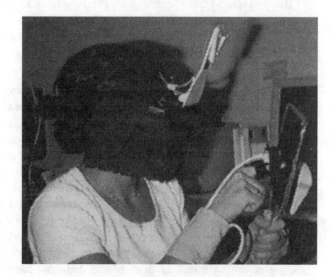

Figure 1: The HARP System

EXPERIMENTAL METHOD

This section describes the experimental design used in the first empirical studies conducted with the HARP system testbed. These experiments were designed to compare interfaces that combine the presence or absence of passive-haptic feedback (i.e. a physical work surface) with hand-held and world-fixed windows. We use quantitative measures of proficiency, such as mean task completion time and mean accuracy, as well as qualitative measures, such as user preference, to compare the interfaces. Two experiments, one involving an open-loop task, and one involving a closed-loop task, were administered. In the interest of space, we present them together.

Experimental Design

These experiments were designed using a 2 × 2 within-subjects approach, with each axis representing one independent variable. The first independent variable was whether the technique used hand-held (H) or world-fixed (W) windows. The second independent variable was the presence (P) or absence (N) of passive haptic feedback.

Four different interaction techniques (treatments) were implemented which combine these two independent variables into a 2 × 2 matrix, as shown in Table 1.

	Hand-Held (H)	**World-Fixed (W)**
Passive Haptics (P)	HP Treatment	WP Treatment
No Haptics (N)	HN Treatment	WN Treatment

Table 1: 2 × 2 Design

Each quadrant is defined as:

HP = Hand-Held Window, with Passive-Haptics.
WP = World-Fixed Window, with Passive-Haptics.
HN = Hand-Held Window, No Haptics.
WN = World-Fixed Window, No Haptics.

For the **HP** treatment, subjects held a paddle-like object in the non-dominant hand (Figure 2), with the work surface defined to be the face of the paddle. The rectangular work surface measured 23cm × 17cm (W × H). The paddle handle radius was 2.8cm, and the handle length was 12.5cm. Subjects could hold the paddle in any position that felt comfortable, but that allowed them to accomplish the tasks quickly and accurately. Subjects were presented with a visual avatar of the paddle that matched exactly the physical paddle in dimension (Figure 3). For the **WP** treatment, a panel with the same dimensions as the work surface of the **HP** treatment was mounted on a rigid, floor-standing mounting frame in front of the dominant-hand side of the body of the subject. The panel was mounted on a rigid Styrofoam box attached to the surface of the mounting frame. When the subjects explored the panel with their hands, they was supposed to get the impression

that it was "floating" in space in front of them. This matched the visual feedback, which was an avatar of the panel floating in front of the subject.

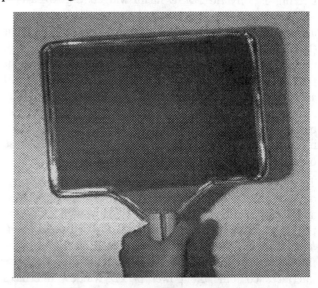

Figure 2: The Physical Paddle

Before the experiment began, each subject was asked at which height the panel should be mounted, and this remained fixed for the duration of the experiment. Each subject was free to move the chair to a comfortable location before each task. For the **HN** treatment, the subjects held only the handle of the paddle in the non-dominant hand (no physical paddle head), while being presented with a full paddle avatar. Again, subjects were free to hold the paddle in any position that allowed them to work quickly and accurately. The **WN** treatment was exactly the same as **WP**, except that there was no physical panel mounted in front of the subject.

Using a diagram-balanced Latin squares approach, four different orderings of the treatments were defined, and subjects were assigned at random to one of the four orderings. We had each subject perform 20 trials on two separate tasks for each treatment. Four different random orderings for the 20 trials were used. The subjects were seated during the entire experiment.

Each subject performed two tasks (experiments) using the treatments. Task one was a docking task. Subjects were presented with a colored shape on the work surface, and had to slide it to a black outline of the same shape in a different location on the work surface, and then release it (Figure 3). Subjects could repeatedly adjust the location of the shape until they were satisfied with its proximity to the outline shape, and then move on to the next trial by pressing a "Continue" button, displayed in the center at the lower edge of the work surface. This task was designed to test the component UI action of "Drag-and-Drop," which is a continuous task. The trials were a mix between horizontal, vertical, and diagonal movements.

Figure 3: The Docking Task

The second task was a shape selection task. For this task, a signpost was displayed in the VE (Figure 4), upon which one shape was chosen at random to be displayed. For the right-handed subjects, the signpost was positioned in front and to the left of the subject. For the left-handed subjects, it was positioned in front and to the right of the subject. In addition, four shapes were arranged horizontally on the work surface, one of which matched the shape and color of the one on the signpost. The subject had to select the shape that matched the one on the signpost, and then press the "Continue" button to move on to the next trial. The subject could change the selection before moving to the next trial. This task was designed to test the component UI action of "Button Press," which is a discrete task.

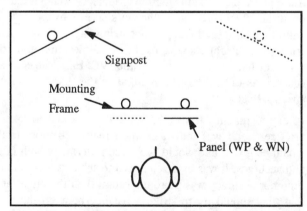

Figure 4: Overhead View of Physical Layout (dashed lines denote object positions for left-handed subjects)

The subject was required to press the "Continue" button after each trial for several reasons. First, this provided a clear distinction for when the trial was over. Subjects had to actively signal that they were through with the trial, so mistakes could be avoided because they could make adjustments before continuing on to the next trial. Second,

this forced the user to return to a known "home" position prior to each trial, eliminating timing differences that could have arisen because of trial order. If the target location for one trial was close to the start position of the next trial, and subjects were not required to begin the trial at a home position, then they could acquire the shape for the next trial more quickly than for trials where the target and start position for successive trials were further apart. Finally, this gave a clear cut event which signaled the end of one trial and the start of the next, which is necessary for timing purposes.

Shape Manipulation

Five different shapes were used for these experiments: a circle, a square, a diamond, a triangle, and a five-pointed star. In addition, each shape could appear in any one of three colors: red, green, or blue. The bounding box used for intersection testing was the same for all shapes, so the only difference was their shape in the VE; each one was as easy to select as every other one.

Subjects selected shapes simply by moving the fingertip of their dominant-hand index finger to intersect the shape. A shape was released by moving the finger away from the shape, so that the fingertip no longer intersected it. For movable shapes (docking task), this required the subject to lift (or push) the fingertip so that it no longer intersected the virtual work surface, as moving the finger tip along the plane of the work surface translated the shape along with the fingertip. For immovable objects (selection task), the subjects were free to move the fingertip in any direction in order to release the object. Once the fingertip left the bounding box of the shape, the shape was considered released.

System Characteristics

The HARP software was running on a two-processor SiliconGraphics (SGI) Onyx workstation equipped with a RealityEngine[2] graphics subsystem, two 75MHz MIPS R8000 processors, 64 megabytes of RAM, and 4 megabytes of texture RAM. Because of a lack of audio support on the Onyx, audio feedback software (see below) was run on an SGI Indy workstation, and communicated with the HARP system over Ethernet. The video came from the Onyx, while the audio came from the Indy. We used a Virtual I/O i-glasses HMD to display the video and audio, with a Logitech ultrasonic tracker mounted on the front to track 6-DOF head motion. For the index-finger and paddle, we used an Ascension Flock-of-Birds magnetic tracker. The mounting stand for the panel was constructed using only wood and PVC tubing, so as to avoid introducing noise to the magnetic trackers. The work space was calibrated once, and the computed values were used for all subsequent runs of the software. All the software ran in one Unix thread. A minimum of 11 frames per second (FPS) and a maximum of 16 FPS were maintained throughout the tests, with the average being 14 FPS.

Subject Demographics

A total of 32 unpaid subjects were selected on a first-come, first-served basis, in response to a call for subjects. Most of the subjects were college students (20), either undergraduate (8) or graduate (12). The rest (12) were not students. The mean age of the subjects was 27 years, 5 months. In all, 30 of the subjects reported they used a computer with a mouse at least 10 hours per week, with 22 reporting computer usage exceeding 30 hours per week. Three subjects reported that they used their left hand for writing. 15 of the subjects were female and 17 were male. 19 subjects said they had experienced some kind of "Virtual Reality" before. Each subject passed a test for colorblindness. 15 subjects reported having suffered from motion sickness at some time in their lives, when asked prior to the experiment.

Protocol

Each subject signed an "Informed Consent for Human Subjects" form, and was given a copy to keep. Before beginning the actual experiment, demographic information was collected. The user was then fitted with the dominant-hand index finger tracker, and asked to adjust it so that it fit snugly. The user then chose between two different heights for the mounting position of the world-fixed work surface. Six subjects chose to use the higher mounting location of the panel (103cm above the floor) and 26 chose the lower position (94cm). The subjects were free to move the chair forward or back during the experiment. The chair surface was 46cm from the floor. Each subject was read a general introduction to the experiment, explaining what the user would see in the virtual environment, which techniques they could use to manipulate the shapes in the environment, how the paddle and dominant-hand avatars mimicked the motions of the subject's hands, and how the HMD worked.

After fitting the subject with the HMD, the software was started, the visuals would appear, and the audio emitted two sounds. The subjects were asked if they heard the sounds at the start of each task. To help subjects orient themselves, they were asked to look at certain virtual objects placed in specific locations within the VE. A blue cube was stationed on the ground plane of the VE at approximately 45° to the left of, and 3 meters away from, the subject. A green cone was placed at 45° to the right of, and 3 meters away from, the subject. Subjects were told that if they turned their head to the left, they should see a blue cube, and the same for the green cone to the right.

The subjects' location within the VE was such that they were in the center of a horizontal plane, texture-mapped with a beige, repeating pattern. Above the subject was a sky plane, which was texture-mapped with a blue sky and clouds. The subject was told to look up to see the blue sky, and to look down to see the patterned ground. This sequence of having the subject look left, right, up, and down was done before each task during the experiment, in order to orient the user each time.

At the beginning of the first task, the subject was instructed to move their dominant hand into the field of view, and that they would see the hand avatar (Figure 5). After moving their hand around for a few moments to get used to the mapping of hand movements to avatar movements, for the **H** treatments they were then asked to hold out their non-dominant hand, into which the paddle was placed, and they were given a few moments to get used to its movement. For the **W** treatments, it was pointed out that the panel in front of them was the panel that had been described in the introduction.

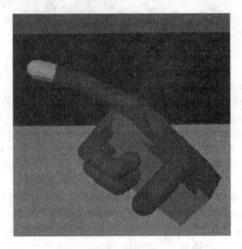

Figure 5: The Dominant-Hand Avatar

The work surface displayed the message, 'To begin the first trial, press the "Begin" button.' Subjects were asked to press the "Begin" button on the work surface by touching it with their finger. Five practice trials were then given, during which subjects were read a verbal description of the task they had to perform within the IVE. Each subject was coached as to how best to manipulate the shapes for each specific treatment.

After the practice trials, the subject was asked to take a brief rest, and was told that when ready, 20 more trials would be given, and would be scored in terms of both time and accuracy. It was made clear to the subjects that neither time nor accuracy was more important than the other, and that they should try to strike a balance between the two. Trial time for both tasks was measured as the total time between successive presses of the "Continue" button. Accuracy for the docking task was measured by how close the center of the shape was placed to the center of the target position, and for the selection task, accuracy was simply whether the correct shape was selected from among the four choices. After each treatment, the HMD was removed, the paddle was taken away (for **H**), and the subject was allowed to relax as long as they wanted to before beginning the next treatment.

Additional Feedback

In addition to visual and (in some cases) haptic feedback, the HARP system provided other cues for the subject, regardless of treatment. First, the tip of the index finger of the dominant-hand avatar was colored yellow (Figure 6a). Second, in order to simulate a shadow of the dominant hand, a red drop-cursor, which followed the movement of the fingertip in relation to the plane of the paddle surface, was displayed on the work surface (Figure 6b). The location of the drop-cursor was determined by dropping a perpendicular from the fingertip to the work surface, and drawing the cursor centered at that location. When the fingertip was not in the space directly in front of the work surface, no cursor was displayed. To help the subjects gauge when the fingertip was intersecting UI widgets, each widget became highlighted, and an audible CLICK! sound was output to the headphones worn by the subject (Figure 6c). When the user released the widget, it returned to its normal color, and a different UNCLICK! sound was triggered.

Figure 6: Manipulation Cues:
(a) Yellow Fingertip; (b) Red Drop-Cursor,
(c) Widget Highlighting and Audio Feedback

Data Collection

Qualitative data was collected for each treatment using a questionnaire. Four questions, arranged on Likert scales, were administered to gather data on perceived ease-of-use, arm fatigue, eye fatigue, and motion sickness, respectively. The questionnaire was administered after each treatment.

Quantitative data was collected by the software for each trial of each task. This data varied for the two tasks. For the docking task, the start position, target position, and final position of the shapes were recorded. In addition, the total trial time and the number of times the subject selected and released the shape for each trial was recorded. For the selection task, the total trial time, number of selections made for each trial, the correct answer, and the answer given by the subject were recorded.

Results

In order to produce an overall measure of subject preference for the four treatments, we have computed a composite value from the qualitative data. This measure is computed by averaging each of the Likert values from the four questions posed after each treatment. Because "positive" responses for the four characteristics were given higher numbers, on a scale between one and five, the average of the ease-of-use, arm fatigue, eye fatigue, and motion sickness questions gives us an overall measure of preference. A score of 1 would signify a lower preference than a score of 5. Table 2 shows the mean values for each question, as well as the composite value, for all four treatments ($N = 32$, standard-deviations in parentheses).

	Preference Factor				
	Ease of Use	Arm Fatigue	Eye Fatigue	Motion Sickness	Composite Value
HP	4.53 (0.671)	4.13 (0.942)	4.28 (0.851)	4.91 (0.296)	4.46 (0.445)
WP	4.28 (0.851)	3.19 (1.091)	4.25 (0.842)	4.84 (0.448)	4.14 (0.466)
HN	2.88 (1.070)	3.44 (0.914)	4.03 (0.999)	4.72 (0.683)	3.76 (0.638)
WN	2.84 (1.019)	2.25 (0.803)	3.78 (1.039)	4.75 (0.622)	3.41 (0.487)

Table 2: Mean Subject Preference by Treatment
(standard-deviations in parentheses)

In terms of the main effects, a within-subjects, 2×2 analysis of variance (ANOVA) for the composite value of subject preference showed that subjects significantly preferred **H** over **W** ($f = 23.02$; $df = 1/31$; $p < 0.001$) and **P** over **N** ($f = 86.178$; $df = 1/31$; $p < 0.001$). There was no interaction effect ($f = 0.09$; $df = 1/31$; $p > 0.760$).

An analysis of the mean trial completion time measure (in seconds) for the docking task yields the following descriptive statistics ($N = 32$ for all treatments): **HP** ($m = 6.71$; $sd = 2.582$), **WP** ($m = 6.60$; $sd = 3.284$), **HN** ($m = 12.78$; $sd = 5.832$), and **WN** ($m = 10.98$; $sd = 4.495$). In terms of the main effects, a within-subjects, 2×2 ANOVA showed that subjects performed significantly faster on **W** than **H** ($f = 6.63$; $df = 1/31$; $p < 0.050$) and on **P** than **N** ($f = 67.61$; $df = 1/31$; $p < 0.001$). There was also an interaction effect ($f = 9.42$; $df = 1/31$; $p < 0.005$). Figure 7 shows a box plot of the trial times by treatment, where the boxes represent the middle 50% of the values, the thick line represents the median, and the whiskers represent lines to the highest and lowest values. A comparison of the means tells us that subjects had particular manipulation problems with hand-held windows when no passive-haptic feedback was present. We postulate that precisely coordinating two movable objects (i.e. the paddle and the dominant hand) in free-space proved challenging for subjects, but that when either the user only had to manipulate the dominant hand (**W**), or when the physical work surface constrained the motion of the dominant hand (**P**), subjects were more capable of working efficiently.

Recall that accuracy on the docking task was measured as the distance the center of the shape was from the center of the target location at the end of the trial; lower values being better. Looking at the mean trial accuracy measure (in centimeters) we see ($N = 32$ for all treatments): **HP** ($m = 0.15$; $sd = 0.079$), **WP** ($m = 0.17$; $sd = 0.072$), **HN** ($m = 0.25$; $sd = 0.194$), and **WN** ($m = 0.28$; $sd = 0.205$). In terms of the main effects, a within-subjects, 2×2 ANOVA showed that subjects were significantly more accurate on **H** than **W** ($f = 6.16$; $df = 1/31$; $p < 0.050$) and on **P** than **N** ($f = 17.87$; $df = 1/31$; $p < 0.001$). There was no interaction effect ($f = 0.29$; $df = 1/31$; $p > 0.590$). Figure 8 shows a box plot of the accuracy by treatment. Intuitively, it comes as little surprise that **P** allowed subjects to be more precise than **N**, as **P** provided physical support for fine motor control. Also, because **H** allowed subjects to hold the work surface in any position that was comfortable, subjects seemed to choose positions that allowed them to steady their hands, whereas with **W**, subjects were forced to work in a fixed location, similar to using a touch-screen interface.

For the selection task, the statistics for the trial time measure (in seconds) were as follows ($N = 32$ for all treatments): **HP** ($m = 2.83$; $sd = 0.791$), **WP** ($m = 3.49$; $sd = 0.614$), **HN** ($m = 3.35$; $sd = 0.736$), and **WN** ($m = 4.31$; $sd = 0.876$). In terms of the main effects, a within-subjects, 2×2 ANOVA showed that subjects performed significantly faster on **H** than **W** ($f = 34.42$; $df = 1/31$; $p < 0.001$) and **P** than **N** ($f = 35.50$; $df = 1/31$; $p < 0.001$). There was a slight interaction effect ($f = 3.96$; $df = 1/31$; $p > 0.050$). Figure 9 shows a box plot of the trial times by treatment. Recall that the signpost was positioned outside the field of view of the subject when looking straight ahead. Because the subject could position the work surface in line with the signpost for **H**, these treatments were significantly faster than **W**. Accuracy on this task was measured as whether the correct choice was selected by the subject. For this measure, all treatments had a mean score of at least 99%, and no significance was found.

Discussion

The addition of passive-haptic feedback to IVE interfaces can significantly decrease the time necessary to perform UI tasks. Subjects performed 44% faster on the docking task, and 17% faster on the selection task when passive-haptic feedback was present. Interfaces which implement a 2D pen-and-tablet metaphor within 3D worlds can provide better support for both precise and ballistic actions by registering a physical surface with the virtual tablet. Docking task accuracy was significantly better, increasing by over 38%, when passive-haptic feedback was present. Furthermore, we have shown that hand-held windows

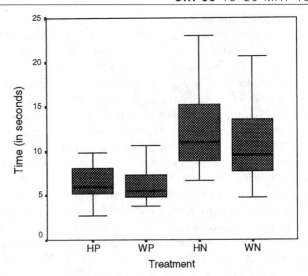

Figure 7: Docking Task Trial Time × Treatment

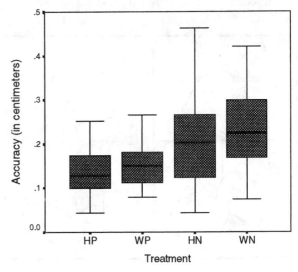

Figure 8: Docking Task Accuracy × Treatment

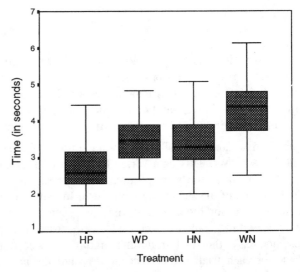

Figure 9: Selection Task Trial Time × Treatment

provide the freedom of movement necessary for working effectively in IVEs. On the selection task, which required looking around the IVE, subjects performed 21% faster using hand-fixed as opposed to world-fixed windows.

These quantitative findings are in line with our qualitative results. Users prefer interfaces that allow them to work efficiently and effectively. The use of passive-haptic feedback, coupled with a hand-held device, can greatly aid interaction in immersive virtual environments.

During our analysis, we found that some learning effects were present. Specifically, for the docking task, **HN** and **WN** trial times improved and accuracy increased over time, while **HP** and **WP** stayed fairly constant. This suggests that the **P** treatments presented subjects with the feedback they expected from real-world experience (i.e. that objects don't simply pass through other objects), and that the **N** treatments required more training. All treatments showed a general improvement trend over time on the selection task.

CONCLUSIONS AND FUTURE WORK

Our results show that the addition of passive-haptic feedback for use in precise UI manipulation tasks can significantly increase user performance. In addition, users prefer interfaces that provide a physical surface, and that allow them to work with UI widgets in the same visual field of view as the objects they are modifying.

In our work, we have tried to provide data to help IVE designers produce interfaces that allow users to perform real work. Because of the complexity of user interaction in IVEs, much work still needs to be done. We have shown that the HARP testbed is an effective environment for performing future studies. We will look at ways of improving non-haptic interfaces for those systems where it is impractical to provide passive-haptic feedback. Possible modifications include the use of 3D representations of widgets instead of 2D representations, and the imposition of simulated physical surface constraints by clamping user movement to the virtual surface of the paddle. Also, we would like to explore other component interaction techniques, such as cascading menus, within the HARP testbed.

ACKNOWLEDGEMENTS

This research was supported in part by the Office of Naval Research. Thanks to Jim Templeman for his insight.

REFERENCES

1. Angus, I., Sowizral, H., "VRMosaic: Web Access from within a Virtual Environment," *IEEE Computer Graphics and Applications*, 16, 3, (1996), pp. 6-10.

2. Billinghurst, M., Baldis, S., Matheson, L., Philips, M., "3D Palette: A Virtual Reality Content Creation Tool," *Proc. of VRST '97*, (1997), pp. 155-156.

3. Bowman, D., Wineman, J., Hodges, L., "Exploratory Design of Animal Habitats within an Immersive Virtual Environment," *GA Institute of Technology GVU Technical Report GIT-GVU-98-06*, (1998).

4. Bryson, S., Levit, C., "The Virtual Windtunnel: An Environment for the Exploration of Three-Dimensional Unsteady Flows," *Proc. of Visualization '91*, (1991), pp. 17-24.

5. Cutler, L., Fröhlich, B., Hanrahan, P., "Two-Handed Direct Manipulation on the Responsive Workbench," *1997 Symp. on Interactive 3D Graphics*, Providence, RI, (1997), pp. 107-114.

6. Deering, M., "The HoloSketch VR Sketching System," *Comm. of the ACM*, 39, 5, (1996), pp. 55-61.

7. Feiner, S., MacIntyre, B., Haupt, M., Solomon, E., "Windows on the World: 2D Windows for 3D Augmented Reality," *Proc. of UIST '93*, (1993), pp. 145-155.

8. Fels, S., Hinton, G., "Glove-TalkII: An Adaptive Gesture-to-Format Interface," *Proc. of SIGCHI '95*, (1995), pp. 456-463.

9. Fisher, S., McGreevy, M., Humphries, J., Robinett, W., "Virtual Environment Display System," *1986 Workshop on Interactive 3D Graphics*, Chapel Hill, NC, (1986), pp. 77-87.

10. Fuhrmann, A., Löffelmann, H., Schmalstieg, D., Gervautz, M., "Collaborative Visualization in Augmented Reality," *IEEE Computer Graphics and Applications*, 18, 4, (1998), pp. 54-59.

11. Mine, M., Brooks, F., Séquin, C., "Moving Objects in Space: Exploiting Proprioception in Virtual-Environment Interaction," *Proc. of SIGGRAPH '97*, (1997), pp. 19-26.

12. Mine, M, "ISAAC: A Meta-CAD System for Virtual Environments," *Computer-Aided Design*, 29, 8, (1997), pp. 547-553.

13. Poupyrev, I., Weghorst, S., Billinghurst, M., Ichikawa, T., "A Framework and Testbed for Studying Manipulation Techniques for Immersive VR," *Proc. of VRST '97*, (1997), pp. 21-28.

14. Shneiderman, B., *Designing the User Interface*, (3rd Edition), Addison-Wesley: Reading, MA, (1998).

15. Sowizral, H., "Interacting with Virtual Environments Using Augmented Virtual Tools," *Stereoscopic Displays and Virtual Reality Systems*, Fisher, S., Merrit, J., Bolas, M., Eds. Proc. SPIE 2177, (1994), pp. 409-416.

16. Stanney, K., "Realizing the Full Potential of Virtual Reality: Human Factors Issues that Could Stand in the Way," *Proc. of VRAIS '95*, (1995), pp. 28-34.

17. Stoakley, R., Conway, M., Pausch, R., "Virtual Reality on a WIM: Interactive Worlds in Miniature," *Proc. of SIGCHI '95*, (1995), pp. 265-272.

18. Sturman, D., Zeltzer, D., Pieper, S., "Hands-on Interaction With Virtual Environments," *Proc. of UIST '89*, (1989), pp. 19-24.

19. van Teylingen, R., Ribarsky, W., and van der Mast, C., "Virtual Data Visualizer," *IEEE Transactions on Visualization and Computer Graphics*, 3, 1, (1997), pp. 65-74.

20. Wloka, M., Greenfield, E., "The Virtual Tricorder: A Uniform Interface for Virtual Reality," *Proc. of UIST '95*, (1995), pp. 39-40.

Socially Translucent Systems: Social Proxies, Persistent Conversation, and the Design of "Babble"

**Thomas Erickson, David N. Smith, Wendy A. Kellogg,
Mark Laff, John T. Richards, Erin Bradner[1]**

IBM T.J. Watson Research Center

P.O. Box 704

Yorktown Heights, NY 10598, USA

+1 914 784-7826

snowfall@acm.org, dnsmith@watson.ibm.com, wkellogg@us.ibm.com,
mrl@us.ibm.com, jtr@watson.ibm.com, ebradner@ics.uci.edu

ABSTRACT

We take as our premise that it is possible and desirable to design systems that support social processes. We describe Loops, a project which takes this approach to supporting computer-mediated communication (CMC) through structural and interactive properties such as persistence and a minimalist graphical representation of users and their activities that we call a social proxy. We discuss a prototype called "Babble" that has been used by our group for over a year, and has been deployed to six other groups at the Watson labs for about two months. We describe usage experiences, lessons learned, and next steps.

Keywords

Conversation, Discourse, Awareness, Social Activity, Computer-Mediated Communication, CMC, IRC, Chat, CSCW, Social Computing, Design, Visualization

INTRODUCTION

In the building where our group works there is a door that opens from the stairwell into the hallway. This door has a small design flaw: opened quickly, it is likely to slam into anyone who is about to enter from the other direction. In an attempt to fix this problem, a small sign was placed on the door: it reads, "Please Open Slowly." As you might guess, people soon ceased noticing the sign and its effectiveness decreased markedly.

We would like to contrast this solution with one of a different sort: putting a glass window in the door. The glass window approach means that the sign is no longer required. As people approach the door they can see whether there is anyone on the other side. This is effective for three reasons: First, as humans, we are *perceptually attuned* to movement and human faces and figures, and notice and react to them more readily than we notice and interpret a printed sign. Second, the glass window supports a perceptually based

awareness: I don't open the door quickly because *I know* that you're on the other side. This *awareness* brings our social rules into play to govern our actions: we have been raised in a culture which frowns upon slamming into other people (except in narrowly defined, culturally recognized situations). Finally, there is a third, and somewhat subtler reason for the efficacy of the glass window. Suppose that I don't care whether I harm others: nevertheless, I am still likely to open the door slowly because *I know that you know that I know* you're there, and therefore I will be held *accountable* for my actions. This distinction is useful because, while accountability and awareness are generally entwined in the physical world, they are not necessarily coupled in the digital realm.

We call systems which provide perceptually-based social cues which afford awareness and accountability "Socially Translucent Systems." In such systems we believe it will be easier for users to carry on coherent discussions; to observe and imitate others' actions; to engage in peer pressure; to create, notice, and conform to social conventions. We see social translucence as a fundamental requirement for supporting communication and collaboration. This brings us to the issue of translucence. Why Socially *Translucent* Systems? Because there is a vital tension between privacy and visibility. Neither is inherently good or bad: each supports and inhibits certain types of behavior (for example, the perceived validity of elections depends crucially on keeping certain aspects very private, and others very visible).

The basic premise of our work is that it is possible and desirable to build digitally based, socially translucent systems which allow our socially based processes to operate. In this paper we describe a system that takes this approach to supporting computer-mediated conversation.

---

[1] Also CORPS (Computing Organizations, Policy, and Society) program, UC Irvine.

Related Work

A concern with making the activity of users of digital systems visible to others dates back to at least the Finger program on UNIX. More recently, a number of investigators have explored ways of portraying socially-salient information in human computer interfaces. Ackerman and Starr [1] have argued for the importance of social activity indicators, particularly in synchronous CMC systems. Hill and Hollan have discussed the creation of persistent traces of human activity [14]. And many researchers have constructed systems which attempt, in various ways, to provide cues about the presence and activity of their users (for example, [3, 6, 15, 16, 18, 20]). Closest in spirit to our approach are the Out to Lunch system [5], and the AROMA [19] and Chat Circles [7] systems, which use abstract representations (sonic and visual, respectively) to portray social activity.

THE LOOPS PROJECT

Our goal is to design systems that support smooth, reflective, and productive conversations through synchronous and asynchronous computer-mediated communication. We believe that social translucence is particularly applicable to the design of CMC systems. After all, conversation is a fundamentally social process. Face to face conversation relies heavily on social cues: facial expressions, gestures, postures, and other socially-relevant actions are used in the initiation and conduct of conversation [12, 13, 17]. That is, we speak *to* an audience: nods and eye contact convey one message, yawns and fidgeting another, and watching people slip out of the room during a presentation is a powerful motivator to either change course or wrap up.

This raises the question of what sorts of social cues might be useful in supporting CMC, and how they might be presented. An obvious answer is to explore the use of video or high resolution virtual reality to depict the subtleties of facial, gestural and postural expressions. We have rejected this approach for two reasons. First, we believe that systems which attempt to leverage social processes need to be developed through a process of creating and deploying working systems, and studying their use in ordinary work contexts. This intent to deploy, in and of itself, argues against a 'radical technology' approach such as VR. Second, using video (or pictures) of participants' faces takes up significant screen space, and doesn't scale to larger groups. We also find the prospect of digital environments populated by floating heads to be aesthetically unappealing. So, instead, we decided to take a minimalist approach to providing socially salient cues.

"Loops" is the project name and serves as a catch all for the assumptions, design rationales, and conceptual and working prototypes developed in this project. Loops is not an acronym, but is taken from the idiomatic phrase, "keep me in the loop," which refers to keeping participants aware of what is going on. The premise of Loops is that conversation is a powerful tool for creating, developing, and sharing knowledge. The ability to carry out coherent, productive conversations among many participants distributed in time and space is likely to become an increasingly important organizational skill. The goal of Loops is to make it easy and practical to initiate, conduct, and share such conversations, and the knowledge developed through them.

A Brief Project History

Although we will focus on the working prototype and its long-term usage, it is useful to situate it in a larger context. Of particular import is the fact that Loops was developed and used within a closely knit work group (aka "the lab"). The work group had two remote members and a number of other members who were 'locally mobile' [2], i.e. often not at their desks.

The Loops concept was initially developed using storytelling, scenarios, and rough prototypes [8]. Beginning with stories about mailing list use (e.g., floods of "Please unsubscribe me messages" as cues of audience dissatisfaction) and conjectures based on studies of the use of a bulletin board system [9, 10], the initial Loops scenario was developed using a prototype consisting of a stack of hand drawn index cards. The initial vision of Loops was akin to a lightweight mailing list that could be started by an ordinary user, and which allowed potential participants control over their degree of involvement in the conversation. The idea was that users could be *aware* of the activities of other participants with respect to the conversation, so that a gathering crowd might entice others to join. Similarly, since this awareness would be shared by all participants and thus enhance accountability, phenomena such as a dispersing crowd might provide a way of shaping a conversation's content, style, or etiquette. Other scenarios and paper prototypes followed, and Loops was widely discussed by members of the lab.

About six weeks after the initial Loops scenario, one of our remote members appeared in the lab with his own prototype. The prototype, which he had named "Babble," was a functioning server and client system. Babble implemented some of the basic Loops concepts, albeit in a form that more closely resembled a combination of chat and bulletin boards than the initial concept's melding of mailing lists and bulletin boards. The adoption of Babble was gradual, taking at least six weeks. Nevertheless, Babble came to play three important roles in the design process. First, it became both the subject and locus of design discussions. Second, it served as a testbed, with new ideas being tried out both in the original client, as well as in two clients being developed for other platforms (these being part of an effort to infect other, cross-laboratory projects with 'Loops ideas'). Finally, after about ten months of use and design evolution, Babble was deployed to six other groups who, as of this writing, have been using it for about two months.

The Design Rationale of Loops

The design of Loops has been shaped by the following assumptions:

- Cues from content— e.g., the ability to see how a conversation has unfolded across time and participants — can enable newcomers to recognize the norms and conventions in a particular conversation, thus enabling them to contribute more effectively.
- Social cues — e.g., audience size, who is listening, how actively people are participating — can focus participation and make conversations more engaging.
- Relatively small groups, whose members all know one another, or know *of* one another, are most likely to draw on social and content cues as a result of their shared activities and social dynamics.

The first two assumptions are embodied in the design of Loops; the last in the selection of its target audience.

The Conversation as a Single Document

A conversation is represented as a single, persistent document with the oldest items first (e.g., Figure 1). Each comment is preceded by a header which has a time stamp and the participant's name. New comments are appended to the end of the document. This approach is employed by some types of asynchronous bulletin boards.

As discussed elsewhere [9, 10], this type of representation has a number of advantages both for readers and for writers. Readers, whether they be newcomers or simply infrequent participants, can get an overview of social norms that govern the conversation by skimming through it. For example, the length of comments is apparent, as is the informality of the conversation (inferable from the simplified syntax and the absence of punctuation), and degree of humor and politeness. By scanning the name and time stamp headers that precede each comment, the tempo of the conversation, the number of participants, and the presence or absence of frequent participants can be inferred. Representing conversation as a single, shared, persistent stream has consequences for authoring as well. The fact that the conversation is persistent and shared increases the potential for accountability. Unlike chat, where conversation is ephemeral, or like mailing lists where the

```
===Friday 12 Dec 97 3:43:44 From: Bill
Hi Steven!
===Friday 12 Dec 97 3:44:49 From:  Steven
Hellooo Bill. A little guidance please?
Is the [...] summary we're preparing for [...]
supposed to be an exercise in feeling
good, or are we supposed to be giving
him hard-headed guidance?
===Friday 12Dec 97 3:56:55 From:  Bill
yes :-)
```

Figure 1. A segment of conversation displayed as a single document.

past becomes buried in message archives, accessing the conversation's history is just a matter of scrolling.

Another important element of this representation of the conversation is its single, shared sequential structure: if someone responds to comment A by posting comment B, B will appear immediately after A (except in rare cases when two postings are submitted at about the same time), and that adjacency will be seen by all viewers. This shared sequential structure means that participants can and do participate with short, indexical utterances like "Yes!", "Thank you," and "Great idea!". This type of response is less likely to occur in a mailing list because since there is no shared, sequential structure it is necessary to quote the text being referred to, and because participants are often annoyed at opening a message and finding only an 'insignificant' comment in it. Yet, while such indexical comments may not extend the conceptual boundaries of the conversation, they can make it more convivial and inviting by providing a low overhead way for participants to signal agreement, encouragement, and empathy.

This portrayal of the conversation as a single, sequential document provides a variety of cues for making people aware of the norms and customs in force that are less visible in other, more hierarchical representations of conversation. The conversation's persistence is a boon to asynchronous interaction, and supports accountability as well. However, we also think it is important to provide a synchronous portrayal of social cues.

The Social Proxy

In Loops, synchronous cues for a given conversation are provided by a social proxy, a minimalist graphical representation of users which depicts their presence and their activities *vis à vis* the conversation (Figure 2). This social proxy portrays the conversation as a large circle, and the participants as colored dots, referred to, hereafter, as marbles. Marbles within the circle are involved in the conversation being viewed; marbles outside the circle represent those who are logged on but are in other

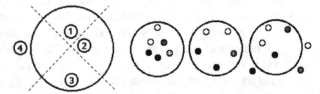

Figure 2. A schematic of the social proxy and, to its right, three instances of it. The schematic shows two people (dots 1 & 2) actively involved in a conversation, one inactive person (dot 3), and one person involved in a different conversation (dot 4). Each dot occupies a (virtual) wedge; wedges are created and destroyed as people log on and off. The first instance shows a 'hot' conversation; the second, a dormant one; the third a mixture of activity, idleness, with three people in other conversations.

conversations. The marbles of those who are active in the current conversation, either contributing or 'listening' (that is, interacting with the conversation window via clicks and mouse movements) are shown near the circle's center; with inactivity marbles drift out to the periphery. When people leave the current conversation their marbles move outside the circle; when they enter the conversation, their marbles move into the circle. In our current prototype these activities have optional sonic cues.

Although simple, this social proxy gives a sense of the size of the audience, the amount of conversational activity, as well as indicating whether people are gathering or dispersing, and who it is that is coming and going. Also, because the portrayal is visual, it has a perceptual directness (like the glass window) that a list of written names lacks. Experientially, the social proxy is interesting because it focuses attention on the group as a whole, and the coherence (or lack thereof) of its activity.

THE WORKING PROTOTYPE: BABBLE

While stories, scenarios, and rough prototypes are invaluable for getting a quick handle on design ideas, we believe that designing CMC — particularly systems in which social mechanisms play a central role — necessitates moving ideas into a usable prototype as quickly as practical. Thus, having laid out the initial design rationale, we shift our attention to a working prototype called Babble. Initially developed about six weeks into the project, Babble

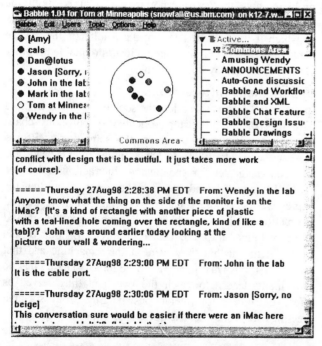

Figure 3. A screenshot of Babble. At the moment shown, all participants are in the same conversation (Commons Area), and most have recently 'spoken' or 'listened'. The two marbles near the periphery of the circle are participants who have not been active recently.

has gone through considerable evolution over the ensuing year. Here we describe the Babble interface as it is now; next, we discuss our experiences from our year-long use of Babble.

Babble, as it has evolved through design and usage, is a CMC system that allows conversation to be threaded (by user-defined topics) and persistent (held on the server until the topic is deleted), and that provides a social proxy that shows the participants and their activities with respect to the conversation (Figure 3). Babble also allows participants to open private, one-to-one chats which are not persistent, so that a completely private channel of communication is available. Written in Smalltalk, it uses TCP/IP and a client-server architecture to transmit both conversation and social information.

A Tour of the Interface.

The Users List

In the upper left pane of the Babble window (Figure 3) is a list of the names of all users who are logged on, each shown with his or her marble (i.e. the colored dots).

The Social Proxy

The upper middle pane contains the social proxy (usually called 'the cookie'), which here shows that all 8 participants are in the current conversation (in this case, the "Commons Area"). Two of these participants have not been recently active; the other six have all 'spoken' or 'listened' (i.e. interacted with the Babble window) recently. Over the course of several minutes of inactivity, a participant's marble drifts towards the periphery.

The Topics List

The upper right pane shows a list of all topics (i.e. conversations), with the currently viewed topic highlighted. Clicking on a topic moves the user to that topic, resulting in the conversation being displayed in the bottom pane of the window, and in the user's marble moving out of the circle (from the perspective of the other participants). Miniature icons to the left of each topic name indicate how many people are in it (to a maximum of 10), and the topic changes color when new material is added. Topics can be created or deleted by anyone.

Talking via the Topic Window and Chat

The bottom pane holds the topic's conversation which consists of a shared sequential structure in a single, persistent document. People 'talk' by typing into an entry window; if they select text before beginning, the selected text is 'quoted' and displayed in the entry window. In either case, once the text is composed, the user clicks a "Done" button and the comment is appended to the end of the conversation, with a name and time stamp.

Babble also supports private, one-to-one chat. By right-clicking on a participant's name or marble, a user can initiate a private chat. One experimental feature is that soft key click sounds are transmitted in real time, giving the chat partner cues as to whether and how extensively the chatter is responding; the actual text of the comment is not sent until the chatter clicks "Done." Although chats are not persistent, participants can, and sometimes do, copy portions of private chats into public conversations.

Other Features

The Babble interface also includes a second, very small window called "the spot" (not shown), which turns green whenever a new message appears in the current conversation. This allows users to minimize the Babble window, using the spot as a monitor for conversational activity while they perform other tasks on their workstations. Clicking on the spot brings up the Babble Window, with new comments temporarily highlighted.

Another feature is the ability to get information about users' activities by right-clicking on their marbles and choosing "Get Info...". This reveals where the user is, and when they were last present in the current topic. This is another way of supporting awareness and accountability.

Babble in Our Lab

Babble began running in our own lab on August 4, 1997. It took 4-6 weeks for the conversational structure that is used today to emerge. That structure consists of a "Commons Area" which is the default entry point, and a set of topics created by Babble users. Figure 4 shows the growth of participants and topics over the first 6 months of use in our lab.

The Deployment of Babble to Other Groups

Both because of interest from non-members of the lab, and because of our conviction that designing solely for one's own use is a mistake, we began deploying Babble to six other groups in July of 1998. The groups included two computer science research groups, two other working groups (technical recruiting and marketing groups), and two cohorts (a social cohort of summer interns, and a professional cohort of HCI professionals).

As of this writing (about two months after deployment), three of the deployment groups are using Babble on a daily basis (one CS group, and the two cohorts). Two are making sporadic use of Babble. One group has abandoned Babble after sporadic attempts at use, though the group has so far resisted efforts to "take it away".

DISCUSSION

In this section we will provide a distillation of our experience using Babble. We will primarily draw upon the year long experience of our lab's usage as reported in interviews and visible in the (persistent) Babble conversations and logs. We will occasionally refer to the usage practices in the deployed Babbles derived from observations and interviews, although we believe that the six weeks to eight weeks of their use is too short a period for group behaviors to stabilize (note that in the growth

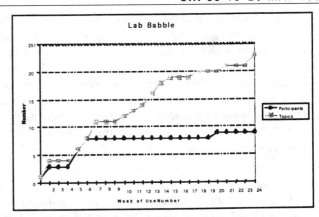

Figure 4. Growth of participants and user-created topics in the first 6 months of Babble use.

trajectory of the Lab Babble, six to eight weeks of use was really just the beginning).

We are well aware of the drawbacks of reflecting on our own use of our own tool. Two problems, in particular, stand out: first, there is the possibility that we will act in such a way as to fulfill our own expectations; second, there is the possibility that we are overly motivated to use our own technology. In view of the first problem, we will primarily focus on ways in which our use of Babble has diverged from our expectations, as embodied in our initial paper prototypes and scenarios; we will supplement these reports, where appropriate, with observations from the Babbles deployed to other groups. In view of the second problem, note that we are not making claims about the degree of usability of Babble, *per se*, but rather about ways in which it used. Note also that the results of the Babble deployment show that there are no insurmountable usability barriers to its use by other groups.

Opportunistic Interactions

In the initial Loops scenarios, the social proxy was depicted as a way of initiating topic-oriented synchronous chats. People who happened to be in the same topic, it was reasoned, would be likely to have similar intents, and thus be good candidates for spontaneous interactions (also see [16]). While this did indeed occur, it also turned out that the expressiveness of the social proxy triggered more general interactions. That is, when someone's marble moved abruptly (either into the center of circle, or out of the circle), it meant that they were at their machine and that their attention was focused on Babble. These marble movements tended to catch the eye, and thus served as effective triggers for interactions ranging from sociable greetings to work-oriented questions, either via the topic (e.g., as in Figure 1) or in a private chat. Marble movements also triggered phone calls and office drop ins, although we did not track the frequency of these occurrences. In this regard, the social proxy's ability to indicate activity via marble movement and position seems superior to purely textual ways of representing activity.

Group Awareness

Another unexpected effect of using Babble has been its usefulness in maintaining and expanding group awareness. As noted, the social proxy provides synchronous awareness of who is on the system, and who is active. And, obviously, examining the persistent conversation traces (particularly that in the Commons Area) reveals who has been around. What is less obvious is how much awareness comes through the content of the conversation, often as an unintended side effect. Sign offs ('I have to go to the [project] meeting now'), asides ('Dave is right, the Network Nation was published in '78'), questions ("Does anyone know how to do a screen capture"), reveal that one participant is still involved in a particular project, remind the group that a paper is underway, and suggest that another participant is beginning to document a prototype. Furthermore, the more one knows about the group and its activities, the more that can be inferred from such talk. Because this awareness grows incrementally over days, weeks, and months, and is essentially a side effect of witnessing comments and conversations among other group members, it feels very lightweight. Lab members commented that one of the things they did upon returning from a trip or vacation was to read through the commons area to see what had happened during their absence.

Informality and Sociability

One of our intentions for Loops was that it should bring a more sociable dimension to workplace discussion. We hoped that the persistent sequential representation of conversation would lower the overhead for jokes, puns, thanks, and affirmations, and that the group activity expressed through the social proxy would heighten the awareness of the group as a group. This did appear to happen, in that it provided a venue for sociable talk that — outside of face to face interaction — did not take place via other communication systems.

Similar feelings were expressed in interviews with members of the groups to which Babble was deployed. Our informants told us that they were less careful about punctuation, spelling, and other mechanical aspects of writing when using Babble as compared with email.

> "When you are in Babble, it seems like a more relaxed atmosphere and you don't have to watch your spelling, you don't have to have your sentence structure perfect and all that. The [email] system we are using, … you feel like everything has to be correct because you feel like someone might print out that note and show someone else."
>
> —Recruiter

> "I think [Babble is] less formal. I treat it less formal. I wouldn't write mail about someone else's bug unless I check very very carefully that it is indeed in their code. … It's funny but it's OK to write things that are not 100% finished. … It's not that thought through … half-baked ideas are OK. Somehow it's much more like conversation."
>
> —Software Engineer

They saw the (perceived) informality of Babble as an advantage – allowing them to express ideas which were not yet fully formed or to make statements that they were not sure were wholly accurate, without offending others. Their comments are reminiscent of Fanderclai's remarks about MUDs [11]:

> The novelty and playfulness inherent in the environment blur the distinctions between work and play, encouraging a freedom that is often more productive and more enjoyable than the more formal exchange of other forums. It is perhaps something like running into your colleagues in the hallway or sitting with them in a cafe; away from the formal meeting rooms and offices and lecture halls, you're free to relax and joke and exchange half-finished theories, building freely on each other's ideas until something new is born.

Babble as a Place

We were taken unawares by the degree to which Babble turned into a place. While we had talked about how to make Babble more MUD-like (indeed, one topic is called "MOOifying Babble"), we viewed this as future development awaiting the ability to use embedded graphics, rich text and complex page layouts. Nevertheless, Babble came to feel considerably more like a place than we had imagined was possible in a client which permitted only the creation of sequences of (non-rich) text.

One element which made Babble seem place-like had to do with the way different topics developed different feels. In the lab's Babble, several different types of 'places' developed. One was the "Commons Area," a place for people to hang out and talk. The Commons was where most people spent most of their idle time (and for that matter, most of their conversational energy) and became a place for social chit-chat that sometimes segued into work issues ranging from design to administrative announcements. Other topics (e.g. "Babble Problems," "Book Recommendations," "Bad Jokes") were places for general postings with occasional side chat or Q&A. Still yet a different sort of place was the private office or notebook. In early July, one lab member started a topic intended to be, according to its opening comment, "a combination of an on-line office and notebook." The comment continued with "You're welcome to leave me a message, or to comment on things I put here" thus becoming an assertion of ownership and control. This assertion was generally complied with, and the topic became characterized by fairly long essay-like comments by 'the owner,' interspersed with comments from and conversations with 'visitors.' The creation of this topic was soon followed by that of other 'offices'.

The place-like nature of Babble was also entwined with that nature of the language used within it. As noted previously, conversation was typically frank and unguarded. Babble was regarded as a semi-private place. This became apparent when several 'visitors' showed up over a short period (access to Babble requires only possession of a client, a server name, and a port number, and thus may be 'granted' by any current Babble user). One inhabitant of the Lab Babble wrote:

> "In the last week or so, D, G, S, and K have shown up. I know the first three, but don't think I know who (or at least which K), K is, and that feels a little weird because to me Babble feels a bit like my office and there are now strangers in it! (Nothing personal, K)."

A similar instance occurred in one of the deployment groups, where a non-group member was invited into Babble. In an interview, one of that group's members said:

> "So I think to myself, 'is she listening to every word?' Since it is such a group thing, I would have expected someone to ask the group before inviting someone outside to join..."

Notice that this concern about strangers — those from outside the group's social context — is another manifestation, this time negative, of the accountability supported by the Babble environment.

CONCLUSIONS

Babble is not a bulletin board, a chat system, a MUD, an email system, or a newsgroup. It merges elements of many of these systems, but it is not quite any of them. Babble combines the persistence and shared sequentiality of asynchronous bulletin boards, with the immediacy and informality of MUDS and chat, and presents these along with a perceptually-based social proxy that shows not just those who are speaking but those who are active (i.e. interacting with the interface). In our view, Babble is more akin to a MUD [4] than anything else. However, unlike a MUD where conversation is ephemeral and built objects have persistence, in Babble it is the conversations that persist and the cues that shape interaction (embodied as rooms and objects in MUDS) that are either ephemeral, as in the social proxy, or at least much more tacitly embedded in the persistent conversation

Our experience with Babble suggests that informal, persistent conversation systems fill a communications niche that is currently lacking in many work contexts. Many members of the lab, as well as informants in the deployment groups, felt that having an electronic place including "just the right crowd" was useful for communicating things that they would not communicate in

other written forms. We believe that this is one of the most important aspects of Babble: it can be used as a place for unguarded discussion among people who know one another, who understand the contexts within which their remarks are being made. Hyperbole, misattribution, inaccuracy, etc., are a fundamental part of how people talk with one another, and they play an important role: they promote response, and cause people to push ideas farther than they would otherwise. Creative and out-of-the-box thinking arises from playful struggle, from exaggeration, from jumping up and down on top of a soap box, from trying to reconcile contrary ideas, tensions, etc. With an important proviso: All this has to take place in a safe and trusting place.

The notion of a conversational environment as a 'trusted place' is an interesting and challenging one. How — technically, socially, and organizationally — can we balance the need for a safe and trusting place with the organizational imperative to share information? One decision facing us as designers is how and to what extent we "design in" norms and social conventions. For example, if we build in technical mechanisms to provide privacy, in addition to the usability impact, we also eliminate opportunities for participants to show that they may be trusted, or to rely on others to respect their privacy. The Babble prototype has no technical features for controlling access: anyone who has access to the client could, in theory, enter any Babble space. But, because Babble makes users visible (synchronously and, through the "Get Info..." command, asynchronously), this resulted in the group noticing, commenting on, and ultimately discussing how to deal with this issue. We believe that a greater understanding of how to design socially translucent systems which permit social mechanisms to come into play is of great importance in designing CMC and CSCW applications.

Next Steps

We intend to continue deploying Babble to other groups, and studying those deployments as they evolve over time. We expect that groups which adopt Babble will evolve considerably different ways of using it. We hope that a close examination of these cases can provide some insight on how group needs and social dynamics interact with social translucence and the structure of the system to determine practice. We also hope to better understand how to design CMC systems to facilitate adoption in a landscape of shifting institutional needs and practices.

We see a number of future research issues. One obvious issue — since we have considerable difficulty (re)finding valuable nuggets of conversation — is providing tools for structuring conversations (both on the fly and after the fact), as well as tools for navigating, searching, and visualizing large conversations. Another issue is to pursue the development of the social proxy. Our current portrayal, while useful, is extremely simple. We intend to explore ways to make it richer, as well as looking at ways of supporting less synchronous behavior such as recording traces of social behavior over time.

ACKNOWLEDGMENTS

The work described herein is highly collaborative, and we acknowledge the substantive contributions of our Babble colleagues: Jonathan Brezin, Brent Hailpern, Amy Katriel, Cal Swart, and Jason Ellis. We thank our users for their assistance, both tacit and explicit. Thanks to Dave Curbow, Allen Cypher, Niklas Damiris, Paul Dourish, Jed Harris, Austin Henderson, Charlie Hill, and Shah Xin Wei, Randall Smith, Rachel Bellamy, and John Thomas for great conversations. This paper benefited from comments by five anonymous reviewers and Noboru Iwayama.

REFERENCES

1. Ackerman, M.S. and Starr, B. (1995). Social activity indicators: Interface components for CSCW systems. In *Proceedings of the ACM Symposium on User Interface Software and Technology* (UIST '95), New York: ACM, pp. 159-168.

2. Bellotti, V. and Bly, S. (1996). Walking Away from the Desktop Computer: Distributed Collaboration in a Product Design Team. *Proceedings of CSCW '96*. ACM Press, 1996, pp. 209-218.

3. Benford, S., Bowers, J., Fahlen, L., Mariani, J., & Rodden, T. Supporting Cooperative Work in Virtual Environments. *The Computer Journal*, Vol 38, No. 1.

4. Bruckman, A. MOOSE Crossing: Construction, Community, and Learning in a Networked Virtual World for Kids. PhD dissertation, Massachusetts Institute of Technology, 1997.

5. Cohen, J. Monitoring Background Activities. *Auditory Display* (ed. G. Kramer). Addison-Wesley, 1994, pp. 439-531.

6. Dieberger, A. (1997). Supporting social navigation on the World Wide Web. *International Journal of Human-Computer Studies*, 46(6), pp. 805-825.

7. Donath, J., Karahalios, K., & Viegas, F. (1999). Visualizing Conversation. *Proceedings of the Thirty-Second Hawai'i International Conference on Systems Science.* (ed. J. F. Nunamaker, Jr. R. H. Sprague, Jr.) IEEE Computer Society Press, 1999.

8. Erickson, T. (1995) Notes on Design Practice: Stories and Prototypes as Catalysts for Communication . In *Scenario-Based Design: Envisioning Work and Technology in System Development.* (ed. J. Carroll). New York: Wiley & Sons, 1995, pp. 37-58.

9. Erickson, T. (1997) Social Interaction on the Net: Virtual Community as Participatory Genre. In *Proceedings of the Thirtieth Hawai'i International Conference on Systems Science.* (ed. J. F. Nunamaker, Jr. R. H. Sprague, Jr.) Vol 6. IEEE Computer Society Press: Los Alamitos, CA, 1997, pp. 23-30.

10. Erickson, T. (1999) Rhyme and Punishment: The Creation and Enforcement of Conventions in an On-Line Participatory Limerick Genre. *Proceedings of the Thirty-Second Hawai'i International Conference on Systems Science.* (ed. J. F. Nunamaker, Jr. R. H. Sprague, Jr.) IEEE Computer Society Press: Los Alamitos, CA, 1999.

11. Fanderclai, T. (1996). "Like Magic, Only Real." L. Cherny and E. Weise (Eds.), *Wired Women: Gender and New Realities in Cyberspace.* Seattle: Seal Press.

12. Goffman, E. (1963) *Behavior in Public Places: Notes on the Social Organization of Gatherings.* Macmillan Publishing Co., New York, 1963.

13. Goffman, E. (1967) *Interaction Ritual*, Anchor Books, New York, 1967.

14. Hill, W., Hollan, J.D., Wroblewski, D., McCandless, T. (1992). Edit wear and read wear text and hypertext. In *Proceedings of ACM CHI '92 Conference on Human Factors in Computing Systems*, pp. 3-9.

15. Hill, W., Stead, L., Rosenstein, M., and Furnas, G. (1995). Recommending and evaluating choices in a virtual community of use. In *Proceedings of ACM CHI '95 Conference.*

16. Isaacs, E.A., Tang, J.C., and Morris, T. (1996). Piazza: A desktop environment supporting impromptu and planned interactions. In M.S. Ackerman (Ed.), *Proceedings of the ACM 1996 Conference on Computer Supported Cooperative Work*, pp. 315-324.

17. Kendon, A. (1990) *Conducting Interaction: Patterns of Behavior in Focused Encounters.* Cambridge University Press, Cambridge, 1990.

18. O'Day, V.L., Bobrow, D.G., and Shirley, M. (1996). The social-technical design circle. In M.S. Ackerman (Ed.), *Proceedings of the ACM 1996 Conference on Computer Supported Cooperative Work*, pp. 160-169.

19. Pedersen, E. R., & Sokoler, T. AROMA: Abstract Representation of Presence Supporting Mutual Awareness. *Human Factors in Computing Systems: CHI 97 Conference Proceedings.* ACM Press, 1997, pp. 51-58.

20. Roseman, M. and Greenberg, S. (1996). TeamRooms: Network places for collaboration. In M.S. Ackerman (Ed.), *Proceedings of the ACM 1996 Conference on Computer Supported Cooperative Work*, pp. 325-333.

The Elements of Computer Credibility

BJ Fogg
Persuasive Technology Lab
CSLI / Stanford University
Cordura Hall, Stanford, CA 94305
bjfogg@stanford.edu

Hsiang Tseng
Quattro Consulting
1 Harbor Drive
Sausalito, CA 94965
tseng@med.stanford.edu

ABSTRACT

Given the importance of credibility in computing products, the research on computer credibility is relatively small. To enhance knowledge about computers and credibility, we define key terms relating to computer credibility, synthesize the literature in this domain, and propose three new conceptual frameworks for better understanding the elements of computer credibility. To promote further research, we then offer two perspectives on what computer users evaluate when assessing credibility. We conclude by presenting a set of credibility-related terms that can serve in future research and evaluation endeavors.

Keywords

credibility, trustworthiness, expertise, persuasion, captology, trust, influence, information quality, psychology of HCI

INTRODUCTION

Like many aspects of our society, credibility is becoming increasingly important for computer products. In the not-too-distant past, computers were perceived by the general public as virtually infallible [31, 39]. Today, the assumption that computers are credible seems to be eroding. As a community of HCI professionals, we should be concerned about the credibility of the computer products we create, research, and evaluate. But just what is *credibility*? And what makes *computers* credible?

This paper addresses these and other issues about computer credibility. In doing so, we don't suggest easy answers; we certainly don't offer a "how to" checklist for credible computer products. Instead, this paper (1) outlines key terms and concepts that relate to credibility, (2) synthesizes the existing literature on computer credibility, (3) provides new conceptual frameworks for understanding computer credibility, and (4) suggests approaches for further addressing computer credibility in research, evaluation, and design efforts. By doing these things, this paper can serve as a key step toward more credible computer products—that is, more credible desktop applications, web sites, specialized computing devices, and so on.

WHAT IS "CREDIBILITY"?

What is "credibility"? Simply put, *credibility* can be defined as *believability*. Credible people are believable people; credible information is believable information. In fact, some languages use the same word for these two English terms. Throughout our research we have found that *believability* is a good synonym for *credibility* in virtually all cases. The academic literature on credibility, which dates back to the 1930s (see [32, 38] for a review), presents a more sophisticated view of credibility, although the essential meaning is similar to what we propose. Virtually all credibility scholars describe credibility as—

- a perceived quality
- made up of multiple dimensions [3, 9, 32, 38, 40]

First, credibility is a perceived quality; it doesn't reside in an object, a person, or a piece of information. Therefore, in discussing the credibility of a computer product, one is always discussing the *perception* of credibility.

Next, scholars agree that credibility perceptions result from evaluating multiple dimensions simultaneously. Although the literature varies on how many dimensions contribute to credibility evaluations, the vast majority of researchers identify two key components of credibility:

- trustworthiness
- expertise

What this means is that in evaluating credibility, a person makes an assessment of both trustworthiness and expertise to arrive at an overall credibility assessment.

Trustworthiness, a key element in the credibility calculus, is defined by the terms *well-intentioned, truthful, unbiased*, and so on. The trustworthiness dimension of credibility captures the perceived goodness or morality of the source. Rhetoricians in ancient Greece used the terms *ethos* to describe this concept.

Expertise, the other dimension of credibility, is defined by terms such as *knowledgeable, experienced, competent*, and so on. The expertise dimension of credibility captures the perceived knowledge and skill of the source.

Taken together, these ideas suggest that *highly credible computer products will be perceived to have high levels of both trustworthiness and expertise*.

Semantic problems in discussing credibility

Unfortunately, English seems to be a difficult language for discussing credibility. Often in the academic literature—both in psychology and in HCI—writers have used the terms *credibility* and *trust* imprecisely and inconsistently. We hope the following paragraphs can help clarify the semantic issues.

First of all, *trust* and *credibility* are not the same concept. Although these two terms are related, *trust* and *credibility* are not synonyms. *Trust* indicates a positive belief about the perceived reliability of, dependability of, and confidence in a person, object, or process [36, 37]. For example, users may have trust in a computer system designed to keep financial transactions secure. We suggest that one way to interpret the word *trust* in HCI literature is to mentally replace it with the word *dependability*. One helpful (though simplistic) summary is as follows:

- *credibility* → "believability"
- *trust*→ "dependability"

The semantic issues get slightly more complicated. A number of studies use phrases such as "trust in the information" and "trust in the advice" (e.g., see [13, 27]). We propose that these phrases are essentially synonyms for credibility; they refer to the same psychological construct. Table 1 shows some of the most common phrases in HCI research that refer to credibility:

Various phrases refer to credibility
• "trust the information"
• "accept the advice"
• "believe the output"

Table 1: Various phrases describe the credibility construct.

As a result of these semantic issues, those who read the research on trust and machines must note if the author is addressing "trust"—*dependability*—or if the author is addressing "trust in information"—*credibility*. We suspect that the confusing use of these English terms has impeded the progress in understanding credibility as it applies to computer products.

WHEN DOES CREDIBILITY MATTER IN HCI?

Now that we have defined key terms relating to credibility, we next outline when credibility matters in human-computer interactions. Quite frankly, in some cases computer credibility does not seem to matter—such as when the computer device is invisible (in automobile fuel-injection systems, for example) or when the possibility of bias or incompetence is not apparent to users (such as in using a pocket calculator). However, in many situations computer credibility matters a great deal. We propose that credibility matters when computer products—

- act as knowledge sources
- instruct or tutor users
- act as decision aids
- report measurements
- run simulations
- render virtual environments
- report on work performed
- report about their own state

The above eight categories are not exhaustive; we anticipate that future work on computer credibility will add to and refine our categories. Furthermore, these categories are not mutually exclusive; a complex computer system, such as an aviation navigation system, might incorporate elements from many categories: presenting information about weather conditions, measuring airspeed, rendering a visual simulation, and reporting the state of the onboard computer system. Many, but not all, of the above eight categories have been the focus of research on computers and credibility, as synthesized in the following section.

HCI RESEARCH ON CREDIBILITY

Given the wide applicability of credibility in computing, a relatively small body of research addresses perceptions of credibility in human-computer interactions. What follows is our synthesis of the previous research, clustered into six domains.

#1: The credible computer myth

One cluster of research investigates the idea that people automatically assume computers are credible. In framing these studies, the authors state that people perceive computers as "magical" [2], with an "'aura' of objectivity" [1], as having a "scientific mystique" [1], as "awesome thinking machines" [31], as "infallible" [14], as having "superior wisdom" [39], and as "faultless" [39]. In sum, researchers have long suggested that people generally are in "awe" of computers [12] and that people "assign more credibility" to computers than to humans [1].

But what does the empirical research show? The studies that directly examine assumptions about computer credibility conclude that—

- Computers are not perceived as more credible than human experts [1, 12, 22, 31].
- In some cases computers may perceived as less credible [19, 41].

Although intuition suggests that people may perceive computers as more credible than humans in some situations, no solid empirical evidence supports this notion.

#2: Dynamics of computer credibility

Another cluster of research examines the dynamics of computer credibility—how it is gained, how it is lost, and how it can be regained. Some studies demonstrate what is highly intuitive: Computers gain credibility when they provide information that users find accurate or correct [10, 13, 27]; conversely, computers lose credibility when they provide information users find erroneous [13, 17, 27]. Although these conclusions seem obvious, we find this research valuable because it represents the first empirical evidence for these ideas. Other findings on the dynamics of credibility are less obvious, which we summarize in the following paragraphs.

The effects of computer errors on credibility

A few studies have investigated the effects of computer errors on perceptions of computer credibility. Although researchers acknowledge that a single error may severely damage computer credibility in certain situations [13], no study has clearly documented this effect. In fact, in one study, error rates as high as 30% did not cause users to dismiss an onboard automobile navigation system [10, 13]. To be sure, in other contexts, such as getting information from an automated teller machine, a similar error rate would likely cause users to reject the technology completely.

The impact of small errors

Another research area has been the effects of large and small areas on credibility. Virtually all researchers agree that computer errors damage credibility—at least to some extent. One study demonstrated that large errors hurt credibility perceptions more than small errors but not in proportion to the gravity of the error [17, 18]. Another study showed no difference between the effects of large and small mistakes on credibility [13]. Findings from these studies and other work [27] suggest that—

- Small computer errors have disproportionately large effects on perceptions of credibility.

Two paths to regaining credibility

Researchers have also examined how computer products can regain credibility [18]. Two paths are documented in the literature:

- The computer product regains credibility by providing good information over a period of time [10, 13].
- The computer product regains some credibility by continuing to make the identical error; users then learn to anticipate and compensate for the persistent error [27].

In either case, regaining credibility is difficult, especially from a practical standpoint. Once users perceive that a computer product lacks credibility, they are likely to stop using it, which provides no opportunity for the product to regain credibility [27].

#3: Situational factors that affect credibility

The credibility of a computer product does not always depend on the computer product itself. Context of computer use can affect credibility. The existing research shows that three related situations increase computer credibility:

- In unfamiliar situations people give more credence to a computer product that orients them [25].
- Computer products have more credibility after people have failed to solve a problem on their own [42].
- Computer products seem more credible when people have a strong need for information [10, 13].

Indeed, other situations are likely to affect the perception of computer credibility, such as situations with varying levels of risk, situations with forced choices, and situations with different levels of cognitive load. However, research is lacking on these points.

#4: User variables that affect credibility

Although individual differences among users likely affect perceptions of computer credibility in many ways, the extant research allows us to draw only two general conclusions:

User familiarity with subject matter

First, users who are familiar with the content (e.g., an experienced surgeon using a computer simulation of surgery) will evaluate the computer product more stringently and likely perceive the computer product to be less credible [12, 13, 19]. Conversely, those not familiar with the subject matter are more likely to view the computer product as more credible [41, 42]. These findings agree with credibility research outside of HCI [9, 38, 43].

User understanding of computer system

Next, researchers have investigated how user acceptance of computer advice changes when users understand how the computer arrives at its conclusions. One study showed that knowing more about the computer actually *reduced* users' perception of computer credibility [2]. However, other researchers have shown the opposite: Users were more inclined to view a computer as credible when they understood how it worked [17, 19, 23, 25]. In this line of research users either learned about the computer product before using it [25, 42], or the computer justified its decisions in real time through dialog boxes [23].

#5: Visual design and credibility

Another line of research has investigated the effects of interface design on computer credibility [15]. These experiments have shown that—at least in laboratory settings—certain interface design features, such as cool color tones and balanced layout, can enhance users' perceptions of interface trustworthiness. Although these design implications may differ according to users, cultures, and target applications, this research sets an important precedent in studying the effects of interface design elements on perceptions of trustworthiness and credibility.

#6: Human credibility markers in HCI research

An additional research strategy has been investigating how credibility findings from human-human interactions apply to human-computer interactions. Various researchers have advocated this approach [7, 15, 25, 34, 35]. The following paragraphs explain key findings using this research strategy, while the final paragraph in this section outlines additional possibilities.

Common affiliation leads to credibility

Psychology research shows that in most situations people find members of their "in-groups" (those from the same company, the same team, etc.) to be more credible than people who belong to "out-groups" [21]. Researchers demonstrated that this dynamic also held true when people interacted with a computer they believed to be a member of their "in-group" [28]. Specifically, users reported the "in-group" computer's information to be of higher quality, and users were more likely to follow the computer's advice.

Similarity leads to credibility

Psychology research has shown that we perceive people who are similar to us as credible sources [4, 6, 44]. One type of similarity is geographical proximity. In researching this phenomenon in HCI, an experiment showed that computer users perceived information from a proximal computer to be more credible than information from a distal computer [24]. Specifically, users adopted the proximal computer's information more readily, and they perceived the information to be of higher quality.

Labels of expertise give more credibility

Titles that denote expertise (e.g., *Dr.*, *Professor*, etc.) make people seem more credible [6]. Applying this phenomenon to the world of technology, researchers labeled a technology as a specialist. This study showed that people perceived the device labeled as a specialist to be more credible than the device labeled as a generalist [29, 35].

Additional H-H dynamics in HCI

In addition to the above three lines of research, other human-human credibility dynamics are likely to apply to HCI. Outlined elsewhere [7], the possibilities include the following principles to increase computer credibility:

- Physical attractiveness [5] - Making the computing device or interface attractive.
- Association [6] - Associating the computer with desirable things or people.
- Authority [9, 44] - Establishing the computer as an authority figure.
- Source diversification [9, 11] - Using a variety of computers to offer the same information.
- Nonverbal cues [16] - Endowing computer agents with nonverbal markers of credibility.
- Familiarity [9, 38, 43] - Increasing the familiarity of computer products.
- Social status [6] - Increasing the status of a computer product.

Researchers have yet to specifically show how the above principles—which are powerful credibility enhancers in human-human interactions—might be implemented in computing systems [8].

THREE NEW VIEWS OF CREDIBILITY

So far, our paper has defined key terms and reviewed the relevant research on computers and credibility. We now change focus somewhat. In this next section we offer three new conceptual frameworks for viewing computer credibility. They are (1) the four types of credibility, (2) the two credibility evaluation errors, and (3) the three strategies for evaluating credibility. We believe that having new ways to think about—and a greater vocabulary for—computer credibility will enhance our HCI community's ability to research, evaluate, and design credible computers.

Four types of credibility

The first conceptual framework we propose outlines four different types of computer credibility. The overall assessment of computer credibility may rely on aspects of each of these four types simultaneously.

Presumed credibility

Presumed credibility describes how much the perceiver believes someone or something because of *general assumptions* in the perceiver's mind. For example, people presume that most people tell the truth, but we also presume car salespeople may not be totally honest. Presumed credibility relies on the assumptions and stereotypes of our culture. Assumptions and stereotypes also exist for computers [41]. In general, people presume computers have expertise and are trustworthy (they are "basically good and decent" [25]).

Reputed credibility

The next type of credibility, *reputed* credibility, describes how much the perceiver believes someone or something because of what *third parties have reported*. This applies very much to computer technologies. For example, a nonprofit consumer magazine may run tests that show Company XYZ makes highly accurate tax software. This third-party report would give Company XYZ's computer products a high level of reputed credibility.

Surface credibility

The third type of credibility is *surface* credibility, which describes how much a perceiver believes someone or something based on *simple inspection*. (In other words, with surface credibility people *do* judge a book by its cover.) For example, a web page may appear credible just because of its visual design [15]. Or the solid feel of a handheld computing device can make users perceive it as credible.

Experienced credibility

The last type of credibility is *experienced* credibility. This refers to how much a person believes someone or something based on *first-hand experience*. For example, over a period of time a fitness enthusiast may determine that her computerized heart rate monitor is highly accurate.

Two credibility evaluation errors

For each type of credibility listed above, computer users can make various types of evaluations [17, 25, 39]. Some of these evaluations are appropriate, while others are erroneous. Table 2 shows four possible evaluation options:

	User perceives product as <u>credible</u>	User perceives product as <u>not credible</u>
Product is <u>credible</u>	appropriate acceptance	**Incredulity Error**
Product is <u>not</u> <u>credible</u>	**Gullibility Error**	appropriate rejection

Table 2: Four evaluations of credibility

The most notable aspects of this conceptual framework are the two errors. The first type of error is what we call the "Gullibility Error." In this error, even though a computer product (such as a web page) is not credible, users perceive the product to be credible. Various individuals and institutions, especially those in education, have taken on the task of teaching people to avoid the Gullibility Error. Often this is under the heading of "information quality." (For example, see www.vuw.ac.nz/~agsmith/evaln/evaln.htm.)

The second type of error is what we call the "Incredulity Error." In this error, even though a computer is credible, users perceive the product to be not credible. Of the two types of errors, the Incredulity Error is likely to be of greater concern to those of us who design, research, and evaluate computer products. In general, reducing the Incredulity Error without increasing the Gullibility Error should be a goal of HCI professionals.

Three models of credibility evaluation

The conceptual framework in Table 2 outlines two types of evaluation errors, but it doesn't account for different evaluation strategies people might use for assessing credibility. For most people, evaluations of credibility are not simply accept or reject decisions, as Table 2 may imply. Adapting previous work [32, 33], we now propose three prototypical models for evaluating computer credibility: Binary Evaluation, Threshold Evaluation, and Spectral Evaluation. Figure A illustrates these three models by making the level of user acceptance a function of the theoretical credibility of the computer product.

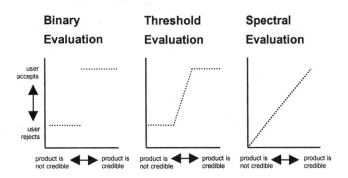

Figure A: These three models represent different approaches to evaluating credibility.

Binary Evaluation of credibility

The simplest strategy for evaluating a computer product is what we call "Binary Evaluation"; users perceive the product as either credible or not credible—no middle ground. Users are more likely to adopt the Binary Evaluation strategy when users have—

- low interest in the issue
- low ability to process information, either due to cognitive abilities or situational factors
- little familiarity with the subject matter
- no reference points for comparison

Any one of the above elements can lead to Binary Evaluations. An example of someone likely to use this strategy would be an unmotivated student seeking information on the Web for a history paper due the next day.

Threshold Evaluation of credibility

The Threshold Evaluation strategy includes upper and lower thresholds for credibility assessments. If a computer product exceeds the upper threshold, users deem it credible; if it falls below the lower threshold, it is deemed not credible. If the product falls between the two thresholds, then the perceiver may describe the product as "somewhat credible" or "fairly

credible." We propose that people use a threshold strategy in evaluating computer credibility when they have—

- moderate interest in the issue
- moderate ability to process information, either due to cognitive abilities or situational factors
- partial familiarity with the subject matter
- moderate ability to compare various sources

An example of someone likely to use a Threshold Evaluation strategy would be a tourist using an information kiosk in order to find a suitable restaurant for dinner.

Spectral Evaluation of credibility

The most sophisticated—and most difficult—evaluation strategy is what we call Spectral Evaluation. This model offers no black or white categories; each evaluation is a shade of gray. We propose that people use a spectral strategy for evaluating computer credibility when users have—

- high interest in the issue
- high ability to process the information, including favorable cognitive and situational factors
- high familiarity with the subject matter
- considerable opportunity to compare various sources

All the above elements must be present to facilitate Spectral Evaluation. One example of a person adopting this strategy would be an individual who is searching for a solution to his or her own terminal illness.

ELM and designing for credibility

Most people use all three credibility evaluation models in different situations, with the threshold model being the most flexible and the most common. But what determines which model people follow? The bullet-point guidelines we offer above are adaptations of the Elaboration Likelihood Model (ELM) [32, 33]. According to the ELM, people can process information through two routes: central and peripheral. People opt for the peripheral processing route when they have little personal involvement with the issue or when they lack ability or motivation to process the information. In contrast, people process centrally when they have high personal involvement in the issue and are able to devote adequate cognitive resources.

The models of credibility evaluation and the ELM have design implications for computer products. For example, if the computer product is intended for users with low involvement or limited cognitive ability, then designers concerned about credibility need only focus on peripheral cues such as attractiveness of source, number of arguments, likability of source, and so on. If, on the other hand, the computer product is one that is highly involving and very important to the user, then users will tend toward spectral evaluations of credibility. In this case, users are likely to focus heavily on the content and less on peripheral cues when assessing trustworthiness or expertise.

TOWARD NEW RESEARCH IN COMPUTER CREDIBILITY

To this point, we have defined key terms, synthesized previous research, and proposed three new frameworks for computer credibility. We next aim to facilitate new research in this domain (1) by outlining two perspectives on what users evaluate when assessing computer credibility, and (2) by providing a set of key terms for researching and evaluating computer credibility.

What do users evaluate when assessing credibility?

Throughout this paper we have discussed users evaluating the credibility of "computer products," a general phrase we use to describe many types of computer devices, systems, and applications. So now we ask, "What precisely are users focusing on when they evaluate the credibility of a 'computer product'?" No existing research fully answers this question, so below we offer two perspectives: a systems perspective and a psychological perspective.

The systems perspective on credibility assessment

In assessing credibility, we hypothesize that people can evaluate four different aspects of a computer product: the device, the interface, the functionality, and the information.

Device credibility relates to the physical aspect of the computing product. For example, a pocket calculator can have a physical design, a density, and button detents that induce perceptions of credibility.

Interface credibility relates to the display of the computer product as well as to the interaction experience. For example, an interface is likely to be perceived as less credible when it contradicts user expectations or mental models.

Functional credibility relates to what a computer product does and how it is done. This includes performing calculations, services, or processes. Functional credibility is most closely related to a strict definition of *trust*, as discussed earlier.

Information credibility relates to how believable the information is from the computing product. For example, information that contradicts what a user views as "correct" (even typographical errors) will reduce credibility.

By pairing these four aspects of a computer product with the two dimensions of credibility, one can isolate specific issues for research, evaluation, and design (see Table 3).

Device Credibility	Interface Credibility	Functional Credibility	Information Credibility
Trustworthiness Issues	Trustworthiness Issues	Trustworthiness Issues	Trustworthiness Issues
Expertise Issues	Expertise Issues	Expertise Issues	Expertise Issues

Table 3: Aspects of computer credibility from a systems perspective

People who research, evaluate, or design computer products with credibility in mind can benefit from differentiating aspects of a computing system, as shown in Table 3. For example, hardware designers may accept the challenge of making the device seem trustworthy, one cell in the matrix. Web site evaluators would likely target other issues, such as the six cells that relate to the interface, the function, and the information. HCI researchers may focus on just a single cell of Table 3 (for example, Kim and Moon [15] focus exclusively on trustworthiness perceptions of interfaces).

Although HCI professionals can—and should—parse out different aspects of a computer product's credibility, people who use computers are unlikely to make these distinctions easily. Research suggests that people may not naturally separate the credibility of one aspect of a computer product from another [27]. Subsequently, the credibility perceptions about one part of the computer—good or bad—will likely affect credibility perceptions of the entire product. For a common and anecdotal example, consider perceptions of the early Macintosh computer. The industrial design was perceived as "cute." Because cuteness does not likely correlate with credibility, many people dismissed the entire Macintosh computing system.

The psychological perspective on credibility assessment

In addition to the systems perspective, we also propose that computer users adopt a psychological perspective in evaluating credibility. For example, if a computer product provides information, who or what is the perceived source of the information? Below we propose four "psychological targets" for credibility assessments, listed from the most psychologically immediate to the least:

On-screen characters - If on-screen characters are part of a computing product, they are likely the most immediate psychological target for credibility evaluation [20, 35].

Computer *qua* computer - The next most immediate target of credibility evaluation is the computer itself. Research shows that people make credibility assessments about computers [34, 35] and that evaluations of the computer are more natural for users than evaluations of the person who created the computer product [35].

Brand - The brand of the computer product may be the next psychological target for evaluation. This includes the company or institution that promotes the computer product.

Expert creator - The expert who created the computer product is perhaps the most rational target for credibility evaluation, but we propose that for most computer users the expert creator may be the least immediate psychological target of the four.

By pairing these four psychological targets of credibility evaluations with the two dimensions of credibility, one can isolate specific issues for research, evaluation, and design (see Table 4).

Credibility of on-screen character	Credibility of computer *qua* computer	Credibility of brand	Credibility of expert creator
Trustworthiness Issues	Trustworthiness Issues	Trustworthiness Issues	Trustworthiness Issues
Expertise Issues	Expertise Issues	Expertise Issues	Expertise Issues

Table 4: Psychological targets for credibility evaluations.

As Table 4 shows, people can target different psychological sources in making credibility assessments about a computer product. One resulting design strategy would be to emphasize the psychological target that has the greatest perceived trustworthiness and expertise. This may mean highlighting the product brand, if the brand has a high reputation for credibility, or it may mean highlighting the experts who created the product. How to enhance the credibility perception for each cell in Table 4 is an important area for additional research and design.

Key terminology for investigating credibility

We hope this paper has suggested profitable areas for discovery about computers and credibility—and we hope to inspire others to join us in these endeavors. To this end we now suggest terminology that can serve in evaluating and researching credibility. Table 5 offers specific terms for assessing credibility of computer products, as well as assessing the two dimensions of credibility: trustworthiness and expertise.

Terms for assessing credibility	Terms for assessing trustworthiness	Terms for assessing expertise
credible	trustworthy	knowledgeable
believable	good	competent
reputable	truthful	intelligent
"trust the information"	well-intentioned	capable
"accept the advice"	unbiased	experienced
"believe the output"	honest	powerful

Table 5: Basic terms for assessing the credibility of computer products

In using the above terminology, investigations into computer credibility can either examine the credibility of the computer product as a whole, or they can probe the credibility of a specific aspect (e.g., device, interface, functionality, information). In doing so, investigators can use the terminology in Table 5 in a variety of ways—as Likert-type scales (with the responses of *strongly agree, agree, neutral, disagree, strongly disagree*) or as semantic differentials (e.g., with "capable" and "not capable" on two ends of a scale). Although the items in Table 5 do not comprise a standard scale, most of the terms in the table have proven successful in HCI research [7, 30]. As an HCI community, we do not yet have a standard credibility scale for our work in evaluation, design, and research; therefore, we suggest using the items in Table 5 as a step toward creating a valid and reliable "Computer Credibility Scale."

LOOKING FORWARD

Our intent in this paper has been to raise awareness in the HCI community about the elements of computer credibility in order to encourage additional work in this area. To the best of our knowledge, this paper makes a unique contribution to the field of human-computer interaction because it is the first document to synthesize the previous research in computer credibility, to suggest new frameworks for understanding this domain, and to propose various issues for continued research, evaluation, and design of credible computing products.

The scope of this paper has been as broad as possible in order to capture credibility issues common to most computer products. We hope that this paper can help lay a foundation

for future work that focuses on increasingly specific issues, expanding and revising topics we have addressed here. In this way, our HCI community can not only increase our understanding about the elements of computer credibility, but we can also use this understanding to enhance our research, evaluation, and design efforts.

REFERENCES

1. Andrews, L.W. & Gutkin, T.B. (1991). The Effects of Human Versus Computer Authorship on Consumers' Perceptions of Psychological Reports. *Computers in Human Behavior*, 7, 311-317.

2. Bauhs, J.A. & Cooke, N.J. (1994). Is Knowing More Really Better? Effects of System Development Information in Human-Expert System Interactions. *CHI 94 Companion*, p. 99-100. New York: ACM.

3. Buller, D.B. & Burgoon, J.K. (1996). Interpersonal Deception Theory. *Communication Theory*, 6(3) 203-242.

4. Byrne, D. (1971). *The Attraction Paradigm*. New York: Academic.

5. Chaiken, S. (1979). Communicator Physical Attractiveness and Persuasion. *Journal of Personality and Social Psychology*, 37, 1387-1397.

6. Cialdini, R.B. (1993). *Influence: Science and Practice*. (3rd ed.). New York: HarperCollins.

7. Fogg, B.J. (1997). *Charismatic Computers: Creating more likable and persuasive interactive technologies by leveraging principles from social psychology*. Doctoral thesis. Stanford University.

8. Fogg, B.J. (1998). Persuasive Computers: Perspectives and research directions. *Proceedings of the CHI98 Conference of the ACM/SIGCHI*, 225-232. New York: ACM Press.

9. Gatignon, H., & Robertson, T.S. (1991). Innovative Decision Processes. T.S. Robertson & H.H. Kassarjian (Eds.), *Handbook of Consumer Behavior*. Englewood Cliffs, NJ: Prentice-Hall.

10. Hanowski, R.J., Kantowitz, S.C., & Kantowitz, B.H. (1994). Driver Acceptance of Unreliable Route Guidance Information. *Proceedings of the Human Factors Society 38th Annual Meeting*, p. 1062-1066.

11. Harkins, S.G., & Petty, R.E. (1981). Effects of Source Magnification of Cognitive Effort on Attitudes: An information processing view. *Journal of Personality and Social Psychology*, 40, 401-413.

12. Honaker, L.M., Hector, V.S., & Harrell, T.H. (1986). Perceived Validity of Computer Versus Clinician-Generated MMPI Reports. *Computers in Human Behavior*, 2, 77-83.

13. Kantowitz, B.H., Hanowski, R.J., & Kantowitz, S.C. (1997). Driver Acceptance of Unreliable Traffic Information in Familiar and Unfamiliar Settings. *Human Factors*, 39(2) 164-176.

14. Kerber, K.W. (1983). Attitudes Towards Specific Uses of the Computer: Quantitative, decision-making and record-keeping applications. *Behavior and Information Technology*, 2, 197-209.

15. Kim, J. & Moon, J.Y. (1997). Designing Towards Emotional Usability in Customer Interfaces: Trustworthiness of cyber-banking system interfaces. *Interacting with Computers*, 10, 1-29.

16. Larson, C. (1995). *Persuasion: Reception and responsibility*. (7th ed.). Belmont, CA: Wadsworth.

17. Lee, J. (1991). The Dynamics of Trust in a Supervisory Control Simulation. *Proceedings of the Human Factors Society 35th Annual Meeting*, p. 1228-1232.

18. Lee, J. & Moray, N. (1992). Trust, Control Strategies and Allocation of Function in Human-Machine Systems. *Ergonomics*, 35(10), 1243-1270.

19. Lerch, F.J. & Prietula, M.J. (1989). How Do We Trust Machine Advice? Designing and using human-computer interfaces and knowledge based systems. *Proceedings of the Third Annual Conference on Human Computer Interaction*. p. 411-419. Amsterdam: Elsevier.

20. Lester, J.C., Converse, S.A., Kahler, S.E., Barlow, S.T., Stone, B.A., & Bhogal, R.S. (1997). The Persona Effect: Affective impact of animated pedagogical agents. *Proceedings of CHI 97*. p. 359-366. New York: ACM.

21. Mackie, D.M., Worth, L.T., & Asuncion, A.G. (1990). Processing of Persuasive In-group Messages. *Journal of Personality and Social Psychology*, 58, 812-822.

22. Matarazzo, J.D. (1986). Response to Fowler and Butcher on Matarazzo. *American Psychologist*, 41, 96.

23. Miller, C.A. & Larson, R. (1992). An Explanatory and "Argumentative" Interface for a Model-Based Diagnostic System. *Proceedings of the ACM Symposium on User Interface Software and Technology, 1992*, 43-52.

24. Moon, Y. (1998). The Effects of Distance in Local Versus Remote Human-Computer Interaction. *In Proceedings of CHI 98*, p. 103-108. New York: ACM.

25. Muir, B.M. (1988). Trust Between Humans and Machines, and the Design of Decision Aids. *Cognitive Engineering in Complex Dynamic Worlds*. p. 71-83.

26. Muir, B.M. (1994). Trust in Automation: Part I. Theoretical issues in the study of trust and human intervention in automated systems. *Ergonomics*, 37(11) 1905-1922.

27. Muir, B.M. & Moray, N. (1996). Trust in Automation: Part II. Experimental studies of trust and human intervention in a process control simulation. *Ergonomics*, 39(3) 429-460.

28. Nass, C., Fogg, B.J., & Moon, Y. (1996). Can Computers Be Teammates? *International Journal of Human-Computer Studies, 45*, 669-678.

29. Nass, C., Reeves, B., & Leshner, G. (1996). Technology and Roles: A tale of two TVs. *Journal of Communication*, 46(2).

30. Nass, C., Moon, Y., Fogg, B.J., Reeves, B. & Dryer, D.C. (1995). Can Computer Personalities Be Human Personalities? *International Journal of Human-Computer Studies*, 43, 223-239.

31. Pancer, S.M., George, M., & Gebotys, R.J. (1992). Understanding and Predicting Attitudes Toward Computers. *Computers in Human Behavior*, 8, 211-222.

32. Petty, R. and Cacioppo, J. (1981). *Attitudes and Persuasion: Classic and contemporary approaches*. Dubuque, IA: Brown.

33. Petty, R., Cacioppo, J., Goldman, R. (1981). Personal Involvement as a Determinant of Argument-Based Persuasion. *Journal of Personality and Social Psychology*, 41(5) 847-855.

34. Quintanar, L., Crowell, C., Pryor, J. (1982). Human-Computer Interaction: A preliminary social psychological analysis. *Behavior Research Methods and Instrumentation*, 14(2) 210-220.

35. Reeves, B. & Nass, C. (1996). *The Media Equation: How people treat computers, television, and new media like real people and places*. New York: Cambridge University.

36. Rempel, J.K., Holmes, J.G, & Zanna, M.P. (1985). Trust in Close Relationships. *Journal of Personality and Social Psychology*, 49 (1) 95-112.

37. Rotter, J.B. (1980). Interpersonal Trust, Trustworthiness, and Gullibility. *American Psychologist*, 35 (1) 1-7.

38. Self, C.S. (1996). Credibility. In M. Salwen & D. Stacks (Eds.), *An Integrated Approach to Communication Theory and Research*. Mahway, NJ: Erlbaum.

39. Sheridan, T.B., Vamos, T., and Aida S. (1983). Adapting Automation to Man, Culture and Society. *Automatica*, 19(6) 605-612.

40. Stiff, J. (1994). *Persuasive Communication*. New York: Guilford.

41. Waern, Y. & Ramberg, R. (1996). People's Perception of Human and Computer Advice. *Computers in Human Behavior*, 12(1) 17-27.

42. Waern, Y., Hagglund, S. et al. (1992). Communication Knowledge for Knowledge Communication. *International Journal of Man-Machine Studies*, 37, 215-239.

43. Zajonc, R.B. (1980). Feeling and Thinking: Preferences need no inferences. *American Psychologist*, 35, 151-175.

44. Zimbardo, P. & Leippe, M. (1991). *The Psychology of Attitude Change and Social Influence*. New York: McGraw-Hill.

A Better Mythology for System Design

Jed Harris
Pliant Research
978 Cragmont Ave.
Berkeley, CA 94708
+1 510 524 4350
jed@pliant.org

Austin Henderson
Pliant Research
PO Box 334
La Honda, CA 94020
+1 650 747 9201
henderson@pliant.org

ABSTRACT

The past decades have seen huge improvements in computer systems but these have proved difficult to translate into comparable improvements in the usability and social integration) of computers. We believe that the problem is a deeply rooted set of assumptions about how computer systems should be designed, and about who should be doing that design.

Human organizations are continually evolving to meet changing circumstances of resource and need. In contrast, computers are quite rigid, incapable of adaptation on their own. Therefore when computer systems are incorporated into human organizations, those organizations must adapt the computers to changing circumstances. This adaptation is another human activity that technology should support, but our design philosophies are oddly silent about it.

This paper explores the origins of these problems in the norms developed for managing human organizations, proposes partial solutions that can be implemented with current systems technology, and speculates about the long-term potential for radical improvements in system design.

Keywords
System evolution, accommodation, mythology, pliant systems.

PROBLEM
The social value of computing is so great that use of computers in developed countries is already pervasive and well on its way to becoming universal. Computer systems are increasingly part of our interaction with most companies and many individuals; indeed, they shape our experience in these interactions.

From 1980 through 1998, the performance of personal computers has increased by at least a factor of 1000, and the size of typical personal computer applications has increased by about a factor of 16. Communication between computers has speeded up by a factor of more than 400, and changed from a difficult, occasional act to a largely transparent and often continuous process.

However, in spite of the enormous improvements in computer performance and functionality, computers, both

personal and institutional, are still very difficult for most people to use, and are becoming more, rather than less, difficult to manage as they become more complex.

Institutional computer systems present apparently intractable problems of ossification, as highlighted by the recent "Year 2000" problem, and the spectacular failure of multi-million dollar projects to upgrade the US air traffic control system, the Internal Revenue Service, and major systems at the Bank of America, among many others [2].

Even when institutional systems are "successful", they often cause serious problems. For example, while workflows mechanized by computers may be greatly accelerated and made more reliable, they are also largely "frozen". Because they are often frozen before experience is gained they are often wrong from the start. Because the world changes, the frozen workflows tend to quickly diverge from the real demands of the business process.

Personal computer systems are subject to another sort of ossification. Most people have great difficulty updating their computer systems, or figuring out how to fix them if an update goes wrong. People become very cautious about changing or updating their environment, with good reason. As a result, users are trapped in a network of assumptions and practices that they cannot easily change.

Because computer systems are pervasive, on the way to becoming universal, the social effects of these problems with computing are also pervasive and will be universal. This is a situation that deserves deeper consideration.

Why are we having such a hard time?
Fortunately, there is a research community of computer scientists, designers, cognitive scientists, and others, who are working on the general problem of "making computers easier to use."

Unfortunately, this research effort is not moving nearly as quickly as the underlying technology. While our hardware technology has improved by orders of magnitude, and our software has grown comparably more complex, the relationship between people (individually or in groups) and computers has only improved incrementally. In some cases, it has even deteriorated.

Why have the huge improvements in computer systems proved so difficult to translate into comparable improvements in the usability (and more generally, the social integration) of computers? We believe that the problem is a deeply rooted set of assumptions about how computer systems should be designed, and about who should be doing that design.

In this paper we propose an explanation for this odd state of affairs, and suggest a research agenda and design approach that can begin to bring our computer systems into better alignment with our social context.

MYTHOLOGY OF SYSTEM DESIGN

Any community, including communities of practitioners, has stories it tells within its ranks about how its activities are conducted. In a community of practice these are largely stories about how the practice is conducted, when it succeeds and when it fails. As with any stories, these are selective and emphasize especially significant or unusual aspects of the practice. They do not directly drive the practice, but they do shape it by helping each participant construct and frame their account of their practice.

We are calling this set of stories the *mythology* of the practice. To understand how our mythology as system designers affects our practice, and how it might be improved, we need to examine our mythology more closely, and briefly examine its roots.

Standard Mythology of System Design

Our mythology of system design takes some basic principles for granted—so much so that they are rarely stated. The following principles are widely accepted:

- Define clear system requirements.

- Define a clean architecture that can meet all the system requirements.

- Define clear choices for users at each point where they interact with the system.

- Maintain consistency throughout the design, for both ease of maintenance and ease of learning.

Underlying these principles are even more fundamental assumptions:

- The parts of the system must interact according to a pre-established harmony defined during its design.

- The job of a designer is to discover, clarify, and when necessary invent the rules that define that harmony, and then embed them into the computer system.

- The users must interact with the system in terms of the language or ontology that these rules create.

Our first—and probably most important—point is that these **are** assumptions, and that they could be **different**. We have some proposals about specific **better** assumptions, but before we get to those, let's look at how we got our **current** assumptions.

Coordination

People working together are always caught in the tension between their particular ways of understanding the world, and the explicit shared regularities they must maintain in order to coordinate their activities.

We must respond to *particularities*—the details of the case at hand—to achieve appropriate, creative action in response

to a changing world and changing goals. These responses can generate unpredictable and unbounded diversity.

Humans in groups depend on shared *regularities* —expectations, norms, conventions, assumptions—to coordinate their activities. To maintain group coordination in spite of adverse circumstances, such as distance, many participants, external hostility, and so forth, we need to support these shared regularities through discussion, teaching, monitoring and enforcement. In other words, the regularities must be made *explicit*. We most often encounter these explicit regularities as various sorts of "rules", including organizational regulations, rules of thumb, and "manners".

Particularities and explicit regularities tend to conflict, because individuals can often see ways to respond to particular circumstances that are not anticipated by or compatible with the regularities required for coordination.

Bureaucratic Organizations

Since at least the advent of large-scale agriculture and armies, over 5,000 years ago, people have been struggling with this tension between particularities and regularities, especially in large groups.

Over these thousands of years people have codified this struggle in military, religious, governmental, and business organizations. Relatively recently this continuing codification has produced *bureaucracy* as we know it today. As Joanne Yates has shown,

> During the period from 1850 to 1920, formal internal communications emerged as a major tool of management, exerted toward the goal of achieving system and, thus, efficiency. By the end of that period, control through communication was a fact of life in the workplace [7].

In such a bureaucracy, all "official" activity is viewed as being conducted according to explicit regularities, captured in rules, guidelines, etc. Bureaucrats are trained and monitored to make sure that they "follow" the rules and interpret them consistently. More precisely, they must obey the following key norms:

- Focus exclusively on **identified** regularities in situations.

- View all the particularities in a situation in terms of these regularities.

- Consistently act in terms of pre-defined rules about these regularities.

- Keep records to allow management and enforcement of the bureaucratic norms.

By respecting these norms, a well-run bureaucracy can coordinate the work of huge numbers of people and can minimize corruption, disorder and mistakes.

Computer Systems: Perfect Bureaucratic Tools!

Viewed in terms of the standard mythology of system design, computer systems ought to be the perfect support for bureaucrats. Computers can only work in terms of the regularities they have been built to handle. They can only respond based on the way situations fit these pre-defined regularities. They always follow pre-defined rules, and they do not (at least in the myth) make mistakes. Finally, computers do not change spontaneously, and so they do not require constant management and enforcement of these bureaucratic norms—they obey them automatically.

All of this is no coincidence. Computer design practice and mythology arose from practices such as telephone systems engineering, ballistics calculation and metamathematics which were pursued by communities intensely dedicated to the bureaucratic norms.

PROBLEMS WITH THE STANDARD MYTHOLOGY

It's hard to get perspective on design assumptions embedded in the mythology and practices of such a pervasive tradition. To create a vantage point from which we can see potential alternatives, let's take a more careful look at how bureaucracies actually work.

Bureaucratic norms arose in the process of trying to control people's tendencies to creativity, subjectivity, and "excessive" responsiveness to particularities. These tendencies may be exercised in the service of self-interest, but they may also be simply the result of trying to do a better and more fulfilling job.

These efforts at control are never completely successful, and in fact total success would be disastrous for the organization. The *ad hoc* elaboration of rules in use" to fit them to individual cases requires a significant level of human creativity and responsiveness to particularities [6, 9]. We call this process *accomodation*. Furthermore, changes in the explicit regularities will be required, and successful change will also demand these abilities.

As a result, real bureaucratic behavior is a dynamic balance shaped by both the underlying human tendencies and the norms. The norms themselves have evolved to make this dynamic balance effective.

Bureaucratic Organizations, Reconsidered

The dynamic balance found in real bureaucracies has several important characteristics that are not captured by the standard mythology:

- Particularities are observed and accommodated.

- The practices of fitting particularities into the rules evolve, changing the interpretation of the rules.

- Practices of rule application are accumulated and codified, often leading to explicit changes in the rules.

- Changes in the rules are designed and implemented. Each change triggers a new round of accommodation as workers adjust their practices to the new regularities.

All of these activities take place in the context of common purposes or missions, which help to guide the accommodation and change, and allow the individual bureaucrats to act appropriately even in the absence of explicit regularities. When members of a bureaucracy do not subscribe to common purposes, the norms can only be maintained by enforcement. Since enforcing obedience to the norms is costly, those who maintain the integrity of an organization must be sensitive to dissent and must make pragmatic tradeoffs to keep the organization viable.

The mission of the organization underpins several further norms that are often important in real bureaucracies:

- Apply the rules with the mission in mind.

- Notice conflicts between the rules and the mission.

- Change the rules so that they serve the mission better.

Computer systems: Less Than Perfect...

Unfortunately all of these additional characteristics of real bureaucracies, and the corresponding demands they place on bureaucrats, are not supported by current computer systems, precisely because computer systems were created using the standard mythology of system design.

In particular, computer systems require their users to map particularities into regularities, and only then can the systems proceed entirely based on the regularities. The systems never deal with the particularities themselves or with the process of accommodation. This has unfortunate consequences:

- Particularities cannot be accommodated by the systems or discussed within them.

- New regularities and difficulties with old ones cannot even be noticed by the systems, since these arise in the process of mapping particularities into regularities.

- Changes are very difficult, slow, and expensive since the system will not notice or accommodate to problems, so all the implications of new regularities must be anticipated by the system designer.

- Most profoundly, computer systems don't share the mission of the organization; all they have is their explicit regularities. The burden of adapting as necessary to carry out the mission falls entirely on users of the systems.

All of this is no coincidence. Practices of accommodation and change are rarely if ever discussed explicitly in bureaucratic mythology, perhaps because the norms are focused on constraining human tendencies, not enabling them. In Yates' extensive study, for example, there is essentially no discussion of the practices through which organizations handled accommodation or change, although some of the technological mechanisms are mentioned in passing [8].

NEED FOR A NEW MYTH

Thus the standard story of bureaucratic rationality that is built into our design practices for computer systems is a story which provides a very partial and rather damaging view of how "good," "rational" organizations work.

Once we recognize the limited and inaccurate perspective on work and technology imposed by the standard myths of both organization and system design, we can start to search for more effective approaches and write better myths around them. That is the focus of the next major section.

However, before we leave our analysis of the problem, let us briefly deal with one seductive alternative.

Smart Systems are Not the Answer

Many have found it very tempting to try to solve the problems described above by making systems "smart"—so that they can notice new regularities, for example. We believe that this is a fatal blind alley. Not only are current "smart" system technologies grossly inadequate to the task, but the mythologies behind many of these "smart" technologies tend to simply reinforce the standard bureaucratic mythology that caused the problems in the first place. They do little or nothing to integrate systems with the mission and values of the organization, or to support the continual reassessment, reinterpretation, and reconciliation that are necessary in a changing world.

Classical Artificial Intelligence (AI) is the source of most ideas about how to make systems "smart." However, AI was founded on the conjecture that a sufficiently large, complex, and well-designed "perfect bureaucracy" could duplicate human flexibility and adaptability. Not surprisingly, it has run into intractable problems that are essentially variations on the ones mentioned above. For example, typical AI systems require examples to be "translated" into an appropriate input format—which conveniently maps the particularities of the examples into the regularities the system is designed to handle. As we might expect, such systems cannot be extended to deal with the untidiness of real situations.

In the last fifteen years, various forms of "soft computing" (for example, neural networks) have been explored as alternatives to classical AI. These techniques can indeed help in some areas where flexibility and accommodation are required, such as handwriting, speech recognition, and recommending books and CDs. However as yet no one knows how to build large systems using these techniques, and in fact we believe that there are deep problems with "scaling" these approaches. As a result, these techniques tend to be used as "rubber bumpers" on systems otherwise built according to the standard mythology.

As we shall see in the next section, a much more realistic and fruitful alternative is not to make systems smart, but to make them better vehicles for the **users'** intelligence.

A BETTER DESIGN MYTHOLOGY FOR TODAY

We believe it is feasible to do much better in designing computer systems if we aim to better integrate human organizations and computer systems, by making the computer system help the humans do the **whole** job, not just the part that fits the standard myth of bureaucracy.

In this section we will explore whether we can move toward such integration without radical changes to the current technology of computing. Perhaps surprisingly, our tentative answer is that we can actually move quite far. In the subsequent section, we speculate on what might be possible with radical changes in computing technology.

To help humans do their whole job, we need to honor the particularities they must handle, the accommodations they must make in nearly every case, the organizational purposes that underpin the coordination, and the process of negotiation and change that keeps the organization viable. Let us examine each of these in turn.

We Must Honor Particularities

The standard mythology simply assumes away particularities that do not fit the regularities. The designer's motto might be "If it's not captured by the regularities, it's not important." As a result, whenever the computer system fails to capture important particularities, users must create parallel records to capture what the system ignores, and then they must coordinate the computer system with their separate records.

For example, in a British printing shop studied by Graham Button [3, 4], a "complete" workflow system was put in place. As we would expect, it could not record any information about jobs beyond its predefined attributes (i.e. its regularities). Of course, these predefined attributes were nowhere near rich enough to capture everything the people working in the print shop needed to remember about a job—in case, for example, it needed to be re-run "the same way." Even if, by some miracle of design, the predefined attributes **had** been adequate, new jobs or work practices would have demanded new attributes very soon.

As a result, the print shop workers maintained the old manual job-tracking system **in parallel** with the computerized workflow system, and coordinated the two systems themselves. The old manual system had a job tracking form similar to the computer system, but in the manual system, the form had **margins**—workers could write notes whenever important features of the job didn't fit into the predefined fields. Unfortunately, typical electronic forms don't have margins, so the workflow system, far from helping the workers, imposed an extra burden.

Fortunately, there are many ways to extend computer system designs so that users can track particularities **within** the system. Simply allowing annotation or "margins" on electronic forms, for example, moves a long way in this direction. Recording annotations and displaying them when the form was retrieved would have greatly aided the workers in Button's print shop. Furthermore, once annotations are captured in machine-readable form, extensions like content search, summarization, etc. become relatively easy to add. Moreover, the accumulated annotations are a valuable resource for suggesting and evaluating extensions to the system's regularities that will allow it to support more of the particularities its users actually encounter.

Margins are only an example, though a very useful one. There are many ways to help users to track the particularities they need to handle, and often they arise fairly naturally from the way a given computer system is used. The key is simply to remember that the system will never be able to capture all the important particularities in terms of its regularities.

We Must Honor Accommodation

Typical computer systems require users to translate particularities into the regularities that the system can handle, and then apply predefined behaviors based on that translation. This translation must produce terms that will lead the system to "do something reasonable." To produce "good" translations, users must "reverse engineer" the system's behavior to come up with encodings that produce the right results. Any particularities that can't be so encoded must be handled outside the system.

In Button's print shop, for example, while workers often ran portions of the same job on multiple machines, the workflow system had no way to describe this, so users had to find ways to convert the actual machine usage, operator time, etc. into terms that the system could handle.

Another example, with more fruitful system design implications, comes from Fikes and Henderson's discussion of the work in an order center for copier supplies [5]. At one point a clerk, attempting to get a "ship to" address for an order, was told that the copier was on an ocean-going barge which called at several different ports, and therefore the address depended on the date the supplies would arrive. Not surprisingly, there was no pre-defined way to fill in the "ship to" field with an address that would produce the correct results.

The clerk invented an ingenious solution on the spot. Instead of a valid address (from the system's perspective), the clerk entered a phone number, and instructions to "Call Bob". This solution highlights several troubling issues, but it also suggests an approach to supporting accommodation.

This solution depended on two things. First, the "ship to" field was flexible enough to accept what was clearly not a valid address. Second, the field ended up being interpreted by a human being on the shipping dock, who could understand the instructions.

If the supply center had been using a "sophisticated" computer system, this accommodation would probably have failed for two reasons. First, the clerk probably would not have been allowed to put the order into the system with a "Ship To" field that the system thought was invalid. Second, the field would probably have been used to automatically generate a shipping label, quite possibly with bar-coded routing information, and no human would have had an opportunity to notice and interpret the instructions.

Note that in this case, annotations could be helpful but they are not sufficient. At a minimum, the system must allow information in essential fields to be incomplete or invalid, and must "call for help" when it needs to carry out some operation that depends on the "invalid" information.

Of course this sort of accommodation mechanism may interfere with the functioning of the system if it is used inappropriately, and it may be subject to abuse. This is just the sort of concern that the standard bureaucratic mythology tends to raise.

However, in reality, building mechanisms for accommodation into a computer system is much more likely to solve problems than to create them. People **must** make these accommodations somehow, unless they are willing to violate or severely limit the mission of the organization. In the print shop it was not feasible to run every job on only one machine, and in the supply center the supplies could not always be shipped to a fixed address. The alternative to system support is for people to cobble

together accommodation mechanisms that are completely outside the system, and are effectively invisible from within the system.

If the system supports accommodation, accommodation activities will generally be much more available for audit than the methods outside the system that will otherwise be used. Furthermore, the record of cases where accommodation was necessary can help system maintainers to identify places where more automated support is needed. Overall, accommodation support is likely to produce a net improvement in system performance and security.

Again, even the most basic support for accommodation moves us a long way, but it opens the door to further improvements based on analysis of the accommodation that is actually being done, semi-automatic codification of accommodations, and so forth.

We Must Honor Purposes

In the standard bureaucratic myth, purposes are not **part of** the system. The designers of the system lay down rules, and the bureaucrats follow them. The designers need not explain their purposes, and the bureaucrats don't need to understand the purposes, since they just have to follow the rules. The purposes, just like the rules, are not affected by the activities of the bureaucracy.

Actually, of course, any viable system, including a functioning bureaucracy, depends on broad agreement on purposes, and this agreement evolves over time. Accommodation, for example, is guided by the underlying purposes of the regularities it is interpreting and extending, at the same time that it also extends and reinterprets those very purposes.

In computer systems, purposes show up mainly in the context of help systems, templates, wizards, etc. These mechanisms are designed to support users who have a purpose they are seeking to fulfill, but don't know how to map this desire into the system's regularities. These user support mechanisms provide various types of maps from purposes to system behavior.

These mechanisms typically provide one way communication, from the system designer to the user, consistent with the standard mythology. However this need not be the case, especially in a networked world. Since we are looking for ways to make the system a better vehicle for users' intelligence, we can see that it **should** not be the case. Once we have shifted our point of view, we can see that there are many opportunities to do better.

One useful option is suggested by email support forums, which typically have FAQs (lists of Frequently Asked Questions, and their answers). These forums are typically excellent vehicles for users' intelligence. Users ask questions, and system experts (in many cases more experienced users) answer the questions. Over time, the questions and answers are gradually codified into a FAQ.

If we extend a typical help system with a support forum, and consolidate answers provided in the forum into the help system, we get a mechanism that has the potential to honor purposes within the system. User questions that cannot be answered within the help system become part of an ongoing conversation about the structure of the system and how it supports its users' needs.

As with honoring particularity and honoring accommodation, this type of mechanism also supports the evolution of the system itself.

We Must Honor Change

The most fundamental of these four issues is support for change. Change is extremely difficult to handle effectively in systems designed using the standard mythology, since it is completely outside the mythology. Computer systems designed using this mythology create an impermeable wall between the users of the system—who know "where it squeaks"—and the maintainers of the system—who see only the (by definition) consistent view from inside. The need for change, the reasons for the need and the specific situations where the need arises have to be communicated entirely outside the system, creating another parallel activity that must be coordinated with the computer system, primarily by social means.

As a result of this exclusion of change management from the computer system, the process of changing the system is severely hobbled. Decisions about changes are not directly driven by the needs of the users, so changes tend to be relatively slow and poorly matched to users' priorities. Even more seriously, design decisions are decoupled from the specific knowledge of the users, so design tends to be based on an inadequate understanding of how the system is really used, and how changes will affect users.

The other three areas we have discussed—particularities, accommodation, and purposes—could be considered specific mechanisms to support change. Each one captures information from the users of the system in a form that bears directly on the changes needed in the system. In some cases, such as aggregating accommodations, a computer system might be able to flag and even mechanically abstract needed changes largely automatically.

Undoubtedly, using this perspective, we can come up with many more ways to incorporate the change process into the system itself, and help the users and designers collaborate effectively on evolving the system to better support their joint purposes.

However, the ability to support change in the use of the system is not enough. Change raises the original challenge that drove the development of bureaucracy in the first place: How can the institution ensure that the local changes combine to support the mission and maintain enough coherence to preserve the organization? In the examples above we have left this burden on the shoulders of the system maintainers. In the following section we consider how computer systems can help deal with the tension between change and maintaining coherence.

A BETTER MYTHOLOGY FOR THE LONG TERM

In the previous section, we accepted the basic concept of bureaucracy, although we adopted a new view of what really goes on in bureaucracies. We observed that the standard bureaucratic myths failed to deal with the need for accommodation or change, because they were focused entirely on constraining people's natural tendencies, which might otherwise result in the organization sliding toward chaos. We suggested that once we recognize this, we can find ways for computer systems to help people manage accommodation and change.

In this section, we question the long-term value of organizations as we know them today. Bureaucracy reflects the inherent problems of building large organizations entirely out of humans. Socio-technical systems composed of both computers and people have problems too, but they are very different problems, and we believe such systems can become dramatically superior to any purely human organization. To achieve such superior systems we will need radically new myths.

However, our entire view of the world is filtered through concepts rooted in organizational structures and concepts designed to constrain and regularize human tendencies—from scientific "laws", to the great chain of being, to "canonical" works in literature, art, and music. Such a pervasive framework makes imagining radical alternatives very hard.

To begin this difficult process, we can observe that evolving systems need to maintain both agility and coherence. If a system isn't agile, it cannot respond effectively to local variations or global change. If it loses its coherence, it cannot act effectively as a system at all.

The bureaucratic solution is to maintain coherence by imposing rules that guarantee coherence through pre-established harmony. Bureaucratic logic then requires managing all proposed changes through a central authority (designers, the systems department). This attempt to preserve coherence implicitly depends on underlying human tendencies to provide adequate agility. Unfortunately, as organizations grow, this approach tends to greatly reduce agility, and over time it also loses the ability to maintain coherence, since it becomes incapable of meeting the organization's needs.

Our goal is to find new *pliant* modes of human organization that can sustain high levels of both agility and coherence as they grow. While we are still far from an engineering theory for creating such pliant organizations, we do see four transitions in computer technology that we believe will help us move in this direction:

From Programs to Patterns

Computer systems today typically execute programs which specify processes completely deterministically. The set of programs in a system must mesh according to a pre-established harmony, since the programs have no ability to adapt to each other. This leads to a system that is incredibly coherent while it works, but also incredibly lacking in agility. Furthermore, this coherence is fragile, since systems that depend on pre-established harmony descend abruptly into chaos if the harmony fails.

In pliant systems programs will be augmented or replaced with process descriptions using *patterns*, as described by Christopher Alexander [1]. (Note that this is very different from using patterns to help people design and build software, and will be much harder to implement.) Such patterns specify processes partially and open-endedly. Any actual process is the result of many overlapping and interacting patterns. The interaction of the patterns is not based on pre-established harmony, but is worked out in the process of using them and sometimes requires search and discovery. The system may need to request help if it cannot get its patterns to mesh well enough; conversely, people may intervene to push the patterns into specific relationships.

From Execution to Enaction

In today's systems, programs are executed —deterministically elaborated in a pre-specified relationship to a pre-defined context. Again, this has all the problems of pre-established harmony. In particular, it assumes that the structure of the context for executing a program can be completely known in advance.

In pliant systems patterns will be *enacted*—interpreted by finding a fruitful way to relate the patterns to the specifics of the case at hand. The process of enaction determines what aspects of the case are relevant and how they should be organized to the meet the needs of the patterns being enacted. As a result, enaction can support accommodation much more effectively than can program execution in current systems. Again, a pliant system may ask for human help if it encounters problems in enacting patterns, and people may intervene to influence the way the system enacts patterns in specific cases.

From Monoliths to Collaborating Activities

A computer system based on current technology defines a single, consistent, monolithic perspective which encompasses all of its information and actions. Once again, this provides incredible coherence while suffering from very poor agility and extreme fragility. However, all organizations contain multiple shifting points of view whose interplay is vital to the actual work underway. As a result, the apparent coherence imposed by the computer system is illusory and stands in the way of assessing and responding to the factors that affect coherence in the organization.

Pliant systems will consist of multiple *collaborating activities*—both cooperating and competing—which contain many partially reconciled perspectives that are only consistent enough for the purposes at hand. Enaction of patterns can continue to function effectively in a partially inconsistent environment, but excessive inconsistency will ultimately lead to loss of coherence. To maintain adequate coherence, enaction must also monitor the consistency of the process being enacted, at many different scales, and work to increase consistency if coherence becomes inadequate. Users have partially reconciled perspectives of their own and will need to be active participants in the process of maintaining coherence.

From Design to Evolution

Current computer systems are updated through re-design and re-implementation, resulting in a transition from one universal perspective to another. Designers usually must maintain some compatibility between the old perspective and the new one, to allow existing data and applications to survive the transition. However, in practice, because of the strong requirements of pre-established harmony, implementing changes and maintaining compatibility are often in deep conflict, and sometimes necessary updates become impossible.

In pliant systems, collaborating activities will evolve largely by incrementally consolidating enaction of their patterns. Such consolidation is similar to just-in-time compilation—once an activity has successfully enacted some patterns it can succeed more quickly in future similar cases, and may gain the ability to handle some more difficult cases. If the system needs help to succeed in one case, it may be able to succeed in subsequent similar cases without help. The knowledge acquired through successful enaction of patterns can be recorded by extending and differentiating the patterns themselves. In addition to this incremental consolidation, the system will need to refactor its patterns as it evolves, to prevent unbounded growth in complexity and to improve its ability to generalize to new cases.

SUMMARY AND CONCLUSION

Let us review some broad characteristics of this shift in mythology:

Different Stance

We begin by recognizing that no attempt to fit the world into a neat set of categories can succeed for long. We will always encounter inconsistent, ambiguous, messy bits that don't fit. Standard system design, which depends on making the world fit a neat set of categories, will naturally have trouble.

Co-Production

Trying to solve this problem by making machines "smart" isn't feasible. It's a lot easier and more fruitful to help **people** be smart, and make machines a better vehicle for **human** intelligence. Working together, people and machines can handle problems better than either can alone, but only if they honor each other's strengths.

Multiple Truths

There is no single consistent perspective within which we can frame all the information or activity in any given complex system, much less the wide variety of systems that we encounter daily. Instead, we are always faced with multiple interacting perspectives which cannot be reduced to one another. We need to find ways for machines to help us work with these multiple perspectives.

Dynamic Balance of Change and Coherence

Effective systems must be sensitive to needs for local change and at the same time must maintain adequate coherence, at many different scales. The dynamic balance between change and coherence is driven by, and judged against, each organization's need to achieve its mission.

We Can't Get Out of the River

There is no way for a designer to stand above the fray, as an observer standing on the bank of the river. Even reflection is a part of the action. Ultimately there cannot be a role of designer prior to and distinct from user. We are all in this together, and designers will be more successful if they see themselves as part of the whole socio-technical system.

ACKNOWLEDGMENTS

Early work leading to these ideas was done at Apple Computer, and we appreciate its support. The other members of the team at Apple were Dave Curbow, Alan Cypher, Paul Dourish, Tom Erickson and Don Norman. In addition, we benefited from consulting by Niklas Damiras, Xin Wei Sha and Brian Cantwell Smith.

Since May, 1997, some members of this team have continued to work on these ideas as Pliant Research http://www.pliant.org/.

REFERENCES

1. Alexander, C. The Timeless Way of Building, Oxford University Press, New York, 1979.

2. Flowers, S. Software Failure: Management Failure: Amazing Stories and Cautionary Tales, John Wiley & Sons, 1996.

3. Bowers, J., Button, G. and Sharrock, W. Workflow from Within and Without: Technology and Cooperative Work on the Print Industry Shopfloor, in Proceedings ECSCW'95, (Stockholm, Sweden), European Foundation for Cooperative Work Technology, 1995

4. Button, G. and Sharrock, W. The production of Order and the Order of Production, in Proceedings ECSCW'97, (Lancaster, UK), European Foundation for Cooperative Work Technology, 1997

5. Fikes, R.E. and Henderson, D. A. Jr. On Supporting the Use of Procedures in Office Work, in Proceedings of the First Annual National Conference on Artificial Intelligence, American Association of Artificial Intelligence, Menlo Park, CA, 1990.

6. Suchman, L. Plans and Situated Action: The Problem of Human-Machine Communication, Cambridge University Press, Cambridge, 1987.

7. Yates, J. Control Through Communication: The Rise of System in American Management, The Johns Hopkins University Press, Baltimore, 1989; pp. xvi-xvii.

8. Yates, J. Op cit. pp. 68, 72.

9. Zimmerman, D. H. and Wieder, D. L. Ethnomethodology and the problem of order: Comment on Denzin. In J. D. Douglas (ed.), Understanding Everyday Life: Toward the Reconstruction of Sociological Knowledge (pp. 285-298) Chicago, Aldine, 1970. Cited in Suchman, L. and Trigg, R. Artificial intelligence as craftwork In Chaiklin, S. and Lave, J. Understanding practice: Perspectives on activity and context Cambridge University Press, 1993.

Nomadic Radio: Scaleable and Contextual Notification for Wearable Audio Messaging

Nitin Sawhney and Chris Schmandt

Speech Interface Group, MIT Media Laboratory

20 Ames St., Cambridge, MA 02139

{nitin, geek}@media.mit.edu

ABSTRACT

Mobile workers need seamless access to communication and information services on portable devices. However current solutions overwhelm users with intrusive and ambiguous notifications. In this paper, we describe scaleable auditory techniques and a contextual notification model for providing timely information, while minimizing interruptions. User's actions influence local adaptation in the model. These techniques are demonstrated in *Nomadic Radio*, an audio-only wearable computing platform.

Keywords

Auditory I/O, passive awareness, wearable computing, adaptive interfaces, interruptions, notifications

INTRODUCTION

In today's information-rich environments, people use a number of appliances and portable devices for a variety of tasks in the home, workplace and on the run. Such devices are ubiquitous and each plays a unique functional role in a user's lifestyle. To be effective, these devices need to notify users of changes in their functional state, incoming messages or exceptional conditions. In a typical office environment, the user attends to a plethora of devices with notifications such as calls on telephones, asynchronous messages on pagers, email notification on desktop computers, and reminders on personal organizers or watches. This scenario poses a number of key problems.

Lack of Differentiation in Notification Cues

Every device provides some unique form of notification. In many cases, these are distinct auditory cues. Yet, most cues are generally *binary* in nature, i.e. they convey only the occurrence of a notification and not its urgency or dynamic state. This prevents users from making timely decisions about received messages without having to shift focus of attention (from the primary task) to interact with the device and access the relevant information.

Minimal Awareness of the User and Environment

Such notifications occur without any regard to the user's engagement in her current activity or her focus of attention. This interrupts a conversation or causes an annoying disruption in the user's task and flow of thoughts. To prevent undue embarrassment in social environments, users typically turn off cell-phones and pagers in meetings or lectures. This prevents the user from getting notification of timely messages and frustrates people trying to get in touch with her.

No Learning from Prior Interactions with User

Such systems typically have no mechanism to adapt their behavior based on the positive or negative actions of the user. Pagers continue to buzz and cell-phones do not stop ringing despite the fact that the user may be in a conversation and ignoring the device for some time.

Lack of Coordinated Notifications

All devices compete for a user's undivided attention without any coordination and synchronization of their notifications. If two or more notifications occur within a short time of each other, the user gets confused or frustrated. As people start carrying around many such portable devices, frequent and uncoordinated interruptions inhibit their daily tasks and interactions in social environments.

Given these problems, most devices fail to serve their intended purpose of notification or communication, and thus do not operate in an efficient manner for a majority of their life cycle. New users choose not to adopt such technologies, having observed the obvious problems encountered with their usage. In addition, current users tend to turn off the devices in many situations, inhibiting the optimal operation of such personal devices.

Nature of Interruptions in the Workplace

A recent observational study [4] evaluated the effect of interruptions on the activity of mobile professionals in their workplace. An interruption, defined as an asynchronous and unscheduled interaction, not initiated by the user, results in the recipient discontinuing the current activity. The results revealed several key issues. On average, subjects were interrupted over 4 times per hour, for an average duration slightly over 2 minutes. Hence, nearly 10 minutes per hour was spent on interruptions. Although a majority of the interruptions occurred in a face-to-face setting, 20% were due to telephone calls (no email or pager activity was analyzed in this study). In 64% of the interruptions, the recipient received some benefit from the interaction. This suggests that a blanket approach to prevent interruptions, such as holding all calls at certain times of the day, would prevent beneficial interactions from occurring. However in 41% of the interruptions, the recipients did not resume the work they were doing prior to it. But active use of new communication technologies makes users easily vulnerable to undesirable interruptions.

These interruptions constitute a significant problem for mobile professionals using tools such as pagers, cell-phones and PDAs, by disrupting their time-critical activities. Improved synchronous access using these tools benefits initiators but leaves recipients with little control over the interactions. The study suggests development of improved filtering techniques that are especially light-weight, i.e. don't require more attention from the user and are less disruptive than the interruption itself. By moving interruptions to asynchronous media, messages can be stored for retrieval and delivery at more appropriate times.

NOMADIC RADIO: WEARABLE AUDIO MESSAGING

Personal messaging and communication, demonstrated in *Nomadic Radio*, provides a simple and constrained problem domain in which to develop and evaluate a contextual notification model. Messaging requires development of a model that dynamically selects a suitable *notification strategy* based on message priority, usage level, and environmental context. Such a system must infer the user's attention by monitoring her current activities such as interactions with the device and conversations in the room. The user's prior responses to notifications must also be taken into consideration to adapt the notifications over time. In this paper, we will consider techniques for *scaleable auditory presentation* and an appropriate parameterized approach towards *contextual notification*.

Several recent projects utilized speech and audio I/O on wearable devices to present information. A prototype augmented audio tour guide [1] played digital audio recordings indexed by the spatial location of visitors in a museum. *SpeechWear* [11] enabled users to perform data entry and retrieval using speech recognition and synthesis. *Audio Aura* [10] explored the use of background auditory cues to provide serendipitous information coupled with people's physical location in the workplace. In *Nomadic Radio*, the user's inferred context rather than actual location is used to decide when and how to deliver scaleable audio notifications. In a recent paper [13], researchers suggest the use of sensors and user modeling to allow wearables to infer when users should be interrupted by incoming messages. They suggest waiting for a break in the conversation to post a message summary on the user's heads-up display. In this paper we describe a primarily non-

visual approach to provide timely information to nomadic listeners, based on a variety of contextual cues.

Nomadic Radio is a wearable computing platform that provides a unified audio-only interface to remote services and messages such as email, voice mail, hourly news broadcasts, and personal calendar events. These messages are automatically downloaded to the device throughout the day and users can browse through them using voice commands and tactile input. The system consists of Java-based clients and remote servers (written in C and Perl) that communicate over wireless LAN, and utilize the telephony infrastructure in the Speech Interface group. Simultaneous spatial audio streams are rendered using a HRTF-based Java audio API. Speech I/O is provided via a networked implementation of AT&T *Watson* Speech API.

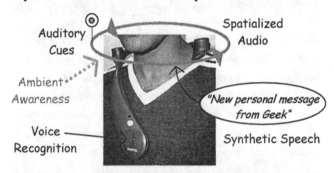

Figure 1: The primary wearable audio device, the *SoundBeam Neckset*. Messages are browsed in a unified manner via speech, auditory cues and spatial audio. The interface is controlled via voice and tactile input.

To provide a hands-free and unobtrusive interface to a nomadic user, the system primarily operates as a wearable audio-only device. The *SoundBeam Neckset*, a research prototype patented by Nortel for use in hands-free telephony, was adapted as the primary wearable platform in *Nomadic Radio*. It consists of two directional speakers mounted on the user's shoulders, and a directional microphone placed on the chest (see figure 1). Here information and feedback is provided to the user through a combination of auditory cues, spatial audio rendering, and synthetic speech. Integration of a variety of auditory techniques on a wearable device provides hands-free access and navigation as well as lightweight and expressive notification.

An audio-only interface has been incorporated in *Nomadic Radio*, and a networked infrastructure for unified messaging has been developed for wearable access [12]. The system currently operates on a Libretto 100 mini-portable PC worn by the user. The key issue addressed in this paper is that of handling interruptions to the listener in a manner that reduces disruption, while providing timely notifications for contextually relevant messages.

USAGE AND NOTIFICATION SCENARIO

The following scenario demonstrates the audio interface and presentation of notifications in *Nomadic Radio* (no voice commands from the user are shown here).

It's 1:15 PM and Jane is wearing *Nomadic Radio*. She has a meeting in a conference room in 15 minutes. The system gives her an early notification via an auditory cue and synthetic speech.

NR: <auditory cue for early event reminder> *"Jane, you have a scheduled event at 1:30 PM today."* <pause> *"Meeting with Motorola sponsors in the conference room for 30 minutes."*

Jane scans her email messages to hear one about the meeting and check who else is coming. A new group message arrives.

NR: <ambient sound speedup and slows down> *"New group message from Chris Schmandt about lost my glasses?"*

Jane ignores the message and heads over to the conference room. At this point, since Jane has been inactive for some time and the conversation level in the room is higher, the system scales down notifications for all incoming messages. Moments later a timely message arrives (related to an email Jane sent earlier) and the conversation level is lower. The system first plays an auditory cue and gradually speeds up the background sound of water to indicate to Jane that she will hear a summary soon.

NR: <auditory cue for timely message> + <faster ambient sound>

Jane is now engrossed in the meeting so she prevents the system from playing a summary of the message, by pressing a button on *Nomadic Radio* (she does not speak to avoid interrupting the meeting). The sound of water slows down and message playback is aborted. The system recognizes Jane is busy and turns down the notification level of all future messages in the next hour.

Its 1:55 PM and the meeting is nearly over. The system is currently in *sleep* mode. A very important voice message from Jane's daughter arrives. It recognizes the priority of the message and despite the high conversation level and low usage, it plays auditory cues to notify Jane. The ambient sound is speed-up briefly to begin playing a preview of the message in 3.5 seconds.

NR: <audio cue for voice message "telephone ringing" sound> + <VoiceCue of Jane's daughter>

Jane hears her daughter's voice and immediately presses a button to play the message. The system starts playing the full voice message in the foreground (instead of just a preview), two seconds earlier than its computed latency time.

NR: <human voice> *"Hi mom, its Kathy. Can you pick me up early from school today?"* <audio cue for end of message>

Jane excuses herself from the meeting and browses her email on *Nomadic Radio* while walking back to get her car keys.

Figure 2: A scenario showing Jane using *Nomadic Radio* to listen to notifications while engaging in other tasks.

SCALEABLE AUDITORY PRESENTATION

A scaleable presentation is necessary for delivering sufficient information while minimizing interruption to the listener. Messages in *Nomadic Radio* are scaled dynamically to unfold as seven increasing levels of notification (see figure 3): silence, ambient cues, auditory cues, message summary, preview, full body, and foreground rendering. These are described further below:

Silence for Least Interruption and Conservation

In this mode all auditory cues and speech feedback are turned-off. Messages can be scaled down to silence when the message priority is inferred to be too low for the message to be relevant for playback or awareness to a user, based on her recent usage of the device and the conversation level. This mode also serves to conserve processing, power and memory resources on a portable device or wearable computer.

Ambient Cues for Peripheral Awareness

In *Nomadic Radio*, ambient auditory cues are continuously played in the background to provide an awareness of the operational state of the system and ongoing status of messages being downloaded (see figure 4). The sound of flowing water provides an unobtrusive form of ambient awareness that indicates the system is active (silence indicates sleep mode). Such a sound tends to fade into the perceptual background after a short time, so it does not distract the listener. The pitch is increased during file downloads, momentarily foregrounding the ambient sound. A short e-mail message sounds like a splash while a two-minute audio news summary is heard as faster flowing water while being downloaded. This implicitly indicates message size without the need for additional audio cues and prepares the listener to hear (or deactivate) the message before it becomes available. Such *peripheral awareness* minimizes cognitive overhead of monitoring incoming messages relative to notifications played as distinct auditory cues, which incur a somewhat higher cost of attention on part of the listener.

Related Work in Auditory Awareness

In *ARKola* [5], an audio/visual simulation of a bottling factory, repetitive streams of sounds allowed people to keep track of activity, rate, and functioning of running machines. Without sounds people often overlooked problems; with auditory cues, problems were indicated by the machine's sound ceasing (often ineffective) or via distinct alert sounds. The various auditory cues (as many as 12 sounds play simultaneously) merged as an auditory texture, allowed people to hear the plant as a complex integrated process. Background sounds were also explored in *ShareMon* [3], a prototype application that notified users of file sharing activity. Cohen found that pink noise used to indicate %CPU time was considered "obnoxious", even though users understood the pitch correlation. However, preliminary reactions to wave sounds were considered positive and even soothing. In *Audio Aura* [10], alarm sounds were eliminated and a number of "harmonically coherent sonic ecologies" were explored, mapping events to auditory, musical or voice-based feedback. Such techniques were used to passively convey the number of email messages received, identity of senders, and abstract representations of group activity.

Auditory Cues for Notification and Identification

In *Nomadic Radio*, auditory cues are a crucial means for conveying awareness, notification and providing necessary assurances in its non-visual interface. Different types of auditory techniques provide distinct feedback, awareness and message information.

Feedback Cues

Several types of audio cues indicate feedback for a number of operational events in *Nomadic Radio*:

1. *Task completion and confirmations* - button pressed, speech understood, connected to servers, finished playing or loaded/deleted messages.

2. *Mode transitions* - switching categories, going to non-speech or ambient mode.

3. *Exceptional conditions* - message not found, lost connection with servers, and errors.

Priority Cues for Notification

In a related project, "email glances" [7] were formulated as a stream of short sounds indicating category, sender and content flags (from keywords in the message). In *Nomadic Radio*, message priority inferred from email content filtering provides distinct auditory cues (assigned by the user) for group, personal, timely, and important messages. In addition, auditory cues such as telephone ringing indicate voice mail, whereas an extracted sound of a station identifier indicates a news summary.

VoiceCues for Identification

VoiceCues represent a novel approach for easy identification of the sender of an email, based on a unique auditory signature of the person. *VoiceCues* are created by manually extracting a 1-2 second audio sample from the voice messages of callers and associating them with their respective email login. When a new email message arrives, the system queries its database for a related *VoiceCue* for that person before playing it to the user as a notification, along with the priority cues. The authors have found *VoiceCues* to be a remarkably effective method for quickly conveying the sender of the message in a very short duration. This technique reduces the need for synthetic speech feedback, which can often be distracting.

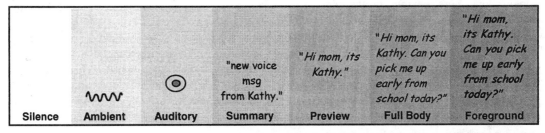

Figure 3: Dynamic scaling of an incoming voice message during its life cycle based on the interruptability of the listener. The message is presented at varying levels: from a subtle auditory cue to foreground presentation.

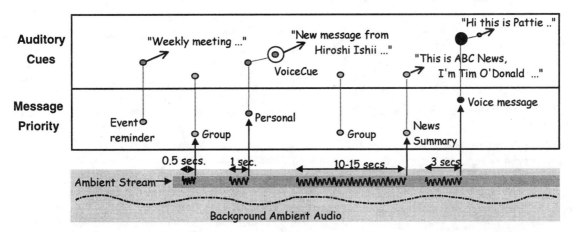

Figure 4: Ambient auditory stream speeded-up while downloading incoming messages. Audio cues indicate priority and *VoiceCues* identify the sender. A few seconds later, the message is foregrounded or spoken as synthetic speech.

Message Summary Generation

A spoken description of an incoming message can present relevant information in a concise manner. Such a description typically utilizes header information in email messages to convey the name of the sender and the subject of the message. In *Nomadic Radio,* message summaries are generated for all messages, including voice-mail, news and calendar events. The summaries are augmented by additional attributes of the message indicating category, order, priority, and duration. For audio sources, like voice messages and news broadcasts, the system plays the first 2.5 seconds of the audio. This identifies the caller and the urgency of the call, inferred from intonation in the caller's voice or provides a station identifier for news summaries.

Message Previews using Content Summarization

Messages are scaled to allow listeners to quickly preview the contents of an email or voice message. In *Nomadic Radio*, a preview for text messages extracts the first 100 characters of the message (a default size that can be user defined). This heuristic generally provides sufficient context for the listener to anticipate the overall message theme and urgency. For email messages, redundant headers and previous replies are eliminated from the preview for effective extraction. Use of text summarization techniques, based on tools such as *ProSum*[1] developed by British Telecom, would allow more flexible means of scaling message content. Natural language parsing techniques used in *ProSum* permit a scaleable summary of an arbitrarily large text document.

A preview for an audio source such as a voice message or news broadcast presents a fifth of the message at a gradually increasing playback rate of up to 1.3 times faster than normal. There are a range of techniques for time-compressing speech without modifying the pitch, however twice the playback rate usually makes the audio incomprehensible. A better representation for content summarization requires a structural description of the audio, based on annotated or automatically determined pauses in speech, speaker and topic changes. Such an *auditory thumbnail* must function similar to its visual counterpart. A preview for a structured voice message would provide pertinent aspects such as name of caller and phone number, whereas a structured news preview would be heard as the hourly headlines.

Full Body: Playing Complete Message Content

This mode plays the entire audio file or reads the full text of the message at the original playback rate. Some parsing of the text is necessary to eliminate redundant header information and format tags. The message is augmented with summary information indicating sender and subject. This message is generally spoken or played in the background of the listener's audio space.

---

[1] *http://transend.labs.bt.com/prosum/on_line/*

Foreground Rendering via Spatial Proximity

An important message is played in the foreground of the listening space. The audio source of the message is rapidly moved closer to the listener, allowing it to be heard louder, and played there for 4/5th of its duration. The message gradually begins to fade away, moving back to its original position and amplitude for the remaining 1/5th of the duration. The *foregrounding* algorithm ensures that the messages are quickly brought into perceptual focus by pulling them to the listener rapidly. However the messages are pushed back slowly to provide an easy fading effect as the next one is heard. As the message moves its spatial direction is maintained so that the listener can retain a focus on the audio source even if another begins to play.

Hence a range of techniques provide scaleable forms of background awareness, auditory notification, spoken feedback and foreground rendering of incoming messages.

CONTEXTUAL NOTIFICATION

In *Nomadic Radio*, context dynamically scales the notifications for incoming messages. The primary contextual cues used include: *message priority* from email filtering, *usage level* based on time since last user action, and the *likelihood of conversation* estimated from real-time analysis of the auditory scene. In our experience these parameters provide sufficient context to scale notifications, however data from motion or location sensors can also be integrated in such a model. A linear and scaleable auditory notification model is utilized, based on the notion of estimating costs of interruption and the value of information to be delivered to the user. This approach is similar to recent work [6] on using perceptual costs and a focus of attention model for scaleable graphics rendering.

Message Priority

The priority of incoming messages is explicitly determined via content-based email filtering using *CLUES* [9], a filtering and prioritization system. *CLUES* has been integrated into *Nomadic Radio* to determine the timely nature of messages by finding correlation between a user's calendar, rolodex, to-do list, as well as a record of outgoing messages and phone calls. These rules are integrated with static rules created by the user for prioritizing specific people or message subjects. When a new email message arrives, keywords from its sender and subject header information are correlated with static and generated filtering rules to assign a priority to the message. Email messages are also prioritized if the user is traveling and meeting others in the same geographic area (via area codes in the rolodex). The current priorities include: group, personal, very important, most important, and timely. Priorities are parameterized by logarithmically scaling all priorities within a range of 0 to 1. Logarithmic scaling ensures that higher priority messages are weighted higher relative to unimportant or uncategorized messages.

$$\text{Priority}\,(\,i\,) = (\,\log\,(\,i\,)\,/\,\log\,(\text{Priority Levels}_{Max}\,)\,)$$

Usage Level

A user's last interaction with the device determines her usage level. If users are engaged in voice commands to the system or browsing messages on it (or have been in the last few minutes), they are probably more inclined to hear new notifications and speech feedback. Each user action is time-stamped and an active timer compares the time since the last action with default values for state transitions at every clock tick. When a new message arrives, its time of arrival is compared with the *Last Action$_{Time}$* and scaled based on the *Sleep$_{Time}$* (default at 15 minutes). High usage is indicated by values closer to 1 and any message arriving after *Sleep$_{Time}$* are assigned a zero usage level. Logarithmic scaling ensures that there is less variance in usage values for recent actions relative to usage levels computed for any duration closer to the *Sleep$_{Time}$* (no activity). Hence, the user not responding for 10-60 seconds has less effect on notification than a response delay of over 10-15 minutes.

$$\text{Idle}_{Time} = \log (\text{Current}_{Time} - \text{Last Action}_{Time})$$

$$\text{Usage} = ((\log (\text{Sleep}_{Time}) - \text{Idle}_{Time}) / \log (\text{Sleep}_{Time}))$$

One problem with using last actions for setting usage levels is that if a user deactivates an annoying message, that action is again time-stamped. Such negative reinforcements continue to increase the usage level and the related notification. Therefore negative actions such as stopping audio playback or deactivating speech are excluded from generating actions for computing the usage.

Likelihood of Conversation

Conversation in the environment can be used to gauge whether the user is in a social context where an interruption is less appropriate. If the system detects the occurrence of more than several speakers over a period of time, that is an indication of a conversational situation.

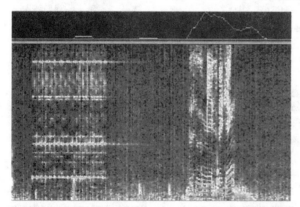

Figure 5: Bottom panel shows a spectrogram (~ 4 secs) with telephone ringing and a speech utterance. The top panel is the output probability (log likelihood) of an HMM trained on speech (which it correctly identified here).

Auditory events are first detected by adaptively thresholding total energy and incorporating constraints on event length and surrounding pauses. The system uses mel-scaled filter-bank coefficients (MFCs) and pitch estimates

to discriminate, reasonably well, a variety of speech and non-speech sounds. HMMs (Hidden Markov Models) capture both the temporal characteristics and spectral content of sound events. The techniques for feature extraction and classification of the auditory scene using HMMs are described in a recent workshop paper [2]. The likelihood of speech detected in the environment is computed for each event in a short window of time. In addition, the probabilities are weighted, such that most recent time periods in the window are considered more relevant for computing the overall *Speech Level*. We are evaluating the classifier's effectiveness by training it with a variety of speakers and background sounds.

Notification Level

A weighted average for all three contextual cues provides an overall notification level (*Notify$_{Level}$*). The conversation level has an inversely proportional relationship with notification i.e. a lower notification must be provided during high conversation.

$$\text{Notify}_{Level} = ((\text{Priority} \times P_{wt}) + (\text{Usage} \times U_{wt}) + ((1 - \text{Speech}) \times S_{wt})) / 3$$

Here P_{wt}, U_{wt} and S_{wt} are weights for priority, usage and conversation levels. This notification level must be translated to a discrete scale to play the messages. There are currently 7 notification levels: *foreground, full message, preview, summary, audio cue, ambient,* and *silence*. The *Notify$_{Level}$* computed must be compared to the thresholds for each of 7 scales to play the message appropriately. The *Notify Levels$_{Max}$* are scaled by two to produce thresholds with a greater range that accommodates notification levels computed under varying interruption. This provides a reasonable *Notification$_{Scale}$* for each message.

$$\text{Threshold}_{Level} (i) = (\log (i) / \log (\text{Notify Levels}_{Max} \times 2))$$

If (Notify$_{Level}$ (i) > Threshold$_{Level}$ (i)) then
assign Notification$_{Scale}$ = i, where i = {1 .. Notify Levels$_{Max}$ =7}

Presentation Latency

Latency represents the period of time to wait before playing the message to the listener, after a notification cue is delivered. Latency is computed as a function of the notification level and the maximum window of time (*Latency$_{Max}$*) that a lowest priority message can be delayed for playback. The default maximum latency is set to 20 seconds, but can be modified by the user.

$$\text{Latency} (i) = (1 - \text{Notify}_{Level} (i)) \times \text{Latency}_{Max}$$

A higher *Notify$_{Level}$* will cause a shorter latency in message playback and vice versa. An important message will play as a "preview" within 3-4 seconds of arrival, whereas a group message may play as a "summary" after 11-13 seconds of arrival (given high usage and low conversation levels). The use of latency primarily allows a user sufficient time to interrupt and deactivate an undesirable message before it is played.

Dynamic Adaptation of the Notification Model

The user can initially set the weights for the notification model to high, medium, or low (interruption). These weight settings were selected by experimenting with notifications over time using an interactive visualization of message parameters. This allowed us to observe the model, modify weights and infer the effect on notification based on different weighting strategies. Pre-defined weights provide an approximate behavior for the model and help bootstrap the system for novice users. The system also allows the user to dynamically adjust these weights (changing the interruption and notification levels) by their implicit actions while playing or ignoring messages.

The system allows *localized* positive and negative reinforcement of the weights by monitoring the actions of the user during notifications. As a message arrives, the system plays an auditory cue if its computed notification level is above the necessary threshold for auditory cues. It then uses the computed latency interval to wait before playing the appropriate summary or preview of the message. During that time, the user can request the message be played earlier or abort any further notification for the message via speech or button commands. If aborted, all weights are reduced by a fixed percentage (default is 5%), a negative reinforcement. If the user activates the message (positive reinforcement) within 60 seconds after the notification, the playback scale selected by the user is used to increase all weights. If the message is ignored, no change is made to the weights, but the message remains active for 60 seconds during which the user's actions can continue to influence the weights.

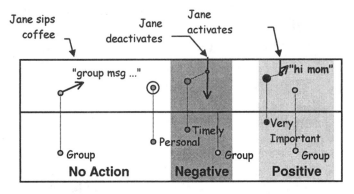

Figure 6: Adaptation of notification weights based on Jane's actions while listening to messages.

Figure 6 shows a zoomed view of the extended scenario introduced earlier, focusing on Jane's actions that reinforce the model. Jane received several messages and ignored most of the group messages and a recent personal message (the weights remain unchanged). While in the meeting, Jane interrupted a timely message to abort its playback. This reduced the weights for future messages, and the ones with low priority (group message) were not notified to Jane. The voice message from Kathy, her daughter, prompted Jane to reinforce the message by playing it. In this case, the weights

were increased. Jane was notified of a group message shortly after the voice message, since the system detected higher usage activity. Hence, the system correctly scaled down notifications when Jane did not want to be bothered whereas notifications were scaled up when Jane started to use the system to browse her messages.

EFFECTIVENESS OF THE NOTIFICATION MODEL

The nature of peripheral awareness and unobtrusive notification on a wearable device requires a usage evaluation that must be conducted on an ongoing and long-term basis. However, the predictive effectiveness of the notification model must first be evaluated on a quantitative basis. Hence, all message and notification parameters are captured for such analysis. Lets consider two actual examples of notification computed for email messages with different priorities. Figure 7 shows an auditory cue generated for a group message (low priority).

```
Last Action: Mon Apr 27 00:54:28 1998
IdleTime: 340 secs - Activity: 0.143104

Message Priority: group
Priority: 0.266667 Activity: 0.143104 Speech: 0
Notify Level: 0.46992
Mode: audio cues - Threshold:0.41629
```

Figure 7: Notification computed for a group email. The user has been idle; hence it is heard as an auditory cue.

The timely message (in figure 8) received greater priority and consequently a higher notification level for summary playback. A moderate latency time (approx. 6 secs.) was chosen. However when the user interrupted the notification by a button press, the summary playback was aborted. The user's action reduced overall weights by 5%.

```
Last Action: Mon Apr 27 04:02:35 1998
IdleTime: 21 secs - Activity: 0.552434

Message Priority: timely
Priority: 0.654857 Activity:0.524812  Speech:0
Notify Level: 0.70989
Mode: full body - Threshold: 0.67893
Computed Latency: 5802 ms

Key Server Command: Stop Audio
Undesirable Interruption - Reset activity time!

Reducing weights:
{Priority:0.722 Activity:0.9025 Speech:0.9025}
```

Figure 8: Notification level and latency computed for a timely email message. The user's action of stopping audio before it plays reduces all the current weights.

Continuous local reinforcement over time should allow the system to reach a state where it is somewhat stable and robust in converging to the user's preferred notification. Currently the user's actions primarily adjust weights for subsequent messages, however effective reinforcement learning requires a model that generalizes a notification policy that maximizes some long-term measure of reinforcement [8]; this will be the focus of our future work.

PRELIMINARY EVALUATION

Although the authors have been using and refining these techniques during system development, a preliminary 2-day evaluation was conducted with a novice user, who had prior experience with mobile phones and 2-way pagers. The user was able to listen to notifications while attending to tasks in parallel such as reading or typing. He managed to have casual discussions with others while hearing notifications; however he preferred turning off all audio during an important meeting with his advisor. People nearby sometimes found the spoken feedback distracting if heard louder, however that also cued them to wait before interrupting the user. The volume on the device was lowered to minimize any disruption to others and maintain the privacy of messages. The user requested an automatic volume gain that adapted to the environmental noise level.

In contrast to speech-only feedback, the user found the unfolding presentation of ambient and auditory cues allowed sufficient time to switch attention to the incoming message. Familiarization with the auditory cues was necessary. He preferred longer and gradual notifications rather than distinct auditory tones. The priority cues were the least useful indicator whereas *VoiceCues* provided obvious benefit. Knowing the actual priority of a message was less important than simply having it presented in the right manner. The user suggested weaving message priority into the ambient audio (as increased pitch). He found the overall auditory scheme somewhat complex, preferring instead a simple notification consisting of ambient awareness, *VoiceCues* and spoken text.

The user stressed that the ambient audio provided the most benefit while requiring least cognitive effort. He wished to hear ambient audio at all times to remain reassured that the system was still operational. An unintended effect discovered was that a "pulsating" audio stream indicated low battery power on the wearable device. A "pause" button was requested, to hold all messages while participating in a conversation, along with subtle but periodic auditory alerts for unread messages waiting in queue. The user felt that *Nomadic Radio* provided appropriate awareness and its expressive qualities justified its use over a pager. A long-term trial with several nomadic users is necessary to further validate these notification techniques.

CONCLUSIONS

We have demonstrated techniques for scaleable auditory presentation and message notification using a variety of contextual cues. The auditory techniques and notification model have been refined based on continuous usage by the authors, however we are currently conducting additional evaluations with several users. Ongoing work explores adaptation of the notification model based on reinforcement from user behavior over time. Our efforts have focused on wearable audio platforms, however these ideas can be readily utilized in consumer devices such as pagers, PDAs and mobile phones to minimize disruptions while providing timely information to users on the move.

ACKNOWLEDGMENTS

Thanks to Brian Clarkson for ongoing work on the audio classifier and Stefan Marti for help with user evaluations. We also thank Lisa Fast and Andre Van Schyndel at Nortel for their support of the project.

REFERENCES

1. Bederson, Benjamin B. Audio Augmented Reality: A Prototype Automated Tour Guide. *Proceedings of CHI '95*, May 1995, pp. 210-211.

2. Clarkson, Brian, Nitin Sawhney and Alex Pentland. Auditory Context Awareness via Wearable Computing, *Workshop on Perceptual User Interfaces*, Nov. 1998.

3. Cohen, J. Monitoring Background Activities. Auditory Display: Sonification, Audification, and Auditory Interfaces. Reading MA: Addison-Wesley, 1994.

4. Conaill, O' Brid and David Frohlich. Timespace in the Workplace: Dealing with Interruptions. *Proceedings of CHI `95*, 1995.

5. Gaver, W.W., R. B. Smith, T. O'Shea. Effective Sounds in Complex Systems: The ARKola Simulation. *Proceedings of CHI '91*, April 28-May 2, 1991.

6. Horvitz, Eric and Jed Lengyel. Perception, Attention, and Resources: A Decision-Theoretic Approach to Graphics Rendering. *Proceedings of Uncertainty in Artificial Intelligence,* Aug. 1-3, 1997, pp. 238-249.

7. Hudson, Scott E. and Ian Smith. Electronic Mail Previews Using Non-Speech Audio. *Proceedings of CHI '96*, April 1996, pp. 237-238.

8. Kaelbling, L.P. and Littman, M.L. Reinforcement Learning: A Survey. *Journal of Artificial Intelligence Research*, vol. 4, 1996, pp. 237-285.

9. Marx, Matthew and Chris Schmandt. CLUES: Dynamic Personalized Message Filtering. *Proceedings of CSCW '96*, pp. 113-121, November 1996.

10. Mynatt, E.D., Back, M., Want, R. Baer, M., and Ellis J.B. Designing Audio Aura. *Proceedings of CHI '98*, April 1998.

11. Rudnicky, Alexander, Reed, S. and Thayer, E. SpeechWear: A mobile speech system. *Proceedings of ICSLP '96*, 1996.

12. Sawhney, Nitin and Chris Schmandt. Speaking and Listening on the Run: Design for Wearable Audio Computing. *Proceedings of the International Symposium on Wearable Computing*, October 1998.

13. Starner, Thad, Mann, S., Rhodes, B., Levine, J., Healey, J., Kirsch, D., Picard, R., and Pentland, A. Augmented Reality through Wearable Computing. Presence, Vol. 6, No. 4, August 1997, pp. 386-398.

Tangible Progress:
Less Is More In Somewire Audio Spaces

Andrew Singer, Debby Hindus, Lisa Stifelman*, and Sean White+
Interval Research Corporation
1801 Page Mill Road, Building C
Palo Alto, CA 94304
+ 1.650.424.0722
{singer, hindus}@interval.com

ABSTRACT
We developed four widely different interfaces for users of Somewire, a prototype audio-only media space. We informally studied users' experiences with the two screen-based interfaces. We prototyped a non-screen-based interface as an example of a novel tangible interface for a communication system. We explored the conflict between privacy and simplicity of representation, and identified two unresolved topics: the role of audio quality and the prospects for scaling audio spaces beyond a single workgroup. Finally, we formulated a set of design guidelines for control and representation in audio spaces, as follows: GUIs are not well-suited to audio spaces, users do not require control over localization or other audio attributes, and awareness of other users' presence is desirable.

KEYWORDS
Audio, speech interactions, mediated communication, computer-mediated communication, CMC, user interfaces, representations, media space, audio space, audio-only, tangible interactions, active objects, design guidelines.

INTRODUCTION
Although the technology for Internet telephony is developing rapidly, most of its interfaces and the interactions that they provide are currently tied to the physical model of the telephone. As the technology improves and the underlying systems offer the full flexibility of digital audio, the possible interactions expand and new kinds of group communication systems become practical.

One promising example of these new systems is the audio space. An *audio space* is an audio communication system for a group, the members of which are in disparate physical locations; the audio space creates the auditory illusion for each member that its users share a common acoustic space.

To explore such audio spaces, we developed the **Somewire** system. Somewire allowed us to look at design issues and the workplace influence of a high-quality, audio-only group communication system. One or more versions of Somewire

were in continuous use by 8 to 16 people within Interval Research Corp. from 1993 to 1995.

A previous paper presented the findings from a Somewire-related field study [1]. This study examined usage, conversational content, and social norms within a single workgroup. The findings clearly show the value and utility of the Somewire audio space. Another significant finding of this study is that audio spaces can lead to social spaces.

The current work looks at the user interface aspects of Somewire, rather than at the social aspects. We built four interfaces to Somewire; each embodies a different approach to the central matters of representation and interaction in such a communication space. We conducted user studies and evolved the interfaces based on the results. Two interfaces are screen-based GUIs, one is a device interface with no software controls, and one is a tangible user interface that used physical objects. This first application of a tangible user interface to a media space is by far the most novel and engaging of the four; we describe it in detail.

In this paper, we first review prior work that informed the design of our audio-only media space. We describe Somewire briefly, then examine the four interfaces, emphasizing representation and interaction. We discuss what we learned from the user studies, and how we applied that knowledge in evolving our designs.

These interfaces entail a conflict between the need for privacy mechanisms and the need for simplicity of representation. We discuss how the conflict arises and some of the difficulties in resolving it. We present the novel tangible interface in detail. Finally, we offer a set of guidelines for the design of audio space systems, and identify areas that require further investigation.

DESIGN CONSIDERATIONS FOR AUDIO SPACES
Empirical data support the hypothesis that audio alone is sufficient to create a usable media space system. Audio has been found to have a primary role in communication [15,17].

---
* Author's current address: AudioVelocity, Inc., 312 Stearns Hill Road, Waltham, MA 02451, +1.781.894.1402, lisa@audiovelocity.com.
+ Author's current address: WhoWhere, Inc., 1675 N. Shoreline Blvd., Mountain View, CA 94043, +1.650.938.4400, sean@whowhere.com.

Somewire's primary characteristics are that it is *persistent, lightweight,* and has *high-quality, spatialized audio.* Persistency refers to communication being available continuously, in contrast to telephone calls which are explicitly started and stopped. Lightweightness refers to the lack of effort required to initiate or end communication; again, the telephone is not lightweight because of the need to pick up the handset, dial a number, and so on.

In support of the importance of the first two characteristics, several office-share studies (e.g., [7]) found continuous open audio to be important to creating and maintaining long-term interaction patterns between colleagues. Gaver [10] pointed out the importance of ambient audio in the workplace for subtly informing people of activities around them. Similarly, Whittaker and colleagues [25] studied informal workplace communication and characterized workplace interactions as one long intermittent conversation, made up of numerous, very short interactions. They predicted that persistent audio and video links could support frequent, brief, lightweight interactions at minimal cost.

The value of high-quality audio has been documented by studies that examined the audio-only condition in media spaces with multiple media. These studies demonstrated the value of providing high-quality full-duplex audio with no transmission lag. For example, Gale [9] found that high-quality audio resulted in faster group task completion times than did low-quality audio combined with video. There is also evidence that low-quality audio adversely affects communication [12].

Spatialized audio uses stereo to create an audio image around the user, like that created by high-fidelity entertainment systems. Spatialized audio is closely related to high-quality audio. Buxton's Hydra system [4], which used small audio-video units for teleconferencing, is particularly interesting in that it allowed users to configure spatially their conference space.

Our use of the term *spatialized* does not imply true three-dimensional (3D) audio, which applies complex signal processing to a mathematical model of the listener's head; such work informed our appreciation of some kind of spatialization, but 3D audio requires headphones to work well. Of interest here is Aoki, Cohen, and Koizumi's [2] audio conferencing system, which has true spatialization, a rich set of audio controls, and a screen interface that supports spatial positioning. That system, however, appears to be primarily a platform for audio spatialization research, rather than a system for workaday use.

One important point is that an audio-only system is considerably less complex, and therefore more practical, than a system that includes video. Somewire is such an audio-only system, and it is described in the next section.

THE SOMEWIRE AUDIO SPACE SYSTEM

Somewire is an audio-based communication system that connects multiple users in separate offices to one another in a manner conceptually similar to a telephone party line or conference call. Connections are continuous rather than transient, and no handset or connection setup is required after an initial configuration.

The goal of the system is to support persistent, lightweight and serendipitous communication among people located in separate physical spaces. Users hear one another's speech and office sounds continuously. This persistency creates and supports serendipitous communication of a kind that rarely occurs with telephone interaction; however, users are free to disconnect themselves from Somewire at any time.

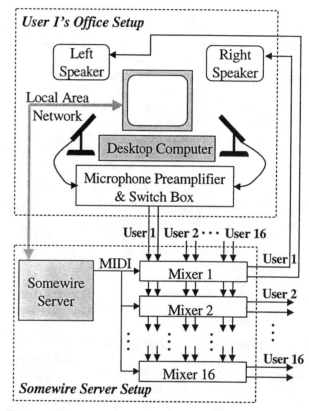

Figure 1. The overall Somewire system for the Faders, Vizwire and ToonTown user interfaces.

Each user's office contains stereo desktop microphones, a pair of speakers, and a hardwired box with an on–off switch that also contains the microphone preamplifiers. The communication process is lightweight. There is no call to place and no switch to throw; users simply speak. Somewire uses analog audio to connect up to 16 users through a central server (Figure 1). The underlying machinery of the system is a set of digital audio mixers, under the control of a networked server [18]. Each mixer is dedicated to creating and maintaining the acoustic space for a single user's office.

The audio is high quality, such that users can easily distinguish one another's voices and clearly hear each other's utterances, even when several users talk simultaneously. The sound quality makes it possible to hear every noise that you might hear if you were sitting in a person's office, including keyboard sounds, telephone conversations, body noises, and background noise.

Unlike other audio conferencing systems, e.g., the one created by Aoki, Cohen, and Koizumi [2], headphones are not necessary in the three Somewire systems that use stereo speakers. With speakers, feedback howl can result if a user's own audio signal is fed back to her system; headphones provide a simple solution to this problem in the fourth Somewire system. The other three versions of Somewire use mixing technology to produce an audio signal that eliminats the local microphones from each office's signal.* Most users work in private offices, so speakers are not problematic for them.

The audio managed by Somewire is not directly connected to the user's computer, although, in two versions, the user controls Somewire via an interface program running as a client application on his computer. The system's model enables widely varying interfaces to operate simultaneously and to interact with one another smoothly. The client programs could modify audio parameters—volume, panning, bass, and treble—for each source sound in the user's local input mix by sending requests to the server. These sound sources are primarily other Somewire users; compact disks and radio broadcasts are also available.

Two of the client application programs, Faders and Vizwire, are screen-based user interfaces. The third, ToonTown, is a physical interface that uses only tangible objects supplemented by auditory indicators. A fourth, Thunderwire, is based on a simpler implementation with just physical controls and headphones.

We shall describe these user interfaces in terms of the system setup, the interfaces' affordances, and users' reactions to the interfaces.

SCREEN-BASED INTERFACES TO SOMEWIRE
Initially, the system designers were predisposed towards conventional graphical user interfaces for controlling Somewire. The first two interfaces we built took this form.

Faders: A Literal Representation
The first interface is **Faders,** which presents a metaphor of the underlying mixing technology, with sound sources represented by bands of sliders.

In Faders (Figure 2), each user on Somewire is represented by a name and a set of audio controls. The sliders indicate the state of the system in relation to each associated user. *Volume* sets the loudness of each associated remote user's microphone in the local user's mix; *Pan* similarly sets the relative balance of the left and right channels, and *Bass* and *Treble* set these signal characteristics. The *Master Volume* control sets the overall volume of the local user's speakers. The *On–Off* button controls the whole mixer

This literal interface has the advantage of directly presenting controls for the audio parameters that the user can

---

*At the time, this required racks of sound apparatus. Now the same task could be accomplished much more easily, due to advances in digital audio mixing technology.

manipulate. It has the disadvantage of requiring that users understand the system's implementation and determine how to manipulate the audio parameters to achieve a desired end.

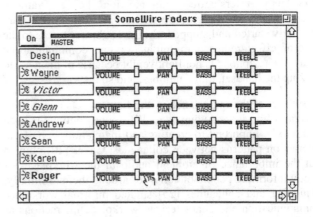

Figure 2. A Faders display. The local user, Roger, is listening to all users except 'Design', the name denoting a group meeting room.

Vizwire: A Social Representation
The mixer paradigm in Faders provides a view into the system machinery itself. **Vizwire,** on the other hand, presents a model that emphasizes the social and physical aspects of audio communication.

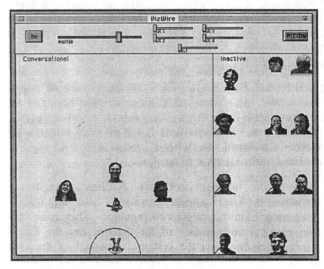

Figure 3. A Vizwire display. The local user, the Rabbit, is talking to four remote users.

In Vizwire (Figure 3), the local user is represented by a fixed icon in a semicircle at the bottom of the left-hand (conversational) region of the display. Each remote Somewire user is represented by a draggable icon on the screen. The Vizwire display is divided into three regions. The top *control region* contains overall settings for the system. Remote users whose icons are in the *inactive region* on the right side of the display are not included in the local user's mix. Users whose icons are in the *conversational region* on the left side of the display are heard in the local user's mix. An exception is a remote user whose microphone is turned off. In this case, the remote user is not heard and a red slash appears over his icon.

The conversational region employs a user-centric presentation. As a remote user's icon moves around the local user's icon, Vizwire moves the remote user's apparent audio position correspondingly. It does this by manipulating the remote user's stereo pan and volume in the local user's mix. Volume is thus represented as a vertical distance between icons, rather than as a linear slider as in the Faders interface. Just as the vertical position of the remote user's icon determines its volume; its horizontal position determines its stereo panning, that is, its left-right relative loudness.

One user can also "whisper" to another—that is, create a temporary private audio space for the two of them—by clicking on the other user's icon.

The advantage of Vizwire's social representation is that it enables users to concentrate on creating a desired social situation. This is a considerable improvement over the Faders interface, which requires users to translate device operations into the corresponding social situation.

User Reactions to Faders and Vizwire

To understand how users perceived the interfaces to Somewire, we conducted interviews after the system had been stable and running continuously for about 6 months. The user community consisted of Somewire project team members and several other researchers, for a total of 17 current and former users.

We formulated two dozen semi-structured questions to elicit users' positive and negative reactions to Somewire; the social influence of use of Somewire; memorable incidents; the way that users operated and conceptualized the system, and typical daily usage. Each user was asked all relevant questions. We also asked users to demonstrate how they operated their Somewire systems and to explain the system's current state. The interviews lasted 10 to 25 minutes; they were videotaped, transcribed, coded independently, and entered into a database for analysis.

The results highlight both the system's strengths and weaknesses. Users almost universally like the form of communication that Somewire provides. They praise both the physical convenience of the system, and the ease of social interaction via the system. One-half of the users, however, are concerned that the system intrudes on their privacy. Not knowing who is listening on the system is a frequent privacy complaint. Users also complain of being occasionally distracted by sounds from their Somewire system, and they find the two GUIs to be awkward to use.

Surprisingly, the hardware on–off switch is the control mechanism that users prefer once the system is configured to their liking. Users do not want to devote screen space to a function that they perceive as being like that of a telephone. An important research idea that emerges from these interviews is the notion of a nongraphical interface—one that is neither screen-based nor computer-based, but rather is like a freestanding physical device.

NON-SCREEN-BASED INTERFACES TO SOMEWIRE

We built two interfaces that were not standard graphical user interfaces: Thunderwire and ToonTown.

Thunderwire: A Physical User Interface

In **Thunderwire**, we eliminated the display and almost all of the user controls.

System Setup

Each user has a pair of desktop microphones, headphones, and a control switch with three settings: off, listen only, and on. There is an on–off indicator light for the microphones, and the sound volume can be adjusted. The overall system design is considerably simpler than the other Somewire systems. Because headphones are used, up to 10 Thunderwire users can be mixed together via a single audio mixer, rather than requiring one mixer per user. Furthermore, there is no software client application, so there is no need for the Somewire server or users' computers to be connected to the Thunderwire system.

Affordances

Thunderwire is like an old-fashioned party line telephone; users share an acoustic space, and they can only control whether their own microphone is active or not. All utterances and sounds from each active user's office or cubicle are heard by all users currently on the system. System use is fluid; people can connect or disconnect from Thunderwire at any time simply by flipping a switch.

Thunderwire is a purely audio medium. Except for the control switch, on–off light and volume control, it has no other visual interface or cues. Connection or disconnection by any user is indicated only by a barely audible click; in fact, there is no way to know exactly who is listening except by asking users to identify themselves.

ToonTown: A Tangible User Interface

Our choice of a tangible user interface for Somewire was greatly influenced by Bishop's marble answering machine [14] and by the emergence of augmented environments as an approach to computationally assisted interaction [24]. Bishop's prototype is an early example of an augmented environment. In the prototype, identification hardware is glued onto ordinary marbles, and a holder that could read a marble's ID is connected to a computer. The marbles could be treated as if they contained voice messages. In Bishop's scripted demonstration, the altered marbles readily afforded message replay, segregation by recipient, and reuse.

ToonTown makes use of similar *active objects*—that is, physical instantiations of computer-based objects that can be manipulated in the same manner as other objects in the physical world. In ToonTown, a user can manipulate physical representations of other users to control their acoustic space. The controls are moved off the screen and into the user's physical space. ToonTown can be described as an *body-syntonic interface*, that is, an interface that allows users to draw on their body knowledge directly [13].

Left pan	S	O	F	T	E	S	T	Right pan	
Left pan				Center Pan				Right pan	
Left pan				Center Pan				Right pan	Info Zone
Left pan	L	O	U	D	E	S	T	Right pan	Assign Zone

Figure 4. ToonTown prototype (top) and the meaning of each position on the board (bottom)

System Setup

The system setup is identical to that used by the screen-based interfaces, except that the display and GUI are replaced by the ToonTown active objects board and pieces. The board is connected to the user's computer and communicates with the ToonTown client software, which in turn controls the Somewire server.

The ToonTown object board and pieces are shown in the photo in Figure 4. This same board is also used in the Logjam system [5]. The prototype object board uses a microprocessor to sense the presence and location of the active object pieces. Each piece is a wooden block, about 1 inch square that contains a unique identification chip. The board has 48 locations arranged in four rows and 12 columns. Pieces are designed to sit on the board like blocks in a Scrabble™ tray, making contact in two places—the bottom and back of each row.

Tangible representations for the pieces are made from toy cartoon and action figures. The figures can be attached interchangeably to the active object pieces. A writable surface can be affixed to the front of each piece, so users can write labels or reminder notes on the pieces.

Afffordances

ToonTown differs from the graphical interfaces in that the user is not represented at all. It feels natural to users to project themselves into the screen when using Vizwire; that is, they are represented by their own icon on the screen and they move other users' icons in relation to their own iconic representation. However, it quickly becomes evident that self-representation is no longer appropriate once the interface moves off the screen and into a physical form; it is not natural for users to have a physical self-representation in addition to their actual physical selves.

The ToonTown object board is shown in Figure 3. Each column on the board, except the rightmost one, represents a spatial location from leftmost to rightmost in pan. Each row represents a volume; the front row is loudest and the back row is softest. The rightmost column is a control area. Placing a piece in the AssignZone causes a list of users to be displayed on the computer screen so that the piece can be assigned to a specific user. Placing a piece in the InfoZone causes an audio segment of the user speaking his or her name to be played, followed by a status message and an optional personalized message. The message is played only when a piece is initially placed in this location; the user can interrupt it by picking up the piece.

Audio feedback, in the form of a rising or falling pitch, indicates whenever an object is moved on or off the board.

User Reactions to Thunderwire and ToonTown

The Thunderwire system is robust and has been in use periodically for over a year. Nonetheless, as we report elsewhere [1], the field study clearly suggests user interface improvements. Users would prefer to know who is present in the audio space, and to have an automatic mechanism for turning off microphone input during an incoming telephone call. Furthermore, they would like the ability to set up two-way, private conversations.

With respect to ToonTown, users consider its tangible interface to be a highly engaging means of interaction. When they first see the object board and characters, several users have remarked that they feel irresistibly drawn to play with the pieces, and users enjoy being represented by a character. Because only a single prototype board exists for interacting with the Somewire system, we have not rigorously investigated usability and collaborative use.

PRIVACY, REPRESENTATION, AND PRESENCE

Previous media space research (see Bly, Harrison and Irwin [3] for a contemporaneous summary) has highlighted the importance of privacy. Privacy is of concern to us, in the design of the Somewire system and in the nature of users' social experiences with one another via Somewire.

In particular, the persistency and lightweightness that enables Somewire's key benefit, casual communication, also makes privacy violations almost inevitable. Privacy violations, group norms, and related social effects are addressed at length in a previously published study [1]. Here, we look at Somewire's privacy model, the implications for user interactions with the system, and the need for interface mechanisms that can provide users with an awareness of who else might be using the audio space.

Privacy Model

Somewire's privacy model emphasizes each user's control over his own acoustic space, and over the information about him that is available to other users. A user can control only what he hears and who can hear him; he cannot control the volume at which other people hear him, or his spatial position in another user's acoustic space.

This approach ensures that the system does not allow any user to be made audible to any other user without express action by both of them. This constraint is valuable in fostering trust in the system machinery. However, it turns out to complicate the representation of system configuration, and therefore to complicate a user's ability to understand and control that configuration.

Individual Control and Lack of Symmetry

All the Somewire interfaces except Thunderwire use a personal point of view—each user on the system controls his or her own acoustic space, moving people to the left or right, making each person louder or softer. The representations ware asymmetric in that user A might place user B to her left, and user B might place user A on her left as well—there is no global coordinate system.

A single global display would have eliminated the asymmetry, at the unacceptable cost of also eliminating each user's control over her own space. Furthermore, the privacy model does not support sharing of configuration information about users other than the two involved in any specific active or inactive state of connection. Even if this were not the case, it is not clear how the multi-way configurations among 16 users could be clearly presented.

In Thunderwire, point of view is irrelevant because there is no representation or control over anything other than the status of a user's own microphone. This solution works remarkably well.

Presence Awareness

Users of all the different interfaces have expressed a strong desire to know who is present on the system and thus potentially listening to them. Knowing whom they had *allowed* to listen is insufficient to forestall perceived violations of personal privacy.

Somewire can only indicate the status of a user's microphone. For example, in Vizwire a red slash indicates that a user's microphone is muted. In ToonTown, a user can determine whether another user's microphone is open by placing that user's piece in the InfoZone space on the board. Somewire cannot determine or indicate a user's actual attentiveness to Somewire, although it is technically feasible to indicate who has recently spoken aloud and who is physically present in their offices.

TANGIBLE USER INTERFACES FOR COMMUNICATION

ToonTown focuses on using tangible interfaces for communication, and users are represented as tangible objects. This section discusses social implications of representing people as objects, as well as how ToonTown is related to recent work in tangible user interfaces.

Social Implications of Representations of People

The ToonTown interface explores a novel use of active objects, where the objects represent people rather than software tools or computer-stored media.

Such a representation of people has social implications. For the ToonTown interface, each user selects his representations for the other users. Thus, it is possible that a person would not like the representations that other users select for her. In Vizwire, by contrast, each person is represented throughout the system with a self-selected icon. In one multi-user chat system studied by Schiano and White, women were more conscious of their representation than were men, and they were more concerned about having control over their representation [16].

Other social implications can result from using physical objects to represent people. How will users feel about picking up people by their heads? Would they 'flick' people off the board when they don't want to listen to them? What kinds of interactions would become acceptable practice?

Related Work

Our exploration of tangible interfaces for communication is a significant contribution to research in tangibility. Fitzmaurice, Ishii and Buxton [8] laid out a taxonomy for tangible interfaces, based on their graspable bricks. This taxonomy identified numerous aspects of tangible interactions, but concentrated on the object's interaction with the technology and so cannot be generalized to communication between users or to a specific application such as control of a communication system.

Ishii and Ullmer [11] reported on their metaDESK system, in which a flat display surface contained hardware for optically recognizing and tracking the location of physical objects on the display surface. For instance, metaDESK users could interact with a displayed campus map by moving an object shaped like a specific building. MetaDESK's use of semantically meaningful objects is similar to ToonTown's use of cartoon figures, but metaDESK did not involve communication, representations of people, or a virtual space shared by multiple users.

MediaBlocks [22], the successor to metaDESK, is similar in appearance and affordances to the ToonTown object board and pieces. However, the blocks referred to digital media content rather than to people, and the blocks did not indicate their contents. The mediaBlocks system extends beyond its ToonTown-like grid board to a range of media containers and operations, such as sequencing video clips. However, it did not address multi-user communication or the representation of people in tangible interfaces.

MediaBlocks suggests a possible extension to ToonTown, in which ToonTown users could add content to pieces that are not attached to any given user. For example, audio reminders could be represented by small alarm clocks.

CONCLUSIONS

We drew two sets of conclusions from our experience with, and study of, these four interfaces. The first set are design guidelines for audio space systems. The second set are questions for future research on audio space systems.

Design Guidelines

> **GUI interfaces are a poor choice for audio spaces.**
> In retrospect, it is not surprising that a graphical user interface is not optimal for interacting with an auditory experience. Audio communication does not demand visual attention. Furthermore, an audio space works like a utility and thus calls for a simple interface. With Thunderwire, we took simplicity too far by eliminating all forms of control and display. Some kind of tangible representation, building on a simpler version of the ToonTown model, might be the more appropriately balanced interaction mechanism.

> **Users do not need control over audio localization, or, by inference, over other audio attributes.**
> We were inspired by user reactions to build successive interfaces with less and less control for audio characteristics. Bass and treble controls available in Faders were dropped from subsequent interfaces; left–right panning, which is a prominent aspect of Vizwire and ToonTown, was dropped with Thunderwire.

> Our experience with localization is particularly instructive. With each of the interfaces that represented position—left–right relative position in Faders and Vizwire, and grid location in ToonTown—localization is a source of user confusion. Furthermore, when it was removed altogether in Thunderwire, users did not complain about its absence.

> This elimination of functionality leaves a system distinct from audio conferencing systems, which typically feature numerous audio controls [2]. Our discovery that here too, less is more, is particularly salient now that digital signal processing is becoming commonplace on personal computers. Designers of interfaces to general-purpose audio environments should be encouraged to resist the temptation to make every possible control available to the user.

> **Awareness of other users' presence is desirable.**
> One way to represent presence in the audio itself is through the use of auditory feedback. Cohen's 'Out to Lunch' [6] system provided auditory feedback about the presence of other workgroup members. Users could get abstract information about other users' activities (e.g., audio feedback of keyboard and mouse activity), but could not converse. The low-disturbance audio explored by Smith and Hudson [19], where users can hear who is speaking without hearing the words themselves, is another way to indicate whether other users are active in an audio space.

Matters for Further Investigation

> **What is audio quality's role in audio spaces?**
> Much of Somewire's attractiveness and utility resulted from its clean audio signal. Based on our experiences, we believe that the use of stereo microphones and speakers affords a spatialization effect that is critical to creating the illusion of an acoustic space. The space illusion is completely distinct from specific control over localization, which is not a necessary feature.

> It may also be that the role of audio quality in a successful audio space is less significant than we originally thought; Strub's study of two-way radio use over a weekend by groups of teenagers [21] showed that even low-quality, persistent audio could enable behavior indicative of social closeness.

> **How can audio spaces scale beyond a workgroup?**
> The Vizwire interface provided a single acoustic space and contained one representation of each user. However, what if users want to be in multiple spaces at once (e.g., to listen to multiple conversations)? One approach would be to have doppelgangers, that is, multiple representations of users.

> The voice-loop systems used by space mission controllers provide additional insight into how we might meet this need. In these systems, multi-layered, complex audio spaces are made usable through constraints on who is allowed to speak to whom, on the use of foreground and background volume levels, and on language use. The applicability of these approaches when the audio system is not the user's primary work task is unknown [23].

Through our work in creating a variety of interfaces to the Somewire audio space system, we have explored representation and control in collaborative shared audio environments. We have not made an exhaustive inquiry, however. We look forward to seeing how audio space interfaces will evolve, and how they will converge with the widespread availability of Internet-based audio communication.

ACKNOWLEDGMENTS
The authors thank the rest of the Somewire team and users, especially Glenn Edens for architecting Somewire and Roger Meike for creating the client and server software infrastructure. Wayne Burdick and Don Charnley built the Somewire hardware and the Vizwire software, respectively.

Bill Verplank crafted the board and pieces, which were instrumented by Scott Wallters and others. Jonathan Cohen provided helpful input to the design of ToonTown. We also thank the many reviewers of earlier versions of this paper, and Lyn Dupré for her editing assistance.

REFERENCES

1. Ackerman, M., Hindus, D., Mainwaring, S. and Starr, B. Hanging on the 'wire: A field study of an audio-only media space. *ACM Transactions on Computer-Human Interaction*, March 1997, 4(1):39-66.

2. Aoki, S., Cohen, M. and Koizumi, N. Design and control of shared conferencing environments for audio telecommunication using individually measured HRTFs. *Presence*, 1994, 3(1):60-72.

3. Bly, S.A., Harrison, S. R. and Irwin, S. Media spaces: Bringing people together in a video, audio, and computing environment. *Communications of the ACM*, January 1993, 36(1):28-47.

4. Buxton, W. Telepresence: Integrating shared task and person spaces. In *Proceedings of Graphics Interface'92,* (Vancouver Canada, May 1992), Morgan Kaufman Publishers, San Francisco, 123-129.

5. Cohen, J., Withgott, M. and Piernot, P. Logjam: A tangible multi-person interface for video annotation. To appear in *Proceedings of CHI'99* (Pittsburgh PA, May 1999), ACM Press.

6. Cohen, J. Out to lunch: Further adventures monitoring background activities. In *Proceedings of ICAD'94, International Conference on Auditory Display.* (Sante Fe NM, November 1994), Sante Fe Institute, 15-20.

7. Dourish, P., Adler, A., Bellotti, V. and Henderson, A. Your place or mine? Learning from long-term use of video communications. *Computer Supported Cooperative Work,* 1996, 5(1):33-62.

8. Fitzmaurice, G., Ishii, H. and Buxton, W. Bricks: Laying the foundations for graspable user interfaces. In *Proceedings of CHI'95* (Denver CO, May 1995), ACM Press, 442-449.

9. Gale, S. Human aspects of interactive multimedia communication. *Interacting with Computers*, 1990, 2(2):175-189.

10. Gaver, W. W. Sound support for collaboration. In *Proceedings of European CSCW'91* (Amsterdam The Netherlands, September 1991), Kluwer Academic Publishers, Boston, 293-308.

11. Ishii, H. and Ullmer, B. Tangible bits: Towards seamless interfaces between people, bits and atoms. In *Proceedings of CHI '97* (Atlanta GA, March 1997), ACM Press, 234-241.

12. O'Conaill, B., Whittaker, S. and Wilbur, S. Conversations over video conferences: An evaluation of the spoken aspects of video-mediated communication. *Human-Computer Interaction*, 1993, 8(4):389-428.

13. Papert, S. *Mindstorms: Children, Computers and Powerful Ideas*. Basic Books, 1980.

14. Poynor, R. The hand that rocks the cradle. *I.D. Magazine*, May/June 1995, 60-65.

15. Rutter, D. R. *Communicating by Telephone*. Pergamon Press, New York NY, 1987.

16. Schiano, D. and White, S. The first noble truth of cyberspace: People are people (even when they MOO). In *Proceedings of CHI'98* (Los Angeles CA, April 1998), ACM Press, 352-359.

17. Sellen, A. J. Remote conversations: The effects of mediating talk with technology. *Human-Computer Interaction*, 1995, 10(4):401-444.

18. Singer, A., *et al.*, Methods and systems for creating a spatial auditory environment in an audio conference system. Patent pending, United States Patent Office.

19. Smith, I. and Hudson, S. E. Low disturbance audio for awareness and privacy in media space applications. In *Proceedings of Multimedia'95* (San Francisco CA, November 1995), ACM Press, 91-97.

20. Stifelman, L. Augmenting real-world objects: A paper-based audio notebook. In *CHI'96 Conference Companion* (Vancouver Canada, April 1996), ACM Press, 199-200.

21. Strub, H. ConcertTalk: A weekend with a portable audio space. In *Proceedings of INTERACT'97* (Sydney Australia, July 1997), Kluwer Academic Publishers, Boston, 381-388.

22. Ullmer, B., Ishii, H. and Glas, B. mediaBlocks: Physical containers, transports, and controls for online media. In *Proceedings of SIGGRAPH'98* (Orlando FL, July 1998), ACM Press, 379-386.

23. Watts, J., Woods, D. D., Corban, J. M., Patterson, E. S., Kerr, R. L. and Hicks, L. C. Voice loops as cooperative aids in space shuttle mission control. In *Proceedings of CSCW'96* (Boston MA, November 1996), ACM Press, 48-55.

24. Wellner, P., Mackay, M. and Gold, R. (eds). Computer augmented environments. *Communications of the ACM*, July 1993, 46(7) (entire issue).

25. Whittaker, S., Frohlich, D. and Daly-Jones, O. Informal workplace communication: What is it like and how might we support it? In *Proceedings of CHI'93* (Amsterdam The Netherlands, April 1993), ACM Press, 131-137.

Whisper: A Wristwatch Style Wearable Handset

FUKUMOTO, Masaaki
fukumoto@mml.yrp.nttdocomo.co.jp

NTT DoCoMo Multimedia Labs.

3-5 Hikari-no-oka, Yokosuka-shi
Kanagawa-ken, 239-8536 JAPAN

TONOMURA, Yoshinobu
tonomura@nttvdt.hil.ntt.co.jp

NTT Human Interface Labs.

1-1 Hikari-no-oka, Yokosuka-shi
Kanagawa-ken, 239-0847 JAPAN

ABSTRACT

"Whisper" is a new wrist-worn handset, which is used by inserting the fingertip into the ear canal. A received signal is conveyed from a wrist-mounted actuator to the ear canal via the hand and a finger by bone conduction. The user's voice is captured by a microphone mounted on the inside of the wrist. All components of Whisper can be mounted on the wrist, and usability does not decrease if the size of components is miniaturized. So, both wearability and usability can be achieved together. The way Whisper is operated is similar to that of an ordinary telephone handset. Thus, onlookers may not look upon Whisper's operation as "talking to oneself", even if the associated PDA is controlled by voice commands. Whisper is especially effective in a noisy environment. Signals received via bone conduction can be heard clearly in the presence of noise without raising the volume (-12 dB at noise = 90 dB(A) in comparison to cellular phone handset). Whisper is also effective in avoiding the annoying problem of the user's voice being raised in a noisy situation. Feedback of the user's utterance is boosted by bone conduction when covering the ear canal with a fingertip, then the user's voice does not need to raised in the presence of noise (-6 dB at noise = 90 dB(A) in comparison to cellular phone handset). Whisper is useful as a voice interface for a wrist-worn PDA and cellular phone.

Keywords

handset, wearable computer, PDA, cellular phone, interface device, Whisper, UbiButton

INTRODUCTION

The recent advances in mobile information systems such as PDAs or wearable computers have been remarkable, and some "wearable" interface devices have been proposed for improving both of portability and usability. Many of these interfaces, however, have been designed as character and graphical interfaces, leaving the area of audio (voice) interfaces relatively untouched.

The audio (voice) interface can be used every time even if both hands are occupied. It also can be used with no or little practice. Moreover, both wearability and usability can be achieved by attaching a simple earphone-microphone unit onto the helix or into the ear canal. Therefore, the technical merits of designing a new interface device seem to be insignificant and unnecessary. Despite the many merits of the voice interface, its proliferation into the public and everyday use has been met with a certain degree of apprehension. Only in special business situations or some science-fiction dramas have the actual implementation of the voice interface been apparent. We think that the main reason for this stems from a general societal sense of apprehension not from technical problems.

Talking alone

Obviously, in information systems that have a voice control interface, voice commands must be uttered for operation. Today's earphone-microphone unit is still large and requires some electrical wires, so the surrounding people can easily notice that it is being used. However, with the advances in technology and the downsizing of components, the "Ear Plug" style device integrating telephone or PDA functions will be realized. Thus it can be easily overlooked by surrounding people. Therefore, it will appears to these people as if the user is "talking to himself" or what we refer to as "talking alone", when the user operates the PDA or makes a telephone call. This notion of "talking alone" is not considered socially acceptable to many people and this behavior seems very strange. This type of behavior will most likely become common place, if the voice interface comes into general use in the future and earphone-microphone style interface proliferates into the public. However, this style is currently not accepted in society. It is thought that the stigma attached to talking alone has hindered the spread of the wearable voice interface. Therefore, the important issue that must be addressed originates not from a technical aspect but rather the social aspect when designing and implementing the wearable voice interface.

However, the "talking alone" style of operation does not seem strange, when a person talks into an object grasped in the hand such as a telephone handset or handheld transceiver, even when the grasped object is too small to see directly. Furthermore, this effect can be achieved when the hand is used to mimic holding the object (hereafter called the grasping posture) even though no object is really held. Therefore, to help proliferate the voice control interface while retaining the benefits of the technological advances, devices that use the grasping posture should be implemented.

Wearable telephone

Some voice interfaces that use the grasping posture have been proposed in the field of cellular phones. Miniaturizing cellular phones using conventional technology has reached its practical limit. Further miniaturization is possible but speaking becomes difficult, because the basic distance between the user's mouth and ear is fixed. Thus, further downsizing is difficult while retaining a conventional handset shape. To overcome this problem, some wearable telephones were proposed[1]. A wristwatch-type telephone[2][3] has a speaker mounted at the end of an arc-shaped boom, which composes a part of the wristband when it is not in use. To operate this device, the boom is rotated and the speaker is moved to the center of the palm. Then the hand is used to cover the ear. The microphone is mounted on the inside of the wrist. When this device is operated, it mimics the posture of holding an ordinary telephone handset. Moreover, interference from outside noise can be eliminated because the speaker is covered by the hand.

There is another device called the "Parasite Phone[4]". The microphone is mounted on the tip of the thumb and the speaker is mounted on the tip of the little finger. This posture pantomimes the use of the conventional telephone. However, because the mechanism and an electrical cord must be attached at the fingertips, it hinders other daily activities.

Loud voice problem

These two devices reap the benefits of the technological advancements while incorporating the grasping posture. The distance between the microphone and the speaker is moderately extended, and the miniaturizing problem in a small sized handset can be resolved. However, these devices have not solved another important problem concerning the voice input interface. A PDA and a cellular phone are often used in noisy outdoor environments such as on a street or in a train station. This has lead to another social problem that has come to light over recent years with the popularization of cellular phones. Often times, the user's voice becomes excessively loud in a noisy environment, and as a result, it is annoying to surrounding people. In recent cellular phones, a part of the utterance voice signal is electrically fed back to the receiver of the handset to suppress the utterance volume, but additional electrical power is required. It is more desirable to boost the feedback of the uttered voice without the need for an electrical amplification. Therefore, a novel voice interface mechanism is desired by which all these problems can be solved in one stroke.

Fingertip into ear canal

In a noisy environment, users often cover their ears with their hands or insert a fingertip into the ear canal to shut out noise. From a distance, this posture is similar to that of grasping a small cellular-phone handset. Especially

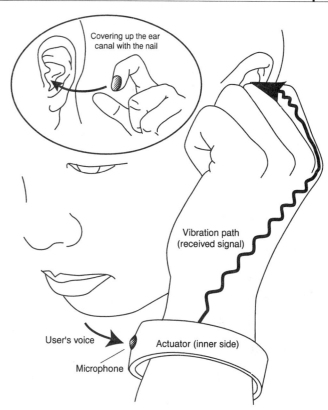

Figure 1: How Whisper works.
The received signal can be transmitted clearly with little force added to the fingertip when covering up the ear canal with the nail.

from the view of surrounding people, this posture can be regarded as "making a telephone call" when the user mumbles to himself. This posture not only shuts out the outside noise but also boosts the feedback of the user's utterance because of the bone conduction effect.

That is, the following effects can be achieved at the same time by inserting the fingertip into the ear canal.

1. The grasping posture is used.
2. Outside noise can be shut out.
3. The feedback of the utterance increases.
   (thus decreasing the need to speak loudly
   in a noisy environment.)

Moreover, the received signal will become clearer under noisy conditions, if the received signal can be transmitted through the finger inserted in the ear canal using bone-conduction. Furthermore, this method enables mounting the receiver mechanism at the wrist or the base of the finger to increase wearability.

This paper proposes a new wearable handset called "Whisper", which is used by inserting the fingertip into the ear canal. Some variations of Whisper are also described. The performance of Whisper is evaluated in comparison with the conventional cellular phone handset, especially with respect to the receiving performance and loudness of utterance in a noisy environment.

WHISPER

Whisper is a full-time wearable voice interface, which is used by inserting a fingertip into the ear canal. An actuator (= electric to vibration converter) is mounted on the wrist or the base of the finger, and is driven by the received audio (voice) signal. The received signal is conveyed from the actuator to the ear via the hand and finger through bone conduction (**Figure 1**). Whisper uses the grasping posture and simulates the use of an ordinary telephone handset. The bone conduction receiver in Whisper provides clear sound even under noisy conditions. Moreover, feedback of the user's utterance is boosted by covering the ear canal with the fingertip, therefore the user's voice does not need to be raised in a noisy environment. The bone conduction method enables the receiver mechanism to be mounted at the wrist or the base of the finger, which has better wearability than the fingertip. The microphone is attached on the inside of the wrist, so the microphone is naturally close to the user's mouth when the unit is in use. Moreover, the distance between the wrist (input) and the fingertip (output) is not changed when the device is miniaturized. Then Whisper can be downsized without decreasing usability. Therefore, Whisper can deal with the all problems mentioned earlier.

There are several variations of Whisper, each has the actuator in a different place. The prototype of Whisper for each variation is shown below.

Ring actuator

A ring shaped actuator is mounted at the base of the index or middle finger. Transmission efficiency of the receiving signal is the best. However, it is necessary to mount the control circuit on the wrist or other position, because it is difficult with current technology to mount all circuits on the ring. Then, some electrical wires are needed to connect the actuator and control circuit. This may be inconvenient to wear all the time. For instance, a cord-reel mechanism is equipped into the wrist-worn module, and makes contact with the ring part when in use (**Figure 2**). This system increases the wearability, especially when the unit is not in use. The Whisper with ring actuator will become an all-in-one style ring-PDA or ring-telephone, if all of the circuits including the bone conduction microphone can be packed into the finger ring in the future.

Boom actuator

For this version of Whisper, the actuator is placed at the end of the boom, which is mounted on the wrist-worn module. When using the unit, the boom is pulled out, and the user's hand is bent backwards. The actuator makes contact with the back of the hand, and vibrations are conveyed to the fingertip (**Figure 3**). For good transmission the actuator should make contact with the tendon (extensor digitorum superficialis) connected to the index or the middle finger. Some users, may feel fatigue because the hand must be bent backwards when using the unit. When not in use, the boom is accom-

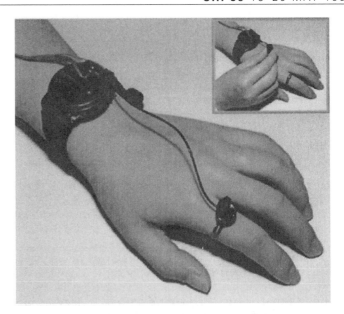

Figure 2: Whisper (ring actuator)
Hook switch is built into the cord-reel, and it turns on when the electrical wire is pulled.

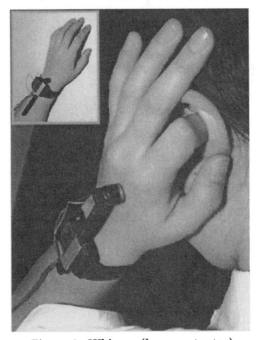

Figure 3: Whisper (boom actuator)
When operating, the boom is pulled out, and the user's hand is bent backwards.

modated into wrist module, to making it more comfortable to wear. For simple implementation, the manually handled boom mechanism, which doubles as the hook switch, is suitable. Of course, an automatic boom extension mechanism would increase the ease of use, however, a large electrical supply is required. The volume and tonal quality of the transmitted signal changes depending on the contact pressure between the actuator and the hand. Thus, the contact force should be detected using a pressure sensor, and the signal characteristics should be adjusted for stable receiving.

Table 1: Variations of Whisper

Position of actuator	Efficiency	Wearability	Notes
Ring	good	poor	future: all in one telephone
Boom(back of hand)	normal	normal	hand bent backwards
Wrist	poor	good	wristwatch style

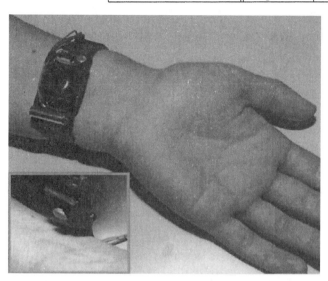

Figure 4: Whisper (wrist actuator)
The actuator is mounted at the center of inside of the wrist, and the microphone is located beside the actuator.

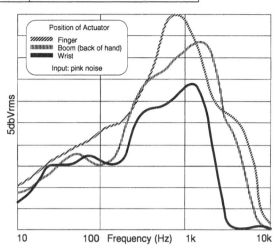

Figure 5: Frequency spectrum at fingertip
The ring actuator has the best transmission efficiency.

Wrist Actuator

In the all-in-one style handset version of Whisper, the actuator and the microphone are mounted on the inside of the wrist (**Figure 4**). For good transmission, the actuator should make contact with the tendon (flexor digitorum superficialis) connected to the index or the middle finger. People in this present age seem to resist attaching machines onto the skin except for the wristwatch. This version of Whisper can simulate the shape of an ordinary wristwatch, and it is most suitable for the general public. However, transmission efficiency is worse than that of other methods (-15dB compared to the ring actuator). Moreover, an echo canceling circuit is required to avoid interference from the actuator to the microphone, because the actuator and the microphone are adjacent.

The characteristics of the three versions are shown in **Table 1**, and the frequency spectrum of each method is shown in **Figure 5**. The ring actuator has the best transmission efficiency, and can transmit typical voice signals (200Hz - 4kHz) sufficiently. Efficiency of the boom actuator is almost the same as that of the ring actuator. However, the performance of the wrist actuator is worse than that of the other methods, especially in the high frequency band. Because the connections among the bones in the wrist (ossa carpi) are weaker than those of the bones in the fingers, so the bone conduction effect becomes weaker.

Despite the lower transmission efficiency of the wrist actuator, it has many merits considering wearability. All circuits can be mounted at the wrist, and no sharply pointed module such as boom is included. In particular, the wrist actuator version can be modeled as a wristwatch, thus it is familiar to people and enable them to wear it comfortably. Therefore, we selected this version of Whisper in the following evaluations. A special actuator, which was originally developed for the bone-conducting headphone, is used to improve transmission efficiency. This actuator has another good characteristic, which is suppressing the amount of spilled sound overheard by other people. Moreover, a tone controller is used to improve the tonal quality of the received sound.

PERFORMANCE

The voice interface of a wearable PDA which is usually used outdoors, should have good performance under noisy conditions. Moreover, it is necessary to be able to operate the device at the lowest speech level possible to avoid annoying surrounding people. Then, the receiving performance and the volume of utterance in a noisy environment were evaluated compared with the conventional handset of a cellular phone.

Receiving performance in a noisy environment

First, the receiving performance in a noisy environment was evaluated. It is necessary to raise the volume of the received signal when operating in a loud noise environment. The smaller the rate of increase in the volume when the surrounding noise is increased, is the better the performance rating. The experiment was conducted by testing the rate of increase in the amplification level of the received signal when the surrounding noise level is changed.

The procedure of the experiment is shown below.

1. The subject is exposed to pink noise from a large speaker that is placed 1m in front of the subject. The noise level generated facing the subject is set from 30 dB(A) to 90 dB(A) in 10 dB increments.

2. [PS1]: A cellular phone handset is held to the subject's left ear with the left hand. The right hand is not used (placed on the knee).

3. A human voice is heard through the receiver of the handset. When beginning the experiment, the volume is inaudible, and then it is gradually increased.

4. The subject indicates when the content (a phrase) of what is said is understandable by pushing a foot switch. The amplification ratio at that time is recorded.

5. The noise level is changed, and phases (3) to (5) are repeated.

6. [WS1]: An experiment similar to [PS1] is repeated using Whisper worn on the subject's left wrist instead of using the cellular phone handset. The index or middle finger (selected by each subject) of the left hand is inserted into the left ear canal. The right hand is not used (placed on the knee).

7. [PD1]: An experiment similar to [PS1] is repeated with the right ear covered by the right hand.

8. [WD1]: An experiment similar to [WS1] is repeated with the right ear covered by the right hand.

The size of the noise attenuation room was 2.2m(W) x 3.2m(D) x 2.5m(H). The size of the cellular phone handset used in the experiment[1] was 39 mm (W) x 19 mm (D) x 113 mm (H), and length between the receiver and microphone is 94 mm. The sound source was a recorded tape of a lecture[2] and came from the receiver of the handset and Whisper. The recorded tape is about 50 minutes long and used repeatedly. An experimental time is about 60 minutes per one subject. Then same phrase of the tape is appeared at most twice through the experiment. The number of subjects is ten, and all subjects are adult. It was necessary to make adjustments to the difference in each subject's audibility and efficiency of the speaker unit. Then, the reference level (0 dB) of amplification for experiments [PS1] and [PD1] was set to the result at the noise level = 30 dB(A) of [PS1] for each subject. Similarly, the reference level (0 dB) of [WS1] and [WD1] was set to the result at the noise level = 30 dB(A) of [WS1] for each subject. Each trial is repeated more than three times for each noise level.

The results of the experiments are shown in **Figure 6**. Graph [PS1] of this figure indicates that the receiving volume should be raised by about 41 dB, when the surrounding noise is raised from 30 dB(A) to 90 dB(A) using the handset. For Whisper ([WS1]), the receiving volume should be raised by about 28 dB, and the difference is 13 dB compared with the use of the handset ([PS1]). At the noise level = 70 dB(A) which is the average noise on a

[1]NTT-Personal(PHS) Paldio T331
[2]Kumiko, MUKOUDA: "I'm scary a word", Shinchousha ISBN 4-10-803101-6

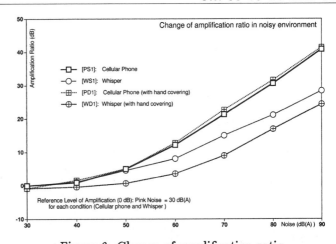

Figure 6: Change of amplification ratio in a noisy environment
Whisper can be audible well under the noise compared with the cellular phone handset.

street, Whisper (WS1) has an advantage of about 6 dB. This experiment indicates that Whisper can be clearly audible without significantly increasing the volume under noisy conditions as compared with the handset.

Moreover, graph [PD1] shows that covering the ear with the hand has little effect when the handset is used. Many people often cover their ears with their hands when using a cellular phone in a noisy environment. However, this result indicates that this posture will not directly improve the audibility. On the other hand, graph [WD1] shows that this posture can decrease the receiving volume by about 4 dB at all noise levels when using Whisper. It is said that audibility can be further increased by closing the opposite ear with the hand when Whisper is used. From this experiment, Whisper is more suitable for operation in a noisy environment than an ordinary cellular phone handset.

In addition, the posture for covering the right ear with the right hand was left to the discretion of each subject. There were three kind of postures: covering the entire ear with the hand (3 subjects), inserting the fingertip into the ear canal (5 subjects), and folding antitragus with the fingertip (2 subjects). In this experiment, no difference of audibility is observed among these three postures.

Voice loudness in noisy environment
As mentioned earlier, the volume of utterance often becomes excessively high when using a cellular phone under noisy conditions. The microphone of the handset can sufficiently capture low volume utterances of a user, even in a noisy environment. Thus, the reasons for this problem are considered to be the following.

- Uneasiness of the user: "The other party may not hear my voice?" when the other party's voice can not be heard easily in a noisy environment (We call this the hearing effect).
- Uneasiness of the user: "The microphone is far from my mouth, therefore I must talk louder" (We call this the microphone effect).

- Decrease of feedback: the user cannot easily hear his own utterance in a noisy environment (We call this the feedback effect).

As mentioned earlier, the trouble caused to surrounding people (especially in a noisy public space) can be decreased, if the utterance volume can be suppressed using Whisper. The volume of utterance under ambient noise at various levels is compared between Whisper and the conventional cellular phone handset. The procedure of the experiment is shown as follows.

1. The subject is exposed to pink noise from a large speaker that is placed 1m in front of the subject. The noise level generated facing the subject is set from 30 dB(A) to 90 dB(A) in 10 dB increments.
2. The throat microphone is attached to the subject's larynx.
3. [PS2]: A cellular phone handset is held to the subject's left ear with the left hand. The right hand is not used (placed on the knee).
4. The subject has a short conversation with the user through the handset. The output level of the throat microphone in this talking session is recorded.
5. The noise level is changed, and phases (4) to (5) are repeated.
6. [WS2]: An experiment similar to [PS2] is repeated using Whisper worn on the subject's left wrist instead of the cellular phone handset. The index or middle finger (selected by each subject) of the left hand is inserted into the left ear canal. The right hand is not used (placed on the knee). Whisper's microphone is placed at the inside of the subject's wrist.
7. [PD2]: An experiment similar to [PS2] is repeated with the right ear covered by the right hand.
8. [WD2]: An experiment similar to [WS2] is repeated with the right ear covered by the right hand.

It is difficult to extract only the volume of the subject's utterance using a conventional microphone under loud noise conditions. A throat microphone is used that captures only the subject's utterance regardless of the surrounding noise. In this experiment, the volume of the received voice is set at an audible level in each trial. All other conditions are the same as the last experiment. The number of subjects is ten, and all subjects are adult. Each trial is repeated more than three times for each noise level.

The results of the experiments are shown in **Figure 7**[3]. Graphs [PS2] and [WS2] of this figure indicate that the utterance volume using Whisper (77 dB(A)) can be decreased about 6 dB(A) as compared with the conventional handset (83 dB(A)), when the surrounding noise level is 90 dB(A). At the noise level = 70 dB(A) which is the average noise on a street, Whisper (WS2) has about a 5 dB advantage. It is said that humans can clearly

---

[3]The value of the utterance volume is converted into dB(A) using the relationship between the output level of the throat microphone and the utterance volume (1m in front of the subject) measured beforehand.

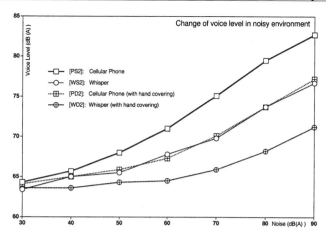

Figure 7: Change of utterance level
in a noisy environment
The utterance volume can be suppressed using Whisper.

recognize a volume difference of 5 dB. Thus, the suppression of utterance volume using Whisper is effective.

Lines [PD2] and [WS2] of this figure almost overlap showing that covering the opposite ear with the hand when using a handset is effective in reducing the utterance volume. These two experiments can be thought as having the same condition from the viewpoint of "covering one ear with the hand or fingertip". The user's own utterance can be heard with a high volume when inserting the fingertip in the ear canal. It is thought that the "feedback effect" is decreased by covering the ear, and the utterance volume can be suppressed. Moreover, when using Whisper, the utterance volume can be decreased further by about 5 dB(A) under loud noise conditions by closing the opposite ear. In this operating style, the receiving voice can also be heard clearly, then the effect of the Whisper method can be enhanced even further.

The last set of experiment results indicates that covering the opposite ear with the hand has little effect in enhancing the audibility of a received voice when using a handset (cf. [PD1] of **Figure 6**). Then, the main reason for the increase in utterance volume in a noisy environment is caused by the "feedback effect". From these two sets of experiments, it is clear that the Whisper method has good audibility and can suppress the utterance volume in a noisy environment.

DISCUSSION

Efficiency of transmission

The transmission efficiency of a received signal of Whisper changes greatly depending on the contact condition of the fingertip and ear canal. Stronger insertion of the fingertip will bring louder and clearer sound, especially for the high frequency band. However, this forceful insertion causes user fatigue, and is not suitable for long-time operation. In general, to improve the transmission efficiency of bone conduction, hard body parts should be touching. Clear sound can be heard with only a slight amount of additional insertion force to the fingertip when covering up the ear canal with the nail. In the future, regulating the volume and tone of the received signal will be realized regardless of changes in the contact condition, if a wrist-mounted sensing device which can detect the contact condition is developed.

User fatigue

The following are possible reasons for user fatigue, excluding when exerting force with the fingertip.

Hand posture

As mentioned earlier, the user becomes fatigued by bending the hand backwards for a long time when using the boom actuator version of Whisper. This action is not required for the ring and wrist actuator versions of Whisper. However, since the microphone is mounted on the inside of the wrist, the user's voice cannot be captured clearly when the wrist is away from the user's mouth. This problem can be solved by using a bone conduction microphone. The user's voice is transmitted from the head to the wrist mounted bone conduction microphone via a finger and the hand, in the reverse order of the received signal. This method frees the position of the wrist when the device is in operation, and it can improve the performance of capturing the user's voice in a loud noise environment. However, this method needs a powerful echo canceller mechanism to separate sending and receiving signals, both of which are transmitted with the same bone conduction route.

Tightening of wrist

For the wrist actuator version of Whisper, the receiving signal is transmitted by contacting the actuator to the tendon on the inside of the wrist. Increasing the contact pressure of the actuator improves the transmission efficiency. However, this may cause the user fatigue and excess stress on the wrist. It would be quite meaningless to tighten the wristband when the device is not in use, which would represent long periods in daily activity. It is possible to improve wearability by adopting a mechanism that increases the contact pressure only while the unit is in use. Usability can be improved at the same time by combining into one lever or knob the main function switch (or hook switch) with the mechanism that presses the actuator against the wrist[4].

Moreover, an after-mark sometimes remains on the surface of the skin when the actuator is in prolonged contact at the same position on the wrist. Changing the contact location of the actuator each time the unit is used would solve this problem. Fatigue associated with long-time operation should be examined.

Another wrist-worn input method

It is effective to combine a wrist-worn input interface with Whisper for some simple operations that do not require interaction, such as controlling the PDA's own state for example "activate" or "inactivate". "UbiBut-

---

[4]An automatic pressure control mechanism employing an air pump or motor can significantly improve the usability, however, it requires a large electrical supply.

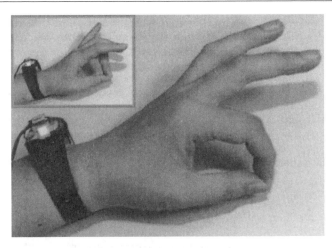

Figure 8: Sensor part of UbiButton
The shape of the finger is an example of "OK tapping".

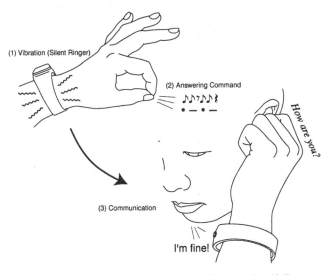

Figure 9: Application example of Whisper & Ubibutton
A sample operation by the combination of Whisper and UbiButton (answering a telephone).

ton" is a wrist-worn command input device[5]. It has one accelerometer mounted on the upper part of the wrist, and detects tapping actions performed by the fingertips on any support object. Commands are represented from the combination of tapping rhythms. Over 10 commands can be input by using UbiButton when the tapping sequence of 2 to 4 strokes is used, and it can cover major PDA commands such as menu selection. UbiButton can also be operated by an "OK tapping" action, i.e., touching the thumb and other fingertip even when a support object does not exist such as when walking. **Figure 8** shows the sensor part of the prototype of UbiButton. UbiButton can be operated by the hand on which it is worn, thus the usability in daily life can be improved.

CONCLUSION

Whisper achieved a "telephone style" natural voice input / output function with good wearability. The wrist mounted PDA or wearable computer can adopt the voice interface by using Whisper. In addition, Whisper has good receiving performance and can suppress the user's utterance volume, in a noisy environment.

We are making a testbed of wrist mounted PDAs that use the Whisper voice I/O, command input with UbiButton, and small LCD display, to test command structures and the feedback method. This testbed also has the function of a cellular phone and infrared remote controller. **Figure 9** shows a sample of cellular-phone operation employing the combination of Whisper and UbiButton. The actuator of Whisper vibrates in the very low-frequency to notify the user when the telephone rings without an audible alarm. The user issues the "answer telephone" command by "OK tapping", and starts conversing immediately. Since all operations can be done with just one hand, this style PDA can be used in many daily situations even when walking or carrying luggage.

The size of the current actuator is still large. Especially, the thickness of the actuator is important for improving wearability, because it is mounted on the inside of the wrist. The conversion efficiency of the actuator is an-other problem, it causes increased power consumption and spilled sound. We are developing a small and thin actuator that has good conversion efficiency. We are also planning to use the bone conduction microphone to improve the uttered voice quality in a noisy environment, and to realize operation that is more comfortable where the user can freely position the wrist. Our goal is to realize an all-in-one wrist (or ring) mounted PDA.

REFERENCES

[1] Yoshitake Suzuki et al. Development of an Integrated Wristwatch-type PHS Telephone. *NTT Review*, Vol.10, No.11, 1998.

[2] Greg E. Blonder et al. Sound Port for a Wrist Telephone. *US Pat. No.5381387*, 1994.

[3] Greg E. Blonder et al. On Hook / Off Hook Mechanism for Wrist Telephone. *US Pat. No.5499292*, 1994.

[4] Takahiro Kudo, "Parasite Phone", *Mobile Computing & Communications*, June, p79, 1998.

[5] Fukumoto, Masaaki et al. UbiButton: A bracelet style fulltime wearable commander. *Trans. of IPSJ*, Vol.40, No.2, 1999 (In Japanese).

i-LAND:
An interactive Landscape for Creativity and Innovation

Norbert A. Streitz, Jörg Geißler, Torsten Holmer, Shin'ichi Konomi, Christian Müller-Tomfelde,
Wolfgang Reischl, Petra Rexroth, Peter Seitz, Ralf Steinmetz

GMD – German National Research Center for Information Technology
IPSI – Integrated Publication and Information Systems Institute,
Dolivostr. 15, D–64293 Darmstadt, Germany
streitz@darmstadt.gmd.de, phone: +49 6151 869 919

ABSTRACT

We describe the i-LAND environment which constitutes an example of our vision of the workspaces of the future, in this case supporting cooperative work of dynamic teams with changing needs. i-LAND requires and provides new forms of human-computer interaction and new forms of computer-supported cooperative work. Its design is based on an integration of information and architectural spaces, implications of new work practices and an empirical requirements study informing our design. i-LAND consists of several 'roomware' components, i.e. computer-augmented objects integrating room elements with information technology. We present the current realization of i-LAND in terms of an interactive electronic wall, an interactive table, two computer-enhanced chairs, and two "bridges" for the Passage-mechanism. This is complemented by the description of the creativity support application and the technological infrastructure. The paper is accompanied by a video figure in the CHI'99 video program.

Keywords

Integrated design, interactive landscape, architectural space, virtual information space, augmented reality, ubiquitous computing, roomware, cooperative rooms, creativity support, dynamic team work, CSCW, workspaces of the future

INTRODUCTION

In this paper, we present an approach for the design and implementation of innovative workspaces that are based on an integrated design of virtual information spaces and – with equal weight – real architectural spaces. While the general approach for the *workspaces of the future* is applicable to a wide range of application scenarios, we will focus in this paper on a specific example, the support for creative teams. The first results of our approach will be presented in terms of the i-LAND environment: an interactive landscape for creativity and innovation.

We approach the issues involved from the following four perspectives. First, we discuss the relationship between the affordances provided by real, physical objects in the architectural space and digital information objects in the virtual information space. Second, we discuss the implications of new work practices resulting from organizational innovations and their requirements for the design of collaborative workspaces. These two perspectives represent the general conceptual framework. In order to make our ideas more concrete, we illustrate them by two example scenarios which had a guiding function for our design. A third perspective is provided by the technological framework, considering developments in augmented reality and ubiquitous computing. The fourth perspective is provided by the results of an empirical requirements study informing our design by current work practices of existing teams and their expectations about future work environments. These four perspectives set the stage for the central part of this paper: the introduction of our 'roomware' concept and the description of the first prototype implementation in terms of the i-LAND environment. The paper ends with a discussion of our approach with respect to related work and directions for future work.

CONCEPTUAL FRAMEWORK

It is our vision of the workspaces of the future – for individuals as well as groups – that the environment around us becomes more of an interface to information which can and should be (re)presented in many more different forms than it is currently the case.

Integrated Design of Information and Architectural Spaces

The advent of information technology resulted in a shift to a situation where information is being created, stored and communicated by means of computers resulting in virtual worlds as the places of information. As a consequence, interfaces to information are being realized as – and in our perspective reduced to – displays of desktop computers or via virtual reality gadgets. On the other hand, our day-to-day living and working environments are highly determined by the architectural space around us. Buildings with their rooms, walls, floors, ceilings, doors, windows, furniture, etc. constitute rich information spaces due to their inherent affordances – either as concrete and direct information sources or by providing ambient peripheral information [7].

Examples are the distribution and availability of physical objects as, e.g., books, magazines, drawings, notepads, photo copies placed on desks, tables, or window shelves; diagrams, pictures, and calendars hanging on the walls. Another example is the physical layout of the workplace in an office or a meeting room and how it is embedded in the overall architectural environment. The positioning of desks, chairs, tables, shelves in offices results from existing work practices. At the same time, these characteristics constrain current group activities in terms of possible changes of their structure. For example, the ease of forming subgroups of a team working in a meeting room is very much dependent on the flexibility of the furniture and the access to multiple information devices. Architectural spaces are and serve as information and cooperation spaces.

With the spread of desktop computers in offices, the situation changed dramatically. The monitor of the desktop computer became the primary, almost "holy" entrance to up-to-date information. There is a tendency that information is more or less available only via the computer. At the same time, the desktop computer turned out to be a bottleneck. There are limitations for parallel access to different sources and types of information and limited screen space results often in complex handling of windows.

We are convinced that - also in the age of information technology - physical objects and their placement in the architectural space provide valuable "affordances" for organizing content information and meta information for the work process of individuals as well as for groups. These affordances should be complemented by augmenting the physical environment by the rich information available in digital information spaces. In some cases, this requires to present this "invisible" information via (dynamic) physical objects in correspondence with the (changing) underlying digital information. There are many ways to approach this overall design goal. For related approaches see [1] and [7].

New Work Practices
In the future, work and cooperation in organizations will be characterized by a degree of dynamics, flexibility, and mobility that will go far beyond many of today's developments and examples. On demand and ad hoc formation of teams, virtual organizations, physically distributed and mobile workers, desk sharing are only initial examples of the work practices and organizational innovation to be expected. Contents and participants as well as contexts, tasks, processes and structures of collaboration will be changing frequently, in various ways and with an increasing rate of the innovation cycle. The role of physical office space will change. It is time to reflect these developments in the design of equally dynamic, flexible, and mobile work environments.

On demand and ad hoc formation of teams requires powerful methods and tools for the support of different work phases in teams. In one of our empirical studies [8],

where we evaluated our previously developed meeting support system [18], we found that the provision of hypermedia functionality facilitates the division of labor in team work. This resulted in better results in the group problem solving activities [8]. In another empirical study [22], we investigated different combinations of personal and public information devices (four networked computers mounted in a table, one interactive electronic whiteboard) and their role for collaboration in meetings. These results show that the groups which developed a balanced proportion of individual work, subgroup activities, and working in the full group achieved better results than those groups which stayed most of the time in the full-group work configuration. The degree of flexibility to work in different modes was largely determined by the range and combination of information devices provided to the team.

While these results were obtained in "standard" electronic meeting rooms, these constellations do not provide the necessary flexibility of assigning different workspace areas within a meeting room to subgroups and individuals. Standard electronic meeting rooms usually employ one large static table and computers on top of it or mounted in the table [e.g., 10, 11, 17] as we also did in the past [18, 22]. So far, it was not possible to (re)configure the combination of furniture and computer devices in a very flexible way. It is a high priority design goal for i-LAND to provide an environment with high spatial flexibility and mobility of the employed information devices.

Two Sample Scenarios
In order to have concrete examples of how we can transform our general approach into working prototypes, we developed sample scenarios guiding our ideas of how to work and cooperate in the future. We present two of them.

First scenario
Meeting a colleague by chance in the hallway and starting a discussion might result in the intention to explain something by drawing a sketch on the wall and annotate it by some scribbles. Besides the fact that this is usually not accepted in office buildings, traditional walls do not support to store and later modify these elements of the discussion. It is also not possible to search for related information in a background information base and to link this information to the sketch and the scribbles on the wall. In the future, we like to be able to turn to the wall and do just this. Think of the wall as an "interactive wall" or as one being "covered" by a high resolution electronic wallpaper providing the functionality needed. A wall like this is also of great use for informal communication in other places, e.g., the cafeteria.

Second scenario
It often happens in group work, that a team divides the work by assigning subtasks and breaks up so that individuals and subgroups can go off to do their work. After some time, e.g., on the next day, the full team meets again and discusses the results which form the basis for the next phase of cooperation. In a time-critical situation, it would be very useful if one can reduce this cycle time of full team

meeting/ subgroup meetings. An alternative is to provide ways for subgroups to split off *during the meeting in the same work space*, do their work, rejoin and then immediately merge the results. Providing adequate IT support for this scenario requires a team or project room which is equipped with components and resources which are so flexible that they can be reconfigured dynamically and on-demand in order to meet the different requirements of changing team work situations. From our analysis of this scenario, we came up with a plenary situation and different subgroup constellations. The plenary is characterized by the full team sitting in chairs and facing a (large) public display. One example of subgroup work is that some people move their chairs and group them in one corner of the room, discuss their task and exchange ideas. Another subgroup might walk over to an ad hoc meeting table, stands around it, views and edits tables and diagrams. A third subgroup walks up to a large whiteboard, draws sketches and annotates them with scribbles.

It is our vision that the chairs, the table, and the whiteboard are all interactive electronic devices providing adequate IT support for these interaction and cooperation situations. We also suggest places for individual work, e.g., searching for background information, called 'Columns of Knowledge'. Furthermore, we think that there will be always paper in one way or another. Thus, we suggest a device, the mobile 'ScanTable', for scanning paper documents so that the content is immediately available in the network. Fig. 1 presents a first visualization of our ideas when we started the i-LAND project (in spring 1997) showing parallel work of three subgroups and two individuals.

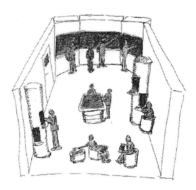

Fig. 1   A first visualization (spring 1997) of our vision of the i-LAND environment

TECHNOLOGICAL FRAMEWORK

We are convinced that we have to go *beyond desktops* in order to realize our vision of the 'workspaces of the future' presented above. It is obvious that this goal requires a different technological setup as usually available in offices. In particular, two areas of recent developments are relevant: *augmented reality* and *ubiquitous computing*.

Augmented Reality

This area reflects our view that the real world around us should be more of an interface to information than it is currently. Rather than sitting in front of the monitor of your

desktop computer and "diving" into cyberspace or wearing helmets, head-mounted displays, goggles, etc. in order to immerse in a virtual world, augmented reality is concerned with the use of computational devices in order to augment our perception and interaction in the physical world. For an overview of initial work see [27]. Early examples are the DigitalDesk [26], Chameleon [3], and the NaviCam [15]. A related but different approach is the notion of 'graspable' user interfaces [4] and 'tangible bits' [7].

Ubiquitous Computing

Pursuing the approach of augmented reality at a larger scale requires to have many, loosely spread and networked information devices around, with displays of different sizes, providing functionality everywhere. This is the concept of ubiquitous computing [24, 25] and – related – of ubiquitous media [1]. The size of these devices can range from very small to very large. Some of the devices will stand out and be recognized as computers, others will be "invisible" as they are embedded in the environment. Once the physical space is filled with multiple devices, two set of issues come up. First, how can one transfer information between them in an intuitive and direct way and, more general, how to interact with them. Second, it is desirable to know the position of the devices and their state wherever they are in a room or a building. The first issue is addressed, e.g., by the 'pick-and-drop' technique [13, 14] and by our concepts of 'take-and-put' and 'Passage' described later on. The second issue requires to set up an infrastructure of sensing and localization technology. We are aware that collecting information on where the devices and especially where the users are raises problems with respect to privacy issues. A combination of ideas from augmented reality and ubiquitous computing is employed in the approach of so called Reactive Environments [2].

REQUIREMENTS ANALYSIS

While innovative concepts, visions about possible scenarios and advances in basic technologies are important to make progress, we know from the principles of user- and task-oriented design that this is not sufficient for the development of new systems. We have to inform our design also by the requirements of anticipated user groups. Therefore, we conducted an empirical study in order to investigate the current work situation of teams and their requirements for future environments.

Method of the empirical study

We selected five companies from the automobile and oil industry and the advertising and consulting business. These companies were selected because they had special work groups which were called "creative teams" or could be labeled as such. They are working in the areas of strategic planning, identifying future trends, designing and marketing new products, etc. We expected these teams to be good candidates for working already with innovative tools and being creative when asked about their ideas and requirements of future work environments for team work.

We interviewed at least one, sometimes more representatives of the teams, visited the project team rooms where they usually hold their meetings, and distributed a questionnaire to all team members. The total number of people in these five teams was 80. The age range was from 28 to 55 years. They usually had an academic education and came from various educational and professional backgrounds: engineering, computer science, business administration, psychology, and design. Unfortunately, only 20 % of the distributed questionnaires were returned but together with the interviews and site visits they provided valuable information.

Results of the empirical study

Due to limited space, we report only selected results relevant for the design of i-LAND. For details see [23]. In most cases, the facilities were traditional meeting rooms furnished with standard equipment as, e.g., large solid tables and chairs, flip charts, whiteboards, and overhead projectors. In only one case, there were a couple of computers, a scanner and a printer permanently installed in the meeting room. In another case, people would bring a laptop and a beamer in order to project computer displays on the wall. This configuration was only used for prepared presentations. No active creation of content during the meeting was done with the aid of computers. Different creativity techniques (e.g. brainstorming, Metaplan,..) were used but only in a paper-based fashion. These results on the current state of the rooms were contrary to our expectations. We had expected more (active) usage of computer-based technology in the meetings.

The situation changed when we asked about the requirements for the future. Usually, a large room was required with a flexible setup and mobile components that would allow different configurations. The room should have the character of a market place or a landscape providing opportunities for spontaneous encounters and informal communication. Quote (translated from German): "Team meetings are not anymore conducted by meeting in a room but by providing an environment and a situation where encounters happen". The furniture should be multifunctional and flexible. Although the current situation was rather low-tech, there was a great openness for computer-based support in the following areas: support for information gathering while preparing meetings by accessing internal and external data bases; in a special case, "pools of ideas" were mentioned - in an advanced version so called "idea spaces"; computer-based support for a wide range of creativity techniques allowing for flexible configuration or tailoring of the underlying rules; support for presentation styles deviating from the traditional situation and involving the attendees in an active fashion labeled as "participatory presentation"; support for visualizations inspiring and enhancing the creative process; support for communicating and experiencing content also via other channels than only visual, e.g., acoustic, tactile. There was less emphasis on videoconferencing. The teams stressed the importance of personal presence being essential for creating a stimulating and productive atmosphere. It was also mentioned that "creative teams" are not only busy being creative all the time but they also have to plan and organize their work. This motivated the request for computer- and video-based support for (on-line) documentation of meetings and preparation of the minutes. While computer-based support was strongly requested, the computer should be in the background. Quote (translated from German): "We have the creative potential, not the computers." Another issue was the creation of a certain atmosphere described with labels as freedom, room for individuality, flexibility, etc. In summary, the teams wanted to have much freedom in (re)configuring their physical environment and their information environment.

THE ROOMWARE-COMPONENTS

Our approach to meet the requirements of flexible configuration and dynamic allocation of resources in integrated physical and information environments is based on the concept we call *roomware*. By *roomware,* we mean computer-augmented objects resulting from the integration of room elements, e.g., walls, doors, furniture (tables, chairs, etc.) with computer-based information devices. The general goal of developing roomware is to make progress towards the design of integrated real architectural spaces and virtual information spaces from the perspective of augmenting reality. In the context of supporting team work, roomware components can be tailored and composed to form flexible and dynamic "cooperation landscapes" serving multiple purposes: project team rooms, presentation suites, information foyers, etc. These goals have in common that they require also to develop new forms of multi-user, multiple-displays human-computer interaction. We will present examples as we go along. The current focus is on designing workspaces for collocated teams but the i-LAND environment can easily be extended to provide support for global cooperation of distributed teams.

We have designed and implemented an initial set of *roomware* components. So far, it consists of an interactive electronic wall (*DynaWall*), an interactive electronic table *(InteracTable),* and mobile and networked chairs with integrated interactive devices *(CommChairs)*. They are assembled in the AMBIENTE-Lab at GMD-IPSI in order to form the first version of the i-LAND environment.

The DynaWall

The objective of the *DynaWall* is to provide a computer-based device that serves the needs of teams, e.g., in projects rooms where large areas of assembled sheets of paper covering the walls are used to create and organize information. The DynaWall can be considered an "interactive electronic wall" represented by a touch-sensitive information device. Our current realization provides a total display size of 4.5 m width and 1.1 m height. It covers one side of the room completely (Fig. 2). The software we developed (BEACH) enables teams to display and interact with large information structures collaboratively on the DynaWall.

Fig. 2   Two people cooperating at the DynaWall

Two or more persons are able to either work individually in parallel or to share the whole display space. The size of the DynaWall provides new challenges for human-computer interaction. For example, it will be very cumbersome to drag an object or a window holding down a mouse over a distance of more than 4 m. Therefore, we have developed two mechanisms addressing these problems. Our "take and put" feature allows to take information objects at one position, walk over (without being in contact with the DynaWall) and put them somewhere else on the display. "Shuffle" allows to throw objects (with different accelerations) from one side to the opposite side where it can be caught by another team member. The initial design idea was presented in [19] and as a late-breaking result in [6]. Now it is implemented and working.

Fig. 3 Usage of two CommChairs

The CommChairs

The *CommChairs* (Fig. 3) are mobile chairs with built-in slate computers. They represent a new type of furniture combining the mobility and comfort of armchairs with high-end information technology.

Fig. 4   Two versions of the CommChairs

Currently, there are two versions: one with a docking facility so that people can bring their laptop computer and drop them into the swing-up desk which is part of the armrest. The other version has an integrated pen-based computer built into the swing-up desk (see Fig. 4).

Fig. 5   Remote annotations from CommChair to DynaWall

The CommChairs allow people to communicate and to share information with people in other chairs, standing in front of the DynaWall or around the InteracTable. They can make personal notes in a private space but also interact remotely on shared (public) workspaces, e.g., making remote annotations at the DynaWall (see Fig. 5). The cooperative functionality is provided by our BEACH software. For maximum flexibility and mobility each chair is provided with a wireless network and independent power supply. The initial design idea was presented in [19] and as a late-breaking result in [8]. Now it is implemented.

The InteracTable

The *InteracTable* is a mobile interactive table that is designed for creation, display, discussion and annotation of information objects by a group of two to six people standing around it. The current stand-up version (1.15 m high) of the InteracTable is built as a vertical bottom-up projection unit (Fig. 6). An LCD beamer projects a high-resolution image to the top of the table providing a horizontal touch-sensitive display of 65 cm x 85 cm.

Fig. 6   Discussion of a subgroup at the InteracTable

People can write and draw on it with a pen and interact via finger or pen gestures with information objects. There is also a wireless keyboard for more extensive text input. The InteracTable, with its horizontal set-up display and people standing around it at each side, is an example of an interaction area with no predefined orientation as top and bottom, left and right at the desktop computer. Therefore, horizontal and round or oval-type displays require new forms of human-computer interaction. As a first step, we developed gestures for rotating and shuffling individual and groups of information objects across the surface. This accommodates easy viewing from all perspectives (Fig. 7).

Fig. 7   Rotating windows on the InteracTable

The Passage Concept

Passage describes an elegant mechanism of connecting information structures in the digital, virtual world of computers with a real-world object. Such a detectable object, a so-called *Passenger*, can be seen as a physical bookmark into the virtual world. One can assign information to it, take it, carry it physically to a new location, and simply by putting it on a device called *Bridge*, the information is displayed immediately at the new location. It is no longer necessary to open windows, browse hierarchies of folders, worry about mounted drives, etc.

Passage is a concept for ephemeral binding of content to an object. It provides an intuitive way for the "transportation" of information between computers/ roomware components, e.g., between offices or to and from meeting rooms.

A Passenger does not have to be a special physical object. Any uniquely detectable physical object may become a Passenger. Since the information structures are not stored on the Passenger itself but only linked to it, people can turn any object into a Passenger: a watch, a ring, a pen, glasses, or other arbitrary objects. The only restriction Passengers have is that they can be identified by the Bridge and that they are unique. Fig. 6 and Fig. 7 show a small wooden block as an example of a Passenger placed on the margin of the InteracTable where the Bridge device is embedded. The current Passage implementation uses the weight of physical objects for identification and computer-controlled scales built in the Bridge for detection.

THE APPLICATION: SUPPORT FOR CREATIVE WORK

The current application for i-LAND is to support team work with a focus on creativity and innovation. The software we develop supports different types of creativity techniques and related generic functionality as, e.g., visualization of knowledge structures. The BEACH software provides the new forms of human-computer interaction, e.g., take-and-put, throw, shuffle, rotate, etc.

We focus on support for different brainstorming techniques and for project organization. It has been shown that computer-supported brainstorming results in more number of ideas than verbal brainstorming [5]. There are limitations with existing brainstorming systems (e.g., [10]) we like to overcome. Our software enables teams to work with networked hypermedia structures providing adequate representations for their ideas. This is based on our earlier hypermedia work [18] combined with new concepts. The possibility to display large information structures at once, e.g., on the DynaWall, provides new opportunities for innovative idea creation and concept presentation modes. Our development includes new visualization metaphors for presenting content and structures of our 'thoughtscapes'.

THE TECHNOLOGY INFRASTRUCTURE

While each of the roomware components presented above has a value of its own, the full benefit is only available via a comprehensive integration and combined use. This integration requires a network infrastructure providing the connectivity between the components and a software infrastructure providing a wide range of cooperative sharing capabilities. For extending the mobility of team members and roomware components within the Lab and later on in the whole building it is necessary to identify them in different locations. This requires a sensing and localization infrastructure planned for the near future.

Network infrastructure

In the current implementation, we use a combination of the local area network already installed in the building and an RF-based wireless network. For maximum flexibility all mobile roomware components are connected to the wireless network. The CommChairs are equipped with an antenna which comes along with a PC-Card. Laptops with a wireless adapter are carried along (e.g., when returning from a business trip), plugged into the docking station of the CommChair and the team member can join the meeting without reconfiguration. The computers of fixed roomware components as, e.g., the DynaWall are connected via cables to the LAN. The network connection for the wireless access to the LAN is realized by a 2-channel access-point which acts as a bridge between the cable-based and the RF-based Ethernet. The transfer rate of one RF channel is currently 2 Mbps, soon to be upgraded to 10 Mbps.

Software infrastructure

In order to meet the functional and integration requirements for i-LAND, we have developed BEACH. It provides the software infrastructure for cooperative sharing of information between the devices in combination with new forms of human-computer interaction required and enabled by the roomware components. BEACH is designed as a layered architecture. The lowest level is the COAST framework [16] previously developed also at GMD-IPSI. It provides the functions necessary for distributing, replicating and synchronizing information objects. This framework was used to create shared information spaces between different roomware components and, in addition, to couple several physically separate roomware components to a logically homogenous workspace. This is also important for large interaction areas as the DynaWall which is currently build from three separate segments because of the limitations of displays currently available.

The next level of BEACH covers the interaction of one user with a roomware device. Here, the software must take care of the different input and output characteristics of the roomware components: Display sizes vary from rather small (as in a CommChair) to the huge display of the DynaWall. The user's orientation might be fixed with respect to the display (as with a "traditional" desktop PCs) or it might be arbitrary and can change over time at the InteracTable. The available input devices are keyboard, mouse, and pen, resp. touch in general. Gesture recognition is crucial for realizing the interaction forms.

On top of this, BEACH provides mechanisms to structure collaboration. The basic metaphor is the "virtual location", which defines who is working together on which topic and which data are used. The virtual location is the virtual counterpart of a physical meeting room: a meeting room is attached to a virtual location during a meeting – it might be associated with another virtual location at another time for another task or project. There is a strong correspondence between the physical places and virtual locations. If, for example, a team decides within a meeting to split up into subgroups, each subgroup might go to a different area of the meeting room or the building to continue their collaboration there. The software must be able to recognize such situations, to decouple the previous homogenous

workspace, and to automatically create shared workspaces for each subgroup. This is achieved by creating a new sublocation for each subgroup within the team's virtual location, corresponding to the different areas, the physical sublocations. BEACH is developed in Smalltalk using Parc Place Systems' Visual Work environment.

DISCUSSION AND FUTURE WORK

We have presented the design and implementation of innovative collaborative workspaces based on an integrated design of real architectural and virtual information spaces. Our approach is related to and was inspired by different developments in human-computer interaction, augmented reality, ubiquitous computing and computer-supported cooperative work, in particular meeting support systems. We developed new ideas for human-computer interaction and applied them to the design of collaborative work environments. On the other hand, we extended interaction techniques by cooperative functionality to create ubiquitous and collaborative workspaces. Since there is not enough space to discuss the relationship to other work in detail, we do this only for a few examples.

Compared to work in augmented reality, e.g., the DigitalDesk [26], the *InteracTable* provides a touch-sensitive interactive display with a bottom-up projection. This avoids the problems of shadows caused by the overlay of video projections on the real surface of the DigitalDesk. Our *Passage* mechanism was inspired by the idea of the "marble answering machine" [12] but extends it by using physical objects not only as representatives for voice or, more general, digital information. It is also used as means for physical transport between different roomware components. Re ubiquitous computing, our roomware approach concentrates on devices that are embedded in furniture, like chairs and tables, as well as in architectural elements of buildings, such as doors or walls. The 'take-and-put' technique for the DynaWall is related to the 'pick-and-drop' mechanism in [13, 14] but it does not require a special pen. It is based on gestures. Compared to work in CSCW, especially meeting support systems [10, 11, 17], including our own previous work [18, 22], our new approach is different due to the flexibility and mobility of the *roomware* components. It allows flexible and dynamic creation and allocation of workspaces in different parts of a room or a building in correspondence with different modes of the group activity instead of having a fixed setup, e.g., a set of chairs around a static table with computers. This enables new methods of establishing cooperation and sharing of information. For example, a subgroup is formed by simply moving chairs in close spatial proximity (see also below). The reactive environments described in [2] are different due to their focus on the special issues of video conferencing rooms.

The i-LAND environment introduces new forms of human-computer interaction. Thus, we have to evaluate their usefulness and their usability. This will be done in the spirit of our previous evaluation studies in a systematic fashion with controlled empirical experiments. Furthermore, we plan to sense and track the position of roomware components and people. Thus, "the room will know" the position and orientation of each component and who is interacting with which device. The i-LAND software mentioned above will process this information and, for example, automatically initiate a coupled session with shared displays between two or three CommChairs when they are moved together to form a subgroup and their distance is below a defined threshold.

The i-LAND environment is a first implementation of the roomware approach which is part of a more general framework called "cooperative buildings" which was introduced in [19, 21] and further discussed on a panel at CSCW'98 [20]. It represents a more global vision about the design of the "workspaces of the future".

ACKNOWLEDGEMENTS

We would like to thank Michele Gauler, Jochen Denzinger, and Daniel Warth for their valuable contributions to various parts of the i-LAND project and in the AMBIENTE division. Furthermore, we like to thank Dan Russell for very fruitful discussions in an early phase of our work and several anonymous reviewers for useful comments on the submitted version.

REFERENCES

1. Buxton, W. (1997). Living in augmented reality: Ubiquitous media and reactive environments. In: K. Finn, A. Sellen, S. Wilber (Eds.), *Video-Mediated Communication*. Erlbaum, 363-384.

2. Cooperstock, J., Fels, S., Buxton, W. & Smith, K. (1997). Reactive environments: Throwing away your keyboard and mouse. *Communications of ACM*, 40 (9), 65-73.

3. Fitzmaurice, G. (1993). Situated information spaces and spatially aware palmtop computers. *Communications of the ACM*, 36 (7), 38-49.

4. Fitzmaurice, G., Ishii, H., Buxton, W. (1995). Bricks: Laying the foundations for graspable user interfaces. *Proceedings of CHI'95 Conference*, ACM, 442-449.

5. Gallupe, R.B., Bastianutti, L.M. & Copper, W.H. (1991). Unblocking brainstorming. *Journal of Applied Psychology*, 76, 137-142.

6. Geißler, J. (1998). Shuffle, Throw or Take It!: Working Efficiently with an Interactive Wall. *CHI '98 Summary*, 265-266.

7. Ishii, H., and Ullmer, B. (1997). Tangible Bits: Towards seamless interfaces between people, bits and atoms. *Proceedings of CHI'97 Conference*, ACM, 234-241.

8. Mark, G.; Haake, J.; Streitz, N. (1997). Hypermedia Use in Group Work: Changing the Product, Process, and Strategy. *Computer Supported Cooperative Work: The Journal of Collaborative Computing*, 6, 327-368.

9. Müller-Tomfelde, C., Reischl, W. (1998). Communication Chairs: Examples of Mobile Roomware Components. *CHI'98 Summary*, 267-268.

10. Nunamaker, J.F. Briggs, R.O. & Mittleman, D.D. (1995). Electronic Meeting Systems: Ten Years of Lessons Learned. In: Coleman, D. and Khanna, R. (Eds.), *Groupware: Technology and Applications*. Prentice-Hall Inc., 149-193.

11. Olson, J., Olson, G., Storrosten, M., and Carter, M. (1993). Groupwork close up: A comparison of the group design process with and without a simple group editor. In: T. Malone, N. Streitz (Eds.), *Special Issue on CSCW of ACM TOIS*. 11 (4), 321-348.

12. Poynor, R. (1995). The hand that rocks the cradle. *I.D. - The International Design Magazine*. May-June.

13. Rekimoto, J. (1997). Pick-and-Drop: A direct manipulation technique for multiple computer environments. *Proceedings of UIST'97*. ACM, 31-39.

14. Rekimoto, J. (1998). Multiple-Computer User Interfaces: A cooperative environment consisting of multiple digital devices. In: [21], pp. 33-40.

15. Rekimoto, J., Nagao, K. (1995). The world through the computer: Computer augmented interaction with real world environments. *Proc. of UIST'95*. ACM. 29-36.

16. Schuckmann, C., Kirchner, L., Schümmer, J., and Haake, J.M. (1996). Designing object-oriented synchronous groupware with COAST. *Proceedings of CSCW '96 Conference*. ACM Press. 30-38.

17. Stefik, M., Foster, G., Bobrow, D., Khan, K., Lanning, S., Suchman, L. (1987). Beyond the chalkboard: Computer support for collaboration and problem solving in meetings. *Comm. of the ACM*, 30 (1), 32-47.

18. Streitz, N., Geißler, J., Haake, J., and Hol, J. (1994). DOLPHIN: Integrated meeting support across LiveBoards, local and desktop environments. *Proceedings of CSCW '94 Conference*, ACM Press. 345-358.

19. Streitz, N., Geißler, J., Holmer, T. (1998). Roomware for Cooperative Buildings: Integrated Design of Architectural Spaces and Information Spaces. In: [21], pp. 4-21.

20. Streitz, N, Hartkopf, Ishii, H, Kaplan, S., Moran, T. (1998). Cooperative Buildings. *Proc. of CSCW '98*. 411-413.

21. Streitz, N., Konomi, S., Burkhardt, H. (Eds.) (1998), *Cooperative Buildings – Integrating Information, Organization and Architecture*. First International Workshop on Cooperative Buildings (CoBuild'98), Darmstadt, Germany, February 1998. Lecture Notes in Computer Science 1370. Springer: Heidelberg.

22. Streitz, N., Rexroth, P., Holmer, T. (1997). Does "roomware" matter? Investigating the role of personal and public information devices and their combination in meeting room collaboration. *Proceedings of E-CSCW'97*, Kluwer Academic Publishers. 297-312.

23. Streitz, N., Rexroth, P., Holmer, T. (1998). Anforderungen an interaktive Kooperations- landschaften für kreatives Arbeiten und erste Realisierungen. *Proc. of D-CSCW'98*. Teubner, 237-250. (in German).

24. Weiser, M. (1991). The Computer for the 21st Century. *Scientific American*, 1991, 265 (3), 94-104.

25. Weiser, M. (1993). Some computer science issues in ubiquitous computing. *Comm. of ACM*, 36 (7), 75-84.

26. Wellner, P. (1993). Interacting with paper on the DigitalDesk. *Comm. of the ACM*, 36 (7), 86-96.

27. Wellner, P., Mackey, W., Gold, R. (Eds.) (1993). Computer-Augmented Environments: Back to the Real World. *Communications of the ACM*, 36 (7).

Logjam: a Tangible Multi-Person Interface for Video Logging

Jonathan Cohen, Meg Withgott[1], and Philippe Piernot[2]
Interval Research Corporation
1801 Page Mill Road
Palo Alto, CA 94304
+1-650-424-0722
cohen@interval.com

ABSTRACT

This paper describes the evolution, implementation, and use of *logjam*, a system for video logging. The system features a game-board that senses the location and identities of pieces placed upon it. The board is the interface that enables a group of people to log video footage together. We report on some of the surprising physical and social dynamics that we have observed in multi-person logging sessions using the system.

KEYWORDS

Tangible user interfaces, TUI, CSCW, video ethnography, video logging, user experience, 2D sensing/tracking

INTRODUCTION

In the summer of 1994, a group of video ethnographers from Interval Research accompanied the Lollapalooza concert tour to venues around the USA. They collected about a hundred hours of videotape of attendees visiting the "Electric Carnival," a tent on the concert site containing about sixty high technology interactive kiosks. The ethnographers were interested in the attendees' reactions to the technology, and their tapes include interviews and observations.

At the end of the summer, the group confronted a massive video logging problem. Video logging is exacting and solitary work. How could the logging process be made less tedious, and how could the ethnographers share their knowledge of the video they logged so they had the best choice of clips when they presented this material? Could a group-based logging approach facilitate this process?

Independently but simultaneously, other Interval researchers constructed an electronic game-board, which detects the 2D position and can identify a number of domino-like pieces placed upon it.

This paper describes *logjam*, a prototype system for video logging, which features the game-board as the interface to enable a group of people to log footage together. We report on the surprising physical and social dynamics that we have observed in multi-person logging sessions using

the system.

BACKGROUND

Before describing logjam itself, this section explains the logging task, presents an example of group-logging, and describes tangible user interface (TUI) work that influenced the design of logjam.

The Logging Task

The task of the video ethnography project (VEP) was to influence researchers—technology inventors and designers—by acquainting them with future consumers' stories, lifestyles, goals, needs and desires [6]. VEP distributed questionnaires, and conducted interviews, focus groups, and visited the homes of people representing potentially interesting segments of society. VEP videotaped much of their research.

These tapes, forming a collection on the order of a hundred hours per study, were then logged and annotated in a process that familiarized several members of the VEP team with the footage. With the help of the logs, the footage was used and reused to construct differently edited videotapes aimed at technologists' various interests.

Logging the Electric Carnival footage was seen as a process of finding and marking various locations, events, and behaviors in the video, collectively called "categories." Some categories seen in the tapes included:

- places: revival tent, main stage, kiosk, etc.
- VEP team activities: interviewing, observing, etc.
- number of people in shot: group, crowd, couple, etc.
- behavior: computer-use, dancing, etc.
- shot description: pan, close-up, zoom, etc.

At any given instant in the video, several categories might apply, and the start and end times of one particular category were mostly independent of the start and end times of another category.

A timeline seemed like the best representation for this style of logging, since it could offer a visual presentation of the duration and overlap of categorized events. Of the

[1] Author's present address: Electric Planet . 1900 O'Farrell Street, Suite 200, San Mateo, CA 94403. withgott@e-planet.com

[2] Author's present address: Mirvo Toys, Inc. 1900 O'Farrell Street, Suite 100, San Mateo, CA 94403. piernot@mirvo.com

commercial and experimental logging software available then, including CVideo™, FileMaker™, Marquee [15], MediaStreams [3], and Timelines [8], only the latter two supported timeline representations that displayed the duration of an annotation. None of the systems supported group-logging such as described in the next section.

Passage to Vietnam: A Group Logging Experience

Bonnie Johnson [personal communication] described the sorting and categorization process Rick Smolan and his company, Against All Odds, undertook in making their work *Passage to Vietnam* [12]. She wrote that the company brought:

...70 photographers, 15 videographers, and crews from NBC and a Japanese television production company (who shot HDTV ...) to Vietnam for a week. ... In ten days, ten editors from major publications watched 200,000 pictures and reduced the candidates for publication to 1000. Each editor looks at the work of 7 photographers; then the whole group looks at everything and they vote out loud with what should be kept. ... A list of 10 or so categories such as "food" and "war" was developed out of this process... Everyone watched the 50 hours of tape. They thus arrived [at] 380 potential clips...

We found that their system works for them to the limit of the ability to remember the pictures and the clips. ... It was the process of a group of people watching footage together, no doubt spinning stories about what they were seeing that "fixed" the pictures in their minds, helped them develop the stories.

What was striking about the Passage to Vietnam editorial process, as Johnson noted, was the rapid and transitory group effort it required. The group agreed to a decision and recorded it, then moved on to the next decision. Perhaps most important, the group established a common perspective on, and categorization of, the raw input. This kind of group effort is not unusual in rapid media production efforts.

Would a similar process work for VEP's logging efforts? What kind of interface could we build to support such a group of loggers? We would not want it to replace conversation, merely to augment and focus the dialogue.

Tangible Influences

Durrell Bishop's marble answering machine prototype [9] was the strongest influence on the tangible design of logjam. Also important was the emphasis on the mixture of the physical and the virtual found in the special issue of *Communications of the ACM* devoted to Computer Augmented Environments [1]. Wellner's DigitalDesk was particularly inspiring in its aim "to go beyond so-called 'direct manipulation' with a mouse (which in fact is not direct at all) and to explore the possibilities of tactile interaction with real and electronic objects using the fingers." [p. 92] DigitalDesk, and Mackay's related Video Mosaic—tailored to editing and controlling video—, used

video cameras to enable the integration between paper and data. Mitchel Resnick's article [pp. 64 –71], about moving computation into small objects, was also a source of inspiration.

THE INTERFACE MEETS THE TASK

At the same time as Interval's ethnographers were coming to terms with the Electric Carnival logging task, another group at Interval, influenced by the TUI work described above, constructed an electronic game-board, which could detect the position and identity of a number of domino-like pieces, or "blocks," placed upon it. The board could send "board events" to a host computer (see figure 1).

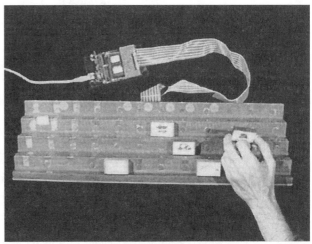

Figure 1. The game-board with a few blocks. The hand shows scale. The board-event processor and the serial line to the host computer are visible at the top.

A further development involved the realization that a block could represent a category, and that a block's presence on the board while a videotape was playing could mean that the category applied to the video at that timecode.

Thus arose the notion of building "logjam," a system for group-logging video that employed a game-board. We imagined a scenario where loggers, watching a videotape playing at normal speed, would quickly plop different blocks on the board, representing different categories that applied to the tape at that moment. The loggers would just as quickly remove blocks from the board when that category no longer applied.

LOGJAM SYSTEM OVERVIEW

The main components of the system were a host computer (Macintosh) with a monitor, keyboard and mouse; a VTR (Sony VDeck) and video monitor; the game-board and its associated board-event processor, and a pair of footpedals for controlling the VTR (see figure 2).

The VDeck was a computer controllable, frame-searchable Hi-8 (analog) VTR. The computer sent commands to the VDeck, for example, to play, stop, or go to a particular frame.

When a logger dropped a block on the game-board, or picked it back up again, the board-event processor recorded the event. The computer continuously polled the board-event processor for new events. The computer also continuously polled the VDeck for the current timecode of the video, so it could be associated with the board events.

Footpedals were used to control the VDeck. Pressing down on the pedals generated keystrokes that the Mac converted into VDeck commands.

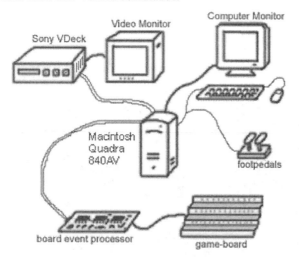

Figure 2. Logjam system diagram. Double lines represent serial I/O; thin lines represent ADB.

Logjam Hardware

The logjam board was able to detect when a block made contact with it. The blocks were designed to sit on the board like on a Scrabble™ tray, making contact with the board in two places—the bottom and back of each row. The board was arranged in a matrix of 4 rows and 12 columns for a total of 48 possible locations.

The blocks and the board were constructed out of a variety of hardwoods. The board was about 22¼ inches wide by 7 inches long by 1 inch high, and the blocks approximately 1¾" by 1¼" by ½". There was room to put 12 blocks across a row. The rows, built of mahogany, were arranged in four parallel 45° "valleys" on the board. Thus, when a block was placed on the board it rested face-up and out (see figure 1).

Each wooden block contained a Dallas Semiconductor DS2401 "silicon serial number" [10]. Each chip held a unique 48-bit ID, and had a ground and a data line. Sending a pulsed signal with the correct protocol over the data line resulted in a return signal, along the same line, containing the 48-bit ID. A copper strip on the *bottom* of the block was connected to the ground line of the chip, and a second copper strip on the *back* of the block was connected to the data line of the chip (see figure 3).

Electrical layout on the board matched that of the blocks. Ground was at the base of the row, and data was at the back. Thus, when a block was placed on the board, the proper electrical contacts were made.

In several early tests, we found that people often placed the blocks on the board so the contacts did not quite line up. Magnets were inserted into each block and into each

board location to pull a block into good alignment when it was placed on the board. The magnetic attraction also added power to the clicking sound made on contact.

The ground and data lines ran from the board to the board-event processor, a Motorola M68HC11 ("6811") microprocessor running custom firmware. Looking for block-IDs, the 6811 could poll all 48 locations on the board from five to ten times per second, depending on the number of blocks on the board. Internally, the 6811 kept a map of which block-IDs were present at which board location. Whenever a block was put down or picked up, the internal map was updated, and the 6811 added a new block down or block up event to a list.

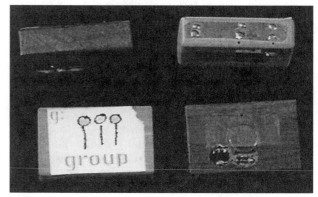

Figure 3. Close-ups of a block. Counterclockwise from lower left: front with "group" category label; back with DS2401, diode, magnet and copper strip for data; bottom with copper strip for ground; hardwood top.

Unreliability and Variable Latency

We never completely solved two major problems with the logjam prototype.

First, the board was not completely *reliable*. We did not engineer a tight enough coupling between the physical action of dropping a block on the board (or picking it up), and the computational action that was supposed to follow. Sometimes the electrical connection did not quite occur, or was so "bouncy" that the system interpreted a single event as several quick drop-and-pick-up events.

Second, the system had a *variable latency*. Because there were two polling architectures involved (both on the 6811 and the Macintosh), and because the Lisp software took time out for garbage-collection, there were occasional delays of one to fifteen seconds before an event was registered.

We will return to these two problems later in the paper.

Mapping Board Locations to Functions

With two exceptions, placing a block on any location in the front three rows of the board meant "create an annotation starting at the current video timecode in the category represented by this block." Picking up a block meant "end the annotation being created in this category at this timecode."

The two exceptions were found at the left side of the board (see figure 4). These "binding" locations gave loggers a way to create or change a binding between a block and a category. Dropping a block on these locations did not affect the log.

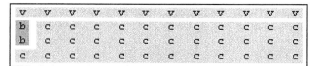

Figure 4. Function map of the 48 locations on the board. Legend: c = create annotation; b = bind category, v = video speed control (see that section below). Placing a block on a "c" location is a different kind of event than placing it on a "b" or "v" location.

Logjam Software

The logjam software, written in Macintosh Common Lisp (MCL) version 2.0.1, kept track of the bindings between blocks and categories, synchronized board events with videotape timecode, offered a screen-based palette for video control, and gave loggers an editable timeline representation of the ongoing log. At the time (1994), we chose MCL because it was a fast prototyping environment and because there was a large code base and an active community of programmers in-house.

The timeline representation was very similar to that used in MediaStreams [3] or Timelines [8]. Time marched along the horizontal axis, and the vertical space was broken up into rows, one per category. A single annotation or "snippet" on the timeline represented a span of time on the videotape to which a particular category applied (see Figure 5).

When a block was dropped on the board, a "block-down" (falling-pitch) sound played and several graphical events took place in the timeline view. First, the row containing

the category bound to that block scrolled so it was visible in the window. Second, an "open snippet" icon was displayed in the row near left edge of the window. Third, a new snippet, represented by a small rectangle, was created ("opened") in that row. The left edge of the snippet was fixed at the starting time code—the time that the block was dropped. As long as the block stayed on the board, the right edge of the snippet was tied to the changing timecode of the video. When a block was picked up, a "block-up" (rising-pitch) sound played, the open snippet icon in that category's row disappeared, and the open snippet in that category "closed", that is, its right edge was fixed at the current timecode.

(Note that the block event sounds were originally designed for ToonTown, another prototype that used the game-board, in this case to control a shared audio space [11].)

Using the keyboard and mouse with the timeline window, a logger could type text beneath a snippet to explain it more fully, move snippets around, create them, delete them, or change their starting or ending times. A logger could also click in the timecode ruler area at the top of the window to get the VDeck to scan forward or back until it reached that timecode on the tape.

A logger could change the time scale of the view using a scrollbar at the bottom left of the timeline. Since text display (not text entry) was clipped to the length of a snippet, zooming in ensured that all a snippet's text could be read. Zooming out gave a good overview of the log so far.

Another important function was the ability to create a new category on the fly. If a logger dropped a new (unbound) block on one of the board's binding locations, it brought up a dialog box on screen, which allowed text entry of a new category name. This category was bound to the silicon serial number in the block.

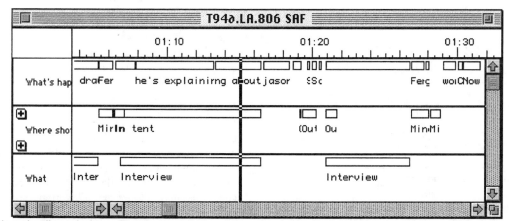

Figure 5. Logjam timeline window. The time scale, spanning about 30 minutes, is across the top. The central black vertical line shows the current video timecode, at about 01:15:00:00. Category names run down the left side. "Where shot" is the currently selected category. The other two categories visible are "What's happening" and "What." Rectangles in the rows are the logged snippets. Using the leftmost scroll bar to zoom the view in further, clipped text annotations can be seen in full.

If a logger dropped an *unbound* block on one of the "create-snippet" locations, it brought up the same dialog box, but the video was paused so the timecode of the event was saved. Thus loggers did not miss any footage while they were filling out the dialog box. Once the dialog was dismissed, the video was returned to its former playback speed, a new row was added to the timeline, and the new snippet was opened in that row at the saved timecode.

If a logger dropped a *previously bound* block on a binding location, the dialog box displayed the block's current binding. This could be purely for checking, or the logger could edit the information, changing the binding.

VIDEO SPEED CONTROL

Because loggers may wish to specify precisely the timing of annotations for later editing, it was important to provide accurate and simple video control.

The VDeck only operated at a set number of speeds (seven forward and seven reverse). These speeds did not have a clear incremental relationship, so true analog speed control (like a jog-shuttle) was not possible, and faking it would not fool loggers.

To give loggers a choice, logjam provided three different interfaces for controlling VDeck speed: blocks-and-board, a pair of footpedals, and a mouse-clickable palette on the computer screen. None of these interfaces allowed loggers to use all of the available VDeck speeds—by consensus, we left out the slower ones.

Each footpedal had two positions, "down" and "way down." With the right pedal, down meant "play forward" and way down meant "fast forward." With the left pedal, down meant "reverse play" and way down meant "rewind." Stepping off the pedals meant "stop."

On the screen, the palette had nine buttons, each representing a different speed. Clicking a button set the speed of the VDeck (see figure 6).

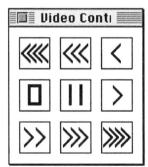

Figure 6. The video control palette

In the blocks-and-board interface, the back row of the board was devoted to video speed control. The location at the center of the row meant "pause," and locations to the right of center signified increasing forward speed: slow, normal play, 2X, etc. To the left of center, the speed increased, but the tape played in reverse. To play the VDeck at a particular speed, a logger dropped any block onto that board location (whether the block was bound to a category or not.) To stop the VDeck, the logger dropped a block on the pause location.

For loggers, dropping and picking up blocks to control video was very clumsy when compared to pressing a footpedal or clicking a mouse, particularly when the variable latency of the logjam event software was taken into account.

Multi-Person Video Speed Control

The board interface was an attempt to implement a multi-person video speed control. In practice, however, our loggers improvised their own system. First, there was no lack of feedback about speed. They had all watched enough video to tell the speed just by seeing and hearing the playback. Furthermore, the VDeck was usually set to overlay a graphic on the video representing the speed. So, any speed change effected by the person with the mouse or footpedals was immediately obvious.

Second, to change the speed, loggers just shouted. For example, "Whoa!," "Stop!," and "Go back!" The latency was comparable to that of the board, and it was physically easier. Before anyone started the VDeck playing again, they alerted the others.

We had wanted the state and control of the VDeck to be "open"—that is, public and accessible to all of the loggers simultaneously, whereas both screen palette and footpedals were only accessible to one person at a time. What we found was just working together in the same location provided openness[3].

MULTI-PERSON LOGGING

A team of VEP members agreed to use logjam to log some of the Electric Carnival footage. The VEP group quickly arranged themselves for working with the system. The board was placed on a table, with the video monitor behind it. One person used the keyboard while three or four others sat near the game-board, picking up and putting down blocks. One of these others also used the footpedals (see figure 7).

The task of the person at the keyboard was to transcribe the video, as well as clean up mistakes, control the VDeck, and occasionally reassure the others that their blocks were recognized correctly by the program.

Group members assigned disjoint sets of categories to themselves (and to each other, like trading-cards), so they could log in *parallel*. The board supported this style of activity because the software could handle multiple block events, and because there were plenty of block locations available. In practice, the number of blocks on the board simultaneously seldom exceeded more than a dozen.

The loggers had no trouble switching between parallel and group activity. The group would quickly focus to discuss

---

[3] Our use of the term "open" comes from Suzuki, et al. [13], describing their tangible programming system for children. Children could inspect, manipulate, and talk about this representation together.

the meaning of a particular category; or a suggestion for a new category, or whether the event on screen was sufficiently "illustrative" to warrant categorizing with a particular block.

Figure 7. A logging session. From the right, C watches the video and waits for the right moment to drop a block; D has his blocks arrayed in front of him; J observes; and S, just out of frame at the left, handles the logjam GUI.

It proved valuable that loggers could create and bind new categories as they identified new events, locations, or behaviors in the video. In the end, they defined more than eighty categories for the Electric Carnival footage, though only around twenty were used with any frequency.

When loggers defined a new category, they attached a sticky label to the block to differentiate it. In the heat of the moment, the label was hand-written, but later they replaced these labels with printed ones. Eventually, even labels with printed text were not sufficiently distinguishable when a logger was trying to grab a block at speed. At first, icons were added to the labels, but later they were also color-coded to emphasize related categories.

An important observation is that the location of the blocks mattered when they were *not* on the board. All participants arranged their own sets of category blocks on the table in front of them, and loggers had individual layout styles and methods for grouping their own blocks, making it easy to find one's own blocks during logging. The blocks' constant physical presence also reminded loggers of the categories they were seeking.

Some other interactions took place with the blocks that are not easily imaginable with GUIs. For example, *snatching*: if one logger took too long to log an event in a category she was responsible for, a second logger might grab that block from the first logger's space on the table and drop it for her. *Sweeping* occurred if the group had been logging a particular scene, and there were a number of category blocks on the board. When the scene changed suddenly (or the tape ended), so that the categories no longer applied, then everyone reached out, sometimes with both hands, to sweep the blocks off the board.

In all, the group used logjam to log eight one-to-two-hour tapes, and spent around fifteen to twenty-five hours—two to three times video duration. In our original scenario, we had naively imagined that group-logging video would not take much more time than just watching it, since group members would be annotating different categories in parallel. But talking things over, or waiting for a person who needed to review the tape or type in a long description, took additional time.

Nonetheless, loggers informally reported that group-logging sessions seemed to take less time than individual logging sessions because they were more fun. Even some self-professed "logging-loathers" dropped in for a couple of the group sessions.

SOLO LOGJAM

One person continued to use logjam for solo logging after the group-logging effort ended. This was a surprise, particularly since the system was only a prototype. Over time this person logged more tapes than the group did, and even built up entirely different sets of categories for logging different sets of tapes. However, she did not use the board and blocks. Instead, she relied on a number of keyboard-and-mouse shortcuts to accomplish the same functions. Why did she not use the logjam board?

First, there was not room on her desktop. Group logging took place on a big cleared-off table in a shared work area, not squeezed into a little space on a filled-up desk in a small cubicle. Second, her hands were already on the keyboard and it was easier to click or type a shortcut key than to reach over, pick up a block, and place it on the board. Third, the keyboard interface bypassed the board's reliability problems. Fourth, although group logging was useful, and even enjoyable, by this point she had a clear idea of how to apply the categories and just wanted to get on with the job, sans discussion.

Thus the logjam interface was not the answer to all logging problems—it only worked well in a specific context. For example, it was no improvement on other systems if a logger was only after a text transcription.

But the group-logging process had several clear benefits. First, it was typical that one of the loggers in the group had shot the tape being logged. That person could cue the others—for example when something interesting was coming up, or when the next section of tape could be skimmed. Second, the process was a way to show logging newcomers the ropes, integrating them with the whole group at once. Third, this process enforced a consensus about the meaning of particular categories. As one logger reported, since the resumption of individual logging, people use categories more idiosyncratically. This makes it difficult to use other people's logs when collecting footage for a new edit. Fourth, the group accumulated a shared knowledge of the videos they logged together, thereby gaining a common reference.

COUPLING THE PHYSICAL AND THE VIRTUAL

Fitzmaurice, et al., define "tightly coupled" systems as those that keep their "physical and virtual representations perfectly synchronized [4]." This section addresses some of the issues of tight coupling that came up with logjam, where the configuration of the blocks on the board was coupled with the state of the video annotation.

At the lowest level, one unintended disparity between these representations made the system less useful. Because the board was occasionally unreliable, and the system had a variable latency, a block event would occur on the board but would not immediately (or sometimes not ever) register at the computer.

This confusion led loggers to doubt whether they had really marked the video when they dropped a block. It made them a little tentative, and they would look over at the computer screen to see if the snippet had appeared in the timeline window, or they would ask the person closest to the screen whether the snippet was displayed. This interrupted the flow of work—loggers were focusing their attention on the tool rather than the task. This is an old CHI response-time lesson repeated on a new platform.

At a higher level, the potential for a great disparity existed, but it never seemed troublesome in practice. The board and blocks could only represent the state of annotations as the video was being logged the first time. If the video was rewound to a section that had already been logged, there was no way for the board to reconfigure its blocks to match. So when people wanted to review or edit video annotations, they used the GUI and ignored the TUI. This shift took place naturally.

CONCLUSION

We hypothesized that group logging could solve three problems: how can we speed up the logging process and make it less tedious, and how can loggers share their knowledge of the video they log? The speed-up would occur because loggers could work in parallel. Working in a group promised to be more fun and create a shared knowledge of the footage.

The logjam interface relied on a game-board that could sense the location and identity of pieces placed upon it. This interface supported group logging by being easily shared among group members. However, one unresolved engineering issue had major repercussions for the quality of the experience. Sometimes there was a latency or disconnection between a block event and the action it was supposed to trigger. As a result, loggers never completely trusted the board.

Still, logjam supported some group processes, for example, lively and probing discussions about the meaning of a category. Also, since people were logging together, they were able to build a common knowledge of the video and the categories. For those who had previously logged or transcribed recorded media with traditional tools, group logging was a welcome relief from a tedious process.

Logjam did not speed up the work, however. Although loggers worked in parallel, whatever time this saved was soon spent in discussions, or waiting on the slowest logger.

There were aspects of the interface that would be difficult to replicate with a GUI. For example, sweeping and snatching, or the individual arrangements of the category blocks on the table with the ability to select one item from 80 (without having to scroll or pop up a menu).

We did not anticipate actions like these before building the prototype; the loggers improvised them. Buxton suggests that the ability to improvise with an instrument is a mark of its worth [2]. While snatching and sweeping actions are probably specific to logjam[4], we think users of other TUIs will improvise actions within those systems because one of the great strengths of TUIs is that they allow people to take advantage of all the degrees of freedom available in the physical world.

Furthermore, all the ways people make use of the physical world may not have to be mirrored in the virtual one—just as the logjam system did not need to "know" how the category blocks were arranged when they were not on the board, though that was important to the loggers. In a TUI system, this kind of capability comes without extra programming.

Another significant dimension of TUIs is the wonderful, high-resolution quality of objects in the world. Ishii and Ullmer remind us of the rich character of historical scientific instruments [7], and Buxton describes the material refinement and careful craft inherent in artist's tools [2]. Though logjam did not aspire to such estimable heights, the board and blocks did express a sturdy physical presence. Hardwood and copper made a pleasing combination, and the blocks, with a nice heft and a domino-like size, felt good in the hand. There was an unmistakable sense of physical contact when a block was dropped on the board (and the electronics worked). Such physical sensations do not exist on the screen.

Logjam's method of binding a physical container to its virtual content was similar to the method used in the ToonTown prototype, where a special board location was used for binding a block to one of the people sharing the audio space [11]. Contrast Bishop's answering machine prototype, in which one of the marbles in a reservoir was automatically assigned to an incoming phone message [9]. In the mediaBlocks system, placing a block in the slot of a media recording device begins recording the media, and picking up the block halts the recording—the block is bound to that chunk of media data [14]. Binding seems like a basic activity for TUIs.

---

[4] Though perhaps snatching behavior isn't so specific to logjam. Hughes, et al., describe the use of paper strips by air traffic controllers: "Anyone [of the controllers] who notices a problem with a strip … can 'cock-out' the strips— move them noticeably out of alignment in the racks."

The game-board interface succeeded best when physical actions were well-matched to functions but failed when they were not. Dropping and picking up blocks worked for creating snippets, but video speed was best controlled by other means. A GUI seemed better suited for the tasks of editing the logs and for solo logging because it was more efficient than the TUI.

Yet even when a TUI seems called for, some people argue that the work is doable "virtually," all within a GUI. They will say "I don't want any more stuff in my life" or "What happens if I lose the pieces?" Though we respond by pointing out their own successful real-world practice with "stuff," we suspect their arguments are not really intended to be answered. Perhaps they are simply reluctant to change interfaces, like those who balked at the introduction of the desktop metaphor.

Nevertheless, we believe logjam succeeded on two levels. 1) Transforming the logging problem from a solo labor to a group activity was powerful because it supported the emergence of consensus, allowed the task to be parallelized, and mitigated the tedium. 2) The equating of a set of categories with a set of blocks, and the direct association of logging actions with physical actions allowed a simple system to serve as a platform for a complex group activity.

ACKNOWLEDGEMENTS

Thanks to Bill Verplank for designing and building the board; Bob Alkire et al., for 6811 programming and foot pedals; Scott Wallters for wiring and magnetizing the board; Durrell Bishop for inspiration; Brian Williams and Neil Mayle for writing the timeline-scaling code, Baldo Faieta for the diagram; and Bonnie Johnson for helping to start and continuing to support the work. Special thanks to the logging crew, especially Sue Faulkner. Finally, thanks to the readers of various drafts for their helpful suggestions, including the anonymous CHI reviewers.

REFERENCES

1. [ACM]. Communications of the ACM. *Computer Augmented Environments: Back to the Real World.* July 1993 Vol. 36, Number 7.

2. Buxton, W. (1997). Artists and the Art of the Luthier. *Computer Graphics: The SIGGRAPH Quarterly,* 31(1), 10-11.

3. Davis, Marc. "Media Streams: An Iconic Visual Language for Video Representation." In: *Readings in Human-Computer Interaction: Toward the Year 2000,* ed. Baecker, R., et al. 854-866. 2nd ed., San Francisco: Morgan Kaufmann Publishers, Inc., 1995.

4. Fitzmaurice, G., et al. "Bricks: Laying the Foundations for Graspable User Interfaces," *Proceedings of the Conference on Human Factors in Computing Systems (CHI '95),* ACM, Denver, May 1995, pp. 442-449

5. Hughes, J., et al. "Faltering from Ethnography to Design," *Proceedings of the Conference on Computer-Supported Cooperative Work (CSCW '92),* ACM, Toronto, October 1992, pp. 115-122.

6. Ireland, C., and Johnson, B. "Exploring the Future in the Present", *Design Management Journal,* Spring 1995.

7. Ishii, H. and Ullmer, B., "Tangible Bits: Towards Seamless Interfaces between People, Bits and Atoms," *Proceedings of Conference on Human Factors in Computing Systems (CHI '97),* ACM, Atlanta, March 1997, pp. 234-241.

8. Owen, R., et al. "Timelines, A Tool for the Gathering, Coding and Analysis of Temporal HCI Usability Data," *Proceedings of the Conference on Human Factors in Computing Systems (CHI '94),* May 1994, pp. 7-8.

9. Poynor, R. "The Hand That Rocks the Cradle." ID Magazine, May/June 1995, pp. 60-65.

10. Silicon Serial Number. Available at http://www.dalsemi.com/DocControl/PFDs/pdfindex.html

11. Singer, A., et al. "Tangible Progress: Less is More in Somewire Audio Spaces," *Proceedings of the Conference on Human Factors in Computing Systems (CHI '99),* ACM, Pittsburgh, May 1999.

12. Smolan, R., and Erwitt, J. *Passage to Vietnam,* Against All Odds Productions, Hong Kong, 1994.

13. Suzuki, H. & Kato H. "Interaction-Level Support for Collaborative Learning: AlgoBlock—An Open Programming Language," *Proceedings of the Computer Supported Collaborative Learning Conference (CSCL '95),* University of Indiana, 1995.

14. Ullmer, B., et al., mediaBlocks: Physical Containers, Transports, and Controls for Online Media, in *Proceedings of SIGGRAPH '98,* (Orlando, Florida USA, July 1998), ACM Press, pp. 379-386.

15. Weber, K., and Poon, A. "Marquee: A Tool For Real-Time Video Logging," *Proceedings of Conference on Human Factors in Computing Systems (CHI '94),* ACM, Boston, April 1994, pp. 58-64.

Time-Compression: Systems Concerns, Usage, and Benefits

Nosa Omoigui, Liwei He, Anoop Gupta, Jonathan Grudin, and Elizabeth Sanocki

Microsoft Research, Redmond, WA 98052

{nosao,lhe,anoop,jgrudin,a-elisan}@microsoft.com

ABSTRACT

With the proliferation of online multimedia content and the popularity of multimedia streaming systems, it is increasingly useful to be able to skim and browse multimedia quickly. A key technique that enables quick browsing of multimedia is *time-compression*. Prior research has described how speech can be time-compressed (shortened in duration) while preserving the pitch of the audio. However, client-server systems providing this functionality have not been available.

In this paper, we first describe the key tradeoffs faced by designers of streaming multimedia systems deploying time-compression. The implementation tradeoffs primarily impact the granularity of time-compression supported (discrete vs. continuous) and the latency (wait-time) experienced by users after adjusting degree of time-compression. We report results of user studies showing impact of these factors on the average-compression-rate achieved. We also present data on the usage patterns and benefits of time compression. Overall, we show significant time-savings for users and that considerable flexibility is available to the designers of client-server streaming systems with time compression.

Keywords

Time-Compression, Video Browsing, Multimedia, Latency, Compression Granularity, Compression Rate.

1   INTRODUCTION

With the Internet now a mass medium, digital multimedia content is becoming pervasive both on corporate Intranets and on the Internet. For instance, Stanford University makes the video content of 15 or more courses available online every quarter [25]. Similarly, corporations are making internal seminar series available on Intranets. With so much content available, it is very desirable to be able to browse it quickly.

Several techniques exist for summarizing and skimming multimedia content [1, 2, 14]. Of these, time-compression-- compressing audio and video in time, while preserving the pitch of the audio--is very promising. Time-compression allows multimedia to be viewed or listened to in less time. People read (and thus comprehend) faster than they speak; studies have shown that as long as compressed speech remains intelligible, comprehension is not affected [2, 11].

Although time-compression has been used before in hardware-

device contexts [1] and telephone voicemail systems [15], it has not been available in streaming video client-server systems. This paper describes studies that can guide the design of such systems supporting time compression.

In client-server systems, designers have three choices: 1) A system with multiple pre-time-compressed server-side files, leading to discrete-granularity (e.g., 1.0, 1.25, 1.5) time-compression and long latency (wait-time) for end users. This requires essentially no client-side changes, but has large server-side storage overhead. 2) A simple real-time client-side solution, leading to continuous-granularity time compression, but still with long-latency for end-users. 3) A complex real-time client-side solution, leading to continuous granularity time-compression and negligible latency for end-users.

We have studied the impact of these choices on use patterns, and also attempted to quantify the benefits achieved. We tracked the change over time in the average speedup-factor and the number of adjustments, across users and videos. These measures are compared with the users' perception of the value of time-compression, the amount of time they saved using the feature.

At a high level, our results show time-savings of 22% for the tasks we studied. Coarse granularity and long latency do not seem to deter the benefits of time compression, but can affect user satisfaction. This suggests that considerable flexibility is available to the designers of client-server streaming systems with time compression.

The paper is organized as follows. Section 2 provides a brief introduction to time-compression. Section 3 focuses on the system-level options and tradeoffs involved in building a client-server time-compression system. Section 4 describes the prototype system used in our study, and Section 5 describes experimental procedure and task. Results are presented in Section 6, related work in Section 7, and concluding remarks in Section 8.

2   TIME COMPRESSION BASICS

Time-compression reduces the time to listen to or watch multimedia content. In general, there are two kinds of time-compression: linear time-compression and skimming [2]. With linear time-compression, compression is applied consistently across entire media streams, without regard to the multimedia information contained therein. With skimming, the content of the media streams is analyzed, and compression rates may vary from one point in time to another. Typically, skimming involves removing redundancies – such as pauses in audio –

from the original material. This paper focuses only on linear time-compression.

2.1 Time Compression of Audio

The time it takes to listen to a piece of audio content can be reduced by playing the audio at a lower sampling rate than that at which it was recorded–for instance, by dropping alternate samples. However, this results in an increase in pitch, thereby creating less intelligible and enjoyable audio. One would like to time-compress the audio and preserve pitch, to maximize the intelligibility and quality of the listening experience.

Audio content may comprise of speech and/or music. We focus on the former in this paper. The most basic technique for achieving time-compressed speech involves taking short fixed-length speech segments (e.g., 100ms segments), and discarding portions of these segments (e.g., dropping 33ms segment to get 1.5-fold compression), and abutting the retained segments [5, 7, 8, 16]. The main advantage of this technique is that it is computationally simple and very easy to implement. However, discarding segments and abutting the remnants produce discontinuities at the interval boundaries and produce clicks and other forms of signal distortion.

To improve the quality of the output signal, a windowing function or smoothing filter–such as a cross-fade–can be applied at the junctions of the abutted segments [21]. A technique called *Overlap Add (OLA)* yields signals of very good quality. OLA is relatively easy to implement and is computational inexpensive---the algorithm can be run on a Pentium 90 using only a small fraction of the CPU.

Other techniques for achieving time-compression of speech include *sampling with dichotic presentation* [18, 24], *selective sampling* [17], and improvements to OLA such as *SOLA* and *P-SOLA* [10]. Trading off output quality and computational complexity, we employed OLA in this study.

2.2 Time Compression of Video

Compared to audio, time-compressing video is more straightforward. There are two techniques to time-compressing video linearly. The first involves dropping video frames on a regular basis, consistent with the desired compression rate. For instance, to achieve a compression rate of 50% (i.e., a speedup-factor of 2.0), every other frame would be dropped. In the second technique, the rate at which video frames are rendered is changed. Thus to get a 2.0-fold speed-up, the frames are rendered at twice this rate. The main negative of this scheme is that it is computationally more expensive for the client, as the CPU has to decode twice as many frames in the same amount of time.

3 TRADEOFFS IN BUILDING CLIENT-SERVER TIME-COMPRESSION SYSTEMS

Time-compression has not been employed in client-server multimedia streaming environments. There are several ways to build time-compression into streaming systems in client-server environments, each with advantages and disadvantages.

3.1 Multiple Pre-Processed Server-Side Files

In this model, the server stores separate pre-processed media files for each speedup-factor. The author chooses a set of speedup-factors and encodes different files at each factor. As a user switches between speedup-factors, the client switches to the media file corresponding to the new factor. For example, an hour-long documentary could be time-compressed at rates of 1.0, 1.25, 1.5, 1.75, and 2.0. Users would then have the option of choosing among the resulting files.

This technique has several advantages: (1) Minimal changes to the client and server. (2) No extra bandwidth is required because the time-compressed media files are also encoded at the appropriate bit-rate. (3) It does not affect server scalability, since no complex processing is done on the server. (4) Because time-compression is performed offline, computationally expensive and high quality time-compression algorithms can be used.

The disadvantages are: (1) Latency is incurred when switching between files (when user changes time-compression) and if video is not at a key-frame boundary. (2) Additional storage is required at the server for the different speed media files. (3) The time-compression feature cannot be provided with existing media files. New files have to be encoded. (4) It allows for only discrete speedup-factors, forcing all users to rely on the author's judgment as to speedup granularity.

3.2 Simple Real-Time Client-Side Solution

In this scheme, the client time-compresses the incoming data in real time. Changes to the server are minimal: it must be able to accept a speedup-factor request from the client. To achieve time-compression for a specified speedup-factor, the client sends a message to the server, informing it to stream data to the client at N times the bit-rate at which the data was encoded, where N is the speedup factor. The client then time-compresses the data on the fly.

This technique has several advantages: (1) Time-compression can be achieved with existing media files. (2) No additional storage is needed on the server. (3) It allows for both discrete and continuous speedup-factors. (4) It does not affect scalability, since no complex processing is done on the server. (5) Most importantly, it is simple to implement, as complex buffering and flow-control to eliminate latency are not needed.

The disadvantages are: (1) It requires extra network bandwidth, since the server must send data at a faster rate than that at which it was encoded. This might be feasible on corporate/LAN environments, but not over existing dial-up networks. (2) Time-compression is performed after the audio is decompressed on the client, leading to worse audio quality than in the previous scheme, where time-compression occurs before encoding audio.

3.3 Sophisticated Real-Time Client-Side Solution

The scheme described above can be improved by having the client perform flow-control in order to drive the rate at which the server streams data to it. For example, the client can monitor its buffer and have the server send data at a rate such that its buffer remains in steady state. The client could also have the server tag incoming data samples with the rate at which they were sent. Then, when the user switches speedup-factors, the client tells the server to send at the new rate, and only invoke time-compression when it receives the data for that rate. In addition, the client would track I-frames so that speedup-factor transitions occur at "clean" boundaries.

The net effect of these optimizations is that the client would eliminate – or at least minimize – startup latency that results from buffering. This technique shares all the advantages of the previous method. However, it is much more complicated than the simple client-side solution; potentially complex changes to both the client and the server are required. The characteristics of the three methods are summarized in Table 1 below.

Table 1: Alternatives for Building Time-Compression into Client-Server Multimedia Streaming Systems.

	Multiple Pre-Processed Server-Side	Simple Real-Time Client-Side Solution	Sophisticated Real-Time Client-Side Solution
Allowed Speed-up Factor Granularity	Discrete only	Discrete and Continuous	Discrete and Continuous
Additional Storage Demands?	Yes	No	No
Additional Bandwidth Demands?	No	Yes	Yes
Added Complexity?	Minimal	Yes, on client	Yes, significantly, on client
Limits Scalability?	No	No	No
Works with Existing Media Files?	No	Yes	Yes
Preserves audio signal quality?	Yes, very well	Yes, reasonably well	Yes, reasonably well
Latency while Switching Speedup-Factors?	Yes	Yes	No

4 TIME-COMPRESSION SYSTEM USED IN STUDY

We built the time-compression system by modifying an existing multimedia streaming system, the Microsoft® NetShow™ product. To enable user control of time-compression, the client was changed to correspond to the "simple real-time client-side" solution. The interface and implementation were changed to support full control of the granularity of time-compression and the latency experienced by the user. Figure 1 and Figure 2 show the user interface.

5 EXPERIMENTAL METHOD

5.1 Subjects

To explore user responses to time-compression and the tradeoffs described, fifteen subjects participated in two study sessions in the Microsoft Usability Labs. They were recruited from a pool of participants previously indicating interest in participating in usability testing at Microsoft. Subjects were intermediate or better Windows users who indicated interest in the topic areas of the videos to be presented. They were given software products for their participation.

5.2 Experimental Procedure

5.2.1 Conditions Tested

All subjects completed five conditions. The first was the control condition, where no time-compression was available. The other four were derived from two values for each of two control parameters. The first parameter was *latency*, i.e., the time following a speedup adjustment before the video resumed playing. The values used for this were 0 and 7.5 seconds, the latter chosen to reflect typical latency for NetShow today. The second parameter was *granularity*, representing the step-size for possible speedup adjustments. The two settings used were

continuous and discrete. For the continuous case we use granularity of 0.01, and for the discrete case granularity of 0.25 (allowing speedup factors of 1.0, 1.25, 1.5, etc.)

Figure 1. The modified interface for Microsoft® NetShow™ with time-compression UI elements. The status bar shows the current speedup-factor.

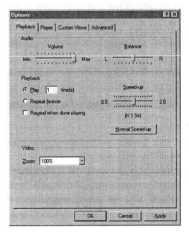

Figure 2. The interface for the "Options" dialog box. Note the slider control for speedup-factor and the "normal speed-up" button that returns users quickly to the regular viewing speed.

The five conditions we study thus are: *CG-LL, CG-NL, DG-LL, DG-NL* (CG/DG for continuous vs. discrete granularity, and LL/NL for long-latency vs. no-latency), and *no-TC* (no time-compression). Based on Section 3, the three conditions of primary interest are CG-LL, CG-NL, and DG-LL.

5.2.2 Subject Tasks

The subjects watched five 25 - 40 minute videos. Two were Discovery Channel™ videos on sharks and grizzly bears, and three were talks from ACM's 50th Anniversary Conference "The Next 50 Years of Computing" held in March 1997. We used talks by Raj Reddy, Bran Ferren and Elliot Soloway. The videos ranged from being easy to watch and visually stimulating to being more intellectually challenging and requiring concentration.

Subjects were asked to assume that they were in a hurry and would have to summarize the videos' contents during a meeting scheduled for later that day. After watching each video, a subject did give a 3-5 minute verbal summary. The videos were viewed in the same sequence by all subjects, but we counterbalanced the four latency-granularity and control conditions; subjects experienced conditions in different orders.

The subjects watched the videos over two days/sessions. The first session began by filling out a background questionnaire. After completing a training session where they familiarized themselves with the operation of the software, they watched the first two videos (the ACM talk by Raj Reddy and the Discovery Channel™ video on sharks). During the second study session, the subjects watched the remaining three videos: an ACM talk by Bran Ferren, a Discovery Channel™ documentary on grizzly bears, and another ACM talk by Elliot Soloway. The second study session ended with the subjects completing a post-study questionnaire and participating in a debriefing session where they discussed their impressions of the time compression feature.

While watching the videos, subjects had full control. They could play, pause, stop, adjust the volume, and move to specific parts of the video via a "seek" bar. The client computer logged these actions: "Open," "Play," "Pause," "Stop," "Seek," "Change Speedup-Factor," and "Close." Also recorded were the "Seek" positions and the "Change Speedup-Factor" rates.

A few caveats: We did not specifically focus on subjective experience of fatigue or confidence in their comprehension, and only obtained general impressions of their preferences. And we recognize that the preliminary interface to the prototype could have some effect on performance.

6   RESULTS

We now report on how the use of time-compression varied with the control conditions, the subjects' usage behavior across time and videos, number of adjustments made, and the savings in task-time.

6.1   Use of Time Compression

The first measure of interest is the average-compression-rate used by the subjects as a function of the conditions. It is calculated based on the amount of time spent at each compression factor:

$$average\_compression\_rate = \frac{\sum_i usertime(i) * speedup\_factor}{\sum_i usertime(i)}$$

Equation 1: Average compression rate.

$usertime(i)$ is length of the ith contiguous playing time at a given compression factor. A new interval begins when the compression-factor is changed. All pause times to take notes, etc are excluded in this measure (we will look at them later, when we consider the total-task-time).

Our thinking before the study was as follows:

Continuous vs. Discrete granularity: On one hand we felt that continuous granularity would lead to greater savings in time, because subjects would move to the highest intelligible speedup factor for that specific video segment. E.g., if a video segment was not understandable at 1.5-fold speedup (feasible in the discrete case), they could watch it at 1.4 rather than having to drop to 1.25 (the next option in the discrete case).

On the other hand, we could see how that discrete granularity could lead to greater savings in time. If a video-segment could be watched with extra-concentration at 1.5-fold speedup, then in the discrete case users might continue to watch at that higher speed rather than switch down to 1.25. In contrast, for the continuous case, they might drop to 1.4.

No-latency vs. Long latency: Here also, our intuition was conflicting. On one side, we felt that no-latency would lead to higher overall speed-up, as subjects would be more prone to making frequent adjustments to match the current video segment. As in the continuous-vs.-discrete case, however, the fixed speed that the long-latency subjects use could be faster than what the no-latency subjects were using (at the cost of more concentration), so the outcome is unclear.

Table 3 presents the average-compression-rate across all subjects and conditions. The first thing that we observe is that the average-compression-rate, across all subjects and conditions, is quite substantial (avg=1.42). If one considers the total length of all five videos (~2.5 hours), this implies a savings of about 45 minutes.

Table 3. Average Compression Rate Across Subjects and Conditions.

Subject No.	CG-LL	CG-NL	DG-LL	DG-NL	Average	Std Dev
1	1.45	1.31	1.48	1.37	1.40	0.08
2	1.47	1.5	1.34	1.4	1.43	0.07
3	1.68	1.71	1.5	1.5	1.60	0.11
4	1.32	1.37	1.36	1.25	1.33	0.05
5	1.42	1.35	1.33	1.25	1.34	0.07
6	1.57	1.71	1.58	1.51	1.59	0.08
7	1.06	1.18	1.36	1.14	1.19	0.13
8	1.37	1.43	1.42	1.41	1.41	0.03
9	1.43	1.43	1.46	1.48	1.45	0.02
10	1.41	1.42	1.46	1.27	1.39	0.08
11	1.44	1.39	1.48	1.42	1.43	0.04
12	1.52	1.44	1.35	1.4	1.43	0.07
13	1.28	1.24	1.26	0.92	1.18	0.17
14	1.36	1.61	1.49	1.71	1.54	0.15
15	1.61	1.82	1.7	1.46	1.65	0.15
Avg.	1.43	1.46	1.44	1.37		
Std Dev	0.15	0.18	0.11	0.18		

Quite to our surprise, we found that there are no significant differences in the average-compression-rate achieved (repeated measures ANOVA, p = n.s.).[1] We found the subjects to be quite diverse in their usage patterns. For example, considering latency effects, while 6 of the 15 subjects (1, 5, 9, 11, 12, 13) perform faster under CG-LL, the rest operate faster under CG-NL. Similarly, considering granularity affects, while

---

[1] Statistically, we do find a significant interaction between latency and granularity factors (repeated measures ANOVA, F = 6.286, p = 0.025). The average-compression-rate for DG-NL was lower than that for other conditions, but since that condition is not of interest to us (based on Section 3) we do not comment here on the result.

5 of the 15 subjects perform faster under CG-LL, the rest are faster under DG-LL. It appears that the counter-acting factors considered before the study seem to be balance out in practice.

Looking at the individual subjects, we see considerable variation in the speed-up factors they used (averaged across all conditions). The fastest three averaged 1.65, 1.60, and 1.59, while the slowest three averaged 1.18, 1.18, and 1.32. This is not too surprising given the variation in the subjects---e.g., the 16-year old high-school student (subject 3) averaging 1.60 speed-up to the 60-year old retired person (subject 13) averaging 1.18 speed-up.

So, what are the implications for designers? The key implication is that implementers should feel free to choose the simplest solution, DG-LL, barring the storage overhead on the server side. If this storage overhead is not acceptable, then CG-LL should provide similar benefits to end-users at much less complexity than CG-NL.

6.2   Usage Over Time and Across Videos

Another question for us was "How does users' behavior change as they watch a video?" Previous work [19, 29] suggests that training on time-compressed speech increases people's ability to use higher speed-up factors. We wanted to see if those observations would apply in our case within the same video, and also across videos (i.e., greater speed-up factor used for videos later in the sequence).

Figure 3 shows the speed-up factor across time for the five videos. The videos appear in the same order in which they were watched by the subjects.

Looking first at change in speed-up used within a video, we see some interesting results. For the Reddy and Shark videos (these two videos were watched on the first day of the subjects' visit to the Usability lab) we clearly see that the subjects are watching them faster as they get deeper into the video. There is some slowdown right at the end, an area that corresponds to the concluding remarks.

Surprisingly, for the latter three videos, which were watched on a subsequent day (their second visit), the pattern is quite different. The subjects start watching the video at a higher speed-up factor (between 1.35-1.4, in contrast to 1.23-1.28), but overall there is no consistent pattern over the duration of the session. Our hypothesis is that on the first day, time-compression was a novel feature for the subjects, and they tried to push their limits. As indicated by past literature, they started conservatively and by end got to quite high speed-up factors. In contrast, on the second day, time-compression was already a familiar feature. The subjects started at a higher compression-rate based on their previous day's experience, and only made local adjustments over the duration of the session. This suggests that in the long-term, when time-compression feature is more universally available, we are more likely to observe the latter behavior.

We look next at change in speed-up across videos. From Figure 3, the numbers are 1.43, 1.46, 1.44, 1.43, and 1.34 respectively. Clearly, there is no increase across videos (repeated means ANOVA = n.s.), as may have been predicted based on the literature [18, 29].

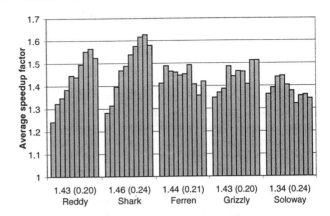

Figure 3: Average speed-up factor as function of time offset within the video. Each bar corresponds to 10% of the length of the video. The average speedup factors and standard deviations for each video are shown below the x-axis.

6.3   Number of Adjustments

One of the things we wanted to learn from the study was "How many adjustments do the subjects make?" Will they just make 2-3 in the beginning and settle in with no more adjustments for the rest of the talk, or will they make tens of adjustments, fine-tuning all along the talk. We did not have any strong predictions before the study (other than there are likely to be more at the beginning of the talk), and we did not know of any previous work to guide our thinking.

Figure 4 shows the distribution of adjustments made by subjects (averaged across conditions) over the length of the session for each video. The mean number of adjustments is quite small (between 2.5 and 4.5). As expected, they tend to occur more in the beginning, though subjects do adjust throughout a session. If almost all adjustments are near the beginning, a design implication might have been to avoid all client modifications, and just provide the end-users with multiple URLs for different speed videos. The data indicate that it is indeed important to allow adjustments throughout the video rather than just a pre-selection mechanism.

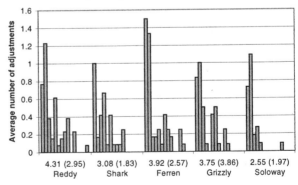

Figure 4: Average number of adjustments to speed-up factor over time. Each bar corresponds to 10% of the length of the video.

At a finer level, we were also interested in understanding how these numbers changed with the latency-granularity conditions. Here we expected more adjustments for the lower-latency condition, as it was less disrupting to the viewer. The continuous-versus-discrete granularity cases present counter-acting factors--continuous provides opportunity for fine-grain adjustments, whereas discrete could cause people to switch back-and-forth frequently when pushing their limits.

Table 4 shows the average number of adjustments the subjects made as a function of the conditions. The averages are quite similar (3.1, 3.7, 3.5, and 3.9 respectively) and we found no statistically significant differences (repeated measures ANOVA, p = n.s.). At least for the limited number of subjects we used, our expectation that no-latency condition would lead to higher adjustments is not borne out here. On the whole, we see no particular systems design implications, as the magnitudes are small and similar (3-4 adjustments over a period of 45 minutes).

Table 4: Average Adjustments across Subjects and Conditions

Subject No.	CG-LL	CG-NL	DG-LL	DG-NL	Average	Std Dev
1	3	3	4	9	4.8	2.9
2	3	13	12	9	9.3	4.5
3	5	3	1	3	3.0	1.6
4	3	2	3	2	2.5	0.6
5	5	8	6	3	5.5	2.1
6	6	8	6	6	6.5	1.0
7	2	1	4	3	2.5	1.3
8	5	7	1	6	4.8	2.6
9	2	2	3	5	3.0	1.4
10	2	1	2	2	1.8	0.5
11	3	2	1	6	3.0	2.2
12	3	1	2	1	1.8	1.0
13	2	2	2	2	2.0	0.0
14	1	1	1	1	1.0	0.0
15	2	1	4	1	2.0	1.4
Avg.	3.1	3.7	3.5	3.9		
Std Dev	1.5	3.6	2.9	2.7		

Interestingly, although the data indicate that neither latency nor speedup-factor granularity affected user behavior, several subjects commented in post-study debriefing that the long latency and discrete granularity conditions had affected their use of the time compression feature. The subjects felt that they made fewer adjustments and watched at a lower compression rate when long latency and discrete granularity were used. This indicates that from a product-design (marketing) perspective, these psychological factors may be the primary driving forces to push for the lower-latency continuous-granularity functionality.

6.4　Savings in Task Time

A bottom-line measure of the utility of the time-compression feature is the amount of time it saves in performing the task. For example, a subject using time-compression may find himself/herself reviewing the content more often due to decreased comprehension, thus negating some of the benefits from the use of time compression. In this subsection we quantify these factors.

We decompose task-time into five components: view-time, review-time, pause-time, seek-time, and latency-time. View-time is when a user is watching the video content for the first time. Review-time is the time a user spends reviewing already watched portions of video (this was time spent throughout the session rather than just at the end of the session). Pause-time is

when the player is paused, e.g., while taking notes. Seek-time is due to the stall (e.g., for buffer fill) that occurs each time the subject seeks to a different point in the video. Latency-time is due to stall after each change in time-compression adjustment.

Table 5 lists the components of task time for the different granularity-latency conditions. As we expected, we find that the review time does go up when time-compression is used---mean of 157 seconds across all conditions with time-compression versus 126 seconds with no time-compression. Overall, subjects seemed to be spending about 9-11% of their time reviewing the videos with time compression. The data show that pause time was also quite substantial (4-13%), but varied widely across the conditions. The contribution of the buffering latency to overall task-time was minor (for both video-seeks and time-compression adjustments).

Table 5: Components of task time under different conditions.

Time	CG-LL		CG-NL		DG-LL		DG-NL		NO-TC	
	seconds	%	seconds	%	seconds	%	seconds	%	seconds	%
View	1289	81	1325	77	1349	81	1393	85	1883	88
Review	150	9	173	10	175	11	161	10	126	6
Pause	92	6	216	13	68	4	92	6	122	6
Seek/Play	20	1	0	0	37	2	0	0	0	0
Latency	40	3	0	0	35	2	0	0	0	0
Total	1591		1714		1664		1646		2131	
Speedup	1.34		1.24		1.28		1.29		1.00	

The need to review content also brought us some valuable user-interface feedback from the subjects. When using high speed-up factors, the subjects would find that they had just gone past some interesting statement that they did not follow. They would want to back-up in the video (say 15 seconds), but the seek-bar in the interface provided only a *very* blunt control for that (e.g., 30 minutes represented over 3 inches). As a result, users would end-up backing too much most of the time. Specific controls/buttons that would say back-up 5/10/15/30/60 seconds would have been quite valuable.

6.5　User Feedback and Comments

6.5.1　Perceived Value of Time-Compression

In a post-study questionnaire, subjects rated several aspects of the time compression feature. Table 6 summarizes the results of these questions.

Table 6: Average subject ratings for time compression feature.

Ave Rating*	Question
6.53	I liked having the time compression feature.
6.67	I found the time compression feature useful.
6.40	I would use this software to watch videos again.
6.33	I feel that I saved a significant amount of time by using the time compression feature.

* where 1 = not useful, strongly disagree, etc., and 7 = very useful, strongly agree.

The questionnaire suggested that most subjects liked the feature very much, a finding reported by others. One subject noted "I think it will become a necessity if introduced on a large scale; once people have experienced time compression they will never want to go back. Makes viewing long videos much, much easier." Another said "Many times you spend a lot of time wading through information that is not related to your needs. This speeds up that process." Yet another wrote "Sure, it saves time and people are always short on time."

In our survey, 87% of the subjects reported that they either loved the feature or found it very useful. However, several subjects wrote that they would use the time compression feature at work or at school for information-related content but not at home for entertainment.

Two subjects mentioned that paradoxically, at rates they paid more attention to the videos than at lower rates. One subject noted "My attention span was kept intact. With the slower pace, my attention span actually wavered, and I focused on too much detail. For summarizing, the faster pace is helpful and forces me to concentrate on the major points."

6.5.2 Perceived Time Savings

On the questionnaire, we asked the subjects whether they actually saved time by using the time-compression feature. Surprisingly, most subjects said they were not sure of whether they saved time or not. One wrote "I'm not sure if I actually saved a significant amount of time, but it sure felt like I did."

Possibly, once users get used to the time-compression feature, they regard the compressed time as though it were normal time. This is supported anecdotally by the fact that one subject insisted that the time compression feature was broken and he had just viewed the video at the recorded speed.

6.5.3 Features Requested by Subjects to Complement Time-Compression

About a third of the users said that they also needed bookmarks or a table of contents in order to quickly browse the videos. In general, they implied that time-compression in and of itself is not enough to give users the ability to browse and skim videos effectively.

This suggests that time-compression should be employed in concert with other features to give users the power to quickly interact with multimedia content.

7 RELATED WORK

Signal processing aspects of time-compression algorithms, such as *OLA*, *SOLA*, and *P-SOLA*, have been studied since the 1950s [1, 5, 7, 8, 14, 16, 17]. These studies are complementary to our work, which focuses on issues that arise in integrating these algorithms into client-server systems. They do not address issues of latency, granularity, scalability of servers, and constraints of constant-bandwidth channels for multiple streams.

Considerable research addresses intelligibility and comprehension of time-compressed speech [1, 3, 6, 11, 12, 28]. In a discrete-granularity study, Harrigan [11] found that students used average speed-up of ~1.3, similar to our ~1.4. Tarquin et al. [28] found that for compression-rates up to 70% (corresponding to a speedup-factor of about 1.4), student performance with time-compressed tutorial tapes was at least as good as that with tapes played at normal-speed. Some researchers have suggested that the limiting factor in comprehension and intelligibility is the word rate, not the

compression rate or speedup-factor. Foulke and Sticht [6] discovered that the mean preferred compression rate was 82% (i.e., a speedup-factor of 1.25) corresponding to a word rate of 212 wpm. Although we have not measured the word-rate in our videos, they are quite diverse, yet we saw a comparable compression-rate for the videos, a finding supported by. Heiman et al [13].

It has been observed in other studies that exposure to time-compressed speech increases both intelligibility and comprehension. Orr [18] noticed that listeners with no prior exposure to time-compression could tolerate speedup-factors of up to 2.0 but that with 8-10 hours of training, significantly higher speedup-factors are possible. Voor [29] also found that comprehension levels of speech increased with practice. Our results are somewhat different. For the first day subjects used higher speed-ups within a video as time progressed. On the second day, however, no such trends were observed. The subjects seemed to find their preferred speedup range quickly and failed to move much from there.

There have been several studies on applications of time-compression technology as small hardware devices (like voice-mail systems) [23]. More recently, work has also been done on speech-skimming hardware devices [1, 2, 4, 22, 27]. In addition, several classroom educational studies have been performed [11, 26]. Of these, the closest study to ours is Harrigan's [11] wherein he offered students time-compressed lectures at three distinct speedups, 1.0, 1.18, and 1.36 and found that 75% of the time, the students preferred the lectures at 1.36 times speed. Stifelman's [26] study included an examination of the educational use of time-compression but the goal of her work was less on time-compression and more on issues relating to speech annotations. None of the studies have looked at the tradeoffs in use of time-compression from a latency and granularity perspective, as done here.

8 CONCLUDING REMARKS

A key feature in future client-server streaming-media solutions will be time-compression. From an implementation perspective, designers of such systems will have three choices. First, a simple system with multiple pre-processed server-side files, leading to discrete-granularity and long latency access (DG-LL) for end users. Second, a simple real-time client-side solution, leading to continuous granularity, but long latency (CG-LL) for end-users. Third, a complex real-time client-side solution, leading to continuous granularity, but negligible latency (CG-NL) for end-users. In this paper we presented results that will enable designers to make these tradeoffs.

Our data show that under all three conditions, users obtain a substantial compression rate of ~1.4. Quite surprisingly though, there are no significant differences in the time-savings under the three conditions. Thus implementers are free to choose the simplest solution, DG-LL, barring the storage overhead on the server side. If this storage overhead is not acceptable, then CG-LL should provide similar benefits to end-users at much less complexity than CG-NL. While some may feel that the results are negative from a study perspective (in that there are no significant differences across conditions), the news is very good for the implementers.

We also presented results regarding usage patterns and benefits of time compression. Across all five videos, the savings in task-time was 22%. The subjects made only a small number (3-4) of time-compression adjustments during the course of the video, the majority made towards the beginning of video. Overall, the subjects liked the time-compression feature very much (47% voting "loved it" and 40% voting "very useful"). One subject quoted "I think it will become a necessity if introduced on a large scale; once people have experienced time compression they will never want to go back. Makes viewing long videos much, much easier."

ACKNOWLEDGMENTS

Thanks to Microsoft Usability Laboratory for use of their facilities, our user study subjects for their time and efforts, and Mary Czerwinski for her assistence in our study designs.

REFERENCES

1. Arons, B. "Techniques, Perception, and Applications of Time-Compressed Speech." In *Proceedings of 1992 Conference, American Voice I/O Society,* Sep. 1992, pp. 169-177.

2. Arons, B. "SpeechSkimmer: A System for Interactively Skimming Recorded Speech." *ACM Transactions on Computer Human Interaction, 4,* 1, 1997, 3-38.

3. Beasley, D.S. & Maki, J.E. "Time- and Frequency-Altered Speech." In N.J. Lass (Ed.), *Contemporary Issues in Experimental Phonetics,* 419-458. NY: Academic Press, 1976.

4. Degen, L., Mander, R., & Salomon, G. "Working with Audio: Integrating Personal Tape recorders and Desktop Computers." *Proc. CHI '92,* ACM, Apr. 1992, pp. 413-418.

5. Fairbanks, G., Everitt, W.L., & Jaeger, R.P. "Method for Time or Frequency Compression-Expansion of Speech." *Transactions of the Institute of Radio Engineers, Professional Group on Audio AU-2* (1954): 7-12. Reprinted in G. Fairbanks, Experimental Phonetics: Selected Articles, University of Illinois Press, 1966.

6. Foulke, W. & Sticht, T.G. "Review of research on the intelligibility and comprehension of accelerated speech." *Psychological Bulletin,* 72: 50-62, 1969.

7. Garvey, W.D. "The intelligibility of abbreviated speech patterns." *Quarterly Journal of Speech,* 39: 296-306, 1953. Reprinted in J. S. Lim (Ed.) *Speech Enhancement,* Prentice-Hall, Inc., 1983.

8. Garvey, W.D. "The intelligibility of speeded speech." *Journal of Experimental Psychology,* 45:102-108, 1953.

9. Gerber, S.E. "Limits of speech time compression." In S. Duker (Ed.), Time-Compressed Speech, 456-465. Scarecrow, 1974.

10. Griffin, D.W. & Lim, J.S. "Signal estimation from modified short-time fourier transform." *IEEE* Transactions *on Acoustics, Speech, and Signal Processing,* ASSP-32 (2): 236-243, 1984.

11. Harrigan, K. "The SPECIAL System: Self-Paced Education with Compressed Interactive Audio Learning," *Journal of Research on Computing in Education,* 27, 3, Spring 1995.

12. Harrigan, K.A. "Just Noticeable Difference and Effects of Searching of User-Controlled Time-Compressed Digital-Video. Ph.D. Thesis, University of Toronto, 1996.

13. Heiman, G.W., Leo, R.J., Leighbody, G., & Bowler, K. "Word Intelligibility Decrements and the Comprehension of Time-Compressed Speech." *Perception and Psychophysics 40,* 6 (1986): 407-411.

14. Hejna Jr, D.J. "Real-Time Time-Scale Modification of Speech via the Synchronized Overlap-Add Algorithm." MS thesis, *MIT, 1990. Electrical Engineering and Computer Science.*

15. Maxemchuk, N. "An Experimental Speech Storage and Editing Facility." *Bell System Technical Journal 59,* 8 (1980): 1383-1395.

16. Miller, G.A. & Licklider, J.C.R. "The intelligibility of interrupted speech." *Journal of the Acoustic Society of America,* 22(2): 167-173, 1950.

17. Neuburg, E.P. "Simple Pitch-Dependent Algorithm for High Quality Speech Rate Changing." *Journal of the Acoustic Society of America 63,* 2 (1978): 624-625.

18. Orr, D.B. "A perspective on the perception of time compressed speech." In P. M. Kjeldergaard, D. L. Horton, & J. J. Jenkins, (Eds.) *Perception of Language,* 108-119. Merrill, 1971.

19. Orr, D. B. Friedman, H.L., & Williams, J.C. "Trainability of listening comprehension of speeded discourse." *Journal of Educational Psychology,* 56: 148-156, 1965.

20. Portnoff, M.R. "Time-scale modification of speech based on short-time fourier analysis." *IEEE Transactions on Acoustics, Speech, and Signal Processing,* ASSP-29 (3): 374-390, 1981.

21. Quereshi, S.U.H. "Speech compression by computer." In S. Duker (Ed.), *Time-Compressed Speech,* 618-623. Scarecrow, 1974.

22. Resnick, P. & Virzi, R.A. "Skip and Scan: Cleaning Up Telephone Interfaces." *Proc. CHI'92 (May 1992),* ACM.

23. Schmandt, C. & Arons, B. "A Conversational Telephone Messaging System." IEEE Transactions on Consumer Electronics CE-30, 3 (1984): xxi-xxiv.

24. Scott, R.J. "Time Adjustment in Speech Synthesis." *Journal of the Acoustic Society of America 41,* 1 (1967): 60-65.

25. Stanford Online: Masters in Electrical Engineering, 1998. http://scpd.stanford.edu/cee/telecom/onlinedegree.html

26. Stifelman, L. "The Audio Notebook: Paper and Pen Interaction with Structured Speech" *Ph.D. dissertation, MIT Media Laboratory,* 1997.

27. Stifelman, L.J., Arons, B., Schmandt, C. & Hulteen, E.A. "VoiceNotes: A Speech Interface for a Hand-Held Voice Notetaker." *Proc. INTERCHI'93 (Amsterdam, 1993),* ACM.

28. Tarquin, A., Craver, L., & Schroder, D. "Time-Compression Effects of Video-tapes on Students," *Journal of Professional Issues in Engineering,* Vol. 110, No. 1, January 1984.

29. Voor, J.B. & Miller, J.M. "The effect of practice upon the comprehension of time-compressed speech." *Speech Monographs,* 32: 452-455, 1965.

SWEETPEA: Software Tools for Programmable Embodied Agents

Michael Kaminsky[*]**, Paul Dourish, W. Keith Edwards,**
Anthony LaMarca, Michael Salisbury and Ian Smith

Computer Science Laboratory
Xerox Palo Alto Research Center
3333 Coyote Hill Road
Palo Alto CA 94304 USA
{dourish,kedwards,lamarca,salisbur,iansmith}
@parc.xerox.com

[*]Laboratory for Computer Science
Massachusetts Institute of Technology
545 Technology Square
Cambridge MA 02139
kaminsky@lcs.mit.edu

ABSTRACT

Programmable Embodied Agents are portable, wireless, interactive devices embodying specific, differentiable, interactive characteristics. They take the form of identifiable characters who reside in the physical world and interact directly with users. They can act as an out-of-band communication channel between users, as proxies for system components or other users, or in a variety of other roles. Traditionally, research into such devices has been based on costly custom hardware. In this paper, we report on our explorations of the space of physical character-based interfaces built on recently available stock consumer hardware platforms, structured around an initial framework of applications.

Keywords

Interaction hardware, tangible media, augmented reality, ActiMates Barney, Mattel Talk-With-Me Barbie.

INTRODUCTION

Although Human-Computer Interaction, as a field, is focussed primarily on the needs of human users, it is also highly responsive to technological developments. Increasingly over the last few years, fuelled on the one hand by the wider availability of computational power in smaller and lower-power units, and on the other by a series of innovative and insightful reconsiderations of the nature of interaction with technology and the everyday world, a new form of interactive devices has emerged based on a very different interaction paradigm than the traditional desktop interfaces with which we are familiar.

In this paper, we report on our early experiences with the development and use of a general platform for developing these new forms of interactive device. We call these devices *Programmable Embodied Agents* or PEAs. A Programmable Embodied Agent is a portable, wireless, interactive

device embodying specific, differentiable characteristics for interaction. The typical form these devices take is as recognizable embodied and often caricatured "characters"; toys and dolls that can be augmented with computational behaviors. Although specific individual devices of this sort have been explored as research prototypes in the past (e.g. Druin's Noobie [5]), we are interested in diversifying the forms of experimentation possible by exploiting a range of commodity platforms. Examples of these platforms are Microsoft ActiMates Barney, and Mattel's "Talk With Me" Barbie[1].

Programmable Embodied Agents lie at the intersection of three recent trends in interactive system exploration.

1. *Embodied Interaction.* A PEA device is not only a site for interaction, but is portable, outside the computer, in the world. Most of the applications we will show here focus on the boundary between the real world (including human activities) and the computational world. PEAs provide a natural way to move back and forth across this boundary, as well as providing an opportunity to exploit human skills (such as spatial discrimination, peripheral perception and haptic interaction) in a way that conventional devices cannot.

2. *Character-based Interfaces.* Since the interactive presentation of a PEA is some form of anthropomorphic character, the character of the agent can provide a context for the activity. Barney, for instance, is generally happy, friendly and helpful. The "helpful Barney" character provides a context for understanding why Barney agent is explaining that the network is down. Being able to recognise and exploit individual characteristics can smooth interaction, and make it more compelling.

3. *Unified multi-purpose interactive devices.* The fact that we are used to the idea that individuals may have multiple concerns embodied in a single activity can be

---

1. "ActiMates" is a trademark of Microsoft Corp. "Barney" and the Barney character are trademarks of The Lyons Group, L.P.. "Talk-With-Me" , "Barbie" and the Barbie character are trademarks of Mattel, Inc.

exploited in the design of PEA applications. The PEA may take on the role of advisor, assistant or gatekeeper, and so may comment on a wide range of different issues (the availability of software services, communication attempts by other individuals, meeting times, and so forth). The character-based interface helps make this "channel-switching" behaviour seem more natural.

The goals of the work outlined in this paper have been two-fold. First, we want to explore the use of Programmable Embodied Agents in our everyday work setting, using them to begin to move aspects of our computational environment into the real world that we all inhabit. We have been less concerned with the use of PEA tools for completely new forms of application functionality and more concerned with supporting existing activities. In general, we want to consider how to use these tools to smooth and assist in the accomplishment of tasks we already perform every day, to assist us in understanding the progress of on-line work, and to support workplace interactions. Second, we want to explore the use of new consumer devices as PEA platforms, rather than developing novel hardware devices. We hope that this will help make PEA tools more widely accessible, and support the development and deployment of PEA technologies more widely than has been possible previously.

The structure of the rest of this paper is as follows. In the next section, we consider related work from the research literature, and present the lessons we have drawn as the basis for the work presented here. We follow that with a discussion of our an exploration of ActiMates Barney as a platform for PEA development. Next, we introduce a framework for organising potential PEA applications, and explore a range of applications we have developed so far. Finally, we present some idea for future development.

RELATED WORK

Our work on Programmable Embodied Agents is inspired by recent developments in non-traditional interactive forms.

A variety of researchers have, in recent years, begun to explore the opportunities for computation in the world. Weiser's "Ubiquitous Computing" proposal [17] was an early articulation of the idea that, since people already interact with artifacts in the everyday world, HCI should take the form of interaction with physical devices augmented with computing power, rather than interaction with computers that mimic or track the everyday world. Related work such as that of Wellner [18, 12], Fitzmaurice [5, 6] and Cooperstock et al. [3] has further explored the "augmented reality" design space.

More recently, Ishii at the Media Lab has been spearheading the development of a program of research into "Tangible Bits", which focuses on how interaction and computation can be brought into the real world and so can capitalise upon everyday human skills [9].

Research efforts such as these have emphasised the power of computation harnessed to the world, and in particular the value of moving the site of interaction out of the *"box on the desk"* and into the world to which it refers. What we draw from this perspective is the argument that, since the site of the user's concern and activity is typically outside the com-

puter, it makes sense to move the site of computational interaction outside the computer too, and to locate it along with the user, rather than forcing the user to interact with a keyboard, mouse and graphical display. At the same time, by moving out into the world, computational interaction can take advantage of the specialized context in which activity takes place, rather than adopting the "one size fits all" approach of graphical interfaces and UI widget sets. For us, then, Programmable Embodied Agents are sites of interaction that can be located "where the (inter-)action is."

In a variety of domains, the idea of characters as interactive proxies has attracted considerable interest. This idea has a long history – Laurel et al.'s work on "Guides" at Apple is an early example [10, 11] – but lately it has come to considerably greater prominence as the computational power for interactive agents has become widely available (see, for example [1, 9, 14]). Perhaps the best-known example of this style of interaction in current products is the "dancing paperclip" (the Office Assistant) of Microsoft Office, one of a variety of help agents available in Microsoft applications.

These explorations hold two lessons that have informed our work. The first is that these characters embody a stronger sense of identity and agency than can be conveyed by a typical graphical interface. As a result, then, they can serve better as channels for carrying particular sorts of information, since they take on the aspect of "messengers." Caricatures of conversational nuance (style of vocal delivery, movement, etc.) provide an opportunity to deliver both information and a context for understanding in a more natural style than could be done with textual messages, pop-up windows and so forth. This idea points us towards a set of opportunities for exploring the areas in which PEAs as specific communication channels, separate from the desktop interface and alongside it, can help manage the variety of information that we deal with in our everyday environments. So, for example, we can use a PEA to convey information about events outside our immediate view (e.g. in distributed systems); messages from other users; and so forth. We will later present a characterization of the styles of interactions for which we have built applications. First, however, we will explore the technical opportunities and challenges that consumer-unit PEAs present.

TECHNICAL BASIS

At the start of our project, we chose two potential platforms for PEAs – Microsoft ActiMates Barney [15] and Mattel's "Talk With Me" Barbie (figure 1).

Barbie is a free-standing Barbie doll who can be programmed to talk on a variety of topics. The necessary speech information is downloaded to Barbie via an infrared interface as Barbie sits at her workstation; Barbie's necklace is an IR receiver, while the screen on her computer is is an infrared transmitter. A child can use the supplied software to select a topic for conversation, and also provides names for the child and friends, which Barbie will drop into the conversation. Once Barbie has been programmed, she can be picked up and carried around like any other doll. Pressing a button on her back will cause her to speak one of the downloaded phrases.

ActiMates Barney is an educational toy based on the children's television character. In addition to being a plush purple dinosaur, this Barney is a radio-controlled device, who can also be programmed to talk and to sing; the Barney toy can also move its arms and head, and has input sensors in his paws (as well as a light sensor in his eye for playing Peek-a-Boo). In "stand-alone mode," Barney can interact with a child in various ways, singing songs and playing games. Additionally, and more significantly for our purposes, Barney can receive instructions from a radio transmitter connected to a television set or personal computer, and controlled by suitably-enabled software or instructions encoded in the television signal. When operating "on-line" to a transmitter, Barney has a wider range of behaviours, which come from the software or television signal. We chose to start our experiments with Barney because of the wider range of functionality available, and in fact we have yet to turn our attention to Barbie

Barney and Barbie are both widely available in toy stores. Indeed, this is what made them attractive to us; we were interested in the use of standard consumer platforms for research on Programmable Embodied Agents, rather than custom platforms which are not only costly to develop, but difficult to deploy in numbers. Developing on standard platforms such as these opens up new opportunities for exploring the use of PEAs in everyday settings.

On the other hand, there are two down-sides to the use of these standard platforms. The first is that we are constrained by the technology we are offered. Barbie can talk, but she can't move; Barney can move, but only in particular ways. Since our goal is to explore the "standard platform" approach, we chose not to modify the devices, although of course that is frequently appealing. (Actually, we introduced one minor modification. Since our Barney development was going on in a public space, we modified Barney so that his audio output could be sent to headphones rather than a loudspeaker. His cheery exclamations of "Let's have some fun!" are not greeted with quite the same joy and surprise when you hear them coming from the desk next to you seventy times a day.)

The second down-side is that the devices are sold in toy stores as end-user platforms, not development platforms. In

FIGURE 1: Barney and Barbie.

line with our "commodity device" principle, our work involved discovering as much as possible about the remote operation of Barney without the benefit of developer documentation.

Exploring Barney's Technology

In "PC Mode," ActiMates Barney communicates with desktop computer software via a radio transceiver connected to the computer's MIDI port. Traditionally, these software titles are educational games, such as "Fun on the Farm with Barney" or "Barney Goes to the Circus," designed as learning experiences for children ages two and up. Building our own applications suitable to using Barney as a Programmable Embodied Agent required uncovering the details of the Barney MIDI protocol.

The challenge we were faced with, then, was to experimentally determine the protocol by which Barney is programmed and controlled. The details of our investigations are not relevant here; primarily, we spent time watching how the existing Barney programs communicate with the doll. Using both hardware and software approaches, we were able to record "conversations" between the two entities that eventually we were able to study and understand. We could then use these mechanisms in our own applications.

Barney's Wireless Protocol

Essentially, the Barney protocol consists of various different packets, each encoded as MIDI messages. Barney packets range in length from three to thirteen bytes, each of which has a clearly defined structure. Examples of outgoing (to Barney) messages are system reset, packets controlling the doll's movements, voice data, as well as flow control and protocol handshaking packets. In the opposite direction, Barney also uses flow control and handshaking packets, in addition to packets describing the state of the sensors in his eye and paws.

In trying to decode the protocol to build our own application framework, one frustrating feature of the Barney protocol is that all packets, particularly those containing data (i.e., motion and voice) contain checksums. Making any changes to the recorded packets produces invalid ones that the Barney hardware simply ignores, so understanding the checksums was a necessary precursor to controlling Barney's behaviour. Furthermore, because the Barney checksums are different for each type of packet, we had to work out each one individually

Challenge/Response Handshaking

Perhaps the most interesting feature of the Barney protocol is a challenge-response that Barney initiates as part of the handshaking sequence that takes him from "stand-alone mode" to "PC mode." The controller device broadcasts a signal looking for Barney devices, and each Barney device within range responds with a 4-byte "challenge" sequence. When the controller responds with the correct response for the offered challenge, a connection is established between the two and the Barney doll is "on-line." Before we could develop software to drive Barney, we had to derive the correct algorithm for generating appropriate responses for the challenges our Barneys would generate.

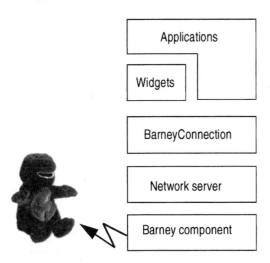

FIGURE 2: The Barney "Protocol Stack"

As it happens, calculating the 4 byte response is mostly a matter of reordering the challenge bits (also 4 bytes), a simple procedure. We speculate that the challenge/response is unlikely to be meant as a security precaution, but rather as a way to allow multiple Barneys to coexist in the same room. The Barney software only completes the handshake with one Barney, so another child can continue to play with his toy in "stand-alone mode" (besides, all Barney's responding to the software in unison, singing the same song and making the same motions, might be rather frightening).

Once Barney is "on-line" (in communication with a transmitter), a periodic "keep-alive" signal is required from the transmitter; if Barney does not receive this signal for a period of time, then he will revert to "stand-alone" mode.[2]

Voice Encoding
The voice encoding is the one feature of the Barney protocol that we were unable to understand fully. Various clues led us to conclude that the doll uses Linear Predictive Coding (LPC) for its speech; however, without knowing how the LPC parameters are encoded into the Barney protocol's voice packets, we could not make Barney say arbitrary sentences[3]. Our solution for PEA applications is to use words and phrases that Barney already knows. One advantage of this is that it preserves the character. Using the stock words and phrases means that Barney not only always sounds like Barney, but he always says the sorts of things that Barney would say.

---

2. Conversely, as long as this signal is sent, Barney does *not* go into standalone mode. This means that an application can be written which explicitly prevents Barney from singing songs and playing games. People seem to find this "Barney Cone-of-Silence" a highly compelling application.

3. Linear Predictive Coding is a means of encoding speech information using a predictive mechanism that allows the next sample to be derived in part from the preceeding ones, resulting in a high compression factor. LPC coefficients are based on formant modelling. However, unravelling the precise encoding of the LPC coefficients into the speech control packet format was beyond the scope of this project.

Programming Barney
Based on what we learned about the Barney protocol, we built several layers of software infrastructure on which to construct PEA applications. The structure of the software system is shown in figure 2.

We implemented the low-level control protocol as a Borland Delphi component. The component provides a simple interface to the application programmer who can move Barney's arms and head, ask him to speak a pre-recorded sound file, and be notified of events such as Barney's eyes being covered or a hand being squeezed.

One such application used for debugging exercises all the aspects of the protocol in the form of a Barney control panel (see Figure 3). The "Init" button performs the handshake, the sliders move Barney's limbs, and the remaining buttons play sound files in various formats. Sensor events appear in the "Messages" text field as they occur.

Using the Barney component, we also wrote a "Barney server" which provides access to Barney's functionality remotely through a TCP/IP network stream. Though the server allows direct connections through programs such as telnet, it serves primarily as a gateway for applications written in other high-level languages.

In fact, all of our PEA applications are written in Java using a Barney Connection class and listener interface, which speak to the Delphi server over the network. The Barney-Connection class encapsulates Barney's control behaviour and allows applications to control Barney's output functions (movement and speech), while the Listener interface allows applications to be informed of input activity (use of the paw sensors and covering or uncovering his eyes). With this framework in place, the PEA applications are lightweight, portable, easy to build, and seamless to integrate—like the agent itself—into one's computing environment.

The Barney Widget Set
When we started building PEA applications for Barney, we encountered certain common idioms that could be applied across a range of applications. This discovery should perhaps not have come as a surprise; since our intuition was that PEAs could be used as generic I/O devices, then it makes sense that certain application behaviours could be factored into "widgets."

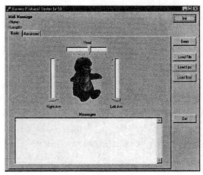

FIGURE 3: The Barney Control Panel

Notifications

Frequently, our applications use Barney to notify the user that something has happened. In order to be sure to attract the user's attention, a number of our applications would use a generic behaviour that essentially caused Barney to move about randomly. Here, we are taking advantage of the limited range of motion in which Barney can engage. Since he can only move his arms and head, and since their motion and range is highly constrained, pretty much any motion looks "Barney-like" and maintains the "character" that we are attempting to exploit. The randomness does lend an air of agitation, however, which was the effect we wished to achieve.

Indicating Values

In some applications, we wanted Barney to be able to notify the user not only of some particular event, but also to give a sense of a quantity. To give a rough quantitative indication visually, we would use Barney's arms to indicate a value, moving them up for large values, and down for smaller ones. Barney's arms move apart as they move up, and together as they move down, so the effect is to give a visual indication of size with his paws.

Counting

To use Barney to control devices, we frequently wish to use him as an input device. The sensors in his eye and paws can be used to trigger events, but we also needed to be able to group these events into more meaningful events. For instance, one widget is a counter for inputting numbers. As you squeeze Barney's left hand, he counts the squeezes out loud. Once you reach the number you want, you squeeze his right paw ("return") to select the number. Squeezing his foot will count back down again ("backspace").

Waiting

Sometimes the events we want to have Barney tell us about concern the completion of some task. Essentially, we delegate the responsibility of watching the task to see when it is complete to the PEA, who waits for completion and the signals it to the user. If the PEA is completely motionless while it's waiting, this can cause confusion. We wanted to give unambiguous feedback of a task in progress. Our "processing" widget involves moving Barney's from side to side slowly until the task is done; normally, when the task is completed there will be some explicit acknowledgment of success.

Exploiting the Character

Some common behaviours come not from our design, but from the character itself. This was an important aspect of our original approach. We wanted to be able work with and exploit the inherent and identifiable elements of the character the PEA presents. In the case of Barney, this means not only his generally cheery outlook on life (although none of our applications have so far involved singing songs), but also certain characteristic phrases. For instance, Barney likes to say, "Super-dee-duper"[4] and so a number of our applications use this phrase to indicate success.

	Channel (synchronous)	Proxy (asynchronous)
Person	*e.g. Barney Pals*	*e.g. Office Guardian*
Device	*e.g. Printer Monitor*	*e.g. Telephone Minder*
Event	*e.g. Build Manager*	*e.g. Meeting Minder*

FIGURE 4: An Application Framework

Although these widgets emerged as an unanticipated side-effect of our implementation efforts, we have found them to be of considerable value in at least two sense. The first is that they provide a convenient encapsulation of application behaviour that makes it easier for application developers to get their applications integrated with Barney as an I/O device. The second is that they ease interactions for end-users by providing identifiable output behaviours and input interactions which are common across applications. These are, of course, the sorts of benefits which we would associate with conventional widgets in a UI toolkits (scroll bars, menus, etc.); what was unexpected to us was the extent to which these same notions would carry over to an unconventional interaction device like Barney.

A FRAMEWORK OF APPLICATIONS

We have developed a range of applications of Barney as an example of a Programmable Embodied Agent. In doing this, we have been using an informal framework of applications which helps us organise and explore the space of applications. The framework is outlined in figure 4.

The framework is organised across two dimensions. The first concerns the style of communication in which Barney engages, either synchronous or asynchronous. The synchrony does not concern Barney's interaction with the user, which is clearly always synchronous, but with the occasion of the information conveyed. This distinction will be seen in more detail as we go through examples. We characterise those occasions on which Barney conveys synchronous, current information as ones when he acts as a *channel*, and those in which the information is presented asynchronously as ones when he acts as a *proxy*.

The table presented in figure 4 gives examples of applications that fit into each of these categories. We will encounter these and other applications as we step through the various cases.

Channel/Person

The "channel/person" category covers those occasions when the PEA acts as a proxy for another user in real-time. It can convey information directly from another person. For example, we have implemented two-way communication in the channel/person category in an application called "Barney Pals."

Two Barney PEAs, in separate offices, are connected via a network[5]. The software is configured so that input on one

---

4. "Super-dee-duper" is a trademark of The Lyons Group, L.P.. No, really, it is.

5. More accurately, two Barney radio controllers are driven by network-connected applications.

FIGURE 5: Barney as an interface to Document Services provides a link to otherwise invisible network processes.

doll is mirrored as output on the other doll. For instance, if Mike squeeze the right paw on the doll in his office, the right arm on the doll in the Anthony's office will move up; if he squeeze the right foot, then the hand moves down. The left side can be controlled similarly, and eye covering can be used to cause speech generation at the remote side. Communication is bidirectional; Anthony can control the doll in Mike's office in a similar way.

The result of this is an abstract communication channel, such as the "rollers" (In-Touch) of Brave and Dahley [2] or the "HandJive" device of Fogg et al. [8] supporting synchronous communication between two users at a distance.

Channel/Device

Although most office work is centered in at desks and workstations, we all make use of and rely upon devices spread throughout the building. Perhaps the most obvious is a printer, although many other devices, both physical and virtual, populate the working world. Barney can provide a way of making these remote and virtual devices accessible within the immediate office environment.

One simple case is the Print Monitor. The PEA software detects when a user sends a job to the printer, and then monitors the printer device to watch the progress of the job. Barney's head moves from side to side while the job is waiting in the printer queue, and a speech message signals when my print job is complete. Another signal warns if a problem develops with the printer that requires the user's attention. Since our current infrastructure does not provide for arbitrary speech generation, we rely on digitised samples; in context, however, phrases such as "Why, thank you," "That was fun!" and "Please try again" function effectively as cues for submission feedback, success and failure.

As another example, we have configured a Barney to act as a feedback channel for part of our internal document management infrastructure ("Burlap"). One form of portal to this infrastructure is a digital scanner which will automatically scan and OCR input documents, placing the results in

a file in my home directory. The virtual device – the OCR engine – has no local embodiment when people are standing at the scanner. The "Burlap Barney" application acts as a feedback device, informing them about changes to the status of their scan job, so they can be sure it is complete before walking away. Since users generally interact with this system through a document device (rather than a desktop computer), we can use Barney as an extra I/O channel (figure 5). This provides a route into the otherwise invisible technology behind the device; covering Barney's eyes causes him to report on the state of the network of servers comprising the Burlap service.

Channel/Event

As an extension of the device model, a PEA can also act as a channel for becoming aware of events that happen at random in my computational environment – ones which are not associated with a particular device or action taken by a user. One simple example of this is an email monitor ("Barney Biff") in which the PEA monitors an email inbox and informs the owner when email has arrived. This application uses the "arms-signal-quantity" widget behaviour, but also provides other notifications if any of the mail appears to be important. Another example is the "Build Master" application, which allows Barney to monitor a source code repository containing the up-to-date version of a large software project. In this application, Barney plays two roles. First, he can act as a channel to inform users of new changes that have been checked into the repository by their colleagues; whenever new code is checked in, Barney announces its arrival. Barney's second role is to perform automated tasks; once code has been checked in, the Build Master application attempts to verify the code that has been checked in, and reports success or failure to tell me whether the new code is good or not.[6] In terms of our framework, this application begins to blur the distinction between channels and proxies, since by informing me of activity on a device (the code repository), it also provides me with information about the activities of others, helping individuals to coordinate my activity with them [4].

One feature of all of these "channel"-based applications is that they report essentially *out-of-band* information. In other words, the information that these applications convey does not arise in synchronous response to a specific user action, but rather results from changes in the environment. These are the sorts of events for which pop-up windows on the computer screen are particularly annoying. A PEA, separate from the computer system but acting in concert with it, can provide a valuable "second channel" which need not divert someone from whatever they are doing on their workstation at the time.

Proxy/Person

The "proxy" side of the framework refers to asynchronous information-passing. In these cases, the PEA will typically act as an interface to some kind of mechanism for relaying information across time.

---

6. This is another case where we can take advantage of the particular character of the PEA (in this case, Barney). When Barney tells you that the build has broken, he can sound really personally hurt.

As an example of the "proxy/person" combination, a PEA can be configured to deliver a message to people who visit an office while it's empty(acting as a proxy for the office's owner). In the case of Barney, this can be triggered by a change in light level when people come to the office (since Barney has a light sensor in his eye). In our current framework, this use is limited by the fact that arbitrary speech generation is not yet supported.

Proxy/Device

As well as acting as a proxy for other people, a PEA can also act as a proxy for other devices. For example, one application allows Barney to monitor the telephone system. The telephones already maintain a log of missed calls, although in practice we rarely remember to check it. However, under the "Telephone Minder" application, when someone returns to their office, Barney's raised arms indicate the number of missed telephone messages; squeezing his paw, causes him to speaks the phone numbers of the callers.

Proxy/Event

The final component of the framework is the area where the PEA acts as a proxy for events, delivering them asynchronously. One opportunity here is for the PEA to report who has visited a user's office while they were away, or to let the visitors record messages. These applications require integration with other components in our environment, such as location sensors or portable devices (such as an IR-equipped PDA to "beam" a signal to the PEA); portable wireless devices such as the PEA prototypes become more powerful when placed in an environment rich in them.

Our application focus has been on the "channel" applications, although some others (such as the Telephone Minder) have been prototyped. We are convinced, though, that the use of a PEA as a means to interact not only with people but also with other devices in the environment, and to act as a site of asynchrnous communication, is a rich source of

FIGURE 6: PEA applications exploit both tactile interaction and the use of a computational channel that is separate from the desktop workstation.

potential new applications, and we are interested in exploring this area of the framework in more detail.

FURTHER WORK AND OPPORTUNITIES

The work described in this paper was conducted as a brief exploration of the opportunities offered by a set of newly available consumer devices. In the space of only a few months during the summer of 1998, we were able only to begin this exploration, especially since a sizeable amount of work was required to uncover the protocols by which Barney could be controlled, and assemble a software infrastructure over which applications could be constructed.

This leaves a number of avenues as yet unexplored. Our biggest disappointment was that, in the time available, we could not decode enough of the LPC mechanism to get Barney to speak arbitrary phrases. This is the single most significant potential advance for the development of future PEA devices, and we hope to be able to work more on this in the future, building on the groundwork laid so far.

At the same time, of course, we have yet to explore the control and use of the Barbie device. Although Barbie a less versatile device than Barney (both because she must be sitting at her workstation to receive signals, and because she cannot move her limbs), we are interested in the potential for a combination of devices. Meantime, a new range of ActiMates devices have become available. We are particularly interested in exploring this because we believe that having multiple devices allows us to move further along the route of associating specific characters with different channels of information or different styles of interaction in a single workplace.

Our primary focus now, however, is on exploring the space of potential applications. The true test of this technology lies in its deployment in everyday working settings. We are investigating opportunities to deploy and study these devices in settings amongst our own colleagues, in particular as part of an ongoing research investigation into augmented reality and interfaces exploiting novel forms of direct, tactile interaction.

CONCLUSIONS

Although there has been considerable interest over the past few years in the opportunities for direct physical interaction with computational proxies and in the use of character-based interface agents, attempts to combine the two have been confounded by a variety of practical factors. Physical character-based interactive devices, or *Programmable Embodied Agents*, are expensive to develop and to deploy. However, recently a range of consumer devices have come onto the market that hold considerable promise as platforms for research into this new style of interaction.

We are interested in the potential uses of these devices as research platforms, and have been working to create a software infrastructure for the development of PEA applications. So far, we have been working particularly with Microsoft's ActiMates Barney. We have developed a set of tools for controlling Barney, and for developing applications which exploit Barney as a generic interaction device. Using these tools, we have been exploring an initial framework of potential applications that can take advantage of the fact that PEA devices embody specific "personality traits," afford direct physical interaction, and constitute a computational channel that is separable from the traditional desktop computer.

In this paper, we have introduced and explained the ideas behind this line of research, and presented Programmable Embodied Agents as arising at the nexus of two recent lines of HCI research, on tangible physical interaction and on character-based interfaces. We have demonstrated that we can build applications that capitalise on the values of each of these lines of investigation, integrating the immediacy and physicality of tangible interaction with the compelling interaction style of character-based interfaces. We have presented an initial framework for exploring the space of potential applications and have populated this space with a range of working prototypes.

We have begin to open up opportunities to exploit "consumer platforms" for PEA research. Although there is much work still be done, our applications show early promise. In particularly, they demonstrate that these cheap consumer devices can be used as research platforms for studies of embodied interaction, and hope that these results will provide a basis for a broader-based investigation of Programmable Embodied Agents.

ACKNOWLEDGMENTS

The work described in this paper was conducted while Michael Kaminsky was a summer intern in the Computer Science Lab of the Xerox Palo Alto Research Center. We would like to thank Karin Petersen and John White for their enlightened tolerance, Ron Frederick, Ralph Merkle and Roy Want for their contributions of expertise, and Melinda Stelzer for the inspired gift that started all this in the first place.

REFERENCES

1. Beth Adelson, "Evocative Agents and Multimedia Interface Design", *Proc. Human Factors in Computing Systems CHI'92* (Monterey, CA), ACM, New York, 1992.

2. Scott Brave and Andrew Dahley, "inTouch: A Medium for Haptic Interpersonal Communication", *Proc. Human Factors in Computing Systems CHI'97 – Extended Abstracts* (Atlanta, GA), ACM, New York, 1997.

3. Jeremy Cooperstock, Koichiro Tanikoshi, Garry Beirne, Tracy Narine and William Buxton, "Evolution of a Reactive Environment", *Proc. Human Factors in Computing Systems CHI'95* (Denver, CO), ACM, New York, 1995.

4. Paul Dourish and Victoria Bellotti, "Awareness and Coordination in Shared Workspaces", *Proc. Computer-Supported Cooperative Work CSCW'92* (Toronto, Canada), ACM, New York, 1992.

5. Allison Druin, "Building an Alternative to the Traditional Computer Terminal", Masters Thesis, MIT Media Laboratory, Cambridge, MA, 1987.

6. George Fitzmaurice, "Situated Information Spaces and Spatially Aware Palmtop Computers", *Communications of the ACM*, 36(7), 38–49, 1993.

7. George Fitzmaurice, Hiroshi Ishii and William Buxton, "Bricks: Laying the Foundations for Graspable User Interfaces", *Proc. Human Factors in Computing Systems CHI'95* (Denver, CO), ACM, New York, 1995.

8. BJ Fogg, Larry Cutler, Penny Arnold and Chris Eisbach, "HandJive: A Device for Interpersonal Haptic Entertainment", *Proc. Human Factors in Computing Systems CHI'98* (Los Angeles, CA), ACM, New York, 1998.

9. Hiroshi Ishii and Brygg Ulmer, "Tangible Bits: Towards Seamless Interfaces Between People, Bits and Atoms", *Proc. Human Factors in Computing Systems CHI'97* (Atlanta, GA), ACM, New York, 1997.

10. David Kurlander and Daniel Ling, "Planning-Based Control of Interface Animation", *Proc. Human Factors in Computing Systems CHI'95* (Denver, CO), ACM, New York, 1995.

11. Brenda Laurel, "Interface Agents: Metaphors with Character", *The Art of Human Computer Interface Design* (ed. Laurel), Addison-Wesley, Reading, MA, 1990.

12. Brenda Laurel, Tim Oren and Abbe Don, "Issues in Multimedia Interface Design: Media Integration and Interface Agents", *Proc. Human Factors in Computing Systems CHI'90* (Seattle, WA), ACM, New York, 1990.

13. William Newman and Pierre Wellner, "*A Desk Supporting Computer-Based Interaction with Paper Documents*", Proc. Human Factors in Computing Systems CHI'91 (New Orleans, LO), ACM, New York, 1991.

14. Byron Reeves and Clifford Nass, "*The Media Equation*", Cambridge University Press, 1996.

15. Thomas Rist, Elisabeth Andre and Jochen Muller, "Adding Animated Presentation Agents to the Interface", *Proc. Intelligent User Interfaces IUI'97* (Orlando, FL), ACM, New York, 1997.

16. Erik Strommen, "When the Interface is a Talking Dinosaur: Learning Across Media with ActiMates Barney", *Proc. Human Factors in Computing Systems CHI'98* (Los Angeles, CA), ACM, New York, 1998.

17. Mark Weiser, "The Computer in the 21st Century", *Scientific American*, 256(3), 94–104, 1991.

18. Pierre Wellner, "The DigitalDesk Calculator: Tactile Manipulation on a Desktop Display", *Proc. Symp. on User Interface Software and Technology UIST'91* (Hilton Head, NC), ACM, New York, 1991.

Sympathetic Interfaces: Using a Plush Toy to Direct Synthetic Characters

Michael Patrick Johnson[♦]**, Andrew Wilson**[∗]**, Bruce Blumberg**[♦]**,**

Christopher Kline[♦] **and Aaron Bobick**[∗]

The Media Laboratory, MIT

Synthetic Characters Group[♦] & Vision and Modeling Group[∗]
20 Ames St.
Cambridge, MA USA 02139
{aries, drew, bruce, ckline, bobick}@media.mit.edu

ABSTRACT

We introduce the concept of a *sympathetic interface* for controlling an animated synthetic character in a 3D virtual environment. A plush doll embedded with wireless sensors is used to manipulate the virtual character in an iconic and intentional manner. The interface extends from the novel physical input device through interpretation of sensor data to the behavioral "brain" of the virtual character. We discuss the design of the interface and focus on its latest instantiation in the *Swamped!* exhibit at SIGGRAPH '98. We also present what we learned from hundreds of casual users, who ranged from young children to adults.

Keywords

Sympathetic interface, plush toy, synthetic characters, physically-based interface, virtual worlds.

INTRODUCTION

Our group's main research goal is to make interactive *synthetic characters*, 3D virtual creatures whose simple intelligence and emotion make them seem sentient and alive. This paper presents one aspect of the *Swamped!* research testbed being developed under the direction of Prof. Bruce Blumberg. The research problem that this paper addresses is how a user can interact with such a character in the most compelling, immersive manner possible. In particular, we wanted to allow a child to assume the role of one character in an interactive cartoon experience.

Any interface for controlling a complex virtual character needs to address several important problems:

- Many degrees of freedom need to be controlled.

- Context-specific actions should be simple to do (same input can map to different actions).

- The character should always remain "in character" and believable in its role.

- Navigation through the environment should be easy.

- The control mapping needs to be open-ended and easily scalable to new interactions

The characters we build have many degrees of freedom (such as arms and legs and heads) which can be animated, all of which potentially can be controlled. The interface must allow this complexity of motion. It must also allow actions that are context-specific in a simple manner. For example, if we have a chicken character, the same input from the user could mean "fly around" or it could mean "fly onto that raccoon's head and scratch him." The interface should use context to disambiguate the input rather than forcing the user to do so. To keep the illusion of life and personality, the characters need to remain "in character," moving and behaving in a compelling and believable manner as designed by the artists. For example, if the character is sad, he should respond to user input in a sad manner. Also, the user simply needs to be able to get around in the virtual world. Finally, the interface should easily allow new types of interactions to be added as simply as possible without adding cognitive complexity to the user (learning new controls, for example).

Since we want the interface to be used by children, it also needs to be friendly and simple to learn. Additionally, we want it to be haptically engaging since children enjoy touching objects. Previously, we discovered that touch was important when participants complained about not being able to "hug" a character in a project that used computer vision input [9].

We argue that a plush toy[1] embedded with sensors is a natural and novel solution to this problem. Children are often already familiar with plush toys and acting out stories with them. They are enjoyable to hold and are cuddly. They allow many degrees of freedom to be sensed, and the

---

[1] A soft doll for children

mapping from the doll to a similar virtual character is simple and often obvious. By augmenting this input device with gesture recognition technology and the character's "brain," we can allow the character to remain in character and allow it to disambiguate user input based on its perceptual and motivational context. We call this collection of technology a *sympathetic interface,* which we describe shortly.

We demonstrated this interface in an interactive cartoon experience called *Swamped!* which was used by hundreds of people at SIGGRAPH '98 and internally within our lab. The participant assumes the role of a chicken that is trying to protect its eggs from a hungry raccoon in a barnyard setting. The chicken has various behaviors such as squawking to get the raccoon's attention and make him angry, scratching his head, kicking him and setting a trap for him. The raccoon is fully autonomous, choosing what actions to take based on his desires, perceptions, and emotional state. The chicken is semi-autonomous and is controlled by the user. The participant stands in front of a projection screen showing the virtual world and the virtual chicken and directs the chicken by making appropriate gestures with the doll (see Color Plates 1 and 2). For example, wobbling the doll back and forth makes the virtual chicken walk and flapping the doll's wings will make him fly. The participant's attention is meant to focus on interactions in the virtual world and not on the doll itself.

The goal of this paper is to introduce the concept of a *sympathetic interface* and one implementation – using a plush toy to control a virtual character. We will also describe design decisions in developing the interface and our lessons from many users experiencing the *Swamped!* exhibit.

SYMPATHETIC INTERFACE
We use the term *sympathetic interface* to describe this type of physical interface. The plush toy interface is sympathetic in several senses of the word:

- the effect of an action resembles its cause (sympathetic magic, sympathetic vibration)

- it is inviting and friendly

- it tries to help the user by understanding what they are trying to do given the context

The first aspect describes the coupling between the physical and the virtual instantiations of the character. Sir James Frazer used the term *sympathetic magic* to describe one of the common ritual magic principles he discovered in various primitive cultures [5]. In sympathetic magic, an effect can be created by performing an iconic version of it. The classic, well-known example of sympathetic magic is that of the *voodoo doll*. A voodoo doll is often a wax or cloth effigy that is somehow associated with a person. The voodoo practitioner then manipulates the doll to cause an effect on that person, such as sticking pins in the doll's arm

to cause pain (theoretically). We often use this "voodoo doll metaphor" to describe the iconic nature of the interface – "Do to the doll what you would like the virtual character to do."

Secondly, a plush doll is inviting and friendly to a child. Children are not afraid to pick it up and manipulate it. Also, they can develop an emotional contact with the doll, which is not the case for a traditional input device such as a mouse or keyboard.

Furthermore, we designed the interface to be sympathetic to what the user is trying to do. It tries to understand the *intentions* of the user's input in the current context of the virtual environment and tries to help them achieve it. For example, if the user is clearly heading for the henhouse in the virtual world, the chicken should realize this and help navigate there rather than forcing the user to make fine control adjustments.

Intentional Control
We call this iconic mapping *intentional control.* Intentional control is an interface control mapping from the input device to the character where there is an interpretation layer between the raw data and character response which tries to infer the user's intent of the input rather than mapping it onto the character directly. The user is influencing the character at the *behavioral* level as opposed to the *motor* level.

Intentional control offered us a solution to the problem of "direct drive." In an early tethered version of the doll (see below), the sensor data were hooked directly to a virtual character's animated degrees of freedom, leading to a direct, continuous mapping of doll motion to character motion. Although this mapping made the nature of the interface immediately obvious to a user, the generated motion tended to be jerky due to noisy data or people moving the sensors quickly. Also, if the virtual character did not do *exactly* what the doll did, users complained. This fact makes the sensor problem much harder since you need to sense every available degree of freedom in the doll.

Furthermore, a major motivation for researching intentional control was our need to let the character "remain in character." Our experience with the direct drive version made us aware that animating a character well was hard. We wanted to keep artistic control over the animation of the character so that it moved believably according to the artist's vision of the character and maintained the illusion of life. Relying on the raw sensor data produced very robotic and lifeless motion, even in the hands of skilled puppeteers. Finally, we did not want to force users to have to make very fine control adjustments with the interface when the task they wished the virtual character to do was obvious in context. For example, the chicken will fly onto the raccoon's head if the wings are flapped anywhere near the raccoon rather than making the user laboriously steer onto his head. This fact also allows the virtual character to act out the action in a dramatic fashion, much like a real actor being directed by a director.

The facts that our characters have a behavior system, or "brain," and are embedded in a virtual world allow them to disambiguate potentially conflated inputs by using perceptual, motivational and emotional context. In the absence of behavioral disambiguation, the perceptual problem is much harder since the gesture recognition needs to do the disambiguation out of context. We discuss this further shortly.

RELATED WORK AND INFLUENCES

Physically-based user interfaces allow a user to manipulate a familiar physical object to achieve a desired effect in a virtual environment, be it a 2D desktop or a 3D application. The concepts of graspable user interfaces [4] and tangible user interfaces [8] center on this idea. To use the parlance of Fitzmaurice, we leverage the affordances of both the physical and virtual instantiations of the character. The physical character affords passive haptic feedback (the cuddly nature of the doll, the feeling of actually moving the parts) and a simple, iconic way to manipulate many degrees of freedom. The fact that the character exists in a virtual world, however, means that anything is possible. We can do anything that we can imagine and program.

Applications demonstrating physically-based interfaces have focused mostly on drawing and data manipulation tasks, however, and often involved an extremely direct coupling between the physical and virtual [4,8,7]. Our work differs from these in that we avoid a *direct* coupling of device input to output in favor of an *intentional* coupling.

Alison Druin's Noobie was influential in our research [3]. Noobie was a large stuffed animal with a computer monitor in its stomach and touch sensors around its body which children could use to design animals. Our work differs in that Noobie was meant to be a softer computer terminal interface, not a synthetic character interface.

Microsoft's ActiMates Barney doll is a plush toy embedded with pressure and light sensors, a wireless data connection, voice output and simple arm motors [12]. Barney is designed to be a social agent, not a transparent interface to a character. The focus of the interaction is on the Barney doll itself, not a virtual representation of him. Barney's main role is to comment on computer media at crucial moments to facilitate learning. Our work is designed to be an interface for controlling a virtual character where the focus of the interaction is on the virtual world. Similar to Barney is the Rosebud system [6] in which a plush toy is used to facilitate and focus a child's storytelling.

We initially evaluated the *Monkey 2* kinematic keyframe input armature from Digital Input Design, Incorporated (www.didi.com). A physical skeleton structure consisting of links and sensor-equipped joints is carefully manipulated to pose a corresponding 3D model in animation software. The *Monkey* was not suitable for our purposes since it is too large and unwieldy to manipulate simply in real-time by an experienced adult puppeteer, let alone a child. It has many degrees of freedom, and it is hard to keep it upright without making the joints very stiff to move.

EARLY TETHERED PROTOTYPE

An early prototype of the plush toy interface was a beaver plush doll which had flex sensors in the legs, tail and arms and an Ascension Flock of Birds magnetic sensor in its head and torso which gave accurate position and orientation data. These sensors were all tethered to the computer, making it hard to move the doll in certain ways, like upside down. The application we tested involved swimming around in a lake with fish and other items to see, but no explicit goal. The user controlled the direction and speed of swimming and could make the character stop and tread water in order to look around by manipulating the head and limbs in a direct drive mode. Many users tried this system and enjoyed using the plush doll to steer the beaver through the water saying it was a "great idea," but most complained about the wires. Several users thought the character was robotic and lifeless at times. We feel that this was because he was controlled with a direct mapping from sensors to animation during these times (direct drive). Many tired quickly of the scenario, also, asking "what else can I do?" or "what's the goal?" The *Swamped!* exhibit was designed to have a wireless interface, an intentional control mechanism and a more compelling interaction in response to these criticisms.

WIRELESS INTERFACE DESIGN

This section describes the design and functionality of the latest wireless version of the interface as demonstrated in the *Swamped!* exhibit at SIGGRAPH '98. The raw sensor data is first interpreted using gesture recognition techniques. The behavioral system then interprets these gestures in the context of the character's current environment and state (see Figure 1).

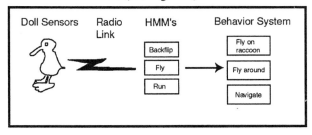

Figure 1: Data flow from sensors over wireless link to gesture recognition (HMM's) which are inputs to the character's behavioral system (brain).

This section is divided into several parts: physical construction, sensing technology, gesture recognition, and behavioral interpretation.

The Doll

The physical doll was fabricated to match the virtual character, which was modeled first. We feel that this similarity is important for making the sympathetic connection between the doll and character clear to the user.

An armature made of plastic, brass tubing and wire holds a sensor package, sensors and provides an articulated structure (see Color Plate 4). The doll's exterior is fleece fabric and molded latex (see Color Plate 3). The latest incarnation of the doll embeds a variation of a wireless sensor package designed by Joe Paradiso *et al* [10]. The sensor package includes an array of 13 sensors, including those relating to the doll's attitude and various configuration aspects:

- two pitch and roll sensors

- one gyroscope sensing roll velocity

- three orthogonally mounted magnetometers sensing orientation with respect to magnetic north

- two flexion (FSR) sensors for wing position

- three squeeze (PVDF) sensors embedded in the body and beak

- one potentiometer to sense head rotation about the neck

See Color Plate 4 for a photo illustrating how the sensor package is embedded in the doll's armature. On board the sensor package, a PIC micro-controller with analog to digital conversion packetizes the sensor values which are then transmitted via radio frequency at a rate of at least 30 Hz. The receiving station then relays the sensor records via a serial connection to the host computer. The commercially available radio transmitter/receiver pair uses the 418 MHz or 433 MHz frequencies which do not require a license from the FCC. Depending on the type of antenna used, the transmitter has a range of several hundred yards. The sensor package does not produce any radiation known to be harmful. The on-board electronics are powered by a 9 volt lithium battery, lasting several hours.

When the *Swamped!* setup is moved, magnetometer readings must be calibrated to account for any change in the direction of magnetic north. To read heading information from the magnetometer, it is important that magnetic north lie somewhat along the plane of the floor; this can be an issue in some buildings, where the earth's magnetic field is distorted in many ways.

Unlike the Ascension or Polhemus unit, the wireless sensor array does not give true 6 degree of freedom position and orientation data: there is no world-coordinate position data, and the orientation data from the magnetometers is complete only up to a roll about magnetic north. At first this fact may appear to be a significant drawback; however, we do not necessarily need accurate position and orientation since we are not using direct control. The gesture recognition techniques for implementing intentional control do not necessarily require complete 6 DOF data. In fact, the variety of sensors on board permits the interpretation software great flexibility in detecting events.

For example, many different styles of "walking" may be detected with the gyroscope alone.

Gesture Interpretation

Raw data from the doll is processed in real-time on the host computer to recognize gestures that are taught to the system in a learning phase as described in this section.

Action Primitives

Our goal is to provide the user with a high level of direction over the synthetic character. It is undesirable from aesthetic and usability points of view to have the user explicitly plant one foot in front of the other to make the character walk. For example, the system should respond to a motion that most users agree evokes "walking" without concern for how the motion would look if rendered in a literal fashion. *Swamped!* uses machine learning and gesture recognition techniques that complement the wireless sensor array to provide a high-level iconic, or intentional, style of control, as described above. The system can detect a variety of actions of the doll under user control, such as *walk*, *run*, *fly*, *squeeze-belly*, *hop*, *kick* and *back-flip*. Each of these action primitives has at least one associated gesture recognition model. Multiple models are used in cases where users tend to use one of a number of styles to accomplish an action. For example, users tend to have two ways of making the character walk: rolling the doll back and forth in a cyclic fashion or a similar motion about the vertical (yaw) axis. By using machine learning techniques, we have avoided the difficulty of writing *ad hoc* routines to identify each of the action primitives. Models of the actions are computed in an automated fashion from a set of examples collected using the actual doll. In this training phase, we use a footswitch to indicate to the system the exact start and duration of a new example. In this way, examples can be collected quickly and easily.

Hidden Markov Models

We use hidden Markov models (HMMs) to learn and recognize action primitives. HMMs were originally developed for speech recognition applications [11] and have been applied to automatic gesture recognition problems [13]. HMMs provide a sound probabilistic framework for modeling time-varying sequences for later recognition. We omit the details of how HMMs work (see [11]) but note that in practice, the designer must specify a Markov model which describes the overall temporal structure of the action (e.g., A to B to C, then back to A in the case of a cyclic gesture). Given this Markov model, the HMM training algorithm takes as input the set of example sequences and associates each state of the Markov model with a particular region of the feature space (the sensor readings). The resulting HMM may be used during runtime to determine the similarity of an input sequence to the set of training sequences. Once the HMM is trained, the training sequences are no longer needed. The set of training sequences must be chosen to span the variation of how different users execute the gesture. In *Swamped!* typically no more than 10 to 20 examples were necessary to train an HMM for a given action primitive. During runtime, each of the HMMs are fit to a sliding window of the past 2 seconds of data returned from the sensors. The HMM testing algorithm returns a continuous value indicating how well the model fit the data. If this value exceeds some threshold, the system concludes that the user performed the action corresponding to the HMM. These thresholds are chosen empirically so as to not allow too many false positives. The testing process is computationally efficient and is well within the computational power of today's computers.

Representational Choices

In the application of HMM's for gesture recognition, it is important to pick features that are appropriate to the action. One approach in the application of HMM's for gesture recognition is to provide all features to the HMM and hope that the set of examples covers the variation that is reasonable to expect. In the case of *Swamped!*, it is sometimes difficult to guess what people are going to do with the doll to indicate some action. For example, a given user may hold the doll differently than the person that trained the system, and so the trained model may not generalize to the new user. While the system allows the addition of training examples and subsequent retraining, it is often easier to restrict the model to a subset of features so that the models generalize appropriately. For example, the *run* primitive is an HMM built solely on the vertically mounted accelerometer. When the user shakes the doll up and down in a large and deliberate manner, the *run* HMM fires, regardless of the value of the other sensors.

HMM's must also be supplied with an initial Markov model which has a topology that is appropriate to the action to be recognized. In *Swamped!* there are two basic topologies used: a periodic or cyclic topology used for *walk*, *run*, and *fly* and a two-phase topology (out and away from some rest position and then a return) for all other primitives. We suspect that because of the physical constraints of holding a doll these are the two most useful topologies in describing how users interact with the doll.

Character Behavior System

Intentional control requires that the character designer decide beforehand which behaviors that the character will perform and program the character to perform the associated sequence of sub-actions when the appropriate gestural and/or contextual signals are received. This allows the character designer to change the complexity of the character's behavior without changing the interface or burdening the user.

Motivated by these concerns, we chose to implement this component of the interface as a reactive behavior system similar to the work of Blumberg [1,2]. In *Swamped!*, the chicken's behavior system treats the gesture threshold value from each HMM as a proprioceptive sensory input to a corresponding consummatory behavior. For example, when

the user flaps the chicken's wings, the HMM for the flying gesture surpasses its threshold and stimulates the flying behavior. If it is the most appropriate behavior at the time, the flying behavior will become active, which will cause the virtual chicken to begin flying. Similarly, when the user ceases to flap the wings on the doll, the feature information from the doll no longer matches the gesture for flying, the HMM will fall below threshold, and the flying behavior will become inactive. This type of system also has the advantage that it can handle noisy sensor data robustly and not "dither," or switch between two behaviors very quickly.

At any moment during the interaction the incoming feature data may closely match more than one gestural model and therefore several behaviors may wish to become active. We resolve such ambiguities by organizing mutually exclusive behaviors into groups within which they compete for dominance in a winner-take-all fashion. While the primary discriminant for determining the dominant action (and consequently the "intention" of the user) is the magnitude of the HMM, context can also play an important role, as described above. In *Swamped!*, the dominant action is dependent on context when the gesture is active. For example, when the user specifies the *fly* gesture near the raccoon, the chicken attempts to land on the raccoon's head. Otherwise, he flies in a navigational manner. Also, the *kick* behavior will not fire unless the chicken is near the raccoon. This disambiguation was useful for filtering out spurious *kick* gestures that were often conflated with *run* or *hop*.

To aid navigation, the chicken will also try to infer which object in the world the user is trying to steer towards. The chicken will then bias his heading towards this object (ideally) to reduce the complexity of navigation.

DISCUSSION

The *Swamped!* system currently runs on a dual processor Pentium computer, with graphics being rendered on a Silicon Graphics Onyx2 Infinite Reality system. Sound and music are also rendered on separate machines. The entire system is written almost exclusively in Java, including the gesture recognition and behavior system, but with the exception of the underlying graphics and sound rendering (which use C++). Rendering speed was the bottleneck, but we achieved framerates of 30Hz.

Over 400 users interacted with the *Swamped!* installation in the *Enhanced Realities* exhibit at SIGGRAPH (see Video Figure). Users were told the cartoon scenario and that the goal was to keep the raccoon busy so he did not eat any eggs by engaging in the chicken's various behaviors. The main behaviors available were:

- Squeeze the torso or beak to squawk and make the raccoon angry

- Walk or fly around the world or on the raccoon's head to make him angry. Continuous direction control was provided by pointing the chicken left or right to steer

- Walk into various buildings to set a trap for the raccoon or get catapulted to the other side of the world

- Kick the raccoon to make him angry

- Stand on head to do backflips

When the raccoon was angry he would chase the chicken, keeping him away from the eggs.

This section will discusses problems we discovered and lessons we learned during this experience.

User Classification

In general, we encountered three categories of users: teachable, ideal and skeptical, in order of approximate group size. The ideal users were often children who would pick up the doll, start manipulating it and immediately understand the concept of the interface. One girl of about six years old became an expert user within minutes (better than the designers, in fact) and played for a half hour. The teachable users were by far the largest group. The typical member of this group would pick up the doll and try to manipulate one part, such as one wing or a foot, expecting a direct mapping. After we demonstrated a *walk* gesture and explained the "voodoo doll" metaphor, many of these users could quickly learn to use the doll and enjoyed the experience. Several users, however, never understood how the doll controlled the character and were convinced that there was no connection.

We informally asked users what they thought of the interface. Most responses were positive. Users said that it was "very cool," "magical," "a great idea," and "beautiful." Several users asked "how much?" thinking we were selling prototypes for videogame systems. Children, in particular, loved playing with the system and many came back to try again. Although adults would often tire of woggling the doll continually, children thought that this was great. One excited girl said, "you mean I can keep moving him like this?" One four-year old child tried to control the character with a plush toy he had with him and was disappointed that it did not work. We feel that the haptic feedback and normal play style associated with a plush toy allowed people to form a more emotional contact with our characters, making them seem more alive.

Most of the complaints involved steering and navigational problems (see below) and wanting more actions available to perform, which is not a function of the interface design.

Navigation

Navigation to desired locations in the scene often proved difficult to users. One problem we noticed is that the turning radius of the character is fairly large, making it difficult to make sharp turns. Also, there was no continuous way to adjust the walking speed of the character in order to compensate for this. The chicken either walked at constant speed or ran at a higher constant speed. We discovered that there was no simple way of inferring the user's desired speed for the chicken using the gesture-based input. We

plan to look at the frequency at which the user makes the walking gesture as a possible parameter to infer speed. Another navigation problem was over-steering, which we describe below.

Camera

The automatic camera control algorithms were originally written for fully autonomous characters with no user inputs and were designed to show off the content of a scene, including action and emotions. When the interaction was added, however, it was often difficult to navigate the chicken based on the camera angles that were chosen and impossible when the chicken was off-screen. The camera system was redesigned to take into account the need of the user to navigate by trying to keep the viewpoint behind the virtual chicken so that the user could steer left and right easily, while also cutting to show important actions that the autonomous raccoon was taking off-screen.

Users were still often frustrated when the camera "cut when I was about to do something." This problem of stealing control from the user in order to display relevant information about the narrative is still an open research question.

Users often would "over-steer" the chicken since they could not see enough of where the chicken was headed when he was taking a sharp turn. The virtual character's heading at this point was somewhere off-screen. By the time the desired location appeared on-screen, the user had already steered too far. This problem also occurs with novice airplane pilots who eventually learn to reduce control input before reaching the desired attitude. We noticed that some users became better at this, but we need to look at ways to avoid this problem, such as wider angle of view or more anticipatory camera angles.

These experiences argue that the camera algorithms for a virtual world cannot be made separately from the input and user interface decisions. The camera is intimately coupled to the user interface in the same way that the behavior system is.

Gesture Recognition

The gesture recognition system uses models automatically derived from training examples recorded while the designer manipulates the doll. It is important that the examples exhibit the same kinds of variation that the system is likely to encounter with naive users, or the system will sometimes miss the user's gesture. While it is very easy to collect training examples and retrain a gesture model with the current system, the designer can never be sure that the training examples will work for all users. Furthermore, it can be difficult or impossible for the designer to reproduce a variant on a gesture seen during runtime.

With *Swamped!* we found that it was indeed difficult to span the entire range of variation of some gestures. Much of this variation is due to differences in the user's style of control. For example, some users manipulate the doll with small, subtle movements, while others make broad, quick gestures. The tendency of users to repeat the misunderstood gesture more boldly and deliberately (a habit borrowed from speech?) will sometimes take the user further away from the gesture model. We found it very difficult, for example, to train a model of the *kick* gesture to satisfy all users. One approach is to simply raise the gesture acceptance threshold; unfortunately, the gesture may then mask the activity of some other gesture. As previously mentioned, we addressed this problem by using mutual exclusion groups in the behavior system. Longer gestures such as *walk* were less problematic. This is most likely because long gestures include more movement information and are thus more unique among the set of gestures.

Wireless vs. Tethered

The users who had experienced the previous tethered interface were much happier with the wireless version, saying that it seemed "magical" without the wires. It was unencumbering and could be carried around the room and used as a normal plush doll away from the context of the screen. It also allowed a wider set of gestures, such as an energetic shaking, which we interpret as *run*.

Strengths and Weaknesses of Sympathetic Interfaces

We feel that our initial evaluation of the plush toy as a sympathetic interface was a success. Users responded positively to the device and intentional control concept. One of the biggest weaknesses with an intentional control mechanism was navigation. Most people are used to more direct control from videogames and have little patience when it is difficult to navigate. This is an issue we will address in future work, perhaps by mixing some direct control with intentional control.

Many people, including children, learned to use the multiple degrees of freedom of the doll very quickly. This implies that we succeeded in making the device easy to learn and use. The designers found it fairly easy to add new gestures and behaviors, suggesting that the system will be scalable. We demonstrated some simple context-dependent disambiguation of gesture, but we cannot make any strong claims yet about the success of this until we add many more such examples.

CONCLUSIONS AND FUTURE DIRECTIONS

We demonstrated the concept of a sympathetic interface in the form of a novel plush toy control interface for a virtual character. Over 400 participants successfully used the system and offered positive comments. Our initial success with sympathetic interfaces suggests that they are a fruitful new research direction for animated character control.

We plan to add actuators to the doll to create simple active haptic feedback. Rather than trying to animate the doll in a robotic sense, we will choose actuators that will convey the emotional and physical state of the virtual character to complement the visual and audio cues. Simple examples of

this are a variable-rate breathing actuator to convey exertion, a heater to make the doll warm, and a motor that can make the doll shiver when the character is afraid or being attacked.

ACKNOWLEDGEMENTS

We would like to acknowledge the significant contributions made by the rest of the *Swamped!* team, without which this paper would not be possible: Michal Hlavac (art design and chicken model), Ken Russell (graphics engine), Bill Tomlinson (camera control and armature design), Song-Yee Yoon (sound), Dan Stiehl (doll fabrication), Zoe Teegarden (electronics), Jed Wahl (animation) and Teresa Marrin (music). Special thanks to Dr. Joe Paradiso and his group for the wireless sensors package. Additional thanks to Bill Tomlinson for photos and video. This work was partially supported by the Toys of Tomorrow and Digital Life Consortia.

REFERENCES

1. Blumberg, B. and Galyean, T. Multi-level Direction of Autonomous Creatures for Real-Time Virtual Environments. In *Computer Graphics*, SIGGRAPH '95, (Los Angeles, CA, August 1995), ACM Press, 47-54.

2. Blumberg, B. *New Dogs, Old Tricks: Ethology and Interactive Creatures*. PhD Dissertation, MIT Media Lab, 1996.

3. Druin, A. Building an Alternative to the Traditional Computer Terminal. Master's Thesis, Media Laboratory, MIT, 1987.

4. Fitzmaurice, G.W., Ishii, H., and Buxton, W. Bricks: Laying the Foundations for Graspable User Interfaces, in *Proceedings of CHI '95* (Denver, CO, May 1995), ACM Press, 442-449.

5. Frazer, Sir J. G. *The Golden Bough*. The MacMillan Company, New York, 1922.

6. Glos, J. and Cassell, J. Rosebud: A Place for Interaction between Memory, Story and Self. In *Proceedings of the Second International Conference on Cognitive Technology* Los Alamitos, CA, 1997.

7. Hinckley, K., Pausch, R., Goble, J.C., and Kassell, N.F. Passive Real-World Interface Props for Neurosurgical Visualization, in *Proceedings of CHI '94* (Boston, MA, April 1994), ACM Press, 452-458.

8. Ishii, H. and Ullmer, B., Tangible Bits: Towards Seamless Interfaces between People, Bits and Atoms, in *Proceedings of CHI '97*, (Atlanta, GA, March 1997), ACM Press, pp. 234-241.

9. Maes P., T. Darrell, B. Blumberg, A. Pentland, The Alive System: Full-body Interaction with Autonomous Agents. In *Proceedings of Computer Animation '95 Conference*, Switzerland. IEEE Press, April 1995.

10. Paradiso, J., Hu, E. and Hsiao, K-Y. Instrumented Footwear for Interactive Dance. To be presented at the XII Colloquium on Musical Informatics, Gorizia, Italy, September 24-26, 1998.

11. Rabiner, L.R. and Juang, B.H. *Fundamentals of Speech Recognition*. Prentice Hall, Englewood Cliffs, 1993.

12. Strommen, E. When the Interface is a Talking Dinosaur: Learning Across Media with ActiMates Barney, in *Proceedings of CHI '98* (Los Angeles, CA, April 1998), ACM Press, 288-295.

13. Wilson, A.D. and Bobick, A.F. Nonlinear PHMMs for the Interpretation of Parameterized Gesture. *Computer Vision and Pattern Recognition*, 1998.

Principles of Mixed-Initiative User Interfaces

Eric Horvitz

Microsoft Research

Redmond, WA 98025 USA

+1 425 936 2127

horvitz@microsoft.com

ABSTRACT

Recent debate has centered on the relative promise of focusing user-interface research on developing new metaphors and tools that enhance users' abilities to directly manipulate objects *versus* directing effort toward developing interface agents that provide automation. In this paper, we review principles that show promise for allowing engineers to enhance human–computer interaction through an elegant coupling of automated services with direct manipulation. Key ideas will be highlighted in terms of the LookOut system for scheduling and meeting management.

Keywords

Intelligent agents, direct manipulation, user modeling, probability, decision theory, UI design

INTRODUCTION

There has been debate among researchers about where great opportunities lay for innovating in the realm of human—computer interaction [10]. One group of researchers has expressed enthusiasm for the development and application of new kinds of automated services, often referred to as interface "agents." The efforts of this group center on building machinery for sensing a user's activity and taking automated actions [4,5,6,8,9]. Other researchers have suggested that effort focused on automation might be better expended on exploring new kinds of metaphors and conventions that enhance a user's ability to *directly manipulate* interfaces to access information and invoke services [1,13]. Innovations on both fronts have been fast paced. However, there has been a tendency for a divergence of interests and methodologies versus focused attempts to leverage innovations in both arenas.

We have pursued principles that provide a foundation for integrating research in direct manipulation with work on interface agents. Our goal is to avoid focusing solely on one tack or the other, but to seek valuable synergies between the two areas of investigation. Surely, we should avoid building complex reasoning machinery to patch fundamentally poor designs and metaphors. Likewise, we

wish to avoid limiting designs for human–computer interaction to direct manipulation when significant power and efficiencies can be gained with automated reasoning. There is great opportunity for designing innovative user interfaces, and new human–computer interaction modalities by considering, from the ground up, designs that take advantage of the power of direct manipulation and potentially valuable automated reasoning [2].

PRINCIPLES FOR MIXED-INITIATIVE UI

Key problems with the use of agents in interfaces include poor guessing about the goals and needs of users, inadequate consideration of the costs and benefits of automated action, poor timing of action, and inadequate attention to opportunities that allow a user to guide the invocation of automated services and to refine potentially suboptimal results of automated analyses. In particular, little effort has been expended on designing for a *mixed-initiative* approach to solving a user's problems—where we assume that intelligent services and users may often collaborate efficiently to achieve the user's goals.

Critical factors for the effective integration of automated services with direct manipulation interfaces include:

(1) **Developing significant value-added automation**. It is important to provide automated services that provide *genuine value* over solutions attainable with direct manipulation.

(2) **Considering uncertainty about a user's goals**. Computers are often uncertain about the goals and current the focus of attention of a user. In many cases, systems can benefit by employing machinery for inferring and exploiting the uncertainty about a user's intentions and focus.

(3) **Considering the status of a user's attention in the timing of services.** The nature and timing of automated services and alerts can be a critical factor in the costs and benefits of actions. Agents should employ models of the attention of users and consider the *costs and benefits of deferring action* to a time when action will be less distracting.

(4) **Inferring ideal action in light of costs, benefits, and uncertainties**. Automated actions taken under uncertainty in a user's goals and attention are associated with context-dependent costs and benefits.

The value of automated services can be enhanced by guiding their invocation with a consideration of the *expected value of taking actions.*

(5) **Employing dialog to resolve key uncertainties.** If a system is uncertain about a user's intentions, it should be able to engage in an efficient dialog with the user, *considering the costs* of potentially bothering a user needlessly.

(6) **Allowing efficient direct invocation and termination.** A system operating under uncertainty will sometimes make poor decisions about invoking— or not invoking—an automated service. The value of agents providing automated services can be enhanced by providing efficient means by which users can directly invoke or terminate the automated services.

(7) **Minimizing the cost of poor guesses about action and timing.** Designs for services and alerts should be undertaken with an eye to *minimizing the cost of poor guesses*, including appropriate timing out and natural gestures for rejecting attempts at service.

(8) **Scoping precision of service to match uncertainty, variation in goals.** We can enhance the value of automation by giving agents the ability to *gracefully degrade* the precision of service to match current uncertainty. A preference for "doing less" but doing it correctly under uncertainty can provide user's with a valuable advance towards a solution and minimize the need for costly undoing or backtracking.

(9) **Providing mechanisms for efficient agent–user collaboration to refine results.** We should design agents with the assumption that users may often wish to complete or refine an analysis provided by an agent.

(10) **Employing socially appropriate behaviors for agent–user interaction.** An agent should be endowed with tasteful default behaviors and courtesies that match *social expectations* for a benevolent assistant.

(11) **Maintaining working memory of recent interactions.** Systems should maintain a memory of recent interactions with users and provide mechanisms that allow users to make efficient and natural references to objects and services included in "shared" short-term experiences.

(12) **Continuing to learn by observing.** Automated services should be endowed with the ability to continue to become better at working with users by continuing to learn about a user's goals and needs.

A TESTBED FOR MIXED-INITIATIVE UI
The LookOut project has focused on investigating issues with overlaying automated scheduling services on Microsoft Outlook, a largely direct-manipulation based messaging and scheduling system. LookOut automation identifies new messages that are opened and brought to focus and attempts to assist users with reviewing their calendar and with composing appointments.

Value-Added Service: Calendaring and Scheduling
When invoked, LookOut parses the text in the body and subject of an email message in focus and attempts to identify a date and time associated with an event implied by the sender. The system then invokes Outlook's calendaring subsystem, brings up the user's online appointment book, and attempts to fill in relevant fields of an appointment record. The system displays its guesses to the user and allows the user to edit its guesses and to save the final result.

LookOut's scheduling analysis centers on a goal-specific parsing of the text contained in the email message that has focus. The system notes when a new message is being read, or when a message comes into focus that has not yet been analyzed. The system first establishes the date a message was sent as an *anchor date* and attempts to normalize its view based on the composition date. For example, if a message was written yesterday and contains text referring to scheduling a meeting for "tomorrow," the system will understand that the message is referring to "today."

If LookOut cannot identify an implied date and time, the system degrades its goal to identifying a span of time that is most relevant given the text of the message (i.e., a specific day, week, or month), and then displays a scoped view of the calendar to the user. The user can directly manipulate the proposed view and, if appropriate, go on to schedule appointments manually.

LookOut has knowledge about typical patterns of expression in email about meetings and times. Beyond understanding the variety of ways that people refer to dates and times, the system understands the temporal implications of suggestions about information in email messages about holding meetings at various times in the future (*e.g.,* "sometime tomorrow," "later in the week," "next week," "within a couple of weeks," "in May," etc.), at prototypical times during the day (*e.g.,* "morning," "afternoon," and "evening"), as well as during typical recurrent events (*e.g.,* "at breakfast," "grab lunch," and "meet for dinner," etc.).

LookOut analysis reduces the number of interactions and complexity of navigation required of the user. Without LookOut, users must navigate to the appropriate graphical button or menu item to open their calendar, search for the appropriate day, input the appropriate times and fill in the subject of the meeting. LookOut performs this operation automatically or via a single interaction, depending on the modality selected. Even when LookOut guesses incorrectly, the user is placed in an approximately correct position in the calendar and can refine an approximate guess about the implied appointment.

Decision Making Under Uncertainty
Users can directly invoke LookOut by clicking on an icon that is always present on the system tray of the Microsoft

Windows shell. However, the system also works to automatically identify a user's goals by considering the content of messages being reviewed. LookOut processes the header, subject, and body of the message and, based on this information, assigns a probability that a user would like to view the calendar or schedule an appointment, by employing a probabilistic classification system that is trained by watching the user working with email. The system makes decisions about appropriate actions as a function of an inferred probability that the user has a goal of performing scheduling and calendaring operations. In particular, the inferred probability that service is desired is used by LookOut to make a decision about whether to apply a second phase of analysis that provides the user with automated calendaring and scheduling.

Depending on the inferred probability—and on an assessment of the expected costs and benefits of action— the system decides to either (1) do nothing but simply wait for continued direct manipulation of Outlook or manual invocation of LookOut, (2) to engage the user in a dialog about his or her intentions with regards to providing a service, or (3) to go ahead and attempts to provide its service by invoking its second phase of analysis.

Multiple Interaction Modalities

LookOut can be configured to be operated in a solely manual modality or can be placed in one of several automated-assistance modalities. In manual operation, the system will only take action if a user clicks on the small LookOut icon appearing in the system. When invoked, LookOut analyzes the email message that has system focus. Users can tell the system to display an alerting symbol (red check mark) on the system-tray icon when LookOut would have taken action if it had been in an automated-assistance modality. By hovering the cursor over the icon on the system tray, a summary of the intended action appears. Figure 1 displays the direct invocation of LookOut. As shown in the figure, a menu with dynamically populated options pops up, letting the user schedule or organize a meeting, or schedule from text on the system clipboard.

When placed in a basic automated-assistance mode, LookOut works by launching and populating fields in Outlook windows. In this mode, the system also employs traditional dialog boxes to request additional information from users when appropriate. LookOut can also operate in a *social-agent modality* projecting an explicit social presence in the form of animated characters, drawn from the MS Agent social user-interface package. When in this mode, the system issues queries to users and announces the results of analyses with an anthropomorphic presence.

When LookOut is in the social-agent modality, it operates in a handsfree manner, establishing an audio channel for interacting with LookOut, further reducing mouse and keyboard interaction with the Outlook system. In the handsfree mode, the system employs a text-to-speech (TTS)

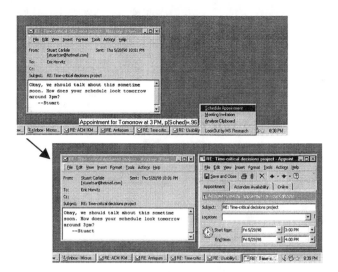

Figure 1. Manual invocation of LookOut. By hovering a cursor over the LookOut icon, a user can examine LookOut's guess. By clicking on the LookOut icon on the system tray, the user invokes the appointment service.

system and automated speech recognition system developed by Microsoft Research to engage users in a natural dialog about their intentions. If LookOut is confident enough in its assessment of a user's goals, a character appears and mentions that it has readied a calendar view to show the user or has created a tentative appointment before displaying the results. At lower levels of confidence, LookOut inquires about a user's interest in either seeing the calendar or scheduling an appointment, depending on the system's analysis of the message being viewed. After asking the user, the system listens for an answer without requiring additional keys or buttons to be pressed.

Figure 2 displays a sequence of screens demonstrating LookOut's operation within the social-agent modality. After a message is analyzed behind the scenes, the system decides it is worthwhile to engage the user in a dialog about creating an appointment. An animated assistant appears and engages the user with speech (a text balloon option is turned on in this case to relay the content of the speech with text). The user can indicate via speech that an appointment is desired with one of several natural acknowledgments, including "yes," "yeah," "sure," "do it." Given a go ahead, LookOut creates an appointment and reviews it with the user with text-to-speech, before evaporating, leaving the result behind for refinement and saving. If the user had expressed disinterest in going ahead with the appointment by simply closing the message or by responding with a variety of natural phrases including "no," "not now," "nah," and "go away," the agent would have immediately nodded to confirm an understanding and disappear.

LookOut dynamically scopes the calendar view to its best guess, given uncertainty or indications about an appropriate view from the message text. For the case captured in Figure 3, LookOut cannot confidently identify a specific time and day. Rather than making a poor guess, LookOut brings up an appropriate week view on the user's calendar.

Handling Invocation Failures

As LookOut is expressly continuing to reason under uncertainty about the value of taking action, or engaging the user in a dialog as messages are opened and closed, the system can make guesses that simply turn out to be wrong. If the LookOut system fails to automatically infer that users wish to see their calendar or schedule an appointment, the system can be directly invoked by clicking on the LookOut icon on the system tray. If LookOut guesses that it is worthwhile to engage the user in a dialog about scheduling but the user is busy or disinterested in interacting with the service, the system will pose a question, wait patiently for a response, and then make a respectful, apologetic gesture and evaporate. The amount of time the system waits before timing out is a function of the inferred probability that a user desires the service. Also, the system increases its dwell on the desktop if it detects signs that the user is thinking, including "hmmm…", "uh…," etc. The design of LookOut's behaviors for handling delays with responses and for reacting to signs that service is being declined was guided by the goal of giving LookOut the sensibility of an intuitive, courteous butler, who might make potentially valuable suggestions from time to time, but who is careful to note when the user is simply too busy to even respond— and to get out of the user's way with minimal disturbance.

INFERRING BELIEFS ABOUT A USER'S GOALS

If we wish to assist users with potentially complex services, it can be valuable to consider how such automation can be provided effectively in light of the uncertainties agents may have about users goals. Thus, developing machinery that endows a system with the ability to explicitly assign likelihoods to different feasible user intentions can be critical in mixed-initiative systems. Such machinery can extend from sets of rules linked to tables of probabilistic information to more complex, real-time inference.

In related work in user modeling, probabilistic models of a user's goals have been employed to continue to perform real-time inference about the probability of alternate feasible goals as a function of observables including the current program context, a user's sequence of actions and choice of words used in a query [4,6]. Some of this work has leveraged recent successes in building and reasoning with Bayesian network models [7,11].

LookOut leverages work in automated text classification for making decisions about actions. Alternate text classification methodologies were explored, including a naïve Bayesian text classifier and text classification based on the Support Vector Machine (SVM) analysis [3]. The current version of LookOut assigns probabilities of user intention by employing an SVM text classification based on an efficient linear SVM approximation method developed by Platt [12]. The method was coupled with a methodology

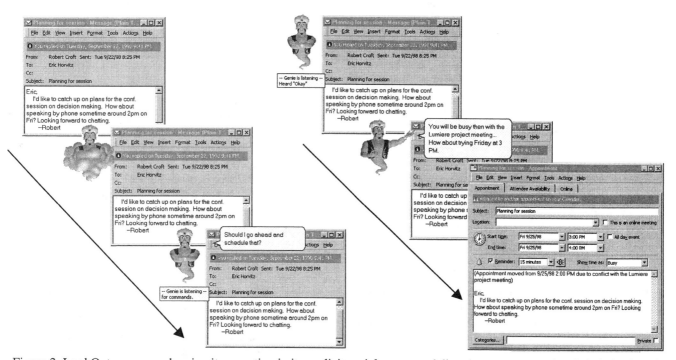

Figure 2. LookOut sequence showing its operation in its explicit social-agent modality. A new message (top left) is analyzed and a decision is made to engage the user in a dialog (left). After receiving confirmation via speech input, the system creates an appointment and presents its guess to the user for refinement (right).

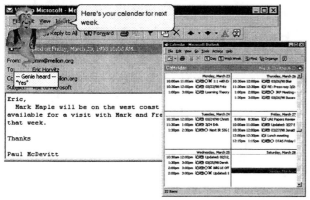

Figure 3. Automated scoping of calendar. If LookOut cannot establish a specific day and time, it attempts to select a most appropriate span of time to display to the user for review or refinement through direct manipulation.

for including custom-tailored, task-specific sets of text features. Rather than employing text classification in the classical manner for tasks such as labeling or categorizing documents, we harness the methods for learning and reasoning about the likelihood of user goals or tasks within a context. For the assumed context of a user reviewing email, we wish to assign a likelihood that an email message that has just received the focus of attention is in the *goal category* of *"User will wish to schedule or review a calendar for this email"* versus the goal category of *"User will not wish to schedule or review a calendar for this email"* based on the content of the messages.

A linear SVM text classifier is built by training the system on a set of messages that are calendar relevant and calendar irrelevant. At runtime, for each email message being reviewed, the linear SVM approximation procedure outputs the likelihood that the user will wish to bring up a calendar or schedule an appointment. The current version of LookOut was trained initially on approximately 1000 messages, divided into 500 messages in the relevant and 500 irrelevant messages.

FROM BELIEFS TO ACTIONS

Given uncertainties about a user's goals, what automated actions should be taken? We shall consider the case of a decision about whether or not to invoke the services performed by an intelligent agent. From the perspective of decision theory, decisions about action versus inaction should be directed by *expected utility*. Autonomous actions should be taken only when an agent believes that they will have greater expected value than inaction for the user,

	Desired Goal	Not Desired
Action	$u(A,G)$	$u(A,\neg G)$
No Action	$u(\neg A,G)$	$u(\neg A,\neg G)$

Table 1. Four outcomes considered in decisions about whether to engage an intelligent agent to provide service.

taking into consideration the costs, benefits, and uncertainties in the user's goals.

Actions, Intentions, and Outcomes

Let us assume an agent has access to inference about the likelihood of a user's goals given observed evidence, written $p(G|E)$. In LookOut, the probability that a user wishes to schedule is computed from evidence in patterns of text contained in a message that has been recently opened or brought to focus.

For decisions about action versus inaction, we must consider four deterministic outcomes: Either the user indeed has the goal being considered or does not have the goal and, for each of these states of user intention, the system either can take an action or not take the action. We map a measure of the value associated with each outcome to a *utility* on a zero to one scale, and define utilities as follows:

- $u(A,G)$: the utility of taking action A when goal G is true

- $u(A,\neg G)$: the utility of taking action A when goal G is not true

- $u(\neg A,G)$: the utility of not taking action A when goal G is true

- $u(\neg A,\neg G)$: the utility of not taking action A when goal G is not true

These outcomes are summarized in Table 1.

The expected utility of taking autonomous action to assist the user with an action given observed evidence, $eu(A|E)$, is computed by combining the utilities of the outcomes for the case where the user desires service and does not desire a service, weighted by the probability of each outcome, as follows:

$$eu(A|E)=p(G|E)u(A,G) + p(\neg G|E) u(A,\neg G) \qquad (1)$$

We can rewrite this equation in terms of $p(G|E)$, by noting that $p(G|E)=1-p(\neg G|E)$. Thus, the expected utility of providing autonomous service is,

$$eu(A|E)=p(G|E)u(A,G) + [1-p(G|E)] u(A,\neg G) \qquad (2)$$

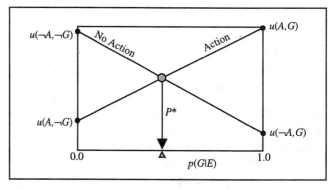

Figure 4. Graphical analysis of the expected utility of action versus inaction, yielding a threshold probability for action.

The expected utility of *not* taking autonomous action to assist the user, $u(\neg A | E)$, is

$$eu(\neg A | E) = p(G|E)u(\neg A, G) + [1 - p(G|E)]u(\neg A, \neg G) \quad (3)$$

We can visualize the implications of these equations by plotting the expected utility as a function of probability. Figure 4 displays a graph where the horizontal represents the probability the user has a goal, ranging from zero to one. The vertical axis indicates the expected value of the system's response. The two outcomes displayed on the right vertical axis have an expected utility associated with $p(G|E)=1.0$—the user indeed having the goal under consideration. The outcomes listed on the left vertical axis indicate the value of the outcomes when $p(G|E)=0$. The expected value of acting for intermediary probabilities of $p(G|E)$, as dictated by Equation 2, is a line joining the two deterministic outcomes associated with taking action. The expected value of not acting as dictated by Equation 3 is a similar line joining the two outcomes associated with inaction.

Expected Utility and Thresholds for Agent Action

The lines representing expected utility cross at a specific inferred probability of the user having a goal. At this threshold probability, referred to as p^*, the expected value of action and inaction are equal. The best decision to make at any value of $p(G|E)$ is the action associated with the greatest expected utility at that likelihood of the user having the goal. By inspecting the graph, it is easy to see that it is best for the system to take action if the probability of a goal is greater than p^* and to refrain from acting if the probability is less than p^*.

The threshold probability can be computed for any four utilities by setting Equations 2 and 3 equal to one another and solving for $p(G|E)$. Given four utilities associated with the four outcomes of interest, a system needs only to check whether the probability of the goal is greater or less than such a threshold probability to decide on whether it is in the best interest of the user to invoke a service.

The threshold probability, p^*, can be influenced by context-dependent changes of the utilities associated with one or more of the outcomes. For example, the utility, $u(A, \neg G)$, associated with the situation where a system takes action when a goal is not desired, can be significantly influenced by the status of a user's attention. The utility of unwanted action can diminish significantly with increases in the depth of a user's focus on another task. Such a reduction in the value of action leads to a higher probability threshold. In contrast, the utility, $u(A, \neg G)$, associated with the situation where a system takes action when a goal is not desired, might be greater when more screen real estate is made available. Increased screen real estate can diminish the perceived cost of the needless operation of a scheduling service that might bring up an appointment that obscures items at a user's focus of attention. As another example of

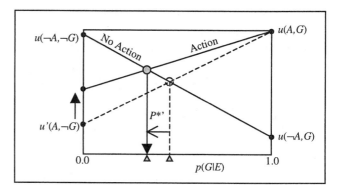

Figure 5. The result of increasing the value of taking erroneous action. Context-dependent shifts in any of the utilities can change the probability threshold for action.

a context-dependent outcome, the utility, $u(\neg A, G)$, representing the situation where a system does not take action when a user indeed has the goal, may decrease as a user becomes more rushed. Diminishing the value of this action reduces the threshold probability for action.

Figure 5 displays geometrically how p^* can change with context. In this case, increasing the utility (decreasing the cost) of outcome $u(A, \neg G)$ of acting when service is not desired leads to a lowering of the threshold probability that must be crossed before action occurs.

Dialog as an Option for Action

Beyond reasoning about whether to act or not to assist a user with an autonomous service, we can also consider the action of asking users about their goals. We can integrate action for dialog into the expected utility framework by considering the expected value of asking the user a question. We now consider the utility of two additional outcomes: the case where an agent initiates dialog about a goal and the user actually desires the goal under consideration, $u(D, G)$, and the case where the user does not have the goal, $u(D, \neg G)$. We compute the expected utility of performing dialog under uncertainty with an equation analogous to Equation 3.

Figure 5 displays a graph with the addition of a line representing the expected utility of engaging in a dialog. As highlighted in the graph, the utility of engaging in a dialog with a user when the user does not have the goal in question is typically greater than the utility of performing an action when the goal is not desired. However, the utility of *asking* a user before performing a desired action is typically smaller than the utility of simply performing a desired action when the user indeed has the goal. In such circumstances, if we follow the rule of selecting the option with the greatest expected utility, we see that action can be guided by two new threshold probabilities: the threshold between inaction and dialog, $p^*_{\neg A, D}$, and the threshold between dialog and action, $p^*_{D, A}$. These two thresholds provide an instant index into whether to act, to engage the

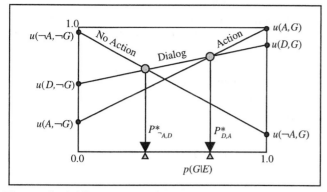

Figure 6. Adding a second action option consisting of dialog with users about their goals. In this case, the graphical analysis highlights the origin of two threshold probabilities for guiding the action of autonomous services.

user in a dialog about action, or to do nothing, depending on the assessed likelihood of the user having a goal.

Systems for guiding autonomous service do not necessarily need to perform explicit computations of expected value. Thresholds can be directly assessed by designers or users. Such directly assessed thresholds for action imply a deeper implicitly assumed expected-utility model.

The LookOut system employs default utilities for guiding dialog and action. However, the system also allows users to specify the utilities for outcomes. Given a set of assessed utilities, the system computes and uses modified threshold probabilities. LookOut also allows users to simply specify two key threshold probabilities for controlling dialog and action. At run time, LookOut considers whether the inferred probability that users desires service is above threshold for dialog or action, versus being consistent with inaction.

USER ATTENTION AND THE TIMING OF SERVICE
Automated activity occurring before a user is ready or open for the service can be distracting. On the other hand, delays in the provision of service can diminish the value of automation. We have found that the value of services and alerts can be enhanced through building and applying models of attention that consider the temporal pattern of a user's focus of attention.

Given the potential value of approaching users with dialog or actions when users are most ready for a service, we performed studies to identify the most appropriate timing of messaging services as a function of the nature of the message being reviewed by the user. We added instrumentation to LookOut to monitor the length of time between the review of messages and the manual invocation of messaging services and collected data from several users with a goal of building a default temporal-centric model of attention. We identified a nonlinear relationship between the size of the message being reviewed and the amount of time users prefer to dwell on the content of the messages before accepting automated calendaring and scheduling operations. We found that the relationship between message

size and the preferred time for deferring offers of service can be approximated by a sigmoid function as represented by the sample data from a user displayed in Figure 7. Continuing studies on timing within the LookOut project are aimed at examining other factors that can explain dwell time including ambiguity and complexity of dates and times mentioned in the message.

In the general case, we can construct a model of attention from such timing studies and make the utility of outcomes time-dependent functions of message length. Alternatively, we can use timing information separately to defer service until a user is likely ready to receive it.

The current version of LookOut employs a predetermined default automated-service timing model based on user studies. However, the system can also be instructed to build a custom-tailored timing model by watching a user interacting with email. The system records the size of each message being reviewed and the amount of time spent on each message before scheduling operations are invoked and stores cases when it is used in a user-directed manner. When the system enters a learning mode, the system performs a regression analysis on the data and fits a piecewise linear model to the data. Alternatively, users can tell the system to delay for a fixed amount of time before the service is invoked.

MACHINERY FOR LIFE-LONG LEARNING
LookOut contains a pretrained probabilistic user model and timing model. However, the system is designed to continue to learn from users. Methods for embedding the capability for life-long learning is a key challenge in Artificial Intelligence research [14]. LookOut continues to store messages as calendar relevant and irrelevant, by watching the user working with email. If a calendar or scheduling facility is invoked within a predetermined time horizon, the system saves the message as schedule-relevant. The system also continues to record the time users dwell on schedule-relevant messages before invoking a calendaring operation.

User can specify a policy for continual learning. Users can dictate a training schedule that guides the learning component of the system periodically to incrementally refine the probabilistic user model and time-based attention model. The ongoing model continues to hone the models used for guessing about the relevance of the automated scheduling services as well as to become a better estimator of the best time to invoke the services.

SUMMARY AND CONCLUSIONS
We reviewed key challenges and opportunities for building *mixed-initiative* user interfaces—interfaces that enable users and intelligent agents to collaborate efficiently. We first presented a set of principles for designing mixed-initiative user interfaces that address systematic problems with the use of agents that may often have to guess about a user's needs. Then, we focused on methods for managing the uncertainties that agents may have about users' goals

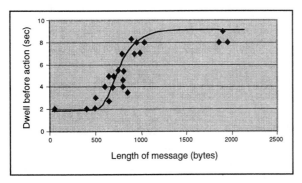

Figure 7. Sigmoid fit on sample of data from a user displaying the relationship between dwell time on schedule-relevant messages and the quantity of text in the message being reviewed.

the uncertainties that agents may have about users' goals and focus of attention. We discussed the consideration of uncertainty, as well as the expected costs and benefits of taking autonomous action in different situations. We highlighted methods and design principles with examples drawn from the LookOut system. Research on LookOut has elucidated difficult challenges and promising opportunities for improving human–computer interaction through the elegant combination of reasoning machinery and direct manipulation. We believe continuing efforts to address problems with the design of mixed-initiative user interfaces will likely yield fundamental enhancements in human–computer interaction.

ACKNOWLEDGMENTS

Andy Jacobs has served as the primary software engineer on the LookOut prototype. John Platt developed the linear SVM text-classification methodology used in the current version of LookOut. Mehran Sahami assisted with the early studies of the use of Bayesian text classification for identifying schedule-relevant messages. Jack Breese, Mary Czerwinski, Susan Dumais, Bill Gates, Ken Hinckley, Jim Kajiya, Dan Ling, and Rick Rashid provided valuable feedback on this research.

REFERENCES

1. Ahlberg, C., and Shneiderman, B. Visual information seeking: Tight coupling of dynamic query filters with starfield displays. *Proceedings of CHI '94 Human Factors in Computing Systems* (April 1994) ACM, 313-317.

2. Birnbaum, L., Horvitz, E., Kurlander, D., Lieberman, H., Marks, J. Roth, S. Compelling Intelligent User Interfaces: How Much AI? In *Proceedings of the 1997 ACM International Conference on Intelligent Interfaces* (Orlando, FL, January 1996).

   http://www.merl.com/reports/TR96-28/index.html

3. Dumais, S. T., Platt, J., Heckerman, D., and Sahami, M., Inductive learning algorithms and representations for text categorization. *Proceedings of CIKM98.* (Bethesda MD, November 1998). ACM Press, 148-155

4. Heckerman, D., and Horvitz, E. Inferring Informational Goals from Free-Text Queries: A Bayesian Approach, *Fourteenth Conference on Uncertainty in Artificial Intelligence* (Madison WI, July 1998), Morgan Kaufmann Publishers, 230-237.

   http://research.microsoft.com/~horvitz/aw.htm

5. Horvitz, E., and Barry, M. Display of Information for Time-Critical Decision Making. *Proceedings of the Eleventh Conference on Uncertainty in Artificial Intelligence* (Montreal, August 1995). Morgan Kaufmann Publishers, 296-305.

   http://research.microsoft.com/~horvitz/vista.htm

6. Horvitz, E., Breese, J., Heckerman, D., Hovel, D., Rommelse, D. The Lumiere Project: Bayesian User Modeling for Inferring the Goals and Needs of Software Users, *Fourteenth Conference on Uncertainty in Artificial Intelligence* (Madison WI, July 1998). Morgan Kaufmann Publishers, 256-265.

   http://research.microsoft.com/~horvitz/lumiere.htm

7. Horvitz, E.J., Breese, J., and Henrion, M. Decision theory in Expert Systems and Artificial Intelligence. *International Journal of Approximate Reasoning*, Special Issue on Uncertainty in Artificial Intelligence, 2:247-30.

   http://research.microsoft.com/~horvitz/dt.htm

8. Lieberman, H., Letizia: An Agent That Assists Web Browsing, *International Joint Conference on Artificial Intelligence* (Montreal, August 1995). IJCAI.

9. Maes, P. Agents that Reduce Work and Information Overload. *Commun. ACM* 37,7, 31-40

10. Maes, P., and Shneiderman, B., Direct Manipulation vs. Interface Agents: A Debate. *Interactions*, Vol. IV Number 6, ACM Press, 1997.

11. Pearl, J. *Probabilistic Reasoning in Intelligent Systems: Networks of Plausible Inference*, Morgan Kaufmann Publishers: San Francisco, 1991.

12. Platt, J. Fast training of SVMs using sequential minimal optimization. To appear in: B. Scholkopf, C. Burges, and A. Smola (Eds.) *Advances in Kernel Methods – Support Vector Learning*, MIT Press, 1999.

13. Schneiderman, B. *Designing the User Interface: Strategies for Effective Human-Computer Interaction*, ACM Press. 1992.

14. Selman, B. Brooks, R.A., Dean, T., Horvitz, E., M. Mitchell, T., Nilsson, N.J. Challenge Problems for Artificial Intelligence, In: *Proceedings of AAAI-96, Thirteenth National Conference on Artificial Intelligence* (Portland, OR, August 1996). AAAI Press, 1340-1345.

An Exploration into Supporting Artwork Orientation in the User Interface

George W. Fitzmaurice, Ravin Balakrishnan, Gordon Kurtenbach, Bill Buxton

Alias|wavefront

210 King Street East

Toronto, Canada, M5A 1J7

<gf, ravin, gordo, buxton>@aw.sgi.com

+1 416 362-9181

ABSTRACT

Rotating a piece of paper while drawing is an integral and almost subconscious part of drawing with pencil and paper. In a similar manner, the advent of lightweight pen-based computers allow digital artwork to be rotated while drawing by rotating the entire computer. Given this type of manipulation we explore the implications for the user interface to support artwork orientation. First we describe an exploratory study to further motivate our work and characterize how artwork is manipulated while drawing. After presenting some possible UI approaches to support artwork orientation, we define a new solution called a *rotating user interface* (RUIs). We then discuss design issues and requirements for RUIs based on our exploratory study.

KEYWORDS: rotating user interfaces, RUI, pen-based computers, GUI toolkits, tablets, LCDs, two-handed input.

INTRODUCTION

The human act of drawing or sketching is a rich technique for entering data into a computer. The notion of sketching as a means of computer input has been around as early as 1945 [4] and 1960 [14]. As display and input technologies evolve systems can be created which approach the quality and style of sketching on paper. Computers have become very adept at emulating the myriad of non-computer drawing effects and properties. For example, displays can show millions of colors and draw at high resolutions, computer "paint brushes" can simulate lead pencils, ink pens, oil brushes, air brushes. Flat panel display technologies are allowing displays to be placed flat on the desk or held in the hand. Input technologies also emulate traditional art tools. For example, computer pens can be made in the same shape as pens, pencils, or brushes and operated without batteries or a tether cord. Finally, the combination of these technologies makes it possible to produce a computer display input system which functions like a drawing tablet where one can draw directly on the display [16].

This combination of display and input surface is extremely appealing to traditional artists. First, up until recently, computer drawing was generally performed by having an input tablet which was separate from the display surface. The displacement of the display and drawing surface produces an eye-to-hand coordination problem (although highly experi-

enced tablet and display users report that this problem can be overcome with experience). However, the problem nonetheless causes many traditional artists to avoid computer drawing. Also, for an artist switching between paper drawing and computer drawing the displacement may be irritating.

Another appealing aspect of combined display and input surfaces is that they approach the form factor of paper and are graspable user interfaces [7]. Because of this, these systems can be manipulated very much like a piece of paper: the drawer can rotate and move the system to either make themselves more comfortable or to facilitate certain kinds of drawing strokes. One need only attempt to draw a cross-hatch pattern on a small piece of paper to realize that moving and rotating the piece of paper can be an integral and almost subconscious act of drawing.

When artists work at a desk, they rotate their drawing paper while the desk top remains fixed. This arrangement has been embodied in a specialized desk called an "animator's turntable" which is the inspiration for our work. Figure 1 shows such a turntable used by an animator for creating drawings for cel based animation. The artwork which is positioned on the turntable in the center of the desk can be rotated while the "UI" (the pencil tray, desktop, etc.) remains fixed.

This type of manipulation gives rise to the following question: if the display and input surface can be rotated, does the user interface need to adapt to the rotation?

Figure 1: Animator's turntable.

In this paper we present a study of the characteristics of how artwork is manipulated while drawing and discuss how these characteristics place new requirements on the user interface. While we propose a variety of solutions to facilitate artwork orientation, we mainly focus on introducing the concept of a *rotating user interface* and associated design issues.

EXPLORATORY STUDY

In order to gain insight into how and why artists rotate and manipulate their drawing surface while they work, we conducted an exploratory study. The inspiration for this study is based partially on Guiard's [8] study on paper orientation and translation for handwriting tasks and builds upon Hinckley's circle sketching study [9].

Why Rotate?

Based on traditional practices of artists and the literature, we expected to observe some amount of rotation. First, studies have been conducted on characterizing stroke orientation during simple drawing tasks and found that subjects operate within an articulation comfort range [13, 15]. These ranges are consistent when we examine the bio-mechanics of the fingers, wrist, and arm. Secondly, there are perceptual issues to be factored into the drawing process. Rotating the artwork may facilitate a drawing task simply by preventing the hand from obscuring a key area of the drawing. Finally, traditional artists working outside the computer medium are trained to factor into the drawing process the characteristics of the raw materials being used. For example, oil paint or ink will smear if an artist is not careful. Thus, the motor skills, perceptual issues, and artist's traditional practices will likely influence computer mediated drawing processes.

Description of Study

The exploratory study consisted of 3 main drawing configurations with 5 representative tasks.

Conditions: Paper, Tablet and 6D

The first condition, *Paper*, had artists draw on a piece of paper with a mechanical pencil on a tabletop (Figure 2a). Fixed on the tabletop was a large piece of white paper. Carbon paper was laid on top of this white paper, and tissue paper laid on the carbon paper. Artists drew on a smaller piece of paper which they could freely move on top of this three layered work surface. This setup allowed us to capture the stroke patterns based on a fixed "user" orientation relative to the table (from the marks on the large white paper under the carbon paper). The paper condition served as a reference condition involving no computer technology to capture traditional drawing patterns.

The second condition, *Tablet*, required artists to draw on a tethered Wacom digitizing tablet [16] measuring 9.5 by 13 inches. This condition roughly reflects the computer configuration of a portable, combined display and digitizer surface (Figure 2b). The stylus was a mechanical pencil with an embedded Wacom stylus sensor. A 6 degree of freedom sensor (the Bird [1]) was attached to the top left corner of the tablet. Paper was affixed to the active digitizing surface (6.5 by 8.5 inches). Artists were instructed to use the tablet on the tabletop. This configuration allowed us to track both the orientation and translational manipulations of the tablet as well as track all pencil strokes.

The third condition, *6D*, was the same as the *Tablet* condition except that artists were not allowed to use the tabletop. Instead they started the task with the tablet in their lap and could move the tablet in 3D space (Figure 2c).

The rationale for these three conditions was to see if the cord on the tablet and the weight/form-factor of the tablet had any impact on subjects drawing styles and manipulation of the drawing surface.

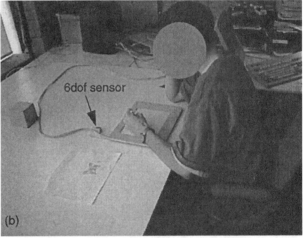

Figure 2: Three drawing conditions: (a) *Paper*, (b) *Tablet* and (c) *6D* conditions.

Tasks

A total of five representative pencil tasks were defined (Figure 3). Two were handwriting tasks, three were drawing tasks. The first task, *Text*, asked subject to transcribe a text passage onto a sheet of 8x11 inch college ruled paper. Subjects were asked to "double-space" their handwriting to fill their page quickly. The second task, *Label*, required subjects to transcribe labels from a master graphical template onto an empty graphical template in a variety of orientations. The task was designed to encourage a great deal of rotation. The third and fourth task, *Ship* and *Butterfly*, asked subjects to reproduce the provided line drawings of a ship and butterfly respectively. The fifth task, *Freeform*, asked subjects to sketch their favorite drawing in under 5 minutes.

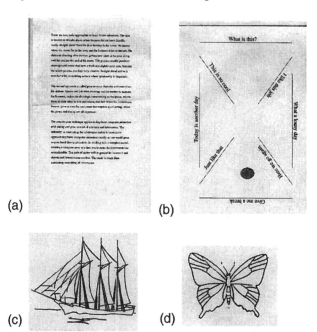

Figure 3: Pencil tasks consisting of (a) *Text*, (b) *Label*, (c) *Ship*, and (d) *Butterfly*.

All tasks were designed to take no more than five minutes to complete. Artists were told they could move and rotate the paper/tablet throughout the task.

Note that for all conditions and tasks, artists used the same mechanical pencil with integrated Wacom stylus sensor. Artists sat in a non-rotating seat to preserve their orientation relative to the drawing table. Subjects were video recorded throughout the exploratory studies.

A total of six artists participated in our exploratory study. Four were right handed, and two were left handed. They performed the five pencil tasks for all three equipment conditions. To reduce transfer effects, the conditions were presented to subjects in a completely counterbalanced order. Within each condition, the order of presentation of each task was randomized. In summary, each subject performed a total of fifteen pencil tasks taking a total of approximately ninety minutes. To minimize fatigue, subjects took short breaks between each task.

Results

As this was a holistic exploratory study, we were mainly interested in observing general patterns of behavior instead of measuring performance with rigorous metrics (e.g., speed and accuracy). Although we did record task completion times, the large individual differences in drawing style and ability we observed amongst the subjects precludes any meaningful conclusions being drawn from this timing data.

We now present separate analyses for the *Text*, *Label*, and three drawing tasks. Due to apparent large individual differences, we present views of the data for individual subjects rather than summarizing across all subjects. We then discuss the issues pertaining to the effects of the three conditions (*Paper*, *Tablet*, and *6D*). Due to the difficulty in extracting data via videotape analysis, we only present detailed data for the *Paper* condition for the *Label* task.

Text Task

As shown in Figure 4, subjects demonstrated two main styles of articulation in the *Text* transcription task. In the first style (Figure 4a,b), subjects first oriented the paper to their preferred orientation and subsequently kept adjusting the paper with their non-dominant hand. As such, the effective working area was limited to a small band of writing (Figure 4b). This result replicates Guiard's [2, 8] observations of people's writing behavior.

Relative to Paper   **Relative to Table**

Figure 4: Sample results of exploratory study in the *Paper* condition with the *Text* task. The left column, figures (a) and (c), show the results of the text transcription output of 2 subjects. The right column, figures (b) and (d), shows the results relative to the physical table. This was captured using carbon paper as described in the "Description of Study" section of this paper.

In the second style (Figure 4c,d), subjects only oriented the paper to their preferred orientation. Unlike the first style, they did not make substantial adjustments. As a result, they used a much larger work space. We hypothesize that this behavior is due to the nature of the transcription task which sometimes caused subjects to use the index finger of their non-dominant hand to keep their place in the source text. Their non-dominant hand is thus not available to easily reposition the writing paper.

Label Task

This task was included in our study as a "control" condition. Essentially, we wanted to observe subjects behavior when presented with a task that would be relatively hard to perform without rotating the paper (e.g., it is practically impossible to write text upside down). However, this is not a completely contrived task: architectural and engineering drawings often require that text be written at varying orientations on the page.

This is the only task where we present detailed analysis for the *Paper* condition. This data was derived from manual analysis of videotapes of the study.

As expected, we found that most subjects rotated the drawing surface to at least eight orientations (Figure 5). This corresponded to the need to write text in the required eight orientations (Figure 3b). The only anomaly was subject S5 who only made four major rotations in the *Paper* condition, but, like the other subjects, made multiple rotations in the *Tablet* and *6D* conditions. We also note that the amount of time spent at each orientation is about equal and that the rotations are well distributed across the full 360 degree range of possible rotations.

The Three Drawing Tasks

As with the *Text* task, subjects exhibited a range of drawing behaviors in the three drawing tasks. We showcase three common styles in Figure 6 within the *Ship* drawing task in the *Paper* condition. Similar behavior was observed in the *Butterfly* and *Freeform* tasks. In the first style (Figure 6a,b), subjects oriented the drawing surface to their preferred orientation and then kept it fixed for the duration of the task.

In the second style (Figure 6c,d), subjects oriented the drawing surface to their preferred orientation, and subsequently made a small number of adjustments to the orientation and position of the drawing surface.

In the third style (Figure 6e,f), subjects made numerous adjustments to the orientation and position of the drawing surface throughout the duration of the task.

We note that only one subject (S1, and also a subject in an earlier pilot study) exhibited the third style (Figure 8). Given that this subject and the pilot subject are professional artists who work under serious time constraints on a daily basis and are perhaps trying to optimize for speed, whereas the other subjects were art school students who may have deemphasized speed, we hypothesize that the amount of rotation may be coupled to the speed of drawing. However, we need more data to definitely confirm this.

Detailed analyses of the magnitude and duration of rotation for the *Tablet* conditions are shown in Figure 8. This data illustrates our earlier observation of three main styles of drawing. We also computed the number of major rotations

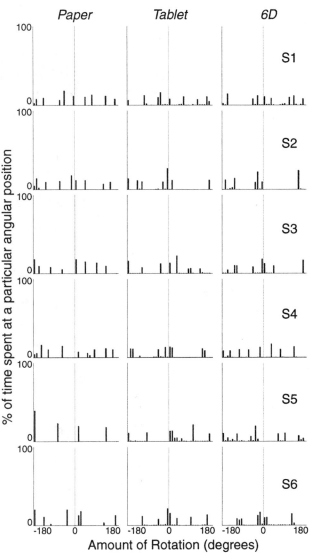

Figure 5: Graphs showing the percentage of time spent by each subject at particular angular positions for the *Label* task in the *Paper*, *Tablet*, and *6D* conditions. The faint dotted line in the centre of each graph denotes the "zero" position, where the drawing surface was perpendicular to the subject's body. Negative angles indicate counterclockwise rotation, positive angles indicate clockwise rotation. The angle of rotation is measured about the axis perpendicular to the drawing surface, and is summarized in increments of 10 degrees.

performed by each subject in each task. This number is usually larger than the number of orientations used, which indicates that subjects rotate back and forth between a few primary orientations. Analysis for the *6D* conditions shows similar results.

Differences Between Paper, Tablet, and 6D

In designing this study, we included three conditions to see if the cord on the tablet, and the weight/form-factor of the tablet had any impact on subject's drawing styles and manipulation of the drawing surface. Aside from the few anomalies discussed previously, the only major difference

Relative to Paper   **Relative to Table**

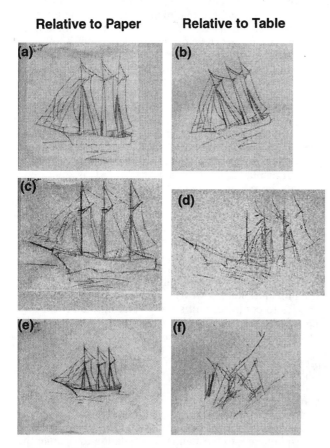

Figure 6. Sample results of exploratory study in the *Paper* condition with the *Ship* drawing task. The left column shows the results of the drawing of 3 subjects. The right column shows the respective results relative to the table. This was captured using carbon paper as described in the "Description of Study" section of this paper.

we observed was between the *Paper* and *Tablet/6D* conditions for the *Label* task. As shown in Figure 7, in the *Paper* condition some subjects performed a series of rotations all in the same direction. We refer to this as the "corkscrew" effect. This "corkscrew" behavior was not observed in the *Tablet/6D* condition. We believe that the cord on the tablet inhibited this behavior. However, subjects did not complain about this issue and the task completion time for all three conditions were similar – indicating that while different styles of rotation were employed, one was not dramatically better than the other. Also, this effect was not apparent in the *Text* and the three drawing tasks.

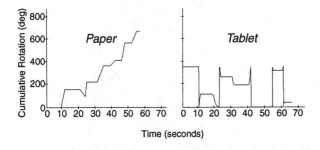

Figure 7: Progression of rotation for the duration of the *Label* task for Subject #6 in the *Paper* and *Tablet* conditions.

Subjects did not mention, nor did we expect or observe, any adverse effects attributable to the weight/form-factor of the tablet. This could be due to the fact that tablet used was lightweight (< 1 pound) and fairly thin (< 0.5 inch).

Discussion

While we observed the need for artwork rotation, we can speculate on reasons for not rotating while drawing. If an artist is using another image as a guide to drawing, they may want to keep both images at the same orientation. Rotating the drawing makes it more difficult to copy a non-rotated source image. This "alignment" may be critical when initially copying the basic shape and proportions of

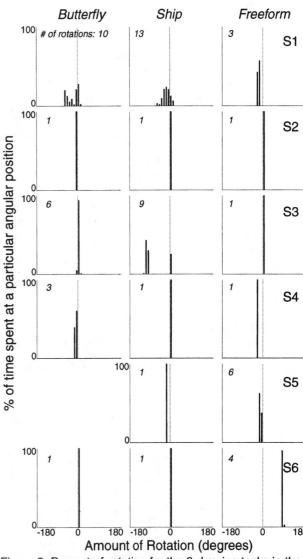

Figure 8: Percent of rotation for the 3 drawing tasks in the *Tablet* condition. The faint dotted line in the centre of each graph denotes the "zero" position, where the drawing surface was perpendicular to the subject's body. Negative angles indicate counterclockwise rotation, positive angles indicate clockwise rotation. Note that the number of rotations may not be equivalent to the number of bars in the corresponding graph since back and forth rotations between two or more positions would result in a small number of bars but a large number of rotations. Subject #5's *Butterfly* task data was lost due to a technical problem.

an image. Alignment may not be so critical later when shading the drawing. Indeed, our study provided some observations of subjects "aligning" the source image with their drawing. The subject in Figure 2c exhibits this behavior.

Another reason for not rotating is the ability to rotate or adjust one's body rather than rotating the artwork. We observed some subjects turning themselves at an angle to the artwork rather than rotating the artwork. Similarly, if artwork has been rotated to an angle to facilitate physical comfort or drawing in a particular direction, the artist doesn't necessarily have to rotate the artwork back to a normal orientation to evaluate it. The artist can align their head or body with the artwork or not move at all if the angle of rotation is not significant enough to hinder perception of the drawing.

An artist's skill level may also play a factor in rotation. As mentioned earlier, we observed that one subject (S1) who is a professional artist rotated more than the other subjects and was faster and more relaxed. We made a similar observation with a pilot subject who was also a professional artist. Our non-professional artists appeared to be a bit intimidated by our study paraphernalia (drawing on the Wacom tablet/sensor combination, being recorded by an overhead video camera). We suspect than this nervousness might have affected their drawing behavior. We don't have enough data to make any solid conclusions, but we are interested in pursuing this issue.

SUPPORTING ARTWORK ORIENTATION

Given our exploratory study where we were able to characterize manipulation behavior for drawing tasks, we now consider possible solutions for supporting artwork orientation in the user interface. The primary issue is how do we present, manage, and preserve UI operability while the interface changes orientation.

Imagine using an interactive drawing surface where the traditional GUI user interface is rotated 90 degrees. The menus don't pop-down, they pop sideways, and the text is vertical (e.g., Figure 9a,b). There are similar problems with most GUI elements. We now present a few UI solutions to facilitate artwork orientation.

Separate displays. One option is to provide multiple displays to the user where one display contains the artwork and a second contains the UI controls. In this configuration, the artwork canvas can be oriented independently from the UI controls. This, however, results in larger workspaces and perhaps a bit more clutter. It also results in divided attention issues where the eye and hand must move back and forth from the control display to the artwork display. Also, this approach eliminates the capacity for context-sensitive UIs such as marking menus[10], tool glass and magic lenses[3].

Software canvas rotation. An alternate solution is to allow the artwork canvas to be rotated via the software while the physical display and UI remain fixed [6]. This solution is used in a few commercially available packages but there are several problems with this approach. First, rotating the artwork is generally a computationally intensive task that often introduces annoying delays while drawing. Second, for artwork consisting of rasters of pixels, the aliasing that results when rotating a raster of pixels by anything other than increments of 90 degrees can be annoying. Advances in graphics hardware and texture memory have largely alleviated this problem, however, it is still hard for these technologies to compete with simply rotating the artwork by rotating the display. Thirdly, given that the canvas is the same size as the display, the software rotation will clip portions of the canvas depending on the orientation. Thus, this approach potentially suffers from a great deal of wasted display space.

Do nothing. This sounds like a silly and unfriendly solution but doing nothing is very easy to implement. The idea is that the user will adapt to slight orientation offsets or rotate the display back to the standard orientation to operate the UI controls. We believe this solution will hinder professional artists who want to actively orient their drawing canvas as they draw as well as efficiently issue UI commands.

Rotating User Interface. There may be a need for a UI which is "self righting", or rather, maintains its orientation relative to the user. This is a new approach which we are calling "rotating user interfaces" (RUIs). We now discuss this solution in detail along with design issues.

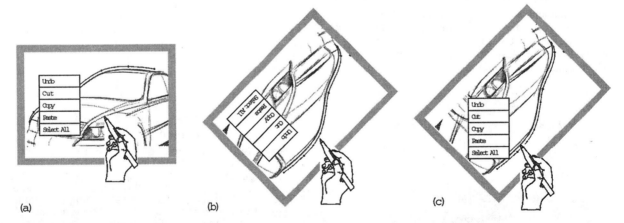

Figure 9: The concept of a rotating UI. a) shows a pen-based computer at normal orientation. Rotating the artwork (b) may give a drawing advantage but the UI becomes hard to use. (c) shows how rotating the UI relative to the user solves the problem.

ROTATING USER INTERFACES

We define a rotating user interface as a system where the display rotates around an axis perpendicular to the center of the display. However, the UI remains fixed relative to the user while the artwork rotates. Note that this requires a system where the display can sense its rotation and display the UI so that it remains fixed relative to the user (Figure 9).

RUIs can be discrete or continuous. Discrete RUIs allow the UI to be rotated in discrete steps, typically 0 and 90 degrees. For example, the PenPoint [5] user interface could be rotated 0 degrees for a portrait display orientation or 90 degrees for landscape orientation (however, in this case the artwork also rotates so it is not a RUI by our definition).

Design Issues for Rotating UIs

Given this simple definition, we have discovered numerous design issues concerning RUIs. One issue is with the rotation sensitive UI components. Some common UI widgets maintain their usability despite severe rotation. We call this property "rotation insensitive." In contrast, some UI widgets are "rotation sensitive" and are severely compromised by rotation. Figure 10 shows examples of both types. A set of color palettes are rotation insensitive. Rotation sensitive widgets are those widgets whose graphics or interaction have some sense of orientation. For example, text and some icon legibility are severely affected by rotation. Other examples are widgets which are directional (e.g., a horizontal slider that is labeled "left" and "right"). Input to a widget can be sensitive to orientation as well. This generally occurs when a widget has no visuals to indicate orientation. For example, marking menus [10] use directional strokes to select menu items from a radial menu without displaying the menu. This runs into problems when the display is rotated. For example, an "up stroke" will select a different item depending on the orientation of the display. Similar problems can occur in UIs that recognize handwriting or gestures.

There are several temporal issues concerning widget rotation. Pop-up UI widgets may be more suitable to RUIs than static widgets. For example, as shown in Figure 9, a pop-up menu need only reorient itself to the current rotation when it is popped up. However, a static widget may have to update itself constantly as the display is being rotated. This may produce annoying flashing or slow system perfor-

mance. This problem could possibility be controlled by delaying the reorientation of the static graphics until the user stops rotating. However, this solution may still produce performance delays when the user stops rotating. Note that pop-up widgets may have to address the issues of interactive rotation as well if the display is rotated while the widget is popped up. However, a reasonable simplifying assumption might be that a user will not significantly rotate the display while interacting with a temporary pop-up widget. This assumption requires further investigation.

All of these issues indicate a RUI, at best, would have to support arbitrary rotation of standard GUI widgets. This is extremely problematic because standard GUI toolkits do not support arbitrary rotation transformations of their primitive objects or input events. For example, primitive graphics like text fonts and rectangles are assumed to be non-rotatable. However, 3D graphics toolkits like OpenGL [12] are capable of arbitrary orientation of primitives and could be used as the basis for a RUI toolkit. The research prototype T3 [11] is a UI that is based entirely on transformational 3D graphics primitives and therefore can very easily be adapted to a RUI system.

In addition to being able to rotate graphics primitives, widget layout routines may have to be more sophisticated. Figure 11 shows a case where, when the display is rotated, the widgets cannot just simply rotate but need to reformat themselves to suit the angle of the rectangular display. This will be especially true for GUI designs that use widgets along the perimeter of the display, such as menubars and toolbars. This is yet another issue for a RUI toolkit to address. One possible solution is to design better layout algorithms. Another, perhaps simpler, solution would be only to use widgets which don't track the perimeter of the display (e.g., pop-up menus). These issues require further investigation.

Also, the technology for sensing the rotation of the display/input system needs to be developed. Current solutions usually require a reference point [1], or complicated mechanical contraptions. Furthermore, this orientation information needs to be fed to the RUI toolkit.

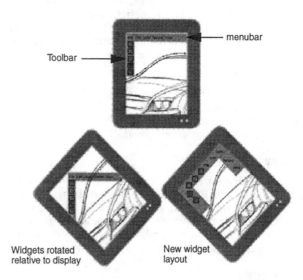

Figure 11. Not only do UI graphics have to be able to draw at arbitrary orientations in a RUI, perimeter widgets like menubars and toolbars may have to adopt different layout schemes depending on the rotation.

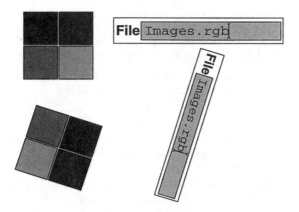

Figure 10. Some widgets are rotation insensitive while others are not. The color pallet on the left is still usable despite the severe rotation. The file name text prompt on the right however becomes very difficult to use at the similar rotation.

Finally, viewing angle of the display can also be an important issue for RUI systems. Image quality on most flat panel displays (e.g., LCD or TFT displays) changes depending on the user's viewpoint. Thus, a rotatable display would have to be of a type that does not suffer from severe image degradation when rotated.

CONCLUSIONS

Lightweight, flat displays are inevitable and this relatively new form factor places new requirements on traditional GUI designs. Moreover, the combined display and digitizer tablets will place additional demands on the UI as this configuration will be used like paper due to its affordances. The goal of this research is to anticipate future UI needs and identify related design issues as early as possible given these new input and output configurations.

We knew a priori from everyday experience and the "animator's turntable" (Figure 1), that rotating the artwork while drawing is important. Before embarking on designing a user interface for such rotatable displays, we thought it was important to understand the nature and the way in which the artwork is rotated when drawing. We conducted an exploratory study to investigate the range of behaviors inherent in drawing tasks.

Our study showed a wide range of individual differences when performing typical drawing tasks. However, three general behaviors emerged. In one case, the artwork is oriented once to a comfortable position and subsequently kept static for the duration of the drawing. In the second case, the artwork is oriented once initially, and a small number of adjustments are made while drawing. In the third case, the artwork is adjusted numerous times while drawing.

These general findings indicate the need for freely rotatable drawing surfaces (not ones that have discrete steps such as 45 or 90 degrees). Given the range of rotation sometimes performed by users, a rotation sensitive user interface (RUI) will likely be necessary.

Our work has unearthed the design issue that currently available GUI toolkits are unsuitable, nor can they be easily modified, to support RUIs. We believe a better approach would be to develop a new user interface paradigm and toolkit that supports rotation in its core architecture. This is clearly a challenging user interface toolkit research problem.

Even if we do not consider systems explicitly designed to support the rotation of artwork, the issues presented in this paper have implications for the broader field of mobile, pen-based, and slate computer systems.

ACKNOWLEDGEMENTS

The original idea for RUIs as embodied in this work came from Jeff Bell and Bill Buxton. We also thank Russell Owen, Thomas Baudel and Yves Guiard for their invaluable comments and assistance, and all the participants in our user study. This work was done under the auspices of the User Interface Research Group at Alias|wavefront.

REFERENCES

1. Ascension Technology, Inc. The Flock of Birds - Position and Orientation Measurement System. URL: www.ascension-tech.com

2. Athenes, S., "Contribution de la main droite a l'acte graphique chez le scripteur gaucher adulte: une comparaison entre postures 'inversee' et 'non-inversee" (*Contribution of the right hand in handwriting for left-handed adults: a comparison of the 'inverted' and 'non-inverted' postures*). Universite de Provence, France. Yves Guiard, thesis advisor, June 1983.

3. Bier, E.A., Stone, M.C., Fishkin, K., Buxton, W. and Baudel, T. (1994). A Taxonomy of See-Through Tools. *Proceedings of ACM CHI'94 Conference on Human Factors in Computing Systems*, 358-364.

4. Bush, V. (1945) As We May Think. *Atlantic Monthly*, July, 1945. 101-108.

5. Carr, R., and Shafer, D. The Power of Penpoint. Reading, MA. Addison-Wesley, 1991.

6. Fekete, J., Bizouarn, E., Cournarie, E., Galas, T., and Taillefer, F. (1995) TicTacToon: A Paperless System for Professional 2D Animation. *Proceedings of the ACM SIGGRAPH '95*, 79-89.

7. Fitzmaurice, G., Ishii, H., and Buxton, W. (1995). Bricks: Laying the Foundations for Graspable User Interfaces. *Proceedings of the ACM CHI'95 Conference on Human Factors in Computing Systems*, 442-449.

8. Guiard, Y. (1987). Asymmetric division of labor in human skilled bimanual action: The kinematic chain as a model. *Journal of Motor Behavior, 19,* 486-517.

9. Hinckley, K. (1997). Haptic Issues for Virtual Manipulation. Ph.D. dissertation, University of Virginia, Dept. of Computer Science.

10. Kurtenbach, G., and Buxton, W. (1993). The limits of expert performance using hierarchical marking menus. *Proceedings of CHI '93 Conference on Human Factor in Computing*, 482-48.

11. Kurtenbach, G., Fitzmaurice, G., Baudel, T., and Buxton, W. (1997). The Design of a GUI Paradigm based on Tablets, Two-hands, and Transparency. *Proceedings of the ACM CHI'97 Conference on Human Factors in Computing Systems*, 35-42.

12. Neider, J., Davis, T., and Woo, M. (1993). *OpenGL programming guide*. Addison-Wesley.

13. Rosenbaum, D. A., van Heugten, C. M., and Calwell, G. E. (1996). From cognition to biomechanics and back: The end-state comfort effect and the middle-is-faster effect. *Acta Psychologica, 94,* 59-85.

14. Sutherland, I. E. (1963). Sketchpad: A man-machine graphical communication system. *AFIPS Conference Proceedings, 23,* 329-346.

15. Van Sommers, P. (1984). *Drawing and Cognition: Descriptive and experimental studies of graphic production processes*, Cambridge, England. Cambridge University Press.

16. Wacom Technology Inc., ArtZ II 6X8 tablet. PL-300 display tablet. URL: www.wacom.com.

An Alternative Way of Drawing

Roope Raisamo

Department of Computer Science

University of Tampere

P.O. Box 607 (Kehruukoulunkatu 1)

FIN-33101 Tampere, Finland

rr@cs.uta.fi

ABSTRACT

Current object-oriented drawing programs have an established way of drawing in which the shape of an object is controlled by manipulating control points. While the control points are intuitive in their basic use, it is not clear whether they make more complex drawing tasks manageable for the average user. In this paper we describe an alternative way of drawing and editing a drawing using new direct manipulation tools. Our approach resembles sculpting in two dimensions: the user begins with a large block and uses different tools to give it the desired shape. We also present a user evaluation in which the users could try our new tools and compare them to their previous experience of control points. The users claimed to understand the operations better with our tools than if they had needed to use curves and control points. However, our tools were better suited for sketching the artwork than for making very detailed drawings.

Keywords

Drawing programs, direct manipulation, two-handed interaction, interaction techniques, sculpting

INTRODUCTION

Direct manipulation has widely been accepted as one of the preferred styles of interaction. Drawing programs were among the first applications that made use of direct manipulation, and are strongly based on its principles. Still, many operations that the user carries out using direct manipulation are based on the interaction techniques that were first suggested when the programs were developed [1, 12]. It is not clear whether they are the best in all situations.

We have suggested an alignment tool that is based on direct manipulation and two-handed interaction [15]. The use of this *alignment stick* has been observed to make some alignment tasks more efficient than carrying them out with

the command-based alignment menus and palettes [16]. The users also learned the purpose of the tool quickly and did not have any conceptual problems with it. Here we explore the stick metaphor further by introducing four new tools with which the user can edit drawings and diagrams. We show how the use of these tools allows an alternative way of drawing.

The final implementation of the alignment stick has been used as the base of our new tools, each of which has its own design considerations and problems. All the tools follow the same interaction style; thus learning one helps learning the others. The choice of the new tools was inspired by the tools that craftsmen and sculptors use, namely planes, drills, chisels, scissors, different carving sticks and cutting wire. Using these tools is like working on wood, shale or other raw material and combining several tools to make the final artwork. There are some volume sculpting systems that are based on a similar kind of metaphors [7, 21], but these systems are used for 3D modeling. Our system was independently developed for 2D drawing in which the sculpting metaphor has not been studied before.

This paper is organized as follows. First, we will present the previous work in the area. After that we briefly describe the alignment stick and explain the current state of its design and functionality. Next we describe the new tools that we have developed together with some implementation details, and show an example of their use. This is followed by a brief user evaluation and discussion of the suggested interaction style. We conclude with suggestions for developing this interaction style further.

BACKGROUND

The way the user draws a picture is almost identical in all current drawing programs. First he or she selects a drawing tool, then uses the tool to draw a number of objects and starts manipulating them. This process can be repeated many times and may require the use of many different drawing tools. The objects can be modified by manipulating so-called "control points" that act as handles and are normally placed at the corners of an object. With the standard shapes, for example rectangles and ellipses, this procedure is clearly based on direct manipulation. It is also easy to understand when drawing rectangles and polygons. Drawing an ellipse may be a little more difficult to grasp, but real problems arise when the shape should be extensively reshaped. Then we usually have to deal with some sort of splines [6, 9, 14, 19, 20] and their control points.

Splines and related curves are mathematically manageable and well suited for free-form drawings. There are many kinds of splines that allow different kind of drawings to be constructed. Although most of the spline types are equivalent in theory, their individual properties suggest that different input strategies depend on the underlying mathematics, and thus the possible results and the user interfaces differ from each other [2]. In the basic case the control points are not within the curve being manipulated, but somewhere near it. For most ordinary users the result that they get by adjusting these points is not clear at all, as indicated in [3, 6, 9, 14, 20]. In order to understand the behavior they should know how the underlying mathematical model behaves. This is clearly something that we can't expect from an average user. The design is more focused on technology than users' needs.

Naturally this problem has been observed repeatedly and the computer graphics community has developed various solutions to the problem. Hsu *et al.* [10] present a direct manipulation technique that lets the user manipulate the object directly. Any part of the object can be adjusted using a cursor, and the system calculates the necessary alterations to the control points. This is a simple example of abstracting the control points so that the user need not manipulate them directly. Many researchers have accomplished the same goal by adding physical effects to the interface [14, 19, 20] or letting the user change geometric properties rather than just control points [6]. Another line of research is based on developing geometric representations of modeling operators, as in [8, 18].

The common object-oriented way of drawing resembles drawing on paper, but the metaphor breaks when the user is allowed to select the objects and alter their shape, color, size and depth level. The fact that most novice users find a bitmap-based painting program much easier to learn than an object-oriented drawing program shows that the currently chosen interaction style may have some shortcomings. It does not mean that the current style is wrong, but suggests that we should not be content with it and stop exploring other alternatives that might be better in some circumstances.

THE STICK METAPHOR

The *alignment stick*, seen in Figure 1, is based on the stick metaphor. It can be thought of as a ruler or simply as a straight stick that can align objects. It is one example of using the stick metaphor in drawing programs, but there are potentially many more uses for it. In this section we first describe the alignment stick and then generalize the stick metaphor to be used in our new tools.

The Alignment Stick

The alignment stick works as follows. When the stick is pushed, it aligns every unlocked object that it touches. The orientation of the stick can be changed between horizontal, vertical, and free angle stick. Also, the length of the stick can be varied so that the stick does not touch unwanted objects. The stick is implemented as a large mouse cursor, which changes to the normal pointer when moved outside of the drawing area. Further discussion of the functionality included in the stick can be found in [15].

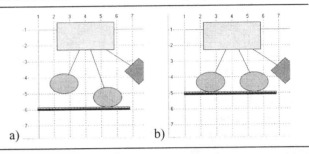

Figure 1: The alignment stick in use: a) The stick is activated and moved upwards. b) The stick is in its intended position aligning the ellipses by their bottom sides.

Normally the stick aligns the objects by their borders. However, it is possible to set so-called *alignment points* for each object, and when they have been set, the alignment is made using these points, not the borders. The most commonly used of these points is the center point that allows carrying out the center alignment in the same way as the border alignment. The points also enable new kinds of alignment operations. For example, the user could align the center point of one object with the right border of another. If several objects are grouped, they behave as one object and have only one set of alignment points for the whole group.

Two methods prevent accidental errors with the stick. First, every stick operation is reversible, following Shneiderman's [17] definition for direct manipulation. An operation is defined so that it begins when the user activates the stick and ends when the user deactivates the stick. Second, objects can be locked, and in the locked state they are not affected by the stick tools. Locking is a property of each object and can be selected from its pop-up menu or by pressing the appropriate button in the toolbar.

Generalizing the stick metaphor

Clearly the only purpose for a real stick is not to align objects. Thus we envision other uses for the stick metaphor. To have the necessary consistence for the user, the different sticks have to be similarly controlled. They also need to have similar undo mechanisms. When we generalize the stick metaphor, we will vary two properties: the visual appearance of the stick, and the effect that the stick has on the objects that it touches. Differences in visual appearance help users recognize the current tool, which is important when there are many sticks in a drawing program. The tools are recognized from their pattern, size and color. In effect, some of the new tools need not be sticks at all. They can be available in different forms to have a broader range of tools.

We have made small changes in the stick controls that were presented in [15]. The assignment of the devices to different tasks was explained in detail there. Figure 2 shows the controls that all of the current stick tools respond to. The stick is moved with the mouse. Rotating the trackball changes the length of the stick. The left button activates the stick and the middle button enables changing the orientation of the stick. If it is clicked, it switches between horizontal and vertical sticks. If it is kept down, the user can rotate the stick to any angle using the trackball. The most important change from the previous implementation is keeping grip of the manipulated objects as long as the left mouse button is pressed, for example, when the stick is used to push objects upwards and then moved downwards.

There are some general issues that need to be addressed when implementing new stick tools. Maybe the most important of them is, what is the extent of the effect of the stick. If an object is only partly touched with the stick, should it be included in the operation completely, partly or not at all? Another general design issue is what happens when the stick is being rotated? It is not clear whether in every case the stick should do something or even what that something is. With the alignment stick the objects are included completely in the operation and they are aligned to the rotated stick but they are not changed in their appearance. We will address these issues when we describe the new tools.

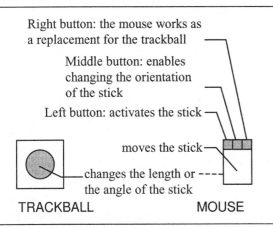

Figure 2: The controls of the stick tools.

THE NEW TOOLS

The new tools that are presented in this section are all based on the same interaction technique that was used in the alignment stick. The way of controlling the tool is the same; the differences are in what the tool does and in the visual appearance of the tool. Next we briefly describe each tool and the specific design problems that are related to it.

The carving stick

The use of the carving stick (Figures 3, 7 and 8) is like sculpting in two dimensions. When the stick is active and touches an object, the portion being touched is removed. This way drawing an object can be started by drawing a large enough rectangle. After that, the carving stick can be used to shape it in any way the user likes. The stick behaves as an efficient plane that can be used to shape the outer boundaries of an object, or as a drill or chisel when it is used to shape the inside of the object.

The carving stick has one obvious design problem: what happens if the user pushes the stick all over the object? Should that object completely disappear or remain on screen in minimal size? The answer is not clear, but we chose to delete the object in this case. Leaving something small on screen would not be consistent with the real world metaphor. For example, in the real world one can use a plane and end up having no object at all, but a pile of chips.

The "chips" are another issue in this tool. If the metaphor were very accurate, we would end up with having a pile of garbage on screen. Fortunately, we can choose not to produce garbage when implementing the sculpting metaphor.

The nature of the carving stick requires that the stick have an effect on only that part of the object that it touches. This is different from the operation of the alignment stick, in which the whole object is affected. Also, the carving stick can be active during rotation. This allows carving round shapes.

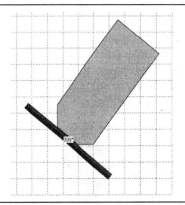

Figure 3: The carving stick in use. The stick is being pushed to northeast direction, and it changes the shape of an initially rectangular object.

The shrinking stick

The shrinking stick (Figure 4) is used to resize the objects that it touches. When the objects are pushed with the stick, they get smaller, but their shape remains the same. This tool replaces the resizing handles that are commonly offered in drawing programs.

The operation of the shrinking stick is not very different from the resizing handles, but allows simultaneous resizing of many objects in many ways. The user can decide which side of the objects will be affected by moving the tool. In a way this is an alternative alignment operation, in which the objects are aligned by adjusting their size, not position.

The shrinking stick shares a problem with the carving stick: what happens if the object is pushed so that it becomes too small and it disappears? The solution here is consistent with the carving stick, so this kind of operation leads to deletion of the object, but this can be cancelled with the undo operation.

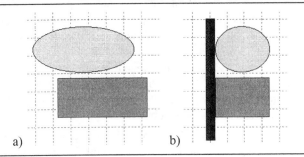

a)   b)

Figure 4: The shrinking stick in use. The stick is used to make the two objects equally wide. Their basic shape and height are preserved.

The cutting stick

The cutting stick (Figures 5 and 9) takes its metaphor from scissors or a knife. When the stick is placed over one or more objects, each object is cut in two pieces along the stick. This operation is clearly something that current drawing programs do not allow, but can prove useful in some cases. For example, if the user wanted to split a complex object in two pieces using current drawing programs, he or she should make a copy of it and try to remove the unwanted parts of both objects in some way. With the cutting stick all that needs to be done is to choose the cutting position and use the left mouse button.

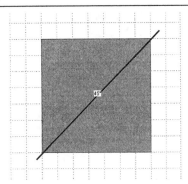

Figure 5: The cutting stick in use. The resulting objects are two triangles.

We decided to choose the take-off strategy (similar to the one used with touchscreens, e.g. [13]) as the signal that the object(s) should be cut. This was because the mouse can move slightly when a button is pressed down, and this way the user can still change his or her mind when the tool has been activated. The final cutting position and direction is selected when the user lifts the left mouse button up. If the operation needs to be cancelled, the user just moves the stick outside of the object before releasing the button. This take-off strategy is motivated by the fact that the cutting stick shares some problems of exact positioning with touchscreen input. If the cutting were made when the button is pushed down, it could result in cutting in the wrong place.

The rotating stick

When the original alignment stick is rotated, the orientation of the objects does not change, but they align to the stick in their original orientations. This decision was motivated by the choice that the alignment stick should not make any changes in the shape or orientation of the objects.

Since the user may still need to rotate some objects to a certain angle, the rotating stick (Figure 6) was developed for this purpose. When the stick touches objects, they align to the stick just like real objects would do if they were pushed with a ruler or another straight object. The rotating stick is another natural application of our stick metaphor, since all of the sticks allow rotation to any angle. This functionality could have been added to the alignment stick, but it would have made it more complicated and thus more difficult to use.

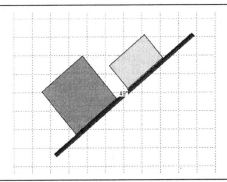

Figure 6: The rotating stick in use. Two rectangles have been rotated 49° from the horizontal level, and they are aligned to the stick.

IMPLEMENTATION

The prototype implementation has been done in the Microsoft Windows environment using C++. The carving and cutting operations are based on the use of regions, free-form objects that are internally composed of a set of rectangles. Regions were good prototyping tools for us since Windows offers operations that, for example, join regions or subtract a region from another. Most common GUI's have similar region structures. Unfortunatrely, the regions are also the reason for the fact that the implementation slows down when there are many complex objects on screen. They are clearly not the optimal implementation for our tools, but still their use helps us in prototyping and testing new ideas. The implementation can be made more efficient by implementing a custom data structure for complex objects and calculating the points at which the stick crosses a boundary of an object instead of the expensive subtract operation between regions.

In detail, the carving operation is done with the regions by taking the initial area of the object and subtracting the stick region from it. Cutting is done by dividing the bounding rectangle of the object in two parts along the stick. Then the new objects are created by subtracting first one and then the other half from the initial object. The Windows API also offers operations for scaling and rotating these complex region objects. These operations enable the use of the shrinking and rotating sticks with region objects. The alignment stick has always been based on regions, so it need not be changed because of the complex region objects.

A DRAWING EXAMPLE

In this section we show an example of how the tools can be used in drawing. This example is aimed at giving a practical demonstration of combining the tools. It is illustrative to try to picture how this example would be done with current drawing tools. Most likely it would take much more time and require many more steps to be certain that the result is exactly what it was meant to be.

In Figure 7, a rectangle has been drawn on screen, and the carving stick has been selected and activated. We want to shape the rectangle so that there is a new edge in the object that is at a 45° angle to the edges that it connects to.

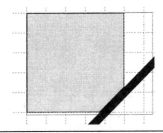

Figure 7: The starting phase in shaping new objects. The carving stick has been activated.

Next we make the object symmetrical so that it has two parallel edges at a 45° angle, while the rest of the edges remain as they were in the initial rectangle. The parallelism is guaranteed by not rotating the stick between the two carving operations. The result is presented in Figure 8, and has been accomplished with just two gestures. The first gesture started in Figure 7 and was extended as far as can be seen in Figure 8. The second gesture is in its final position in Figure 8. Note that the grid is used to accomplish the symmetry.

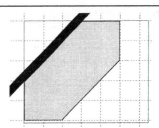

Figure 8: The object is being shaped with the carving stick. In this case, the symmetry is preserved by utilizing the grid.

After the object has been shaped as we wanted, we decide to divide the object in two symmetrical parts. We switch to the cutting stick and use the grid to make the objects of equal size. Figure 9 shows the cutting stick in position just before it is activated.

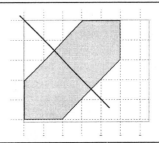

Figure 9: The cutting stick is being used to divide the object in two parts.

Finally, after cutting we have two new objects. In Figure 10 they have been rearranged to make a new type of form in the drawing. The resulting objects can be grouped together to act as one object again. They can also be aligned using the alignment stick or further reshaped with the new tools.

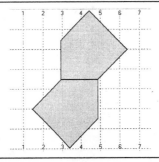

Figure 10: The resulting objects have been rearranged.

The versatility of the new stick tools can be observed in this example. The presented set of operations is not the only one that results in the shape that is presented in Figure 10. One alternative is to shape just one of the objects with the carving tool, make a copy of it, and rotate the copy 180 degrees with the rotating stick. Still another alternative is to use just the carving tool and shape the rectangle to be the form that is composed of the two resulting objects in Figure 10. The shape can then be cut in two objects with the cutting stick. This last alternative is somewhat more complex than the method that was presented in this section. These alternatives illustrate the fact that the user has many parallel alternatives when creating a drawing with the new stick tools.

EVALUATION

We have evaluated the new tools with six users. All of them are experienced in computing, but their knowledge of drawing programs differed from basics to comprehensive, including two pretty confident spline users. One of the users is a sculptor and three of the others consider themselves as artists or talented in drawing. Five of the users use spline or Bezier curves at least occasionally, but only one of them claimed to understand their behavior in all cases. The users had no previous experience in using the stick tools.

The evaluation was qualitative and focused on testing the potential use of our new tools. All trials were videotaped in our usability laboratory and the tapes were analyzed to find out usage patterns and potential problems with the new tools. The evaluation began with a five-minute introduction to the alignment stick, to make the users familiar with the stick controls. This stage was followed by a demonstration of the other new tools. After a short rehearsal the users started to prepare their drawings. The task was to draw whatever they wanted and use only the new stick tools after creating the initial objects. Examples of the drawings can be seen in Figures 11-13. Each evaluation session lasted 45-60 minutes in total. The users could make comments during the drawing and each session concluded with an interview.

The users could use the tools any way they liked. All of them started the process by drawing one or more large blocks on screen. Then they selected the carving stick and worked on the drawing until it was satisfying. The unlimited undo operation proved very useful since the users tended to make movements that were too extensive at the beginning of the trial.

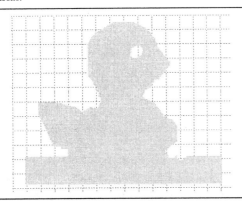

Figure 11: A bird that was made from a few blocks using the carving stick.

The bird seen in Figure 11 was created by our sculptor. In her opinion the carving stick and the cutting stick act very closely like their real counterparts and make the sculpting process understandable. She wished for different kinds of heads to the carving tool to match more closely the different stick tools that sculptors use. She also wanted to be able to use her hands directly to shape the object, as she normally does when working on shale. This may be possible with a drawing tablet that has a built-in display, and will be taken into account in our later studies.

The alignment stick was used to align wheels when working on the cars in Figure 12. In these kinds of drawings the cutting stick, rotating stick and shrinking stick were not needed, but they can be used when working on more complex drawings that include many structures.

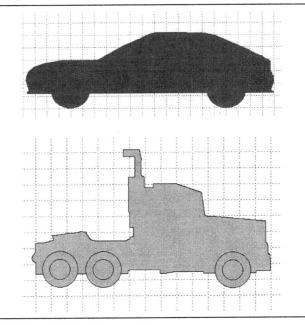

Figure 12: Two examples of the drawings that were made during the user evaluation.

Most of our users chose to create a single structure that was shaped with the tools. One user, however, wanted to create something more. Even though the evaluation period was pretty short, she managed to build a simple scene using just object creation and the stick tools. Especially in this kind of drawing, the possibility to lock objects outside the effect of the stick proved very useful. When, for example, the skyline in Figure 13 was finished, it was locked, and all subsequent changes left it untouched.

The users found the stick tools natural, but the naturalness was partly hampered by the slowdown that the complex drawings caused in our prototype. The purpose here was to test the metaphor and functionality of the new tools, not what they would be in a final consumer product.

Figure 13: A different kind of drawing that was made using our tools.

Interestingly, one of our users commented that he normally does not draw much with computers since the drawing style of current drawing programs does not match the one that he uses with the paper. He said that our tools are much closer to his sketching process.

With all of the users it was noticed that sometimes they would prefer an increased level of accuracy, but usually the carving stick was appropriate for sketching the form. Accuracy can easily be increased with a zooming feature that enables careful shaping of details. Also, it became evident that a triangular variation of the carving stick will be useful when working in detail. In some cases the users also wanted to change the width of the stick in addition to its length. This is allowed in our latest prototype by using the x- and y-values of the trackball to change each dimension.

All of the users used their two hands naturally to control the stick tools and commented that the large-sized trackball was well suited for the second hand. They also said that given more time to practice they would perform much better than in their first trial.

DISCUSSION

The tools that were presented in this paper allow an alternative and new way of drawing. Instead of trying to draw exact forms at the time of their creation, the user can begin with a general form (like a pile of raw material) and start working on it with the tools. The main difference from current tools is the way of working: building a drawing from individual components vs. sketching the structure by reshaping larger objects. Our new tools can be used to sketch something that the user is not sure of when he or she starts working on a drawing. In our evaluation this happened especially with the user that produced the drawing seen in Figure 13. For example, she started to draw clouds, but later decided to make them pools of water. The new tools may thus be better suited for artistic drawing than the previous tools in drawing programs.

Gross and Do discussed the same issue in their paper on electronic cocktail napkins [9]. Their argument was that the precisely defined graphical elements eliminate the suggestive power of sketches that helps being creative.

Another powerful feature that is present in all of the new stick tools is the range of their effect. Usually drawing programs require changing each of the objects separately, unless they have been grouped or simultaneously selected. With the stick tools the user can implicitly select which objects to manipulate by changing the length of the stick and moving it. For example, resizing all the objects so that their right borders are at the same level is just one gesture when the shrinking stick is used. Normally each of the objects would have to be selected and resized from its resizing handles, since this kind of action is not possible for grouped objects.

The power of not needing to explicitly select the objects has the potential for making operations more efficient. It can also be a disadvantage in some circumstances, such as when the user accidentally touches objects that were not meant to be changed. Sometimes a drawing may also be arranged so that it is not possible to manipulate just those objects that are desired. Because these shortcomings may have serious consequences, we provided two solutions to this problem, undo operations and object locking. They seemed to be enough for the users that evaluated the new tools.

The new tools are highly based on direct manipulation. The alignment stick pushes the objects directly on the same line and does not require selecting each of them. The carving stick changes the shape of the objects directly, and requires no other tools or menu commands in the process. The cutting stick follows the same idea by dividing the objects with the tool, and the rotating stick directly rotates one or more of the objects to a certain orientation. The second pointing device was used to make the mouse less modal and allow changing different properties of the tools at the same time. This design decision was supported by our test users; this gives support to the use of two-handed interfaces in drawing programs that was introduced by Bill Buxton and Brad Myers in 1986 [4].

As Hutchins *et al.* [11] have suggested, direct manipulation has an inherent problem of accuracy. This problem did not seem to hinder our test users, since they were not working with accurate drawings. The stick tools seem to work well in this kind of sketching tasks. However, it seems plausible that supplemented with a zooming function the tools can be used to polish these sketches. Another option to finalize the drawing is to automaticly convert the shapes to splines after sketching the drawing, as is done in many sketching systems, for example in [3].

The alternative way of drawing that was presented in this paper gets additional support from Helaman Ferguson [5]. As a sculptor his process involves direct carving and cutting away material. He prefers this method over the construction or addition process since the method is more interesting and challenging to him. This difference in sculpting is analogous to the difference between the common object-oriented drawing style and the way presented in this paper.

CONCLUSIONS AND FUTURE WORK

This paper described an alternative way of drawing. Instead of building drawings consisting of many objects that are manipulated with control points, we start with larger blocks and use different tools to sculpt them the way we wish. This closely resembles sculpting in two dimensions.

The brief user evaluation suggests that our two-dimensional sculpting metaphor suits well for sketching creative drawings, even though the tools are somewhat different from the basic drawing tools. Further studies are needed to make more accurate comparisons between the current and proposed interaction styles and to find out the tasks that our metaphor suits best for.

Until now our tools have been different kinds of sticks. The sticks have performed well in their tasks, but the stick shape is not a requirement for these tools. We are currently designing alternative shapes to make the interface even more expressive. The new tools will be available for public testing in a new Java version of our prototype system.

ACKNOWLEDGMENTS

I want to thank professor Kari-Jouko Räihä for his support and the volunteer group that participated in user evaluation.

REFERENCES

1. Ronald M. Baecker and William A. S. Buxton, Case study D: The Star, the Lisa, and the Macintosh. In *Readings in Human-Computer Interaction, A Multidisciplinary Approach*, R. M. Baecker and W. A. S. Buxton (Eds.), Morgan Kaufmann, 1987, 649-652.

2. Richard H. Bartels, John C. Beatty, Kellogg S. Booth, Eric G. Bosch, and Pierre Jolicoeur, Experimental comparison of splines using the shape-matching paradigm. *ACM Transactions on Graphics*, 12 (3), July 1993, 179-208.

3. Thomas Baudel, A Mark-based interaction paradigm for free-hand drawing. *ACM UIST'94 Symposium on User Interface Software and Technology*, ACM Press, 1994, 185-192.

4. William Buxton and Brad A. Myers, A study in two-handed input. *Human Factors in Computer Systems, CHI'86 Conference Proceedings*, ACM Press, 1986, 321-326.

5. Helaman Ferguson, Computer interactive sculpture. *Computer Graphics*, 26 (1), March 1992, 109-116.

6. Barry Fowler, Geometric manipulation of tensor product surfaces. *Computer Graphics*, 26 (1), March 1992, 101-108.

7. Tinsley A. Galyean and John F. Hughes, Sculpting: an interactive volumetric modeling technique. *Computer Graphics*, 25 (4), July 1991, 267-274.

8. Cindy Grimm, David Pugmire, Mark Bloomenthal, John Hughes, and Elaine Cohen, Visual interfaces for solids modeling. *ACM UIST'95 Symposium on User Interface Software and Technology*, ACM Press, 1995, 51-60.

9. Mark D. Gross and Ellen Yi-Luen Do, Ambiguous intentions: a paper-like interface for creative design. *ACM UIST'96 Symposium on User Interface Software and Technology*, ACM Press, 1996, 183-192.

10. William M. Hsu, John F. Hughes, and Henry Kaufman, Direct manipulation of free-form deformations. *Computer Graphics*, 26 (2), July 1992, 177-184.

11. Edwin L. Hutchins, James D. Hollan, and Donald A. Norman, Direct manipulation interfaces. In *User Centered System Design*, D. A. Norman and S. W. Draper (Eds.), Lawrence Erlbaum, 1986, 87-124.

12. *MacDraw Manual*. Apple Computer, Inc., 1984.

13. Richard L. Potter, Linda J. Weldon, and Ben Shneiderman, Improving the accuracy of touchscreens: an experimental evaluation of three strategies. In *Sparks of Innovation in Human-Computer Interaction*, Ben Shneiderman (Ed.), Ablex Publishing, 1993, 157-166.

14. Hong Qin and Demetri Terzopoulos, Dynamic manipulation of triangular B-splines. *Proceedings of the Third Symposium on Solid Modeling and Applications (SMA'95)*, ACM Press, 1995, 351-360.

15. Roope Raisamo and Kari-Jouko Räihä, A New Direct Manipulation Technique for Aligning Objects in Drawing Programs. *ACM UIST '96 Symposium on User Interface Software and Technology*, ACM Press, 1996, 157-164. An extended version is available online at [ftp://ftp.cs.uta.fi/pub/reports/A-1996-5.ps.Z].

16. Roope Raisamo and Kari-Jouko Räihä, Design and evaluation of the alignment stick. Report A-1999-1, University of Tampere, Department of Computer Science. [ftp://ftp.cs.uta.fi/pub/reports/A-1999-1.ps.Z].

17. Ben Shneiderman, The future of interactive systems and the emergence of direct manipulation. *Behaviour and Information Technology 1*, 1982, 237-256.

18. Scott S. Snibbe, Kenneth P. Herndon, Daniel C. Robbins, D. Brookshire Conner, and Andries van Dam, Using deformations to explore 3D widget design. *Computer Graphics*, 26 (2), July 1992, 351-352.

19. Demetri Terzopoulos and Hong Qin, Dynamic NURBS with geometric constraints for interactive sculpting. *ACM Transactions on Graphics*, 13 (2), April 1994, 103-136.

20. Demetri Terzopoulos, John Platt, Alan Barr, and Kurt Fleischer, Elastically deformable models. *Computer Graphics*, 21 (4), July 1987, 205-214.

21. Sidney W. Wang and Arie E. Kaufman, Volume Sculpting. *1995 Symposium on Interactive 3D Graphics*, ACM Press, 1995, 151-156.

The Strategic Use of CAD:
An Empirically Inspired, Theory-Based Course

Suresh K. Bhavnani
HCI Institute
Carnegie Mellon University
Pittsburgh, PA 15213 USA
Tel: +1-412-363-8308
E-mail: suresh@andrew.cmu.edu

Bonnie E. John
HCI Institute
Carnegie Mellon University
Pittsburgh, PA 15213 USA
Tel: +1-412-268-7182
E-mail: Bonnie.John@cs.cmu.edu

Ulrich Flemming
School of Architecture
Carnegie Mellon University
Pittsburgh, PA 15213 USA
Tel: +412-268-2368
E-mail: ujf@andrew.cmu.edu

ABSTRACT

The inefficient use of complex computer systems has been widely reported. These studies show the persistence of inefficient methods despite many years of experience and formal training. To counteract this phenomenon, we present the design of a new course, called the Strategic Use of CAD. The course aims at teaching students efficient strategies to use a computer-aided drafting system through a two-pronged approach. *Learning to See* teaches students to recognize opportunities to use efficient strategies by studying the nature of the task, and *Learning to Do* teaches students to implement the strategies. Results from a pilot experiment show that this approach had a positive effect on the strategic behavior of students who did not exhibit knowledge of efficient strategies before the class, and had no effect on the strategic behavior of those who did. Strategic training can thus assist users in recognizing opportunities to use efficient strategies. We present the ramifications of these results on the design of training and future experiments.

Keywords

CAD, strategy, training, GOMS, learning, efficiency

INTRODUCTION

Several longitudinal and real-world studies have reported widespread inefficient use of complex computer systems such as computer-aided drafting (CAD), spreadsheets, word processors, and operating systems [4, 7, 8, 11]. Given the tremendous leverage that computers can provide if used efficiently, this situation seriously limits the overall productivity of human-computer interaction.

The causes and persistence of inefficient methods to perform various tasks have been explored for many decades. Early work identified the *Einstellung* effect, which demonstrated not only the powerful influence of prior experience on novel tasks, but also how it prevented users from exploring other methods [10]. In more recent work on

knowledge transfer within the ACT* production framework [14], Singley and Anderson note that "productions [a representation of knowledge] which produce clearly inappropriate actions contribute to poor initial performance on a transfer task but are quickly weeded out. Productions which produce actions which are merely nonoptimal, however, are more difficult to detect and persist for longer periods" (p. 137).

These experimental results have been validated in our studies of real-world CAD usage. In data collected during an ethnographic study [2], we found that despite formal training in CAD and several years of experience, many users missed opportunities to use efficient methods in routine CAD tasks. Although the users had mastered basic commands and could complete their tasks, they used inefficient strategies that resulted in an increase of low-level inputs and errors, both of which led to an increase in execution time [1, 4, 5]. Furthermore, many of these inefficient methods appeared to be directly transferred from manual drafting methods that still worked in the new medium.

The above empirical findings point to the difficulty that users have in moving from a sufficient use to a more efficient use of computer applications. We have argued that neither good interface design nor experience guarantee that this transition will occur [4]. Instead, we have come to believe that *strategic knowledge* holds the key to efficient usage and that this knowledge must be explicitly taught. This contrasts with traditional training, which focuses on the use of commands to complete simple tasks. We hypothesized that if users were taught to use efficient strategies in the context of tasks, they would be able to recognize opportunities to use them also in new tasks. To test this hypothesis, we developed and implemented a new approach to training called the Strategic Use of CAD. This paper presents initial findings that demonstrate the effects of this approach on the ability of users to recognize opportunities for using efficient CAD strategies.

We begin by describing the nature of strategic knowledge in the context of complex computer tools. We then explain the role it played in the design of the Strategic Use of CAD course offered in the School of Architecture at Carnegie

Mellon University (CMU). The course content and structure were based on a two-pronged approach: *Learning to See* taught students how to recognize opportunities to use efficient strategies; *Learning to Do* taught students how to implement these strategies to complete a task. We present the results of a pilot experiment to explore the efficacy of this approach. We conclude by discussing the ramifications of these results for the design of training and future experiments.

THE NATURE OF STRATEGIC KNOWLEDGE

Complex computer applications such as CAD systems typically offer more than one way to perform a given task. Consider the task of drawing the three shapes shown in Figure 1. One way of doing this is to draw the outline of *all* the outer shapes, then to outline the inner shapes, and finally to pattern *all* the inner-shapes individually (Figure 1A). An alternate way to do the same task, shown in Figure 1B, is to draw all the elements of the first shape (Detail), to group these elements using an appropriate command like FENCE (Aggregate), and then to make multiple copies of the fence contents to create the other shapes (Manipulate).

Both of these methods allow a user to complete the task. We have called such *non-obligatory* and *goal-directed* methods strategies [4, 13]. The Sequence-by-Operation and Detail-Aggregate-Manipulate (DAM) methods illustrated in Figure 1 are prime examples of CAD strategies. When we refer to *strategic knowledge,* we refer to knowledge of such alternate methods and of how to choose between them.

To arrive at a precise understanding of the knowledge required to use various strategies, we modeled them using GOMS [6]. The DAM strategy, for example, was represented by a combination of a selection rule and a method as shown below:

IF   CURRENT-TASK IS DRAW MULTIPLE OBJECTS
          AND COMPOSITION IS REPLICATION
THEN ACCOMPLISH GOAL: DETAIL-AGGREGATE- MANIPULATE.

METHOD FOR GOAL: DETAIL-AGGREGATE-MANIPULATE.
        STEP 1. ACCOMPLISH GOAL: DETAIL.
        STEP 2. ACCOMPLISH GOAL: AGGREGATE.
        STEP 3. ACCOMPLISH GOAL: MANIPULATE.
        STEP 4. RETURN WITH GOAL ACCOMPLISHED.

The selection rule connects the nature of the task (replication) to a strategy label (Detail-Aggregate-Manipulate); the method decomposes the label into subgoals (Detail, Aggregate, Manipulate). This representation shows that the knowledge required to use the DAM strategy is fairly abstract in that it does not include knowledge of explicit CAD commands. In fact, we have shown that strategies such as DAM are useful in other applications such as word processors and spreadsheets [4]. We therefore call them *abstract strategies.* Abstract strategies such as DAM are used in combination with *concrete strategies,* which capture the knowledge of how to

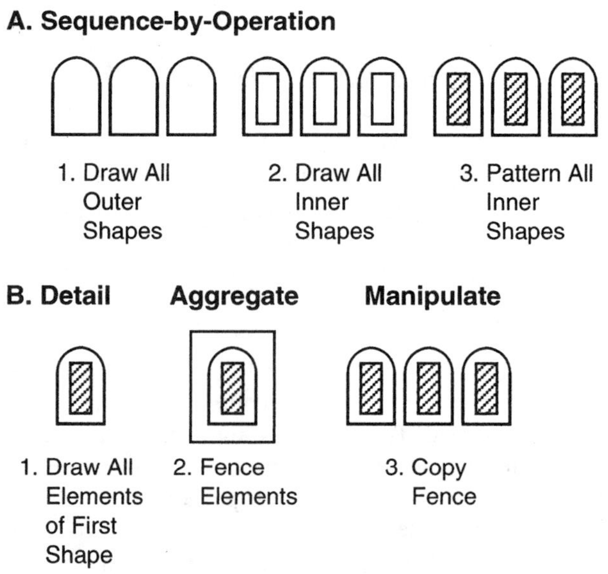

A. Sequence-by-Operation

1. Draw All Outer Shapes   2. Draw All Inner Shapes   3. Pattern All Inner Shapes

B. Detail   Aggregate   Manipulate

1. Draw All Elements of First Shape   2. Fence Elements   3. Copy Fence

Figure 1. A comparison of the steps required for the Sequence-by-Operation strategy and the Detail-Aggregate-Manipulate (DAM) strategy.

select and execute appropriate commands in a particular application in order to actually execute a task. Concrete strategies are important because CAD systems provide in many cases more than one command to achieve a result.

The GOMS analysis of a real-world task using the DAM strategy estimated a reduction of almost 40% in execution time when compared to the Sequence-by-Operation strategy [1, 4]. The strategy furthermore reduced low-level mouse interactions, which tend to be error-prone. Such performance variables are important to users [1, 4]; the DAM strategy is therefore more efficient than the Sequence-by-Operation strategy for the analyzed task.

The main reason why the DAM strategy is more efficient than the Sequence-by-Operation strategy is that it exploits the iterative power of the computer through aggregation commands (such as FENCE). By aggregating the first shape and then applying the copy operation to the aggregate, the *computer* performs the iterative actions of copying each element. In contrast, the Sequence-by-Operation strategy requires the *user* to perform the iterative task of drawing and patterning multiple copies of the same shape, which leads to time-consuming and error-prone actions. Such analyses of strategic knowledge helped us understand the sources and consequences of different strategies; they led us in the end to the formulation of a general theory of efficient strategies (see [1, 5] for an explication of this theory).

Using the theory of efficient strategies, we identified other strategies that exploit the power of iteration provided by computers. Figure 2A shows the Aggregate-Drop-Modify-Strategy (ADM), which is useful for the modification of multiple elements with exceptions. Figure 2B shows how

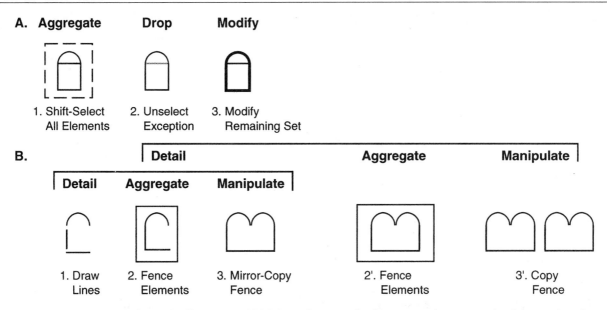

Figure 2. The Aggregate-Drop-Modify strategy (ADM) is another example of an aggregation strategy that delegates iteration to the computer. Aggregation strategies such as DAM can be used recursively to create complex drawings (B).

the DAM strategy described earlier can be used recursively to create complex drawings that have more than one level of symmetry or replication. Because the DAM and ADM strategies exploit iteration through aggregation tools, we have called them *aggregation strategies* (see [1, 4, 5] for a description of other aggregation strategies). The theory furthermore guided us in the identification of other computer powers such as precision and of strategies to exploit them [1, 5].

Several experimental and real-world studies have shown that strategic knowledge is not easily acquired by computer users in command-based training or through many years of experience [4, 7, 8, 11]. Furthermore, we have argued that even well-designed interfaces cannot express this knowledge unambiguously [4]. We therefore hypothesized that the most effective way to make users efficient is to teach them strategic knowledge explicitly. The GOMS representation and the theory of efficient strategies led directly to the design of the Strategic Use of CAD course.

THE STRATEGIC USE OF CAD COURSE
The goal of the Strategic Use of CAD course was to teach architectural graduate students how to use MicroStation™, a complex CAD package. While the students were taught how to use a wide range of commands to complete complex drawings, the course focused on how to use efficient abstract strategies that are useful in any CAD system.

Course Content
The course concentrated on teaching six classes of strategies. These strategies exploited the powers of calculation, precision, iteration, propagation, visualization and generation provided by CAD systems in various degrees. For example, an abstract precision strategy is to set

up the grid units of a drawing and appropriate snap locks *before* attempting to draw any object. A concrete precision strategy specifies how to choose between various snap locks and how to use them in combination with other commands (see [1, 5] for a discussion of strategies to exploit the other powers). Figure 3 shows how the presentation of abstract and concrete strategic knowledge was interleaved throughout the course, which moved from 2-D and 3-D drawing to rendering and finally macro development.

Individual classes were held in a computer cluster. They were structured around the demonstration of abstract and concrete strategies using MicroStation™. Demonstrations were supported by lectures focussing on the underlying concepts or background knowledge, such as the mathematics of b-spline curves. Students were allowed to choose their own midterm and final projects (upon approval of the instructor) to demonstrate their understanding and mastery of efficient strategies.

Pedagogical Approach
The GOMS representation of strategies discussed earlier made salient two important knowledge components necessary to use a strategy. The selection rule suggested that a student must learn to recognize when a task offers an opportunity to use a particular strategy. We call the process of acquiring this knowledge *Learning to See*. The method component suggested that a student must learn how to implement the strategy by decomposing the task into temporally-ordered subgoals. We call the process of acquiring this knowledge *Learning to Do*.

We realized early on that it was not possible to gauge whether a student actually used an efficient strategy just by inspecting a completed drawing. For example, by looking

Week	1	2	3	4	5	6	7	8	9	10	11	12	13	14	15
Lectures	Overview Motivation	Cognitive modeling Theoretical frame-work	Action sequences Euclidean transform.					Iteration (summary)	Orthogr. views		Curves Surfaces			Generative systems	
Abstract Strategies	Pre-test DAM (as illustration)	*Calculation* *Precision*	*Iteration* *Recursion*	LAMM		Propagation Reuse Data stratification		Other aggregation strategies (AM,ADM, AMM,etc.)	*Visualization* Multiple views					Generation Programming	Post-test Discussion
Concrete Strategies	Getting started Grid set-up Snap modes Basic constructions	Aggregation Manipulation	Modification	Advanced constr./ modification	Cells Levels	Patterns Plotting		Advanced aggregation	3D display Rendering	3D constructions Depth control	Advanced 3D constructions	Surface modification Output from 3D models	Misc. commands	Macros	

Figure 3. A time-line for the semester-long Strategic Use of CAD course showing the interleaving of abstract and concrete strategic training. Powers of CAD are italicized, and aggregation strategies are in upper case.

only at step 3 in Figure 1A, it is not possible for an instructor to know which strategy was used to draw the three arched figures. While designing exercises to help students in the process of Learning to See and Learning to Do, we therefore asked students to describe in words and figures the steps they plan to use in completing their homework exercises, mid-term and final projects. We called these descriptions *action sequences*. The steps shown in Figures 1 and 2 are examples of very simple action sequences.

Previous research has shown that users have substantial difficulty in recognizing and using efficient abstract strategies [4, 7, 11]. We therefore required students to describe the abstract strategies they intended to use explicitly and completely in their action sequences. Students were not required to specify the concrete strategies (command selection and execution) they planned to use. Figure 4 shows the various types of knowledge taught by the Learning to See and Learning to Do components. The gray cells represent the knowledge captured in action sequences.

	Abstract Strategies	**Concrete Strategies**
Learning to See	Knowledge to see the structure in a task and select a strategy	Knowledge to select appropriate commands
Learning to Do	Knowledge to decompose a task based on a strategy	Knowledge to execute and combine commands

Figure 4. The types of knowledge required in the Learning to See and Leaning to Do components for abstract and concrete strategies. The gray cells represent the knowledge expressed in action sequences.

Action sequences are pedagogically important because they make the *process* public and therefore open for inspection. Furthermore, it allows the instructor to provide timely feedback to students. To motivate students to think about the process as well as their final products, they were informed that their final grade would depend on their action sequences as well as the quality of the final drawings. This approach is a significant departure from traditional training approaches, which concentrate on giving feedback mainly on the final product. To understand the efficacy of this approach, we tested its effect in a pilot experiment.

EXPERIMENTAL DESIGN

The Strategic Use of CAD course was offered in the graduate program in the School of Architecture at CMU in the spring semester of 1998; it was open to advanced undergraduates. Eight students (seven graduates and one undergraduate) took the course for credit. The small size of the class is typical of graduate-level courses offered at the university. Six of the students were architecture majors and two of them were HCI graduate students. While all the students took part in the experiment, one student had to be dropped from the analysis as she had attended some lectures when the course was offered in the previous year, which invalidated her pre-test scores. Taking part in the experiment did not affect the students' course grade.

The experiment consisted of a pre-test conducted on the first day of classes and a post-test conducted on the last day of classes. The goal of the experiment was to investigate how the course affected the students' ability to decompose a drawing task so that efficient CAD strategies could be applied. As the experiment was not a test of command knowledge, the students were asked to describe with words and pictures the steps they would take to perform a drawing

A. Pre-test Task

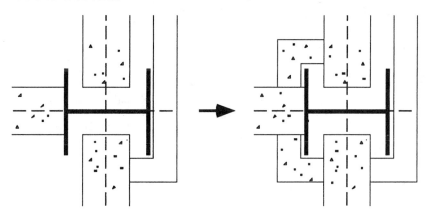

Imagine you are using your favorite drawing package. By using words and sketches, please describe the steps you would use to change the figure on the left to the figure on the right. Try and be as explicit as possible for each step.

B. Post-test Task

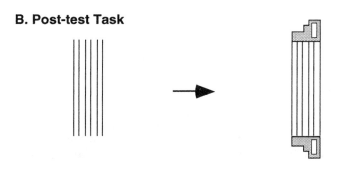

Imagine you are using MicroStation. By using words and sketches, please describe the steps you would use to change the figure on the left to the figure on the right. Try and be as explicit as possible for each step.

Figure 5. A pre-test task (A) and its isomorph in the post-test (B). The pre-test task is identical to a task that a user performed inefficiently in our ethnographic study (see [1, 4, 9] for a detailed analysis of this task). This task requires an application of the DAM strategy described in Figure 1B. The drawings presented here are half the size of the original tasks presented to the students.

task when using their favorite CAD or drawing application. Students were instructed to use 8-1/2"x11" sheets of unruled paper provided by us to describe the steps. Students could choose their own writing instruments to perform the experiment.

The pre- and post-test each consisted of three drawing tasks[1]. The first task required the DAM strategy, the second required the ADM strategy, and the third task was designed to test if the students could use the DAM strategy recursively. The post-test drawing tasks were isomorphs of those in the pre-test. Figure 5 shows an example of a task

---

1. A fourth task, which tested knowledge of a strategy called LAMM [4], had to be dropped from the analysis because the difference between the before and after drawings in the pre-test was too subtle; this caused five of the seven students to misunderstand the pre-test task.

and instruction in the pre-test, and an isomorph of the same task in the post-test. These tasks were similar to those observed in our ethnographic study [2] where real-world architects missed opportunities to use aggregation strategies. The students were given no time limit, but all completed the tasks within the 80 minute time slot of the class.

DATA ENCODING

We established the following criteria for the successful application of each strategy.

1. The DAM strategy was used successfully if all details were completed in the first drawing before it was aggregated and mirror-copied to create any subsequent copies. The Detail stage itself did not have to be correct, but any attempt to draw elements in the copy was considered a non-use of the strategy.

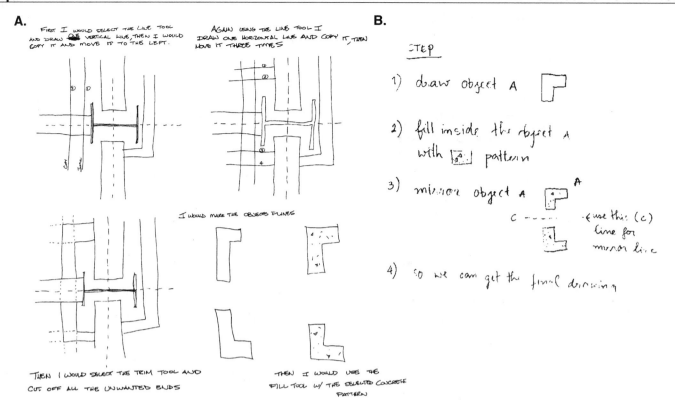

A.

FIRST I WOULD SELECT THE LINE TOOL AND DRAW ONE VERTICAL LINE, THEN I WOULD COPY IT AND MOVE IT TO THE LEFT.

AGAIN USING THE LINE TOOL I DRAW ONE HORIZONTAL LINE AND COPY IT, THEN MOVE IT THREE TIMES

I WOULD MAKE THE OBJECTS PLANES

THEN I WOULD SELECT THE TRIM TOOL AND CUT OFF ALL THE UNWANTED ENDS

THEN I WOULD USE THE FILL TOOL W/ THE SELECTED CONCRETE PATTERN

B.

STEP

1) draw object A

2) fill inside the object A with [a] pattern

3) mirror object A — use this (c) line for mirror line

4) so we can get the final drawing

Figure 6. Two attempts by students in the experiment to do the pre-test task (described in Figure 5A) requiring the DAM strategy. A score of 0 was given to the attempt shown in (A), and a score of 1 was given to the attempt shown in (B).

2. The ADM strategy was used successfully if there was any attempt to aggregate elements in such a way as to exclude the exceptions. Attempts to modify each element individually to avoid the exceptions was considered a non-use of this strategy. The type of commands to perform the aggregation was irrelevant.

3. The recursive use of the DAM strategy was considered successful if the strategy was used in at least two levels as shown in Figure 2B.

Based on the above criteria, a score of 1 was given if the appropriate strategy was used, and a score of 0 if the strategy was not used. This coarse-grained analysis reflected the main goal of the experiment, which was not so much to see if the students could execute commands or draw accurately, but rather to determine if the students could recognize opportunities to use abstract strategies and plan a course of action. The criteria also reflected the temporal aspect of the aggregation strategies (do A before B). Our GOMS analysis of similar tasks has shown that when such temporal criteria are violated, low-level interactions proliferate leading to many errors and an increase in execution time [1, 4, 5].

Figure 6A shows an example of how a student decomposed the task requiring the DAM strategy described in Figure 1B. The steps show how he planned to draw both the "L" shapes using lines similar to those that would be drawn using a T-square in manual drafting. This is similar to the Sequence-by-Operation strategy shown in Figure 1A. As the student did not recognize the opportunity to use the DAM strategy, he was given a score of 0 for that task. Figure 6B shows how another student attempted the same pre-test task. Here she correctly saw the symmetrical composition of the task and demonstrated the use of the DAM strategy by first drawing all the details in the first "L" shape, and then aggregating and mirroring the shape to create the copy. She was therefore given a score of 1 for that task.

DATA ANALYSIS

As shown in Figure 7, two (S4 and S7) of the seven students demonstrated knowledge of all the strategies in the pre-test, while one student (S5) demonstrated knowledge of none. The rest of the students showed knowledge of at least one aggregation strategy, but not of all. To determine if there was an overall positive effect of the class, the Wilcoxon test[1] was performed on the data collapsed over tasks. A one-tailed test showed a significant improvement of the post-test scores over the pre-test scores ($p < 0.05$).

Of the 11 cases where students did not exhibit knowledge of a strategy in the pre-test, only 2 did not display that

---

1. The Wilcoxon test is a distribution-free, non-parametric test designed for nominal data and is similar to the paired sample T-test designed for continuous data.

Studnt	DAM Task		ADM Task		Rec. DAM Task	
	Pre	Post	Pre	Post	Pre	Post
S1	0	1	1	1	0	1
S2	1	1	0	0	0	1
S3	0	1	0	0	1	1
S4	1	1	1	0	1	1
S5	0	1	0	1	0	1
S6	0	1	1	1	0	1
S7	1	1	1	1	1	1
Total	**3**	**7**	**4**	**4**	**3**	**7**

Figure 7. The pre- and post-test scores for seven students performing three tasks. The scores represent the unsuccessful (0) and successful (1) use of aggregation strategies.

knowledge in the post-test. These cases show up in the table as a pair of 0s in the pre- and post-test scores for the same task (S2 and S3 in the ADM task). Furthermore, there was only one case where a strategy known by a user in the pre-test was not used in the post-test (S4 in the ADM task). It is interesting to note that all three cases occurred in the task requiring the ADM strategy. We therefore performed a more detailed analysis to determine whether the ADM strategy was taught differently from the DAM strategy.

The analysis revealed that the DAM strategy was introduced in the first week and emphasized for homework assignments throughout the course. Furthermore, the recursive DAM strategy was explicitly taught in the third week. In contrast, the ADM strategy was taught for only a small portion of the eighth week. Therefore, the DAM and ADM strategies received proportionately different times in lectures, demonstrations, and practice in homework assignments.

DISCUSSION OF RESULTS

The results provide encouraging evidence that the Strategic Use of CAD course improved the students' ability to recognize opportunities for the use of efficient strategies. While the students came into the course with mixed abilities to recognize these opportunities, the post-test scores show a far more uniform ability at the end of the course. Furthermore, with the exception of one student in one task, all students who could recognize opportunities to use strategies at the start of the course did not loose that ability at the end of the course. The course therefore helped those who did not know the strategies and did not hurt those who knew them. Because students had no discernible problems showing the steps they would use to do the pre-test task, we are confident that these results were not caused by an improved ability to describe action sequences over the semester.

Because we had carefully chosen the DAM task to be identical to the one we had observed in our ethnographic study (as shown in Figure 5A and described in [4, 9]), the

study helped confirm our long-standing belief that the carry-over of manual drafting strategies to CAD was not unique to our ethnographic data. In fact, four of the seven students failed to use the DAM strategy in the pre-test while all used it in the post-test. We found the same proportion of pre-test and post-test scores in the recursive DAM task.

The three missed opportunities to use the ADM strategy and subsequent analysis suggest that students may not have learned the conditions for its use because we did not spend enough time in describing and demonstrating the ADM strategy. This has been observed in other studies that taught strategies. For example, several strategies in Shoenfeld's [12] experiments on teaching problem-solving strategies in mathematics were also not used in transfer experiments. Singley and Anderson [14] suggest that the strategies which were least used in Shoenfeld's study lacked explicit conditions for their use, and therefore did not provide the information important for their selection. Thus, if either explicit conditions for strategy selection do not exist (as in Shoenfeld's study), or sufficient time is not taken to teach them (as seems to be the case in our course), students may fail to use the strategies. In the next iteration of the course, we intend to provide explicit conditional information for the ADM strategy.

Clearly, our pilot experiment is limited by the small number of students that registered for the graduate-level course, a constraint beyond our control. In addition, the pilot experiment was limited by the absence of a control condition. This could lead to the rival hypothesis that the observed improvements in recognizing opportunities to use strategies could have occurred just by virtue of learning how to use a CAD system for a semester, irrespective of the training approach. However, we have evidence against such a claim. First, although one of the students in the experiment had taken a command-based AutoCAD™ (another sophisticated CAD system) course at CMU in the preceding semester, he still used the inefficient Sequence-by-Operation strategy in the pre-test (as shown in Figure 6A). While he had mastered the use of aggregation commands in AutoCAD™, the command-based course had not helped him to recognize opportunities to use them with efficient strategies. Second, our ethnographic study also demonstrates the ineffectiveness of command-based training to make users efficient: despite formal training through their CAD vendor, the users in the study exhibited similar forms of inefficient usage.

Both limitations of this pilot experiment (the small number of participants and the lack of a control condition) will be addressed in our current research that aims to design and test a strategy-based course for other complex applications (such as word processors and spreadsheets). This new course will be taught to approximately 130 incoming freshmen next year with the same number of students in a traditional command-based control condition.

CONCLUSION

Based on converging evidence starting from the Einstellung effect down to our own studies on experienced CAD usage, we have begun to recognize the widespread and persistent occurrence of inefficient methods and their negative effects on performance. Our research over several years has explored different approaches to counter-act this phenomenon. We have focused on the systematic identification of strategic knowledge and the dissemination of that knowledge to users. Insights from the research led directly to the design of the Strategic Use of CAD course.

The course design made two departures from conventional training. The first was to focus on the teaching of strategies in addition to commands as neither can achieve efficient usage on its own. The second departure was to make students think consciously about process before they attempted their tasks. Both relied on a pedagogical device we called action sequences.

The results of our pilot experiment suggest that the strategic approach had a positive effect on the students' ability to recognize opportunities for using efficient abstract strategies and to develop a plan to use them. Furthermore, the course did not negatively affect existing knowledge of strategies. While the experimental tasks tested the learning of abstract strategies for relatively small drawings, future experiments should investigate whether the strategic approach also helps users apply abstract strategies in the context of large complex drawings requiring deep decompositions. In addition, future research should investigate the link between abstract strategies which are general to any CAD package, and concrete strategies which are specific to a particular package. Finally, we need a systematic understanding of trade-offs between strategies because we have observed situations where the choice between competing strategies is not as clear-cut as those we have discussed in this paper.

Although we have explored other ways to disseminate strategic knowledge, such as active assistance as well as better management and peer interaction [1, 2, 3], we believe that there can be no replacement for the explicit training and practice of strategic knowledge to use complex computer systems. Our current research extends the strategic approach to the teaching of other complex computer applications. We intend to study if users are able to transfer abstract strategies across applications and if they retain this knowledge over time. The hope is that this research will provide a way to counter-act the persistence of inefficient usage, which has plagued modern computer usage for many years.

ACKNOWLEDGMENTS

This research was supported by the National Science Foundation, Award# IRI-9457628 and EIA-9812607. The views and conclusions contained in this document are those of the authors and should not be interpreted as representing the official policies, either expressed or implied, of NSF or the U. S. Government. The authors acknowledge the contributions of students who took part in the experiments, in addition to A. Corbett, M. Lovett, and G. Vallabha. Bentley Systems, Inc. supplied the academic edition of MicroStation™.

REFERENCES

1. Bhavnani, S. K. *How Architects Draw with Computers: A Cognitive Analysis of Real-World CAD Interactions*, unpublished Ph.D. dissertation, 1998, Carnegie Mellon University, Pittsburgh.

2. Bhavnani, S.K., Flemming, U., Forsythe, D.E., Garrett, J.H., Shaw, D.S., and Tsai, A. CAD Usage in an Architectural Office: From Observations to Active Assistance. *Automation in Construction* 5 (1996), 243-255.

3. Bhavnani, S.K., and John, B.E. Exploring the Unrealized Potential of Computer-Aided Drafting. *Proceedings of CHI'96* (1996), 332-339.

4. Bhavnani, S.K., and John, B.E. From Sufficient to Efficient Usage: An Analysis of Strategic Knowledge. *Proceedings of CHI'97* (1997), 91-98.

5. Bhavnani, S.K., and John, B.E. Delegation and Circumvention: Two Faces of Efficiency. *Proceedings of CHI'98* (1998), 273-280.

6. Card, S.K., Moran, T.P., and Newell, A. *The Psychology of Human-Computer Interaction*. Hillsdale, NJ: Lawrence Erlbaum Associates, 1983.

7. Cragg, P.B. and King, M. Spreadsheet Modeling Abuse: An Opportunity for OR? *Journal of the Operational Research Society* 44 (1993), 743-752.

8. Doane, S.M., Pellegrino, J.W., and Klatzky, R.L. Expertise in a Computer Operating System: Conceptualization and Performance. *Human-Computer Interaction* 5 (1990), 267-304.

9. Flemming, U., Bhavnani, S.K., and John, B.E. Mismatched Metaphor: User vs. System Model in Computer-Aided Drafting. *Design Studies* 18 (1997), 349-368.

10. Luchins, A. S. Mechanization in Problem Solving. *Psychological Monographs*, (1942), 54 (248).

11. Nilsen, E., Jong H., Olson J., Biolsi, I., and Mutter, S. The Growth of Software Skill: A Longitudinal Look at Learning and Performance. *Proceedings of INTERCHI'93*. (1993), 149-156.

12. Schoenfeld, A. H. Mathematical Problem Solving. New York: Academic Press, 1985.

13. Siegler, R.S., and Jenkins, E. *How Children Discover New Strategies*. Lawrence Erlbaum Associates, New Jersey, 1989.

14. Singley, M.K., and Anderson, J. R. *The Transfer of Cognitive Skill*. Harvard University Press, Cambridge, Massachusetts, 1989.

Implementing Interface Attachments Based on Surface Representations

Dan R. Olsen Jr., Scott E. Hudson, Thom Verratti, Jeremy M. Heiner, Matt Phelps
Human Computer Interaction Institute
Carnegie Mellon University
Pittsburgh, PA 15213
{dolsen, hudson}@cs.cmu.edu

ABSTRACT

This paper describes an architecture for supporting interface *attachments* – small interactive programs which are designed to augment the functionality of other applications. This architecture is designed to work with a diverse set of conventional applications, but require only a minimal set of "hooks" into those applications. In order to achieve this, the work described here concentrates on what we will call *observational attachments*, a subclass of attachments that operate primarily by observing and manipulating the *surface representations* of applications – that is the visual information that applications would normally display on the screen or print. These attachments can be thought of as "looking over the shoulder of the user" to assist with various tasks. By requiring very little modification to, or help from, the applications they augment, this approach supports the creation of a set of uniform services that can be applied across a more diverse set of applications than traditional approaches.

Keywords: User interface architectures, observational attachments, surface representations, linking and embedding.

INTRODUCTION AND MOTIVATION

In an increasingly diverse digital world, the ability to provide services uniformly across a range of applications or information sources can be very valuable. By providing one service (e.g., a text searcher, a spelling checker, a translation service, or an annotation manager) that can be applied to many different applications, the availability of the service in whatever context it is needed in can be ensured. More importantly, the learning burden created by including similar services, each with a somewhat different user interface, in each application can be avoided. Further, if they are separated from monolithic applications, various services can typically afford to be much more specialized, and in some cases can be very customized to specific users, or even their current task.

There is a long-standing challenge in user interface

architecture to create independently developed tools – what we call *attachments* – that can work on any application [1]. The problem lies in finding a general medium of communication between the application software and such independent tools. This paper presents an architecture that provides a useful general approach to that challenge.

Component architectures such as Visual Basic [2], or JavaBeans [3], as well as lower level application linking and automation facilities such as AppleEvents [4] or OLE Automation [5] are an attempt to provide some of the benefits of such a non-monolithic approach. However, these systems have suffered from a number of drawbacks. Perhaps the most important being that the application programmer must make (often substantial) provisions for these features in order to make them useful. This "extra work" to create components or export capabilities is often peripheral to the main goals of the application. As a result these facilities are often left out of larger applications, or provide only limited access. Further, even when special effort is made to create applications that can be accessed "from the outside", one is often limited to activities that were anticipated by the programmer and it is often difficult or cumbersome to use them in unanticipated ways.

Most existing systems for providing access to application facilities can be thought of as *model based*, because they operate in terms of the internal or underlying model (or even data structures) used by the application. While this tends to allow powerful forms of access, it also presents a barrier to the creation of uniformly applicable attachments since each application tends to use a specialized model or data structure. While one might hope for standardization over time, in fact we believe precisely the opposite will happen because in most cases market forces are driving towards increased incompatibility and diversity (in order for example, to differentiate products from their competitors and to provide incentives to purchase new versions).

In this paper we consider a different approach, one that places a premium on wide applicability (perhaps at some cost in overall power for the attachments created). This approach works primarily in terms of the surface representations of the application – the information it already presents to the user. Because these representations must exist for other purposes, they do not represent an additional burden to the application programmer. As a

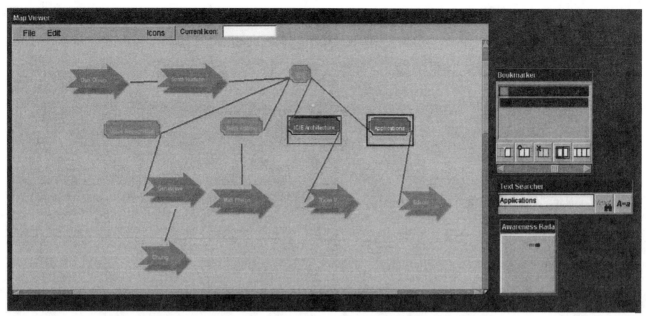

Figure 1 – Application with Attachments

result, using surface representations allows the creation of much more widely applicable and reusable attachments. Further, because these attachments operate in terms of the same information that user sees and manipulates, their normal means of discourse is typically closer to the user's conceptual model. In many cases this will make them easier to understand and control than attachments that work in terms of internal representations not seen by the user. This is an important property for attachments that are designed to work cooperatively with the user.

OBSERVATIONAL ATTACHMENTS

In this work we are primarily interested in attachments that work collaboratively with the user to assist in various tasks. These attachments can be thought of as "looking over the shoulder of the user". We employ the term *observational attachments* to refer to a class of attachment that works in this fashion, primarily observing and manipulating the human consumable information presented by an application directly to a user.

Observational attachments have the important advantage that they share a common frame of reference with the user. This allows them to work directly with what the user sees, referring to the same objects in the same terms. This eliminates the translation between internal structures and end-user terms that is necessary with model-based approaches. As a result, the gulf between user interface concepts and the user's conceptual space can be more easily narrowed.

Figure 1 shows an example situation of an organization chart application augmented by three attachments (appearing in the small windows at the right edge). The primary attachment in this case is one that searches the surface for strings of text. (In this case we have searched first for "architecture" and then for "applications", thereby highlighting two objects.) When the text search attachment

finds text it creates a reference to all located instances and gives them to a second *bookmarker* attachment. The bookmarker remembers references from any number of sources, manipulates them and modifies the application's display to show where they are located. It acts as a general highlighting or pointing device, working by blending non-selected object with gray and drawing colored boxes around selected objects. (The highlight rectangle to the left is drawn in red, and the one on the right is drawn in blue, matching the colors of the first and second bookmarks respectively.) In the example shown in Figure 1, the bookmarker attachment also communicates with a third *radar* awareness attachment [6]. The radar attachment monitors the bookmark references and monitors the location of objects on the application surface so that it can present a global view of all bookmarks (again employing colors that match various bookmarks).

Each attachment in this example is independent of the application implementation and independent of the other attachments. This allows a very modular implementation. The text search attachment uses another attachment (in this case the bookmark) to accept references to what it has found and display them to the user. Similarly the radar attachment needs an attachment to supply it with object references to display. Neither, however, cares which attachments they work with or exactly how they are being implemented.

Although observational attachments offer a number of advantages when attachments are designed to act as collaborators, the use of surface representations does also impose some limitations. In particular, it is somewhat harder to make observational attachments proactive since they normally work only with what the user sees (or could see given a larger display surface) and do not normally have the ability to communicate with the application about its presentation. In addition, observational attachments in some cases need to recreate semantic concepts that are directly represented in an underlying model, but only indirectly represented in surface presentations. This can make some more algorithmic oriented tasks more awkward than they might be in a model based setting.

SURFACE REPRESENTATIONS

The key challenge in developing a ubiquitous attachment architecture is the communication of information between the application and the attachment. A second challenge is for the attachment to communicate with the user in the same space and in the same terms as the user is currently working.

Let us first consider the problem of communicating information to an attachment. For this communication to work ubiquitously, it must have a form that is general across all applications. In order to reduce the burdens placed on application programmers, this attachment communication must not involve substantial additional programming, and any small additions that are required must be applicable to the support of all attachments. It is unacceptable to require application programmers to make special modifications for each new attachment.

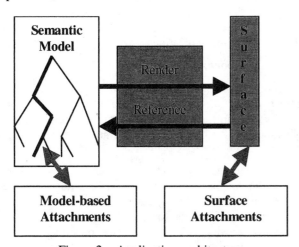

Figure 2 - Application architecture

As illustrated in Figure 2, the model-based approaches for supporting independent tools function by exposing some variant of an object model with fields and actions. By exposing the model to external entities, scripting tools can manipulate the application programmatically. The problem lies in the fact that general tools (other than scripting tools) are very difficult to write on top of the many different interfaces presented by many different application.

Consider the problem of our text search attachment which must find all strings in any application and check them individually against the search pattern. The general object interface of Java Beans or OLE can in principle supply all such strings but writing the general code to extract words from many different data structures would be very painful.

Our second key challenge is the problem of communicating with the user. For example, our text searcher must have a

mechanism for showing the user where the located words are in the application. The object/action model for accessing application information is again very unsuited for this. The text searcher (assuming that one could write the general code for touring the object space looking for a string) might keep track of where it is in the application's object space but still have no effective means to draw the user's attention to the object containing the located word. Applications each provide highlighting and selection in their own way and for their own purpose. Again, an attachment would be forced to operate in terms particular to each application it deals with.

In order to meet these key challenges a number of specific capabilities are needed, including at least the following:

- The ability to extract information (such as text strings and geometric containment relationships) from the application's presentation,

- the ability to identify meaningful units within the application presentation (such as those that represent the presentation of a single "object" in the presentation),

- a mechanism for changing and/or augmenting application output in order to highlight objects or express new information, and finally,

- the ability to monitor the application to detect changes of interest.

In order to make these capabilities truly ubiquitous, it is important to also realize that we cannot realistically expect the application programmer to do much to help us. To the extent possible, an observational attachment system must operate on the basis of actions the programmer must already take in order to implement the application. For this reason the work presented here strives to intrude on application programs as little as possible. Some of the techniques presented here can work with no additions or changes to an application. However, to take advantage of the full potential of observational attachments, applications typically must provide some very simple capabilities and remain within some reasonable limits.

For this work, we have assumed that each application meets the following requirements:

- The application presents information to the user on a collection of uniquely identifiable graphical planes. We expect that this requirement will be met by almost all modern applications without modification. For the prototype presented here we assume that the application presents all of its information on one large (conceptual) surface, only some of which is visible at any given time. The use of a single surface simplifies our prototype implementation, but is not a hard requirement for the techniques being described.

- Each application works with a conventional damage/redraw cycle. That is, when an application needs to update its display it tells the toolkit, window, or operating system about the region that needs to be redrawn, and the application is capable of redrawing any portion of its presentation when requested. Further, the application's access to the screen is done through normal toolkit, window, or operating system mechanisms. We expect that this requirement will also be met by almost all modern applications without modification. For our prototype, we have also assumed that some sort of graphics or device context object is used to access the drawing operations, and that this object is controlled by the toolkit, window, or operating system. However, as will be discussed later, this is not essential to the concepts presented here.

- Further each application must be capable of reporting damage and performing redraw operations for all portions of its display, even parts that might not be currently visible. We expect that most applications will already do this. It is possible that some applications may have "optimized away" this capability. However, since basic damage and redraw capabilities must already be provided, even in these cases we would expect little impact on the application to meet this requirement (the potential performance implications of this will be considered later).

- A more intrusive requirement is that meaningful units within the presentation be delimited by special calls. This will require additions to the application. However, as will be considered below, in many cases these additions can be hidden from the programmer by placing them within the existing code of a toolkit. Even when this is not possible, these changes require only the equivalent of annotations to the existing drawing code and should never require any reorganization of the control or data structures involved.

In addition to these basic requirements, several optional application capabilities – which are still easy to provide – can further enhance the capabilities of attachments. These include:

- The ability to report information that identifies the currently selected object(s) of an application on demand.

- The ability to report the portion of the overall application surface(s) that is currently being displayed.

- Finally, the ability to move the display (e.g., the position of a scrolled window) to make a particular identified object visible on demand.

Again, each of these capabilities is designed to piggyback on actions the application is very likely to already perform, and hence each is designed to represent a minimal intrusion on the application.

The following sections will consider the details of providing for each of these requirements and using these capabilities to implement observational attachments.

Accessing the interactive surface

All graphical user interfaces function by drawing user-relevant information on the screen. In modern systems there is normally an object-oriented abstraction (device context, graphics object, etc.) which the application uses to draw. This insulates the application from the details of screen interfaces and also unifies other drawing chores, such as printing. In modern windowing systems the application must support the ability to redraw any portion of its surface representation on demand in order to properly support overlapping and resizable windows.

Our work is built in Java using the subArctic toolkit [7]. In the subArctic system, much like other modern toolkits, all drawing is performed through an object which maintains a graphical context and encapsulates access to drawing surfaces (in this case a *drawable* object). Every interactive component (subArctic *interactor* object) must provide a method for redrawing its appearance that accepts a drawable object.

Every piece of user-relevant information must pass through such a drawable object in order to appear on the screen. This means that all of the context information – all information that the user sees – is accessible to the drawable in a user consumable form and in a form that is uniform across all applications. Our surface attachments work by substituting their own drawable objects. This not only allows attachments to capture and consume application information but also to modify how that information is communicated to the user. Further, this capability is uniform across all applications. (Other applications of this general technique are described in [7] and [8].)

Note that in cases where the equivalent of a drawable object is not available, or attachments do not have the ability to substitute those objects within applications, it is still possible to achieve the same effects. This can be done by catching drawing calls made to the operating system drawing or printing API and modifying their actions. (For example on the Apple Macintosh, these capabilities can be accessed via the grafProcs field of a GrafPort object). As we will see below, a few other small augmentations to this API (or addition of a small separate API) are required. However, overall this approach allows observational attachments to be implemented with very little intrusion on the application and provides basic access to all the information presented to the user.

Discovering a semantic/surface mapping

Defining new classes that support the drawable interface gives an attachment access to all surface information. Such simple surface information can be used to implement a number of useful attachment services. In many cases, however, the attachments could make use of information about the underlying semantic structure that the surface is presenting. For example, suppose that the text searcher has found the string "Applications" in the organization chart in Figure 1 and has created a bookmark for it, which the radar is watching. If the user drags that element around the screen the radar view wants to follow it wherever it goes. This means that the bookmark must have some description of the semantic object being referenced so that it can maintain the reference while editing is going on. This requires some map between the surface and the underlying semantic model.

In order to provide a mechanism for determining which parts of the surface presentation correspond to a meaningful semantic unit in the application, a set of methods for "object bracketing" have been added to the system:

> groupStart(interactor toolkitObject)
>
> groupStart(String name, String type)
>
> groupStart(int index, String type)
>
> groupEnd()

Whenever the redraw method begins drawing some object on the screen the application calls groupStart using one of the APIs listed above. When it is through drawing the object it calls groupEnd.

The first form of groupStart is used in the most common case where the presentation is implemented by interactor objects in our toolkit. In this case, the interactor object reference passed to the startGroup method provides a convenient identifier for reference to the semantic object.

It is important to note that the toolkit can supply groupStart and groupEnd calls of this form automatically without any effort (or change) on the part of the programmer. This is done by "hiding" these calls within toolkit base class code which already performs per-interactor drawing setup such as establishing a local coordinate system translation and setting the proper clipping rectangle. (A similar approach should be possible in most modern object-oriented toolkits.)

Only in the case where the application implements multiple conceptually separate objects within one toolkit object does the programmer need to explicitly add calls to groupStart and groupEnd. In this case, the programmer supplies either a name or an index, along with type information. This information (partially) identifies the object in question. As we will see below, this information does not have to be unique for each object, because we employ a sequence of such (partial) identifiers to establish object identity.

While addition of these calls involves a modification to the application, their nature is still designed to be as unobtrusive as possible. In particular, adding these calls will not normally require any modifications to the control or data structures used to implement application presentations. Instead they represent simple, independent statements that can be added to existing code (typically at the start and end of a drawing method) without otherwise disturbing its implementation. Further, the form of identification used here is designed to be general and application independent in nature, and to present little burden on the programmer.

This bracketing of drawing calls with object identity information is enough to support the observational attachments that we are interested in. Because groupStart/groupEnd pairs can be nested, a tree-like map is defined between the surface and the semantic model. Individual objects can be identified in this tree by a path or sequence of interactor references, names, and indices from the root to any object. Such a path defines the *identity* of an object and is employed as a *reference* to that object.

Consider the example of the bookmarker which needs to highlight objects for which it holds a reference. The bookmark attachment uses the generalized pointing technique described in [9]. Under this technique any unreferenced object has its colors blended with gray (to reduce its visual contrast) and any referenced object is drawn unchanged. By using the identification information in the reference, and by interposing its own version of drawable, the bookmarker can use the groupStart and groupEnd calls to know when to turn blending on and off. This allows its highlighting mechanism to be employed across applications. In fact, it operates without the application's knowledge at all.

As a more detailed example of how attachments operate consider the text search attachment from Figure 1. In our prototype system when an attachment is initialized and attached to an application it is given access to the top level interactor object of the application (applications which are aware of the attachment system are also given opportunity to specify a different object to represent their surface). When the user requests a search, the text search attachment will create a special object that is a subclass of drawable. This object ignores all of the drawing calls except those that draw text and the groupStart/groupEnd calls. The text search attachment takes the application's surface interactor and calls its draw_self method passing in the specialized object as the drawable. This forces the application to draw itself, not to the screen, but into our special class designed to glean information from the application's drawing.

The actual text searching is performed in the specialized drawable object while the surface interactor is drawing itself as it normally would. Whenever groupStart is called the specialized drawable object pushes the reference, name, or index onto a stack. Whenever groupEnd is called the stack is popped. When any text drawing call is made the string to be drawn is checked against the search string. If a match is found then a reference to the object currently being drawn is generated.

As discussed earlier, object references are paths from the root of a drawing down to the object being referenced. At the time that a matching text draw is detected the stack created by groupStart/groupEnd calls will contain just such a path. A reference is created from this stack and is added to the reference set of all matching objects. This reference is returned to the text search attachment when the matching process is complete.

It is very important to note that the application cannot distinguish between normal drawing requests from the windowing system and those used to search for text. The text search attachment requires no additional work on the part of the application other than the inclusion of groupStart/groupEnd calls to provide structure to the display.

Although the overhead of redrawing the entire application display (potentially including off-screen areas) could in some cases be a problem, in practice this have not been a significant issue because no actual drawing is performed. Instead this serves as a mechanism for searching application data without the assistance of the application, and has a cost that is not too much different from other simple traversals of that data to do a similar search.

As a second detailed example, consider a dictionary lookup attachment. In this case, only selected objects are of interest. References to such selected objects can be provided in several ways. References could come from another attachment on the basis of a search (using the same approach as the text search attachment above). References could also be provided directly by the application if it implements the optional capability of reporting its currently selected object set on demand. Finally, it is possible to perform object selection without additional assistance of the application.

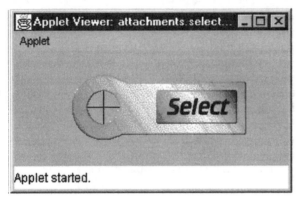

Figure 3. – A Selection Attachment

One way in which this is done is using an object selection attachment like the one shown in Figure 3. This attachment works like other attachments by performing a special draw of the application using its own drawable object (whenever its "select" button is pressed). In this case, the attachment sets a very small clipping rectangle surrounding the point of its crosshairs and records the reference path associated with any object which falls within that small area. Since the clipping rectangle is set to a small region, most applications will perform trivial rejection to eliminate most drawing, making this operation very fast in practice.

Given a selected object set, the dictionary lookup attachment operates in a similar fashion to other attachments – it performs a specialized drawing operation over the application. In this case the special drawable object used is one which extracts text only from drawing

that occurs as part of an object within the selected set. In order to optimize this specialized redrawing, the startGroup method returns a boolean value on each call. If the value is returned as false this indicates that the application may safely skip the drawing of the object (since, based on its identifying path it is known not to contain any selected objects). Applications which care to be attachment aware may choose to use this information to optimize their redraw. For startGroup/endGroup calls made automatically by a toolkit, this optimization is automatically applied with no effort by the programmer.

Manipulating output

In our example, the text search attachment itself does not do any modification of the application display. As described above, this is delegated to the bookmark attachment. The specifics of this delegation process will be discussed later. The bookmark attachment, however, is an example of an attachment that modifies the display of an application. The role of the bookmark attachment is to implement the generalized pointing or highlighting facility that can be employed by a range of other attachments. The bookmark attachment maintains a list of reference sets, each of which is associated with a color. In addition the bookmark maintains a control which sets the strength of the highlighting to be applied. The actual highlighting technique is shown in Figure 4. In this example the red bookmark is highlighting April 2-3 while the blue bookmark is highlighting April 3. The calendar application shown does not know of the existence of either bookmark.

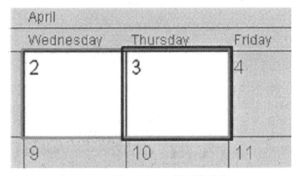

Figure 4 – Bookmark Highlighting

In order to implement the shading (dimming) of non-selected objects, the bookmark attachment must intercept and modify the drawing calls of the application as outlined above. To draw the colored borders the attachment must obtain access to the drawable being used by the application after the application has completed its drawing so that the borders can be drawn over the top. Similarly, it can also be useful to allow an attachment to draw before the application. (This can be used, for example, to create "halo" effects which place a highlight color behind and around an object.)

A mechanism for supporting each of these types of drawing is provided by our prototype attachment system. Each attachment may request to draw before, during, or after a particular application. Drawing modifications performed during application drawing are done by means of drawable *filters*. These filters are implemented as wrappers which may be placed around another drawable object and intercept and modify its drawing actions (see [7] for a complete discussion of this approach and [8] for related approaches).

The approach described for bookmarks could also be applied to an annotation attachment. The annotation attachment might want to draw a note icon next to any object that has an attached note. Such drawing would be done after the application without interfering with the behavior of the application itself.

These mechanisms also support attachments that manifest themselves as magic lenses™ [7, 8, 10]. In that case the attachment is simply placed over the top of the application itself (possibly leaving most of its area transparent). Any modifications to the application image (via wrapping the drawable, and/or drawing under or over the normal application output) are limited to the area covered by the attachment by setting the clipping rectangle to the attachment's current location. Once the modified application image has been created at the proper location, the attachment draws its own appearance (e.g., borders and controls for the lens) over the top of the lens contents.

Monitoring changes

Some attachments must also monitor what is happening on the application surface. Take for example the organization chart in Figure 1. The radar attachment is showing a representation of the application's entire surface with the bookmarks being highlighted on that representation. The radar provides a global view of the application's surface beyond what is seen in the application's window. In Figure 1 two nodes containing previously searched for text are selected and highlighted. A corresponding rectangle for each appears in the radar view. The radar view is not concerned with drawing on the application's surface because it is maintaining its own separate view of the world. If, however, the user were to drag one of the selected nodes to a different location, the radar view would need to update itself to display this change. The bookmark attachment must also update how it displays its highlighting.

As in other areas, the problem is that we do not want attachments to have application specific hooks into the semantics of applications and we do not want applications programmers to implement lots of special code to support the attachments. To accomplish this we make use of the fact that, at least in an observational setting, any significant semantic change that the user should know about will manifest itself at some point by a change in the application's presentation.

In modern graphical user interfaces changes to the display are forced by invalidating or declaring *damage* to the relevant portions of the display. When a portion of the display is damaged, redraw requests are propagated to get the new information drawn. Attachments can monitor all surface changes by monitoring the requests for areas of the screen to be redrawn. The only potential change that we make to an application is to require it to declare damage for all of its surface and not limit itself to the areas currently visible.

This same mechanism also provides the coordination needed to implement attachments displayed as lenses over the application. In that case, any redraw request that intersects the currently displayed area of the lens attachment can be monitored to request a redraw of the lens object as well.

THE ATTACHMENT/ATTACHMENT INTERFACE

All of the discussion so far has focused on the relationships between attachments and the application to which they are connected. In this section, we consider connections between attachments. As shown in our examples, in order to increase modularity and decrease the complexity of individual attachments, some attachments rely upon others to perform their tasks. The text search attachment for example, relies upon a bookmark attachment to highlight the objects that contain the specified text. The radar attachment also relies upon a bookmark attachment to provide the references and colors that the radar is to display.

When an attachment such as the text search or radar attachments are connected to an application, they must have their supporting attachments available. They must be able to locate the supporting attachments and establish communications with them.

Every attachment that provides a service to other attachments, does so by means of a Java interface declaration. This allows supporting attachments to be dealt with by categories instead of requiring specific attachments. For example, the text searcher does not care about the user interface that the bookmark implements, nor does it care about the particular style of highlighting used by the bookmark attachment. All that it cares about is that such an attachment is available to perform the service.

When an attachment is registered with the system it indicates the set of attachment interfaces that it supports. Attachments like text search and radar that require support of other attachments, indicate to the system the names of the interfaces that they require. For example the bookmark attachment implements the RefHighlighter interface and so indicates when it is registered with the system. The text search attachment and the radar attachment each indicate that they require an attachment with the RefHighlighter interface in order to function properly. If the user connects the text search attachment to an application, the system will check its list of connected attachments to see if there is already one that implements the required RefHighlighter interface (this approach is similar to the one pioneered in the CyberDesk system [11]). If the system does not find a suitable attachment already connected to the application, it will consult a registry of known attachment types to obtain such an attachment. It is possible that there is more than one registered attachment type that implements RefHighlighter. In that case the system employs a simple priority mechanism to use the type that is designated as preferred.

Selection of supporting attachments is done automatically at the time an attachment to an application is made. In addition, the system provides a mechanism for shutting down and detaching supporting attachments when they are no longer needed.

The interface between, for example, the text search and bookmark attachments is quite simple, but it is indicative of the kind of relationships that exist between modular attachments. Whenever a search is performed, the text search attachment calls the appropriate method to create a bookmark from the reference and the bookmark attachment does the display. The relationship between radar and bookmark is not quite as simple because the radar needs to know when new bookmarks are added or old bookmarks are changed. In this case, a protocol similar to the Java Beans event listeners is implemented. Using this technique the radar can register itself as a listener on the bookmark. The methods for registration are part of the RefHighlighter interface. There is no additional machinery required within the attachment system to establish such a relationship.

IMPLEMENATION STATUS

Our prototype attachment system currently runs in Java 1.1.5 on Windows/NT and a variety of other platforms as a part of the ICIE environment. We have implemented four demonstration applications in the ICIE environment, which we use to test our techniques. We have implemented the bookmark, text search and radar attachments shown in Figures 1 and 4, as well as the selection attachment shown in Figure 3. In addition we have implemented scrollbar-like awareness attachments that complement the radar by providing awareness in the vertical or horizontal dimension only. Finally, we have implemented a primitive (very small dictionary) spell checking attachment and a dictionary lookup attachment. By far the most interesting attachment being developed is one which supports speech navigation and inquiry on ICIE applications. At present the facilities for launching applications and attaching agents within the environment are somewhat primitive. However, other more sophisticated models for such services have already been considered at length in the form of operating system desktop interfaces.

CONCLUSIONS

The attachment architecture described here provides a general mechanism for users to interactively connect attachments to applications so that attachments can provide universal services across applications. Our observational attachments provide their functionality by extracting information from the surface drawings of the application. Such attachments not only provide informative and useful services based on application information, but also can modify the application's visible behavior in response to user requests. By exploiting surface information the attachments are independent of any application and do not require the application to perform more than minor additional work beyond the mechanisms it already uses for drawing. We believe that the techniques presented here are an important next step in architectures for interactive environments because they work in a much more application independent and ubiquitous manner than previous techniques.

ACKNOWLEDGEMENTS

This work was supported in part by grants from DARPA and Microsoft Corporation, as well as NSF grants IRI-9500942 and IIS-9800597.

REFERENCES

[1] Olsen, D. R., Buxton, W., Ehrich, R., Kasik, D. J., Rhyne, J. R., and Sibert, J., "A Context for User Interface Management" IEEE Computer Graphics and Applications (4), 12 (December 1984)

[2] Microsoft Corp. "Visual Basic 5.0 Programmers Guide", *Microsoft Press*, 1997.

[3] Sun Microsystems, "JavaBeans", Sun Microsystems Technical Documentation (available electronically as http://java.sun.com/beans/spec.html).

[4] Apple Computer, "Inside Macintosh: Interapplication Communication", *Addison Wesley Publishing*, Reading, Mass, 1993.

[5] Microsoft Corp. "OLE 2 Programmer's Reference Volume 2: Creating Programmable Applications with OLE Automation", *Microsoft Press*, 1996.

[6] Gutwin, C., Greenberg, S., "Workspace Awareness Support with Radar Views", *CHI '96 Conference Companion*, 1996, pp. 210-211.

[7] Edwards, W.K., Hudson, S., Rodenstein, R., Smith, I., and Rodrigues, T., "Systematic Output Modification in a 2D UI Toolkit", *Proceedings of the ACM Symposium on User Interface Software and Technology*, October 1997.

[8] Bier, E., Stone, M. and Pier, K., "Enhanced Illustration Using Magic Lens Filters", *IEEE Computer Graphics and Applications*, Vol. 17, No. 6, Nov. 1997.

[9] Olsen, D., Boyarski, D., Verratti, T., Phelps, M., Moffett, J., and Lo, E., "Generalized Pointing: Enabling Multiagent Interaction" Human Factors in Computing Systems (CHI '98), April 1998.

[10] Bier, E.A., Stone, M.C., Pier, K., Buxton, W., DeRose, T.D., "Toolglass and Magic Lenses: The See-Through Interface", *Proceedings of ACM SIGGRAPH '93 Conference on Computer Graphics and Interactive Techniques*, 1993, pp. 73-80.

[11] Wood A., Dey, K., Abowd, D., "CyberDesk: Automated Integration of Desktop and Network Services", *Proceedings of the 1997 Conference on Human Factors in Computing Systems (CHI '97)*, pp. 552-553. 1997.

A Visual Medium for Programmatic Control of Interactive Applications

Luke S. Zettlemoyer and Robert St. Amant
Department of Computer Science
North Carolina State University
EGRC-CSC Box 7534
Raleigh, NC 27695-7534
{lszettle | stamant}@eos.ncsu.edu

ABSTRACT

The VisMap system provides for "visual manipulation" of arbitrary off-the-shelf applications, through an application's graphical user interface. VisMap's API-independent control has advantages for tasks that can benefit from direct access to the functions of the user interface. We describe the design goals and architecture of the system, and we discuss two applications, a user-controlled visual scripting program and an autonomous solitaire-playing program, which together demonstrate some of the capabilities and limitations of the approach.

Keywords

Interaction techniques, agents, demonstrational interfaces, development tools

INTRODUCTION

In modern software environments, interactive applications often control one another in an arrangement that can lead to increased modularity, improved software reuse, and more coherence in the user interface, among other benefits. Rather than building special-purpose, standalone utilities, a developer can extend an application's functionality by way of its application programming interface, or API. This approach is followed by many commercial applications such as Netscape Navigator.

Unfortunately, current techniques for the programmatic control of interactive applications have subtle shortcomings. Suppose that I have devised a set of application-independent methods for computer-assisted tutoring for word processing, methods that depend on close interaction (perhaps at the mouse gesture level) with the user. As a developer, I face a number of obstacles. I must either limit my development to a single application or be forced to develop several versions of my software, one for

the API of each different application—sometimes for each different version of a single application. I must hope that the developers of each API have had the foresight to support the types of interaction I require. I must hope that the functions in each API are appropriate for the abstractions that will appear in my extensions to the user interface of the application. Even if my project appears trivial, from a user interface design viewpoint, a variety of such technical issues may bring it to a halt.

The problem lies with the mismatch between the functionality of an application as seen through its user interface and as seen through its API. The functionality of an interactive application is most naturally defined by its user interface: its capabilities have been carefully developed to offer specific coverage of tasks, to act at an appropriate level of abstraction, to accommodate the cognitive, perceptual, and physical abilities of the user. The API, on the other hand, is much more closely tied to the software architecture, with only an indirect relationship to the user interface. For some tasks, this indirection rules out the most appropriate means of managing interaction with the user. In some situations, we want to be able to control an interactive application directly, through the same medium that users rely on—its user interface.

We have developed a system, called VisMap (for "visual manipulation"), that supports the control of an application through its graphical user interface, bypassing its API. VisMap takes its input from the screen display, runs image processing algorithms over its contents to build a structured representation of interface objects, and passes this representation to a controller program. Responses from the controller are output by VisMap as mouse and keyboard gestures that control the application. VisMap allows a broad range of interaction with an application in this way, through the same medium as the user.

At first glance this approach may seem a profligate waste of processing power. Consider, however, that much of the time the processor would otherwise sit idle; much of the additional processing cost is hidden. Visual manipulation has potential advantages as well. For various reasons some applications lack an API; others allow only limited control through their API. In some cases (e.g. online tools for layout and task analysis) an API cannot substitute for direct access to the events and appearance of the interface. In general we hope that VisMap will contribute to the development of systems for programming by demonstration, improved macro recorders, wizards, help systems, tutorials, advisory systems, visual scripting systems, and agent-based systems—opportunities to extend off-the-shelf interactive systems that one cannot modify directly as a developer.

VisMap is a relatively new system, and thus we have not yet built applications in all these areas. Instead, we describe two applications that give the flavor of the approach, demonstrating its feasibility and some of its generality. The first, VisScript, gives users a simple facility for running visual scripts. Though as yet a simple prototype, VisScript promises greater flexibility and coverage than existing macro definition utilities. The second application, VisSolitaire, allows an artificial intelligence planning system to play solitaire. As a problem domain, solitaire poses few conceptual difficulties; rather, the task highlights VisMap's ability to control an application that has non-standard interface controls and no API. In both applications, VisMap is responsible for low-level interaction with the application, while the relevant domain knowledge is provided by easily interchanged controller modules.

Our work benefits the CHI community in two ways. From a developer's perspective, the direct benefit is a flexible complement to API-based control of interactive applications. Imagine for example building a tutorial or walkthrough for an arbitrary suite of applications, including tasks in the operating system, and being able to work at a consistent level of abstraction and with the same vocabulary across all the diverse components of the system. A designer need not be constrained by software architecture limitations when tasks can be accomplished through the user interface. The potential benefit for users is equally great, if less direct. The potential applications for VisMap, as described above, can extend the functionality and coherence of direct manipulation interfaces. Our early experience with the system and its applications has shown the approach to have considerable promise.

DESIGN GOALS

VisMap acts as an intermediary between a controlling application and an application to be controlled, which we will call the "controller" and the "application" respectively. Informally, VisMap provides the controller with the eyes and hands (the sensors and effectors) necessary to manage the application. The user may even act in the role of a controller, when appropriate. An earlier version of VisMap [13] has given us a good deal of insight into the design goals for this kind of system. Three sets of goals arise from the need to interact with applications, controllers, and users.

An enormous effort goes into the development of application user interfaces [6], toward the implicit goal of matching the abilities and limitations of human users. In interacting with applications through such interfaces, the ideal system accommodates and exploits this bias toward human-like perception, action, and cognition wherever possible.

1. Sensors: At the "physical" level, the system must process input from the joint human-computer system. This includes monitoring the mouse and keyboard as well as distinguishing visual and temporal patterns in the contents of the screen.

2. Effectors: At the same level, the system must be able to control an application through its user interface, via mouse and keyboard gestures.

3. Information processing: The system must be able to recognize the patterns in its input stream as constituting specific types of information, and to combine these patterns into known structures and relationships.

A second set of goals arises from the need to support controller programs. From a controller's perspective, the ideal system has these properties:

4. Coverage: It must provide the functions necessary to control a variety of applications, but in an application-independent manner.

5. Extensibility: It must support extensions, possibly application-dependent, beyond the basic coverage functions.

6. Representational flexibility: It must support a means of adjusting the amount and level of detail—setting the appropriate level of abstraction—in the information exchanged.

Finally, the ideal system cannot neglect the user, who is interacting with an otherwise direct manipulation environment. The system adds an element of autonomy to the environment: it may in some cases take actions not explicitly specified by the user. While this can be managed without subverting the benefits of direct manipulation [11], the ideal system must at a minimum address these issues:

7. User control: The system must respond continuously to user control, when it is available.

8. User awareness: It must be clear at all times whether the system is taking autonomous action in the interface.

The system we present in the next section does not meet all of these goals; it does however approach our ideals in its design. Even an ideal system, however, will encounter several limitations. First, the benefit of API-independence is offset by dependence on an application's user interface. If an interface supports extreme variations in look and feel layered over the same functionality, this can result in less generality for a visual system rather than more. Second, a purely visual system will have no access to the internal data

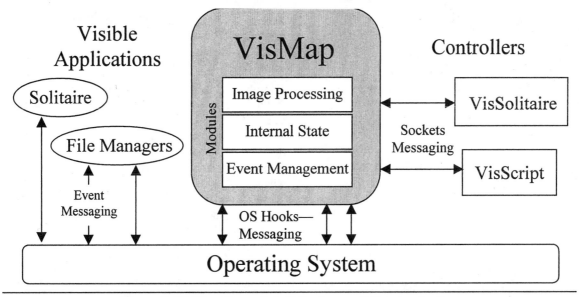

Figure 1. VisMap General Architecture and Communication

structures of an application. Others have demonstrated [9] that a good deal of information can be derived directly from the screen, information that would be difficult to gain otherwise, but not all useful information appears on the screen. Third, a visual system has no choice but to work through the interface. Even if a task might be better carried out behind the scenes, without the user's knowledge, this option is not available. These implications are unavoidable for a visual system and limit the range of its application.

SYSTEM DESIGN

We have described the general architecture of VisMap elsewhere [14]. Here we give a brief recap and discuss how it meets the design goals identified in the last section. VisMap is divided into three separate modules: the event management module, or EMM, the image processing module, or IPM, and the internal state representation module, or ISRM. These three modules provide all of VisMap's processing. VisMap's architecture and methods of communication can be seen in Figure 1.

The EMM handles events as both a sensor and an effector. It manipulates the operating system's event queue, able both to observe user-initiated events as they pass through the queue and to insert its own events into the queue. In its sensor role the EMM supports the first design goal by maintaining an internal variable-length queue of user-generated events for processing in later stages. In its effector role the EMM meets the second design goal: its event insertions are indistinguishable from user-generated events. The EMM can be used to select icons, click buttons, pull down menus, turn on radio buttons, and carry out all other standard operations we have experimented with. These are implemented as sequences of low-level events: *move-mouse, mouse-down, mouse-up, key-down,* and *key-*

up. Some useful higher-level abstractions, such as *click-button*, which requires a sequence of these more primitive events, have been implemented, but the issue of deciding on an appropriate level of abstraction currently remains open.

The IPM rounds out support for the first design goal and partially meets the third, in a conventional sequence of image processing stages [1]. The IPM begins with a two-dimensional image of the screen. In the *segmentation* stage, the module breaks the image into pixel groups by color. The white background of a list box, for example, would end up in a single group. In the *feature computation* stage the module attaches features to each group that describe its internal structure and its relationship with other groups. Figure gives an example that shows how the "area" feature of an pixel group would be computed. Note that these computations are data-driven, bottom-up—there is no guarantee that a feature will be useful for the interpretation of a given group. In the *interpretation* stage, features are iteratively combined via rules to build structures that correspond to "meaningful" objects. In contrast to the second stage, interpretation is top-down. Rules are hypotheses that must be verified in their identification of objects in the interface. Figure shows an interpretation rule for identifying a list box.

The ISRM is responsible for integrating the information provided by the IPM and the EMM over time. It maintains a representation of the temporal and spatial changes observable through the screen buffer. This information is then available to controllers so they can observe changes in their applications. The ISRM completes our coverage of the sensor/information processing design goals.

Operation GetArea()
MaxPossibleNumPixels = GetWidth() * GetHeight()
Area = ActualNumPixels() /MaxPossibleNumPixels
Return Area

Figure 2. A feature computation of area

If there exists a downArrow()
That is containedIn() a raisedButton()
That is toTheRightOf() a rectangularTextArea()
Which is recessed() and has a width()
greater than its height()
Then we have found a list box

Figure 3. An interpretation rule to identify a list box

In pursuing the first set of design goals we have in effect defined a simple artificial user, a kind of programmable user model. A system limited to our description so far, however, is incomplete: it is entirely independent of an operating environment. This issue is addressed by the second set of design goals, which require that we flesh out the feature computation and interpretation rule libraries of the IPM until they have sufficient coverage of functionality in a real user interface (Microsoft Windows in our current implementation.)

The IPM contains in total 29 feature computation functions and 80 interpretation rules of the types shown in Figure 2 and Figure 3. A sample of the IPM's processing is shown in Figure 4. The top picture shows the original interface, the bottom picture all of the widgets that the IPM has identified. Given the performance of its libraries across a variety of applications, VisMap can claim good coverage (the fourth design goal) in interacting with the user interface.

The fifth design goal requires that a controller be able to extend VisMap's capabilities to handle special-purpose processing. For example, an application may include specialized controls that are not commonly found in other domains and are not be available thorough any APIs. Server-side image maps displayed in web browsers are a common example. Visual representations of interactive widgets are not accessible to the browser or the local system; processing is handled remotely by the server. To a VisMap controller, however, a button graphic with the appropriate appearance, however generated, is treated no differently than an actual widget in a local application.

The sixth design goal entails giving a controller the ability to tailor its interaction with VisMap to an appropriate level of abstraction. For example, should every mouse movement event, every mouse up and mouse down, be passed to the controller? Perhaps common abstractions, such as selection? The current implementation of VisMap is relatively inflexible in this regard. The level of representation is programmable, but cannot be varied at run time. Controllers connect to VisMap through standard TCP

sockets to communicate with a fixed set of commands and responses. The interaction, though limited, supports the necessary range of communication for our prototype controllers.

To summarize VisMap's coverage of the design goals up to this point, the sensor/effector design goals are met. VisMap can reliably recognize all the user interface controls we have worked with: buttons, scroll bars (including the scroll box, scroll arrows, and background regions), list boxes, menu items, check boxes, radio buttons and application windows. VisMap also meets the fourth and fifth design goals by providing a basic set of functions, which can be extended at the cost of a nontrivial programming effort. The sixth design goal of variable abstraction is not met.

User interaction issues, touched on in the final two design goals, raise a number of unsolved problems. VisMap essentially adds another player to the user interface environment. Depending on the controller, a VisMap-based system may exhibit a high degree of autonomy or none at all. (Examples of these two extremes are described in the sections below.) Mixed-initiative interaction with an automated system raises a number of elementary HCI questions: Will users know where they are in the interaction

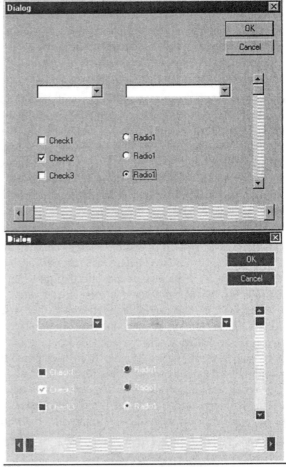

Figure 4. IPM results

Screen Resolution	Sample Execution Time
640x480	2.32 seconds
800x600	3.72 seconds
1024x768	5.85 seconds
1152x864	7.81 seconds

Figure 5. Screen Processing Execution Times

process? Will they know how they arrived there, what they can do, where they can go from there? These questions cannot be answered for VisMap in isolation, but must be considered in the context of its integration with a specific controller and application.

In VisMap's current state of development, we must sidestep these and related questions until we have gained more experience with its use. VisMap does nevertheless ensure that its autonomous actions are accompanied by strong visual cues that control has temporarily shifted away from the user, and that its activity can easily be interrupted and turned off.

VisMap comprises 2,800 lines of C++ code. Runtime efficiency has been considered for different screen resolutions and effort is being put into increasing the speed of execution. Current sample running time for various screen resolutions on a 300 megahertz Pentium II processor with 128 megabytes of RAM are given in Figure 5.

Notably, only about 3% of the system is specific to the Windows operating system. This lends support to our claim that VisMap is largely platform-independent and operating system-independent (e.g., VisMap should easily port to a Windows emulator running on a Macintosh or a Unix machine.) Another 40% is specific to Windows interface conventions for visual display: the appearance of buttons, list boxes, and other controls. This latter point may seem to contradict our earlier claim; however, one of the strengths of VisMap is that it separates operating system issues from user interface issues. A port to the Macintosh and its native environment, to test the degree of dependence on the user interface, is in planning.

VisSolitaire

Building a system that allows a computer to play solitaire without the intervention of a human user—in other words, to waste time all by itself—has more serious underpinnings than it might initially appear. A great deal of work in agent-based systems, demonstrational interfaces, and other AI-driven approaches to improving user interaction could benefit from a stronger connection to commercial applications, to gain leverage from market pressures that constantly increase the power and flexibility of interactive software. Many (even most) interactive AI systems, however, never leave the research laboratory.

We believe that a contributing factor is the difficulty in developing a tight integration with existing applications at the user interface. Solitaire represents applications that pose obstacles to such an integration:

- The application uses non-standard icons in its interface, which means that a controller cannot simply ask for, say, the positions of the windows or buttons in the interface.

- The application has no API, which means that conventional programmatic control is not possible in any case.

- The internals of the application are not available to us as developers; we cannot simply rewrite it to accommodate external control.

- Assistance in the application can reasonably take the form of direct action, rather than advice to the user (e.g., "In order to accomplish your task, follow steps X, Y, and Z.")

VisSolitaire, an exemplar of a VisMap-based system, has three components. The first component is the application, an unmodified version of Microsoft Solitaire. VisMap is the second component, responsible for the visual and physical aspects of the game, such as interpreting layout and screen icons, and moving the mouse. The third component is an AI planning system (UCPOP [8]) which handles the strategy of solitaire through an abstract game-playing representation.

The integration of these components is straightforward. The application generates an initial game state, displayed as card images the screen. For the initial move and each thereafter, VisMap identifies the cards and groups them in their layout, the stock, waste, tableau, and foundation piles. This process occurs through the segmentation, feature computation, and interpretation stages described above; it leads to a screen-coordinate representation of all cards in play. From the Cartesian representation VisMap constructs a symbolic abstraction and passes it to the planner. The planner processes the game state, selects a move, and passes it back to VisMap to be executed.

The planner maintains most of the relevant knowledge about the problem, represented in a set of plan operators, or a domain. The planner analyzes the state representation supplied by VisMap and constructs a plan to satisfy the top-

```
(:operator tableau-to-foundation
  :parameters (?tn ?tr ?s ?fn ?fr)
  :precondition (and (tableau-last ?tn ?tr ?s)
                     (foundation-last ?fn ?fr ?s)
                     (previous-rank ?tr ?fr))
  :effect (tableau-to-foundation ?tn ?tr ?s ?fn ?fr))
```

Figure 6. Solitaire operator

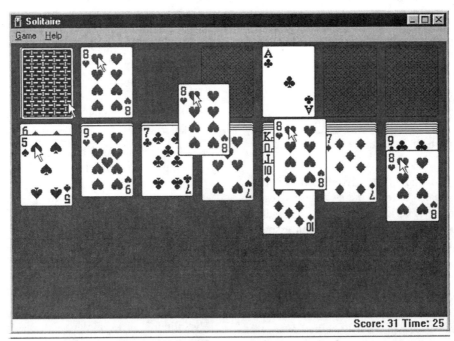

Figure 7. VisSolitaire playing solitaire

level goal of making a move. In actuality, because we are not especially concerned with solitaire-playing strategies, there is very little planning involved. A sample operator, of ten in total, is shown in Figure 6. Parameters in the operator shown contain numerical identifiers for the tableau and foundation piles and the suits and ranks of the cards. If the precondition of this operator holds in the current environment, the effect specifies that the card of suit *s* and rank *tr* should be moved from tableau pile *tn* to foundation pile *fn*, to end up on the card with suit *s* and rank *fr*. The top-level goal for the planner, in all initial states, is simply the disjunction of the effects of all its operators.

In this implementation, the planner returns operators that are specified down to the level of commands to press and release the mouse button and to move the mouse from one location to another (though these locations are in an abstract representation independent of screen coordinates.) We could easily have arranged for interaction to occur at a higher level of abstraction: "Drag 4S to 5H," for example, ignoring the lowest level of mouse event processing, or even "Move 4S to 5H," abstracting away the relationship between mouse gestures and card movement altogether. Our decision was to retain a high degree of detail at the planner level, rather than adding what could be considered domain knowledge to VisMap. A sample interaction sequence between VisMap and VisSolitaire is shown in Figure 8. An important issue remains open: how the level of abstraction of the interaction can be modified, ideally on the fly, for conceptual clarity and efficiency.

VisSolitaire plays a reasonable game of solitaire, from the starting deal to a win or loss. The planner maintains a minimal amount of state information between moves,

including a record of the sequence of its moves. On encountering the same cards after working through the stock, with no intervening moves that have changed the tableau or foundation, the system stops with the loss.

VisSolitaire is implemented in Harlequin Lispworks and communicates with VisMap via sockets. The VisMap feature recognition rules required some time and effort to build, enough to motivate future work on support tools for their development.

VisScript

Researchers on both sides of the direct manipulation/autonomous agents debate recognize the importance of visual scripting to the future of direct manipulation interfaces. Shneiderman calls graphical macro tools his favorite project to advance general computing [12]. Myers describes a wide range of benefits to incorporating scripting into the interface [6]: the automation of repetitive tasks, the addition of useful levels of abstraction, the delegation of

VisSolitaire COMMAND:

    (GET-CARDS-LAYOUT)

VisMap RESPONSE:

    ((((8 :HEARTS) 2 1)

    ((:ACE :CLUBS) 5 1)

    ((6 :DIAMONDS) 1 2)

    ((5 :SPADES) 1 2)

    ...

    ((9 :CLUBS) 7 2))

Figure 8. Sample interaction sequence

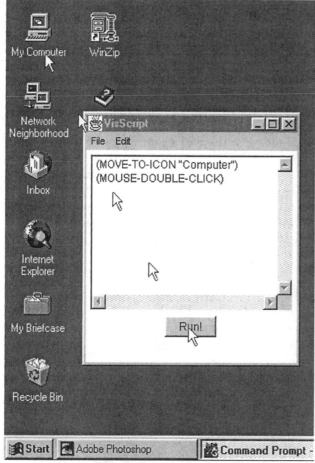

Figure 9. VisScript executing a simple script

responsibility for low-level activities. Unfortunately, a visual scripting tool based on current technology, even if it were able to provide all these benefits, would still suffer a number of drawbacks:

- Application-dependence: Some scripting tools can only be used within a single application (e.g. macro definition in Microsoft Word.)

- System-dependence: Some tools can exist only within a specialized interface framework (such as Garnet or Amulet [7].)

- Interoperability: Existing scripting tools that can move between the interfaces of different applications, as well as the operating system, can access only a limited subset of the available functionality.

Another necessary element of a scripting tool is user control—users should be able to write scripts and execute them on demand. We have designed these considerations into VisScript, an early prototype for executing scripts through the user interface. VisScript is an attempt to provide a tool with which users can simplify their interactions with standard pre-existing user interfaces. While VisScript is not a general purpose visual macro system, we have taken important first steps towards reaching the above goals.

VisScript allows users to enter commands and add them to a script to be executed. The current list of commands includes *move-mouse*, *singe-click*, *double-click*, and *move-mouse-to-text*. These commands are combined in Figure 9, which shows a script that allows the system to open a file manager for the top level directory. During execution, the progression through the script is entirely linear; VisScript does not incorporate programming constructs to control its flow. The commands are sent to VisMap to be executed one at a time and the user can watch as the are performed.

VisScript is implemented in Java and communicates with VisMap through TCP sockets. VisScript can run on the same machine as VisMap or remotely. Working with VisMap as a foundation, we were able to develop VisScript in less than two days of programming effort. We consider this evidence of the generality of VisMap and its potential for building other useful tools.

RELATED WORK

A recent paper describes an earlier prototype of the VisMap system, along with an application in usability testing [14]. The system presented at that time had a number of limitations that are addressed in the current version. The most significant step forward is conceptual: the earlier system presented evidence that a visual manipulation system *could* be built; in this paper we have presented our perspective on how a visual manipulation system *should* be built. More concretely, unlike the earlier system, the current system can run fast enough to handle interaction with users, although not at high rates of speed. Its interpretation rules encompass a broad range of patterns that appear in the user interface, not simply limited to standard controls. It supports multiple simultaneous controllers, for a planned application in cooperative computing environments.

The VisMap effort draws on three main areas of research: user interface agents, programming by demonstration, and programmable user models.

Lieberman outlines a number of areas relevant to the VisMap approach [4]. His discussion emphasizes the importance of granularity of event protocols, styles of interaction with the user, and parallelism considerations. Event granularity determines the level of abstraction at which an agent interacts with an interface. For example, should mouse movements be included in the information exchanged? If not all mouse movements (possibly a very large number, depending on the sampling rate), then which ones are important? An interaction style describes the way in which an agent interacts with the user. That is, it may not always be sufficient for an agent to execute commands in an interface; it may be necessary to communicate directly with the user. This can force a different interaction style, for example, on an agent designed mainly for direct manipulation interactions. Issues of parallelism can enter the picture when the agent and the user both try to manipulate the same interface object. System performance can also be affected by the activities of an agent. As discussed earlier, VisMap does not address these issues in detail. For its current applications, it works at a system event granularity, though its controllers operate at a higher level of abstraction. As yet it has no mechanisms for communicating directly with the user or managing parallel activities.

Potter's TRIGGERS system [9] is an early example of an approach similar to ours. TRIGGERS is an example of a system for programming by demonstration, one of only a few examples that work with off-the-shelf software. TRIGGERS performs pattern matching on pixels on the computer screen in order to infer information that is otherwise unavailable to an external agent. A "trigger" is a condition/action pair. Triggers are defined for such tasks as surrounding a text field with a rounded rectangle in a drawing program, shortening lines so that they intersect an arbitrary shape, and converting text to a bold typeface. The user defines a trigger by stepping through a sequence of actions in an application, adding annotations for the TRIGGERS system when appropriate. Once a set of triggers have been defined, the user can activate them, iteratively and exhaustively, to carry out their actions. From TRIGGERS VisMap adopts the notion that the screen itself is a powerful source of information for an agent, if it can be properly interpreted.

The third area, programmable user models, has contributed only indirectly to VisMap's development. In Young's original description [13], PUMs were engineering models, not to be executed directly. The intention was to provide designers with an engineering model that could give predictions at an early stage in user interface development. This approach has shown significant promise, especially in the recent work of Kieras and Meyer [3]. A natural extension, which VisMap pursues, is the construction of executable PUMs that can be applied directly to implemented systems as well as those in the design stage. The architecture of VisMap has no strong foundation in cognitive theory, but could accommodate such a foundation in an appropriate controller.

CONCLUSION

We view our work as facilitating technology. Many of the most interesting extensions of graphical user interfaces have been demonstrated in isolated research systems, and have failed to make the transition to commercially available software. We believe that the general layer VisMap provides will allow such work (e.g. in visual scripting [7], demonstrational interfaces [6], mixed-initiative interfaces [10], and agents that interact directly with users [5]) to reach the mainstream.

ACKNOWLEDGMENTS

We wish to thank Derrick Foley, who contributed significantly to the development of character recognition rules in VisSolitaire. Support for this work was provided by North Carolina State University and the William R. Kenan Institute for Engineering, Technology, and Science.

REFERENCES

1. Gentner, D., and Nielsen, J. The Anti-Mac Interface, *Communications of the ACM*, 39:8 (August, 1996), 70-82.

2. Gonzales, R.C. and Woods, R.W. *Digital Image Processing*. Addison-Wesley, Reading, MA. 1992.

3. Kieras, D. and Meyer, D. E. An overview of the EPIC architecture for cognition and performance with application to human-computer interaction. *Human-Computer Interaction*.

4. Lieberman, H. Integrating User Interface Agents with Conventional Applications. *Proceedings of Intelligent User Interfaces '98*. (San Francisco, CA, January, 1998.) ACM Press, 39-46.

5. Maes, P. Agents that Reduce Work and Information Overload. *Communications of the ACM*, 37:7, (July 1994), 31-40.

6. Myers, B. Demonstrational Interfaces: A Step Beyond Direct Manipulation, *Watch What I Do: Programming by Demonstration*, Allen Cypher, et. al., eds. MIT Press Cambridge, MA. 1993. pp. 485-512.

7. Myers, B. Scripting Graphical Applications by Demonstration. Proceedings of CHI '98. (Los Angeles, CA, April, 1998.) 534-541.

8. Penberthy, J. and Weld, D. UCPOP: A sound, complete, partial-order planner for ADL. *Proceedings of the Third International Conference on Knowledge Representation and Reasoning*. 1992. Morgan Kaufmann, 103-114.

9. Potter, R. Triggers: Guiding Automation with Pixels to Achieve Data Access. In *Watch What I Do: Programming by Demonstration*. MIT Press, Cambridge, MA. 1993.

10. Rich, C. and Sidner C. L. Adding a Collaborative Agent to Graphical User Interfaces, *Proceedings of UIST'96*, (1996), 21-30.

11. Shneiderman, B. Direct Manipulation for comprehensible, predictable, and controllable user interfaces. *Proceedings of Intelligent User Interface'97*. (Orlando, FL, January, 1997.) ACM Press, 33-39.

12. Shneiderman, B., and Maes, P. Debate: Direct Manipulation vs. Interface Agents. *Interactions*, 4:6 (November and December, 1997), 42-61.

13. Young, R. M., Green, T. R. G., and Simon, T. Programmable User Models for Predictive Evaluation of Interface Designs. *Proceedings of CHI '89*. 15-19.

14. Zettlemoyer, L. S., St. Amant, R., and Dulberg, M. S. Application control through the user interface. *Proceedings of Intelligent User Interfaces '99*. (Redondo Beach, Los Angeles, CA, January, 1999.) To appear.

Should We Leverage Natural-Language Knowledge?
An Analysis of User Errors in a
Natural-Language-Style Programming Language

Amy Bruckman and **Elizabeth Edwards**
College of Computing
Georgia Institute of Technology
Atlanta, GA 30332-0280 USA
asb@cc.gatech.edu, lizzie@cc.gatech.edu

ABSTRACT

Should programming languages use natural-language-like syntax? Under what circumstances? What sorts of errors do novice programmers make? Does using a natural-language-like programming language lead to user errors? In this study, we read the entire online interactions of sixteen children who issued a total of 35,047 commands on MOOSE Crossing, an educational MUD for children. We counted and categorized the errors made. A total of 2,970 errors were observed. We define "natural-language errors" as those errors in which the user failed to distinguish between English and code, issuing an incorrect command that was more English-like than the correct one. A total of 314 natural-language errors were observed. In most of those errors, the child was able to correct the problem either easily (41.1% of the time) or with some effort (20.7%). Natural-language errors were divided into five categories. In order from most to least frequent, they are: syntax errors, guessing a command name by supplying an arbitrary English word, literal interpretation of metaphor, assuming the system is keeping more state information than is actually the case, and errors of operator precedence and combination. We believe that these error rates are within acceptable limits, and conclude that leveraging users' natural-language knowledge is for many applications an effective strategy for designing end-user-programming languages.

Keywords

Natural language, novice programming, programming language design, end-user programming.

A HISTORICAL PERSPECTIVE

Since the very beginning of computing, the use of natural-language-like syntax for programming languages has been controversial. In fact, the use of words of any kind was initially hotly debated. Admiral Grace Murray Hopper, speaking at the history of programming languages conference in 1978, told this story:

"In the early years of programming languages, the most frequent phrase we heard was that the only way to program a computer was in octal. Of course a few years later a few people admitted that maybe you could use assembly language. But the entire establishment was firmly convinced that the only way to write an efficient program was in octal. They totally forgot what happened to me when I joined Eckert-Mauchly. They were building BINAC, a binary computer. We programmed it in octal. Thinking I was still a mathematician, I taught myself to add, subtract, multiply, and even divide in octal. I was really good, until the end of the month, and then my checkbook didn't balance! [Laughter] It stayed out of balance for three months until I got hold of my brother who's a banker. After several evenings of work he informed me that at intervals I had subtracted in octal. And I faced the major problem of living in two different worlds. That may have been one of the things that sent me to get rid of octal as far as possible." [1]

A somewhat puritanical spirit pervaded the early days of computing. Computers were astronomically expensive, and many argued that their resources shouldn't be squandered to cater to the weakness of human programmers. If coding in octal was time-consuming or error-prone, the coders were simply not working hard enough. It took time to recognize that those delays and errors are inevitable, and better accommodating the needs of the human programmer is not indulgent coddling but simply good business sense. Today, computers are no longer so expensive, but elements of the underlying attitude remain: technologies that are too user-friendly are often denigrated as "not serious."

In 1959, a committee with representatives from industry and government was formed to design a "Common Business Language"—what eventually became COBOL. At one of their first meetings, they made a list of desired characteristics of the new language. It began with these two points:

"a) Majority of the group favored maximum use of simple English language; even though some participants suggested there might be advantage from using mathematical symbolism.

b) A minority suggested that we steer away from problem-oriented language because English language is not a panacea as it cannot be manipulated as algebraic expressions can." [2]

As these early observations indicate, how natural-language-like to make a programming language is a matter of trade-offs. The COBOL committee was concerned primarily with *manipulability*—in other words, expressive power for mathematical applications. A second common concern is *ambiguity*: words may mean something different in typical English usage than in a program [3, 4]. Another key issue and the primary concern of this paper is *learnability* and the slippery slope of natural language: will novice programmers be able to draw a distinction between English and code? Will they try to insert arbitrary English sentences into programs?

More than twenty-five years after the design of COBOL, the designers of Hypertalk had similar goals and strategies. When asked about the language ancestors of Hypertalk, designer Bill Atkinson replied "The first one is English. I really tried to make it English-like" [5]. Ted Kaehler, another member of the Hypertalk design team, comments that "One principle was 'reads as English, but does not write as English.' Like an ordinary programming language, it depends on exactly the right syntax and terms" [6]. English-like scripting languages are becoming more common, but few empirical studies have addressed the pros and cons of this design approach.

A NATURAL-LANGUAGE-STYLE LANGUAGE

Work on the MOOSE programming language began in mid-1993, and it has been in public use since October 1995. The language was designed for one restricted application: for children to create places, creatures, and other objects that have behaviors in a text-based multi-user virtual world (or "MUD"[1]). The fundamental goal is for children to learn reading, writing, and computer programming through the process of creating such objects [13]. This is an unusual design goal: the process of programming and what is learned from that process is more important than the product (the program created).

The design of MOOSE borrows liberally from the MOO language (on top of which it is built [14-16]) and from Hypertalk. Another significant influence is Logo, the first programming language designed explicitly for kids [17]. The designers[2] deliberately tried to make the MOOSE language as natural-language-like as possible while

maintaining a regular syntax. While some researchers are investigating the use of free-form natural language [18], we felt that a natural-language-like approach which still maintained a degree of formal syntax was a more promising compromise. The following is a MOOSE program written by Wendy (girl, age 10-12)[3], one of the randomly selected subjects of this study. The program choreographs a sequence of events as a magical book is opened:

```
on read blue book
    tell context "You take an old and musty blue
        book off of the shelf. As you blow the dust
        off the cover, a symbol painted in gold
        appears. It resembles a circle with a ~ in
        the middle" + "."
    announce_all_but context context's name +
        "carefully takes an old,large,and musty
        blue volume off of the shelf" + "." +
        context's psc + " blows gently. The dust
        swirls up in a flurry of gray mysts⁴. A
        symbol imprinted in gold on the cover
        emerges. It resembles a circle with a ~ in
        the middle" + "..."
    fork 5
        tell context "You hesitantly open this
            strange book. As you peer inside, you see
            a life like painting of a brook behind a
            poppy field and infront of an apple
            orchard...."
        announce_all_but context context's psc + "
            hesitantly opens the strange book."
        fork 15
            announce "A strong wind blows in from the
                open windows. It grows stronger and
                stronger and STRONGER....."
            fork 5
                announce_all_but context context's name
                    + "Is suddenly lifted up into the
                    air, and carried off...."
                tell context "You are lifted off your
                    feet and are carried off...Up over
                    the     trees,     houses,     lakes,
                    meadows...."
                fork 3
                    move player to #4551
                endfork
            endfork
        endfork
    endfork
end
```

---

[1] "MUD" stands for "Multi-User Dungeon." The first MUDs were violent adventure games [7]. More recently, the technology has been adapted for a variety of purposes including professional communities [8-10] and educational applications [11, 12].

[2] The MOOSE language was designed by Amy Bruckman with guidance from Pavel Curtis, Mitchel Resnick, and Brian Silverman, and assistance from MIT students Austina DeBonte, Albert Lin, and Trevor Stricker.

---

[3] The children's online pseudonyms have been changed to protect their identities.

[4] Children's spelling and grammar have been left unchanged.

When you run this program by typing "read blue book," you are magically transported to a babbling brook. This is what you see:

```
You take an old and musty blue book off of the
shelf. As you blow the dust off the cover, a
symbol painted in gold appears. It resembles a
circle with a ~ in the middle.
```

[pause]

```
You hesitantly open this strange book. As you
peer inside, you see a life like painting of a
brook behind a poppy field and infront of an
apple orchard....
```

[pause]

```
A strong wind blows in from the open windows.
It grows stronger and stronger and
STRONGER.....
```

```
You are lifted off your feet and are carried
off...Up over the trees, houses, lakes,
meadows....
```

[pause]

```
Babbling Brook
```

```
You are in a small meadow filled with poppies.
As the breeze frolicks above the flowers, the
dance and sway like the sea. Behind you is a
forest of apple trees, pear trees, orange
trees, and peach trees.Underneath them is a
carpet of green green moss, soft and springy.
Beside you is a babbling brook which giggles
and laughs as it slides down over the sMOOth
pebbles. As you stick your foot in you are
suprised. This stream is not cold like all the
others, but warm, and soothing. Tiny mare's
tails walts across the sky.Can this last
forever? It is late-afternoon summer. A
bright sunny day with few clouds.
```

The syntax of a basic MOOSE command is a verb followed by some number of arguments. Arguments can be string constants, numbers, or references to objects. Quoting of strings is optional as long as those strings don't contain words that function as logical operators (such as "and"). The environment includes both a command-line language and scripting language, which were designed to be as nearly identical as possible. This allows the learner to try most commands out at the command line, and later use them in programs. A more complete description of the language and principles that underlie its design appears in [13].

The language was designed with eight basic heuristics:

1. Have a gently-sloping learning curve.
2. Prefer intuitive simplicity over formal elegance.
3. Be forgiving.
4. Leverage natural-language knowledge.
5. Avoid non-alphanumeric characters wherever possible.
6. Make essential information visible and easily changeable.
7. It's OK to have limited functionality.
8. Hide nasty things under the bed. [13]

Are these heuristics useful? Under what circumstances? Of particular interest is rule four, "Leverage natural-language knowledge." The designers felt that a natural-language-like programming language would increase accessibility to young children. However, we worried about the slippery slope of natural language: would children understand the differences between MOOSE and English? This paper attempts to address that question systematically.

NAME	AGE	TIME OF ACTIVE MEMBERSHIP	COMMANDS ISSUED	OBJECTS CREATED	SCRIPTS PROGRAMMED	SCRIPTING LEVEL ACHIEVED
Percy	6	7 min.	15	1	0	
Jessica	7	3 days	79	1	0	
Wowzers	8-9	7 mo.	190	11	1	Basic
Snickers	9-10	15 days	2398	31	12	Basic
Hope	10	2 days	145	5	0	
Liono	10	2 mo.	217	4	0	
Reebok	10-11	6 mo.	1379	17	10	Basic
Wendy	10-12	21 mo.	15719	56	49	Advanced
Sheriff	11-12	2 mo.	609	17	0	
Mike	11-15	33 mo.	40182 (1275)	129	234	Expert
Oracle	12	7 days	467	1	2	Basic
Darcy	13	3 days	158	7	0	
Altair	15	49 min.	68	1	0	
Lucy	15	2.5 mo.	70	2	2	Basic +
Pedro	15-16	6 mo.	3617	17	21	Advanced
Sven	16	1 mo.	8641	21	12	Intermediate

Table 1: Randomly selected study subjects

Note that this paper addresses the risks and possible downsides of natural-language-style programming, but not the benefits. Three years of observation of children using the MOOSE language in the virtual world called MOOSE Crossing have led us subjectively to believe that it has significant benefits. Children as young as seven have been able to program in MOOSE. Kids can immediately read other children's programs and use them as examples to learn from. The intuition that reliance on natural language is part of what makes this possible is based on years of participant observation, clinical interviews, and log file analysis. A systematic analysis of the benefits of natural-language-style programming would be desirable. However, that is beyond the scope of this study, and is left for future work. In this study, we attempt to examine the downside risks systematically.

THE STUDY

At the time of this writing, the MOOSE language has been used for almost three years by 299 children and 211 adults. All input to and output from the system is recorded, with written informed consent from both parents and children. A total of 1.1 Gb of data has been recorded as of July 31st, 1998.[5] To re-evaluate the language's design and principles underlying it, we randomly selected 16 children, and categorized every error each child made. While this retrospective analysis is not a controlled study, the data is intriguing and we believe sheds light on general questions of programming language design for children.

Data about the random sample of children appears in Table 1. The children range in age from six to fifteen at the start of their participation. Their length of involvement ranges from seven minutes to thirty-three months. The total number of commands they typed into the system (which ranges from 15 to 40,182) is perhaps a better measure of their varying degrees of involvement. Seven of the children wrote no programs; five attained basic or slightly above basic programming knowledge; one, intermediate knowledge; two, advanced knowledge; one, expert knowledge. Definitions of coding categories are:

Basic	Simple output.
Intermediate	Conditionals, property references, variables.
Advanced	List manipulation, control flow.
Expert	Complex projects using all language features and constructs.

The children's level of achievement is based on what language constructs they were able to use independently in original programs. For example, Snickers has a number of programs with intermediate language constructs;

---

[5] Most data for one roughly six-month period (6/10/97-12/1/97 was lost due to a technical problem. Most of Lucy's participation was during this time. The other subjects are less directly affected.

however, he received significant assistance in writing that code and never demonstrated that he understood everything he was shown. Consequently, he is listed in the Basic category.

For each child, Elizabeth Edwards read the child's entire online experiences, and categorized each error the child made. (With one significant exception: Mike's degree of participation was so high that it was logistically impossible for us to read his entire log file. Instead, we sampled his participation by randomly selecting one month per year for a total of 1,275 of his 40,182 commands typed.) "Errors" most typically are times when the system returned an error message; however, we also subjectively inferred situations in which the output from the system was likely not what the child desired. For example, Wendy typed:

```
describe here as the way it was
before!!
```

We can reasonably infer that the outcome (the room was described literally as "the way it was before!!") was not what she intended.

NUMBER OF ERRORS	NUMBER OF COMMANDS TYPED	ERROR RATE (ERRORS/TOTAL COMMANDS)
2970	35047	8.5%

Table 2: Over-all error rate observed

KID NAME	ERRORS	PERCENT NATURAL LANGUAGE (NAT.-LANG. ERRORS/TOTAL ERRORS)	SCRIPT LEVEL
Percy	1	0.0% (0)	
Jessica	3	0.0% (0)	
Wowzers	22	9.1% (2)	Basic
Snickers	394	15.2% (60)	Basic
Hope	29	10.3% (3)	
Liono	67	7.5% (5)	
Reebok	148	7.4% (11)	Basic
Wendy	975	11.3% (110)	Advanced
Sheriff	134	12.7% (17)	
Mike	155	12.3% (19)	Expert
Oracle	27	3.7% (1)	Basic
Darcy	45	6.7% (3)	
Altair	3	33.3% (1)	
Lucy	12	0.0% (0)	Basic +
Pedro	432	13.7% (59)	Advanced
Sven	523	4.4% (23)	Intermediate

Table 3: Errors for each child

For the sixteen children, a total of 2,970 errors were observed (see Table 2). They are broken down per child in Table 3. There is no apparent correlation between the child's age or level of programming achievement and the number of natural language or other errors they make.

Errors are divided into seven basic categories (see Table 4). From most to least frequent, they are: object manipulation, command-line syntax, typos, scripting syntax, movement, system bugs, and communication/interaction errors. A more detailed breakdown appears in Table 5.

Interaction in the virtual world takes place at the interactive command-line prompt. Scripts are written in a separate window, in a client program (MacMOOSE or JavaMOOSE) designed to give the child a supportive programming environment. Clicking "save" in the client compiles the script and returns feedback to the user. Note that command-line errors are counted per individual line typed; however, scripting errors are counted *per compile*.

In each of these error categories, some errors can be categorized as natural-language errors, and some can not. Examples appear in Table 6. Generally speaking, we define natural-language errors as those errors in which the incorrect command is more English-like than the correct.

In total, 10.6% of errors found were judged to be natural-language related. A total of 314 natural-language errors were found. Of those, 73% (229/314) were command-line syntax errors. In most cases, such errors involve a child guessing at a command's name or the syntax of its arguments. The "examine" command will tell you what commands are available for a particular object and what their exact syntax is; however, children frequently guess rather than use "examine."

In a study of novice Pascal programmers, Jeffrey Bonar and Elliot Soloway found error rates attributable to "step by step natural-language knowledge" from between 47%

to 67% [19]. Certainly the measures used in the two studies are not directly comparable, and the definitions of "natural-language errors" differ. However, if it were the case, broadly speaking, that natural-language errors were less common in MOOSE than Pascal, this finding wouldn't be surprising. In an English-like language such as MOOSE, relying on natural-language knowledge is often a successful strategy. In a more formal language like Pascal, this approach is more likely to lead to errors.

ERROR	DETAILED BREAKDOWN
Object manipulation	Assuming presence of object that doesn't exist (243)
	Assuming script that doesn't exist (240)
	Incorrect number of arguments (128)
	Trying to run script that never compiled (98)
	Ambiguous object reference (35)
	Permissions errors (31)
	Wrong type of argument (24)
Command-line syntax	Syntax errors (336)
	Guessing at commands (263)
	Errors creating objects (67)
	Difficulties with tutorial system (26)
	Disallowed characters in object names (9)
Typos	Misspellings (440)
	Forgotten "say" or "emote" (174)
	Key banging (87)
Scripting syntax	Quoting errors (117)
	Scripting syntax errors (111)
	Mismatch of script name (38)
	Nonexistent property or variable (38)
	Missing script structure ("on", "end", returns) (28)
	Problems with alternate line editor (7)
Movement	Assuming exit which doesn't exist (201)
	Teleporting to random non-existent room name (64)
	Type room name instead of exit name (53)
System bugs	Mail system problems (39)
	Other system bugs (15)
Communication and interaction errors	Saying something instead of doing it (15)
	Typing desired output instead of command to generate desired output (12)
	Talking to non-player characters (9)
	Talking to person not in the room (7)
	Addressing person by real rather than character name (2)

Table 5: Detailed error breakdown

TYPE OF ERROR	NUMBER OF ERRORS	PERCENT NATURAL LANGUAGE (NAT.-LANG. ERRORS/TOTAL ERRORS)
Object manipulation	799	7.6% (61/799)
Command-line syntax	701	32.7% (229/701)
Typos	701	0% (0/701)
Scripting syntax	352	2.0% (7/352)
Movement	318	5.3% (17/318)
System bugs	54	0% (0/54)
Communication and Interaction errors	45	0% (0/45)
TOTAL	2970	10.6% (314/2970)

Table 4: Categorization of errors

Roy Pea comments:

"[Students'] default strategy *for making sense* when encountering difficulties of program interpretation or when writing programs is to resort to the powerful analogy of natural language conversation, to assume a disambiguating mind which can understand. It is not clear at the current time whether this strategy is consciously pursued by students, or whether it is a tacit overgeneralization of conversational principles to computer programming "discourse." The central point is that this personal analogy should be seen as *expected* rather than bizarre behavior, for the students have no other analog, no other procedural device than "person" to which they can give written instructions that are then followed. Rumelhart and Norman have similarly emphasized the critical role of analogies in early learning of a domain—making links between the to-be-learned domain and known domains perceived by the student to be relevant. But, in this case, mapping conventions for natural language instruction onto programming results in error-ridden performances." [20]

Pea's conclusions are based on his analysis of student errors in traditional programming languages. One approach to countering this problem is deliberately to leverage students' natural-language knowledge in the programming-language design.

Table 7 sorts the 314 natural language errors into different categories—categories more descriptive of the nature of natural-language errors we observed. The most common

OBJECT MANIPULATION:	
NON-NL	`set Rocky's following 1` (Correct command would be: set Rocky's following to 1)
NL	`feel Napoleon`
COMMAND-LINE SYNTAX:	
NON-NL	`create #100 josephine` (Correct command would be: created #100 named josephine)
NL	`examine me more`
SCRIPTING SYNTAX:	
NON-NL	Missing end, endif, etc.
NL	`if number < 20 and > 10`
MOVEMENT:	
NON-NL	Trying to use exit that doesn't exist.
NL	Back `Go to tree house` (There are no such commands.)

Table 6: Examples of non-natural language (Non-NL) and natural language (NL) errors

are again syntax and guessing errors. Many of these errors demonstrate a lack of understanding of underlying computer-science concepts. In the first example, Wendy apparently wants to make her pet follow her around the virtual world. She expresses that in an English-like fashion ("set Roo to follow me"). However, she evidently fails to understand that making a pet follow you involves setting a property on the pet's object (the correct command would be "set Roo's following to me".) Wendy demonstrates an understanding of the use of properties in other contexts, but not in this instance.

Perhaps the most intriguing category of error is literal interpretation of metaphor. For example, to get rid of an object that you no longer want, you "recycle" it. Recycling is a metaphor for a process that can be more precisely described as deleting a database entry. Interpreting that metaphor somewhat literally, a number of participants have tried to "reuse" objects.

The next most prevalent category is assuming the system tracking or aware of state more than it is. When travelling through the virtual world, children will often type "back" to try to retrace their steps. No such command exists, (though implementing one is not hard and actually might be a good idea.)

TYPE	INSTANCES (ERRORS OF TYPE/TOTAL ERRORS)	EXAMPLE
Syntax	46.8% (147/314)	`set Roo to follow me` (To make a pet follow you, you need to set its "following" property. Correct command is: set roo's following to me.)

Guessing	21.7%
	 (68/314)
		`make new thing`
		
		 (Correct command would be to type "create" and wait for prompts or type "create \<parent> named \<object name>")
		
		 `tie hair with ribons`
		
		 (Child has created an object called "ribons" but not programmed any scripts on it.)

Literal interpretation of metaphor	18.5% (58/314)	`reuse Harper` (You can "recycle" an object, but not "reuse" it.)

Assuming system is tracking/ aware of state	4.5%
	 (14/314)
		`back`
		
		 `describe here as the way it used to be`

Operator precedence or combination	2.2% (7/314)	`if number < 20 and > 10`

Table 7: Types of natural language errors

Interestingly enough, the least common category is the one we were most worried about before we began data analysis: operator precedence and combination. The conditional clause "if A is B or C" is parsed by the computer as equivalent to "if (A is B) or (C is true)"; however, it's often the case that the user meant "if (A is B) or (A is C)".

Another type of operator error involves the insertion of extra operator words. For example, children often write statements of the form "if x is member of y," inserting an extra "is" before the "member of" operator. This particular problem can be automatically detected and is corrected by the MOOSE compiler. However, the compiler currently is not able to correct the error in the example "if number < 20 and > 10."

Concern about operator errors was the original motivation for undertaking this study. However, only seven of 314 natural language errors and 2,970 total errors fell into this category. It's worth noting that only four of sixteen children demonstrated an understanding of the use of conditionals. Those four children had a total of 2125 errors. Operator precedence and combination errors represent only 0.3% of the total.

ERROR RECOVERY?

But how serious are these natural language errors? Certainly an error that is immediately corrected is quite different from one that causes the child to abandon a project in frustration. We divided error recovery into six categories:

Immediate As soon as feedback is received, the next command directed towards the problem solves it.

Short The problem takes more than one attempt but is solved in that particular sitting.

Long The child doesn't solve the problem in the initial attempt, but returns to it later (time ranging from minutes to days) and solves the problem then.

Workaround Child does not determine how to execute this particular command, but constructs a different string of commands that produce the desired results.

Interrupted Child is interrupted by a message, arrival of another child, parental threat of grounding if they don't get off the computer, etc., and does not appear to return to the problem.

Never Problem not solved.

For each of the 314 natural language errors observed, we categorized the recovery time. This data appears in Table 8. Table 9 analyzes how quickly errors were recovered by type, grouping them into easily recovered (immediate and short), recovered with difficulty (long and workaround), not recovered (never), and unclear (interrupted). Error recovery rates were not calculated for non-natural-language errors. This would be an interesting topic for future work.

At first glance it surprised us that guessing errors were the most "serious"—aren't operator errors, for example, conceptually deeper? However, it's likely that this is simply a reflection of the depth of the child's engagement with the task at hand. A guessing error may often be a whim—if the task isn't easy, it is readily abandoned. An operator error, on the other hand, occurs in the context of

	IMMEDIATE	SHORT	LONG	WORK-AROUND	INTER-RUPTED	NEVER	TOTAL
Syntax	42	27	32	13	2	61	177 (56.4%)
Guessing	10	9	10	2	0	37	68 (21.7%)
Metaphor	21	6	1	1	0	19	48 (15.3%)
State	6	7	0	0	1	0	14 (4.5%)
Operator	1	0	0	6	0	0	7 (2.2%)
Total	80 (25.5%)	49 (15.6%)	43 (13.7%)	22 (7.0%)	3 (1.0%)	117 (37.3%)	314

Table 8: Error recovery times for natural language errors

	EASILY RECOVERED (IMMEDIATE + SHORT)	RECOVERED WITH DIFFICULTY (LONG + WORKAROUND)	NOT RECOVERED (NEVER)	UNCLEAR (INTERRUPTED)
Syntax	39.0% (69/177)	25.4% (45/177)	34.5% (61/177)	1.1% (2/177)
Guessing	27.9% (19/68)	17.6% (12/68)	54.4% (37/68)	0.0% (0/68)
Metaphor	56.3% (27/48)	4.2% (2/48)	39.6% (19/48)	0.0% (0/48)
State	92.9% (13/14)	0.0% (0/14)	0.0% (0/14)	7.1% (1/14)
Operator	14.3% (1/7)	85.7% (6/7)	0.0% (0/7)	0.0% (0/7)
Total	41.1% (129/314)	20.7% (65/314)	37.3% (117/314)	1.0% (3/314)

Table 9: Recoverability of natural language errors

a project in which the child has already invested significant time and effort. Consequently, the child is more likely to spend the time to solve the problem or in most cases find a workaround. It makes sense then too that syntax errors are more likely to be successfully resolved than guessing errors: with a syntax error, the child has found a command and simply needs to learn to use it correctly. In the case of a guess, no such command or concept may exist.

CONCLUSIONS

Is it advisable to "leverage natural-language knowledge" in designing programming languages? The question of course can't be answered in the general case, because different applications and target audiences have different needs. A more focused question might be: is it wise to leverage natural-language knowledge in the design of a programming language for children designed to promote learning? We began in 1993 with the intuition that the answer was "yes." This study supports that conclusion.

This work primarily addresses the risks of natural-language-style programming. A formal analysis of its benefits of would be desirable, but is beyond the scope of this study.

In total, we found that 16 children made a total of 2,970 errors. Of those, 314 were natural-language-related. Most of those errors were easily recovered (41.1%) or recovered with some difficulty (20.7%). Those that were not recovered represent 37.3% of the natural language errors and only 4.2% of total errors. We believe these rates to be within acceptable limits. Leveraging users' natural-language knowledge does not appear to cause serious problems. We believe that making use of people's pre-existing natural language knowledge is an effective strategy for programming language design for children, end users, and others new to coding.

In future work, we hope to continue to analyze this set of data to shed light on other aspects of programming-language design for novice users.

REFERENCES

1. Hopper, G.M., *Keynote Address,* in *History of Programming Languages,* R.L. Wexelblat, Editor. 1981, Academic Press: New York. p. 7-20.

2. Sammet, J., *The Early History of COBOL,* in *History of Programming Languages,* R. Wexelblat, Editor. 1981, Academic Press: New York.

3. Spohrer, J. and E. Soloway, *Analyzing the High Frequency Bugs in Novice Programs,* in *Empirical Studies of Programmers,* E. Soloway and S. Iyengar, Editors. 1986, Ablex Publishing: Norwood, NJ.

4. Boulay, B.D., *Some Difficulties of Learning to Program,* in *Studying the Novice Programmer,* E. Soloway and J.C. Spohrer, Editors. 1989, Lawrence Erlbaum Associates: Hillsdale, NJ. p. 283-299.

5. Goodman, D., *The Complete HyperCard Handbook.* 2nd ed. 1988, New York: Bantam Books.

6. Kaehler, T., 1996, personal communication.

7. Bartle, R., *Interactive Multi-User Computer Games.* 1990, MUSE Ltd:
   ftp://ftp.lambda.moo.mud.org/pub/MOO/papers/mudreport.txt

8. Bruckman, A. and M. Resnick, *The MediaMOO Project: Constructionism and Professional Community.* Convergence, 1995. **1**(1): p. 94-109.

9. Glusman, G., E. Mercer, and I. Rubin, *Real-time Collaboration On the Internet: BioMOO, the Biologists' Virtual Meeting Place.,* in *Internet for the Molecular Biologist.,* S.R. Swindell, R.R. Miller, and G.S.A. Myers, Editors. 1996, Horizon Scientific Press: Norfolk, UK.

10. Van Buren, D., *et al., The AstroVR Collaboratory,* in *Astronomical Data Analysis Software and Systems IV,* R. Hanish and H. Payne, Editors. 1994, Astronomical Society of the Pacific: San Francisco.

11. O'Day, V., *et al., Moving Practice: From Classrooms to MOO Rooms.* Computer Supported Cooperative Work, 1998. **7**: p. 9-45.

12. Bruckman, A., *Community Support for Constructionist Learning.* Computer Supported Cooperative Work, 1998. **7**: p. 47-86.

13. Bruckman, A., *MOOSE Crossing: Construction, Community, and Learning in a Networked Virtual World for Kids.* 1997, MIT, Ph.D. dissertation:
    http://www.cc.gatech.edu/~asb/thesis/

14. Curtis, P. *Mudding: Social Phenomena in Text-Based Virtual Realities.* in *DIAC.* 1992. Berkeley, CA:
    ftp://ftp.lambda.moo.mud.org/pub/MOO/papers/DIAC92.txt

15. Curtis, P., *LambdaMOO Programmer's Manual.* 1993:
    ftp://ftp.lambda.moo.mud.org/pub/MOO/ProgrammersManual.txt

16. Curtis, P. and D. Nichols. *MUDs Grow Up: Social Virtual Reality in the Real World.* in *Third International Conference on Cyberspace.* 1993. Austin, Texas:
    ftp://ftp.lambda.moo.mud.org/pub/MOO/papers/MUDsGrowUp.txt

17. Papert, S., *Mindstorms: Children, Computers, and Powerful Ideas.* 1980, New York: Basic Books.

18. Miller, L.A., *Natural language programming: Styles, strategies, and constrasts.* IBM Systems Journal, 1981. **20**(2): p. 184-215.

19. Bonar, J. and E. Soloway, *Preprogramming Knowledge: A Major Source of Misconceptions in Novice Programmers,* in *Studying the Novice Programmer,* E. Soloway and J. Spohrer, Editors. 1989, Lawrence Erlbaum Associates: Hillsdale, NJ.

20. Pea, R.D., *Language-Independent Conceptual "Bugs" in Novice Programming.* Journal of Educational Computing Research, 1986. **2**(1): p. 25-36.

Testing Pointing Device Performance and User Assessment with the ISO 9241, Part 9 Standard

Sarah A. Douglas and Arthur E. Kirkpatrick
Computer and Information Science Dept.
University of Oregon
Eugene, OR 97403 USA
douglas@cs.uoregon.edu
ted@cs.uoregon.edu

I. Scott MacKenzie
Dept. of Computing and Information Science
University of Guelph
Guelph, Ontario, Canada N1G 2W1
smackenzie@acm.org

ABSTRACT

The ISO 9241, Part 9 Draft International Standard for testing computer pointing devices proposes an evaluation of *performance* and *comfort*. In this paper we evaluate the scientific validity and practicality of these dimensions for two pointing devices for laptop computers, a finger-controlled isometric joystick and a touchpad. Using a between-subjects design, evaluation of performance using the measure of *throughput* was done for one-direction and multi-directional pointing and selecting. Results show a significant difference in throughput for the multi-directional task, with the joystick 27% higher; results for the one-direction task were non-significant. After the experiment, participants rated the device for comfort, including operation, fatigue, and usability. The questionnaire showed no overall difference in the responses, and a significant statistical difference in only the question concerning force required to operate the device—the joystick requiring slightly more force. The paper concludes with a discussion of problems in implementing the ISO standard and recommendations for improvement.

Keywords

Pointing devices, ergonomic evaluation, ISO 9241 standard, isometric joystick, touchpad, Fitts' law

INTRODUCTION

During the past five years the International Standards Organization (ISO) has proposed a standard entitled *ISO 9241 Ergonomic Requirements for Office Work with Visual Display Terminals, Part 9 Non-keyboard Input Device Requirements* [3]. The primary motivation of the standards effort is to influence the design of computer pointing devices to accommodate the user's biomechanical capabilities and limitations, allow adequate safety and comfort, and prevent injury. Secondarily, the standards establish uniform guidelines and testing procedures for evaluating computer pointing devices produced by different manufacturers. Compliance can be demonstrated through testing of user *performance*, *comfort* and *effort* to show that a particular device meets ergonomic standards or that it

meets a de facto standard currently on the market.

Crafting and adopting any set of standards for the evaluation of pointing devices raises a number of questions:

- Are the standards consistent with accepted scientific theory and practice?

- Do the standards allow practical implementation and conformance?

- Are the expected results reliable and ecologically valid in order to predict behavior and evaluate devices?

The goal of our present study is to answer these questions for the ISO proposed standard for the evaluation of *performance* and *comfort*. We first implement the proposed testing procedures using a case study experiment of a finger-controlled isometric joystick and of a touchpad. Secondly, we reflect upon that experience. To that end, we are specifically interested in problems that arise in replication, interpretation and reliability of results.

ISO 9241 - Part 9

ISO standards are written by committees drawn from the research and applied research communities. As of September 1998 the *ISO 9241-Part 9* is in Draft International Standard version and is currently awaiting a vote of member organizations. If adopted, certification of conformance to this standard will be legally required for devices sold in the European Community. The general description of the Standard and the particulars of Part 9 are described in Smith [6].

The proposed standard applies to the following hand-operated devices: mice, trackballs, light-pen & styli, joysticks, touch-sensitive screens, tablet-overlays, thumb-wheels, hand-held scanners, pucks, hand-held bar code readers, and remote-control mice. It does not cover eye-trackers, speech activators, head-mounted controllers, datagloves, devices for disabled users, or foot-controlled devices.

Part 9 specifies general guidelines for physical characteristics of the design including the force required for operating them as well as their feedback, shape, and labeling. In addition to these general guidelines, there are requirements for each covered device.

ISO 9241 defines evaluation procedures for measuring user *performance*, *comfort* and *effort* using an experimental protocol which defines subject samples, stimuli, experimental design, environmental conditions, furniture adjustments, data collection procedures, and data analysis recommendations.

Performance is measured by task performance on any of six tasks: one-direction (horizontal) tapping, multi-directional tapping, dragging, free-hand tracing (drawing), free-hand input (hand-written characters or pictures) and grasp and park (homing/device switching). The tasks selected for testing should be determined by the intended use of the device with a particular user population.

For the tapping tasks which are essentially basic point-select tasks, the ISO recommends collection of the following performance data. The primary ISO dependent measure is *Throughput* (*TP*).

$$Throughput = ID_e / MT \qquad (1)$$

where

MT is the mean movement time, in seconds, for all trials within the same condition,

and

$$ID_e = \log_2(D/W_e + 1) \qquad (2)$$

ID_e is the effective index of difficulty, in bits, and is calculated from D, the distance to the target and W_e, the effective width of the target. W_e is computed from the observed distribution of selection coordinates in participants' trials:

$$W_e = 4.133 \, SD \qquad (3)$$

where SD is the standard deviation of the selection coordinates. Throughput has units bits per second (bps).

Readers will note that Equation 1 for throughput is the usual Fitts' Index of Performance (*IP*) except that effective width (W_e) replaces actual measured size of the target (*W*). Using effective width incorporates the variability observed of human performance and includes both speed and accuracy [4]. Thus, throughput precludes a separate computation of error rate.

The ISO 9241 standard also argues that evaluating user performance using a short-term test is not enough for a complete evaluation of a device. Consequently, the ISO 9241 requires assessment of *effort* as a biomechanical measurement of muscle load and fatigue during performance testing. Finally, *comfort* is ascertained after performance testing by having participants subjectively rate the device using a questionnaire form which assesses aspects of operation, fatigue, comfort, and overall usability.

METHOD

An experiment was designed to implement the performance and comfort elements of the ISO testing. The third element, effort, was not tested due to our inability to obtain the sophisticated equipment and technician for measuring biomechanical load.

Performance testing was limited to pointing and selecting using both a one-direction test (1D Fitts serial task) and a multi-directional test (2D Fitts discrete task). The testing environment was modeled on the ISO proposal as described in Annex B [3]. Comfort was evaluated using the ISO

"Independent Questionnaire for assessment of comfort". The design attempted to follow as reasonably as possible the proposed description in Annex C [3].

Testing was conducted for two different pointing devices, a finger-controlled isometric joystick and a touchpad, both connected to the same computer.

Participants

Twenty-four persons participated in this experiment, twelve for each device. For the touchpad, all participants were right-handed. For the joystick, eleven participants were right-handed and one left-handed.

Participants were unpaid volunteers recruited through posters and personal contact. They were offered the opportunity to win a dinner for two selected randomly from among the participants. All participants were screened using a questionnaire which assessed their prior experience with computers and pointing devices. All participants had prior computer experience and extensive experience with the mouse pointing device. Participants were assigned to the device for which they had no prior experience. If they had no experience on either, they were randomly assigned to one. They all signed an informed consent document informing them of the goals and activities of the study, their rights to terminate, and the confidentiality of their performance.

Apparatus

An IBM Thinkpad® laptop computer was fitted with a separate 21 inch color display monitor. The tested device for the joystick was the installed Trackpoint® III located on the keyboard between the "G" and the "H" key. For the second device, a Cirque Glidepoint® Touchpad 2 Model 400 was connected through the PS/2 port. For both devices, the "gain" was set to the middle value in the standard NT driver software for setting pointing device speed.

Experimental tasks were presented by two different programs. For the one-direction test (1D Fitts task), the *Generalized Fitts Law Model Builder* was used [7]. This program, written in C, runs under Windows 95® in MSDOS mode. Figure 1 illustrates the screen as presented by the software. For each block of trials, the software presented a pair of rectangular targets of width *W* and

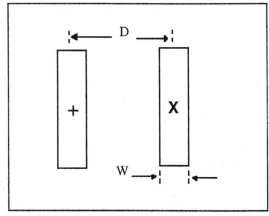

Figure 1. One-direction task.

distance *D*. For this experiment, the target rectangle was varied by three different widths, and three different distances. There were 30 trials in each block.

At the beginning of a trial, a crosshair pointer appeared in the left rectangle and a red X appeared in the opposite rectangle denoting it as the current target. For the next trial the location of crosshair and X were reversed. This allows the participant to move quickly back and forth between the two targets.

The multi-directional test was implemented by software written at the University of Oregon HCI Lab. The basic task environment has been used for prior evaluation work on pointing device performance assessment [1, 2]. It is written in C++ and runs under Windows NT.

Figure 2 illustrates the screen as presented by the software. A trial starts when the participant clicks (selects) in the home square, and ends when the participant clicks in the target circle. The time between these clicks is recorded as the trial time. The cursor is automatically repositioned in the center of the home square at the end of each trial. Combinations of width, distance and angle are presented randomly.

For this experiment, the target circle was varied by three different widths, three different distances, and eight different angles.

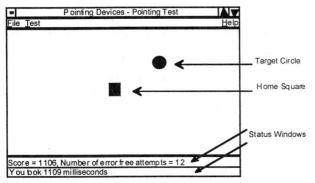

Figure 2. Multi-directional task.

All software is available from the authors.

Procedure

Participants were given the multi-directional task first. The task was explained and demonstrated to the participant. They were instructed to work as fast as possible while still maintaining high accuracy. Participants were instructed to continue without trying to correct errors. Participants performed ten blocks of multiple combinations of target width, distance and angle trials, and were informed that they could rest at any time between trials. Participants using the touchpad were instructed to use the button for selection rather than multiple taps.

After completion of the multi-directional task, participants rested for a few minutes before receiving instruction on the one-direction task. The one-direction task was run for blocks of multiple combinations of target width and distance. Participants were allowed to rest briefly between blocks, but not between trials.

At the conclusion of the performance portion of the experiment, participants were asked to respond to a written questionnaire asking them to rate their experience in using the device. The questionnaire consisted of thirteen questions covering issues of physical operation, fatigue and comfort, speed and accuracy, and overall usability. Participants were asked to respond to each question with a rating from low to high. Figure 3 illustrates this device assessment questionnaire.

DEVICE ASSESSMENT

Please circle the x that is most appropriate as an answer to the given comment.

1. The force required for actuation was
   x   x   x   x   x
   too low   too high

2. Smoothness during operation was
   x   x   x   x   x
   very rough   very smooth

3. The mental effort required for operation was
   x   x   x   x   x
   too low   too high

4. The physical effort required for operation was
   x   x   x   x   x
   too low   too high

5. Accurate pointing was
   x   x   x   x   x
   easy   difficult

6. Operation speed was
   x   x   x   x   x
   too fast   too slow

7. Finger fatigue:
   x   x   x   x   x
   none   very high

8. Wrist fatigue:
   x   x   x   x   x
   none   very high

9. Arm fatigue:
   x   x   x   x   x
   none   very high

10. Shoulder fatigue:
    x   x   x   x   x
    none   very high

11. Neck fatigue:
    x   x   x   x   x
    none   very high

12. General comfort:
    x   x   x   x   x
    very   very
    uncomfortable   comfortable

13. Overall, the input device was
    x   x   x   x   x
    very difficult   very easy
    to use   to use

Figure 3. Device Assessment Questionnaire.

The total time spent by each participant ranged from slightly less than an hour to one hour and 30 minutes. The performance section took between 45 minutes to one hour to complete.

Design

Pointing Performance

The design for the experiment used a mixed design, with device as a between-subjects factor, and task-type (one-direction or multi-directional tapping) as a within-subjects factor. For the one-direction task, we have the following independent variables:

Target Width (2 mm, 5 mm, 10 mm)

Target Distance (40 mm, 80 mm, 160 mm)

Trial (1 to 30)

Block (1 to 9)

The three target sizes approximated the width of a "o" in 8 pt. Helvetica, the height of a character or word, and the width of an icon in the Microsoft Windows environment. These widths and distances represent Fitts' Index of Difficulty values from 2.3 to 6.3 bits. (We have given the widths in actual physical distance rather than pixels since pixel sizes vary from monitor to monitor.)

In the one-direction case, a block consists of 30 trials of the same width-distance combination. A total of 270 trials were run (30 trials per block x [3 widths x 3 distance] blocks).

For the multi-directional task we have the following independent variables:

Target Width (2 mm, 5 mm, 10 mm)

Target Distance (40 mm, 80 mm, 160 mm)

Target Angle (0°, 45°, 90°, 135°, 180°, 225°, 270°, 315°)

Trial (1 to 72)

Block (1 to 10)

Note that a block of the multi-directional task is defined as the 72 fully crossed combinations of target distance, width and angular location from the starting position (3 widths x 3 distances x 8 angles). A total of 720 trials were run (72 trials per block x 10 blocks). Since the multi-directional task was more complex, it was performed before the one-direction task to bring the participants to a criterion level of practice in a much more realistic and ecologically valid task environment for computer users.

Dependent variables are movement time (*MT*) for each trial, throughput (*TP*), and error rate (*ER*). Error rate is the percentage of targets selected when the pointer is outside the target and is not an ISO recommended measure. However, we have found it useful piece of information when assessing performance.

Device Assessment Questionnaire

The Device Assessment questionnaire consisted of thirteen questions taken from the ISO standard. Participants were asked to give a response to each question as a rating on a five point scale from low to high. The data were considered ordinal.

ANALYSIS

The data for movement time (*MT*), and selection point (*x*, *y*) were collected directly by the software which presented the experimental tasks. The data were then prepared for further statistical analysis by computing values for throughput and error rate in addition to *MT* for each trial. Finally, basic statistics and ANOVA were performed using commercial software.

Adjustments to Data

We did not make any adjustments to the data and excluded none of the trials.

Computed Formulas

For the one-direction task, the computation for *throughput* begins by computing W_e according to Equation 3. To achieve this, for each trial the *x* coordinate of the participant's final selection point is recorded. For all participants in a *D* x *W* condition, these constitute a distribution of points. The sample mean can be computed in the usual manner. Then the difference between the participant's selection point and the mean is computed and squared; this can also be interpreted as the square of the distance between the selection point and the mean. For all subjects and all trials, the standard deviation (*SD*) is then computed as

$$SD = \sqrt{\left(\frac{\sum_{i=1}^{n} (x_i - \bar{x})^2}{n-1} \right)} \tag{4}$$

W_e, ID_e and *throughput* are then computed by Equations 3, 2 and 1, respectively.

For the multi-directional task, the computation of W_e must be modified because selection points are now located in a two-dimensional plane. The "difference" between each actual selection point and the mean is computed now as the Euclidean distance between the selection point and the mean point ($\bar{x}$, $\bar{y}$).

$$Dist = \sqrt{(x_i - \bar{x})^2 + (y_i - \bar{y})^2} \tag{5}$$

In the *SD* computation, we square the distance and hence obtain

$$SD = \sqrt{\left(\frac{\sum_{i=1}^{n} \left[(x_i - \bar{x})^2 + (y_i - \bar{y})^2 \right]}{n-1} \right)} \tag{6}$$

W_e, ID_e and *throughput* are then computed by Equations 3, 2 and 1, respectively.

Device Assessment Questionnaire

The mean and standard deviation of the ratings for each of the thirteen questions was computed. Given the ordinal nature of the data, the Mann-Whitney non-parametric statistic was computed to test for significant differences between participants in the two device groups.

RESULTS

Pointing Performance

Multi-directional Task

The mean movement time for the joystick was 1.975 seconds with a standard deviation of .601 seconds. For the touchpad, the mean movement time was 2.382 seconds and a standard deviation of .802 seconds. These differences were statistically significant ($F_{1,22}$ = 11.223, p= .0029). From this we can conclude that the pointing time for the joystick is 17% faster on average.

Error rates were 2.1% (sd = 5.68) for the joystick and 5.4% (sd = 10.5) for the touchpad. These differences were statistically significant ($F_{1,22}$ = 7.604, p= .0115), with the joystick having a 61% lower error rate.

Throughput was computed for the joystick at 2.15 bps (sd = .40). For the touchpad, it was 1.70 bps (sd = .53). These differences are statistically significant ($F_{1,22}$ = 20.458, p = .0002), and indicate that throughput for the joystick is 27% higher than for the touchpad.

Although the ISO standard does not discuss learning effects, this obviously must be considered when designing and evaluating performance data. In this experiment, participants performed the multi-directional task for ten blocks of 72 trials each. We hypothesized, based on other similar experiments, that they would have achieved a criterion level of practice by block ten. In other words, no significant improvement in performance would be shown in the final blocks.

This was confirmed by the data analysis. Helmhert contrasts show the differences between blocks become non-significant at block 6. For throughput, the effect of Block*Device was significant ($F_{9,198}$ = 2.726, p = .0051). Graphing the Block*Device effect shows only a mild effect (see Figure 4). The main contributor is that the difference between Block 1 and 2 is greater for the pad than the joystick.

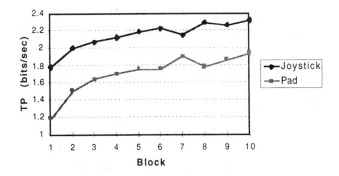

Figure 4. Learning shown for Throughput by Device and Block.

The effect of learning on the task suggests that examining Block 10 alone will give us a good measure of practiced performance.

For Block 10 trials the mean movement time for the joystick was 1.770 seconds (sd = .458). For the touchpad, the mean movement time was 2.132 seconds (sd = .583). These differences are statistically significant ($F_{1,22}$ = 14.462, p = .010). From this we can conclude that the pointing time for the joystick is 17% faster on average.

Error rates were 3.4% (sd = 6.8) for the joystick and 3.8% (sd = 7.7) for the touchpad. These differences are not statistically significant ($F_{1,22}$ = .123, p > .05).

Throughput was computed for the joystick at 2.33 bps (sd = .32). For the touchpad, it was 1.94 bps (sd = .46). These differences are statistically significant ($F_{1,22}$ = 15.873, p < .0006), and demonstrate slightly higher throughput due to practice for both devices—the joystick now 20% higher. (The change in relative performance is due to the steeper slope of the learning curve for the touchpad.)

One-direction Task
The mean movement time for the joystick was 1.544 seconds (sd = .305). For the touchpad, the mean movement time was 1.563 seconds (sd =.285). These differences are not statistically significant ($F_{1,22}$ = .024, p > .05).

Error rates were 17.5% (sd = 13.8) for the joystick and 25.6% (sd = 22.5) touchpad. These differences are not statistically significant ($F_{1,22}$ = 1.136, p > .05).

We were surprised by the high error rates for both devices. In post-experiment interview, many participants commented on the difficulty of the one-direction task with the small targets. A closer examination of the data revealed that many of the errors occurred on the 2 mm target widths. Error rate means for the 2 mm widths were 29.6% (28.5); 5 mm were 20.4% (26.4); and 10 mm were 14.7% (22.1). An ANOVA testing error rate by width shows a significant effect ($F_{2,44}$ = 7.565, p = .0015). We speculate that this difference in error rate might be due to the serial nature of the one-direction task, and the ballistic nature of the initial pointing movement which promotes increased momentum causing overshoot. Further analysis of errors will be needed to confirm that.

Throughput was computed for the joystick at 2.07 bps (sd =.39). For the touchpad, it was 1.81 bps (sd = .62). These differences are not statistically significant ($F_{1,22}$ = 1.469, p > .05).

Overall Pointing Performance
Table 1 illustrates the various computations of throughput. It is clear from these results that the joystick is consistently superior in performance in both overall and practiced analysis of multi-direction pointing. Results for one-direction are non-significant, although the joystick is, again, slightly higher in throughput.

Throughput	Joystick mean (sd)	Touchpad mean (sd)
Multi-direction: All Trials	2.15 bps (.40)*	1.70 bps (.53)*
Multi-direction: Block 10 only	2.33 bps (.32)*	1.94 bps (.46)*
One-direction: All Trials	2.07 bps (.39)	1.81 bps (.62)

*Significant at p < .005

Table 1. Comparison of throughput.

Finally, how do these results compare with other published data of performance for the same or similar devices? On the multi-direction task, the throughput for Block 10 can be compared with published data for the mouse at 4.15 bps and another finger-controlled isometric joystick, the Home-

Row J key, at 1.97 bps [2]. Note, however, that these latter values are throughput computed using W instead of W_e.

Similarly, our results for the one-direction task can be compared with the study of MacKenzie and Oniszczak [5] on selection techniques for a touchpad. Their results indicate a throughput of .99 bps for another button selection touchpad versus our results of 1.81 bps. However, our value is for a one-direction task after the participants received a great deal of practice on the multi-directional task. Their value is an overall value for a task environment in which participants learned the device on one-direction tasks only, and repeated each condition 60 times (20 trials x 3 blocks). Our experiment had participants performing each condition 30 times (30 trials x 1 block). Practice could account for the higher values we observed.

Device Assessment Questionnaire

The means and standard deviations of the responses on the thirteen questions on the questionnaire are shown in Table 2. The results of the questionnaire analysis show that these responses are not statistically significant overall (Mann-Whitney $U = 11653$, $p = .5180$). Individual question analysis showed only Question 1, on the amount of force required for actuation, had significant differences in response between the two devices (Mann-Whitney $U = 33.000$, $p = .0243$). The joystick participants rated the force required slightly higher (3.583) than the touchpad participants (2.833).

Question	Joystick	Touchpad
1	3.583 (.996)	2.833 (.835)
2	2.583 (1.084)	2.000 (.739)
3	3.583 (1.165)	3.333 (.651)
4	3.667 (.888)	3.917 (.669)
5	4.083 (.996)	4.000 (.739)
6	3.583 (.515)	3.500 (.522)
7	3.083 (1.564)	3.167 (1.193)
8	3.500 (1.382)	3.667 (1.371)
9	3.167 (1.337)	2.250 (1.422)
10	2.000 (.953)	2.000 (1.651)
11	1.833 (2.167)	2.167 (1.337)
12	2.333 (.985)	2.667 (.985)
13	2.417 (.793)	2.583 (.900)

Table 2. Results of the Device Assessment Questionnaire.

Since each response was rated on a five point scale, a value of 3 is the mid-point. Indeed, the overall question mean was 3.032 for the joystick and 2.929 for the touchpad, indicating participants rated both devices in the midpoint range. Questions 7-11 regarding fatigue rated both devices in the same range, with finger and wrist fatigue higher than shoulder and arm. Even Question 12 on overall comfort

and Question 13 regarding usability of device were rated near the midpoint for both devices (2.417 for the joystick; 2.583 for the touchpad).

We can conclude from these questionnaire data that the ISO subjective comfort assessment shows little difference between the two devices. Given that the throughput difference was 27% favoring the joystick and that both devices were laptop devices, we might suggest that the difference was not enough to be reflected in differences in subjective evaluation.

DISCUSSION

At the beginning of our paper, we posed three questions concerning the ISO standards. We will now discuss these issues using our experience in implementing this case study.

- Are the standards consistent with accepted scientific theory and practice?

Much of the ISO standard for pointing performance is based on the accepted use of Fitts' law as a basis for the evaluation of pointing performance [1, 4]. Throughput is essentially Fitts' Index of Performance. The human factors literature is filled with studies of pointing device performance based on this scientific theory. In keeping with current practice, the ISO formula for throughput uses W_e (the effective target width) rather than W. Thus throughput incorporates both the speed and accuracy of users' behavior.

Our case study focused on pointing performance evaluation for both one-direction and multi-directional (2D) tasks. The one-direction task has been widely used in human factors work on pointing devices; the multi-directional task less so.

As the standard recommends, in recent years effective width (W_e) has replaced measured width (W) in the computation of *Index of Performance* or the ISO term, *throughput*. While this allows a single measure of both speed and accuracy, we feel that it does not replace separate measures of speed as movement time and accuracy as error rate. Consequently, we recommend computing both movement time and error rate as separate dependent variables.

A serious flaw in the standard is its failure to incorporate learning into the analysis. Existing studies of pointing devices show a significant effect due to learning [2]. The standard does not recommend experimental designs that reach a criterion level of practice nor discusses controls for transfer of training. In our study we applied a repeated measures paradigm and tested for learning effects. We recommend that others do so as well.

Concerning experimental design, the standard recommends a participant sample that is representative of the intended user population, and recommends at least 25 participants. We only used 12 for each between-subjects condition. This is standard practice for pointing device performance experiments, and psychological testing in general.

Finally, we did not agree with the recommended design of the Questionnaire. The standard recommends a 7 point rating scale which it claims is an interval scale. We substituted a 5 point rating scale after pilot tests showed that participants could not make finer distinctions. We also consider the data ordinal rather than interval.

- Do the standards allow practical implementation and conformance?

In general, the standard is very vague concerning the implementation of the Fitts' concepts into experimental designs for testing environments. No discussion of Index of Difficulty is made, i.e., there are no explanations of how the task conditions should vary as a function of target width and distance to produce a range of difficulties. (We recommend *ID* range from 2 to 6 bits.) Computations for throughput and W_e are not explained in enough detail to implement the data analysis. As our study has shown, extension of the computation of W_e to the multi-direction case is not straight-forward. We propose that our experiment be used as a paradigm.

- Are the expected results reliable and ecologically valid in order to predict behavior and evaluate devices?

In other words, do they really help us evaluate devices? Given the general recommendations of the ISO standard for evaluating *performance* which is based on sound scientific foundations and the proper implementation of an experiment as we have described in this paper, we believe the results are reliable and can successfully predict user behavior. While we implemented both the one-direction and multi-directional tasks, we believe that the multi-directional task is more ecologically valid, presenting a complex task environment closer to what is observed with modern user interface tasks. As we observed, one-direction tasks performed by well-practiced participants gave us non-significant results.

As with other Fitts' law results, we adamantly assert caution in comparing results across experiments: It is critical that exactly the same experimental design, task environment, instructions and data analysis be given [1, 4]. The ISO standard does not make this clear. Given these limitations, it is useful to have standardized software such as that used in this experiment for presenting experimental environments, namely the *Generalized Fitts Law Model Builder* [7] available from author MacKenzie which runs both 1D and 2D Fitts' tasks, or the 2D Fitts' task software written at the University of Oregon HCI Lab available from authors Douglas and Kirkpatrick.

We have no means to compare *comfort* which is done through a post-experiment questionnaire. From our interviews with participants after the experiment, the questions were too vague to pick up specific problems with a device. We recommend an additional open-ended questionnaire with the following questions:

- Did you have any trouble moving the cursor to the target? If so, please describe.

- Did you have any trouble selecting (clicking) a target? If so, please describe.

- Do you have any comments in general about using this device for pointing?

- Comparing the tested device to your usual pointing device (which is ____), could you imagine a situation in which you would prefer the tested device?

- Do you have any suggestions how to improve this device?

This will allow the testers to more fully evaluate specific problems with the device.

CONCLUSIONS

Our goal in conducting this study is to assess the ISO 9241, Part 9 standard as a tool to evaluate pointing device performance and comfort by implementing a case study. We have done this by examining the scientific and practical issues. On its scientific merits, the standard appears sound; on practicality, it sorely needs improvement. A major contribution we have made in this paper is to define the experimental design in sufficient detail so as to allow others to replicate it. Finally, we have contributed to the growing evaluation of pointing devices through our study of the joystick and touchpad.

We note that while the ISO standard assesses user performance, comfort and effort, it does not address other issues of interest to users such as footprint, cost or integration of the pointing device with the rest of the hardware and software. These must be evaluated by other means if a broader analysis is needed.

As of the writing of this paper (January 1999) the ISO organization members are in the process of deciding whether the 9241, Part 9 will be adopted or not. Voting began last summer and lasted until October 21, 1998. Members had a choice of four options: approved as written, approved with attached comments, not approved with attached comments, and abstain. To the best of our knowledge and even given the fact that one of the authors (MacKenzie) is an ISO representative for Canada, the results are not known yet. If the Standard is adopted it will have major impact on device manufacturers in terms of cost, time for development, and final marketability of the product.

ACKNOWLEDGMENTS
We thank Katja Vogel who, as a visiting research intern from the Psychology Dept. at the University of Regensburg, made many valuable suggestions on the experimental design and helped us begin the initial data collection. We also thank Chris Hundhausen for providing the initial version of the multi-directional experiment code. Finally, we thank Steve Fickas for the extended loan of his IBM Thinkpad.

REFERENCES
1. Douglas, S.A. and Mithal, A.K. *The ergonomics of computer pointing devices*. Springer-Verlag, New York, 1997.

2. Douglas, S.A. and Mithal, A.K. The effect of reducing homing time on the speed of a finger-controlled isometric pointing device. *Human Factors in Computing Systems, CHI '94 Conference Proceedings*, ACM Press, New York, pp. 411-416.

3. ISO. *ISO/DIS 9241-9 Ergonomic Requirements for Office Work with Visual Display Terminals, Non-keyboard Input Device Requirements, Draft International Standard*, International Organization for Standardization, 1998.

4. MacKenzie, I. S. Fitts' law as a research and design tool in human-computer interaction. *Human-Computer Interaction, 7*, (1992), pp. 91-139.

5. MacKenzie, I. S. and Oniszczak, A. A comparison of three selection techniques for touchpads. *Human Factors in Computing Systems, CHI '98 Conference Proceedings*, ACM Press, New York, pp. 336-343.

6. Smith, W. *ISO and ANSI ergonomic standards for computer products: A guide to implementation and products*, Prentice Hall, New York, 1996.

7. Soukoreff, W. and MacKenzie, I.S. Generalized Fitts' law model builder. In *Companion Proceedings of the CHI '95 Conference on Human Factors in Computing Systems*, ACM Press, New York, pp. 113-114.

Touch-Sensing Input Devices

Ken Hinckley and Mike Sinclair
Microsoft Research, One Microsoft Way, Redmond, WA 98052
{kenh, sinclair}@microsoft.com; Tel: +1-425-703-9065

ABSTRACT

We can touch things, and our senses tell us when our hands are touching something. But most computer input devices cannot detect when the user touches or releases the device or some portion of the device. Thus, adding touch sensors to input devices offers many possibilities for novel interaction techniques. We demonstrate the *TouchTrackball* and the *Scrolling TouchMouse*, which use unobtrusive capacitance sensors to detect contact from the user's hand without requiring pressure or mechanical actuation of a switch. We further demonstrate how the capabilities of these devices can be matched to an implicit interaction technique, the *On-Demand Interface*, which uses the passive information captured by touch sensors to fade in or fade out portions of a display depending on what the user is doing; a second technique uses explicit, intentional interaction with touch sensors for enhanced scrolling. We present our new devices in the context of a simple taxonomy of tactile input technologies. Finally, we discuss the properties of touch-sensing as an input channel in general.

Keywords

input devices, interaction techniques, sensor technologies, haptic input, tactile input, touch-sensing devices.

INTRODUCTION

The sense of touch is an important human sensory channel. In the present context, we use the term *touch* quite narrowly to refer to the cutaneous sense, or *tactile perception* [16]. During interaction with physical objects, pets or other human beings, touch (physical contact) constitutes an extremely significant event. Yet computer input devices, for the most part, are indifferent to human contact in the sense that making physical contact, maintaining contact, or breaking contact provokes no reaction whatsoever from most software. As such, touch-sensing input devices offer many novel interaction possibilities.

Touch-sensing devices do not include devices that provide active tactile or force feedback [22]. These are all *output* modalities that allow a device to physically respond to user actions by moving, resisting motion, or changing texture under software control. Touch sensing is an *input* channel; touch sensing allows the computer to have greater awareness of what the user is doing with the input device.

Fig. 1   *Left*: The TouchTrackball (a modified Kensington Expert Mouse) senses when the user touches the ball. *Right*: The Scrolling TouchMouse (a modified Microsoft IntelliMouse Pro) senses when the user is holding the mouse by detecting touch in the combined palm/thumb areas. It can also sense when the user touches the wheel, the areas immediately above and below the wheel, or the left mouse button.

Of course, certain input devices (such as touchpads, touchscreens, and touch tablets) that require touch as part of their normal operation have been available for many years. In all of these devices, one cannot specify positional data without touching the device, nor can one touch the device without specifying a position; hence touch sensing and position sensing are tightly coupled in these devices. Yet once it is recognized that touch sensing is an orthogonal property of input devices that need not be strictly coupled to position sensing, it becomes clear that there are many unexplored possibilities for input devices such as mice or trackballs that can sense one or more independent bits of touch data (*Fig. 1*).

We present two examples of interaction techniques that match these new input devices to appropriate tasks. The *On-Demand Interface* dynamically partitions screen real estate depending on what the user is doing, as sensed by implicit interaction with touch sensors. For example, when the user lets go of the mouse, an application's toolbars are no longer needed, so we fade out the toolbars and maximize the screen real estate of the underlying document, thus presenting a simpler and less cluttered display. By contrast, we use the touch sensors located above and below the wheel on the *Scrolling TouchMouse* to support explicit, consciously activated interactions; the user can *tap* on these touch sensors to issue Page Up and Page Down requests. Touch sensors allow this functionality to be supported in very little physical real estate and without imposing undue restrictions on the shape or curvature of the region to be sensed. We conclude by enumerating some general properties of touch sensors that we hope will prove useful to consider in the design of touch-sensing input devices and interaction techniques.

PREVIOUS WORK

Buxton proposes a taxonomy of input devices [3] that draws a distinction between input devices that operate by touch (such as a touchpad) versus input devices that operate via a mechanical intermediary (such as a stylus on a tablet). Card, Mackinlay, and Robertson [5] extend this taxonomy but give no special treatment to devices that operate via touch. These taxonomies do not suggest examples of touch-sensing positioning devices other than the touchpad, touchscreen, and touch tablet. Buxton et al. provide an insightful analysis of touch-sensitive tablet input [4], noting that touch tablets can sense a pair of signals that a traditional mouse cannot: *Touch* and *Release*. Our work shows how multiple pairs of such signals, in the form of touch sensors, can be applied to the mouse or other devices.

For the case of the mouse, we have already introduced one version of such a device, called the TouchMouse, in previous work [10]. This particular TouchMouse incorporated a pair of contact sensors, one for the thumb/palm rest area of the mouse, and a second for the left mouse button. This TouchMouse was used in combination with a touchpad (for the nonpreferred hand) to support two-handed input. The present paper demonstrates the TouchTrackball and a new variation of the TouchMouse, matches these devices to new interaction techniques, and discusses the properties of touch-sensing devices in general.

Balakrishnan and Patel describe the PadMouse, which is a touchpad integrated with a mouse [1]. The PadMouse can sense when the user's finger touches the touchpad. The TouchCube [12] is a cube that has touchpads mounted on its faces to allow 3D manipulations. Rouse [21] uses a panel with 4 control pads, surrounding a fifth central pad, to implement a "touch sensitive joystick." Rouse's technique only senses *simultaneous* contact between the thumb on the central pad and the surrounding directional pads. Fakespace sells *Pinch Gloves* (derived from ChordGloves [17]), which detect contact between two or more digits of the gloves.

Harrison et al. [7] detect contact with handheld displays using pressure sensors, and demonstrate interaction techniques for scrolling and for automatically detecting the user's handedness. Harrison et al. also draw a distinction between explicit actions that are consciously initiated by the user, versus implicit actions where the computer senses what the user naturally does with the device.

The Haptic Lens and HoloWall do not directly sense touch, but nonetheless achieve a similar effect using cameras. The Haptic Lens [23] senses the depression of an elastomer at multiple points using a camera mounted behind the elastomer. The HoloWall [18] uses an infrared camera to track the position of the user's hands or a physical object held against a projection screen. Only objects close to the projection surface are visible to the camera and thus the HoloWall can detect when objects enter or leave proximity.

Pickering [20] describes a number of technologies for touchscreens (including capacitive, infrared (IR) detection systems, resistive membrane, and surface acoustic wave detection); any of these technologies could potentially be used to implement touch-sensing input devices. For example, when a user grabs a Microsoft Sidewinder Force Feedback Pro joystick, this triggers an IR beam sensor and enables the joystick's force feedback response.

Looking beyond direct contact sensors, a number of non-contact proximity sensing devices and technologies are available. Sinks in public restrooms activate when the user's hands reflect an IR beam. Burglar alarms and outdoor lights often include motion detectors or light-level sensors. Electric field sensing devices [26][24] can detect the capacitance of the user's hand or body to allow deviceless position or orientation sensing in multiple dimensions. Our touch-sensing input devices also sense capacitance, but by design we use this signal in a contact-sensing role. In principle, an input device could incorporate both contact sensors and proximity sensors based on electric fields or other technologies.

The following taxonomy organizes the various tactile input technologies discussed above. The columns are divided into *contact* and *non-contact* technologies, with the *contact* category subdivided into touch-sensing versus pressure or force sensing technologies. The rows of the table classify these technologies as either *discrete* (providing an on / off signal only) or *continuous* if they return a proportional signal (e.g., contact area, pressure, or range to a target). A technology is *single-channel* if it measures touch, pressure, or proximity at a single point, or *multi-channel* if it includes multiple sensors or multiple points of contact. The table omits the position and orientation-sensing properties of input devices as these are handled well by previous taxonomies [3][5]. The table also does not attempt to organize the various technologies listed within each cell.

		CONTACT		NON-CONTACT
		Touch-sensing	Pressure / Force	Proximity
DISCRETE	Single channel	Touchpad touch tablet touchscreens (except IR) touch-based switches PadMouse [1]	push button membrane switch Palm Pilot screen (pressure required) supermarket floor mats car seat: weight sensors for airbag	motion detectors electro-magnetic field sensor [11] Light-level sensor Sidewinder force-feedback joystick (IR beam sensor) IR touchscreens
DISCRETE	Multi-channel	TouchMouse TouchCube [12] touch-sensitive joystick [21] Pinch Gloves [17]	Psychic Space [13] (A grid of floor tiles that can sense which tiles a user is standing on.)	
CONTINUOUS	Single channel	contact area (e.g. some touchpads & touchscreens)	pressure-sensitive touch tablet [4] vector input touchscreen [9] torque sensor isometric joystick	laser rangefinder stud finder
CONTINUOUS	Multi-channel		Multi-touch tablet w/ pressure [15] pressure sensors on handhelds [7] Haptic lens (deformation at multiple points) [23]	HoloWall [18] Field-sensing devices [24][26]

Table 1 : Classification of tactile input technologies.

TOUCH SENSING: HOW IT WORKS

The touch-sensing input devices described in this paper employ the circuitry shown in Fig. 2, which senses contact from the user's hand– no pressure or mechanical actuation of a switch is necessary to trigger the touch sensor. The "touch sensors" are conductive surfaces on the exterior of the device shell that are applied using conductive paint (available from Chemtronics [6]). The conductive paint is then connected internally to the touch sensing circuitry.

The internal circuitry generates a 30 Hz square wave that is present on the conductive paint pad. The parasitic capacitance of the user's hand induces a slight time delay in this square wave. When this time delay passes a critical threshold, a *Touch* or *Release* event is generated. A potentiometer (shown in the circuit diagram) allows adjustment of this threshold to accommodate conductive surfaces of various sizes; this only needs to be set once when the circuit is constructed (no calibration step is required for individual users). To provide a good coupling with the tactile feedback that the user feels, the capacitance sensors are set to generate *Touch / Release* events only and exactly when the user's hand actually makes (or breaks) contact with the surface. Our current prototype sends the touch data to the host PC's parallel port.

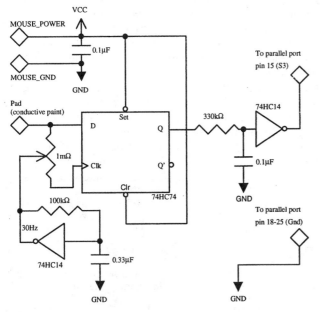

Fig. 2   Circuit diagram for a single touch sensor.

When providing *multiple* touch sensors with the circuit described above, the 30 Hz square wave can pass through the user's body and be picked up by another touch sensor as a false *Touch* or *Release* signal. Thus, to avoid interference, all devices that the user may be touching at a given time should be synchronized to the same square wave.

Software Emulation

One could attempt to emulate *Touch* and *Release* events from software based only on the events provided by a normal mouse. Although this approach may be "good enough" for some interaction techniques or to support situations in which a touch-sensing device is not available,

it suffers from two significant drawbacks. First, one cannot distinguish a user holding the mouse still from a user that has let go of the mouse; this also implies that one cannot know with certainty that subsequent mouse motion occurs because the user just touched the mouse, or because the user moved the mouse after holding it stationary for some period of time. A second limitation of software emulation is that only a single *Touch / Release* event pair for the entire input device can be inferred in this way. Without using actual touch sensors, it is impossible to know precisely which part(s) of the input device the user is touching, or to integrate multiple touch-sensitive controls with a device.

TOUCH-SENSITIVE INTERACTION TECHNIQUES

We now discuss specific interaction techniques that use touch sensors to good advantage. These techniques can be broadly categorized as implicit techniques, which passively sense how the user naturally uses an input device, versus explicit techniques, which require the user to learn a new way of touching or using the input device.

Implicit Actions Based on Touching an Input Device

Touch sensors can provide applications with information about the context of the user's work, at the level of which input devices the user is currently holding. Implicit actions use this information to improve the delivery and timeliness of user interface services, without requiring the user to learn a new way to use the input device. The user can benefit from touch sensing without necessarily even realizing that the device senses when he or she touches it. The following section demonstrates how this style of implicit interaction can be used to support the On-Demand Interface, and presents initial usability testing results for this technique.

The On-Demand Interface

Limited screen real estate is one of the most enduring design constraints of graphical user interfaces. Display resolutions are creeping upward, but quite slowly when compared to advances in memory and processor speed. Current market research data suggest that 66% of PC users are still restricted to a 640x480 pixel display surface [19].

The On-Demand Interface uses touch sensors to derive contextual information that can be used to make decisions about the relative importance of different parts of a graphical interface display. We use the touch sensors provided by the TouchTrackball and the Scrolling TouchMouse to determine changes to the current task context, and thus to dynamically shift the focus of attention between different layers or portions of the display. It may be possible to use traditional input events such as mouse motion or clicks to emulate some aspects of the On-Demand Interface, but given that the signals from the touch sensors are reliable, unambiguous, and require little or no overhead to use, we believe these provide a superior information source upon which to base the technique.

For example, toolbars can make a large number of functions "discoverable" and easy to access for the user, but they have often been criticized because these benefits come at the cost of permanently consuming screen real estate

Fig. 3: When the user releases the mouse, the toolbars fade out to maximize screen real estate for the document.

[14]. Although some toolbars do provide visual indications of state (e.g. the current font and point size), most toolbars display no useful state information when the user is just looking at a document or entering text with the keyboard.

In the On-Demand Interface, when the user touches or releases the TouchMouse, the toolbars fade in or fade out on an as-needed basis using smooth alpha-transparency animation[1]. Touching the mouse causes the tool bars to fade in quickly, while releasing the mouse causes the toolbars to fade out gradually. The end result is that when the user is not actively using the toolbars, the screen appears simpler and less cluttered, while the display real estate allocated to the document itself is maximized (*Fig. 3*). In the current prototype, we leave the toolbar slightly transparent even when it is faded in so that the user can maintain awareness of parts of the document that are underneath the toolbar.

We chose to use animations of alpha-transparency rather than animated motion such as sliding or zooming. Motion draws the user's attention, and our design goal is for the interface to change in a manner that is minimally distracting. Fading in takes place quickly (over 0.3 seconds) because the user may be grabbing the mouse with the intent to select an item from the toolbar; fading out takes place more gradually (over 2.0 seconds) because we do not want to draw the user's attention to the withdrawal of the toolbars. The toolbars could appear instantaneously, but we find that instantaneous transitions seem very jarring and unpleasant, especially given that such a transition will occur every time the user grabs the mouse.

Note that although it would be possible to fade out *all* menus and toolbars, this may not always be appropriate. Menus serve as reminder for keyboard shortcuts during text entry, and some toolbars do provide visual indications of state. However, one can distinguish the size of the toolbar that is best for interaction with the mouse versus the size of the toolbar that is necessary to visually display the desired state information. As seen in Fig. 3, the On-Demand Interface fades in a *compact* toolbar, scrollbar, and menu representation while the toolbars fade out. During our usability tests, most users did not notice or comment on this change in appearance, although one user did mention that "I would expect the Bold icon to stay in the same place."

We also use the touch sensors on the wheel and on the mouse button of the Scrolling TouchMouse to support a *reading mode* of interaction when the user engages the wheel. Rotating the wheel on a standard IntelliMouse scrolls the document line-by-line, and we have observed that users will often keep their finger perched on the wheel when they pause to read the document. Since the user does not need the toolbars while using the wheel, the On-Demand Interface senses initial contact with the wheel and uses this signal to gradually fade out the toolbars and again maximize the display real estate allocated to the document. In our current design, a faint trace of the toolbars remains visible while in reading mode so that the user can see where the toolbars will appear upon return to normal mouse usage. The interface reverts to normal mouse usage when the user's index finger returns to and touches the mouse button, which quickly fades the toolbars back in. Although accidentally touching the wheel and thus switching to reading mode might seem to be a problem, during our usability tests we found this was not a significant issue. Regarding this point, one test user commented that "I like that it fades back in kind of quick. So if you had accidentally touched [the wheel] it's no big deal."

Fig. 4   When the user touches the trackball, the ToolGlass fades in quickly; the toolbars simultaneously fade out.

We use the TouchTrackball to apply the On-Demand Interface concept to the ToolGlass technique [2], which provides the user with a set of movable semi-transparent "click-through" tools that are controlled with a trackball in the nonpreferred hand. When the user touches the trackball, the ToolGlass fades in quickly over 0.3 seconds; if the user is also touching the mouse, the toolbars simultaneously fade out (*Fig. 4*). When the user releases the trackball, after a brief time delay[2] the ToolGlass fades out gradually, and if the user is touching the mouse, the toolbars simultaneously fade in (over 1.0 second). If the user clicks-through a tool

---

[1] We implemented this prototype using a 3D graphics accelerator to provide alpha-blending of texture maps; it is not a fully functional implementation of Microsoft Word.

[2] This time delay (0.5 seconds) allows one to "reclutch" the trackball (release and recenter one's hand on the ball) without undesired changes to the display.

to initiate a command with the ToolGlass, it fades out immediately (over 0.2 seconds) and does not fade back in unless the user moves the trackball or releases and touches the trackball again.

Informal Usability Evaluation

We conducted informal usability tests of the On-Demand Interface, which were intended to explore user acceptance of this technique and to identify usability problems with our current implementation. We recruited 11 users from an internal pool of administrative assistants for this study. All users were familiar with Microsoft Word but none had seen or tried our touch-sensing input devices before.

For the testing, we implemented the On-Demand Interface technique in a prototype that fully supported the various fade in / fade out transitions in response to interacting with the input devices, but only supported limited interaction with the document itself (users could click and drag with the mouse to circle regions of text) and limited keyboard text entry (as the user typed, text actually appeared in a small separate box below the main window). Nonetheless, we feel that this functionality was sufficient to test the utility of the On-Demand interface concept.

In particular, since we felt that *transitions* between the different task contexts recognized by the On-Demand Interface might result in usability problems, we tried to test interleaving of the various task contexts as much as possible. For example, we asked users to highlight a word with the mouse; then type in some text to replace this; then click on the Bold icon in the toolbar; then switch back to typing again, and so on. After performing several structured tasks of this sort, users were also encouraged to play around with the interface to get a more thorough feel for what they did or did not like.

Test users were quite enthusiastic about the ability to see more of the screen during typing and scrolling tasks, while at the same time having the toolbar available on short notice. One user explained that "I like that [the toolbar] comes up quickly when you need it and you can control how long it stays up" and that "all the extra stuff isn't there when I don't need it." Subjective questionnaire ratings on a 1 (disagree) to 5 (agree) scale confirmed these comments: users reported that the TouchMouse was easy to use and that they liked seeing more of the document at once (average rating 4.5 for both questions).

Most users also liked the fading animations that transitioned between screen layouts. Two users did feel that the transition from the toolbars to a "clean screen" for text entry was too slow. One user wanted the toolbar to slide into place instead of fading. However, it was clear that transitions between the toolbars and the "clean screen" were well accepted overall and were not the source of any significant usability problems; when asked if "switching between the keyboard and mouse is disconcerting," users clearly disagreed (average rating 1.9). Users also felt that the touch sensors provided an appropriate way to control these transitions, offering comments such as "I really like the touch-sensitive – I really like that a lot."

As noted above, in this prototype we experimented with leaving the toolbars slightly transparent even when they were fully faded in to allow some awareness of the occluded portions of the document. We felt this was a useful feature, but *all 11 users* reported that they disliked the slightly transparent toolbar, and often in no uncertain terms: one user described it as looking "like a wet newspaper" while another simply stated, "I hate that!" Users clearly felt the display should always transition to fully opaque or fully invisible states. In retrospect, we realized that this dissatisfaction with semi-transparent toolbars on top of a text editing application perhaps should have been expected given that studies of transparent interfaces have shown text backgrounds lead to relatively poor performance [8], and we may not have chosen the icon colors, styles, or transparency levels with sufficient care.

With regard to the TouchTrackball and ToolGlass, users also generally liked that the ToolGlass faded in when they touched the trackball: "That's cool when the ball takes over the hand commands." One user did comment that the appearance of the ToolGlass, and simultaneous disappearance of the toolbars, was the only transition where "I felt like too much was going on." Perhaps the toolbars should stay put or fade out more slowly in this case. Interestingly, in contrast to the strongly negative response to the slightly see-through toolbars, most users had no problem with the semi-transparency of the ToolGlass; it was probably easier to visually separate the foreground and background layers in this case because the user can move the ToolGlass. For example, one user mentioned that "It's good to see where an action would be and what it would look like." A couple of users commented that using two hands "would definitely take some getting used to," but in general users seemed to agree that that "using the trackball was easy" (average 4.3).

The On-Demand Interface demonstrates a novel application of touch sensors that dynamically adjusts screen real estate to get unnecessary portions of the interface out of the user's face. Since the initial user feedback has been encouraging, we plan to add these capabilities to a more fully functional application and perform further studies of the technique to determine if additional issues might arise with long-term use. We are also investigating the appropriateness of the technique for other interface components such as floating tool palettes or dialog boxes.

Explicit Actions Based on Touch Sensors

A second general class of interaction techniques uses touch sensors to allow an input device to express an enhanced vocabulary of explicit actions, but the user must learn these new ways of touching or using the input device to fully benefit from them. Clearly, such actions should have minimal impact on the way one would normally use the device, so that the new capabilities do not interfere with the user's existing skills for controlling the input device.

The Scrolling TouchMouse

The Scrolling TouchMouse (*Fig. 1, right*) is a modified Microsoft IntelliMouse Pro mouse. This mouse includes a wheel that can be used for scrolling, and an oblong plastic basin that surrounds the wheel. The wheel can also be clicked for use as a middle mouse button.

In the previous section, we described how several of the touch sensors on the Scrolling TouchMouse could be used for implicit sensing of the user's task context. In this section, we describe the use of two touch sensors that we have added to the basin, one above and one below the wheel. In addition to the usual line-by-line scrolling supporting by rolling the wheel, these touch sensors enhance scrolling actions with several new behaviors:

- *Tapping*: Tapping the top part of the basin triggers a Page Up command; tapping the bottom of the basin triggers a Page Down. The wheel is good for short-range scrolling, but is less effective for long range scrolling [25]; the tapping gesture provides an effective means for discrete scrolling at a larger scale of motion.

- *Roll-and-hold*: This extends the gesture of rolling the wheel to support smooth scrolling. Rolling the wheel until the finger contacts the top touch sensor or the bottom touch sensor initiates continuous up scrolling or continuous down scrolling, respectively. The scrolling starts after a brief delay (0.15 seconds) to prevent accidental activation from briefly brushing the sensor.

- *Reading sensor*: We already use the wheel touch sensor in the On-Demand interface to sense when the user begins a scrolling interaction. Since IntelliMouse users often leave their finger perched on the wheel while reading, an intriguing possibility is that dwell time on the wheel may prove useful as a predictor of how much time the user has spent reading content on a web page, for example. We have not yet tested the wheel sensor in this role.

We performed informal evaluations with ten test users recruited from the Microsoft Usability pool; 3 of the 10 users had previously used a mouse including a scrolling wheel. Test users were asked to scroll to various points within a long web page containing approximately 10 pages of content. For this informal study, we did not control the distances to the various scrolling targets, nor did we test the interleaving of scrolling with other common mouse tasks; a future study should address these issues. Our main goals were to observe user responses to the device, discover some potential usability problems, and see if touch sensors were effective for these kinds of interactions.

Users found the tapping feature extremely appealing. When asked to respond to the statement "Paging up and down with the TouchMouse was easier than paging with my current mouse" user responses averaged a 4.6 (again on a 1-5 scale). One user commented "I really like this, it's pretty cool... just tap, tap, tap, done!" while another commented that "I didn't really see a reason for the wheel. Just touching the gold [sensor] was easy enough." One user did feel that "the tap surface should be larger."

Several users expected the tapping sensors to support an additional gesture that we currently have not implemented, the *tap-and-hold*. Tapping and then holding one's finger would trigger a paging command followed by more rapid continuous up or down scrolling. One potential problem with the tap-and-hold is that simply resting one's finger on the basin after tapping would now trigger an action. We plan to experiment with a tap-and-hold gesture to see whether or not it is genuinely useful.

Problems with the device related to the wheel itself and the roll-and-hold behavior. When asked to respond to "I liked the way the wheel on the TouchMouse felt while scrolling," user responses averaged a 3.2 (with 3 = neither agree nor disagree). Several difficulties led to this lukewarm response. Our touch-sensing modifications to the wheel made it slightly slippery and harder to turn; this problem also made it more likely that users would click the wheel by mistake, and due to a technical glitch, the roll-and-hold did not work correctly when this happened. Also, the "continuous" scrolling implemented in our prototype was jerky and moved too slowly. Users did not like this. Fortunately, these are not inherent problems and will be improved in our next design iteration.

Despite the problems with the roll-and-hold mentioned above, users felt that overall "The TouchMouse was easy to use for scrolling" (responses averaged 4.1). Users also clearly liked the concept of having additional scrolling or paging commands on the mouse (responses averaged 4.8). In combination with the enthusiastic user response to the tapping feature, this demonstrates that the Scrolling TouchMouse successfully employs touch sensors to support new functionality while occupying a minimum of device real estate, and without making the device look significantly more cluttered with physical buttons.

PROPERTIES OF TOUCH-SENSING DEVICES

We now consider the properties of touch sensors and touch sensing input devices in general. Based on our design experience, we feel these are useful issues to consider when designing touch-sensing input devices and interaction techniques, and hope that they may be suggestive of additional possibilities.

Similarities between Touch Sensors and Touch Tablets

Although the touch sensors that we use do not sense positional information, since the geometric arrangement of sensors is known ahead of time, one can potentially confer to the mouse properties that, in the past, have normally been associated with touch tablets. Thus touch sensors have some properties similar to those of touch tablets as enumerated by Buxton, Hill, and Rowley [4]. For example:

- *No moving parts:* Touch sensors have no moving parts.

- *No mechanical intermediary:* Touch sensors require no mechanical intermediary to activate them.

- *Operation by feel:* Touch sensors can be arranged into regions that act like a physical template on a touch tablet. The user can *feel* the touch-sensing regions (e.g., the Page Up / Down controls on the Scrolling TouchMouse) without looking at the device or at the screen. This can reduce the time that would be required to switch between devices or widgets on the screen.

- *Feedback:* Touch sensors differ from traditional pushbuttons in the amount and type of feedback provided. Compared to a mouse button, for example, the user does not feel or hear a distinct "click" when a touch sensor is activated. For cases where a touch sensor is being used in an implicit role and is not being used to simulate such devices, however, such feedback may not be needed or even desired.

Other Properties of Touch Sensors

Touch sensors have a number of additional unique properties that can be useful to consider in the design of devices and interaction techniques:

- *Accidental activation:* Because touch sensors require zero activation force, they may be prone to accidental activation due to inadvertent contact. In particular, when touch sensors are used to trigger explicit actions, care needs to be taken so that the user can rest his or her hand comfortably on the device without triggering an undesired action. Of course, for implicit sensing applications, "accidental" activation is precisely the property that makes touch sensors useful.

- *Flexible form factor:* Unlike a touchpad, which generally requires a planar form factor, touch sensors can have an extremely flexible shape; curved surfaces, uneven surfaces, or even moving parts such as wheels and trackballs can be touch sensitive. Touch sensors also have a near zero vertical profile (assuming the touch-sensing electronics can be located elsewhere), which allows them to be used in tight spaces that may not readily accommodate a traditional pushbutton.

- *Unobtrusive:* Touch sensors can be added to a device without necessarily making it *look* complex and cluttered with buttons. The user may not even have to be aware that the device incorporates a touch sensor.

- *Low overhead to disengage:* Some input devices, such as a puck on a Wacom tablet, can provide *In Proximity* and *Out Of Proximity* signals when the puck is placed on or removed from the tablet. Although this pair of events is similar to the *Touch* and *Release* events generated by touch sensors, they are useful for different things. For example, removing one's finger from a touchpad requires considerably less overhead than lifting a puck from a tablet. Thus, the proximity signals provided by a tablet and the touch signals provided by a touch sensor support logically distinct device states [10].

- *Deactivation from software:* Touch sensors lend themselves to deactivation from software, because a touch sensor does not respond to user input with a physical "click." Thus, unlike a pushbutton, a disabled touch sensor does not offer any false physical feedback when it is touched, which is useful if the user is in a context where the action is not valid or if the user does not want an added feature.

- *Additional physical gestures:* Some gestures that are not captured well by pushbuttons, such as tapping or simply maintaining contact with a portion of the device, can be captured by touch sensors. A pushbutton that includes a touch sensor [10] can capture these gestures, in addition to the traditional *click* and *drag*.

Intentional Control vs. Cognitive and Physical Burden

Touch-sensing and proximity-sensing technologies offer an inherent tradeoff in intentional control versus the cognitive and physical burden of an input transaction. The progression from button-click, to touch, to hand-near-device is potentially accompanied by a decrease in intentional control by the user, and hence increases the inferential burden (and error rates) of interpretation. This means that, although error rates can be minimized by good design, accidental activation will occur and thus actions triggered by touch or proximity sensors should have a low cost from errors of interpretation.

Yet this apparent weakness is also a strength, as a reduction of intentional control also implies a potential decrease in the cognitive burden of making explicit decisions to perform an action. Thus, when used in an implicit role, touch sensing can provide enhanced device functionality with little or no added cognitive burden. Touching or letting go of the device is an inherent part of *what the user would have to do anyway to use the input device*, so nothing new has to be learned by the user in terms of operating the input device. Touch-sensing devices are capable of sensing the *Touch* and *Release* events that in a manner of thinking have always been available, but were ignored by traditional devices such as mice and trackballs.

CONCLUSIONS AND FUTURE WORK

The present work has demonstrated that touch-sensing is an orthogonal property of input devices that does not necessarily have to be coupled with position sensing. This observation suggests new possibilities for touch-sensing input devices, exemplified by the TouchTrackball and Scrolling TouchMouse presented herein. We have also described the hardware needed to actually build touch sensors in the hope that this will encourage other interface designers to experiment with our techniques and explore additional possibilities for touch-sensing devices.

Touch sensors allow some properties that have normally only been associated with touch tablets to be integrated with other input devices such as the mouse. Thus, the touch-sensing mouse provides a set of design properties that neither traditional mice nor traditional touch tablets can match. Touch sensors also provide a number of other unique properties, perhaps the most important of which are (1) zero activation force, allowing implicit sensing of "accidental" contact, and (2) great flexibility of form factor which allows touch sensors to be applied to tight spaces, curved surfaces, or even moving parts.

When matched to appropriate interaction techniques these unique properties of touch-sensing input devices allow user interfaces to effectively support a number of new behaviors. Our initial usability testing results of the On-Demand Interface and the Scrolling TouchMouse demonstrate that touch-sensing devices can provide new behaviors that users find compelling and useful.

However, much future work is still required. We need to refine and more formally evaluate the specific interaction techniques that we have described. Additional study is needed to better understand and characterize the strengths and weaknesses of touch sensors. Also, we feel that a more detailed taxonomy of touch sensing and proximity sensing devices could help to better understand and explore the design space. A good taxonomy of such devices should probably include both sensors and actuators. For that matter, a more unified treatment including audio I/O (microphones and speakers), visual I/O (cameras and displays), and the haptic channels (tactile, force, and kinesthetic I/O) might be useful to describe a wider range of existing devices and suggest future possibilities.

ACKNOWLEDGEMENTS
We would like to thank the Microsoft Hardware Group for ideas and discussions; Hunter Hoffman, Barry Peterson, and Mary Czerwinski for assistance with usability studies; Bill Gaver for thoughtful comments on touch-sensing; Matt Conway for suggested improvements to the paper; Dan Robbins for the photographs; and George Robertson for managerial support and design discussions.

REFERENCES
1. Balakrishnan, R., Patel, P., "The PadMouse: Facilitating Selection and Spatial Positioning for the Non-Dominant Hand," CHI'98, 1998, 9-16.

2. Bier, E., Stone, M., Pier, K., Buxton, W., DeRose, T., "Toolglass and Magic Lenses: The See-Through Interface," SIGGRAPH 93, 1993, 73-80.

3. Buxton, W., "Touch, Gesture, and Marking," in *Readings in Human-Computer Interaction: Toward the Year 2000*, R. Baecker, *et al.*, Editors. 1995, Morgan Kaufmann Publishers. p. 469-482.

4. Buxton, W., Hill, R., Rowley, P., "Issues and Techniques in Touch-Sensitive Tablet Input," Computer Graphics, 19 (3): p. 215-224, 1985.

5. Card, S., Mackinlay, J., Robertson, G., "The Design Space of Input Devices," CHI'90 Conf. on Human Factors in Computing Systems, 117-124.

6. Chemtronics, CircuitWorks Conductive Pen, : http://www.chemtronics.com/.

7. Harrison, B., Fishkin, K., Gujar, A., Mochon, C., Want, R., "Squeeze Me, Hold Me, Tilt Me! An Exploration of Manipulative User Interfaces," CHI'98, 17-24.

8. Harrison & Vicente, "An Experimental Evaluation of Transparent Menu Usage," CHI'96, 391-398.

9. Herot, C., Weinzapfel, G., "One-Point Touch Input of Vector Information from Computer Displays," Computer Graphics, 12 (3): p. 210-216, 1978.

10. Hinckley, K., Czerwinski, M., Sinclair, M., "Interaction and Modeling Techniques for Desktop Two-Handed Input," UIST'98, 49-58.

11. Infusion Systems, "Reach" electromagnetic field sensor: http://www.infusionsystems.com/.

12. ITU Research, TouchCube: www.ituresearch.com.

13. Krueger, M., "Artificial Reality II". 1991, Reading, MA: Addison-Wesley.

14. Kurtenbach, G., Fitzmaurice, G., Baudel, T., Buxton, B., "The Design of a GUI Paradigm based on Tablets, Two-hands, and Transparency," CHI'97, 35-42.

15. Lee, S., Buxton, W., Smith, K., "A Multi-Touch Three Dimensional Touch-Sensitive Tablet," Proc. CHI'85, 1985, 21-25.

16. Loomis, J., Lederman, S., "Tactual Perception," in *Handbook of Perception and Human Performance: Vol. II*, K. Boff et al., eds. 1986, John Wiley and Sons: New York. Chapter 31.

17. Mapes, D., Moshell, J.M., "A Two-Handed Interface for Object Manipulation in Virtual Environments," Presence, 4 (4): p. 403-416, 1995.

18. Matsushita, N., Rekimoto, J., "Holo Wall: Designing a Finger, Hand, Body, and Object Sensitive Wall," UIST'97, 209-210.

19. Media Metrix Inc., HardScan Report, 1998, p. 4.

20. Pickering, J., "Touch-sensitive screens: the technologies and their application," International J. Man-Machine Studies, 25 (3): p. 249-69, 1986.

21. Rouse, P., "Touch-sensitive joystick," Radio & Electronics World, Feb. 1985, p. 23-26.

22. Ruspini, D., Kolarov, K., Khatib, O., "The Haptic Display of Complex Graphical Environments," SIGGRAPH'97, 345-352.

23. Sinclair, M., "The Haptic Lens," SIGRRAPH'97 Visual Proceedings, p. 179.

24. Smith, J.R., White, T., Dodge, C., Allport, D., Paradiso, J., Gershenfeld, N., "Electric Field Sensing for Graphical Interfaces," IEEE Computer Graphics and Applications, May, 1998.

25. Zhai, S., Smith, B.A., Selker, T., "Improving Browsing Performance: A study of four input devices for scrolling and pointing tasks," Proc. Interact '97: The 6th IFIP Conf. on HCI, 286-92.

26. Zimmerman, T., Smith, J, Paradiso, J., Allport, D., Gershenfeld, N., "Applying Electric Field Sensing to Human-Computer Interfaces," CHI'95, 280-287.

The Hotbox: Efficient Access to a Large Number of Menu-items

Gordon Kurtenbach, George W. Fitzmaurice, Russell N. Owen and Thomas Baudel[*]

Alias | Wavefront

210 King Street East

Toronto, Ontario, Canada, M5A 1J7

<gordo, gf, rowen>@aw.sgi.com

1+ 416 362-9181

ABSTRACT

The proliferation of multiple toolbars and UI widgets around the perimeter of application windows is an indication that the traditional GUI design of a single menubar is not sufficient to support large scale applications with numerous functions. In this paper we describe a new widget which is an enhancement of the traditional menubar which dramatically increases menu-item capacity. This widget, called the "Hotbox" combines several GUI techniques which are generally used independently: accelerator keys, modal dialogs, pop-up/pull down menus, radial menus, marking menus and menubars. These techniques are fitted together to create a single, easy to learn yet fast to operate GUI widget which can handle significantly more menu-items than the traditional GUI menubar. We describe the design rationale of the Hotbox and its effectiveness in a large scale commercial application. While the Hotbox was developed for a particular application domain, the widget itself and the design rationale are potentially useful in other domains.

KEYWORDS: menus access, menubars, two-handed input, transparency, marking menus

INTRODUCTION

In this paper we describe the design of a menu access widget in Alias |Wavefront's professional 3D computer animation and design application, Maya [14]. Because Maya is a professional's tool it presents many challenging user interface requirements. First and foremost, Maya allows complex and sophisticated controls over 3D data and the behavior of 3D data over time. For example, Maya is used for computer graphics special effects in blockbuster Hollywood movies like "Jurassic Park" and "Toy Story". This sophisticated functionality results in an application with hundreds of commands. Professional users also require efficient access to commands since they may spend a huge number of hours operating the application under strict deadlines. Therefore even small performance improvements (like menu selection speed) can dramatically affect user efficiency and their perceived efficiency of the application. Another major design requirement for this class of application is to reduce the complexity of the user interface whenever possible. The nature of data and the operations on

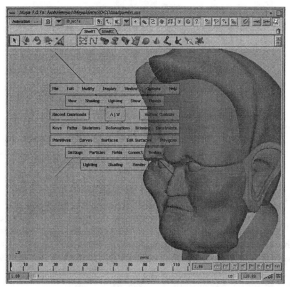

Figure 1: Maya application with Hotbox widget in the center

the data is, by itself, complex. Adding in a complicated user interface would only further increase complexity of the application.

These challenges produce three basic problems for the traditional GUI design:

Quantity: Maya has approximately 1200 commands which would be typically found in the menubar. This number of commands will increase with subsequent versions. Roughly speaking, at the very most 20 menus can be placed in a menubar that span the entire length of a high resolution screen (1280 pixels across). With 1200 commands this results in menus that on average have 60 items in them. In practice this results in information overload.

Speed: Users want fast access to frequently used commands. In traditional GUIs, hotkeys (also called "menu accelerators"), are used for the frequently used functions. In Maya, a default set of hotkeys are used to access frequently used functions, however, this allows access to only a small fraction of the 1200 commands. Increasing the number of hotkeys creates problems. First, as the number of hotkeys assignments increases the hotkey mappings become hard to remember ("why is ctrl-d mapped to "Create IK Joint?").

[*] Thomas Baudel is now at Ilog, thomas@lri.fr 33+149082965, http://www.lri.fr/~thomas

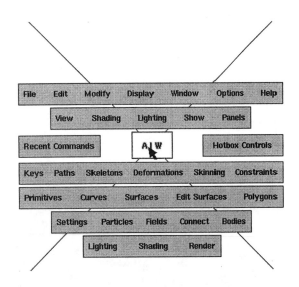

Figure 2: Hotbox widget in "Show All" rows mode.

Second, the keystrokes themselves become slow to articulate (for example, ctrl-alt-P). We also support user-definable hotkeys, however, this still has the same limitations.

Unification: In a traditional GUI, commands may get distributed between toolbars and the menubar. Typically GUIs place functional modes into toolbars and one-shot actions into the menus. However, from a functional point of view, some particular modes and actions are closely related and therefore should be found close together in the interface. We believe this aids the user in learning the application and in finding commands in the interface especially when there are numerous commands. Thus we developed the requirement of "unification": modes and actions should be grouped together in the interface according to function.

We also wanted to create a menu access technique that would unify novice and expert behaviors. In a traditional GUI, novice and expert operation of the interface can be dramatically different. For example, a novice user may exclusively use only the menubar while an expert may almost exclusively use hotkeys. The radical difference between these two behaviors makes graduating from novice to expert behavior an explicit (and extra) effort. We wanted to produce a menu access technique where novice operation was a rehearsal of expert behavior. Essentially, we wanted novices and experts to use the same menu access technique perhaps differing only in speed of operations (much like Marking Menus [8]).

OTHER POSSIBLE SOLUTIONS

Our default solution in Maya makes use of the traditional menubar. Due to the sheer number of menu-items, we divide the menu-items into separate menubars which roughly reflect the high-level tasks of our users. Therefore we have "Modeling", "Animation", "Dynamics" and "Rendering" menubars. The first six menus of a menubar are common to all menubars so we refer to this subset of menus as the "Common" menu-set. These four menubars cannot be displayed simultaneously so a user can switch between menubars by selecting from a popup menu containing the four menubar names which is located directly underneath the main menubar. The menu items in this modal menubar can also be accessed with other standard GUI techniques:

predefined hotkeys and user definable "drag and drop" toolbars and hotkeys.

This default solution does address some problems mentioned in the previous section. The multiple menubars increase the virtual capacity of the menubar by a factor of four. Hotkeys do provide fast access to functions in the menubars but as mentioned earlier the number of hotkeys is limited and the mappings are confusing. The problem of breaking functional groupings by distributing functions between toolbars and menubars is eliminated by simply placing all functions in the menubars and having no predefined static toolbars.

However, there are some major drawbacks to this solution. Direct menu access (not using hotkeys) is slower when a user has the extra step of switching between menubars. Also, our user base finds menubar and toolbar selection slow since selection requires having to move the cursor from their working area in the center of screen to the menubar or toolbar at the edge of the screen and back. Relative to hotkeys and in-context pop-up menus this "cursor round trip" is perceived as slow.

This solution also has unification problems. Novice and expert behaviors are radically different: novices use the menubars while experts use hotkeys and user defined toolbars. Drag and drop toolbars further erode unification, since favorite commands and unfavorite commands get placed in different spots over time breaking functional groupings.

Given the problems with this "status quo" solution we began work on alternate solutions. Some solution approaches we ruled out early in our design process. Our solution space was narrowed down dramatically by the fact that we were designing for a commercial product not a research system. For example, text command line entry was ruled out for the usual arguments that apply concerning GUI versus command line systems. Speech input was ruled out because systems support for speech isn't ubiquitous and guaranteed like keyboard and mouse input.

Other solutions such as menu modes which present fewer menu-items to novices than to experts [3] were not suitable because they only aid novices not experts who need to deal with the complete set of menu-items and also require fast access.

Essentially we had to construct a solution out of the basic interaction techniques of GUIs: popup, pulldown menus, different mouse buttons, hotkeys, etc. None of these techniques used in the traditional sense provided a satisfactory solution. The main problem with these techniques was handling the sheer number of menu items without producing heavily nested menus (nesting menus has been shown to degrade menu selection performance [7][10]) or forcing the user to learn many different hotkey or button mappings. However, the solution we did develop is built using a combination of these GUI components.

Ultimately, we had to develop a new technique which our users would prefer over the traditional default technique. Use of the new technique would be optional (both the new technique and the traditional technique would be available in the application simultaneously), so if users elected to use the new technique instead the traditional we would consider this a success.

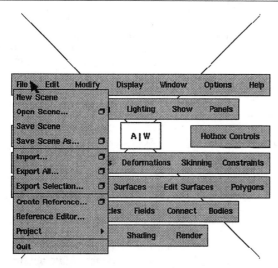

Figure 3: Hotbox widget with linear popup menus.

HOW THE HOTBOX WORKS

This section outlines how the Hotbox widget works. The next section will discuss rationale behind this design.

The HotBox works as follows. To display the Hotbox the user holds down the space-bar (with their non-dominant hand) when the cursor is in any of Maya's windows. The Hotbox instantly appears, centered at the location of the cursor. The "rows" of the Hotbox (see Figure 2) behave like traditional menubars. Individual menus can be popped down like menubar menus by moving the mouse (with the dominant hand) so the cursor is over a menu label and pressing any mouse button (Figure 3).

Each row of the Hotbox corresponds to a particular set of menus (Figure 4). The top row, is referred to as the "common" row. This corresponds to menus commonly found in most applications' main window menubar (e.g., File, Edit,...). The next row down shows the items in the menubar for the window that the cursor is currently in. Below the center row of the Hotbox are rows of menus specific to certain computer graphics tasks.

The center row's menu label "Recent Commands" displays a list of recent commands issued by the user and allows a user to repeat a command without having to relocate the command in the menus. (Figure 5). The other menu in the center row, "Hotbox Controls" allows the user to control which rows of the Hotbox are displayed. This menu is a marking menu [8]. In Figure 2, all the rows of the Hotbox

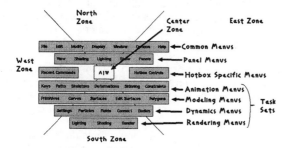

Figure 4. Hotbox rows and marking menu zones for widget

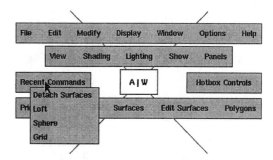

Figure 5. Recent commands history.

are displayed. Using the marking menu a user can quickly display and hide specific rows. Figure 6 shows an example of changing the display of rows.

Besides presenting the user with rows of menus the HotBox divides the entire screen into five zones (Figure 4)[1]. Each one of these zones has a different marking menu which can be accessed simply by pressing down a mouse button when the cursor is in the zone. These marking menus are used for user defined menus.

The Hotbox remains displayed as long as the space-bar is kept pressed. This allows a user to perform a series of commands without having to re-invoke the Hotbox.

DESIGN ISSUES AND RATIONALE

In this section we present major design issues and rationale in the development of the Hotbox. We have grouped these issues and rationale into five main categories: Quantity, Speed, Unification, Graphic Design, and Interaction Design.

1 Quantity

The Hotbox project actually started off with the goal of simply increasing the number of marking menus we could make available in our applications and perhaps capturing all the menu-items in Maya in these marking menus. Traditionally, a user can access marking menus in our older product (Power Animator) by holding down both the shift and ctrl key (the "trigger key") and pressing a mouse button to popup a marking menu. Each mouse button has a different marking menu associated with it. If the user configures each menu to have eight items, this results in fast access to 24 items.

This configuration of marking menus in Power Animator is extremely popular--most expert Power Animator users make heavy use of this feature. In Maya we wanted to improve the situation:

- use the space-bar instead of the awkward "shift-control" keys.
- have the same menu for each mouse button (to avoid "wrong mouse button" errors and to support use with a tablet and stylus device instead of a mouse).
- get access to many more items.

Based on these requirement we developed the idea of using different "menu zones" to access different menus as

---

1. The center zone label, "AlW", is simply a graphic for Aliaslwavefront, the manufacturer of the application.

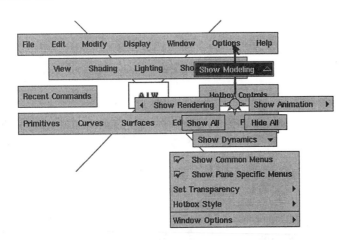

Figure 6. A marking menu is used to control the visibility of rows in the Hotbox. Here the user is about to access a submenu which controls the visibility of the modeling row.

opposed to different mouse button or trigger keys. To get a feel for this solution approach we built several working prototypes and let expert users test them. Figure 7, shows variations on the configurations of zones.

Our expert users reported that this approach allowed efficient access to menus. However, we still realized that 4 or 5 zones were not enough to capture all the menu-items in Maya without severe menu nesting. To solve this problem, we then generalized the concept of zones to have overlapping zones and developed the basic configuration of the Hotbox. With this new approach we realized we could begin considering handling the number of menu-items in Maya.

The next question was how to organize the menu-items in the Hotbox.

Menubar compatibility. In designing the Hotbox widget, we wanted to be sensitive to users who worked with the traditional GUI menubar and then wanted to transition to the Hotbox. To support learning, we designed the Hotbox command set rows to match the menu organizations in the traditional GUI menubar.

Hide/show command sets. While the original intent for the Hotbox was to house and present all of the command functions to the user, we learned early on that users did not want to see all of the command sets all of the time. Therefore, we created a marking menu (Hotbox controls) to allow the user to quickly toggle the visibility of individual rows or to specify the viewing of specific rows (which hides all other rows).

Pane specific command set. Besides the main menubar, each window in Maya may have its own menubar. The Hot-

box provides access to these menus as well. The "pane specific" row in the Hotbox changes its contents depending on the position of the cursor within different views at the time the Hotbox is invoked. This design provides context specific access to command sets which automatically change as the user changes views.

2 Speed

Large menu targets. With the layout of the Hotbox, there is a design tension between speed of access (making the menu rows tall and wide) versus the overall size of the Hotbox widget (which interferes with seeing the underlying application data). We know from Fitts' law [12] that speed of target acquisition is a function of the distance to the target from the cursor and the width of the target. In our case, the width of the target is broken up into two components: the length and height of the menu label. To provide fast access, we increased the height of our menu rows which is the true effective width of our Fitts' Law targets while not distorting the visual appearance of the Hotbox widget.

Popup at cursor or center of screen. Having chosen a popup design, we considered two strategies. First, we could pop the Hotbox widget centered around the current cursor location. This reduces the average distance between the cursor and a given menu label. Also, it guarantees that the center marking menu zone will be immediately active for invoking a marking menu. Alternatively, we considered popping up the Hotbox widget in the center of the screen. This design would provide a constant, absolute positioning of menu items as well as marking menu zones. In terms of cursor travel distances, this approach is more costly than the first approach where the menus come to the user instead of the user going to the menus.

Issuing multiple commands in a single posting. Many popup widgets are designed to dismiss themselves when a user selects an item. We designed the Hotbox widget to handle issuing multiple commands in a single posting. This provides a more efficient interaction (often saving mouse clicks and cursor travel time).

Marking zones. The 5 marking zones (North, South, East, West and Center) are designed to provide a user with quick access to a large number of their own personal custom menus. These customizeable marking menus are extremely useful for an expert user. For example, a user that very frequently invokes the "show surface normals" menu-item (which is nested 2 levels deep in the menubar menus), can place this item in one of the zone marking menus for fast access.

These zone menus can be built by a user using a GUI menu builder in Maya. Not only can they contain menu-items from Maya's menubars but a user can also write their own custom menu-item commands using Maya's embedded programming language. This level of customizability is extremely useful for expert users.

Quick access is supported in two of ways. First, a menu zone is an extremely large target (almost 1/4 of the screen). This makes moving the cursor into it extremely fast. Second, the use of marking menus provides fast command access compared to traditional linear menus [8]: once in the correct zone a user can simply press down the mouse button and "flick" the cursor in the direction of the desired menu-item.

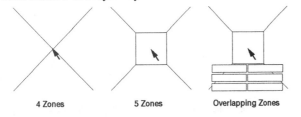

4 Zones   5 Zones   Overlapping Zones

Figure 7. Early prototypes of Hotbox with marking zones.

Within each zone, a marking menu set can be defined for each of the three mouse buttons. This provides the user with the potential for 15 custom marking menu sets. While this may seem a bit excessive, we believe it is a reasonable size if users have a preference for single level menus. By default, the Maya application has five default marking menu (one in each zone). The center marking menu zone has been designed for the quickest access as it does not require any cursor travel before a user can start issuing a mark.

By its design, the Hotbox creates a hierarchy of access speed. The center zone provides the fastest access. When the space bar is pressed it can be accessed without having to move the cursor. The next level of access is the north, east, south and west zones. These zones don't pop-up under the cursor but since they are very large they can be moved to very quickly. Finally, the menu row items are the next level of access. Like the zones, they require cursor movement but are slower to access since they are much smaller targets than the zones. Also, within the menu rows, items closer to the center are faster to access.

3 Unification

Everything in menubar. Early versions of Maya had two main widgets to house commands: the menubar and toolbox. Our users never realized that the toolbox contained moded items. Instead they would ask us why the functions were separated into two places. Given this, we wanted to provide "one-stop-shopping" for our users where the commands were organized by function not by interaction style (e.g., moded tools are in the toolbox while one-shot actions are in the menus). Placing the tools into the menus had a side benefit of using text labels instead of icons to describe a command function.

Menus under one key. To simplify the interaction model, we wanted to define a single mechanism for accessing the menus. While Maya uses the Motif toolkit, which has it's pop-up menus under the right mouse button, many of our users found this fatiguing and wanted to use the left mouse button. We could not use modifier keys (ctrl, alt, shift) as these were already assigned to standard keys for managing selection and camera controls. Thus, we needed to find another key and we chose the space bar for its ease of access. Using a single key to access menus within the application provides a gestural unification and simplification to the overall interaction model.

Customizeable menus. Strictly speaking, our customizeable zone menus violate our design principle of unification. Like a drag and drop toolbar a user can relocate functions and this results in different novice and expert behaviors. We have two observations concerning this. First, because of the capacity of the Hotbox zones, our default zone menu set is quite large and we have observed that many expert users don't find a need to create custom menus--they simply use the defaults and perceive these menus as the functional location for these menu-items. In this situation novice and expert behavior remains the same. Second, when a user creates fast access to some menu items by placing them in a zone menu, the basic access behavior remains the same (i.e., through the Hotbox). This is in contrast with traditional drag and drop customization where a menu-item is dragged from the menubar to a toolbar after which access is through the toolbar not the menubar.

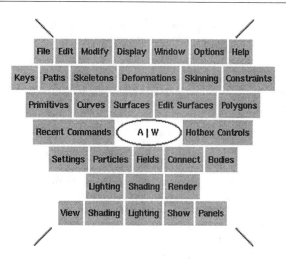

Figure 8. Early Hotbox layout with rows centered.

4 Graphic Design

Visual & organizing theme. We considered a variety of layouts for the menu sets (e.g., column based, cluster based, etc.). In the end, we chose a row based approach which was easy to implement, offered a compact layout, and visually reflected the common menubar concept.

Row presentation. Presenting multiple menu rows to the user without overwhelming them was a major challenge in our design. Initially we had the rows left justified. Next we prototyped a center justification approach to reduce the travel distance to the various menus (see Figure 8). Still, graphically, this was hard to visually parse and identify command sets based on row length. We considered coloring each row separately but realized that some of our machines only have 3 colors in the overlay window in which the Hotbox widget is drawn so this solution would not work. Finally, we came up with a layout algorithm which we call "stair-step justify" which quantizes row lengths to various uniform step increments and center justifies the row. This provides visual order to the Hotbox widget (see Figure 2). In addition, we placed a border around the rows to further reinforce their menubar likeness and to reduce visual interference from the application data. Lastly, we preserved the row ordering (Common, Pane specific, Hotbox specific, Animation, Modeling, Dynamics, Rendering) and made the Hotbox specific row visually distinct to provide a visual grouping of rows. This final design is much more visually balanced while still offering the same degree of interaction efficiency as in our earlier designs.

Marking menu zones. Delimiting the five marking menu zones also provided a challenge. We quickly settled on using the cross (X) but found it difficult to determine visual rules for the length of the lines. This was specially awkward for Hotbox configurations with an even number of rows. This is truly a subtle graphical design issue which was noticeable and visually disturbing in our early designs but has been rectified in our current design (which keeps the cross length balanced above and below the Hotbox specific row, such that the cross is perfectly square).

Transparency. To reduce obscuring the underlying application data, the Hotbox widget employs transparency (see Figure 1) to allow the user to see through the widget (similar to systems like ToolGlass [1] or T3 [9]). This is especially useful as the Hotbox can be quite large when all of the rows are being displayed. The user can adjust the degree of transparency from fully opaque to clear.

Anti-alias fonts. When the Hotbox is drawn with 100% transparency (i.e., clear), a great deal of interference occurs between the textual menu labels and the underlying application data. To reduce this interference, we use anti-alias fonts [4] which surrounds each character with an "opposite" contrasting color to ensure its legibility.

No need for traditional menubars. Users also quickly realized the benefit of transitioning to the Hotbox widget in that they can hide the traditional GUI menubars (both the main menubar and the pane specific menubars) to free up more screen space for their application data. This can be a very significant saving if there are many windows displayed with a menubar in each one.

5 Interaction Design

No Hotbox warping. We do not warp the position of the Hotbox if portions of it fall off the screen. This is to produces the benefit of having the center marking menu zone always popping-up under the cursor. The cost is, of course, to have some inaccessible menu-items when popping up near the edge of the screen. We have found in practice that this isn't a major problem since users prefer to generally work near the center of the screen.

Menubar functionality. Since the Hotbox widget can be viewed as a collection of menubars, users expect the same degree of functionality as traditional menubars. Thus, we need to provide the usual functions of posting individual menus, browsing multiple menus within a single drag operation, the ability to tear-off menus, and offering roll-over help for individual menu items. Nothing in the design of the Hotbox prevents these features, however, time constraints prevented us from implementing these features in the first commercial release of the Hotbox.

HOTBOX USAGE

At the time of this writing, the Hotbox has been used on a daily basis by about 10 in-house users for 16 months, by about 100 beta customers for 13 months, and has now been shipping in the *Maya* product for 6 months, available to thousands of users. At each stage, we find approximately the same usage pattern: some users just ignore it and use the regular GUI elements instead. Some use it as part of their workflow but not to its full extent. Finally, some users use it extensively and exclusively (that is, they hide the traditional menubars, toolbars and make heavy use of the zone menus).

One useful method we have for gauging the success of a product feature is through unsolicited comments from our users, either directly sent to us, published in internet newsgroups or addressed to our customer service. As an example, Table 1 shows some representative comments found on the comp.graphics.apps.alias and comp.graphics.apps.wavefront newsgroups (notes: PA and Wavefront are our previous products, MAX is a competitor, all comments are from different contributors, misspellings are not corrected)

This data is by no means a formal proof of the efficiency of the Hotbox but it is evidence that there is strong acceptance of the hotbox from a portion of our customers.

A more formal survey of 12 of our most experienced in-house users revealed that 5 of them are intensive users, removing all menu bars from their display to gain screen real estate, 5 are frequent users (using it for about half of their menu selections but not removing all menubars from their screen) and 2 use it very rarely or never.

We should point out that the use of the hotbox is optional and users can choose to use many other standard GUI techniques in Maya instead of the Hotbox (e.g., drag and drop toolbars, user definable hotkeys, traditional menubars and popup menus). Thus, we believe that users are using the Hotbox because of some perceived benefit.

> With all the missing Tools, is anyone happy about what they got > a paid for in Maya? Can you give me 5 good reasons to buy it? 1) Semi-Procedural Modeling and Animation (makes PA look barbaric) 2) FAST UI interactivity for modeling 3) Incredible work-flow improvements over PA, Wavefront 4) Hotbox! 5) Hardware rendering particles.
Does anyone who's used Maya for more than a few days ever use the regular menus? The hotbox seems so handy (if visually chaotic) I can't imagine using the traditional menus much.
I tried to do some work in PA the other day only to find that I had almost forgotten how to use it. Maya's way of doing things has taken over my brain. I was on my Mac using AfterEffects and tried to use the Hotbox, and was confused momentarily as to why it wasn't working (about 2 or 3 se onds of confusion).
As I have said I have used Maya just for 10 or 15 hrs or so, and when I come back to PA I feel really bad and I start to press Space for my hotbox menu.
"This other animator here who uses MAX was a hard sale on PA (Oh yeah, we can do that for less is basically his line) was also impressed. I heard him say, Hmmmm.....now that's nice!!! He was referring to the HotBox, general workflow issues, hardware rendered particles etc. and that sort of compliment from him is a rarity. Anyway, I can't wait to see where this is all going with MAYA.".

Table 1: Unsolicited comments from users.

CONCLUSIONS

We believe the Hotbox design produces the following benefits to a user and these benefits are responsible for its acceptance:

- Access to multiple menu bars without having to switch menubar modes.
- Fast access to up to 15 user definable marking menus. Up to 3 of these menus are available directly under the cursor after pressing the space-bar.
- Multiple commands can be issued in a single posting.
- Commands normally distributed between the toolbox, menubar, window menus and user definable marking menus are in the same spot.
- The user can free up more screen space by hiding the traditional menubars.

We believe the following features aid in learning and using the Hotbox:

- Mimicking the structure of the traditional menubar menus eases learning of the Hotbox menu rows.
- The simple and consistent access method for all menus (i.e., press the space bar and press a mouse button to pop-up a menu) is easy to learn and habituate.

- Supporting both novice and experts without requiring customization or radically different behaviors.

We also believe the Hotbox design and rationale can be applied to other domains. First it could easily be applied to other applications where the number of commands overload the traditional GUI elements. Furthermore, many of the benefits of the Hotbox are still applicable even if the application's command set isn't overly large.

Finally, we hope that other UI designers will apply some of the unique design principles and techniques used in the Hotbox (unification, a single, habituating access mechanism, large, radial zones for fast menu access, marking menus and transparency).

ACKNOWLEDGEMENTS

We gratefully thank our expert users most notably Jeff Bell, Chris Ellison and Corban Gossett for their relentless feedback. Beth Goldman, Ravin Balakrishnan and Bill Buxton also provided valuable comments on the design. We would also thank Venu Venugopal, product manager for Maya, for supporting the development and deployment of the Hotbox.

REFERENCES

1. Bier, E., A.,Stone, M., C., Fishkin, K., Buxton, W., Baudel, T., (1994) A Taxonomy of See-Through Tools. *Proceedings of the ACM CHI'94 Conference on Human Factors in Computing Systems,* 358-364.

2. Brooks, P. (1994). Adding Value to Usability Testing. in *Usability Inspection Methods,* Nielsen, J. & Mack R. (Eds). John Wiley. 255-271. see p. 262.

3. Carroll, J., M., & Carrithers, C. (1994) Training Wheels in a User Interface. *Communications of ACM,* 27, 800-806.

4. Harrison, B. & Vicente, K. (1996) An Experimental Evaluation of Transparent Menu Usage.*Proceedings of the ACM CHI'96 Conference on Human Factors in Computing Systems,* 391-398.

5. Gould, John (1988). How to Design Usable Systems. in *Handbook on Human-Computer Interaction, M. Helander (Editor), North-Holland. Elsevier. 1988.* pp. 757-789. Reprinted In *Readings in Human Computer-Interaction: Towards The Year 2000.* Baecker, R., Gru-din, J. Buxton, W. & Greenberg, S. (Eds), Morgan Kaufmann, 1995. 93-121. see p. 113.

6. Jeffries, R. (1994). Usability Problems Reports: Helping Evaluators Communicate Effectively with Developers. in *Usability Inspection Methods,* Nielsen, J. & Mack R. (Eds). John Wiley. 273-294. see p. 278.

7. Kiger, J.L. (1984) The Depth/Breadth Tradeoff in the Design of Menu Driven User Interfaces. *International Journal of Man Machine Studies,* 20, 210-213.

8. Kurtenbach, G., Buxton, W. (1993) The limits of expert performance using hierarchical marking menus. *Proceedings of CHI '93 Conference on Human Factor in Computing,* 482-487.

9. Kurtenbach, G., Fitzmaurice, G., Baudel, T. & Buxton, B. (1997) The Design of a GUI Paradigm based on Tablets, Two-hands, and Transparency. *Proceedings of the ACM CHI'97 Conference on Human Factors in Computing Systems,* 35-42.

10. Landauer, T.K. & Nachbar, D.W. (1985) Selection from Alphabetic and Numeric Trees Using a Touch Screen: Breadth, Depth and Width. *Proceedings of the ACM CHI'85 Conference on Human Factors in Computing Systems,* 73-78.

11. Lewis, C. & Rieman, J. (1993). Getting to Know Users and Their Tasks. in *Task Centered User Interface Design, a practical introduction.* Reprinted In *Readings in Human Computer-Interaction: Towards The Year 2000.* Baecker, R., Grudin, J. Buxton, W. & Greenberg, S. (Eds), Morgan Kaufmann, 1995. 122-127. see p. 124, col. 2.

12. Mackenzie, I.S., & Buxton, W. (1992) Extending Fitts' Law To Two-dimensional Tasks. *Proceedings Of Acm Chi '92 Conference On Human Factors In Computing Systems,* 219-226.

13. Sears, A. & Shneiderman, B. (1994) Split menus: Effectively using selection frequency to organize menus. *ACM Transactions on Computer-Human Interaction, vol. 1, #1 (March 1994), 27-51.* also available online at ftp://ftp.cs.umd.edu/pub/papers/papers/2997/2997.ps.Z.

14. http://www.aw.sgi.com, Maya product brochure

Combining Observations of Intentional and Unintentional Behaviors for Human-Computer Interaction

Yoshinori Kuno, Tomoyuki Ishiyama, Satoru Nakanishi and Yoshiaki Shirai

Department of Computer-Controlled Mechanical Systems, Osaka University

Suita, Osaka 565-0871, Japan

+81 6 6879 7332

kuno@mech.eng.osaka-u.ac.jp

ABSTRACT

Human interfaces are usually designed to respond only to intentional human behaviors. However, humans show unintentional behaviors as well. They can convey useful information to realize user-friendly human interfaces. This paper presents how to combine observations of both types of behaviors by taking two human-machine systems: a gesture-based interface and an intelligent wheelchair. In the first system, intentional hand gestures are chosen using unintentional behaviors. In the second system, near unintentional behaviors following intentional behaviors can be used to control the wheelchair motion. Experimental systems working in real time have been developed. Operational experiments prove our approach promising.

Keywords

Vision-based interface, gesture-based interface, wheelchair, face direction, intention

INTRODUCTION

Human behaviors can be classified into two groups: intentional behaviors and unintentional behaviors. When we want to do a particular thing, we exhibit behaviors that are required to carry out the purpose. We do such behaviors intentionally and are aware of what we are doing. These behaviors belong to the first group. Conventional human interfaces use only behaviors in this category. However, we move our hands, heads, bodies and other parts unconsciously even when we do not have any intention to inform others of certain things. Still, such behaviors convey information about our attention, emotion, and so on. This information may be helpful to realize more user-friendly human interfaces.

This paper presents how to combine observations of both types of behaviors by taking two human-machine systems.

One is a gesture-based human interface system where users can design objects by combining parts and changing the sizes of parts through such hand movements that they might do in the real world. When we use this kind of system, we may move our hands when we do not intend to manipulate objects in the virtual world. We use face direction so that the system cannot respond to such unintentional movements. The assumption here is that we watch the object when we manipulate it. This watching behavior is so strongly connected with the intention of manipulating the object that it happens almost unconsciously without any intentional thinking process. Chino et al. [1] have proposed a similar method in their multimodal interface. It recognizes speech only when the user is looking at the display. Although their assumption is reasonable, we sometimes talk without looking at each other. However, it is rare to manipulate an object without watching it.

The other is an intelligent wheelchair based on behavior observations. The proposed wheelchair uses intentional behaviors and near unintentional behaviors to lessen the user's burden of operation. It recognizes the user's face direction, controlling its direction of travel based on the recognition result. Thus, when the user wants to turn to the left or right, he/she needs to see in the direction by turning the head intentionally. As the turn is getting completed, the user should turn back the head to the frontal position to adjust the wheelchair's direction. However, this behavior is so natural that it happens almost unconsciously. If we use a steering lever or wheel to control the vehicle motion, we need to move it consciously all the time. Our interface by face direction is more user-friendly than such conventional methods. The problem, however, is that we may move our head when we do not intend to make turns. We have the intentional part selection problem in this system, too. In this wheelchair, we solve the problem just by ignoring quick movements because we can expect that behaviors for turning are done intentionally, thus they are slow and steady.

This paper presents the above two systems, showing how intentional and unintentional behaviors are used. Experimental systems working in real time are also presented.

GESTURE-BASED INTERFACE

Intentional Gesture Selection

We propose a gesture-based human interface system that has the capability to respond only to intentional gestures. Conventional gesture-based human interface systems [2] assume that we move our hands only when we want to issue commands to these systems. However, in real situations, we often move our hands for other purposes than issuing commands, sometimes even unconsciously. These movements might be understood as some motion commands and objects in the virtual world might move accordingly. Thus, we need to be careful not to move our hands when we do not intend to issue commands with conventional systems. To overcome this inconvenience, we introduce the capability to choose and to recognize only hand motions by which we intend to control objects in the virtual world. This can be done by observing face direction. If we want to move an object in the virtual world, we will watch the object on the display screen. In other cases, we may not watch the screen. For example, if anyone enters the room and we want to say hello, we will turn toward the person. Based on this assumption, the system observes our face direction, choosing hand motions only when our face is directed toward the screen. Then, the chosen motions are recognized by the method described below.

Hand Gesture Recognition

This section briefly describes our gesture recognition method. Details can be found in [4].

The purpose of our research is to develop a human interface system that enables us to manipulate objects in a virtual 3D world. In the virtual space, we may point at an object, grasp it, move it, bring it into the work space, and may change its sizes or put it down on another object. These actions will not happen independently. We can narrow down the possible action candidates following each action to the small number. We represent these relationships by a state transition diagram. Since this diagram limits the number of possible recognition classes, the system can recognize the next gesture using simple image features.

In order to obtain hand features, hand regions need to be extracted. Each hand region can be extracted by a simple color segmentation method based on hue information. In the current implementation, we have to wear a green glove and a red one on each hand to realize fast reliable feature extraction. Fig. 1 shows an example of hand region extraction.

For each segmented hand region, the system calculates a feature vector consisting of simple features such as the region area, the region centroid, and the index finger tip position. We use two cameras placed upper front of the user and above for gesture recognition. The feature vector is calculated for each hand in each image.

Fig. 2 shows the state transition diagram used in the system. The transition condition from each state is represented by the feature values and their changes. Except pointing gestures such as Direct and Move, the system mainly uses feature vectors over several frames to recognize gestures. To cope with the variation of motion speed, the system examines in most cases whether particular feature values are increasing or decreasing rather than checks their exact values.

(a) Original image.   (b) Extracted hand regions.

Figure 1: Hand region extraction.

In Fig. 2, the transitions from and to the Rest state are shown by broken lines. If a new observation does not match any possible state transition conditions from the current state, the system changes it to the Rest state. While in the Rest state, if the system observes a feature vector that satisfies one of the possible transition conditions from the previous state, it changes the state according to the condition.

Human manipulative gestures are often conducted with the two hands. Thus, vision-based interfaces should have the capability to recognize collaborative gestures with both hands. In this system, we allot a state for each manipulative gesture with both hands. This solves the combinatorial problem that arises when a state is given for each hand and manipulative gestures are represented by combinations of both hand states. For example, Hold_together is assigned to the manipulative gesture for holding an object with both hands as shown in Fig. 2.

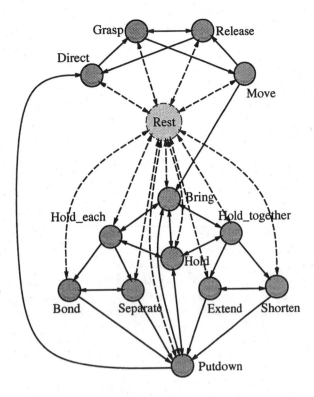

Figure 2: State transition diagram.

Use of Face Direction

Although we have introduced the Rest state into our recognition method so that the system can respond only to intentional gestures, we have found this insufficient. Thus, we consider to use other nonverbal behaviors to extract intentional parts of hand motions. In this system, we choose gaze and eye contact information.

When we manipulate an object, we usually do this while watching it. Thus, it is a reasonable assumption that if we are not watching the object, the hand motions then are not intentional gestures for its manipulation. Although the reverse is not necessarily true, the use of this assumption with the introduction of the Rest state can help to solve the problem.

In the current implementation, the system uses face direction instead of actual gaze direction. We need only rough gaze direction because we do not use gaze information to point at an object on the screen but to check whether or not the user is looking at the screen. In addition, the system should work in real time. Thus, we consider only the rotation of the head around the vertical axis and calculate the face direction using the following simple processes.

First, the system extracts a large skin color region as the face region as shown in Fig. 3. Second, it extracts face features such as the eyes and the eyebrows from the face region by thresholding. Third, it computes the pro-

jection onto the vertical axis to determine the vertical range of the eye-eyebrow region as shown in Fig. 4 (a). If two peaks located closely are found in the projection result, they are considered for the eyes and the eyebrows. Fourth, the system computes the projection onto the horizontal axis to determine the horizontal range of the eye-eyebrow region as shown in Fig. 4 (b). In this region, it examines the black parts, considering the lower two as the eyes. Then, it measures the distance between the tail of the right eye and the right edge of the face on the line connecting the centroids of the eyes as denoted by Lr in Fig. 5. It also calculates the counterpart to the left eye Ll.

If the following value D is smaller than 4, which means that the face direction is approximately within 20 degrees from the normal of the screen plane, the system considers that the user is facing the screen, thus recognizing the hand motions as intentional gestures.

$$L_{min} = min\{L_l, L_r\} \qquad (1)$$

$$D(L_l, L_r) = \frac{|L_l - L_r|}{L_{min}} \qquad (2)$$

(a) Original image.   (b) Face region.

Figure 3: Face region extraction.

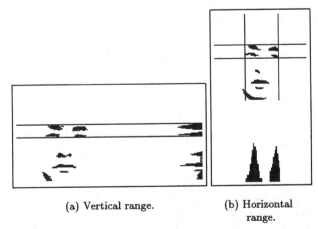

(a) Vertical range.   (b) Horizontal range.

Figure 4: Eye-eyebrow region extraction.

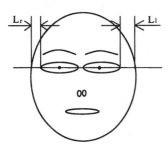

Figure 5: Face direction computation.

Experimental System

We have developed an experimental human interface system using the proposed recognition methods. Fig. 6 shows the system configuration. It has three cameras: two for gesture recognition and the other for face direction computation. The current system uses two personal computers. One carries out face and gesture recognition with the aid of a real-time image processing board consisting of 256 processors developed by NEC [6]. The other displays two views for the user as shown in Fig. 7. They are a usual perspective view of the virtual world and a top view of the virtual world to help the user to understand the positional relationships of objects.

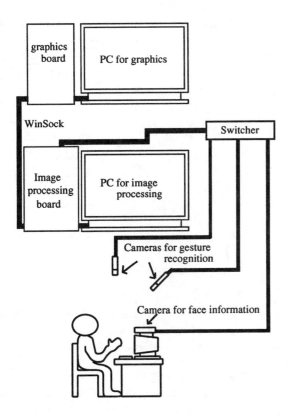

Figure 6: System configuration.

We consider the following scenario for operational experiments. There is a palette space (PS) in the virtual world where object components are floating. We Direct (point at) a desired object in PS and Grasp it by hand gestures. Then, we Move it and Bring it to the work space (WS), which is a space on the desk in the virtual world. We hold the object with both hands (Hold_together) and Extend it or Shorten it to change its sizes to desired ones. Then, we bring another object component from PS and put it down on the first object (Putdown).

We carried out operational experiments according to the above scenario. We were able to design objects such as the one in Fig. 7 by hand gestures even if we added any unintentional movements of our hands during operation.

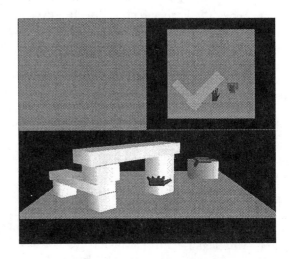

Figure 7: Operational experiment.

INTELLIGENT WHEELCHAIR

Motion Control by Face Direction

As the number of senior citizens has been increasing year by year, demand for human-friendly wheelchairs as mobility aids has been growing. Recently, robotic wheelchairs have been proposed to meet this need [5][8][9]. These wheelchairs help humans with the aid of ultrasonic, vision, and other sensors to avoid obstacles, to go to pre-designated places, and to pass through narrow or crowded areas.

A wheelchair with a human in it can be considered as a system consisting of the human and the machine. Conventional robotic wheelchairs see the outside of the system, realizing the autonomous movement functions mentioned above. Although these functions are indispensable, we would like to point out the importance of seeing the inside of the system, that is, looking at the user to realize a human-friendly system. For example, if the machine can tell the user's intention of turning left in advance by observing his/her behaviors, it can give helpful information to him/her, such as a caution message when he/she is not paying necessary attention around him/her. Or if it is certain about the user's intention, it will turn left autonomously. Pentland et al. [7] have proposed the use of recognizing unintentional movement patterns as the aid to car driving.

Our ultimate goal is to realize a wheelchair that can move as the user wishes even though the user does not intentionally show his/her wish. However, this is difficult to be achieved. Thus, we consider to use human behaviors which are done intentionally but so naturally that the user may not feel any burden. We use face direction. The wheelchair moves in the direction of the user's face. For example, it turns left if the user turns the face to the left. The user should know this fact and needs to move the head intentionally. However, it is a natural behavior to look in the direction where he/she intends to go. It is also a natural behavior turning back the head to the frontal position as the turn is getting completed. Although this behavior can be done almost unconsciously, it can control the wheelchair appropriately. When we use a steering lever or wheel to control the vehicle motion, we need to operate it intentionally all the time. Using face direction can remove a considerable part of such intentional operations, realizing a user-friendly interface.

The problem, however, is that we move our head in various other occasions than in controlling the wheelchair's direction. The intelligent wheelchair system needs to separate wheelchair-control behaviors from others. This is the intention understanding problem in the current system. We assume that we move our head slowly and steadily when we are told that the wheelchair moves in our face direction. Thus, the current system ignores quick head movements, only responding to slow steady movements.

There are, however, cases that we look in a certain direction steadily without any intention of controlling the wheelchair. For example, when we notice a poster on a corridor wall, we may look at it by turning our face in its direction while moving straight. The environmental information around the wheelchair can be helpful in such cases. In the example case, even if we turn our face to the left to look at the poster, the system can consider this not to show a left-turn intention if it knows that a wall exists on the left and that it cannot turn left. We have made a simple experiment on this.

System Configuration

We have developed an experimental wheelchair system that can move in the user's face direction computed from video camera images. Figs. 8 and 9 show an overview of the system and the configuration, respec-

tively. The system has ultrasonic sensors to see the outside of the system. We are planning to use the sensor data to realize autonomous capabilities such as avoiding obstacles and detecting intersections. The system has a video camera to see the inside of the system. That is, the camera is set to look at the user's face. The system understands the user's intentions from the sensor data, using them for user-friendly interface.

Figure 8: System overview.

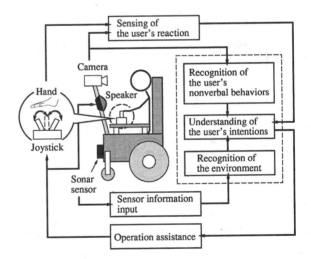

Figure 9: System configuration.

The face direction computation method developed for the gesture-based interface can be used for this purpose. In the current implementation, however, we use another method because of the hardware available to us. The wheelchair system has a Tracking Vision [3], which can track features at frame rate. Thus, we use a method based on feature tracking. We assume all facial features such as eyes and mouth are on the same plane.

Table 1: Experimental evaluation for response time by six subjects (A-F)

Frames(n)	A	B	C	D	E	F	Total	(shown by the number of *'s)
1	1	2	3	3	2	3	14	**************
3	2	2	3	3	3	2	15	***************
5	3	3	2	3	3	3	17	*****************
6	1	3	2	2	2	2	12	************
7	1	3	2	2	2	2	12	************
8	1	3	3	2	1	2	12	************
9	1	2	2	1	2	1	9	*********
10	1	2	2	1	2	2	10	**********
12	1	1	2	1	2	2	9	*********
14	1	1	1	1	1	2	7	*******
16	1	1	1	1	1	2	7	*******
18	1	1	1	1	1	1	6	******
20	1	1	1	1	1	1	6	******

Table 2: Experimental evaluation for unintentional head movements

Frames(n)	Level 1					Level 2					Level 3				
5	×	×	×	×	×	×	×	×	×	×	×	×	×	×	×
10	O	O	O	×	×	×	×	×	×	×	×	×	×	×	×
15	O	O	O	O	×	O	O	O	O	×	O	×	×	×	×
20	O	O	O	O	O	O	O	O	O	O	O	O	O	O	×
30	O	O	O	O	O	O	O	O	O	O	O	O	O	O	O

O: the movement was not affected;   ×: the movement was affected.

Also we assume that the feature positions in the frontal face image are given. They can be obtained by asking the user to look forward when getting in the wheelchair. The parameters of affine transformation can be calculated from the current feature positions and those in the frontal face image. The normal vector of the plane with the features on, that is, the face direction, can be calculated from the affine transformation parameters.

Experiments

The system can compute face direction 30 frames per second. We apply a filter to the direction data to separate wheelchair-control behaviors from others. The filter that we use is a simple smoothing filter by averaging the values over a certain number of frames. If this number is large, the system will not be affected by quick unintentional head movements. However, the user may feel uneasy at the slow response of the system. We made actual running experiments by changing the number of frames n used in the filter.

First, we examined the degree of uneasiness about the slow response. We used six subjects. They were male students at our university and not regular wheelchair users. We told them that the wheelchair would move in

their face direction. They drove the wheelchair without any problem. This confirms that face direction can be used for the wheelchair operation. They were asked to give their subjective evaluation score for each smoothing filter condition from the viewpoint of the system's response to their head movements: 1 for not good, 2 for moderate, and 3 for good. Table 1 shows the result. When n is small, the wheelchair responds sensitively to any head movements. Thus, the scores are a little small. When n is large, the wheelchair does not respond soon even when the user turns the head intentionally. The scores in these cases are considerably small. The highest score is obtained for $n = 5$.

Second, we examined whether the system would be affected by quick unintentional head movements. We consider three levels of movements: quick movements with duration less than 0.5 second (level 1), moderate speed movements with duration from 0.5 to 1 second (level 2), and slow movements with duration from 1 to 1.5 seconds (level 3). At the level 3, we turn our head and can read characters. Simple filtering cannot discriminate such movements from wheelchair-control movements. Thus, the purpose here is to make the system not to be affected by up to the level 2 movements. We asked a subject to move his head five times for each level while the wheelchair was moving straight. Then, we examined whether or not the wheelchair motions were affected. Table 2 shows the result. It suggests that n should be equal to or larger than 15 for the system not to be affected by movements at the levels 1 and 2.

The subjects commented as follows after the experiments. When they turned the wheelchair to the left/right, they did not mind the slow response. However, when the turn was getting completed and they turned back their head to the frontal position, they felt uneasy if the response was slow. In the former case, they did turning-head behaviors intentionally. Thus, they did not mind the slow response because their movements themselves were slow and steady. However, in the latter case, their behaviors were almost unconscious and quick. Thus, the slow response caused their uneasiness.

Based on this observation, we have modified the system to use 5 frames for smoothing for center-oriented face directions and 15 for left/right directions. The six subjects have given the same high scores as in the case of n=5 to this modified version wheelchair. Also, experimental runs have shown that it has the same degree of stability against unintentional quick head movements as in the case of n=15.

Fig. 10 shows an experimental scene. The left column displays the images used for face direction computation. The small white squares show the feature tracking results. The right column displays the wheelchair motion. The user turned the wheelchair to the right in the second and third rows and to the left in the fifth and sixth rows. Fig. 11 shows the computed face direction during the experimental run displayed in Fig. 10.

Although the filtering process solves the problem of quick unintentional movements, there are times that we look in a direction for a while even though we do not intend to turn in the direction. An example case is that we notice a poster on a wall and examine it. In such cases, the environmental information around the wheelchair can be useful. In the example case, even if we turn our face to the left to look at the poster, the system can consider this not to show a left-turn intention if it knows that a wall exists on the left and that it cannot turn left.

We made a simple experiment on this idea. We gave map data to the system. The system was able to tell the existence of walls and other obstacles using the dead reckoning data and the map data. The experiment was successful. In this experimental run, the user turned his face to the right twice: to look at a poster on the wall and to show his intention of turning right. The wheelchair responded only to the second movement of the user's head.

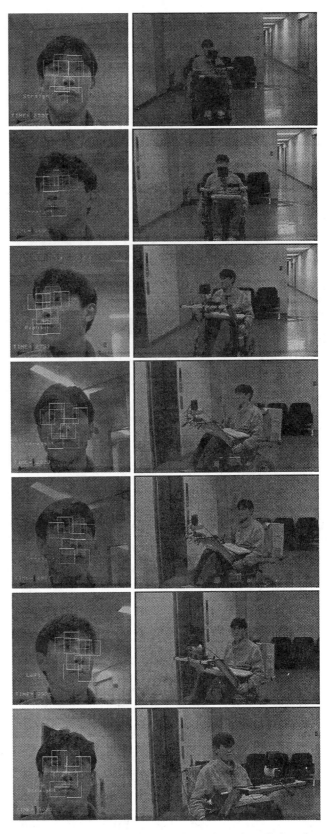

Figure 10: Experimental run: face direction (left column) and wheelchair motion (right column).

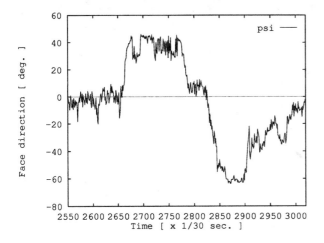

Figure 11: Face direction during the experimental run.

We made several other running experiments. These experimental results confirm that we can control the wheelchair by face direction. Owing to smoothing, the system does not respond to quick head movements. Thus, if we look for a while in the direction where we want to go, we can move the wheelchair to meet our intention. However, this slow response means that we cannot make quick precise control of the wheelchair. We may not be able to avoid an obstacle if it suddenly comes close. Thus, to make the system practical, we need to introduce an autonomous motion function for obstacle avoidance. The idea is that we show our intention by our face direction and after that the system can navigate autonomously while avoiding obstacles. We are now developing such a function using ultrasonic sensors. The sensor information around the wheelchair can also be helpful to choose intentional head movements. Instead of map data, we are working on the use of ultrasonic and vision sensors.

CONCLUSION

We have presented two human-machine systems: a gesture-based interface and an intelligent wheelchair. In these systems, we have proposed the importance of observing both intentional and unintentional behaviors to realize user-friendly interfaces. Experimental systems working in real time have confirmed our approach promising.

We use only face direction as an unintentional behavior in the current systems. Humans exhibit various nonverbal behaviors. The use of these behaviors are left for our future work.

ACKNOWLEDGEMENTS

This work has been supported in part by the Ministry of Education, Science, Sports and Culture under the Grant-in-Aid for Scientific Research (09555080), the Kurata Foundation under the Kurata Research Grant, and the Kayamori Foundation of Informational Science Advancement.

REFERENCES

1. Chino, T., Fukui, K., Yamaguchi, O., Suzuki, K., and Tanaka, K. GazeToTalk: A nonverbal interface system with speech recognition, gaze detection, and agent CG output, in *Proceedings of Interaction '98* (Tokyo, Japan, March 1998), 169-176 (in Japanese).

2. Huang, T.S. Hand gesture modeling, analysis, and synthesis, in *Proceedings of International Workshop on Automatic Face- and Gesture-Recognition* (Zurich, Switzerland, June 1995), 73-79.

3. Inoue, H., Inaba, M., Mori, T., and Tachikawa, T. Real-time robot vision system based on correlation technology, in *Proceedings of International Symposium on Industrial Robots* (1993), 675-680.

4. Jo, K.H., Kuno, Y., and Shirai, Y. Manipulative hand gesture recognition using task knowledge for human computer interaction, in *Proceedings of 3rd IEEE International Conference on Automatic Face and Gesture Recognition* (Nara, Japan, April 1998), 468-473.

5. Miller, D.P., and Slack, M.G. Design and testing of a low-cost robotic wheelchair prototype. *Autonomous Robotics 2* (1995),77-88.

6. Okazaki, S., Fujita, Y., and Yamashita, N. A compact real-time vision system using integrated memory array processor architecture. *IEEE Transactions on Circuits and Systems for Video Technology 5* (1995), 446-452.

7. Pentland, A., and Liu, F. Towards augmented control systems, in *Proceedings of IEEE Intelligent Vehicles '95* (Detroit MI, September 1995), 350-355.

8. Simpson, R.C., and Levine, S.P. Adaptive shared control of a smart wheelchair operated by voice control, in *Proceedings of 1997 IEEE/RSJ International Conference on Intelligent Robots and Systems 2* (Grenoble, France, September 1997), 622-626.

9. Yanco, H.A., and Gips, J. Preliminary investigation of a semi-autonomous robotic wheelchair directed through electrodes, in *Proceedings of Rehabilitation Engineering Society of North America 1997 Annual Conference* (1997), 414-416.

Manual And Gaze Input Cascaded (MAGIC) Pointing

Shumin Zhai   **Carlos Morimoto**   **Steven Ihde**

IBM Almaden Research Center
650 Harry Road
San Jose, CA 95120 USA
+1 408 927 1112
{zhai, morimoto, ihde}@almaden.ibm.com

ABSTRACT

This work explores a new direction in utilizing eye gaze for computer input. Gaze tracking has long been considered as an alternative or potentially superior pointing method for computer input. We believe that many fundamental limitations exist with traditional gaze pointing. In particular, it is unnatural to overload a perceptual channel such as vision with a motor control task. We therefore propose an alternative approach, dubbed MAGIC (Manual And Gaze Input Cascaded) pointing. With such an approach, pointing appears to the user to be a manual task, used for fine manipulation and selection. However, a large portion of the cursor movement is eliminated by warping the cursor to the eye gaze area, which encompasses the target. Two specific MAGIC pointing techniques, one conservative and one liberal, were designed, analyzed, and implemented with an eye tracker we developed. They were then tested in a pilot study. This early-stage exploration showed that the MAGIC pointing techniques might offer many advantages, including reduced physical effort and fatigue as compared to traditional manual pointing, greater accuracy and naturalness than traditional gaze pointing, and possibly faster speed than manual pointing. The pros and cons of the two techniques are discussed in light of both performance data and subjective reports.

Keywords

Gaze, eye, computer input, eye tracking, gaze tracking, pointing, multi-modal interface, Fitts' law, computer vision.

INTRODUCTION

Using the eyes as a source of input in "advanced user interfaces" has long been a topic of interest to the HCI field [1] [2] [3] [4]. Reports on eye tracking frequently appear not only in the research literature, but also in the popular press, such as the July 1996 issue of Byte magazine [5]. One of the basic goals that numerous researchers have attempted to

achieve is to operate the user interface through eye gaze, with pointing (target acquisition) as the core element. There are many compelling reasons to motivate such a goal, including the following:

1. There are situations that prohibit the use of the hands, such as when the user's hands are disabled or continuously occupied with other tasks.

2. The eye can move very quickly in comparison to other parts of the body. Furthermore, as many researchers have long argued [3] [6], target acquisition usually requires the user to look at the target first, before actuating cursor control. Theoretically this means that if the eye gaze can be tracked and effectively used, no other input method can act as quickly. Increasing the speed of user input to the computer has long been an interest of HCI research.

3. Reducing fatigue and potential injury caused by operating keyboard and pointing devices is also an important concern in the user interface field. Repetitive stress injury affects an increasing number of computer users. Most users are not concerned with RSI until serious problems occur. Utilizing eye gaze movement to replace or reduce the amount of stress to the hand can be beneficial.

Clearly, to replace "what you see (and click on) is what you get" with "what you look at is what you get" [4] [6] has captivating appeal. However, the design and implementation of eye gaze-based computer input has been faced with two types of challenges. One is eye tracking technology itself, which will be briefly discussed in the Implementation section of the paper. The other challenge is the human factor issues involved in utilizing eye movement for computer input. Jacob [7] eloquently discussed many of these issues with insightful observations.

In our view, there are two fundamental shortcomings to the existing gaze pointing techniques, regardless of the maturity of eye tracking technology. First, given the one-degree size of the fovea and the subconscious jittery motions that the eyes constantly produce, eye gaze is not precise enough to operate UI widgets such as scrollbars, hyperlinks, and slider handles on today's GUI interfaces. At a 25-inch viewing distance to the screen, one degree of arc corresponds to 0.44 in, which is twice the size of a typical scroll bar and much greater than the size of a typical character.

Second, and perhaps more importantly, the eye, as one of our primary perceptual devices, has not evolved to be a control organ. Sometimes its movements are voluntarily controlled while at other times it is driven by external events. With the target selection by dwell time method, considered more natural than selection by blinking [7], one has to be conscious of where one looks and how long one looks at an object. If one does not look at a target continuously for a set threshold (e.g., 200 ms), the target will not be successfully selected. On the other hand, if one stares at an object for more than the set threshold, the object will be selected, regardless of the user's intention. In some cases there is not an adverse effect to a false target selection. Other times it can be annoying and counter-productive (such as unintended jumps to a web page). Furthermore, dwell time can only substitute for one mouse click. There are often two steps to target activation. A single click selects the target (e.g., an application icon) and a double click (or a different physical button click) opens the icon (e.g., launches an application). To perform both steps with dwell time is even more difficult.

In short, to load the visual perception channel with a motor control task seems fundamentally at odds with users' natural mental model in which the eye searches for and takes in information and the hand produces output that manipulates external objects. Other than for disabled users, who have no alternative, using eye gaze for practical pointing does not appear to be very promising.

MAGIC POINTING

Are there interaction techniques that utilize eye movement to assist the control task but do not force the user to be overly conscious of his eye movement? We wanted to design a technique in which pointing and selection remained primarily a manual control task but were also aided by gaze tracking. Our key idea is to use gaze to dynamically redefine (warp) the "home" position of the pointing cursor to be at the vicinity of the target, which was presumably what the user was looking at, thereby effectively reducing the cursor movement amplitude needed for target selection. Once the cursor position had been redefined, the user would need to only make a small movement to, and click on, the target with a regular manual input device. In other words, we wanted to achieve Manual And Gaze Input Cascaded (MAGIC) pointing, or Manual Acquisition with Gaze Initiated Cursor. There are many different ways of designing a MAGIC pointing technique. Critical to its effectiveness is the identification of the target the user intends to acquire. We have designed two MAGIC pointing techniques, one liberal and the other conservative in terms of target identification and cursor placement.

The liberal approach is to warp the cursor to every new object the user looks at (See Figure 1). The user can then take control of the cursor by hand near (or on) the target, or ignore it and search for the next target. Operationally, a new object

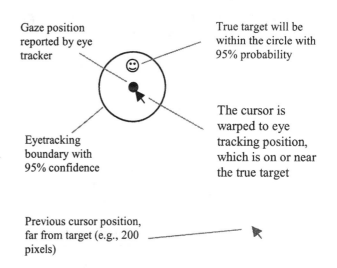

Figure 1. The liberal MAGIC pointing technique: cursor is placed in the vicinity of a target that the user fixates on.

is defined by sufficient distance (e.g., 120 pixels) from the current cursor position, unless the cursor is in a controlled motion by hand. Since there is a 120-pixel threshold, the cursor will not be warped when the user does continuous manipulation such as drawing. Note that this MAGIC pointing technique is different from traditional eye gaze control, where the user uses his eye to point at targets either without a cursor [7] or with a cursor [3] that constantly follows the jittery eye gaze motion.

The liberal approach may appear "pro-active," since the cursor waits readily in the vicinity of or on every potential target. The user may move the cursor once he decides to acquire the target he is looking at. On the other hand, the user may also feel that the cursor is over-active when he is merely looking at a target, although he may gradually adapt to ignore this behavior.

The more conservative MAGIC pointing technique we have explored does not warp a cursor to a target until the manual input device has been actuated. Once the manual input device has been actuated, the cursor is warped to the gaze area reported by the eye tracker. This area should be on or in the vicinity of the target. The user would then steer the cursor manually towards the target to complete the target acquisition.

As illustrated in Figure 2, to minimize directional uncertainty after the cursor appears in the conservative technique, we introduced an "intelligent" bias. Instead of being placed at the center of the gaze area, the cursor position is offset to the intersection of the manual actuation vector and the boundary of the gaze area. This means that once warped, the cursor is likely to appear in motion towards the target, regardless of how the user actually actuated the manual input device. We hoped that with the intelligent bias the user would not have to actuate input device, observe the cursor position and decide in which direction to steer the cursor. The cost to this method is the increased manual movement amplitude.

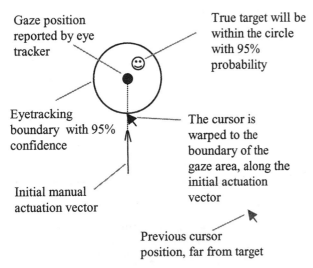

Figure 2. The conservative MAGIC pointing technique with "intelligent offset"

To initiate a pointing trial, there are two strategies available to the user. One is to follow "virtual inertia:" move from the cursor's current position towards the new target the user is looking at. This is likely the strategy the user will employ, due to the way the user interacts with today's interface. The alternative strategy, which may be more advantageous but takes time to learn, is to ignore the previous cursor position and make a motion which is most convenient and least effortful to the user for a given input device. For example, on a small touchpad, the user may find it convenient to make an upward stroke with the index finger, causing the cursor to appear below the target.

The goal of the conservative MAGIC pointing method is the following. Once the user looks at a target and moves the input device, the cursor will appear "out of the blue" in motion towards the target, on the side of the target opposite to the initial actuation vector. In comparison to the liberal approach, this conservative approach has both pros and cons. While with this technique the cursor would never be over-active and jump to a place the user does not intend to acquire, it may require more hand-eye coordination effort.

Both the liberal and the conservative MAGIC pointing techniques offer the following *potential* advantages:

1. Reduction of manual stress and fatigue, since the cross-screen long-distance cursor movement is eliminated from manual control.

2. Practical accuracy level. In comparison to traditional pure gaze pointing whose accuracy is fundamentally limited by the nature of eye movement, the MAGIC pointing techniques let the hand complete the pointing task, so they can be as accurate as any other manual input techniques.

3. A more natural mental model for the user. The user does not have to be aware of the role of the eye gaze. To the user, pointing continues to be a manual task, with a cursor conveniently appearing where it needs to be.

4. Speed. Since the need for large magnitude pointing operations is less than with pure manual cursor control, it is possible that MAGIC pointing will be faster than pure manual pointing.

5. Improved subjective speed and ease-of-use. Since the manual pointing amplitude is smaller, the user may perceive the MAGIC pointing system to operate faster and more pleasantly than pure manual control, even if it operates at the same speed or more slowly.

The fourth point warrants further discussion. According to the well accepted Fitts' Law [8], manual pointing time is logarithmically proportional to the A/W ratio, where A is the movement distance and W is the target size. In other words, targets which are smaller or farther away take longer to acquire. For MAGIC pointing, since the target size remains the same but the cursor movement distance is shortened, the pointing time can hence be reduced.

It is less clear if eye gaze control follows Fitts' Law. In Ware and Mikaelian's study [3], selection time was shown to be logarithmically proportional to target distance, thereby conforming to Fitts' Law. To the contrary, Silbert and Jacob [9] found that trial completion time with eye tracking input increases little with distance, therefore defying Fitts' Law.

In addition to problems with today's eye tracking systems, such as delay, error, and inconvenience, there may also be many potential human factor disadvantages to the MAGIC pointing techniques we have proposed, including the following:

1. With the more liberal MAGIC pointing technique, the cursor warping can be overactive at times, since the cursor moves to the new gaze location whenever the eye gaze moves more than a set distance (e.g., 120 pixels) away from the cursor. This could be particularly distracting when the user is trying to read. It is possible to introduce additional constraint according to the context. For example, when the user's eye appears to follow a text reading pattern, MAGIC pointing can be automatically suppressed.

2. With the more conservative MAGIC pointing technique, the uncertainty of the exact location at which the cursor might appear may force the user, especially a novice, to adopt a cumbersome strategy: take a touch (use the manual input device to activate the cursor), wait (for the cursor to appear), and move (the cursor to the target manually). Such a strategy may prolong the target acquisition time. The user may have to learn a novel hand-eye coordination pattern to be efficient with this technique.

3. With pure manual pointing techniques, the user, knowing the current cursor location, could conceivably perform his motor acts in parallel to visual search. Motor action may start as soon as the user's gaze settles on a target. With MAGIC pointing techniques, the motor action computation (decision) cannot start until the cursor appears. This may negate the time saving gained from the MAGIC pointing technique's reduction of movement amplitude.

Clearly, experimental (implementation and empirical) work is needed to validate, refine, or invent alternative MAGIC pointing techniques.

IMPLEMENTATION

We took two engineering efforts to implement the MAGIC pointing techniques. One was to design and implement an eye tracking system and the other was to implement MAGIC pointing techniques at the operating systems level, so that the techniques can work with all software applications beyond "demonstration" software.

The IBM Almaden Eye Tracker

Since the goal of this work is to explore MAGIC pointing as a user interface technique, we started out by purchasing a commercial eye tracker (ASL Model 5000) after a market survey. In comparison to the system reported in early studies (e.g. [7]), this system is much more compact and reliable. However, we felt that it was still not robust enough for a variety of people with different eye characteristics, such as pupil brightness and correction glasses. We hence chose to develop and use our own eye tracking system [10]. Available commercial systems, such as those made by ISCAN Incorporated, LC Technologies, and Applied Science Laboratories (ASL), rely on a single light source that is positioned either off the camera axis in the case of the ISCAN ETL-400 systems, or on-axis in the case of the LCT and the ASL E504 systems. Illumination from an off-axis source (or ambient illumination) generates a dark pupil image. When the light source is placed on-axis with the camera optical axis, the camera is able to detect the light reflected from the interior of the eye, and the image of the pupil appears bright [11] [12] (see Figure 3). This effect is often seen as the red-eye in flash photographs when the flash is close to the camera lens.

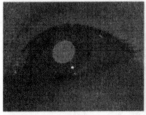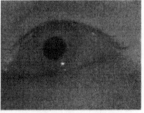

Figure 3. Bright (left) and dark (right) pupil images resulting from on- and off-axis illumination. The glints, or corneal reflections, from the on- and off-axis light sources can be easily identified as the bright points in the iris.

The Almaden system uses two near infrared (IR) time multiplexed light sources, composed of two sets of IR LED's, which were synchronized with the camera frame rate. One light source is placed very close to the camera's optical axis and is synchronized with the even frames. Odd frames are synchronized with the second light source, positioned off-axis. The two light sources are calibrated to provide approximately equivalent whole-scene illumination. Pupil detection is realized by means of subtracting the dark pupil image from the bright pupil image. After thresholding the difference, the largest connected component is identified as the pupil. This technique significantly increases the robustness and reliability of the eye tracking system. After implementing our system with satisfactory results, we discovered that similar pupil detection schemes had been independently developed by Tomono et al [13] and Ebisawa and Satoh [14]. It is unfortunate that such a method has not been used in the commercial systems. We recommend that future eye tracking product designers consider such an approach.

Once the pupil has been detected, the corneal reflection (the glint reflected from the surface of the cornea due to one of the light sources) is determined from the dark pupil image. The reflection is then used to estimate the user's point of gaze in terms of the screen coordinates where the user is looking at. The estimation of the user's gaze requires an initial calibration procedure, similar to that required by commercial eye trackers.

Our system operates at 30 frames per second on a Pentium II 333 MHz machine running Windows NT. It can work with any PCI frame grabber compatible with Video for Windows.

Implementing MAGIC pointing

We programmed the two MAGIC pointing techniques on a Windows NT system. The techniques work independently from the applications. The MAGIC pointing program takes data from both the manual input device (of any type, such as a mouse) and the eye tracking system running either on the same machine or on another machine connected via serial port.

Raw data from an eye tracker can not be directly used for gaze-based interaction, due to noise from image processing, eye movement jitters, and samples taken during *saccade* (ballistic eye movement) periods. We experimented with various filtering techniques and found the most effective filter in our case is similar to that described in [7]. The goal of filter design in general is to make the best compromise between preserving signal bandwidth and eliminating unwanted noise. In the case of eye tracking, as Jacob argued, eye information relevant to interaction lies in the *fixations*. The key is to select fixation points with minimal delay. Samples collected during a saccade are unwanted and should be avoided. In designing our algorithm for picking points of fixation, we considered our tracking system speed (30 Hz), and that the MAGIC pointing techniques utilize gaze information only once for each new target, probably immediately after a saccade. Our filtering algorithm was designed to pick a fixation with minimum delay by means of selecting two adjacent points over two samples.

EXPERIMENT

Empirical studies, such as [3], are relatively rare in eye tracking-based interaction research, although they are particularly needed in this field. Human behavior and processes at the perceptual motor level often do not conform to conscious-level reasoning. One usually cannot correctly describe how to make a turn on a bicycle. Hypotheses on novel interaction techniques can only be validated by empirical data. However, it is also particularly difficult to conduct empirical research on gaze-based interaction techniques, due to the complexity of eye movement and the lack of reliability in eye tracking equipment. Satisfactory results only come when "everything is going right." When results are not as expected, it is difficult to find the true reason among many possible reasons: Is it because a subject's particular eye property fooled the eye tracker? Was there a calibration error? Or random noise in the imaging system? Or is the hypothesis in fact invalid?

We are still at a very early stage of exploring the MAGIC pointing techniques. More refined or even very different techniques may be designed in the future. We are by no means ready to conduct the definitive empirical studies on MAGIC pointing. However, we also feel that it is important to subject our work to empirical evaluations early so that quantitative observations can be made and fed back to the iterative design-evaluation-design cycle. We therefore decided to conduct a small-scale pilot study to take an initial peek at the use of MAGIC pointing, however unrefined.

Experimental Design

The two MAGIC pointing techniques described earlier were put to test using a set of parameters such as the filter's temporal and spatial thresholds, the minimum cursor warping distance, and the amount of "intelligent bias" (subjectively selected by the authors without extensive user testing). Ultimately the MAGIC pointing techniques should be evaluated with an array of manual input devices, against both pure manual and pure gaze-operated pointing methods (in the case of large targets suitable for gaze pointing). Since this is an early pilot study, we decided to limit ourselves to one manual input device. A standard mouse was first considered to be the manual input device in the experiment. However, it was soon realized not to be the most suitable device for MAGIC pointing, especially when a user decides to use the push-upwards strategy with the intelligent offset. Because in such a case the user always moves in one direction, the mouse tends to be moved off the pad, forcing the user adjust the mouse position, often during a pointing trial. We hence decided to use a miniature isometric pointing stick (IBM TrackPoint IV, commercially used in the IBM Thinkpad 600 and 770 series notebook computers). Another device suitable for MAGIC

pointing is a touchpad: the user can choose one convenient gesture and to take advantage of the intelligent offset.

The experimental task was essentially a Fitts' pointing task. Subjects were asked to point and click at targets appearing in random order. If the subject clicked off-target, a miss was logged but the trial continued until a target was clicked. An extra trial was added to make up for the missed trial. Only trials with no misses were collected for time performance analyses. Subjects were asked to complete the task as quickly as possible and as accurately as possible. To serve as a motivator, a $20 cash prize was set for the subject with the shortest mean session completion time with any technique.

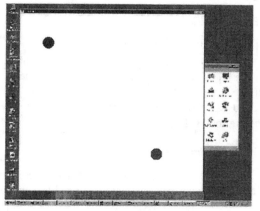

Figure 4. Experimental task: point at paired targets

The task was presented on a 20 inch CRT color monitor, with a 15 by 11 inch viewable area set at resolution of 1280 by 1024 pixels. Subjects sat from the screen at a distance of 25 inches.

The following factors were manipulated in the experiments:

- two target sizes: 20 pixels (0.23 in or 0.53 degree of viewing angle at 25 in distance) and 60 pixels in diameter (0.7 in, 1.61 degree)

- three target distances: 200 pixels (2.34 in, 5.37 degree), 500 pixels (5.85 in, 13.37 degree), and 800 pixels (9.38 in, 21.24 degree)

- three pointing directions: horizontal, vertical and diagonal

A within-subject design was used. Each subject performed the task with all three techniques: (1) Standard, pure manual pointing with no gaze tracking (No_Gaze); (2) The conservative MAGIC pointing method with intelligent offset (Gaze1); (3) The liberal MAGIC pointing method (Gaze2). Nine subjects, seven male and two female, completed the experiment. The order of techniques was balanced by a Latin square pattern. Seven subjects were experienced TrackPoint users, while two had little or no experience.

With each technique, a 36-trial practice session was first given, during which subjects were encouraged to explore and to find the most suitable strategies (aggressive, gentle, etc.). The practice session was followed by two data collection sessions.

Although our eye tracking system allows head motion, at least for those users who do not wear glasses, we decided to use a chin rest to minimize instrumental error.

Experimental Results

Given the pilot nature and the small scale of the experiment, we expected the statistical power of the results to be on the weaker side. In other words, while the significant effects revealed are important, suggestive trends that are statistically non-significant are still worth noting for future research.

First, we found that subjects' trial completion time significantly varied with techniques: $F(2, 16) = 6.36$, $p < 0.01$. The total average completion time was 1.4 seconds with the standard manual control technique (No_Gaze in Figure 5), 1.52 seconds with the conservative MAGIC pointing technique (Gaze1), and 1.33 seconds with the liberal MAGIC pointing technique (Gaze2). Note that the Gaze1 technique had the greatest improvement from the first to the second experiment session, suggesting the possibility of matching the performance of the other two techniques with further practice.

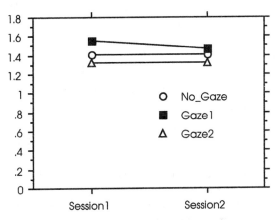

Figure 5. Mean completion time (sec) vs. experiment session

As expected, target size significantly influenced pointing time: $F(1,8) = 178$, $p < 0.001$. This was true for both the manual and the two MAGIC pointing techniques (Figure 6).

Pointing amplitude also significantly affected completion time: $F(2, 8) = 97.5$, $p < 0.001$. However, the amount of influence varied with the technique used, as indicated by the significant interaction between technique and amplitude: $F(4, 32) = 7.5$, $p < 0.001$ (Figure 7). As pointing amplitude increased from 200 pixels to 500 pixels and then to 800 pixels, subjects' completion time with the No_Gaze condition increased in a non-linear, logarithmic-like pace as Fitts' Law predicts. This is less true with the two MAGIC pointing techniques, particularly the Gaze2 condition, which is definitely not logarithmic. Nonetheless, completion time with the MAGIC pointing techniques did increase as target distance increased. This is intriguing because in MAGIC pointing techniques, the manual control portion of the movement should be the distance from the warped cursor position to the

true target. Such distance depends on eye tracking system accuracy, which is unrelated to the previous cursor position.

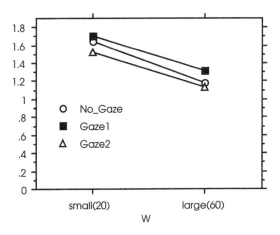

Figure 6. Mean completion time (sec) vs. target size (pixels)

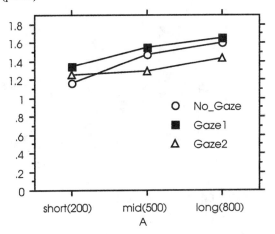

Figure 7. Mean completion time (sec) vs. pointing amplitude (pixels)

In short, while completion time and target distance with the MAGIC pointing techniques did not completely follow Fitts' Law, they were not completely independent either. Indeed, when we lump target size and target distance according to the Fitts' Law Index of Difficulty $ID = \log_2(A/W + 1)$ [15], we see a similar phenomonon.

For the No_Gaze condition:

$$T = 0.28 + 0.31\ ID\ (r^2 = 0.912)$$

The particular settings of our experiment were very different from those typically reported in a Fitts' Law experiment: to simulate more realistic tasks we used circular targets distributed in varied directions in a randomly shuffled order, instead of two vertical bars displaced only in the horizontal dimension. We also used an isometric pointing stick, not a mouse. Considering these factors, the above equation is reasonable. The index of performance (IP) was 3.2 bits per second, in comparison to the 4.5 bits per second in a typical setting (repeated mouse clicks on two vertical bars) [16].

For the Gaze1 condition:

$$T = 0.8 + 0.22 \; ID \; (r^2 = 0.716)$$

$$IP = 4.55 \text{ bits per second}$$

For Gaze2:

$$T = 0.6 + 0.21 \; ID \; (r^2 = 0.804)$$

$$IP = 4.76 \text{ bits per second}$$

Note that the data from the two MAGIC pointing techniques fit the Fitts' Law model relatively poorly (as expected), although the indices of performance (4.55 and 4.76 bps) were much higher than the manual condition (3.2 bps).

Finally, Figure 8 shows that the angle at which the targets were presented had little influence on trial completion time: $F(2, 16) = 1.57$, N.S.

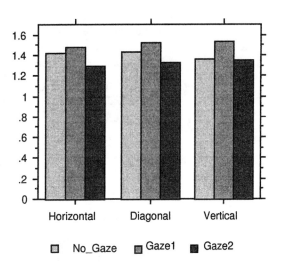

Figure 8. Mean completion time (sec) vs. target angle (degrees)

The number of misses (clicked off target) was also analyzed. The only significant factor to the number of misses is target size: $F(1,8) = 15.6$, $p < 0.01$. Users tended to have more misses with small targets. More importantly, subjects made no more misses with the MAGIC pointing techniques than with the pure manual technique (No_Gaze – 8.2 %, Gaze1 –7%, Gaze2 – 7.5%).

DISCUSSIONS AND CONCLUSIONS

The performance data from this pilot study shows both promises and shortcomings with the very first implementation of MAGIC pointing techniques. First, the MAGIC pointing approach actually worked. All subjects were able to operate the two novel techniques with minimal instruction. By the end of the experiment, subjects had less than 10 minutes of exposure to each technique, but were able to perform at a speed similar to their manual control skills. In the second session of the experiment, on average, subjects using the liberal MAGIC pointing technique performed slightly faster (6.8%) and those using the conservative technique slightly

slower (4.3%) than those using pure manual pointing (1.41 seconds). The US$20 cash prize was claimed by a subject whose shortest mean completion time was 1.03 second, achieved with the Gaze2 technique. The closest runner up was 1.05 second, also achieved with the Gaze2 technique. Although some users performed in fact slower with the new techniques, subjectively they tended to feel faster with MAGIC pointing techniques. On a –5 (most unfavorable) to +5 (most favorable) scale, subjects gave an average rating of 1.5 (spread from -1 to +3) to the Gaze1 technique and 3.5 (from 2 to 4.5) to the Gaze2 technique. The overall positive reaction from the users could be due to any of the following factors: 1) The novel experience, which may or may not be fundamentally beneficial; 2) the reduced physical effort. Users might have liked the fact that a big chunk of the physical task was done automatically. Some subjects were disappointed after the MAGIC pointing sessions when they realized that the cursor would no longer move to the vicinity of the target "by itself."

The targets used in the experiment varied from small (0.53 degree) to large (1.6 degree), resembling realistic targets in practice. Notably, the traditional gaze pointing technique works well only for large targets (2.0 by 1.6 degree in [3] and deteriorated rapidly when target was smaller than 1.5 degree.

The reduced fatigue from pure manual pointing is self-evident, simply because less cursor movement is needed.

On the other hand, the speed advantage, when there was one, was not obvious. It is undoubtedly possible to improve the performance of the MAGIC pointing techniques. First, many aspects of the proposed techniques can be refined, including optimizing the parameters in the gaze system's filter and in the MAGIC pointing techniques themselves. The input device transfer function was designed to accommodate both large and small cursor movements. It is possible to optimize the transfer function for MAGIC pointing techniques. Second, the engineering aspects of the eye tracking system may also be improved. Many subjects commented that the eye tracker performance varied over time, probably due to their head motions during the session. In order to achieve the best results, we turned off the camera's servo mode and used a chin-rest. Some subjects did not stay steady in the chin rest as asked. Some subjects also noticed the delay in the tracking system, which depended on how quickly a pair of samples was detected, which in turn depends on noise in the system. In the ideal case, the delay can be as small as one sampling period (33 ms). Other times it may take several samples to find a pair of adjacent points.

In summary, the pros and cons of the two techniques were demonstrated both in the performance data and in subjects' comments. The conservative MAGIC pointing method was truly "conservative." Its average speed was slower than the "liberal" and the manual technique, although such a difference tended to shrink with practice. Some subjects commented that the conservative technique required more effort to coordinate the timing of eye-hand cooperation.

Others found it less distracting and more "discreet" than they found the liberal technique. Some also pointed out that it took them several trials to get used to the conservative technique, specifically the uncertainty of not knowing exactly where the cursor would appear. Interestingly, the intelligent offset, designed to reduce the directional uncertainty, was not unnoticed by some users who pointed out that the conservative technique had greater "tracking error": the cursor was farther from the target. Clearly we need to further test the conservative technique without the offset.

Overall subjects liked the liberal technique better for its responsiveness. This may change in a more realistic setting where pointing is mixed with other tasks, in which case the more discreet conservative technique may become more favorable.

Based on the results of this pilot experiment, we are refining the proposed MAGIC technique. Alternative techniques may also be designed in future research.

The IBM Almaden Gaze tracker described in the paper points to the rapid improvement in eye tracking technology. The price (and size) of commercial eye tracking equipment has dropped significantly in the last decade, from over US$100k to around US$20k. Our system hardware cost was around US$2000 (US$200 for camera and US$1500 for frame grabber), in addition to the computer (which also ran the applications used by subjects). As computer power and the price of cameras and video processing hardware continue to exponentially improve, it is conceivable that in the future mainstream computers will all be equipped with technology similar to that which we used in this experiment. Such a prospect calls for continued, in-depth research on eye-based interaction techniques. This work attempts to serve as one stepping stone in this process.

ACKNOWLEDGMENTS

This study was conducted as part of the IBM Blue Eyes project, led by Myron Flickner, who provided us great support. Barton Smith developed the Fitts' Law testing program used in the experiment. Dragutin Petkovic was a constant source of support and inspiration. Dave Koons, Rob Barrett, and Arnon Amir contributed to brainstorming discussions; and Johnny Accot provided much-needed help with data processing and analysis.

REFERENCES

1. Levine, J.L., *An Eye-Controlled Computer*, . 1981, IBM TJ Watson Research Center: Yorktown Heights, New York.

2. Bolt, R.A. *Eyes at the interface*. in *Human Factors in Computer Systems*. 1982. Gaithersburg, Maryland: ACM.

3. Ware, C. and H.H. Mikaelian. *An evaluation of an eye tracker as a device for computer input*. in *CHI+GI: ACM Conference on Human Factors in Computing Systems and Graphics Interface*. 1987. Toronto.

4. Jacob, R.J.K. *What You Look At is What You Get: Eye Movement-Based Interaction Techniques*. in *CHI'90: ACM Conference on Human Factors in Computing Systems*. 1990: Addison-Wesley/ACM Press.

5. Joch, A., *What Pupils Teach Computers*. Byte, 1996(July): p. 99-100.

6. Jacob, R.J.K., *The Use of Eye Movements in Human-Computer Interaction Techniques: What You Look At is What You Get*. ACM Transactions on Information Systems,, 1991. **vol. 9**(no. 3): p. 152-169.

7. Jacob, R.J.K., *Eye Movement-Based Human-Computer Interaction Techniques: Toward Non-Command Interfaces*, in *Advances in Human-Computer Interaction*, H.R. Hartson and D. Hix, Editors. 1993, Ablex Publishing Co.,: Norwood, N.J. p. 151-190.

8. Fitts, P.M., *The information capacity of the human motor system in controlling the amplitude of movement*. Journal of Experimental Psychology, 1954. **47**: p. 381-391.

9. Silbert, L. and R. Jacob, *The Advantage of Eye Gaze Interaction*, . 1996: Unpublished manuscript.

10. Morimoto, C., *et al.*, *Pupil detection and tracking using multiple light sources*, . 1998, IBM Almaden Research Center: San Jose.

11. Young, L. and D. Sheena, *Methods & designs: Survey of eye movement recording methods*. Behavioral Research Methods & Instrumentation, 1975. **7**(5): p. 397--429.

12. Hutchinson, T.E., *et al.*, *Human-computer interaction using eye-gaze input*. IEEE Transactions on Systems, Man, and Cybernetics, 1989. **19**(Nov.Dec): p. 1527--1533.

13. Tomono, A., I. Muneo, and Y. Kobayashi. *A TV camera system which extracts feature points for non-contact eye movement detection*. iSPIE vol. 1194. Optics, Illumination, and Image Sensing for Machine Vision IV. 1989.

14. Ebisawa, Y. and S. Satoh. *Effectiveness of pupil area detection technique using two light sources and image difference method. 15th Annual Int. Conf. of the IEEE Eng. in Medicine and Biology Society*. 1993. San Diego, CA.

15. MacKenzie, I.S., *Fitts' law as a research and design tool in human computer interaction*. Human Computer Interaction, 1992. **7**: p. 91-139.

16. MacKenzie, I.S., A. Sellen, and W. Buxton. *A comparison of input devices in elemental* pointing *and* dragging *tasks*. in *CHI'91: ACM Conference on Human Factors in Computing Systems*. 1991. New Orleans, Louisiana.

Inferring Intent in Eye-Based Interfaces:
Tracing Eye Movements with Process Models

Dario D. Salvucci
Department of Computer Science
Carnegie Mellon University
Pittsburgh, PA 15213
+1 412 268 8102
dario+@cs.cmu.edu

ABSTRACT

While current eye-based interfaces offer enormous potential for efficient human-computer interaction, they also manifest the difficulty of inferring intent from user eye movements. This paper describes how *fixation tracing* facilitates the interpretation of eye movements and improves the flexibility and usability of eye-based interfaces. Fixation tracing uses hidden Markov models to map user actions to the sequential predictions of a cognitive process model. In a study of eye typing, results show that fixation tracing generates significantly more accurate interpretations than simpler methods and allows for more flexibility in designing usable interfaces. Implications for future research in eye-based interfaces and multimodal interfaces are discussed.

Keywords

Eye movements, eye-based interfaces, tracing, hidden Markov models, user models, cognitive models.

INTRODUCTION

In the quest for efficient human-computer interaction, researchers have recently begun to explore how to use eye movements to improve user interfaces. Work on eye movements and user interfaces falls into two broad categories. First, researchers have analyzed user eye movements as cognitive protocols to study and evaluate interface design and layout [e.g., 1]. Such analysis helps manifest fine-grained details of user interaction that are often hidden in other types of analysis. Second, researchers have developed eye-based interfaces in which users communicate information to a computer by means of their eye movements [e.g., 5, 7, 12]. These interfaces can act upon either intentional eye movements that actuate specific commands or natural eye movements that arise from normal screen scanning [8]. Such interfaces have proven

useful for hands-free operation, especially for people with physical disabilities [7].

While work with eye movements has achieved moderate success in understanding and developing interfaces, this success has been tempered by the difficulty of interpreting eye movements accurately [6]. Just as speech or handwriting analysis requires accurate interpretation of user speech or pen movements, eye-movement data analysis requires accurate interpretation of user eye movements—that is, mapping observed eye movements to the user intentions that produced them. Unfortunately, interpreting eye movements is often complex and tedious due to eye-tracking equipment noise, user variability in visual and cognitive processes, and the size of typical eye-movement data sets.

Recent work has shown that a new analysis technique, *fixation tracing*, facilitates the analysis of eye movements as cognitive protocols [11]. Tracing is the process of inferring intent by mapping observed actions to the sequential predictions of a process model [2, 4, 9]. Fixation tracing, a tracing method designed specifically for eye movements, interprets protocols by means of hidden Markov models, probabilistic models that have been used extensively in speech and handwriting recognition. Fixation tracing can interpret eye-movement protocols as accurately as human experts and can help in the creation, evaluation, and refinement of cognitive models [11].

This paper demonstrates how fixation tracing can facilitate eye-movement analysis in eye-based interfaces. To illustrate the benefits of fixation tracing for eye-based interfaces, this paper presents a study of an eye-typing interface in which users type characters by looking at letters on an on-screen keypad. The results show that, for an interface with minimal restrictions, fixation tracing can significantly improve the accuracy of eye-movement interpretations over existing methods. In addition, the results show that users type faster in the less restrictive interface and improve their performance with even small amounts of practice.

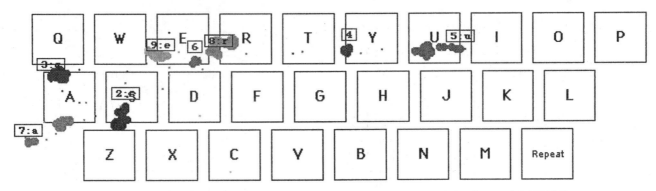

Figure 1. Eye-typing keypad with sample eye-movement protocol for the word *SQUARE*.

DIFFICULTIES IN INTERPRETING EYE MOVEMENTS

Eye-based interfaces encounter two major difficulties in the interpretation of user eye movements:

- Incidental fixations: As users fixate various targets to actuate commands, they also produce incidental fixations (e.g., during search) that are not intended to actuate commands. This so-called "Midas touch" problem [8] requires that interfaces distinguish intended command fixations from incidental non-command fixations.

- Off-center fixations: Observed fixations as recorded by eye trackers are often not centered over visual targets for two reasons: users can fixate within 1° visual angle of the target and still encode information in the fovea, and eye trackers have a typical accuracy of approximately 1°. This problem requires that interfaces recognize off-center fixations and map them to the correct intended targets.

These two problems present a significant challenge for eye-based interfaces in mapping user actions to user intentions—that is, determining what users are thinking based on where they are looking.

Figure 1 shows a sample eye-movement protocol that illustrates these two major difficulties. The protocol is taken from an eye-typing task (to be detailed later) in which users type words by looking at the appropriate letters. For each trial, users read a word at the top of the screen, fixate each letter in the word, and look down at an output box to signal the end of the trial. Figure 1 shows the keypad portion of the screen along with a protocol for a user typing the word *SQUARE*; the protocol is plotted as a sequence of points where larger points represent fixations and lighter points represent later samples. The user first fixated the word to type (fixation 1, not shown) and then fixated the letters *S* (2) and *Q* (3); note that the fixation on *Q* falls more on *A* than on *Q*. After undershooting the next target with a fixation near *Y* (4), the user fixated the letter *U* (5). The user then fixated the letter *A* (7) with an intermediate fixation near *E* along the way (6). Finally, the user fixated the letters *R* (8) and *E* (9), and the output box beneath the keypad (not shown).

This protocol illustrates how incidental and off-center fixations can cause confusion in interpretation. The most straightforward approach to interpreting user protocols would simply map fixations to their closest targets. Using this approach, the two incidental fixations (4 and 6) would be included in the interpretation as the letters *Y* and *E*. Also, off-center fixations that occur between targets could be interpreted as either target; for instance, the fixation intended for *Q* (3) would be mapped to its actual closest target *A*. Clearly, such simple approaches cannot adequately handle the complexity of typical eye-movement protocols.

The approach presented in this paper—tracing user eye movements with cognitive process models—helps alleviate the problems of incidental and off-center fixations. The process models incorporate the likelihood of expected sequences of user actions, allowing tracing to favor more likely interpretations over less likely ones. For instance, consider an eye-typing model that represents the likelihood of typing various letter sequences. In analyzing incidental fixations such as (4), tracing would use statistical information that *Q* almost always precedes *U* to determine that the fixation between *Q* and *U* (4) is most likely incidental. In analyzing off-center fixations such as (3), tracing would determine that the entire letter sequence corresponds to *SQUARE* and that *Q* is the most likely interpretation for (3), even though the fixation falls more on *A*. Thus, tracing with process models employs information about predicted user actions to form correct interpretations of complex eye-movement protocols.

FIXATION TRACING

Fixation tracing [11] describes a class of automated algorithms for mapping eye movements to process model predictions by means of hidden Markov models (HMMs). HMMs are probabilistic finite state machines that have been widely employed in speech and handwriting recognition systems [10]. In fact, tracing eye movements is conceptually very similar to speech and handwriting recognition: These recognition systems translate a user's speech or handwriting input to the most likely

Table 1. Full grammar for {*RAT, TRAP, PART*}.

start	→	**word** *rat*	.33
start	→	**word** *trap*	.33
start	→	**word** *part*	.33
rat	→	**R A T** *end*	1.00
trap	→	**T R A P** *end*	1.00
part	→	**P A R T** *end*	1.00
end	→	**out**	1.00

interpretation given a model of the person's possible intentions. Fixation tracing performs the analogous task for eye movements, translating a user's eye movements to the most likely sequence of intended fixations.

Fixation tracing operates in two stages: finding fixation centroids from raw eye movement data, and mapping fixation centroids to process model predictions. After specifying the inputs and outputs of the fixation tracing algorithm, this section provides a description of each stage along with a cost analysis of the two stages.

Inputs and Outputs

Fixation tracing algorithms take three inputs: eye-movement data, target areas, and a process model grammar. The eye-movement data comprise sampled points of the form $<x, y, v>$, where x and y indicate the location of the point and v indicates the velocity at that point (calculated as point-to-point distances). The target areas include the name and location of possible fixation targets on the experiment screen; for instance, for the eye-typing task, the targets would include the letters on the keypad, the **word** target that shows the word to be typed, and the **out** target where users look to signal the end of a trial.

The process model grammar represents the cognitive steps undertaken in a task and the eye movements generated in the execution of these steps. The grammar may be written directly or derived from models implemented in other systems, such as ACT-R [3] or GOMS [4]. The grammar comprises regular production rules where the left-hand side contains a non-terminal (placeholder) and the right-hand side contains a sequence of terminals (symbols) followed optionally by a non-terminal; the non-terminals represent cognitive subgoals and the terminals represent target fixations. For instance, Table 1 contains a sample process model grammar for eye typing one of the words *RAT*, *TRAP*, or *PART*. The model first fires the rule for the subgoal *start*, generates a fixation on the target area **word**, and proceeds to one of the word subgoals *rat*, *trap*, or *part*. For the word subgoals, the model fixates the letters for the word and moves to the subgoal *end*. Finally, the model fixates the **out** target area, thus ending the trial. The rules in the grammar include probabilities to model the likelihood of each rule firing for a particular subgoal; for

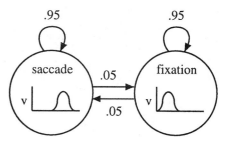

Figure 2. Saccade-fixation model HMM.

the sample grammar, the rules for the *start* subgoal are equally likely.

Fixation tracing produces two outputs: a model trace and a model evaluation. The model trace represents a mapping from eye movement data points to the fixation sequence predicted by the best corresponding model strategy. The model evaluation represents the probability of the model trace, which can be used to evaluate the fit of the model to the data. In this paper, we will use only the model trace and ignore the model evaluation. However, future work on eye-based interfaces could utilize the model evaluation to determine the likelihood that its interpretation of observed eye movements is correct.

Stage 1: Finding Fixation Centroids

Given the three inputs described above, the first stage of fixation tracing converts raw eye-movement data tuples into a sequence of fixation centroids—that is, $<x, y>$ tuples that indicate fixation locations. This stage[1] employs a two-state *saccade-fixation model* that represents the two alternating phases of saccadic eye movements: the saccade, or rapid eye movement from one location to another; and the fixation, or stationary positioning over one target. The saccade-fixation model HMM is shown in Figure 2. The HMM has two states with a single probability distribution to represent velocity. The first state models points that represent saccades; its velocity distribution is weighted toward high velocities to model high-velocity saccadic movement. The second state models points that represent fixations; its velocity distribution is weighted toward low velocities to model near-stationary fixations. Thus, as we determine the most likely interpretation for a given protocol, high-velocity saccade points will likely match to the first state of the submodel while low-velocity fixation points will likely match to the second state. The HMM's velocity distributions and transition probabilities can be estimated using standard HMM parameter training [10].

Given the saccade-fixation HMM, we find fixation centroids by determining the most likely state sequence for

---

[1] While a number of alternative methods exist for finding fixation centroids, this discussion uses the saccade-fixation model to illustrate similarities with HMM use in the second stage of fixation tracing.

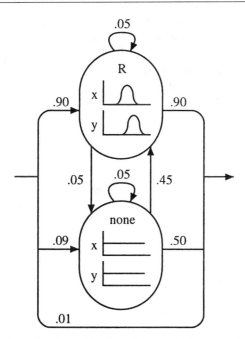

Figure 3. Centroid submodel HMM for target **R**.

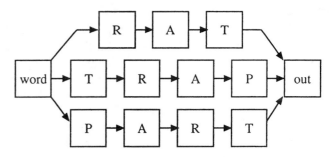

Figure 4. Sample eye-typing tracer model, where each square represents a centroid submodel for that target.

the eye movements using the Viterbi HMM decoding algorithm [10]. This decoding process finds the mapping from eye movement tuples to HMM states such that the probability of the sequence (including observation and transition probabilities) is maximized. The mapping thus describes which points represent saccades and which represent fixations. We then convert this mapping into a sequence of $<x, y>$ fixations where the location represents the centroid of the data points associated with the fixation.

Stage 2: Finding the Model Trace

After the first stage of fixation tracing determines the sequence of fixation centroids, the second stage of fixation tracing maps these centroids onto the predictions of the process model. This process begins with the construction of a *centroid submodel* for each target area. Each submodel is an HMM that specifies the x and y distributions for possible centroids over its respective target area. A sample centroid submodel for the **R** target area is shown in Figure 3. The submodel has two states: the first represents a fixation, with x and y means centered over the target; the second represents incidental fixations before or after target fixations. The transitions shown allow the submodels to bypass or repeat fixations with certain probabilities; the transitions have been informally preset to reasonable values.

Next, we use the submodels to construct a *tracer model* that incorporates the predicted fixation sequences of the model grammar. We use the model grammar to build the tracer model in two steps. First, we create an HMM for each rule that comprises a serially-linked sequence of submodels for each of the rule's terminals. Second, we connect the rule HMMs together according to the non-terminals: If a rule

has a particular non-terminal on its right-hand side, its HMM is linked to all rule HMMs with that non-terminal on the left-hand side. If the model grammar includes rule probabilities, these probabilities can be used in this linking phase; otherwise, equal probabilities are used. The tracer model for the eye-typing grammar in Table 1 appears in Figure 4.

Finally, we generate the model trace by decoding fixation centroids with the tracer model using the Viterbi algorithm. The model trace thus represents the most likely interpretation of the given eye movements: It describes the path through the model grammar followed by the eye movements and the most likely assignment of fixation centroids to their corresponding predicted fixations.

Cost Analysis

The primary cost of the fixation tracing algorithm arises in HMM decoding in the two stages. The Viterbi decoding algorithm decodes sequences in $O(N^2T)$ time, where N is the number of HMM states and T is the length of the decoded sequence [10]. In its first stage, fixation tracing uses a two-state HMM to decode fixations and find fixation centroids. Although T, the length of the decoded sequence, may be large, N is fixed at 2. In its second stage, fixation tracing decodes centroids using its tracer model. Here, N may be large (depending on the model grammar) but T—the number of fixation centroids—is often small. Thus, both stages of fixation tracing are typically fast, resulting in efficient yet accurate interpretation of eye movements.

EYE-TYPING STUDY

To illustrate how fixation tracing benefits eye-based interfaces, this section considers in detail an experimental study of an eye-typing task. In the task, users type characters by looking at letters on an on-screen keypad, such as that shown in Figure 1. The section first motivates the study by discussing how the task interface eliminates restrictions imposed by existing eye-typing systems. It then describes the task and data collection. Finally, it discusses data analysis with a variety of process models and shows how fixation tracing alleviates the major problems in interpreting the data.

Motivation

Existing eye-typing systems [e.g., 7, 12] have demonstrated the great potential for such systems to facilitate hands-free typing. However, these systems include two major restrictions that limit their usefulness. First, the systems require large distances—approximately 4° visual angle—between visual targets. The coarse spacing alleviates off-center fixations but limits the amount of information presented on the screen. Second, the systems require users to fixate visual targets for long durations—750 ms to a few seconds—to trigger an action. These long durations alleviate incidental fixations but result in extremely slow input times. Thus, the restrictions of large distances and long durations seriously limit the design and use of these interfaces.

This study aims to determine the implications of eliminating these restrictions to allow for more freedom in the design and use of eye-based interfaces. The study has two primary goals. First, the study evaluates how eliminating the restrictions hinders interpretation of user eye movements. Because existing systems impose these restrictions to facilitate interpretation, it is important to see how difficult interpretations become when the restrictions are removed. Second, the study tests how well fixation tracing can interpret protocols in the context of a less restrictive interface. The performance of fixation tracing is compared with that of the typical algorithm in existing systems to measure any potential improvement offered by fixation tracing. In addition, the study has several secondary goals, including analysis of user improvement with practice and comparison with manual typing by hand.

Eye-Typing Task

In the eye-typing task, users encounter a screen containing the word to be typed at the top, the typing keypad in the middle, and the output box at the bottom. Each trial begins with the user reading the word to be typed. To type the word, the user fixates the letters of the word in sequence on the on-screen keypad, as shown in Figure 1. For repeated letters, the user first fixates the letter and then fixates the "Repeat" key at the bottom-right of the keypad. After fixating the final letter, the user looks down into the output box displayed beneath the keypad; this look triggers the fixation tracing algorithm, which interprets the user's eye movements and outputs the resulting word in the output box.

The task interface eliminates both the spacing and time restrictions mentioned earlier. First, the interface spaces keypad letters by approximately 1° visual angle to reflect the size of the fovea; this tight spacing provides a rigorous test for the fixation tracing algorithm to handle off-center fixations. Of course, we would expect better end results with a looser spacing, but the 1° spacing better tests the limits of the algorithm. Second, the interface allows the user to fixate visual targets for an arbitrary duration—that is, the user can move her/his eyes as quickly as desired. This allowance also provides a rigorous test for the tracing algorithm: The system can no longer rely on duration to discriminate incidental from command fixations, but instead must employ the user model to make this discrimination.

Data Collection

Seven Carnegie Mellon students participated in the study. Each student eye-typed 12 words four times (a total of 48 words) and hand-typed the same 12 words once. Eye-movement data was collected using an IScan (Cambridge, MA) corneal-reflection eye tracker running at 60Hz. The eye tracker has an accuracy of approximately 1° visual angle. Two additional participants were excluded because of technical problems with the experimental software.

Data Analysis

We analyzed the data set using four models of user behavior for the eye-typing task:

- Full: represents each word separately
- 2nd-order: represents transitions from letter pair to letter
- 1st-order: represents transitions from letter to letter
- Simple: maps each fixation to the nearest letter

These four models provide varying amounts of sequential information: the full model gives a full description of possible action sequences, the simple model gives no information about action sequences, and the 1st-order and 2nd-order models fall in between these two extremes. As we shall see, models with more sequential information produce more accurate interpretations but require more time to generate interpretations.

The full model contains a single rule for each word in the vocabulary, as shown in Table 1 for the words *RAT*, *TRAP*, and *PART*. The model first fixates **word** and moves to one of the word subgoals with equal probability. The model then types the word letters and finally fixates the **end** target. In actual implementation, the grammar can be compacted so that words with the same prefixes use the same subgoals; this modification results in smaller HMMs, especially for large vocabularies.

The 2nd-order model represents 2nd-order transitions from letter pairs to letters, as shown in Table 2. After fixating word, the model moves to the subgoal for a letter with the probability of that letter starting a word. The model then moves to 2nd-order rules that, for each letter pair, fixate the second letter and transition to a new letter pair. This type of encoding can contain very useful sequential information, such as the fact that consonant clusters like *TR* almost always precede vowels. However, the 2nd-order is not as fully specified as the full model because it allows for both English and non-English words not in the vocabulary—for instance, *RAP* and *TRAT*.

Table 2. 2nd-order grammar for {*RAT*, *TRAP*, *PART*}.

start	→	**word** *p*	.33
start	→	**word** *r*	.33
start	→	**word** *t*	.33
p	→	**P** *pa*	1.00
r	→	**R** *ra*	1.00
t	→	**T** *tr*	1.00
ap	→	**P** *end*	1.00
ar	→	**R** *rt*	1.00
at	→	**T** *end*	1.00
pa	→	**A** *ar*	1.00
ra	→	**A** *ap*	.50
ra	→	**A** *at*	.50
rt	→	**T** *end*	1.00
tr	→	**R** *ra*	1.00
end	→	**out**	1.00

Table 3. 1st-order grammar for {*RAT*, *TRAP*, *PART*}.

start	→	**word** *p*	.33
start	→	**word** *r*	.33
start	→	**word** *t*	.33
a	→	**A** *p*	.33
a	→	**A** *r*	.33
a	→	**A** *t*	.33
p	→	**P** *a*	.50
p	→	**P** *end*	.50
r	→	**R** *a*	.67
r	→	**R** *t*	.33
t	→	**T** *r*	.33
t	→	**T** *end*	.67
end	→	**out**	1.00

The 1st-order model represents 1st-order transitions from one letter to another, as shown in Table 3. As for the 2nd-order model, the 1st-order model starts by moving to a letter subgoal with the appropriate probability. Then, the model simply transitions from letter to letter with the probability observed in the vocabulary. Again, this type of model can encode useful information about the vocabulary, such as the fact the *Q* almost always precedes *U*. However, this model contains even less information than the 2nd-order model; for instance, it can produce the words *RAP* and *TRAT*, like the 2nd-order model, and can also produce *PAT* and *TRT*, unlike the 2nd-order model.

The simple model maps each fixation to its nearest letter target. This model, or a similar form thereof, represents the data analysis method typically used in existing eye-based interface [e.g., 7, 12]. The simple model can be represented as a 1st-order grammar with uniform transition probabilities for every letter. However, this analysis uses a much more efficient implementation: after finding fixation centroids, it simply computes the nearest target to each centroid and labels the fixations with these nearest targets. The simple model contains essentially no sequential information and is thus the antithesis of the full model.

Given these four models, fixation tracing was employed to form an interpretation of each protocol in the data set. Of the four models, only the full model is guaranteed to produce a model trace that actually represents a word in the vocabulary. For this reason, after interpreting each protocol with fixation tracing, the system determined the closest word to its interpretation using string-edit distance—that is, the number of insertions and/or deletions

needed to modify the interpretation to the vocabulary word. String-edit distance can be computed efficiently using a standard dynamic programming algorithm [4].

The following results include analyses of the four models and three sizes of vocabularies: 12, 100, and 1000. Vocabulary size was varied to determine how well fixation tracing scales to large sets of words in terms of both interpretation accuracy and speed. All vocabularies included the 12 words tested in data collection.

Results

Interpretation Accuracy and Time

Interpretation accuracy measures how often the interpretation generated by fixation tracing matches the word given to be typed in a particular trial. Table 4 shows the accuracy results for the various models and vocabularies. As expected, models with more sequential information give the highest accuracy while those with less information give the lowest. The full model is highly accurate for all vocabularies. The simple model performs modestly for the smallest vocabulary and quite poorly for the largest vocabulary. The 1st-order and 2nd-order model results fall in between those of the full and simple models.

The interpretation results bring up an important issue concerning how interpretation accuracy should be viewed. Some protocols have so much variability and tracker noise that even human experts have difficulty interpreting them. Because of this difficulty, we often compare interpretation accuracy not to a "perfect" score of 1.0 but rather to the accuracy of human expert coders. Recent work [11] has shown that fixation tracing with full models can code protocols as accurately as, if not better than, human coders. Thus, we can view the full model results in Table 4 as (approximately) the best possible for the given protocols

Table 4. Interpretation accuracy.

Words	Model			
	Full	2nd-order	1st-order	Simple
12	.997	.98	.94	.90
100	.98	.91	.87	.80
1000	.92	.80	.76	.74

Table 5. Interpretation times, in milliseconds.

Words	Model			
	Full	2nd-order	1st-order	Simple
12	142	119	81	55
100	891	602	203	124
1000	9276	3701	834	777

and compare the other models' results to this standard.

Because of an inevitable speed-accuracy tradeoff, it is important to examine interpretation time along with accuracy. Table 5 shows the time in milliseconds needed to interpret a single protocol. Again as expected, models with more information take more time to interpret protocols than those with less information. Most of the times are faster than real-time, that is, they are faster than the time taken to generate the protocols. The two slowest times (full and 2nd-order times for 1000 words) could realistically be sped up to near real-time with better HMM representations and search algorithms. Overall, fixation tracing thus allows interface designers to choose an appropriate model given specific accuracy and time constraints. For interfaces with few strategies or for which high accuracy is critical, the full model provides good results. For interfaces with many strategies or for which fast response is critical, the simple, 1st-order, or 2nd-order model may be preferable.

User Performance and Improvement
Because eye-based interfaces are new to most users, we are interested in determining how well they perform and how quickly their performance improves. This analysis examines performance and improvement for two measures: average typing time and average number of incidental fixations.

Typing time is the average time needed to type one character, not including time needed to read the word and fixate the output box (as interpreted by the full model for the 12-word vocabulary). Overall, users registered 822 ms per character on average; the fastest user averaged 430 ms, while the slowest user averaged 1272 ms. These times are significantly faster than those reported for other eye-typing systems [e.g., 7: 85 min/page, 12: 1870 ms/char]. Users also showed a modest improvement over the two halves of

the experiment, averaging 871 ms in the first half and 773 ms in the last half, $F(1,7)=1.47, p>.2$.

The number of incidental fixations is another measure that captures user performance, since we expect more experienced users to eliminate complex search procedures and thus produce fewer incidental fixations. This measure was computed using the interpretations of the full model for the 12-word vocabulary. On average, users reduced their incidental fixations dramatically during the experiment, producing 1.62 incidental fixations in the first half and 1.01 in the second half. This difference is highly significant, $F(1,7)=35.78, p<.001$. Again, we have strong evidence that users can improve their performance in eye-based interface tasks even after a small number of trials.

Eye Typing versus Hand Typing
Another interesting aspect of the eye-typing interface involves comparing eye-typing performance with hand-typing performance. Naively, we might expect eye typing to correlate highly with hand typing, simply because better hand-typists have better working knowledge of the keyboard. However, it is far from clear whether this motor-oriented knowledge transfers to eye movements. In fact, we might even expect so-called "hunt-and-peck" hand-typists to perform better in eye typing because they often use their eyes to search the keyboard.

Eye-typing times (as described earlier) were compared with hand-typing times on the hand-typing trials. Not surprisingly, eye typing was significantly slower than hand typing: Eye typing averaged 822 ms per character, while hand typing averaged 342 ms. Interestingly, eye-typing times were highly correlated with hand-typing times, $R=.95$. Thus, the expertise and skills involved in hand typing apparently transfer readily to eye typing.

DISCUSSION
This research offers great promise for unimodal and multimodal interfaces that utilize eye-based input. Significant effort has gone into developing more accurate, less expensive, and less intrusive eye-tracking devices [e.g., 13]. However, even an accurate, inexpensive, non-intrusive eye tracker is not sufficient for building effective eye-based interfaces; the systems would still need robust algorithms to interpret eye movements in the face of equipment and individual variability. This work helps to bridge the gap between a user's eye movements and his/her intentions. In addition, while eye movements can serve as the sole input modality for certain applications (e.g., assistive technology for disabled users), greater potential arises in the integration of eye movements with other input modalities—for instance, an interface in which eye movements provide pointer or cursor positioning while speech allows typing or directed commands.

While the eye-typing interface provides a good illustrative domain for this exposition, fixation tracing is applicable to a wide variety of systems. For instance, by incorporating fixation tracing to interpret eye movements, intelligent tutoring systems could potentially disambiguate solution strategies which cannot be inferred solely from other observable data. Also, systems could implement eye-driven menu selection with process models that predict likely menu choices given some prior history of user actions. Of course, the power of any tracing algorithm is closely tied to the quality of the given process model, so the applicability of fixation tracing to a particular domain depends highly on how easily one can model eye movements and cognitive processes within the domain.

This work has at least two important implications for future eye-based interfaces. First, user performance in eye-based interfaces can improve with even small amounts of practice. Analysis of the eye-typing data illustrates that, with repeated trials, users type words faster and produce fewer incidental fixations. In addition, cognitive and motor skills from similar domains (e.g., hand typing) can potentially transfer to eye-based interfaces. Second, removing limiting restrictions found in past eye-based interfaces—such as long dwell times and large spacing between visual targets—can significantly improve interface usability and flexibility. However, fewer restrictions inevitably lead to reduced accuracy, emphasizing the necessity for more powerful interpretation algorithms such as fixation tracing.

Clearly this research represents only one step in the pursuit of better eye-based interfaces. There are a number of promising directions for future work. First, systems could incorporate language models for eye-typing or similar interfaces to provide likelihood estimates of particular word pairs or triplets [10]. Second, automated methods such as cluster analysis [6] could help determine likely target areas of attention. Third, implementations could utilize more sophisticated algorithms to produce efficient HMMs for larger vocabularies. Fourth, systems could extend the current the off-line fixation tracing algorithm to a more on-line algorithm, allowing the system to interpret user eye movements as they are being generated.

ACKNOWLEDGMENTS

I would like to thank John Anderson and several anonymous reviewers for helpful comments on previous drafts. This work was supported in part by a National Science Foundation Graduate Fellowship awarded to Dario Salvucci and Office of Naval Research grant N00014-95-10223 awarded to John R. Anderson.

REFERENCES

1. Aaltonen, A., Hyrskykari, A., & Räihä, K. (1998). 101 spots, or how do users read menus? In *Human Factors in Computing Systems: CHI 98 Conference Proceedings* (pp. 132-139). ACM Press.

2. Anderson, J. R., Corbett, A. T., Koedinger, K., & Pelletier, R. (1995). Cognitive tutors: Lessons learned. *The Journal of the Learning Sciences*, 4, 167-207.

3. Anderson, J. R., & Lebiere, C. (1998). *The atomic components of thought*. Hillsdale, NJ: Erlbaum.

4. Card, S., Moran, T., & Newell, A. (1983). *The psychology of human-computer interaction*. Hillsdale, NJ: Erlbaum.

5. Frey, L. A., White, K. P., & Hutchinson, T. E. (1990). Eye-gaze word processing. *IEEE Transactions on Systems, Man, and Cybernetics*, 20, 944-950.

6. Goldberg, J. H., & Schryver, J. C. (1995). Eye-gaze determination of user intent at the computer interface. In J. M. Findlay, R. Walker, & R. W. Kentridge (Eds.), *Eye Movement Research: Mechanisms, Processes, and Applications* (pp. 491-502). New York: Elsevier Science Publishing.

7. Hutchinson, T. E., White, K. P., Martin, W. N., Reichert, K. C., & Frey, L. A. (1989). Human-computer interaction using eye-gaze input. *IEEE Transactions on Systems, Man, and Cybernetics*, 19, 1527-1534.

8. Jacob, R. J. K. (1995). Eye tracking in advanced interface design. In W. Barfield & T. A. Furness (Eds.), *Virtual Environments and Advanced Interface Design* (pp. 258-288). New York: Oxford University Press.

9. Lohse, G. L., & Johnson, E. J. (1996). A comparison of two process tracing methods for choice tasks. *Organizational Behavior and Human Decision Processes*, 68, 28-43.

10. Rabiner, L. R. (1989). A tutorial on hidden Markov models and selected applications in speech recognition. *Proceedings of the IEEE*, 77, 257-286.

11. Salvucci, D. D., & Anderson, J. R. (1998). Tracing eye movement protocols with cognitive process models. In *Proceedings of the Twentieth Annual Meeting of the Cognitive Science Society* (pp. 923-928). Hillsdale, NJ: Erlbaum.

12. Stampe, D. M., & Reingold, E. M. (1995). Selection by looking: A novel computer interface and its application to psychological research. In J. M. Findlay, R. Walker, & R. W. Kentridge (Eds.), *Eye Movement Research: Mechanisms, Processes, and Applications* (pp. 467-478). New York: Elsevier Science Publishing.

13. Yang, J., Stiefelhagen, R., Meier, U., & Waibel, A. (1998). Visual tracking for multimodal human computer interaction. In *Human Factors in Computing Systems: CHI 98 Conference Proceedings* (pp. 140-147). ACM Press.

Direct Combination

Simon Holland
Department of Computer Science
Open University, Milton Keynes
MK 7 6AA, England
+44 1908 653148
s.holland@open.ac.uk

Daniel Oppenheim
Computer Music Center
IBM TJ Watson Research Center
PO Box 218, Yorktown Heights
NY10598 USA
+1 914 945 1989   music@watson.ibm.com

ABSTRACT

This paper reports on Direct Combination, a new user interaction technique. Direct Combination may be viewed variously as: a systematic extension to Direct Manipulation; a concise navigational framework to help users find the operations they need; and as a framework to make a greater range and variety of operations available to the user, without overburdening user or interface designer. While Direct Combination may be seen as an extension of Direct Manipulation, it may also be applied to a wide range of user interaction styles, including even command line interfaces. Examples from various hypothetical systems and from an implemented system are presented. This paper argues that Direct Combination is applicable not just to problem seeking or design oriented domains (where the technique originated) but is generally applicable. A variety of new interaction styles for Direct Combination are presented. The generalisation of Direct Combination to the n-dimensional case is presented.

Keywords

Interaction technique, interaction styles, interaction design, navigating large operator spaces, novel interaction objects, n-tuples, creating new operations, interaction theory.

INTRODUCTION

In direct manipulation and graphical user interfaces from the Xerox Star [5] onwards, the form of many, though not all, user interactions may be characterised loosely in terms of the following pattern.

interactionObject operator [arguments]

That is to say, user interactions often consist of the user selecting some interaction object, then using a menu, button, keystroke, mouse or similar means to specify an operation on that object. A dialog box or other mechanism may be used to allow the user to qualify the operation with one or more arguments. This interaction pattern can be re-stated metaphorically in the following way:

noun verb - with optional qualifying terms.
Direct Combination is a way of extending Direct Manipulation by focusing systematically not on single interaction objects but on *pairs* of interaction object. The essential requirement for Direct Combination is that for *every pair* of interaction objects in a system, there should be at least one or more operators defined and available to the user. To explore this idea, we will consider some examples. Direct Combination can be afforded using a variety of interaction techniques: we will begin by focusing on a style using a toolglass or magic lens [1]. (These terms are explained in the following section.)

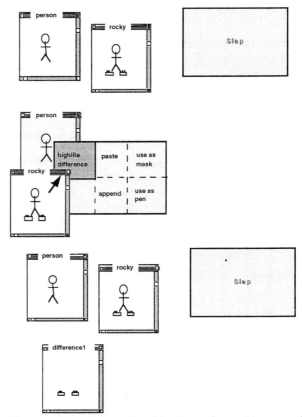

Figure 1: A Direct Combination of two bitmaps. One bitmap is dropped through a toolglass onto the other to produce a difference bitmap.

Introducing Direct Combination

Figure 1 shows two windows (labelled 'Rocky' and 'Person') in a hypothetical desktop environment. These windows contain similar, but not quite identical bitmaps. If the user drags one window over, or partly over another window, nothing of interest happens; the first window is simply left lying over the other. But the situation can be transformed by using a toolglass (figure 1). A toolglass [1] is typically a transparent but shaded pane (here labelled 'Slap') which can be slid around independently over the other interaction objects. The user moves a toolglass by using a pointing device operated by the second (usually the left) hand. Tool glasses, and the closely related magic lenses, are generally used to modify the effect of some tool wielded by the other hand, or to provide specialised views of interaction objects underneath them. In Direct Combination, the toolglass can be used to modify the effects of drag and drop. For the following examples, we will introduce some terminology to improve clarity. In cases of drag and drop, we will refer to the item being dragged as the **'visitor'**, and the item it is dropped on as the **'target'**. We will refer to the tip of the arrow used to drag the visitor as the **probe.**

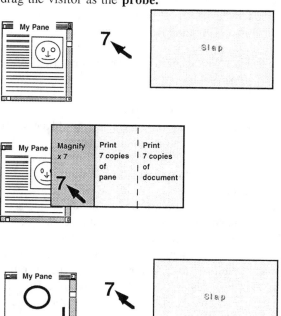

Figure 2: Direct Combination of the integer 7 with a bitmap.

To continue with our first example, when the tool glass by itself is slid partially or wholly over the window labelled 'Person', this has no particular effect. But if the user drags the visitor, 'Rocky', over the target, 'Person', with the tool glass sandwiched in-between, something different happens. As in conventional drag and drop, the target becomes highlighted when the visitor is held over the target. At the same time, the toolglass divides into labelled regions each representing a different operation that can be performed on the ordered pair of visitor and target object. In the present case, the visitor and target both happen to be of the same

type, namely they are both windows open on a bitmap. Accordingly, the toolglass divides itself into regions corresponding to the following operations specific to two bitmap windows: *paste, append, highlight differences, use as mask, use as pen.* (Of course, many other operations could be defined on pairs of bitmap windows.) The region of the toolglass labelled with the default option (*'highlight differences'*) is distinguished from the other regions by bold dividing lines. By sliding the toolglass around with the left hand between target and probe, the user can choose one operation from those on offer. Specifically, the tip of the arrow icon (the probe) used to drag the visitor object is taken to define the selection point. When a toolglass region is selected but before it is executed, it is highlighted (just like a menu choice). If the help system is switched on, a brief summary of each operation is displayed as the operation is selected. When the visitor is dropped, the highlighted operation is executed. In our first example, a third bitmap window is created containing just the differences between the two bitmaps (figure 1).

Diversity of Interaction Objects

Direct Combination (DC) is not limited to dragging and dropping windows or icons: it can be applied to any kind of interaction object. Indeed, the wider the range of interaction object available, the more expressive direct combination can be. Our second example (figure 2) deals with a hypothetical implementation of Direct Combination in Self [6], where all system objects, including numbers, are draggable interaction objects. In this second example, dragging the integer 7 onto the window labelled 'My Pane' has no effect, but placing the toolglass between visitor and target elicits three possibilities, *magnify by 7, print 7 copies of pane dump, or print 7 copies of full document.* Figure 2 shows the effect of dropping the number 7 through the 'magnify by 7' region of the tool glass. Note that all options differ from those in the first example. The options are determined neither by the integer alone nor by the window alone - they are determined by the context of the *ordered pair* of interaction objects *(number, window).*

An Alternative DC Interaction Style: Portals

The tool glass makes it possible to retain the ordinary functionality of drag and drop (e.g. moving files) while keeping direct combination interactions straightforward. But direct combination can be implemented without the complication of two pointing devices. One alternative interaction style that requires only a single pointing device uses *portals.* Figure 3 shows a desktop environment with a document and a folder. In this example, dragging the document icon over the folder icon causes the target icon to be highlighted and to expand, if legibility demands, revealing two portals labelled *move* and *other choices.* The default operation, **move** is shown in bold. If the user wishes to choose the default operation, the visitor object can simply be dropped down the default portal as a continuation of the gesture used to highlight the target. Alternatively, if the user drops the visitor down the *other choices* portal, a menu of choices is offered. In this case, the choices specific to the file and folder ordered pair include the following: *copy the file to the folder; move the file to the folder (default); find all files in the folder of the same type as the sample file; find all files in the same folder created at the same time (minute, hour, day, week, month or year) as the sample file; find all duplicates of the file.* To cancel the operation, the user need only move the cursor away from the menu, which then vanishes, and the target flies back to its original position. In figure 3, the user has chosen the *find all files of the same type* option, which creates a new folder on the desktop containing the aliases of the found files.

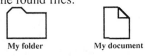

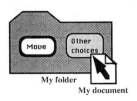

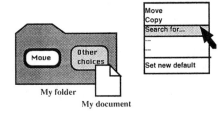

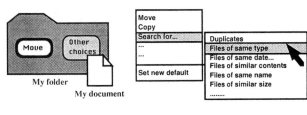

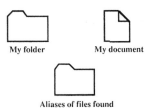

Figure 3: Direct Combination via a Portal.

DIRECT COMBINATION Vs DIRECT MANIPULATION

One way to view Direct Combination is as an extension of Direct Manipulation. We noted earlier that many (though not all) direct manipulation user interactions may be characterised loosely in terms of the following pattern.

interactionObject operator [arguments]

Direct Combination requires the following additional interaction pattern to be made available.

(visitorObject targetObject) operator [arguments]

In other words, Direct Combination requires (in the ideal case) that the system permit *any* pair of interaction objects to interact meaningfully. As noted earlier, this capacity should not be limited to icons. Interaction objects can include: graphic elements, diagrams, selections of text, items on a list, collections of cells, hotlinks, parts of a pane, numbers, characters, files, folders, or entire windows or panes. As the second example suggested, the scope of direct combination is greatest in systems with the widest range of interaction objects. An ideal example of such a system, noted earlier, is Self [6], which is both a programming language and a user interface construction environment. In Self, every internal object is potentially visible, and every visible item has the potential to take part in user interactions. In its drag and drop manifestation, Direct Combination requires that every object in the system can meaningfully be dragged and dropped on any other object. Direct Combination can be characterised by the following principles.

Principles of Direct Combination

• Every object of interest in the system should be visible (or more generally perceptible).

• Every object of interest in the system should be capable of treatment as an interaction object.

• Every interaction object should be capable of useful interaction, in one or more ways, with any other interaction object. The interactions available should be diverse, and should be well-suited to each *ordered pair* of object types.

Of course, there is nothing new about dragging and dropping, sometimes with a limited choice of operations (e.g. Windows non-default drag-and-drop). The key requirement in Direct Combination, that differentiates it from other interaction strategies is that *every pair* of objects of interest must have its own set of useful operations defined, well-suited to that particular pair. Conversely, Direct Combination is not limited to drag and drop. Some other interaction styles for direct combination will be examined later in this paper that do not involve drag and drop at all.

Treatment of Argument Objects

The objection might be raised that the 'new' interaction pattern is already implicitly present in the optional arguments of the existing pattern

interactionObject operator [arguments]

This may be true in some abstract mathematical sense, but not from a user interaction viewpoint, since the direct combination pattern gives rise to distinctly new affordances and new usability issues. However, focusing on the treatment of *arguments* in the pattern does bring to light some interesting issues, as we shall now consider. In many direct manipulation systems implemented using the *noun verb* pattern, dialog boxes are used to specify any needed arguments. Such dialog boxes create a context which restricts the freedom of the user. Indeed, many dialog boxes are *modal,* requiring the user to specify certain information or to cancel the entire interaction before being permitted to take part in any other interaction. Conversely, dialog boxes (i.e. the parts of the system dealing with arguments to a command) are often *not accessible to the user* until the primary interaction object and the operator have been determined. Both of these restrictions violate the principle of direct manipulation that the items of interest should be visible and open to manipulation at all times. Thus, some styles of interaction characterised by the pattern *noun, verb, dialog-box* prevent users from manipulating primary objects (or operators) of interest while dealing with arguments, and vice versa. This can be irritating to users. For example, a dialog box may require the user to specify a pathname for a file, but provide no convenient means from within the dialog box to find it. Outside of the dialog box, the file may be directly selectable, but to no avail. Direct Combination provides a way around some of these violations of direct manipulation principles imposed by dialog boxes. This issue arises even more acutely in the n-dimensional case, treated later in the paper.

IMPLEMENTATION AND FEASIBILITY

To simplify discussion of implementation issues, it will help to introduce further terminology. Since direct combination is not limited to drag and drop, it is useful to have a common term for the *user action* of whatever kind used to interact two objects. This is referred to as a *slap* [4]. The resulting operation carried out on the two objects of interest in the underlying system is called the *mix* operation. If there is a choice of operation, then the mix operator incorporates a set of *submix* operations. At first sight, it might appear that direct combination must be arduous to implement, in terms of the amount of work required to specify the semantics of the mix operations for each *pair* of interaction object classes. This need not be so, as can be seen from the case where direct combination is implemented in a *single-rooted, uniformly object-oriented* operating system or environment such as Smalltalk, Omega or Self. In fact, Direct Combination can be applied irrespective of how the underlying system is implemented, but the method of implementation is particularly straightforward in such systems. The implementation strategy can be outlined as follows. Firstly, note that every visible (or more generally, every perceptible) object in the interface should correspond to a more or less well-defined computational object in the underlying object-based system. Secondly, note that in a single-inheritance class hierarchy, every object in the system will inherit its behaviour from

one or more abstract classes (or prototypes in a prototype system) ultimately commonly rooted in the most general category *Object*. By exploiting inheritance, and assuming there are n classes of interaction object, it is clear that there is no need to define mix and submix operations explicitly for all n^2 possible pairs of classes. We need only define distinct mix operations for the much smaller number of appropriate abstract classes, and for some leaf classes. Provided these classes and their mix operations are suitably chosen, the mechanism of inheritance will insure that all other classes will inherit appropriate mix and submix operations. Note that for most pairs of interaction object, there will be several submix operators defined, with one operator marked as the default, subject to user customisation. Note that in a Smalltalk implementation, the mix operator will typically contain a method dictionary of submix operators, each of which can be implemented using double dispatch.

ORIGINS OF DIRECT COMBINATION

Direct Combination is a broader version of 'Slappability' [4]. Slappability is essentially the systematic exploitation of pair-wise interactions, together with an object-oriented architecture to facilitate this, as outlined in the previous section. The first system to support this idea systematically was DMIX [4], an object-oriented environment for music composition. See the next section for an example of pairwise interaction as implemented in DMIX. The original motivation behind slappability was to manage conversions between different musical representations. Holland extended slappability to the broader form presented here, Direct Combination[2]. In this paper we present these extensions in detail, including: new interaction techniques using toolglasses and portals; the generalisation to the n-dimensional case; analyses, definitions, principles, and characterisations suitable for HCI purposes; terminology such as 'direct combination', 'visitor', 'probe', 'portal', and 'command needle'; and example applications and scenarios outside of the musical domain, to illustrate the general usefulness of the technique.

USES OF DIRECT COMBINATION
Musical Uses

As mentioned in the previous section, Oppenheim's implemented system, DMIX [4] offers numerous examples of Direct Combination using a simple menu-based technique. As also mentioned, the original motivation for providing such a facility was to help users convert between the diverse representations encountered in music systems. A simple example of direct combination in DMIX is shown in figure 4. This involves slapping a mathematical function (here a sine function) onto a Bach prelude. The middle part of Figure 4 shows a sine function displayed in the standard graphical representation for function objects in DMIX. The top part of Figure 4 shows Bach's Prelude No. 1 as a DMIX music object displayed using piano roll notation.

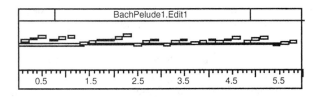

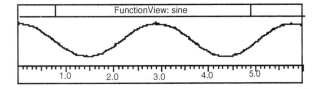

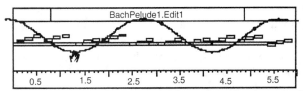

Figure 4: A musical use of Direct Combination. A sine function is slapped onto Bach's Prelude No. 1 to modify the pitches (or the dynamics, timbre or micro-timing).

In piano roll notation, the y-axis represents pitch and the x-axis represents time. The horizontal bars scattered on the diagram represent notes, each an object with various attributes in its own right. The duration of a note is indicated by its length. In DMIX, a slap is initiated by keying command-S when the cursor is over the visitor (in this case the sine function shown in figure 4). The cursor changes shape into a hand holding a sine curve (see bottom part of figure 4). The new cursor shape both indicates that a slap has been initiated, and identifies the visitor. By dragging the cursor in this state over the target (in this case the Prelude) and releasing the mouse button, the slap is executed. The default effect of a slap on an ordered pair consisting of a mathematical function and a music object in DMIX is that the music object takes new pitches from the function. If the user does not want the default mix operation, a menu of alternatives can be provided by initiating the slap using Shift-S instead of command-S, in which case a hierarchical menu of non-default operations is popped up (not shown). In principle, a wide range of alternatives operations could be provided for the interaction of a function and a music object. For example, the function might be applied not to the pitch, but to the rhythm, the dynamics, the timbre, or the micro-timing. Similarly, the function need not simply overwrite the previous values, it could be used to add to them, or to multiply them, or to vary them using any suitable mathematical relationship. To appreciate the power of Direct Combination in DMIX, it helps to realise that music objects can originate from a wide variety of sources; from a file, an algorithm, a music editor, or from a live performance. Direct Combination allows musicians to craft performance nuances (via successively applied functions) onto a piece of music (the music object)

originating from whatever source. A key benefit is that users need know nothing about the originating format, or about the tools normally required to work with that specific format.

Uses In Problem-Seeking Domains

One interesting feature of Direct Combination discovered by Oppenheim in the musical domain [4] was that the inheritance of mix operations sometimes gave rise to useful operations between pairs of object that had not been explicitly foreseen by the system designer. In open-ended, problem-seeking [3] or design-oriented domains, this is a desirable property for fostering creative approaches. It suggests that Direct Combination has considerable potential as a design support framework for use in open-ended, problem-seeking or design-oriented domains. On the other hand, in safety-critical or enterprise-critical applications, the existence of interactions with unforeseen behaviours might be highly undesirable. However, designers who did not want to permit unforeseen interactions could simply enumerate and audit all possible combinations of object types and then explicitly block any undesired interactions. The Direct Combination principle demanding that all interaction objects should be able to interact with each other is of a heuristic and polemical nature rather than an absolute requirement. A wealth of other musical examples can be found in Oppenheim[4]. Oppenheim's DMIX and the papers written about it and the pieces composed with it furnish an existence proof that Direct Combination is implementable, usable, and produces useful results in at least one domain. Direct Combination clearly excels at managing conversions and interactions between different representations. Note that the user interaction gestures used in DMIX are control key, drag and drop, and menu mechanisms, rather than the toolglass or portal mechanisms introduced here.

Exploring Large Spaces Of Operators

One purpose of this paper is to demonstrate that Direct Combination is a widely applicable strategy, and not limited to uses in design-oriented domains. In particular, Direct Combination appears to be useful in more or less any application where there are very many operations defined on a variety of objects, and where the classification system for these operations may not be immediately apparent to the user. In such situations, users tend to experience navigation problems, and have difficulties in finding the relevant operations quickly. This is especially true when the name of the operation may be unknown, hard to guess, or when it is unclear even whether the operation exists. These problems can apply to more or less any large application program, such as well-known word processors. For example, when dealing with an unfamiliar word processor under an unaccustomed operating system, it may be unclear how to convert a document to HTML. Similarly, it may be hard to know how to itemise automatically the differences between two drafts of a document originating from an unfamiliar word processor. In both cases, Direct Combination makes it possible to cut down the search space simply by considering pairs of relevant objects. A user wishing to carry out either operation might 'browse' the direct combination interactions available between two relevant document files, as shown in figure 5.

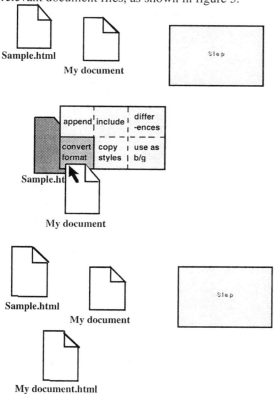

Figure 5: Converting the format of one document to the format of another by Direct Combination through a toolglass.

In the case of the format conversion, a sample document in the desired format could be employed by the user to indicate to the system which destination format is desired. In our example, to carry out the conversion, the user simply drops the document 'My document' through the 'convert format' region of the toolglass onto the sample target document Sample.html. A third document is thereby created, namely the first document converted to HTML format (figure 5).

ISSUES FOR DIRECT COMBINATION
Light Weight User Interfaces
Direct Combination can be implemented without the expense of a second pointing device or the graphical complication of the portals mechanism. For example, figure 6 revisits the interaction between two documents explored in figure 5 (the HTML conversion), but this time using a simple menu-enhanced drag-and-drop. This interaction style need not get in the way of ordinary drag and drop, since the control key can be used to elicit Direct Combination on dragging. Direct Combination can be implemented in even more rudimentary interaction styles.

For example, a command line user interface parser could be designed to make use of the techniques outlined in the section on implementation to process commands with two initial 'nouns' such as the following.

> *myDocument sample.html convertFormat*

Similarly, Direct Combination can, if desired, be implemented as a systematic extension of cut and paste, rather than as a variant of direct manipulation.

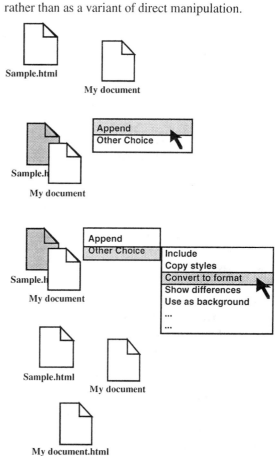

Figure 6: The same interaction as in figure 5, using an easily implemented, menu-based drag-and-drop version of Direct Combination.

Design Of Space Of Mix Operations
There are several approaches for system designers to determine which particular set of mix operations should be made available for a particular ordered pair of classes of interaction objects. One approach is to catalogue existing operations and make them available via additional routes as mix operations. This approach does not necessarily make any new operations available, except perhaps to some classes of interaction objects by inheritance, but it may make these operations accessible in new ways. This conservative approach is called *Operator Re-use*. By contrast, the more constructive *Operator Synthesis* involves systematically looking for new operations suitable for defining on ordered pairs of objects. This approach can make many new operations available. The search may be carried out informally, on an intuitive basis of what

operations appear to be useful, or more systematically. For example, one more systematic technique is to list the attributes of each object, and then to look for ways in which the state of one object can be used to alter the state of another object. Similarly, one can use attribute lists to look for ways in which new objects can be formed from two given objects. Note that operator sets may depend on the state of operands, as well as on their class. Where these processes produce too many candidate mix operators, the numbers can be reduced by expert pruning, or by conventional usability techniques such as task analysis and considerations of relative frequency of use.

N-DIMENSIONAL DIRECT COMBINATION

One of the key ideas of direct combination is to systematically extend the number of direct manipulation operations that are defined (and conveniently accessible) for *pairs* of interaction objects. But there is no reason to stop with pairs. In this section we show how Direct Combination can be extended to deal with arbitrary *n-tuples* of interaction objects simply and consistently. One important constraint on the interaction design is that we do not want any new elements of the interaction design to interfere with existing ordinary direct manipulation actions, or ordinary pairwise direct combination actions. So, for example, it might be confusing if the simple selection of a collection of interaction objects was taken as the invocation of an n-fold direct combination. Such a selection might be intended by the user simply as the first step in sending a single menu command to the selected collection of objects, which is a widely recognised direct manipulation idiom. A better candidate interaction design uses the *command needle,* described below (figure 7). The *command needle* is a new interaction object that looks like a spike on a base. When an interaction object is dropped on the needle, the object is highlighted to show that the object is *spiked,* and not merely placed close to the needle. The needle responds to the spiking by displaying a menu showing available commands. Of course, the commands displayed will vary depending on the number and class of objects spiked on the needle. This is best understood by means of an example. This example is intended to illustrate the interaction style and may not be an ideal example of a well-designed n-fold direct combination operator set. Figure 7 shows a cut and pasted area from a bitmap that has been pasted onto the needle. This elicits a needle menu with several relevant operations, including one shaded as a default (in the example, **Print...**). The user may ignore the available options, or may, in help mode, consult displayed information about any selected option, or may execute a selected option using the *do it* button. Note that in our example, the **Print** operation happens to be accessible via several routes from a variety of n-fold combinations using one, two, three or four objects. The user should not be expected to exhaustively catalogue all arguments to a

potential operation just to be offered that operation. Much as conventional drag-and-drop operations may sometimes provoke a dialog box or other intervention to solicit additional parameters from a user, so it is with n-fold direct combination. To continue with our example (figure 7), the user chooses to spike a second object, namely a printer icon. This alters the choice of operations on the needle menu, any of which can be browsed for details, executed, or ignored, as before. When two or more objects are spiked, the *spatial* ordering of the objects top to bottom may, in some circumstances, make a difference to the operations evoked. This is because the designer may arrange for differently ordered n-tuples to evoke different sets of operations. However, the *temporal* order in which the items are spiked does not matter. One of the (hidden) needle preference controls allows the user to opt for the spatial order of spiked items to be ignored, in which case all relevant operations, irrespective of tuple order are made available. It was noted earlier that the simple selection of a collection of objects is not, by itself, an appropriate interaction design for invoking direct combination operations. Indeed, this observation led to the devising of the command needle. However, a collection of interaction objects may be selected together and then dropped as a group on a command stick. In such a case, the temporal order of selection *is* translated into spatial order of spiking, i.e. temporal order becomes tuple order. To make it easier for users to read the labels of items put on the needle, the needle is by default arranged vertically. This tends to aid legibility for labels in horizontally flowing languages (e.g. European languages). But the needle may be rotated through ninety degrees, if preferred. Continuing with our example, two more items are spiked next, the integers 7 and 2 (figure 7). As it happens, this does not alter the choice of operations offered. Selecting the 'print' operation now displays a dialog box for printing 7 copies of the graphics clip with a magnification of 2 at the specified printer. The dialog box and its contents provides feedback on how the selected operation is being interpreted. To alter this interpretation, the dialog box could be edited, or alternatively the order or identity of items on the spike could be altered by direct manipulation, in which case the changes would be reflected immediately in the dialog box. Note that this close coupling between the contents of the command needle and the dialog box avoids the restriction of the user's freedom identified in the earlier section on argument objects. Indeed, in some respects, a command needle is an open-ended direct manipulation version of a dialog box. To complete our example, in figure 7, the user finishes by changing some of the objects on the spike, ending up with the original graphics clip, an email address, a number, and a graphics document. In our example, just one operation is finally offered on the needle menu for this particular combination of objects. Selecting this operation discloses via the dialog box the interpretation - namely to email the bitmap clip to the given email address, at half size, and converted to the format represented by the sample PICT file. The *do-it* button causes this command to be executed. When a command is executed, all icons fly back to their original locations. Note that the implementation of the n-fold case in languages like Smalltalk is much as in the two-fold case, but with double dispatching on multiple arguments. In CLOS, the implementation is even more direct using multi-methods. The n-fold version of Direct Combination may not have the immediacy of pairwise direct combination, but it does appear to have applications in helping users to constrain searches for operations in large and unfamiliar command sets by considering the objects involved.

CONCLUSIONS

We have presented a novel interaction strategy, Direct Combination, that builds on traditional direct manipulation techniques. Several Direct Combination styles using drag and drop through a toolglass, portals, and other techniques have been presented. We have shown how, in situations where it is hard to locate commands from a large command set, users may constrain their search space by an intuitive consideration of what kind of objects are involved. By focusing systematically on direct manipulation interactions between two or more objects, we have identified a framework that may have the potential to make a greater range and variety of operations available to the user, without overburdening user or interface designer. We have demonstrated a variety of interaction styles that make these strategies available without interfering with conventional drag and drop or cut and paste. Novel interaction objects such as the portal and command needle have been presented. We have demonstrated that the strategy has plausible applications much wider afield than design-oriented areas

such as music composition, in which the basic idea was first devised and implemented. We have shown how the idea can be usefully generalised to the n-dimensional case.

ACKNOWLEDGEMENTS

We thank Bill Gaver, who provided deftly targeted advice and was a first-rate mentor. Mark Blurton-Jones and Rob Griffiths took part in useful discussions. Tom Carey created a much needed space to think about the problem.

REFERENCES

1. Bier E. A., Stone M.C., Pier K., Buxton,W., and DeRose T. D. (1993). Toolglass and Magic Lenses: The See Through Interface. Proceeding of SIGGRAPH 1993, Computer Graphics Annual Conference Series, ACM, 1993, Pages 73-80.

2. Holland, S. (1998). Direct Combination: novel user interaction strategies. Technical Report 98/20. Department of Computing, Open University, Milton Keynes, England.

3. Holland, S. (1999). Artificial Intelligence in Music Education: a Critical Review. In Miranda, E.R. (Ed.) Readings in Music and Artificial Intelligence. Contemporary Music Series, Vol. 20, Harwood Academic Publishers, Amsterdam, Netherlands.

4. Oppenheim, D. (1996). DMIX: A Multi Faceted Environment for Composing and Performing. Computers and Mathematics with Applications, Volume 32, Issue 1, pages 117-135, 1996.

5. Smith D., Irby C., Kimball R., Verplank B. and Harslem E. (1982). Designing the Star User Interface. Byte, 7(4), 242-82.

6. Ungar, D. And Smith, R.B. (1987). Self: The Power of Simplicity. ACM SIGPLAN Notices 22 (12), December 1987.

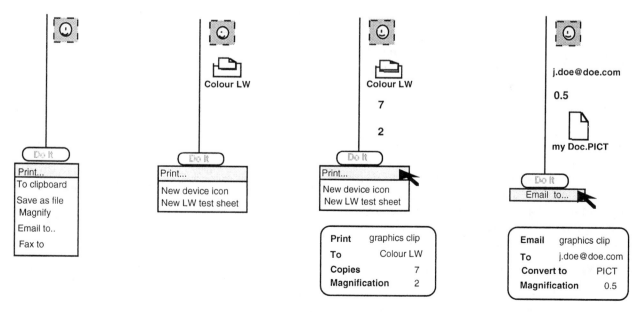

Figure 7: An example of n-dimensional Direct Combination using a Command Needle.

Footprints: History-Rich Tools for Information Foraging

Alan Wexelblat, Pattie Maes

MIT Media Lab

20 Ames St.

Cambridge, MA 02139 USA

{wex, maes}@media.mit.edu

ABSTRACT

Inspired by Hill and Hollan's original work [7], we have been developing a theory of interaction history and building tools to apply this theory to navigation in a complex information space. We have built a series of tools — map, paths, annotations and signposts — based on a physical-world navigation metaphor. These tools have been in use for over a year. Our user study involved a controlled browse task and showed that users were able to get the same amount of work done with significantly less effort.

Keywords

information navigation, information foraging, interaction history, Web browsing

INTRODUCTION

Digital information has no history. It comes to us devoid of the patina that forms on physical objects as they are used. In the physical world we make extensive use of these traces to guide our actions, to make choices, and to find things of importance or interest. We call these traces *interaction history*; that is, the records of the interactions of people and objects. Physical objects may be described as *history-rich* if they have associated with them historical traces that can be used by people in the current time. For example, if you are driving your car down an unfamiliar highway and approach a curve, you may notice that the guardrail has a number of black streaks on it. Realizing that these streaks have been formed from the "interaction" of the guardrail and the bumpers of other cars, you slow down. You are able to negotiate the curve safely because you can take advantage of the interaction history.

Interaction history is the difference between buying and borrowing a book. Conventional information retrieval theory would say they were the same object, given the same words, same pictures, same organization, etc. However, the borrowed book comes with additional information such as notes in the margins, highlights and underlines, and dog-eared pages. Even the physical object reflects its history: a book opens more easily to certain places once it has been used.

In Norman's terms [15], the history-rich object acquires new affordances and we can use these affordances to interact with the object in new ways. We make use of interaction history every day in dozens of different ways without conscious reflection; we think it is natural. In fact, car bumpers and guardrails are man-made artifacts that we have come to understand and read as a part of becoming adults in our society. The fact that we undergo such extensive learning suggests that interaction history is highly valuable. Our project, called "Footprints" by analogy with the footprints we leave in the world, is an attempt to understand what is valuable about interaction history in the physical world, and to find ways to capture history for use with digital information. We believe that the lack of interaction history information represents a significant loss. Work done by users to solve problems in information systems should leave traces. These traces should be accessible to future users who could take advantage of the work done in the past to make their own problem-solving easier.

For example, recently Maes found herself shopping for a new car on the Web. She visited a number of car manufacturer sites, car dealer sites, read reviews on-line, and looked at various independent reports and tests of a number of different vehicles. At the end of this process, she had not picked a particular car to buy — in fact, her list of possible choices was longer than when she began. But all the work done in this process was lost when she finished. If Wexelblat wanted to take advantage of her work, he might ask her, because he happens to know she has done this task, and she might remember some of what she had done and learned. But for anyone who did not know she had done this work there is no way to recover any of the things she found, nor to avoid any of the mistakes she made.

In the digital realm, problem-solvers must approach situations as though they were the first and only people ever to make use of the information. Maes' digital footprints are unavailable, so we all must become information foragers — in the sense of Pirolli and Card [17][18] — over and over again. The Footprints project tries to alleviate some of this kind of problem by allowing users to leave traces in the virtual environment, creating history-rich digital objects.

The term history-rich object and its association with records of the interaction of people and digital information derives from work by Will Hill and Jim Hollan [7][8]. We have taken their initial insight and expanded it into a theoretical framework that allows us to talk about a wide variety of history systems. The next section of this paper gives a basic introduction to the theoretical framework. We then describe the tools we have built to enable history-rich navigation in complex information spaces, particularly the World Wide Web. Finally, we describe our experiment in having people use these tools in a controlled task and discuss our ongoing work in expanding and improving the tools.

INTERACTION HISTORY FRAMEWORK

We have developed a framework for talking about interaction history. This framework presents six properties that characterize interaction history systems. The goal of the framework is to bound a space of all possible interaction history systems, and to give designers of such systems guidance as to what things are important in building history-rich interfaces. We use six properties to describe this space.

Property 1 — Proxemic versus Distemic

Urban planning and social anthropology use the words *proxemic* and *distemic* to describe the closeness relationship of people and spaces. We consider proximity to be a function of both the physical distance and the cognitive distance between the person and the space. A proxemic space is one that is felt by users to be transparent, in that the signs and structures can be easily understood. People feel close to, or part of, the space. Conversely, distemic spaces are opaque to users. Signals go unseen, usually because the people in the space lack the required background or knowledge to translate or comprehend what they experience. We feel "close" to our bedroom even when far away from it and experience a certain "distance" when we sleep in someone else's guest bedroom.

Interaction history systems may be more or less proxemic based on how well they relate to their users and how well they take advantage of users' past experiences and knowledge. For example, the personal computer desktop interface pioneered with the Xerox Star was intended to be proxemic in that it attempted to recreate a space with which the user would be familiar.

Property 2 — Active versus Passive

Most interaction history is passive; it is recorded and made available without conscious effort, usually as a by-product of everyday use of objects. Conversely, when we stop to think about leaving a record, we are creating an active history element. The active/passive distinction is concerned with the user's mental state and relationship to history-rich objects.

The most common example of this distinction is in Web browser software, e.g. Netscape Navigator. The "history" or "go to" list is passive history because it is recorded for the user as she browses; the "bookmarks" or "favorites" list is active history because the user must stop to think that she may want to return to this location in the future. The challenge for history-rich computer systems is to find ways to allow interaction history to be passively collected when necessary so that users are not constantly thrown out of the cognitive state necessary to getting their tasks done.

Property 3 — Rate/Form of Change

History moves forward, building as more interactions take place. This "accretion" process is how history builds up. However, interaction history does not only accrete, it also fades out. One of the challenges for history-rich interfaces is deciding how to deal with this accretion. Just as a complete video playback of a meeting is usually not as useful as a summary, the total accumulation of history must be summarized so that it can be observed and used quickly. A good real-world example of this are patient charts in hospitals. These charts are annotated and added to by many different personnel under different situations over time, yet a physician must be able to come into the room, pick up the chart, and understand essential facts of the patient's current state at a glance.

In the digital realm, Hill and Hollan's "Editwear" tool [7] used a modified scrollbar to show areas within a source file which had been more or less heavily modified. Dozens or hundreds of accesses were summarized by an unobtrusive thickening of the "thumb" component of the scrollbar.

Property 4 — Degree of Permeation

Permeation is the degree to which interaction history is a part of the history-rich objects. History may be inseparable from the object, as in a flight of worn stairs, or it may be completely separate, as in records of stolen art. In a history-rich interface, we must decide how closely to link the objects of interaction and the history information. Digital data will only retain that history information that we choose to keep; therefore, any record of this information must be captured and displayed by tools that we create explicitly for that purpose, or by display systems built into existing tools; for example, the mode-line modification to Emacs described above. The tools we have built to display interaction history information are described in the next section of this paper.

Property 5 — Personal versus Social

History can be intimate to a person: what have I done? Or it can be social: what has been done here? Many tools focus on personal histories; for example, bookmarks in Web browsers that allow users to revisit sites they have noted. Group histories, such as knowledge repositories and shared digital libraries are more rare but, we believe, more valuable because most problem-solving tasks are collaborative in nature. One of the primary benefits of interaction history is to give newcomers the benefit of work done in the past. In fact, the slogan for the Footprints project is:

We all benefit from experience,

preferably someone else's

Property 6 — Kind of Information

There are an infinite variety of kinds of interaction history information that can be captured. What kinds of information are important are, to a large degree, dependent on the task that the observer is trying to accomplish. Since we cannot possibly characterize all the kinds of information available, we focus on the uses to which interaction history might be put. We categorize the kind of information available loosely into *what, who, why,* and *how.*

Knowing *what* was done can be useful if users are *searching for value,* particularly among clutter, or if they are in need of reassurance. This is particularly helpful for novices who lack the kind of practice that helps them know what is reasonable to do with a given computer system. Knowing what was done can also *give guidance;* that is, the process of directing someone in a task or journey.

Knowing *who* has done something is important for reasons of *companionability* (doing things with friends), *sociability* (doing things with people who are similar to me), and for establishing *authority* and possibly *authenticity.*

Knowing *why* something was done can be important for reasons of *similarity of purpose.* I may care a great deal about something that was done by people with a goal similar to mine. A related reason is *goal discovery,* the process of starting off on one task and realizing that it relates to, or can be co-accomplished with, another task. Finally, knowing why something happened is crucial for *explanation and learning.*

Knowing *how* some bit of interaction history was done can be important for issues of *naturalness.* For example, Microsoft Office's assistant has a "show me" mode in which it will show the user how to select the correct options from menus, how to fill in dialog boxes, and so forth.

APPLICATION TO THE WEB

To validate the theoretical framework, we built a series of tools applying interaction history to the problem of navigation in a complex information space. Earlier versions of these tools have been described in [20] [23]. The Footprints tools assume that people know what they want but may need help finding their way to the information and may need help understanding what they have found. Therefore, we do not use history to make recommendations. Instead we provide tools that use history information to contextualize Web pages that the user is seeing. This is information foraging: exploration combined with exploitation.

Our architecture is based on a proxy server (front end) and a database (back end). Both parts are written in Java and work on any platform with standard Web browsers. The front end controls the user interface tools, and records logs that are sent to the back end once per user session and incorporated into the database overnight. Interaction history information seen by users changes as they move from Web page to Web page, but the database itself changes only slowly. The one exception to this is user comments, as noted below.

Our tools are based on a metaphor of navigation — maps, paths and signposts — familiar from the physical world that we have implemented in the digital realm. There are, of course, many other tools that could have been implemented, but these both fit our metaphor and allowed us to explore interesting points in the space of possible interaction history systems described above.

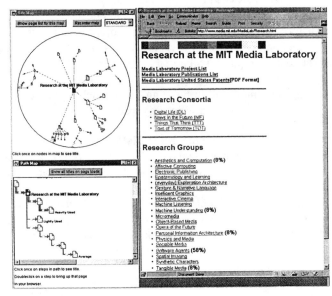

Figure 1 — Screen Shot of Footprints in Use

Each tool visualizes interaction history information in a different way, but they are active aids to navigation rather than static visualizations. The tools act in coordination. Selecting a document in one tool highlights it everywhere; focus is also coordinated. Tools also have some control buttons for manipulating document titles and helping users who get lost; these are explained below.

On start-up Footprints provides a control panel window that allows the user to show or hide each of the tools separately. Users can also shut down Footprints from the control panel. The Map and Path tools appear in separate windows alongside the Web browser. Figure 1 shows a screen shot of a user visiting the Media Lab Research Web page with all three tools turned on.

Over the course of the project, we have designed, tested and implemented several different versions of these tools. Our goals have always been to test our theories and to make systems that people will actually use. As a result, our designs have changed significantly over time, though our basic metaphor has stayed the same. All our tools use Web navigation transitions as their basic information — the "what kind" of information from our framework. Footprints validates that the pages it displays are accessible, so the rate of change of all Footprints is the rate of change of the Web itself. Footprints does not have a notion of user identity; all user data is anonymized and merged with the data of other users. This has the advantage of protecting users' privacy — no one can tell what Web sites you have visited — but it has the disadvantage of not allowing users to see each others' paths. This is a deliberate trade-off; other, equally valid trade-offs could be made but the focus of our research is on the interaction history itself and not on mechanisms for personal privacy.

The first tool is the map, pictured in Figure 2. This map shows the traffic through a Web site. Nodes are documents and links are transitions between them. Note that this is not all the documents and transitions, only the ones that people have actually visited or used. This is, typically, only a fraction of the actual site content. Additionally, we track all transitions made by the user, whether they come from selecting a link on the page, typing in a URL, selecting a bookmark, etc. The result of this is that links on the map often do not correspond directly to links embedded in the Web page.

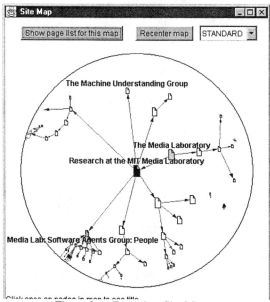

Figure 2 — Footprints Site Map

In Footprints these user-created transitions are considered to be as important as the transitions (i.e. links) provided by Web-page designers. In some sense they are more important, since they reveal user's models of how information *should* be connected. As we described in earlier publications ([20] [23]) the patterns shown in the maps and paths are an externalization of users' mental models. This theory is reinforced by our experiment, described below.

The map visualization we use is derived from [13]. Users can drag the display in any direction to bring nodes from the edge towards the center. Individual nodes can be single-clicked to show their titles, or double-clicked to bring that document up in the Web browser. Titles might overlap, so the user may right-drag to rotate the map.

Popularity of documents is shown by shades of red — the hottest documents are in red, then shades of pink down to white (shown here as shades of grey). The document currently displayed in the browser is shown in black. Because users can get lost while viewing the map, there is a "Recenter map" button that redraws the map centered around the node in which the user expressed the most recent interest, either by single-clicking it or double-clicking it.

The titles of all nodes in the map can be viewed by clicking on the "Show Page List for this Map" button. Since many titles would clutter the display, the titles are shown in a separate window. This window presents the titles alphabetized, with the current document highlighted. Clicking on any title shows the title in the map view; double-clicking on a title brings up the document in the Web browser.

In the terms of our framework, the map view is social, combining data from all users. It is passive in that the data are added without requiring user intervention. It is distemic in that it requires users to learn new rules for interaction, and unpermeated in that the data are kept and displayed separately from the Web documents to which they refer.

The second tool is the path view, shown in Figure 3. If we think of the map as the high-level view, the path view is "lower" level in that it shows the user what paths have been followed by other people.

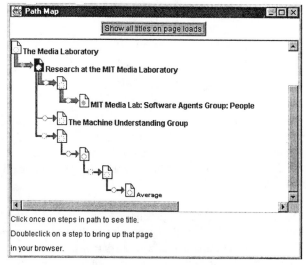

Figure 3 — Footprints Paths

Paths are coherent sequences of nodes followed by an individual. The map is much like a real-world map, with each document appearing once just as a city would appear once. The Path view is like a list of routes that go through these cities. A city appears at least once on each highway; likewise, a document in the Path view appears at least once on each path.

The number of paths formed this way is very large, of course, so we only show the paths that are relevant to (include) the current document. Note that paths with common starting points are merged, so users can see branching — forks in the road — more easily. For example, imagine that the following sets of paths are in the database.

$$A \rightarrow B \rightarrow C \rightarrow D$$
$$A \rightarrow B \rightarrow C \rightarrow E$$
$$A \rightarrow B \rightarrow D \rightarrow F$$

Then if the user was looking at page B, the representation would be:

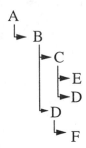

The two representations of 'D' are not collapsed since they represent different paths through the space. The multiple representations of A and B are collapsed, however, since their positions in the path space are identical. If the user now selects page C, the representation would change to:

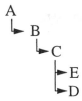

The $A \rightarrow B \rightarrow D \rightarrow F$ path is removed from the display because it is no longer relevant. Other paths containing page C (that do not also contain page B) would be shown if they were in the database. If the user backtracks, the previous path is redisplayed.

Paths also respond to single clicks — by showing titles — and double-clicks, by taking the user to the new document. There is also a button that allows users to see or hide all titles at once. Since the path view is arranged in a stair-step fashion, titles can be shown in the same window. Paths are coded for degree of use. The thickness of the line representing the path increases as the path is more heavily used; we also use a text string to give an approximate level of use. Paths are social, passive and unpermeated in the same way as maps; however, they are intermediate between distemic and proxemic because they take advantage of users' familiarity with tools such as outline listings and hierarchical file browsers.

The next tool is annotations, seen on the Web page in Figure 1. These are our only inactive aids. Annotations are marks — in our case numbers — inserted in the Web page that show what percentage of users have followed each link on the page. Footprints parses the HTML of the page in order to insert the annotations; therefore, we cannot annotate links that are "inside" imagemaps, applets, etc. Annotations are social and passive as with maps and paths. However, they are proxemic and permeated as they represent the "wear" directly in the page.

The final tool is signposts, or comments. These are the means by which users can enter feedback on the interaction history they have seen. Figure 3 shows a path view both with comments (filled circle, upper left) and without comments (open circles). Unlike other systems that only allow comments on pages, Footprints allows users to comment on both pages and paths. This can be useful, for example, in marking forks in the road. One of our beta test users provided an annotation that said "Go this way for software agents; go that way for artificial life." Users can click on the circles to bring up a simple text window. If comments already exist for that path, they are shown and the user has the option to add a comment. Clicking on an "Add Comment" button takes the user to a text input widget. Comments are social, active, proxemic and permeated.

Unlike the passive history information, comments are entered into the database immediately. Once the user clicks "OK" on the add comment window, the path view updates so that the circle is filled if it was not before. Clicking on the filled circle brings up the comments, including the new one, sorted so that the most recent comment is at the top. Older comments appear below. We do not delete comments; users can read the entire history and can converse or exchange ideas. With our small user population this has worked; as Footprints is used by larger groups, we will investigate whether any editorial policies are necessary.

USE OF THE TOOLS
Earlier versions of our tools have been in use for over a year. The first version was used only by alpha testers in-house, and at two Media Lab sponsor companies. The first public beta version of Footprints occurred in October 1997 via our Web site (footprints.media.mit.edu) and improved versions were released to sponsors for internal use. The third major release, described in this paper, occurred in August 1998. Each release has been used by a wider audience.

Although, as noted above, we have been guided both by a navigation artifact metaphor, and by a desire to explore the space of possible interaction history systems, we have also been fortunate to have continual feedback from our users. Many of the features found in the current implementation are a result of requests from users; for example, the recenter button.

EXPERIMENTAL RESULTS

We also performed a controlled experiment to evaluate both the subjective and objective usefulness of the tools. Subjects performed a timed (20 minute) browsing task, one group unaided and one group with the Footprints tools. Subjects were told that they had approximately $20,000 to spend on a car and were to find cars that might be interesting to them. They were encouraged to use their normal Web browsing patterns and tools. The second group had available the interaction history generated by the first group, and received a 5-minute instruction on how to use the Footprints tools based on a data set we created around the Media Lab Web site.

In testing a system that is designed to help people with an imprecise task such as browsing, it is hard to find useful measures. We settled on two objective and two subjective measures. Objective measures were the number of alternatives generated (that is, how many car makes/models they found), and the number of pages visited to generate those alternatives. Subjective measures were the users' sense of satisfaction and judgement of how easy the task was.

Twenty subjects participated in each of the two conditions. Subjects were volunteers given a token reward for participation. All subjects were expected to be familiar with Netscape Navigator before the experiment. Full details of the experimental conditions and evaluation can be found in [21]. Our pre-test hypotheses were that Footprints tools would increase the number of alternatives generated and reduce the number of pages visited. We also hoped that users would find it easier to find and understand relevant information, and would have a greater sense of satisfaction. The available interaction history information could lead people to a greater sense of having explored the problem.

The experiment partially supported our first hypothesis and gave a surprising result on our second. The number of alternatives generated by the two subject groups was not significantly different; however, the mean number of pages required to reach the same alternative level was significantly less for the Footprints group: 24.8 pages for the unaided group versus 18.75 pages for the Footprints group ($p < .05$).

In measuring the subjective responses, no significant differences were observed, with one exception. There was a significant interaction effect across conditions for those subjects who had, prior to the experiment, looked for car information

on the Web, as shown in the ANOVA below. In this table, we test the interaction of user's previous activity (*looked* means that they have looked for car information on the Web before this experiment) with their response to a question about their satisfaction with the experience. Satisfaction was measured on a scale of 1-5, with 1 representing "Totally Satisfied" and 5 representing "Totally Dissatisfied." The table shows that while there is no significant effect for either effect considered separately, the two-way interaction of experimental condition (unaided vs. Footprints) and previous experience (looked vs. has not looked) was significant ($p < .01$).

TABLE 1. Interaction of Previous Experience with Satisfaction

Variation Source	Sum of Squares	DF	Mean Square	F	Sig of F
Main Effects	1.607	2	.803	1.5	.237
Expmt #	.207	1	.207	.385	.539
Looked	1.079	1	1.079	2.014	.164
2-Way Interacts					
Expmt # / Looked	4.872	1	4.872	9.093	.005

This was surprising as we had been assuming that interaction history models would help naive users; instead we seem to have found a situation in which past users' models are recognized and used by experienced browsers. In fact, naive users — in our case users who do not have experience with the domain — find themselves less satisfied when seeing these models. This most likely relates to our notion of proxemic/distemic, and reminds us that all naive Web users are not alike. Those who had a mental model of what car information on the Web was like found the Footprints representations much more proxemic and were able to make much better use of them. This conclusion was reinforced by other subject-reported experiences. In particular, subjects who rated their level of Web expertise lower reported having a harder time finding information that was relevant to their problem and less satisfaction with the solutions they found.

At this writing we are doing more detailed analyses of how subjects used the Footprints tools. Informal observation and post-test conversation suggested three patterns of use were in evidence. Some subjects simply took off in directions we had not seen before and so received little or no help from Footprints. This suggests that our test data set could be improved. Other subjects started off using Footprints information then went off in new directions since their tastes in vehicles differed from those of our first group of subjects. These subjects usually started with a popular site such as Yahoo! or Edmund's for which we had lots of history data from the first group. This variety of use patterns was expected; we cannot possibly cover all the possible car makes and models in which subjects might be interested.

The third group of subjects did not start out using the Foot-prints information. They had different search strategies. However, they ended up using Footprints information once their searches brought them near to popular car-related sites. At this point, the map proved particularly useful; as one subject put it: "As soon as I got there, the map had a bunch of alternatives and I used those."

RELATED WORK

Our theoretical work derives from two major influences. The first is ethnographic studies of how people work in teams in real situations, primarily research from Hutchins [11], Orr [16], and Suchman [19]. The second is urban studies, particularly the work of Lynch [14] and Brand [1]. From these we have developed our theory of how interaction history information can be used by people involved in their normal problem-solving tasks.

Hill and Hollan's original work [7] involved a series of tools, called "editware," "readware," and so on that were oriented toward helping people on a software development project keep track of which portions of the code and documentation were being the most heavily modified, most heavily read, etc.

Chalmers and his collaborators [3] have also been applying history (or activity-centrism as they call it) to tracing users' paths through the Web. Their tools are oriented towards providing recommendations for possible Web pages to visit, based on differences between the current user's paths and paths recorded in the system's history database.

The notion of paths through digital information and their use is at least as old as Bush's famous MEMEX essay [2]:

> The owner of the memex... runs through an encyclopedia, finds an interesting but sketchy article, leaves it projected. Next, in a history, he finds another pertinent item, and ties the two together. Thus he goes, building a trail of many items. [H]is trails do not fade.

Hypertext systems have used map and path mechanisms for many years. However, these are typically top-down created artifacts put in the system by the designer for guidance or pedagogical purposes. Zellweger's "Scripted Documents" [24] are an excellent example of this. This notion is also being carried into the Web domain by projects such as CMU's *WebWatcher* [12], a tour-guide agent for the Web, and *Walden's Paths* [6], a K-12 educational application of scripted paths.

Some related work falls into the category of assisting social navigation. Dieberger [5] describes an enhanced MOO system, which keeps track of how many people use passages between rooms in the MOO and augments textual descriptions with information on how heavily used the passages appear. Dahlback, Hooks and others in the PERSONA

project [4] have been exploring a number of different aspects of social and personal navigation, including the uses of artifacts in these processes and individual differences in the navigation process.

Other related work has been done in the area of community-created information sources. Hill and Terveen, particularly in their PHOAKS project [9][10], have been active in creating new techniques for mining existing information — on the Web and in Usenet newsgroups — for traces that can be collected and made available to future users. PHOAKS collects URLs that have been positively mentioned from postings and Frequently Asked Questions documents. These URLs are then provided as recommendations on a central server to people interested in the topic of the newsgroup from which they were extracted. Alexa (www.alexa.com) provides a real-time local Web-page recommendation system. They use history information as part of their input in determining what pages to recommend; however, it is unclear just how history is used or how it is integrated with the keyword matching that forms the basis for their recommendations.

CONCLUSIONS AND FUTURE WORK

We have built a set of tools to support undirected Web browsing. The tools are based around the concepts of interaction history and the notion that the work done by past users can be important to helping current users solve problems such as navigation in a complex information space. Our tools have been in use and available on the Web for over a year. The user community is small but growing. Our tools have been popular with Web information users and designers.

The experiment reported here showed that our tools are successful in two respects:

- they enable users to get the same work done with significantly less effort, and

- experienced users were able to recognize the information models left behind by other users and reported a significantly higher sense of satisfaction when working with these models.

More work remains to be done in testing the use of active history tools, as well as scaling up our user community. Applications of these ideas to areas such as electronic commerce and information management are also being investigated.

Finally, we set out to take something pervasive in the physical world, characterize it, and extract use from it for the digital realm. We have begun to show success in this endeavor; we have given history to digital information.

Thanks

Work on Footprints has been funded by the MIT Media Laboratory's News in the Future consortium. Code for the Footprints tools was written by Felix Klock, Alex Lian, and James Matyszak. Jennifer Smith provided statistical help.

REFERENCES

1. Brand, Stuart. *How Buildings Learn: What happens after they're built*, Penguin Books, 1994.

2. Bush, Vannevar. "As We May Think," *Atlantic Monthly*, July 1945.

3. Chalmers, Matthew, K. Rodden & D. Brodbeck. "The Order of Things: Activity-Centred Information Access," *Proceedings of the 7th International World Wide Web Conference* (WWW7), 1998.

4. Dahlback, Nils (ed.) *Exploring Navigation: Towards a Framework for Design and Evaluation of Navigation in Electronic Spaces*, Swedish Institute of Computer Science TR98:01, 1998.

5. Dieberger, Andreas. "Supporting Social Navigation on the World-Wide Web," *International Journal of Human-Computer Studies*, Vol. 46, 1997.

6. Furuta et al. Hypertext Paths and the World-Wide Web: Experiences with Walden's Paths, *Hypertext'97 Proceedings*, ACM Press, 1997.

7. Hill, Hollan, Wroblewski & McCandles. "Edit Wear and Read Wear," *Proceedings of CHI'92 Conference on Human Factors in Computing Systems*, ACM Press, 1992.

8. Hill, Will & Jim Hollan. "History-Enriched Digital Objects," *Proceedings of Computers, Freedom, and Privacy (CFP'93)*, available from http://www.cpsr.org/dox/conferences/cfp93/hill-hollan.html

9. Hill, Stead, Rosenstein & Furnas. "Recommending and Evaluating Choices in a Virtual Community of Use," *Proceedings of CHI'95 Conference on Human Factors in Computing Systems*, ACM Press, 1995.

10. Hill, Will & Loren Terveen. "Using Frequency-of-Mention in Public Conversations for Social Filtering," *Proceedings of CSCW'96 Conference on Computer-Supported Cooperative Work*, ACM Press, 1996.

11. Hutchins, Edwin. *Cognition in the Wild*, MIT Press, 1995.

12. Joachims, Freitag & Mitchell. "WebWatcher: A Tour Guide for the World Wide Web," *Proceedings of IJCAI97*, 1997.

13. Lamping, Rao & Pirolli. "A Focus+Context Technique Based on Hyperbolic Geometry for Visualizing Large Hierarchies," *Proceedings of CHI'95 Conference on Human Factors in Computing Systems*, ACM Press, 1995

14. Lynch, Kevin. *What Time is this Place?* MIT Press, 1972.

15. Norman, Don. *The Psychology of Everyday Things*, Basic Books, 1988.

16. Orr, Julian. *Talking About Machines: An Ethnography of a Modern Job*, Cornell University Press, 1996.

17. Pirolli, Peter & Stuart Card. "Information Foraging in Information Access Environments," *Proceedings of ACM CHI'95 Conference on Human Factors in Computing Systems*, ACM Press, 1995.

18. Pirolli, Peter. "Computational Models of Information Scent-Following in a Very Large Browsable Text Collection," *Proceedings of ACM CHI 97 Conference on Human Factors in Computing Systems*, ACM Press, 1997.

19. Suchman, Lucy A. *Plans and Situated Actions*, Cambridge University Press, 1987.

20. Wexelblat, Alan. "Communities through Time: Using History for Social Navigation," in *Community Computing and Support Systems*, Toru Ishida (ed.), Lecture Notes in Computer Science, Volume 1519, Springer Verlag, 1998.

21. Wexelblat, Alan. *Footprints: Interaction History for Digital Objects*, Ph.D. Thesis, MIT Program in Media Arts & Sciences, 1999.

22. Wexelblat, Alan. "History-Based Tools for Navigation," *Proceedings of the 32nd Hawaii International Conference on Systems Sciences (HICSS-32)*, IEEE Computer Society Press, 1999.

23. Wexelblat, Alan & Pattie Maes. "Visualizing Histories for Web Browsing," *RIAO'97: Computer-Assisted Information Retrieval on the Internet*, Montreal, 1997.

24. Zellweger, Polle. "Scripted Documents: A Hypermedia Path Mechanism," *Hypertext'89 Proceedings*, ACM Press, 1989.

Design Guidelines for Landmarks to Support Navigation in Virtual Environments

Norman G. Vinson
Institute for Information Technology
National Research Council, Canada
Ottawa, ON K1A 0R6
+1 613 993 2565
norm.vinson@iit.nrc.ca

ABSTRACT

Unfamiliar, large-scale virtual environments are difficult to navigate. This paper presents design guidelines to ease navigation in such virtual environments. The guidelines presented here focus on the design and placement of landmarks in virtual environments. Moreover, the guidelines are based primarily on the extensive empirical literature on navigation in the real world. A rationale for this approach is provided by the similarities between navigational behavior in real and virtual environments.

Keywords

Guidelines, navigation, wayfinding, landmarks, virtual reality, virtual environments.

INTRODUCTION

Follow the road until you get to the church, then turn right. Then continue past two intersections. You'll see a gas station on one side of the road and a big apple tree on the other. Right after that, make your first left. At the stop sign, turn left again. I'll meet you in front of the house at the end of the road.

Add the objects mentioned above to an environment you know well. Then imagine following the above directions in that context. Which objects stand out? The church, intersections, gas station, apple tree, stop sign, and the 'end of the road' probably stand out because they are reference points. Such distinctive environmental features functioning as reference points are **landmarks**. When associated to navigational actions (such as turn right), landmarks ease navigation by indicating when and where these actions should be taken.

Because of their navigational function, it is important to include landmarks in virtual environments (hereafter "**VEs**"). One can wonder though how to design and place landmarks in a VE to maximize their utility to the navigator. Research from the fields of urban planning (e.g. [19]), geography (e.g. [15]), and psychology (e.g. [3]) has explored the roles of landmarks in real world navigation. This empirical research can be applied to the development of design guidelines for VE landmarks to effectively support navigation. VEs designed according to these guidelines would facilitate users' navigation by permitting them to apply their real world navigational experience. The intent of this paper is therefore to provide landmark design guidelines to support navigation in large-scale VEs.

The guidelines herein focus on the structural elements and content of VEs because the virtual reality literature already contains many articles on specific navigational interfaces like input devices (e.g. [32]), motion control (e.g. [27]), and maps (e.g. [24]).

Before the guidelines themselves are presented, the necessity of supporting navigation in VEs is discussed, as is the justification for using research on real world navigation to create guidelines facilitating VE navigation.

The Need for Navigational Support

The need for navigation design guidelines exists for three reasons: many VEs require the user to navigate, navigation in VEs is difficult, and disorientation is upsetting [18]. The first two reasons are discussed more fully below.

VEs Often Require Navigation

Navigation becomes necessary in environments that are so large that the navigator's viewpoint does not encompass the environment in its totality [3][7]. Such environments, whether virtual or real, are commonly termed "**large-scale environments**" (e.g. [3][26]). This scale forces the navigator to integrate the information provided by successive viewpoints into a coherent mental representation of the traversed environment, often termed "**cognitive map**" [3]. The navigator then relies on this cognitive map to navigate in the environment [25].

Current examples of large-scale VEs include simulators (flight, ship, or car) and some forms of telerobotics. As computers become more powerful and 3D visualization more common, fly-throughs of networks (electronic or biological) and complex molecular structures, simulations, and data visualizations will also pose navigational

CHI '99 Pittsburgh PA USA
0-201-48559-1/99/05

problems. The guidelines presented here are applicable to these types of large-scale VEs.

VE Navigation Is Difficult

Most of us have little difficulty navigating in the real world most of the time. The reason is that we mainly navigate in environments that are quite familiar. Even when environments are not completely familiar, we can often keep to familiar routes, for instance, by taking the same roads or buses. The difficulties arise when navigating unfamiliar environments. In these cases, we rely on navigational aids like written directions or maps. In urban environments, or on highways, we follow roads and signs that guide our travel. However, in unfamiliar environments these guides are often insufficient, and sometimes confusing [23]. Even maps can lead to navigational errors [35]. In natural environments, hikers use maps, and follow paths and signs. However, when a natural environment is devoid of such human artifacts, navigation is so challenging that it constitutes the competitive sport of orienteering [5].

The difficulty of navigating in unfamiliar real world spaces suggests the need to support navigation in VEs. A VE will always be unfamiliar when the user first encounters it. Gaining sufficient familiarity for successful navigation without any navigational support can take several hours that users may not be willing to provide [26]. Other differences between real and virtual environments increase the need to support navigation in VEs.

VEs contain fewer spatial and locomotive cues than real environments. Because of computational limitations, there is often less visual detail presented in VEs [26]. This means there may be fewer landmarks to support navigation, and fewer depth cues (such as occlusion and texture gradients (see [35])) to help with distance estimation. Locomotive and proprioceptive cues normally provided by walking, and turning one's body or head are often absent, especially from desktop virtual reality [26]. Finally, peripheral vision, absent from many forms of VE, has also been shown to provide navigational information [26]. These factors heighten the need for VE navigational support.

Moreover, the spatial structure of VEs may represent information. For example, a VE could contain objects whose spatial properties (e.g. shape, position, size) represent data values on different dimensions. Here, it is necessary for the navigator to quickly develop accurate representations of those spatial properties in order to understand the relationships in the data. In contrast, real environments typically do not represent data. Accordingly, in real environments, the most important function of navigators' spatial knowledge is to get them from here to there. This kind of navigation can be accomplished by remembering a string of associations between landmarks and their corresponding navigational actions (e.g. at the church, turn right) [17][29]. More accurate spatial knowledge is useful, for example to recover from navigational errors [35], but is not essential to navigation.

Thus, VEs that represent data demand greater accuracy of the navigator's cognitive map than do real environments. Guidelines promoting this accuracy are presented in the final section.

There is evidence that, despite these differences, the *way* in which we navigate is the same whether the environment is virtual or real. For instance, the development of spatial knowledge and its relation to navigation are the same for real and virtual environments [26]. Another example is that navigational experience with a virtualized environment has been found to transfer to the corresponding real environment [5]. Finally, principles and techniques coming out of real-world navigation research have been successfully applied to VE navigation research [1] [7]. This evidence provides a strong rationale for basing VE design guidelines on real-world navigation research.

In sum, it is clear that users of large-scale VEs require some navigational support. Moreover, it is reasonable to use research on real world navigation to generate guidelines for supporting navigation in VEs. The following section presents and explains such guidelines.

GUIDELINES

VEs should be easy to navigate, to leave cognitive resources available for the processing of any concurrent tasks. Because it is expected that people will navigate in unfamiliar VEs [7], VE design should promote rapid learning of the information necessary to navigate successfully. When information is represented by the relative size, orientation, or position of virtual objects, it is desirable that navigators develop accurate spatial information as quickly as possible.

These goals can be met by placing in the VE the types of objects that people use as cues for navigating in the real world: landmarks. Landmarks and their layout are critical for navigation [8][14][19]. In addition, the VE can be designed to be consistent with the way people remember large spaces. Cognitive maps are often distorted, but in predictable ways [3][35]. A designer who anticipates these distortions can minimize them by structuring the VE according to people's mnemonic predispositions.

In many cases, some features of the VE will be constrained by factors not under the designer's control. An example is provided by VEs with virtual objects that represent data. Designers have no control over such data objects, so the design guidelines cannot be applied to them. However, designers can add artificial landmarks to the environment, as long as they can be easily discriminated from the features and objects representing data. Those artificial landmarks can be designed and located according to the guidelines presented below. In this way, the designer can support navigation, while allowing the data objects to just represent data.

The first subsection contains explanations of how people use landmarks to learn the layout of an environment. This not only highlights the importance of landmarks, but also provides VE designers with a basic understanding of how cognitive maps are formed. In the following subsection, several abstract categories of landmarks and their role in navigation are presented. With this information, designers can review their VEs to ensure that all the landmark types are present. Guidelines on composing and placing landmarks to optimize their usefulness are then presented. These are followed by descriptions of environmental arrangements that minimize distortions in cognitive maps.

Learning about an Environment

Newcomers to an environment rely heavily on landmarks as points of reference [8][14]. As experience with the environment increases, navigators acquire *route knowledge* that allows them to navigate from one point in the environment to another [29]. Route knowledge is acquired and expanded by associating navigational actions to landmarks, such as turning right (action) at the corner (landmark). An ordered series of such action-landmark associations constitutes a route [12][17]. In following a route, the landmark (e.g. the corner) serves as the cue to recalling the associated action (e.g. turning right) [3].

In sum, landmarks support initial orientation in the new environment, they support the subsequent development of route knowledge, and they are essential to navigation using route knowledge. Thus, the first guideline is:

- **Guideline 1: It is essential that the VE contain several landmarks.**

Generally, additional experience with the environment increases the representational precision of route distances, and of the relative orientations and positions of landmarks [9][22]. Additional experience may also transform the representation from route knowledge to *survey knowledge* [29]. Survey knowledge is analogous to a map of the environment, except that it does not encode a typical map's top-down or bird's-eye-view perspective. Rather survey knowledge allows the navigator to adopt the most convenient perspective on the environment for a particular task [29][31]. Survey knowledge acquired through navigational experience also incorporates route knowledge [29].

In comparison to route knowledge, survey knowledge more precisely encodes the spatial proprieties of the environment and its objects [29]. Nonetheless, survey knowledge also contains distortions of the environment. Such distortions are especially problematic in VEs containing data objects (i.e. objects whose spatial properties represent data). The final subsection presents guidelines to minimize these distortions. Immediately below, the types of landmarks and their functions are discussed. The subsection following that contains guidleins on the construction and placement of landmarks.

Landmark Types and Functions

To include landmarks in a VE, one must know what constitutes a landmark. In his seminal work on urban planning and cognitive maps, Kevin Lynch found that people's cognitive maps generally contained five types of elements: paths, edges, districts, nodes, and landmarks. Each element *type* serves a particular function, though an *individual* element can serve more than one function[1] (see Table 1) [19].

Because these elements are used as landmarks (in the general sense[1]), and people make use of landmarks to navigate, the inclusion of Lynch's elements in a VE will support navigation through that VE. Moreover, since each type of element supports navigation in its own way, a VE designer should endeavor to include all five types of elements in the VE. Hence:

- **Guideline 2: Include all five types of landmarks (from Table 1) in your VE.**

Table 1: Landmark/Element Types and Functions.

Types	Examples	Functions
Paths	Street, canal, transit line	Channel for navigator movement
Edges	Fence, river	Indicate district limits
Districts	Neighborhood	Reference point
Nodes	Town square, public bldg.	Focal point for travel
Landmarks[1]	Statue	Reference point into which one does not enter

Landmark Composition

It is important to include objects intended to serve as landmarks in a VE. However, it is also important that those objects be designed so that navigators will choose them as landmarks. There are two issues regarding the way in which landmarks should be constructed. One issue relates to the landmark's physical features. The other issue relates to the ways in which landmarks should be distinctive.

Landmark Features

A VE designer has the opportunity to create landmarks that are noticeable and help navigators remember their positions in the environment. Such landmarks support the use, and possibly the development of survey knowledge. For instance, a navigator can determine her position in the environment through her knowledge of the position of landmarks. Consequently, using particular features in designing landmarks can support navigation.

Evans and colleagues, expanding the work of Appleyard and Kaplan, empirically examined the relationship between building features and recall [11]. These studies produced a

---

[1] Note that Lynch refers to these items as "elements" and reserves a specific meaning for the term "landmark" (see Table 1). In this paper, we use the term landmark more generally to refer to Lynch's elements and other features of an environment that provide information on navigator position and orientation.

set of features that make a building more memorable, and a set of features that make the building's location easier to recall. Many of the features from both sets enhance a building's distinctiveness (see Table 2 and Guideline 3). Evans and colleagues found that the functions of buildings, their socio-cultural significance and their surrounding traffic patterns also affect their memorability. However, these types of features are more difficult to reproduce in a VE.

- **Guideline 3: Make your landmarks distinctive with features from Tables 2 and 3.**

Table 2: Building Features Contributing to Memorability.

Significant height [m]	Expensive building materials & good maintenance [l]
Complex shape [m]	Free standing (visible) [lm]
Bright exterior [l]	Surrounded by landscaping [m]
Large, visible signs [m]	Unique exterior color, texture [l]

[m] Increases memorability of building.
[l] Improves memory for building location.

- **Guideline 4: Use concrete objects, not abstract ones, for landmarks.**

A study of VE landmarks also suggests that memorable landmarks increase navigability [26]. Landmarks consisting of familiar 3D objects, like a model car and a fork, made the VE easier to navigate. In contrast, landmarks consisting of colorful abstract paintings were of no help. It was felt that the 3D objects were easier to remember than the abstract art and that this accounted for the difference in navigability.

Table 3: Landmarks in Natural Environments.

Manmade Items	Land Contours	Water Features
roads	hills	lakes
sheds	slopes	streams
fences	cliff faces	rivers

While Lynch and Evans studied urban environments, Whitaker and colleagues examined the landmarks used in navigating natural environments. In a natural environment, any large man-made object stands out. Accordingly, experts in orienteering (natural environment navigation) relied most on manmade objects as cues when navigating [34]. They also used land contours and water features. However, they tried not to rely on vegetation since it is a rapidly changing, and therefore unreliable, feature in natural environments [33].

- **Guideline 5: Landmarks should be visible at all navigable scales.**

Finally, one can consider environment scales that differ from that of a city [12]. For instance, on a larger scale, a cognitive map of a country could have cities themselves as

landmarks. It is not unusual for a user to have the ability to view a VE at different scales by "zooming in" or "zooming out". In such cases, it is important for the designer to provide landmarks at all the scales in which navigation takes place.

It is important to remember that the distinctiveness of an object is a crucial factor in its serving as a landmark. Consequently, it is important to apply the features from Tables 2 and 3 selectively. In the following section, this issue of distinctiveness is explored further.

Distinctiveness

- **Guideline 6: A landmark must be easy to distinguish from nearby objects and other landmarks.**

- **Guideline 7: The sides of a landmark must differ from each other.**

Objects intended to serve as landmarks must be distinctive in several ways. First, they must be distinctive in regard to nearby objects. Accordingly, Evans and colleagues note that a building that stands out from others on the same street is significantly more likely to be remembered [11]. Second, a landmark must be easy to distinguish from other landmarks, especially nearby ones. Otherwise, a navigator could confuse one landmark with another, and, as a result, select the wrong navigational action (e.g. make a wrong turn). This error is so common in the sport of orienteering, which involves navigation in natural environments, that it has been given a name: a parallel error [5]. Third, the sides of each landmark should differ from one another. These differences can help navigators determine their orientation. In contrast, consider a pine tree that is fairly symmetrical around the vertical axis. Because of its symmetry, the tree looks the same whether one is facing it from the East, from the West, or from any other direction in that plane. Consequently, navigators cannot use the tree to determine their orientation around the vertical axis (yaw). Without knowing one's own orientation, selecting a direction of travel to reach a destination becomes impossible. Navigation, other than aimless wandering, is therefore impossible. Accordingly, informal observation of navigators of a VE has revealed the superiority of asymmetrical landmarks in supporting navigation [6].

- **Guideline 8: Landmark distinctiveness can be increased by placing other objects nearby.**

Where a single object is not distinctive enough, a pair of objects may suffice. Consider again the radially symmetrical pine tree. Due to the tree's symmetry around the vertical axis, it is difficult to tell from which direction one is viewing it. However, by inserting a lamppost next to the tree, the viewing direction is disambiguated. From one direction, the lamppost is in front of the tree. From the opposite direction, the tree hides the lamppost. Viewed from another direction the tree is to the *left* of the lamppost, while viewed from the opposite direction the tree is to the *right* of the lamppost. This technique can also differentiate the views from directions falling around the horizontal axes. Moreover, it can be used to differentiate two similar landmarks. Here, one need only insert a different object near one (or each) landmark. The designer should keep in mind however that it is likely to be more difficult for navigators to determine their positions or orientations under these circumstances. With several objects, the spatial relationships between them must be considered in order to determine the viewpoint's orientation or position. This processing is not required when a single object provides unambiguous position or orientation information. It is the additional processing required with several objects that probably makes it more difficult for navigators to estimate their positions and orientations from several objects. Nevertheless, some VE navigators have been observed relying on configurations of landmarks to obtain orientation information [6].

- **Guideline 9: Landmarks must carry a common element to distinguish them, as a group, from data objects.**

Finally, consider VEs whose features are constrained by the underlying data, such as the human circulatory system. Although some of the objects in these VEs can serve as landmarks, it is possible to further assist navigation by augmenting the VE with additional objects that only function as landmarks. However, navigators must easily recognize these objects as landmarks and realize that they are *only* landmarks. To continue the circulatory example, navigators should not take an artificial landmark for a blood cell. Otherwise, navigators could develop misconceptions about blood cells (e.g. about their motion, position, or shape). Consequently, in such VEs it is important for landmarks to carry some common element that distinguishes them from the other virtual objects. For instance, artificial landmarks in the circulatory system could appear solid and angular, like a truck, in contrast to the soft, bulbous objects shown travelling through the blood. Nonetheless, these artificial landmarks must still be distinctive as described above.

In sum, it is possible to compose VE landmarks with the features navigators use to select landmarks in the real world. Thus, navigators' experience and navigational abilities can transfer from real environments to virtual ones. The common theme in the selection of landmarks seems to be their distinctiveness. However, not only the appearance of landmarks is important to navigation. Their placement must also be carefully considered, as we see below.

Combining Paths and Landmarks: Landmark Placement
- **Guideline 10: Place landmarks on major paths and at path junctions.**

Evans and colleagues found that the memorability of a building and its position was also affected by the building's location in the environment [11] (Table 4). In short, memorability is enhanced when the building is located on a major path or at a path junction (see also [14]). These

findings highlight the importance of including paths in a VE to provide a structure for placing landmarks. The correct placement of landmarks enhances their memorability and consequently, eases navigation.

Table 4: Building Positions Contributing to Memorability.

Located on major path [m]	Visible from major road [lm]
Direct access from street (esp. no plaza or porch) [lm]	
Located at important choice points in circulation pattern [m]	

[m] Increases memorability of building.
[l] Improves memory for building location.

Paths can also facilitate navigation by guiding the navigator to points of possible interest. Moreover, paths provide a way for the designer to minimize the number of landmarks in the VE while still supporting navigation. The recommendation to use to landmarks to support navigation can be problematic for a designer of large-scale VEs. To maintain an acceptable level of interactivity, a VE designer will want to limit the number and complexity of virtual objects in the environment. On the other hand, to support navigation, especially the acquisition and use of route knowledge, the designer must include many landmarks in the VE. Specifically, when at least two landmarks can be seen from each viewpoint, navigators can represent a route from one place to another as a string of landmarks. This allows navigators to follow the whole route by moving from one landmark to the next. Supporting all possible routes through a VE in this way would require a vast number of landmarks. Paths allow the designer to minimize the number of landmarks, thus enhancing interactivity, while still supporting navigation. Here, many of the landmarks are placed at path junctions, and a few others are placed along the paths themselves. Navigators use the landmarks along the paths for distance estimation and course verification [33][34]. When navigators reach a path junction, they select the appropriate navigational action (e.g. turn left) via landmark recognition. Thus, paths support the acquisition and use of route knowledge with fewer landmarks.

In sum, it is important to use both paths and landmarks to support navigation; especially navigation based on route knowledge. Nonetheless, when the spatial properties of virtual objects represent data, route knowledge is insufficient to provide an understanding of the relationships in the data. Survey knowledge is needed for this purpose. The common distortions in survey knowledge must also be minimized. Guidelines for this are presented in the following section.

Minimizing Distortions in Cognitive Maps
The term "cognitive map" is misleading in that it suggests that mental representations of environments are very much like images. In reality, our cognitive maps contain many features that are not image-like. Cognitive maps contain categorical and hierarchical structures [3][16][31], and many spatial distortions, some of which cannot even be

represented in an image [15][20][30][35]. Distance asymmetry is an example of such a distortion. A distance asymmetry involves representing two different distances between two points, e.g. A and B, wherein the A to B distance is different from the B to A distance. Both of these distances cannot be represented in a single image. Since people use their cognitive maps to navigate [25], distortions in their cognitive maps can be confusing and lead to navigational errors. Moreover, such distortions will warp a navigator's understanding of data represented by data objects. For these reasons, it is important to minimize these distortions. Studies have shown that these distortions diminish with increased navigational experience [9][13][22]. However, it is possible to structure an environment to minimize the development of these distortions in the first place. This requires an understanding of the types of distortions and their causes. Accordingly, this is presented first, followed by an examination of the design guidelines.

Sources of Distortions

Many distortions seem to result from the hierarchical structure of cognitive maps [3][16]. These hierarchies can be formed by clustering objects that fall within identifiable boundaries to form districts (see Table 1). For instance, all the cities in one state (a district) can form a cluster. When there are no objective boundaries, clusters can form around anchor points, which can be important landmarks [4][6][16]. A multi-level hierarchy can develop wherein districts themselves are clustered at a higher level [16]. An example of a hierarchy-induced distortion is provided by Stevens and Coupe [28]. Participants in one experiment reported that San Diego California is west of Reno Nevada. This response resulted from an inference based on the hierarchical relationship between the cities and their containing states. People reasoned that since San Diego is in California, Reno is in Nevada, and that California is west of Nevada, then San Diego must also be west of Reno. Distances can also be distorted. Here, people underestimate the distances between objects in the same district, while overestimating distances between objects from different districts [16]. In sum, cognitive map hierarchies can produce distortions of relative directions and distances.

Distortions are also produced by mental heuristics that help us remember the layout of objects [30]. One heuristic aligns the main axes of nearby objects. Main axes are provided by an object's shape and/or its most salient features. For example, people drew a map of Palo Alto California showing familiar streets as being more parallel than they are in reality. Another heuristic is to rotate an object relative to its background, so the object's main axes line up with the background's [30]. For example, residents of Umeå Sweden misrepresented the northern direction so that it corresponded with Umeå's street grid [13]. Tversky speculates that an environment's axes (e.g. the axes of Umeå's street grid) provide a possible framework on which to construct the type of hierarchy described above. She also

notes that the alignment and rotation heuristics could be responsible for rectilinear normalization, the tendency to distort environmental features into a grid [30][35].

In sum, hierarchical structures and Tversky's heuristics can explain several, though not all, of the distortions found in cognitive maps. By understanding how distortions come about, we can design VEs to minimize them. Three guidelines for doing so are discussed in the following section.

The Grid

- **Guideline 11: Arrange paths and edges (see Table 1) to form a grid.**

- **Guideline 12: Align the landmarks' main axes with the path/edge grid's main axes.**

- **Guideline 13: Align each landmark's main axes with those of the other landmarks.**

To minimize the distortions, the designer must create a VE that induces a hierarchical representation whose districts form a grid. A consequence of the grid's spatial regularity is that the spatial relationships between districts are a good approximation of the spatial relationships between objects in those districts. For instance, if district A is to the left of district B, then all objects in A are to the left of all objects in B. Consequently, judgments about the relative positions of objects are not so distorted, even though these judgments are based on the spatial relationships between districts. Figure 1 shows theoretical direction distortions for districts forming a grid and an irregular shape. (The irregular districts correspond to the California and Nevada example from the Sevens and Coupe study discussed previously.) A grid structure still produces some distortions, but they are smaller than those produced by an irregular structure.

Figure 1: Cognitive Map Direction Distortions in Grid-Form and Irregular Districts.

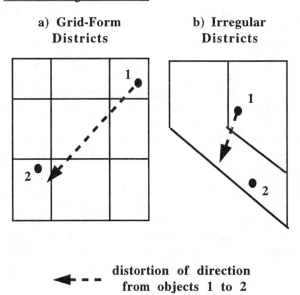

a) **Grid-Form Districts**   b) **Irregular Districts**

◀- - -   **distortion of direction from objects 1 to 2**

Accordingly, it has been shown that distance and direction judgements are more accurate in environments with street grids [10][13]. The question then is how to encourage the navigator to construct a grid-like representation? It appears that people use cues in an environment to structure their spatial hierarchies [6][16][30]. Consequently, the designer should arrange the environment's paths and edges to form a grid.

Each landmark's main axes should be aligned with the other landmarks' main axes and the path/edge grid's too. This will reinforce the grid-like districting. Moreover, it will substantially reduce distortions due to rotation and alignment. Since the landmarks are already aligned, the navigator will not need to bring them into alignment by distorting their position. Since the landmarks' axes and the environment's axes already coincide, the navigator will not need to rotate the landmarks or the environment. Finally, rectilinear normalization does not need to be performed since the objects in the environment are already rectilinear.

Darken and Sibert placed a generic grid on the surfaces of their VEs. However, the grid's structure was incompatible with the environments' (i.e. the above guidelines were violated). The grid did improve navigability, but statistical comparisons between the grid and no grid conditions were not computed. Some analyses revealed that the grid could *interfere* with the acquisition of survey knowledge [7]. This most likely occurred because of the structural incompatibility between the grid and VEs. These results reveal the importance of following the guidelines presented above.

CONCLUSION

This paper focused on the use of landmarks in human navigation. Landmarks not only indicate position and orientation, but also contribute to the development of spatial knowledge. Therefore, a VE containing distinctive landmarks supports navigation by facilitating the acquisition and application of spatial knowledge.

The substantial research on human navigation in real environments was used to formulate guidelines for landmark design. Guidelines to increase the accuracy of a navigator's spatial knowledge were also presented. Because the guidelines are based on real-world navigation, VE navigators are encouraged to transfer their real-world navigational abilities. Consequently, following these guidelines in constructing VEs will make them more navigable.

The guidelines presented here can be considered design rules-of-thumb – untested generalizations from one domain to another. Brooks notes that VE designers are in need of such rules-of-thumb [2]. Accordingly, these guidelines can be of use to VE designers who have little research interest in navigation. Specifically, navigational problems can interfere with concurrent tasks that are the topics of research. The VE designer can follow these guidelines to ease navigation and thus allow users to focus on the tasks

of interest. On the other hand, where navigation is the research topic, these guidelines can be used as starting points for empirical testing or further hypothesis generation.

ACKNOWLEDGEMENTS
The author thanks Janice Singer and Marceli Wein for their comments.

REFERENCES

1. Billinghurst, M. & Weghorst, S. The use of sketch maps to measure cognitive maps of virtual environments, in *Proceedings of IEEE 1995 Virtual Reality Annual International Symposium*, IEEE Computer Society: Los Alamitos, CA, 1995, 40-47.

2. Brooks, F. P. Jr. Grasping reality through illusion — Interactive graphics serving science, in *Proceedings of CHI '88 Conference on Human Factors in Computing Systems*, ACM Press, 1988, 1-11.

3. Chase, W. G. Visual information processing, in *Handbook of perception and human performance, Vol II: Cognitive processes and performance*, K.R. Boff, L. Kaufman, & J.P. Thomas (Eds.), John Wiley and Sons, 1986, pp. 28-1 to 28-71.

4. Couclelis, H., Golledge, R. G., Gale, N. D., & Tobler, W. R. Exploring the anchor point hypothesis of spatial cognition, *Journal of Environmental Psychology*, 7, 1987, 99-122.

5. Darken, R. P. & Banker, W. P. Navigating in natural environments: A virtual environment training transfer study, in *Proceedings of IEEE 1998 Virtual Reality Annual International Symposium*, IEEE Computer Society: Los Alamitos, CA, 1998, 12-19.

6. Darken, R. P. & Sibert, J. L. A toolset for navigation in virtual environments, in *Proceedings of UIST '93* (Atlanta GA, Nov. 1993), ACM Press, 158-165.

7. Darken, R. P. & Sibert, J. L. Navigating large virtual spaces. *International Journal of Human-Computer Interaction*, 8, 1, 1996, 49-71.

8. Evans, G. W. Environmental cognition, *Psychological Bulletin*, 88, 1980, 259-287.

9. Evans, G. W., Marrero, D. G., Butler, P. A., Environmental learning and cognitive mapping, *Environment and Behavior*, 13, *1981*, 83-104.

10. Evans, G. W., Skorpanich, M. A., Gärling, T., Bryant, K. J., & Bresolin, B., The effects of pathway configuration, landmarks, and stress on environmental cognition, *Journal of Environmental Psychology*, 4, 1984, 323-335.

11. Evans, G. W., Smith, C. & Pezdek, K., Cognitive maps and urban form, *Journal of the American Planning Associations*, 48, 1982, 232-244.

12. Gärling, T., Böök, A, & Lindberg, E., Cognitive mapping of large-scale environments: The

interrelationship of action plans, acquisition, and orientation, *Environment and Behavior*, *16*, 1984, 3-34.

13. Gärling, T., Lindberg, E., Carreiras, M. & Böök, A. Reference systems in cognitive maps, *Journal of Environmental Psychology*, *6*, 1986, 1-18.

14. Golledge, R. G, Smith, T. R., Pellegrino, J. W., Doherty, S., & Marshall, S. P. A conceptual model and empirical analysis of children's acquisition of spatial knowledge, *Journal of Environmental Psychology*, *5*, 1985, 125-152.

15. Golledge, R. G. & Stimson, R. J. *Spatial Behavior.* The Guilford Press: New York, NY, 1997.

16. Hirtle, S. C., & Jonides, J., Evidence of hierarchies in cognitive maps, *Memory & Cognition*, *13*, 1985, 208-217.

17. Kuipers, B., Modeling spatial knowledge, *Cognitive Science*, *2*, 1978, 129-153.

18. Lawton, C. A. Gender differences in way-finding strategies: Relationship to spatial ability and spatial anxiety, *Sex Roles*, *30*, 11/12, 1994, 765-779.

19. Lynch, K. *The Image of the City.* MIT Press: Cambridge, MA, 1960.

20. Moar, I., & Bower, G. H., Inconsistency in spatial knowledge, *Memory & Cognition*, *11*, 1983, 107-113.

21. Montello, D. R. A new framework for understanding the acquisition of spatial knowledge in large-scale environments, in *Spatial and Temporal Reasoning in Geographic Information Systems*, M. J. Eganhofer & R. Golledge (Eds.), Oxford University Press, 1998, 143-154.

22. Moore, G. T., Developmental differences in environmental cognition, in *Environmental Design Research*, W Preisser (Ed.), Dowden, Hutchinson, and Ross: Stroudsburg, PA, 1973.

23. Passini, R., Way-finding in complex buildings: An environmental analysis, *Man-Environment Systems*, *10*, 1980-31-40.

24. Pausch, R., Burnette, T., Brockway, D., & Weiblen, M. E. Navigation and locomotion in virtual worlds via flight into hand-held miniatures, in *Proceedings of ACM Siggraph '95, Computer Graphics*, July 1995.

25. Rovine, M. J., & Weisman, G. D., Sketch-map variables as predictors of way-finding performance, *Journal of Environmental Psychology*, *9*, 1989, 217-232.

26. Ruddle, R. P., Payne, S. J., & Jones, D. M. Navigating buildings in "desk-top" virtual environments: Experimental investigations using extended navigational experience. *Journal of Experimental Psychology: Applied*, *3*, 2, 1997, 143-159.

27. Song, D. & Norman, M. Nonlinear interactive motion control techniques for virtual space navigation, in *Proceedings of IEEE 1993 Virtual Reality Annual International Symposium*, IEEE Computer Society: Los Alamitos, CA, 1993, 111-117.

28. Stevens, A., & Coupe, P., Distortions in judged spatial relations, *Cognitive psychology*, *10*, 1978, 422-437.

29. Thorndyke, P. W., & Hayes-Roth, B. Differences in spatial knowledge acquired from maps and navigation, *Cognitive Psychology*, *14*, 1982, 560-589.

30. Tversky, B., Distortions in memory for maps, *Cognitive Psychology*, *13*, 1981, 407-433.

31. Tversky, B., Franklin, N., Taylor, H. A., Bryant, D. J. Spatial mental models from descriptions. *Journal of the American Society for Information Science, 45*, 9, 1994, 656-669.

32. Ware, C. & Slipp, L. Using velocity control to navigate 3D graphical environments: A comparison of three interfaces, in *Proceedings of the Human Factors Society 35th Annual Meeting*, (San Francisco, CA, Sept. 1991), Human Factors Society: Santa Monica, CA, 300-304.

33. Whitaker, L. A. Getting around in the natural world. *Ergonomics in Design*, *4*, 3, 1996, 11-15.

34. Whitaker, L. A., & Cuqlock-Knopp, G. Navigation in off-road environments: Orienteering interviews. *Scientific Journal of Orienteering*, *8*, 1992, 55-71.

35. Wickens, C. D. *Engineering Psychology and Human Performance, 2nd ed.* Harper Collins Publishers Inc.: New York, 1992.

Single Display Groupware:
A Model for Co-present Collaboration

Jason Stewart
Computer Science Dept.
University of New Mexico
Albuquerque, NM 87106
jasons@cs.unm.edu

Benjamin B. Bederson
Computer Science Dept. / UMIACS
Human-Computer Interaction Lab
University of Maryland
College Park, MD 20742
+1 301 405 2764
bederson@cs.umd.edu

Allison Druin
College of Education / UMIACS
Human-Computer Interaction Lab
University of Maryland
College Park, MD 20742
+1 301 405 7406
allisond@umiacs.umd.edu

ABSTRACT

We introduce a model for supporting collaborative work between people that are physically close to each other. We call this model Single Display Groupware (SDG). In this paper, we describe the model, comparing it to more traditional remote collaboration. We describe the requirements that SDG places on computer technology, and our understanding of the benefits and costs of SDG systems. Finally, we describe a prototype SDG system that we built and the results of a usability test we ran with 60 elementary school children.

Keywords

CSCW, Single Display Groupware, children, educational applications, input devices, Pad++, KidPad.

INTRODUCTION

In the early 1970's, researchers at Xerox PARC created an atmosphere in which they lived and worked with technology of the future. When the world's first personal computer, the Alto, was invented, it had only a single keyboard and mouse. This fundamental design legacy has carried through to nearly all modern computer systems. Although networks have allowed people to collaborate at a distance, the primary assumption still remains that only a single individual would need to access the display at any time.

Is this a valid assumption? Do we really work in isolation, without the desire to interact with one another around a computer? When designing technology for elementary school children, we frequently observed two, three, and four children crowded around a computer screen each trying to interact with the computer application [7]. It also appeared to us that children enjoyed their experiences with the computer more if they had control of the mouse and were actively controlling the application. Since there are times when multiple people would like to each interact with

a computer application, how does the lack of technological support affect people's collaborative behavior? Could we as technology designers improve collaboration by explicitly designing computer support for collaboration at a single computer display? We believe that we can, and in this paper, we introduce a model for doing so.

We define Single Display Groupware (SDG) to be computer programs that enable co-present users to collaborate via a shared computer with a single shared display and simultaneous use of multiple input devices. We have focused on the use of a single display because it most accurately reflects how computers are used today.

Recent work including our own has begun to explore SDG. In this paper, we attempt to create a framework that ties together these different approaches, and motivate future system designers to include low-level support for SDG.

Scenarios

Let us imagine ourselves in the computing environment of the not-so-distant future where there is universal support for co-present collaboration:

At work, you are visiting the office of a co-worker to get feedback on your latest project. Since the Personal Data Assistant (PDA) you carry uses wireless networking technology, you can easily communicate with your co-worker's computer. After she approves your log-on request, you start up your demo on her monitor, and use the touch screen of the PDA to control a cursor on her workstation. While she uses her workstation's mouse to use your program, you gesture with your cursor indicating the areas you had questions about. As you expected, she finds a number of bugs in your code. But since you are both able to interact with the software, you work around the bugs without interrupting her or taking the input device out of her hand.

At the designer's office, you review the plans for the renovation of your living room. After going over some of the paper sketches, the designer offers to show you the 3D model of the renovation on his computer. He thinks it will give you a better idea of how his plans fit in with the rest of the house. As he guides the program into the living room, he encourages you to pick up the extra mouse and investigate the layout yourself. You have some trouble navigating with the unfamiliar software at first, but the designer demonstrates the navigation tools with his mouse and you quickly learn to mimic him. Together you both relocate furniture and experiment with different room layouts and color schemes.

At school, your daughter is finishing work on her latest geometry project. She's having difficulty with the Pythagorean theorem and asks the teacher for help. The teacher is busy helping a group of students working at the other collaborative learning station, so your daughter's friend comes over to help. Her friend picks up one of the unused mice and together they explore the problem. They work together moving around the squares and triangles and measuring the results until they both feel more comfortable with the Pythagorean theorem.

Despite the fact that Computer-Supported Cooperative Work (CSCW) is a thriving field, and networked computing is one of the biggest selling points of computers today, the scenarios described above are not part of today's world of computing. What is missing is that the forms of collaboration we suggest here are *co-present* collaboration. Most research in CSCW today focuses on supporting people that are working apart from each other. Computers and networks are very well suited to supporting remote collaboration, but supporting people that are working together requires solutions to new problems.

Based on the computer paradigm discussed in this paper, Single Display Groupware (SDG), we suggest an increase in effort that investigates technology that brings people together and enhances the interaction of people working together.

Related Work

Several projects support people collaborating in the same room. The CoLab project, like other electronic meeting rooms, provided each member with a desktop computer which allowed private work as well as control of a shared display at the front of the room [17]. Earlier shared rooms were built by Krueger as installation art pieces [13]. One drawback of electronic collaborative rooms is that they require expensive, specialized hardware that is prohibitive to many people who could benefit from enhanced support for co-present collaboration, for example school children.

The Liveboard digital whiteboard and the Tivoli application enabled multiple simultaneous users (both co-present and remote) to interact with the shared digital whiteboard [17]. The authors point out that simultaneous use of the whiteboard rarely occurred and they speculated that the lack of adequate software level support for co-present collaboration (of the kind presented in this paper) may have been the cause. Given the publicly available information on this project, it is not clear to what extent SDG was supported.

The Pebbles project [15], investigates the use of handheld Personal Digital Assistants (PDAs) as portable input devices in an SDG setting. They have also explored the limitations of current GUI application toolkits and what is needed to make toolkits support SDG.

Another implementation of SDG was MMM [3]. It enabled multiple co-present users to interact with multiple editors on the same computer display by providing each user with an independent input device. The system was never made available to the research community, and no user studies were conducted to investigate the limitations of the idea. MMM was not pursued, but some of the researchers working on it transferred this technology to study the use of multi-handed input for single users.

Other researchers have investigated how SDG technology could influence groups in a learning environment. Work by Inkpen showed that by providing each user with a separate input device gave significant learning improvements, even when only one device could be active at a time. The active device could be toggled through a predetermined access protocol [10]. This is an important result because it indicates that SDG could benefit tasks in which both users are not expected to work simultaneously, such as editing a paper.

Bricker built software architectures that enable building SDG applications that teach collaborative skills [4]. The guiding metaphor of applications built with her SDG architecture is the 3-legged race: the goal is not only to run the race faster, but also to require participants to learn to cooperate in order to be able to run at all. Example applications include a color-matcher in which 3 users must find the RGB values for a given color, and a chord matcher where users find the notes for a given chord.

Rekimoto's multi-device approach enables users to create work on a palmtop computer and then move the data onto a shared public computer, such as a digital whiteboard, using the Pick and Drop protocol [18]. Work by Greenberg and Boyle has also been investigating the boundaries between public and private work by designing applications that can be used collaboratively in both an SDG setting using PDAs or over a network using a workstation [8].

McGrath and Hollingshead conducted a critical review of empirical studies to date of how technology impacted group interaction [14]. An important contribution of this work was a comprehensive listing of variables that should be evaluated when testing the effect that any technology has on group processes. For example, McGrath lists three outcome variables that can be measured: task performance, user reactions, and member relations. The first two outcome variables are commonly measured, but the third, how using technology influences how group members feel about one another, was not commonly measured.

There are other examples of technological support for co-present collaboration that we place in the category of hardware interfaces. Included in this category are vehicles with multiple steering mechanisms, such as aircraft flight controls and driver education cars. Although these systems enable simultaneous co-present users through multiple input devices, they have little or no software interfaces and can teach us little about the design of more general-purpose SDG systems. Other examples of SDG systems include some multiplayer video games. While these are software based, they primarily support users navigating through scenes and shooting things, playing ball, or fighting. They do not support shared creation of information. And, aside from spatial navigation, they do not support much information retrieval. So, while the social issues of video games are interesting to SDG designers, they do not offer us much guidance for interface development.

Input Channels and Output Channels

To better understand the implications that SDG will have on computer system design we need to investigate how SDG applications differ from other applications. User Interfaces consist of *input channels* – which enable users to communicate with the computer, and *output channels* – which enable the computer to communicate with its users.

We define an input channel to be an input device that provides *independent* input to the computer. So for example, in current computer systems the mouse and the keyboard would not be considered separate input channels since the keyboard input is dependent upon the mouse for setting keyboard focus. Future computer systems may support an independent mouse and keyboard but current ones do not, so the *typical* current system will be described as having only a single input channel. In some cases, such as laptop computers, a computer has multiple pointing devices, *i.e.,* an external mouse and a trackpad. These devices are also dependent and share the same input channel—either both share control of the system cursor, or only one can be active at a time. This definition covers the observation that dividing up tasks by giving one user the mouse and another the keyboard is not likely to result in a good collaborative experience [16 p. 89].

We define an output channel as a part of the computer interface that uses an independent modality to provide user feedback. Examples would be a display for visual feedback, speakers for audio feedback, and a force-feedback joystick for haptic feedback. Most current computers have the potential of using both visual and audio feedback, but most UIs use little or no audio feedback and rely almost exclusively on visual feedback. There are exceptions to this, such as audio systems for blind users, but these are in the overwhelming minority of existing systems. This could change with future systems, but the *typical* current system will be described as providing a single output channel.

Single Display Groupware and Traditional Groupware

Most computer applications written today are single user applications – they have no special support for multiple users. In contrast, groupware applications are *group aware*, they have a fundamental knowledge of multiple users. SDG

is a subset of groupware that focuses on co-present collaboration: multiple users at the same time and place.

Traditional groupware systems create applications that are intended to be run on multiple workstations and can communicate with one another across a computer network. They either communicate in a distributed fashion where each database is synchronized, or with a single centralized server. Similar to a single user application (Figure 1), a traditional groupware application provides both a single input channel and a single output channel for each user (Figure 2).

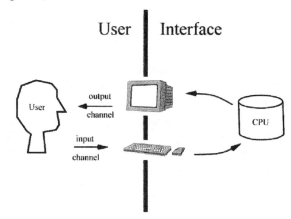

Figure 1: The User Interface for Single User Applications

In contrast, SDG applications provide an input channel for each user through the use of a separate input device, but each must share the single output channel (see Figure 3). These are the qualities that give SDG applications their unique character: the combination of multiple independent input channels together with a single shared output channel. There have been traditional groupware systems which chose to use a shared user interface, or coupled navigation, but the conclusions were that doing so limited the functionality of the application for no apparent gain when the users were *remote* [6, 19].

The Model-View-Controller (MVC) language of the Smalltalk community provides another way of expressing this concept. The Model corresponds to the underlying information of the program, the data. The View corresponds to that part which controls the output channels of the system, while the Controller corresponds to the part that handles the input. Traditional groupware systems have a single shared Model, and since each user has a separate computer, each has a separate View-Controller pair that communicates with the shared Model. SDG systems also have a single shared Model, but differ from traditional groupware systems by only having a single shared View through which the computer must give feedback to all users, and a single shared Controller through which all users interact with the computer. SDG applications could have multiple controllers if an application wanted to replicate all user interface elements and provide every user with a unique copy. This solution seems unlikely to scale as it would quickly take up all available screen space for the user interface.

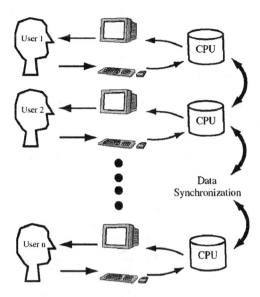

Figure 2: Traditional groupware

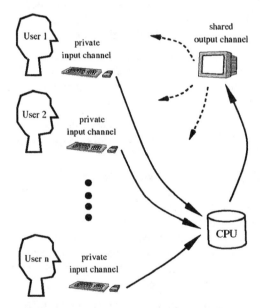

Figure 3: Single Display Groupware

Both the MVC model and the previous discussion about input channels and output channels, help bring out some of the central differences between designing SDG and traditional groupware systems which are:

Shared User Interface. Even though users have separate input devices, the user interface elements that are used to communicate with the computer (menus, palettes, buttons, etc.) must be designed to handle multiple simultaneous users. This restriction corresponds to the single shared Controller in the MVC description.

Shared Feedback. The user interface elements used by the computer to communication state information to users (buttons, palettes, etc.) will likewise be shared by all users and must be capable of relaying information to all users simultaneously. This is a consequence of the shared View from the MVC discussion.

Coupled Navigation. Whenever one user navigates to a different part of the Model the other users will be affected. If the coupling is tight, then all users will navigate together when one navigates. If the coupling is loose, then other users may have part of their Views obscured by one user navigating to a different area of the Model.

Why Single Display?
We could have chosen to expand the scope of this model to include multiple output devices, and called it Co-Present Groupware (CPG). The goal of this work, however, was to study the architectural concerns that arise while supporting multi-user collaboration around a single Personal Computer (PC). The overwhelming majority of current PC systems provide only a single display, and rely almost solely on that display for output. Some feedback is given using an audio channel, but almost never are touch, taste, or smell used [5, 11]. When users collaborate around a single computer, they consider themselves to be collaborating around the display and not the CPU, hard drive, or CD-ROM drive. For these reasons we chose the single shared display as the central metaphor for this new paradigm.

The single display metaphor is also intended to connote several properties of applications that are designed for co-present use. Not only do such groupware systems have shared data, they also possess a shared UI and shared or coupled navigation. What constitutes a single display? If a single computer has multiple displays, does that mean it is not using SDG? What about full wall projection devices that use three projectors to create a single *seamless* display? What constitutes a display? A blind person may use a computer whose only feedback is sound, is SDG therefore not for blind people?

While Co-Present Groupware is a more general form of SDG, we decided to focus on the use of a single display because it most accurately reflected current computer use. Therefore we will not include examples which relax the strict conditions imposed by having multiple co-present users at a single display. For example, by using a two-monitor computer each user could be given their own UI, and the shared user interface restriction no longer applies. However, if the use of the second monitor is solely to provide extra physical screen space and not to provide an independent UI, then the conditions still apply and the system could still be considered SDG.

TRADEOFFS IN SINGLE DISPLAY GROUPWARE
Current computer systems do little to encourage collaboration of multiple users. Single user systems provide only one explicit input channel for all users, so if multiple users attempt to collaborate using such a system it is up to the users to develop a sharing mechanism for utilizing that

channel. In contrast, SDG applications will have an inherent notion of multiple co-present users and will provide each user with an equivalent input channel. This could have an impact on many aspects of using computers together. Some possible benefits are:

- Enabling collaboration that was previously inhibited by social barriers. For example, in many cultures there is often a reluctance to invade the personal space of another person. The personal space surrounding close friends is smaller than that surrounding co-workers and acquaintances, and the space surrounding strangers is the largest of the three [9; Chapter X]. Due to these proximate effects, many people may be inhibited from attempting to share a computer when another person is sitting in front of it. By explicitly providing for a separate input channel, the personal space around the person may be decreased enough to allow another person to comfortably interact with the computer at the same time.

- Enabling types of interaction that require multiple users. Bricker has explored a number of collaborative interactions that require multiple simultaneous users at a single computer. The goal of her research was to create tools that would strengthen collaborative learning [4].

- Enriching existing collaboration at a computer. For example, turn taking is often viewed as unnecessary and cumbersome [19]. Enabling multiple input devices will in some cases enable work to be done in parallel, making the collaboration both more efficient and more enjoyable in the eyes of the users [7, 22]. Also, a number of studies have indicated the benefit of shoulder-to-shoulder collaboration due to the collaborators enhanced verbal and nonverbal communications [9 p. 108–111, 20].

- Reducing or eliminating conflict when multiple users attempt to interact with a single application. Often it is difficult to create an appropriate sharing mechanism for the shared channels, or it is difficult to obey the mechanism created [22]. By providing separate channels, potential conflicts are pushed one step further away.

- Encouraging peer-learning and peer-teaching. When existing single user technology is used in a collaborative learning setting, the competition between users to interact with the application can inhibit the learning benefits of collaboration [22]. By providing applications with multiple communication channels, it is possible to enrich learning by diminishing competition for access to the input channels [16 p. 89].

- Strengthening communication skills. Because strong willed users can no longer monopolize a task by merely controlling the input device, users may *have* to communicate more with each other to resolve conflicts.

Along with the potential benefits of the new computer paradigm comes the potential for negative effects:

- New conflicts and frustrations may arise between users when they attempt simultaneous incompatible actions. Working in parallel can be an advantage, but it could also be a disadvantage if users each have separate conflicting agendas. One serious concern in this area is navigation. Since there is only a single shared output channel (the display), if one user decides to navigate elsewhere in the data space, it may negatively affect the other users.

- SDG applications must squeeze functionality into a very limited screen space, which may result in reduced functionality compared with similar single-user programs.

- Due to increased processing requirements, SDG applications might be slower than a single user version, or a traditional groupware version.

- Because successful SDG implementation depends on low-level operating system and windowing system issues, applications may not be very portable and might exist for only the most popular OSs.

- Completing tasks might take more time, because it is no longer possible for a strong willed user to direct the collaboration by controlling the input device.

- Users may actually collaborate less. Because they can do work in parallel, they may set about completing their own tasks and never communicate with the other users.

In order to build successful SDG applications, these tradeoffs will have to be carefully balanced for each application.

POTENTIAL APPLICATION DOMAINS

SDG is presented to complement the existing single user paradigms, not to replace them. Even so, it is anticipated that there will be collaborative situations in which co-present interaction at a single display will not be as useful as networked synchronous collaboration or asynchronous collaboration. We expect SDG to be potentially useful in at least the following domains:

Creative Domain where users are involved in a creative, expressive, or constructive task such as writing, drawing, artistic expression, programming, and brainstorming. Creative projects often benefit from group activity and input, but the restrictive nature of current systems can limit expression. The potential benefits of using SDG in this domain include being able to work more effectively by working in parallel and eliminate unnecessary turn taking.

Learning Domain where users are involved in the exploration of new material such as a problem solving environment, learning new technology, debugging, or simulations. Learning has been shown to be a domain in which group activity is important [12]. Learning around current computer systems can create an inequality in the partners due to the difference in their skills and the restrictions of only having a single input device [7, 10, 22]. Potential benefits of using SDG in this domain include more effective learning by being able to work at the same time with the same objects, reducing the cognitive difference between partners by giving each parallel access.

Instruction Domain where one user is more experienced than the other and has skill or knowledge to impart such as training to use software, peer teaching in a classroom, or informal help from an instructor.

Sales Domain where a sales person and customer could configure items together. The crucial point is that by allowing customers to play an active role in the selection and configuration process they may be more inclined to choose one product supplier over another.

One area not likely to benefit from SDG is any application that can be best accomplished using a divide-and-conquer approach, such as data entry. Because Inkpen's work shows that adding multiple input devices can benefit tasks in which users are not expected to work simultaneously, there are many areas in which it is unknown how effective SDG could be. For example, when collaboratively editing a paper for a conference, would it be effective to use multiple keyboards, or would it be better to provide the second user with highlighting and gesturing tools instead.

LOCAL TOOLS

In order to investigate how SDG affects group interactions at a single display, we implemented a general-purpose architecture to build SDG applications, the Local Tools architecture. The underlying operating system and event model was built using the Linux operating system, and the X Window System. The application layer was built using the Tk toolkit and Pad++ [2], and was written in Perl. This section will describe some of the important high level issues. While a complete description of the architecture and its implementation are provided elsewhere [21], the following discussion is intended as a motivation for why future systems should include low-level support for SDG.

The current Windows, Icons, Menus, and Pointers (WIMP) metaphor for building GUI applications has a number of limitations when used to build SDG applications. Many toolkits have implemented widgets that do not work in the SDG paradigm (e.g., they use global variables that assume single users). Many applications store user state information in global variables leading to shared interface state such as a single pen color or font. Even if these applications were to store state per user, many feedback techniques are insufficient for displaying multi-user state (e.g., applications would have to be redesigned to have an entire interface per user).

At a high level, the interaction semantics of many widgets are designed for single users. Should locking mechanism be used to prevent multiple users from interacting with the same menubar or scrollbar? Should modal dialog boxes apply to all users or only the user who activated the dialog? What happens when one user interacts with another user's selection handles?

Because of these reasons, we chose a different metaphor that appeared to be more appropriate for use in SDG applications. We developed the "local tool" metaphor that represents tools as separate icons that lie on the data surface along with user data [1]. The goal was to represent all of the applications functionality as tools.

For example, a user chooses a crayon tool for creating freehand lines. The tool has its own pen color and line width. Once the user has chosen the tool, he/she is the only person who can configure the tool to behave differently. By clicking the crayon on the color tool, the crayon's drawing color is changed (the tool changes color to provide feedback), and by clicking on the sharpen tool, the crayon's line width is modified (the tool tip changes size to provide feedback). In the tool approach, feedback is made simpler because each user's cursor is already an enlarged tool icon, whereas more traditional approaches to feedback in SDG systems have required the use of home areas or unattractive looking cursor constructs [3, 15].

KIDPAD

In order to test the Local Tools architecture, it was necessary to build a multi-user application. Our earlier work with building a collaborative drawing program for children indicated that it would be a rich source of potential conflict and interaction and it would likely provide a task that could benefit from SDG [7].

Our earlier work also showed the importance of using an iterative design process involving children as design partners when building applications for kids. We felt that iterative design would be even more important when building applications for co-present collaboration. 72 children from a local elementary school helped design and test the KidPad application over a period of 7 months. The starting application consisted of only 3 tools, one crayon for each user, and a shared eraser. By the end of the design process the kids had helped create over 20 different tools.

Since this was to be an application that enabled users to *collaboratively* create drawings, it was important to pay attention to how the application affected user relations and their collaborative behavior more than how efficiently drawings could be created [14 p. 95]. One such example is the evolution of the eraser tool. The original eraser was overly simplistic, it would erase the entire drawing. The kids quickly got frustrated not being able to erase small mistakes without the need to start over from scratch, and asked for a better eraser. The second generation eraser allowed users to erase individual line segments, instead of the entire drawing. Upon addition of the new eraser tool, however, the collaborative behavior of the groups changed fairly dramatically. They became overly critical of each other's work ("that's ugly, get rid of it") and they spent the majority of their time erasing.

A good solution to the problem of erasing took about 3 weeks of iterative testing, and involved the creation of 3 different tools: a bomb tool for erasing all of one users work; an eraser with two modes, a rub-out mode that would only erase lines drawn by the current user and a click mode that would erase any line clicked on; and a hand tool for picking up and moving lines. Although none of these tools are new concepts for a drawing program, it was the careful combination of tools and their functionality which enabled users to perform all the desired tasks while minimizing the amount of conflicts they experienced.

Usability Test

To evaluate the success of our ideas we conducted a usability test involving 60 students in the 3rd, 4th and 5th grades of Hawthorne Elementary School in Albuquerque, NM. Students were grouped into same-sex pairs, and were randomly assigned to either a single input device condition, or an SDG condition.

Earlier pilot studies demonstrated the need to have a positive interdependence on collaborating partner's goal structures [22] as was indicated by Johnson and Johnson [12]. Therefore, the children involved in the study were told that they and their partner were a team in a design contest sponsored by the University of New Mexico. The researchers were building technology for kids and they wanted to know what kids thought about the technology they used, and what they wanted the technology of the future to look like. The teams were asked to complete a series of three drawings that would be entered as a team effort into the contest, in which all teams would compete against one another for prizes.

The children were given access to KidPad with one or two mice depending on the condition they were assigned to. They used KidPad once a week for 15 minutes during their regularly scheduled computer lab for a period of four weeks. At the final session they were given a switched condition: groups that had been using KidPad with only a single device were given multiple devices, and vice versa. All interaction with the application was logged, and each session was observed by the investigators as well as recorded on videotape for later verification of any observations. After the final session, the teams were given an informal verbal debriefing, to see how they felt about their ability to work together as a group in each condition. They were asked which condition they felt was the easiest to do drawings, which condition was the most fun, and which condition they would choose for use in other applications. Due to scheduling difficulties only 46 of the 60 students were able to complete the final session.

Results

One initially surprising result was the data for the post evaluation debriefing. We anticipated that the groups would be split as too which environment would be considered the easiest to use, a single input device or multiple input devices. Only 7 children (15%) thought that one device was easiest to complete the drawings, while 37 (85%) felt the

two device condition was easiest, and 2 children (4%) were undecided. 45 children (98%) answered that they felt that it was most fun using two devices. Only one child (2%) thought that one device was more fun. The answers for the final question (which condition kids would like to use for other computer applications) were identical to the answers for the first question (which condition was most fun). This suggests that having fun may be more important for kids than efficiency of task completion.

The children were also given the opportunity to say why they felt either condition was better. The one girl who preferred the one-input device condition did not say why. The others described why they preferred the SDG condition. A summary of the most frequent responses are:

Response	Frequency	Examples
No turn taking	49%	"We didn't have to share"
Parallel work	35%	"We can do different stuff at the same time"

Some comments worth highlighting follow. In response to our question of why they preferred SDG, one child commented "because there's two mouses!" Many of the kids thought it was obvious that two had to be better than one. Another said "if [my partner was stuck and] I wanted to help there's another mouse" – peer-teaching was an advantage that even the kids were aware of. One girl said "[with two mice] you could do whatever you want" – KidPad didn't enforce collaboration, kids could work individually if they chose.

The majority of kids (20 kids, 77%) who had used the two mouse condition complained loudly when they were only given a single mouse for the final session: "Hey! Where's the other mouse?" and "If there's only one mouse, I'm going back to work at my other computer" were typical reactions. The opposite reaction was common in groups that had only used a single mouse and were now given two mice: "Coool!" was the nearly unanimous response (18 kids, 90%). One girl didn't want to complete the final session because she was frustrated over having to share. When told she didn't need to share anymore her attitude changed completely, and she didn't want to leave the computer when their session was over.

CONCLUSION

This paper describes a model for co-present collaboration that we call Single Display Groupware. Several research groups have recently developed forms of SDG. We have tried to describe a framework for these projects to help understand common problems, and to suggest ways that technology developers should incorporate low-level support for SDG into their systems so that the scenarios we started this paper with could become a reality.

The usability studies conducted to date, both by ourselves and others, have indicated that existing technology has a number of shortcomings when used for co-present collaboration. It appears that SDG technology enables new interaction modalities and can reduce some of the shortcomings observed with existing technology. It also may create new interaction problems. To better understand the overall impact that SDG can have, and to better design SDG applications, longer-term naturalistic studies are needed, and we hope that many people will continue to develop and evaluate SDG technologies and systems.

ACKNOWLEDGEMENTS

We would like to thank Angela Boltman and the children from Hawthorne elementary school in Albuquerque, NM for making the user study of KidPad possible. In addition, we appreciate the CHIkids at CHI 96 and CHI 97 who evaluated early versions of KidPad. Finally, this work could not have been done if it weren't for the other members of the Pad++ team, especially Jim Hollan and Jon Meyer. This work, and Pad++ in general has been largely funded by DARPA to whom we are grateful.

REFERENCES

1. Bederson, B. B., Hollan, J. D., Druin, A., Stewart, J., Rogers, D., & Proft, D. (1996). Local Tools: An Alternative to Tool Palettes. *In Proceedings of User Interface and Software Technology (UIST 96)* ACM Press, pp. 169-170.

2. Bederson, B. B., Hollan, J. D., Perlin, K., Meyer, J., Bacon, D., & Furnas, G. (1996). Pad++: A Zoomable Graphical Sketchpad for Exploring Alternate Interface Physics. *Journal of Visual Languages and Computing, 7*, 3-31.

3. Bier, E. A., & Freeman, S. (1991). MMM: A User Interface Architecture for Shared Editors on a Single Screen. *In Proceedings of User Interface and Software Technology (UIST 91)* ACM Press, pp. 79-86.

4. Bricker, L. J. (1998). *Collaboratively Controlled Objects in Support of Collaboration.* Doctoral dissertation, University of Washington, Seattle, Washington.

5. Buxton, W. (1994). The Three Mirrors of Interaction: A Holistic Approach to User Interfaces. L. MacDonald, & J. Vince (eds.), *Interacting With Virtual Environments.* New York: Wiley.

6. Cockburn, A., & Greenberg, S. (1996). Children's Collaboration Styles in a Newtonian Microworld. *In Proceedings of Extended Abstracts of Human Factors in Computing Systems (CHI 96)* ACM Press, pp. 181-182.

7. Druin, A., Stewart, J., Proft, D., Bederson, B. B., & Hollan, J. D. (1997). KidPad: A Design Collaboration Between Children, Technologists, and Educators. *In Proceedings of Human Factors in Computing Systems (CHI 97)* ACM Press, pp. 463-470.

8. Greenberg, S., & Boyle, M. (1998). *Moving between personal devices and public displays.* Tech Report 98/630/21, Department of Computer Science, University of Calgary, Calgary, Canada.

9. Hall, E. (1968). *The Hidden Dimension.* Anchor.

10. Inkpen, K., Booth, K. S., Klawe, M., & McGrenere, J. (1997). The Effect of Turn-Taking Protocols on Children's Learning in Mouse-Driven Collaborative Environments. *In Proceedings of Graphics Interface (GI 97)* Canadian Information Processing Society, pp. 138-145.

11. Ishii, H., & Ullmer, B. (1997). Tangible Bits: Towards Seamless Interfaces Between People, Bits and Atoms. *In Proceedings of Human Factors in Computing Systems (CHI 97)* ACM Press, pp. 234-241.

12. Johnson, D. W., & Johnson, R. T. (1991). *Learning Together and Alone, 3rd Edition.* Prentice Hall.

13. Krueger, M. (1991). *Artificial Reality II.* Addison-Wesley.

14. McGrath, J. E., & Hollingshead, A. B. (1994). *Groups Interacting With Technology.* Sage.

15. Myers, B. A., Stiel, H., & Gargiulo, R. (In Press). Collaboration Using Multiple PDAs Connected to a PC. *In Proceedings of Computer Supported Collaborative Work (CSCW 98)* ACM Press,

16. Pappert, S. (1996). *The Connected Family: Bridging the Digital Generation Gap.* Longstreet Press.

17. Pedersen, E. R., McCall, K., Moran, T. P., & Halasz, F. G. (1993). Tivoli: An Electronic Whiteboard for Informal Workgroup Meetings. *In Proceedings of Human Factors in Computing Systems (InterCHI 93)* ACM Press, pp. 391-398.

18. Rekimoto, J. (1998). A Multiple Device Approach for Supporting Whiteboard-Based Interactions. *In Proceedings of Human Factors in Computing Systems (CHI 98)* ACM Press, pp. 344-351.

19. Shu, L., & Flowers, W. (1992). Groupware Experiences in Three-Dimensional Computer-Aided Design. *In Proceedings of Computer Supported Collaborative Work (CSCW 92)* ACM Press, pp. 179-186.

20. Smith, R. B., O'Shea, T., O'Malley, C., Scanlon, E., & Taylor, J. (1989). Preliminary Experiments With a Distributed, Multi-Media, Problem Solving Environment. *In Proceedings of First European Conference on Computer Supported Cooperative Work* Slough, UK: Computer Sciences House, pp. 19-34.

21. Stewart, J. (In Press). *Single Display Groupware.* Doctoral dissertation, University of New Mexico, Albuquerque, NM.

22. Stewart, J., Raybourn, E., Bederson, B. B., & Druin, A. (1998). When Two Hands Are Better Than One: Enhancing Collaboration Using Single Display Groupware. *In Proceedings of Extended Abstracts of Human Factors in Computing Systems (CHI 98)* ACM Press, pp. 287-288.

The GAZE Groupware System: Mediating Joint Attention in Multiparty Communication and Collaboration

Roel Vertegaal
Cognitive Ergonomics Department
Twente University
The Netherlands
roel@acm.org

ABSTRACT

In this paper, we discuss why, in designing multiparty mediated systems, we should focus first on providing non-verbal cues which are less redundantly coded in speech than those normally conveyed by video. We show how conveying one such cue, gaze direction, may solve two problems in multiparty mediated communication and collaboration: knowing who is talking to whom, and who is talking about what. As a candidate solution, we present the GAZE Groupware System, which combines support for gaze awareness in multiparty mediated communication and collaboration with small and linear bandwidth requirements. The system uses an advanced, desk-mounted eyetracker to metaphorically convey gaze awareness in a 3D virtual meeting room and within shared documents.

KEYWORDS: CSCW, multiparty videoconferencing, awareness, attention, gaze direction, eyetracking, VRML 2.

INTRODUCTION

With recent advances in network infrastructure and computing power, desktop video conferencing and groupware systems are rapidly evolving into technologically viable solutions for remote communication and collaboration. Video conferencing is no longer limited to expensive circuit-switched ISDN networks and is starting to be used over standard internet connections in conjunction with groupware software. The central premise for the use of video mediated communication over traditional telephony has been that video images improve the quality of communication between individuals by increasing the available sensory bandwidth. In a face-to-face situation, auditory, visual and haptic expressions are freely combined to convey messages and regulate interaction. It has been presumed that by adding video to an audio-only communication link, mediated communication would bear a significantly closer resemblance to face-to-face communication. Firstly, we will show why this is not necessarily so. Secondly, we will show how designing mediated systems is a problem of conveying the least redundant cues first. We will show that by providing the right cues, one problem emerging from usability studies into multiparty video mediated communication may be solved: the difficulty of establishing who is talking or listening to whom in multiparty communication. With regard to cooperative work, we extend this notion to the problem of knowing who is talking about what. The central issue here is that regardless of whether audio or video is used, in multiparty communication and collaboration one should provide simple (i.e., unobtrusive and low-bandwidth), yet effective means of capturing and

metaphorically representing the attention participants have for one another and their work [21, 30]. We will demonstrate that gaze direction is a good way of providing such information and review candidate solutions. Finally, we present the eye-controlled GAZE Groupware System, a virtual meeting room which supplements multiparty audio conferencing with gaze awareness, allowing users to see where other participants look, be it at each other or within documents.

CONVEYING THE RIGHT CUES

Face-to-face communication is an extremely rich process in which people have the ability to convey an enormous amount of information to each other. In mediating the process of human communication, it is not obvious that such information richness is easily replicated by adding video images to standard telephony. Indeed, empirical studies [23] show the difference between face-to-face communication and video mediated communication to be significantly greater than the difference between video mediated communication and audio mediated communication. We may indeed attribute such findings to the large difference in sensory bandwidth between face-to-face and mediated conditions. Sensory bandwidth is characterized by the number of cues (actions which convey information from one human to another) conveyed by the different media. Verbal cues are the actual words spoken in a conversation, non-verbal cues include the way in which these words are spoken (paralinguistic speech), facial expressions, gaze, gestures, bodily movement, posture and contact, physical proximity and appearance [2]. Theoretically, the notion that we can simulate face-to-face situations under mediated conditions is a correct one. In practice, however, it seems that the number of cues that need to be conserved in order to accomplish a complete replication is far greater than one would expect. Simply adding video is only a minor step. And in conditions where much of the information is redundantly coded it seems to actually be an insignificant step where it comes to improving regulation of conversations or task performance [23]. The notion that the addition of video images should make mediated communication significantly more like face-to-face communication may have been based on a misinterpretation of Short et al.'s Social Presence Theory [24]. In this theory, communication media are ranked according to the degree in which participants feel co-located. Face-to-face communication would provide the greatest sense of social presence, followed by video, multispeaker audio and monaural audio. This ranking was based on a factor analysis of subjective ratings of dyadic (two-person) conversations using the various media, and does indeed suggest that the amount of social presence is improved by increasing the number of cues conveyed. So why then does the addition of video images to audio-only communication seem to be an insignificant step towards replicating face-to-face conditions where it comes to regulation of conversations or task performance? We believe this may, to a large extent, be attributed to a typical redundant coding scheme for those visual cues that are conveyed by a single stream of video. As Short et al. themselves pointed out, when cues are redundantly coded, we can no longer predict the effects of a communication system upon interaction by listing differences in the number of cues conveyed by different media. For example, a speaker preparing to yield the floor to a listener may use a combination of the following expressions: completion of a grammatical clause; a sociocentric expression such as 'you know'; a drawl on the final syllable; a shift in pitch at the end of the phonemic clause; a drop in loudness; termination of a hand gesture; relaxation of body position; and resumption of eyegaze towards the listener [9, 15, 24]. Note that we see a merging of verbal, paralinguistic, gestural, postural, and gaze-related cues, all indicating the same thing. When confronted with a different medium, speakers may easily adapt their behaviour by using different combinations of cues or by simply dropping several cues without failing to yield the floor. Indeed, half of the non-verbal cues in the above example are auditory, and five of the total of eight cues could be conveyed by telephone. This makes it extremely hard to find differences between video mediated communication and audio mediated communication in terms of performance in a joint task or, for that matter, more objective variables of conversational structure such as number of interruptions, duration of simultaneous speech or number of utterances. Indeed, empirical studies have so far failed to find clear differences in terms of conversational structure or task performance between video- and audio mediated communication (for an excellent overview, see [23]). When improving mediated communication, should we therefore aim to model face-to-face conditions even closer? We agree with Dennett [7] that it is not very realistic to think that face-to-face situations can, or indeed should be substituted by modeling the world on a one-to-one basis (a question already raised by Descartes [8]). We conclude that we should avoid putting *too* much research emphasis on improving mediated communication by means of increasing the bandwidth for video, and first focus on providing non-verbal cues which are less redundantly coded in speech, thereby hoping to provide some essential characteristics of face-to-face communication without intending to substitute it completely.

PROBLEMS WITH MEDIATING MULTIPARTY COMMUNICATION

In multiparty conditions (in which more than two persons communicate), gaze direction may well serve as a good example of such a cue. Multiparty conversational structure is much more complicated than its dyadic equivalent. As soon as a third speaker is introduced, the next turn is no longer guaranteed to be the non-speaker. When the number of participants rises beyond three, it becomes possible to have side conversations between subgroups of people. This can pose problems for the regulation of, for example, turntaking. When we consider the above example of a speaker yielding the floor in a multiparty situation, the question arises to whom he would like to yield the floor. With the notable exception of gaze direction (or rather the general orientation of body, head and eyes) and perhaps pointing gestures, such attention-related information is not coded by the eight cues listed in the above example. It can only be conveyed by telephone by means of explicit verbal references (e.g., calling someone by name) or the internal context of conversation. We believe turntaking problems with current multiparty conferencing systems (regardless of whether they use video or audio) may be attributed to a lack of cues about other participants' attention.

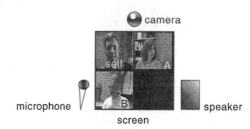

Figure 1. A single-camera video conferencing system.

Isaacs and Tang [13] performed a usability study of a group of five participants using a typical desktop video conferencing system. They found that during video conferencing, people needed to address each other by using each other's names and started to explicitly control the turntaking process by requesting individuals to take the next turn. In face-to-face interaction, however, they saw many instances when people used their eyegaze to indicate whom they were addressing and to suggest a next speaker. Often, when more than one person started speaking at the same time, the next speaker was determined by the eyegaze of the previous speaker without the need for conventions or explicit verbal intervention. Similarly, O'Connaill et al. [19] found that in video conferencing more formal techniques were used to achieve speaker switching than in face-to-face interaction. They too attribute this to the absence of certain speaker-switching cues. This suggests that multiparty communication using video conferencing is not necessarily easier to manage than using telephony. Single-camera video systems such as the one shown in figure 1 do not convey deictic visual references to objects (such as the computer screen) or persons (such as the other participants) outside the frame of reference of the camera any more than telephony. To some extent, the participants' presumption that video conferencing is more like face-to-face interaction than telephony may actually lead to inappropriate use of such visual cues. Isaacs and Tang [13] show how, when a participant points to one of the video images on her screen, it is difficult for the others to use spatial position to figure out whom is being addressed. Similarly, subjects may try to establish eye contact by gazing at the video image of a participant. Although the large angle between the camera and the screen usually prevents looking each other in the eyes (as one would need to look at the camera and the video image simultaneously), even if they were to establish eye contact, they would establish it with every participant in the group.

With respect to the conservation of gaze direction, we therefore identified the following incremental requirements for conferencing systems [29, 31]:

1) Relative position: Relative viewpoints of the participants should be based on a common reference point (e.g., around a shared workspace), providing basic support for deictic references. One may add a corresponding spatial separation of audio sources (e.g., by means of stereo panning) in order to ease selective listening, for example during side conversations.

2) Head orientation: Conveying the general orientation of looking may help participants in achieving deixis (e.g., "What do you think?"), and may provide basic support for knowing who is attending to whom.

3) Gaze (at the facial region): Conveying the exact position of looking within each other's facial region may also help in achieving deixis, and may provide support for knowing whether others are still attending. Mutual gaze constitutes eye contact.

THE CASE FOR CONVEYING GAZE DIRECTION IN MULTIPARTY COMMUNICATION

According to Argyle and Kendon, in two-party communication, looking at the facial region of the other person (gaze) serves at least five functions [2, 3, 15]: to regulate the flow of conversation; to provide feedback on the reaction of others; to communicate emotions; to communicate the nature of relationships; and to avoid distraction by restricting input of information. Due to technological and methodological complications, most studies into the role of gaze direction in communication were limited to two-person (dyadic) situations. In the early seventies, Argyle [2] estimated that when two people are talking, about 60 percent of conversation involves gaze, and 30 percent involves mutual gaze (or eye contact). People look nearly twice as much while listening (75%) as while speaking (41%). The amount of gaze is also subject to individual differences such as personality factors and cultural differences. For example, an extrovert may gaze more than an introvert. Also, there is more gaze in some kinds of conversations than others. If the topic is difficult, people look less in order to avoid distraction. If there are other things to look at, interactors look at each other less, especially if there are objects present which are relevant to the conversation [4]. In general, however, gaze is closely linked with speech. According to Kendon [15], person A tends to look away as she begins a long utterance, and starts looking more and more at her interlocutor B as the end of her utterance approaches. This pattern should be explained from two points of view. From the first point of view, in looking away at the beginning, person A may be withdrawing her attention from person B in order to concentrate on what she is going to say. When she approaches the end of her utterance, the subsequent action will depend largely upon how person B is behaving, necessitating person A to seek information about her interlocutor. From the second point of view, these changes in gaze can come to function as signals to person B. In looking away at the beginning, person A signals that she is about to begin an utterance, forestalling any response from person B. Similarly, in looking at person B towards the end of her utterance, she may signal that she is now ceasing to talk yet still has attention for him, effectively offering the floor to person B.

So how do these results hold in a multiparty condition? We conducted a study into the synchronization between auditory/articulatory attention and gaze at the facial region in four-person conversations [31]. When someone is listening or speaking to an individual, there is indeed a high probability that the person she looks at is the person she listens (88% chance) or speaks to (77% chance). In this more or less dyadic condition we found percentages of gaze similar to those found by Argyle, with about 1.6 times more gaze while listening than while speaking. However, when a person starts speaking to all three listeners, she will typically distribute her gaze over all of them. In this condition we found that the total percentage of gaze (while speaking) rises to 59% of the time. We may therefore conclude that gaze is indeed an excellent cue for establishing who is talking or listening to whom in multiparty face-to-face communication. In the next section, we investigate whether a representation of this cue can improve multiparty mediated communication.

Empirical Evidence in Multiparty Mediated Conditions

Very few, if any, studies exist in which the isolated effect of representing gaze direction in multiparty mediated communication has been empirically evaluated. Sellen [22] examined the differences in conversational structure between three multiparty conditions: using face-to-face communication; using a single-camera desktop video conferencing system (similar to the one depicted in figure 1); and using a Hydra system: a setup with multiple cameras, monitors and speakers which preserves relative position (including separation of audio), head orientation and, according to Sellen, gaze (Hydra [23] will be discussed further on in this paper). Although Sellen found differences in terms of objective measures (such as amount of simultaneous speech) between face-to-face and mediated conditions, she did not detect any differences between the two mediated systems. Sellen attributed this, in part, to the small screens of Hydra and their separation. As Heath and Luff [12] pointed out, movements in the periphery of vision which appear on a screen lose their power to attract attention. In addition, the still-present angle between camera and monitor in Hydra, albeit small, may have inhibited correct perception of gaze at the facial region [31]. Qualitative data did indicate subjects preferred the Hydra system over single-camera video conferencing. Reasons given included the fact that they could selectively attend to people, and could tell when people were attending to them. They also confirmed that keeping track of the conversation was the most difficult in the single-camera video conferencing condition. However, such conclusions may, in part, also be attributed to the separation of audio sources in the Hydra system.

We investigated the isolated effect of representing gaze directional cues on multiparty mediated communication, relative to the availability of other nonverbal upper-torso visual cues (see [31] and future publications). Groups of three participants (2 actors and 1 subject) solved language puzzles under three mediated conditions (all of which conveyed audio):

1) Motion video only, showing actor gaze 14% of time.
2) Motion video with head orientation, showing actor gaze 7% of time.
3) Head orientation and appearance only, showing actor gaze 32% of time. Actors manually selected one of three still images for display: looking at subject; looking at other actor, and looking at a computer terminal.

We found no effect of gaze directional cues, or any other nonverbal upper-torso visual cues, on task performance. However, gaze directional cues in the form of head orientation caused the number of deictic verbal references to persons used by the subjects to increase significantly by a factor two. We found a significant increase in turn frequency of about 25% in condition 3. A significant positive linear relationship between the amount of actor gaze at the facial region of subjects and the number of subject turns ($r=.34$, $p<.02$) and speaker switches ($r=.37$, $p<.01$) accounted for this finding. Thus, representing the gaze direction of the actors increased turn frequency, but only if it could be recognized by subjects as being aimed at themselves (i.e., as gaze at their facial region). We found no effect on turntaking of other nonverbal upper-torso visual cues. These findings suggest that all our requirements for multiparty conferencing systems should be met (i.e., they should preserve relative position, head orientation and gaze).

We conclude that although there have not been enough studies into the isolated effect of gaze directional cues on mediated multiparty communication, our evidence suggests that conveying gaze direction — especially gaze at the facial region — eases turntaking, allowing more speaker turns and more effective use of deictic verbal references. Depending on the task situation, however, this does not necessarily result in a significant performance increase. In the next section, we will investigate the role of gaze directional cues in collaboration.

THE CASE FOR CONVEYING GAZE DIRECTION IN COOPERATIVE WORK

We have so far examined the role of gaze direction in multiparty communication. Although some studies have investigated the role of looking at things during face-to-face collaboration, there are, to our knowledge, few empirical studies examining the effect of conveying gaze direction during computer supported cooperative work. Argyle and Graham [4] found that if a pair of subjects were asked to plan a European holiday and there was a map of Europe in between them, the amount of gaze dropped from 77 percent to 6.4 percent. 82 percent of the time was spent looking at the map. Even when they presented a vary vague, outline map, subjects looked at it for 70% of the time, suggesting that they were keeping in touch by looking at and pointing to the same object, instead of looking at each other. They also found there was little attention for the map if it was irrelevant to the topic of conversation.

Within the realm of computer supported cooperative work, Ishii and Kobayashi [14] demonstrated how the preservation of relative position and the transfer of gaze direction could aid cooperative problem solving through their ClearBoard system. They conducted an experiment in which two participants were asked to solve the "river crossing problem", a puzzle in which two groups of people (typically missionaries and cannibals) should reach the other side of a river with certain restrictions on who can join whom in the boat. According to the authors, the success of this game depends heavily on the point-of-view of the players. Participants could see video images of each other through a shared drawing board on which they could also sketch the problem. Ishii and Kobayashi concluded that it was easy for one participant to say on which side of the river the other participant was gazing and that this information was useful in jointly solving the problem. Colston and Schiano [6] describe how observers rated the difficulty people had in solving problems, based upon their estimates of how long a person looked at a particular problem, and how his or her gaze would linger after being told to move on to the next problem. They found a linear relationship between gaze duration and rated difficulty, with lingering as a significant factor. This suggests that people may use gaze-related cues as a means of obtaining information about the cognitive activities of a collaborator. Velichkovsky [27] investigated the use of eyetracking for representing the point of gaze during computer supported cooperative problem solving. Two people were asked to solve a puzzle represented on their screen as a random combination of pieces which had to be rearranged using the mouse. The two participants shared the same visual environment, but the knowledge about the situation and ability to change it on the way to a solution were distributed between them. One of the partners (the expert) knew the solution in detail but could not rearrange the pieces. The other (the novice) could act and had to achieve the goal of solving the puzzle without having seen more than a glance of the solution. In the first condition, they could only communicate verbally. In the second condition, the gaze position of the expert was added by projection into the working space on the screen of the novice. In the third condition, the expert used his mouse instead to show the novice the relevant parts of the task configuration. Both ways of conveying the attention of the partners improved performance. The absolute gain in the case of gaze position transfer was about 40%. Approximately the same gain was obtained with mouse pointing. In a second experiment, the direction of gaze position transfer was reversed from the novice to the expert. Here too, a significant gain was found in the efficiency of distributed problem solving. Apparently, experts could see the types of barriers novices confront in their activity and were therefore able to give more appropriate advice. This shows that gaze position transfer may be useful in situations where manual deixis is impossible: the novices could not use their mouse for pointing because they needed it to manipulate puzzle pieces.

We conclude that although the effect of providing a representation of gaze direction in cooperative work may be highly dependent on the task situation, a closer coordination between the communication and cooperation media with respect to conserving such deictic cues can be considered beneficial. In the next section, we will review existing systems in which gaze directional cues are preserved.

PREVIOUS SOLUTIONS

Over the years, a number of multiparty conferencing systems have been developed which complied with the earlier presented design recommendations. Such systems preserved relative position (including spatial separation of audio), head orientation and gaze. Negroponte [18] describes a system commissioned by ARPA in the mid-1970s to allow the electronic transmission of the fullest possible sense of human presence for five particular people at five different sites. Each of these five persons had to believe that the other four were physically present. This extraordinary requirement was driven by the government's emergency procedures in the event of a nuclear attack: the highest ranking members of government should not be hiding in the same nuclear bunker. His solution was to replicate each person's head four times, with a life-size translucent mask in the exact shape of that person's face. Each mask was mounted on gimbals with two degrees of freedom, so the 'head' could nod and turn. High-quality video was projected inside of these heads. In this rather humorous setup, each site was composed of one real person and four plastic heads sitting around a table in the same order. Each person's head position and video image would be captured and replicated remotely. According to Negroponte, this resulted in lifelike emulation so vivid that one admiral told him he got nightmares from these 'talking heads'. A technical advantage of this system was that only one camera was needed at each site to capture the video image of the participant's head, resulting into only one stream of video data from each participant (we will further address this issue below). It may, however, be difficult with this system to capture gaze at the facial region correctly. A technical disadvantage was the elaborate setup of the talking heads: the total number of heads required is almost the square of the number of participants ($n^2 - n$; in which n is the number of participants).

Sellen [23] describes the Hydra system, a setup of multiple camera/monitor/speaker units in which relative position (including spatial separation of audio), head orientation and gaze might be preserved during multiparty videoconferencing. Hydra simulates a four-way round-table meeting by placing a box containing a camera, a small monitor and speaker in the place that would otherwise be held by each remote participant. Each person is therefore presented with his own view of each remote participant, with the remote participant's voice emanating from his distinct location in space. This way, when person A turns to look at person B, B is able to see A turn to look towards B's camera. According to Sellen, eye-contact (i.e., mutual gaze) should be supported because the angle between the camera and the monitor in each unit is relatively small. The separation of audio in the Hydra system may ease selective listening, allowing participants to attend to different speakers who may be speaking simultaneously. Although Hydra is of course a very elegant alternative to Negroponte's system, it has some disadvantages. One disadvantage seems to be that the system does not preserve gaze at the facial region accurately enough [23]. Another disadvantage is that although participants can see when someone is looking at a (shared) workspace, their estimation of where this person looks within that workspace would probably be worse than possible with, e.g., Negroponte's system. A more technical drawback is that each camera in the setup provides a unique video stream, and that the number of cameras required is almost the square of the number of participants ($n^2 - n$; in which n is the number of participants). For three participants, only six Hydra units are needed, but when this number rises to five, twenty Hydra units are required. In a Multicast network [10], the bandwidth requirements of traditional single-camera video conferencing systems are greatly reduced. With Multicasting, a video stream of an individual user is not sent to individual remote participants by means of multiple connections. Instead, that video stream is 'broadcast' to all other participants simultaneously, requiring only one unit of the total network bandwidth at any time. With the Hydra system, such compression cannot be achieved, causing the amount of network bandwidth used to convey video to rise with almost the square of the number of participants ($n^2 - n$). This may have an effect on usability, as it may lead to problems with proper conveyance and synchronization of audiovisual information.

Okada et al.'s MAJIC system uses a rather more elaborate setup in an attempt to achieve a seamless integration of life-size images of the other participants with each participant's real work environment [20]. In essence, it is a bigger version of the Hydra system, with a more precise positioning of cameras, behind the monitors (i.e., a big video tunnel [1]). In each office, a thin half-transparent curved projection screen is placed behind a computer terminal in front of the user. On this screen, life-size video images of the other participants are projected. Behind each projection screen, video cameras are located at the center of the projected facial region of the other participants, one camera for each participant. This way, head orientational information is conveyed, and users may achieve eye-contact by looking at each other's faces, as long as those faces do not move too much relative to the camera lens behind them [1, 31]. A corresponding placement of microphones and speakers is used to ease selective listening. We may well consider the MAJIC system the closest we will get to replicating a face-to-face situation without holographic projection. However, the disadvantages of MAJIC are similar to those of the Hydra system. In addition, due to the large image size, each video stream will require considerably more bandwidth than with the Hydra system, assuming resolution is maintained.

A more recent development has been the embodiment of chat participants in virtual environments [5, 17]. Although such systems do include ways to pictorially represent users in a spatial formations, we will not elaborate upon them as they do not include a direct way of capturing gaze direction. For a discussion on the issues concerning such Collaborative Virtual Environments, we refer to [11].

We conclude that most systems which convey gaze direction in multiparty communication have difficulties preserving gaze at the facial region under all circumstances, and suffer from an inefficient use of network resources. They may also have difficulties preserving gaze awareness in the workspace. In the next section, we will describe our own candidate solution based on a direct measurement of gaze direction.

THE GAZE GROUPWARE SYSTEM

Based on our design recommendations we developed a prototype multiparty mediated communication and collaboration system which provides awareness about the participants' gaze position without some of the drawbacks of earlier systems. Instead of conveying gaze direction by means of multiple streams of video, the GAZE Groupware System (GGS) measures directly where each participant looks using an advanced desk-mounted eyetracking system [33]. The system represents this information metaphorically in a 3D virtual meeting room and within shared documents. The system does this using the Sony Community Place [26] plug-in, which allows interactive 3D scenes to be shared on a web page using a standard multiplatform browser such as Netscape. The GAZE Groupware System can be used in conjunction with any multiparty speech communication facility such as an internet-based audio conferencing tool, or standard telephony.

The Virtual Meeting Room

The GAZE Groupware System simulates a four-way round-table meeting by placing a 2D image (or *persona*) of each participant around a table in a virtual room, at a position that would otherwise be held by that remote participant. Using this technique, each person is presented with a unique view of each remote participant, and that view emanates from a distinct location in space. Each persona rotates around its own x and y axes in 3D space, according to where the corresponding participant looks. Figure 2 shows the system in use in a four-way situation. When Robert looks at Roel, Roel sees Robert's persona turn to face him. When Robert looks at Harro, Roel sees Robert's persona turn towards Harro. Based on our earlier findings, this should effectively convey whom each participant is listening or speaking to.

When a participant looks at the shared table, a lightspot is projected onto the surface of the table, in line with her persona's orientation. The color of this lightspot is identical to the color of her persona. This "miner's helmet" metaphor enables a participant to see exactly where the others are looking within the shared workspace. With their mouse, participants can put document icons on the table representing shared files. Whenever a participant looks at a document icon or within the associated file, her lightspot will be projected onto that document icon. This allows people to use deictic references for referring to documents (e.g., "Here, look at these notes"). Shared documents are opened by double clicking their icon on the table. When a document is opened, the associated file contents appears in a separate frame of the web page (see figure 2). In this frame, an editor associated with the file runs as an applet. When a participant looks within a file, all participants looking inside that file can see a lightspot with her color projected over the contents. This lightspot shows exactly what this person is reading. Again, this allows people to use deictic references for referring to objects within files (e.g., "I cannot figure this out"). We realize, that providing such information may invade the privacy of individual users. By (annoyingly) projecting their own gaze position whenever it is shared, we hope to ensure that individuals are aware their

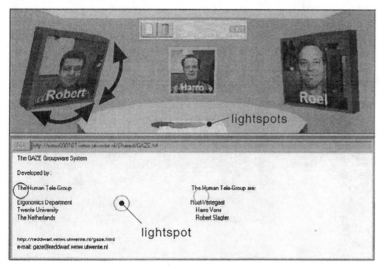

Figure 2. Personas rotate according to where users look.

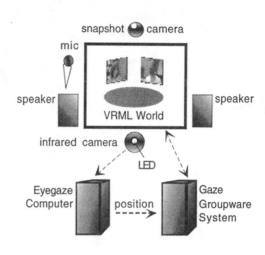

Figure 3. The GAZE hardware setup.

gaze position is transferred to others. Although files can be referred to by URL, they are currently restricted to ascii text.

HARDWARE SETUP

Each participant has a hardware setup similar to the one shown in figure 3. The GAZE Groupware System consists of two key components: the Eyegaze system, which determines where the participant looks; and the GGS computer, a Windows '95 Pentium running Netscape, the GAZE Groupware System, a web server, frame grabbing software and an internet-based audio conferencing tool. The Eyegaze system, which is discussed in detail below, reports the gaze position of the user over a serial link to the GGS computer. The GGS computer determines where the participant looks, manipulates her persona and lightspot, and conveys this information through a TCP/IP connection via a server to the other GGS computers. The Eyegaze system is not required. Participants can also switch to using their mouse to indicate point of interest. The video conferencing camera on top of the monitor is currently used to make snapshots for the personas (future versions will also incorporate motion video). When making a snapshot, it is important that users look into the video conferencing camera lens, as this will allow them to achieve a sense of eye contact during meetings.

THE LC TECHNOLOGIES EYEGAZE SYSTEM

When the eye remains relatively still for more than about 120 milliseconds, we speak of a fixation [28]. For determining where the user is looking, it is these fixation points that we are interested in. Our system measures the eye fixation points of a user by means of the Eyegaze System [16], an advanced, desk-mounted, imaging eyetracker with a spatial resolution of approximately 0.5 degrees of arc and a temporal resolution of 50-60 Hz. The Eyegaze system consists of a 486 computer processing the images of a high-resolution infrared video camera. This camera unit is mounted underneath the screen of the user (see figure 3), and is aimed at one of his eyes (see figure 4). On top of the camera lens, an infrared light source is mounted which projects invisible light into the eye. This infrared light is reflected by the retina, causing a bright pupil effect (the large circle in figure 5) on the camera image. The light is also reflected by the cornea of the eye, causing a small glint to appear on the camera image (the small dot in figure 5). Because the cornea is approximately spherical, when the eye moves, the corneal reflection remains roughly at the same position. However, the bright pupil moves with the eye. By processing the image on the computer unit, the vector between

the center of the pupil and the corneal reflection can be determined. In order to correctly translate this vector into screen coordinates, the user needs to calibrate the Eyegaze system once before use. This calibration procedure takes about 15 seconds. When the coordinate remains within a specified range for approximately 120 msec (3 complete camera frames), the Eyegaze system decides that this is a fixation. It then starts reporting the coordinates over a serial link to the GAZE Groupware System running on a separate computer (see figure 3). The GAZE Groupware System uses this coordinate to determine at which object or participant on the screen the user is looking.

SOFTWARE IMPLEMENTATION

The GAZE Groupware System was implemented using the *Virtual Reality Modeling Language 2.0* [25]. This cross-platform standard separates 3D graphic descriptions (rendered natively) from their dynamic behaviour (running on a JAVA Virtual Machine). Sony Community Place [26] is a plug-in for Netscape which implements the VRML 2 standard and adds a client-server architecture for sharing 3D graphics and behaviour over TCP/IP. For each dynamic object a user sees in the virtual meeting room, there is a corresponding JAVA object. Whenever such an object does something, its behaviour is broadcast via the Community Place Server by means of messages to the other systems. This way, all participants' copies of the meeting room are kept in sync. Eyetracker input is obtained from a small native driver application polling the serial port or the mouse. Document editors are JAVA applets running separately from the VRML world, although they do communicate with it to obtain eyetracking data and URLs. All code, graphics, and documents are shared using web servers running on each GGS computer.

EVALUATION OF THE SYSTEM

Informal sessions with several hundred novice users at ACM Expo'97 indicated our approach to be a promising one. Most participants seemed to easily interpret the underlying metaphors. The eyetracking technology was, in many cases, *completely* transparent. Users would sit behind the system and immediately start chatting, without calibration or instruction. As we spent most of our time empirically evaluating the underlying assumptions of the system (as discussed earlier, and in [31]), the prototype has not yet been tested for usability.

Figure 4. Participant using the GAZE Groupware System

Potential usability issues include:

*   *No spatial separation of audio or visual encoding of speech activity.* Although it is not necessary for audio sources to be exactly co-located with the visual representation of users, spatial separation of their voices may ease selective listening [23]. This feature is not yet integrated into the prototype. Users currently need to depend on auditory discrimination of voices for identifying the source of individual speech activity. Spatial separation of audio and visual encoding of speech activity (using the animation techniques demonstrated in [32] or by using motion video) may solve this issue.

*   *No option for motion video.* Although this is the subject of further investigation, the capturing of gaze at the facial region and the conveyance of motion video seem to be conflicting demands. This is because humans seem extremely sensitive to parallax [31]. Even when video tunnels are used, it is difficult to keep cameras and eye regions aligned at all times [1, 31]. Evidence presented in this paper suggests one should typically choose to convey gaze at the facial region. However, in future versions we hope to resolve this conflict, and convey both gaze and motion video in a network-scalable fashion.

*   *Color coding and lightspot confusion.* Lightspots can only be attributed to a persona by color and synchronized movement. We would like to devise a more redundant coding scheme. When there are many lightspots, novices may get confused or distracted. It should at the very least be possible to turn lightspots off.

*   *Privacy.* Although knowing what others are reading may be beneficial during a joint editing process, there are many task situations where this could be detrimental. Users should always be aware when their gaze is being transmitted, and when not. Currently, we hope to ensure this by (annoyingly) projecting the user's own gaze whenever she looks at shared objects. This is not a satisfactory solution.

*   *Eyetracker limitations.* Although the eyetracker works well while talking, head motion is still limited to about 5-10 cm in each direction in order for gaze to be conveyed correctly (if the eye moves out of range, the eyetracker stops sending coordinates until it is back in range). However, similar restrictions apply to most other conferencing systems which convey gaze by means of

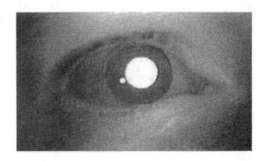

Figure 5. The infrared camera image.

video tunnels [1, 31]. In addition, a version of the Eyegaze System which allows 30 cm of head movement in each direction is almost ready for release. Although the eyetracker works fine with most glasses and contact lenses, a small percentage of users has problems with calibration. Eyetracking is still expensive, but current developments lead towards eyetrackers which are just another input device: inexpensive and transparent in use.

*   *Meeting room restrictions.* Although this is not an intrinsic limitation, the system currently allows only four users in the meeting room. Users are currently not allowed to move freely through space or control their point of view, as this complicates the mapping of their gaze coordinates.

CONCLUSIONS

Designing multiparty mediated systems is a problem of conveying the least redundant cues first. Many of the cues conveyed by video are redundantly coded in speech. Less redundantly coded cues such as gaze direction are, however, usually not conveyed. We have shown how conveying gaze direction may solve a problem in multiparty mediated communication: establishing who is talking or listening to whom. Gaze direction is an excellent cue for providing such information. Evidence suggests that conveying gaze direction — especially gaze at the facial region — eases turntaking, allowing more speaker turns and more effective use of deictic verbal references. However, this does not necessarily result in a significant task performance increase. Depending on the task situation, gaze direction may also help establishing who is talking about what in cooperative work. Our GAZE Groupware System combines support for gaze awareness (preserving relative position, head orientation and gaze) in multiparty mediated communication and collaboration with small and linear bandwidth requirements. The system measures directly where each participant looks using a desk-mounted eyetracker. It represents this information metaphorically in a 3D virtual meeting room and within shared documents.

ACKNOWLEDGEMENTS

Thanks to Harro Vons, Robert Slagter, Gerrit van der Veer, Nancy and Dixon Cleveland, the LC Technologies team, Boris Velichkovsky, and Robert Rathbun of Cyberian Outpost for their important contributions to this project.

REFERENCES

1. Acker, S. and Levitt, S. Designing videoconference facilities for improved eye contact. *Journal of Broadcasting & Electronic Media* 31(2), 1987.

2. Argyle, M. *The Psychology of Interpersonal Behaviour.* London: Penguin Books, 1967.

3. Argyle, M. and Cook, M. *Gaze and Mutual Gaze.* London: Cambridge University Press, 1976.

4. Argyle, M. and Graham, J. The Central Europe Experiment - looking at persons and looking at things. *Journal of Environmental Psychology and Nonverbal Behaviour* 1, 1977, pp. 6-16.

5. Benford, S., Greenhalgh, C., Bowers, J., Snowdon, S., and Fahlén, L. User Embodiment in Collaborative Virtual Environments. In *Proceedings of CHI'95.* Denver, Colorado: ACM, 1995.

6. Colston, H. and Schiano, D. Looking and Lingering as Conversational Cues in VMC. In *Proceedings of CHI'95.* Denver, Colorado: ACM, 1995.

7. Dennett, D. *Conciousness Explained.* London: Penguin, 1991.

8. Descartes, R. *Discours de la méthode.* Leiden: Jean Maire, 1637.

9. Duncan, S. Some signals and rules for taking speaking turns in conversations. *Journal of Personality and Social Psychology* 23, 1972.

10. Ericksson, H. MBONE: The Multicast Backbone. Communications of *ACM* 37(8), 1994, pp. 54-60.

11. Harrison, S. and Dourish, P. Re-Place-ing Space: The Roles of Place and Space in Collaborative Systems. In *Proceedings of CSCW'96.* Cambridge, MA.: ACM, 1996, pp. 67-76.

12. Heath, C. and Luff, P. Disembodied conduct: Communication through video in a multi-media office environment. In *Proceedings of CHI'91.* New Orleans: ACM, 1991.

13. Isaacs, E. and Tang, J. What video can and can't do for collaboration: a case study. In *Proceedings of Multimedia'93.* Anaheim, CA: ACM, 1993.

14. Ishii, H. and Kobayashi, M. ClearBoard: A Seamless Medium for Shared Drawing and Conversation with Eye Contact. *Proceedings of CHI'92.* Monterey, CA: ACM, 1992.

15. Kendon, A. Some Function of Gaze Direction in Social Interaction. *Acta Psychologica* 32, 1967, pp. 1-25.

16. LC Technologies. *The Eyegaze Communication System.* Fairfax, VA, 1997. *http://www.lctinc.com*

17. Nakanishi, H., Yoshida, C., Nishimura, T., and Ishida, T. Freewalk: Supporting Casual Meetings in a Network. In *Proceedings of CSCW'96.* Cambridge, MA.: ACM, 1996, pp. 308-314.

18. Negroponte, N. *Being Digital.* New York: Vintage Books, 1995.

19. O'Connaill, B., Whittaker, S., and Wilbur, S. Conversations Over Video Conferences: An Evaluation of the Spoken Aspects of Video-Mediated Communication. *Human Computer Interaction* 8, 1993, pp. 389-428.

20. Okada, K., Maeda, F., Ichikawaa, Y., and Matsushita, Y. Multiparty Videoconferencing at Virtual Social Distance: MAJIC Design. In *Proceedings of CSCW'94.* Chapel Hill, NC.: ACM, 1994, pp. 385-393.

21. Raeithel, A. and Velichkovsky, B.M. Joint Attention and Co-Construction of Tasks: New Ways to Foster User-Designer Collaboration. In Nardi, B. (Ed.), *Context and Conciousness.* Cambridge, MA: MIT Press, 1996.

22. Sellen, A.J. Speech Patterns in Video-Mediated Conversations. In *Proceedings of CHI'92.* Monterey, CA: ACM, 1992, pp. 49-59.

23. Sellen, A.J. Remote conversations: the effects of mediating talk with technology. *Human Computer Interaction* 10(4), 1995.

24. Short, J., Williams, E., and Christie, B. *The Social Psychology of Telecommunications.* London: Wiley, 1976.

25. Silicon Graphics, Sony and ISO. The Virtual Reality Modeling Language — Part 1: Functional specification and UTF-8 encoding. *ISO/IEC 14772-1:1998,* 1998. *http://www.iso.ch/*

26. Sony. *Sony Community Place,* 1997. *http://vs.spiw.com/vs/*

27. Velichkovsky, B.M. Communicating attention: Gaze position transfer in cooperative problem solving. *Pragmatics and Cognition,* 3(2), 1995, pp. 199-222.

28. Velichkovsky, B.M., Sprenger, A., and Unema, P. Towards gaze-mediated interaction: Collecting solutions of the "Midas touch problem". In *Proceedings of INTERACT'97.* Sydney, Australia, 1997.

29. Vertegaal, R. Conversational Awareness in Multiparty VMC. In *Extended Abstracts of CHI'97.* Atlanta, GA: ACM, 1997, pp. 6-7.

30. Vertegaal, R., Velichkovsky, B.M., and Van der Veer, G. Catching the Eye: Management of Joint Attention in Cooperative Work. *SIGCHI Bulletin* 29(4), 1997.

31. Vertegaal, R. *Look Who's Talking to Whom.* PhD Thesis. Cognitive Ergonomics Department, Twente University, The Netherlands, 1998. ISBN 90 3651 1747.

32. Vertegaal, R. GAZE: Visual-Spatial Attention in Communication. Video Paper. In *Proceedings of CSCW'98.* Seattle, WA: ACM, 1998.

33. Vertegaal, R., Vons, H., and Slagter, R. Look Who's Talking: The GAZE Groupware System. In *Summary of CHI'98.* Los Angeles, CA: ACM, 1998.

Video Helps Remote Work:
Speakers Who Need to Negotiate Common Ground Benefit from Seeing Each Other

Elizabeth S. Veinott
Judith Olson, Gary M. Olson
The Collaboratory for Research
on Electronic work (CREW)
University of Michigan
Ann Arbor, MI 48109-1234
+ 1 734 647 4948
{veinott, jsolson, gmo} @umich.edu

Xiaolan Fu
Institute of Psychology
Chinese Academy of Sciences
Beijing, China
+ 86 10 6487 9856
fuxl@ht.rol.cn.net

ABSTRACT
More and more organizations are forming teams that are not co-located. These teams communicate via email, fax, telephone and audio conferences, and sometimes video. The question often arises whether the cost of video is worth it. Previous research has shown that video makes people more satisfied with the work, but it doesn't help the quality of the work itself. There is one exception; negotiation tasks are measurably better with video. In this study, we show that the same effect holds for a more subtle form of negotiation, when people have to negotiate meaning in a conversation. We compared the performance and communication of people explaining a map route to each other. Half the pairs have video and audio connections, half only audio. Half of the pairs were native speakers of English; the other half were non-native speakers, those presumably who have to negotiate meaning more. The results showed that non-native speaker pairs did benefit from the video; native speakers did not. Detailed analysis of the conversational strategies showed that with video, the non-native speaker pairs spent proportionately more effort negotiating common ground.

Keywords: Video-mediated communication, remote work, common ground, communication, negotiation

INTRODUCTION
As organizations become more global, co-workers and collaborators are no longer housed down the hall from each other. More and more often, people are remotely located.

Not only are collaborative interactions now crossing geographic boundaries, they also are crossing language and cultural boundaries. Traveling to meetings is expensive in both time and money, so companies have been turning to using audio and video conferencing systems. Since high-quality video-plus-audio connections are more costly than audio-only conferencing systems, the question arises as to the value of the video connection. Does it improve the quality of the work? How does it affect the communication process?

Over twenty-five years of research, beginning with the classic studies of Chapanis, has shown very little advantage of video over audio-only connections for remote communication. [3, 5, 6, 10, 12, 13, 14, 17]. It is not surprising that if one is discussing a complex artifact, video helps [11]. However, it is surprising that although people are more satisfied conversing by video than by audio only, video has been shown to add nothing to the outcome performance of people engaged in variety of different tasks. It seems that the only tasks for which video has been shown to add value are certain kinds of negotiation tasks [19], where presumably people benefit by being able to read important cues from each other's faces and adjust their strategies accordingly.

We believe that negotiation is more ubiquitous than commonly thought. Everyday conversations regularly involve negotiation of meaning, especially when two people do not have similar backgrounds or experiences [7]. The mutual understanding and beliefs that arise from similar backgrounds and experiences is referred to as common ground [8]. Because achieving common ground involves numerous mini-negotiations, we expect achievement of common ground will be *more successful* when the two people can see each other [7]. This success may account for the consistent result that people are more satisfied with remote conversations when they have video.

In this paper we explore the role of video in the negotiation of meaning in conversation. Although these negotiations go on in everyday conversations between friends and colleagues, they are not nearly as frequent nor potentially as important as in conversations between strangers. These negotiations are even more likely to appear between people who are not only culturally dissimilar, but do not share the same native language [20]. Detailed analysis of the content of conversations in the Varonis and Gass study showed that this negotiation serves to clarify information rather than to correct it. Although negotiations are essential for successful communication when people do not share common ground, they may also disrupt the flow of conversation and might be thought of as side episodes to the main conversational thread. The more clarification needed, the less efficient the overall communication.

Examination of the details of conversations over various communication media show that even though performance is often no different, conversational structures differ when conversants are using video in addition to audio. Participants verbally check each others' understanding more when they have just audio compared to audio plus video [9].

We hypothesized, based on the results in the literature to date, that video would not affect the performance of pairs who have greater common ground, here defined as those who share a common language and culture. For those people who do not share a native language and culture, however, we expected that video would improve their performance and satisfaction as well as change the structure of their conversations. This hypothesis is supported by psychological literature that shows that when there is significant processing difficulty, people supplement audition with vision [18].

We expected further that video would change the details of how common ground is negotiated. Specifically, we predicted that pairs in the video condition would have fewer clarification questions (because their speech is more clearly understood), and need to check for mutual understanding less often (because the pairs will be able to visually monitor understanding). We expected these differences to be greater for those that are culturally dissimilar. Video allows for gestures, facial expressions, and head nods to enrich the communication between pairs.

METHOD

In this study, we compared the performance, subjective ratings of satisfaction, and communication patterns of thirty-eight pairs of students. We further varied the base level of common ground by having pairs be either native speakers of English (NS) or non-native speakers (NNS). The pairs sat in different rooms, simulating remote work situations, connected either by a high quality audio connection or by audio plus video with no delay. Each pair was to reproduce the path shown on the instructor's map onto the follower's map. A previous short paper [21] reported a preliminary analysis of the performance data; this paper adds the analysis of the conversational structure.

Participants

Thirty-eight pairs of students attending the University of Michigan participated in the study for pay. Twenty pairs were native English speakers (NS), and eighteen were non-native English speakers (NNS). For each non-native pair, the two native languages differed. They all conversed in English. None of the pairs knew each other prior to participating in the study. Pairs were assigned to media conditions randomly.

To be considered a NNS in the study, one had to have a native language other than English and have lived in an English speaking country for less than four years. Most were enrolled in courses at the English Language Institute at the University of Michigan. On average, NNS pairs had been living in the United States 1.2 years and reported having studied English in their native country for 10 years. Their average score on the Test of English as a Foreign Language (TOEFL) was 600.[1] Pairs assigned to the video condition did not differ from those in the audio condition in any of these measures, nor did their partner's ratings of their English proficiency, taken at the end of the session, differ across conditions.

Task

The fictional map task reported in [1, 4] was adopted for this study because it requires effective communication for good performance. This task reflects real life in that the task goals are shared, people have different information, and they must effectively share this information in order to accomplish their goals. In this task, one person was the instruction-giver (instructor) and the other was the instruction follower (follower). Each person received a copy of the map, but only the instructor's map had the path drawn on it (See Figure 1). The follower's task was to accurately draw the path on his or her own map based on the instructor's directions. In order to make the task

---

[1] A score of 600 is a common threshold for acceptance of foreigners to US graduate schools. Possible scores range from 200 to 680.

more difficult and encourage communication and clarification, the two maps were similar, but not exactly the same. Each set of maps contained items in common (e.g., bicycle, boat, turtles in Figure 1), items that were on one map, but not the other (e.g., blimp, footsteps in Figure 1) and items that were in the same location on both maps, but not the same items (e.g., palm tree, oak tree in Figure 1). Each pair worked on four maps of approximately equal perceived difficulty, as measured by ratings on a post-experimental questionnaire. Furthermore, overall performance on each map was the same. However, there was a difference with respect to map order, with the first map being the hardest. $(F(3,93)=3.06, p<.05)$.

Figure 1. The instructor's and follower's maps showing a path on one, not on the other, and a few differences between objects on the maps.

Setting and Procedure

Pairs worked in different rooms connected with a full-duplex audio connection or audio plus high fidelity video. Both audio and video had no delay.[2] The video was an analog connection between a camera and a monitor in the adjacent room. In the video condition, the face, shoulders, and hand gestures of the remote participant were visible. Both participants could see each other.

In order for the pair to become familiar with the communication mode, pairs participated in a short interactive task prior to the map task. Before commencing with the set of map tasks, the participants were told that: 1) each person's map would have the same starting point on it, 2) only the instructor's map would have the entire route and end point marked, 3) there were some differences in landmarks between the two maps, 4) the instructor's task was to communicate the direction of the route as accurately as possible to the follower so that he or she could draw the route on his or her map, and 5) they could use any strategy they wished in order to accomplish

---

[2] This is not equivalent to commercial video conferencing systems, which often have a delay of ½ to 1 sec.

the task with the exception of holding the map up to the camera (in the video condition). Each pair worked on four maps, counterbalanced for order across all conditions. Participants switched roles of instructor and follower in an ABBA format. The pairs were not given any feedback about their performance until after they had completed all four maps.

Following the four maps, participants filled out a questionnaire, described below.

Performance Score

We used a video tape of each session to calculate the time to complete each map. The accuracy of the drawing of the map was measured by the discrepancy between the instructor's and follower's paths. This was calculated by overlaying the two maps and counting the number of cm^2 by which they deviated. Because the assumption of equal variance was violated for the accuracy and time data, the raw scores for each map were transformed using natural logarithms. Both the time and quality data were normalized across all subjects and added together to produce a combined performance score. Combining these two measures was possible because there was no evidence of a speed/accuracy tradeoff (Pearson r = -.08, n.s.). Pairs showed good or poor performance by either time, accuracy, or both.

Communication Coding

Verbatim transcripts were made of the 152 discussions associated with each of the map tasks (four maps for each of 38 pairs). We coded each speaker turn as new information, previously mentioned information being clarified, discussion about how to approach the task, or digression. The codes blended the scheme developed in Conversational Games Analysis [3] and discussion categories [16]. The list of categories is shown in Table 1.

Two independent raters categorized each utterance in each speaker's turn into the speech categories in Table 1. The coding categories and these definitions were developed iteratively on a subset of the data until sufficient reliability could be achieved. The two raters achieved an inter-rater reliability of Cohen's Kappa=.77 for the final coding scheme. Each rater then coded half of the transcripts for each condition.

Since the individual map sessions differed in the total elapsed time and the number of ideas spoken, we report the communication analyses two ways: (1) the proportion of spoken units that were each category and (2) the number of units spoken in a category, normalized by time on that task. The first adjusts for the likely differences in rate at which NNS speak. The second counts the

Table 1. Categories and their definitions for the conversation analysis.

Category	Definition
Instruction	A *new* request for action or strategy to be done in the near future. "Do this."
Align/Check	Explanations and statements that check the status of something, that does not call for action. "Are you here?"
Clarification	Statements that clarify or restate information already presented. "So you have a beach umbrella, you say."
Answers	Simple responses or agreements to clarification or align/check. "Yep."
Acknowledg-ment	Simple utterances of receipt of information. "OK." "Uh huh."
Meeting management	Statements that orchestrate the overall activity, move things head, etc. "Let's see now." "Now what."
Digression	Statements not related to the task or progress, usually humor or side topics.

proportion of individual things said, factoring out how many words each utterance required.

Questionnaire

At the end of the four map sessions, participants were given a 22-item questionnaire. They were asked to rate the communication process (e.g., its efficiency and how understandable it was), map difficulty, and for the appropriate conditions, the usefulness of the video and the English proficiency of one's partner.

RESULTS

Performance

We predicted that native speaker pairs would not benefit from the video channel, whereas the non-native pairs would. The results showed that on average, the pairs took about 12 minutes to complete each map, and deviated from the path on average approximately 36cm^2. Overall, NS performed better than NNS ($F(1,34)=16.48$, $p<.001$, $\eta^2=.32$). Native speaker and NNS pairs were affected by video differently as indicated by the significant interaction between communication media and pair type, shown in Table 2 ($F(1,34)=5.65$, $p<.05$, $\eta^2=.14$). NS pairs did not differ significantly in the audio and video conditions ($F(1,18)=.56$, n.s.), consistent with past research. However, the difference between audio and video for the NNS pairs was significant, $F(1,16)=6.07$, $p<.025$), with NNS pairs performing better with video. In fact, the NNS with video were indistinguishable from the NS with video ($F(1,17)=2.34$, n.s.).

Table 2. The raw scores of time and accuracy of the drawn path in four conditions, plus the combined normalized performance score. The higher the performance scores, the worse the performance (longer times and greater deviation).

	Audio	**Video**
Native Speakers	731 sec 24.7 cm^2 -0.84 perf	701 sec 28.64 cm^2 -0.52 perf
Non-Native Speakers	875 sec 44.4 cm^2 1.44 perf	640 sec 37.85 cm^2 0.06 perf

Table 3. Proportion of units spoken that occurred in each category.

Category	NS Audio	NS Video	NNS Audio	NNS Video
Instruction	.26[a]	.26[a]	.20[b]	.22[b]
Acknowledg-ment	.24[a]	.22[a]	.19[b]	.18[b]
Align/Check	.19	.22	.20	.20
Clarification	.15[b]	.14[b]	.24[a]	.24[a]
Answers	.12[b]	.11[b]	.14[a]	.14[a]
Meeting management	.03	.03	.03	.03
Digression	.02	.02	.01	.01

Table 4. Number of units in each category normalized by time in the task.

Category	NS Audio	NS Video	NNS Audio	NNS Video
Instruction	5.69[b]	6.11[a]	4.53[c]	5.90[a]
Acknowledg-ment	5.93[a]	6.05[a]	4.11[b]	4.49[b]
Align/Check	4.94[b]	5.63[a]	4.44[b]	5.21[a]
Clarification	3.55[b]	3.73[b]	5.23[a]	6.31[a]
Answers	2.83	2.80	3.06	3.68
Meeting management	0.66	0.85	0.77	0.80
Digression	0.16	0.20	0.13	0.09

Communication Analyses

Total time in communication was the same for NS and NNS pairs across all conditions ($F(1,34)=2.26$, n.s.). The total number of units spoken overall was 293 per map; again these were not different across the four conditions.

Tables 3 and 4 show the details of the proportion and rate of units in each of the 7 categories for NS and NNS in both media conditions. Different superscripting indicates significant differences across conditions within a category (within a row). Most differences are single main effects, e.g. Clarifications being lower for NS than for NNS. Table 4's Instruction category illustrates the one case where there are two main effects.

Giving Instructions
Instructions are defined as the first offering of new information to the partner. Although we had no a priori hypotheses regarding instructions, we found that NS pairs had proportionally more instructions than NNS pairs (26% vs. 21%; $F_{(1, 34)} = 5.78$, $p < .05$, $\eta^2 = .14$). For instructors, not only did the relative proportion of instructions differ, so did the rate. There was a main effect for both pair type ($F_{(1,34)} = 12.39$, $p < .01$, $\eta^2 = .27$) and communication medium ($F_{(1,34)} = 4.88$, $p < .05$, $\eta^2 = .13$). On further analysis, it is only in the audio condition ($F_{(1,17)} = 17.68$, $p < .005$) and not the video condition ($F_{(1,17)} = 2.465$, n.s.) that the NS instructed more than the NNS. The fewer instructions for the NNS in the audio condition may explain their poorer performance. In addition, instructors in the video condition instructed their partners more than their counterparts in the audio condition. The puzzle is why this is. Perhaps the instructor picks up confusion in the follower's facial gestures and instructs in more detail to be clear.

Acknowledgements
Acknowledgments are simple auditory signals confirming receipt of information and often follow instructions. It stands to reason that more instructions would result in more acknowledgments, and indeed this was true. Consequently, as NS pairs instructed proportionately more, so did they acknowledge proportionately more than NNS pairs ($F_{(1,34)} = 10.18$, $p < .005$, $\eta^2 = .23$). The same results appeared in examining the rate ($F_{(1,34)} = 8.82$, $p < .01$, $\eta^2 = .21$).

Align and Check
Alignments and checking statements are those initiated by either the instructor (Align) or follower (Check) to seek confirmation that the other is where they should be. It is a clear episode of seeking to establish or increase the common ground. Because the pairs were able to visually monitor understanding, we expected the need to check for mutual understanding to be less in the video condition. In contrast to this expectation, no differences between the proportion of aligning and checking were found between native and non-native speakers nor across media type. However, there was a clear increase in the rate of align/checks in the video condition for both NS and NNS pairs ($F_{(1,34)} = 4.14$, $p = .05$, $\eta^2 = .11$).

Clarifications and Answers
We predicted that pairs in the video condition would have fewer clarification questions because their speech would be more clearly understood. The results showed that the number of clarifications differed with respect to pair type. Overall, NNS pairs asked proportionately more clarification questions than their NS pairs ($F_{(1,34)} = 58.68$, $p < .001$, $\eta^2 = .61$). We were expecting more clarification in the non-natives' audio condition, but that was not the case. Answers were similarly proportionately higher in for NNS ($F_{(1,34)} = 8.39$, $p < .01$, $\eta^2 = .19$).

Meeting management and digressions.
Neither of these categories differed across conditions.

Questionnaire responses
Post-experiment questionnaire data provided some additional support for these results. NNS pairs in the video condition reported finding the video more useful than NS pairs ($F_{(1,34)} = 4.53$, $p < .05$). In addition, there were two significant interactions between pair type and communication medium: namely, self-reported ratings on the ability of pairs to communicate with each other in an efficient ($F_{(1,63)} = 7.301$, $p < .01$), and an understandable manner ($F_{(1,63)} = 4.92$, $p < .03$). Oddly, NS pairs in the *audio* condition reported that the communication was more efficient and understandable than NS pairs in the video condition. In contrast, NNS pairs in the audio condition reported that the communication was less efficient and understandable than NNS pairs in the video. Furthermore, there was a marginally significant negative correlation between ratings of the partner's English and the usefulness of the video (Pearson $= -.39$, $p < .06$). The correlation indicates that the more proficient one rated his or her partner's English, the less useful they rated the video.

Although NS pairs perceived that their communication was more efficient in the audio condition, their performance did not support this perception. NS pairs had the same performance whether they communicated by audio or video. NNS pairs, on the other hand, perceived their communication as more efficient and understandable in the video condition than NNS pairs in the audio condition, and this perception reflected their performance differences.

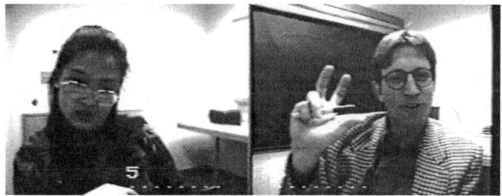

Figure 2. A pair of NNS using the video connection to communicate. The instructor is on the right, the follower on the left.

Summary of results

Consistent with past research, native speaker pairs showed no performance difference in the presence of video. However NNS pairs performed significantly better with video. Overall, pairs did not differ in the amount of time they communicated, independent of whether they were native speakers or not and independent of whether they spoke through audio only or audio plus video. Native speaker pairs *instructed* in a larger proportion of their communication than NNS pairs. Consequently, they also spent proportionately more of their communication acknowledging. This difference was most marked in the NNS audio condition.

Overall NNS pairs spent proportionately more of their time clarifying. The performance loss in NNS audio seems to be associated with less instructing and checking of their mutual understanding.

In the post-experimental questionnaire, NNS pairs rated the video as more useful than NS pairs. Surprisingly, NS pairs rated the *audio* condition as more efficient. The less proficient a person rated his or her partner's English, the more video was valued.

DISCUSSION AND CONCLUSION

Video clearly helped the NNS pairs communicate. Their performance was significantly better than with audio only, and they preferred it. What might be a reason for that? What are the NNS pairs doing with the video?

The analysis of their communication showed that the non-native English speakers with video had a higher rate of instructions and checked their mutual understanding more. What is the video doing to help them here?

Video helps assess the state of understanding

Instructors may pick up signals about whether an instruction is understood or not, by being able to see their partner's face. They could respond to a look of puzzlement on the follower's face and provide more detail, whereas their counterparts in the audio condition would not be able to adjust their instructions as easily. Video could also reduce the need for side negotiations to clarify the meaning of instructions. It could be the case that, in the video condition, the detail in the instructions was provided at an appropriate level for the partner and task. Another possible response to a look of puzzlement from the follower would be to check for understanding by checking his or her current location. As a result there is less confusion, less need for explicit repair, and common ground is more easily negotiated.

Figure 2 illustrates this idea. The man on the right is the instructor, and the woman on the left is the follower. He is engaged in instructing, using his hands to describe the shape of some object, and monitoring both her attention (i.e., by whether she is looking at him) and her degree of understanding. The woman on the left is paying attention to the instructor through the video channel, and displays a mild degree of puzzlement.

Without the visual feedback, non-native pairs might engage in useless instruction, by continuing to the next instruction when the follower is lost. This suggests that when people with little common ground use audio, they should check whether or not they are understood more often, since the visual clues to this state are missing.

Video offers clarifying information through hand gestures

There is another potential benefit to the video channel, partly illustrated in Figure 2 as well. The video not only provides a way to monitor understanding, it also provides an additional way to communicate via gestures. Hand gestures serve many roles in conversation from accompanying speech, to indicating speaker turns, to pointing to a common referent and finally being a substitute for speech (e.g., iconic). [2]. The former two types of gestures facilitate the flow of the conversation, while the latter two types contribute to the content of the conversation.

We noted that NNS pairs often used iconic gestures. For example, in the map task NNS pairs were at times at a loss for how to describe particular objects or the path direction because they could not find the appropriate word (e.g., distinguishing between two types of trees or boats). They begin to draw in the air (e.g., fingers pointing up in the air to signify palm fronds, or fists representing lakeshore and the other hand drawing the path direction around the lake). This is another use of the "air board" [15].

Interestingly, participants seemed unaware of the difficulties they experienced using audio-only. The limited channels may limit one's ability to notice and identify errors in communication. For simple tasks, this difference may not be detected, but the present findings suggest that more for complex tasks, or when communication clarity is strained or the communication is difficult to understand, video provides a significant advantage in performance.

Conclusions

Video does matter, not only in formal negotiation tasks, but also in the more subtle and daily negotiations of meaning in ordinary conversations. We examined a situation in which meaning is negotiated frequently, in pairs whose proficiency in the language is low. Without video, they can exchange neither iconic gestures to help specify what they are talking about, nor facial expressions to signal attention and understanding. As a result, their performance suffers. However, when these pairs are provided with a video connection their performance improves to the point of being equal to those who have more basic common ground. They can gesture and attend, pick up signals of confusion right away and make repairs to their mutual understanding. Consequently, they achieve mutual understanding by more efficiently negotiating a shared meaning.

These results have very important practical implications as more and more organizations demand that their employees serve on multiple teams where people are not co-located, do not share a common native language, and are not familiar with each other. Commonly, with budget restrictions, people find themselves unable to travel as much as they wish. They experience misunderstandings in conversations with remote colleagues because they share little common ground. These are the situations in which

people will benefit most from video. It is for these situations that the investment in video-conferencing pays.

ACKNOWLEDGEMENTS

This work was supported in part by a grant from the National Science Foundation IIS-9320543. We are grateful to the English Language Institute at Michigan for their help in this research and to our second coder, Ben Leroi, for his diligence, care and patience.

REFERENCES

1. Anderson, A. H., Bader, M., Bard, E., Boyle, E., Doherty, G., Garrod, S., Issard, S., Kwotko, J., McAllister, J., Miller, J., Sotillo, C., & Thompson, H. (1991). The HCRC MAP Task corpus. *Language and Speech, 34,* 351-360.

2. Bekker, M. M., Olson, J., & Olson, G. M. (1995). Analysis of gestures in face-to-face design team provides guidance for how to use groupware in design. *Proceedings of the Symposium on Designing Interactive Systems, DIS'95,* 157-166.

3. Boyle, E. , Anderson, A. & Newlands, A. (1994). The effects of visibility on dialogue performance in a cooperative problem solving task, *Language and Speech, 37,1,* 1-20.

4. Brown, G., Anderson, A. H., Yule, G., & Shilcock, R. (1984). *Teaching talk.* Cambridge, England: Cambridge University Press.

5. Chapanis, A. (1975). Interactive human communication. *Scientific American, 232,* 36-42.

6. Chapanis, A. Ochsman, R.B., Parrish, R. N.& Weeks, G. D. (1972). Studies in interactive communication: The effects of four communication modes on the behavior of teams during a co-operative problem solving. *Human Factors, 14,* 487-509.

7. Clark, H. H. (1996). *Using language.* (pp. 92-125) Cambridge England: Cambridge University Press.

8. Clark, H. H. & Wilks-Gibbs, D. (1986) Referring as a collaborative process. *Cognition, 22,* 1-39.

9. Doherty-Sneedon, G., Anderson, A., O'Malley, C., Langton, S., Garrod, S., & Bruce, V. (1997). Face-to-Face and video mediated communication: A comparison of dialogue structure and task performance, *Journal of Experimental Psychology: Applied, 3, 2,* 105-123.

10. Edigo, C. (1990). Teleconferencing as a technology to support co-operative work: Its possibilities and limitations. In J. Gallegher, R. E. Kraut, & C. Edigo (Eds.) *Intellectual teamwork: Social and technological foundations of cooperative work* (pp. 351-371). Hillsdale, N.J.: L. Erlbaum Associates.

11. Farmer, S. M. & Hyatt, C. W. (1994). Effects of task language demand and task complexity on computer-mediated work groups, *Small Group Research, 25, 3*, 331-336.

12. Finn, K., Sellen, A., & Wilbur, S. (1997). *Video-mediated communication.* Hillsdale NJ: Lawrence Erlbaum Associates.

13. Green & Williges, R. C. (1975). Evaluation of alternative media used with a groupware editor in a simulated telecommunication environment. *Human Factors, 37(3)*, 283-289.

14. O'Connaill, B., Whittker, S. & Wilbur, S. (1993). Conversations over video conferences: An evaluation of video mediated interaction. *Human-Computer Interaction, 8,* 389-428.

15. Olson, G. M. & Olson, J. S. (1991). User Centered design of collaboration technology. *Journal of Organizational Computing, 1*(1), 61-84.

16. Olson, G. M., Olson, J.S., Carter, M. & Storrosten, M. (1992). Small group design meetings: An analysis of collaboration. *Human Computer Interaction, 7,* 347-374.

17. Olson, J., Olson, G. & Meader, D. (1995). What mix of video and audio is useful for remote real-time work. In *Proceedings of Computer and Human Interaction'95*, (Denver, CO, May 1995), ACM Press, 362-368.

18. Reisberg, D., McLean, J. & Goldfield, A. (1987). Easy to hear but hard to understand: A lip-reading advantage with intact auditory stimuli. In R. Campbell & B. Dodd (Eds.) *Hearing by Eye: The psychology of lip-reading.* Hillsdale, N. J.: Lawrence Erlbaum Associates.

19. Short, J., Williams, E., & Christie, B. (1976) *The social psychology of telecommunications.* London: Wiley.

20. Varonis, E. M. and S. M. Gass (1985) "Non-native/Non-native Conversations: A Model for Negotiation of Meaning", *Applied Linguistics* 6(1): 71-90.

21. Veinott, E. S., Olson, J. S., Olson, G. M. & Fu, X. (1997). Video Matters! When communication is stressed video helps. In *Extended Abstracts of Computer and Human Interaction '97*, (Atlanta, GA, April 1997), ACM Press, 315-316.

Designing Multimedia for Learning:
Narrative Guidance and Narrative Construction

Lydia Plowman
Scottish Council for Research in Education
15 St. John Street
Edinburgh EH8 8JR UK
+44 (0)131 557 2944
Lydia.Plowman@scre.ac.uk

Rosemary Luckin
School of Cognitive & Computing Sciences
University of Sussex
Brighton BN1 9PH UK
+44 (0)1273 678647
rosel@cogs.susx.ac.uk

Diana Laurillard, Matthew Stratfold, Josie Taylor[1]

ABSTRACT

Narrative is fundamental to the ways we make sense of texts of all kinds because it provides structure and coherence, but it is difficult to see how this works in the context of multimedia interactive learning environments (MILEs). We tested our hypotheses about the form and function of narrative in MILEs by developing three versions of material on CD-ROM which had different narrative structures and analysed the impact of the different versions on learner behaviour. We present a theoretical framework in which we explain the concepts of narrative guidance and narrative construction and their application to the design of MILEs.

Keywords

Narrative, multimedia design, education

NEW NARRATIVES AND LEARNING

Narrative is not simply an aesthetic issue. It is fundamentally linked to cognition and understanding, so an understanding of how it works is particularly relevant to the design of multimedia for learning. The introduction of hypertexts has seen a resurgence of interest in the form and function of narrative because the authorial process and how it is understood by the reader or user accentuates the roles which are frequently left unstated in other media [1, 9, 19, 21]. There has, however, been less interest in the role of narrative in non-literary texts and, particularly, of educational media. Our aim is to develop an approach which emphasises the importance of structure but recognises that narrative cannot be studied in isolation from the dynamic processes of interaction if it is to be applied to multimedia interactive learning environments (MILEs). We discuss the relationship between narrative and usability and how MILEs can provide the narrative guidance necessary to facilitate the user's construction of narrative.

There are precedents for suggesting that books, films, drama and other narrative media can inform the design and usability of multimedia [5, 10, 15] but we focus on how the form and function of narrative facilitates or impedes *learning*, heeding the ways in which prior exposure to other narrative forms shapes our understanding but also examining how it works in a specifically interactive medium.

Because narrative can be suspended or altered at various decision points, or foci of interactivity, the rearrangement of discrete elements generates new texts and new meanings [24]. Narrative structures as traditionally understood are not therefore appropriate for interactive multimedia but an Aristotelian concept of narrative (at its simplest, the concept that texts should have a beginning, a middle and an end) is locked into western European thought and shapes our expectations. Students can discern narrative more easily when using textbooks or video because these media generally conform to generic narrative expectations. There is not yet this heritage to draw on for MILEs and so students often have problems engaging with materials and making sense of them [25].

The two main forms of MILEs observed in use in the early phase of this study and previously [12, 23] are those presented in an *encyclopaedia* format, designed to support both free exploration and specific information enquiries, and those which use a more guided and focussed *tutorial* approach. Both formats have structures, the issue is the extent to which they are perceptible to users. Although encyclopaedia-style software is more commonly supposed to be lacking in structure, at least at the highest level it is recognisably an encyclopaedia, even if the specifics of navigation are not clear. Tutorial-style multimedia software does not have a comparable provenance because it is based on live interaction with a teacher, so although it may seem to lend itself to a narrative structure, the lack of precedents makes design decisions difficult, especially given the lack of empirical work in this area. Either way, comprehension problems can be exacerbated for users when compared to books, videos or live tutors, mainly because the procedures and operations involved in using them get in the way of understanding. Where teachers are not on hand to provide guidance, it is even more important that it is provided by the software.

NARRATIVE AND COGNITION

Narrative is typically thought of as being synonymous with 'story', but whereas 'story' implies both form and content our observations suggest that, for MILES, it is generally the structure rather than the content which is problematic. Narrative can be seen as a macro-structure which creates global coherence, contributes to local coherence and aids recall through its network of causal

---

[1] All at Open University, Milton Keynes, MK7 6AA, UK

links and signposting. The structure provides a linear dynamic which can accommodate diversions and tangents and allows learners to maintain their plans and goals. It has both cognitive and affective impact, performing an essential organising function for the learner by shaping the creation of meaning from texts of all kinds.

Whether we have a predisposition to finding and creating narrative [3, 17] or whether we are enculturated into it, the role of narrative is central to our cognition from earliest childhood [6, 20]. It helps us think, remember, communicate, and make sense of ourselves and the world. More specifically, previous research [2, 22, 28] suggests that texts which are unfamiliarly structured because they do not conform to mental models of narrative make excessive demands on our cognitive processes. Learners constantly adjust their understanding in accordance with their exposure to conventional narratives, making the construction of narrative a central cognitive goal.

Learners favour clearly structured and navigable texts so MILEs generally produce cognitive costs in terms of narrative construction. The very nature of a medium which brings with it the benefits of interactivity and a multimedia format also results in a fragmentation of the narrative which is normally present in linear media such as books: the narrative can be suspended and altered and may thwart or confuse our expectations, producing a multiplicity of pathways and disruption of the flow of the user's experience. The freedom to explore the material and choose its pace and sequence is liberating but it can also be confusing because it results in frequent, sometimes gratuitous, interactions with the computer. This can mean that the interactions which are integral to the experience of using MILEs impede learning. In such contexts narrative not only exists in the software with which students interact but must take account of the interactants, what they bring to its interpretation, and the processes of interaction. We describe the two main interdependent processes as narrative *guidance* and narrative *construction*.

Background to the study

The focus of the research reported here is how students make sense of their learning with multimedia by constructing their own narratives in conjunction with the narrative guidance presented by the text. Previous observations [26] of school use of commercially available CD-ROMs showed that group discussion was associated with operations and procedures rather than the educational content, meaning that students were unable to construct a sustained narrative because their learning was so fragmented. One of the problems in designing MILEs is the tension between providing integral learning activities and providing information and resources for externally provided tasks. This can manifest itself as a series of units with varying degrees of relationship to each other and to the overall structure. We have characterised this in terms of the macro-narrative of the global structure and the micro-narratives of the lower-level task units.

Some software is designed with an explicit narrative which operates at a macro-level to give coherence to the content. An example of this is *Clémentine*, a CD-ROM designed to teach French to poorly motivated teenagers. The macro-narrative involves Clémentine having to raise a million francs to save the Bengali tigers and all the sub-tasks, such as designing posters, arranging coverage on the local radio station, and Clémentine's appearance on a TV charity quiz show, relate to this. The structure is relatively linear because this was seen as more appropriate for the guided progression needed for language skills.

But an explicit macro-narrative does not necessarily lead to a coherent learning experience. *School Disco* had a strong narrative of organising a school disco but the tasks involved (such as calculating cumulative frequency) did not always bear a clear relationship to the narrative, or were so complex and time-consuming that it became forgotten. In such an example there is a tension between the macro-level of the narrative and the lower-level task units. Students need to be able to relate the constituent units to the high level structure but also perceive the relationship between sub-units.

NARRATIVE GUIDANCE AND NARRATIVE CONSTRUCTION

The design elements presented by the software constitute narrative *guidance* and can be a combination of features specific to interactive media, such as the need for clear navigational procedures, with features associated with traditional media, such as recognisable narrative and a clear relationship between tasks and the macro-narrative. We have observed ways in which teachers compensate for its absence by providing their own narrative guidance. They mediate its use for the classroom context by constraining the range of responses, offering interpretative possibilities and elaborating the task. An example of this is a task in which students aged 11 had to use *Encarta* to find information relevant to a forthcoming trip to a Roman site. They were going to act out, in costume, a play they had written based on a newspaper account of the discovery of a skeleton at the site; they were able to locate and use information more purposefully than others who did not have this guidance.

This example of the teacher providing narrative guidance is unusual because it involves a lot of preparation and familiarity with the materials. More often, students use MILEs in a context where they do not enjoy such committed teacher input and the narrative guidance needs to be embedded in the software design.

Narrative *construction* is the active process of meaning-making, stimulated by the text and the environment, combined with the vast reservoir of knowledge that each person brings with them to the experience. It is a process of both discerning and imposing a structure on the materials, making links and connections in a personally meaningful way.

Although this active process of meaning-making is cognitive, it cannot be divorced from cultural context, whether this is the classroom or exposure to other media. Narrative is a way of connecting what goes on 'in the head' (internal representations in fig.1) with what goes on in the world (external representations in fig.1), hence our shift in emphasis from the text itself to the process of constructing narrative. Prior knowledge may prove to be counter-productive if, for example, learners' experiences of paper-based texts lead them to assume they can interact with multimedia in ways which do not translate from one medium to another or if they expect the strong narrative typical of computer games. Or prior knowledge may be beneficial if learners are able to make meaningful links to other texts and sources of knowledge.

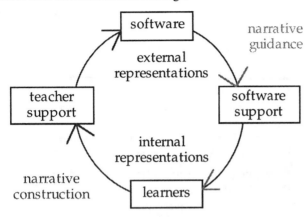

Figure 1: The cycle of narrative guidance and narrative construction

Although we have separated them for the purposes of explication, narrative guidance and narrative construction are not discrete processes but, in a productive learning experience, a dynamic cycle. The construction of narrative is a collaboration between designers, teachers and learners.

The learner's inclination to supply narrative continuity, to bridge the gaps at the foci of interactivity, is based on their own input in addition to what is presented by the software and their co-learners. The relationship between the designer and learner is symbiotic, each dependent on the other, and not so different from Steiner's description of the 'full act' of reading books as being one of 'dynamic reciprocity' [27]. In this sense, there is little difference from books and other media with which narrative is more closely associated. The notion of an active reader is nothing new: Sterne played with such conventions in his eighteenth century novel *Tristram Shandy* and, more recently, reader response theory [8] has promoted an understanding of the ways in which author and reader jointly construct narrative. In an educational context, teachers are also included in this process.

THE DESIGN OF *GALAPAGOS*

We have developed three versions of *Galapagos* as a research tool, based on extended observation of students using commercially available CD-ROMs in schools. We hypothesised that students need some form of presented narrative guidance from the software because the narrative in MILEs is not easily discernible and there may be multiple narratives depending on the route taken. Students also require support for narrative construction as this increases understanding of the material. The purpose of the manipulations was to see to what extent different

forms of narrative guidance affect learner behaviour, including the ease with which they accomplish the task and how well they can recall their learning, and to establish implications for the design of multimedia for learning.

Galapagos is a CD-ROM in which we have manipulated the type of narrative guidance in each version and provided a model answer, script of the audio track, notepad and easily accessible statement of the task to support learners in their narrative construction. *Galapagos* uses Darwin's experiences in the Galapagos Islands to teach the principles of natural selection and aims to stimulate users to think about how wildlife arrived on the newly formed volcanic islands given they are so distant from the nearest land mass. This in turn stimulates thinking about how variation in the islands' bird population has arisen and all learners are given the task of explaining the variation in the wildlife observed by Darwin and constructing their answer to this task using the on-line notepad. All learners have access to a model answer once some text has been saved in the notepad. All versions have the same content (eight sections, each of which deals with a different aspect of the Islands such as their formation, location, or the effects of trade winds), use the same video sequences and audio tracks, but have different structures.

The linear version was designed to present an easily identifiable narrative so we could explore the extent to which MILEs should emulate more familiar narrative structures. The resource-based learning version was designed to reflect existing commercially available CD-ROMs we had observed in classroom use, and the guided discovery learning version was designed to combine guidance of the type offered by classroom teachers with the benefits of an interactive medium.

The linear version

The linear version is designed in such a way that students are led through the eight sections of the CD-ROM in sequence and it is closest to a traditional narrative as presented in, say, educational television. There are no search mechanisms and users cannot change section, except by going backwards or forwards, until they have seen all eight sections once. The interface is active compared to the other versions: video segments start as soon as they are on the screen and learners are relatively passive. After the voice-over welcome users are invited to proceed by selecting the 'Next' button. The educational rationale for this design was that it would be more suitable for novice users as the scope for machine interaction was limited and it would encourage them to see enough resources to be able to answer the set question; left to their own devices, they may not see everything available. There is no explicit external support for narrative construction other than that provided by all versions; narrative guidance is provided by the familiarity of a traditional linear structure.

The resource-based learning (RBL) version

The resource-based version offers no guidance through the CD-ROM sections and leaves students to define their own route. Although on a smaller scale, its closest equivalent is a multimedia encyclopaedia. The eight sections of the RBL version can be accessed from a main menu or the simple word-search mechanism at the top level. When resources appear on screen, they are not activated until the user clicks on them. The style is exploratory and users are free to go where they want; the only constraint is that they cannot access the model answer before they have entered some notes in the notepad, as is true for all versions. The interface is static and more complex as learners have to make selections for control and navigation. This could mean a cluttered and intimidating screen, so we provided sufficient features to enable effective RBL but from a clean and attractive interface. The educational rationale for this version was to encourage independent learners who are able to search through the resources to research their answers and complete the task. In this design manipulation learners need to construct their own questions in order to decompose the task into manageable chunks. There is no additional support for narrative construction and no explicit narrative guidance.

The guided discovery learning version

The guided discovery (GDL) version offers guidance in breaking down the task by providing paths through the material, questions to stimulate enquiries, and direction to specific resources. Of the three versions, this is closest to the support given by a teacher. It does not present the narrative as strongly as the linear version but provides more guidance than the RBL version. The eight sections can be accessed from one of three text guides which focus on aspects relevant to completing the task such as formation and location of the Islands, effects of trade winds and ocean currents, and Darwin's exploration of the

islands and the bird populations. The guides are not animated or intelligent agents although this is an area for future development. Users do not have the same freedom to move around as provided by the RBL menu but, as with the RBL version, users are expected to be active, although the range of choices they can make at any given point is constrained. After the voice-over welcome and introduction to the package, task, and toolbar buttons, attention is drawn to the 'Guides' button. The educational rationale for this version was to encourage and support learners in locating appropriate resources to complete the task. There is explicit support for narrative construction through the provision of this guidance.

The approach learners adopt to complete the given task is therefore determined partly by the version they use. In addition to the narrative guidance manipulations which are outside the learners' control, other features such as the availability of a model answer and notepad editor scaffold the task [14] at different points in the narrative construction process. Use of these supports depends on whether students choose to adopt them because, as table 1 shows, they are available in each version.

DESIGN OF THE STUDY

Four groups of three students, aged between 15 and 21 years, used each of the three versions of *Galapagos*. The 36 students were based in two different institutions and all were studying for a national examination in Biology. A session using *Galapagos* to complete the task to their own satisfaction typically took about 45 minutes. The study maintained ecological validity inasmuch as use of the CD-ROM was integrated into their studies at an appropriate point in curriculum delivery and provided an authentic task within the syllabus. It took place in their own environment and their teachers both introduced the

	NARRATIVE GUIDANCE	SUPPORT FOR NARRATIVE CONSTRUCTION	STUDENT RESPONSES
LINEAR	recognisable, linear structure easy navigation limited interaction	notebook model answer easily accessible statement of task script	**navigation**: access all sections, do not alter sequence **task**: do not take notes during 1st linear sequence, then become more like other groups; write chunks in notepad w/o reference to sections; all access model answer and subsequently make revisions **talk**: talk low during 1st linear sequence, then both procedural & task increase slightly
RESOURCE-BASED LEARNING (RBL)	no explicit narrative guidance some implicit guidance in interface design (eg order of items)	notebook model answer easily accessible statement of task script	**navigation**: do not access some sections; use menu or search for navigation **task**: start written response before completing access to content; low level of text revisions; all access model answer - not all revise subsequently **talk**: less talk relating to answer construction
GUIDED DISCOVERY LEARNING (GDL)	three text guides offer routes through material and stimulate enquiry some implicit guidance in interface design	notebook model answer easily accessible statement of task script	**navigation**: access all sections; use online guide as navigational tool **task**: start response before completing access to content; high level of text revision; text entered in small sections; frequent reference back to content **talk**: low level of talk in early stages; increases after access to guides

Table 1: Summary of design and use of different versions of *Galapagos*

topic and debriefed them afterwards. However, each group was randomly assigned to one version of the CD-ROM and none of the students was aware of the different versions. It was not our intention to measure learning (as there are too many variables if studying a naturalistic environment is prioritised) but to identify ways in which learning can be supported.

Data collection

Every session had two video-recorded sources: one recorded the group of learners at the computer to capture talk, movement, gesture and machine interaction; the other was the screen image, taken from the computer via a scan converter. The videotapes were mixed in an editing suite, transcribed, and used for very detailed analysis of learners' talk and behaviour and their path through the material [13]. The three-way software design manipulation has enabled us to analyse similar events across versions to see how design features, such as the narrative structure and provision of software support for learners, interact with and support students' learning.

Following completion of the task, individual learners were given a tape-recorder and asked to record their responses to questions which ranged from checking on accuracy of factual recall to asking them to recount the lesson for an absent friend. We analysed the notepad answers constructed during use of *Galapagos*, as they provide the most accessible means of insight into their emerging understanding, and a teacher evaluated how well they fulfilled the task requirement of explaining the variations in wildlife. We also collected information about each learner's prior experience with computers, their predicted examination grades for Biology and the teacher's assessment of their oral abilities.

STUDENTS USING *GALAPAGOS*

Because the students used *Galapagos* in groups their experience is most clearly revealed through their talk. This is particularly useful for illuminating the processes of narrative construction, especially discussion involved in producing an answer to fulfil the task requirements. This data is supplemented by navigational information from the video recordings. As the route taken is determined to some extent by the version used, this gives us information on narrative guidance, although neither source of data can be analysed in isolation.

For analytical purposes, each group was conceived of as a small case study and we did not attempt to find quantitatively defined relations between groups and the version used. Our focus of interest was in local relations between design features and behaviour for the various sources of data we had. Some of these were generated by the group (talk, notepad responses), others were generated by individuals (self-recorded responses to probes). The following discussion is based on very detailed analyses [13] of learners' interactions with the software and with each other but has been simplified for illustrative purposes.

Interacting with *Galapagos*

The linear version presents a high degree of narrative guidance and little opportunity for learners to decide their own narrative path so they have relatively little control. This is more apparent in the early part of a session as all eight sections were viewed in sequence, even though learners were able to move backwards and forwards. Once they had seen all eight sections learners exercised more control but still retained a fairly linear path through the material.

For the RBL version, the reverse is true. There is very little narrative guidance offered and learners have to construct a narrative by making decisions about sequence, so there is a high degree of user control and heavy use of the menu to decide the route. In some cases, this meant that they did not access all available sections. The GDL version was designed to offer a balance between narrative guidance and support for narrative construction and this is reflected in a more even balance between user and system control: learners are able to determine sequence and their course of action but are offered guidance in doing so.

Given that the main purpose of *Galapagos* was for students to represent their knowledge in a written response to a question, one measure of difference between the versions is how many sections they access in composing their answer. There is a total of eight subject-related sections and a model answer available. Attempts to open the model answer before sufficient text has been entered into the notepad results in learners being advised that they can only access the model answer when they have typed 50 words into the notepad. Analysis of video recordings shows how many sections of *Galapagos* were accessed from the point at which they started composing the answer, ie after first opening the notepad, and before accessing the model answer.

The mean for students using the linear version was only two sections (two groups did not revisit any sections at all) and they did not return to any sections subsequently. Students using this version did not take notes, and they did not interrupt the flow of the narrative or alter the order of the presentation, although their behaviour often changed when they reached the end of the sections with its reminder of the task. At this point they began to behave more like students using the other versions, going back over other material and focusing on the construction of their answer.

Most sections (seven) were accessed by the GDL users because the guide had encouraged them to be interactive in their approach and to use the material to support their response. This was confirmed by teacher analysis of the completed written responses. The RBL users accessed a mean of three sections. This could be because they were forced to be more interactive than the linear version users but did not receive the guidance of the GDL users.

Interacting with each other

All group talk was transcribed and utterances were classified using NUD*IST but quantitative results across versions and different talk categories show no regular pattern. Task talk was highest for linear version users at 73% of the total number of utterances, but there was no difference between RBL (65%) and GDL (63%) users. For procedural talk about navigation and operations there was no difference across versions, all three being between 17% and 20% of the total number of utterances. We cannot read too much into this given the small number of groups, but the minimal difference in procedural talk could be attributed to the fact that all versions featured the same explicit learner support and this may have overridden problems inherent in different structures. The same features appeared in each version so as not to favour a particular narrative structure. By doing this, however, we lost some of the clear differences in the types of talk we had identified in earlier classroom observations of commercial CD-ROMs which did not offer such support. Analysing simple differences in the amounts of talk generated by different versions also risks eliding the role of individuals and, in some cases, individuals were a more important factor in group behaviour than the version to which they were exposed.

The points at which talk takes place and the effortfulness involved are more revealing. There was a low initial level of procedural talk for users of the *linear* version because there were fewer procedural and operational decisions (where to go, what to do next, how to do it) to be made. However, there was also a relatively low level of task talk (relating to completion of the task and relevant information) early in the session as the students simply sat back and watched the multimedia sequences unfold. During this time there was minimal student collaboration. The level of procedural talk increased once they had seen all eight sections because they had to assume some control, but this subsequently levelled off.

Although the level of procedural talk was similar for the *resource-based* (RBL) students they spent less time on answer construction and we have already noted that they referred back to fewer sections. This is reflected in an initial analysis of their self-recorded individual accounts after the event, with RBL students using less than half as many words (an average of 31) than either the GDL or linear users (76 and 77, respectively). Procedural talk tended to relate to using either the search or the menu facility as a central spine around which navigation to other sections of the CD-ROM was managed.

The *guided discovery* (GDL) users demonstrated low levels of talk in the early stages, but once the guides had been identified procedural talk decreased and task talk increased because the written guidance helped them to focus on the task and suggested routes. There was a tendency for the text to be entered in small sections, none longer than two short sentences, and to refer back frequently to other material, whereas some of the linear system users constructed large parts of their answer without referring back, an approach which was only observed with the linear version.

DISCUSSION

We are not basing universal design guidelines on these findings because narrative is constructed both by learners as individuals and within groups, is culturally defined [4, 7], and there are important gender differences [18]. Because the subject matter of *Galapagos* was evolution, there are also religious differences of interpretation. We have not, so far, analysed our findings from these perspectives although support for narrative construction should provide for individual differences to some extent.

The presence or absence of narrative affects whether learners interact productively with MILEs and so affects usability. Teachers provide narrative guidance and support for narrative construction because they are able to assimilate digressions, repeat points and tie up threads in a highly interactive way which takes account of the individuality of learners, the social context, relevant artefacts and the environment. They are able to elicit knowledge from students and respond to what they say, to initiate, confirm, evaluate, reformulate, and give feedback. They provide what Mercer [16] calls the guided construction of knowledge. Narrative guidance and narrative construction are interdependent because the guidance provides the means for learners to construct their own narratives and the additional support for narrative construction leads to greater engagement with the narrative guidance (fig.1). MILEs are not as sophisticated as teachers in this respect but our findings suggest that improved design and awareness of this interdependence would lead to benefits for learning.

Narrative guidance

The linear version of *Galapagos* demonstrates a relatively traditional narrative structure but this is not necessarily a solution to the design of MILEs. Although navigation is straightforward and learners access all parts of the content, this design encourages students to enter text in the notepad without reference to other sections, thus undermining a potentially beneficial feature of interactivity - being able to move easily between different sections.

A strong narrative can be motivational and contribute to the dynamic of the text but it can also detract from the real learning content. A previous example is *Stowaway*, a CD-ROM which provides a database of information about fighting ships in the 18th century. One observed problem was that the game of trying to spot the stowaway became a diversion from the information even though it provided a strong narrative link [23].

The presence or absence of the teacher is also a key variable. Students are more able to cope with multimedia encyclopaedias, for instance, if the teacher is available to offer guidance. Where teachers provide a strong narrative structure for the task, we observed fewer problems and noted that low-level interface and navigational problems can be more easily accommodated [23]. If more effort is involved in interacting with the text, mental resources available for comprehension are reduced. Low narrative guidance leads to problems with narrative construction: even though the resources were very limited compared to a multimedia encyclopaedia the RBL group did not access all the sections and started answer construction before viewing all the sections. Not all groups made revisions after accessing the model answer. This suggests less involvement and the possibility that the procedural overhead meant that their attention was diverted from the task, as demonstrated by the minimal narratives offered to explain their experiences after the event.

It is not usually possible to design a software-embedded narrative structure similar to the linear or GDL versions for multimedia encyclopaedias but it is possible to provide the means for learners to develop narratives which encompass the task and the route required to complete it satisfactorily. The role of teachers in mediating the information can also be critical.

Narrative construction

The design dilemma is that building in support for narrative construction requires more tools and a more complex interface. The three versions varied in the amount and type of guidance offered but they all offered similar help for narrative construction (model answer, notepad, script, statement of task) as we hoped that comparisons could be more easily drawn. The existence of a model answer motivated learners to start constructing an answer of their own and, once opened, the model answer itself prompted revisions.

Even though all versions have the same features supporting narrative construction, the take-up of these features varies according to the version used. For instance, users of the linear version do not access the notepad until they have seen the whole sequence of eight sections and do not use the back/forwards buttons, even though they are clearly accessible and their function is described in the spoken introduction. It is not that the linear version precludes them from using these features, but the interface design affects their responses so they do not actively engage with the task. The design also affects their interaction with each other, as a lower level of collaborative talk was observed for this group.

Although users of the linear version did not need to do as much work at narrative construction they did not seem to use their cognitive resources to tackle the task more effectively than other groups. It is as if a strong, recognisable narrative structure encourages users to jump aboard and be transported to the final destination but they can't easily get off. This narrative seduction works well in traditional linear media such as films but is less appropriate for MILEs because it doesn't maximise the potential benefits of an interactive medium or the interactivity offered by a good teacher and so is less suitable for learning.

The impetus to narrativise is so strong that in the RBL version cognitive resources are directed at constructing a route and finding structure rather than a content-rich narrative. The GDL version offers the same support for

narrative construction as the other versions, balanced by a presented narrative which offers guidance to scaffold users' learning [14]. It appears to level out some of the individual differences noted with other versions, giving support most consistently. Design features which we identified as effective in engaging learners, supporting meaning-making processes and eliciting effortful activity included:

- a clearly defined goal to encourage productive collaboration;

- a balance between narrative guidance provided by software design and the provision of facilities which allow learners to determine their route and construct a meaningful narrative;

- easy access to the task and notepad enabling learners to search for information relevant to their task and use it to construct a narrative of their emerging understanding;

- a model answer which motivates learners both to start constructing an answer of their own and, once opened, prompts revisions.

CONCLUSIONS

These are small-scale, exploratory studies and we do not claim a simple causal relation between a version of *Galapagos* and effective learning. Rather, we have explored a dynamic relationship in which the learners' experiences of design features affect both group and individual behaviour and this, in turn, affects their experience of design features. We have explored this relationship with particular reference to the cyclical processes of narrative guidance and narrative construction because they are central to learning.

The generation of narrative is an active process of meaning-making. It is a process through which we create a structure for interpreting and understanding connections and links between people, texts and events. But although we are skilled at imposing order in this way, this is not necessarily an efficient use of cognitive resources when engaging with complex texts. Texts which appear to have a strong surface narrative can be problematic if there is no support for narrative construction.

Even for more experienced users, if effort is involved in interacting with the material, mental resources available for comprehension and achievement of the learning goal are reduced. MILEs do not yet accommodate diversions, interruptions and repetitions as human teachers do, so although students are usually able to follow individual units of content they are not given the help they need in getting the bigger picture of how units interrelate. Productive learning experiences benefit from the interplay between the processes of narrative guidance and narrative construction. Multimedia interactive learning environments need to be designed so learners are able to both *find* narrative coherence and *generate* it for themselves.

ACKNOWLEDGEMENTS

This research has been conducted as part of MENO (Multimedia, Education and Narrative Organisation), funded by the Economic and Social Research Council's Cognitive Engineering Programme, grant no. L127251018. The *Galapagos* CD-ROM was developed by Matthew Stratfold. We are indebted to the schools, teachers and students who made this research possible and to the reviewers, for detailed and valuable comments.

REFERENCES

Publications marked with an asterisk are available from http://meno.open.ac.uk/meno/

1. Bolter, J.D. (1991). *Writing Space: the Computer, Hypertext and the History of Writing*. LEA, Hillsdale, NJ.

2. Bower, G. H., & Morrow, D. G. (1990). Mental models in narrative comprehension. *Science*, 247(4938), 44-48.

3. Bruner, J. (1996). *The Culture of Education*. Harvard University Press, Cambridge MA.

4. Chafe, WL (ed.) (1990). *The Pear Stories: Cognitive, Cultural and Linguistic Aspects of Narrative Production*. Ablex, Norwood NJ.

5. Clanton, C., F. Iannella & E. Young (1992). Film craft in user interface design. Tutorial Notes, *CHI'92*, Monterey, Ca. May 3-7, 1992.

6. Engel, S. (1995). *The Stories Children Tell: Making Sense of the Narratives of Childhood*. New York: WH Freeman.

7. Heath, S. (1983). *Ways with Words: Language, Life and Work in Communities and Classrooms*. CUP, Cambridge.

8. Iser, Wolfgang (1989). *Prospecting. From Reader Response to Literary Anthropology*. John Hopkins University Press, Baltimore.

9. Landow, G. (1992). *Hypertext: the Convergence of Contemporary Critical Theory and Technology*. Johns Hopkins University Press, Baltimore.

10. Laurel, B. (1993). *Computers as Theatre*. Addison-Wesley, Reading, Mass.

11. Laurillard, D. (1998). Multimedia and the learner's experience of narrative. *Computers & Education* 31 pp.229-242.*

12. Laurillard, D., L. Baric, P. Chambers, G. Easting, A. Kirkwood, L. Plowman, P. Russell & J. Taylor (1994). *Teaching and Learning with Interactive Media*. National Council for Educational Technology: Coventry. ISBN 1 85379 302 7.*

13. Luckin, R., L. Plowman, L. Gjedde, D. Laurillard, M. Stratfold & J. Taylor (1998). An evaluator's toolkit for tracking interactivity and learning. In M. Oliver, ed. *Innovation in the Evaluation of Learning Technologies*, pp.42-64. University of North London, London.*

14. Luckin, R., L. Plowman, D. Laurillard, M. Stratfold, J. Taylor (1998). Scaffolding learners' constructions of narrative. In A. Bruckman et al. (eds.) *Proceedings of Third International Conference on the Learning Sciences* (ICLS-98), pp. 181-187. Georgia Tech, Atlanta, GA.*

15. McKendree, Jean & John Mateer (1991). Film techniques applied to the design and use of interfaces. In *Proceedings of the IEEE Twenty-Fourth Annual Hawaii International Conference on System Sciences*, (pp.32-41). IEEE, NY.

16. Mercer, N. (1995). *The Guided Construction of Knowledge*. Multilingual Matters, Clevedon.

17. McNeil, L. (1996). Homo inventans: the evolution of narrativity. *Language and Communication*, 16(4), pp.331-360.

18. Millard, E. (1997). *Differently Literate: Boys, Girls and the Schooling of Literacy*. Falmer Press, London.

19. Murray, J. (1997). *Hamlet on the Holodeck. The Future of Narrative in Cyberspace*. Free Press, NY.

20. Nelson, K. (1996). Emergence of the storied mind. In *Language in Cognitive Development*, ed. K. Nelson. CUP, Cambridge.

21. O'Donnell, J. (1998). *Avatars of the Word: From Papyrus to Cyberspace*. Harvard University Press, Cambridge, MA.

22. Olson, DR (1990). Thinking about narrative. In *Narrative Thought and Narrative Language*, eds. Bruce Britton & Anthony Pellegrini, LEA, Hillsdale, NJ.

23. Plowman, L. (1996). What's the story? Narrative and the comprehension of educational interactive media. Proceedings of the *8th European Conference on Cognitive Ergonomics* (ECCE8), Granada, Spain, eds. T. Green, J. Cañas, C. Warren, pp.167-172.*

24. Plowman, L. (1996). Narrative, linearity and interactivity: making sense of interactive multimedia. *British Journal of Educational Technology*, 27(2) pp.92-105.*

25. Plowman, L. (1994). The 'Primitive Mode of Representation' and the evolution of interactive multimedia: some design issues for group use. *Journal of Educational Multimedia and Hypermedia* 3 (3/4) pp.275-293.*

26. Plowman, L. (1992). An ethnographic approach to analysing navigation and task structure in interactive multimedia. In *People and Computers VII*, eds. A. Monk et al., pp. 271-287. CUP, Cambridge.*

27. Steiner, G. (1996). 'The Uncommon Reader'. In *No Passion Spent, Essays 1978-1996*. Faber & Faber, London.

28. Thorndyke, P. (1977). Cognitive structures in comprehension and memory of narrative discourse. *Cognitive Psychology*, 9, pp.77-110.

Interactive 3D Sound Hyperstories for Blind Children

Mauricio Lumbreras §
Department of Computer Science
University of Chile
Blanco Encalada 2120, Santiago
CHILE
mlumbrer@dcc.uchile.cl

Jaime Sánchez
Department of Computer Science
University of Chile
Blanco Encalada 2120, Santiago
CHILE
jsanchez@dcc.uchile.cl

ABSTRACT

Interactive software is currently used for learning and entertainment purposes. This type of software is not very common among blind children because most computer games and electronic toys do not have appropriate interfaces to be accessible without visual cues.

This study introduces the idea of interactive hyperstories carried out in a 3D acoustic virtual world for blind children. We have conceptualized a model to design hyperstories. Through AudioDoom we have an application that enables testing cognitive tasks with blind children. The main research question underlying this work explores how audio-based entertainment and spatial sound navigable experiences can create cognitive spatial structures in the minds of blind children.

AudioDoom presents first person experiences through exploration of interactive virtual worlds by using only 3D aural representations of the space.

Keywords

Virtual acoustic environment, space representation, blind children, audio-based navigation, hyperstory, 3D sound, audio interface.

INTRODUCTION

Interactive computer games have been used for entertainment purposes for some time. However, it has been during the last years that these games have been available to a wider population of children. Today, most youth worldwide have had some type of experience with computer games delivered mainly through video-based devices [6]. This scenario is not the case for children with disabilities [1] who do not have interactive entertainment software available in quantity and variety. The case turns more critical with blind children, because they cannot take advantage of visual games.

This study reacts to this growing need through a two-fold approach: present a way to introduce interactive and immersive edutainment for blind children, and demonstrate that 3D auditory experiences can render spatial environmental images.

An image is a two dimensional representation of an n-dimensional referent; it is not visual by nature. Since vision plays a preponderant role in our knowledge of the world, the majority of image representations are created from visual perception. This seems to exclude people who lack the sense of vision. A small number of psychologists do research in the field of drawings and spatial image representation for the blind. Kennedy [10] let blind individuals draw spatial scenes and concluded that they do not represent images with perspective, maintaining a flat bidimensional projection in their drawings. Burton developed a system called Rose [3] that imitates children's drawings based on spatial models. However until now no systematic approach has been developed to design perceptual image maps of three-dimensional objects and scenes without visual cues.

Our approach tries to extend these concepts by testing the hypothesis that a 3D sound navigable environment can create some mental images and serve as an aural representation of the space and surrounding entities such as the ones explored in previous studies [13,15,16,20]. Kobayashi [11] explores the idea of sound-space association to enable simultaneous speaker listening, but spatial navigation is not included. To deal with this topic we have created a framework to describe and implement virtual acoustic navigable environments.

The application introduced here stems from a design model for generic hyperstories. A hyperstory is defined by the combination of a navigable virtual world, a character manipulated by the user, a set of dynamic objects and characters, and traces of interaction among these entities given by the plot of the story [14].

The main research question underlying this work explores how audio-based entertainment and spatial sound navigable experiences can create cognitive spatial structures in the minds of blind children. We also propose a model to describe an acoustic navigable environment. In addition, we asked whether spatialized acoustic modality combined with haptic manipulation of the environment may allow blind children to construct mentally associated structures

---

§ Also, LIFIA, Universidad Nacional de La Plata, ARGENTINA.

such as haptic/acoustic correlation, spatial navigation without visual cues, or object permanence in time through the hyperstory metaphor. Furthermore, we examined interface and usability issues related to interactive software for blind children.

WHAT IS A HYPERSTORY?

A hyperstory is a story that occurs in a hypermedia environment. It is the hypermedia version of literary stories. The concept of hyperstory is derived from MUDs (Multi-User Dungeons), their variations (MOO, MOOSE, etc.) and adventure games. Our model extends these ideas by including the elements of a story. These elements are: plot, roles, and characters. The main idea is to capture these elements in the hyperstory representation [8]. Plot is a temporal sequence of actions involving a set of individuals. A plot and its constituent actions may be quite abstract, i.e.: A meets B, A loves B, A loses B, A wins B. Role is the class of individuals whose prototypical behaviors, relationships, and interactions are known by both actors and audience. This plot is ordinarily illustrated with alternative roles, for instance: the boy in love and the girl he loves. Character is a personality defined as a coherent configuration of psychological trait, for instance, any of the characters in the present scenario might be shy and sensitive, silly and affectionate.

We first introduce the definition of a Story Virtual Environment (SVE) as:

$$SVE := navigable\ world + dynamic\ objects\ + characters$$

Eq. (1)

The navigable world is composed of several environments (nodes) connected by physical links. Each node of the virtual world represents a container of objects and a potential scenario of the hyperstory [5]. Physical gates, portals and doors represented as links render the connectivity. Dynamic objects are in charge of representing objects within the virtual world. They are entities that have behavior in time and react to the events produced by the user or other virtual objects. The characters are special cases of dynamic objects, which are critical to the central plot and elicit the content of the story. The characters are entities carrying on the main course of events involving a complex behavior. For example, in a film the most interesting events happen to the characters and trigger the actions that emotionally impact the audience. There is also a distinguished character called the protagonist manipulated by the child and representing the user-system connection. Due to the sound rendering, the protagonist is acted in a first person representation.

But at this point an adventure computer game could be in some way similar to the previous definition. We add a narrative component to SVE. This is a necessary condition for a HS which is not so in the case of adventure games. Then a Hyperstory (HS) is an extension of a SVE and structurally can be defined as:

$$HS = SVE + narrative$$

Eq. (2)

As depicted, our model extends the idea of a SVE by introducing the idea of narrative. Differences of hyperstories from standard MUDs rely on an intentional sequence of events based on plot, roles and characters. Also, a HS differs from a MUD because the design includes a closure or an explicit end, described as a good feature of a narrative [12].

The added value of hyperstories

A hyperstory is an interactive story guided by an intentional argumentative structure rather than a casual scenario. The plot in a hyperstory is not linear, it is a hyper-plot; here, action, object activation and dialog can trigger a change in the flow of the story. Thus, we borrow ideas from hypertext/hypermedia technology by including narrative in a virtual environment context [2]. Hyperstories have improved conventional literary stories by allowing a "dynamic binding" between characters, the world in which they move, and the objects they act upon [19]. The child develops this binding through a greater flexibility in the learning/exploration process. In other words, a hyperstory is a combination of a navigable virtual world, a set of interactive objects, and the pattern of interaction between entities [14].

In a particular execution of a hyperstory, two children may experience different views of the same virtual world, extending the ideas of Joiner [9]. Slight changes introduced by a child to the object's behavior can produce different hyperstories in the same world. Children when manipulating a character can also interact with other characters to solve a given problem. Familiar environments such as schools, neighborhoods, squares, parks, and supermarkets can be interesting metaphors for building virtual worlds. It is critical to notice that conventional computer authoring tools do not provide an adequate set of facilities for building acoustic hyperstories as we have conceptualized them here.

THE MODEL

Our model is a design model based on object oriented concepts, providing a framework to describe the diverse building blocks of the hyperstory. The model supplies a framework composed by four foundational classes as described in Object Oriented Design (OOD) techniques [18]. These classes are context, link, entity, and channel. Contexts model the static world and links model the connectivity between contexts. Entities are the abstract class that capture any object or character definition, and channels work as a broadcast media of events in a fan-in or fan-out fashion to the subscribed entities. The definition of these classes allows a scheme for designing virtual worlds. Environments such as Virtual Reality Modeling Language, VRML, does not inherently include these high level concepts.

Each fundamental class has a predefined behavior and a set of attributes that makes them different from each other (e.g. a link knows about the transportation of entities between contexts). Another example of specialized behavior arises from contexts: if an entity sends an event to a context, it does so to all contained objects. Thus, a context works as a diffuser of events. All these fundamental classes have behavior, based on modal programming. We used ObjectCharts as the formalism to specify behavior [4]. ObjectCharts are a well-suited tool to describe environments based on events and actions as in hyperstories.

The structure of the world

Hyperstories with several scenarios organize them according to their physical linking or connectivity. For this purpose, we can describe the virtual world as a type of nested context model. A virtual world is defined as a set of contexts that represent different environments. Each context contains an internal state, a set of contained contexts, a set of objects, links to other contexts, and a specific behavior. Different relationships may be held between two different contexts, such as:

- Neighborhood (there is a link from one context to the other),

- Inclusion (one context is included in the other), or

- None (contexts are "disjoints").

Different "real world" metaphors such as a town, a house, houses within a town, and rooms within a house can be described easily with this simple model. All these metaphors are built in such a way that can be freely navigated. Another important concept about context is perception: a context is a spatial container that can be perceived as a whole rendered as a unity at the interface level. In the case of an acoustic HS the context presents some attributes as echoes, background music or atmosphere sound. At this point of the design, we are dealing with the navigable world, the first term of the Eq. (1).

The activity in the world

In order to bring life to the hyperstory, we populate the environments with objects, some active and some passive. This is the behavioral dimension. Another dimension is the navigational one. To avoid confusion we briefly define some terms concerning objects in a virtual world.

- **Passive**: the object answers only to simple events such as "Who am I?"

- **Active**: the object has a noticeable behavior while the time progresses -continuous or discrete- or they respond to events with some algorithm that reflects some behavior.

- **Static**: the object always belongs to the same context.

- **Dynamic**: the object can be carried between contexts by some entity or travel autonomously.

Any object or character (even the protagonist) is a subclass of an entity. Therefore we need to extend the basic attributes and behavior of the entity class. Basically, an entity can be viewed as an object with a set of attributes that define an internal state and a behavior. Using especially made state-based scripts we are able to describe the object's behavior. In each state there are a set of rules containing a triggering event, a pre-condition, and a list of actions that must be performed when the event arrives and the pre-condition is satisfied. Each rule plays the role of a method in OOD. But, if we try to capture the nature of the narrative and the diverse branches of a hyperstory, the model must consider this requirement: certain entities in a story can respond to the same event (message in OOD) in a different way according to the story stage. For example, according to the stages of the hyperstory a character can respond "fine" or "tired" related to the question "How are you?" In short, an object can behave differently to the same message received depending on its life stage. This concept is called programming with modes [21] or state-based programming. To capture this feature the rules are not specified in a standard way. Instead they are blocked and grouped according to the entity's life stage. In short, we use state-based scripts in order to deal with a variable response to the same event. By embedding narrative in the behavior of entities we are satisfying the components of a HS as depicted in the Eq. (2).

AUDIODOOM: A HYPERSTORY FOR VISUALLY IMPAIRED CHILDREN

Visual imagery may be loosely defined as visual mental processing that resembles the perceptual mental processing normally induced by the eyes. AudioDoom tries to test the hypothesis that claims that a 3D sound interactive, navigable aural environment can create these mental images in the absence of direct sensory stimuli from the eyes.

Sound serves as the output media of the system. However, the transient nature of the sound imposes a bias in the interface design, leaving it tightly linked to temporal constraints. For this reason, the conceptual idea of an interactive narrative combined with challenging features of game and story must be organized and rendered in a very simple way to model our target user, blind children between 8-12 years old.

AudioDoom is the prototype designed to test our ideas about interactive hyperstories for visually impaired children. With AudioDoom the child can navigate in a set of corridors where he obtains and interacts with virtual objects, resembling in some way the classic Doom game. AudioDoom is based on a fantastic story about an extraterrestrial invasion to the earth, developing the action inside an extraterrestrial flying-source. The child must save the planet in order to get a successful story ending. While playing AudioDoom, the child encounters characters, objects, and challenges that may change the plot of the story.

The structure of the flying-source is presented as a set of perpendicular corridors of different lengths (see Fig. 1). These corridors are connected by doors that can appear at the end or at the side as an optional exit to other corridors. In each case the user can activate the desired door in order to access the a specific corridor. Related to the physical navigation inside a corridor, the user is allowed to move in the forward direction step-by-step. Certain entities can appear suddenly after a current step has finished. If this happens, before progressing the user must solve a challenge depending on the type of entity found. For example, the monster is simple to destroy -three shots- but the mutant moves in the space jumping between neighborhood voxels, minimal discrete units of volume. This type of behavior enforces the child to localize the entity as soon as possible and then shoot immediately. It must be clear that each user action or entity appearance is rendered with spatialized sound.

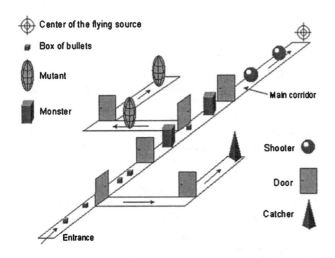

Fig 1. Graphical representation of the spatial environment rendered by AudioDoom

Typical actions in AudioDoom involve getting objects (box of bullets), shooting an entity (monster and mutant), or localizing and interacting with a determined character (the catcher) in a position of the space. The soul of the story presents multiple branches, but some of them are not deterministic, because some story entities may or may not be encountered, depending on the casual user-entity encounter. This scenario brings new alternatives in each session with AudioDoom. The spatial sequencing of the space enables the user to get involved in the story, resolving challenges *in crescendo*, increasing the level of complexity.

The added value of AudioDoom comes from the fact that we have used the hyperstory metaphor to evaluate how a virtual acoustic representation can build a mental spatial representation in blind children. For this reason, we have built some tasks where the child interacts several times with AudioDoom and then tries to describe the taxonomy, organization, entity locations, and space organization of the environment by using LEGO blocks. In short, AudioDoom serves as an argument to test our hypothesis.

Interacting with AudioDoom

To interact with AudioDoom the child operates through the surrounding space, acting on voxels. The voxel concept determines a discreteness of the space, simplifying the surrounding positions of interaction and creating a concrete repository for an entity (see Fig. 2). For example, in a given moment a voxel can be empty or contain an entity. This entity usually is a virtual object represented acoustically, a door, a box, a character, etc. This entity can receive some events from the child depending on the entity: take, activate, open, and so on. AudioDoom presents a modal interface where the same physical event can be interpreted according to the context, mode, and entity located in the target voxel. We must take into account that an entity can have a kinetic behavior, a movement in space through time. This activity involves several voxels because a voxel is an atomic space container. This approach may appear slightly restrictive, but we can divide the environments into the desired quantity of voxels until we obtain the desired granularity.

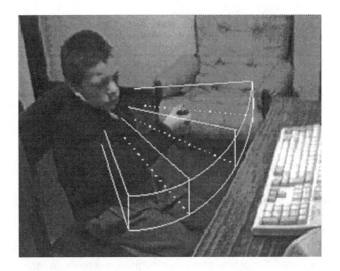

Fig 2. The child explores AudioDoom by interacting with entities located in virtual voxels (drawn artificially over the photography).

In an exploratory study with AudioDoom, first the child constructs a mental representation based on casual encounters of objects. Then, as the use of the software continues, the child tries to locate special items using a goal-directed mental navigation framework.

From the child's point of view, AudioDoom is manipulated by using a wireless ultrasonic joystick called The Owl [17]. Through this device, the child can interact and move in the environment by clicking in different voxels of the surrounding space.

According to the position of the sound, the child must coordinate the haptic/kinestetic device with the perceived sound position. This scheme of action-reaction is strongly stimulated in the child, because of the strong haptic-acoustic correlation embedded in the system. To deal with this issue we designed AudioDoom to be mainly used with both an ultrasonic joystick with 3 degrees of freedom (X,Y,Z) and spatialized sound. The child can also use AudioDoom by interacting with a standard keyboard or a mouse.

How AudioDoom works?

The basic idea of AudioDoom is to split the navigable space into small atomic environments. This is the minimal scenario of action in a given moment. In this environment the child can interact with entities in different voxels. The linear connection of the atomic environments renders a corridor. This structure organizes the space into several corridors, giving a semantic and argumentative connection of the hyperstory and the space. These corridors are modeled as contexts and the doors as links.

The child can perform different types of activities in an atomic environment such as:

- To move forward to the next atomic environment by taking a step,
- To open a door,
- To make a turn, or
- To interact with an entity in a certain way

When we consider the type of presentation media and the interaction with a strong physical metaphor, we highlight three key points to be at the interface of AudioDoom: the structuring of elements at a given moment, the location of objects, and the dynamics of selection and interaction. In general, the system presents one or several entities at a given moment, each localized in a voxel. The child then, after the acoustic localization, tries to locate the entity and elicits a reaction. According to the type of entity, the interaction can be reduced to a discrete event -take a box of bullets or hit a door to be opened. It also can be synthesized to a chain of events with a given purpose: i.e. to shoot three times to destroy an alien, to shoot several times to destroy a mutant moving randomly between contiguous voxels.

Inside AudioDoom

AudioDoom was conceptualized with the following constraints. AudioDoom must:

- Stimulate spatial relations by exploiting the physical environment surrounding the child,
- Be capable of presenting disjoint and distinguishable acoustic entities, located in some point of the space,
- Clearly distinguish isolation between the input-output media in order to test various concepts according to each device, and
- Reflect a real time response related to the child's action.

Our implementation follows the idea that if some entity can move between n possible voxels, then we can take the monophonic sound of this entity. By combining different sets of Head Related Transfer Functions or HRTF's -one pair from each position- to the monophonic sound, we obtain n clips of 3D sound. This processing is done off-line. The result is a large set of 3D sounds requiring only a cheap soundboard to be played. To deal with real time sound mixing -background music, sound effects, entity sound, etc.- we use the Dynamic Link Library *wavemix.dll*, included in MS Windows. Thus the execution hardware platform requires only a PC, Windows 3.1, and a stereo soundboard. In this version of AudioDoom, the sounds are only presented at ear level. This means that we do not include elevational cues.

THE EVALUATION OF AUDIODOOM

The evaluation of AudioDoom was predominantly qualitative in the sense that we tried to establish relevant usability elements of the interactive applications used by children without visual cues. They will give us enough data to determine if our hypothesis was well grounded.

The testing scenario

AudioDoom was tested with seven Chilean children aged 8-11 in a blind school setting. The children ranged from total blindness since birth to other children with light and dark discrimination (see Table 1).

Subject	Sex	Age	Blind from age	Actual vision loss degree	Current degree at the school
FAF	M	11	0	Total	3
JOH	M	8	0	Light/shadow	2
MAR	M	8	0	Total	2
FRA	M	8	3	Total	2
ROC	F	11	6	Total	5
EDS	M	7	0	Light/shadow	2
JOM	M	9	0	Light/shadow	2

Table 1. Profile of each child involved in the testing

After a short oral explanation about how the software works the child explored the interface and began the hyperstory. In the first session the child interacted with AudioDoom by getting confidence with the joystick and developing simple actions in the first corridor. To talk with the child we used external speakers at this stage. The localization is preferentially perceived by the sound intensity played from each speaker. The child interacted with AudioDoom several times and then we set the first evaluation. After this training the child used headphones to deliver full 3D sound.

By using LEGO blocks the child tried to represent the environment structure of AudioDoom as he imagined and perceived. To accomplish this task, each type of LEGO block had an assigned semantic: long blocks represented a part of one corridor, cubes represented mutants, small cubes represented boxes of bullets, etc. Small plastic doors represented the perceived doors (see Fig. 3).

Corridor   Door   Monster   Box of
segment   bullets

Fig 3. Each LEGO block had a specially assigned meaning in order to evaluate and interpret the structure built by the child.

The testing involved two sessions following this cycle:

1. Getting confidence with the interface of AudioDoom by running the software several times.

2. Exploring the main corridor and some hyperstory branches.

3. Building the perceived structure with LEGO blocks by following these steps:

- The child recognizes the objects separately.

- As the construction goes on, the child establishes an order of complexity (objects, scenes, contexts).

- The child constructs a model by assembling the pieces.

- The child represents the whole structure.

4. Orally describing decisions and testing errors.

5. Re-exploring AudioDoom by navigating the same path or exploring new branches.

6. Restarting the cycle in step 3.

The experiment with AudioDoom performed in the Chilean School for Blind Children consisted of two sessions of two hours each. In each session the child tried at least five times the software. Both sessions were separated by one or two weeks.

As a result, the children made a model of the environment and entity locations (see Fig. 4). It is interesting to note that when the children interacted with AudioDoom in the second session they remarkably remembered clearly the former structure built in the first session.

A very motivating aspect of this experience is reflected by the fact that the children expressed a notable satisfaction in the independent discovery of the environment. They orally communicated their feelings about this experience as a performance with self-efficacy and self-efficiency. This kind of sensation elicited in the children has few comparisons with previous experiences. Parents and teachers of the school where AudioDoom was tested assured this view.

1. After several attempts with AudioDoom, the child began the navigated space representation.

2. After trying AudioDoom at least five times, the child extended the main corridor, locating doors and singular entities.

3. This is the child's last LEGO model.

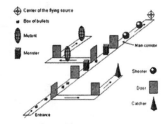

4. Compare this ideal version of the AudioDoom space with the child's LEGO model (**3.**)

Fig 4. After some back-and-forth model building, the child is able to "draw" the environment experienced. Amazingly, the child never saw the last picture.

DISCUSSION

After a preliminary user evaluation of AudioDoom with

blind children we have demonstrated that it is possible to render a spatial navigable structure by using only spatialized sound. This mechanism of acoustic representation of the environment preserves with a notable precision the structure, topology, orientation, navigation, and mobility. The result is preliminary because we have not included free navigation in open places within the virtual environment. This is due to the restriction of navigating in straight corridors with divergent branches connected at 90° angles. Some children showed some difficulties, especially with mapping transversal corridors. This problem apparently arises from the fact that the turn disorientates the user, because the real surrounding space is fixed such as chair, table, etc. For this reason, we face as a key issue the representation of distinguishable milestones in the environment to facilitate the orientation of the player. The use of some artificial auditory rotational beacons may help to ameliorate this issue.

One important observation collected at the evaluation arises from the possible impact of the child's previous experiences with testing materials on the fidelity of LEGO model. We infer that with appropriate training we can control for independent variables such as confidence with LEGO blocks and previous computer experience, leaving the intellectual ability/capacity of the children as the dependent variable without any contamination (see Table 2).

Subject	Confidence with LEGO Blocks	Previous computer experience	Fidelity of the last LEGO model
FAF	😞	😐	😞
JOH	😀	😀	😀
MAR	😀	😀	😀
FRA	😀	😀	😀
ROC	😐	😞	😐
EDS	😐	😞	😞
JOM	😀	😐	😐

Key ———————————————
Poor   Fair   Good

Table 2. The correlation of the child's previous experiences with the materials used in the intervention and the fidelity of the last LEGO model.

The process of building the LEGO models by the children shows that first they represent navigable structures preserving the taxonomy. Then they try to locate each

entity. This process resembles the map drawing from a visually capable person: first sketch the structure and then describe the singular details. We can infer from these patterns that acoustic navigable environments recreate spatial structures similar to those acquired by first person navigation and visual environment recognition.

Even though we use 3D sound with several limitations such as no head tracking and limited quantity of voxels, children usually preferred external speakers. Children were not so clear about the reasons for this preference but one reason could be that the headphones impose the isolation, limiting the oral interaction with the evaluator. The discomfort imposed by the headphone used (a Sony MDR CD30) appears to be another reason. We detected this pattern of preference at the beginning, so we adapted the HRTFs to be used to external speakers by reprocessing the amplitude of the signal of each channel. This result triggered the use and study of transaural audio, which enabled us to spatialize sound with external speakers [7].

Furthermore, we carefully observed the mechanism of interaction in AudioDoom. We tested AudioDoom by using the keyboard as input device. Children get better confidence because there is no ambiguity of the selected voxel. The use of ultrasonic joystick presented some difficulties due to erroneous voxel selection and undetected clicking due to misalignment of the joystick related to the ultrasonic sensors. But children reported a higher level of satisfaction with joysticks. It seems that the child's arm movement increases the level of immersion. In addition, the haptic-acoustic correlation is an excellent mechanism to stimulate the available skills in visually impaired children. This result imposes opposing design decisions.

One key element in the further improvement of AudioDoom is the construction of an editor, because currently AudioDoom has a hardwired solution. The editor will help teachers and parents to adapt tasks to their own needs. Finally, we propose the possibility to go beyond the concrete construction with LEGO blocks and the mental representation of the spatial environment. We propose to the use motor skills to represent the LEGO model built by the blind child through an interactive motor skill play.

FINAL REMARKS

One of the most promising benefits of AudioDoom stems from the fact that virtual acoustic environments can not only serve as entertainment worlds but also can be used to deliver an ample variety of educational materials. It is well known that blind children need assistance to know and mentally map their neighborhood, school, downtown, etc. In this way we are exploring the possibility to go beyond the rendering of fantastic environments by including virtual representations of real and familiar places. These representations can be modeled with the hyperstory model by including motivating elements to capture the attention of the children. The results gathered at this point are not completely categorical but they serve as a proof-of-concept that spatialized sound environments rendered without visual cues can bring spatial structures into the minds of blind children.

We have presented a conceptual model for building highly interactive stories for blind children. Our past experiences with hyperstories indicate to us that learners tend to have control over these stories and they enjoy having free access to diverse tools and materials constructively in order to develop strategies and test hypotheses. Hyperstories were used with the implicit idea of fostering the development and use of the cognitive skills such as spatial relationships and laterality. Our preliminary results with 3D aural hyperstories support our belief that they can contribute to make the interaction with computers much more enjoyable and learnable. Children like stories and remember them easily. When children are engaged in a story, they can identify, retrieve and use relevant data to solve a challenge by having rapid and flexible access to the story sequence. From our experience with AudioDoom we have learned that hyperstories highly motivate learners, facilitate free navigation, and promote active constructivist learning by providing blind children with the power to construct virtual environments through dynamic learning materials with audio cues.

REFERENCES

1. Blind Children Center. *First Steps, a Handbook for teaching young children who are visually impaired.* Los Angeles, California, USA, 1993.

2. Bernstein, M. Conversation with friends: hypertext with characters. *Lectures on Computing.* Springer-Verlag, 1996.

3. Burton, E. Thoughtful Drawings: A Computational Model of the Cognitive Nature of Children's Drawing, in: *Proc. EUROGRAPHICS '95*; Maastricht, NL August 28 - September 1, C159-C170, 1995.

4. Coleman D., Hayes F., Bear S. Introducing ObjectCharts or how to use StateCharts in object-oriented design. *IEEE Transactions on Software Engineering*, Vol.18, No.1: 9-18, 1992.

5. Dieberger A. Browsing the WWW by interacting with a textual virtual environment: A framework for experimenting with navigational metaphors, in *Proceedings of ACM Hypertext '96*, pp.170-179, 1996.

6. Druin A., Solomon C. *Designing Multimedia Environments for Children.* John Wiley & Sons Inc., USA, 1996.

7. Gardner W. Transaural 3-D audio, *PhD Thesis.* MIT, 1997.

8. Hayes-Roth B., Gent R., Huber D. Acting in character. *Technical report KSL-96-13, Knowledge Systems Laboratory*, USA, 1996.

9. Joiner D. Real Interactivity in Interactive Entertainment. *Computer Graphics*, Vol 28, number 2: 97-99, 1994.

10. Kennedy, J. M. *Drawing & the Blind. (pictures by touch).* New Haven, London: Yale University Press, 1993.

11. Kobayashi M., Schmandt C. Dynamic soundscape: Mapping time to space for audio browsing, in *Proceedings of ACM CHI 97*, pp. 224-228, 1997.

12. Landow G. *Hypertext: the Convergence of Contemporary Critical Theory and Technology.* Baltimore: The John Hopkins University Press, 1992.

13. Lumbreras M., Sánchez J., Barcia M. A 3D sound hypermedial system for the blind, in *Proceedings of the First European Conference on Disability, Virtual Reality and Associated Technologies,* pp.187-191, Maidenhead, UK, 1996.

14. Lumbreras M., Sánchez J. Hyperstories: A model to specify and design interactive educational stories, in *Proceedings of the XVII International Conference of the Chilean Computer Science Society*, Valparaiso, Chile. Published by IEEE, 1997.

15. Lumbreras M., Rossi G. A metaphor for the visually impaired: browsing information in a 3D auditory environment, in *Proceedings Companion CHI 95,* Denver, Colorado, May 1995, pp. 261-262, 1995.

16. Mereu. S., Kazman R. Audio enhanced 3D interfaces for visually impaired users, in *Proceedings of ACM CHI 96*, pp. 72-78, 1996.

17. Pegasus., Pegasus Web Site, *http://www.pegatech.com.*

18. Rumbaugh J., Blaha M., Premerlani W., Eddy F., Lorensen W. *Object-Oriented Modeling and Design.* Englewood Cliffs, NJ: Prentice Hall, 1991.

19. Sánchez, J., Lumbreras, M. HyperHistoires: narration interactive dans des mondes virtuels. En Balpe, J., Lelu, A., Nanard, M. & Saleh, I.(editors). *Hypertextes et Hypermédias.* Paris: Editorial Hermes, Vol. 1, 2-3-4, pp. 329-338, 1997.

20. Savidis A., Stephanidis C., Korte A., Crisipie K., Fellbaum K. A generic direct-manipulation 3D-auditory environment for hierarchical navigation in non-visual interaction, in *Proceedings of ACM ASSETS 96,* pp. 117-123, 1996.

21. Taivalsaari A., Object-Oriented programming with modes. *Journal of Object Oriented Programming*, Vol. 6, 3, pp. 25-32, 1993.

Designing PETS:
A Personal Electronic Teller of Stories

Allison Druin, Jaime Montemayor, Jim Hendler, Britt McAlister,
Angela Boltman, Eric Fiterman, Aurelie Plaisant, Alex Kruskal*, Hanne Olsen*,
Isabella Revett*, Thomas Plaisant Schwenn*, Lauren Sumida*, & Rebecca Wagner*

Human-Computer Interaction Lab, Institute for Advanced Computer Studies
University of Maryland, College Park, MD 20742
http://www.umiacs.umd.edu/~allisond/kidteam/robot-index.html
allisond@umiacs.umd.edu

ABSTRACT

We have begun the development of a new robotic pet that can support children in the storytelling process. Children can build their own pet by snapping together the modular animal parts of the PETS robot. After their pet is built, children can tell stories using the *My Pets* software. These stories can then be acted out by their robotic pet. This video paper describes the motivation for this research and the design process of our intergenerational design team in building the first PETS prototypes. We will discuss our progress to date and our focus for the future.

Keywords

Children, design techniques, educational applications, cooperative inquiry, intergenerational design team, PETS, robotics.

A CHILD'S WORLD

Real and imaginary animals fill children's storybooks, television, film, amusement parks, and zoos. In books, they are drawn with words or ink. In television or movies, they can take the furry form of *Muppets, Disney* characters, or animated creatures. In amusement parks or zoos, real or imaginary animals can be visited, touched, or ridden. These animal-filled activities continue to sustain children's attention, fill their imagination, and pique their curiosity [8].

It is interesting to note however, studies have shown that in settings where there are both things to observe and things to interact with, (e.g., in science museums, zoos, aquariums) children show a predictable pattern. Young people are attracted to activities that let them become physically involved. In the zoo for example, they prefer to interact with pigeons and squirrels, than more exotic animals isolated behind bars [9].

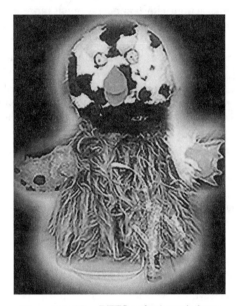

Figure 1: The PETS robot prototype

Therefore, our research goal is to take animals out from behind those bars. We are developing new learning opportunities for children to physically explore their animal interests with stories and robots. Storytelling has long been considered an important learning experience. Throughout generations, storytelling has been a way to preserve culture and history, communicate ideas and feelings, and educate learners young and old [2, 7, 11]. Storytelling continues to be a critical part of children's playtime, school time, and home life [8].

Therefore, we believe that these two important childhood ingredients, storytelling and animals, should be brought to the world of robotics for children. Robots don't have to be hard and plastic. They can be soft and huggable, like animals. Robots don't have to be complex and tedious to build, but can be enjoyably created by children. And robots don't just have to live in factories or fly to Mars, robots can simply act out the stories that children tell them.

---

*These authors are "junior" members of our lab and are currently attending local Maryland elementary schools.

THE RESEARCH LANDSCAPE

Significant work has been done by researchers at the MIT Media Lab in bringing together the worlds of robotics and children [12]. Computationally-enriched LEGO bricks have been their robotic building blocks. From *programmable bricks* to *crickets*, children can build everything from fanciful animals to physical simulations of viruses. While these robotic constructions do not focus on the storytelling experience, other research initiatives at the Media Lab do. SAGE: the Storyteller Agent Generation Environment [14] uses a programmable stuffed animal to tell stories. Children can listen to stories or tell their own with SAGE. However, the robotic storyteller is minimally configurable. Different characters can be "created" when the animal's hat is changed by the child, or the sensors from the animal are detached and placed on another object.

Other researchers at the MIT Robotics Lab have been developing KISMET, a robot for social interaction [1]. This robot displays behaviors and emotions, though it is not for the purposes of storytelling, but learning. The learning is not necessarily for the person who interacts with the robot, but for the robot itself. Similar research in the form of a 4-legged robotic pet named MUTANT was recently developed by researchers at the Sony Corporation [6]. Again, storytelling was not a goal in this research, but the purposes of entertainment and companionship were. On the other hand, researchers at Carnegie Mellon University have been developing OZ, an environment that supports interactive drama [10]. While this is a rich world to explore and tell stories with, it is a virtual one that lives behind a computer screen. In recent years, however, the HCI community has come to recognize the importance of physical interfaces to our computational environments [15]. In particular, stuffed animal interfaces have become more common over the years, from Druin's NOOBIE in 1987 [3] to Microsoft's Barney in 1998 [13].

THE PETS ENVIRONMENT

Our research in this area has come to be called PETS: A Personal Electronic Teller of Stories (Figures 1, 2). Using this robotic storytelling environment, elementary-school-age children can tell stories about how they feel (e.g., excited, sad, lonley). Children can build a robotic pet by simply snapping together special robotic animal parts (e.g., dog paws, a fish tail, duck feet). After a robotic pet is built, children can tell stories with the *My PETS* software, giving their robot emotions and behaviors throughout the story. An example below was created by a 7-year old girl in Maryland. This story was entitled *Michelle*:

"There once was a robot named Michelle. She was new in the neighborhood. She was HAPPY (robot behaves happy) when she first came, thinking she would make friends. But it was the opposite. Other robots threw rocks and sticks. She was SAD (robot behaves sad). No one liked her. One day she was walking down a street, a huge busy one, when

another robot named Rob came up and asked if she wanted to have a friend, but then realized she was HAPPY (robot behaves happy). The other robots were ANGRY (robot behaves angry) but knew that they had learned their lesson. Michelle and Rob lived HAPPILY (robot behaves happy) ever after. No one noticed the dents from rocks that stayed on Michelle" (Research notes, August 1998).

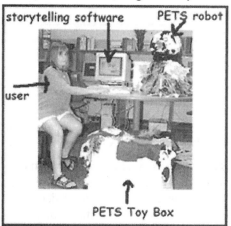

Figure 2: The PETS storytelling environment

The PETS robotic animal parts were built with LEGO bricks covered in fur, feathers, felt, etc. Each part can be snapped into place on the body and is also plugged into a plugbox embedded in the animal's torso. This plugbox is an interface to a Handyboard controller also in the animal's body, which controls servos and motors, and can read inputs from sensors that are attached throughout the robot's body. This controller has a serial connection to a Macintosh computer. In the Macintosh, the application software layer, *My PETS*, takes a story written by children, translates and transfers it to the system software layer that resides in the Handyboard.

THE INTERGENERATIONAL DESIGN TEAM PROCESS

The name, concept, and the development of our PETS prototypes came about because of children. We develop new technologies for children, with children in an *intergenerational design team*. This team consists of children (ages 7-11 years old) and adult professionals, with experience in computer science, education, art, and robotics. Together we use the methodology of *cooperative inquiry* to understand what children want in new technologies, today, tomorrow and in the future [4]. From this understanding we have begun to interatively design and prototype the PETS robotic storytelling environment.

Cooperative Inquiry

We began our work in March of 1998, by examining and exploring a robotics lab at the University of Maryland. Children and adults tried out robots, asked questions of researchers, and took notes about the experience. When we returned to our HCI lab, each child and adult researcher wrote down on Post-It notes what they liked and didn't like about the robots they saw. Each researcher privately wrote their comments before sharing them with the group. The table below summarizes these results.

What we Liked:	Number of comments
They have sensors	4
Seeing the robot examples in the lab	4
They move	2
They look like robots	2
What we didn't like	
What they looked like (e.g., plastic, ugly, brains showing)	9
They moved slow	1
They talked funny	1
They seem unreliable	1

Table 1: Summary of what we liked and didn't after visiting a robotics lab at the University of Maryland

What was most interesting, turned out to be the number of children and adult researchers who described the robots as "ugly." One child wrote on their note, "I don't like the way the brains show when you look at it." Another child wrote, "They're plastic and they should be furry like an animal" (Research notes, March 1998).

After our field research and analysis, we began to create numerous low-tech prototypes, using participatory design techniques [5]. Essentially, what we built were animal robots that didn't move. They were made out of LEGO bricks with fur, feathers, clay, socks and more. They represented our first ideas for animal robots.

In addition, the research team went to a local zoo to conduct research on how real animals look and move. We took notes and pictures of our experience back to the lab.

Iterative Prototyping

In the beginning of August 1998, the team met for two weeks, eight hours a day. During that time, we split into three groups. Each group consisted of two adults and two children, and focused on one important part of the prototype design. The *skeleton group* was responsible for creating the robotic skeleton of LEGO bricks, gears, motors, and servos. This group developed the plugbox interface to the Handyboard controller and the modular parts that could be put together to create an animal. In addition, they also created the connections for the sensors. One of the most difficult parts to build seemed to be the neck. It had to be redesigned six times so that it could properly hold the weight of the head. The wheel base also had to be redesigned three times so that it could properly move the weight of the entire animal.

What the skeleton group made, the *skins and sensors group* covered in fur, feathers, felt and fabric. This group started out by sketching on paper the kinds of animal parts they wanted to make. Ultimately, they decided to make a fish tail, dog paws, cow head, bear body, duck feet, and bird tail. The "skins" they created were either sewn, glued, tied, or attached using velcro to the LEGO bricks. The skins were redesigned many times, primarily due to weight. Heads would fall over, tails would not move, and paws would fall off. The skins and sensors group was also responsible for embedding light sensors into the eyes and touch sensors into the paws.

The third group focused on software. The *software group* was responsible for designing the software that children could use to tell stories. They began by looking at what software had already been made and decided what they liked and didn't like about it. Then they brainstormed and discussed what feelings they wanted to give the robot. From this list of feelings, a chart was made that showed all the actions the robot would need to perform to show each feeling. At times, questions were asked of the skeleton group to find out what robot actions were possible given the skeleton they were creating. This group then went out and "tested" these actions by having one child play the part of the robot. If their audience could not guess the feeling from the robot's actions, then revisions were made in the final database of feelings and actions. Finally, the group sketched on paper the design for the screens. These screens were scanned and used for the initial prototype software.

Each day, the three groups would meet together in the morning and afternoon to go over the progress of each group. Design issues were hashed out, questions were resolved, directions were discussed. Everything from the weight of the latest head, to the possibilities for motion were questioned. At times, team dynamics were reflected upon, and depending upon the issue, team process procedures were developed or changed. For example, one 10-year old team member raised the issue that the adults in the skins and sensors group were being noisy and disrupting the software team. This was addressed by changing the location of the software team.

At the end of this two-week intensive work session, a working prototype was developed and presented to a group of 40 local daycamp children (ages 7-14 years old). During this presentation, we received positive feedback and suggestions for future directions. Currently, we are working to better integrate the system software with the application software. In addition, we are developing ways to designate different behaviors for different animal parts. Currently only one behavior can be given to the whole animal. At this time, we are also considering replacing the LEGO brick skeleton with a more stable metal one. Our work continues on PETS during the school year, with the team meeting two afternoons a week.

REFLECTIONS ON THE DESIGN PROCESS

It has been almost a year since we began our research team. During that time, we have learned a few things, not just about technology, but about the process of how we make it. As our work together has progressed, three guiding principles have emerged as critical to our design process. They are simple, but difficult to make happen: (1) New power structures between adults and children must be developed; (2) All design partners must have a voice in the design process; (3) A comfortable design environment must be created.

In order to support new power structures or relationships between adults and children, we have attempted to "undo" what schools teach children. An example of this, is a rule we have made: no one raises his or her hand to talk. Children easily seem to raise their hands when they want to talk with adults in a group setting. When children raise their hands, it brings on thoughts of school, where teachers are in charge and children are called upon for "right" answers. Instead, children in our team have learned to challenge adults' ideas, questioning what is done and making suggestions. In addition, we have supported adults in learning to hear what child partners have to say. And that does not mean relegating adults to a corner where they sit and take notes about everything a child does. Instead, we believe in facilitating discussions where children and adults each feel comfortable contributing ideas.

Finding ways to give each design partner a voice in the process is no small challenge. Sharing ideas needs to happen in numerous ways, since people, young and old, feel comfortable communicating in various forms. We have found that there are times when drawing or writing or even building can and should be used to capture ideas. These artifacts become a catalyst and bridge for discussion in large or groups.

Not only should communication opportunities be diverse, but the design environment needs to feel comfortable. A common ground can not truly be found without physical surroundings that accommodate all design partners. One way we have made this possible is being strict about our informality. No child or adult dresses formally in a skit or tie. Design experiences take place in informal settings sitting on the floor or in bean-bag chairs. We capture our ideas in low-tech prototypes made of LEGO bricks and clay rather than yellow pads and design specifications. This all takes a commitment of time and a willingness to change by all design partners. There have been times of frustration, differences among team members, and questioning of goals. It may be those times that have taught us the most.

ACKNOWLEDGMENTS

This research could not have been accomplished without the generous support of the Institute for Advanced Computer Studies, the Sony Corporation, Intel Research Council, and The Army Research Laboratory. In addition, we thank Ben Bederson and Catherine Plaisant for their lab resources and continued help over the last year.

REFERENCES

1. Breazeal, C. (1998). A motivational system for regulating human-robot interaction. *In Proceedings of AAAI'98*. AAAI Press, pp.126-131.

2. Bruchac, J. (1987). *Survival this way: Interviews with American Indian poets*. Tuscson, AR: University of Arizona Press.

3. Druin, A. (1987). NOOBIE: The Animal Design Playstation. *SIGCHI Bulletin, 20*(1), 45-53.

4. Druin, A. (1999). Cooperative inquiry: Developing new technologies for children with children. *In Proceedings of Human Factors in Computing Systems (CHI 99)*. ACM Press.

5. Druin, A., Bederson, B., Boltman, A., Miura, A., Knotts-Callahan, D., & Platt, M. (1999). Children as our technology design partners. A. Druin (Ed.), *The design of children's technology*. (pp.51-72) San Francisco, CA: Morgan Kaufmann.

6. Fujita, M., & Kitano, H. (1998). Development of an autonomous quadruped robot for robot entertainment. *Autonomous Robots, 5*(1), 7-18.

7. Gish, R. F. (1996). *Beyond bounds: Cross-Cultural essays on Anglo, American Indian, and Chicano literature*. Albuquerque, NM: University of New Mexico Press.

8. Goldman, L. R. (1998). *Child's play: Myth, mimesis, and make-believe*. New York: Berg Press.

9. Greenfield, P. M. (1984). *Mind and Media*. Cambridge, MA: Harvard University Press.

10. Loyall, A. B., & Bates, J. (1997). Personality-rich believable agents that use language. *In Proceedings of First Annual Conference on Autonomous Agents*

11. Ortiz, S.(Ed.), (1998). *Speaking for generations: Native writers on writing*. Tuscson, AR: University of Arizona Press.

12. Resnick, M., Martin, F., Berg, R., Borvoy, R., Colella, V., Kramer, K., & Silverman, B. (1998). Digital manipulitives: New toys to think with. *In Proceedings of Human Factors in Computing Systems (CHI 98)*. ACM Press, pp.281-287.

13. Strommen, E. (1998). When the interface is a talking dinosaur: Learning across media with Actimates Barney. *In Proceedings of Human Factors in Computing Systems (CHI 98)*. ACM Press, pp.288-295.

14. Umaschi, M. (1997). Soft toys with computer hearts: Building personal storytelling environments. *In Proceedings of Extended Abstracts of Human Factors in Computing Systems (CHI 97)*. ACM Press, pp.20-21.

15. Wellner, P., Makay, W., & Gold, R. (1993). Computer augmented environments: Back to the real world. *Communications of the ACM, 36*(7), 24-26.

Visual Profiles: A Critical Component of Universal Access

Julie A. Jacko[1], Max A. Dixon[2], Robert H. Rosa, Jr.[3], Ingrid U. Scott[3], and Charles J. Pappas[3]

[1]Department of Industrial
Engineering
University of Wisconsin-Madison
1513 University Avenue
Madison, WI 53706
+1 608 262 3002
jacko@engr.wisc.edu

[2]Department of Industrial &
Systems Engineering
Florida International University
10005 W. Flagler Street
Miami, FL 33174
+1 305 348 3036

[3]Bascom Palmer Eye Institute
Department of Ophthalmology
University of Miami School of
Medicine
900 NW 17th Street
Miami, FL 33136
(305)326-6000

ABSTRACT

This research focuses on characterizing visually impaired computer users' performance on graphical user interfaces by linking clinical assessments of low vision with visual icon identification. This was accomplished by evaluating user performance on basic identification and selection tasks within a graphical user interface, comparing partially sighted user performance with fully sighted user performance, and linking task performance to specific profiles of visual impairment. Results indicate that visual acuity, contrast sensitivity, visual field and color perception were significant predictors of task performance. In addition, icon size and background color significantly influenced performance. Suggestions for future research are provided.

Keywords

universal access, low vision, visual icons, disabilities

INTRODUCTION

The ability to operate within our environment is a function of our capacity to detect, interpret, and respond appropriately to sensory information [12,17].   Just as a large portion of the information in our environment is visual, so is the majority of the information presented during a computer task. Thus, our ability to utilize a computer effectively is largely dependent upon the complex chain of visual processes that begin at the ocular media of the eye and extend to high-level perceptual processes in the brain.

Advances in the computational power of personal computers have led to an increased use of graphics. Today's graphical representations provide vivid details and colors to the "normal" eye. The use of graphics has been exploited for representing numerical and pictorial information. Moreover, graphical symbols, or icons have become mainstream in the graphical user interface (GUI) environment of today's computing systems.

Icons serve as a means through which users can initiate higher level actions and concepts without the use of complex syntax [20]. Icon use requires a pointing device, most frequently a mouse. When using a mouse, two interaction tasks are critical to successful icon activation: *selection* and *position* [9]. In selection tasks, the user chooses from a set of items displayed on the screen. In position tasks, the user chooses a point in a one- two- or three-dimensional space. Completion of these tasks requires complex interactions of the visual and tactile senses. In fact, successful use of iconic representations within GUIs places considerable demands on the human visual system.

Given that visual displays are the dominant medium for human-computer interactions, visual impairment can significantly influence a user's ability to perceive graphical and textual information in a GUI. No matter how well the interface is developed or the quality of the visual medium of presentation, reduced visual capability results in poorly perceived image quality.

This paper describes novel research that focuses on basic interaction strategies and their link to the visual capabilities of the user. This research couples frequently cited anecdotal evidence with empirical evaluations of partially sighted users' performance with GUIs. It also serves as a solid foundation for future investigations.

BACKGROUND

Direct manipulation tasks

Direct manipulation has been characterized [5] as a "visual interface which emphasizes eye-hand coordination skills as a prime requisite for successful and efficient interaction" (p.116). Direct manipulation is attractive because its use often results in faster performance, fewer errors, easier learning, and user satisfaction [3]. Physical, spatial, or visual representations also appear to be easier to retain and manipulate than textual or numeric representations [1]. However, for people with low vision, there are inherent limitations associated with the use of direct manipulation interfaces [7].

Characterizing human vision

A comprehensive determination of one's ability to visually perceive the state of a computer system lies in the discrimination of light, space, and color. This is the foundation upon which this research lies.

An assessment of visual limitations includes baseline data on visual acuity, contrast sensitivity, field of vision, and color perception. Visual acuity refers to a person's ability to resolve fine spatial detail [12]. Traditionally, visual acuity is measured using a Snellen visual acuity chart, a standard letter-based chart. The Bailey-Lovie style chart is favored when the patient's visual acuity does not permit reading of the largest letters on the Snellen chart at the standard distance [2,8].

Contrast sensitivity tests a person's ability to detect pattern stimuli at low to moderate contrast levels. The contrast sensitivity function provides an extensive representation of the spatial discriminating abilities of the visual channels [21]. The Pelli-Robson chart [16] consists of a series of letter-charts of different contrasts. This chart enables mapping of a contrast-sensitivity function for letters.

The useful field of view is the total area over which effective sight is maintained relative to a constant straight-ahead fixation point [12]. Ophthalmologists most commonly use standardized, automated perimetry to evaluate visual field. A human's ability to discern and identify color within their useful field of view is called color vision. The Farnsworth D-15 color vision test can be administered to assess color perception [13].

Traditional approaches to accommodation

We focus on partially sighted users because this group of computer users has been largely overlooked. Extensive research has focused on developing GUIs that can be used effectively by fully sighted users. Recognizing the difficulties GUIs create for blind users, researchers and developers recently began exploring alternatives that would allow blind computer users to work with GUIs. The lack of attention to partially sighted users is ironic given that there may be as many as three times more partially sighted people than fully blind people (e.g., [15]).

Partially sighted people cannot use traditional GUIs without alteration. Further, partially sighted people will not choose to use a device that does not allow them to make use of their residual visual processes [6]. Therefore, interfaces that are designed for fully blind computer users hold little value for partially sighted individuals. As a result, it is important to understand the difficulties partially sighted users experience when utilizing GUIs and how these difficulties can be overcome.

While systematic approaches exist for developing standard GUIs and researchers continue to explore new alternatives for fully blind users, little research has focused on partially sighted users. Most existing designs for partially sighted users appear to be grounded in the philosophy that minor enhancements to existing GUIs allow partially sighted users to function as if they were fully sighted. An exception is UnWindows, which serves as a tool for low vision users of X Windows and centers on improving the usability of existing graphical user interfaces [11].

In contrast, Accessibility Options in Windows®95 allow limited manipulation of keyboard mappings, sounds, screen colors, and text enlargement. Because the Accessibility Options do not allow for minute adjustments of enlargement settings, color, and contrast that are sometimes necessary for persons with partial vision, it appears they were not constructed with an accompanying knowledge of the physiology of partial vision. At present, there appear to be no published reports documenting the benefits of these options. How effective are these enhancements? What portion of the partially sighted community really benefits from these options? Do they have appeal or functional value for partially sighted users? We assert that more extensive knowledge of the physiology of partial vision will allow more effective accessibility aids to be developed.

Beyond simply determining whether someone is fully blind, functionally blind, or partially sighted, designers must understand the degree of visual impairment with respect to four characteristics of vision: visual acuity, contrast sensitivity, field of view and color perception. These characteristics determine where a person resides on a vision continuum ranging from fully sighted to completely blind.

In addition, there is a system configuration continuum that users with low vision have adopted in the interest of usability. For example, some people with low vision are able to be productive as long as they use large monitors. People with more advanced impairments may use enlargement software. Others may employ a hybrid system that is composed of enlargement software and voice. Our long-term mission is to have the capability to match a user, given their visual profile, to a system configuration that will best support their unique needs. In order to accomplish this goal, we must understand how visual profiles drive the interaction strategies that are adopted during task execution [10].

OBJECTIVE

There is a lack of knowledge about how an individual's visual profile determines the strategies and behaviors exhibited while using computers. Furthermore, there is no data that considers how combinations of impaired visual processes affect preferences for, and performance with graphical user interfaces. The premise of this research is that fundamental investigations will expand our knowledge of how visual profiles determine the strategies and behaviors exhibited by partially sighted users. This, in turn, will allow the design of more effective enabling technologies.

This essential knowledge is even more critical when you consider the nature of partial vision. Many visual disorders cause declines in vision over time [4]. This phenomenon results in accessibility needs that also change with time. To accommodate these changes, the enabling technologies must be able to shift in accordance with changes in visual function.

The specific objectives of this research are to evaluate partially sighted computer user performance (PSU) on basic identification and selection tasks within a graphical user interface, to compare PSU performance with fully sighted user (FSU) performance, and to link task performance to specific aspects of visual impairment.

HYPOTHESES

This investigation will be accomplished by testing the following hypotheses:

1) There will be significant differences between PSUs and FSUs with respect to the time required to identify visual icons in a GUI.

2) Contrast sensitivity, visual field, visual acuity and color perception will have a significant influence on the time required to identify visual icons in a GUI.

3) There will be a significant effect of icon size on the time required to identify visual icons in a GUI.

4) There will be a significant effect of set size on the time required to identify visual icons in a GUI.

5) There will be a significant effect of background color on the time required to identify visual icons in a GUI.

METHODOLOGY
Participants

To examine differences along the full range of vision, subjects were selected from two pools: persons who have been diagnosed with an uncorrectable ocular disease (PSU) and persons who possess no known uncorrectable ocular diseases and who have fully corrected vision (FSU). Ten PSU participants were identified with assistance from the Low Vision Clinic at Bascom Palmer Eye Institute and the Computer Systems Coordinator at the Miami Lighthouse for the Blind in Miami, Florida. Thus, all PSU participants were prescreened and known to possess knowledge of the utility of computers. In addition to their ocular status, information was also gathered from the PSU participants concerning age (μ=36 years), gender (3 males and 7 females) and computer experience (μ=4.85 years). The ten FSU participants were experience-, age- and gender-matched to the PSU participants so that valid comparisons could be made between the two groups.

The relatively small sample size is justified in several ways. First, this is a preliminary inquiry intended to motivate a larger research agenda in this area, if the results of this study are fruitful. Second, in this study we are interested in engaging experienced subjects who understand the utility of computers and recognize their value in the marketplace. Our access to partially sighted people who met these criteria was limited despite the fact that Bascom Palmer Eye Institute has one of the largest low vision clinics in the country.

PSUs were provided with a clinical asessment of their vision at the Low Vision Clinic at Bascom Palmer Eye Institute to ensure that the experimenters had knowledge of their current visual status and that corrective eyewear could be provided during experimentation that would enable performance under conditions of best-corrected vision.

Assessments of visual acuity were made using a Bailey-Lovie Chart. A Pelli-Robson Chart was used to assess contrast sensitivity. Field of view was assessed using the Esterman projection perimetry technique to evaluate binocular field of view and the Humphrey Visual Field-SITA 60 was used to evaluate monocular visual field. Color perception was evaluated using the Farnsworth D-15 color vision test. As an incentive to participate, PSUs were provided this clinical assessment free of charge. FSU participants were paid an incentive for their participation.

Experimental tasks and environment

A computer interface was designed to test the ability of the subjects to correctly identify and select icons common in a Microsoft® Windows environment. The apparatus consisted of an IBM compatible PII/266 running Microsoft Windows NT 4.0®. The interface was designed with Microsoft® Visual Basic® 5.0. A total of six icons were employed throughout the experiments: Print, Paste, Save, Copy, New, and Open. These icons were chosen because they have been shown to be the most identifiable to Microsoft® Word® users [19].

The following is a description of the interface employed in this experiment. The user was presented with instructions that read "Select the Following Icon". Accompanying this instruction was one of the six icons. This stimulus icon was randomly chosen and displayed on the screen at 58.3 mm to maximize the probability of detection by all participants. Then, presented on the target presentation screen were a set of two to six icons which were randomly chosen from the icon set described. On each trial the size of the icons varied from 9.2 to 58.3 mm. However, the collection of icons on a single display were identical in size. The sizes of the icons were proportional to the sizes of the letters on the Bailey-Lovie acuity chart. For example, an acuity level of 20/100 is represented by letters 29.19 mm wide on the Bailey-Lovie chart. The color of the background upon which the icons were presented was also manipulated. Five colors: black, white, blue, red, and green were employed at the fully saturated level. Table 1 summarizes the icon sizes and corresponding acuity levels.

A timer was necessary to record two events during experimentation. Within each trial, event 1 was defined to be the onset of the stimulus interface (time=0). Event 2 was defined to be the moment of target identification. The difference in time between events 1 and 2 was the reaction time (RT).

Table 1. Icon Sizes

Icon Size (mm)	Corresponding Acuity Level
9.2	20/32
14.6	20/50
23.2	20/80
36.8	20/125
58.3	20/200

In order to capture event 2, the subjects were instructed not to move the cursor until they had identified the target to which they wanted to move the cursor. Upon target identification, the subjects were instructed to execute a mouse click to mark event 2. The participants then moved the mouse to the target icon and clicked on their selection. This second click triggered the onset of another trial.

The distance from the center of the home position to the center of the target icon was identified for each trial. The home position was a circular area located at the bottom center of the screen with an outside diameter of 58.3 mm and an inner diameter of 38.3 mm. The outside diameter was filled with a 60% gray tone and the inner diameter was completely filled black. The distance from the center of the home position to the bottom of the bottom row of icons was 90 mm for every trial. The icons were arranged in a 3 x 2 matrix. The space between icons was the same distance as the size of the icons used. This configuration allowed all icons to be visible to the user on every trial when using a 21" monitor.

Experimental design

A 5 x 5 x 5 repeated measures design was utilized to test the hypotheses of this study. Five set sizes of icons, five background colors, and five icon sizes were examined, yielding 125 conditions. Each condition was repeated two times, resulting in a total of 250 trials per subject.

The dependent variable in the experiment was reaction time (event 1 through event 2). The independent variables were set size, background color, icon size, and subjects' visual profiles. Other demographics that were collected were age, gender, and years of computer experience.

Procedure

The study was conducted in two parts. In the first part, PSUs' vision was assessed at the Low Vision Clinic of the Bascom Palmer Eye Institute. Visual acuity, contrast sensitivity, color perception, and visual field of each subject was assessed. Total time for this assessment was approximately one hour. The second part of the experiment involved the execution of the computer-based tasks. Subjects performed the tasks with the assistance of corrective eyewear (glasses, contacts, field glasses) if necessary, to allow experimentation under best-corrected vision. Illumination levels in the study room were low during the initial stages, to allow for dark adaptation of the eyes, while the experimenter gathered demographic information from the subject. The lights were then turned off in the room so that the only source of illumination came from the monitor. This was done to eliminate glare and other confounding effects due to ambient light. The subjects then positioned themselves such that the distance from the monitor to their eyes was approximately 20 inches. The mouse was the only input device used by the subjects. The first fifty trials were used as practice, which allowed the subjects to become familiar with the experimental environment. Upon completion of the practice trials, the subject rested for 5 minutes before beginning the actual

experimentation and data collection. Subjects were given the opportunity to discontinue the experiment at any time if they desired. Conditions were blocked by background color. Background color blocks were randomly ordered. After the completion of one color block, subjects were allowed a 5-minute break. The estimated duration of the computer-based evaluation was one hour. In the second part, FSUs were engaged in the computerized task. The same procedure was used for the FSUs as was used with the PSUs, with the exception that the FSUs did not receive clinical visual assessments and instead were paid for their time.

RESULTS

Clinical assessments of PSU vision

Table 2 summarizes the results of the visual profiles of the PSUs. Acuity is represented as the logarithm of the minimum angle of resolution (LogMAR) for each eye. Contrast sensitivity scores are represented as summations across both eyes for the number of letters identified correctly. Color perception is represented by a categorical variable where 2=deutan (green deficient), 3=tritan (blue deficient), 4=anomalous (a more general color confusion), and 5=normal vision. Visual fields are depicted by Esterman Efficiency Scores representing the percentage of stimulus points detected.

FSUs did not have accompanying ocular diagnoses and were able to document by report that best-corrected vision was 20/20 with no known ocular diseases. Thus, FSUs were assigned maximum contrast sensitivity scores of 48, Esterman Efficiency Scores of 100, and a normal rating of color vision.

Visual icon identification performance

The aims of this research are to explain sources of variation in performance on computer-based tasks among patients with impaired vision. Given vast differences from individual to individual, variability in visual capabilities will be expected between PSU and FSU. Thus, Analysis of Covariance (ANCOVA) was used for the statistical analyses in order to control for this variability. In addition, ANCOVA enabled us to treat the visual profile parameters of acuity, contrast sensitivity, field of view, and color perception as covariates in the analyses. The covariance technique integrates regression and analysis of variance and is used to adjust the data for effects due to covariates.

The assumptions for the ANCOVA were met [14]. Further attempts to reduce the error term, ε, were made by selecting FSUs with the same gender, age and level of computer experience as the PSUs. In doing so, the ANCOVA model, incorporating these demographics, may reduce differences in the treatment effects. ANCOVAs, however, only provide an indication that not all the adjusted means are equal. As a result, further analysis of the differences among sets of adjusted means is warranted. Hence, post hoc comparisons using pairwise comparisons of adjusted means were conducted using Fisher's Least Significant Differences (LSD) post hoc tests.

Table 2. Visual assessments for PSU (A=acuity*, CS=contrast sensitivity, VF=visual field, C=color perception, (L)=left eye, (R)=right eye)

	Ss #	A (L)	A (R)	CS (L)	CS (R)	VF	C	Diagnosis
PSU	26	+0.2	+0.4	36	32	15	4	Retinitis Pigmentosa
	29	+1.0	+0.9	32	36	100	5	Albinism
	30	0	+1.0	0	17	27	2	Optic Neuritis
	33	+1.1	+1.0	18	18	13	3	Retinitis Pigmentosa
	44	+0.9	+1.1	32	27	93	5	High myopia
	49	+0.9	+0.6	32	35	90	5	Congenital Cataract, Nystagmus
	54	+1.2	+1.1	21	24	71	3	Age-related Macular Degeneration
	56	+0.4	+0.5	24	15	1	4	Retinitis Pigmentosa
	63	+0.8	+0.9	32	28	100	4	Congenital achromotopsia
	65	+0.8	+0.8	29	30	100	4	Congenital achromotopsia

*Visual acuity status was summarized for the analyses in terms of weighted average LogMAR (WMAR) with the better eye given a weight of 0.75 and the worse eye given a weight of 0.25 [18].

A repeated measures ANCOVA of RT on vision, set size, background color and icon size was performed with the visual profile measurements of acuity, contrast sensitivity, visual field and color perception as covariates. The between group variable, Vision, was significant after covariate adjustments ($F= 5.18$, $p< .001$). This result supports Hypothesis One. The four covariates, acuity ($F=18.13$; $p<.001$) contrast sensitivity ($F= 19.47$, $p< .001$), visual field ($F= 14.49$, $p< .002$) and color perception ($F= 17.14$, $p< .001$) were significant in predicting RT. This result supports Hypothesis Two.

Icon size
Mean RT data after covariate adjustment are shown in Figure 1. The main effect of icon size was significant ($F=7.88$, $p< .001$). This result supports Hypothesis 3. The two-way interaction of vision with icon size was significant

($F=12.05$, $p< .001$). The two-way interaction indicates that there exist differences in mean reaction time between PSU and FSU on at least two levels of icon size. Further analyses using LSD post hoc comparisons (adjusted for covariates) were examined. In the case of PSUs, all pairwise comparisons were significant. In the case of FSUs, none of the comparisons were significant. Figure 1 illustrates the influence of icon size on RT for both groups of participants.

Set size
The main effect of set size was not significant on RT. Thus, Hypothesis 4 was not supported. However, the interactions, set size by vision ($F=3.50$, $p< .043$) and icon size by set size ($F=3.05$, $p< .029$), had significant effects on RT.

Background color
There was a significant main effect due to background color on RT ($F=7.82$, $p< .001$). This result supports Hypothesis 5. In addition, there were several two-way interactions and a three-way interaction: background color by vision ($F=5.12$, $p< .017$), background color by icon size ($F=4.43$, $p< .018$), and background color by set size by vision ($F=3.12$, $p< .028$). The interaction between background color and vision suggests that at least one pair of mean RTs for background color and vision differ from the rest. LSD post hoc comparisons revealed no differences in RT between red and white backgrounds for both the FSUs and PSUs. All other pairwise comparisons for both groups were significant. However, black yielded best performance for the PSUs and blue yielded best performance for the FSUs. Figure 2 illustrates the influence of background color on RT for both groups of participants

CONCLUSIONS

Evidence in support of hypothesis 1
Hypothesis 1 was supported in this study. The partially sighted subjects, on average, required significantly more time to identify visual icons within a graphical user interface than the fully sighted subjects. This result is intuitive, as we would expect this task to be more challenging for visually impaired users. However, this is the first empirical evidence that documents the degree of difference between the two groups of users.

Evidence in support of hypothesis 2
Hypothesis 2 was supported in this study. The four visual characteristics, visual acuity, contrast sensitivity, visual field, and color perception, had significant effects on determining reaction time.

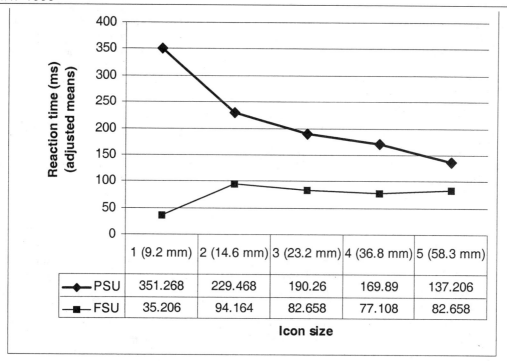

	1 (9.2 mm)	2 (14.6 mm)	3 (23.2 mm)	4 (36.8 mm)	5 (58.3 mm)
PSU	351.268	229.468	190.26	169.89	137.206
FSU	35.206	94.164	82.658	77.108	82.658

Icon size

Figure 1. Relating Icon Size and Reaction Time (adjusted means)

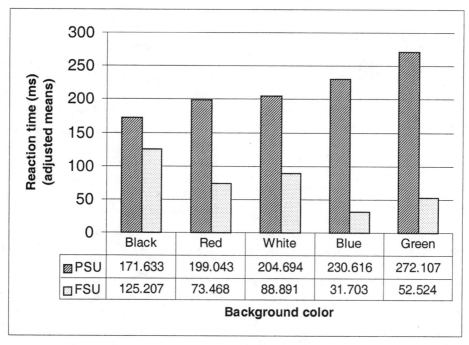

	Black	Red	White	Blue	Green
PSU	171.633	199.043	204.694	230.616	272.107
FSU	125.207	73.468	88.891	31.703	52.524

Background color

Figure 2. Relating Background Color and Reaction Time (adjusted means)

Evidence in support of hypothesis 3

Hypothesis 3 was fully supported by the data. Icon size had a significant effect on performance. In fact, for the smallest size icon (9.2 mm), the PSUs were, on average, ten times slower identifying icons than the FSUs. The gap between the two groups decreased as icon size increased. For the largest size icon (58.3 mm), the PSUs were only 1.7 times slower, on average, than the FSUs. There is a point of diminishing returns associated with increasing icon size, however. A maximum of six, 58.33 mm icons are able to fit on a 21" monitor without occluding each other. Recall, that these results reflect average performance. Icon enlargement is less effective for people with diseases like Retinitis Pigmentosa (RP) because RP causes losses in visual field, beginning with peripheral vision. Thus, portions of enlarged icons may not be visible if they happen to reside in a portion of the user's visual field that is impaired. While this research suggests that, in general, larger icons are preferred for PSUs, and smaller icons are preferred for FSUs, more research, with more subjects, is needed that focuses on the characteristics of specific diagnoses so that more focused guidelines and designs can be developed.

Evidence in support of hypothesis 4

Set size did not have a significant main effect on performance. Thus, Hypothesis 4 was not supported. FSU and PSU performance were no different in the presence of 2 to 6 icons on the screen at one time. An extension of this research will include investigating additional set sizes.

Evidence in support of hypothesis 5

There was a significant main effect due to background color on performance which supported Hypothesis 5. PSUs performed best with a black background and FSUs performed best with a blue background. The biggest performance disparity between FSUs and PSUs was for the green background color. PSUs were five times slower than FSUs in the presence of a green background. In contrast, PSU and FSU performance were closest when using a black background. When asked, participants generally agreed that black backgrounds provide the most contrast. Of the seven participants who had impaired color perception, three were either blue or green deficient and the other four experienced varying levels of general color confusion. In order to make definitive recommendations to designers; additional investigations need to be conducted. However, this research provides documented evidence that PSUs and FSUs have very different needs with respect to background color.

Additional discussion

The visual abilities of the participants in this study varied considerably. Due to this large variability as well as the relatively small number of participants, caution should be heeded when interpreting these results. However, we can conclude from these results and their accompanying post hoc comparisons that we must account for specific visual capabilities like visual acuity, contrast sensitivity, field of view, and color perception when designing and evaluating basic interaction tasks like visual icon identification. Furthermore, we can conclude that PSUs perform very differently depending upon the size of the icons in the interface and the background color of the interface. Knowledge of the influence of visual profile on performance contributes in a substantial way to the existing knowledge base in the field of human-computer interaction. Such information will also serve to influence critical design decisions made by software and hardware developers so that GUIs can more closely accommodate a wide range of visual capabilities.

This study generates empirical evidence that the visual profiles of partially sighted users must be considered when evaluating task performance in fundamental interaction tasks within a GUI like visual icon identification. This research establishes a solid foundation for future investigations whose aims are to couple clinical assessments of low vision with psychomotor task performance. In addition, this study serves as a launching point for a larger, more comprehensive research agenda in this area for the authors.

Future research will focus on further delineating the respective roles of visual acuity, contrast sensitivity, visual field, and color perception on psychomotor task execution. This will enable specific design recommendations given a user's visual profile and moves us closer to accomplishing the goal of universal accessibility.

ACKOWLEDGMENTS

This research was supported by a Research Planning Grant awarded to the first author by the Bioengineering and Research to Aid Persons With Disabilities Division of the National Science Foundation (BES 9714555).

A portion of this research was submitted in partial satisfaction of the requirements for Master of Science in Industrial Engineering by the second author. His participation was made possible through a grant awarded by the 1997 NASA Graduate Students Researchers Program (NGT10-52614).

The authors gratefully acknowledge the contributions of Dr. Elly du Pre' at the Miami Lighthouse for the Blind and Dr. Paulette Johnson, Department of Statistics, Florida International University.

REFERENCES

1. Arnheim, R. (1972) *Visual Thinking*. University of California Press, Berkely, CA.

2. Bailey, I. L., & Lovie, J. E. (1976) New design principles for visual acuity letter charts. *American Journal of Optometry & Physiological Optics, 53* (11), 740-745.

3. Buxton, W. (1985) There's more to interaction than meets the eye: some issues in manual input. In Norman, D.A. & Draper, S.W. (Eds.), *User Centered Design: New Perspectives on Human-Computer Interaction* (pp.319-337). Hillside, NJ:Laurence Erlbaum Associates.

4. Czaja, S.J., (1988) Computer technology and the older adult. In M.G. Helander, T.K. Landauer, and P.V. Prabhu (Eds.), *Handbook of Human-Computer Interaction (*pp.797-812). North Holland: Elsevier.

5. Eason, K.D., Johnson, C., & Fairclough, S. (1991) The interaction of sensory modalities in the man-machine interface. In J.A.J. Roufs (Ed.), *Vision and Dysfunction: The Man-Machine Interface.* Boca Raton, FL: CRC Press.

6. Edwards, A. (1995) Computers and people with disabilities. In A. Edwards (Ed.), *Extra-Ordinary Human-Computer Interaction* (pp.19-43). New York: Cambridge University Press.

7. Farrell, F. E. (1991) Fitting physical screen parameters to the human eye. In J.A.J. Roufs (Ed.), *Vision and Visual Dysfunction: The Man-Machine Interface.* Boca Raton: CRC Press.

8. Ferris, F. L., Kassoff, A., Bresnick, G. H., & Bailey, E. (1982). New visual acuity charts for clinical research. *American Journal of Ophthalmology*, 94, 91-96.

9. Foley, J. D., Wallace, V. L. & Chan, P. (1984). The human factors of computer graphics interaction techniques. *IEEE Computer Graphics and Applications*, 89(8), 13-48.

10. Jacko, J. A., & Sears, A. (1998) Designing interfaces for an overlooked user group: Considering the visual profiles of partially sighted users. *The 3rd ACM/SIGCAPH Conference on Assistive Technologies (ASSETS 98),* Marina del Rey, California, April 15-17, 75-77.

11. Kline, R. L., & Glinert, E. P. (1995) Improving GUI accessibility for people with low vision. Proceedings of the ACM Conference on Human Factors in Computing Systems (CHI 95), 114-121.

12. Kline, D. W., & Schieber, F. (1985) Vision and Aging. In J. E. Birren & K.W. Schaie (Eds.), *Handbook of the Psychology of Aging* (pp.296-331). New York: Von Nostrand Reinhold Company.

13. Kraut, J. A. & McCabe, C. P. (1994) The problem of low vision. In D. M. Albert, F. A. Jakobiec, & N. L. Robinson (Eds.), *Principles and Practices of Ophthalmology*, 3664-3683.

14. Lindman, H.R. (1992) *Analysis of variance in experimental design*. New York: Springer-Verlag.

15. Newell, A. F., & Gregor, P. (1997) Human computer interfaces for people with disabilities. In M.G. Helander, T.K. Landauer, and P.V. Prabhu (Eds.), *Handbook of Human-Computer Interaction* (pp.813-824). North Holland: Elsevier.

16. Pelli, D. G., Robson, J. G., & Wilkins, A. J. (1988) The design of a new letter chart for measuring contrast sensitivity. *Clinical Vision Science*, 2(3), 187-199.

17. Proctor, R. W. & Van Zandt, T. (1994) *Human Factors in Simple and Complex Systems*. Boston: Allyn and Bacon.

18. Scott, I. U., Schein, O. D., West, S., Bandeen-Roche, K., Enger, C., & Folstein, M.F. (1994) Functional status and quality of life measurement among ophthalmic patients. *Arch Ophthalmol*, 112, 329-335.

19. Sears, A., Jacko, J. A., Brewer B., & Robelo, L. (1998) A framework for visual icon design. *Proceeding of the 42nd Annual Meeting of the Human Factors Society*. Santa Monica, CA: Human Factors Society, in-press.

20. Shneiderman, B. (1998) *Designing the User Interface: Strategies for Effective Human-Computer Interaction*. Reading, MA: Addison-Wesley.

21. Wood, J. M., & Troutbeck, R. J. (1994) Effect of age and visual impairment on driving and vision performance. *Transportation Research Record,* n1438, Oct. 1994, 84-90.

NotePals: Lightweight Note Sharing by the Group, for the Group

Richard C. Davis[1], James A. Landay[1], Victor Chen[1], Jonathan Huang[1], Rebecca B. Lee[1], Francis C. Li[1], James Lin[1], Charles B. Morrey III[1], Ben Schleimer[1], Morgan N. Price[2], Bill N. Schilit[2]

[1] Group for User Interface Research
EECS Department
University of California
Berkeley, CA 94720-1776 USA
+1 510 643 7354
{rcdavis, landay}@cs.berkeley.edu

[2] FX Palo Alto Laboratory
3400 Hillview Avenue, Bldg. 4
Palo Alto, CA 94304 USA
+1 650 813 7220
{price, schilit}@pal.xerox.com

ABSTRACT

NotePals is a lightweight note sharing system that gives group members easy access to each other's experiences through their personal notes. The system allows notes taken by group members in any context to be uploaded to a shared repository. Group members view these notes with browsers that allow them to retrieve all notes taken in a given context or to access notes from other related notes or documents. This is possible because NotePals records the context in which each note is created (e.g., its author, subject, and creation time). The system is "lightweight" because it fits easily into group members' regular note-taking practices, and uses informal, ink-based user interfaces that run on portable, inexpensive hardware. In this paper we describe NotePals, show how we have used it to share our notes, and present our evaluations of the system.

Keywords

CSCW, PDA, pen-based user interface, digital ink, mobile computing, informal user interfaces, NotePals

INTRODUCTION

Communication of ideas and experiences is one of the biggest challenges facing a workgroup. Group members spend much of their time alerting colleagues to new information, explaining ideas to them, or searching for a person who has needed information. The NotePals system attempts to give group members more direct access to their colleagues' thoughts and experiences by allowing them to view each other's personal notes. By automatically capturing notes taken in any context and making those notes accessible to an entire workgroup via the web, we have found that group members can more easily benefit from their collective experience.

The NotePals system operates by capturing group member's notes and some of the context in which those notes were written (e.g., the author, the topic, and the time the note was created). These notes are then uploaded to a shared note repository that all group members can access through note "browsers." These browsers allow group members to retrieve all notes taken in a given context or to access notes through other related notes or documents.

Shared notes from meetings can capture group members' detailed thoughts and differing perspectives. If one person in the meeting creates an important diagram or list of ideas in his personal notes, all group members have easy access to that information. This information can be retrieved by listing all notes taken by that person during the meeting and browsing for the desired pages. Alternatively, if a presentation was given during the meeting, group members can browse for the slide that was visible when the desired pages were created and find them next to the slide.

At a conference, shared notes that one group member takes during a session can benefit other members that did not attend that session. Group members may take more detailed notes than they would without NotePals, because they know that other group members will be looking at their notes. When the group reviews the conference later, they can retrieve the notes taken during each presentation and discuss them in detail. Group members may also discover each other's impressions months after the conference, because their notes can be shown next to the conference paper in an on-line proceedings.

NotePals can capture group members' thoughts and experiences because it is "lightweight," fitting easily into groups' existing processes. Note taking is a natural activity that nearly all people engage in to record their ideas and experiences. NotePals captures this natural activity with an informal ink-based user interface [8]. This lets users focus on taking notes, instead of correcting a handwriting recognition system. Also, NotePals runs on Personal Digital Assistants (PDAs) that are inexpensive and very portable.

This paper gives a detailed description of the NotePals system and shows how it can be used to share notes as in the above examples. We begin by describing the NotePals user interface. Then, we will describe usage experience that has shown us the value of shared notes. The next section presents two user studies we conducted, and this is followed by a description of two task-specific NotePals browsers that we built as a result of one of the studies. We finish with related work, future plans and conclusions.

NOTEPALS USER INTERFACE

The NotePals system, first described in [4] and demonstrated in [6], includes a PalmPilot-based interface for taking notes and a web browser-based interface for viewing notes. Each interface had its own requirements and challenges, and we discuss them here separately.

Note-taking Interface

We wanted the note-taking interface to run on a device that was as inexpensive as possible, usable in almost any environment, and capable of uploading notes to a central repository with little effort. We considered using paper-based notes that could be copied or scanned. Although paper may be natural to use, copying would require collation of the notes for sharing and scanning excludes performing handwriting recognition on the notes due to the lack of timestamps on the ink.

Instead of paper, we chose to use PDAs. In particular, we chose the 3Com PalmPilot, a pen-based PDA that over a million people already use for personal information management [1], and which currently sells for under $300. In addition, the PalmPilot has a simple mechanism for exchanging information with other computers. Placing the Pilot in a docking cradle connected to a desktop PC and pressing the HotSync button causes an application-specific data exchange program to run. This platform enabled us to create an informal, electronic ink-based note-taking system that allows users to share notes with little effort.

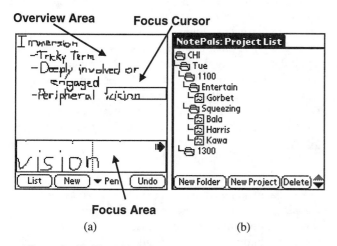

Overview Area   **Focus Cursor**

Focus Area

(a)   (b)

Figure 1. (a) The NotePals note-taking interface on a Pilot. Ink can be drawn in the Overview Area or the Focus Area. Erase and undo are also supported. (b) The NotePals interface for selecting a project name.

The Pilot's size makes it easy to carry, but also difficult to draw on. An unrecognized, ink-based interface is hard to design for a two-inch square screen. A user's hand can obstruct her view of words on the screen. Resolution is also a problem. Even if users can write very small words, the 160x160 pixel resolution makes them hard to read.

The interface we created to deal with these problems is shown in Figure 1(a). Users write in their own handwriting directly on the page at the top of the screen (the "overview area") or in the box at the bottom of the screen (the "focus area"). Words drawn in the focus area appear in the overview area inside the "focus cursor," shrunk to 40% of their original size. Once the user has filled up the focus area with text, a quick right to left swipe of the pen moves the focus cursor forward, clearing space for the next word. This interface allows many words to fit on one page, despite the small screen.

Each page of notes in NotePals is created within a "project." Projects are organized in a hierarchical set of folders, as in Figure 1(b), which gives users a way to group notes into topics. New project names are entered using Graffiti (the Pilot's text shorthand) rather than using digital ink, but it is also possible to pre-load a list of project names. To give extra context, users can assign each page of notes a "Type" that indicates what kind of information it contains (e.g., action item or new meeting header). Other contextual information, such as the author's name and the time the note was created, are recorded automatically.

Users can also control who has access to their notes. By default, notes are public, but they can either be marked private so that only the author can view them or they can be marked group-visible, which makes the notes visible only to the author's workgroup.

With this system, group members can take personal notes in any environment and make those notes available to their entire group, if they wish. In order for this sharing to take place, all they have to do is remember to dock their Pilots with their desktop PCs once in a while. Docking causes the NotePals data exchange program, or "conduit," to upload their notes to the group's web repository.

Browsing Interface

Shared notes are accessed on networked computers through conventional web browsers. This makes notes viewable at most group members' desks and in many meeting rooms.

When group members wish to review notes, they point a web browser to the group's web repository. After entering their name and password, they can view a subset of notes by selecting note properties (project, author, date, type, and keyword). The notes are sorted by the time they were created, with notes from different authors interleaved (see Figure 2[1]). Users can sort notes by their properties (such as

---

[1] This browser can be viewed at the following web site: http://guir.berkeley.edu/notepals/guir

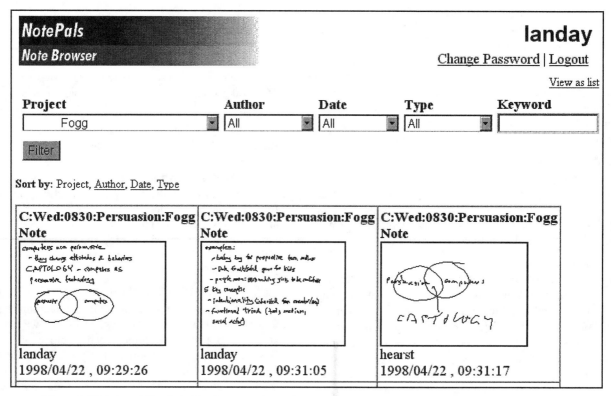

Figure 2. Web-based NotePals Note Browser shows thumbnails of the notes matching the selected properties.

author or type) and change the subset of notes viewed by selecting a new set of properties. Clicking on a thumbnail shows individual notes at full size, as shown in Figure 3.

The NotePals system made it possible for our research group of about 10 people to take shared notes regularly. The following section shows how we use our shared notes.

USAGE EXPERIENCE

We have been using NotePals for sixteen months and taken over 3000 pages of notes. The ability to share notes has proven quite useful in conference settings and shown great promise in classroom settings as well. Many of us also find NotePals useful for our own private notes, which indicates that the system can fit easily into our existing note-taking practices. Here we describe these usage patterns in detail.

Note Taking at Conferences

We began to see the real value in shared notes at the UIST '97 conference. Two of the authors took a combined 128 pages of notes during talks at this conference. Afterwards, at a conference review meeting, the entire group viewed the shared notes through a web browser projected onto a large screen. The easy accessibility of these notes enabled us to have a very detailed review, because participants asked questions about things written in the notes, and the authors used their notes to recall details.

Inspired by this experience, we prepared for a greater challenge, the CHI '98 conference. Since this conference has multiple, simultaneous tracks, it was not possible to determine which notes went with which talk by time alone.

Therefore, we pre-loaded the list of talks into NotePals as projects. Six members of our research group took over 350 pages of notes at the conference.

After the conference, we had an even more detailed review that extended over three group meetings. Notes were displayed on a large screen, as before, and each talk was discussed in detail. This review was important for those who were unable to attend the conference and for those who attended but could not be in every session of interest.

For group members that were not present at the review, their notes served as their "voice" in the meeting, though notes were occasionally too hard to read. Group members that were present used their own notes to jog their memory (as before), and other group members asked them questions about the content of their notes. After this review, many of those present felt that they had a better understanding of what happened at the conference than they would have had without the shared notes. This benefit appears to be due mostly to the fact that the notes were displayed in the same place at the same time, and partially to the fact that they were visible to all group members.

Since the conference review, we have found new value in these shared notes. Though an individual may not have attended a certain talk and may have forgotten about the review of that talk, she can easily access other group members' impressions of that talk. This effectively gives the entire group access to an impression of a talk just because one group member attended it. Such knowledge may be useful when one of us is writing a paper and wants

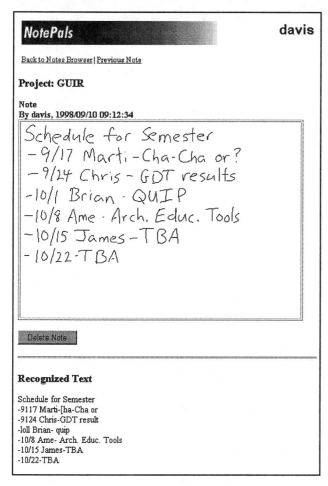

Figure 3. A note shown at full-size. The recognized text was added as a result of our group note taking study.

to quickly check out a reference from this conference. We explore this possibility further below.

More recently, we have taken notes at the UIST '98 and CSCW '98 conferences, as well as in medium to large-sized grant proposal meetings. In particular, we have had success taking NotePals notes on the paper-based CrossPad [3]. This portable device digitizes ink as it is drawn and is more natural to use than a PDA. The digital ink is uploaded to a desktop PC and a transfer utility, written using a Java API [9], transfers the ink and attributes to the NotePals web repository, and allows the user to specify a project for the notes.

Note Taking in Class

Three group members, two of whom have not worked on NotePals, have also successfully used shared notes in their graduate operating systems course. This course requires students to read research papers that are discussed in class. The goal of the course is to teach them how to analyze these papers critically and how to recognize common themes. As such, much of the "content" of the course is contained in the discussions that the professor leads during each class.

These students said that there was more information presented in class than they could record alone. Not all of this information is important, but it is hard to determine which points are worth remembering. Each did his best to record the important points presented in class, but all relied on each other to improve their coverage of the topics. The students used NotePals so that they could benefit from each other's notes after lectures or when preparing for exams.

Right before the midterm, the three students met for a total of six hours over two evenings for a study session. They found that projecting their NotePals notes was a productive and an effective way to study as a group. Many times during their discussion the notes helped them recall information they had forgotten. Often, viewing a note would lead to questions and discussion to clarify a particular concept, and sometimes this would lead them to look at other information such as the papers themselves, on-line summaries, or the instructor's lecture notes.

NotePals was valuable in this class environment because the students felt a strong need to recall as many important ideas as possible from class discussions. It is unlikely that the notes would be so valuable if all of the lecture content were contained in distributed lecture slides, or if there were not exams driving these students to pool their resources.

Personal Note Taking

It is worth noting that several group members prefer taking all of their personal notes with NotePals, regardless of whether or not they *need* to be shared. Some simply like taking all of their notes on a device that fits in their pocket. Others like the fact that notes are automatically stored in a computer format that is easy to retrieve, duplicate, and share if needed.

For example, one of the authors uses NotePals to take notes during weekly meetings with students. He makes the notes accessible to the student so that both can have a shared record of work plans. Though students seldom need to refer to these notes, this author is assured that the plans are available to the students if they should ever need them.

Few of us ever make our notes private, preferring instead to make notes accessible to the rest of the group, in case they *might* one day prove useful. This may however be due to the inconvenience of changing the note property from the default value of public.

USER STUDIES

As we were beginning to use NotePals in our everyday lives, we also conducted two studies to evaluate the strengths and weaknesses of the NotePals system. The first of these studies measured the quality of the note-taking interface and revealed some problems that we have since addressed. The second study looked at how meeting notes could be shared after a large group meeting and showed us the value of making shared notes accessible from other documents, such as meeting minutes. Here, we describe these findings.

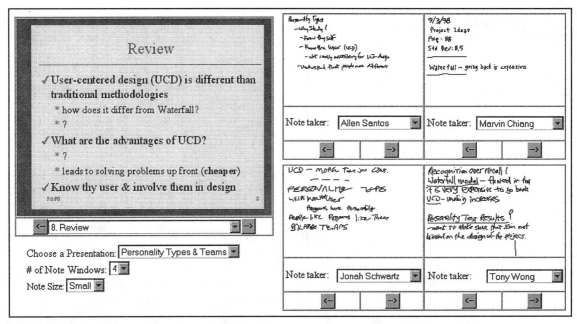

Figure 4. A web interface for browsing presentation slides along with multiple users' notes.

Note Reading/Writing Speed Study

Our first evaluation of NotePals, reported in [4], compared the speed of creating and reading NotePals notes versus paper notes. The study found that it took 64% longer on average to write NotePals notes because users had difficulty moving the focus cursor and often lost track of its location on the page. Another group of participants who read these paper notes and the on-line NotePals notes could do so with almost no errors, but NotePals notes took on average 37% longer to read. These results indicated that creating legible notes with NotePals was possible but slow, and the interface tended to make bad handwriting worse.

This study made it clear that providing ink-based note-taking interfaces on small PDAs would be challenging, and we have tried several approaches to improve the situation. First, we allowed the right-to-left swipe to be drawn in the focus area[2], and made the cursor snap to a grid so that it could easily be dragged and centered on a line of text. Also, users often lost track of the cursor's position on the page because their attention was directed to the focus area. To alleviate this problem, we enhanced the focus area with the two position cues shown in Figure 1(a). A vertical line indicates that the end of the page is ½ a screen-width away, and tic-marks similar to those on a ruler give a coarse indication of horizontal position. We believe these changes improved writing speed and legibility.

We are in the process of adding Graffiti support to NotePals so that Pilot experts can add ASCII text to their notes using this recognized shorthand alphabet. We are also experimenting with new methods for creating ink-based notes on small screens. Finally, we are continuing our exploration of note taking on the CrossPad. With a combination of these approaches, we hope to improve the ease of taking notes on portable, inexpensive devices.

Group Meeting Study

Our second evaluation, described in [5], focused on the use of shared notes to create meeting minutes from a real meeting. Each member of a research group of about 15 people was given small paper pads that simulated the ideal NotePals interface. We used paper so that problems with the existing interface would not affect the study. For three consecutive weekly meetings, about half the group took their personal notes on these pads.

Since our focus was to provide a shared meeting record and we did not know what form these records would take, we worked with a participant from each meeting to assemble the notes into a useful meeting record. After each meeting, participants were asked to compare their regular, scribed meeting minutes with our group record.

We made several interesting discoveries. First, we found that many participants had difficulty reading each other's handwriting, especially in records that changed handwriting styles every few lines. (A participant performed this interleaving of notes to imitate meeting minutes.) This discovery led us to separate individuals' notes into distinct, non-overlapping regions in later systems (see Figure 4). It also led us to add off-line handwriting recognition[3] to the NotePals browser, as shown in Figure 3. This recognized text is not accurate enough to provide an exact transcript of all notes, but it catches enough

---

[2] This gesture was originally made in the "Graffiti" area below the display.

[3] NotePals uses ParaGraph's CalliGrapher handwriting recognition SDK when notes are uploaded [16].

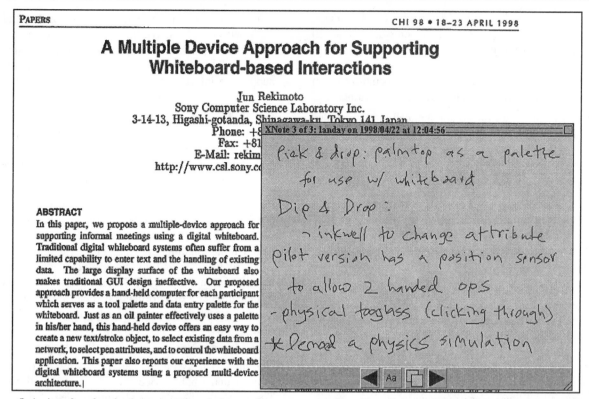

PAPERS

CHI 98 ● 18–23 APRIL 1998

A Multiple Device Approach for Supporting Whiteboard-based Interactions

Jun Rekimoto
Sony Computer Science Laboratory Inc.
3-14-13, Higashi-gotanda, Shinagawa-ku, Tokyo 141 Japan
Phone: +8...
Fax: +81...
E-Mail: rekim...
http://www.csl.sony.c...

ABSTRACT

In this paper, we propose a multiple-device approach for supporting informal meetings using a digital whiteboard. Traditional digital whiteboard systems often suffer from a limited capability to enter text and the handling of existing data. The large display surface of the whiteboard also makes traditional GUI design ineffective. Our proposed approach provides a hand-held computer for each participant which serves as a tool palette and data entry palette for the whiteboard. Just as an oil painter effectively uses a palette in his/her hand, this hand-held device offers an easy way to create a new text/stroke object, to select existing data from a network, to select pen attributes, and to control the whiteboard application. This paper also reports our experience with the digital whiteboard systems using a proposed multi-device architecture.

Figure 5. An interface for viewing notes taken during conference presentations. Hyperlinks can be made between ink in the note and portions of the underlying paper. The recognized text corresponding to the handwriting can be displayed by clicking on the "Aa" icon.

keywords to make searching for text faster than browsing through hard to read notes. Note that the lack of timestamps and stroke data would have made this almost impossible with scanned notes.

Second, we discovered that participants did not like "minutes" that were automatically created from their personal notes, because the large group size made the jumble of personal perspectives incoherent. They began to see real value, however, in *combining* personal notes and presentation slides with the regular minutes. The key insight appeared to be that a single, unifying document is needed to provide a structure when there are too many sources of notes to make sense of them all. This caused us to begin looking at the possibility of combining outside documents with shared notes.

TASK-SPECIFIC NOTEPALS BROWSERS

This drive to combine shared notes with unifying, outside documents has resulted in two new browsers that we have recently started to use. The first is specific to the task of finding shared notes in the context of presentation slides, and the second, to finding shared notes from on-line conference proceedings.

Browsing Notes and Presentation Slides

With the new goal of making shared notes accessible from contextually related documents, we developed a browser interface that combines notes with presentation slides. In this system, presenters start their PowerPoint presentations with a special tool that logs when each slide is visible,

while the audience takes notes with NotePals. After the meeting, slides and personal notes are uploaded to the system. The browsing interface, shown in Figure 4, allows users to see the notes of up to five people synchronized with the presentation slides. Cycling through slides or notes changes all other views to keep them in sync.

Recently, a prototype version of this system was used in an undergraduate UI course taught by the author. Each of the fifty students was provided with an IBM WorkPad (equivalent to a Pilot) for taking notes. Students could view lecture slides next to the notes taken by other members of their project groups. We felt NotePals would prove useful to these students because much of the learning in this class happens through class discussions, and lecture slides are used mostly to frame these discussions. The value of NotePals appeared limited in this situation because the students reported that the slides were "very complete."

Browsing Notes and Conference Papers

We also developed a new browser for conference proceedings and notes that may make our conference notes useful far into the future. The notes taken during CHI '98 were combined with on-line proceedings to create the interface shown in Figure 5. This interface shows personal notes attached to conference papers and also allows viewing of recognized versions of the notes[4].

---

[4] This browser can be viewed at the following web site: http://guir.berkeley.edu/notepals/chi98

This browser was built on top of the Multivalent Document architecture (MVD) [17]. MVD documents are composed of "layers" of related data and dynamically loaded "behaviors." For example, each note is comprised of the original handwriting image layer and a recognized text layer, allowing the user to manipulate the handwriting.

Because these notes are linked automatically to conference papers, this interface can make group members aware of others' impressions of a presentation long after the presentation has taken place. In the future, we will experiment more with this interface.

RELATED WORK

NotePals was inspired by many previous systems. Here we compare and contrast our work with similar research in two main areas: computerized meeting rooms and personal ink-based note-taking systems.

Computerized Meeting Rooms

Some meeting room systems seek to improve specific kinds of meetings by structuring meeting activities. The Electronic Meeting System, for example, leads a group through brainstorming, idea organization, voting, and comment phases [14]. These tools can improve the quality and number of ideas generated by a group, but they are inappropriate for other styles of meetings.

Other meeting room systems make no attempt to structure meetings, but instead give participants new means to communicate and record meeting activities. These systems often give participants access to traditional applications that have been group-enabled [11, 15, 18]. Some of these systems have been shown to help groups create documents that better reflect a group's ideas and decisions.

These meeting room systems share some problems. They may shift a meeting's focus to document creation, redirect some of the group's attention to complex computer interfaces, and they often require participants to type during meetings, which can be disruptive.

Another class of meeting room systems tries to enhance natural interaction styles or record keeping methods, without shifting the meeting focus or process. WeMet [23], for example, provides access to a shared drawing space running on multiple workstations. Tivoli [12] allows users to manipulate handwritten text in structured ways on a LiveBoard [7]. Tivoli notes and meeting audio can be captured together, allowing participants to access the audio from the notes after the meeting [13]. Similarly, the Classroom 2000 project [2] records classroom audio, presentation slides, and the professor's LiveBoard notes, and provides ways to browse through them after class. An early prototype of this system merged handwritten notes taken on Apple MessagePad PDAs with lecture slides. Unlike Classroom 2000, we do not assume classroom settings, and we focus on the sharing of notes between meeting participants.

These more natural systems have been influential in our work with NotePals. We have implemented many of these ideas in cheaper, more portable systems than the traditional computerized meeting room. This is important for supporting informal meetings or conferences. Unlike these systems, we also focus on the *sharing* of personal notes and information between group members.

Dolphin allows co-located and remote groups to link personal notes and documents in shared spaces [19]. NotePals also links notes and documents, but we make these links automatically when possible.

Personal Freehand Note-taking Systems

Since typing can interfere with many note-taking situations, we have also taken inspiration from research in informal, personal note-taking systems. Freestyle allows personal, handwritten notes and annotated documents to be shared using electronic mail [10]. NotePals also takes advantage of the simplicity of informal, personal note taking, but has more automated sharing and supports note taking *away* from the desktop.

The PARCTab [20] was an early handheld CSCW system that supported a simple shared drawing application. This showed that small devices could be used collaboratively. There has also been research in portable, handwritten note taking and audio recording systems, such as Filochat [21] and Dynomite [22]. Handwritten notes written with these systems can be used to access audio that was recorded when they were created. The simplicity of these note-taking interfaces and the automatic recording of audio context makes these systems very similar, in spirit, to NotePals. NotePals, however, uses even cheaper hardware and allows personal notes to be shared. Interviews of Dynomite users showed that free-form ink can be lighter weight and more expressive than text entry.

FUTURE WORK

For some users, the PalmPilot is simply too small and can be uncomfortable for ink-based note taking. We plan to extend NotePals in the immediate future by exploring more natural methods for entering notes. This includes improving our initial support for the paper-based CrossPad [3], evaluating solutions based on scanning-in handwritten notes, and creating a better PDA interface. We have also recently implemented text search of the ASCII text generated by our off-line handwriting recognizer.

Our long-term goal is to add inexpensive systems that capture audio and whiteboard notes so that we can support meeting environments without expensive equipment, such as the LiveBoard [7]. We will also continue to look for useful ways to share personal notes and to explore methods for linking these notes with related documents and captured information. Finally, we will continue to evaluate how sharing can be beneficial to workgroups.

CONCLUSIONS

NotePals is a lightweight note sharing system that gives group members easy access to each other's experience through their personal notes. The system captures notes and related documents of interest to a workgroup and provides a central repository for this information. NotePals fits easily into a workgroup's regular practices and uses portable, inexpensive hardware. We have built a note-taking client on a handheld device using a novel focus plus context user interface, as well as a paper-based system using the CrossPad. A field study found that shared notes are more valuable if retrieved using task-specific browsing interfaces that group related pieces of information and make them accessible from each other. Usage experience with NotePals has shown that shared notes can add value to meeting, conference, and class records.

ACKNOWLEDGMENTS

Thanks go to Jason Brotherton, who implemented the first NotePals Browser. Thanks also to Gene Golovchinsky, Jason Hong, Chris Long, Mark Newman, and Steve Whittaker who provided valuable feedback on this paper.

REFERENCES

1. PalmPilot Sets Record, *Pen Computing Magazine*, vol. 5(20): pp. 12, 1998.

2. Abowd, G.D., *et al.* Teaching and Learning as Multimedia Authoring: The Classroom 2000 Project. In Proceedings of *Multimedia '96*, p. 187-198, November 1996.

3. Company, A.T.C., *CrossPad*, 1998. http://www.cross-pcg.com/products/crosspad/pad.html

4. Davis, R.C., J.A. Brotherton, J.A. Landay, M.N. Price, and B.N. Schilit, *NotePals: Lightweight Note Taking by the Group, for the Group*. Technical Report CSD-98-997, CS Division, EECS Department, UC Berkeley, Berkeley, CA, February 1998.

5. Davis, R.C. and J.A. Landay, *An Exploration of Lightweight Meeting Capture*. Technical Report CSD-98-1015, CS Division, EECS Department, UC Berkeley, May 1998.

6. Davis, R.C., J. Lin, J.A. Brotherton, J.A. Landay, B.N. Schilit, and M.N. Price. A Framework for Sharing Handwritten Notes. Formal Demonstration. In Proceedings of *UIST '98: 11th Annual Symposium on User Interface Software and Technology*. San Francisco, CA. pp. 119-120, Nov. 1-4 1998.

7. Elrod, S., *et al.* Liveboard: A Large Interactive Display Supporting Group Meetings, Presentations and Remote Collaboration. In Proceedings of *Human Factors in Computing Systems*. Monterey, CA. pp. 599-607, May 3–7 1992.

8. Hearst, M.A., M.D. Gross, J.A. Landay, and T.E. Stahovich, Sketching Intelligent Systems. *IEEE Intelligent Systems*, 1998. **13**(3): p. 10-19.

9. IBM, *The IBM Ink Software Development Toolkit*, 1998. http://www.research.ibm.com/electricInk/introduction.html

10. Levine, S.R. and S.F. Ehrlich, *The Freestyle System: A Design Perspective*. Human-Machine Interactive Systems, ed. A. Klinger. Plenum. pp. 3-21, 1991.

11. Mantei, M.M., Observation of Executives Using a Computer Supported Meeting Environment. *International Journal of Decision Support Systems*, 1989. **5**(June): p. 153-166.

12. Moran, T.P., P. Chiu, W. van Melle, and G. Kurtenbach, Implicit Structures for Pen-Based Systems within a Freeform Interaction Paradigm, in *Proceedings of ACM CHI'95 Conference on Human Factors in Computing Systems*. p. 487-494, 1995.

13. Moran, T.P., *et al.* "I'll Get That Off the Audio": A Case Study of Salvaging Multimedia Meeting Records. In Proceedings of *Human Factors in Computing Systems*. Atlanta, GA. pp. 202-209, March 22-27 1997.

14. Nunamaker, J.F., A.R. Dennis, J.S. Valacich, D.R. Vogel, and J.F. George, Electronic Meeting Systems to Support Group Work, *Communications of the ACM*, vol. 34(7): pp. 40-61, 1991.

15. Olson, J.S., G.M. Olson, M. Storrosten, and M. Carter, Groupwork Close Up: A Comparison of the Group Design Process With and Without a Simple Group Editor. *ACM Transactions on Information Systems*, 1993. **11**(4): p. 321-348.

16. ParaGraph, *CalliGrapher SDK*, 1998. ParaGraph, a division of Vadem: 1960 Zanker Road, San Jose, CA 95112. http://www.paragraph.com

17. Phelps, T.A. and R. Wilensky. Toward Active, Extensible, Networked Documents: Multivalent Architecture and Applications. In Proceedings of *Digital Libraries '96*. Bethesda, Maryland, March 20-23 1996.

18. Stefik, M., D.G. Bobrow, G. Foster, S. Lanning, and D. Tatar, WYSIWIS Revised: Early Experiences with Multiuser Interfaces. *ACM Transactions on Office Information Systems*, 1987. **5**(2): p. 147-167.

19. Streitz, N.A., J. Geissler, J.M. Haake, and J. Hol, DOLPHIN: Integrated Meeting Support Across Local and Remote Desktop Environments and LiveBoards, in *Proceedings of ACM CSCW'94 Conference on Computer-Supported Cooperative Work*. p. 345-358, 1994.

20. Want, R., *et al.*, An overview of the PARCTAB ubiquitous computing experiment. *IEEE Personal Communications*, 1195. **2**(6): p. 28-43.

21. Whittaker, S., P. Hyland, and M. Wiley, Filochat: Handwritten Notes Provide Access to Recorded Conversations, in *Proceedings of ACM CHI'94 Conference on Human Factors in Computing Systems*. p. 219, 1994.

22. Wilcox, L.D., B.N. Schilit, and N.N. Sawhney. Dynomite: A Dynamically Organized Ink and Audio Notebook. In Proceedings of *Human Factors in Computing Systems*. Atlanta, GA. pp. 186-193, March 22-27 1997.

23. Wolf, C.G., J.R. Rhyne, and L.K. Briggs, Communication and Information Retrieval with a Pen-Based Meeting Support Tool, in *Proceedings of ACM CSCW'92 Conference on Computer-Supported Cooperative Work*. p. 322-329, 1992.

Flatland: New Dimensions in Office Whiteboards

Elizabeth D. Mynatt[1], Takeo Igarashi[2], W. Keith Edwards[3], and Anthony LaMarca[3]

[1]College of Computing
Georgia Institute of Technology
Atlanta, GA 30332-0280
+1 404-894-7243
mynatt@cc.gatech.edu

[2]University of Tokyo
7-3-1 Bunkyo-ku, Hongo
Tokyo 113-8656, JAPAN
+81 3 3812 2111 ext. 7413
takeo@mtl.t.u-tokyo.ac.jp

[2]Xerox Palo Alto Research Center
3333 Coyote Hill Road
Palo Alto, CA 94304, USA
+1 650-812-4405
[kedwards,lamarca]@parc.xerox.com

ABSTRACT

Flatland is an augmented whiteboard interface designed for informal office work. Our research investigates approaches to building an augmented whiteboard in the context of continuous, long term office use. In particular, we pursued three avenues of research based on input from user studies: techniques for the management of space on the board, the ability to flexibly apply behaviors to support varied application semantics, and mechanisms for managing history on the board. Unlike some previously reported whiteboard systems, our design choices have been influenced by a desire to support long-term, informal use in an individual office setting.

Keywords: pen-based computing, whiteboards, ubiquitous computing, light-weight interaction, Flatland

INTRODUCTION

Whiteboards are ubiquitous tools in informal office work. By this description, we envision a whiteboard in a private office with four principal characteristics based on observations of whiteboards in an office setting [16]. First, the whiteboard acts as a working area and repository to support *thinking* tasks such as sketching out a paper as well as quick *capture* tasks such as jotting down a reminder. As an interface for thinking, whiteboards are often used for *pre-production* tasks where the emphasis is on understanding ideas, tasks or concepts and the production work based on that thinking is accomplished in a different arena. Examples are sketching out an algorithm that is later coded using a computer, planning out a set of tasks whose schedule is captured in a planner or email message, drafting ideas for a web page or organizing concepts that are later put into prose using a word processor. These pre-production artifacts would not even be thought of as drafts, but as what comes before a draft. Due to its large visual surface and simple input capabilities, the whiteboard can be appropriated for many pre-production activities It lacks, however, mechanisms to support specific tasks, such as managing to-do lists or organizing an outline, that be found in many desktop and PDA tools.

Second, the content on the whiteboard, whether a sketch or a reminder, has particular characteristics stemming from its creation and use. We refer to this type of content as *everyday content* and loosely define it as the continually shifting set of information in your office that you use to do the majority of your tasks. This flow of information is often incomplete, unnamed, informal, heavily context-dependent and transient. Examples are notes, to-do lists, drafts, reminders, sketches and the like that are in sharp contrast to archival material typically filed either electronically or physically. As an interface for everyday content, common whiteboards afford quick creation of material with an informal look-and-feel without the overhead of naming, filing and formatting. However, the context surrounding its creation (e.g. "What was I thinking when I wrote down "Rosebud"?") must be remembered by the user.

Third, whiteboard material is generally clumped into various clusters on the whiteboard. Some clusters, such as an important phone number or a sketch, may be long-lived compared to other clusters, such as an illustration for a visitor or a quick calculation that is erased within a day. Often there are "hot spots" that are erased while bordering content persists. Since whiteboard content is rarely obscured and quite visible in the office, its presence acts as a reminder. Some people depend on this informal awareness. As an interface for clusters of content, the whiteboard's large visual space affords delegating portions for longer-lived content. Additionally, its vertical orientation makes it less likely to be obscured in contrast to the horizontal orientation of a desk that affords stacking and obscuring layers of content.

Fourth, in an individual office, the whiteboard functions as a personal device, but it also has a semi-public role for office visitors and informal meetings. Whiteboards are typically visible to an office visitor, and can be the focal point for an informal office discussion whether one person is illustrating ideas for the other, or multiple people are contributing to the board's content. The placement of the whiteboard significantly affects its public role, whether it is visible and writable for the typical office visitor. Since the whiteboard can be easily erased, private material can be quickly deleted when an office visitor arrives, although the material would then be lost.

These four characteristics—thinking or pre-production tasks, everyday content, clusters of persistent and short-lived content, and semi-public to personal use—underlie our model of informal whiteboard use in an individual office. This use of whiteboards is quite distinct from the use of desktop computers, and still varies significantly from the use of personal, pen-input devices given a whiteboard's public role and large, continually visible surface.

Although the whiteboard is a flexible tool for quickly capturing input with an informal look-and-feel and its large visible surface supports parallel tasks including awareness, its utility past that point is limited. Its content cannot be saved and retrieved, or even moved out of the way. As simple strokes on a board, all input is treated the same whether it is a to-do list, a series of calculations or an illustration. Additionally, writing may be illegible and the visual quality of drawings poor.

While there has been previous research in computer-augmented whiteboards, these efforts have principally focused on the use of whiteboards in meeting or classroom settings [1][12]. Our goal in this work is to create an augmented whiteboard called "Flatland" to better support typical whiteboard use in the setting of an individual office. In our design, we attempt to extend the existing whiteboard look-and-feel with an interface whose feel and aesthetics match its role in informal office work. Our initial hardware configuration is a SmartBoard™ coupled with a projector. The SmartBoard is a touch-sensitive whiteboard that accepts normal whiteboard marker input as well as stylus input. Captured strokes are then projected onto the board. Given this platform and our characterization of whiteboard use, our design goals were:

- To support a low threshold for initial use while making increasingly complex capabilities available. At the simplest level, Flatland should act like a normal whiteboard where you can walk up to it and write on it. In general, its look-and-feel should remain simple and informal to support the nature of pre-production tasks.

- To provide a look and feel appropriate for informal whiteboard tasks and distinct from production-oriented tools such as a desktop computer.

- To support informal office pre-production tasks such as to-do lists and sketching.

- To support clusters of content on the whiteboard. These clusters, or segments, may be created for different purposes, at different times and by different people.

- To support the use of everyday content by creating context-aware interaction and infrastructure. As unnamed material, content could be stored and retrieved based on its salient context (spatial location on board, time of creation, people present) instead of requiring a file name.

- To support the flexible management of a dynamic whiteboard space such as freeing up whitespace for new input while maintaining the visibility of current content.

- To support a range of use from semi-public to private use, such as providing a means to get a clean board without losing current content.

This paper is organized as follows. In the following section we introduce the basic concepts in Flatland to give the reader a sense of its functionality and feel. We then discuss Flatland's design in three parts. First, we describe facilities for managing the virtual projected space on the physically constrained board. Key concepts here are automatically segmenting user input as well as mechanisms for shuffling whiteboard segments while maintaining visibility of those segments.

Second, we describe how we support different tasks on the whiteboard by allowing the user to apply different "behaviors" to input strokes. While behaviors provide specific interpretation of input strokes, the whiteboard maintains a unified appearance and feel. To support concurrent tasks and flexible reuse of content, behaviors can be composed, in parallel or sequentially.

Third, we describe how whiteboard segments are stored based on their context, and strategies for retrieving those segments. Each segment is tagged with context markers (e.g. spatial location on board, people present, time of day) that can be used as the basis for later retrieving that segment. Since time is often a key contextual clue, we provide a strategy for searching segments across time where the search "snaps" to interesting points in the timeline.

We then discuss related work, paying particular attention to other whiteboard and pen-input interfaces as well as general work in blurring the boundaries between the physical and virtual realms. We close the paper by detailing the status of the current system, summarizing the key contributions of this work, and discussing potential avenues for future work.

FLATLAND BASICS

In this section, we give a general description of Flatland. We shall describe many of these features in greater detail in later sections. As Flatland is designed for long-term use, this scenario illustrates using Flatland over a period of days.

On Monday, Ian walks up to his new Flatland board and jots down some quick notes using the stylus just as if he were using an old-fashioned whiteboard. Flatland automatically groups his notes into a segment and draws an informal border around them. On Tuesday, he writes down a to-do list creating another segment. On Wednesday afternoon, he sketches a map to his house for an office visitor. On Thursday, he uses the time slider to replay items that he has checked off so that he can write his status report. (See Figure 1).

There are two modes of stylus input. The primary mode is for drawing strokes on the board. The secondary mode is activated by holding a button and is used to create meta-strokes. These meta-strokes form gestures[1] that are used for managing the board's visual layout as well as for applying behaviors to segments. The tap gesture causes a pie menu to be displayed and directional gestures are short cuts for the pie menu (i.e. a marking menu). (See Figure 2)

---

1. Although we took great care in designing a small gesture set, we will not discuss this process in detail due to space constraints.

FIGURE 1. Using Flatland

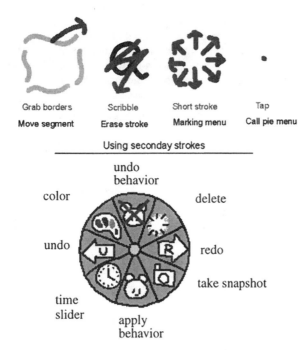

| Grab borders | Scribble | Short stroke | Tap |
| Move segment | Erase stroke | Marking menu | Call pie menu |

Using seconday strokes

FIGURE 2. Gestures and Pie Menus

MANAGING SPACE

As a computationally-enhanced whiteboard, Flatland provides a flexible and dynamic writing surface. Since the presence of material on the whiteboard often acts as an informal reminder, we opted for strategies that allow users to acquire whitespace while still ensuring the visibility of existing content.

The basic conceptual building block here is that of a whiteboard *segment*—a cluster of content. Flatland creates segments automatically when users write on the board. The segments are not allowed to overlap and can be moved by the user or the system. Flatland also automatically shrinks segments to create more whitespace on the board.

Auto-Segmenting

Most whiteboard users manage multiple clusters of content on their whiteboard. By taking advantage of the large visual surface, they use different parts of the board for different tasks at different times. Since this process of dividing up the board is a lightweight, implicit interaction, we wanted to provide *automatic* mechanisms for generating these clusters or segments. Although users do not *need* segments to write on the board, these segments are the basic building block for managing the board's spatial layout, adding additional behaviors to the whiteboard, and retrieving content.

Given a fresh, clean board, when the user begins writing a border appears, denoting a new segment. The border grows to encompass additional strokes of input if the subsequent strokes seem to fall in the same segment. Several factors could determine into what segment strokes belong:

- Ink Density: Given a new stroke, the system could balance maximizing ink density in each segment while minimizing the number of segments on the board.

- Active Segment: If the user has been interacting with the board recently, there could be an active segment that expects subsequent input.

- Time: The system could be biased to creating a new segment if significant time has passed since input in that area of the board.

- Content: Similar content could be kept together.

- Spatial Arrangement: The system could expect subsequent input following cultural norms. For example, lists would proceed top to bottom, left to right per Western writing norms.

We explored these factors in our design, interaction mock-ups, and implementation. We opted for a simple design where existing segments are grouped into bounding boxes.[1] The bounding box for the active segment is expanded to anticipate new strokes to that segment. If new strokes cross the border of the expanded segment, they are included. Currently the extra space in the active segment only follows Western writing conventions with additional space to the right of and below existing strokes. Pen input in an inactive segment, makes it active with an expanded input area. Input to the "root" space of the board (called the *root segment*)) generates a new segment.

We opted for this simpler mechanism since it seemed to do "the right thing" most of the time and the interaction is predictable. We also provide simple facilities for joining and splitting segments that act as error-recovery mechanisms. In general, automatic segmenting does not significantly raise the threshold for initial use, and it does provide a base for supporting interaction tailored to natural clusters of content.

Our design differs from other whiteboard interfaces [13] as users do not have to explicitly group material and clusters are not recognized by their content (e.g. recognizing a list or a table). Although the system is working in the background, the feel in Flatland is that the user is driving the interaction

---

1. Although aesthetically marked as thick, wavy lines, the segments are rectangles easing coding complexity and performance costs. The discrepancy has not been problematic.

since the auto-segmenting mechanism is simple and the user can easily activate segments to add more content, or create a new segment by tapping on the root segment.

Active and Inactive Segments

Flatland supports active and inactive segments where there can be one or zero active segments at a time. Active and inactive segments differ in their behavior and appearance. First, the border of the active segment is much brighter and visibly noticeable than the lighter borders of the inactive segments (see Figure 3). We experimented with a number of approaches in delineating segments, including not showing borders at all, and only showing the border for the active segment. Our informal use favored showing borders for all segments since they convey a great deal of information about the state of the board. Since Flatland is biased to including new strokes in the active segment, visually marking the active segment informs the user where the bias resides.

Inactive segments are sized to take as little screen real estate as possible while still showing their content. In contrast, active segments expand to include white space. This expansion visually marks the bias for new input to fall into the active segment. When the segment becomes inactive, it shrinks to remove the surrounding whitespace.

One lesson from informal use pertains to deleting strokes in an active segment. In our first design, the active segment would shrink based on the deleted material. This behavior was disturbing when followed by more pen input since the input area was now smaller, and new strokes in the area of the deletion, which was the last location of the pen, might now fall outside of the active segment. Currently, the active segment can only become larger, taking the more compact presentation when made inactive

Moving, Squashing and Flipping

Users can move segments with a standard select and drag motion. To reduce the complexity of working on the whiteboard, and to ensure visibility of each segment, segments are not allowed to overlap. As other segments are *bumped*, they move out of the way. According to [16], many people use their whiteboard as a surrogate memory. If segments were allowed to overlap, important reminders might be completely obscured.

Although we did not want users to obscure content via overlapping segments, we still needed mechanisms for creating more whitespace. To meet this need, Flatland automatically squashes segments as they bump into the border of the board. With each bump the segment is scaled down until it reaches a minimum size. (see Figure 3) Flatland is biased to squashing segments that have been inactive the longest. With further user testing, we will determine if users need to ever explicitly squash segments or if the automatic squashing is sufficient. To gain more space, users can also explicitly remove segments from the board.

Users can also flip to a new board by dragging the right or left border of the board [17]. The metaphor is a long roll of paper partitioned into *flip charts*. This mechanism provides

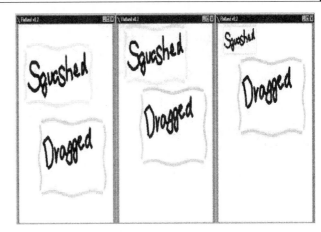

FIGURE 3. Segments squash to reduce size

a fast way to get a clean board, and perhaps quickly hide content from an office visitor.

In interviews regarding how users thought a virtually-extended whiteboard should be organized [16], they expressed two main desires. First they did not want to lose material given the whiteboard's role of surrogate memory and reminder. Some explicitly asked for the ability to squash existing content out of the way so they could gain more whitespace. Second, they wanted a constrained virtual space only four to eight times larger than their existing whiteboard. Flatland's design addresses these needs and concerns. In its principal use as a single board, the borders provide an intuitive affordance for scaling segments to gain space. The flip charts are a quick way to acquire a clean board for an office visitor or to create secondary boards for particular projects and activities. We opted against using a scrolling or zooming space (a la Pad++ [2]) to minimize the potential for losing track of whiteboard clusters.

APPLYING BEHAVIORS

One of the primary design philosophies of Flatland is that the whiteboard should be usable exactly like a normal, physical whiteboard, and yet should be able to provide powerful assistance with everyday tasks as needed. To retain the simplicity of a whiteboard, in Flatland, the user's input is always freehand strokes on the board with no pull-down menus, buttons, handles and the like. At the simplest level these freehand strokes are inked as they are drawn on to the board. As previously discussed, these strokes are grouped into segments.

Flatland supports specific tasks by allowing the user to apply *behaviors* to segments. Behaviors interpret input strokes, potentially adding strokes and replacing existing strokes. For example with the map behavior, a single line is replaced by a double line to depict a road. Behaviors, however, do not render the strokes themselves, they just modify the strokes belonging to a segment. The segments then paint the strokes creating a unified appearance for the entire board.

Behaviors are implemented so that the behavior only observes strokes, not lower-level mouse events. Thus, behaviors must wait until a stroke is completed before it interprets the stroke. This design helps provide a unified interface similar to stroking a normal whiteboard as all strokes look the same.

Users apply behaviors by selecting from a set of behavior icons. These animal figures indicate a working behavior at the top of the segment. To dismiss a behavior, one taps on the animal figure and chooses "Good-bye" from the resulting menu. This design helps maintain an informal feel without menus bars while providing a handle to behavior-specific functions. The metaphor is of an assistant or muse that interprets user input and personifies the behavior.

FIGURE 4. Flatland Behaviors

Sample Behaviors

We have designed and implemented a few behaviors to support typical office whiteboard tasks (see Figure 4). Flatland's design goals of simple, informal interaction extend past the general look-and-feel of the interface into the design of individual behaviors themselves. Since the purpose of the behaviors is to support informal, pre-production tasks, ease-of-use is strongly favored over providing features for producing a detailed artifact. Common themes in designing individual behaviors are:

- There are few explicit commands; but strokes are interpreted on-the-fly.

- Generated output is rendered in a "handdrawn" style.

- Minimal (in any) control widgets are added to the segment.

- Handwriting recognition is generally not used to limit the need for error correction and recovery. This design choice limits some potential uses of the system but

significantly simplifies user interaction[1]. The one current exception is the calculator behavior that favors handwriting in lieu of push buttons.

- "Infinite" undo-redo supports easy error recovery.

To-Do Lists The to-do behavior manages a series of strokes as a single-column list. The items are not recognized per se, but remain individual inked strokes. A handdrawn checkbox is rendered to the left of each item. Subsequent strokes across the checkbox checks off the item. Strokes across an item removes it from the list. A simple gesture allows users to move an item to a new location in the list. After any change to the list's contents (e.g. add, remove, reorder) the list is reformatted.

2D drawing The 2D drawing behavior is a port of Pegasus[9], an interactive beautifier, to the Flatland architecture. The typical frustration users have drawing illustrations on their whiteboards motivates the inclusion of this behavior. Strokes are neatened to create simple formatted line drawings. To create an efficient and intuitive drawing process, Pegasus offers potential new strokes based on the current structure of the drawing. Without explicit commands, the user can quickly author compelling and useful line drawings.

Map Drawing Another common drawing task is sketching maps for other people. Like the 2D drawing behavior, the map behavior replaces input strokes with improved strokes. Single lines become roads with double lines and open intersections. Again, there are no explicit controls for creating detailed production quality maps to get in the way of quickly sketching sufficient and powerful illustrations.

Calculator In the calculator behavior, strokes are interpreted as columns of numbers to be added or subtracted. Output is rendered in a hand-drawn style. Successive calculations can be appended for further interpretation. Likewise input can be modified at any point to trigger re-interpretation. Instead of supplying a calculator widget with push buttons and a display, this behavior leaves a persistent, editable trail that is more easily shared with others and reused.

Combining Behaviors

The difference between behaviors and traditional applications is more apparent when one combines multiple behaviors over time. For example, starting first with the map behavior, a user can sketch out the relevant streets and intersections. After removing the map behavior and applying the 2D drawing behavior, the user can now sketch relevant buildings and other landmarks. Now with no behaviors present, the user can label the map. In the future a writing behavior that cleans up letters might be used (see Figure 5).

RETRIEVING SEGMENTS

One obvious limitation of current whiteboards is that once material on the whiteboard is erased it can no longer be

---

1. We are experimenting with off-line handwriting recognition that makes best guesses at recognizing the content of segments. Recognized keywords at a reasonable level of confidence can be used for later retrieval of the segment.

FIGURE 5. Combining Behaviors

recovered. In our design, we sought to enable users to retrieve past whiteboard content without adding to the complexity and overhead of using the whiteboard.

Naming a file and deciding on its location is a common, albeit heavyweight task, too heavyweight for informal interaction with a whiteboard. Simply determining a name for content that is loosely associated with any product or deliverable is difficult. In contrast to production artifacts, whiteboard content is heavily context-dependent (e.g. "the outline I was working from last month," "the diagram that Amy and I worked on a few days ago," "my latest to-do list").

To support lightweight, context-rich storage and retrieval of whiteboard content, Flatland uses the Presto [5] document repository. By default, each segment in Flatland is automatically saved as a Presto document without requiring an explicit action or input from the user. The document is identified by its surrounding context (date, time, color(s), spatial location, active and past behaviors). Other forms of context, such as people present in the office, are possible but not yet implemented.

With saving as an automatic process that doesn't require explicit attention from the user, we still must provide a means for retrieving saved segments. When whiteboard users were asked to describe past segments, as well as strategies for retrieving segments, time and visual recognition were the two most cited cues that would aid them in retrieval [16]. We are currently experimenting with a number of context-based retrieval methods for Flatland segments. Two are described below:

Semantic Time Snapping

Time is a powerful cue in retrieving context-rich information. In [16], most whiteboard users could not say exactly when they had written something on their board, but they had a good idea for a general range in time (e.g. few days ago, sometime last week, couple months ago). To support time-based retrieval in Flatland, users can attach a time slider to any segment. The slider can be used as expected, to change the display backward and forward in time for that segment (see Figure 6). Touching the endpoints of the slider makes the slider jump to the next *interesting* point in that timeline. Interesting points are states prior to long periods of no input, prior to input to another segment, prior to removing that segment, as well as explicit snapshots by the user. These states are automatically tagged and stored via Presto.

The history mechanism used to implement the time slider also provides infinite undo/redo capability. With a leftward

FIGURE 6. Snapping to an Interesting Point in Time

gesture, users can undo strokes in a segment and quickly access a past version. Undo strokes on the root segment *play back* the whole board including the creation and deletion of segments. This history mechanism is based on Timewarp [6], a system to support autonomous collaboration through the use of multiple, editable timelines.

Context Queries

Visual recognition via thumbnails is another powerful method for retrieving files [16]. The Find behavior will allow users to scan and retrieve past segments. To constrain the search, users select context attributes for a desired segment such as "the map behavior was used," "about last week," and "Ian was in the room," "Icons corresponding to the choices (query terms) are visually depicted in the segment and can be furthered modified (e.g. negated). When the number of matching segments is small (20), thumbnails of the segments are displayed. To retrieve a segment, the user drags it out of the search segment and onto the root segment. This retrieval interface is not fully implemented, but the underlying storage and retrieval mechanisms are in place.

RELATED WORK

Tivoli

One of the major examples of previous work in this area is Tivoli [12][13][13][14], a pen-based interface designed to run on a LiveBoard. Tivoli is principally designed for a specific task—supporting meetings. It has been most used and studied in the context of supporting PARC intellectual property management.

Although there are many surface similarities, the interaction styles in the two systems are significantly different. As a tool for meetings, Tivoli's interface is geared for sorting, categorizing and annotating whiteboard content. Different types of content such as tables and lists are implicitly recognized although not explicitly marked. At any time, however, the strokes on the board are simple strokes that must be reparsed to support subsequent operations. To support application-specific controls, Tivoli provides "domain objects"—packaged data and controls that can be freely interspersed with freeform ink strokes[14].

In contrast, Flatland is designed to support ongoing, continuous work across a host of domains, rather than a series of meetings. Content is clustered automatically as the user moves among different segments. In general, the basic interface is simpler with a smaller gesture set that makes accidental interaction less likely. Further, Flatland engenders a kind of fine-grained persistence, in which the entire history of a user's experience with the whiteboard is captured and available for retrieval and use, as opposed to the potentially more coarse persistence of Tivoli, where, although meeting records may be kept indefinitely and indexed for second-by-second playback, history is largely "chunked" by particular meeting or topic. In contrast to the use of domain objects and continuously reparsed strokes, Flatland provides behaviors that can be associated with any content region building persistent application state for those strokes. This ability to dynamically associate an application's interpretation of content with the representation of that content is much closer to Kramer's notion of Translucent Patches[10].

Translucent Patches and Magic Lenses

Kramer's work [10] identified the importance of separating representation from perceived structure and the interpretation of that structure, especially in the creative design process. Kramer's work focused on the "window system" issues around this free-form association, in the form of "translucent patches." These patches are non-rectangular regions which allow users to associate interpretations of content area with regions on the screen.

Kramer's work applied translucency as a way to preserve context. Arbitrarily-shaped patches were a way to allow spatial multiplexing of interpretations—different nearby regions of the screen could have different interpretations applied to them.

Our work takes a different approach. Our dynamic behavior infrastructure does not require translucency to preserve context, because the user is *always* working in the context of the representation. That is, the user does not need to work "through" the translucent patch to acquire the new interpretation of the content. Second, instead of spatial multiplexing of interpretations, we use temporal multiplexing. In Flatland, a given region of content can have multiple interpretations over the course of its lifetime. These interpretations can be added and removed over time. The focus on temporal multiplexing relieves the user from the tasks of spatial management of interpretations (such as patches) in addition to the spatial management of content. To describe the Flatland model in terms of Translucent Patches, Flatland supports one interpretation layer at a given time, instead of multiple "onion skins" layers at the same time.

Magic Lenses[3], much like Translucent Patches, provide a way to view and manipulate data in different ways. Many of the distinctions between Behaviors and Patches are the same distinctions that can be drawn between Behaviors and Magic Lenses: spatial versus temporal multiplexing, no need for special "see through" presentations, etc.

Further, Lenses provide a way to temporarily modify the presentation or interaction with the data in a non-persistent way. That is, the transformation is in effect during the time when the lens is over the data area. While Flatland behaviors affect input and output only while they are applied, they "annotate" the back-end structure of the data they have been applied to with persistent information. That is, if a set of strokes has ever been interpreted as a map (by having a Map Behavior applied to it), that information is stored in with the strokes in a way specific to the semantics of the Map Behavior. Now, if the Map Behavior is ever removed and then reapplied, those strokes are able to regain their "mapness" as a result.

DynaWall

DynaWall is one or the *roomware* components developed within the i-LAND project [7]. It has an active area of 4.5 meters by 1.1 meters with a resolution of 3027x768. Using multiple computers and projectors, it is clearly designed for a setting quite different than Flatland's intended setting. Its gestures for "throwing, shuffling and taking" whiteboard content are designed for its large size and collaborative use.

Rekimoto

In [18], Reikimoto investigated how to combine multiple pen-based devices. With the Pick-and-Drop interaction, users could move content from one tablet to another. In [19], he demonstrated pick-and-drop and other techniques for using multiple personal tablets with shared whiteboard in a collaborative setting. In the future, we would like to investigate coupling tablets to Flatland as a means to connect Flatland with existing tablet and desktop interfaces as well as to support personal spaces in conjunction with the shared whiteboard space.

Sketching ++

Saund and Moran's perceptual sketch editor (Persketch)[20], Gross and Do's work on an "intelligent cocktail napkin" [8] and Landay and Myer's work on sketching user interfaces (SILK)[11] are good examples of interpreting sketched input while maintaining the look and inherent ambiguity of sketches. SILK recognizes GUI layouts while the Cocktail napkin recognized shapes from a number of domains (furniture layout, circuit diagrams). Persketch extracts perceptual structure out of a collection of strokes. We clearly share the same design ideas of using free strokes to support creative thinking, but our focus is on an environment to support those tasks. Additionally, both SILK and the Cocktail Napkin were tablet interfaces similar to using a notepad. Flatland is designed for long-term use of a whiteboard with heterogeneous content and context-based storage and retrieval of content.

STATUS

The Flatland system has been implemented in Java using JDK1.1.6 and the Swing UI toolkit. The current implementation is approximately 42,000 lines of code. The system uses the Presto document management system as the basis for saving and retrieving "documents" that represent the histories of segments. All of the behaviors described in this paper have been implemented; the Calculator behavior uses the Calligrapher online handwriting recognizer from Paragraph Corporation; this is the only native code in the system.

CONTRIBUTIONS

This work has investigated approaches to building an augmented whiteboard in the context of continuous, long term office use. In particular, we have pursued three avenues of research based on input from user studies: techniques for the management of space on the board, the ability to flexibly apply behaviors to support varied application semantics, and mechanisms for managing history on the board.

Unlike some previously reported systems, our design choices have been influenced by a desire to support informal work in an office setting, rather than heavy-weight "production" tasks. In particular this focus manifests itself in the four characteristics of use mentioned in the introduction: whiteboards provide interfaces for thinking through pre-production problems; they are useful for organizing and managing "everyday content;" information is implicitly clustered on the board; and office whiteboard use spans the range from private to semi-public. Our designs have attempted to address these characteristics, to make the augmented whiteboard fit easily into existing office work practices.

FUTURE WORK

One obvious area of future work is in the creation of additional behaviors for the Flatland system. There are a number of common tasks in office preproduction work that have been suggested by users and could profitably be supported by behaviors: paper outlining, rough budget analysis, communications, and so on. One of our goals is to evolve the system into a development environment for the creation of light-weight pen-based tools for whiteboard settings.

Although our work has been informed by usage studies of whiteboards in actual offices, we plan to validate our designs via several additional studies: first, an evaluation of the specific UI techniques presented here, and second, an in situ evaluation of the board in its intended setting.

Finally, one of the goals of our work which we have not begun to address yet is the blurring of the physical and the virtual in the office setting. We plan on extending the notions of ubiquitous computing throughout the office, with a particular focus on integrating physical artifacts.

ACKNOWLEDGMENTS

Numerous groups of people with Xerox PARC have contributed to this work. Thanks to the "Magic Office" team that was the home base for these efforts. Thanks to EDT and CSL for funding for people and equipment. Also thanks to the Tivoli team for design discussions and an initial gesture code base to get us going.

REFERENCES

[1] Abowd, G., Atkeson, C., Feinstein, A., Hmelo, C., Kooper, R., Long, S., Sawhney, N. and Tani, M. Teaching and learning as multimedia authoring: the classroom 200 project. Proceedings of ACM Multimedia '96. New York: ACM.

[2] Bederson, B.B., & Hollan, J.D. Pad++: A zooming graphical interface for exploring alternate interface physics. Proceedings of UIST'94. New York: ACM.

[3] Bier, E.A., Stone, M.C., Pier, K., Buxton, W., and DeRose, T. Toolglass and magic lenses: The see-through interface. In James T. Kajiya, editor, Computer Graphics (SIGGRAPH '93 Proceedings), volume 27.

[4] Communications of the ACM, Special Issue on Augmented Environments, 36 (7), 1993.

[5] Dourish, P. Edwards,W.K., LaMarca, A., Salisbury, M. Uniform document interaction using document properties. Submitted to CHI'99.

[6] Edwards, W.K, Mynatt, E.D. Timewarp: techniques for autonomous collaboration. Proceedings of CHI'97. New York: ACM.

[7] Geissler, J., Shuffle, throw or take it! Working efficiently with an interactive wall. Proceedings of CHI'98. New York: ACM.

[8] Gross, M.D., & Do, E.Y. Ambiguous intentions: a paper-like interface for creative design. Proceedings of UIST '96. New York: ACM.

[9] Igarashi, T., Matsuoka, S., Kawachiya, S., & Tanaka, Hidehiko. Interactive beautification: A technique for rapid geometric design. Proceedings of UIST'97. New York: ACM.

[10] Kramer, A. Translucent patches - dissolving windows. Proceedings of UIST '94. New York: ACM.

[11] Landay, J.A. and Myers, B.A. Interactive sketching for the early stages of interface design. Proceedings of CHI'95. New York: ACM.

[12] Moran, T.P., Chiu, P., Harrison, S., Kurtenbach, G., Minneman, S. & van Melle, W. Evolutionary engagement in an ongoing collaborative work process: a case study. Proceedings of CSCW'96. New York: ACM.

[13] Moran, T.P., Chiu, P., van Melle, W., & Kurtenbach, G. Implicit structures for pen-based systems within a freeform interaction paradigm. Proceedings of CHI'95. New York: ACM.

[14] Moran, T.P., van Melle, W., & Chiu, P. Tailorable domain objects as meeting tools for an electronic whiteboard. Proceedings of CSCW'98. New York: ACM.

[15] Moran, T.P., Chiu, P., & van Melle, W. Spatial interpretation of domain objects integrated into a freeform electronic whiteboard. Proceedings of UIST '98. New York: ACM.

[16] Mynatt, E. D. The writing on the wall. Unpublished technical report. www.cc.gatech.edu/~mynatt.

[17] Nakagawa, M., Oguni, T., Yoshino, T. Human interface and application on IdeaBoard. Published in Interact '97.

[18] Rekimoto, J. Pick-and-drop: a direct manipulation technique for multiple computer environments. Proceedings of UIST'97. New York: ACM.

[19] Rekimoto, J. A multiple device approach for supporting whiteboard-based interactions. Proceedings of

Palette: A Paper Interface for Giving Presentations

Les Nelson, Satoshi Ichimura,
Elin Rønby Pedersen
FX Palo Alto Laboratory
3400 Hillview Avenue
Pal Alto, CA 94304 USA
+1 650 813 7473
{nelson,satoshi,pedersen}@pal.xerox.com

Lia Adams
Lia Adams Consulting
P O Box 194
Palo Alto CA 94302
Lia_Adams@ieee.org

ABSTRACT

The Palette is a digital appliance designed for intuitive control of electronic slide shows. Current interfaces demand too much of our attention to permit effective computer use in situations where we can not give the technology our fullest concentration. The Palette uses index cards that are printed with slide content that is easily identified by both humans and computers. The presenter controls the presentation by directly manipulating the cards. The Palette design is based on our observation of presentations given in a real work setting. Our experiences using the system are described, including new practices (e.g., collaborative presentation, enhanced notetaking) that arise from the affordances of this new approach. This system is an example of a new interaction paradigm called *tacit interaction* that supports users who can spare very little attention to a computer interface.

KEYWORDS: Paper interfaces; presentation appliance; interaction design; physically embodied interfaces; tacit interaction.

INTRODUCTION

This paper introduces the Palette, an interface that presenters use to control electronic media without devoting attention to the computer. Presenting material to an audience is a ubiquitous aspect of business life. Presentation software for personal computers (PCs) is well designed for the task of creating and modifying content (e.g., slides). But this same technology can be daunting and awkward to use during times when we can not give it our fullest attention, such as when giving a presentation using electronic media. For example, it is quite common to see a talk where the audience must wait and watch the presenter manipulate the presentation PC, including searching through the file system for the presentation slides, fumbling over the controls (mouse, keyboard, or remote) to find a single slide, and trying to coordinate operation of other

equipment (e.g., video tapes, room lighting).

The introduction of electronic presentation support gave us new capabilities, including multimedia content and removal of the nuisance of overhead projection (e.g., fan noise, misaligned or unfocused slides). However, we have lost the affordances of using physical slides (e.g., transparencies), including being able to select viewing material simply by picking up a slide, and being able to privately rearrange and preview slide sets before showing a slide.

The Palette (Figure 1) supports slide viewing using index cards. Presenters create slides with their chosen presentation software. Cards are generated from these slides with a thumbnail view of a slide, text notes, and a machine-readable code (e.g., barcode or Data Glyph [7]). Each card is encoded with file and slide information permitting presentation by simply sliding a card under the code reader located on a table or lectern. A presenter may keep the cards in hand or spread them out like paint colors on a palette for easy selection of whatever content should be shown next.

The Palette thus uses physical cards to represent presentation content. Physical objects have the property that we can perceive them both focally (for periods of

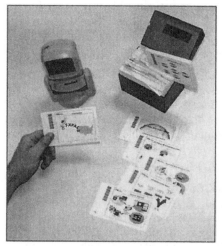

Figure 1. Palette cards are encoded with slide information permitting presentation by simply sliding a card under the Palette code reader. A presenter may compose a talk by selecting cards from one or more sets of previous talks.

concentrated actions) and peripherally (for keeping track of an object's presence without being fixated on it). For example, the commonplace objects on our desks (e.g., clocks, phones) blend into the background of our awareness until we either need them or they call attention to themselves. This strategy of using physical objects for human-computer interaction (HCI) allows the presenter to work with electronic media and retain affordances lost by moving to a graphical user interface (GUI).

Tangible or physically-embodied user interfaces [2, 6] are a recent trend in HCI. Johnson, et al.[7] developed a paper user interface where users physically fill in a paper form on which computer-readable marks are printed to perform operations such as retrieving electronic files. A fax or scanner is used to enter the forms into the system and receive the results. The Digital Desk [10] uses video to observe paper documents on a desktop and allows workers to perform various computer-based interactions on the document text (e.g., retrieval of physical document location by content). More generally, Tangible Bits [6] are examples of the physical instantiation of GUI elements such as windows, icons, and handles in a sensor-based user interface. Applications include using physical objects for navigation of geographic data and controlling the flow of online data [4, 13], and controlling a simulation [14]. Systems such as Video Mosaic [9], PaperLink [1], and the Insight Lab [8] link online information with paper. The Insight Lab uses barcodes in support of analysis of video and audio data by linking paper notes to corresponding multimedia clips. The notes express evidence, patterns of evidence, and electronic whiteboard images created during the analysis. The Barcode Hotel is an interactive art exhibit that presents a shared physical and virtual space where users scan barcodes to modify virtual object behavior and movement [5].

The Palette integrates the use of physical and virtual objects and operations into a system where the physicality is well suited to the needs of the presentation task, including easy slide show initialization, having a private slide overview, preview and selection, keeping supporting notes readily available, and other needs discussed below.

We next describe the system through typical scenarios of its operation and then discuss our iterative, user-centered design and implementation. We describe our experiences of using the system in operation, including new work practices enabled by the system. The Palette is then considered with respect to its implications for HCI, as a specific example of a general interaction paradigm called tacit interaction, and we conclude with our future work in this area.

THE PALETTE AND ITS USE

The following scenarios for using the Palette illustrate the operation and main features of the system.

Before a Talk

Ed, a director in a large, multinational corporation, is planning a presentation for some visiting executives. They represent different divisions of their corporation and so

have a variety of interests and levels of technical expertise. Ed does not need to author a new presentation for these visitors, because he often gives talks about his division and the projects going on there. Thus, Ed already has a large collection of Palette cards representing slides in various presentations that he and his managers have made.

To start assembling the current presentation, Ed draws on some recent materials created for a division-wide project review (Figure 1). There is a detailed set of slides for each project in the division that he may reuse. Ed plans to give only an overview of the projects in his 45-minute talk, but he will need to be prepared to discuss any project in detail. He goes through the project slides selecting just the slides labeled "Vision", "Goals", and "Status" for each project. He also consults a set of slides he presented at the last quarterly meeting, and selects some slides that describe how his division's projects relate to other activities in the company.

Once Ed has collected the slides he wants to present, he may decide to add some new material. The morning newspaper had a headline story relevant to the corporation's business, and so Ed has the story scanned and pasted into a slide in a new presentation. Ed runs the Palette Converter program to create a Palette card for that new slide. The slides are also stored in a central location at this time so they are accessible from the presentation room. Ed reviews what he wants to say in the talk and adds last-minute speech cues in pencil to a few cards.

Since these visitors are all fellow employees, Ed does not have to worry about revealing private corporate information. When Ed selects a slide, it is easy for him to preview and filter the cards before and even during the meeting to make sure he includes or excludes appropriate information.

Before the talk, Ed prints out several sets of the cards he plans to present, to hand out to the audience members to take home with them. He chooses to print only the thumbnail image and barcode for each slide. The cards themselves make useful handout material, either as cards or card images printed several to a page.

Making a Presentation

Right before the talk, Ed brings his deck of Palette cards along with sets of handouts to the presentation room, which is set up with a computer running the Palette software and driving a projection system (Figure 2). A barcode reader is connected to this system. Ed usually stands at the front of the room and has the barcode reader set up on a lectern. Ed often walks around the front of the room, making eye contact with different audience members, and carrying the cards he needs with him so he can advance the slides by walking back to the lectern or using a portable reader he keeps in his pocket.

Ed arranges his cards on the lectern in the categories he has chosen (e.g., overview slides in the center and topic slides off to the left). He starts with the overview slides, face up in

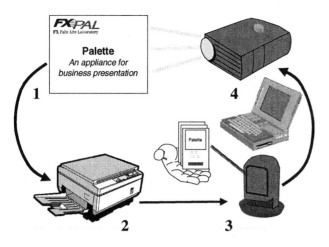

Figure 2. Presenters use their usual authoring software (1) and run the Palette Converter to generate cards (2) for use with a card scanner (3) to display the slides (4).

front of him, keeping them in the center. Even though the cards represent slides from different presentation files, Ed does not have to think about that; each card has enough information to identify the file and the slide within that file. As he finishes talking about a slide, he turns it face down and adds it to the pile of completed slides, in the same way that people stack overhead transparencies. Different spatial arrangements of presentation content are possible, giving Ed a flexible overview of the material.

When he learns from his audience that they attended a detailed seminar about Project X, Ed pulls those slides from his deck and sets them aside to avoid boring the audience. As projects requiring greater detail and questioning arise, Ed switches to the side piles, returning to the overview when detailed discussion concludes. Ed makes notes of the discussion on the back of each card for later use.

At the end of the talk, there is a question and answer session. Susan, one of the visiting executives, has questions about a graph Ed displayed earlier. She asks "What causes that blip in the graph you put up on demographics?" While Ed flips back through the slides looking for the demographics chart, Susan has already found her copy. Susan uses a wireless pen-style reader that is conveniently available to the audience, changing the display to that slide. As further question and answer proceeds, Ed spreads out the related slides face up in front of him, so he can quickly recognize and pull slides that will help him address the questions.

Follow-up Activities

Ed brings his annotated deck of cards back to his office. He later refers to them when summarizing the meeting for his notes and placing action items in his calendar. Each of the attendees may use the handout cards in a similar manner, and they can also incorporate those cards into their own presentations about the results of the meeting.

USER-CENTERED DESIGN FOR PRESENTATION

The current form of the Palette resulted from an iterative process that involved several stages of user study and prototyping to inform the design. In the beginning we had a general vision of being able to make presentations more physical: we compared the presenter with a painter using a palette of colors.

Observations of Users of Presentation Support

The palette vision lead us to observe and interview 14 people giving presentations, to find out which presentation media they prefer, how they like to control their presentation material and equipment, what number and duration of slides they presented, what events occurred to affect the order of the presented material (e.g., questions from the audience), and how they dealt with those events. Once we focused on the idea of replacing GUI control with a more physical mechanism, we paid particular attention to where presenters stood and traveled during the presentation, and what they held or carried. People observed were Xerox staff (managers, researchers, and summer interns) and participating visitors (executives and researchers).

Almost every presenter manipulated some representation of their slides, usually a printed copy of the transparency or electronic slide. They all touched some kind of control device for changing slides, such as a keyboard or mouse for electronic slides, a remote-control for 35-mm slides, or the slides themselves for transparencies. Presenters who used multiple media such as videos controlled that part of the presentation indirectly, by giving verbal commands to an unseen technician.

Most presenters had media other than the slides that they consulted or interacted with during a presentation, including notes written on copies of the slides, notes written on cards or sheets of paper, models to demonstrate, quotations or tables to consult, or materials to hand out during the talk.

Our observations and interviews of people giving presentations identified the following needs that a new presentation support mechanism should accommodate.

Slide initialization. We commonly noticed a long nervous pause in the meeting flow while a slide set was being started, especially when multiple presenters were speaking consecutively. If the slide viewer was not initialized beforehand, presenters manually navigated the files to find their talk.

Slide manipulation and overview. Presenters preferred systems in which they could directly control the change of slides (e.g., transparencies) over systems in which they had to issue an indirect request for the next slide (e.g., verbally). In order to answer a question, a presenter sometimes needed to search for a particular slide. Searching through transparencies was sometimes not done strictly sequentially (i.e., by fanning the slides out and scanning the overlapping title lines); sequential search was the norm for pre-ordered media such as 35-mm and PowerPoint slides.

We did, however, observe one individual use the 'Slide Sorter' view of PowerPoint to provide a selectable overview of slides for questions and answers at the end of a presentation. This usage provided a useful overview even though it had disadvantages: the thumbnails of the slide sorter were low resolution images and difficult to see, the speaker notes were not available, the audience observed the presenter manipulating the internal view of PowerPoint (i.e., menus and toolbars), the audience viewed all thumbnails (even those intentionally left hidden or skipped), and the presenter had to leave the 'Slide Show' presentation view of PowerPoint to see the 'Slide Sorter'.

Slide re-ordering. Presenters indicated a need for re-ordering slides to change emphasis, fit a particular time slot, and omit certain material. With sequential presentation media, if a presenter needed to skip a slide due to lack of time or audience interest, it was common for the audience to see the slide briefly as the presenter passed it by.

Presenter Mobility. Presenters often walked around to engage the audience, gesture at the screen, and use the presentation-control equipment. Some presenters carried their speech notes around with them, so they could refer to notes without staying at a lectern. Many speakers changed their physical position in the space for different activities (e.g., presenting, question and answer, discussion).

Audience (public) and presenter (private) views of material. We noted a number of actions that made the audience wait and watch the control of the presentation mechanics, including: loading slides, skipping slides, exiting to the desktop at the end of a talk, viewing cursor movement for hyperlink navigation and controlling multimedia content, and using the wrong control because of a misunderstanding where the presenter was in the slide sequence or because of forgetting infrequently used controls.

We also observed private views used by a presenter, including reading and making annotations on copies of slide or notes, using notes or transparencies to look ahead or back at slide, and controlling other media (e.g., software demonstration, audio/video equipment, room lighting). Our observations and interviews indicate that if a presenter consulted a private view such as a set of speech notes, they needed to coordinate it with the public material. Of the media seen, overhead transparencies offered the most straightforward coordination mechanism, since the act of moving the old slide and replacing it with the new exposes a separator sheet that is suitable for storing notes for that slide. Presenters using electronic slides that could be flipped forward and backward using control keys often experienced delays in then searching through notes to find the matching place.

Use of hands. Many presenters like to keep their hands occupied. If they are not doing things directly related to the presentation, such as pointing or changing slides, they often fiddle with other things. More than one presenter said they like to keep their hands busy to "burn off excess energy".

Sharing material. Frequently, presenters hand things out to the audience (e.g., full slide sets, particularly interesting slides, or a physical artifact). Full slide sets would sometimes be handed out at the beginning or end of a talk. We have seen a particular slide or artifact handed out or displayed only when the talk reached the appropriate point.

Comparing Presentation Support

The Palette responds well to these presentation support needs. Table 1 compares how the Palette and commonly used presentation methods address these issues, including desktop style PCs (e.g., window-icon-menu-pointer), remotes (e.g., a remote mouse with control buttons), 35 mm slide projection, and document projection (e.g., transparencies and document cameras).

A presentation should start immediately without the presenter having to navigate through file structures and commands. The Palette cards have all the information for initializing the presentation, unlike desktop interfaces and remotes. Projected documents and 35mm slides (once properly adjusted for projection) also physically incorporate the static part of slide content needed for presentation.

Palette cards represent the slide content for the presenter and provide direct manipulation for slide changing. The cards do this in a manner supporting an overview of slides that can be rearranged at any time. The desktop, remote, and 35mm slides all require an intervening control device of some kind, making re-ordering content difficult. While overview is possible to some degree with desktop systems (e.g., 'Slide Sorter' discussed earlier) and to a lesser degree with sophisticated remotes, a display screen is much more limited by total size and resolution than a deck of high quality printed cards. The cards are small enough to be arrayed on a table or flipped through in hand for searching.

Feature Supported	GUI/Desktop	GUI/Remote Control	35mm	Transparency/Camera	Palette
Show initialization	Must navigate	Must navigate	Yes	Yes	Yes
Direct manipulation	No, uses mouse/ keys	No, uses mouse/ button	No, uses button	Yes	Yes
Slide overview	Limited by display	Limited by display	No	Yes	Yes
Slide re-ordering	Limited by input device	No	Awkward	Yes	Yes
Public/private views	Needs multiple windows	Limited by display	No	Yes	Yes
Presenter mobility	Limited by I/O devices	Yes	Limited by equipment	Limited by equipment	Yes
Use of hands	Limited by input devices	Yes	Yes	Yes	Yes
Sharing	Limited by I/O devices	Must share controller	Must share controller	Yes	Yes
Electronic media	Yes	Yes	No	No	Yes

Table 1. Comparison of Presentation Support Systems.

The system control should be mobile, so the presenter can hold it in hand and carry it around while talking, but not be so bulky that s/he is kept from using other objects (e.g., pointers). Using a detection mechanism such as commonly available barcode readers (portable or hands-free) to scan barcodes on the card provides mobility. A card gives the presenter something to hold that provides presentation control, assists them in what they say, and does not cause a distraction to the audience (since the card is only active when under the reader and repeating a card causes no problems). Systems with control devices fixed in a location require a presenter to move back to that location for slide change. The presentation remotes and portable barcode readers avoid this situation.

Presentation support should let the presenter control the accessing and display of public material directly while also keeping a synchronized view of the related private material. The less that the presenter has to do to keep these views together, the better. Systems with separate views of control and private material (desktop, remotes, and 35mm slides) are somewhat more limited in this capacity.

Finally, the audience should be able to use the distributed material to frame questions. The cards are aesthetically appealing when printed with high quality printers, hence easily readable in fine detail, and are shareable with other presenters and the audience.

User Study for Palette Configuration

Prospective users of the first Palette prototype were studied to identify the physical configuration of the design, including the layout of the index card and the kind and orientation of scanning device that will access identifiers on the cards. A variety of photographs of barcode readers with different scanning and physical characteristics were given to users, including forward, downward, and upward looking scanners, a sliding strip scanner, a pen scanner, and a mockup of a "wearable" scanning device. Two mockups of card layouts were constructed that contained a thumbnail of a presentation slide, a barcode, and text of presenter's notes: all three elements on one side, and thumbnail and barcode on one side with notes on the other. Users were then interviewed to determine their preferences and enact

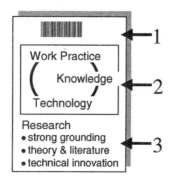

Figure 3: The preferred card configuration identified by presenters contains, all on one side, a code (1), thumbnail image (2), and speaker notes (3).

how they would use the actual scanners and cards represented by the mockups. The seven people observed were all Xerox researchers who were frequent presenters.

The strongest preference was for waving the index card at the barcode reader. However, for less formal, round-table meetings, pen-based systems received strong interest. The motion of reading the barcode must be quick, comfortable, and sure. Consequently, we determined that the first Palette installation include an omni-directional hands-free scanner (to give the greatest location choice and flexibility), and a pen system (to test different presentation scenarios). Two standard templates for card layout for each device were preferred: all elements on the front of the card, and also barcode located on back, thumbnail and notes on front.

EXPERIENCES IN OPERATING THE PALETTE

A study was made using the Palette prototype and equipment where presenters were given an identical presentation task. The 13 people observed were all Xerox employees (research and support staff) who represented a mixture of frequent and infrequent presenters. The goal of this study was to determine actual position and orientation of the reader and arrangement of Palette object elements (identifier, thumbnail, and speaker notes) needed for deploying the system in our own company conference room. We observed how many times a card was flipped or turned by a presenter and the number of times the scanning device failed to read a card. Four sets of four cards in each of the major configurations of elements were used (i.e., three sets with two elements on one side and one on the other, and one set with all on one side). We also noted presenter activity (e.g., gaze and what they did with the cards after using them). Finally, we asked people what card arrangement they preferred from all possible arrangements.

We found that the one-sided card arrangement resulted in by far the fewest card motions and that a majority of people preferred this arrangement (Figure 3). We also noted that there was quite a bit of variation for other styles that the system should accommodate (e.g., horizontal cards, not showing the speaker notes). Speakers who spread the cards out in an orderly spatial arrangement are able to quickly select a slide in response to a question. Keeping the cards in a stack or in hand requires the speaker to thumb through the cards looking for the correct one.

The Palette has been put into use in our own conference room. We have found one situation where a portable GUI system might be considered more appropriate than the Palette, namely in addressing very last minute changes. Like other presentation methods (e.g., transparencies), using the Palette enforces a separation between slide authoring and presentation: the cards must be fabricated. Consequently, there might not be time to print a new card. While it is usually not wise to make such late changes to an important presentation, we have found that this situation may be accommodated with the Palette by a simple workaround. If the change is to an existing slide, the Palette card still functions correctly (i.e., nothing has changed that affects the encoding). If material is to be dropped, the card is just omitted. If new material is to be added, it should be put at the end of a presentation file. A temporary card may be easily fabricated by hand. We have preprinted, adhesive barcode labels for this purpose.

IMPLICATIONS ON PRESENTATION PRACTICE

In addition to providing the affordances we expected, we are finding that having a presentation medium with new capabilities is enabling new practices.

For example, when the Palette is used, the machinery of presentation initialization and slide selection is not visible and, hence, does not impede collaborative presentation (i.e., talks involving material and ideas mixed from several people). The ability to very quickly share, collectively preview, and discuss cards without disturbing the flow of a meeting permits an atmosphere for 'co-presentation' (Figure 4). We have observed this practice happening as spontaneous and brief discussions that arise between presenters during normal pauses in meeting flow (e.g., when questions are asked and at end of a topic).

We are also observing some changes in notetaking and new uses for paper notebooks. Palette cards are often annotated with revisions or used to record interesting questions, comments, or other relevant information. We have seen a paper notebook being used in place of cards. Pointers to supplemental material such as supporting slides, including *ad hoc* sketches and Universal Resource Locators (URLs) for relevant Web pages, are kept in the notebook along with a barcode link to the online information.

IMPLEMENTATION

The selection of barcode reading for card sensing is perhaps the key factor shaping the current Palette implementation. Our rationale for this decision is based on the following reasons: (1) barcode-reading is a mature technology, for which many kinds of devices are widely available that provide good, robust performance in real-world settings; (2) prototyping with barcodes gives us a migration path to other marking technologies (e.g., glyphs).

Another choice that affected the current implementation is the selection of Powerpoint as the supported presentation software. Our rationale for this decision is based on the following reasons: (1) Powerpoint is a mature application that has a large user community; (2) the presentation authoring and slide viewing functions are accessible programmatically through an application programming interface.

Performance tests conducted with our prototype support these system choices. The test configuration was a Pentium II (333 megahertz) running Windows NT 4.0 with 130 megabytes of memory and using a Symbol LS9100 barcode scanner. By adjusting barcode type and size, misreads of barcode scans were reduced to an average of 1 miss every 25 tries. We scanned sets of 100 cards manually in the same manner a presenter would use the device (with the exception of moving as fast as possible) and observed the

Figure 4. Co-presenters decide how to continue discussion based on questions and available material.

Palette response. Times for slide changes using Powerpoint depends on the slide content size. The test presentations were graphics intensive files, averaging 11 slides stored in 2 megabytes files. The average time in which slides from within one file could be switched on the presentation display using the Palette was observed to be 0.83 seconds. Using keyboard control to switch to previously displayed slides requires some small fraction of a second. However, it is difficult to notice or quantify a difference when switching to new slides when compared to the Palette. The average time for consecutively and cumulatively loading slides from 12 unopened files was 2.18 seconds per file. The average time for using the Palette to switch between slides from different files already opened in PowerPoint was 1.31 seconds. This multiple file access is not supported by the Powerpoint slide show viewer, and hence is not comparable with the Palette.

The resulting Palette system is implemented as two programs running under Window 95/NT: the *converter* and the *controller*. Before a presentation is given, the converter is used to create Palette cards from the presentation. The controller runs during a presentation; it is responsible for accepting scanned input from the codes on those printed cards and for displaying the appropriate electronic slides.

The Palette converter is a standalone program that reads a file created by presentation authoring software (currently PowerPoint) and creates a document (currently Microsoft Word) containing the content of the presentation in a layout suitable for printing on card stock. Each card represents the content of one slide and contains up to four elements: a thumbnail of the slide image, speech notes, the slide number in the sequence of the presentation file, and a computer readable identification code (i.e., barcode) indicating the presentation and number for this slide. The converter resizes and positions these elements in the output document so that the image will fit neatly and readably on the card stock. A number of different layouts are provided based on our user observations of card use. The converter also saves a copy of the presentation in a central location (with a filename consistent with the card identification code) and records its actions in a central log. The Palette converter is implemented in Visual Basic for Applications (VBA), using Visual Basic primitives to extract elements from PowerPoint presentations and manipulate them in Word. After the converter runs, the printed cards are used to control a presentation through the Palette controller.

The Palette controller uses a client-server architecture. The client accepts input from a barcode reader; the server carries out commands to operate PowerPoint.

The Palette client is implemented in Java. The client runs remotely and communicates with the server PC through a TCP network interface. The client listens to input from a barcode reader attached to the keyboard port or to the serial input (RS232C) port of the client PC. The data from the reader includes the filename of a PowerPoint file, slide number, or a special control command such as merging multiple slides into one composite slide, changing background color of slides, or stopping a presentation. The client translates the barcoded data into presentation-control commands and sends them to the Palette server.

The Palette server is implemented in VBA. The server runs on a PC and controls a PowerPoint application running on the same PC. The video monitor output from the server PC drives a presentation display screen. The server waits for network connections from Palette clients. Once a client connects, it sends presentation control requests to the server. Visual Basic primitives allow the server to control PowerPoint presentations. For example, the server can direct the presentation to load a specified PowerPoint file, jump to a specified slide, go to the next or previous slide, stop the PowerPoint slide show, and so on.

One consequence of our implementation approach is that manual overrides and fallbacks for equipment problems are well supported. At any time a presenter may use the keyboard/mouse interface to PowerPoint. If the cards are printed with sufficiently high quality (e.g., 300 dpi), the cards provide the same resolution as PowerPoint images, and thus can be used with a document camera as a fallback if a computer-projection interface fails. Finally, if all projection or electrical power fails during a talk, the cards can be used as speech notes for the presenter to continue giving the talk without technological support.

TACIT INTERACTION AND FUTURE WORK

The Palette is one of several efforts to explore a new human computer interface paradigm; we call the paradigm tacit interaction. Tacit interaction combines two concerns: technology should engage a wider range of human perception and it should enable a larger degree of low-intentional interaction than is found in current interfaces. Within this paradigm, the Palette explores ways to "re-physicalize" the human computer interaction (HCI) and thereby allow the user to distribute tasks to less intentional, less intellectual modes of action.

The need for new interaction paradigms, such as tacit interaction, has been growing as the traditional graphical user interface develops and reaches its limit of usefulness. The problems may be classified as concerning intentionality and attention.

Intentionality. Office workers experience an increased need to shift back and forth between multiple applications and communication appliances, but most applications assume the user to be ready and dedicated to whatever interaction they engage in, i.e., these applications appeal to high-intentional interaction. For example, the print spooler tells the user that a print job is ready to print by popping up a modal alert, blocking the user in whatever else s/he was engaged in to "release" the computer from the alert. Many of the devices and appliances we are surrounded and serviced by make similar demands. Rather than forcing a computer-like multiplexing scheme onto the user, we suggest we let the technology adapt to the human way of dealing with parallel demands: by distributing the tasks to automatic and semi-automatic modes of action we involve more of our motor skills and thereby more of our body. The open problem and challenge to HCI is to understand how to "re-physicalize" parts of the human computer interaction, and the Palette is only a first step.

Attention. The focus of our perception is becoming increasingly overcrowded by competing demands for our attention [15]. For example, Microsoft Powerpoint 97 has a pop-up/slide-out menu in its Stage Manager tools (used during a slide show) that has 29 unique functions, including three additional windows for presentation control (see also [3]). Also, in many presentation rooms, there are controls for audio, video, room environment, and commonly a dedicated PC, as well as an audience, demanding a presenter's attention. Rather than continuing to fill up the user's focal space even more, the tacit interaction paradigm suggests we utilize a wider range of perception and include also some peripheral modes of taking in the environment. The Palette offloads the user's attentional focus in several ways, partly by relieving the user from the entanglements of a computer desktop and partly by making the essential objects for manipulation physical, thereby providing all the affordance of the well-known index card. The Palette expands in this way on our previous work on peripheral awareness in the AROMA system [11, 12].

Technology we have developed for tacit interaction currently involves three interface approaches that address off-loading activities from an over-taxed cognitive system to under-utilized areas such as the peripheral ranges of our senses and the motor system.

First, we reduce the need for keeping in mind complex steps for explicitly invoking system operation by using physical objects as tangible representations of interface content or control (physicality strategy). For example, placing a Palette card on the lectern to select a slide is more easily accomplished than finding and adjusting a pop-up/slide-out menu on a control window - in general we observe that direct physical action can be more efficient and reliable than a GUI style interaction. Second, we reduce the need for cognitively demanding decision-making by reducing choice (the appliance strategy). For example, by packaging the Palette as an appliance we provide a powerful, self-contained device suited for a specialized task, namely, selecting and displaying information for an audience. Third and last, we further reduce the need for decision-making by deriving decision data from the environment (the sensor strategy). Sensor technology enables us to detect what actions are in progress and thus, aids the system in responding to a user's intent. While the Palette uses sensors to detect the identity and action a presenter makes with a Palette card, the decision-making aspect has not yet been explored in detail in the system.

We are now focusing our work on long term deployment of the Palette in a busy conference room of a business organization. This experience will help us to refine our physicality strategy as a tacit interaction method and should allow us to generalize the concept to other applications (and hence tasks) that should be accomplished in a similar manner. Such results will be integrated with our findings on peripheral perception and low-intentional interaction as they were explored in the context of the AROMA system. In parallel we are expanding the design space to further include the sensor strategy.

CONCLUSIONS

The Palette is a new interface that allows a user to control electronic slide shows without having to handle a computer and thereby deflect attention away from the primary task of communicating to an audience. The design for the system is based on our observation of presentations given in a real work setting. Using an interaction paradigm based on direct manipulation of physical objects representing slide content overcomes current interface limitations that overtax our focal perception and demand too much of our attention. Our use of the Palette has produced new kinds of presentation work practices (e.g., collaborative presentation) arising from the affordances of a new approach.

ACKNOWLEDGMENTS

We thank Sara Bly for her enthusiasm and advice on assessing the Palette user community and for reviewing drafts of this paper. We thank Bill Schilit for his constructive comments on drafts of this paper. We thank Stephen Smoliar for his inspirations on presentation impact of the Palette. We thank Brian Drummond and Katy Ly for their part in implementing the first presentation prototypes. We thank Jim Baker for supporting this research.

REFERENCES

1. Arai, T., Aust, D., and Hudson, S.E., PaperLink: A Technique for Hyperlinking from Real Paper to Electronic Content, Conference Proceedings on Human Factors in Computing Systems, 1997, pp. 327-334.

2. Fishkin, K.P., Moran, T.P., and Harrison, B.L., Embodied User Interfaces: Towards Invisible User Interfaces, Proceedings of EHCI '98 (to appear).

3. Gibbs, W.W., "Taking Computers to Task", Scientific American (electronic edition), July 1997, http://www.sciam.com/0797issue/0797trends.html

4. Gorbet, M.G., Orth, M., and Ishii, H., Triangles: Tangible Interface for Manipulation and Exploration of Digital Information Topography, A Physical/Digital Construction Kit, in *Proceedings of CHI' 98*, ACM Press, Los Angeles, April 1998, pp. 49-56.

5. Hoberman, P., The Barcode Hotel, Web page, http://www.hoberman.com/perry/php/bch/index.html

6. Ishii, H. and Ullmer, B., Tangible Bits: Towards Seamless Interfaces between People, Bits, and Atoms, *in Proceedings of CHI'97*, ACM Press, Atlanta, March 1997, pp. 234-241.

7. Johnson, W., Jellinek, H., Klotz, L. and Card, S. Bridging the Paper and Electronic Worlds: The Paper User Interface, Proceedings of INTERCHI'93, 1993, 507-512.

8. Lange, B., Jones, M., Meyers, J., Insight Lab: An Immersive Team Environment Linking Paper, Displays, and Data, Proceedingz of Conference on Human Factors in Computing Systems (CHI '98), ACM Press, April 1998, pp. 550-557.

9. Mackay, W-E., and Pagani, D.S. Video Mosaic: Laying Out Time in a Physical Space, in Proceedings of Multimedia '94 (San Francisco, CA, October 1994), ACM Press, 165-172.

10. Newman, W. and Wellner, P, A Desk Supporting Computer-based Interaction with Paper Documents, Proceedings of CHI'92 Conference on Human Factors in Computing Systems, 1992, 587-592.

11. Pedersen, E., and Sokoler, T., AROMA: Abstract Representation Of presence for Mediated Awareness, Proceedings of Conference on Human Factors in Computing Systems (CHI '97), ACM Press, March 1997, pp. 51-58.

12. Pedersen, E., People Presence or Room Activity, Companion proceeding of Conference on Human Factors in Computing Systems (CHI '98), ACM Press, April 1998, pp. 283-284.

13. Ullmer, B., Ishii, H. and Glas, D., mediaBlocks: Physical Containers, Transports, and Controls for Online Media, in Proceedings of SIGGRAPH '98, (Orlando, Florida USA, July 1998), ACM Press, pp. 379-386.

14. Underkoffler, J., and Ishii, H., Illuminating Light: An Optical Design Tool with a Luminous-Tangible Interface, Proceedings of Conference on Human Factors in Computing Systems (CHI '98), ACM Press, pp. 542-549, April 1998.

15. Weiser, M, and Brown, J.S., Designing Calm Technology, *PowerGrid Journal*, v 1.01 (July 1996), http://powergrid.electriciti.com/1.01.

TouchCounters: Designing Interactive
Electronic Labels for Physical Containers

Paul Yarin and Hiroshi Ishii

MIT Media Laboratory

20 Ames Street

E15 {-444, -485}

Cambridge, MA 02139 USA

+1 617 253 {-9708, -7514}

{yarin, ishii}@media.mit.edu

ABSTRACT

We present TouchCounters, an integrated system of electronic modules, physical storage containers, and shelving surfaces for the support of collaborative physical work. Through physical sensors and local displays, TouchCounters record and display usage history information upon physical storage containers, thus allowing access to this information during the performance of real-world tasks. A distributed communications network allows this data to be exchanged with a server, such that users can access this information from remote locations as well.

Based upon prior work in ubiquitous computing and tangible interfaces, TouchCounters incorporate new techniques, including usage history tracking for physical objects and multi-display visualization. This paper describes the components, interactions, implementation, and conceptual approach of the TouchCounters system.

Keywords

Tangible interfaces, ubiquitous computing, distributed sensing, visualization

INTRODUCTION

For decades, research into computing technology has yielded steady improvements in processing power, network bandwidth and availability, and graphical realism. Despite this, objective measures indicate surprisingly minimal gains in productivity [2]. As we continue to invest in computers for schools, homes, and offices, we must face the question: will information systems really improve our ability to work together in the physical world?

Exchanges between people, information, and physical objects (the basic operations of work) are only partially accessible to digital processing and augmentation [Ken Cooper, personal communication]. While interpersonal

communication is increasingly mediated by computers, the hundreds of daily exchanges between people and physical objects are largely unknown and unknowable to information systems. No mechanism exists for tracking the placement, movement, and usage of objects in the typical workplace.

In addition, computing systems are limited in their ability to deliver information in a working environment. Keyboards, mice, and GUI displays tether users to stationary boxes that require close attention to operate. Handheld computers, while mobile, also require direct manipulation that interrupts the flow of work. While these constraints are acceptable for some tasks, they limit the adoption of computer-supported collaboration to highly specialized environments.

Must every working environment be redesigned with computer clusters as focal points of activity? Will wall-sized, handheld, or wearable computers actually improve our ability to work together? In short, what kinds of interfaces will support collaboration in the physical world?

Our direction has been to employ the physical world itself as an interface [9]. By employing things that we can touch—objects, surfaces, and structures—as interface elements, we hope to enable seamless and natural interfacing of physical and digital environments. This vision has motivated the design of various "hybrid" objects that act as containers or controls for digital information, thus providing a means to record and access data through physical interaction.

In this paper, we present our efforts in developing an interface system to support physical-world collaborative work. We named this project "TouchCounters," as in some ways it is a physical analogue to the digital "hit counters" on web pages.

This paper begins with a brief description of our prototype system and the user interactions it supports. We then describe related research efforts and the defining characteristics of our approach. A more detailed discussion of the implementation follows, including reference to the design objectives that informed technical development. We conclude with our plans for further work and a summary of our contribution to HCI.

SYSTEM OVERVIEW: COMPONENTS

The TouchCounters system is comprised of electronic labels, physical storage containers, networked shelving surfaces, and a web server. Together, these components allow information to be gathered from and displayed upon physical objects distributed throughout a working environment.

The electronic labels are palm-sized electronic devices that attach to the front faces of plastic storage containers. The labels display bright, colored patterns on arrays of LED's. Each label module can sense physical motion, as well as the opening and closing of the container.

Fig. 1: Attaching an electronic label to a storage container

The containers are transparent plastic storage boxes with electrical connectors that attach instantly to the shelving surfaces. When a container is placed upon the shelf, it links its label to the server through a local data bus. Through this server, data can then be passed to other networks or to the Internet.

Fig. 2: Attaching a storage container to networked shelves

SYSTEM OVERVIEW: INTERACTIONS

We have implemented a variety of interactions using the above system of components. We present these here without discussion of the usage context; an explanation of the design objectives appears in the implementation section.

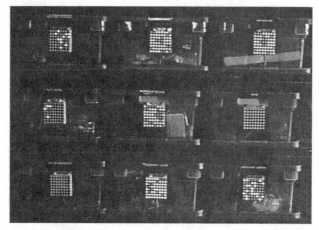

Fig. 3: Usage frequency distribution of multiple containers

Usage frequency visualization

The multiplicity of displays allows the visualization of usage information before even approaching the containers. The label on each box shows a dot pattern that indicates its recent frequency of use. (Each pixel represents a single use of the container during a given period. Just as hit counters display a count of accesses to a web page, these devices display a "count" of physical accesses. This led to the name "TouchCounters.")

When the entire set of containers is viewed from across a room, the aggregated independent displays comprise a spatial map of usage frequency. As one might expect, a small fraction of the containers are subject to much heavier use than the average; these "hot spots" can be used as starting points when searching for a commonly used item. In addition, the relative counts can be used to facilitate the manual task of optimizing box placement. For example, the most active ones can be placed at hand- or eye-level.

Usage correlation visualization

Frequently, *combinations* of particular boxes are used to accomplish a given task. Through analysis of the record of box accesses, the system determines the degree of usage correlation between all possible pairs of boxes. Once a single container is accessed, all of the others display patterns indicating their correlation to the first.

In this way, the search for a related item can often be accelerated by looking at the brightest displays in the area. This information can also be used to improve container placement, as paired boxes can be placed near each other.

Fig. 4: Correlation of usage of multiple containers (relative to container that has been removed)

Object labeling

In addition to displaying automatically recorded data, the system allows users to explicitly annotate the boxes with simple label information. By pointing an infrared remote control at the boxes, users can attach "glyphs" that indicate a common association between several containers.

Like the file "labeling" feature of the Macintosh ™ OS, these glyphs are generic symbols that can be associated with any categorization scheme desired by the user. For example, users indicate that certain boxes belong to a certain user to are related to a certain project. Alternately, a group of users could agree upon certain symbols as indications of the state of completion of a various prototypes.

Fig. 5: Labeling multiple containers with an infrared remote control

Remote browsing

Finally, users can view and modify the entire system remotely. Since data from each label is transmitted to a server, the state of each label can be displayed through a Java-enabled browser. As a demonstration of the

bidirectional interaction, users can also click on these web-based images; this triggers changes to the physical displays. In the future, this capability will allow physical object-based messaging and notification that integrates with traditional PC environments.

Fig. 6: Physical containers displaying frequency-of-use data.

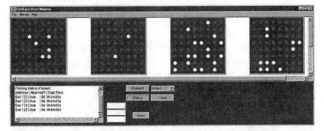

Fig. 7: Java applet displaying identical information on a web page

CONCEPTUAL APPROACH

We next consider the conceptual approach we employed applicable to the design of various physical interface devices. Here, we describe several significant elements of this approach.

First is the binding of *digital attributes with physical containers*. Containers are a means for categorizing physical objects, just as "folders" are a means for categorizing files. Placing a group of items in a box is thus akin to attaching a common attribute to each item. By recognizing the container (and not the individual items contained) as the unit of interest, we were able to link additional attribute information with an existing physical classification system. No modification of the objects themselves was necessary to achieve this.

Eventually, the automated association of attribute information (meta-data) will allow fundamentally digital operations to be performed on physical objects. Physical objects can be digitally indexed, searched, and even located *in situ* through simple physical actions. Clearly, centralized graphical interfaces can offer no comparable functionality.

Another key concept is the tracking of *physical usage frequency to support collaborative work*. Hill and Hollan have noted the effect of thumb smudges in well-worn repair manuals: as indicators of popular pages, these marks index the most useful sections of the book. [8] Of course, physical wear usually occurs too slowly to offer feedback for collaboration. (In addition, such wear is often associated with a loss in functionality or structural integrity.) A physical/digital interface, however, allows physical use to be displayed *without physical wear*.

Records of these interactions can then be used to improve resource allocation, ergonomics, and workflow.

As a visualization mechanism, the simultaneous use of *multiple displays in aggregate* represents a new paradigm for the information visualization community. Because all of the individual displays show the same type of data, they act in concert as a single, room-filling, "meta-display." This type of display allows a qualitatively different style of engagement from graphically complex handheld or wall-sized displays. If the mapping of information to display is persistent, the system can even recede into the "periphery" of awareness, noticed only when sudden changes occur [10].

Finally, the *object-centered interaction* physically situates information in its context of use, and makes unambiguous the association of object, information, and physical location. While general-purpose computers can also display this information visually, the complexity of accessing, configuring, and navigating these systems often renders them unsuitable for assisting physical tasks.

RELATED WORK

Our work draws from a variety of research in augmented reality [3], augmented environments [12], distributed sensing devices [11], information visualization [7], computational learning tools [13], and various interfaces based upon object manipulation [1], [5], [6], [9], [14], [15].

Ubiquitous computing

Ubiquitous Computing [16] anticipated the proliferation of various computational devices throughout the environment, all connected to a distributed network. Wall- and tablet-sized versions of such devices were demonstrated, in addition to a handheld version called the ParcTab.

Although our system fits well with the concept of ubiquitous computing, our approach differs substantially from that of handheld GUI devices like the ParcTab. While handheld devices support closely attended interaction with a single user, our distributed displays are equally well-suited for concurrent multi-user, multi-object interaction.

Spatially aware palmtops

The Chameleon prototype developed by George Fitzmaurice [4] is a handheld device that displayed "situated," or context-sensitive, information. The system's display acted as a window into a virtual workspace, responding dynamically to changes in its physical orientation and position.

Like the Chameleon, TouchCounters provide a spatial visualization of information, but eliminate the need for tilting, panning, and zooming. However, the possibility of integrating portable devices with augmented environments was a key inspiration. Fitzmaurice imagined a computer-augmented library with indicators beneath the shelves: "as we walk through the music section, books on the topic of interest as well as related material will be highlighted by indicator lights..." [4]

There are many issues involved in making such a system operational, and it was never implemented. However, our approach is very much in accordance with this concept.

History-enriched digital objects

Perhaps the most interesting related work connection is the concept of the "history-enriched digital object," or HEDO, by Hill and Hollan [8]. HEDOs are mechanisms for recording use history data onto digital objects. As described in *Edit Wear and Read Wear*, "object-centered interaction histories" allow records of use to be embedded within and displayed upon computational objects. For example the degree of editing or reading of different portions of a document can be indicated on "attribute-mapped scroll bars" accompanying images, documents, or email windows.

We too employ "object-centered interaction histories," but in our case the objects are physical containers. Our objects sense both physical and digital events, and portray them in glyphic form.

IMPLEMENTATION

Design approach

In addition to the TouchCounters system, we have developed several other interaction devices for the augmentation of working environments. Like the TouchCounters modules, each of these devices supports the visualization of a specific type of information. Although a detailed discussion is beyond the scope of this paper, we list some of these devices for reference: electric field sensing modules for non-contact, gestural input, electromagnet arrays with magneto-rheological fluid for tactile output [17], and tag reader interfaces for visualizing information on RFID (radio-frequency identification) tags.

To facilitate the development, deployment, and reconfiguration of these devices, we have emphasized modularity in all aspects of their design. This is evidenced by the electronic components, physical connectors, data protocol, and software used in the TouchCounters system.

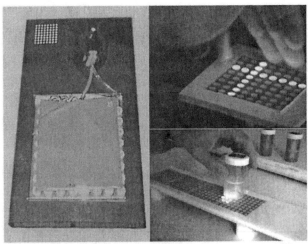

Fig. 8: (clockwise) Tactile output [17], electric field sensing, and RF tag reader interface devices

Electronic Labels

The TouchCounters modules are palm-sized (12x15x3cm) electronic devices. Each is essentially a simple computer equipped with sensing, display, processing, and communications capabilities.

Fig. 9: TouchCounters electronic label modules; one is reversed to reveal the magnetic snap connectors

The sensing capabilities currently include magnetic and infrared detectors. Dual-axis accelerometers have been installed on some modules, but are not yet integrated with our working system. To detect the opening and closing of the container lids, permanent magnets were installed in the front edges of the lids. A magnetic reed switch on each module detects the proximity of this magnet to determine the status of the lid. Thus the system can count the number of container openings as discrete events.

The front of each module is covered by an 8x8 LED matrix display. Originally intended for use in outdoor

electronic signs, these components can portray glyphic graphical patterns composed of bright red, green, and orange pixels. While these are not intended as a replacements for high-resolution monitors, they are well-suited for the dynamic display of simple quantitative information. Simple animations such as rotating lines or oscillating particles can also be rendered, but we felt that motion would be unnecessarily distracting and chose static graphics instead. Unlike liquid crystal displays, LED displays can be viewed easily at a large distance, a key characteristic for our intended use.

The inclusion of a Microchip PIC™ processor on each module greatly enhances the system's flexibility. As the processor is electrically erasable, new code can be rapidly uploaded through a five-pin programming port. To identify each module uniquely, the processor can read a 48-bit ID from a Dallas Semiconductor Silicon Serial Number™ chip. Higher-level identifications, such as descriptions of the container's contents, are added at the server level.

The modules also support infrared and wired communications. Standard TV remote controls can be decoded through an IR receiver module, and IR can be transmitted through a small emitter. In the future, IRDA data transfer may be implemented to allow the direct annotation of information using a PDA.

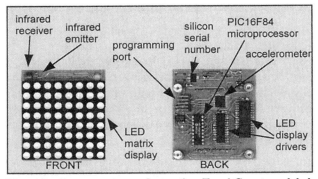

Fig. 10: Components used on the TouchCounters label modules

Containers and Shelves

Data is exchanged with the server through a series of connectors on the modules, storage containers, and shelves. The modules attach to objects using a set of four magnetic snaps located on their back sides; these allow rapid, robust, and single-handed attachment/detachment. As the snaps are electrically conductive, both power and data signals are activated through the act of placing the container upon the shelf. The receptacles on the shelves are hard-wired to a common bus connected to a central server. This architecture allows easy scaling of the number of containers or devices in the system.

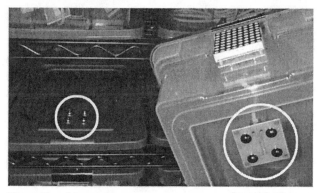

Fig. 11: Magnetic snap connectors connect storage containers to the shelves.

Web Server

The web server is a standard personal computer running Java™ code. Serial I/O classes enable the server to read data from the machine's serial port. To allow remote users to dynamically alter the code executed on this machine, Java's remote method invocation (RMI) routines were employed. All data is exchanged as ASCII text; this facilitated debugging of communications errors by humans.

Usage correlation is measured both through count information relayed from the labels, and by measuring the time that a box unit is *offline* and therefore removed from the shelf. Each access event is stored in a matrix of variables which is updated continually. Likewise frequency of use information is logged in a file available online.

A Java applet displays box status to remote users, and also allows data to be sent to the labels.

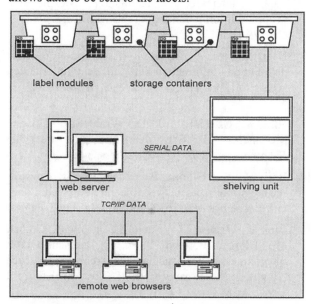

Fig. 12: Network topology of the TouchCounters system

PRELIMINARY OBSERVATIONS

In an effort to optimize its design, we have installed our prototype system in our own facilities for evaluation and integration with our everyday use. Though this is no substitute for controlled user studies, it has allowed us to obtain some qualitative feedback about this system.

This system was installed in a large room used by about a dozen researchers for prototyping and fabrication. Materials in this area, including supplies, materials, and tools, are stored in 50-60 plastic containers. Inevitably, the number of different users results in frequent changes in the positions of each box. The locating of any particular box is challenging, as the boxes span multiple shelving systems across a room. 16 containers were fitted with the labels and networking hardware; the remainder were left unchanged.

Users responded positively to the display graphics, and expressed interest in the complete implementation of the system. In particular, users liked the visual feedback that accompanied labeling with the remote control. It was noted that the electronic modules acted as both *labels* and as *indicators*; that is, they support both passive recording and direct annotation of data.

Some users asked how messages could be left on the containers themselves; for example, a note that an item had been borrowed from a box. Others asked whether the users of each box could be identified. We address these in Future Work section below.

Wire	Solder	Scissors	Velcro
Serial Cables	Ethernet	Serial Adapters	Foam
Fabric	Magnets	Abrasives	Adhesives
Paint	Markers	Tape	Monitor Cables

Figure 13: Sampling of items stored with TouchCounters system

FUTURE WORK

Our plans for further development include user studies, improvements to functionality and visualization, and the application of our approach to new environments.

While preliminary feedback has been encouraging, we plan to implement a complete system for testing under actual working conditions. To do this, we will have to determine which metrics will best quantify user performance and satisfaction, and to compose controlled experiments to test these aspects. This data will inform the refinement of our system's design.

Possible improvements to the system's functionality include PDA-based message annotation, user identification through wearable badges [13], and support for collaboration with geographically distant groups.

Additionally, we plan to implement more sophisticated indications of usage history on the matrix displays, indicating not only the number of accesses but also their temporal distribution. In its glyphic portrayal of temporal distribution such a system would closely parallel the spatial visualizations of TileBars [7].

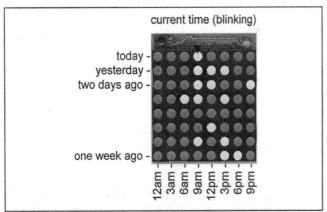

Fig. 14: Temporal distribution of frequency of use represented using glyphic display

Finally, we hope to investigate the extension of our system to accommodate objects which may allured have rich online associations—books, papers, compact disks, videotapes, etc. Recording history of use on such objects may involve very different technologies and visual representations. Nevertheless, we feel that the conceptual approach will be very similar.

CONCLUSION

In closing, we have noted the limitations of current computer interfaces in supporting collaboration, and have designed a lightweight information access system in response to this need. By recording and visualizing *in situ* the history of use of physical storage containers, we promote the use of real-world, distributed interaction systems for the support of physical work.

We have noted a number of parallels between objects in the physical and digital realms, and have enumerated the critical features of our approach towards physical design. In our discussion of technical implementation, we have demonstrated highly modular physical, electronic, and software design that supports easy integration with various devices and physical configurations.

Finally, we have indicated a number of promising directions for future work, including the further qualification and improvement of our system. We hope that our work will improve the collaboration of real people in the physical world by harnessing the power of computation.

ACKNOWLEDGEMENTS

Clay Harmony, James Hsiao, and Chris Leung deserve special thanks for their diligence and ingenuity in implementing this project. In addition, we thank Brygg Ullmer, Joanna Berzowska, and John Underkoffler for their ongoing support, advice, and intellectual curiosity. Thanks to Rich Fletcher, Josh Smith, Tom White, Rob Poor, Victor Su, and Rick Borovoy for making available their considerable collective experience. Finally, we thank all students of the Tangible Media Group for their energy, creativity, and camaraderie. This work was supported in part by fellowships from IBM and Mitsubishi Electric Research Laboratories.

REFERENCES

[1] Fishkin, K., Moran, T., and Harrison, B. Embodied User Interfaces: Towards Invisible User Interfaces, to appear in *Proceedings of EHCI'98*, ACM Press.

[2] Edwards, Paul N. "From 'Impact' to Social Process: Computers in Society and Culture," in Sheila Jasanoff et al., eds., *Handbook of Science and Technology Studies* (Beverly Hills, CA: Sage Publications, 1994), 257-285.

[3] Feiner, S., MacIntyre, B., and Seligmann, D. Knowledge-based augmented reality. *Commun. ACM 36*, 7 (July 1993), ACM Press, 52-62.

[4] Fitzmaurice, G. Situated Information Spaces and Spatially Aware Palmtop Computers. *Commun. ACM, 36*, 7 (July 1993), ACM Press, 38-49.

[5] Fitzmaurice, G., Ishii, H., and Buxton, W. Bricks: Laying the foundations for graspable user interfaces, in *Proceedings of CHI'95,* ACM Press, 442-449.

[6] Gorbet, M., Orth, M., and Ishii, H. Triangles: Tangible interface for manipulation and exploration of digital information topography, in *Proceedings of CHI'98*, ACM Press, 49-56.

[7] Hearst, Marti A. TileBars: Visualization of term distribution information in full text information access, in *Proceedings of CHI'95*, ACM Press, 59-66.

[8] Hill, W. C., Hollan, J. D., Wroblewski, D., and McCandless, T. Edit wear and read wear, in *Proceedings of CHI'92*, ACM Press, 3-9.

[9] Ishii, H., and Ullmer, B. Tangible bits: Towards seamless interfaces between people, bits, and atoms, in *Proceedings of CHI'97,* ACM Press, 234-241.

[10] Ishii, H., Wisneski, C., Brave, S., Dahley, A., Gorbet, M., Ullmer, B. and Yarin, P. ambientROOM: Integrating ambient media with architectural space (video), in *Summary of CHI '98* (Los Angeles, April 1998), ACM Press, 173-174.

[11] Poor, R. The iRX 2.0 ...where Atoms meet Bits. http://ttt.media.mit.edu/pia/Research/iRX2/

[12] Rekimoto, J, and Nagao, K. The world through the computer: Computer augmented interaction with real

world environments, in *Proceedings of UIST'95,* ACM Press, 29.

[13] Resnick, M., Berg, F., et al. Digital manipulatives: New toys to think with, in *Proceedings of CHI'98,* ACM Press, 281-285.

[14] Ullmer, B., Ishii, H., and Glas, D. (1998). "media-Blocks: Physical containers, transports, and controls for online media, in *Proceedings of SIGGRAPH'98,* ACM Press, 379-386.

[15] Underkoffler, J., and Ishii, H. Illuminating light: An optical design tool with a luminous-tangible interface, in *Proceedings of CHI'98*, ACM Press, 542-549.

[16] Weiser, M. "The Computer for the 21st Century." In *Scientific American*, 265(3), 94-104.

[17] White, Tom. Introducing Liquid Haptics in High Bandwidth Human Computer Interfaces. MS Thesis, MIT Media Lab, May 1998.

Bridging Physical and Virtual Worlds with Electronic Tags

Roy Want, Kenneth P. Fishkin, Anuj Gujar, Beverly L. Harrison
Xerox PARC
3333 Coyote Hill Road
Palo Alto, CA 94304 USA
{want, fishkin, agujar, beverly}@parc.xerox.com

ABSTRACT

The role of computers in the modern office has divided our activities between virtual interactions in the realm of the computer and physical interactions with real objects within the traditional office infrastructure. This paper extends previous work that has attempted to bridge this gap, to connect physical objects with virtual representations or computational functionality, via various types of tags. We discuss a variety of scenarios we have implemented using a novel combination of inexpensive, unobtrusive and easy to use RFID tags, tag readers, portable computers and wireless networking. This novel combination demonstrates the utility of invisibly, seamlessly and portably linking physical objects to networked electronic services and actions that are naturally associated with their form.

KEYWORDS: RFID tag, portable computers, wireless networks, ubiquitous computing, tangible interface, phicon, augmented reality.

INTRODUCTION

Six years ago a compelling and provocative vision of the future was presented in Pierre Wellner's video and article on the Digital Desk [24,25]. Physical office tools such as pens, erasers, books, and paper were seamlessly integrated (or at least almost seamlessly!) with computational augmentation and virtual tools, using projection and image processing. His works, and our recent efforts (reported here and [5,10]), are directed at more seamlessly bridging the gulf between physical and virtual worlds; an area which we believe represents a key path for the design of future user interfaces.

Since the Digital Desk, there has been an ever-increasing interest in augmented reality and physically–based user interfaces [5,6,7,8,9,10,12,13,15,17,18,19,20,26,27]. A

goal of these emerging projects is to seamlessly blend the affordances and strengths of physically manipulatable objects with virtual environments or artifacts, thereby leveraging the particular strengths of each. Typically, this integration exists in the form of physical input artifacts [7, 8,10,24,25,26] virtually linked to electronic graphical objects. Manipulation of the physical artifacts signals a related operation on the associated electronic objects. Typically these electronic objects reside within a proximate computer and associated display. With each new prototype comes a wealth of subtle information about how to best design and support these new "invisible interfaces" (see [4] for an analysis).

The goal of this paper is to share our experiences in designing and building a number of new physical prototypes which incorporate key technologies to address issues which limited the use of earlier experimental systems. In particular, we have combined four technologies (RFID identifier tags and readers, RF networking, infrared beacons, and portable computing) in a seamless and tightly integrated way. This combination has not been previously discussed in the literature. We provide several new examples of augmented reality "devices" that we have created using this package and we describe the underlying hardware and software systems used to support this emerging genre for user interaction.

Similar to Wellner [22,23], Fitzmaurice [6], and Ishii [11], a primary goal of our work is to support everyday tools and objects, the affordances of these objects, and to computationally augment them to support casual interaction using natural manipulations and associations. However, unlike this previous work, we have tried to build invisible interfaces that have little reliance on specialized single-user environments and/or display projection, or custom-designed objects. To this end, we start with everyday objects and embed portable, distributed augmentation in them in the ubiquitous computing tradition founded at PARC [20, 21].

SOME ISSUES FROM PREVIOUS WORK

One exciting set of past work has allowed physical manipulation of invisibly augmented objects. However, the manipulation detectors and manipulation environments have been localized prototypes, being expensive, difficult to deploy, non-portable, and restrictive in terms of the range and class of human interactions. For example, the rear-projection [13] or light-emitted projection [24] systems they employ are expensive - typically $35K for the former and $10K for the latter, per prototype.

These systems were built around a model of "time traveling" into the future to better understand these physical/tangible user interfaces by building custom "user workstations". As a result it is usually difficult to establish a wide-scale deployment and to measure their impact in different environments across many users.

Finally, virtually all of these systems assume that the augmented objects must reside upon the display surface area to have interaction meaning. Notable exceptions are work where tethered objects such as Hinckley's doll's head [12] are used. The tether and the location sensor limit the range of object movement or distribution of objects throughout an environment.

A second path has been to augment objects via visible graphical tags, such as bar-codes [2] or glyphs [11]. In the limit case of Barret's "virtual floppies" [1], the augmented object serves solely to house the tag. While these scenarios are much lower-cost, allow many more objects to be augmented, and support multi-location use, the visual obtrusiveness of the tags, and the awkwardness of the readers, has limited their use.

Our approach is to merge these two paths. Like the first path, we try to make the user experience of interacting with the augmented objects as seamless as possible, with unobtrusive tagging. Like the second path, large numbers of existing everyday objects can be easily tagged and used in multiple locales, using a simple and inexpensive infrastructure.

Specifically, our approach is to take everyday objects that already have some useful purpose independent of any electronic system, and to augment those objects via embedded RF ID tags . They are sufficiently inexpensive (as low as $0.20) that they can be considered disposable (or easily recyclable). They are sufficiently small that they do not destroy (or, often, even alter) the aesthetics of the original object. Although custom objects can be augmented, we mainly use everyday items, which have proved to be the most powerful examples. Embedding tags and associating virtual functionality is straightforward (described later). This provides us with a broad range of artifacts to experiment with and an easy deployment scheme.

A tagging system must consider not only the affordances of the tag, but also of the tag detector. RFID tags have three important advantages in this regard. Firstly, RFID tag readers are small enough that they can be unobtrusively "piggy-backed" onto the back of pen computers, plugging into the serial port – the user need not carry a second specialized device. Secondly, they detect RFID tags whenever "waved" in the proximate vicinity of a tag

(roughly 10 cm) – precise alignment and registration is not necessary. Thirdly, they are relatively inexpensive (roughly $80 as a one-of off-the-shelf purchase).

This means that we can instrument a number of tablet computers (e.g., Fujitsu® 1200 & 510), laptops, or even Palm Pilots® thereby deploying the system for many users in many contexts. The technology and interactions are not tied to a particular location or workstation.

The system can operate locally with no network dependencies. However, in practice we found that more interesting scenarios are possible when wireless network connections are incorporated [9]. This enables users to access remote web-based material, digital video sequences (potentially too large to be device-resident), and applications like email. Wireless networking provides more flexibility and seamless integration than previous systems allowed. This too is a relatively low cost item and easy to deploy across many devices (at present, we are using an existing PARC wireless network (Proxim RangeLAN2®), with device PC cards costing $475 each).

Lastly, in some scenarios we have used the IrDA ports on the mobile computers to receive a room ID from strategically placed IR beacons. This allows us to further interpret the context of tagged objects, as the system is now aware of the room in which they reside. To achieve this, we have re-used, and re-coded, the IR transceivers (a.k.a. "deathstars"), built in the early 90's for PARC's ubiquitous computing project [21,22]

In the remainder of the paper, we describe implementation details, scenarios, and applications that we hope will inspire and teach others about this provocative UI domain.

SYSTEM OVERVIEW

The essence of the system is the attachment of one or more electronic identification tags each physical item that we wish to augment. These RFID tags are small transponders comprised of an integrated circuit, storing a unique 39-bit ID, and a small coil. There is no on-board power, thereby reducing the size and weight of the individual tags and eliminating maintenance requirements (see Figure 1).

Figure 1. Three RFID tags compared to an American dime and a ruler for scale.

A tag reader is affixed to a computational device. The tag reader draws power either from the associated computational device or from an externally connected power supply. The reader energizes the tag by inductive coupling between its coil and a tiny coil in the tag. The received energy is stored in a capacitor until there is sufficient energy to transmit its ID modulated on a signal at half the induction frequency. (Figure 2).

Communication between tag and reader only occurs when both are proximate. The actual distance varies based on the size of the antenna attached to the tag and to the transmitter. In our present system, distances range from 5 to 10 cm. Once the ID sequence (transmitted serially) is received, the tag reader passes this on to the computer system as an ASCII string via an RS-232 connection. The system cannot correctly detect multiple tags simultaneously present within its proximity. For this reason, our use scenarios all involve the reader being "waved" near or on a tag of interest.

When the reader detects a tag, our application program interprets the ID input string, determines the current application context, and provides appropriate feedback. In particular, we maintain an ASCII file that maps ID numbers to one or more actions. For example, one common action is to invoke a specified program with some associated parameter(s); others tell programs such as Internet Explorer or Word to display certain documents. The system currently supports 21 such actions. We provide auditory and visual feedback to confirm that an RFID tag was within range and was read by the hardware. If the ID number has not been previously registered, i.e., associated with an action in our tag file, we prompt the user to enter an action(s) and any associated parameters via a dialog box. Network and server connectivity is provided by a separate wireless RF networking system. If the program or the file to be retrieved reside on the network, we can have filenames that are independent of the particular sensing computer.

Figure 2. The tag reader system components

We believe this tag system has some interesting advantages over other methods of tagging documents, such as bar codes [2] or glyphs [11]. Specifically:

- **Unobtrusiveness.** These tags are sufficiently small that, with some care, they can be unobtrusively (or even invisibly) added to most physical objects. This extends beyond tagging paper or printed material. Although we are currently using 3 specific commercially available tags, we are investigating tags with other form factors to further support subtle integration. This flexibility lets us choose many different locations for tag positioning and supports tagging of highly curved 3D shapes, as opposed to the more limited, surface-only space used by glyphs and barcodes.

- **Robustness.** RFID tags don't degrade over the course of normal usage. They are impervious to dust, dirt, and smearing, and are quite physically robust. They are routinely used over long periods of time in very harsh environments, such as in tracking livestock [16].

- **Post-Hoc Augmentation.** RFID tags are easily added as a post-process to many physical objects, a task that can be more difficult with bar codes or especially glyphs.

- **Easily sensed.** Because the tag and the reader have been designed to be loosely coupled during interrogation, the tags do not have to physically contact the sensing device, let alone "dock" in a specific location with a specific orientation. This flexibility makes the tags easier to use, and adds to the unobtrusiveness mentioned above. They are read in tens of milliseconds; we are not restricted by image processing software quality and related processing time, camera hardware or image resolution, camera placement, angular skew, or visual obstruction of objects.

- **Aesthetics.** Bar codes, and in some cases glyphs, are used to label many commercial products. However, we are often less inclined to have a bar code stamped upon certain items because appearance is important. While barcodes appear on any number of products, it is frequently on the packaging that is subsequently discarded. The look of a product in these cases limits the widespread use of visual labels. Furthermore, the size of these labels is often constrained by the scanning technology, print quality and cost, i.e., small labels are, at present, infeasible.

There are two principle disadvantages of the tagging technology we have described:

- **Associating Functionality.** At present our system supports a general binding of tag to semantics. However, this comes at a price. The administrator of the tag system or the user must register actions and maintain this file. Barcode labels and glyph labels, which are produced and subsequently affixed to objects, rely on the same post-hoc process. While printed material can be readily associated with particular barcodes or glyphs at the system level automatically, to execute a particular action, additional instructions must be explicitly provided. In both scenarios, the challenge is to provide easy mechanisms for performing the association of a physically tagged object to a particular set of actions.

- **Knowing what is tagged.** The advantage of

"unobtrusiveness" carries a corresponding disadvantage. Since barcodes and glyphs both rely on being visible, it is clear which objects have these tagging mechanisms. In our scenario, tags can be so unobtrusive that they are invisible. While this can have aesthetic advantages, it has obvious drawbacks – the user cannot, without instruction, guess which objects are tagged, where, and with what semantics. How to best combine unobtrusiveness with obviousness of use is a major focus of our current work.

However, overall the technologies and research area seem both promising and useful. We have explored a variety of applications and prototypes. We briefly outline some of these in the next section.

SOME SAMPLE APPLICATIONS AND PROTOTYPES
Using our prototype system, we have implemented a variety of virtual associations for a variety of physical objects.

Augmenting Books and Documents
By augmenting a physical document or book with an RFID tag, we introduce a virtual linkage between that physical document and an equivalent or related electronic document(s). For example, consider a book consisting of a collection of printed pages, such as a technical manual, a patent application, or a conference submission such as this paper. (It is most natural to associate tags with the document as a whole rather than the individual pages of these documents. This more accurately reflects our cognitive model of that object.)

Figure 3. An augmented book -- tag location is highlighted

Although current RFID tags are too large and thick to invisibly embed within a page, they can be easily accommodated in most forms of document bindings. For example, tags can be located upon or within a document binder as shown in Figure 3, can be embedded within other marks such as an embossing seal (Figure 4) or can even be located in or on the document staple.

When a computational device such as a tablet computer detects the tag, an associated virtual document is displayed. This is particularly useful in the case of collaborative and/or iterated documents, which go through versioning –

no matter which version the user is physically holding, when they bring the document near to their computer, they can see the latest electronic version.

Figure 4. An augmented document -- tag is in the seal.

Augmenting Small Documents: Business Cards
Tags can be associated with any physical document, even those smaller than a book. For example, Figure 5 shows a tag placed on the back of a regular business card. The virtual association for this physical document is the home page of the person so represented – when the business card is brought close to the computer, their home page is displayed. We have also implemented business card tags that automatically generate email messages with the addressing information already filled in.

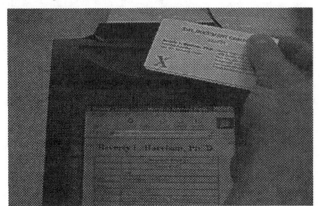

Figure 5. A business card associated with the web page of the person on the card.

Extending Document Functionality: Services
A book or document can be linked to an associated service. For example, in Figure 6 below, we show an augmented book that is linked to the corresponding Amazon.com® web page to order a copy of the book. We could additionally link in the author's home page, the New York Times® reviews of the book, or other correspondence related to the book. We could link all of these sources to a single book by displaying a page of hyperlinks, one for each option.

A tagged item can also be linked to a context-aware service that is to be performed on a document already being displayed. For example, a French dictionary was augmented with a tag (Figure 7).

Figure 6. Augmented book linked to Amazon.com web site for book ordering.

When sensed, the dictionary can invoke a language translation program that translates the currently displayed document. The language of translation can be based upon the physical affordances of the dictionary, in particular the title and content, e.g., a French dictionary will perform French translation. In this way, we can use everyday objects and tools in the office place to invoke electronic *services* upon documents analogous to and synergistic with the real-world services they already perform.

Figure 7. A French dictionary used to translate "the Jabberwocky"

Tags which set context

As shown by the French dictionary example, tag semantics can be a function of the existing context on the sensing computer. Tags can, therefore, have an associated action that sets that context, either instead of, or in addition to, launching applications and services. Two particularly useful examples of this are using tags to establish user ID, and to establish location

User ID

Tags can be imperceptibly added to existing physical artifacts used for user identification, such as ID cards, signet rings, watches, jewelry, or even keys. When such an artifact moves close to the computer, the user specified by the tag has their profile and preferences applied to the current context.

Location

Locations such as tables, chairs, and doorways can be augmented, either by the addition of tags, or additional coil sensors. In the first configuration, the computer senses the location – in the second, the location senses the computer. In either case, the semantics are similar. By automatically detecting context in this way, the device can perform various actions, such as only displaying documents in certain locations, displaying the last document used in this location, etc. We have also augmented the rooms with IR beacons to provide room ID information within this system. The beacons transmit room information either automatically (e.g. every 10 seconds) or upon activation via laser beam (e.g. a hand laser pointer). The IR port on the pen computer detects the room information so transmitted and sets context accordingly.

Augmenting "Bookmarks"

Tags can be used to create ephemeral or transitory associations. For example, we took physical bookmarks and augmented them with two tags, one at each end (Figure 8). Waving the bottom end of the bookmark by the reader binds the bookmark to the current page of the current document. Waving the top end loads the last bound association onto the display.

Figure 8. Augmented bookmark referencing a particular document page.

Any number of user interface mechanisms could be used to signal the "put association" action as opposed to the "go to association" action – tapping on different parts of the computer, reserving one side of the bookmark for each action, having a "write-only" enabler on the bookmark, and so forth.

This example shows that while the tag ID is read-only, the tag can be "conceptually writeable", by using the ID as a pointer to a remote writeable document. This is similar to the work of Barrett and Maglio [1], whose "tags" took the form of floppy disks, with only one action (displaying a document) supported.

Augmenting "Non-Document" Objects: The Photo Cube

Virtual links may be ssociated with any physical container or object and may reference various media, not just textual information. For example, consider a "photo cube" (Figure 9). In this document container, a set of 6 related documents (photographs) are bound together within the same physical object. Each face or side of the cube has its own associated information set, augmented by a unique ID tag. This is one example of a 3D-augmented object.

Figure 9. The augmented photo-cube.

To implement this prototype, we took a small balsa wood cubeoid (5cm by 7.5cm by 7.5cm), and drilled holes in each face such that each face could accommodate a disk-sized tag (see Figure 1). Each face was then covered with a photograph – one photo of each author of this paper. (One co-author did not have an immediately available photograph, therefore the other team members jokingly substituted an image of "Xena, Warrior princess"™, from a popular television program). Each of these graphics had a corresponding Web site link. The virtual association for each face, then, was to the Web home page for the person or organization shown on that face. For example, in Figure 10, a photo of a team member is being touched to the computer. In Figure 11, as a result of this action, the computer is displaying that person's home page. The photo-cube illustrates one mechanism associating particular affordances of a specific physical object with a *set* of virtual documents.

Figure 10. Cube face moved next to computer (just prior to screen change) -- BEFORE.

Figure 11. After the photo-cube is proximal, the image is updated with the currently associated web page -- AFTER.

Augmenting "Non-Document" Objects: The wristwatch

To better illustrate potential links between everyday object associations and virtual functionality, we created a wrist watch application (Figure 12).

Figure 12. Augmented watch linked to calendar.

In this scenario, a tag is embedded in a wristwatch. When the user brings the wristwatch close to the active zone on the computer a calendar application for that particular user is shown for the current day, at the current time. The wristwatch behaves in all other respects exactly as it normally would. When the computer is held and used normally, the watch is not located near the sensor zone and therefore it has no effect. If the watch is deliberately moved over the top of the tablet computer and hence into range, the calendar program is loaded. In this way, we keep all prior uses of the watch, while leveraging its affordances: they are already worn, are already associated with scheduling, and are already easily (but unambiguously) available for moving into a target area of a computer.

Portable Use

By tightly integrating the tag reader into a portable computer with network support, portable use of becomes possible. For example, our workplace has many printers scattered throughout. To print a particular document at one, you have to know the exact pathname of the document, and the exact name of the printer. To make this easier, we have affixed RF tags to a number of these printers. By simply "waving" the portable computer proximal to the printer, the current document is sent to that printer.

CURRENT IMPLEMENTATION

We now briefly outline the hardware we used for the scenarios, and the software we wrote to support this system. We then discuss some of the limitations we discovered in implementing and testing this system.

Hardware Integration

Our system was designed around a pen-based computer, the Fujitsu® 1200, – a tablet computer with a 20cm diagonal and VGA resolution. We integrated the RFID reader electronics onto the back of the housing. To provide wireless network connectivity for these mobile devices, we chose a Proxim Rangelan2® frequency-hop spread-spectrum radio in a Type II PC card format. This type of radio system operates at 2.4GHz. The units we acquired provide up to 500 feet of coverage centered on each network access point. The raw bandwidth of the radio is 1.6Mbps with a data rate of 500kbps available to applications, taking into account the protocol overhead. The Trovan® 656 OEM reader turned out to be ideal for our task (shown in Figure 2). It was easily concealed on the back of the tablet and power was delivered to it by tapping into the internal power supply of the machine, with only minor modifications to the computer's housing. All of the interpretation and storage of the tag-IDs is carried out by our software system and we only rely on the Trovan® reader to deliver valid digital representations of the tags across the RS-232 serial interface. The Trovan® RFID tags use 39 bits for each ID Physically larger tags and coils have a greater read range. The tradeoff between tag size, reader coil size, and read range is governed by the application. For the applications described in this paper, we were always able to find some combination of the many readers, coils and tags to achieve the desired property.

Software Infrastructure

Two threads of a multi-threaded Windows program, written in C++, monitor the serial port and IR port, respectively, for incoming tag IDs. A third thread is notified of each incoming tag. It looks the tag up in the semantics database, and then executes them. . Some application programs are invoked as remote "black box" services via "spawn"-type commands, while others are communicated with at a finer level via OLE.

Sometimes the same tag will be rapidly detected twice: to filter this out, a hysteresis is imposed on each tag. If a tag ID is detected which is not associated with any semantics, the program can either ignore the tag, or launch a dialog box querying the user for the semantics of the tag. The latter mechanism is used to update our system whenever a tag is attached to a new document. We created a shared network database, mapping each tag ID number to its virtual association. By placing this database on the network,

and making the association descriptions generic, we were able to support augmented documents in a portable way and ensure consistent object responses across multiple computers/users.

Some Limitations of the Current Implementation

The reader and the RFID tags communicate by inductive coupling between two coils. The reader coil is large relative to the tag and is responsible for providing energy to it and for reading the small signal that is returned. Placement of the reading coil on the housing of a tablet computer has to be done bearing two issues in mind. First, the reading coil must be in a position that is both convenient and natural for a user interacting with tagged objects. Second, the mounting location must be chosen to minimize interference from the host computer. We found that the pen sensing electronics on a Fujitsu® 1200 generates signals that are directly in competition with the reader system and coil placement is critical. If care is not given to this part of the design, the apparent tag reading range of the system can be reduced to a centimeter or less. In our prototype we could generally rely on a reading range of approximately 5-10 cm.

The Trovan® system can only read one tag at a time and some care needs to be taken beyond a tag separation of 1cm because the tags will interference with each other. However for objects that are large enough to support multiple tagged regions, it is usually possible to final suitable locations for their placement.

Because the positioning of the read coil is critical to the ease of use of the system, we have examined this problem in some detail. The exact dimensions of the read coil affects the overall inductance and the Q value. Dimensions that are optimal for one application are not for another. For example, placing a reading coil on the underside of a tablet computer, where there is lots of space to embed it, gives a designer more flexibility with the coil geometry than if it were on the front, where space is limited. To solve this problem we expanded the original system so that a variety of coils could be positioned around the computer housing. The modifications allowed a user to chose between sensing locales with a manual switch. For some applications it might be desirable to use the physical world to automatically choose the active coil. For instance, if the tablet was placed on a table, a micro-switch could detect the contact pressure and thus disable the coil at the back of the unit and switch in a more useful coil at the front. An alternative approach is to automatically multiplex the various coils onto the reader electronics.

CONCLUSIONS

There has long been a discontinuity between the rich interactions with objects in our physical world and impoverished interactions with electronic material. Furthermore, linking these two worlds has been difficult and expensive. Yet "invisible interfaces" still hold promise to leverage the natural, intuitive manipulations based on a wealth of affordances and everyday skills married with powerful computational and network information and functionality. In this paper, we have described our efforts at bridging this physical-virtual gap by subtly augmenting physical objects, making them computationally sense-able through combining several technologies in a widely deployable manner. We have illustrated a number of examples of how this augmented environment might support coupling physical objects to a virtual form or to representative services (actions). These concepts can clearly be extended further. We have described a software and hardware implementation that supports this system and can be extended and enhanced in a variety of ways to encompass more complex scenarios. The research described in this paper reflects our approach and philosophy of creating what we hope will be "invisible interfaces" for the workscape of the future, leveraging the strengths and intuitiveness of the physical world with the advantages and strengths of computation.

ACKNOWLEDGEMENTS

We thank PARC summer intern Dimitriy Portnov, who implemented the IR "deathstar" component of the system. The physical/virtual concept has been a hot topic at Xerox PARC during the last two years and we wish to acknowledge the many people and conversations that have influenced our thinking: Rob Burtzlaff, Helen Davis, Keith Edwards, David Goldberg, Dan Greene, Anthony Lamarca, Tom Moran, Beth Mynatt, Bryan Preas, Mark Weiser, and Polle Zellweger.

REFERENCES

1. Barrett, R. and Maglio, P. Informative Things: How to attach information to the real world. *Proceedings of UIST '98*, pp. 81-88.

2. Collins D. J, Whipple N. N. Using Bar Code – why its taking over. Data Capture Institute, ISBN 0-9627406-0-8.

3. Dallas Semiconductor. Automatic Identification Databook. 1995-1996

4. Hewkin, P. Smart Tags – The Distributed Memory Revolution, IEEE Review (UK), June 1989.

5. Fishkin, K. P., Moran, T., and Harrison, B. L. Embodied User Interfaces: Towards Invisible User Interfaces. *Proceedings of Engineering for Human-Computer Interaction*, Heraklion, Crete, September 1998. In press.

6. Fitzmaurice, G. Situated Information Spaces and Spatially Aware Palmtop Computers, *CACM*, *36*(7), July 1993, pp.38-49.

7. Fitzmaurice, G., Ishii, H., and Buxton, W. A. S. Laying the Foundations for Graspable User Interfaces. *Proceedings of CHI'95*, pp. 422-449.

8. Gorbet, M. G., Orth, M., and Ishii, H. Triangles: Tangible Interface for Manipulation and Exploration of Digital Information Topography. *Proceedings of CHI'98*, pp. 49-56.

9. Gujar, A.U., Wong, L. Fishkin, K.P., Want, R., and Harrison, B.L. Initial User Experiences with an Integrated Tagging System. Submitted for publication.

10. Harrison, B. L., Fishkin, K. P., Gujar, A., Mochon, C., and Want, R. Squeeze Me, Hold Me, Tilt Me! An Exploration of Manipulative User Interfaces. *Proceedings of CHI'98*, pp. 17-24.

11. Hecht D. L., Embedded Data Glyph Technology for Hardcopy Digital Documents. SPIE -Color Hard Copy and Graphics Arts III, Vol. 2171. Feb 1994, pp341-352.

12. Hinckley, K., Pausch, R., Goble, J. and Kassel, N. Passive Real-World Interface Props for Neurosurgical Visualization, *Proceedings of CHI'94*, pp. 452-458.

13. Ishii, H. and Ullmer, B. Tangible Bits: Towards Seamless Interfaces between People, Bits, and Atoms. *Proceedings of CHI'97*, pp. 234-241.

14. Schilit B. N., Golovchinsky, G and Price M. Beyond Paper: Supporting Active Reading with free-form digital ink annotations. *Proceedings of CHI'98*, pp. 249-256.

15. Small, D., and Ishii, H. Design of Spatially Aware Graspable Displays. *Extended Abstracts of CHI'97*, pp. 367-368.

16. Spencer, H. Non-Contact Imaging Tracks Incoming Cartons, Crowds – and Cattle! *Advanced Imaging*, April 1998, pp. 10-12.

17. Streitz, N. A. Integrated Design of Real Architectural Spaces and Virtual Information Spaces. *Summary Proceedings of CHI'98*. pp. 263-264.

18. Streitz, N. A., Konomi, S., and Burkhardt, H.-J. *Cooperative Buildings: Integrating Information, Organization, and Structure*. Proceedings from the 1st International Workshop CoBuild'98, Springer-Verlag. 1998.

19. Streitz, N. A. and Russell, D. M. Basics of Integrated Information and Physical Spaces: The State of the Art. *Summary Proceedings of CHI'98*, pp. 273-274.

20. Underkoffler, J. and Ishii, H. Illuminating Light: An Optical Design Tools with a Luminous Tangible Interface. *Proceedings of CHI'98*, pp. 542-549.

21. Want R., A. Hopper, V. Falcao, J. Gibbons The Active Badge Location System. ACM TOIS 10(1), Jan 1992 Pages 91-102

22. Want R., Schilit, B. N., Adams, N. I., Gold, R., Petersen, K., Goldberg, D., Ellis, J. R., and Weiser, M. An Overview of the ParcTab Ubiquitous Computing Experiment. *IEEE Personal Communications*, December 1995, pp. 28-43.

23. Weiser, M. The Computer for the 21st Century. *Scientific America*, *265*(3), 1991, pp. 94-104.

24. Wellner, P. Tactile Manipulation on the DigitalDesk. Video in CHI'92 Special Video Program, *ACM SIGGRAPH Video Review 79*.

25. Wellner, P. Interacting with paper on the Digital Desk, *CACM*, *36*(7), July 1993, pp. 86-96.

26. Wellner, P. Mackay, W., and Gold, R. Computer Augmented Environments: Back to the Real World. *CACM*, *36*(7), July 1993

27. Wisneski, C., Orbanes, J. and Ishii, H. PingPongPlus: Augmentation and Transformation of Athletic Interpersonal Interaction. *Summary Proceedings of CHI'98*. pp. 327-329.

Augmented Surfaces: A Spatially Continuous Work Space for Hybrid Computing Environments

Jun Rekimoto
Sony Computer Science Laboratories, Inc.
3-14-13 Higashigotanda, Shinagawa-ku,
Tokyo 141-0022 Japan
Phone: +81 3 5448 4380
Fax: +81 3 5448 4273
E-Mail: rekimoto@acm.org
http://www.csl.sony.co.jp/person/rekimoto.html

Masanori Saitoh
Department of Computer Science,
Keio University
3-14-1 Hiyoshi, Kohoku-ku,
Yokohama, Kanagawa 223 Japan
saitoh@aa.cs.keio.ac.jp

ABSTRACT

This paper describes our design and implementation of a computer augmented environment that allows users to smoothly interchange digital information among their portable computers, table and wall displays, and other physical objects. Supported by a camera-based object recognition system, users can easily integrate their portable computers with the pre-installed ones in the environment. Users can use displays projected on tables and walls as a spatially continuous extension of their portable computers. Using an interaction technique called hyperdragging, users can transfer information from one computer to another, by only knowing the physical relationship between them. We also provide a mechanism for attaching digital data to physical objects, such as a videotape or a document folder, to link physical and digital spaces.

KEYWORDS: multiple device user interfaces, table-sized displays, wall-sized displays, portable computers, ubiquitous computing, architectural media, physical space, augmented reality

INTRODUCTION

These days people can take small yet powerful computers anywhere at anytime. Modern notebook-sized portable computers have of several gigabytes of disk storage, processing power almost equal to desktop computers, and an integrated set of interface devices (LCD screen, keyboard, and pointing device). Therefore, it is not impossible to store and carry almost all one's personal data (documents, presentation slides, or   images) in such a small computer.

In parallel with this tendency, our working environments, such as meeting rooms, are going to be equipped with many computing facilities such as data projectors and digital

whiteboards. It is becoming quite common during a meeting to make a presentation using a video projector to show slide data stored in the presenter's portable computer. It is also very common for meeting attendees to bring their own computers to take notes. In the near future, we also expect that meeting room tables and walls will act as computer displays. Eventually, virtually all the surfaces of the architectural space will function as computer displays [8]. As Lange et al. [5] pointed out, large and multiple display surfaces are essential for supporting collaborative, or even individual, activities. We can simultaneously spread several data items out on these surfaces without hiding each other.

Considering these two trends, the natural consequence would be to support smooth integration between portable/personal and pre-installed/public computers. However, in today's computerized meeting rooms, we are often frustrated by poor supports for information exchange among personal and pre-installed computers. In our physical lives, it is quite easy to circulate physical documents among meeting participants and spread paper diagrams on the table, or hang them on the wall. During a meeting, participants around the table can quickly re-arrange these diagrams. When they are displayed on computer screens, information exchanges between computers often require tedious network settings or re-connection of computers. It is not easy to add annotations to an image on the projector screen while another participant is presenting his data on that screen. When you want to transfer data from your computer to others', you might need to know the network address of the target computer, even if you can physically identify that computer.

In this paper we describe our design and implementation of a computer augmented environment that allows a user to smoothly interchange digital information between their portable computers and a computerized table and wall. Using the combination of camera-based marker recognition and interaction techniques called hyperdragging and anchored cursors, users can easily add their own portable computers to that environment. This intuitive, easy-to-use system is just like dragging icons from on screens to another in a single

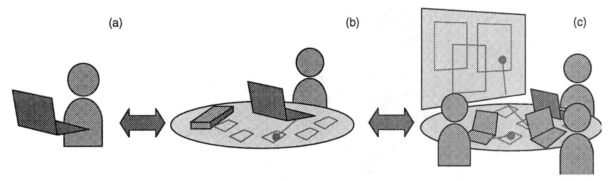

Figure 1: Evolution of spatially continuous workspaces: (a) A user can perform individual tasks with a portable computer. (b) The table becomes an extension of the portable computer. (c) Pre-installed computer displays (table and wall) also serve as shared workspaces for collaborative tasks.

computer supports multiple monitors. People can move information between different computers by only using normal mouse operations and only knowing the physical relationship among them. The system also provides a mechanism for attaching digital data to physical objects, such as a videotape or a document folder, to make tight connections between physical and digital spaces.

A SPATIALLY CONTINUOUS WORKSPACE

While many research systems on augmented physical spaces use pre-installed computers for interaction, we are more interested in how we can smoothly integrate our existing portable computers with the pre-installed ones.

The key features of our system design can be summarized as follows:

Environmental computers as extensions of individual computers

In our design, users can bring their own portable (notebook or palmtop) computers into the environment and put them on the table. Then, the table becomes an extended desktop for the portable computers (Figure 1). That is, the user can transfer digital objects or application windows to the displays on table/wall surfaces. They can use a virtually bigger workspace around the portable computer.

The user manipulates digital objects on the table (or on the wall) using the input devices (such as a track-ball or a keyboard) belonging to the portable computer. Instead of introducing other interaction techniques such as hand-gesture recognition, we prefer to use portable computers because notebook computes already have an integrated set of interaction devices that are enough for most applications. With these interaction devices, users do not have to change user-interface style while dealing with the table or wall. In addition, many recent sub-notebook computers have audio I/O devices, so they can also be used to create voice notes during the task.

If two or more users sit at the same table, the table also becomes a shared workspace among them; the participants can freely interchange information among the participating

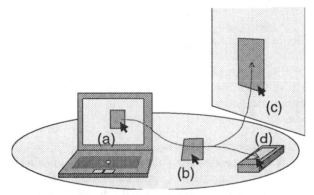

Figure 2: Hyperdragging: A spatially continuous interaction technique for moving information between computers. (a) A user can start moving an object on a computer in the normal manner by dragging it with the pointing device. (b) When the cursor reaches the edge of the screen, it "jumps" to the table surface. (c) The user can continue to drag it to another surface, such as a wall. (d) The user can also drop an item on a physical object, such as a VCR tape, to make a link between real and virtual objects.

portable computers by placing information items on the table/wall.

Support for links between digital information and physical objects

In addition to providing support for portable computers, the system allows users to put non-electronic objects such as VCR tapes or printed documents on the table. By reading an attached visual marker on the object, the system recognizes it and displays digital data that is linked to that object. The user can also add other digital information by simply dragging-and-dropping it onto the object.

Although other systems also support links between physical and digital objects (such as InfoBinder[15], mediaBlocks[18], and Passage[7]), these objects are only for carrying digital data and there are no particular roles in a real world. On the other hand, we are more interested in making a link between digital contents and things *that also have specific roles in the real world*. For example, we can attach editorial instructions

Figure 3: A meeting with InfoTable and InfoWall

to a VCR tape, as a digital voice note. We can also bind physical documents and digital data in a single document folder.

Spatially Continuous Operations

During these operations, we pay special attention to how the physical layout of objects (computers and other real objects) can match the digital manipulations. In other words, the user can use the integrated spatial metaphor for manipulating information in the notebooks, on the table or wall surfaces, and other physical objects placed on the table (Figure 2). For example, when the user wants to transfer data from a notebook computer to the table, he/she can simply drag it from the notebook screen to the table surface across the boundary of the notebooks. At the edge of the notebook screen, the cursor automatically moves from notebook to the table. The user can also attach digital data to the physical object by simply dragging and dropping it onto the physical object.

INFOTABLE and INFOWALL: A PROTOTYPE HYBRID ENVIRONMENT

To explore the proposed workspace model, we developed a computer-augmented environment consisting of a table (called InfoTable) and a wall (called InfoWall) that can display digital data through LCD projectors. Figure 3 shows the system configuration of our environment. In this environment, users can dynamically connect their portable computers to perform collaborative and individual tasks. This section summarizes the user-interface features of the system.

We make some assumptions about the portable computers that can be integrated into the environment. To enable the portable computers to be identified by the pre-installed environmental computers, we attach a small visual marker (printed 2D barcode) to each portable computers and other physical object. Portable computers are also equipped with a wireless network for communicating with other computers.

Hyperdragging

When a user sits at the table and puts his/her portable computer on the table, a video camera mounted above the table finds its attached visual marker and identifies the owner of the computer. At the same time, the location of the computer is also recognized.

When the user wishes to show his/her own data to other participants, he/she can use an interaction technique called hyperdragging (Figure 4). That is, the user presses the mouse cursor on a displayed item and drags it toward the edge of the computer screen. When the cursor reaches the edge of the display, it migrates from the portable computer to the table

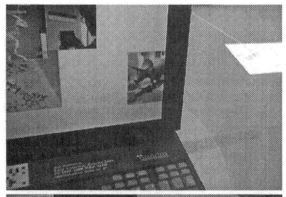

Figure 4: Moving information using "hyperdragging": A user can drag-and-drop a digital object between a notebook PC and a table surface display. During its operation, an "anchored cursor" line connecting the cursor and the notebook appears on the table display.

Figure 5: The anchored cursor shows the link between information on the table and the notebook computer

Figure 6: A recognized object (a VCR tape) with an "object aura": A user can attach a digital item by dropping it onto the object aura.

surface (Figure 4, middle). If the cursor is grabbing an object, the dragged object also migrates from the portable computer to the table surface. By manipulating the cursor, the user can place the object at any location on the table. Furthermore, the user can move the item toward the edge of the table, to cause a hyperdrag between the InfoTable and the nearby InfoWall display (Figure 4, bottom panel).

This hyperdragging technique supports the metaphor of the table being a spatially continuous extended workspace for portable computers. Users can place data items such as text or graphics around the notebook computer, as if they had a virtually bigger computer desktop.

The combination of two different displays -- a high-resolution small display on the portable computer and a low-resolution large display on the table -- represents the user's focal and peripheral information space. While keeping the focal objects on the notebook screen, the user can spread a number of items around the computer. When the user needs one of them, he/she can immediately hyperdrag it back to the notebook screen.

Anchored cursor

While a user is manipulating his/her cursor outside the notebook computer, a line is projected from the portable computer to the cursor position. This visual feedback is called the *anchored cursor*. When multiple users are simultaneously manipulating objects, there are multiple cursors on the table/wall. This visual feedback makes it easy for all participants to distinguish the owner of the cursors. When two or more participants manipulating objects on the table or on the wall, anchored cursors indicate the owner of the cursor in a visual and spatial way.

The anchored cursor is also used to indicate the semantic relationships between different display surfaces. For example, while the user navigates through a large map projected on the

table, a notebook computer continuously displays detailed information related to the current cursor position (Figure 5). The anchored cursor shows the visual connection between them.

Table and wall as shared information surfaces

The InfoTable/InfoWall surfaces can also act as an integrated shared information space among participants. When two or more users sit at the InfoTable, they can freely place data objects on the table from their notebook computers.

Unlike desktop computer's screens, or augmented desk systems [22], there is no absolute notion of the "top" or "bottom" of the screen for table-type computers. Thus the multi-user capability of the InfoTable causes interesting user-interface design issues for determining the above sides. InfoTable uses the recognized spatial position of notebook computers to determine which is the "near" side for each user. For example, when a user brings a diagram from the far side to the near side of the user, the system automatically rotates it so that the user can read it.

Object aura

The system also supports the binding of physical objects and digital data. When an object (such as a VCR tape) with a printed visual marker is placed on the InfoTable, the system recognizes it and an oval-shaped area is displayed at the location of that object. This area, called the "object aura", representing the object's information field (Figure 6). This visual feedback also indicates that the physical object has been correctly recognized by the system.

The object aura represents a data space for the corresponding object. The user can freely attach digital data, by hyperdragging an object from the table surface and dropping it on the object aura. For example, if the user wants to attach a voice memo to the VCR tape, he/she first creates a voice note on his/her notebook computer (using its built-in microphone),

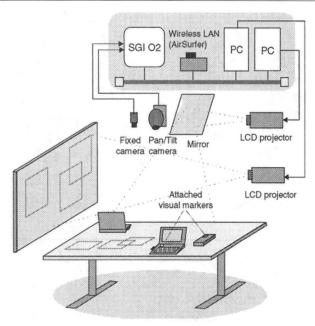

Figure 7: System configuration

and then hyperdrags it from the notebook screen to the VCR tape's aura. When the user releases the mouse button, the voice note is linked to the VCR tape. When someone physically removes the object from the table, the attached data is saved in the network server. This data is re-displayed when the object is placed on any InfoTable.

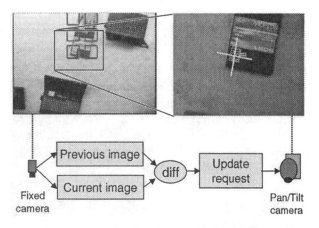

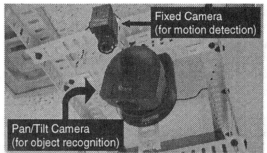

Figure 8: DeskSat uses a combination of two cameras for object recognition

SYSTEM ARCHITECTURE

To enable the interactions described in the previous section, we installed a computer projector and a set of CCD cameras (about 160 cm) above the table. Beside the table, we also installed the combination of a whiteboard and another computer projector as a wall-sized display. Figure 7 shows the device configuration of the system.

Desksat

For the video camera used as an object recognition sensor, there is a tradeoff between camera resolution and the field of view. The camera resolution must be high enough to identify fairly small visual markers that are attached on objects. High-resolution images should also be useful for making a record of the table. However, currently-available video cameras do not cover the entire table surface with the required high resolution. DigitalDesk [22] attempted to solve this problem by adding a second video camera, which is used to capture a fixed sub-part of the desk with higher resolution than the first one. A user is guided to place a document on that focal area.

Our solution is to use a combination of two cameras (Figure 8). The first one is a motor-controlled video camera (Sony EVI-D30) that changes its panning, tilting, and zooming parameters according to commands from the computer. This camera can capture the entire table surface as well as a part of the area with higher resolution (up to 120 dpi) when the camera is zoomed in. Normally, this pan/tilt camera is scanning over the surface of the table by periodically changing the direction and orientation of the camera head. We divided the table surface into a 6-by-6 mesh and the pan/tilt camera is controlled to regularly visit all 36 areas. We called this scheme "Desksat", by analogy to Landsat (land-satellite). In our current setup, it takes about 30 seconds to visit all the areas, including camera control and image processing (marker recognition) times.

The second camera is a fixed camera that is always looking at the entire table surface. This camera analyzes changes on the table from the difference between video images. Then it determines which sub-area has been changed and sends an "area changed" event to the pan/tilt camera. Using this event information, the pan/tilt camera can quickly re-visit the changed area. We choose a threshold value for difference detection so that the fixed camera is not affected by the projected image.

We use a small amount of heuristics to determine the order of visiting these changed areas. Since people normally use the table from the outside, changes in the inner areas are more likely to be object changes. Thus we assign higher priorities to inner areas than to outer areas; when the fixed camera finds several changes simultaneously, the pan/tilt camera checks these areas from inside to outside.

Using these techniques, when a user puts, moves (or removes) objects on the table, this effect will be recognized

Figure 9: Visual marker recognition and obtained position and orientation.

by the system within a few seconds. Although this response time might not be satisfactory for applications that require continuous/realtime object tracking, such as the one in [20], this scheme suits our circumstances quite well where changes occur only intermittently.

Visual marker recognition

Figure 10: The visual marker recognition algorithm: (a) Original image. (b) Binarized image. Connected regions that have the specific second-order moment are selected. These regions become candidates of a guide bar of the marker. (c) Four corners of the marker region are searched based-on the guide bar position/orientation. (d) If the guide bar and the four corners are successfully found, the system finally decodes the bitmap pattern in the marker. Based on the corner positions of the marker, the system estimates and compensates for the distortion effect caused by camera/object tilting. Then the system decodes the code bit pattern. After checking for the error bits, the system determines whether or not the image contains a correct 2D marker.

The printed visual markers (2D matrix code) attached to objects (including portable computers and other non-electronic objects) on the table can identify 2^{24} different objects using the combination of printed matrix patterns (we use a slightly different version of the matrix code system described in [10]). Using the Desksat architecture described above, 2D markers as small as 2cm × 2cm can be recognized from the pan/tilt camera above the table.

In addition to its ID being recognized, the marker's position and orientation are also identified (Figure 9). This information is used to calculate object positions in related to the marker position. For example, the position of the cursor on the table while the user is doing a hyperdrag, is calculated based on the current position/orientation of the marker attached on the portable computer. The marker recognition algorithm is summarized in Figure 10.

Since 2D codes cost virtually nothing and can be printed, there are some uses that could not be achieved by other ID systems. For example, we can use small Post-it notes with a 2D code. This (physical) Post-it can convey digital data such as voice notes or photographs with an attached ID.

Hyperdragging

To enable hyperdragging (when the user moves the cursor of the notebook computer from notebook to the table), the system designates mouse-sensitive areas along all four edges of the notebook screen. When the cursor enters this area, the system re-maps the cursor position to the screen, and calculates the offset of this remapping to maintain the cursor position on the table. While the real (original) cursor stays near the edge of the notebook screen, the user can control the virtual cursor position on the table by continuing to press the pointing device.

To correctly calculate the cursor position on the table, the system also has to know the notebook's position and orientation on the table. The system gets this information from an attached visual marker on the notebook PC. Figure 9 shows how the system finds the PC position/orientation based on the attached marker.

Object migration

As a result of hyperdragging, the system needs to transfer data between two computers (e.g., from a notebook computer to the computer running the table display). All application programs for our environment are written in Java and the system employs Java's object serialization mechanism and the remote method invocation (RMI) method to transfer objects. Currently we support text, sound (voice notes), URLs, file short-cuts, and image data as migratable object classes.

EXPERIENCE AND DISCUSSIONS

Up to the time this paper was written, no formal evaluation had been conducted. However, with this environment, the authors and their colleagues in the laboratory have experimentally tried several collaborative activities including a group meeting.

The concept of hyperdragging was instantly understood by the users and well accepted. Many users were surprised that they could freely move objects between different computers and other physical objects, with a simple drag-and-drop operation. People also appreciated being able to attach data onto the wall surface while sitting at the table. Many wished that they could also move physical objects with the cursor! Anchored cursors were also helpful when two or more users were performing operation simultaneously, especially when the users manipulated object far from their positions. Some users suggested (and we are considering implementing) putting small peripheral devices, such as printers or scanners, on the table and supporting hyperdragging to them. For example, the user could drop an image objet onto the printer for making a hardcopy of it.

Some users felt that moving an object across a larger distance was tiresome. We might be able to incorporate techniques other than dragging, such as described in[2]. We also felt that the mapping scale between pointer movement and the pointing device greatly affects usability. Since the projector resolution on the table (about 20 dpi) is much coarser than the notebook computer's (100-110 dpi), mapping without scaling causes a discontinuous change in cursor speed at the boundary between the notebook and the table.

We also observed that there were interesting differences between hyperdragging and our previous multi-device interaction technique called ''pick-and-drop''[9, 11]. Pick-and-drop uses a digitizer stylus to pick up a displayed object from one screen and drop it on another screen. Pick-and-drop is a more direct and physical metaphor than hyperdragging, because its operation is quite similar to picking up a real object. Hyperdragging allows a user to manipulate objects that are out of the user's physical reach, while pick-and-drop does not. Pick-and-drop requires a stylus-sensitive surface for operation, but hyperdragging works on any display and projected surfaces.

There is also the question of suitability between pointing devices and interaction styles. Apparently pick-and-drop is best suited for a pen, while hyperdragging does not work well with a pen because it forces indirect mapping between the pen position and the cursor position. On the other hand, hyperdragging is more suitable for a track-ball or a trackpoint, and these are common for notebook-sized computers.

RELATED WORK

Research on augmenting face-to-face interactions often assumes pre-installed computer facilities so the configuration of computers is fixed. For example, Colab[17] provides a projector screen and table-mounted computers for participants. There was no support for incorporating other computers that the participants might bring to that environment. However, considering recent trends in mobile computing, it would be more practical to support dynamic connections between mobile and pre-installed computers.

There are several systems that project digital information onto the surface of a physical desk. VIDEODESK[4] consists of a light table and a video camera. The user can interact with the other participant's silhouette projected onto the table. DigitalDesk [21, 22] allows interactions between printed documents and digital information projected on a desk. A recent version of the DigitalDesk series also added a document identification capability based on OCR[13]. Luminous Room[19] (and its underlying "I/O bulb" concept) uses a video projector mounted on a computer-controlled gimbal to change the projection area. Its application called Illuminating Lights[19] helps a holography designer to rapidly layout physical optics devices on the desk. Streitz et al. developed a set of computer augmented elements including a wall, chairs, and a table[7]. Among them, the InteracTable is a table-sized computer supporting discussion by people around it. It also displays information which is carried by a physical block called "Passage". While these systems mainly focus on interaction between non-electronic objects and projected digital information, our system also supports information interchange among portable computers, table/wall surfaces, and physical objects.

The Desksat architecture was partially inspired by the whiteboard scanning system called ZombieBoard[14]. Zombieboard controls a pan/tile camera to capture the mosaic of partial whiteboard images. By joining these images together, a higher resolution image of the entire whiteboard can be produced. The Brightboard [16] is another example of a camera augmented whiteboard system; it recognizes hand-drawn commands made by a marking pen.

As for multi-computer interactions, the Hybrid User Interfaces [1] is an application for a see-through head-mounted display that produces a virtually bigger screen around the screen of the desktop computers. The PDA-ITV system[12] uses a palmtop computer (Apple Newton) as a commander for an interactive TV system. These systems assume a fixed-devices configuration, and are mainly designed for single-user applications.

Ariel [6] and transBOARD[3] support connections between barcode-printed documents or cards and digital contents. Insight Lab[5] is a computer supported meeting room that extensively uses barcoded tags as physical/digital links and commands. These systems normally require a manual ''scan'' of each printed barcode. This may become a burden for users, especially when they have to deal with a number of barcodes. These systems do not recognize the location of each object, so they require other mechanism to achieve spatially continuous operations.

CONCLUSIONS AND FUTURE WORK

We have described our design and implementation of a hybrid work space, where people can freely display, move, or attach digital data among their computers, tables, and walls.

There are a number of features that must be improved. Currently, we only support Java-based applications and users cannot directly interchange information between other applications that are not written in Java (such as PowerPoint) or native desktop environments (such as the Windows desktop).

We are also interested in implementing a smaller version of InfoTable for individual users. In this environment, user can hyperdrag items from their computer to the wall (typically a cubicle partition) in front of them, in the same way that they usually attach a post-it note to it. When the user wants to attach a To-Do item on the schedule, he/she can simply hyperdrag it to the physical calendar on the wall.

ACKNOWLEDGMENTS

We thank Takahashi Totsuka for helpful discussions and we are also indebted to Mario Tokoro for their continuing support of our research.

REFERENCES

1. Steven Feiner and A. Shamash. Hybrid user interfaces: Breeding virtually bigger interfaces for physically smaller computers. In *Proceedings of UIST'91, ACM Symposium on User Interface Software and Technology*, pp. 9-17, November 1991.

2. Jorg Geisler. Shuffle, throw or take it! working efficiently with an interactive wall. In *CHI'98 summary*, February 1998.

3. Hiroshi Ishii and Brygg Ullmer. Tangible Bits: Towards seamless interfaces between people, bits and atoms. In *CHI'97 Proceedings*, pp. 234-241, 1997.

4. Myron W. Krueger. *Artificial Reality II*. Addison-Wesley, 1990.

5. Beth M. Lange, Mark A. Jones, and James L. Meyers. Insight Lab: An immersive team environment linking paper, displays, and data. In *CHI'98 Proceedings*, pp. 550-557, 1998.

6. W.E. Mackay, D.S. Pagani, L. Faber, B. Inwood, P. Launiainen, L. Brenta, and V. Pouzol. Ariel: augmenting paper engineering drawings. In *CHI'95 Conference Companion*, pp. 420-422, 1995.

7. Torsten Holmer Norbert A. Streitz, Jorg Geisler. Roomware for cooperative buildings: Integrated design of architectural spaces and information spaces. In Norbert A. Streitz and Shin'ichi Konomi, editors, *Cooperative Buildings - Integrating Information, Organization, and Architecture*, 1998.

8. Ramesh Raskar, Greg Welch, Matt Cutts, Adam Lake, Lev Stesin, and Henry Fuchs. The office of the future: A unified approach to image-based modeling and spatially immersive displays. In *SIGGRAPH'98 Proceedings*, pp. 179-188, 1998.

9. Jun Rekimoto. Pick-and-Drop: A Direct Manipulation Technique for Multiple Computer Environments. In *Proceedings of UIST'97*, pp. 31-39, October 1997.

10. Jun Rekimoto. Matrix: A realtime object identification and registration method for augmented reality. In *Proc. of Asia Pacific Computer Human Interaction (APCHI '98)*, July 1998.

11. Jun Rekimoto. A multiple-device approach for supporting whiteboard-based interactions. In *Proceedings of CHI'98*, February 1998.

12. Stott Robertson, Cathleen Wharton, Catherine Ashworth, and Marita Franzke. Dual device user interface design: PDAs and interactive television. In *CHI'96 Proceedings*, pp. 79-86, 1996.

13. Peter Robinson, Dan Sheppard, Richard Watts, Robert Harding, and Steve Lay. Animated Paper Documents. In *7th International Conference on Human-Computer Interaction, HCI'97*, 1997.

14. Eric Saund. ZombieBoard project description. http://www.parc.xerox.com/spl/members/saund/zombieboard-public.html.

15. Itiro Siio. InfoBinder: a pointing device for a virtual desktop system. In *6th International Conference on Human-Computer Interaction (HCI International '95)*, pp. 261-264, July 1995.

16. Questin Stafford-Fraser and Peter Robinson. Brightboard: A video-augmented environment. In *CHI'96 proceedings*, pp. 134-141, 1996.

17. M. Stefik, G. Foster, D. Bobrow, K. Khan, S. Lanning, and L. Suchman. Beyond the chalkboard: computer support for collaboration and problem solving in meetings. *Communication of the ACM*, Vol. 30, No. 1, pp. 32-47, 1987.

18. Brygg Ullmer, Hiroshi Ishii, and Dylan Glas. mediaBlocks: Physical containers, transports, and controls for online media. In *SIGGRAPH'98 Proceedings*, pp. 379-386, 1998.

19. John Underkoffler. A view from the Luminous Room. *Personal Technologies*, Vol. 1, No. 2,, June 1997.

20. John Underkoffler and Hiroshi Ishii. Illuminating Light: An optical design tool with a luminous-tangible interface. In *CHI'98 Proceedings*, pp. 542-549, 1998.

21. Pierre Wellner. The DigitalDesk calculator: Tangible manipulation on a desk top display. In *Proceedings of UIST'91, ACM Symposium on User Interface Software and Technology*, pp. 27-34, November 1991.

22. Pierre Wellner. Interacting with paper on the DigitalDesk. *Communication of the ACM*, Vol. 36, No. 7, pp. 87-96, August 1993.

Urp: A Luminous-Tangible Workbench for Urban Planning and Design

John Underkoffler and **Hiroshi Ishii**

MIT Media Laboratory, Tangible Media Group

Cambridge, MA

{jh,ishii}@media.mit.edu

ABSTRACT

We introduce a system for urban planning – called *Urp* – that integrates functions addressing a broad range of the field's concerns into a single, physically based workbench setting. The *I/O Bulb* infrastructure on which the application is based allows physical architectural models placed on an ordinary table surface to cast shadows accurate for arbitrary times of day; to throw reflections off glass facade surfaces; to affect a real-time and visually coincident simulation of pedestrian-level windflow; and so on.

We then use comparisons among *Urp* and several earlier *I/O Bulb* applications as the basis for an understanding of *luminous-tangible interactions*, which result whenever an interface distributes meaning and functionality between physical objects and visual information projectively coupled to those objects. Finally, we briefly discuss two issues common to all such systems, offering them as informal thought-tools for the design and analysis of luminous-tangible interfaces.

Keywords

urban design, urban planning, architectural simulation, luminous-tangible interface, direct manipulation, augmented reality, prototyping tool, interactive projection, tangible bits

SCENARIO

Two urban planners, charged with the design of a new plaza, unroll onto a large table a map showing the portion of the city that will contain their project. They place an architectural model of one of the site's buildings onto the map. Immediately a long shadow appears, registered precisely to the base of the model, and tracks along with it as it is moved. They bring a second building model to the table and position it on the opposite side of a large fountain from the first; it too casts an accurate shadow. "Try early morning," requests one of the planners. Her colleague places a simple clock on the map; a glowing '3pm' appears on the clock's face. The colleague rotates the hour hand around to seven o'clock, and as '3pm' changes to a luminous '7am' the shadows cast by the two models swing around from east to west.

It is now apparent that in the morning the second building is entirely shadowed by the first and will receive no direct sunlight. The urban planners decide to try moving the first building south by eighty yards, and upon doing so can immediately see that this solution restores the second building's view of the sun. The just-moved building is now only

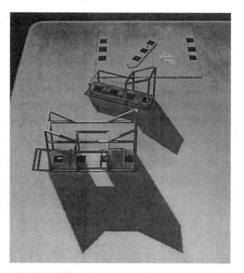

FIGURE 1: URP, SHOWING LATE-AFTERNOON SHADOWS

twenty yards to the north of an east-west highway that borders the plaza on the south; one of the planners places a long road-like strip of plastic on top of the map's representation of the highway, and tiny projected cars begin progressing at various speeds along its four lanes. The other planner brings a wand into contact with the nearby building, and the model's facade, now transformed to glass, throws a bright reflection onto the ground in addition to (but in the opposite direction from) its existing shadow. "We're blinding the oncoming rush-hour traffic for about ninety yards here at 7 AM," he observes. "Can we get away with a little rotation?" They rotate the building by less than five degrees and find that the effect on the sun's reflection is dramatic: it has gone from covering a long stretch of highway to running just parallel to it.

The urban planners position a third building, near and at an angle to the first. They deposit a wind-generating tool on the table, orienting it toward the northeast (the prevalent wind direction for the part of the city in question). Immediately a graphical representation of the wind, flowing from southwest to northeast, is overlaid on the site; the simulation that creates the visual flow takes into account the building structures present, around which airflow is now clearly being diverted. In fact, it seems that the wind velocity between the two adjacent buildings is quite high. The planners verify this with a probe-like tool, at whose tip the instantaneous speed is shown. Indeed, between the buildings the wind speed hovers at roughly twenty miles per hour. They slightly rotate the third building, and can immediately see more of the wind being diverted to its other side; the flow between the two structures subsides.

INTRODUCTION

The scenario above depicts the use of *Urp*, a working application for urban planning. Like *Illuminating Light* (its more primitive predecessor) *Urp* is built atop the *I/O Bulb* infrastructure and employs the *glimpser*-and-*voodoo* vision analysis pipeline [5] to identify and locate its component objects. Both applications also demonstrate *luminous-tangible interaction*, a style in which a participant's relations with the system consist of manipulation of physical objects and the resultant ongoing projection of visual information onto and around these same objects; indeed, *Urp* extends the variety of such interactions, as we will see later.

The paper has two principal parts: in the first, we describe *Urp*. This entails a brief introduction to the collection of concerns in the urban planning domain that motivate the present work, including a review of some traditional means of addressing these concerns; a recapitulation of basic material introduced elsewhere regarding the *I/O Bulb* and *Luminous Room* infrastructures that make the *Urp* application possible; and finally the implementation issues and a function-by-function description of the *Urp* system itself.

The second part begins with short descriptions of several other projects built with *I/O Bulb* technology (some of which have not yet been otherwise published or publicly presented) and uses a comparison among these and *Urp* to suggest two 'Luminous-Tangible Issues', early thought-tools for the design and analysis of systems that subscribe to luminous-tangible interaction styles.

BACKGROUND

The domain of urban planning involves the relationship between architectural structures and existing settings (to harshly distill what is of course a very complex field).

Urban Planning Issues

The work reported here focuses in particular on the arrangement of architectural forms with the goal of fulfilling certain aesthetic goals while at the same time respecting a variety of practical constraints. Among the primary constraints we will consider are the following:

· **shadows:** Does the proposed placement of a tall structure mean that from dawn until 10 AM no direct sunlight will reach an existing building that was formerly able to see the sunrise? Could such a situation be the source of a lawsuit? (Yes, in fact.)

· **proximities:** Is a building too close to a roadway? Is the distance between two adjacent buildings too small to allow adequate pedestrian flow? Is a building too far from an intersection?

· **reflections:** When a building with all-glass sides is erected as proposed, will low-angle sunlight (in early morning or late afternoon) be reflected directly into the eyes of oncoming motorists on a nearby highway? For what distance along the highway will this glare be present?

· **wind:** Does the placement of a building into an existing urban configuration result in a constant 80 km/h airflow over its north face? Does it result in a low-pressure zone on its east side that will make opening doors difficult?

· **visual space:** How will what pedestrians see change with the addition of the new structure? Will the space become visually claustrophobic? Will the new structure introduce a pleasing regularity into the skyline?

Standard Options

A collection of traditional techniques exists for the treatment of these different constraints. Shadow studies are often undertaken by placing a specially-mounted light source above a model of the site in question; the exact position of the source is determined by consulting a table indexed through time of day, season, and latitude. This scheme is somewhat arduous, difficult to adjust, and ultimately not quite correct (the source throws shadows from a finite distance, while the true sun's rays are essentially parallel as they reach our planet). Distances are of course easy to measure by hand. Reflections present further difficulties, however: adapting the shadow-technique (light sources positioned above the models) for reflections requires placing small patches of reflective material the models' various surfaces, but the difficulty of obtaining extreme flatness and full registration of these patches makes accurate results less than likely. Each of these concerns can also of course be addressed solely on paper using drafting techniques that involve tedious constructions and by-hand calculations [7].

Airflow analysis is another proposition altogether. Here, the only viable non-computational approach is to immerse the model or models in a wind tunnel; smoke sources released upstream from the subjects can be used to show overall flow patterns. No matter the level of detail imposed on this kind of setup, however, the actual scale of the phenomenon being tested differs from that of the simulated setting – fluid dynamics is sensitive to scale – so that observations are valid only to a certain extent.

More recently, computational approaches to each of these analyses have become available. There are several CAD-style architectural applications (AllPlan FT, ArchiCAD, 3D Studio Max, AccuRender, etc.) that incorporate on-screen facilities for shadow and reflection studies. Airflow simulation is still a difficult matter; full solutions to the prevailing *Navier-Stokes* equations are always expensive, and no known system allows real-time rearrangement of architectural structures within the ongoing simulated flow field.

IMPLEMENTATION

It was our intent to construct an interactive workbench for urban design and planning that would collect together functions addressing the concerns listed above; the novel aspect of our system would be that its information would all be centered on or attached to actual physical models of the architecture in question. The result of this effort is *Urp*.

I/O Bulb & Luminous Room

The large-scale goal behind the work that has led to *Urp* and its companion systems is the wholesale transformation

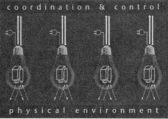

FIGURE 2: I/O BULB (L) AND LUMINOUS ROOM (R) CONCEPTS

of architectural space – to make of each surface an information-display-and-interaction structure. The approach we have been pursuing calls for the conceptual generalization of the familiar lightbulb into the *I/O Bulb*, as follows: if an ordinary incandescent bulb is actually a low-resolution digital projector – specifically, 1x1 pixel(s) – then we increase this resolution, so that the lightbulb is capable of projecting images into the space around it. At the same time we incorporate a tiny video camera that looks out at the world around the bulb. The resulting structure, called an *I/O Bulb*, is capable of simultaneous optical input and output. The work described here makes use of a prototype *I/O Bulb* constructed with commercially available projectors and cameras.

The notion of a *Luminous Room* extrapolates from just one to a collection of many *I/O Bulb*s, computationally interlinked and distributed throughout an interior architectural space. The resulting aggregate of two-way optical nodes addresses every portion of a room, and is thus one way of achieving our original space-transformation goal [6].

Software Components

glimpser & voodoo

Currently, *I/O Bulb* applications like *Urp* that need to identify and locate specific, known objects use an optical tagging scheme in which small colored dots are applied to the surface of each physical implement. A simple, low-level machine vision system called *glimpser* is used to find all colored dots of some specified size within the video input stream supplied to it by the *I/O Bulb*. For each video frame, *glimpser* passes a list of whatever dots it has found to *voodoo*, with which it communicates over the network as a client-server pair. *voodoo* is a software tool whose job it is to recognize among each amorphous collection of dots as many known patterns as possible; these patterns have been defined by the end application that *voodoo* serves (here, *Urp*). Affixing the appropriate pattern of actual colored dots to each object is then all that is required for applications to track it using the *glimpser-voodoo* pipeline [5].

wind simulation

We employ a variety of cellular automaton called a 'lattice gas' [2] to simulate pedestrian-level airflow through *Urp*'s workspace. The lattice gas computation involves a grid of hexagonal cells, each of which can support up to six gas 'particles' – one for each face. The state of each hex-cell is represented at every instant as a modest six bits: if a bit is on it implies the presence of an incoming particle, understood as travelling toward the center of the cell through that bit's corresponding side. At each timestep, every cell is 'reacted' according to a small set of rules that determine whether and how particle collisions occur within a cell; the rules are arranged to preserve momentum. After reaction, the redirected particles from each cell undergo transport to the boundaries of the six surrounding cells, and the cycle then repeats.

We use a 100x100 grid of lattice gas cells to simulate windflow in the workspace. The motions from contiguous 4x4 sub-blocks of cells are averaged to find an aggregate flow: local wind direction and magnitude. Obstacles – i.e. the bases of buildings – are represented by 'filling in' the appropriate cells, disallowing them from containing particles and causing incident particles to bounce directly back from their boundaries. Meanwhile, because such a small grid displays preferential anisotropy along its three major axes, it's not possible to represent arbitrary flow directions

accurately. Instead, the grid is held fixed, with particles injected from the right side flowing leftward, while the world (i.e. building footprints) is rotated opposite the intended wind direction and analyzed into the grid. The resulting simulation is then rotated back once more (so that the airflow is moving in the originally specified direction) and projected down into alignment with *Urp*'s objects.

Functions & Requirements

Shadows

The shadow-casting facility was the first portion of *Urp* to be constructed, and was in fact the original catalyst for thinking about the field of urban planning: we'd asked ourselves "what if little models of buildings could cast adjustable solar shadows?". This function is very simple; any building placed in the working environment continuously casts a shadow, and the sole influence available to the urban planner is a clock, whose instantaneous setting determines the time of day and thus the position of the computational sun (see Fig. 1). If the clock object is removed from the workspace, time is 'locked' at its most recent value.

An early incarnation of the shadow function allowed time to jump instantaneously between different values as the clock – quantized at every-hour-on-the-hour values – was adjusted. The resulting visual discontinuity was somewhat disconcerting, particularly during rapid changes from mid-morning to mid-afternoon: the shadow appeared to flop around in a way that (wrongly) suggested inaccuracy. Particularly when compounded with the inevitable small positional uncertainties that result from (genuine) video-noise-based imprecisions in our machine vision pipeline, this proved fairly confusing. Instead, the current system interpolates from one time value to the next using a cubic spline (the transition lasts about one second). This gives rise to appealing shadow transitions, whose smooth 'swinging' motions strongly recall time-lapse cinematography.

Distance Measurements

An initial test in which every building and road structure constantly displayed its distance from every other left the workspace far too cluttered and visually distracting. Rather,

FIGURE 3: TAKING A DISTANCE MEASUREMENT

Urp now provides a distance-tool (shaped like a pencil but with the image of a ruler stretching between the pencil tip and eraser) that can be used to connect together selected structures. To do this, an urban planner touches the tool's tip to one building, on which one end of a sinuous line is then anchored; pulling the tip-end of the line away and eventually touching a second building or a road then connects the two structures, the line's curves flattening to leave it straight. A display of the line's length floats along and around it, and this number continuously changes as the connected structures are moved. When this display is no longer desired, touching the eraser end of the tool to either connection point disconnects the line.

Reflections

Long, thin *voodoo*-tagged strips represent roads; placing these in the environment engages a traffic simulation, whose automotive components are projected onto the plastic strips. Crossing two strips at any angle automatically generates an intersection with implicit traffic-control signals, so that cars come to a standstill in one direction while cross-traffic flows.

A transparent wand placed onto the table shows a **B** at one end and a **G** at the other. Touching the **G** end of the wand to any building causes its facades to become glass, so that

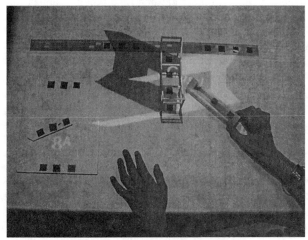

FIGURE 4: A BUILDING BECOMES GLASS

solar reflections are generated and projected onto the ground. It is apparent that reflections are far less intuitive for most people than are shadows – in part because of the angle-doubling that occurs at the bounce surface, and in part because not all of the components of the reflection are necessarily in contact with the object itself: some small 'polygons of light' can be thrown huge distances away from the building that generates them, depending on the angle and orientation of the responsible surface.

Incidence of reflected sunlight onto the various roadways is always immediately evident, and it is easy to experiment with the small angular adjustments that give rise to large changes in these reflected patterns. Finally, touching the **B** end of the wand to a glass building transforms its facades back into brick, and the reflections disappear.

Wind Effects

Urp's airflow simulation is engaged simply by placing the wind-tool – a kind of inverse weather vane – anywhere on the table; orienting the tool selects one of eight quantized directions (the eight major compass points). The simulation is displayed as a regular array of white segments, whose direction and length correspond to the instantaneous direction and magnitude of the wind at that position. In addition, ten red contour lines are shown, generated simply by 'connecting the dots' from location to location according to the local field vectors. These displays take a qualitative form; for more precise measurements, the anemometer-object is available. Placing this arrow-shaped tool within the field samples and numerically displays the flow magnitude at the precise position of the tool's tip. Periodically, these num-

bers break off from the tool and go floating through the field as a further means of depicting larger-scale flow patterns.

Although the airflow simulation is the most computationally expensive part of *Urp*, the entire system remains usably interactive and responsive at a modest eight Hertz – so it's possible to move buildings around the workspace and immediately view the effects on wind flow.

Site Views

The most recently added functionality provides a mechanism for 'previewing' a configuration of buildings from various points of view. Since the model buildings' three-dimensional forms are already resident in the system (necessary for the calculation of shadows), it is a simple matter to render them in perspective and with simple shading parameters. A camera object is provided for this purpose; driving this camera about the workspace results in the updating of a real-time rendering of the current arrangement of buildings in the site, as viewed from pedestrian height and the position and orientation of the camera.

Objects

Irrespective of the range of functions attached to them (investigation of which is the topic of the latter half of this paper), the *forms* of the various physical elements employed in *Urp* rove through a small part of an object-design space. The architectural models, of course, have well-dictated forms: the system is predicated on the idea of attaching variegated graphical information to *pre-existing* models. The road-object, too, must correspond at least in its dimensions to the simulation that will be overlaid on it.

For the remainder of the objects, however, no particular form is necessarily prescribed. Some, like the wind-tool and the distance-measuring-object, attempt to denote their

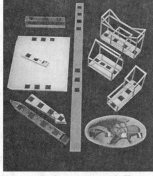

FIGURE 5: WIND   **FIGURE 6: STRUCTURES & TOOLS**

function through suggestive pictorial elements. Others, including the clock-, anemometer-, and material-transformation-objects, are abstract in form and hint only vaguely at their intended use. In short, no specific design methodology has yet emerged or been chosen.

But as we build more and more *I/O Bulb* applications, and as the accessible complexity of each increases, objects will unavoidably multiply. Without yet addressing the problems of this inevitable overpopulation, we acknowledge that the general issue of how object form is related to object meaning is an important one. It may be that a measure of standardization is called for, so that a recognized vocabulary of object appearances imposes some order on design; alternately, the application designer may be free to assemble arbitrary forms, with the understanding that end users of any system are necessarily semi-expert and thus expected to have learned its individual 'language'.

EXPERIENCE & DISCUSSION
Informal Experience

While we have not yet subjected *Urp* to formal user testing (which is planned as part of a future collaboration with architecture students), it is worth noting in the meantime the reactions of the many people who've already been able to experiment with the system: general attitudes toward *Urp*'s new interface style and specific comments about its functionality are already helping us to understand and refine this and other such systems.

Professionals

Close to two dozen architects and urban planners (both practicing and academic) have either watched demonstrations of or directly experimented with *Urp*. Their overall impressions have been uniformly favorable; critically, most of the professional visitors said that they would voluntarily begin using a system like *Urp* immediately if it were available. Academicians affirmed its usefulness for teaching and 'quick turnaround' student prototyping. Practicing architects mentioned that not only would the system aid in their own personal design efforts, but that it could be invaluable for client presentations (in which, at the moment, the activity of viewing physical models and the activity of viewing animations and simulations of light & shadow, windflow, etc. are always separate). Further, several younger professionals stated that such an application would help them to communicate ideas to seasoned, older practitioners within their firm (especially founders!) who have otherwise resisted attempts to 'computerize' aspects of their art.

Many commented that it was unusual and significant to find so many of the field's major concerns addressed by a single application, and all responded excitedly to the use of the architectural models themselves as the system's principal 'interface'. One insider was particularly delighted at seeing wireframe architectural models cast solid shadows, while insisting "and yet it doesn't bother me at all – the shadows are entirely believable".

Others

Perhaps as many as two hundred visitors with no special expertise in the urban planning field have also observed or directly operated *Urp*. The easy and universal familiarity of architecture apparently minimizes the 'domain knowledge hurdle', allowing these nonprofessional experimenters to be strongly (and fearlessly) engaged by the system. Several asked about an expanded functionality that could encompass not just the phenomena of interest to urban planners but also other distinctly nonphysical processes to be simulated and attached to the geometric distribution of structures in *Urp*. Questions arose about economic simulations (what's the effect if the bank or the post office is twice as far away, or is turned wrong-way-round so that the door is on the other side?) and production-flow simulations (can we increase efficiency by building a second warehouse and interposing it between the manufacturing plant and the shipping building?).

Others took a larger conceptual leap, generalizing *Urp*'s capacities to suggest similar treatment of their own domains' problems: "What about a luminous-tangible tool for design of office spaces?", "Could we build a system to interactively simulate ventilation flow patterns throughout a theater?", and so on.

Known Problems

A small shortcoming of our object-mediated interaction style becomes apparent through the use of *Urp*'s site-view camera. Because an object with physical extent (i.e. the camera object) must be employed to designate the desired position and orientation of the view to be rendered, it's simply not possible to get immediately next to an existing structure. That is, if we want to see a rendering of an architectural structure in some proposed location as viewed from, say, the doorway of another building, we'd need to place the camera object closer to the building object than the physical extents of both together will allow. In the real world, of course, this is no problem at all because of the vastly different scales of a building and a camera. Inside our simulation world, however, all objects and tools must be represented at essentially the same scale.

So the same properties of physical objects that are advantageous in some circumstances (e.g. three-dimensional collision detection is computationally expensive, but the impossibility of interpenetrating *Urp*'s architectural models is a convenient constraint that automatically mirrors the desired impossibility in the real situation) can simultaneously be detrimental in other circumstances (our inability to position the *Urp*-camera 'in the doorway' of a building, when that would present no difficulty for a real camera).

The lattice gas used to simulate airflow in *Urp* – while a true Navier-Stokes solution – is admittedly inappropriate in several ways. Most important is that we use a two-dimensional structure to approximate what is ultimately a three-dimensional phenomenon: *Urp* 'air' flows sideways, but can never flow *up*. The scale of the simulation is incorrect as well; with the grid dimensions we are constrained to (in the interests of real-time operation), what is simulated is closer to the micron domain than the meter domain. This scale mismatch then has implications for resulting fluid properties, including viscosity and Reynolds number.

FUTURE

Efforts are already under way to construct two additional *Urp* workspaces for a new design studio in MIT's architecture school, where they are to be used as a teaching tool and for student experiments. We intend to take this opportunity to simultaneously pursue formal user-testing studies.

Based also on comments from professional architects and urban planners, we are considering an expansion of each of *Urp*'s individual functions, by way of bringing the application nearer to 'actual usability'. Many such enhancements are immediately evident: built-in zoning knowledge, so that automatic warnings are generated when proximity or other positional violations occur; additional controls for specifying latitude and season; a light-and-shadow integration tool that will cause the cumulative light incident over a year's time to be calculated and displayed within the workspace, as an aid to landscape architects; and the incorporation of topographic information, so that non-planar sites can be accurately treated.

It will also be important to introduce a facility for projecting 'absent' components into the workspace: buildings that are part of the site but for which no model is available, or whose positions cannot be changed by the planner. These elements would of course still cast shadows and exhibit the various forms of interaction enjoyed by the physically present models.

Such projection-only components may also represent real models manipulated by colleagues at a remote location with whom the urban planner is collaborating. A distributed version of *voodoo* (an important software modification for the *Luminous Room* infrastructure) will allow planners at distributed *Urp* installations to collaborate directly: objects manipulated at each location will be projectively represented at the other. These remote collaboration functions will be incorporated into and tested in the new *Urp* workspaces being constructed for MIT's architecture studios.

OTHER LUMINOUS-TANGIBLE SYSTEMS

We have begun to analyze our observations and experiences in constructing luminous-tangible applications; the issues that seem invariant across these different systems – *Luminous-Tangible Issues*, perhaps – are slowly emerging. We review here several other *I/O-Bulb*-based projects, followed then by a brief introduction to two of these issues.

Context

Illuminating Light

An earlier application constructed with the *I/O Bulb* is *Illuminating Light*, which allows engineers and students to pro-

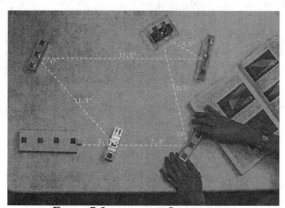

FIGURE 7: ILLUMINATING LIGHT

totype laser-based optical layouts. The system provides an assortment of models representing simple optical elements, including lasers, mirrors, lenses, beamsplitters, recording film, and so on. Each of these objects carefully recapitulates the function of the element of which it's a model, so that a laser placed on the table under the *I/O Bulb* appears to emit a precisely aligned beam; a beamsplitter placed in this beam transmits half and reflects half; and a lens breaks an incident beam into a diverging fan of sub-beams.

Illuminating Light depends, like *Urp*, on the *voodoo*-tagging of its objects with colored dots and on the cooperation of a *glimpser / voodoo* machine vision pipeline. Again, the only 'tools' available in the system are faux optics; and although the display of ancillary qualitative information is automatically projected into the real-world setup, no objects are provided for explicit measurement or 'higher-level' modification of the layout being constructed. In this way the application closely mimics a corresponding real-world optical engineering environment, in which the only access to control of light propagation is through the manip-

ulation of physical optics.

Seep

The first *I/O Bulb* application to be built without the use of *glimpser* and *voodoo* is a simple fluid dynamics workbench called *seep*. The same lattice-gas simulation deployed in *Urp* runs here, but instead of taking as input the position and orientation of structures known in advance (i.e. *Urp*'s various architectural forms), *seep* allows arbitrary objects to be placed in the flow path. The shapes of these objects are extracted from the visual field captured by the *I/O Bulb* using rudimentary frame-differencing techniques; these silhouette shapes then serve as obstacles appropriately positioned within the flow simulation's boundary.

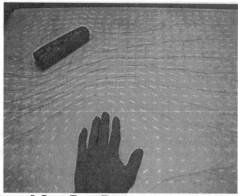

FIGURE 8: SEEP: FLUID FLOW WITH ARBITRARY OBJECTS

The result is a real-time simulation in which fluid appears to flow from right to left across a table surface; any object (non-inanimates like hands are also valid) placed on the table rapidly diverts the flow, which for example exhibits increased field velocities in certain places – as one would expect – in order to maintain the overall right-to-left flux. Moving the obstacle-objects produces beautiful and fluid-dynamically satisfying transient effects, including slipstreams, eddies, sloshing, and all manner of swirls. Although *seep* is in no sense a complete application – there's no facility for extracting quantitative measurements, or for affecting the simulated flow constants, for example – it is a promising new kind of tool for providing intuition for complex physical phenomena and their interaction with real-world objects.

Early Chess & Bottle System

The earliest luminous-tangible application – built with an *I/O Bulb* aimed horizontally to treat an entire wall in a small office – collected together a few 'toy' functions. The

FIGURE 9: WALL CHESS & BOTTLE STORAGE

system recognized a large chessboard that, when brought into the space, would be gradually populated by animated projective chesspieces; the thus-far-unrealized further intent was that physical pieces placed on the board could be identified and located, allowing a half-physical, half-luminous game to be played. Meanwhile (and simultaneously, if desired), a large bottle was able to act as a container for digital information: text, images, and live video could be placed inside the bottle which, irrespective of subsequent movement about the space, could always be made to disgorge these contents. Finally, a colored paddle was available for most of the actual manipulations in the system; it was with this paddle that sample documents could be created, moved, disposed of (in a physical trash can), placed

FIGURE 10: PADDLE CREATES & MANIPULATES DOCUMENT

into or pulled out of the bottle, and so on.

DISCUSSION

Object Meanings

What are the different ways in which a luminous-tangible system can understand or make use of objects? We offer an

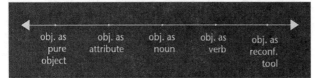

FIGURE 11: CONTINUUM OF OBJECT MEANINGS

analysis space that arrays all possible interpretations along an axis that moves away, in both directions, from a center representing a maximally 'real-world' object reading.

Note that these classifications are intended to apply only to objects considered in the context of a luminous-tangible system – we are not attempting a generic scheme appropriate for arbitrary TUIs (tangible user interfaces) [3]. Moreover, we are not proposing a formal grammar (as does Ullmer in [4]) for the analysis of TUI-based object-to-object interactions; the Object Meanings axis classifies *individual* objects. Finally, it must be understood that we use the words 'noun' and 'verb' merely as a convenient way to suggest certain properties, and not in any attempt to imply a full mapping between luminous-tangible objects and linguistic parts of speech (as is undertaken in [1]).

Object As Noun

These objects occupy the center of the axis and are likely the most obvious in their behavior. They are fully literal, in the sense that they work in their luminous-tangible context very much the way objects 'operate' in the real world – an Object As Noun exists in our applications simply as a representation of itself: an immutable thing, a stand-in for some extant or imaginable part of the real-world. All the objects in the *Illuminating Light* application are of this type – each of the optics models is meant to be understood (in function) as its real-world counterpart. The buildings and roads in *Urp* are also of this variety.

Object As Verb

As we move to the right along the continuum, away from Object As Noun, inherent object meaning is progressively abstracted in favor of further – and more general – functionality. The material-changing wand in *Urp*, for example, is an Object As Verb. It is not understood as 'present' in the

world of *Urp*'s simulation, but exists to act on other components that are, or on the environment as a whole. The clock and wind objects do just this, in affecting ambient conditions like time, solar angle, and wind direction. However, both these tools in fact lie somewhere along the continuum between Object As Noun and Object As Verb, inasmuch as they are each, in part, a metonymic proxy for objects that *do* conceptually occupy the simulation's world – i.e., the sun and the aggregate phenomenon of 'wind'.

Object As Reconfigurable Tool

This variety of object-function is fully abstracted away from 'objecthood', in a way perhaps loosely analogous to a GUI's mouse-plus-pointer. The paddle in the chess-and-bottle system is of this sort, but where a WIMP-style interface typically uses a series of menus to change the function of the mouse, the paddle depends for these meaning-alterations on context and state. Since that single early use of this kind of object, however, we have temporarily avoided its further deployment: to simply transplant some variation on the mouse-and-menu idea into our applications is too easy, and would fly in the face of the basic tenets of building luminous-tangible systems in the first place. We do believe that there exists a proper (non-menu) method for introducing such reconfigurable objects into the world of the *I/O Bulb* – and this solution will soon be required to combat the inevitable proliferation of objects that results from constructing ever more complex applications.

Object As Attribute

As we move to the left away from the center of the axis, an object is stripped of all but one of its properties, and it is this single remaining attribute that is alone considered by the system. The arbitrary objects that act as flow obstacles in the *seep* application are one example: there, nothing matters but the *shape* of what's placed in the workspace; all other attributes of the objects used are ignored. Another system might consider (for some purpose or other) only the color of an object, or the object's size, or its velocity.

Object As Pure Object

This last category is the most extreme, and represents the final step in the process of stripping an object of more and more of its intrinsic meanings. In this case, all that matters to a luminous-tangible system is that the object is knowable as *an object* (as distinct from *nothing*). It may or may not be important that the object be uniquely identifiable; to take an example in which it is, we can imagine extending the digital-storage-in-physical-bottle scenario to a full Luminous Room setting in which information can be stored in arbitrary objects, wherever we may happen to be. Thus, just as we might scribble a phone number on anything nearby – an envelope, a magazine, even a hand – the following scenario would make sense: "Where did you put the directions to the restaurant?" "Oh – they're in the scissors."

The scissors don't matter as scissors; all that's relevant is that they exist and are distinct from other objects that might have been used instead – and that they're where the restaurant directions are.

It is at this far end of the meaning spectrum that we suddenly find that the axis is not linear, but in fact connects to itself, end-to-end: if an object has been shorn of all inherent meaning, then paradoxically it is free to be assigned an arbitrary functionality. So if we move beyond Object As

Pure Object we can find ourselves suddenly back at Object As Reconfigurable Tool.

Straddle-Balance

By definition, every luminous-tangible system locates meaning and functionality simultaneously in two contrasting places: in physical objects, which are directly manipulable by human clients of the application, and in projected digital elements, which are not. It has become apparent that the way in which an application distributes its tasks between corporeal objects and noncorporeal projection – straddling the graspable/corporeal and the digital/projective – has a great deal of bearing on its ultimate behavior and form.

The *Illuminating Light* system, for example, posed little question as to which parts of the application would be projected and which would be physical; in setting out to directly parallel the way in which optics experiments are constructed and carried out in the real world, we automatically obtained an elegant balance: physical models would represent physical optics, and projected *I/O Bulb* light would represent actual laser light. So as the real-world engineering pursuit became a luminous-tangible simulation, noncorporeal remained noncorporeal and manipulable remained manipulable. In a sense, the system very conveniently dictated its own design.

Urp represented a somewhat more complex design circumstance. However, the same pattern of solid-to-solid and nonmaterial-to-projective mappings emerged: light and shadow effects became aligned projective complements to the architectural models, as did the airflow simulation.

It is important to note that the buildings in *Urp*, through their geometric arrangement, carry no less meaning than the more 'exciting' shadows and reflections attached to them – the placement and orientation of structures is, after all, the end goal of urban planning. That is to say: in *Urp* the disposition of physical building models itself contains information; they are not just 'input' but 'output' as well.

A very different kind of meaning distribution is demonstrated by the early 'chess & bottle' system. Here, the scenario's objects carried little specialized meaning: the chessboard was simply an inert stage for the antics of the animated chesspieces, and the bottle – being a container – was essentially unrelated to the digital constructs that it contained. Instead, nearly all the functionality in the system had been concentrated into one physical tool: the color paddle. This single significant instrument was used to create documents, to move them about the space, to associate them with the bottle, to trigger the bottle to absorb them, and so on. To a certain extent, the paddle acted much like the featureless but infinitely assignable mouse of a GUI.

Clearly, applications that have very few projective components and rely mostly on physical objects lean toward 'just being the real world'; while applications that tend to ignore physical objects in favor of complex or standalone graphical components (e.g. the paddle system) encroach on familiar GUI territory. But each extreme can also be appropriate, depending on the needs it addresses and the context in which it's deployed.

Ultimately, we do not yet have a large enough body of telling luminous-tangible applications to formulate general prescriptive rules, but we can state that such straddle-balance issues will remain central to proper luminous tangible design.

CONCLUSION

We have presented *Urp*, an application for working with architectural elements in the context of urban planning and design. This luminous-tangible system attempts to address the primary concerns of this field in a novel way: by using *I/O Bulb* techniques to attach projected forms to physical architectural models, we can provide the urban planner with access to the full efficacy of computational resources in a manner that is comfortable, intuitive, and – ultimately – most appropriate given the spatial and geometric nature of the pursuit.

We have also provided a preliminary examination of luminous-tangible interactions as a general class, identifying two early issues fundamental to every such arrangement. We expect that, as more *I/O Bulb*-based applications add to the set of available examples, the current luminous-tangible issues (joined by others) will mature into a full set of proper *luminous-tangible principles*: appropriate theoretical tools for further design and analysis.

Finally, and as an aside, we are discovering that luminous-tangible interactions, apparently by their very nature, strongly engage nearly everyone. People who've played with one or more of the applications described here evince a delight in that very playing, irrespective of the task at hand. While sheer novelty surely contributes to these reactions, we also believe (for the moment leaving the assertion informal) that the proposition of giving additional meaning and animate life to ordinary inert objects is a cognitively powerful and intriguing one. So: at least as much as do benedictions from professionals in the various applications' fields, visitors' more visceral responses have begun to build a strong case for *I/O-Bulb*-mediated workbench environments, whether physics simulation (*Illuminating Light & seep*), design tool (*Urp* & an as yet unreported filmmaking previsualization tool), or children's construction kit (another to-be-described system).

ACKNOWLEDGEMENTS

We extend heartfelt flying buttresses to Dean William J. Mitchell of MIT's School of Architecture and Planning (high level insight & analysis); Peter Underkoffler & Andy Dahley (model design & construction); Brygg Ullmer (thinking beyond); Dan Chak & Gustavo Santos (future pillars); & Wendy Plesniak (all this & more).

REFERENCES

[1] Fishkin, K., Moran, T., and Harrison, B. Embodied User Interfaces: Towards Invisible User Interfaces, in *Proceedings of EHCI '98*, September 1998.

[2] Frisch, E., Hasslacher, B., and Pomeau, Y. Lattice-Gas Automata for the Navier-Stokes Equation. *Physical Review Letters*, 56, 1505-8

[3] Ishii, H. and Ullmer, B. Tangible Bits: Towards Seamless Interfaces between People, Bits and Atoms, in *Proceedings of CHI '97*: 234-241, March 1997.

[4] Ullmer, B. and Ishii, H. Formal Representations for TUI Primitives: Towards a Theory of Tangible Interfaces, submitted to *CHI '99*

[5] Underkoffler, J. and Ishii, H. Illuminating Light: An Optical Design Tool with a Luminous-Tangible Interface, in *Proceedings of CHI '98*: 542-549, April 1998.

[6] Underkoffler, J. A View From The Luminous Room. *Personal Technologies*, Vol. 1, No. 2, June 1997.

[7] Yee, R. Architectural Drawing. John Wiley & Sons, 1997

PingPongPlus: Design of an Athletic-Tangible Interface for Computer-Supported Cooperative Play

Hiroshi Ishii, Craig Wisneski, Julian Orbanes, Ben Chun, and Joe Paradiso*

Tangible Media Group

*Physics and Media Group

MIT Media Laboratory

20 Ames St., Cambridge, MA 02139, U.S.A.

{ishii, wiz, joules, benchun, joep}@media.mit.edu

ABSTRACT

This paper introduces a novel interface for digitally-augmented cooperative play. We present the concept of the "athletic-tangible interface," a new class of interaction which uses tangible objects and full-body motion in physical spaces with digital augmentation. We detail the implementation of PingPongPlus, a "reactive ping-pong table", which features a novel sound-based ball tracking technology. The game is augmented and transformed with dynamic graphics and sound, determined by the position of impact, and the rhythm and style of play. A variety of different modes of play and initial experiences with PingPongPlus are also described.

Keywords

tangible interface, enhanced reality, augmented reality, interactive surface, athletic interaction, kinesthetic interaction, computer-supported cooperative play.

INTRODUCTION

When an expert plays ping-pong, a well-used paddle becomes *transparent*, and allows a player to concentrate on the task – playing ping-pong. The good fit of grasp is vital to making a paddle transparent [10]. To achieve a "good fit," a user has to choose a paddle of the right size, right form, and right weight for his or her hand and style of play. To achieve a "better fit," the user has to *customize* the tool by scraping the edge of the paddle with a knife and sandpaper. The "best fit" is, however, achieved by using a paddle over a long period of time.

Figure 1 shows the author's paddle and the traces of the body left on it [4]. After twenty years of use, the grip of the paddle has captured the traces of his right hand (marks of the thumb and index finger in front and marks of the middle finger on back). The right-bottom picture shows the dent made on the back of the paddle by a strong grasp with the tip of the middle finger.

The ping-pong paddle, which can co-evolve with a user by changing its physical form and being united with the human hand, suggests an important direction for HCI – transparent physical extensions of our body and mind into both physical and digital worlds.

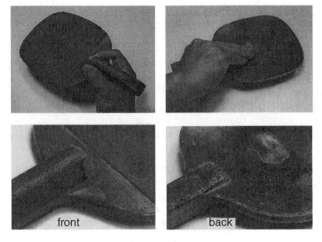

front   back

Figure 1   Traces of grasping hand left on the well-used ping-pong paddle

Moreover, the full-body motion, speed, and rhythm of a ping-pong game make the interaction very engaging and entertaining. Kinesthesia is one of the keys of what makes ping-pong enjoyable.

Modern graphical user interface (GUI) technologies provide very limited, generic physical forms (e.g. mouse, keyboard, and monitor) and allow limited physical motions (only clicking and typing). Thus, the GUI is difficult to adapt to human bodies and to take advantage of kinesthesia.

Goals of the PingPongPlus Project

We have designed PingPongPlus on top of the classic game of ping-pong [21]. Its goals are:

1. to demonstrate an instance of an *athletic-tangible interface,* developed on top of existing skills and protocols of familiar competitive/cooperative play.

2. to develop an underlying technology for an "interactive architectural surface" which can track the activities happening on the surface.

3. to study the impact of digital augmentation on the competitive/cooperative nature of play.

COMPUTER-SUPPORTED COOPERATIVE PLAY

Sport is an activity governed by a set of rules or customs that involves skill and physical exertion. It is often undertaken competitively against opponents, while it is played cooperatively within a team. By playing sports, people can not only learn athletic skills and develop physical strength, but they can also develop social communication and coordination skills.

Computer support is gradually embedding itself in, and transforming the way we play sports and games. Traditional computer games are now extending their reach out from the sole domain of the keyboard, mouse, joystick, and twitch-controllers [8]. Children can create and teach robots, interact with their dolls, and experience complex skiing and motorcycle simulators. With the rise of networks, in the home and in the arcade, play can occur cooperatively more than ever before.

We may give a generic label "CSCP" (Computer-Supported Cooperative Play) to uses of computer technology that enhance physical exertion, social interaction, and entertainment in sport and play. Our research interests in CSCP encompass both the *augmentation* and *transformation* of sports and games. We expect that CSCP research will guide us to design a new form of HCI that we call the "athletic-tangible interface." This refers to a new class of interaction that uses tangible objects and full-body motion in physical spaces with digital augmentation. We believe that a person's physical prowess and sense of kinesthesia can be leveraged to strengthen the quality of a collaborative play experience in physical/digital domain.

Our athletic-tangible interface research looks at augmentation and transformation of *real* sports and games, rather than partial simulations of them. Arcade simulation games, while moving in very promising physically-based directions, can only imitate portions of real experience. Immersive virtual environments, such as VIDEOPLACE [7] and ALIVE [9], allow users to use unencumbered full body motion. Although these systems are engaging, they are designed to provide only a simulated experience and the interaction is limited to simple gesturing.

We see the opportunity to explore the design of new games and play experiences where physical interaction is of central importance. We have begun to explore this by adding digital layers of graphics and sound on top of existing skills and protocols of classic games.

DESIGN OF PINGPONGPLUS

We have chosen ping-pong as a target sport of our athletic-tangible interface research, and have designed a computer-augmented version called "PingPongPlus." PingPongPlus is a digitally enhanced ping-pong game using a "reactive table" that incorporates sensing, sound, and projection technologies. The table displays graphics patterns as a game is played, and the rhythm and style of play drives accompanying sound.

Figure 2 shows a snapshot of PingPongPlus in the water ripples mode, and Figure 3 shows the system architecture of PingPongPlus. In the water ripples mode, a bouncing ball leaves images and the sound of rippling water.

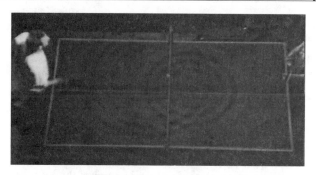

Figure 2   PingPongPlus in water ripples mode

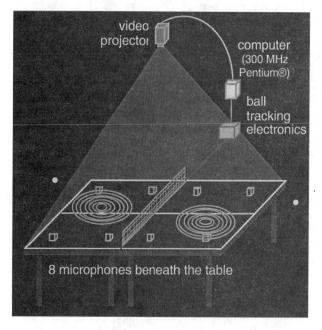

Figure 3   System architecture of PingPongPlus

A series of "tangible interfaces" have been created which give physical form to online digital information [3, 5, 16]. In these projects, users can directly *grasp* and *manipulate* digital information by coupling graspable objects and online digital information. We have also demonstrated the concept of an *interactive surface* that can sense and track the graspable objects on it and project digital shadows [15, 17].

In PingPongPlus, we are extending this notion of tangible interfaces by integrating the kinesthesia of athletic interaction. With PingPongPlus, users experience dynamic and athletic interactions using the full-body in motion, a paddle in hand, a flying ball, and a reactive table. PingPongPlus requires sophisticated realtime coordination among the body, paddle, ball, and digital effects of graphics and sound.

IMPELMENTATION TECHNOLOGY

The PingPongPlus system consists of ball-tracking hardware, software algorithms for ball-hit location detection, and a graphics projection system. The technology behind creating "interactive surfaces" is of utmost importance to this system, and is further described here.

Ball Tracking System

We have developed a sound-based ball tracking system. When a ball hits, the sound travels through the table at roughly twice its speed in air. Eight microphones mounted on the underside of the table pick up the sound. When a microphone detects a hit, a time value is assigned to that microphone, and it is sent to a computer through a custom-made electronic circuit. The time values are evaluated on a 300 MHz PC by an algorithm that determines the location of the hit. The algorithm we have developed can pinpoint the ball's position within a few inches in a matter of milliseconds, which is good enough for our application.

Figure 4 shows a schematic diagram of a ball hit. The four microphones (m1, m2, m3, and m4) on the underside of each table top pick up the ball hit sound at different times (t1, t2, t3, and t4). Given this information, there are a few different algorithms that can determine the original location of a ball hit. We implemented two different methods along with the necessary hardware.

Hardware Implementation

A custom-built hardware circuit connects the ping-pong table to the computer via the serial port (Fig. 5). This circuit only outputs a microphone number (m1, m2, m3, or m4) along with its associated time value (t1, t2, t3, t4). Software running on a host PC does the rest of the work.

The hardware is realized by doing peak thresholding on signals from the microphones. The microphones themselves are electret pickups, which output a voltage around 0.25 volts for a typical hit. First, their signal is passed through an op-amp which increases their gain by a factor of 20, such that there is a signal between 0 and 5 volts, quiescently at 2.5 volts. This signal is sent through two comparators and an or-gate that compare the signal's absolute value (relative to the 2.5 volt center) against a threshold voltage (both high and low). The comparator/or-gate pair returns true to a PIC chip if there is an impact. This PIC chip is running at 20 MHz, and polls its input about 100,000 times a second. If there is a hit, the PIC chip assigns a time value to that microphone input, and sends this information out a serial connection. Fig. 6 shows a photo and a block diagram of the electronic circuit.

Including the microphones, the total cost for this hardware is nominal. A future improvement to this system is to implement peak detection and to match the various incoming waveforms (as opposed to simple thresholding) to more accurately determine the time differences, and perhaps enable us to extract impact characteristics. It is expected that this will produce significant gains in accuracy and reliability.

Software Algorithms for Location Detection

Given the hit timing information from the hardware, the software can calculate a ball-hit coordinate in a number of different ways.

The first algorithm we implemented is by a direct inspection of the time differences. If the ball lands directly

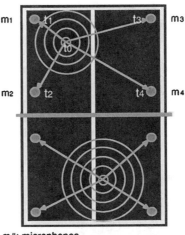

m#: microphones

Figure 4 Ball tracking algorithms

(a) photo of circuit

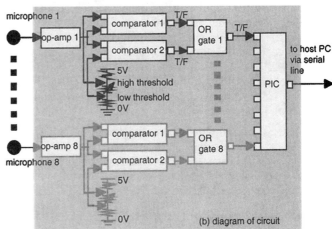

(b) diagram of circuit

Figure 5   Ball tracking electronic circuit

at a midpoint between two microphones, the time differences between the two points will be the same (t1 = t2, for instance), and you can infer that the ball landed on a straight line equidistant from those points. If the ball lands closer to one microphone than another, it can be inferred that the ball landed on a hyperbolic shaped curve between the two points.

The time differences between many microphones can be compared, which results in a system of hyperbolas that intersect at different points. This system of equations can be solved to yield these points. By throwing out intersection points that do not occur on the table, and looking at which points have the largest number of intersecting hyperbolas, a very good approximation of the original hit location can be made. This method is efficient, as no calibration whatsoever is required.

This algorithm, however, has drawbacks. First, it requires solving equations for two variables that go out to infinity. This is computationally expensive. Second, this method is sometimes not accurate. Sometimes there might be multiple intersection points, or possibly, no points at all. In these cases, a best guess must be made based on the data, and the system is fairly prone to error.

While hyperbolic locator algorithms have been further refined in the literature (e.g. [2]), we have developed a much simpler algorithm to calculate the ball hit position that is better suited to this application. This method is based on a comparison of the time-difference data to a set of model parameters that are acquired by a linear least-squares fit of calibration/training data. The model for this method is:

$$AX = Y$$

Where:

Y = the ball landing coordinate vector (x,y)

X = sensor data vector (time differences information)

A = model parameters   (matrix obtained by linear least-squares fit)

When an impact occurs, the sensor values, X, are multiplied by the model parameters, A, which returns a ball landing coordinate, Y. Matrix A, the model parameters, is set through a calibration routine. This calibration routine, however, only needs to be performed once in the life of the table, unless the microphone placement is changed.

Training data is acquired by dropping a ping-pong ball on certain known spots on the table a number of times. In our case, we chose to calibrate the table with 18 distinct points; the A matrix was then calculated through a least-squares fit to this data [14].

Although it involves a linear approximation to hyperbolic relation, this method works well here for a variety of reasons. Since it is a simple matrix multiplication, it is very fast. Also, the linear least-squares fit error metric in the creation of the model parameters makes the system somewhat adaptive to imperfect tables. Performance does not degrade as drastically around edges as compared to the first algorithm (This is important, as most hard surfaces have different kinds of edge effects.). Using this method makes the sensing system more portable to other kinds of tables and surfaces. Although the linear approximation introduces some distortion, it provided accuracy on the order of a few inches, while being fast enough to appear perceptually instant.

At the early stage of this PingPongPlus project, we evaluated the use of computer vision technology for ball tracking, but we concluded that it was slower, more complicated, and computationally more expensive than sound-based tracking technology. Computer-vision, however, is attractive because the system can capture not only the ball but also the motion of players with paddles. Computer vision could be a reasonable and more interesting alternative technology when the computation speed becomes fast enough and the price drops.

Creation and Projection of Graphics

The graphics are created in accordance with the ball tracking information. They are written in Visual C++ with a custom-made graphics package. In the following APPLICATION section, we describe several patterns of graphics we have developed.

A projector suspended 20 ft. above the table displays the graphics on to its surface. We used a Mitsubishi LCD projector LVP-G1A for the experiments, but the brightness of this projector was not enough. To see the graphics on the surface of ping-pong table, we had to darken the room, making it difficult for human eyes to track the ball. We expect the next generation of brighter video projection technology and, potentially, "e-ink" technology [6] to resolve this problem.

In order to make the graphics less "pixelated," we out-focused the video projector slightly so that the image became softer and naturally merged into a wooden table surface.

APPLICATIONS

We have designed and implemented over a dozen different application modes on the PingPongPlus table. The goal of our application design was to explore the design space characterized by the two axes: 1) augmentation vs. transformation, and 2) competition vs. collaboration.

We had two phases of application development.

Phase 1: 1997 Summer-Fall

Artistic and collaborative play modes: water ripples, thunderstorm, spots, painting, comets, etc.

Phase 2: 1998 Spring-Summer

An enhanced artistic mode (school of fish) and a new competitive game mode (Pac-Man®).

PingPongPlus was demonstrated from October 1997 until July 1998 at the MIT Media Lab to the faculty, students, and sponsors. In July 1998, PingPongPlus was exhibited at SIGGRAPH '98 Enhanced Realities in Orlando [20].

Although we have not yet conducted formal experiments to evaluate those applications, informal feedback from casual users was reflected in the iterative design of these applications. In this section, we illustrate and discuss seven examples of those applications.

Water Ripples mode

The *Water Ripple* mode is a simple, causal augmentation. When a ball hits the table, an image of a water ripple flows out from the spot the ball landed (Fig. 2). Players found this to be one of the less distracting applications from the normal game of ping-pong, allowing them to concentrate

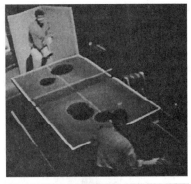

computer
screen
shot

Figure 6   Spots mode

computer
screen
shot

Figure 7   Painting mode

on the game at hand, yet augmenting the game in a non-traditional sense. People often played with curiosity, rather than competitiveness, trying to examine what kinds of interference wave patterns they could create on the table. Once a child even climbed up on the table and created water ripple with his foot. When a player makes an error by hitting a ball into the net, it is usually disappointing. However, in water ripples mode, it turns into an opportunity to enjoy a sequence of small water ripples making a beautiful pattern of interference and sound.

Spots mode

The *Spots* mode was originally intended to be played in a completely dark room where the only light source is the bright white projection on the table. In this mode, a large black spot appears wherever the ball hits, effectively "taking light away" from the other person's side of the table (Fig. 6). The removal of light can be used strategically, changing the strategies employed in a game.

Painting mode

The *Painting* mode was derived from spots mode. The *Painting* mode was designed to explore the collaborative aspects of PingPongPlus. In *Painting* mode, one side of the table is a blank canvas, and the other is a black and white "ink" pallet. When a ball hits the black area of the "ink," it leaves a black spot on the canvas (Fig. 7). Accordingly, when it hits the white "ink," it leaves a white spot on the canvas side of the table. Through collaboration on color choices and placements by expert players, an interactive artwork can be made on the canvas. There is a shift here away from normal ping-pong to a collaborative painting game. The object is not to win a game, but to create an image. This suggests digital augmentation can not only change the nature of the game, but also change the object of the game itself.

In practice, however, the precise control of the ball is too difficult for most users. They could not succeed in painting what they intended. Rather than coordinating the ball movement to create images, they simply enjoy painting visual effects. This motivated us to design the *Comets* mode.

Comets mode

In the *Comets* mode, when a ball hits the table, it "releases a comet" which travels up towards the net (Fig 8). When the comet hits the net, it creates a sound that is mapped to the place on the table from which the comet originated. Experts using this mode could potentially use PingPongPlus to create/play music. We are planning to further explore the integration of playing music and ping-pong by using the speed of play as a metronome that controls the tempo of music being played.

Thunderstorm mode

The *Thunderstorm* mode was designed to encourage collaboration by continuing to rally rather than scoring points. By keeping the ball in play, rallying back and forth, players "build up a thunderstorm." At the beginning of a point, calm, flowing waves appear on the table (Fig. 9 top). As the rally duration increases, a sound of a heartbeat in the background gets faster, wind whips around the sound space, and waves speed up. If the ball is kept in play for a long time, lightning bolts shoot from one side of the table to the other, connecting the ball's last two locations (Fig. 9 bottom).

In this mode, we found that the way people play is changed due to the additional effects of the thunderstorm. When the wind picks up and the heartbeat gets faster, players tend to be more nervous and hit the ball faster and harder. Players try to rally until they see the lightning. The lightning at the end of a long rally encourages players to cooperate.

Pac-Man® mode

In *Pac-Man*® mode, the Namco classic video game is reinterpreted for the PingPongPlus environment (Fig. 10). The ball serves the same functions as Pac-Man® did in the video game; it is controllable by the players and results in the scoring of points, which is the goal of the game. Points are awarded for accuracy in hitting the various fruit targets, and points are taken away for hitting the ghosts.

computer
screen
shot

Figure 8   Comets mode

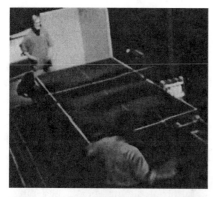

computer
screen
shot

Figure 9   Thunderstorm mode

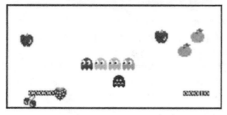

computer
screen
shot

Figure 10 Pac-Man® mode

We designed this *Pac-Man* mode to see if we could transform ping-pong into a very different engaging, competitive game. However, it was found that it was difficult to divide visual attention between tracking a ball and watching the Pac-Man screen on a table. This indicates that highly detailed display elements on the table do not work as well as simple visual patterns. The best results seem to occur when a simple visual pattern is combined with some level of complexity to keep the game interesting. The School of Fish mode is a good example of this concept.

School of Fish mode

The school of fish with water ripples seemed to be the most popular mode for players. In this mode, a school of fish swims on the table (Fig. 11) following a behavior pattern set forth from the algorithms that Craig Reynolds developed for flock behavior [12]. (Top three pictures are the images from a computer screen, and the bottom picture is a picture from the installation.) The ball causes a splash and a ripple in the "water" where it hits, scaring the fish. In time, the fish, following their individual behavior models, school back together. The simplicity of the visual display, combined with the complexity of the emergent activity from a behavior model made this mode continually compelling, even after days of play.

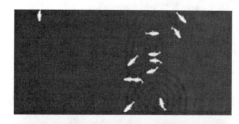

computer
screen
shots

Figure 11   School of fish and water ripples mode

DISCUSSION AND FUTURE WORK

Through the PingPongPlus project, we intended to explore a design space that can be characterized by two axes: augmentation vs. transformation, and competition vs. collaboration. Figure 13 illustrates the seven applications plotted in this 2D design space based on our intention and experiences.

Originally ping-pong is a competitive game, and modes such as water ripples and spots did not change the basic nature of ping-pong play very much; it was still primarily a competitive game.

In contrast, *Comets*, *Painting* and *Thunderstorm* modes added new collaborative goals. For example, *Thunderstorm* and *Comets* encouraged players to keep playing to see the lightning effects or to hear the music of the comets. The *Painting* mode was intended to encourage coordination to paint on a "canvas" table.

Pac-Man® was intended to test the transformation of the game into another competitive game. Originally, we expected that the experienced players could place the ball accurately to score points. This assumption proved to be false, showing that careful design is needed in "target" games.

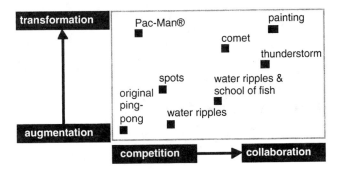

Figure 13   Design Space of PingPongPlus Applications

School of Fish mode was most successful in keeping the attention of both players, and those watching around the table. Even when no one was playing, people enjoyed watching fish swim in a virtual pond.

Although we have focused on the *transformation* of interaction in this paper, we see promising applications in the augmentation of players' performance. We plan to design a ping-pong expert training system using PingPongPlus.

Besides new modes tailored for the PingPongPlus table, there exist a number of extensions that can be made in the realm of *interactive surfaces*. Interactive surfaces absorb information from the physical world, move it into a digital world, process it, and then radiate the results back to a physical world. This is one of the key concepts of the Tangible Bits vision [5]. We plan to use the PingPongPlus sensing system in conjunction with various new wireless sensor technologies to extend the application domain of interactive surfaces.

RELATED WORK

Research in Augmented Reality [1, 19] and Ubiquitous Computing [18] stimulated this work. VIDEOPLACE [7], ALIVE [9], and many other computer-vision based interactive systems have been developed that allow people to use human body motion as a means of interacting with the digital world using vision tracking techniques.

There are also a variety of *virtual reality* (VR) systems [7, 13] which enable people to interact with computational 3D space using a HMD (head-mounted display) and a data glove. AR² Hockey (Augmented Reality AiR Hockey) [11] is a good example of a *mixed-reality* (MR) system for digitally augmented competitive multi-user games. The players of AR² Hockey use physical mallets to hit a virtual puck with a see-through head-mounted display.

CONCLUSION

We have presented the concept of the athletic-tangible interface through the example of PingPongPlus, an augmented ping-pong table. We developed new sound-based ball tracking technology that is robust and inexpensive. Through experiments with various application modes, we explored the design space of interactions with special focus on two axes: augmentation vs. transformation and competition vs. collaboration.

Figure 12   PingPongPlus in use
(SIGGRAPH '98, Enhanced Reality)

We expect PingPongPlus to suggest new directions to integrate athletic recreation and social interaction with engaging digital enhancements. By the augmentation and transformation of physical games, new, engaging interactions can be developed in the physical/digital world.

ACKNOWLEDGMENTS

We thank the members of Tangible Media Group and our colleagues in the Digital Life and Things That Think Consortia at the MIT Media Laboratory for their support and collaboration. Thanks are also due to Rich Gold at Xerox PARC and Michael Naimark at Interval Research for their valuable comments on an early prototype of PingPongPlus.

REFERENCES

1. Azuma, R., A Survey of Augmented Reality, Presence, Vol. 6, No. 4, August 1997, pp. 355-385.

2. Chan, Y.T., A Simple and Efficient Estimator for Hyperbolic Location, IEEE Transactions on Signal Processing, Vol. 42, No. 8, August 1994, pp. 1905-1915.

3. Gorbet, M., Orth, M. and Ishii, H., Triangles: Tangible Interface for Manipulation and Exploration of Digital Information Topography, in *Proceedings of Conference on Human Factors in Computing Systems (CHI '98)*, (Los Angeles, April 1998), ACM Press, pp. 49-56.

4. Ishii, H. "The Last Farewell": Traces of Physical Presence. interactions 5, 4 (July + August 1998), ACM, pp. 55-56.

5. Ishii, H. and Ullmer, B., Tangible Bits: Towards Seamless Interfaces between People, Bits and Atoms, in Proceedings of Conference on Human Factors in Computing Systems (CHI '97), (Atlanta, March 1997), ACM Press, pp. 234-241.

6. Jacobson, J., et al., The Last Book. IBM Systems Journal, Vol. 36, No. 3, 1997, pp. 457-463.

7. Krueger, M., Artificial Reality II, Addison-Wesley, 1990.

8. Levy, Steven., Hackers: Heroes of the Computer Revolution, Delta Books; February 1994.

9. Maes, P., Darrell, T., Blumberg, B., and Pentland, A., The ALIVE System: Wireless, Full-Body Interaction with Autonomous Agents, *ACM Multimedia Systems*, Special Issue on Multimedia and Multisensory Virtual Worlds, ACM Press, Spring 1996.

10. MacKenzie, C. and Iberall, T., The Grasping Hand, North-Holland, 1994.

11. Ohshima,T., Satoh, K., Yamamoto, H., and Tamura, H., AR^2 Hockey, in Conference Abstracts and Applicatinos, SIGGRAPH '98, ACM, July 1998, pp. 110.

12. Reynolds, C. Flocks, Herds, and Schools: A Distributed Behavior Model, in Proceedings of SIGGRAPH '87, ACM Press, pp. 25-34.

13. Rheingold, H., Virtual Reality, Summit Books, 1988.

14. Strang, G., Introduction to Applied Mathematics, Wellesley-Cambridge Press, 1986

15. Ullmer, B. and Ishii, H., The metaDESK: Models and Prototypes for Tangible User Interfaces, in Proceedings of Symposium on User Interface Software and Technology (UIST '97), (Banff, Alberta, Canada, October, 1997), ACM Press, pp. 223-232.

16. Ullmer, B., Ishii, H. and Glas, D., mediaBlocks: Physical Containers,Transports, and Controls for Online Media, in *Proceedings of SIGGRAPH '98*, (Orlando, Florida USA, July 1998), ACM Press, pp. 379-386.

17. Underkoffler, J. and Ishii, H., Illuminating Light: An Optical Design Tool with a Luminous-Tangible Interface, in Proceedings of Conference on Human Factors in Computing Systems (CHI '98), (Los Angeles, April 1998), ACM Press, pp. 542-549.

18. Weiser, M. The Computer for the 21st Century. Scientific American, 1991, 265 (3), pp. 94-104.

19. Wellner, P., Mackay, W., and Gold, R. Computer Augmented Environments: Back to the Real World. *Commun. ACM*, Vol. 36, No. 7, July 1993

20. Wisneski, C., Orbanes, J. and Ishii, H., PingPongPlus, in Conference Abstracts and Applications, SIGGRAPH '98, ACM, July 1998, pp. 111.

21. Wisneski, C., Orbanes, J. and Ishii, H., PingPongPlus: Augmentation and Transformation of Athletic Interpersonal Interaction (short paper), in Summary of Conference on Human Factors in Computing Systems (CHI '98), (Los Angeles, April 1998), ACM Press, pp. 327-328.

Eye Tracking the Visual Search of Click-Down Menus

Michael D. Byrne, John R. Anderson, Scott Douglass, Michael Matessa
Psychology Department
Carnegie Mellon University
Pittsburgh, PA 15213
byrne@acm.org, ja+@cmu.edu, sd3n+@cmu.edu, mm4b+@cmu.edu

ABSTRACT

Click-down (or pull-down) menus have long been a key component of graphical user interfaces, yet we know surprisingly little about how users actually interact with such menus. Nilsen's [8] study on menu selection has led to the development of a number of models of how users perform the task [6, 2]. However, the validity of these models has not been empirically assessed with respect to eye movements (though [1] presents some interesting data that bear on these models). The present study is an attempt to provide data that can help refine our understanding of how users interact with such menus.

Keywords

Menu selection, eye tracking, visual search, cognitive models

INTRODUCTION

Menus of one form or another have been a central feature of the user interface for some time (see [9] for a review). Mouse-based pull-down (requiring that the mouse button be held down) and click-down (which stay open once clicked until another click occurs) menus are more recent advances that have become ubiquitous in the modern graphical user interface. Recently, there has been increased effort devoted to understanding how users interact with click-down or pull-down menus. This research has included computational cognitive modeling [6, 2] and eye tracking research [1, 4]. Detailed approaches have the potential to provide understand interaction with menus at a fine grain.

Nilsen [8, Experiment 2] performed an experiment which provided detailed enough data to constrain computational cognitive modeling. In this experiment, users were presented with a single digit on the screen and a menu button. They clicked the button, and then searched for that digit in a menu of randomly-ordered digits that appeared as a result of the button click. Nilsen's data (shown in Figure 1) shows that users' response time is an approximately

linear function of serial position in the menu, with each successive position being approximately 100 ms slower than the last. The exception is serial position 1, or the first menu position. Time for this position is slightly higher than response time for position 2.

The data suggest that Fitts' Law (see [5], chapter 2, Welford form), while an excellent predictor of mouse movement time, is not a good characterization of the menu search process. Users took much longer and had steeper slope as a function of target position than would be predicted by Fitts' law. Thus, it was argued by Nilsen and others that the bulk of the users time spend on this task is time for visual search.

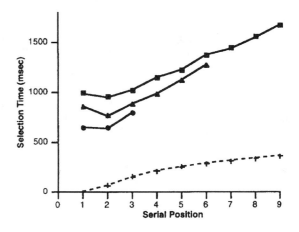

Figure 1. Nilsen's results: Response time as a function of menu size and target position. Lower dotted line is Fitts' Law predicted time[1]

Computational cognitive models that reproduce these results have been produced in both ACT-R [2] and EPIC [6], which are production-system theories that can be used to predict latency, accuracy, and ease of learning for a wide variety of HCI-related tasks. These models are similar in that they both produce response times that approximate the observed data. However, the models differ in the details of eye movement and mouse movement.

---

[1] Serial position 1 required a one-pixel mouse movement, so the Fitts' Law time is very close to zero.

The EPIC model[2] predicts the following:

1) Eye movement patterns should conform to a pattern that consists of 50% sequential top-to-bottom searching, and 50% randomly-ordered searching;

2) In cases of serial top-to-bottom search, the users' eyes should move down the menu a constant distance in each saccade, which is exhaustive in that every item of the menu from item 1 to the target item is examined;

3) The eye should "overshoot" the target item by one saccade with some regularity, since users are examining multiple items in parallel; and

4) No mouse movement occurs until the target has been located.

In contrast, the ACT-R model predicts:

1) Eye movements should be exclusively top-to-bottom;

2) The distance moved on each saccade should vary from trial to trial and menu to menu—items which do not share features with the target will be skipped over and thus the not every item is searched;

3) The eye never overshoots the target item; and

4) Mouse movements trail the saccades in a regular fashion but occur before the target has been located.

So, while these models cannot be differentiated by response time data, it should be possible to assess the validity of each model through careful eye and mouse tracking. While [1] attempted to shed more light on the validity of the EPIC model through an eye-tracking study, their experiment had several problems with respect to distinguishing among the current models. Their menus consisted of non-random arrangements of words where the exact target was sometimes unknown to participants, thus introducing reading, comprehension, memory for location, and the like. While this study is perhaps in some sense more ecologically valid, it is not a good evaluation of either the EPIC or ACT-R models and does not clearly relate to the Nilsen data.

EXPERIMENT
Procedures

The tasks used was essentially the same as the one used in the Nilsen experiment and a subsequent follow-up experiment [2]. Users were first shown a screen containing a rectangle with the word "Target:" followed by a target character. When the user clicked on this rectangle, a menu of characters appeared (see Figure 2). Users then searched

---

2 [6] presents several models. "The EPIC model" referred to here is the final model presented, the "Parallel Processing Dual Strategy Varying Distance Hybrid Model."

for the target item in the menu and clicked on it. Visual point-of-regard (POR) and mouse position were tracked throughout the entire trial, and response time and accuracy were recorded for each trial..

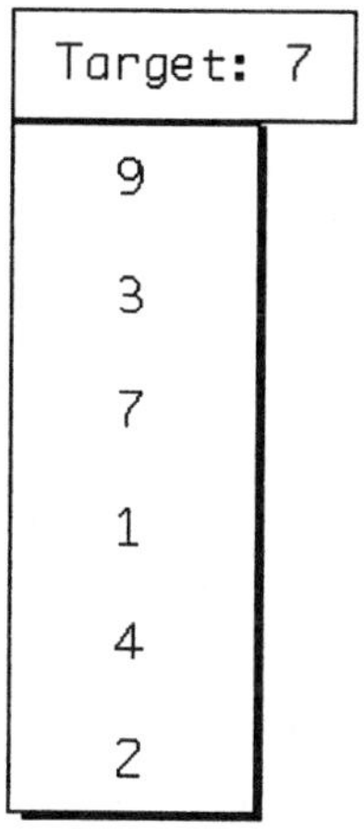

Figure 2. Example menu used

Participants

11 undergraduate participants were paid for their participation in the study. They were paid a base amount for simple participation and additional "bonus" money which was determined by their performance. All participants had normal uncorrected vision and were familiar with the use of computer menus.

Design

There were two primary within-subjects factors in the experimental design: menu length and target location. Three menu lengths were used: 6, 9, and 12 items. We decided to use longer menus than those used in the original Nilsen experiment because pilot data showed a general lack of interesting eye movements for 3-item menus. All target locations were used for each menu length.

The were other within-subjects factors in the design as well: target type and distractor type. Targets could be either letters or digits, as could non-target distractors. Thus, there were a total of 108 trials in the experiment: 6 6-item menu trials (one for each target location) + 9 9-item menu trials + 12 12-item menu trials X 2 target types X 2 distractor types. The 108 trials were randomly ordered by the experimental software. Participants also received 36 practice trials with randomly-chosen values on all factors. There was also a between-subjects manipulation. In one condition, the "Target" field remained on the screen when the menu appeared (as in Figure 2) and in the other, the "Target" button disappeared when it was clicked. The effects of the target type, distractor type, and presence of the target button are beyond the scope of the current presentation and will not be considered further.

Apparatus/Materials

The eye tracker used was an ISCAN RK726/RK520 HighRes Pupil/CR tracker with a Polhemus FASTRACK head tracker. Head-mounted optics and a sampling rate of 120 Hz were used in this experiment. This system, like most other laboratory eye trackers, works by shining an infrared light on the eye and taking a video image of the eye. From that image, it is possible to determine the pupil center and the point on the cornea closest to the camera (the corneal reflection) and take the vector between them. This vector changes as the eye orients to different positions on the screen and with calibration to known points, it is possible to compute visual POR. The magnetic polhemus is used to compensate for head movements. POR reports by the eye-tracking equipment are typically accurate to within one degree of visual angle.

POR and mouse position were recorded approximately every 8 ms by the experimental software. Stimulus and POR/mouse data for each trial were recorded so that all individual trials could be "replayed" at various speeds. An experimenter monitored each experimental trial and recalibrated the eye tracker if there appeared to be sizable disparity between reasonable expectations about where users would look (in particular, users needed to look at the target on each trial) and the position reported by the tracker.

Users were seated approximately 30 inches from a 72 ppi computer display. Characters were 13 pixels high (approximately 0.34° of visual angle) with 26 pixels (approximately 0.69° of visual angle) separating characters. Thus, simultaneously foveating three characters would require a fovea of approximately 2.4° visual angle in diameter. (EPIC assumes that the fovea covers 2° of visual angle and characters must be foveated to be recognized.)

RESULTS

Analysis Technique

Sampling at 120 Hz, despite short trials, generates a great deal of raw data over 108 trials. However, from this raw data it is possible to compute where and when fixations have occurred. This can be done either by assuming that any eye position within a given region for more than some threshold number of milliseconds is a fixation (dwell-based) or assuming that any period of time showing relatively low velocity is a fixation (velocity-based). For the current data set, both methods were initially used and both methods yield approximately the same result. Because the velocity based method yields slightly less noisy data, the results presented here are based on that method of post processing. For each trial, the location of each fixation (with location 1 being the top item in the menu) was recorded. Mouse data were treated similarly; that is, post-processing analysis was used to identify the number and location of mouse "fixations" for each trial.

Response Time

Results for response time are presented in Figure 3. Clearly, response time is a function of target location, with higher locations generating longer response time. This is consistent with the Nilsen data. However, other aspects of Nilsen's data set were not reproduced as clearly. First, the slope of the function for the two larger menu sizes is somewhat shallower, around 75 ms (as opposed to 103 observed by Nilsen) and is even shallower for 6-item menus. Further, there appears to be very little main effect of menu size (controlling for position), as opposed to what Nilsen found. This may be a function of the larger spacing between items used here, which was necessary to make it possible to discriminate fixations on adjacent items. A second distinct possibility is that this is a practice effect; Nilsen's subjects had many more trials (1440) than our participants. Error rates were negligible in all conditions and will not be discussed.

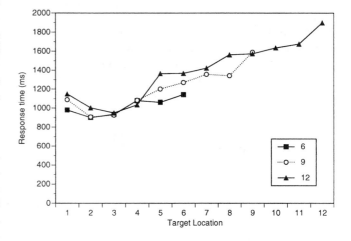

Figure 3. Response time by menu size and target location

Eye fixations

Random search models predict that the number of fixations should not be a function of target position (half of the time for EPIC). Ordered and exhaustive models (the other half of EPIC's trials) predict a strictly-increasing step function in the number of fixations required—for example, if the search takes in three items per fixation, targets locations 1-3 should require 1 fixation, targets at locations 4-6 two fixations, and so on. Ordered selective models (ACT-R) also predict a shallow and graded increase in the number of fixations with target location. Results are presented in Figure 4.

For six-item menus, the number of fixations is relatively insensitive to target location. For both the longer menus, the best-fitting regressions have an intercept of approximately 2.5 fixations and a slope of just under 0.2 fixations per serial position—thus, there is evidence that locations further down the menu do indeed require somewhat more fixations.

This is consistent with both the EPIC mixed top-down/random model and ACT-R's top-down feature search, which is encouraging for both models.

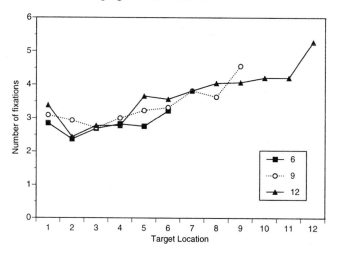

Figure 4. Number of fixations vs. target location by menu size

However, there is considerably more to the story than the raw number of fixations—in particular, the locations of those fixations is quite revealing. If the EPIC model is correct, then on 50% of the trials, every menu item has an equal probability of being foveated in the initial fixation, with the remaining 50% of the trials fixating somewhere in the first two (or perhaps three) items. Thus, the initial fixation would be to one of items 4, 5, or 6 approximately 25% of the time. (Fully random would predict 16.7% for each item; half random predicts 8.3% per item, summed across three items.) It would similarly predict the initial fixation be to items 4 or higher 33% of the time in a 9-item menu and 38% of the time in a 12-item menu. Figure 5 shows that this is clearly not the case.

Users clearly have a non-random preference for the first three menu items with their initial fixation, and a particularly strong preference for the first item. Clearly, the total number of initial fixations on items 4 and higher in the menus is less than what the EPIC model predicts. This is also inconsistent with the ACT-R model, which predicts that users will fixate on the first item in the menu which has a feature in common with the target item. While it is likely that a character in the first three items meets this criterion, the ACT-R model under-predicts the preference shown for the initial item.

Examining only the initial fixation does not, however, provide a complete characterization of the overall search process. Another way of looking at the fixation data is to consider the number of times each location on the menu is visited, on average, as a function of the serial position and the location of the target. These data are presented for 9-item menus only (due to space considerations—the patterns

for 6- and 12-item menus are quite similar) in Figure 6.

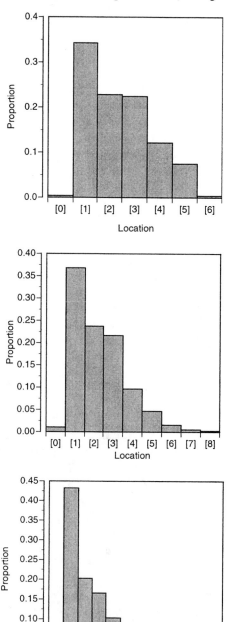

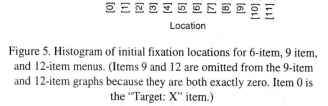

Figure 5. Histogram of initial fixation locations for 6-item, 9 item, and 12-item menus. (Items 9 and 12 are omitted from the 9-item and 12-item graphs because they are both exactly zero. Item 0 is the "Target: X" item.)

These data are especially revealing with respect to the status of random search. A random search would, for example, in a 9-item menu, still occasionally visit items 7-9 of the menu when the target appeared in items 1-3. However, the

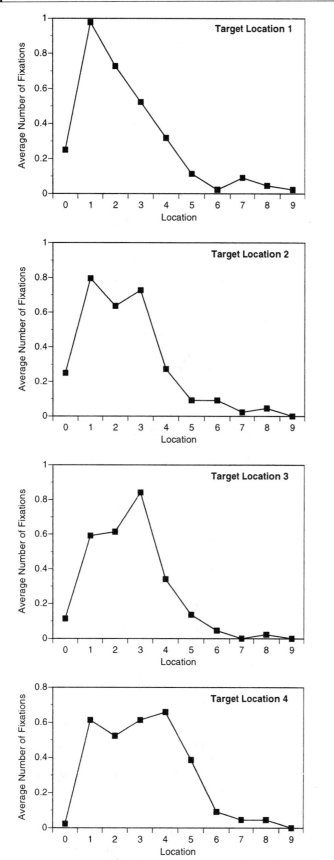

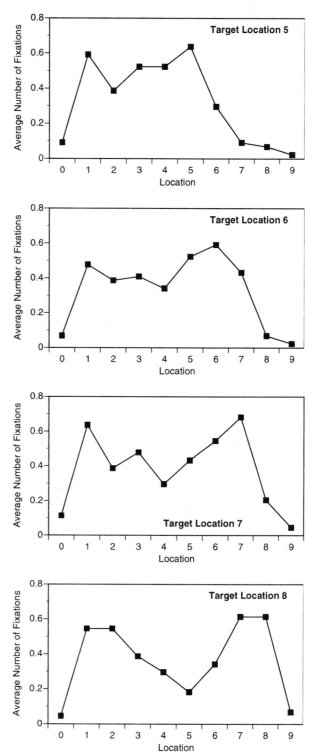

Figure 6 (continued on following page). Fixation frequency as a function of serial position for targets at location 1 through 9. Item 0 is the "Target: X" item.

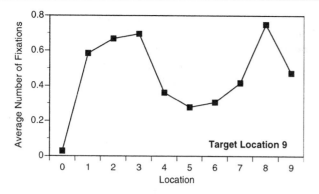

average number of fixations for positions 7-9 when the target is in the upper third of the menu is effectively zero. Even when the target is in the second third of the menu (items 4-6), the number of fixations on locations 8 and 9 is quite small—much smaller than a random search model would predict. Even if a random search model were modified to systematically begin a search with an item in the 1-3 range (as seems the users' pattern), later fixations should still be seen with some regularity on the lower items in the menu—but this is not what appeared in our data.

Instead, the modal fixation location moves systematically down the menu as the target moves down the menu, suggesting a search that is predominantly top-to-bottom. These data further suggest that the search is non-exhaustive; that is, not all menu items with location less than the target item receive full consideration. Since it is unlikely that users can foveate three items at a time, a systematic and exhaustive search of the menu should average 1/2 of a fixation on each item all the way to the bottom (if necessary). However, for targets at the bottom of the menu (items 8 and 9), the middle menu items average less than half a fixation. That is, there is evidence that users skip intermediate items on their way to the bottom of the menu. This is consistent with the ACT-R model but not with the EPIC model.

On the other hand, the data are not wholly consistent with the ACT-R model, either. The ACT-R model predicts that if the item is in position N, none of the items with position greater than N will be examined—that is, search is entirely top-to-bottom with no extra search below the target item. This, too, is clearly not the case. Figure 5 shows that users frequently begin with their first fixation below the initial menu item, which should not happen if the ACT-R model is correct. Further, the first few panels of Figure 6 show that users average well over one fixation in the later part of the menu even when the target is in the first two menu locations, meaning there is at least some search past the target. This is inconsistent with the ACT-R model of menu search.

Interestingly, there is considerable variability both between users and from trial to trial in the each user. There are trials that certainly appear to be top-to-bottom exhaustive searches, trials that appear more or less random (especially for 6-item menus), and trials that appear to be top-to-bottom searches that skip items. However, neither of these models appears to be a good characterization of either the mean or modal behavior of the users.

Mouse Movement

Both the EPIC model and the ACT-R model make predictions about mouse movements as well as eye movements. The EPIC model predicts that there should be a single aimed mouse movement from the initial position to the target item once that target item has been located. Timing of this movement should be governed by Fitts' law. The ACT-R model, on the other hand, predicts that the mouse should "trail" the eyes such that once the target item is located, there should be an approximately constant and short distance between the current mouse location and the target. This predicts multiple mouse movements, directly related to the number of eye movements.

Once again, the data appear inconsistent with both models. Figure 7 depicts the number of mouse "fixations" (as defined by the velocity-based post processing algorithm described earlier) vs. the target location for the three menu sizes used.

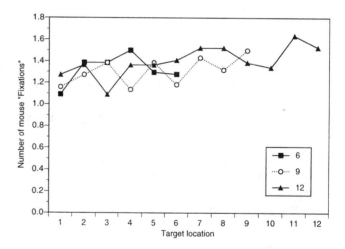

Figure 7. Average number of mouse fixations as a function of target location, by menu length

The EPIC model predicts that this should be a flat function at 1.0. The ACT-R model predicts this should be a monotonically increasing function that should approximate the eye movement data (Figure 4). Instead, the data show that, while users seem to average more than one mouse fixation, they average considerably fewer fixations than they do eye movements. There seems to be a very slight upward trend in the number of mouse movements as the target appears in later menu positions, but this effect appears quite small (approximately 0.03 additional mouse fixations per serial position).

Further information about users' strategies in terms of moving the mouse can be found in Figure 8, which shows the average location of the initial mouse fixation. The EPIC model predicts that users make one fixation on the target item and thus a slope of 1 throughout the full range of serial positions. The average initial mouse position increases linearly with target position until the last few target positions where it tends to flatten off. The slope for the linear portion is approximately 0.65, implying that the initial mouse fixation is often short of the target.

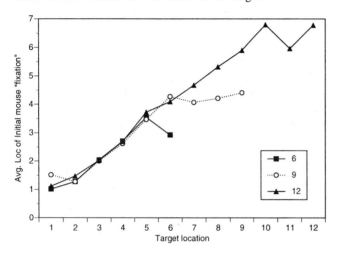

Figure 8. Average location of the initial mouse fixation as a function of target location, my menu size

The ACT-R model predicts that the initial mouse fixation should be relatively insensitive to the target location, particularly for late targets in longer menus. So neither model is consistent with these data. [3]

As with eye movements, both mouse movement strategies (wait until the target is found and trail the eyes with the mouse) quite clearly appear in the data on some trials for some users. The actual data appears to be some mixture of these two (and possibly other) strategies.

DISCUSSION

Despite the fact that both the EPIC and ACT-R models provide good fits to the Nilsen latency data, a finer-grained

---

[3] A secondary issue with respect to mouse movements is the detection of sub-movements, as Fitts' movements have been shown to consist of several sub-movements [e.g. 10]. In order to avoid this problem, the velocity threshold was set conservatively high—high enough that the terminal stop on the target item was occasionally not detected. Thus, we are confident these results are not a function of detection of sub-movements.

analysis at the level of eye and mouse movements reveals that neither of the models accurately characterize the visual search and mouse movement strategies employed by real users. What would more accurately characterize the search? These properties seem to be key:

• The initial eye fixation is modally to the initial menu item and almost always to one of the first three items.

• Search is primarily, though not exclusively, top-to bottom. Search rarely appears to be random.

• Some items are not foveated at all, that is, that they are "skipped" by the top-to-bottom search.

• Though the evidence is not conclusive, examining the individual protocols indicates that most violations of top-to-bottom search come from the target item being skipped by the top-to-bottom search and found by backtracking. Users also occasionally move their eyes down the menu without passing the target, backtrack, and then proceed back down.

One plausible model is a "noisy" top-to-bottom search that sometimes skips items and backtracks, which in some cases would give the appearance of a random search—especially for short menus—but would, particularly for longer menus, produce predominantly top-to-bottom searches.

With respect to mouse movement, the truth appears to lie somewhere in between the EPIC model's single move strategy and the ACT-R model's many-move strategy. Further analysis of the data will be necessary to generate a clear model of the mouse movement data and its relationship to eye movements.

It is interesting to note that other researchers have claimed both entirely random [4] and entirely top-to bottom [7] searches. What we observed is something in between, though not a simple 50/50 mixture of the two. With lower resolution eye-tracking equipment or a slightly different task (perhaps one more like reading, which likely biases the users towards top-to-bottom), it is not difficult to imagine coming to one or the other conclusion. However, as is often the case in studies of human behavior, the story is more complex than it initially appears.

The immediate design implications for this work are not obvious, as the menu task itself is somewhat artificial. However, these data suggest that interface designers should make few assumptions about what items users will and will not process when they make selections from unfamiliar menus. While it is very likely that users will see one of the initial items, it cannot be assumed that users will have seen intermediate items, particularly for longer menus.

The ultimate value of such work lies primarily in its informing of more accurate models of human cognition and performance. Such models are valuable to the field in that they allow the evaluation of interfaces, even ones that have not been constructed yet, without expensive user tests. This work also highlights the utility of advanced data collection methodologies such as eye tracking.

FUTURE WORK

The analyses presented here merely scratch the surface of an incredibly rich data set. We have only begun to examine certain aspects of the data, such as the temporal relationship between the eye and mouse movements. The post-processing algorithms are constantly being improved and may shed more light on the data we already have. We have also not yet examined in great detail the influence of target type, distractor type, and the presence/absence of the initial button during the course of the trial. Clearly, there is a great deal of work yet to be done.

Once we have achieved a clearer understanding of the data, we hope to construct a computational cognitive model of the menu search process using a new extension of ACT-R, ACT-R/PM [3], which incorporates a number of key features of the EPIC system into the original ACT-R architecture. Hopefully, through a clearer understanding of both the data and a more complete model, it will be possible to improve upon current guidelines and tools for evaluating displays used in human-computer interfaces.

ACKNOWLEDGEMENTS

This research was supported in part by the Office of Naval Research (ONR), Award #N00014-96-10491 and by the National Institute for Mental Health (NIMH), fellowship #2732-MH19102. The views and conclusions expressed here are those of the authors and do not reflect the views or opinions of the ONR, the NIMH, or the U. S. government

REFERENCES

1. Aaltonen, A., Hyrskykari, A., & Räihä, K. (1998). 101 Spots, or how do users read menus? In *Human Factors in Computing Systems: Proceedings of CHI 98* (pp. 132–139). New York: ACM Press.

2. Anderson, J. R., Matessa, M., & Lebiere, C. (1997). ACT-R: A theory of higher level cognition and its relation to visual attention. *Human-Computer Interaction, 12,* 439–462.

3. Byrne, M. D., & Anderson, J. R. (1998). Perception and Action. In J. R. Anderson & C. Lebiere (Eds.) *Atomic Components of Thought* (pp. 167–200). Mahwah, NJ: Lawrence Erlbaum.

4. Card, S. K. (1984). Visual search of computer command menus. In H. Bouma & D. G. Bouwhuis (Eds.) *Attention and Performance X: Control of Language Processes* (pp. 97–108). London: Lawrence Erlbaum.

5. Card, S. K., Moran, T. P., & Newell, A. (1983). *The Psychology of Human-Computer Interaction.* Hillsdale, NJ: Lawrence Erlbaum

6. Hornof, A. J., & Kieras, D. E. (1997). Cognitive modeling reveals menu search is both random and systematic. In *Human Factors in Computing Systems: Proceedings of CHI 97* (pp. 107–114). New York: ACM Press.

7. Lee, E., & MacGregor, J. (1985). Minimizing user search time in menu retrieval systems. *Human Factors, 27,* 157–162.

8. Nilsen, E. L. (1991). Perceptual-motor control in human-computer interaction (Technical Report Number 37). Ann Arbor, MI: The Cognitive Science and Machine Intelligence Laboratory, the University of Michigan.

9. Norman, K. L. (1991). *The Psychology of Menu Selection: Designing Cognitive Control of the Human/Computer Interface.* Norwood, NJ: Ablex.

10. Rosenbaum, D. A. (1991). Human motor control. New York: Academic Press.

Cognitive Modeling Demonstrates How People Use Anticipated Location Knowledge of Menu Items

Anthony J. Hornof and David E. Kieras

Artificial Intelligence Laboratory
Electrical Engineering & Computer Science Department
University of Michigan
1101 Beal Avenue, Ann Arbor, MI 48109-2110
+1 734 763 6985
hornof@umich.edu, kieras@eecs.umich.edu

ABSTRACT

This research presents cognitive models of a person selecting an item from a familiar, ordered, pull-down menu. Two different models provide a good fit with human data and thus two different possible explanations for the low-level cognitive processes involved in the task. Both models assert that people make an initial eye and hand movement to an anticipated target location without waiting for the menu to appear. The first model asserts that a person knows the exact location of the target item before the menu appears, but the model uses nonstandard Fitts' law coefficients to predict mouse pointing time. The second model asserts that a person would only know the approximate location of the target item, and the model uses Fitts' law coefficients better supported by the literature. This research demonstrates that people can develop considerable knowledge of locations in a visual task environment, and that more work regarding Fitts' law is needed.

KEYWORDS

Cognitive models, Fitts' law, menus, visual search.

INTRODUCTION

Menu selection is a very common human-computer interaction technique, and has been studied at length (such as in [6, 11, 13]), but models of the low-level cognitive processes and strategies that people use when they select an item from a menu have only been emerging in the last few years. To give human-computer interaction (HCI) practitioners better advice for building better menu systems, more work needs to be done to figure out how people use menus. In a previous CHI paper [6], we presented empirically validated models of the low-level perceptual, cognitive, and motor processing that people use when they select a known target item from a randomly ordered pull-down menu. In this paper, we present similarly detailed models for numerically ordered pull-down menus.

People can select a target from an alphabetically or numerically ordered menu significantly faster than from a randomly ordered menu. This has been demonstrated by Perlman [11] and Somberg [13]. A simple explanation of this phenomenon is that if a menu always contains the same items in the same places, people can learn and remember the exact location of each item. But Somberg's and Perlman's observations only partially support this theory. Both researchers found that, even after practice and even when menu items are selected with a keystroke instead of a mouse, people can select the top items in an ordered menu faster than lower items. This suggests that people cannot learn the location of all menu items equally well. Both researchers left as an open question a more detailed explanation for this phenomenon. The research presented here attempts to fill this void by offering an empirically validated model of the low-level perceptual, cognitive, and motor processing that people use when they select a known item from a numerically ordered pull-down menu.

THE EPIC COGNITIVE ARCHITECTURE

The EPIC (Executive Process-Interactive Control) cognitive architecture [7] provides a general framework for simulating humans interacting with their environment to accomplish a task, and is well-suited to model a menu selection task. EPIC resembles the Model Human Processor [4], but differs in that EPIC is a precise computational model, has a programmable production-rule cognitive processor, and incorporates more specific constraints synthesized from human performance literature.

EPIC consists of a production-rule cognitive processor and perceptual-motor peripherals. To model human performance aspects of accomplishing a task, a cognitive strategy and perceptual-motor processing parameters must be specified. A cognitive strategy is represented as a set of production rules, much the same way that CCT [3], ACT-R [2], and SOAR [8] represent procedural knowledge. The simulation is driven by a description of the task environment that specifies aspects of the environment that would be directly observable to a human, such as what objects appear at what times, and how the environment changes in response to EPIC's motor movements. EPIC computational models are *generative* in that the production rules only represent general procedural knowledge of the task, and when EPIC interacts with the task environment,

EPIC generates a specific sequence of perceptual, cognitive, and motor activities required to perform each specific instance of the task.

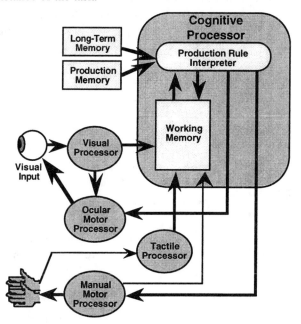

Figure 1. Subset of EPIC architecture, showing flow of information and control. The processors run independently and in parallel. Not shown: Auditory and vocal motor processors, task environment.

EPIC takes as its input:

- The cognitive strategy for accomplishing a task.
- Availability of object features, to represent human perceptual capabilities.
- Details of the task environment, such as when and where objects appear.

EPIC generates as output:

- The time required to execute the task.
- A detailed trace of the flow of information and control.

As shown in Figure 1, information flows from sense organs, through perceptual processors, to a cognitive processor (consisting of a production rule interpreter and a working memory), and finally to motor processors that control effector organs. All processors run independently and in parallel.

The appearance of a visual object in the EPIC task environment produces multiple object-feature outputs from the visual perceptual processor. These object-feature pairs are deposited in visual working memory using a standard delay for each feature. For example, if the visual object "4" appears in the task environment, the *location* feature of this new object will arrive in visual working memory before its *text* feature.

Location information can also be made available to the cognitive processor by defining *named locations* for a particular task environment. Named locations represent knowledge of fixed locations in visual space.

To act upon the environment, a production-rule strategy sends motor commands to the various motor processors. These motor commands specify a movement in terms of its *style*, as well as other characteristics such as direction and extent. Predefined manual movement styles allow EPIC to point with a mouse (the POINT style), press a mouse button (PRESS), point with a mouse while holding down the mouse button (POINT-PRESSING), and release a mouse button (RELEASE). *Compound* movement styles combine multiple movements into a single command. For example, the PUNCH compound movement style executes a PRESS and RELEASE with a single command. A PUNCH of a mouse button is more commonly referred to as "clicking" the mouse button.

A motor movement must be *prepared* and then *executed*. Movement preparation time will be reduced if the previously executed movement had any identical features. The standard 200 msec to prepare a POINT, for example, will be reduced to zero if the previous manual motor command was an identical POINT. Execution time represents the time required for mechanical muscular movements in the physical world, and is thus determined in part by features such as the distance that an effector must travel. Motor movement styles and their associated timing functions and parameters are based on what is available in the human performance literature (such as in [12]). Execution time for a mouse point, for example, is determined by the Welford version of Fitts' law [4], with a minimum execution time of 100 msec enforced:

$$T = \max\left(100\,,\ K \cdot \log_2\left(\frac{\text{Distance}}{\text{Width}} + 0.5\right)\right) \text{ msec}$$

For a POINT movement, the coefficient K is set to 100, as given in [4]. For a POINT-PRESSING movement, the coefficient K is set to 140; this value is derived from data presented in [14].

This provides a cursory overview of the EPIC cognitive architecture. A more thorough description of EPIC is presented in [7]. The task modeled in this paper will be presented next.

THE TASK

The menu selection task modeled in this paper was designed by Nilsen, who presented the task to human participants in an experiment (Experiment 2 in [10]). Nilsen used menus of three, six, and nine menu items. Menu items were the numerical digits from 1 to *n*, where *n* was the length of the menu. Menu items were either randomly re-ordered for each trial or presented in numerical order. Trials were blocked by menu length and ordering. Menus always appeared at the exact same location on a computer screen.

As shown in Figure 2, each trial consisted of the following steps: Using a mouse, move the cursor to the GO box, which causes the precue of the target item to appear above the GO box. Commit the precue to memory. Click on the GO box. The GO box and precue disappear, the menu appears, the cursor is positioned one pixel above the first menu item, and the clock starts. As quickly as possible, click on the target item in the menu. The clock stops.

Two different menu styles were used: Walking and click-open. With walking menus, participants moved the cursor to the GO box, pressed and held down the mouse button, moved the cursor to the target while keeping the mouse button depressed, and then released the mouse button. With click-open menus, participants moved the cursor to the GO box, clicked the mouse button, moved the cursor to the target, and then clicked the mouse button. Within a block, all menus were of the same style.

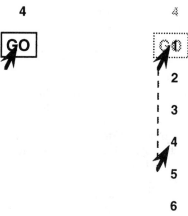

Figure 2. Nilsen's task with a numerically ordered menu and six items in the menu.

Eight experienced mouse users participated in the experiment, and were financially motivated to perform each trial as quickly as possible. Nilsen presented each participant with eighteen trials for every possible combination of target position, menu length, menu ordering, and menu style (walking versus click-open). The final fifteen asymptotic trials are reported in the data.

THE OBSERVED DATA

Figure 3 shows Nilsen's observed data for randomly and numerically ordered menus, averaged across participants, blocks, and menu style (walking versus click-open). Also shown is a Fitts' law movement time prediction, with a coefficient of 120 (an average between the coefficients for the POINT-PRESSING movement required for walking menus and the POINT movement required for click-open menus).

The important features in the numerically ordered menu data include:

- Participants select an item from a numerically ordered menu substantially faster than from a randomly ordered menu. As a result, the visual search strategies presented in the previous CHI paper [6] to explain the randomly ordered menu data will not also explain the numerically ordered menu data. Evidently, extensive visual search is not needed for the numerically ordered menus.

- Participants select the target item from numerically ordered menus very quickly, requiring only 350 to 950 msec to click on the GO box, move the cursor to the target, and click on the target.

- There is no menu-length effect in the numerically ordered menu data. Every serial position takes the same amount of time regardless of the menu length.

- There is a negatively accelerated increase in the numerically ordered menu data; the increase is greater than that of the Fitts' law prediction also shown on the graph.

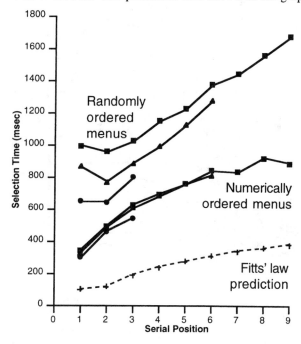

Figure 3. Nilsen's observed data for randomly and numerically ordered menus. Mean selection times as a function of serial position of target item, for menus with three, six, or nine items. Also: Time required to move the mouse to each target position as predicted by Fitts' law with a coefficient of 120.

These features in the data will direct the model-building endeavor that follows. All of the models that follow will compare how well the models' predictions match Nilsen's observed data. But the comparisons will use a more detailed view of the same data presented in Figure 3. Since the observed data points for the different menu lengths are the same, but the menu styles produced different times, the graphs that follow will collapse the observed data and the predictions by menu length, but expand them by menu style (walking versus click-open).

THE MODELS

This section presents two classes of models, the *immediate look, point, and click* models and the *immediate look, point, check and correct* models. Preliminary modeling not discussed here for lack of space demonstrates that waiting for the menu to appear will produce excessive delays. As a result, all of the models discussed in this paper represent the belief that people will use anticipated location knowledge to prepare and execute eye and hand movements to the target without waiting for the menu to actually appear. Anticipated location knowledge is made available to strategies by means of *named locations* in

EPIC that correspond to the actual menu item locations and are available before the actual menu items have appeared.

The difference between the two classes of models is that the *immediate look, point, and click* models assume that the location information will always be correct, so a second eye and hand movement will never be necessary. The *immediate look, point, check and correct* models, on the other hand, allow for imperfect location knowledge; they check to see that the first eye and hand movement landed on the target and make a corrective eye and hand movement if necessary.

The discussion of each model includes a flowchart that summarizes the production rules written in EPIC to represent that model. Production rules were written to maximize performance within the constraints imposed by EPIC, and to be as parsimonious as possible. The production rules send the correct motor commands to interact with the current menu style (such as PRESS, POINT-PRESSING, and RELEASE for the walking menus), but for the sake of brevity, the flowcharts will summarize both sets of motor movements as just click, point, and click.

Immediate Look, Point, and Click Models

The *immediate look, point, and click* models represent a belief that people anticipate a target location before opening a menu, execute an eye movement and a mouse movement to that location immediately upon opening a menu, and then click on that location without confirming that the cursor is actually on the target. This strategy assumes that anticipated target locations are correct. The EPIC production rules to represent this strategy are summarized in Figure 4.

Figure 4. The immediate look, point, and click strategy.

Standard Fitts' Law Coefficients Model

The results from running the *immediate look, point, and click* strategy are shown in Figure 5. Each predicted selection time is averaged from one trial run for every menu length and serial position combination. For these trials, the Fitts' law coefficients in EPIC were set to the standard 100 for a POINT and 140 for a POINT-PRESSING.

The results in Figure 5 demonstrate that the model is wrong. The predicted values are negatively accelerated, as are the observed data, and the difference between the two menu styles is predicted to be the same as the observed data. But the predictions for most positions are much too fast,

the trend in the predicted values does not increase steeply enough, and the prediction for position 1 is much too high.

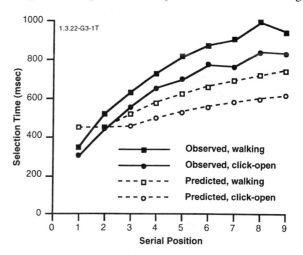

Figure 5. Selection times observed by Nilsen and predicted by the immediate look, point, and click strategy run with standard Fitts' coefficients of 100 and 140.

For positions 2 through 9, the model could be underpredicting for a number of reasons, including (1) participants could not anticipate the exact location of the target, which would imply that (2) this is not the strategy participants really used, or (3) participants took longer to point than is predicted by Fitts' law with the standard coefficients. The next model investigates the third of these possibilities.

Nonstandard Fitts' Law Coefficients Model

The *immediate look, point, and click* strategy run with nonstandard Fitts' coefficients represents the belief that participants could anticipate the exact location of a target item before the menu appears and always execute a correct eye and hand movement to the target, but that mouse points took longer than is predicted by standard Fitts' coefficients. The results from running the *immediate look, point, and click* strategy with exactly known location information and with nonstandard Fitts' coefficients of 175 and 220 are shown in Figure 6. The values of 175 for POINT and 220 for POINT-PRESSING were chosen iteratively to provide a good fit. The implications of these increased values are discussed later.

With the increased Fitts' coefficients, this model now does a very good job of predicting selection times for positions 2 through 9. The difference between the predicted and observed values for the two menu styles is the same, and both the predicted and the observed values follow the same negatively accelerated trend. The overall plausibility of this model and the implications of the nonstandard Fitts' coefficients will be discussed after providing a plausible explanation for position 1.

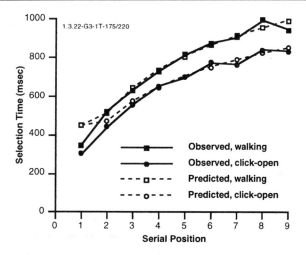

Figure 6. *Selection times observed by Nilsen and predicted by the immediate look, point, and click strategy run with Fitts' coefficients increased to 175 and 220.*

Special Case for Position 1 Model

An explanation as to how participants selected targets in position 1 so quickly requires a detailed analysis of the task. Recall that upon clicking on the GO box, the cursor is automatically positioned exactly one pixel above the first menu item. When the participant knows the target item will be in position 1, all that he or she must do is click on the GO box, make a tiny downward movement with the mouse, confirm that the target has actually appeared, and click again.

Additional production rules were added to the *immediate look, point, and click* strategy to create a *special case for position 1* branch, rules that will only be executed if the precue is a "1". A flowchart summarizing the production rules appears in Figure 7. In the special case production rules, there is no separate POINT movement, but rather the click on the GO box is assumed to produce as a side effect a tiny downward twitch that is prepared in advance along with the click.

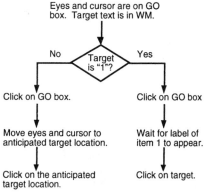

Figure 7. *The immediate look, point, and click strategy with special case for position 1.*

Since a mouse click followed immediately by a deliberate tiny twitch is rarely required in HCI tasks and since it is only proposed here to accommodate an artifact of the experimental procedure that only affects position 1, it seems hardly worthwhile to create a new movement style in EPIC for this model. Instead, in this model, a twitch is assumed to occur with the first click when the target is "1".

EPIC's predictions when running the *immediate look, point, and click* strategy with special case for position 1 and nonstandard Fitts' coefficients are shown in Figure 8. As can be seen, this model predicts the observed data very well, for an average absolute error of 3.0%.[1]

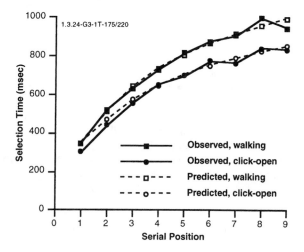

Figure 8. *Selection times observed by Nilsen and predicted by the immediate look, point, and click strategy with special case for position 1 run with nonstandard Fitts' coefficients of 175 and 220.*

Though this model explains the data well and offers a reasonable explanation for how people accomplish the task, there are two aspects of this model that make it questionable. First, it is hard to accept Fitts' coefficients so much higher than the standard values. Second, the model asserts people know exactly where to look and point before the menu even appears.

The first problem, of the increased Fitts' coefficients, actually points to a shortcoming in the HCI literature. Though Fitts' law is often cited as a useful tool for prediction and design in HCI (such as in [4, 5, 9]), the exact form and coefficients of Fitts' law are not settled. Several studies in fact provide evidence for a Welford Fitts' coefficient of about 175 for a mouse point [5, 9]. In addition, the Fitts' equation appears in several forms (compare [4, 5, 9]), which makes some coefficients incomparable. Thus, it may or may not be reasonable to use such large Fitts' coefficients. Much more work needs to be done to determine the correct Fitts' coefficients for various tasks and environments.

---

[1] It should be pointed out that re-running the randomly ordered menu models presented in [6] with the increased Fitts' coefficients of 175 and 220 does not seriously reduce the good fit of the randomly ordered menu models since, as argued in [6], the pointing time effects are very minor compared to the effects due to visual search.

The second problem is that all of the *immediate look, point, and click* models assume that a person has exact location knowledge for all menu items before the menu even appears. This assertion seems to contradict Perlman's [11] and Somberg's [13] findings that, even with numerically and alphabetically ordered menus and a constant time to select an item once it is found, the top menu items can be selected faster than lower menu items. Perlman's and Somberg's findings suggest that some items do take longer to locate even in a known, ordered menu.

So, the *immediate look, point, and click* models provide a good fit and a reasonable explanation for how people select an item from an ordered menu. But the models discussed next provide an equally good fit and perhaps an even more plausible explanation.

Immediate Look, Point, Check & Correct Models

The *immediate look, point, check and correct* models represent a belief that people anticipate a target location before opening a menu, execute an eye movement and a mouse movement to that location immediately upon opening a menu, check to see if the cursor actually landed on the target, make a corrective eye movement and mouse movement if necessary, and then click on the target. These models allow us to explore the possibility that people cannot predict the exact location of the target before it appears, but only an approximate location.

The flowchart in Figure 9 summarizes the production rules written in EPIC to explore the plausibility of this strategy. Note that the strategy carries forward the special case for position 1 discussed in the previous section.

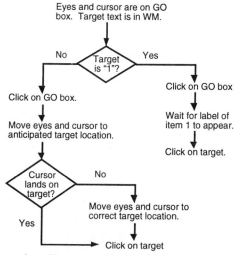

Figure 9. The immediate look, point, check and correct strategy.

For simplicity, the model asserts that a third eye and mouse movement will never be necessary. For the small amount of error introduced in these models, the first movement will rarely fall more than one menu item away from the target, in which case the correct location information will be readily available for the second eye and hand movement.

Exactly Known Location Model

Running the *immediate look, point, check and correct* strategy in EPIC with exactly known location information reveals the baseline prediction of the strategy, before adding any error to the initial eye and hand movement location. The results from running this model are shown in Figure 10. Each predicted selection time is averaged from one trial run for every menu length and serial position combination.

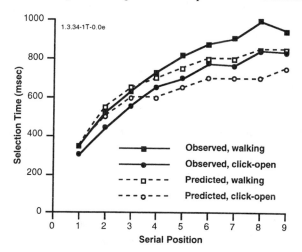

Figure 10. Selection times observed by Nilsen and predicted by the immediate look, point, check and correct strategy run with exact location knowledge.

As can be seen in Figure 10, the model does not account for the data. But the results are informative nonetheless. The model's predictions for the first three serial positions are very close to the observed, and with roughly the same negatively accelerated slope as the data. The model underpredicts for serial positions 4 and above, which might be remedied by adding some error to the model that would sometimes make necessary a second, corrective eye and hand movement.

Approximately Known Location Model

The *immediate look, point, check and correct* model run with approximately known location information represents the belief that people can anticipate the position of a target in a menu before the menu actually appears, but that people can anticipate the location of items higher in the menu more accurately than items lower in the menu. Approximately known locations are introduced to the model by perturbing the vertical coordinate of the named location for the target item at the start of a trial.

To represent the relation between the accuracy of location knowledge and distance, these initially anticipated target locations vary from trial to trial, and are normally distributed around μ, the true distance from the GO box to the correct target location, with a standard deviation σ that is defined as

$$\sigma = e \cdot \mu$$

where *e* is a constant error coefficient. Thus, the further away the target, the less likely that the first eye movement and mouse point will land within the target region. This relationship is actually well-grounded empirically. Abrams et al. [1] observed just such a linear relationship between target distance and standard deviation in endpoints of eye movements directed at a single target that is peripherally visible before the start of the trial. A value of $e = 0.04$ provides a very good fit with the data presented in Abrams et al. [1]. Seeing as how in Nilsen's task there are multiple target locations from trial to trial and the target is not visible at the start of the trial, a higher error coefficient e seems plausible for predicting the error in the initial eye and mouse movement locations when modeling Nilsen's data.

The results from running the *immediate look, point, check and correct* strategy with an initial location error coefficient $e = 0.1$ are shown in Figure 11. The value of 0.1 was chosen iteratively to provide a similar slope as that of the data. Three hundred trial runs were executed for every unique combination of menu length, serial position, and menu style. The predictions in Figure 11 average those results.

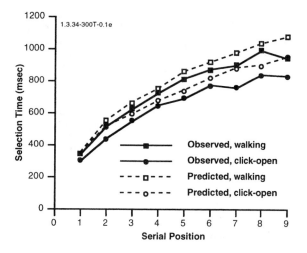

Figure 11. Selection times observed by Nilsen and predicted by the immediate look, point, check and correct strategy run with approximate location knowledge ($e = 0.1$).

As can be seen in Figure 11, the model comes very close to explaining the observed data. The predicted values have almost exactly the same negatively accelerated slope as the observed data, and are very close to the observed data, but the model's predictions are a little too slow for how quickly people accomplished this task.

Perhaps the overall high speed of the observed data is due to extensive overlapping of the motor processing involved. For example, perhaps people can prepare and execute a compound click-and-point movement, a movement style not currently implemented in EPIC. This tentative new compound movement style is introduced in the next model.

Click-and-Point Compound Movement Style Model

Introducing a click-and-point compound movement style to the *immediate look, point, check and correct* model represents a belief that, since the destination of the initial mouse point can be determined in advance, the motor preparation for the point movement can also be partly prepared in tandem with the first mouse click. To see if such a style would help the model, a modification to the existing POINT movement is introduced in these models. A more complete representation would be to introduce a new movement style to the EPIC motor processor, but these modifications are tentative.

The specific modifications are as follows: (1) The existing POINT movement style is modified to allow a POINT to begin during the release of a mouse button rather than waiting for its completion. (2) The existing POINT and POINT-PRESSING movement styles are modified to require only 150 msec of preparation rather than the usual 200 msec if the movement was preceded by a PRESS or PUNCH.

The results from running the *immediate look, point, check and correct* strategy with an initial location error coefficient $e = 0.1$ and a click-and-point compound movement style are shown in Figure 12. The predictions in Figure 12 average the results from three hundred trial runs executed for every unique combination of menu length, serial position, and menu style.

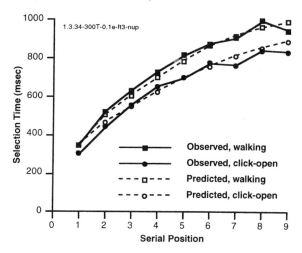

Figure 12. Selection times observed by Nilsen and predicted by the immediate look, point, check and correct strategy run with approximate location knowledge ($e = 0.1$) and with a click-and-point compound movement style.

As can be seen in Figure 12, this model predicts the observed data very well, with an average absolute error of 3.92%. This model demonstrates that two problems with the *immediate look, point, and click* models – increasing the Fitts' coefficients and asserting perfect location knowledge – can be overcome by a more subtle analysis of the task and a more detailed representation of the perceptual-motor activity required to accomplish the task.

CONCLUSION

The models presented here provide a plausible explanation for the low-level perceptual, cognitive, and motor processing required for selecting a known target item from a familiar, ordered pull-down menu. In order to account for such fast selection times, it was necessary to assume that people anticipate the target position and make their initial eye and hand movements to the target even before the menu appears. The models also suggest that people can anticipate the position of items that appear higher in an ordered pull-down menu more accurately than items lower in the menu.

The models presented here also demonstrate that more work needs to be done in the study of human performance to predict simple pointing time with a mouse. A more systematic effort is needed to catalog Fitts' coefficients for specific pointing tasks and mouse environments. And to be truly valuable, aimed movement studies need to report observations in at least as much detail as can be found in Walker et al. [14], as well as all measurable mouse parameters such as weight, drag, and variable gain settings. Perhaps an altogether new model is needed for predicting aimed movement times, such as *Meyer's Law* (See [12], p.213), which relates movement time to width, distance, and the number of submovements required.

FUTURE WORK

Successfully modeling Nilsen's data for both numerically and randomly ordered menus provides evidence that a more general visual search task can similarly be modeled. Future work includes collecting data for a more two-dimensional visual search task, such as icon search, and then carrying forward the strategies developed in the menu selection tasks in an effort to explain the low level cognitive processes involved in more general search tasks.

ACKNOWLEDGMENTS

Many thanks to Erik Nilsen for providing additional details on his experiment and generously sharing a copy of the menu software used in his experiment.

This work was supported by the Advanced Research Projects Agency under order number B328, monitored by NCCOSC under contract number N66001-94-C-6036 awarded to David Kieras.

REFERENCES

1. Abrams, R. A., Meyer, D. E., & Kornblum, S. (1989). Speed and accuracy of saccadic eye movements: Characteristics of impulse variability in the oculomotor system. *Journal of Experimental Psychology: Human Perception and Performance*, 15(3), 529-543.

2. Anderson, J. R. (1993). *Rules of the mind*. Hillsdale, NJ: Erlbaum.

3. Bovair, S., Kieras, D. E., & Polson, P. G. (1990). The acquisition and performance of text editing skill: A cognitive complexity analysis. *Human-Computer Interaction*, 5, 1-48.

4. Card, S. K., Moran, T. P., & Newell, A. (1983). *The Psychology of Human-Computer Interaction*. Hillsdale, NJ: Lawrence Erlbaum Associates.

5. Han, S. H., Jorna, G. C., Miller, R. H., & Tan, K. C. (1990). A comparison of four input devices for the Macintosh interface. *Proceedings of the Human Factors Society 34th Annual Meeting*, Santa Monica, CA: Human Factors Society, 267-271.

6. Hornof, A. J., & Kieras, D. E. (1997). Cognitive modeling reveals menu search is both random and systematic. *Proceedings of ACM CHI 97: Conference on Human Factors in Computing Systems*, New York: ACM, 107-114.

7. Kieras, D. E., & Meyer, D. E. (1997). An overview of the EPIC architecture for cognition and performance with application to human-computer interaction. *Human-Computer Interaction*, 12(4), 391-438.

8. Laird, J., Rosenbloom, P., & Newell, A. (1986). *Universal subgoaling and chunking*. Boston: Kluwer Academic Publishers.

9. MacKenzie, I. S., & Buxton, W. (1992). Extending Fitts' law to two-dimensional tasks. *Proceedings of CHI '92*, New York: ACM, 219-226.

10. Nilsen, E. L. (1991). Perceptual-motor control in human-computer interaction. (Tech. Rep. No. 37). Ann Arbor, Michigan: The Cognitive Science and Machine Intelligence Laboratory, The University of Michigan. Also: Ph.D. dissertation in Psychology, The University of Michigan, 1991.

11. Perlman, G. (1984). Making the right choices with menus. *Proceedings of Interact '84*, Elsevier Science Publishers, 317-321.

12. Rosenbaum, D. A. (1991). *Human motor control*. New York: Academic Press.

13. Somberg, B. L. (1987). A comparison of rule-based and positionally constant arrangements of computer menu items. *Proceedings of CHI '87*, New York: ACM, 79-84.

14. Walker, N., Meyer, D. E., & Smelcer, J. B. (1993). Spatial and temporal characteristics of rapid cursor-positioning movements with electromechanical mice in human-computer interaction. *Human Factors*, 35(3), 431-458.

Learning and Performing by Exploration: Label Quality Measured by Latent Semantic Analysis

Rodolfo Soto

Institute of Cognitive Science

University of Colorado

Boulder, CO 80309-0344, USA

+1 (303) 492-4574

Rodolfo.Soto@Colorado.edu

ABSTRACT

Models of learning and performing by exploration assume that the *semantic similarity* between task descriptions and labels on display objects (e.g., menus, tool bars) controls in part the users' search strategies. Nevertheless, none of the models has an objective way to compute semantic similarity. In this study, Latent Semantic Analysis (LSA) was used to compute semantic similarity between task descriptions and labels in an application's menu system. Participants performed twelve tasks by exploration and they were tested for recall after a 1-week delay. When the labels in the menu system were semantically similar to the task descriptions, subjects performed the tasks faster. LSA could be incorporated into any of the current models, and it could be used to automate the evaluation of computer applications for ease of learning and performing by exploration.

Keywords

Learning by exploration, label-following strategy, cognitive models, semantic similarity, latent semantic analysis, usability analysis

INTRODUCTION

In the interaction between humans and computers, words are the link between users' goals and the actions required to accomplish those goals. For command-based environments, such as UNIX, users must memorize sets of keywords that they type to interact with the system. Likewise, in display-based environments, such as Mac OS or Win 95, users must point at and click on display objects labeled by words (e.g., menu items, tool bars, or dialog boxes). The right choice of words can successfully lead users through novel or rarely used applications such as library databases [1], telephone menu systems [2], or graphics applications [3].

The experiment described in this paper provides empirical evidence supporting the hypothesis that users act on those interface labels that are semantically related to the users' goals. Several cognitive models have been proposed to simulate the exploration and recall of the action sequences required to perform novel tasks using display-based computer applications. All these models emphasize the use of semantic information as a means to successfully discover and recall the correct action sequences. Independently of the details in each model, they all use some version of semantic similarity as an evaluation function to predict the users' searching behavior. However, as shown here, LSA [4] proves to be a reliable technique to compute semantic similarity and it can be used to automate usability testing.

Outline of the paper

The next section describes the searching strategies users employ when learning a new application by exploration. Later, cognitive models of exploration are summarized emphasizing the role of semantic similarity in these models. An introduction of LSA is provided showing its role as an objective technique to compute automatically the semantic similarity between pieces of text. Finally, the experiment is described in detail and its results are discussed. This study has important implications for any cognitive model of exploration and for the design and automatic testing of interfaces that support learning by exploration.

LEARNING BY EXPLORATION

Polson and Lewis [5] analyzed the exploratory behavior of novice users who have a goal in mind, and who have some experience with particular types of applications or operating systems. In this situation, users engage in search through the interface objects for labels that will lead them to the solution of their task. During this process, the application changes from one state to another. For instance, a menu item is pulled down and a pop-up menu is exposed. When the pop-up menu items appear, the application's state changes to a richer one that contains more information that eventually will help the users find the solution of the task. The different states of the application define a problem space [6]. Novel users should employ some domain-independent method to guide their search through the problem space since they cannot anticipate the state shifts that their actions would produce. This kind of method is called a weak method because it does not contain any specific information about the problem, and means-ends analysis is probably its most used variation.

Two versions of means-ends analysis are frequently observed in novice exploration: hill climbing, and back chaining. In both cases, for each state one action is chosen among the available alternatives using "perceptual similarity as a measure of distance" [5, p. 205]. Since novel users do not have complete information about the available actions in each application state, they have to rely on their previous knowledge about the operating system or about display-based applications to select a particular action. In modern display-based applications, the most common actions are pulling down menu items, clicking on tool bars, "dragging and dropping" objects, or using "hot keys".

To accomplish a task, users need to estimate the distance between the current state and the desired state (i.e., the solution of the task). Engelbeck [7] observed that novice users tend to explore those menu labels that share one or more words with the experimenter-supplied description of the tasks (or with the user's goal). Muncher [8] also found this behavior in novice users learning Lotus 1-2-3. This heuristic has been called the *label-following strategy* [5], and it can be classified as a hill-climbing technique that uses semantics to compute distance. Considerable evidence confirms that label following is an effective method for discovering the solution to novel computer tasks [3,5,9].

Ideally, the application interface would have a set of labels that maximizes the semantic similarity between the users' goals, or the task descriptions, and the object labels that have to be followed to perform the tasks. However, given the hierarchical structure of the menu systems, some labels are very general because they have to describe several different tasks at the same time. For instance, many modern applications have a menu item labeled **Tools**. If the users' goal is to perform a mail merge, the semantic similarity between the terms "mail merge" and "tools" is so low that it is unlikely that novice users will pull down the **Tools** menu in their first attempt. In this case users try other more promising labels or, if they are unsuccessful, they backtrack and try other options [5]. This back-chaining procedure allows them to uncover new labels that might be semantically more similar to their goals than the ones they attempted first.

The interaction of the hill-climbing strategy (label following) and back chaining strategy (backtracking to try less promising labels) constitutes the basic searching mechanism that most cognitive models include to explain exploratory behavior. Note that either strategy assumes that users estimate semantic similarity between labels and goals (or task descriptions). The review of the cognitive models of exploration reveals that each model implements semantic similarity very informally, an approach that is both unreliable and time consuming. Researchers have to include manually the necessary semantic information based on their own intuitions. Unless an objective measure of semantic similarity is available, choosing the right semantic features may vary considerably from one person to another [10].

COGNITVE MODELS OF EXPLORATION
SOAR Models
The Task-Action Learning (TAL) model [11] simulates users who are familiar with basic operations of the mouse and keyboard, but unfamiliar with a particular menu structure, object labels, and actions required to accomplish a task. TAL emphasizes the role of semantics, since it assumes that users analyze the experimenter instructions, the semantic features of the tasks, and the labels on the screen, hoping to find a link between them. "Interpreting instructions involves matching the task description to the instruction using a rule base of *semantic links* [italics added] between features of the task and items on the display" [11, p. 313]. The semantic associations are implemented via a function that takes semantic features of the tasks (defined by the experimenter) and lexical items as parameters, and returns a Boolean expression indicating semantic matching.

The IDXL model [12] simulates learning by exploration. Rieman [13] analyzed searching in menu systems and concluded that an effective search algorithm would be a combination of label-following and a hybrid between depth- and breadth-first search called depth-first iterative deepening (DFID). Rieman suggested that this combination of label following and DFID should be called "guided DFID", or gDFID. Rather than using brute force, as in pure DFID, gDFID "heuristically limits its search to items *semantically* [italics added] related to the current task" [12, p. 747]. The IDXL model implements gDFID searching and assumes that the user's attention mechanism focuses on one object at a time.

The model is supplied with a task description in working memory and it has knowledge about Macintosh conventions and about the correct and legal actions that can be taken in the menu system. Scanning is the main operator used during exploration. It allows the visual focus to shift right, left, up, down, and to jump from place to place. Another operator comprehends the items that have been under attention and "may note that the scanned item is a label that *matches* [italics added] some key word in the task" [12, p. 758]. The model considers that a direct match costs less than an indirect match (e.g., a synonym). Thus, it tries those items that have a direct match with the experimenter-supplied task description before trying anything else. All the knowledge about synonyms has to be explicitly given to the model.

A Comprehension-Based Model of Exploration
The LICAI+ model [14,15] simulates the user's comprehension of task instructions and hints, the generation of goals, and the use of these goals to discover correct actions by exploration. This model is based on the CI architecture [16], that was originally developed as a model for text comprehension and extended to action planning by Mannes and Kintsch [17]. LICAI+ predicts that successful exploration and recall require semantic matching between the goal representation (or task description) and the labels on the display objects.

The CI architecture combines propositional knowledge with connectionist spreading activation mechanisms. CI assumes that two propositions are related if they share one or more arguments. For LICAI+, this means that a menu label and the description of a task (or a hint, or a piece of instruction, or the user's goal) are related if there is concept overlap between them. The semantic similarity notion of this model is very crude. If the labels and the task descriptions do not share words, additional knowledge can be provided by long-term memory to establish a link.

In summary, the available models of learning by exploration share the same intuition about the role of semantic similarity: users tend to act on objects with labels that "seem" to be semantically related to their goals. Additionally, some of the models explain how the label-following strategy is frequently combined with other exploratory mechanisms. Although all the simulations confirm the reliability of the label-following strategy, they do not include an objective measure of semantic similarity. This paper proposes that a mathematical model of semantics, such as Latent Semantic Analysis, is a good candidate for computing semantic similarity estimates.

LATENT SEMANTIC ANALYSIS AS A MODEL FOR SEMANTICS

LSA is both a model and a technique to extract semantic information from large bodies of text. LSA was originally conceived as an information retrieval technique [18] that makes use of statistical procedures to capture the similarity of words and documents in a high-dimensional space [4,19]. Once LSA is trained on a corpus of data (consisting of several thousands of documents), it is able to compute similarity estimates that go beyond simple co-occurrence or contiguity frequencies. Although LSA does not have any knowledge about grammar, morphology, or syntax, it mimics humans' use of language in several areas ranging from the rates of vocabulary acquisition by schoolchildren, to word and passage priming effects, to evaluating the performance of students on essay tests.

The collection of documents used to train LSA is arranged in a matrix where the columns correspond to the documents, and the rows correspond to unique word types. An entry in the matrix indicates the number of times the word appears in the document. Using a linear algebra technique called singular value decomposition it is possible to represent each document and each word as a vector of high dimensionality (e.g., 400) that captures the underlying relations of the words and their contexts. To determine how similar two words are, LSA computes the cosine between the vectors that represent the words. A cosine, like a correlation coefficient, ranges between −1 and 1, where 1 represents a perfect match (i.e., the same word), and 0 represents no relationship between the words.

The available evidence suggests that LSA is a plausible theory of learning, memory, and knowledge [19]. All the tests that LSA has performed successfully have been solved using semantic similarity as the main predictor of fitness. For instance, LSA does well on the synonym portion of the Test of English as a Foreign Language (Educational Testing Service) [20,21]. It computes the semantic similarity between the stem word in each item and each of the four alternatives, choosing the one with the highest cosine. Using this method, LSA performed virtually identically to the average of a large sample of non-English speaking students. Since the HCI literature stresses the role of semantics as a measure of distance during hill-climbing-like strategies, LSA should be able to account for the "good-labels effect" observed during exploration. In other words, LSA could be extended to action planning.

Since LSA learns about language exclusively from the training texts, it is very important to choose the right corpus for the specific situation to be modeled. Several corpora have been used to train LSA. One of the most versatile is the TASA (Touchstone Applied Science Associates, Inc.) corpus (see http://lsa.colorado.edu). This group of documents uses a variety of text sources, such as newspaper articles and novels that represent the kind of material students read during the school years. The TASA corpus is broken into grade levels, from third grade to college, using a readability score (DRP-Degrees of Reading Power Scale) that is assigned to each of its 37,651 documents. TASA is a good training corpus to model naïve or inexperienced users, especially because it is assumed that these kinds of users are forced to adapt their "everyday" knowledge about common words to the new context that is imposed by a computer application [11].

THE EXPERIMENT

The main limitation of both the theoretical and the empirical research on the label-following strategy is the lack of a well-defined measure for semantic similarity. In most cases, semantic relationships are established exclusively via some form of literal word overlap. Hence, the only well-defined similarity metric is, in LSA terms, a cosine of 1 (i.e., an exact match). Unless informal intuitive estimates of semantic similarity are included in the models, it is difficult to study situations where there are intermediate degrees of semantic similarity.

This experiment systematically manipulates the interface of Microsoft Excel to show that the semantic similarity (estimated by LSA) between the labels in the menus and the task descriptions predicts the ease of discovering the solution of the tasks. Additionally, a few different degrees and patterns of semantic similarity are used to explore the interaction between label-following and back-chaining strategies.

Methods

Participants

Fifty-five undergraduate students participated in the experiment. Twenty-eight received class credit and twenty-seven received $10 for their participation. The data from seven participants, four from the group that received class credit and three from the group that received $10 were discarded: two of them were not able to follow the instructions correctly, and in the five other cases, technical errors invalidated the results. The remaining forty-eight participants had at least four years of experience with either the Macintosh or the IBM-PC computer, or both. The group that received class credit had significantly more experience than the other group (on average 5.8 vs. 4.3 years, $F(1,47) = 5.21$, $p < .03$). However, the groups did not differ significantly in their years of experience with Microsoft Word, Microsoft Excel (without creating graphics), Mac Draw, and WWW Browsers. Likewise, they did not differ significantly in the number of graphs they had created by hand in their life. None of the participants had experience with graphics applications such as Cricket Graph or with the graphics capabilities of Microsoft Excel.

Materials

Twelve computer tasks were designed manipulating the semantic similarity between the labels of the menu system and the task descriptions. Microsoft Excel was used to administer the tasks, running in a Macintosh Centris 650 with 16 MB in RAM, 500 MB in hard disk, and a page-size grayscale monitor. An Excel *Add-in* was developed to reconfigure Excel's interface. This made it possible to have a fully functional graphics application in which the tasks had the features required by the experiment, and which guaranteed that the application was novel for the participants.

An S-VHS camera and a clip-on microphone were used to record the computer screen and the participant's voice. Each participant received a package containing an informed consent form, a blue pen, and a notebook with the instructions and the task descriptions.

Tasks

There were four warm-up and eight experimental tasks. All consisted of editing a bar graph using a graphics application. Participants received detailed descriptions of the tasks, but no information about how to perform them (Table 1 shows the experimental tasks descriptions). The eight experimental tasks consisted of five steps. (1) Choose a top-level menu item. (2) Choose a submenu item. (3) Choose a sub-submenu item. (4) Click on a radio button or check box (in a dialog box). (5) Click on a button labeled "Ok" to close the dialog and end the task.

Task 1	Change the graph type to column
Task 2	Apply the default format to the graph
Task 3	Hide the graph title
Task 4	Add a third dimension to the graph
Task 5	Change the graph font to bold
Task 6	Delete the values from the bar graph
Task 7	Change the graph background color to green
Task 8	Apply a logarithmic scale to the graph axes

Table 1. Description of the experimental tasks

The labels for the second and third steps were manipulated so that their semantic similarity with respect to the task descriptions varied. These labels were selected using LSA working under the TASA space. The closest 1000 terms to the description of the tasks were computed. From this pool, words were selected and two-word phrases were created for each menu item. Four degrees of semantic similarity were chosen based on the LSA cosines between the labels and the task descriptions. Good (G) labels had an average cosine of .69 (SD .17) with the task descriptions. The other three degrees of similarity had significantly lower cosines than the G labels had. Therefore, they were classified as three degrees of badness (B). B_1 labels had an average cosine of

.25 (SD = .08), B_2 labels had an average cosine of .15 (SD = .02), and B_3 labels had an average cosine of -.05 (SD = .01) with the task description.

For example, a G label for task 1 (*Change the graph type to column*) was **Change Type** (cosine = .64), a B_1 label was **Correct Presentation** (cosine = .22), a B_2 label was **Rendering Practice** (cosine = .18), and a B_3 label was **Troubleshooter Route** (cosine = -.04). Depending on the condition (as explained in the next section) these labels were assigned to either the second or the third step of the task. That is to say, there were four different patterns of semantic similarity for the second and third steps of each task: a G label followed by a G label (G, G), (G, B), (B, G), and (B, B). In the last case, when both the second and the third steps had bad labels, the degree of badness for both labels remains constant: (B_1, B_1), (B_2, B_2), or (B_3, B_3).

Only the labels for the second and third steps were manipulated because they appear in similar contexts: submenus (pop-up menus). The labels for the other three steps had a fixed semantic similarity. The first step (top-level menu item) had a semantic similarity between B_1 and B_2 with respect to the description of the tasks under that menu. The fourth step (radio button or check box in a dialog box) had a semantic similarity of G. Finally, the fifth step ("Ok" button) had a semantic similarity between B_2 and B_3 with respect to any of the task descriptions.

Design

A menu structure template was created having eight top-level items: **File**, **Edit**, **General**, **Assign**, **Transformation**, **Appearance**, and **Tools**. Figure 1 shows the menu structure template under the **Assign** menu. Tasks 1 and 3 were under the **General** menu, tasks 2 and 8 were under the **Assign** menu, tasks 5 and 6 were under the **Transformation** menu, and tasks 4 and 7 were under the **Appearance** menu.

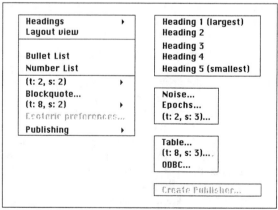

Figure 1. Menu structure template for the **Assign** menu. Data in parenthesis refer to task and step numbers. For instance, (t:2, s:3) is the slot for the third step of task 2.

Different conditions were created so the slots for the second and third steps could be filled out in a balanced way. Four patterns of similarity (G, G), (G, B), (B, G), and (B, B) were equally distributed across tasks, and across conditions. Since the degree of badness (B_1, B_2, and B_3) was fixed for each subject, it was considered a between factor. As an extra experimental factor, four of the eight experimental tasks were explicitly instructed, whereas the other four were explored (see next section). This factor was also balanced across tasks and across conditions. In total, 24 different conditions were created for this experiment.

Procedure

The experiment consisted of two 30-minute sessions: a training session followed by recall 7 days later. Participants were interviewed individually, their responses were recorded, and the computer screen was videotaped. In the training session, participants read and signed a consent form and received a written version of the instructions. During the first 3 minutes, a verbal protocol practice task was administered consisting of a "think aloud" description of the participant parent's house, as recommended by [22]. During both sessions, participants had to think aloud while performing the experiment. The experimenter reminded the participants that they had to think aloud if they remained silent for more than 15 s.

After signing the consent form, participants opened the notebook and read the instructions. At this point, the experimenter answered any question the participants had. Participants were instructed to pay close attention to what they did because they had to repeat it in one week. They were also informed that they would be explicitly instructed in 4 of the 12 tasks. When a task was explicitly instructed, the experimenter gave step-by-step instructions on how to perform the task. When the task was not explicitly instructed, the participant could explore the interface to "figure out" how to perform the task. During this process, users could undo or cancel any incorrect action. If after 60 s the participant did not show progress, the experimenter gave a hint that consisted in revealing the corresponding step of the sequence. The hints were the same as the ones used in the explicitly instructed version. The experimenter gave as many hints as needed in order from the first step to the last step, and allowed 60 s for exploration at each step.

For the recall session, participants had to perform the same training tasks and in the same order. During the recall session, none of the tasks was explicitly instructed, but hints were given if necessary following the same procedure used in the training session. At the end of the recall session, a survey was administered to obtain information about the participants' computer experience. After the questionnaire, the experimenter turned off the computer screen and handed the participants a piece of paper with the task descriptions used during the experiment. Participants were asked to write down as many labels as they could recall from the menus and other screen objects that had to be manipulated to perform each of the tasks.

Scoring and Data Measurement

During the explored part of the training session and during the whole recall session two measures were recorded for each task step: elapsed time, and number of hints. The experimenter recorded the number of hints whereas the VCR's counter was used to measure the time per step from the videotapes of the sessions.

Results

ANOVA tests were conducted for both dependent variables (time and number of hints) to determine the effect of the design factors. On average, no significant differences in performance were found between the group that received $10 for the experiment and the group that did not receive any payment. Additionally, there were no effects related to the configuration of the 24 menu structures that were used. None of these factors was included in further analyses. In this paper, the effects of type of learning: explicit instructed versus explored, and the results from the verbal protocols are not analyzed.

Task Data

The total elapsed time for each task was computed as the sum of the elapsed time for each of the 5 steps. Likewise, the number of hints was computed as the number of steps that could not be performed in less than 60 s and, therefore, required a hint. On average, each task was performed in 87.36 s during training (SD = 15.1), and in 68.1 s during recall (SD = 20.1). This difference was significant, $F(1, 47) = 51.35$, $p < .0001$. Similarly, 0.96 hints per task were given on average during training (SD = .35), and 0.67 during recall (SD = .22). This difference was also significant, $F(1,47) = 29.12$, $p < .0001$.

Time and number of hints were collapsed over the individual tasks, over sessions, and over degree of badness to analyze the effect of similarity pattern: (G, G), (G, B), (B, G), and (B, B). As expected, the pattern (G, G) was performed much faster and required fewer hints than the other three patterns ($F(1, 47) = 195.3$, $p < .0001$, $F(1,47) = 189.8$, $p < .0001$, for time and for hints, respectively). Likewise, the (B, B) pattern was performed much more slowly and required more hints than the other three patterns ($F(1, 47) = 183.9$, $p < .0001$, $F(1,47) = 156.1$, $p < .0001$, for time and for hints, respectively). Finally, there was no significant difference between the (G, B), and the (B, G) patterns ($F(1,47) = 1.71$, $p = .19$, $F(1, 47) = 2.19$, $p = .14$, for time and for hints, respectively). Figure 2 shows the effect of similarity pattern and the effect of degree of badness on task performance time. The interaction between task configuration and degree of badness was not significant.

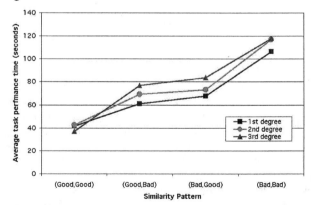

Figure 2. Effects of similarity pattern and degree of badness on **task** performance time. (3rd degree of badness represents the worst semantic similarity)

Step Data

Since only the semantic similarity of the second and third steps was manipulated, the data from those two steps were used to analyze the effects of semantic similarity and degree of badness. Collapsing over task configuration, sessions, and step number (second and third), the more semantically similar the label and the task description were, the faster step was performed and the fewer hints were required. Good steps (average cosine of .67) were performed, on average, in 7.97 s (SD = 4.56) and required .05 hints (SD = .06). On average, bad steps (average cosine of .11) were performed in 20.83 s (SD = 7.71) and required .17 hints (SD = .1). Broken down by degree of badness, bad steps (first degree of badness, cosine of .25) were performed, on average, in 18 s (SD = 7.75) and required .13 hints (SD = .1). Bad steps (second degree of badness, cosine of .15) were performed, on average, in 20.67 s (SD = 8.13) and required .17 hints (SD = .09). Bad steps (third degree of badness, cosine of -.05) were performed, on average, in 23.83 s (SD = 6.47) and required .22 hints (SD = .09).

Figure 3 shows a linear trend in the effect of semantic similarity on performance time. As expected, good steps were performed faster than the average bad step, $F(1,47) = 127.47$, $p < .0001$. Likewise, there was a reliable linear effect of degree of badness on the bad steps performance time, $F(1,47) = 4.86$, $p < .05$. When moving from one degree of badness to another (i.e., moving from more similar to less similar), the performance time increases, on average, by 2.9 s. Good steps required fewer hints than the average bad step, $F(1,47) = 60.69$, $p < .0001$. Additionally, for the bad steps, there was a reliable linear effect of degree of badness, $F(1,47) = 7.5$, $p < .05$. When moving from one degree of badness to another (i.e., moving from more similar to less similar), on average, .04 more hints were required per step.

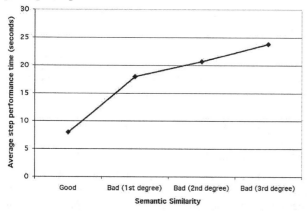

Figure 3. Effect of semantic similarity on **step** performance time. (3rd degree of badness represents the worst semantic similarity)

Free Recall Data

Replicating the literature [23], the correct action sequences necessary to perform the tasks were very poorly recalled when participants did not have access to the application interface. None of the subjects was able to recall a complete sequence of steps, and although 46 out of the 48 participants were able to recall at least one label, on average, only .11 labels were correctly recalled for each task.

DISCUSSION

Semantic similarity between task descriptions and menu labels reliably predicted the ease of discovering and recalling the experimental tasks. The semantic similarity, estimated by LSA cosines, predicted users' performance not only at the task level, but also at the individual step level. Different similarity patterns showed different reaction times: (G, G) was the fastest pattern, whereas (B, B) was the slowest. Additionally, it was shown that all subjects had very poor recall when they were away from the application interface.

Several models of learning by exploration have been reviewed here, all of which describe an attention mechanism that is driven by semantics. They agree that users select actions based on the semantic similarity between the task descriptions (or goals) and the display labels. These models assume that the display can be represented as a collection of objects and labels, and that other information about the objects (e.g., what action can be carried out on them) is stored in long-term memory. Therefore, to decide what object to act on, users semantically match object labels, task descriptions, and long-term memory knowledge. LSA can thus be applied appropriately to any of these models to estimate semantic similarity. Certainly, LSA cannot replace any of the models because there are other issues in exploration and action planning (e.g., backtracking) that could not be explained by a purely semantics based model. However, LSA can be a valuable addition to any of the models and provides a powerful tool to test the usability of applications.

Usability testing

It is impossible to design an application in which, for each task description, only highly semantically related labels are used in the action sequence. The hierarchical structure of the menu forces the designer to select very broad and sometime ambiguous labels at the top of the hierarchy. However, a good interface should guarantee that the correct label is always the one with the highest semantic similarity among the available labels. In order to evaluate the differences in semantic similarity between labels and task descriptions, an objective method, such as LSA, is desirable. So far, theorists and designers have used very informal estimates of semantic similarity. This study suggests that this may not be necessary.

LSA could be used in addition as an "automated" cognitive walkthrough [2]. This is a method for assessing the usability of a system, focusing on ease of learning. It involves hand simulation of the cognitive processes by which users, with no formal instruction, learn an application by exploration. The method takes into account users' elaboration of goals and users' interpretation of the application's feedback. The cognitive walkthrough is very labor intensive, and for this reason it is impractical for large modern applications. However, with LSA it would be possible to construct an automated system to evaluate large applications.

An alternative method is to hire expert designers to evaluate each of the labels of the application and their semantic similarity to the task descriptions. However, this method may be disadvantageous for various reasons. First, it may be highly unreliable because of the variance in opinion between one expert and another [24]. Second, it may be very time consuming, especially when tasks can be described in different ways, or when the application labels suffer minor changes during the design process. Finally, hiring expert evaluators can be very expensive.

LSA offers a more convenient method because it can rapidly estimate the semantic similarity of several alternative task descriptions and labels. When the application interface changes or when tasks are added or reformulated, the re-computation of the similarity estimates can be done very efficiently. Additionally, the estimation of semantic similarity can even be performed over the Internet (http://lsa.colorado.edu).

As stated above, LSA can be trained in any written language and with different corpora of texts. This makes it possible to model users with different backgrounds and skill levels. In the present study, a corpus of very broad and general knowledge was used to train LSA because the participants were mostly college freshmen, and there was no reason to believe they had any advanced technical knowledge. During the construction of the stimuli, it was discovered that one of the closest words to the phrase "hide the legend" (referring to a graph legend) was "dragons", with a cosine value of .41. This result is due to the fact that all the knowledge that the TASA space has about the word "legend" comes from epic novels, rather than from computer manuals ("map" and "heroes" are among the top 5 closest terms to "legend"). LSA has no way of knowing that "legend" also refers to part of a graph. The word "legend" was not used in the present experiment because it does not seem to be a good way to describe a graph legend to a novice user. Using computer manuals or other more technical materials to train LSA may result in better and more accurate models.

Conclusions

This study showed that semantic similarity accurately predicts the ease of learning new computer tasks. The degree of similarity between the object labels to be acted on and the task descriptions drives the exploratory behavior of novel users. LSA proved to be a reliable way to estimate semantic similarity and, therefore, can be applied to any of the cognitive models that has been developed to explain users' exploratory behavior. Eventually, LSA could be used in conjunction with other already available techniques (e.g., the cognitive walkthrough method) to automatically test the usability of computer applications.

ACKNOWLEDGMENTS

Partial support was provided by NASA Grant NCC 2-904. This paper is based on the author's master thesis [25]. The author thanks his thesis committee members, Professor Peter G. Polson (chair), Professor Tomas K. Landauer, and Professor Walter Kintsch, for their help and support in developing this project. Dr. Eileen Kintsch and three anonymous reviewers provided very helpful comments on earlier versions of this manuscript.

REFERENCES

1. Rieman, J., *et al.* (1991). An automated walkthrough. *Proceedings of CHI'91 Conference on Human Factors in Computer Systems*, pp. 427-428. New York, NY: ACM Press.

2. Polson, P.G., *et al.* (1992). Cognitive walkthroughs: A method for theory-based evaluation of user interfaces. *International Journal of Man-Machine Studies, 36*(5), 741-773.

3. Franzke, M. (1995). Turning research into practice: Characteristics of display-based interaction. *Proceedings of CHI'95 Conference on Human Factors in Computing Systems*, pp. 421-428. New York, NY: ACM Press.

4. Landauer, T.K., Foltz, P., and Laham, D. (1998). An Introduction to Latent Semantic Analysis. *Discourse Processes, 24*, 259-284.

5. Polson, P.G. and Lewis, C.H. (1990). Theory-based design for easily learned interfaces. *Human-Computer Interaction, 5*(2-3), 191-220.

6. Newell, A. and Simon, H.A. (1972). *Human Problem Solving*. Englewoods Cliffs, NJ: Prentice-Hall.

7. Engelbeck, G.E. (1986). *Exceptions to generalizations: implications for formal models of human-computer interaction*. Unpublished masters thesis, University of Colorado, Boulder, CO.

8. Muncher, E. (1989). *The acquisition of spreadsheet skills*. Unpublished masters thesis, University of Colorado, Boulder, CO.

9. Kitajima, M. and Polson, P.G. (1997). LICAI+: A Comprehension-Based Model of Learning for Display-Based Human–Computer Interaction. *Proceedings of CHI'97 Conference on Human Factors in Computing Systems*, pp. 333-334. New York, NY: ACM Press.

10. Landauer, T.K., Galotti, K.M., and Hartwell, S. (1983). Natural Command Names and Initial Learning: A study of Text-Editing Terms. *Communications of the ACM, 26*(7), 495-503.

11. Howes, A. and Young, R.M. (1996). Learning consistent, interactive and meaningful device methods: A computational model. *Cognitive Science, 20*, 301-356.

12. Rieman, J., Young, R.M., and Howes, A. (1996). A dual-space model of iteratively deepening exploratory learning. *International Journal of Human-Computer Studies, 44*(6), 743-775.

13. Rieman, J.F. (1994). *Learning Strategies and Exploratory Behavior of Interactive Computer Users*. Unpublished Doctoral Dissertation, University of Colorado, Boulder, CO.

14. Kitajima, M. and Polson, P.G. (1997). A Comprehension-Based Model of Exploration. *Human-Computer Interaction, 12*, 439-462.

15. Kitajima, M., Soto, R., and Polson, P.G. (1998). LICAI+: A Comprehension-Based Model of The Recall of

Action Sequences. In F. Ritter and R.M. Young (Eds.), *Proceedings of the Second European Conference on Cognitive Modelling (Nottingham, April 1-4, 1998)* (pp. 82-89). Nottingham, UK: Nottingham University Press.

16. Kintsch, W. (1998). *Comprehension: A paradigm for cognition.* New York, NY: Cambridge University Press.

17. Mannes, S.M. and Kintsch, W. (1991). Routine Computing Tasks: Planning as Understanding. *Cognitive Science, 15*, 305-342.

18. Deerwester, S., *et al.* (1990). Indexing by Latent Semantic Analysis. *Journal of the American Society For Information Science, 41*(6), 391-407.

19. Landauer, T.K. and Dumais, S.T. (1997). A solution to Plato's problem: The latent semantic analysis theory of acquisition, induction, and representation of knowledge. *Psychological Review, 104*(2), 211-240.

20. Landauer, T.K. and Dumais, S.T. (1996). How come you know so much? From practical problem to theory. In D. Hermann, *et al.* (Eds.), *Basic and applied memory: Memory in context* (pp. 105-126). Mahwah, NJ: Erlbaum.

21. Landauer, T.K. and Dumais, S.T. (1994). Latent semantic analysis and the measurement of knowledge. In R.M. Kaplan and J.C. Burstein (Eds.), *Educational testing service conference on natural language processing techniques and technology in assessment and education* . Princeton, N.J.: Educational Testing Service.

22. Ericsson, A.K. and Simon, H.A. (1980). Verbal Reports as Data. *Psychological Review, 87*(3), 215-251.

23. Payne, S.J. (1991). Display-based action at the user interface. *International Journal of Man-Machine Studies, 35*, 275-289.

24. Nielsen, J. (1992). *Applying Heuristic Evaluation to a Highly Domain-Specific User Interface.* Technical memorandum. Morristown, NJ: Bellcore.

25. Soto, R. (1998). *Learning and Performing by Exploration: Label Quality Measured by Latent Semantic Analysis.* Unpublished master thesis, University of Colorado, Boulder, CO.

MOBILE: User-Centered Interface Building

Angel R. Puerta, Eric Cheng, Tunhow Ou , Justin Min
RedWhale Software and Stanford University
192 Walter Hays Drive
Palo Alto, CA 94303 USA
+1 650 325 4587
puerta@redwhale.com – http://www.redwhale.com

ABSTRACT

Interface builders are popular tools for designing and developing graphical user interfaces. These tools, however, are engineering-centered; they operate mainly on windows and widgets. A typical interface builder does not offer any specific support for user-centered interface design, a methodology recognized as critical for effective user interface design. We present MOBILE (Model-Based Interface Layout Editor) an interface building tool that fully supports user-centered design and that guides the interface building process by using user-task models and a knowledge base of interface design guidelines. The approach in MOBILE has the important added benefit of being useful in both top-down and bottom-up interface design strategies.

Keywords

Model-based interface development, task models, interface builders, user-centered interface design, user interface development tools.

INTRODUCTION

For a good number of years, interface-building tools have gained wide acceptance among developers of graphical user interfaces [1]. Interface builders allow developers to layout and organize, via direct manipulation, the various elements of a graphical user interface (GUI). Typically, these tools include code generators that produce the basic hooks for application developers to write the code to communicate with the user interface. All major commercial software-development environments currently available include interface-building tools.

Although efficient at what they do, interface builders restrict their scope to manipulation of those elements that make up a GUI, such as windows and widgets. They support, in essence, an engineering process. An interface

developer working with an interface builder occupies his or her thoughts with widget selection, layout, and organizational issues. Any connection between the operations made through an interface builder and the requirements of the target users and their tasks must be maintained in the head of the developer without assistance from the interface-building tool.

Separately, the user-interface community has come to accept that one of the best methodologies for user-interface construction is that of *user-centered design* [2]. The basis of this methodology is straightforward: The design of a user interface should be guided principally by the nature of the task that the user needs to accomplish. This differs from so-called engineering-centered approaches where interface design decisions are made according to the requirements of the application being built. The benefits of user-centered design have been clearly demonstrated over the years [2].

It is therefore curious that the clearly effective graphical interface builders do not support the similarly effective user-centered approach. This opens the question of how could interface builders be augmented, enhanced, or modified in order to enable a user-centered approach but without changing the operations in such a way that the original benefits of the tools disappear.

OUR SOLUTION

The approach taken by our group incorporates elements of user-centered design and of model-based interface development into the functionality of an interface builder. From user-centered design we take the idea of building user-task representations as a guide for interface development. From model-based interface development [3] we take the ability to create, edit and refine user-task models. These models are computational units that can be exploited by an interface builder. Finally, from interface builders we take their basic functionality and try to augment it in very specific ways (using user-task models) to enable a user-centered process.

The result is a tool called MOBILE (Model-Based Interface Layout Editor), which enables user-centered interface building. MOBILE allows developers to interactively build user interfaces according to a user-task model. The tool also provides decision-support guidance thanks to knowledge base of interface design guidelines. Users of MOBILE can benefit whether they use a top-down approach (i.e., build a user-task model and then an interface), or a bottom-up one (i.e., build a user interface and construct a user-task model that goes along with it).

The rest of the paper is organized as follows. We first provide some contextual information about model-based interface development. Then, we describe MOBILE and its main functional characteristics. We illustrate the use of the tool via a sample target interface. We proceed by detailing the decision-support capabilities of MOBILE and by describing its use in a bottom-up approach. We conclude by relating our evaluation experiences, the work related to our approach, and the possible directions of future research.

MOBI-D

Model-based interface development [3] is a technology that embraces the idea of designing and developing user interfaces by creating *interface models*. An interface model is a computational representation of all the relevant aspects of a user interface. The components of an interface model include submodels such as user-task models, domain models, user models, presentation models and dialog models. Model-based interface development systems are suites of software tools that allow developers to create and edit interface models. Many model-based systems aim at generating significant parts of a user interface given a partial interface model. Some others aim at interactively guiding developers in building user interfaces using interface models [3].

Over the past three years, our group has been developing MOBI-D (Model Based Interface Designer) [3]. MOBI-D is a model-based interface development environment that enables designers and developers to interactively create user interfaces by defining interface models. The environment integrates a variety of tools including model-editing tools, user-task elicitation tools, and the interface building tool presented here.

A full description of the model-based interface technology and development methodology supported by MOBI-D has been presented elsewhere [3] and it is beyond the scope of this paper. Some of the other individual tools integrated into MOBI-D have also been described in previous publications [4-6]. For our purposes, however, we simply need to note that a component of the interface models constructed in MOBI-D is a user-task model. This component is the essential element for the interface-building tool presented in this paper.

User-Task Models

A user-task model in MOBI-D is a hierarchical representation of a user's task. The model decomposes the user task into subtasks arranged in a tree-like structure. Attributes can be specified for any task as well as procedural information (e.g., whether certain sub tasks must be executed in sequence). Conditions that affect the execution of a task/subtask can also be specified in the model. Domain objects (and their attributes) involved in the completion of a task can also be defined and associated with any task. In general, a user-task model is less complex than a workflow diagram and it can retain a certain informal level to it without losing its usefulness. In MOBI-D, user-task models are elicited from domain experts and then refined by interface developers [4]. Once created, it is available to any of the other tools in the environment.

SAMPLE INTERFACE

For illustration purposes of some of the shortcomings of conventional interface builders, let us consider the partial interface shown in Figures 1 through 3, which has been designed using the MOBI-D tools. These figures show screen snapshots from a military logistics application. This application allows users to perform typical tasks associated with requesting and monitoring supplies in a theater of operations. These tasks include among others: (1) creating and modifying plans for requisitions of materials, (2) reviewing potential suppliers for location, available stocks, and delivery times, (3) requesting supplies and tracking shipments, and reviewing all current stocks of materials

The application supports users of different ranks. The dialog and presentation should adapt to the rank of the user and to the specific task that the user must perform. In the screen snapshots we can observe the following situations:

Figure 1 is the initial screen (after login) for a user of rank Major. Typically, a user of this application needs to see the *authorized stock levels* (ASLs) for the current operation and needs access to a map of the region. The Major can inspect the ASLs via the 3-D viewer shown on the left. She can change the data in the viewer to that of a different location by clicking on the particular location on the map shown on the right. Each row of bars in the 3-D viewer (lengthwise) corresponds to a different class of materials (e.g., subsistence items, ammunition). The user can quickly see in this viewer if any class has a deficiency in ASLs in which case, he is authorized to modify it and does so via the push button shown above the 3-D viewer. We determined from domain experts and from the construction of a user-task model for this interface that this screen fulfills the first activity that a user must perform (overview of operation) and that the data presented was exactly (not more or less) what is needed to complete the overview.

Figure 2 shows the initial screen for a user of rank Sergeant. This user can also inspect ASLs according to location but since her task is different to that of a Major, the dialog and presentation adapt. The central role of a

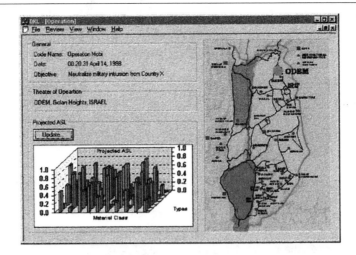

Figure 1. Initial screen in logistics application for a user of rank Major.

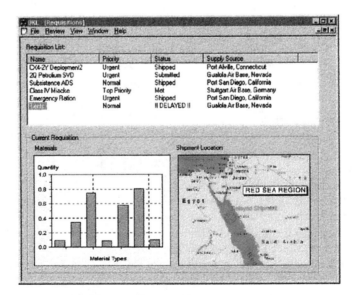

Figure 2. Initial screen in logistics application for a user of rank Sergeant.

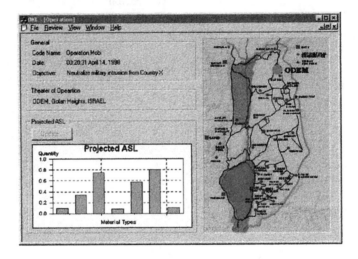

Figure 3. Shipment inspection screen for a user of rank Sergeant.

Sergeant in this scenario is to carry out the requisition plans constructed by the major. The Sergeant observes when supplies are running low and orders new shipments that conform to the levels set by the Major. Because a Sergeant deals only with one specific class of materials (e.g., subsistence items only), the interface uses a 2-D viewer for the ASLs. In addition, since a Sergeant is not authorized to modify ASLs, the pushbutton for access to the ASL modification screens is disabled. The user-task information is again derived from the accompanying user-task model.

Figure 3 shows a shipment inspection screen for a user of rank Sergeant. Once more, the complete information needed to perform the inspection task is included in this screen as dictated by the user-task model. Interestingly, under certain conditions (e.g., shipment delay) this screen must be the initial screen for a Sergeant user (as opposed to that of Figure 2). In such a situation, the decision context of the Sergeant changes from one of *monitoring* (as in Figure 2) to one of *repair* (e.g., request new shipment, wait, reroute other shipment).

Clearly, a conventional interface builder can be used to layout and arrange the elements of any of the screens discussed above. However, such a tool would offer no help with managing any of the user-task requirements. Issues such as how data should be split among the screens, what widgets correspond to what type of user, and how the dialog changes according to the task and user characteristics are well beyond the support of a typical interface builder. In practice, it may be that such user-task information is kept in paper documents, or is viewable through a separate tool, or (worse) it is just in the head of the designer. The result is bound to be a number of mismatches between the designed screens and the user-task specifications. In addition, revisions of the screens or of the specifications can produce even more pronounced mismatches, or at the very least a cumbersome coordination process.

We aim for a much higher level of coordination and support for user-task specifications in the interface building process. This is the central goal of MOBILE.

MOBILE

MOBILE (Model-Based Interface Layout Editor) is an interactive software tool for user-centered interface building. Figure 4 shows the main architectural components of MOBILE. A task/presentation manager communicates with an interface model to obtain and update information related to user-task models and presentation elements of the target interface. The interface model is also used by a knowledge base of interface design guidelines to manage a palette of standard and custom widgets that interface designers use to select elements for layout.

The general philosophy in MOBILE is to guide and facilitate the interface building process. It is never to automate the creative decision facets of that process.

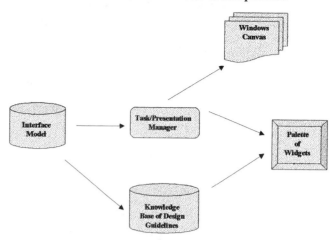

Figure 4. Architectural components of MOBILE.

Functionality

Figure 5 shows the main functional elements of MOBILE during the design of the screen shown in Figure 1. The task/presentation manager is shown to the left as a split-screen view. The palette of widgets (top right) is a toolbar where each icon represents an available widget. The canvas area (bottom right) is the drop target for selected widgets where interface elements are arranged under the direction of the interface designer.

The lower pane of the task manager is the user-task model inspector. Here the interface designer can review the hierarchy of tasks and subtasks. Limited operations are possible in this pane. The designer can add a new task (by clicking on the icon just above the task inspector), delete tasks, or regroup them in a different order. More elaborate operations on the user task model (e.g., setting task attributes) require moving to a separate model-editing tool in MOBI-D. This separation is by design and was determined by our evaluation of MOBILE (see evaluation section). Immediately above the user-task inspector is also the end-user selector pull-down list. Changing the user selected in this list results on the task inspector being updated with the user-task model for the specific user type selected.

The lower pane of the presentation manager is the presentation inspector. Here the interface designer can review the elements of the interface and their relationship to the user-task elements. The top elements in the presentation trees are windows (a window can be a regular window or a dialog panel). Underneath each window, as per the tree hierarchy is the task(s) assigned to that particular window by the designer. Each window can have multiple tasks assigned to it and each task in a window can have any number of subtasks. The leaf elements of the

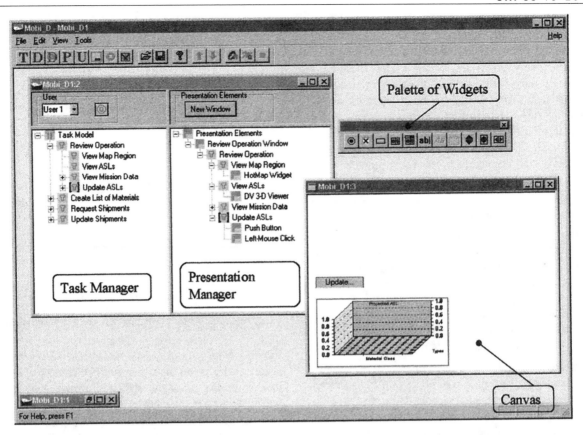

Figure 5. The main functional elements of MOBILE: The task/presentation manager on the left, the palette of widgets on the top right, and a windows canvas area.

presentation tree are found under subtasks and include the widget that allows completion of the subtask (e.g., a push button, a 3-D viewer), and an interaction technique (e.g., a left-mouse click). Immediately above the presentation inspector there is a button to create new windows in the presentation tree. New windows can also be created by dragging a task onto the presentation manager and dropping it at the appropriate level in the presentation tree.

The palette of widgets is a toolbar populated with icons each symbolizing an available widget. The widgets can vary from standard ones, such as checkboxes and text fields, to complex ones, such as the 3-D viewer shown in Figure 1. These widgets are not created and maintained by us. They are strictly third-party elements. For example, the 3-D viewer is an ActiveX control supplied by a company called DataViews [7]. In general, the MOBILE palette can access standard Windows95 widgets and any other widget wrapped as either a Java Bean or an ActiveX control. The canvas areas in MOBILE are identical to those of conventional interface builders.

The various elements of MOBILE are coordinated so that if the designer selects a particular task, the other views are updated automatically to reflect the presentation elements that correspond to that task. Similarly, selection of a widget on the canvas causes the update of the task and presentation managers.

A typical sequence of designer operations in MOBILE is as follows. The designer starts the tool and selects a target end user via the user selector. This updates the user-task inspector with the user-task model corresponding to the selected end user. The presentation inspector appears initially empty (except for the root element). The designer creates one or more new windows that are inserted automatically into the presentation tree. The next step is to assign tasks from the user-task model to specific windows. This is accomplished by simple drag-and-drop operations. If a dragged task contains any subtasks, these are also included in the same window as the parent task (the designer can later change this assignment).

Following task assignment, the designer selects specific windows within the presentation tree. For each window, the designer accepts or modifies the subtasks that are grouped into that window (by visual inspection). This may require merging or splitting windows if changes are desired. Ultimately, the designer reaches a satisfactory arrangement of tasks into windows. At that point, the designer then selects each leaf subtask (i.e., a subtask that has no subtasks of its own) and uses the palette of widgets to select a widget to complete that particular subtask. Additionally, the designer can select an interaction technique(s) to perform the task.

In our example, the sequence looks like this (refer to Figure 5). The designer selects *user1* (of type Major) and the corresponding user-task model is displayed. After creating a *new window*, the designer drags the task *review operation* onto the new window. This window is automatically relabeled *review operation window*. All subtasks of *review operation* are placed under the *review operation window*. For each leaf subtask (e.g., *view map region*, *view ASLs*) the designer selects one widget from the palette to perform the operation (e.g., the 3-D viewer widget for the *view ASLs* subtask).

Note some interesting decisions from the design of the screen in Figure 1. The user-task model in the task inspector of Figure 5 shows four subtasks for the task *review operation*. The subtask update ASLs has some subtasks of its own (as revealed by the "+" sign next to its name). However, no such subtasks appear for *the update ASLs* subtask in the presentation inspector of Figure 5. The designer has noted that the update subtask is optional (this is conveyed by the somewhat different icon next to the task name in the task inspector). Because of its optional nature, the designer decides not to clutter the screen with potentially useless elements and to relegate any subtasks of *update ASLs* to a different screen. The designer simply provides a navigation button for the end user whom will use it, if necessary, to access the update functionality.

Second, the screen in Figure 2 shows that the button for *update ASLs* is disabled for a user of type Sergeant. We already discussed that users of this rank are not allowed to perform updates. In the task inspector window this results in the *update ASLs* subtask not appearing as part of the user-task model when the designer selects a user of this rank. Without any changes by the designer, the consequence would be that the screen of Figure 2 would contain no button at all for the Update of ASLs. Instead, the designer decided to add the *update ASLs* task to the user-task model of *Sergeant* and in place of *left-mouse-click* (as in Figure 5 for users of type *Major*) insert *disabled*. This decision was made for purely aesthetic reasons in this case as it avoided creating a wide blank area within the screen.

This type of close coordination between use-task requirements and interface building is the main benefit of MOBILE. Designers can evaluate at all times their interface building decisions based on the specifications of the user task. They can also effectively manage the links between the various types of users, the user-task specifications for each user, and the widgets and interaction techniques that correspond to each task and subtask. Furthermore, assignment of user-tasks into windows is a direct manipulation operation. None of these important functions are available in conventional interface builders.

DECISION SUPPORT

In addition to the basic functionality offered by MOBILE, a knowledge-based decision support system complements the assistance given by the tool to interface designers.

As we discussed earlier, a user-task model encompasses knowledge about the attributes and nature of user tasks as well as about the domain objects involved in the completion of a given task. When a designer working with MOBILE selects a subtask for which a widget must be assigned, MOBILE can exploit the user-task knowledge to assist in the assignment process.

Based on the attributes of tasks and their related domain objects, MOBILE can consult a knowledge base of interface design guidelines to determine what are the most appropriate widgets to use for a given task. The knowledge base is essentially a decision tree. The inference mechanism looks at attributes of objects, such as data types and value ranges, in order to traverse the tree to find optimal widgets. As a simple example, if a data/domain object to be accessed via the interface is of type Boolean, then the inference mechanism will recommend a checkbox as a suitable widget. The widgets identified in this manner may also be grouped into discrete categories reflecting their relative suitability (e.g., high, medium, or low).

When a designer working in MOBILE sets a preference to work in *guided mode*, the tool reflects its decision-support capabilities via the palette of widgets. As the designer selects a subtask for assignment of a widget, MOBILE disables all widgets in the palette that make no sense according to the knowledge base of interface design guidelines. In addition, MOBILE will highlight the widgets that are considered of high suitability. In this manner the attention of the user is directed towards the optimal widgets and irrelevant choices are removed from consideration.

In addition to widget assignment, MOBILE also exploits the user-task models to provide a *user-task- and domain-specific interface building experience* to the designer. For example, in conventional interface builders when the designer selects a push button from a palette of widgets and places the widget on a window canvas, the widget appears with either a generic label (e.g., "button1") or no label at all. In MOBILE, every widget assigned appears already tailored to the specific task and domains. In the case of Figure 1, the button for updating ASLs first appears on the window with that label as the information is carried directly from the user-task model. This capability serves to further solidify the user-centered design experience for the user of MOBILE.

BOTTOM-UP INTERFACE DESIGN STRATEGIES

The use of MOBILE described so far follows a strict top-down approach. First a user-task model must be built, then MOBILE can be used to lay out a corresponding interface.

It can be easily argued that this limits the freedom of interface designers. Some designers like to immediately jump into an interface builder and informally construct possible designs for a user interface. Having to work out a user model beforehand may be an undesirable burden for these designers.

Fortunately, MOBILE can be used by this type of designer and still potentially provide some of the user-centered benefits of the tool. A bottom-up approach with MOBILE would entail the same kind of free-form interface layout that is available with a conventional interface builder. However, once the designer starts settling with a particular set of layouts, the designer can *annotate* each window (and widget) with a newly created user task and then can arrange the tasks into a skeleton user-task model. In this mode, MOBILE acts as a *design rationale* tool. The initial user-task model can always be refined into a complete one that would be useful in any revision and update of the interface.

EVALUATION

The implementation of MOBILE shown here has evolved through several evaluations that also included an early mock-up and two preceding prototypes. Along the way, we learned what are the functions that designers really want in a tool like MOBILE, and how the on-screen items should be arranged for better efficiency in the interaction.

Our initial mock-up did not include a task/presentation manager. Instead it counted on the existence of a user-task model-editing tool in MOBI-D. MOBILE simply provided canvas areas for windows, each with an attached palette of widgets populated specifically for that window and its associated task. Users were quick to point out that it was cumbersome to continually switch from MOBILE to the user-task model editor. Furthermore, the model editor included lots of functions that were not relevant at interface-building time. The one-palette-per-screen approach also seemed to consume too much screen real estate.

Our first prototype was entirely task-based (i.e., a user-task inspector but no presentation inspector). The user-task inspector included only the functionality for editing user-task models that users felt was relevant (deleting, adding, and regrouping tasks). A single palette was attached to the inspector. The palette changed its widgets according to which task was selected in the user-task model inspector. Designers remarked that it was important for them to be able to see the organization of the presentation elements (this could be done but only by switching to another view within MOBI-D).

The second prototype included a task/presentation manager similar to the current one, and a dynamic palette that changed its widgets with each task/subtask selection in the manager. The main difficulty in this version was

that designers did not want the palette changing continuously. This forced them to visually inspect the palette for every task to see what widgets appeared and in what order.

In the current prototype, we fixed the elements of the palette of widgets. Their location on the palette is always the same. We simply change their enable/disable state and highlight widget icons if necessary, as detailed on the earlier section on decision support. We also don't make any changes to the palette if the user is selecting tasks/subtasks in the user-task inspector (as we did in previous versions). We only modify the palette when the user selects a subtask in the presentation inspector. In the earlier version, it caused confusion for users to be inspecting user tasks in the user-task inspector for possible regrouping (i.e., not an actual interface-building operation) and having the palette change with each selection (a true interface-building operation).

RELATED WORK

There are three areas directly related to our work: interface builders, user-centered design, and model-based interface development. There are excellent comprehensive surveys of existing interface builders and other software tools [1]. We will refer to those surveys but will remark again that we are not aware of any interface builder that exploits interface models to support its operations. Similarly, much has been written about user-centered design [2]. However, no specific implementations have arisen from this field to address the shortcomings of interface builders.

The work closest related to ours is that of other model-based interface development systems. UIDE [8] was one of the first systems to introduce the notion of using interface models to drive interface development. ADEPT [9] used effectively for the first time user-task models in their approach to generate user interfaces. UIDE [8] and Mecano [10], among others, exploited the idea of being able to generate automatically the elements of an interface layout from the attributes of the data/domain objects to be displayed on the interface. A number of other systems have also improved or modified to a certain extent the techniques of user-task modeling and interface generation. In particular, TRIDENT [11] has combined the use of user-task models with a knowledge base of interface design guidelines to guide the generation of an interface.

The key difference between earlier systems and MOBI-D is that the former placed an emphasis on the automated generation of an interface given a partial interface model. For example, generating a concrete interface in ADEPT from a user-task model. Because of the automated approach, these systems did not attempt to incorporate interactive tools, such as an interface builder, directly into their interface modeling approaches. Therefore, efforts such as MOBILE have not been attempted in the past by those systems.

CONCLUSIONS

We have presented a software tool, called MOBILE, which enables user-centered design approaches for interface builders. The tool combines the recognized benefits of user-centered design with the efficient functionality of interface builders. We have, in addition, created knowledge-based techniques for decision support that further augment the capabilities of the tool over conventional interface builders. We have evaluated the tool and made extensive changes to its design based on user recommendations.

One area that we are currently improving is the flexibility of design in the relationship between tasks and presentations. As shown in the example of Figure 5, there has to be a certain isomorphism between tasks and widgets. In the example, there is a one to one mapping. We are now constructing a version of MOBILE that allows a task to encompass multiple domain/data objects. Each domain object can then be mapped to its own widget. This introduces a much higher degree of design flexibility.

MOBILE can serve as an initial step also in demonstrating the value of model-based interface development technologies. We expect to further enhance MOBILE by providing additional decision-support functions, such as layout critics. Our current experience with the tool is of course limited. We do not know yet how it will respond in designs that include large and complex user-task models. Nor do we have an extensive knowledge base of interface design guidelines that will cover a majority of widget assignment situations. However, we feel the MOBILE approach significantly helps in advancing user-centered design principles in practical user interface building, a definite worthwhile goal.

ACKNOWLEDGEMENTS

The work on MOBI-D is supported by DARPA under contract N66001-96-C-8525. We thank Hung-Yut Chen, James J. Kim, Kjetil Larsen, David Maulsby, Dat Nguyen, David Selinger, and Chung-Man Tam for their work on the implementation and use of MOBI-D.

REFERENCES

1. Myers, B., *User Interface Software Tools*. ACM Transactions on Computer-Human Interaction, 1995. 2(1): p. 65-103.

2. Norman, D. and S. Draper, eds. *User Centered System Design.* . 1986, LEA.

3. Puerta, A.R., *A Model-Based Interface Development Environment*, in *IEEE Software*. 1997. pp. 40-47.

4. Tam, R.C.-M., D. Maulsby, and A. Puerta. *U-TEL: A Tool for Eliciting User Task Models from Domain Experts*. In *IUI98: 1998 International Conference on Intelligent User Interfaces*. 1998. San Francisco, CA: ACM Press.

5. Puerta, A. and D. Maulsby. *Management of Interface Design Knowledge with MOBI-D*. In *IUI97: 1997 International Conference on Intelligent User Interfaces*. 1997.

6. Puerta, A. and J. Eisenstein. *Interactively Mapping Task Models to Interfaces in MOBI-D*. In *DSV-IS98: Eurographics Workshop*. 1998. Abingdon, England.

7. Valaer, L. and R. Babb. *Choosing a User Interface Development Tool*, in *IEEE Software*. 1997. pp. 29-39.

8. Foley, J., *et al.*, *UIDE-An Intelligent User Interface Design Environment*, in *Intelligent User Interfaces*, J. Sullivan and S. Tyler, Editors. 1991, Addison-Wesley. p. 339-384.

9. Johnson, P., S. Wilson, and H. Johnson, *Scenarios, Task Analysis, and the ADEPT Design Environment*, in *Scenario Based Design*, J. Carrol, Editor. 1994, Addison-Wesley.

10. Puerta, A. and H. Eriksson. *Model-Based Automated Generation of User Interfaces*. In *AAAI'94*. 1994: AAAI Press.

11. Vanderdonckt, J.M. and F. Bodart. *Encapsulating Knowledge for Intelligent Automatic Interaction Objects Selection*. In *InterCHI'93*. 1993: ACM Press.

The Context Toolkit:
Aiding the Development of Context-Enabled Applications

Daniel Salber, Anind K. Dey and Gregory D. Abowd

GVU Center, College of Computing

Georgia Institute of Technology

Atlanta, GA 30332-0280

+1 404 894 7512

{salber, anind, abowd}@cc.gatech.edu

ABSTRACT

Context-enabled applications are just emerging and promise richer interaction by taking environmental context into account. However, they are difficult to build due to their distributed nature and the use of unconventional sensors. The concepts of toolkits and widget libraries in graphical user interfaces has been tremendously successful, allowing programmers to leverage off existing building blocks to build interactive systems more easily. We introduce the concept of context widgets that mediate between the environment and the application in the same way graphical widgets mediate between the user and the application. We illustrate the concept of context widgets with the beginnings of a widget library we have developed for sensing presence, identity and activity of people and things. We assess the success of our approach with two example context-enabled applications we have built and an existing application to which we have added context-sensing capabilities.

Keywords
Context-enabled or context-aware computing, ubiquitous computing, toolkits, widgets, applications development

INTRODUCTION

Over the last decade, several researchers have built applications that take advantage of environmental information, also called context, to enhance the interaction with the user. The construction of these context-enabled applications is cumbersome, and currently no tools are available to facilitate the development of this class of applications. This paper presents a toolkit for developing reusable solutions for handling context information in interactive applications.

We first define the notion of context, and through a brief review of the literature identify the key challenges of developing applications that sense context, followed by an overview of the paper.

What Is Context?

Environmental information or context covers information that is part of an application's operating environment and that can be sensed by the application. This typically includes the location, identity, activity and state of people, groups and objects. Context may also be related to places or the computing environment. Places such as buildings and rooms can be fitted with sensors that provide measurements of physical variables such as temperature or lighting. Finally, an application may sense its software and hardware environment to detect, for example, the capabilities of nearby resources.

Sensing context information makes several kinds of context-enabled applications possible: Applications may display context information, capture it for later access and provide context-based retrieval of stored information. Of major interest are context-aware applications, which sense context information and modify their behavior accordingly without explicit user intervention.

Why Use Context?

Usage scenarios of typical context-enabled applications found in the literature have led us to identify recurrent challenges, which we further detail below.

Mobile tour guides are designed to familiarize a visitor with a new area. They sense the user's location and provide information relevant to both the user and the location she's at [1, 3, 6, 10]. Likewise, office awareness systems sense users' locations, but are also interested in their activities to help people locate each other, maintain awareness or forward phone calls [12, 17, 18]. In ubiquitous computing systems, devices sense and take advantage of nearby resources: a handheld computer located next to an electronic whiteboard may make use of the larger display surface or allow the user to interact with other nearby handheld users [14, 18]. Finally, context-based retrieval applications gather and store context information and allow later information retrieval based on context information. For instance the user can ask a note-taking application to pull up the notes taken at a previous meeting with the group she's meeting with currently [9, 13].

Why Is Using Context Difficult?

The above usage scenarios raise the following difficulties, which are common to most applications that use context information. These difficulties stem from the very nature of context information:

1) It is acquired from unconventional sensors. Mobile devices for instance may acquire location information from outdoor GPS receivers or indoor positioning systems. Tracking the location of people or detecting their presence may require Active Badge devices, floor-embedded presence sensors or video image processing.

2) It must be abstracted to make sense for the application. GPS receivers for instance provide geographical coordinates. But tour guide applications would make better use of higher-level information such as street or building names. Similarly, Active Badges provide IDs, which must be abstracted into user names and locations.

3) It may be acquired from multiple distributed and heterogeneous sources. Tracking the location of users in an office requires gathering information from multiple sensors throughout the office. Furthermore, context sensing technologies such as video image processing may introduce uncertainty: they usually provide a ranked list of candidate results. Detecting the presence of people in a room reliably may require combining the results of several techniques such as image processing, audio processing, floor-embedded pressure sensors, etc.

4) It is dynamic. Changes in the environment must be detected in real time and applications must adapt to constant changes. For instance, when a user equipped with a handheld moves away from the electronic whiteboard, the user loses the benefit of the wide display surface and the application must modify its behavior accordingly. Also, context information history is valuable, as shown by context-based retrieval applications. A dynamic and historical model allows applications to fully exploit the richness of context information.

Although these problems are recurrent we lack conceptual models and tools to describe solutions to these problems.

Overview Of Paper

This paper presents a context toolkit aimed at developing reusable solutions to address these problems and thus make it easier to build context-enabled applications. The inspiration for this context toolkit is the success of toolkits in graphical user interface (GUI) development. The context toolkit builds upon the widget concept from GUI toolkits. In the same way GUI toolkits insulate the application from interaction details handled by widgets, the context toolkit insulates the application from context sensing mechanics through widgets. We first introduce the concepts underlying the context toolkit and describe applications it allowed us to build. We discuss details of the toolkit implementation that address specific problems of distribution, heterogeneity and dynamism that are not addressed by GUI toolkits. We conclude with future plans for the evolution of the context toolkit.

DESIGNING A CONTEXT TOOLKIT

The context toolkit we have developed relies on the concept of context widgets. Just as GUI widgets mediate between the application and the user, context widgets mediate between the application and its operating environment. We analyze the benefits of GUI widgets, introduce the concept of context widget, detail its benefits, and explain how context-enabled applications are built using these widgets.

Learning From Graphical User Interface Widgets

It is now taken for granted that GUI application designers and programmers can reuse existing interaction solutions embodied in GUI toolkits and widget libraries. GUI widgets (sometimes called interactors) span a large range of interaction solutions: selecting a file; triggering an action; choosing options; or even direct manipulation of graphical objects [11].

GUI toolkits have three main benefits:

- They *hide specifics* of physical interaction devices from the applications programmer so that those devices can change with minimal impact on applications. Whether the user points and clicks with a mouse or fingers and taps on a touchpad or uses keyboard shortcuts doesn't require any changes to the application.

- They *manage the details* of the interaction to provide applications with relevant results of user actions. Widget-specific dialogue is handled by the widget itself, and the application often only needs to implement a single callback to be notified of the result of an interaction sequence.

- They *provide reusable building blocks* of presentation to be defined once and reused, combined, and/or tailored for use in many applications. Widgets provide encapsulation of appearance and behavior. The programmer doesn't need to know the inner workings of a widget to use it.

Although toolkits and widgets are known to have limitations such as being too low-level or lacking flexibility, they provide stepping stones for designing and building user interfaces and developing tools such as User Interface Management Systems (UIMS). With context widgets, we aim at providing similar stepping stones for designing and building context-enabled applications.

What Is A Context Widget?

A context widget is a software component that provides applications with access to context information from their operating environment. In the same way GUI widgets insulate applications from some presentation concerns, context widgets insulate applications from context acquisition concerns.

Context widgets provide the following benefits:

- They *hide the complexity* of the actual sensors used from the application. Whether the presence of people is sensed using Active Badges, floor sensors, video image processing or a combination of these should not impact the application.

- They *abstract context information* to suit the expected needs of applications. A widget that tracks the location of a user within a building or a city notifies the application only when the user moves from one room to another, or from one street corner to another, and doesn't report less significant moves to the application. Widgets provide abstracted information that we expect applications to need the most frequently.

- They *provide reusable and customizable building blocks* of context sensing. A widget that tracks the location of a user can be used by a variety of applications, from tour guides to office awareness systems. Furthermore, context widgets can be tailored and combined in ways similar to GUI widgets. For example, a *Presence* widget senses the presence of people in a room. A *Meeting* widget may rely on a *Presence* widget and assume a meeting is beginning when two or more people are present.

These benefits address issues 1 and 2 listed in the introduction. From the application's perspective, context widgets encapsulate context information and provide methods to access it in a way very similar to a GUI toolkit. However, due to the characteristics of context and notably issues 3 and 4 mentioned in the introduction, distribution and dynamicity, the context toolkit has some unique features. We briefly describe the similarities with GUI toolkits and point out some major differences.

How Applications Use Context Widgets

Context widgets have a state and a behavior. The widget state is a set of attributes that can be queried by applications. For example, an *IdentityPresence* widget has attributes for its location, the last time a presence was detected, and the identity of the last user detected. Applications can also register to be notified of context changes detected by the widget. The widget triggers callbacks to the application when changes in the environment are detected. The *IdentityPresence* widget for instance, provides callbacks to notify the application when a new person arrives, or when a person leaves.

Context widgets are basic building blocks that manage sensing of a particular piece of context. We expect full-fledged context-aware applications to take advantage of multiple types of context information and rely on a rich dynamic model of their operating environment. To this end, our widget toolkit provides means of composing widgets. For example, a widget designed to detect the kind of activity people in a classroom are engaged in could combine the information provided by presence widgets and activity sensing widgets using, for instance, audio and video analysis. Based on information provided by widgets such as the number of people in the room, their location in the room, the speakers, activity in the front of the classroom, the composite widget would detect activities such as lecture, group study, exam, etc.

So far, context widgets are very similar to GUI widgets, however there are important differences:

- Context widgets live in a distributed architecture because context may need to be acquired from multiple distributed sources. Widgets rely on three kinds of distributed components: generators that acquire context information, interpreters that abstract it and servers that aggregate information. Applications, widgets and the components they rely upon may be distributed. This feature of the toolkit addresses issue 3 listed in the introduction

- Context widgets monitor environmental information that may be needed at any time by an application. Thus a context widget is active all the time, and its activation is not, as with GUI widgets, driven by applications. This feature, along with other characteristics of the toolkit described in the implementation section, addresses issue 4.

The context toolkit aims at enabling easier development of context-enabled applications. To assess our objective, we have built context widgets we expect applications to need frequently and have developed applications based on these widgets.

BUILDING CONTEXT WIDGETS

In this section, we describe two of the context widgets that we have built. These context widgets aim at surveying an indoor environment. We show examples of their use in the applications described in the next section. The first widget, *IdentityPresence*, is attached to a specified location and senses the surrounding environment for the presence of people and their identity. The second widget, *Activity*, continuously monitors the surrounding environment for significant changes in activity level.

The *IdentityPresence* Widget

The *IdentityPresence* widget is placed in a pre-specified location and reports the arrival and departure of people at that location. The identities of the people arriving and departing as well as the times at which the events occurred are also made available to applications. The information this widget provides is useful for any location-aware application like tour guide or applications that track people.

The *IdentityPresence* widget provides applications with the attributes and callbacks listed in Table 1.

Widget Class	IdentityPresence
Attributes	
Location	*Location the widget is monitoring*
Identity	*ID of the last user sensed*
Timestamp	*Time of the last arrival*
Callbacks	
PersonArrives (location, identity, timestamp)	*Triggered when a user arrives*
PersonLeaves (location, identity, timestamp)	*Triggered when a user leaves*

Table 1. Definition of the *IdentityPresence* widget.

All widgets acquire context information through generators. *Generators* are components that encapsulate a single sensor or a set of closely related sensors and the software that acquires raw information from the sensor(s).

The *IdentityPresence* widget could be implemented using any number of generators, including voice recognition, Active Badges, video/image recognition, keyboard and login information, or even a combination of these. The generator that is chosen affects neither the definition of the widget nor any application that uses the widget. The attributes and callbacks provided by the widget are independent from the actual implementation, thus sheltering the application from the specifics of the sensors used. Our current implementation of the *IdentityPresence* widget uses Dallas Semiconductor's iButtons [4], passive tags with unique identifiers and storage and computing capabilities or alternatively passive TIRIS RF tags [15].

The *Activity* Widget

The *Activity* widget senses the current activity level at a location such as a room. It may be used to sense the presence of people if they are active in a room. While it can not provide reliable presence information by itself, it provides additional environmental information and can, for example, sense that people are actively discussing in the room. The widget is instantiated at a pre-specified location. Applications that use the *Activity* widget specify parameters for receiving callbacks, as seen in the table below.

The attributes and callbacks supported by the *Activity* widget are listed in table 2.

Widget Class	Activity
Attributes	
Location	*Location the widget is monitoring*
Timestamp	*Time of the last change in activity level*
AverageLevel	*Activity level (none, some, a lot) averaged over a user-specified time interval*
Callbacks	
ActivityChange (location, AverageLevel, timestamp)	*Triggered when the activity level changes from one level to another*

Table 2. Attributes and callbacks of the *Activity* widget.

The *Activity* widget has been implemented with a microphone, but like the *IdentityPresence* widget, it could be implemented with any appropriate generator, such as an infrared sensor, video image analysis, or a combination of these.

Other Context Widgets

We have also constructed other widgets as part of the context toolkit. The *NamePresence* widget is similar to the *IdentityPresence* widget. Instead of providing an artificial user ID for a user whose presence has been detected, this widget provides the user's actual name. The *PhoneUse* widget provides information about whether a phone is being used and the length of use. The *MachineUse* widget provides information about when a user logs onto or off of a computer, his identity, and length of her computing

session. The *GroupURLPresence* widget provides a URL relevant to the research group a user belongs to when her presence is detected. An application describing its use is given in the following section. The completeness and overall structure of the entire context widget library is an interesting open research issue.

BUILDING APPLICATIONS WITH THE CONTEXT TOOLKIT

In this section, we describe three applications we have built to assess the actual benefits of our context toolkit. To reiterate, the expected advantages of the toolkit are to hide complexity, provide appropriate interpretation of context information and ease overall construction through reusable widgets.

In/Out Board

Motivation

The first application we have built is the electronic equivalent of a simple in/out board that is commonly found in offices. The board is used to indicate which members of the office are currently in the building and which are not (see figure 1). In both the academic and corporate world, we often find ourselves trying to determine whether someone is in the office in order to interact with her.

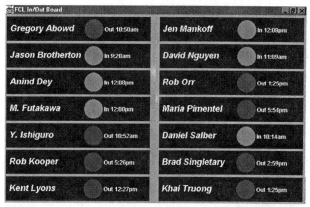

Figure 1. Screenshot of the in/out board application. The dot next to a user name is green if the user is in and red if she is out.

Context Information

The in/out board application is an example of a context-viewing application. It gathers information about the participants who enter and leave the building and displays the information to interested users. The context information is a participant's identity and the time at which they arrived or departed. This application is interested in events when people pass the single entry point into the building. Therefore, only a single instance of the *IdentityPresence* widget is required, and is located at the entrance to the building. Through the use of this widget, the context-sensing infrastructure is successful in hiding the details of how the context is sensed from the application developer.

Future Extensions

With the use of additional *IdentityPresence* widgets located in strategic areas (e.g., offices, meeting spaces) within the building, the in/out board application can easily be extended to a person tracking application. It would display the location of users throughout the building on a map. By adding an *IdentityPresence* widget to sense the identity of the user watching the display, we would be able to tailor the display to show only information relevant for this user, such as close colleagues or members of the same research group.

Information Display

Motivation

For our second application, we built an information display, similar to those found in the literature [7, 19]. We aim to show that the context toolkit can be used to reimplement existing context-enabled applications. This application displays information relevant to the user's location and identity on a display adjacent to the user. It activates itself as someone approaches it, and the information it displays changes to match the user, her research group, and location.

Context Information

The context information used by the information display is the location of the display, the identity of the user, the research group the user belongs to and information that is interesting to that research group. A single *GroupURLPresence* widget is used to supply the information to this application. The widget installed nearest to the display is used. When a user's presence is detected by the widget, it makes a URL about the user's research group available to the interested application. The application shows the contents of the URL on the nearby display.

This application does not deal with the details of how the context information is sensed, meaning the widget is successful at hiding the complexity of the sensing infrastructure. As well, the widget provides the appropriate information and detail to the application. For example, this application could have been implemented with an *IdentityPresence* widget. This would have required the application to determine what research group the nearby user was in and find information relevant to that research group. However, using the *GroupURLPresence* widget alleviated the need to perform these extra steps.

Future Extensions

The information display application provides the beginnings of a simple tour guide application, where the user is mobile and displays are static. Essentially, a basic context-aware tour guide [1, 6] displays information relevant to the location and the identity of the person viewing the information. The information display is a very simple example of a tour guide with only one location of interest, but with additional displays and information providing widgets, it could be extended to build a full tour guide application.

DUMMBO Meeting Board

Motivation

For our third application, we chose to augment an already existing system, the DUMMBO (Dynamic Ubiquitous Mobile Meeting Board) project at Georgia Tech [2]. DUMMBO is an instrumented digitizing whiteboard that supports the capture and access of informal and spontaneous meetings. Captured meetings consist of the ink

written to and erased from the whiteboard as well as the recorded audio discussion. After the meeting, a participant can access the captured notes and audio by indicating the time and date of the meeting.

In the initial version of DUMMBO, recording of a meeting was initiated by writing or erasing activity on the physical whiteboard. In the revised, context-aware version of DUMMBO, we wanted to have recording triggered when a group of two or more people gathered around the whiteboard. We also wanted to use information about when people were present around the whiteboard and their identities to help in visualizing and accessing captured material.

Context Information

This application belongs to the context-aware class of applications. It uses context to modify its own behavior (e.g., automatically starting the recording when enough people are standing around the whiteboard). The context information used is the participants' identities, the time when they arrived at or left the mobile whiteboard, and the location of the mobile whiteboard. The application uses multiple *NamePresence* widgets, one for each location where DUMMBO could be moved to in our research lab, and one on DUMMBO itself to detect the presence of users. Once again, the application could have used *IdentityPresence* widgets but the *NamePresence* widgets provided the appropriate level of detail, requiring fewer steps on the part of the programmer and application.

Adding Context to DUMMBO

This application was augmented on both the capture side and the access side. On the capture side, information about how many people were close to the whiteboard is used to determine when to start the audio and notes recording. During the access phase, participants can use context information such as the location, time and date of the meeting, and the names of participants at the meeting to retrieve the recorded meeting information. This extra context makes it easier for participants to retrieve the meeting information at a later date.

Again, the details of the widget are kept transparent from the programmer. The programmer, another member of our research group, simply needed to determine which widgets he was interested in and handle the information those widgets were providing. In all, the application only required changing/adding 25 lines of Java code (out of a total of 892 lines) and modifications were localized in a single class file. The significant modifications include 2 lines added to use the context toolkit and widget, 1 line modified to enable the class to handle callbacks, and 17 lines that are application specific. Comparatively, the size of the context toolkit is about 12400 lines of Java code.

To achieve such easy retrofitting of context handling capabilities in existing applications, the context toolkit manages the mechanics of context acquisition and abstraction. We now turn to the relevant implementation details of these mechanics.

CONTEXT TOOLKIT IMPLEMENTATION DETAILS

We have previously outlined the application programmer's interface to the context toolkit by describing what is a context widget, giving some examples of widgets and demonstrating context-enabled applications that make use of the widgets. There are some important requirements (points 3 and 4 in the introduction) for the context toolkit having to do with its distribution, composition, heterogeneity and dynamism that we will address in this section.

Distribution

The context infrastructure must accommodate distribution of applications, widgets and the components they rely upon, across a network. Applications may require the services of several widgets distributed across different machines, as described in the DUMMBO application.

In addition, widgets themselves may be distributed. A widget may consist of any number of three types of components: generators, interpreters, and servers (see figure 2). A generator, as described earlier, acquires raw context information from hardware or software sensors and provides it to widgets.

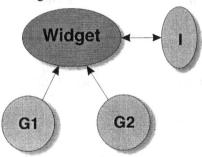

Figure 2. A context widget and supporting components. Arrows represent the data flow. In this example, the widget gets raw context data from two generators G1 and G2 and requests the services of an interpreter I.

An interpreter abstracts raw or low-level context information into higher level information. An example of this was seen in the DUMMBO application where the basic *NamePresence* widget used a generator to obtain a user ID for the user whose presence was detected. An interpreter is used to abstract the raw ID information into an actual user name. Interpreters can be used for more than simply converting between types of data. They play an important role in widget composition.

Composition

Context widgets can be composed to provide richer context information while reusing existing widgets. For example, composing the *IdentityPresence* and *Activity* widgets could provide a simple *Meeting* widget. By combining the information about the presence of people at a location and an estimate of their activity, one can roughly detect if the people are engaged in a meeting or if they are just sitting in the same place and no collaborative activity is taking place. The *Meeting* widget would gather information from the *IdentityPresence* and *Activity* widgets assigned to the room. It would rely on an interpreter to analyze the information

provided by both widgets and deduce if a meeting is taking place. The interpreter could assume a meeting is taking place if the number of people in the room is at least two and the activity level is "a lot". The *Meeting* widget would provide this information to applications through two callbacks: *MeetingStarts* and *MeetingEnds*.

When dealing with generators that provide uncertain information such as video image analysis techniques, interpreters are used to assess the validity of the information provided. They perform either simple filtering (such as rejecting any result whose confidence factor is less than a given threshold) or comparison and consolidation of the results from multiple uncertain generators.

Taking composition one step further, a server is a special kind of widget that collects, stores and interprets information from other widgets. To pursue the GUI widget analogy, it is similar to a container widget like a frame or a dialog box: it maintains a high-level model of related components. Servers are typically used to model context information of real world entities such as users or places. By acting as a gateway between applications and elementary widgets, servers hide even more complexity within the context infrastructure. For example, in the PersonFinder (extended in/out board) application, rather than have the application subscribe to every *IdentityPresence* widget in the building, it simply subscribes to the building server and receives the same desired information.

As well, to address the privacy concerns that are raised by context-sensing, a server can be used to encapsulate a privacy manager for its given domain (whether it is a person, place, or thing). For example, if applications access their desired context information via servers, then users who don't want particular information made public can modify the privacy restrictions for their personal server to keep that information from anyone but themselves or a trusted group.

Communicating Across Heterogeneous Components

To allow easy communication between the components that make up a widget and between widgets and applications, we needed to support a single, simple communications and language model. To allow as many systems as possible to employ our context toolkit, we only assume that the underlying system supports TCP/IP.

To further this goal of platform independence, our communication model uses the fairly ubiquitous HTTP protocol and our language model uses the ASCII-based Extensible Markup Language (XML) [16]. ASCII text is the lowest common denominator available on a wide variety of platforms for data transfer and XML allows us to describe structured data using text. Implementations of HTTP servers and clients libraries that can interpret XML are beginning to appear and have minimal resource requirements, allowing communication across a wide variety of platforms and devices.

Handling Dynamism

Context information is inherently dynamic. As changes in the environment are detected, applications must be given the opportunity to easily adapt to these changes. This requires two components: providing access to the information using a standard mechanism and allowing access to only the desired information. Furthermore, context information history has value for applications as well as widgets and must be preserved.

The communications model just described aids in allowing applications access to the changing information. To ease programmatic access to context information, we provide a standard subscription mechanism, enabling an application to be notified of context changes, and a polling mechanism, enabling an application to inquire about context information.

Context widgets allow applications to specify conditions that must be fulfilled before they will be notified of a change in the context. This shifts the task of filtering unwanted information to the context infrastructure and away from the application. An example of this can be seen in the DUMMBO application. This application needs to know where the mobile whiteboard is at all times, so it must subscribe to all *NamePresence* widgets in the building. However, it is only interested in callbacks where presence of the mobile whiteboard is detected. By specifying this condition in the subscription, the application can more efficiently deal with the information that it is particularly interested in and not have to deal with all the presence detections for other objects and people.

For our context toolkit to be able to support context-based retrieval applications, all context widgets store historical data in a database. Applications or interpreters can retrieve past data from a widget. Aside from context-based retrieval, we expect this feature to be useful for building interpreters that rely on patterns of behavior deduced from machine learning techniques.

RELATED WORK

Previous research efforts have proposed infrastructures for context-enabled applications. We review them in this section and point out the differences with the context toolkit.

Schilit's infrastructure for ubiquitous computing is probably the earliest attempt at providing services for handling context [14]. In this work, context information is primarily location. Location is acquired from an Active Badges infrastructure. Active Map objects gather context information related to a physical spatial area and make it available to client applications. This approach assumes that a location can be assigned to all context information.

The stick-e framework addresses the needs of context-aware notes used, for example, to make up a tour guide [3]. Notes use SGML tags to register interest in context information and set conditions on context values that will trigger the display or execution of the note. Although this model is potentially wide ranging, it is mainly aimed at displaying context information or triggering simple actions. The mandatory use of notes as clients of context information makes it difficult to retrofit an existing application with context sensing or even build an

application that modifies its behavior in response to a changing environment.

The Situated Computing Service (SitComp) has objectives very close to ours: it seeks to insulate applications from sensors used to acquire context [8]. A SitComp service is a single server that encapsulates context acquisition and abstraction and provides both an event-driven and a query interface to applications. The sensors used are location-tracking tags very similar to Active Badges. Our work goes one step further by advocating a modular structure made of several widgets dedicated to handling specific pieces of context information and laying the grounds for reusable context handling building blocks.

Although simply aimed at conveying context information to other users in a CSCW setting, the AROMA prototype shares an interesting feature with our context toolkit [12]. It provides "abstractor" objects that abstract high-level context information from the raw information captured by sensors.

Finally, CyberDesk was inspirational to the work presented in this paper [5]. Although it only deals with one piece of context information, namely the user's current text selection, it proposes a modular structure that separates context acquisition, context abstraction mechanisms and actual client services.

FUTURE WORK

The context toolkit we have presented still needs additional work to accommodate the wide range of context-enabled applications. Areas we want to explore are extending the toolkit capabilities, structuring the widgets design space, and heuristic rules for designing with context widgets.

To extend the toolkit capabilities, we need to address the issue of resource discovery and temporal composition. Resource discovery enables applications to adapt transparently to changes in the infrastructure. Widgets, generators, or interpreters may become active or inactive, migrate from machine to machine and even modify the set of capabilities they provide. Resource discovery will allow us to better handle the dynamism requirement. In the current version of our toolkit, context widgets can be composed to provide richer information. However, we don't provide means to impose temporal constraints within the composition mechanism. In a setting where context information changes rapidly, combination of information from different widgets may need to occur in a guaranteed time frame.

Work on the context widget library we have described in this paper is only in its initial stage. Although it has proved useful in its current state, the number and variety of widgets should be increased to effectively support a wide range of context-enabled applications. An immediate concern is to devise a structure for organizing widget classes in the library. Identifying the basic pieces of context information needed by applications, defining widgets to handle them and then combining these widgets will allow us to enhance the widget library and construct more diverse applications. So far, Presence, Identity, and Activity appear to be core types of context information and we plan to build upon this list.

CONCLUSION

We have presented a toolkit that supports the development of context-enabled applications. The context toolkit was inspired by the success of GUI toolkits and has similar benefits: building blocks called context widgets provide reusable solutions for context handling; by delegating details of context handling to the toolkit, we achieve separation of concerns between context sensing and application semantics.

To assess the validity of our toolkit-based approach, we have developed a small number of context widgets and example applications described in this paper. We were able to build new context-enabled applications, replicate canonical context-enabled applications found in the literature and retrofit an existing application with context capabilities.

More information on the work described in this paper is available on the web at http://www.cc.gatech.edu/fce/contexttoolkit/. The context toolkit software is available from the same web page.

ACKNOWLEDGMENTS

We wish to thank the members of the FCE group at Georgia Tech for helpful feedback and comments. Jen Mankoff's comments inspired the concept of context widget. This work is supported in part by an NSF ESS grant EIA-9806822.

REFERENCES

1. Abowd, G.D., Atkeson, C.G., Hong, J., Long, S., Kooper, R. and Pinkerton, M. Cyberguide: A Mobile Context-Aware Tour Guide. *ACM Wireless Networks 3*, 421-433.

2. Brotherton, J. DUMMBO, Dynamic, Ubiquitous, Mobile Meeting Board. Available at http://www.cc.gatech.edu/fce/dummbo/.

3. Brown, P.J. The Stick-e Document: A Framework for Creating Context-Aware Applications. *Electronic Publishing 9*, 1 (September 1996), 1-14.

4. Dallas Semiconductor. iButton Home Page. Available at http://www.ibutton.com/.

5. Dey, A., Abowd, G.D. and Wood, A. CyberDesk: A Framework for Providing Self-Integrating Context-Aware Services, in *Proceedings of the 1998 Intelligent User Interfaces Conference* (San Francisco CA, January 1998), ACM Press, 48-54.

6. Fels, S., Sumi, Y., Etani, T., Simonet, N., Kobayshi, K. and Mase, K. Progress of C-MAP: A Context-Aware Mobile Assistant, in *Proceedings of AAAI 1998 Spring Symposium on Intelligent Environments* (Palo Alto, CA, March 1998), AAAI Press, 60-67.

7. Finney, J. and Davies, N. FLUMP, The FLexible Ubiquitous Monitor Project. Available at http://www.comp.lancs.ac.uk/computing/staff/joe/papers/flumpdh.html.

8. Hull, R., Neaves, P. and Bedrod-Roberts, J. Towards Situated Computing, in *Proceedings of the 1st International Symposium on Wearable Computers, ISWC '97* (Cambridge MA, October 1997), IEEE Press.

9. Lamming, M. and Flynn, M. Forget-me-not: Intimate Computing in Support of Human Memory, in *Proceedings of FRIEND 21: International Symposium on Next Generation Human Interfaces* (Tokyo, 1994), 125-128.

10. Lancaster University. The Active Badge Tourist Application. Available at http://www.comp.lancs.ac.uk/computing/research/mpg/most/abta_project.html.

11. Myers, B.A. A New Model for Handling Input. *Transactions on Information Systems 8*, 3, 289-320.

12. Pederson, E.R. and Sokoler, T. AROMA: Abstract Representation of Presence Supporting Mutual Awareness, in *Proceedings of CHI '97* (Atlanta GA, March 1997), ACM Press, 51-58.

13. Rhodes, B.J. The Wearable Remembrance Agent, in *Proceedings of 1st International Symposium on Wearable Computers, ISWC '97* (Cambridge MA, October 1997), IEEE Press, 123-128.

14. Schilit, W.N. *System Architecture for Context-Aware Mobile Computing.* Ph.D. Thesis, Columbia University, 1995.

15. Texas Instruments. TIRIS Products and Technology. Available at http://www.ti.com/mc/docs/tiris/docs/rfid.htm.

16. W3C XML Working Group. Extensible Markup Language (XML) 1.0. Available at http://www.w3.org/TR/1998/REC-xml-19980210.

17. Want, R., Hopper, A., Falcao, V. and Gibbons, J. The Active Badge Location System. *ACM Transactions on Information Systems 10*, 1, 91-102.

18. Want, R., Schilit, B., Adams, N., Gold, R., Petersen, K., Ellis, J., Goldberg, D. and Weiser, M. *The PARCTAB Ubiquitous Computing Experiment.* Technical Report CSL-95-1, Xerox Palo Alto Research Center, 1995.

19. Weiser, M. The Computer for the 21st Century. *Scientific American 265*, 3, 66-75.

Getting More Out Of Programming-By-Demonstration

Richard G. McDaniel and Brad A. Myers
HCI Institute, School of Computer Science
Carnegie Mellon University
5000 Forbes Avenue
Pittsburgh, PA 15213 USA
{ richm, bam }@cs.cmu.edu

ABSTRACT

Programming-by-demonstration (PBD) can be used to create tools and methods that eliminate the need to learn difficult computer languages. Gamut is a PBD tool that nonprogrammers can use to create a broader range of interactive software, including games, simulations, and educational software, than they can with other PBD tools. To do this, Gamut provides advanced interaction techniques that make it easier for a developer to express all aspects of an application. These techniques include a simplified way to demonstrate new examples, called "nudges," and a way to highlight objects to show they are important. Also, Gamut includes new objects and metaphors like the deck-of-cards metaphor for demonstrating collections of objects and randomness, guide objects for demonstrating relationships that the system would find too difficult to guess, and temporal ghosts which simplify showing relationships with the recent past. These techniques were tested in a formal setting with nonprogrammers to evaluate their effectiveness.

Keywords
End-User Programming, User Interface Software, Programming-by-Demonstration, Programming-by-Example, Application Builders, Inductive Learning, Gamut.

INTRODUCTION
Gamut is an innovative tool for building interactive software like games, simulations, and educational software. Much of the effort involved in producing software in this domain is not in programming the application's logic but in providing the engaging background, artwork, and gameplay that keeps the users interested. Artists and educators who could produce such material are often unable to program computers. Thus, tools which eliminate the burden of programming while providing a wide range of capabilities are desirable.

Traditional development tools for producing interactive software require extensive programming knowledge. Programming graphics in common environments like Visual C++ or Visual Basic can be difficult even for seasoned programmers. Tools such as interface builders can help developers design the visual appearance of an application but still require programming to make the interface actually work. Application builders such as Click & Create [3] eliminate programming but impose severe limits on the kinds of programs that can be

created. Authoring tools like AuthorWare [1] or Director [8] are similarly limited and cannot produce complex behaviors and player interactions without using their built-in scripting languages.

One method for simplifying the programming process has been programming-by-demonstration (PBD). Rather than using a textual notation, the developer builds the program by providing examples of the intended interactions between the user and the application. Examples are demonstrated using the same interface normally used to create and manipulate the application's data. The system uses the examples to infer the developer's intention and creates the code to execute the program.

Our research is aimed at significantly improving and expanding what can be accomplished using PBD. Gamut has the ability to infer complex relationships through the use of improved interaction techniques. The interaction techniques allow the developer to give Gamut all of the required information without resorting to a written programming language. These interaction techniques provide several benefits:

- A simplified method for producing examples.
- An understandable way to create negative examples.
- The ability to give the system specific and direct hints.
- Objects and metaphors that can describe complex behaviors concisely.

DOMAIN
Gamut can create games and simulations similar to board games. These are two-dimensional games with a board-like background that uses playing pieces to represent the game's state. The domain extends well beyond Chess and Monopoly, however. By having objects react autonomously and by adding player interaction, one can create video game behaviors such as moving monsters and shooting aliens. Educational games like Reader Rabbit [16] and Playroom [6] and video games like PacMan can all be made using Gamut.

The board game domain provides several challenges for a PBD system:

- The created games are interactive and require player input. Some PBD systems only assist in editing static data such as a text document.
- Board games have a large number of states and modes. Game behavior can be triggered by a variety of events and can have complicated relationships.

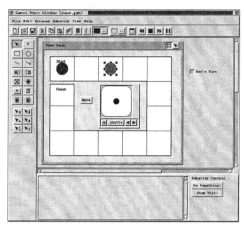

Figure 1: Gamut's main window. On the left are the tool palette and mouse icons. Along the bottom is the behavior dialog area.

- Relationships between objects and actions are often formed as long chains of other relationships which build upon each other.

For example, the destination square where a piece is moved in Monopoly could be described as "the square that is the dice's number of squares away from the square where current player's piece currently resides." This description depends on the configuration of the board, the number on the dice, and the player whose turn it is. Each object in the relation forms a link in the chain. Furthermore, an object such as the turn indicator is not necessarily graphically or temporally connected to the other objects. Current PBD systems cannot infer this form of relationship.

Gamut can be taught the rules of a game, but generally cannot create computer opponents. The difference here is the difference between rules and strategy. Playing a complex game well requires strategy which is often not easily encoded as a set of rules. Gamut is designed to assemble games for humans to play, not to play the games, itself. The developer has to show the system all relationships upon which a behavior depends.

EXAMPLE

To motivate the design of Gamut's interaction techniques, we will show how to build the simple board game application shown in Figure 1. This game was also used as a task in the usability study discussed later. In the game, two pieces colored red and blue follow the path of squares around the edge. The first piece to reach the end wins. The pieces alternate turns and move the number of spaces as shown on the die in the center. As an added complication, whenever one piece lands on another, the landed-on piece must go back to the beginning.

As each of the following interaction techniques is presented, we will show how the developer uses that technique to build this board game.

INTERACTION TECHNIQUES

The key to Gamut's interaction techniques is that the developer can demonstrate not only the surface activity of the interface, but the semantics behind that activity. The tech-

niques allow the developer to express all the relevant relationships of an entire application. The techniques can be divided into three categories: developer generated objects, such as guide objects, cards, and decks of cards; interaction methods, which includes nudges and hint highlighting; and system generated objects, such as temporal ghosts.

Guide Objects

Guide objects are graphical objects and widgets that are visible while the developer is creating an application but are hidden when the application runs. Gamut supports two kinds of guide objects. The first is derived from Maulsby's Metamouse [9] and Fisher *et al*'s Demo II [4] which allowed certain graphical objects to be made invisible on demand. *Onscreen* guide objects show graphical relationships between other objects on the screen, visible or invisible. Onscreen guide objects can be used to demonstrate distances, locations, and even speeds.

For instance, in the example game, the path that each piece follows around the board can be represented with arrow line guide objects as shown in Figure 2. Guide objects are drawn in pastel colors so they will be distinct from application objects. At any time, the developer can make the guide objects invisible by switching a mode. Without the path, the system would not know how the squares around the board were connected, and might not even be able to see that the squares exist at all. Allowing the developer to draw the graphical connections saves the system from having to provide sophisticated machine vision heuristics to achieve the same effects.

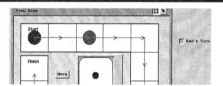

Figure 2: The developer uses arrow lines as guide objects to represent the path the pieces follow.

Other guide objects are placed *offscreen*. The player's view is shown as a blue window frame in the middle of the developer's drawing area as seen in Figure 1. Objects that are drawn outside of the blue frame cannot be seen by the player and are offscreen. Offscreen guides objects are used to represent the application's data that is not stored directly on the board. Timers, counters, toggle buttons, and other widgets are all used as offscreen objects.

In our example game, the developer needs to represent the player turn order. The developer decides to use a checkbox and places one outside of the frame window and labels it "Red's Turn." (In the Motif look-and-feel, a "checkbox" looks like a raised or lowered rectangle next to a text label.) The widget begins with its checkmark on.

The purpose of guide objects is to enable the developer to show relationships that are nearly impossible to infer. In AI, this is called the *hidden object problem* [18]. A hidden object is a dependency or variable upon which a behavior depends that is not included as part of the application's visible state. Gamut cannot infer hidden objects without the developer's help because it has no way to determine what such objects could be. The number of possible things a hidden object could be is virtually infinite. However, it is possible to recognize when a relationship requires more than the developer has shown. Gamut's inferencing algorithm can detect when relationships have not been fully specified and asks the developer to tell the system about missing objects.

Deck Widget

Cards and decks are the two major data structures in Gamut. Many modern board games use decks of cards to simulate a large variety of behaviors. In games like Monopoly, cards are a source of random events like the Chance deck as well as the means for storing game state such as knowing which player owns each property. In Gamut, decks may be used to represent lists of numbers, objects, colors, etc., and they provide a randomization feature (shuffling) which is useful for constructing random behaviors.

A deck may also be used to produce video game behaviors. For example, a deck can provide alternating images for an animated character. To make a character move randomly, its position can be tied to a deck containing an arrow for each direction that gets shuffled each time the character moves.

Gamut's deck of cards is not the same card metaphor found in HyperCard [7]. In HyperCard, cards are the whole application. In general, a HyperCard "stack" is a set of screen displays with links between them to denote the method and order in which displays are presented. A Gamut deck is a widget within the application. To use a deck in Gamut, one drags objects into it. The deck will store and maintain the order of all objects it contains.

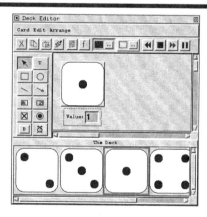

Figure 3: The card and deck editor. This shows the contents of the deck in Figure 1. Each face of a die is presented as a card. The current face is shown in the main drawing area.

Card Widget

Gamut's card widget acts as a large drawing surface, independent from the main window. Naturally, cards may be placed in decks, but they can also be used on their own. The developer uses Gamut's card editor (see Figure 3) to draw on a card. The raised frame in the card's drawing area shows what is visible within the card's widget. Objects drawn outside the visible region act as offscreen guide objects similar to offscreen objects in the main window.

In the example game, the developer uses a deck to represent the die in the center of the board (see Figure 1). The deck editor shows each item in the assembled deck which in this example is a set of cards each representing a face of the die (see Figure 3). The developer can demonstrate "rolling" the die by shuffling the deck. In the drawing portion of the deck editor, the developer draws the pips for each face in the card's visible region. Below the visible region, the developer adds a number box and types the numeric value of the die face. By including the number box, the system will not have to count the dots in order to infer the value of the card.

Demonstrating Behavior

Gamut introduces a new way to demonstrate behavior which we call *nudges*. The idea is that when the system makes a mistake or needs to learn new material, the developer gives the system a "nudge" telling the system immediately where it went wrong. In other words, when the application is supposed to do something but does nothing, or does something when it is not supposed to, the developer nudges the system and corrects the behavior.

Gamut defines two kinds of nudges. The first is called "Do Something." The developer uses Do Something to demonstrate new behaviors. When the developer sees the system miss a cue, the developer pushes the Do Something button. The system then becomes ready to accept the developer's new example permitting the developer to modify the application's state appropriately.

The second nudge is called "Stop That" which tells the system that one or more objects did something wrong. The developer, when noticing a deviant action, selects the affected object and presses the Stop That button. The system immediately undoes all actions just performed on that object. If the object was supposed to do nothing, the developer is finished at this point. If the object was supposed to perform a different action, the author may modify objects to show the system the correct behavior.

In our example, the developer wants to demonstrate that when the player pushes the application's "Move" button, the game will respond by moving the current player's piece. The developer first pushes the Move button (it is to the left of the die in Figure 1). Though the developer pushes the button, the application will do nothing because no behavior has yet been demonstrated. So the developer pushes Do Something at which point the system prepares to accept a new example. The system displays *temporal ghosts* to show how objects have changed from the previous state, activates *hint highlighting* so the developer may give hints, and presents a dialog asking the developer to complete the example and press the Done button when complete.

The application is supposed to roll the die and move the piece the corresponding number of places. It also must update the player turn. The developer pushes the "Shuffle" button on the die's deck, moves the red piece the corresponding number of squares, and toggles the turn indicator to be unchecked. The view would now look like Figure 4a. At this point, before pressing "Done" to finish the example, the developer should give the system *hints*.

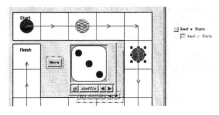

Figure 4a: The developer has just moved the red piece which used to be in the middle of the top row. The red piece's ghost shows where it was.

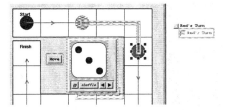

Figure 4b: The developer has highlighted the arrow lines, die, and ghost of the toggle switch as hints.

Hint Highlighting

A "hint highlight" is a special form of selection where the author points out key elements that are important to a demonstration thereby focusing the system's attention on those objects. Maulsby implemented a similar feature in Cima [10] by having the user select a word or phrase and use a menu command to make it a hint. Hints are used to reduce the size of the inferencing algorithm's search space. The number of features upon which a single relationship may depend can be immeasurably large. Finding the correct features can require an exponential amount of search time without hints. Providing hints can reduce the search to near constant time.

In Gamut, the developer highlights objects as hints by pressing the right mouse button over them. Gamut marks hinted objects with green rectangles. Highlight marks around lines are seen as a thin rectangle that follows the line's direction as seen in Figure 4b. Highlighting is different from normal selection which is caused by the left mouse button and presented as a conventional set of square handles. (The circle on the right of Figure 4a and b is selected.) Selection is used to move, resize, and recolor objects. Since it is common for the developer to want to hint highlight an object and still perform other operations, highlighting is made an independent operation from selection.

In the example, the developer knows that the path of the piece is important as well as number shown on the die; so, the developer highlights the lines in the path and the die object. The developer will also need to highlight something that shows what value to set the current player checkbox. The checkbox only toggles back and forth between true and false so its only dependency is its own value. Thus, the new value of the checkbox depends on its original value. To highlight the original value, the developer highlights the checkbox's *temporal ghost* which is shown on the right in Figure 4b.

Temporal Ghosts

A common problem for hint highlighting arises when the objects that need to be highlighted do not exist anymore. Interactive games are dynamic: objects are created, moved, and destroyed constantly. Temporal ghosts are a technique for keeping objects that change onscreen so that they may be highlighted. Ghosts also make the recent past visible so that the author can understand what changes have occurred. Though the concept of ghost objects is not new, Gamut is the first to use it for PBD.

Gamut displays temporal ghosts as dimmed, translucent images of objects seen in their past state. If an object is moved, a ghost will appear in the object's original position. If the object changes color, the ghost will appear directly below the object but offset so the developer can still see it.

When the developer toggles the turn indicator in the example, a ghost appears below it, offset to show that it used to be checked (see the right portion of Figure 4a). The developer highlights this ghost to show that its value is important. Gamut will be able to see that the new value is different from the old value and use that to describe how the toggle changes. Finally, the developer pushes "Done" because the example is finished.

For the second example, the developer pushes the "Move" button again. The system is able to incorporate enough information to know how far to move the pieces but it does not know that it is supposed to move the blue piece and so it moves the red piece. The developer notices that this behavior is wrong, selects the red piece and presses "Stop That." Gamut immediately undoes the move action performed on the red piece. Stop That places the system into the same mode as Do Something so temporal ghosts are displayed once again and hint highlighting is made active. The developer moves the blue piece the correct number of spaces and also changes the player turn indicator if the system did not already do so. When finished, the developer presses "Done." This time, the developer did not highlight any objects. As a result, when the system finds ambiguities, it will ask the developer questions in order to resolve them.

Question Dialogs

Questions occur when the system finds a contradiction or suspects that there is a relationship where an object was not highlighted. The system will generate one question at a time in the behavior dialog region of the window. The questions ask about the objects or values that are immediately affected by the behavior. Developers have three choices for response. First, they may highlight the object upon which relationship depends and press the "Learn" button. The system then tries to incorporate this new information to generate a description. Second, they may choose the "Replace" button in order to directly replace the old value with the new. Replace is used to correct mistakes or to modify a behavior from its original form. Finally, the third button is called "Wrong" and is used in cases where Gamut asks a question that makes no sense. Gamut generates its questions using heuristics which can sometimes fail. The Wrong button tells the computer that it has generated a bad question and that it should try a different line of reasoning.

In the developer's second example in the example application, the system sees the blue piece move instead of the red piece but it does not know why. The system asks the developer to highlight the object that best describes why the blue piece has moved and not the red. The developer highlights the ghost of the turn indicator and presses Learn. Highlighting the turn indicator tells the system that the blue piece moves when the checkbox is unchecked. To finish this portion of the example, the developer would need to test the Move button one more time and correct the system (without needing further highlighting) to complete the behavior.

Mouse Input Icons

The example application does not directly use mouse input in the window since the button widget handles the mouse automatically. However, it is worth mentioning how demonstrating mouse events is accomplished in Gamut. Gamut has a palette of mouse events below the main tool palette (see Figure 1). To create a mouse event, the developer selects an event and drops it onto the window as though it were a graphical object. This allows the developer to demonstrate mouse events without entering a special mode. The system will respond as though the player had just produced the selected event. Keyboard and other sorts of events, though not implemented, could be included in a similar way.

Gamut uses the same icons to represent mouse events as we used in our Marquise system [14]. Clicking events are shown with an arrow pointing up as well as down whereas button down events only point down. Double clicks are shown as two arrowheads pointing down and moving/dragging uses a wavy line. The icons are shown in Figure 5.

Figure 5: Icons that are used to represent mouse events.

Contrasting Nudges With Other Systems' Techniques

In an abstract sense, Do Something and Stop That represent positive and negative examples. New demonstrations are positive examples and are performed using Do Something. Stop That signifies a negative example since it asks that no action be performed in that given instance. Evidence from Frank [5] suggested that developers found negative examples difficult to understand, but we suspect that those users had difficulty with the demonstration techniques in that particular system. Frank's system and others require the developer to demonstrate negative examples using special modes. This requires the developer to understand *a priori* when a negative example is required and it draws attention to the example instead of to the behavior that it represents.

With nudges, the developer stays focused on the behavior of the application. Each nudge provides an incremental improvement to the behavior that the developer is testing. The developer does not have to know whether a particular example is positive or negative, and must only tell the system when objects are not behaving correctly.

Negative examples permit the learning of disjunctive logic statements which in turn permits program structures such as

if-then statements to be learned without the author having to create conditions by manually changing the inferred code.

Another advantage of nudges is that they reduce the number of system modes. Some PBD systems require a separate recording mode to enter stimulus events. This is part of the Stimulus/Response mode distinction used in various system including Pavlov [19]. A Stimulus/Response style interface is normally implemented as an extended macro recorder. With a macro recorder, pressing "record" causes the system to record all subsequent actions. "Playing" the macro later will execute those actions in a new context. An extended macro recorder adds an extra *stimulus* phase where the developer demonstrates the event of the behavior.

Revising behaviors can be more tedious using the extended macro recorder technique than Gamut's nudges approach. Since the macro recorder requires the developer to perform the event during the stimulus recording phase, the developer must know beforehand what he or she intends to demonstrate. If the developer were to find a problem while testing the application, the stimulus event that occurred during the test would have to be recreated for the macro recorder. Furthermore, the initial state for all the objects involved would have to be reset. With the nudges approach, the developer can create new examples as the need occurs. When a problem appears during testing, the developer can immediately nudge the system and use the current application state in the example.

INFERENCING

To manage the various interaction techniques, Gamut needs an inferencing algorithm that can understand them. The algorithms must handle multiple examples incrementally while incorporating hint highlighting of various objects, guide objects, and temporal ghosts. Furthermore, the algorithms must be able to generate the behaviors characteristic of board games like chains of relationships with conditional components. For a more complete description of Gamut's inferencing algorithm see our previous paper [11].

Gamut's action language is based on the *command object* structure found in Amulet [13], the development environment used to implement Gamut. A command object represents an atomic action such as Move, Create, Cut, Copy, and Paste. In Amulet, user actions are queued onto an undo history which Gamut uses as the input to the first stage of inferencing (see Figure 6).

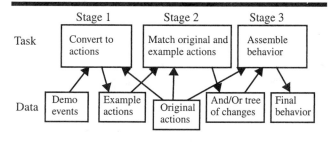

Figure 6: Stages in Gamut's inferencing algorithm.

In the first stage, the commands from the undo history are reduced to a canonical form which removes repetition and order dependencies. The events found in the undo list are often complicated. A group command, for instance, not only creates a group object but also moves and reparents the objects being grouped. This stage converts the events into a small set of basic actions. This reduced set of commands is passed on to the matching stage.

The matching stage uses a plan recognition algorithm as its basis [18]. If the application already has behavior defined for the event being demonstrated, the old behavior is used as a template for recognizing features in the new example. (If there is no previous behavior, the algorithm moves to stage three.) The algorithm can follow chains of descriptions in the original behavior and determine which of the parameters should be changed in order to make the old behavior perform the actions in the new example. Output from this phase is the set of differences from the existing behavior and the new example. The set of changes is captured in an And/Or tree which represents the various ways the changes might be applied. And-nodes represent changes that must occur together while Or-nodes are used to store alternatives.

The final stage of inferencing resolves the differences found in stage two and describes new parameters. This stage uses the objects highlighted by the developer to search for descriptions which resolve differences stored in the And/Or tree. The algorithm employed by this phase is heuristic and is based on the algorithm in Marquise [14]. When Gamut does not find a suitable description, it asks the developer a question in the behavior dialog. The text of the question is based on the current unresolved difference and refers to the value in the original behavior, the new value in the example, and some context information stating what the value affects. The developer is asked to highlight the appropriate objects to answer the question.

If Gamut still fails to find a suitable description, it will use a decision tree to choose between the old and new values. The precise way that Gamut applies decision trees is beyond the scope of this article. The basic idea is that Gamut generates attributes for the decision tree algorithm using the objects the developer highlights. The algorithm (specifically ID3 [15]) will, in turn, decide which attributes to apply and in what order. This allows Gamut to generate conditional expressions with objects that are not directly affected by the behaviors they control.

USER TESTING

We tested Gamut under formal conditions to see how well the techniques would be understood by nonprogrammers. In a short three-hour session, the test participants had to learn the system and build two tasks using Gamut. One participant was also invited back to attempt a third task which was longer and required mouse input. Overall, Gamut performed fairly well. Three of the four participants were able to complete the tasks and the one person who attempted the third task completed it as well.

Participants

The study's participants were contacted through electronic bulletin boards and email at Carnegie Mellon University. The subjects were required to be nonprogrammers. Specifically, the subjects were allowed to have taken a low-level class in programming, but were not allowed to program computers for a living or as a hobby. Participants were required to be familiar with typical computer interface metaphors as well as drawing editors.

Tasks

In the three hour sessions, the participants had to complete an hour-long tutorial and two tasks. We asked the participants to use a "think-aloud" protocol [17] to articulate their thoughts. The sessions were videotaped and an experimenter was present to answer the participant's questions.

The first task was based on a matching test similar to some educational games like Reader Rabbit and is shown in Figure 7. It was called Safari and it consists of two decks of cards. One contained a list of animals like "Zebra," and the other contained a list of questions about animals like "Does it have stripes?" The goal of the task was to put guide objects into the deck that would tell Gamut the correct answers and to demonstrate the behavior of a pair of buttons labelled "Yes" and "No."

The second task was the board game task that we used in this paper as an example and can be seen in Figure 1. The participants did not have to draw the board or create the die, but did have to create guide objects to represent the path the pieces followed, create something to represent the turn indicator, and demonstrate all the behaviors.

The third task which only one participant attempted was based on the video game Q*bert and is also shown in Figure 7. It had a character which jumps from cube to cube in a pyramid and collects objects. There is also an enemy ball which falls down from the top of the pyramid in random directions. The third task required a longer time to complete than the others so it had its own session. The participant was given a shortened tutorial which described the new interaction techniques required in the third task.

Observations

The purpose of the study was to see whether nonprogrammers could use Gamut to demonstrate behavior. Few PBD systems in the past have ever been tested with actual users so we were mostly interested in proving that PBD could actually work.

As shown in Table 1, each participant used a different set of Gamut's techniques in order to complete the tasks. For instance, some participants preferred to use Do Something exclusively, others preferred to use Stop That. Only one participant was unable to learn enough of Gamut's techniques to build the applications.

One of the problems the participants had concerned highlighting ghost objects. Most participants showed a peculiar reluctance to highlight a ghost object. Several preferred to highlight the original object and not its ghost even though the original was modified and displayed a different state from what the participant wanted the system to learn. The "Highlight Ghosts" line on the table shows that only one participant was truly comfortable highlighting ghosts while the others would choose not to most of the time.

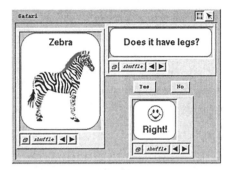

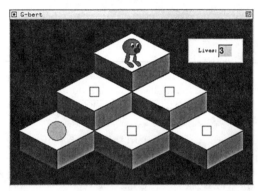

Figure 7: Screenshots of the first and third usability tasks. The top one is Safari which is based on an educational game. The lower one is G-bert which is a video game.

The most significant problem we discovered in Gamut concerns guide objects. Developers were always reluctant to create guide objects to use in their demonstrations. The pilot study showed we had to include specific instructions to tell the participant to draw guide objects. However, once told, participants were usually able to create objects that were suitable for the task they needed to demonstrate. The only successful participant who had difficulty creating guide objects after being told to do so was P4. It turns out P4 eventually did create all the needed guide objects, but only after asking the experimenter so many questions that it was not clear whether P4 had designed the objects herself or whether the experimenter had given away the answers.

A problem that all participants shared (though to different degrees) was highlighting inappropriate objects as hints when Gamut asked a question. Gamut requires that the developer provide a hint when it asks a question, but there seemed to be situations where certain objects were considered too obvious to highlight. Ghost objects seemed to be one instance. Visual paths and lines connected to objects seemed to be another.

When the system needed to have an object highlighted that was too obvious for the participant's taste, the participant would often choose to highlight an object which had a less obvious connection to the behavior. Gamut is designed to be resilient to badly highlighted objects so the participant usually had multiple opportunities to answer the same question, though the system's performance becomes considerably worse each time the participant gives a bad hint. Eventually, most participants would highlight the appropriate object and the system could proceed.

techniques	P 1	P 2	P 3	P 4
Do Something	X		X	X
Stop That		X		X
Highlights Ghosts				X
Guide Objects		X	X	
Cards and Decks		X	X	
Player Mouse Icons*		X		

Table 1: Different participants learned and used different sets of Gamut's techniques. All participants except the first were able to successful complete the tasks.

* Only participant two was given a task that required the Mouse Icons to complete.

The Cards and Decks and Player Mouse Icons lines of the table show that two participants used decks in their tasks and one used the mouse icons. The first two tasks came with decks of cards already prepared. All participants had little difficulty using the decks. However, P2 and P3 created and used an original deck of cards as their own widget. The Player Mouse Icons were only needed for task 3 and were only used by P2 who had little trouble.

It is not entirely clear why P1 was unable to use the system. According to the participant's own comments, he was "too tired" to learn how the system worked. The poor result may have simply been due to fatigue from a long day at work. The sorts of errors P1 would make were mostly caused by forgetting how to demonstrate using nudges. For instance, sometimes he might not demonstrate the event for the example and sometimes he would not push Do Something or Stop That.

RELATED WORK

A number of tools exist for building games. Most construct a specific class of games such as Bill Budge's Pinball Construction Set [2] which makes pinball simulations. A recent product is Click & Create [3] in which the developer first draws the game objects and classifies each as background, characters, or other objects. Then the author assigns behavior to the characters by picking from a list of stock behaviors. These behaviors can be customized by changing some parameters, but the author is limited to the built-in methods.

Gamut most resembles our previous system, Marquise [14]. Like Gamut, Marquise's goal was to create whole applications. Marquise had the ability to recognize palettes of objects and could quickly infer operations such as selecting and dragging. Marquise's major deficiency was an inability to correct guesses by demonstration. It also had a limited set of expressions for describing objects and locations which caused it to make poor inferences. The only means for correcting the system was editing the inferred code using a set of unwieldy dialog boxes.

PBD systems such as Wolber's Pavlov [19] and Frank's Grizzly Bear [5] have shown that simple heuristics can be used to infer many forms of graphical constraints and simple behaviors. Both of these systems infer linear relationships between objects with numeric parameters (like an object's screen position). Unfortunately, linear constraints cannot be used to infer conditional expressions based on modes and many other kinds of behavior needed to build whole applications. Pavlov requires users to annotate their demonstrated behaviors with conditional guard statements in order to overcome these problems.

Gamut's inferencing ability is similar to Maulsby's Cima system [10]. Cima also has the ability to learn from hints and can learn concepts incrementally. Cima's description language is not as powerful as Gamut's. Cima's statements are restricted to logic statements in disjunctive normal form (DNF) which it uses to recognize passages in a body of text. Also, Cima currently cannot do work on behalf of the user: it just recognizes strings of text.

STATUS AND FUTURE WORK

Gamut is implemented using Amulet [12] and will run on Unix, Windows, or the Macintosh. Gamut is a prototype system implemented as the first author's thesis project. It is not a commercial software product and it is not available for release except for research purposes. Though Gamut is functional, more work would be needed to make it usable for typical developers.

We have used Gamut to demonstrate behaviors that other systems cannot produce. For instance, we have created a Turing machine emulation, complete Tic-Tac-Toe and Hangman games, various video game behaviors such as a PacMan-like monster. Behaviors from educational games such as matching words as in Reader Rabbit have also been created. Thus, Gamut has been used to demonstrate a broad range of behaviors without resorting to a written programming language at any point.

Though Gamut's input techniques work well, the interface still needs to provide better feedback. Currently, the system has only the behavior dialog to tell the developer about the behavior being demonstrated. More work is needed to inform the developer about what the system knows and what it can infer. The system needs to note graphical constraints and to have a dialog mechanism for displaying the inferred code in an understandable format.

CONCLUSION

Gamut has the ability to infer complex behaviors which can be used to build complete interactive applications. This new capability derives from an innovative collection of interaction techniques coupled with inductive learning algorithms that can take advantage of the techniques. The nudges interaction simplifies example recording and provides a simple manner to create negative examples. Hint highlighting is a means for improving the system's guessing by allowing the software author to point out important objects in a behavior. The deck-of-cards metaphor allows complicated behaviors to be specified that can involve sets of data and randomness. Guide objects permit demonstration of objects and relationships which the system could not guess by itself. Finally, temporal ghosts allow the author to directly form relationships with the recent past. These techniques were tested in a

usability study where we found that nonprogrammers were able to use them to build realistic application behaviors effectively. Thus, Gamut's techniques are an effective method for demonstrating a broader range of applications with a minimum of programming expertise and would be appropriate for use in a wide range of future PBD systems.

ACKNOWLEDGEMENTS

This research was partially sponsored by NCCOSC under Contract No. N66001-94-C-6037, Arpa Order No. B326, and partially by NSF under grant number IRI-9319969. The views and conclusions contained in this document are those of the authors and should not be interpreted as representing the official policies, either expressed or implied, of the U.S. Government.

REFERENCES

1. *Authorware*. Authorware Inc. 8400 Normandale Lake Blvd., Suite 430, Minneapolis MN 55437, 612-912-8555, 1991.

2. B. Budge. *Pinball Construction Set*. Exidy Software.

3. *Corel Click & Create*. Corel Corporation and Europress Software Ltd. 1996.

4. G. L. Fisher, D. E. Busse, D. A. Wolber. "Adding Rule-Based Reasoning to a Demonstrational Interface Builder." *Proceedings of UIST'92*, pp 89-97.

5. M. Frank. *Model-Based User Interface Design by Demonstration and by Interview*. Ph.D. thesis. Graphics, Visualization & Usability Center, Georgia Institute of Technology, Atlanta, Georgia.

6. L. Grimm, D. Caswell, and L. Kirkpatrick. *Playroom*. Broderbund Software, 500 Redwood Blvd., Novato, CA 94948-6121, 1992.

7. *HyperCard*. Apple Computer Inc., Cupertino, CA, 1993.

8. Macromedia, *Director*, 600 Townsend Street, San Francisco, CA 94103, macropr@macromedia.com, http://www.macromedia.com/, 1996.

9. D. Maulsby, I. Witten. "Inducing Procedures in a Direct-Manipulation Environment." *Proceedings SIGCHI'89*, April, 1989. pp. 57-62.

10. D. Maulsby. *Instructible Agents*. Ph.D. thesis. Department of Computer Science, Univ. of Calgary, Calgary, Alberta, June 1994.

11. R.G. McDaniel, B.A. Myers. "Building Applications Using Only Demonstration." *Proceedings of IUI'98*. pp 109-116.

12. B. A. Myers *et al*. "The Amulet Environment: New Models for Effective User Interface Software Development." *IEEE Transactions on Software Engineering*, Vol. 23, no. 6. June 1997. pp. 347-365.

13. B. A. Myers, D. S. Kosbie. "Reusable Hierarchical Command Objects." *Human Factors in Computing Systems, Proceedings SIGCHI'96*, Denver, CO, April, 1996, pp 260-267.

14. B. A. Myers, R. G. McDaniel, and D. S. Kosbie. "Marquise: Creating Complete User Interfaces by Demonstration." *Proceedings of INTERCHI'93: Human Factors in Computing Systems*, 1993, pp 293-300.

15. J. R. Quinlan. "Induction of Decision Trees." *Machine Learning*, Kluwer Academic Publishers, Boston, Vol. 1, 1986, pp 81-106.

16. *Reader Rabbit*. The Learning Company, 1987.

17. M. Rettig. "Prototyping for tiny fingers." *Communications of the ACM* 37, 4 (April 1994). pp. 21-27.

18. K. VanLehn. "Learning One Subprocedure per Lesson." *Artificial Intelligence*, Vol. 31, 1987, pp 1-40.

19. D. Wolber. "Pavlov: Programming By Stimulus-Response Demonstration." *Human Factors in Computing Systems, Proceedings SIGCHI'96*, Denver, CO, April, 1996, pp 252-259

Navigation as Multiscale Pointing: Extending Fitts' Model to Very High Precision Tasks

Yves Guiard
Mouvement & Perception
CNRS & Université de la
Méditerranée - France
+33 (0)4 91 17 22 57
guiard@laps.univ-mrs.fr

Michel Beaudouin-Lafon
Laboratoire de Recherche en Informatique
CNRS & Université de
Paris-Sud - France
+33 (0)1 69 15 69 10
mbl@lri.fr

Denis Mottet
Faculté des Sciences du Sport
Université de Poitiers
France
+33 (0)5 49 45 33 43
Mottet@mshs.univ-poitiers.fr

ABSTRACT

Fitts' pointing model has proven extremely useful for understanding basic selection in WIMP user interfaces. Yet today's interfaces involve more complex navigation within electronic environments. As navigation amounts to a form of multi-scale pointing, Fitts' model can be applied to these more complex tasks. We report the results of a preliminary pointing experiment that shows that users can handle higher levels of task difficulty with two-scale rather than traditional one-scale pointing control. Also, in tasks with very high-precision hand movements, performance is higher with a stylus than with a mouse.

Keywords

Fitts' law, pointing, navigation, multiscale interfaces, input devices, stylus, mouse, graphical tablet

INTRODUCTION

Interfaces in the 1980's relied heavily on pointing to modify window size, select icons, and choose from menus. Today's user interfaces have moved beyond the desktop metaphor, enabling users to explore far richer information spaces, including virtual offices, libraries and "cities of knowledge" [e.g., 4, 6, 22]. These interfaces can all be considered "zoomable" in one way or another, allowing users to navigate through electronic worlds at different scales [9].

These new interfaces require additional theorizing on the nature of human movement in human-computer interaction (HCI). We believe the distinction between *pointing* and *navigation* is of special importance. Pointing, which involves simple aimed movements of the hand typically performed on the surface of a desktop by a seated individual, has long been understood in HCI in light of Fitts' law [see 17 for a review]. Navigation, unlike pointing, is a metaphor in HCI—that of a living organism moving itself as a whole relative to a complex environment that is only partially accessible to the senses.

So pointing and navigation, two categories of human motion, apparently call for different conceptualizations. Below we discuss some difficulties that seem to hinder the application of Fitts' pointing model to multiscale navigation. We suggest that some apparent obstacles vanish if the abstractness and generality of Fitts' model is fully acknowledged.

The Scale Problem in Graphical User Interfaces

Scale has always been a concern in HCI. The first computer screens showed too few lines to make an entire document visible. An early solution was to provide users with four cursor keys for local movements of the cursor and page-up and page-down keys for large-scale movements. WIMP (Windows, Icons, Menus, and Pointing) interfaces provide a clearer separation between document and desk levels, with the option of either working within the document or manipulating it as a whole on the virtual desktop. The problem remains, however, that windows are typically smaller than the documents they display (all the more so with multiple windowing), hence the scrollbar, widely used in today's applications. The scrollbar represents *all* the space along one dimension while the thumb represents the position, and sometimes the size, of the window. To reach a particular out-of-view target, one first moves the thumb to move the window; when the target is revealed within the window, one positions the cursor to make the selection. This amounts to two-scale pointing with a coarse-grain first component and a fine-grain second component.

Scrollbars represent the document at a scale $s = w/d$ determined by the ratio of window size (w) and document size (d). Moving the thumb by p pixels scrolls the document by p/s pixels. If the document is larger than the square of the window size ($d > w^2$), a problem arises: Moving the thumb by one pixel scrolls the document by more than a full window, making parts of the document inaccessible. Also, when documents are large relative to the window size, even small thumb movements make the contents of the window jump, causing the user to lose context. This occurs frequently, typically with documents that are 20-50 times the size of the display window. One solution is to let the user control the scale. Many drawing programs (e.g., Claris Draw or Adobe Photoshop) allow zooming in and out, usually by a predetermined set of scales. Zooming interfaces (e.g., Pad++) offer continuous control over the scale, allowing elements of the space to be visible or concealed according to viewing scale [semantic zooming, 9].

Attempts to improve the scrollbar device include new mice with a finger device, a wheel (Intellimouse) or a small joystick (Scrollpoint), bound to the scrollbar of compatible applications. These devices allow users to maintain their focus on the document rather than shift attention to the scrollbar.

Because global navigation (e.g., with a scrollbar) and local pointing within a window are used in combination to reach a specified target, we can treat them as the macro and micro components of the same act of selection. This insight enables us to extend the application of Fitts' law from simple pointing to more complex navigation tasks.

Fitts' Law in WIMP Interfaces

According to Fitts [7, 8], movement time (*MT*, the time to reach a target of width *W* placed at a distance *D)* varies linearly with $\log_2(2D/W)$. Better data fits may be obtained with linear [21] or power [19] models, but in this paper we need only to retain the basic, truly important fact acknowledged by all versions of Fitts' law, namely that task difficulty is determined by the dimensionless ratio *D/W*. According to this generic formulation of Fitts' law, $MT = f\ (D/W)$.

Since Card's first demonstration of the suitability of Fitts' model to characterize the user's motor action in HCI [5], Fitts' law has been a very successful tool for designing and evaluating interfaces [17]. The success of Fitts' model is largely due to the fact that most actions carried out with the pointer in a desktop environment amount to, or at least involve, simple target acquisitions. Accot and Zhai [2] recently argued that Fitts' model does not take into account constraints on trajectories such as those imposed by hierarchical menus, but they were able to demonstrate that the law does generalize to the case of motion along paths of arbitrary shapes and widths.

Peter Pan Pointing in Complex, Multiscale Electronic Worlds

Does Fitts' law have any relevance at all to navigation in the first place? Imagine that, like Peter Pan, you can freely move in a purely kinematic 3D space, that is, in a world with time and length but no mass. As you fly in 3D space, you experience none of the constraints of the real world (e.g., gravity, limited speed, limited acceleration). Your only limit is your rate of information intake, since to guide your locomotion, you need to accommodate the flow of optical information induced by your motion.

In such a world, if you started from Paris, you could easily pick up a flower in Central Park, New York City (assuming this is permitted!). You would just rise up to a

sufficient height (zooming out) that you could simultaneously see Europe and North America, then quickly traverse the Atlantic (panning), and finally plummet to the East Coast of the U.S. (zooming in and panning), regulating your progress as your perception of location got finer and finer: New York City, Manhattan, Central Park, a nice flower bed, and, in the end, one particular flower. As you grasped the stem with the tip of your fingers, you would have just executed a pointing movement over a huge distance (*D* > 5,000 km) and, more importantly, with a tremendous accuracy (*W* = about 1 mm) given the distance covered. According to Fitts' index of difficulty (*ID*), this task would involve a spatial difficulty of $\log_2(5*10^6/10^{-3} +1) =$ about 32 bits.[1]

Using the terminology of Furnas and Bederson [9], Peter Pan's world is a 2+1D world with two dimensions of space (latitude and longitude) and one of scale (altitude). Obviously, such a world is no longer as imaginary as it was in 1952, when Walt Disney produced his animated movie. For example, geographical information systems will let you move to any location on the planet, even specific buildings, by panning and zooming. In fact this management of complex navigation characterizes information visualization systems in general [e.g., 4, 6].

So Fitts' pointing model does indeed seem to have relevance to the problem of navigation in complex, multiscale electronic worlds. Yet, navigation is certainly not pointing. Below we examine some apparent and real differences involving the spatial dimensionality of movement, coordinate systems, and task difficulty.

The Spatial Dimensionality of Movements

In a tapping task like Fitts' [7], participants must use the hand to reach a target placed on a tabletop. Although the hand moves typically in 3D space, the task is one-dimensional (1D) in the sense that *D*, *W*, and movement endpoints are measured along a single line. In recent years, cognitively oriented studies [e.g., 19] have often used even simpler mono-articular movements, since a single spatial dimension or a single articular degree of freedom (DOF) suffices to capture the essence of Fitts' law. Whereas the bulk of Fitts' law research has been concerned with 1D space, navigation typically has to do with 2D or 3D space. Fitts' model, however, need not be confined to the 1D world. Fitts' law has already been generalized to the 2D space [18, 20] and accommodating aimed movements in 3D space would require just one more step, presumably using the same logic as in [18]. So the spatial dimensionality of movements should cause no real difficulty when applying Fitts' ideas to multi-dimensional navigation.

---

[1] As is customary in HCI, we define the *ID* as $\log_2$ (D/W +1) (see [17] for justifications).

The Task Coordinate System

Fitts' law has been studied with a variety of tasks involving either hand translations in task space or rotations in the angular space of a single joint. Note that since Fitts' law links MT to the dimensionless ratio D/W, it must hold with any coordinate system, whether Cartesian or articular.

Recourse to single-joint movement to study Fitts' law may look attractive to those interested in rigorous experimental control. However, this simplification takes us one step toward physiology and one step away from the spirit of Fitts' research because of its emphasis on the actor's *body space*. Fitts' law, whose validity is quite independent of the muscular and skeletal means involved in reaching the target, is in essence a relationship within *task space*. To make this clear, let us compare four target-acquisition tasks of increasing complexity in body space.

- Task 1: Moving a cursor to a target by means of a wrist pronation/supination as in [19].

- Task 2: Hand tapping on a tabletop as in Fitts' experiments, with the participant seated.

- Task 3: Same as Task 2 except that $D = 100$ m, so that actual running is required.

- Task 4: Peter Pan pointing with $D = 5,000$ km, so that virtual flying is required.

In body space, Task 1 is the only one that requires a simple movement. The movement in Task 2 is already very complicated: Fitts [7] had his participants cover a distance with the hand that varied from 5 to 40 cm. Considering the body's coordinate system, a 5-cm and a 40-cm hand movement represent strikingly different acts since the former mainly involves the most distal joints of the upper limb (wrist and fingers) whereas the latter heavily involves the proximal joints of the elbow and shoulder [15]. So it is tempting to criticize Fitts' experiment on the grounds that changes in D were confounded with dramatic biomechanical changes.

In fact such a criticism does not apply if one uses the appropriate coordinate system. The task paradigm with which Fitts established his law involves a kind of movement that, however complex in body space, remains quite simple in task space. Importantly, the same argument holds for Tasks 3 and 4. Whether one physically runs in order to move the stylus 100 m or virtually flies to move oneself (or a visualization window) 5,000 km is in no way more problematic than mobilizing all the DOF of one's arm in Fitts' tapping task. In Tasks 2 through 4, the uncontrolled biomechanical complexity is indeed enormous, but irrelevant to Fitts' model. This model, which only considers target distance and target width, has essentially to do, not with movements of arm segments in

body space, but rather with *moves* in task space. [2] In task space, which incorporates the target and the cursor, lengths D and W are measurable for all four tasks and hence an ID can always be computed. Tasks 2 through 4 comply just as rigorously as Task 1 with the operational requirements of Fitts' paradigm.

In sum, the motor activities involved in pointing and navigation are quite different in terms of the usual body-centered view of human movement. However, they can be tackled in the same conceptual framework, provided they are treated as moves in task space—the coordinate system that happens to be most appropriate to Fitts' law.

Scale and Task Difficulty

As first hinted by Fitts, the difficulty of an aimed movement is best estimated as the logarithm of the inverse of a probability ratio—namely, the ratio of the size of the target destination subset and the size of the set of accessible destinations. The best justification for using Fitts' logic here is that it provides an abstract metric of task difficulty, based on Shannon's notion of information, for jointly thinking about pointing and navigation.

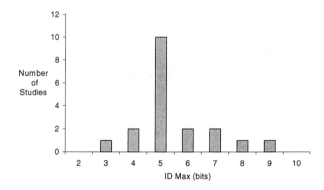

Figure 1. *Distribution of ID_{max} for a random sample of 20 Fitts' law studies. ID's were (re)computed as $log_2 (D/W+1)$.*

Using the metric of information, task difficulty in typical navigation tasks is vastly superior to that seen in traditional pointing. For instance, selection of one Web page from among the 5,000,000 pages made accessible by the Library of Congress [22] involves an ID of about 22 bits. Compare this to Fitts' law research, in which the task ID rarely exceeds 8 bits. Figure 1 shows our estimate of the distribution of the maximum ID used in Fitts' law research,[3] based on a random sample of 20 studies.

---

[2] The game of chess is an exemplary instance in which only moves (piece displacements in the chessboard coordinate system) are considered, the gestural technique of manipulating the pieces (the hand movement) being ignored as irrelevant.

[3] Figure 1 is based exclusively on studies using the classic time-minimization paradigm [19].

It is no surprise that the range of manageable *ID*'s appears so limited in Fitts' law research. In tapping, for example, if one uses only the arm to the exclusion of the trunk and legs, then the hand can cover a maximum *D* of about half a meter, while the smallest workable target size, without the help of a magnifying lens, is about a millimeter. So an *ID* of about 9 bits ($\log_2(0.5/0.001 + 1)$) does indeed represent an upper limit for hand pointing in traditional Fitts' law experimentation. Consistent with this observation, numerous data sets from the literature show dramatic decrements in bandwidth as the *ID* rises beyond 4-6 bits [7, 8, 10, 12, 16].

The reason why the *ID* is strongly limited in traditional pointing is because it involves selection at a *single scale*. As has been occasionally noted [e.g., 9], this limitation must disappear in multiscale navigation. This is most easily understandable in the 1D case, by simply comparing one vs. two levels of scale. Consider a device like an optical microscope with a macro and a micro control knob. Notice that even with a double-knobbed microscope, the task of adjusting the lens/section distance remains in essence a 1D target acquisition task: It is simply a *two-scale*, as well as a two-step, pointing task, and this task must abide by Fitts' law.

Many sophisticated devices have been designed with multi-knob control systems in order to accommodate the limitations of the human perceptual-motor system. Multi-knob controls make it possible to handle very high *D/W* ratios that cannot be achieved with single-scale controls. For example, one regulated power supply of Lambda Electronics Inc. has two concentric knobs for the control of the output voltage. The external, macro knob offers a high-gain control (148 mV per degree of knob rotation), making it possible to cover, with a limited resolution, the whole voltage range (0-40 V for a 270° rotation). The gain of the internal, micro knob is only 4 mV/deg, which allows the user to set the voltage to the nearest 1/100 of a volt. With this two-scale control, a total of 4,000 settings can be differentiated and the information the user can produce is 12 bits, a figure well above the maxima of task difficulty identified in Figure 1.

AN EXPERIMENT ON TWO-SCALE POINTING

We investigated two-scale pointing with an *ID* of 12.2 bits (*D/W* = 4800), a level of task difficulty which, to our knowledge, has not yet been explored in Fitts' law research. Participants were presented with two cursors representing a single input device, a puck or a stylus on a digitizing tablet. One cursor, the macro cursor, provided a complete, but low-resolution view of the task, while the other, the micro cursor, provided a high-resolution view of the target region. The experiment was designed to test two hypotheses.

• *H1*. In standard single-scale pointing, the decay of the rate of information processing makes it difficult to handle *ID*'s greater than 9 bits. This limitation should vanish with a suitable two-scale (if not multiscale) representation of the movement. Not only should users provided with double-scale control be able to successfully handle an *ID* far above the usual maxima of Fitts' law research, but their processing rate should remain similar to that observed in standard single-scale pointing.

The capacity limitation for single-scale pointing obviously reflects the existence of both a numerator maximum and a denominator minimum in the *D/W* ratio. In the present experiment, participants were asked to handle an unusually small *W* by using the equivalent of a magnifying lens, while the *D* to cover remained relatively large. In their famous microscopic pointing experiment, Langolf et al. [16] required very fine-grained movements, but the whole range of the movement was visible within the field of the microscope, making this a single-scale task of standard difficulty ($ID_{\max}$ = 8.2 bits). Our hypothesis was that people can master higher levels of *ID* if they are provided with a two-scale control.

• *H2*. At a high level of task difficulty, the stylus should allow better performance than the puck or the mouse because it more fully exploits the high-resolution movement capability of the fingers.

Card's [5] early demonstration that the mouse was a nearly optimal input device has received much confirmation, even after the introduction of digitizing tablets with a stylus as the pointing device [e.g., 14]. So far, however, authors have only considered relatively easy pointing tasks with single-scale control. We reasoned that the stylus would most clearly surpass the mouse with movements involving a very fine terminal adjustment because the stylus, with its pen shape, elicits a *precision grip* favorable to fine finger motion, whereas the mouse elicits a *power grip* which allows very limited mobilization of joints more distal than the wrist.

We used a Wacom puck with absolute mapping, rather than a mouse with relative mapping, to make shape the only experimental contrast between the puck and the stylus. Note that the Wacom puck, quite similar in shape to a regular mouse, elicits a similar hand posture.

Methods

Participants
Eight unpaid adult volunteers (seven male and one female, all with normal or corrected-to-normal vision) participated in the experiment.

Equipment
The experiment was programmed on an Apple Workgroup Server 7250 connected to a 832 x 634 pixel screen. We used a Wacom A4 digitizing tablet (304 x 304 mm), which discriminates 15,240 positions on each of its two dimensions. The pointing tools were the Wacom puck UltraPoint Ergonomic UC-520 and the Wacom stylus UltraPen Eraser UP-801E.

Screen Display and Task Conditions

The pointing task was one-dimensional, with the pointing tool (either a puck or a stylus) and the screen cursors moving along the horizontal dimension. Because the tablet range (T) was more than 18 times larger than the screen range (S), no one-to-one mapping of the former onto the latter was possible. The screen display offered, on two horizontal lines separated by a distance of 150 pixels, two pointer representations that involved opposite, complementary compromises (see Figure 2). On the lower line, the *macro* cursor represented tool motion over the full range of the tablet at the cost of a poor visual resolution —with a display/control (DC) gain of only 0.05. The equation of the macro cursor was $y = x * S / T$, with y denoting cursor position on the screen and x denoting tool position on the tablet.[4] On the upper line, the *micro* cursor represented tool position with a complete resolution (DC gain = 1), at the cost of an incomplete coverage of the tablet range. This cursor, as if appearing under a magnifying lens, only became visible when the macro cursor below entered its target. The equation of the micro cursor was $z = x - T + S$, with z denoting the position of the micro cursor on the screen. Both the macro and the micro cursors had the form of a vertical line segment 1-pixel thick and 50-pixels high.

The participants were asked to perform the movements as fast as possible, but there was no time pressure between target acquisition and initiation of the next movement. The task involved a discrete pointing movement in alternating directions, rather than a reciprocal movement [12], and in this sense it was more representative of usual pointing in HCI.

In the easy, single-scale (1S) task condition, used as a control, participants had to move the macro cursor back and forth to left and right targets visualized by red-colored rectangles 45-pixels wide (and 40 pixels high, as were all targets of this experiment) separated by a D of 674 pixels from center to center (ID = 4.0 bits). The currently-to-be-acquired target appeared brighter than the other. As soon as the cursor entered one of the two targets on the macro line, the micro cursor popped in above. In this easy condition, however, this event conveyed no information as the micro target (also a red rectangle) covered the whole width of the screen (w' = 828 pixels)—that is, acquisition of the lower, macro target automatically caused acquisition of the upper, micro target. When the macro

---

[4] Below we denote tool position on the tablet as x, macro-cursor position as y, and micro-cursor position as z. For the distance and the tolerance, we use upper-case characters (D and W) for the tablet, lower-case characters (d and w) for the macro cursor, and primed lower-case characters (d' and w') for the micro cursor. Note that all three variables x, y, and z correspond to the horizontal dimension of the tablet and screen.

cursor had stayed in a target for 0.5 s, the alternate target became brighter, an invitation for the participant to start the next move.

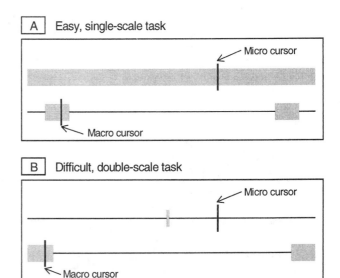

Figure 2. *The screen display in the single-scale (A) and double-scale (B) condition (here targets are represented in gray). In each of the two examples shown, the left target has just been acquired on the lower, macro line, and so the micro cursor above has just popped in from the right. Acquisition of the right macro target would cause the micro cursor to pop in from the left.*

In the difficult, double-scale (2S) task condition, acquisition of the macro target (d = 788 pixels, w = 45 pixels, ID = 4.2 bits) again caused the micro cursor to appear on one end of the upper line, but here the micro target, placed in the middle of the upper line, was very narrow (w' = 3 pixels) and so target approach had to be continued, using the high-resolution visual feedback offered on the upper line. As the distance that remained to be covered on the upper line was ½ S = 414 pixels, the ID for this second component of the movement was 7.12 bits. In tablet units, w' was 3 points (0.060 mm), d' was 14,500 points (289 mm), and hence the overall ID for micro-target acquisition was 12.24 bits. In essence, this task amounted to pointing to a minuscule target with the help of a fixed magnifying lens for the terminal phase of the movement [see 1 for an exploratory experiment on pointing through a mobile 2D magnifying glass].

Procedure

Participants were tested individually in a single session which lasted about 90 min. Each participant executed 32 blocks of movements. The first 16 comprised only four movements each and served as warm-up blocks (the data were not analyzed). The next 16 were experimental blocks, with four blocks for each of the four treatments (1S puck, 2S puck, 1S stylus, and 2S stylus). Each experimental block comprised 15 movements, only the last ten of which were considered for data analysis. So each participant provided 40 *MT*'s per condition, and 160 *MT*'s overall. The order of the four experimental treatments obtained with the two factors were balanced with Latin squares within each group of 16 blocks.

Data Elaboration

MT was measured from the moment hand velocity on the tablet reached a threshold of 50 mm/s to the moment the target-acquisition criterion was satisfied (less 0.5 s, the time required for the system to acknowledge target acquisition). The 2S condition offered the opportunity to decompose *MT* into its macro and micro components, with the former measured from movement initiation to the time when the macro cursor entered the macro target and the latter measured as the remaining time until acquisition of the micro target (less 0.5 s).

To compare 1S and 2S performance across very different levels of *ID* we used Fitts' [8] index of performance (*IP*), simply defined as the ratio of *ID* and *MT* (in bits/s).

Results and Discussion

An analysis of variance (ANOVA) was run on the *MT* and *IP* data with task condition (1S vs. 2S) and tool (puck vs. stylus) as within-participant factors. A further ANOVA was run on the 2S data with movement component (initial macro vs. terminal micro) and tool as within-participant factors.

Movement time

Table 1 shows a strong cross-over interaction between condition and tool ($F(1,7)=53.02$, $p=.0002$). For the easy 1S condition, all participants but one performed faster with the puck than with the stylus (Wilcoxon $T(8)=1$, $p<.02$, two-tailed). However, for the difficult 2S condition all eight participants were faster with the stylus ($T(8)=0$, $p<.01$, one-tailed).

Table 1. *Mean MT (s) for each tool and each task condition (first two columns), with an easy-macro vs. difficult-micro decomposition of MT within the 2S condition (last two columns).*

	1 Scale	2 Scale	2S Macro	2S Micro
Puck (P)	0.804	4.320	0.919	3.402
Stylus (S)	0.944	2.995	0.815	2.180
S *minus* P	0.140	-1.325	-0.103	-1.222

The speed advantage provided by the stylus in the difficult 2S condition was significant for both components of *MT*, but it was much more marked for the difficult micro component than for the easy macro component (for the tool by movement component interaction, $F(1,7)=31.26$, $p=.0008$). So whether one considers the difficulty contrast between the two task conditions or that between the two components of the movement in the 2S condition, the same conclusion obtains: the stylus beat the puck specifically for higher *ID* levels.

Index of Performance

As shown in Figure 3, the effect of task condition on the *IP* was tool dependent ($F(1,7)=46.86$, $p=.0002$). With the puck, 2S pointing yielded an *IP* considerably lower than 1S pointing (3.09 vs. 5.17 bits/s, Wilcoxon $T(8)=0$, $p<.01$). With the stylus, however, there was no significant difference between 1S and 2S pointing (4.30 vs. 4.16 bits/s, respectively, $T(8)=13.5$, non significant). So, even though our 12-bit test was successfully passed with both the puck and the stylus, it was only with the latter tool that participants conserved a normal processing rate.

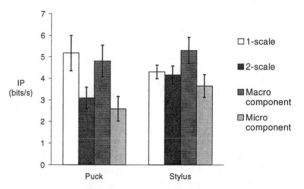

Figure 3. *Mean index of performance (in bits/s) with 1% confidence intervals for each tool and each condition.*

CONCLUSIONS AND PERSPECTIVES

Multiscale Pointing as an Experimental Paradigm for the Study of Navigation

In the 2S pointing condition, all participants successfully handled an *ID* of over 12 bits, accommodating a level of task difficulty far above the maxima seen in Fitts' law literature. We believe our two-scale pointing paradigm can be applied to the experimental study of navigation in electronic worlds. Our main justification is that, using the metric of information, the complexity of a multiscale electronic world is equivalent to task difficulty as defined in a Fitts pointing task. The paradigm may, of course, be extended to more than two levels of scale and to more than one spatial dimension, but the simplest two-scale, one-dimensional version is of special interest, being sufficient for capturing the general problem of navigation while remaining representative of pointing in current graphical interfaces.

With the multiscale pointing paradigm, interesting empirical questions about navigation become tractable. One such question—whose treatment would involve systematic manipulations of *D* and *W*—is whether Fitts' law still holds in the case of multiscale pointing. Our finding that, with the stylus, the information rate was similar for an *ID* of 4 and 12 bits suggests this may be the case. If, as one may suppose, there is an optimal number of scale levels for each level of task difficulty, it would be important to determine empirically how this optimal number increases with the *ID*. Generally speaking, we feel that the multiscale pointing paradigm should help to address the problems of human movement in the new scale-space geometry of Furnas and Bederson [9] (e.g., the optimal path problem).

Implications for the Theory of Motor Control: The Arm as a Multiscale Structure

Our finding that users can easily handle an *ID* of over 12 bits on a digitizing tablet has important implications regarding human motor control. Providing a magnified view of the target region helped the eye but *not* the hand, which still had to select on the tablet a 60 μ wide target at a *D* of 289 mm. Thus, the *ID* was 12.2 bits both in task space and in hand space. Many manual activities (e.g., microsurgery) are successfully accomplished under a microscope. This means that humans manipulating a small tool with their fingers are capable of producing a very low level of motor noise so as to control the position of the tip of the tool within microscopic tolerances (76 μ in Langolf et al.'s [16] microscopic task, 60 μ in the present experiment, and there is no reason to take this figure as a physiological limit). So, in terms of maximal resolution, the hand can be said to beat the eye in human visual-manual tasks and the likely limiting factor for tolerance is vision, not motor control.

The fact that the stylus is more suitable than the puck for an *ID* of 12 bits is consistent with the view that most difficult hand movements can be produced only if one is allowed to *concurrently* exploit the large spatial coverage permitted by one's shoulder, elbow, and wrist and the fine resolution of one's fingers. An arm, with its hierarchy of mechanical gains from proximal to distal joints, represents a multiscale structure *par excellence* [11, 13]. Zhai and collaborators [23] have recently reported data that clearly support the view that the recruitment of the arm's most distal DOF—in addition to its more proximal DOF—enhances the informational capacity of aimed movements. They showed that in a 3D docking task over a *D* of several tens of cm (a *D* that unconditionally involved the proximal joints) performance was better with an input device that fully exploited finger motion (FingerBall) than with one that virtually ignored it (6-DOF Glove).

Scale as a Criterion for Multimodal Division of Labor

One interesting possibility with two-scale interfaces is to assign the macro and micro components of pointing to different parts of the user's effector system, keeping in mind that, in many activities, the division of labor is hierarchically organized with scale as a major criterion [11, 13]. Buxton and Myers [3] showed that right-handers asked to reach target words within a long document perform better, relative to the standard one-handed technique, if they are allowed to scroll with the left hand and select with the right [see 24 for a recent corroboration]. A design that assigns the macro component of the task to the non-preferred hand and the micro component to the preferred hand conforms to the general principles of human manual lateralization [11, 13]. In contrast, ignorance of the above principles might explain why a recent evaluation [24] rated Intellimouse as a mediocre input device for a Web navigation task. One problem with the design of Intellimouse (and Scrollpoint mouse as well) is that it assigns large-scale scrolling to finger joints, which are naturally specialized for fine-grained acts, and fine-scale selection to more proximal arm joints (wrist, elbow, and shoulder), whose natural role is to produce large-scale motion of the hand.

Implications for HCI Design

The need to produce a highly accurate movement of the hand on the tablet in the difficult condition of this experiment made pointing quite different in our two-scale task than in current two-scale graphical interfaces. Because usual interfaces map hand space onto either a complete but coarse-grained or a fine-grained but incomplete view of the world, users must discriminate far fewer positions in hand space than in task space, seldom having to produce more than 4-5 bits with the hand. The present experiment shows that the hand can accommodate much higher levels of movement difficulty provided users are given an appropriate two-scale visual feedback. This could be exploited in current interfaces by using input devices that have a higher resolution than the screen. As noted at the beginning of this article, mouse scrolling generates a discontinuous response if the document is larger than 20-50 times the display window. With a tablet, whose resolution is typically 1/10 of a screen pixel, this limit would be 10 times higher (i.e., 200-500 screen pages) while still allowing a precise positioning of the document via the scrollbar. More generally, the high precision of human manual control could be used in many navigation tasks by providing appropriate visual feedback based on multiscale representation.

ACKNOWLEDGMENTS

We acknowledge the generous financial support of the French Ministry of Defense (DGA Grant # 96.34.058.00.470.75.65 to the first author). We thank Jeff Pressing, Ken Hinckley, and Wendy Mackay for useful discussions and suggestions, Didier Casalta, Rémi Temmos, and Raymond Fayolle for technical help and advice, and Thelma Coyle for help in checking the English.

REFERENCES

1. Accot, J., Yamaashi, K., Zhai, S., & Buxton, W. Elementary, My Dear Fitts: Performance in two-handed pointing with a magnifying glass. CENA internal research report #NR98-831 (1998).

2. Accot, J. and Zhai, S. Beyond Fitts' law: Models for trajectory-based HCI tasks, in *Proceedings of CHI'97* (Atlanta GA, March 1997), ACM Press, 295-302.

3. Buxton, W. and Myers, B. A study in two-handed input, in *Proceeding of CHI'86* (1986), ACM Press, 321-326.

4. Bederson, B. B., & Hollan, J. D. Pad++: a zooming graphical interface for exploring alternate interface physics, in *Proceeding of ACM UIST'94*, (Marina del Ray, CA, November 1994), ACM Press, 17-26.

5. Card, S.K., English, W.K., and Burr, B.J. Evaluation of mouse, rate-controlled isometric joystick, step-keys, and text keys for text selection on a CRT. Ergonomics, 21, 8 (1978), 301-613.

6. Card, S.K., Robertson, G.G., & York, W. The WebBook and the Web Forager; An information workspace for the world-wide web, in *Proceedings of CHI'96* (Vancouver, BC, Canada, April 1996), ACM Press, 111-117.

7. Fitts, P.M.. The information capacity of the human motor system in controlling the amplitude of movement. *Journal of Experimental Psychology 47* (1954), 381-391.

8. Fitts, P.M., and Peterson, J.R.. Information capacity of discrete motor responses. *Journal of Experimental Psychology 67* (1964), 103-112.

9. Furnas, G.W. & Bederson, B.B. Space-scale diagrams: Understanding multiscale interfaces, in *Proceedings of CHI'95* (Denver CO, May 1995), ACM Press, 234-241.

10. Gan, K.C. and Hoffmann, E.R. Geometrical conditions for ballistic and visually controlled movements. *Ergonomics 31* (1988), 829-839.

11. Guiard, Y. Asymmetric division of labor in human skilled bimanual action: The kinematic chain as a model. *Journal of Motor Behavior 19* (1987), 486-517.

12. Guiard, Y. Information and energy constraints in human movement: Fitts' law in the discrete vs. continuous paradigm. *Human Movement Science 16* (1997), 97-131.

13. Guiard, Y. & Ferrand, T. Asymmetry in bimanual skills, in D. Elliott & E. A. Roy (Eds.), *Manual asymmetries in motor performance* (1996). Boca Raton FL: CRC Press, 175-195.

14. Kabbash, P., MacKenzie, I.S., and Buxton, W. Human performance using computer input devices in the preferred and non-preferred hands, in *Proceedings of CHI'93* (Amsterdam, 1993), ACM Press, 474-481.

15. Lacquaniti, F., Ferrigno, G., Pedotti, A., Soechting, J.F., and Terzuolo, C. Changes in spatial scale in drawing and handwriting: Kinematic contributions by proximal and distal joints. Journal of Neuroscience 7, 3 (1987), 819-828.

16. Langolf, G.D., Chaffin, D.B., and Foulke, J.A.. An investigation of Fitts' law using a wide range of movement amplitudes. *Journal of motor Behavior 8* (1976), 113-128.

17. MacKenzie, I.S. Fitts' law as a research and design tool in human-computer interaction. *Human-Computer Interaction 7* (1992), 91-139.

18. MacKenzie, I.S. and Buxton, W. Extending Fitts' law to two-dimensional tasks, in *Proceedings of CHI'92* (Monterey CA, May 1992), ACM Press, 219-226.

19. Meyer, D.E., Smith, J.E.K., Kornblum, S., Abrams, R.A., & Wright, C.E.. Speed-accuracy tradeoffs in aimed movements: Toward a theory of rapid voluntary action. In M. Jeannerod (Ed.), *Attention and performance XIII* (1990). Hillsdale, NJ: Erlbaum, 173-226.

20. Mottet, D., Bootsma, R.J., Guiard, Y., and Laurent, M. Fitts' law in two-dimensional task space. *Experimental Brain Research 100* (1994), 144-148.

21. Schmidt, R.A., Zelaznik, H.N., Hawkins, B., Frank, J.S., & Quinn, J.T., jr. Motor output variability: A theory for the accuracy of rapid motor acts. *Psychological Review 86* (1979), 415-451.

22. Shneiderman, B. Designing information abundant websites: Issues and recommendations. *International Journal of Human-Computer Studies* (1997).

23. Zhai, S., Milgram, P. and Buxton, W. The influence of muscle groups on performance of multiple degree-of-freedom input, in *Proceedings of CHI'96* (Vancouver BC, Canada, April 1996), ACM Press, 308-315.

24. Zhai, S., Smith, B.A., and Selker, T. Improving browsing performance: A study of four input devices for scrolling and pointing tasks, in *Proceedings of INTERACT97* (Sydney, Australia, July 1997), 286-292.

Authoring Animated Web Pages Using 'Contact Points'

Pete Faraday
Multimedia Authoring Product Unit,
Microsoft
Redmond, WA 98052 USA
peterfar@microsoft.com

Alistair Sutcliffe
The Centre for HCI Design,
City University,
London, EC1 0HB, UK
A.G.Sutcliffe@city.ac.uk

ABSTRACT
This paper explores how 'contact points' or co-references between an animation and text should be designed in web pages. Guidelines are derived from an eye tracking study. A dynamic HTML authoring tool is described which supports these requirements. An evaluation study is reported in which four designs of animation in web pages were tested.

KEYWORDS
Web Page Design, Authoring Tools

THE PROBLEM
More and more web pages contain text and animated media, yet little work has addressed how to effectively design such combinations. Existing guidelines give unfocussed and contradictory advice which encourages the use of animation while warning that it can have unspecified, detrimental effects. For instance, Nielsen [3] concludes that animated web pages are useful for providing 'enriching graphical representations', but warns 'unconstrained use of multimedia results in user interfaces that confuse users and make it *harder* for them to understand the information.'

This paper introduces the notion of 'contact points', or co-references between text and animation as a solution to effectively combining the two types of media. Contact points are places in the text where the content needs to be related with the animation. Contact points allow the viewer to integrate the content of the text with a referent in the animation eg for details of an object's appearance, or how to perform an action. The key issues for design concern how to form a 'contact point' :

- How to provide linking references and synchronisation between text and visual streams.

- How to ensure that the message thread can be followed between the text and visual media.

The use of a combination of text and visuals in a

presentation is not entirely novel. Presentation planning systems such as WIP [8] and COMET [7] provide support for adding captions to images. In this paper we explore the trade offs between designing the medium itself for better integration, i.e. segmenting and interleaving animation and text so the topic references are contiguous, and designing user viewing controls to facilitate cross references or allowing less constrained user initiative.

The first part of the paper provides guidelines for designing contact points based on a set of eye tracking studies we performed. The next section then describes how the guidelines were used to design a tool to assist in authoring web pages using contact points. Finally, in order to validate the value of the web pages using contact points, a study of four types of animation control in web pages is presented. The paper is illustrated by an example which explains the formation of cancer.

GUIDELINES
To investigate how viewers form contact points, we performed a number of eye tracking studies upon a range of still and animated presentations [4]. Figure 1 shows an example result set for one of the cancer materials which shows a text title and caption, both with contact points to a static image : the title to the slide as the whole, the caption to the brown coloured highlighted cells.

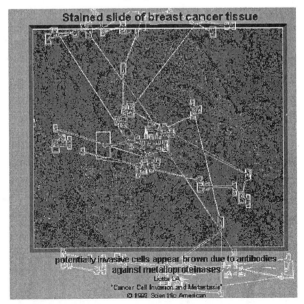

Figure 1 Single subject eye track results

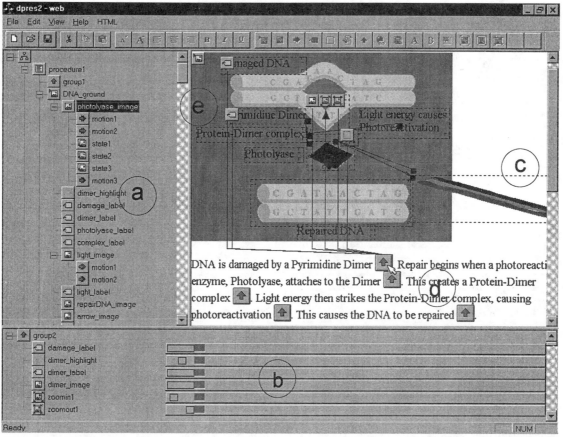

Figure 2 Screen dump illustrating the tool. The content view - marked (a) shows the media script organised in a hierarchy of components and design effects. The time line view, marked (b) sets the sequence of the design effects for the image illustrated in the page view (c). The contact points in the text (d) are connected by direct manipulation to presentation effects (e). In this case one contact point will play six effects when the button is activated.

The eye tracking studies provided evidence for the effect of contact point design techniques :

– *Contact points should be sequenced to avoid overwhelming the reader.* Subjects seemed to process the text as a whole, then rescan the image or play the animation. This may cause problems if the text has several contact points, since references should be resolved in the order given in the text to deliver information effectively. In figure 1, the subjects did not generally return from the lower caption until they had read it all; even though a reference was made to the image by the sentence 'Potentially invasive cells appear brown..', many subjects read the copyright information beneath it before shifting to the image. It should be made explicit to the user at which point in the text reference to visuals is required.

– *Animation should be arranged so as not to compete with surrounding images or text.* Our studies showed that attention is strongly directed to animation, causing subjects to ignore accompanying text or images. It is vital that the animation should be sequenced in time so as not to distract.

– *The referent in the visuals should be easy to locate.* Subjects tended to fixate highlighted, labelled or moving objects. These should be related to the current referent in the text. In figure 1, the brown colouring of the cells provided a highlight which subjects fixated upon after reading the caption.

– *Viewing should be self paced.* The studies showed that inspecting the image and text are serial processes which take time. The number of fixations upon figure 1 varied across subjects, suggesting differences in reading speed.

TOOL SUPPORT

Our study demonstrated the need to design contact points between a text and animation in a systematic way. To meet these needs, a Dynamic HTML authoring tool was developed. The tool is novel in that it encourages the designer to input a representation of the content to be presented and break it up into a number of contact point segments, each relating a part of the text with a particular visual sequence. These are shown as buttons (⬆) in the presentation, which when clicked play back a related segments of the animation. The tool also makes authoring the messages required to start or stop each effect easier by using a direct manipulation approach.

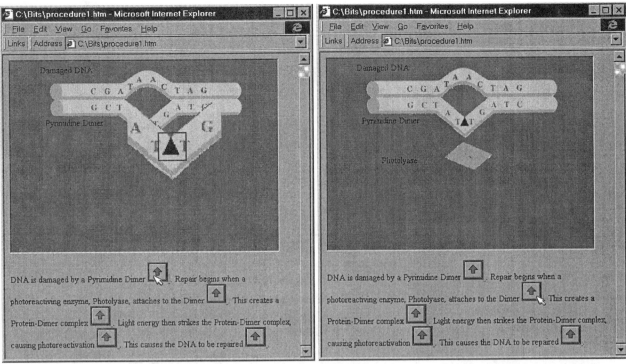

Figure 3   Figure 4

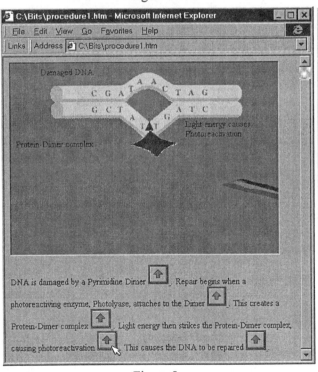

Figure 5

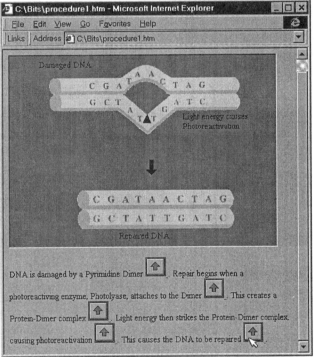

Figure 6

IMPLEMENTATION

The tool was built in Visual C++ under MS Windows 95. It is composed of three main views which will be discussed in the following sections. Figure 2 shows an overview of how these views fit together in the tool. It is illustrated with a more complex cancer example, showing DNA repair by photoreactivation. More details of the tools architecture can be found in [6].

Content View

The content view is represented as a tree which is used by the designer to input the script to be presented. Each procedure in the tree represents one web page. The tree shows all the media and presentation effects which have been defined for the sequence. Presentation effects are used to modify the appearance of a media item; these include animation, highlight, and zoom. These effects provide ways of making the referent of a contact point in the image easy for the user to locate. In figure 2, the content view shows that the photolyase_image has motion and change of state effects defined upon it.

Page View

The page view provides the facilities of a simplified WYSIWYG word processor, and allows images, animation, and labels to be placed on the page. The text editor is used initially to input and format the text, and to position background images. The view can be scrolled, and multiple paragraphs of text and images added within the page.

Contact point buttons (▣) are then placed in the text to represent the point at which a co-reference must be made with the animation. The button makes the reference explicit to the user, and allows reading of the sequence to be self paced. If the user needs to re-read the text, they can click the associated contact point to replay it.

The referents for each contact point are defined in the tool using direct manipulation. An effect can be set by double clicking on the contact point button and dragging a connecting line from the button to the media element or presentation effect which is to be referred to. The elements connected to a contact point can be reviewed by single clicking on the contact point button.

In figure 2, the first contact point 'DNA is damaged by a pyrimidine dimer' is connected to the damaged DNA label, the Dimer image and label, and to a highlight effect (a red box), with a zoom in and out effects on the Dimer image. These will be played when the contact point button is clicked by the user; the end result is shown played in a web browser in figure 3.

Timeline view

The timeline view allows the media elements associated with the contact point to be arranged over time. Sequencing is important because it allows animation to be timed so that it does not compete for the user's attention with other media and presentation effects.

Sequencing is supported in the tool by timeline bars. These can be dragged to change the start or end time, or to set duration. When a contact point is selected in the page view, the timelines for its elements are shown in the timeline view. In figure 2 the timelines for the 'DNA is damaged by a pyrimidine dimer' contact point are shown, it has a zoom in effect is set upon the Dimer, followed by a highlight and then a zoom out.

HTML Output

The presentation is output as a set of web pages. The tool parses the presentation structure and converts it into a set of HTML tags which render the text, contact point buttons, and background images; and uses dynamic HTML layers to float the referent images, labels and animation on top of the page. A JavaScript playback engine is called from the contact point buttons to sequence playback of the DHTML

elements. Clicking on the contact point button plays the presentation in the order set by the designer.

Example

An example of the cancer sequence play back in a browser is shown in figure 3-6. As each contact point button is selected, a part of the animated sequence is played. In figure 3, the damaged part of the DNA is zoomed in, and then the Dimer highlighted and labelled. In figure 4, an animation shows the Photolyase attach to the Dimer and form a Protein -Dimer Complex; then the Photolyase changed shape and colour when it joins with the Dimer. In figure 5, light energy is animated striking the Dimer Complex, which then reacts by splitting apart. In figure 6 the Photolyase moves away, and the repaired DNA is revealed.

DO CONTACT POINTS HELP USERS ?

Having implemented the tool, we were interested in testing out web pages with and without contact points to see if they improved comprehension of the animated cancer sequence.

We believed that presentations produced by the tool with explicit contact points would have several benefits. First, making the reference between the text and a particular segment of the animation explicit, they should improve comprehension. Secondly, by allowing the user to self pace the play back of animation, they should be able to view the text without being disrupted by the animation. If the animation distracted the subjects they would have to replay it to understand the sequence.

STUDY

To test our claims, we conducted a between subject study using four web page designs, comparing comprehension of the cancer sequence in figure 3-6 with contact points against three conditions which varied the integration of the media and play back controls. The study was conducted over the web, with subject's invited to remotely view one of the designs in their browser and then given a comprehension test. It was felt that this provided an ecologically valid approach to studying how a typical the web user would perform with our animations.

Condition	Animation Segmented ?	Type of Play Controls
Contact Points	Yes	Contact Point play buttons related to each segment
Video controls	Yes	Play button, fastforward & rewind to each segment
Single Play Button	No	Play button shows whole sequence each time
Onload animation	No	Plays automatically on page load. Play button shows whole sequence each time

Table 1 Experimental conditions

Materials

Four experimental conditions were designed. Each condition used the same animated sequence, but varied how the animation was integrated with the text. An overview of the conditions is given in table 1 and in more detail below :

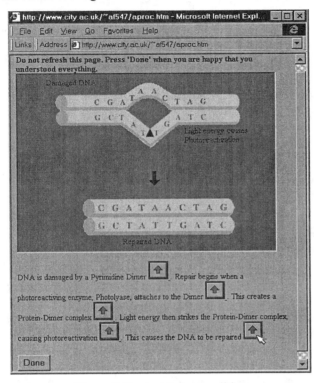

Figure 7 Contact Point condition

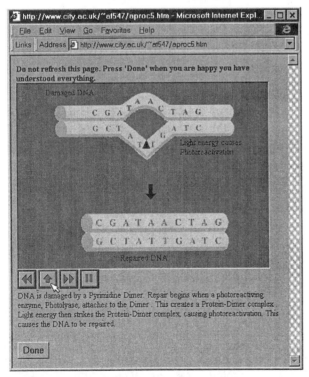

Figure 8 Video controls condition

- Contact Points : The page had five contact point buttons in the text linked to the five separate segments of the animation. The related part of the animation played when a button was clicked. Any part of the animation could be replayed by clicking the appropriate button. This is shown in figure 7.

- Video controls : The page had video control buttons, see figure 8. Clicking the play button played the animation once in a continuous sequence. The fastforward and rewind buttons set the video starting point to the next or previous segment boundary. These controls let the subject browse the animation as they wished.

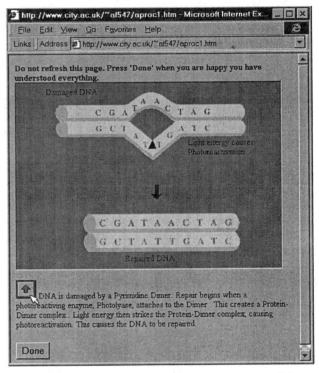

Figure 9 Single Play Button & Play Onload Condition

- Single Play Button : The page had a single play button clicking it played the whole animation. The animation could be replayed by clicking the button again. This is shown in figure 9.

- Onload animation : The whole animation automatically played once in a continuous sequence on page load. A single play button allowed all of the animation to be replayed. In all other ways this appeared as figure 9.

Method

Subjects were recruited from a range of usability and web design listservers, such as UTEST, students.chi, web.chi and web design. In all, 98 subjects were recruited. As the subjects were self selecting their background knowledge and viewing conditions could not be tightly controlled.

Because of a lack of standards for dynamic HTML, the study required users to view the page in Microsoft Internet

Explorer 4. Subjects who noted problems with playing back the animation in their browsers were not included in the study.

The subjects were first directed to a web page which gave instructions on how to use the animation, and split into one of the four conditions based on their surname (eg A-F into condition 1 etc.)

Subjects were then prompted to view the animation as many times as was required in order to fully understand the content. The web pages used are shown in figures 7-9. Once the subjects were happy that they understood the sequence, they hit a 'Done' button at the bottom of the page. A Javascript function in the web page was used to collect all of the play button clicks and record them, via a CGI script, to a file on the server when the 'Done' button was pressed. This produced a trace of how often each part of the animation sequence was played by each subject.

Next, the subjects were given a set of multiple choice questions to test their comprehension, see table 2, presented a set of radio buttons, one of which could be selected as an answer for each question. Subjects who did not answer all the questions were not counted in the study. To prevent cheating, a re-direction in the page made it impossible for the subject to go back and look at the animation again.

Finally, the subjects were asked to provide a subjective rating of 'how well did the animation help you understand the content ?'. They could select from a scale of options 'a lot easier', 'a little easier', 'not sure', 'a little harder', 'a lot harder'. Subjects could also record any comments about the use of animation in a text box.

Question 1	What damages the DNA ?
Choices	Photolyase, Pyrimidine Dimer, Light Energy, None of the above, Do not know
Answer	Pyrimidine Dimer
Question 2	What does the Photolyase do ?
Choices	Attach to the DNA, Use Light Energy, Cause Photoreactivation, None of the above, Do not know
Answer	None of the above
Question 3	What does light energy strike ?
Choices	Pyrimidine Dimer, Dimer Complex, Photolyase, None of the above, Do not know
Answer	Dimer Complex
Question 4	What is needed to create a Protein-Dimer complex ?
Choices	Photolyase, Light Energy, Repaired DNA, None of the above, Do not know
Answer :	Photolyase

Table 2 Multiple choice questions and answers

The multiple choice answers, subjective scores and comments were posted back to the server via a CGI script and saved in a file for analysis.

Results

The results of the study are shown in table 3 and 4. They have three parts : the comprehension score, the number of replays required to understand the sequence (a replay is watching any part of the sequence more than once), and the subjective rating.

Condition	Number of Subjects	Average Multiple Choice Score (/4)	% of Subjects Replaying Any Part of Sequence
Contact Points	28	2.8125	28.6% (8/ 28)
Single Play Button	21	2.809	47.5% (10/ 21)
Video controls	21	1.906	76.2% (16 /21)
Onload animation	28	1.709	85.6% (24 / 28)

Table 3 Average Multiple Choice Score and Percent of subject's replaying any segment.

	Question : 'Did the animation help you understand the content ?'				
Condition	A Lot Easier	A Little Easier	Not Sure	A Little Harder	A Lot Harder
Contact Points	50%	37.5%	6.25%	6.25%	-
Single Play Button	30%	60%	5%	5%	-
Video controls	5.5%	63%	31.5%	-	-
Onload animation	9%	54%	27%	9%	-

Table 4 Subjective ratings for each condition

Overall, the best condition was the contact point design, shown in figure 7. First, it produced the highest comprehension score for the fewest replays, and gave the most positive subjective rating. The contact points provided an improvement in comprehension over the onload animation, video style controls, and single play button. This was statistically significant for the the onload animation and video style controls (p < 0.05 Mann Whitney U).

Second, the contact point buttons required the least replays of all the conditions : only just over a quarter of the subjects had to replay any part of the animation. With the single play button, almost double the number of subjects needed to look at the sequence twice or more. Most of the subjects in the video control and onload animation groups needed to replay the sequence.

Third, the subjective rating was more favourable for the contact point condition than others; 50% of the subjects' found it 'a lot easier' to understand. Subject comments were also positive. One subject praised the ability to control the sequence 'I believe the animation does help especially because it is interactive, not a canned film sequence.' A second wrote 'I feel this was a very powerful use of animation'. Another stated 'The process is still vivid in my mind which demonstrates to me the effectiveness of animation'.

The next best condition was the single play button, shown in figure 9. This was better for comprehension against the onload animation and video controls. Both these results are statistically significant (p <0.05 Mann Whitney U). However, it required many more replays than the contact point design.

A possible explanation for the extra replays might be that the single play button provided a weaker link from the text to the animation. The argument here is that the play button allowed user's to read the text and then play the animation, but because the references between the two media are poor, more replays are needed to resolve them. Subject's comments indicate they had a difficulty in combining the text with animation. One subject complained 'the animation seemed almost context free .. it was hard to keep the text and animation in the same context'. Another stated 'the animation helped though the written explanation was not clear'. A third wrote 'the animation helped me somewhat with seeing the process, but not with remembering the terms'. The subjective rating bear out this analysis, with fewer subjects voting that the single play button animation made the sequence 'a lot easier' to understand than for the contact points condition.

The third place condition was the video controls (see figure 8). This was considerably worse than contact points or the single play button. It provided an improvement in comprehension over the onload animation, but this was not statistically significant.

It was a surprise that the video controls did not produce a better comprehension result than the single play button, since it allowed a greater freedom to view the sequence. However, the subjective ratings show that subjects did not find that it made understanding the animation 'a lot easier' anywhere near as much as the contact point or single play button conditions, and many more subjects were 'not sure' of the value of the animation in this condition.

One reason for this failure may be that using the video controls confused the subject's understanding of how the order of the sequence was related to the controls. Subjects comments suggest this confusion. One noted : 'It would be better to integrate the steps of what is happening in the animation with numbers to describe the process as it is being shown.' Another complained 'It wasn't clear that there were several steps to the animation which could be controlled with the back button'.

Further validation of this hypothesis comes from an analysis of the number of times the segments were replayed, shown in table 5. The cancer animation had five segments, each of which could be played separately in the video control condition. The data shows that the subjects using the video control played more segments, but these tended to be of the latter part of it. In comparison, the single play button enforced the subject to watch the entire sequence each time it was replayed. Taken together with the subject's comments, the results imply that the subjects failed to understand how the rationale for how the segments related to the controls.

Condition	Average Number of Replays for each segment of Cancer Animation				
	1	2	3	4	5
Contact Points	1.13	1.06	1.13	1.13	1.02
Single Play Button	1.38 - Non Segmented Sequence				
Video controls	1.57	1.62	1.81	2.43	3
Onload animation	1.88 - Non Segmented Sequence				

Table 5 Average Number of replays for each segment

The onload animation was the worst of all of the conditions, requiring many replays and having the lowest average comprehension score. A likely explanation for this is that because the animation played as soon as the page finished loading, it distracted the viewer from the text, making it extremely difficult to cross reference between the two media.

This is reflected in the subjective ratings, which has the highest total score for 'not sure' and 'little harder' than any of the other conditions, and in subject's responses. One subject wrote 'When the animation played right away it distracted me so that I had to wait until it was done to read the text then play the animation.' Another added 'In the beginning the animation took my attention away from the text.'

It is also interesting to note that comprehension in the onload animation condition was not improved by replays. This suggests that the viewing the animation first may have confused subjects as to how the animation was related to the text, and this confusion remained even after reading the text and replaying the animation. This may be because the subjects were trying to base their understanding around the animation rather than the text. One subject griped 'I had to re-read the text about six times to get the whole mess straight'. A second concluded 'I think the content was to hard to understand without showing the objective of the animation. For each category of animation there should be a bullet objective'. In all of these cases the text was available, but it did not seem to help as the subjects tried to retro-fit the content of the animation to it even after they had read the text and replayed animation.

DISCUSSION & IMPLICATIONS

The study is important because web pages are more frequently using animation to present their content, and little empirical work has addressed its usability. Taken together, these results suggest that the contact points were indeed effective in improving comprehension for less replays of the animation against the other conditions. The contact points made a strong connection between the text and visuals without the need for the subjects to replay the sequence to establish references between the animation and text.

The good performance of the single play condition probably reflects the advanced organiser function of the text [3]. Mayer & Anderson [1] have noted the need for language to be supplied with animation for similiar reasons. The animation information was integrated into the initial memory schema produced by the text. However, the extra replays suggest that the user has to devote more effort to integration possibly because of working memory overloading. Narayanan & Hegarty [5] propose that replays are required when users' ability to cognitively process animation are overwhelmed : 'less informed or less able users replay a section until the appropriate mental model has been built in memory'. Thus, good comprehension can be achieved with more work, as the replay results show. In contrast, however, our contact points condition promotes effective chunking for less effort.

We ascribe the poor performance of the video controls condition to the hidden model of media segmentation. The users were confused by the opaque effect of rewinding, hence they did not review the earlier segments. This probably hindered schema integration. A future experiment is to compare free form video controls, eg using a slider to allow any part of the sequence to be played, with these results. However, even with such enhancements, the contact point design may well be superior in that it makes it obvious which part of the sequence is being and tightly links the animation to text.

The poor performance of the onload condition is not surprising. This interfered with the advanced organiser role of the text, so even with replays the design did not help the user to chunk information.

The study is also of novelty because it was conducted entirely across the web. The main advantage was that subjects were actually using the web in the way they would in normal life, not sitting in the unusual environment of a usability lab. The downside was that subjects tended to not complete the comprehension test; or sent flame emails because they did not understand that the study had conditions which showed less usable designs. Adding a clearer explanation of the studies aims helped solve these problems.

CONCLUSIONS

This paper has shown how guidelines can be implemented in a tool to support web page design. The tool is a prototype that allows us to explore how explicit support for contact points can be used to assist designers and users. Our tool encourages the designer to consider how the visuals are linked to text by representing contact points within the content itself, and as buttons within the presentation.

The study demonstrated the importance of integrating animation and text both in terms of segmenting components to make the topics clear, and in providing explicit references between media to help memory schema integration. These results are therefore important for tutorial multimedia. Animation may be eye catching (and annoying) in multimedia adverts, but for effective information delivery it needs to be integrated with text following the guidelines we propose.

REFERENCES

1. Mayer, R.E. & Anderson, R.B. The Instructive Animation : Helping students build connections between words and pictures in multimedia. Journal of Education Psychology, 84 (4), 444-452, 1992.

2. Nielsen, J. Guidelines for Multimedia on the Web. `http://www.useit.com/alertbox/`

3. Ausebel, D. The use of advanced organisers in the learning and retention of meaningful verbal language. Journal of Educational Psychology, 51, 267-272, 1962

4. Faraday, P.M. & Sutcliffe, A.G. Designing Effective Multimedia Presentations, ACM CHI 97, 272-279, 1997

5. Narayanan, H. & Hegarty, M. On Designing comprehensible interactive hypermedia manuals. International Journal of Human-Computer Studies, 48, 267-301, 1998.

6. Faraday, P.M. & Sutcliffe, A.G. Making Contact Points between Text and Images. ACM Multimedia 98, `http://www.kom.e-technik.tu-darmstadt.de/Pr/workshops/acmmm98/electronic_proceedings/faraday/index.html`

7. Feiner, S. & McKeown, K. Automating the Generation of co-ordinated Multimedia Explanations. In Intelligent Multimedia Interfaces, AAAI Press, 117-138, 1993

8. Wahlster, W., Andre, E. Finkler, W & Rist, T. Plan-based integration of natural language and graphics generation. AI Journal, 387-427,1993.

Performance Evaluation of Input Devices in Trajectory-based Tasks: An Application of The Steering Law

Johnny Accot[1,2]

[1] Centre d'Études de la Navigation Aérienne
7 avenue Edouard Belin
31055 Toulouse cedex, France

accot@cena.dgac.fr

Shumin Zhai[2]

[2] IBM Almaden Research Center
650 Harry Road
San Jose, CA 95120, USA

zhai@almaden.ibm.com

ABSTRACT

Choosing input devices for interactive systems that best suit user's needs remains a challenge, especially considering the increasing number of devices available. The choice often has to be made through empirical evaluations. The most frequently used evaluation task hitherto is target acquisition, a task that can be accurately modeled by Fitts' law. However, today's use of computer input devices has gone beyond target acquisition alone. In particular, we often need to perform trajectory-based tasks, such as drawing, writing, and navigation. This paper illustrates how a recently discovered model, the steering law, can be applied as an evaluation paradigm complementary to Fitts' law. We tested five commonly used computer input devices in two steering tasks, one linear and one circular. Results showed that subjects' performance with the five devices could be generally classified into three groups in the following order: 1. the tablet and the mouse, 2. the trackpoint, 3. the touchpad and the trackball. The steering law proved to hold for all five devices with greater than 0.98 correlation. The ability to generalize the experimental results and the limitations of the steering law are also discussed.

Keywords

Steering laws, input devices, Fitts' law, human performance modeling, empirical comparison

INTRODUCTION

The unceasing invention of new computer input devices makes a user interface designer's job increasingly perplexing: which device to choose? In some cases the choice becomes obvious due to specific system requirements, including physical characteristics such as mechanical reliability and installation space, application needs such as drawing, and environmental constraints such as those in mobile computing. In other cases, one has to look into the research literature for guidance.

Much research has been conducted to help designers and users choose the input device that best suits to their needs. Yet, due to the rich dimensionality of input device design and the complexity of human capability, adaptability, and limitation, human performance in using various devices can not be reliably predicted from previous research alone. User interface designers therefore often have to conduct empirical comparisons among many candidate devices. In order to make the empirical comparison generalizable to task parameters beyond those tested in the experiment, the experimenters need performance models that provide predictable power. The best known model serving such a purpose is Fitts' law [5], commonly expressed in the following form:

$$T = a + b \log_2(\frac{A}{W} + 1) \qquad (1)$$

where T is the acquisition time of a target of width W that lies at distance A. a and b are empirically determined constants. The log term is called the index of movement difficulty; the reciprocal of b, called the index of performance (IP), is often used as a measure of input device efficiency.

Card and colleagues [3] first applied Fitts' law to computer input device evaluation. They tested a mouse, an isometric joystick, step keys, and text keys in target selection tasks. The study played an important role in the commercial introduction of the mouse as a computer input device. Since then, numerous device evaluation studies have been done under the Fitts' law paradigm. This body of literature is well summarized in MacKenzie's survey [8].

There are at least two advantages to apply models like Fitts' law to empirical studies. First, the model provides predictable power beyond the task parameters, such as a set of target size and distance, tested in the experiment. Second, since Fitts' law transforms the experimental measurements to an index of performance that is independent of the specific task parameters (size and distance), it is possible to compare results across studies that do not use identical settings.

One limitation of Fitts' law paradigm, however, is that target acquisition, or pointing, is no longer the only task a computer input device is used for. Capabilities such as drawing, writing, navigating through nested menus, and moving in 3D virtual worlds all become increasingly desirable. The commonality among these tasks is that they are all based on movement trajectories, not targets. If we only test input devices in the Fitts' law paradigm, the quality of producing trajectories with these devices is overlooked and the choice of input device will be biased by pointing performance alone.

An interesting trajectory-based device evaluation was done by Cohen et al. [4], who tested seven input devices in a star-tracing task which required moving a cursor around a star as fast as possible, while keeping within the boundaries of the figure[1]. However, their conclusions were weakened due to the lack of a formal framework for handling speed/accuracy trade-off in trajectory tasks. For example, the touch-screen was measured faster than the mouse, but was also less precise. How would the two devices compare if they were held at the same accuracy?

Recently we have made advances in overcoming the lack of trajectory-based testing paradigms [1]. We proposed steering, i.e. moving through narrow tunnels, as a study scenario in parallel with Fitts' pointing task. Moreover, we found the existence of a model, dubbed the steering law, that can predict completion time in relation to the tunnel parameters. Such a finding may serve as a theoretical tool for analyzing trajectory-based tasks. Mirroring the Fitts' index of performance for pointing, an index of performance in steering can be similarly defined and applied to input device evaluation.

THE STEERING LAW

A steering task is moving along a normally constrained trajectory[2]. A daily example of the steering task is driving an automobile without going off the road boundaries. For a generic tunnel C, such as the one shown in Figure 1, the steering law [1] that models the relationship between completion time T and the task parameters can be expressed in the following form:

$$T_C = a + b \times ID_C \qquad (2)$$

where a and b are constants; $1/b$ is called the index of performance in steering; ID_C is the index of difficulty of the task and is defined by integrating the inverse of the path width along the trajectory:

$$ID_C = \int_C \frac{ds}{W(s)} \qquad (3)$$

The integration variable s stands for the curvilinear abscissa and $W(s)$ for the path width at abscissa s.

---

[1] The devices tested in the experiment ranked in the following order: mouse, touch-screen, MousePen, large-ball trackball, small-ball trackball, touchpad, and joystick.

[2] The word "normal" is used here with its mathematical meaning: a normal constraint means the constraint is perpendicular to the trajectory.

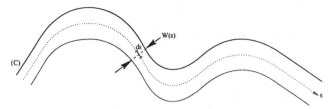

Figure 1: Integrating along a curve

Equation 3 allows the calculation of steering difficulty for a wide range of tunnel shapes. In [1], three shapes were tested: straight, narrowing and spiral tunnels. In all three cases, the steering law calculation correlated with experimental data at greater than 0.96 r^2 value.

The steering law is not without limitation. Analogous to Fitts' law, the independent variables in the steering law are tunnel length and width (see Equation 3). One dimension that may affect steering difficulty but not modeled yet in the steering law is tunnel shape. While we have shown the validity of the law with various tunnel shapes, there is not a generalized law that predicts performance across different shapes of tunnels. This means that when we apply the steering law to input device evaluation, we have to do it categorically. Performance of input devices has to be compared within each category.

Note that the same limitation applies to Fitts' law, although pointing is a much less complicated task than steering. When applying Fitts' law, one typically restricts the target type to two vertical bars (hence modeling one dimensional pointing). Performance data collected with a different or more realistic target shape, such as a word or a circular target, can not be directly compared with those collected in the vertical-bar type of target (see [7]).

Given these limitations, the steering law still provides significant value to input device evaluation, as does Fitts' law. Without the steering law, evaluating input devices in trajectory tasks will be completely dependent on the parameters of the trajectory used, including length and width. With the steering theory, results collected can be generalized and compared with each category across studies due to the predictable power provided by the law.

Although there are un unlimited number of categories of shapes that can be studied, only a few need to be used for practical purposes. We decided to limit ourselves in this study to two shape categories: straight tunnels and circular tunnels[3] (Figure 3). Although they do not necessarily represent all trajectory shapes found while interacting with a computer, these two tasks allow us to evaluate device performance in both linear and non-linear movements: the straight tunnels resem-

---

[3] Note that these two tasks had been suggested long ago as basic tests for input device evaluation in the past [2], but like the star-tracing task they have never been used for device evaluation due to the lack of an adequate formal analysis framework. The steering law provides such a framework.

ble the task of navigating in hierarchical menus (see Figure 2); a circular tunnel examines the ability to move along curved trajectories, which requires more coordination in multiple dimensions. Furthermore, as the radius of the circle changes, the curvature changes accordingly, therefore covering a wide variety of trajectory curvature (Figure 3). The representativeness of the two tasks, as well as the simplicity of their steering models (see next section) made them the ideal candidates for standard evaluation of input devices in trajectory-based tasks.

Figure 2: Navigating in hierarchical menus: a sequence of straight tunnel steering tasks

The goal of the present paper is threefold. First, we set out to test the generalizability of the steering law to various devices, as many authors did to Fitts' law (e.g. isometric device [6]). Our previous study showed that the steering law holds well with a stylus device, but it is not clear if the same is true for other types of devices. Second, by way of example, we illustrate how the steering law can be applied to input device research. Third, we wanted to gain insights into the characteristics of the most common input devices when used for steering tasks. The five devices studied were a mouse, a graphic tablet with a stylus, a trackball, a touchpad and an isometric joystick.

EXPERIMENT

Using the steering law paradigm, we conducted an experiment to investigate users' performance with five common types of computer input devices in constrained trajectory following tasks. In this experiment, we restrict ourselves to the current "reality": even if researchers would ideally like to address the fundamental differences between various classes of device (which is the best device?), studies have to be done with specific products that are resulted from particular hardware and software implementation details, such as resolution, sampling frequency, form factors, sensor technology, transfer functions, etc. And these engineering details often override the general differences between two types of technologies. There are also complex interactions among the multiple dimensions of an input method. For instance, the acceleration function in software driver may have different effects on different input devices. So should we turn off the acceleration while testing? If not, should we

use the most often used transfer function or find the optimal conditions of use of each device and compare them in these conditions? Ideally one should optimize all of these parameters for each individual subject. However, subjects' learning/adaptation phase made this impossible. If a subject needs a few minutes to get use to one setting, a two dimensional (e.g. gain and acceleration) search for each subjects may take hours to complete.

In short, it is nearly impossible to make a definitive performance comparison between different types of input devices. Given such limitations, we nonetheless believe it is valuable to conduct experimental evaluation in steering tasks for the following reasoning: We only attempt to make one estimate of the current devices in performing steering tasks. First we selected one device in each technology category that best represented the state of the art in the easily available market place. Second, we kept all the default values in the system software, assuming they are optimized for the majority of users. This is also most likely what an average user would do: simply plug in the device and use it.

Tasks

Two steering tasks, one linear and one circular, were used in the experiment (Figure 3).

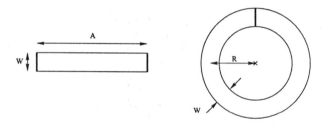

(a) Straight tunnel steering   (b) Circle tunnel steering

Figure 3: Two steering tasks

By applying Equations 2 and 3, it was found that the difficulty for steering through a straight tunnel (see Figure 3.a) is:

$$T = a + b\frac{A}{W} \qquad (4)$$

where A is the length of the tunnel, and W its width.

Through the same procedure, the steering law equation for circle tunnels (see Figure 3.a) was found to take the same form as Equation 4, where the movement amplitude A is equal to the circle circumference $2\pi R$, where R is the circle radius:

$$T = a + b\frac{2\pi R}{W} \qquad (5)$$

Subjects

Fifteen volunteers served as subjects in the experiment. All had experience with using the mouse, but most of them never used the other computer pointing devices tested in the experiment. Unfortunately we could not recruit enough experienced users to have an unbias design against none-mouse devices.

Apparatus

The experiment described below was performed on a Silicon Graphics' indigo with a 19-inch monitor (35×28 cm active view, 1280×1024 pixels resolution). Five input devices were tested:

- Logitech MouseMan 96,
- Wacom ArtZ II 6×8 tablet and stylus,
- Cirque GlidePoint touchpad 2,
- Marcus trackball (ball radius of about 3 centimeters)
- IBM TrackPoint 3.

Figure 4: The five tested input devices

All devices above used relative mapping, except the graphic tablet which was used in absolute mode (the tablet 6×8 in. active area being mapped onto the screen). For pointing devices using relative mapping, the software acceleration provided by the X server was set to its default value (acceleration 2/1, threshold 4)[4]. To minimize the bias that may be introduced by different system settings, the same driver was used for all tested devices with the exception of the wacom tablet, which has its own driver that sends events to the application through an input extension of the X server. Nonetheless, as the tablet uses absolute mapping, the influence of the system is still minimal.

With their dominant hand, subjects used the five input devices given above to control the GUI cursor. All experiments were done in full-screen mode, with the background color set to black.

Procedure

Subjects performed two types of steering tasks: straight tunnel, and circle tunnel steering (see Figure 3). At the

beginning of each trial, the path to be steered was presented on the screen, in green color. After placing the cursor to the left of the start segment and pressing the "left" button of the tested device[5], the subject began to draw a blue line on the computer monitor, showing the stylus trajectory. When the cursor crossed the start segment, left to right, the line turned red, as a signal that the task had begun and the time was being recorded. When the cursor crossed the end segment, also left to right, all drawings turned yellow, signaling the end of the trial. Releasing pressure on the stylus after crossing the start segment and before crossing the second segment would result in an invalid trial (error). Crossing the borders of the path also results in the cancellation of the trial and an error being recorded. Subjects were explicitly asked to minimize errors and not to take risks.

Design

A fully-crossed, within-subjects factorial design with repeated measures was used. Independent variables were the task type (T = straight and circle tunnels), device (D = mouse, stylus, touchpad, trackball, and isometric joystick), movement amplitude (A = 250, and 1000 pixels) and path width (W = 35, 45, and 70 pixels). The amplitudes and widths define 6 different IDs, ranging from 3.6 to 28.6. Steering time was the dependent variable.

The order of testing of the five devices (D conditions) was balanced between 5 groups of subjects according to a Latin square pattern. Within each D condition, subjects performed a practice session, consisting of 10 trials in the easiest and most difficult conditions in both linear and circular steering. The practice session was followed by two identical sets of the 12 T-A-W conditions presented in a random order, during which data was actually collected. Subjects performed 5 trials in each D-T-A-W condition.

RESULTS

Steering time

There was a significant effect of device ($F_{4,56} = 52.2, p < .0001$) upon steering time. Mean steering time for the mouse, stylus, trackball, touchpad, and trackpoint were respectively 768, 880, 2445, 1846, and 1663 milliseconds for linear steering and 2532, 2193, 4092, 4859, and 4158 for circular steering (Figure 5).

Although subjects were given a short practice session, their performance still significantly improved during the experiment from test 1 to test 2 ($F_{1,14} = 22.5, p < .0005$). However, this learning improvement did not significantly affect the relative performance of devices (see Figure 6), as indicated by the insignificant interaction between device and test phase ($F_{4,56} = .59, p = .67$).

Least square means comparison (t-tests) showed that the overall difference between the tablet and the mouse

---

[4] With these settings, a movement of amplitude a results in a cursor movement of amplitude a if a is lower than 4 pixels and $2a$ if greater.

[5] Holding the button down was usually done using the non-dominant hand with the trackball, trackpoint and touchpad. With the tablet, it was achieved by depressing the tip of the stylus.

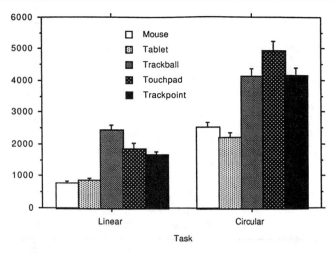

Figure 5: Mean completion time with standard error bars

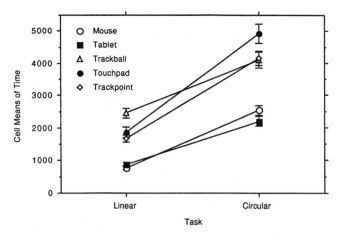

Figure 7: Device and task interaction plot: the relative performance between devices changes with the nature of the task

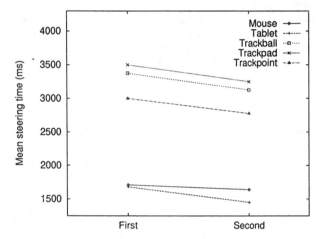

Figure 6: Mean time against test phase

($F_{1,14} = 187$, $p < .0001$). More interesting is the amplitude effect on steering time interacted with devices ($F_{4,56} = 55$, $p < .0001$) (see Figure 8). In particular, while the mean steering times with Touchpad and the Trackball were slightly shorter than that of the trackpoint when amplitude is small (250 pixels), the opposite was true when the amplitude was large (1000 pixels). Both the Touchpad and the trackball are relative position control devices and are intuitive to use, but the drawback is that repeated strokes are needed to make large movements. The overhead (both time and effort) of releasing and re-engaging the control surface reduced the overall performance with these small sized isotonic position control devices. In contrast, the trackpoint works in rate control, which does not require clutching, which is an important advantage for large distance movement.

was insignificant ($p = .52$). These two devices outperformed all other devices significantly ($p < .0001$). The Trackpoint significantly outperformed the trackball and the touchpad ($p < .05$ and $p < .01$ respectively). The overall difference between the trackball and touchpad was insignificant.

The circular steering task was significantly more difficult than the linear task ($F_{1,14} = 396$, $p < .0001$), although the two share the same lengths and widths. Furthermore, there was a significant interaction between task and device ($F_{4,56} = 26.5$, $p < .0001$). As shown in Figure 7, the performance of the tablet was similar to that of the mouse in linear steering, but was higher than the performance of the mouse in circular steering. Given the higher dexterity afforded by the tablet stylus, this is plausible. Note also that while the Touchpad outperformed the Trackball and was close to the Trackpoint in linear steering, it performed much slower than the Trackball or the Trackpoint in the circular steering task.

Longer steering amplitude obviously required more time

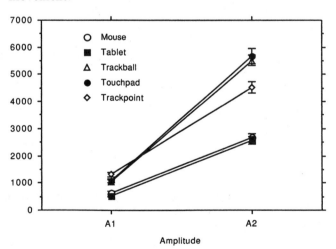

Figure 8: Interaction between steering amplitude and device

Similarly, the significant impact of tunnel width ($F_{2,28} = 104.6$, $p < .0001$) also interacted with devices ($F_{8,112} = 12.87$, $p < .0001$). As shown in Figure 9, the most noticeable effect of this interaction is that while the trackball performed similarly to the touchpad in wider tunnels ($W_2 = 45$ and $W_3 = 70$), it took less time than the touchpad in the narrow tunnel steering ($W_1 = 35$). Another device width interaction effect is that as the tunnel becomes narrower, the tablet shows an increasing advantage over the mouse.

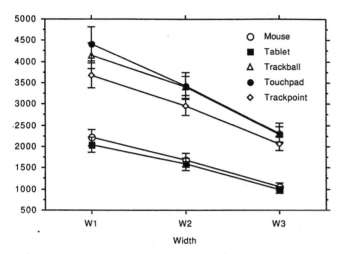

Figure 9: Interaction between path width and device

Having done a factorial analysis of the steering time, let us examine how the steering time followed the steering law outlined earlier. Figure 10 presents the scatter-plots of steering time against index of difficulty for the five devices. All devices proved to fit the steering model with correlations greater than 0.98 (Figure 10). In linear steering, linear regression between steering index of difficulty and steering time (expressed in milliseconds) produced the following equations for each device:

Mouse: $T = 69.6 * ID - 174.8$ $(r^2 = 0.985)$
Tablet: $T = 69.1 * ID - 56.4$ $(r^2 = 0.993)$
Trackball: $T = 188.8 * ID - 104.5$ $(r^2 = 0.986)$
Touchpad: $T = 148.5 * ID - 154.2$ $(r^2 = 0.993)$
Trackpoint: $T = 114.4 * ID + 107.7$ $(r^2 = 0.995)$

For circular steering, the equations were:

Mouse: $T = 181.6 * ID + 72.1$ $(r^2 = 0.999)$
Tablet: $T = 182.3 * ID - 274.0$ $(r^2 = 0.999)$
Trackball: $T = 326.9 * ID - 328.8$ $(r^2 = 0.987)$
Touchpad: $T = 391.0 * ID - 377.3$ $(r^2 = 0.986)$
Trackpoint: $T = 268.8 * ID + 523.1$ $(r^2 = 0.994)$

Note that (see Figure 10) some of the regression lines cross each other. This means some devices are actually better in steering of low difficulty, whereas others perform better (relatively to other devices) when the task difficulty is high. This is the case, for instance, for the trackball and trackpoint in circular steering: the trackball is better than the trackpoint when the task is easy, and the trackpoint is better than the trackball when the task gets more difficult.

By analogy to Fitts' law in pointing, steering law allows us to compute an index of performance $IP = 1/b$ that indicates steering time increase as a function of task difficulty. By such a measure, the devices tested in the experiment ranked in the following order in the linear steering task: the tablet ($IP = 14.4\,s^{-1}$), the mouse (14.3), the trackpoint (8.7), the touchpad (6.7), and the trackball (5.3). For the circular task, the order was slightly different: the mouse (5.5), the tablet (5.4), the trackpoint (3.7), the trackball (3.0) and the touchpad (2.5).

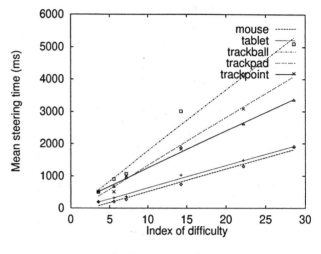

(a) Linear steering

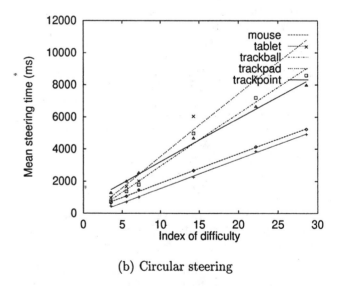

(b) Circular steering

Figure 10: Average steering time for devices as a function of difficulty in both linear and circular steering tasks

It should be pointed out that the steering law predicts the time it takes to "successfully" steer through a tunnel with a given difficulty quantified by ID. If a trial went over the boundaries before completion, the trial was aborted. The number of aborted trials were 9%,

18.8%, 18.7%, 17.5%, 18.9% respectively for the mouse, tablet, trackball, touchpad, and trackpoint in the linear steering task. In the case of circular steering, the number of aborted trials were 14%, 22.9%, 20.9%, 23.7%, 21.9%.

Note that the number of aborted trials is very different in nature from the "error rate" used in Fitts' law studies in [1]. In Fitts' pointing task, the only moment that one can make an error is when the tapping or selection is made. In steering tasks, one can go off the trajectory at any moment. The total chance of making an error therefore accumulates along the trajectory and is far greater than error rate in the Fitts' tapping task. In our experiment, although the subjects were asked to try to stay on track, and despite their effort to do so, the number of aborted trials was still in the range of 10 to 25%.

CONCLUSIONS AND DISCUSSIONS

The experiment presented in this paper is an initial effort in evaluating input devices in trajectory based tasks with a quantitative model: the steering law. Five commonly used computer input devices were tested in the experiment with two steering tasks. Subjects' performance with the five devices can be generally classified into three groups in the following order: 1. the tablet and the mouse, 2. the trackpoint, 3. the touchpad and the trackball. Statistically, the differences between the groups were significant and the differences within each group were not.

However, this general conclusion is only true to the overall performance. The nature of the steering task (linear vs. circular) and the task difficulty factors (amplitude and width) significantly changed the relative performance of the devices. The following exceptions are particularly worth noting: 1. Although very similar to the mouse on average, the steering time of the tablet was slightly shorter than that of the mouse in circular (Figure 4) or narrow steering tasks (Figure 8), presumably due to the higher dexterity afforded by the tablet stylus. 2. The relative performance of the trackball and the touchpad switched order between linear and circular tasks (Figure 4 and 9) 3. The trackpoint is more advantageous than the trackball or the touchpad for longer tunnels, due to the increase of repeated "clutching" in operating the touchpad and the trackball for longer trajectories (Figure 7).

The steering law proved to hold for the five devices tested, all with greater than 0.98 correlation. The steering index of performance not only provides an integrated measure for each device, but also holds predictable power to steering time with new levels of task difficulty.

Like any other theoretical tools, the steering law does not necessarily give answers to all questions. Among other limitations, since the task index of difficulty integrates width and length into one metric as Fitts' law does, the steering law index of performance may conceal some of the subtle differences caused by width and length individually. We suggest users of the steering law always couple the steering law regression with factorial analysis, as we did in this paper.

Finally, we would like to re-emphasize that the conclusions on device difference were based upon the existing representative products and most of these devices have not been developed with the steering law paradigm as a guiding test. We expect different conclusions once the designers and producers of these devices test and refine the properties of their products with consideration to the steering paradigm. For example, the transfer function property of a device could be refined using the steering paradigm. If that happens, it will be a valuable impact of the steering law studies.

ACKNOWLEDGMENTS

We would like to thank the generous support to this study by CENA (Centre d'Études de la Navigation Arienne). Special thanks to Stéphane Chatty of CENA and Thomas Baudel of Alias|Wavefront Inc. for their helpful comments on this paper.

REFERENCES

1. Accot, J., & Zhai, S. (1997). Beyond Fitts' law: models for trajectory-based HCI tasks. *Proceedings of ACM CHI'97 Conference on Human Factors in Computing Systems*, pp. 295–302.

2. Buxton, W. (1987). The haptic channel. Chapter 8 in Baecker, R.M., & Buxton, W., *Readings in Human-Computer Interaction.* Morgan Kaufmann Publishers, pp. 357–365.

3. Card, S.K., English, W.K., & Burr, B. J. (1978). Evaluation of mouse, rate-controlled isometric joystick, step keys and text keys for text selection on a CRT. *Ergonomics*, 21(8), pp. 601–613.

4. Cohen, O., Meyer, S., & Nilsen, E. (1993). Studying the movement of high tech. rodentia: pointing and dragging. *Proceedings of ACM CHI'93 Conference on Human Factors in Computing Systems*, pp. 135–136.

5. Fitts, P.M. (1954). The information capacity of the human motor system in controlling the amplitude of movement. *Journal of Experimental Psychology*, 47, pp. 381–391.

6. Kantowitz, B.H., & Elvers, G.C. (1988). Fitts' law with an isometric controller: Effects of order of control and control-display gain. *Journal of Motor Behavior*, 20(1), pp. 53–66.

7. MacKenzie, I.S., & Buxton, W. (1992). Extending Fitts' law to two-dimensional tasks. *Proceedings of ACM CHI'92 Conference on Human Factors in Computing Systems*, pp. 219–226.

8. MacKenzie, I.S. (1992). Fitts' law as a research and design tool in human-computer interaction. *Human-Computer Interaction*, 7, pp. 91–139.

Symphony: A Case Study in Extending Learner-Centered Design Through Process Space Analysis

Chris Quintana, Jim Eng, Andrew Carra, Hsin-Kai Wu, and Elliot Soloway
Center for Highly Interactive Computing in Education
University of Michigan
1101 Beal Ave.
Ann Arbor, MI 48109 USA
+1 734 763 6988
quintana@umich.edu

ABSTRACT

We are exploring a new class of tools for learners: scaffolded integrated tool environments (or SITEs), which address the needs of learners trying to engage in new, complex work processes. A crucial phase within a learner-centered design approach for SITE design involves analyzing the work process to identify areas where learners need support to engage in the process. Here we discuss the design of Symphony, a SITE for high-school science students. Specifically, we discuss how the process-space model helped us analyze the science inquiry process to help us identify a detailed set of learner needs, leading to a full set of process scaffolding strategies for Symphony.

Keywords

Learner-centered design, process spaces, process scaffolding, scaffolded integrated tool environments

INTRODUCTION: MOTIVATION AND GOALS

Computer technology is becoming more pervasive in everyday work activities. As HCI professionals, we are charged with developing computer tools to support people in their work. Consider, for example, the work of scientists. Scientists perform a wide range of activities when they investigate problems: they do research, collect and visualize data, build models, etc., all in a self-coordinated, dynamic manner. As such, there is now an array of computational tools—search engines, databases, graphing, animation, and modeling tools—to support experts in scientific inquiry.

However, expert scientists are not the only people that need to engage in the process of science inquiry. It is becoming increasingly important for students to engage in and understand the science inquiry process. For example, national education standards (e.g., [10]) state that students

need to develop the ability to do scientific inquiry, to understand and develop the process skills needed to do scientific work. Science activities should not just be homework exercises, but should help students develop the skills needed to think about and affect the world around them.

Students themselves pose complex questions about their world. "Are the air pollution concentrations in my school higher than in other parts of Michigan? If so, will it affect my health?" "Why is the vegetation surrounding the streams in my community suddenly dying?" In order to investigate such questions, students need to engage in the full range of scientific activities that experts do: researching the health effects of pollution, collecting and visualizing pollution data, building models of stream ecosystems, etc. However, the science inquiry process is not so straightforward for students. Students might be able to perform each individual activity, but they lack the expertise for "putting the pieces together," for organizing the activities in the purposeful way needed to answer their questions.

Just as expert scientists have tools that support their scientific activities, so too should students. Our recent work has involved using a *learner-centered design* (LCD) approach [12] to develop tools for learners—a special group of users who are novices in the domain in which they are trying to work and learn. Thus we have developed a range of tools (e.g., [5], [15]) that students can use for individual inquiry activities (e.g., research, data collection, visualization, modeling, etc.) However, giving students such a learner-centered "toolbox" is not enough because students essentially do not know what to do with the tools. While expert scientists have the underlying process knowledge to engage in the inquiry process, students do not. What students lack is overarching support for the inquiry process itself.

We are moving to the next level in learner-centered support to address this. Having developed tools for the individual activities in the inquiry process, we are now putting the tools together in a single environment that offers tools plus *process scaffolding* to help students engage in the inquiry process. By supporting the work process itself, these scaffolded integrated tool environments (or *SITEs*) provide a computational framework to help students engage in complex work processes and meet the objectives outlined in current educational standards.

A challenge for developing a SITE is identifying the necessary process scaffolding that supports both the difficult explicit activities and the less-apparent implicit activities in the process. In order to identify the scaffolding, we must analyze the complex process to determine the areas where students need support. In our previous work, we have had to analyze the domains of the individual inquiry activities (e.g., TheoryBuilder supports the domain of system dynamics modeling [5]). Analyzing a single activity to design an individual tool was challenging. Now, the challenge is greater; we must analyze a process composed of *several* individual activities. We must understand the synergy between the range of activities in the process, and we must understand the dynamic manner in which an expert performs these activities.

Thus in order to develop comprehensive SITEs, we need to understand the complexity of the work process and what support the learner needs to engage in the process. The challenge involves identifying the process complexity along with the implicit expert knowledge and skill to determine the scaffolding needed for the SITE.

We explore these issues here by discussing the design of Symphony, a SITE for high school science students. In particular, our discussion centers on our use of *process spaces* [4] to analyze the complex science inquiry process and help illuminate the areas where learners need support, thus informing the design of effective process scaffolding.

SYMPHONY FOR SCIENCE INQUIRY: AN OVERVIEW

Symphony is a Java-based SITE for high-school students investigating environmental science problems (figure 1). Two students' investigation of the air-pollution question mentioned earlier might proceed as follows:

• Online research: The students use Artemis [15] to search the web for information, such as factors leading to heavy pollution concentrations and the adverse health effects of pollution.

• Problem development and planning: Having done preliminary research, the students decide to investigate both air pollution levels near their school as compared to other areas in Michigan plus possible adverse health effects from the pollution. The students set up a preliminary plan for how they might investigate the problem.

• Data collection: To begin making the analysis needed to address their driving question, the students need to collect data. The students use DataWarehouse (our data collection tool) to collect data about air pollution (e.g., concentrations for various pollutants) and health data

(e.g., respiratory disease rates) for their city and other cities in Michigan.

• Data visualization: Having collected some data, the students graph their data with VizIt (our data visualization tool) to make some sense of their data. They might generate graphs comparing the pollution levels in their city to other cities in Michigan. They may graph pollution and health data to see if there are correlations between pollution and health effects.

• Progress review and plan revision: The students review their results, looking at their graphs in terms of their driving question. They realize that the datasets they collected are incomplete, so their analysis is inconclusive. They now need to decide what new activities to perform.

• More data collection and visualization: Given their inconclusive results, the students collect more data and generate new graphs with the new data.

• Progress review and plan revision: The students now review the new graphs, which seem to show that the air pollution levels in their city are higher than in other cities. Given these new results, the students revise their plan to see what other damage such high pollution levels can cause, and how those levels might be reduced.

• System modeling: The students use TheoryBuilder [5] to model the factors that contribute to pollution concentration. The student run simulations based on their models to discover scenarios resulting in lower pollution concentrations for the community.

This small example describes activities that students perform to investigate science problems. Some activities are tool-based (e.g., data collection, visualization, etc.). Some are more "meta-level" (e.g., planning, reviewing progress, etc.). A SITE needs to support both kinds of activities for the student.

Along these lines, students need to have support for creating and revising their plan throughout the investigation. As an introductory scaffolding example, Symphony displays an inquiry map and a flexible planning grid (figure 1) to allow students to see the possible inquiry activities and drag items from the map to the planning grid. Activities can be moved around in the plan or removed as the plan is revised.

Other tools do not offer the full range of support needed by students. Some tools support a more static, simplified version of the inquiry process (e.g., [7]). Some environments may not integrate a wide range of tools (e.g., [14]). And some environments provide the necessary tools in a realistic representation of the scientist's domain, but lack scaffolding to help student see how to engage in the process (e.g., [11]). These tools certainly have their merits. However, we feel that students need both the tools and a wide range of process scaffolding within a single package to help them effectively engage in the range of scientific activities.

How did we determine the scaffolding that will be necessary for a SITE like Symphony? How can we analyze the work process (i.e., the science inquiry process) in order to understand the process complexity and identify the areas where learners will need support?

We discuss these questions by illustrating how we used the process-space model to identify a more detailed set of learners' needs, and thus develop a more focused set of scaffolding strategies for Symphony.

LEARNER-CENTERED DESIGN AND SITES

Learner-centered design is an evolving design approach for building tools for learners. We can characterize the distinction between learners (i.e., domain novices) and users (i.e., domain experts) along three dimensions: growth, diversity, and motivation [12]. While it is important for designers of learner-centered tools to consider the diversity of learners (i.e., the cultural, gender, and developmental differences), in this paper we focus primarily on growth and motivation:

• Growth: Learners need to grow in their domain expertise. Learner-centered tools should present the work domain in a manner that meets the learners' current level of expertise and supports them in transitioning to more sophisticated, more complex activities. For example, activities like planning and reviewing progress are not apparent to the novice learner. A SITE can thus explicitly represent activities that are new to the learner and structure those activities to help the learner handle initial problems and undertake more complex problems.

• Motivation: Learners do not necessarily have the intrinsic motivation that experts have. Domain complexity can pose obstacles to learners, resulting in frustration and loss of interest. Learner-centered tools should support learners in completing complex (and possibly overwhelming) work activities to keep them focused on their work. For example, activities such as data collection can be difficult for learners to perform. A SITE can reduce the complexity of work activities, putting the activities within the learners' reach, giving them immediate successes, and keeping them motivated to pursue their problem.

Our challenge is to identify the necessary process scaffolding strategies for a SITE to address the growth and motivation of students engaging in science inquiry. Thus within an LCD process, we need to understand the complexity of the work, identify where the learners need support, and identify scaffolding strategies to address those needs. In the following sections, we discuss how we addressed this challenge in designing Symphony. We will first describe the complexity of science problems and the inquiry process to illustrate why learners need support. Next we focus on how we used the process-space model to help identify the set of learners' needs. Finally, we give a more detailed review of Symphony to illustrate the implementation of the process scaffolding.

COMPLEXITY OF SCIENCE PROBLEMS AND THE SCIENCE INQUIRY PROCESS

The domain of science inquiry can be difficult for novices to work in. Much of the complexity in the inquiry process arises from the fact that science problems can have characteristics of so-called "wicked" or "ill-structured" problems [1], leading to a problem-solving process that is described as complex, chaotic, and opportunity-driven [3] (table 1).

SCIENCE PROBLEMS CONTAIN "WICKEDNESS"	CHARACTERISTICS OF THE SCIENCE INQUIRY PROCESS
There are no pre-defined sequences of operations to solve a science problem. Different problem-solvers may perform different activities to investigate the same problem.	**Complex:** The process involves completing a wide range of activities (e.g., planning, data collection, modeling, analysis, etc.)
Science problems can be ill-formulated and non-deterministic. Problem-solvers need to explore and try different alternatives to better define the investigation.	**Chaotic:** There is no linear path through the space of process activities. Rather, problem-solvers iterate (or "bounce around") among the different process activities.
There are no explicit stopping rules to define when the problem is "solved". Accumulated results constantly define the direction of the investigation.	**Opportunity-driven:** In moving through the process, problem-solvers are constantly reviewing progress and selecting activities that they feel will bring them closer to an adequate answer.

Table 1: Complexity of the science inquiry process

Thus, we can begin to see that the nature of the work process we are supporting with a SITE is different from other processes we have designed tools for in previous work. Consider the domain of system dynamics modeling supported by TheoryBuilder [5]. While the modeling process is complex, it has less of the chaotic, opportunity-driven nature than the inquiry process. The modeling process is more straightforward and well-defined.

The challenge in designing a SITE like Symphony is to uncover the difficulty and the "implicitness" in such a complex process to help define the necessary learner-centered support. The complex nature of the process requires that we illustrate all work activities in the process, both explicit (e.g., building graphs) and implicit (e.g., planning). Its chaotic nature requires that we support the learner in charting a path through the non-sequential process activities. Finally, its opportunity-driven nature requires that we describe the tacit knowledge that experts have in selecting appropriate activities to perform and in refining the direction of the investigation.

We need to uncover this information to better understand the areas where learners need support to engage in the process. By identifying a larger, more fine-grained set of learners' needs, we can identify a more complete set of scaffolding strategies and strengthen the learner support in the software. In order to perform this needs analysis, we turn to the process-space model.

USING PROCESS SPACES TO IDENTIFY LEARNERS' NEEDS

The stated goal of the process-space model is to "define the environment in which the work processes take place" to "make many of the tangible and definable aspects of work more visible" [4]. This fits with the LCD approach: we can use process spaces to uncover more components of the complex work process and thus identify the areas where the learner needs support to compose their own path through the process.

A *process space* is defined in terms of the components that comprise the work process, i.e., the roles, activities, artifacts, information objects, and services required to engage in the work [4]. In this section, we discuss how we used this process-space model to analyze the science inquiry process, making some observations about the results of the analysis and noting how the analysis led us to a set of learners' needs.

Defining Process Spaces for Science Inquiry

To perform our analysis of the science inquiry process, we observed expert scientists in their work and looked at other studies of scientists' work (e.g., [13]). Also, we worked with our educational partners (UM School of Education and Ann Arbor high-school teachers) who helped us identify important process activities for high-school students.

We began building the process space for the science inquiry process by identifying the activities, artifacts, information objects, and services used in the process. (While the process-space model allows multiple roles for collaborative work, we only include one role for this work: the learner. Thus, we do not list the role component in our process spaces). The process-space model only identifies the major components, but as we continued our analysis, we refined the model to identify more fine-grained categories for the components. We identified three types of activities: metaprocess, reflective, and tool-based, with metaprocess and reflective activities being the more implicit activities performed by experts. We identified three kinds of information objects needed to perform the activities: explanatory, procedural, and activity-option information. Finally, we identified the services that were used in the process: computational tools, non-computational tools (e.g., a notebook), and none. (We maintained the artifact categories implied in [4]: production and mediation.)

Noting that a process space can itself contain other process spaces [4], we also described the set of process spaces for science inquiry. Looking at the complete set of process spaces, we were able to identify different *levels* of work. The planning level contains the single process space involved with planning the investigation. The

activity level contained two process spaces for reflective activities (develop problem and review progress) and three process spaces for tool-based activities (collect data, visualize data, model data).

The upper portion of table 2 summarizes the results of the process space analysis.

Observations on the Process Space Analysis

The process space analysis helped us understand the inquiry process and uncover a set of specific learners' needs with respect to each process space component (lower portion of table 2):

• Activities: The analysis identified the entire range of metaprocess, reflective, and tool-based activities in the inquiry process. Also, our categorization of activities identified that the metaprocess and reflective activities are implicit to the expert and not necessarily apparent to the learner. It is important to make all work activities visible to help the learner form a conceptual model of the work process [2]. The process space analysis helped identify the "hidden" tasks that learners need to be aware of and that consequently need to be explicitly represented by the SITE.

• Artifacts: The analysis identified the range of artifacts that are produced throughout the investigation: plans, research notes, datasets, graphs, models, etc. In a lengthy investigation (e.g., a fifteen-day investigation by high-school sophomores), the number of artifacts can be quite large. It is important to periodically review the artifacts produced to help define the direction of the investigation [13], so managing the range of artifacts is crucial. But as the number of artifacts grows, it becomes more complex and more time-consuming to organize the artifacts. If experts can have a problem effectively managing their artifacts, learners certainly need artifact organization by the SITE to help focus more on their investigation and less on this "housekeeping chore".

• Information Objects: The analysis identified the large amount of well-organized domain knowledge that scientists employ to plan and conduct their investigation. Learners, being novices, do not know this information, suggesting the need for the SITE to provide this information to help learners complete the activities in the process.

• Services: The analysis identified the functional set of computational tools that need to be incorporated in the SITE. The analysis also identified where experts have minimal tool support. Experts possess process knowledge needed to perform activities with only a notebook or even without tool support. Learners, however, need additional tool support. For example, where an expert can do much of their planning internally without any tool support, learners, lacking the process knowledge of the expert, can benefit from planning services. A SITE should not only

		PROCESS SPACE COMPONENTS			PROCESS SPACE GESTALT
	Activities	Artifacts	Information Objects	Services	
PROCESS SPACE ANALYSIS — Planning Level	• [Metaprocess] Select activities to add to or revise plan. • [Metaprocess] Select a new activity (or sub-activity) from the plan to perform. • [Metaprocess] Review previously logged activities.	[Mediation/Production] • Plan • Log	• [Activity option] List of possible metaprocess activities to perform. • [Explanatory] Rationales and information about the different metaprocess activities. • [Activity option] List of possible inquiry activities to pursue. • [Explanatory] Rationales for the different inquiry activities. • [Activity option] Constraint information describing what inquiry activities are possible.	Scientists' notebook, or internal (experts do it in their heads)	Science inquiry process requires flexible, non-linear movement between the range of process spaces that make up the process
Activity Level: Generalized reflective activity (One each for develop problem and review progress)	[Reflective] Think about and record pieces of information needed in activity (e.g., driving question, hypotheses, research notes, etc.)	[Production] Notes and other pieces of information	[Explanatory] Information describing the different pieces of information the learner should reflect on.	Scientist's notebook, or internal	
Activity Level: Generalized tool-based activity (One each for collect data, visualize data, model data)	• [Metaprocess] Select a sub-activity (e.g., data search is a sub-activity for collecting data.) • [Reflective] Think about the objectives for the activity and the results of the activity. • [Tool-based] Use the tool to perform the activity.	• [Production] Artifacts produced by the tool. • [Production] Notes	• [Explanatory] Descriptions of the sub-activity choices. • [Procedural] Description of the procedure needed to use the tool. • [Explanatory] Rationales for the different activities in the tool procedure.	Computational tools used in the activity (e.g., database, visualization and modeling tools)	
IMPLICATIONS FOR LEARNER-CENTERED DESIGN — Specific learners' needs	Need to make implicit activities explicit: • Metaprocess activities • Reflective activities; Need to make visible the entire collection of activities in the inquiry process • Planning • Reflective (Develop problem, review progress) • Tool-based (Collect data, visualize data, model)	Need to organize artifacts	• Need activity option information to see what metaprocess activities are currently possible ("what can I do now?") • Need activity option information to see what inquiry activities are currently possible ("what can I add to my plan?") • Need procedural information to see how to perform some tool-based activities. • Need explanatory information to see activity rationales. • Need reflective information to see "things to think about" during reflective activities.	Need explicit services for planning and reflection.	Need to support non-linear movement through the process • Between planning and activity level • Among different activities in the activity level
Scaffolding strategies	Explicit workspace for all process spaces • Planning workspace • Activity workspaces	Artifact logging and "table of contents"	• Process maps for illustrating activity possibilities • Flow diagrams for procedural information • Activity-based help text for activity rationales • Reflection prompts to describe reflective information	• Plan/log grid • Reflection areas in workspaces	• Simultaneous views of planning and activity work areas • Tabbed activity workspaces to facilitate movement between activities

Table 2: Process space analysis and the implications for learner-centered design. The categorization of process-space components is shown in brackets.

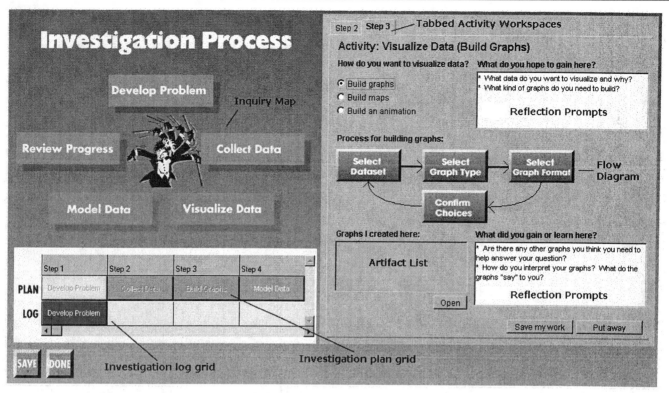

Figure 1: Symphony main screen

include the identified set of computational tools, but also missing tools that learners might need.

Aside from the information that we gained by looking at the individual process spaces, the analysis also identified an overall set of process spaces, (i.e., *the process-space gestalt*). We noted that engaging in the science inquiry process essentially means moving among the different process spaces (e.g., moving from planning to data collection to visualization to planning, etc.) Scientists move among the different process spaces in a chaotic, non-sequential manner. Learners may not be used to such non-linear work, being more familiar with straightforward linear work with a linear series of steps. A SITE needs to support learners in engaging in the non-linear work patterns inherent in the inquiry process.

IMPLEMENTING PROCESS SCAFFOLDING IN SYMPHONY

A review of Symphony illustrates some of the process scaffolding that we incorporated to address the learners' needs identified in the process space analysis. We are currently on the third major iteration of the software. We tested the previous two versions with a small number of high-school students who used Symphony to investigate environmental science questions. Additionally, we performed several design reviews within our group, which consists of members of our computer science department, School of Education, and local high-school teachers. The current version is being tested this school year by high-school students using Symphony to investigate long-term projects.

We include a more detailed list of our scaffolding strategies in table 2. Here, we highlight three scaffolding strategies to demonstrate how process scaffolding can support a learner engaging in the science inquiry process.

Providing information

Recall that students need a wide variety of information to engage in the inquiry process, such as activity-option information to see what possible metaprocess activities they can perform and what possible inquiry activities they can add to their plan. We present activity-option information through process maps.

At the planning level, students need to see what metaprocess activities are possible and what steps to take next in the investigation. Metaprocess activities are illustrated in the *Conductor window* (figure 2). The possible metaprocess activities in the Conductor window include: revising the plan, doing the next activity in the plan, revisiting the log, etc. The space of metaprocess activities is context-sensitive, changing as different metaprocess activities become possible at different points of the investigation. The activity-space information conveyed by the Conductor window thus serves to help students answer the question "what can I do next?"

Another process map is the *inquiry map* on the main screen (figure 1). As students create and revise their plan, they need to see what activities can be added to the plan, e.g., develop problem, collect data, etc. Simple constraint information is displayed on the inquiry map, indicating through color changes which inquiry activity was most

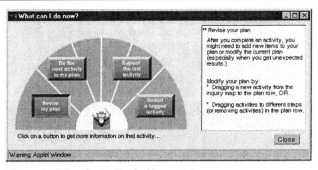

Figure 2: "Conductor" window

recently completed, and which inquiry activities might be logical next steps.

Finally, Symphony uses *flow diagrams* to explain procedural tasks. Figure 1 illustrates the flow diagram describing the procedure for building graphs. The different tool-based activities use flow diagrams to describe the procedure for which the tool is used. Pressing each button in the flow diagram launches the appropriate component of the tool. The computational tools in Symphony lie behind these more "procedurally-oriented" diagrams that both invoke a tool and convey information to help learners see "how do I do this?"

Managing artifacts

As mentioned, learners need support for managing the range of artifacts produced throughout the investigation. One example of how Symphony provides automatic artifact information is the artifact "table of contents" (figure 3).

Artifact Log

List of things you've built

	Artifacts Created
Step 1	
Step 2	Spreadsheet: Carbon Monoxide Data
	Spreadsheet: Nitrogen Dioxide Data
Step 3	Graph: Carbon Monoxide Graph
Step 4	Graph: Nitrogen Dioxide Graph
Step 5	

Close

Warning: Applet Window

Figure 3: Artifact "table of contents"

The table of contents lists and provides quick access to all of the artifacts the students have produced throughout the investigation. In figure 3, we see a small slice of the students' investigation. In the second step of the investigation, the student collected two sets of air pollution data. In the third and fourth steps, they created graphs to illustrate pollution data. The items in the "Artifacts Created" column are actually buttons that bring up the artifact named in the button. This example is

small, only displaying four artifacts, but as investigations become larger, the number of artifacts grows quickly. Being able to easily manage and access artifacts is useful when students need to review their progress, build their argument, and revise their plan. The table of contents removes the burden for the student of having to create and search disk directories for the artifacts that they are interested in.

Supporting non-linear work

Throughout the inquiry process, learners need to iterate between the planning level and the activity level (e.g., complete an activity, refine the plan, complete an activity, refine the plan, etc.). The learner will also have to iterate among activities in the activity level (e.g., develop the problem, visualize data, review the problem to refine hypotheses, visualize more data, etc.)

In order to support iteration, we designed the main screen to display both the planning workspace and individual activity workspaces, thus allowing a simultaneous view of the planning level and activity level (figure 1). In earlier versions, our strategy to support iteration involved having the planning workspace in a window while individual activity workspaces opened in separate windows. However, our student testers had problems with this approach. Students inevitably had several activity workspaces open, resulting in screen real-estate problems that interfered with the work. The activity windows covered the planning window, so it was difficult to move back to the planning level. Also, it was difficult to move between activity workspaces because of the number of windows. Students suggested and have been favorable to the current approach. Both work levels are visible at all times, making it easier to revise the plan and access logged activities as needed throughout the investigation.

Because of this single main window approach, we needed to design a better way of having multiple activity workspaces open simultaneously. We made the activity level area of the main screen a tabbed work area (figure 1), where multiple individual activity workspaces can be accessed by tabs. Again, we are getting favorable feedback from the student testers who have reviewed this version, and in some small tests, we have seen how students begin to keep multiple workspaces open and how they are facilitated in quickly moving between workspaces.

CONCLUDING REMARKS AND FUTURE RESEARCH

With Symphony, we are exploring SITEs and the use of process scaffolding to support learners working on and developing an understanding of complex work processes (e.g., the science inquiry process). With effective scaffolding, we can support the entire range of activities that make up the complex process, both the difficult and implicit activities that learners need to complete. We found that the process-space model provided us with a rich analytic vocabulary to help us analyze the complex science inquiry process and identify a detailed set of learners' needs to be addressed by process scaffolding. Many cognitive analysis methods (e.g., GOMS) focus on tasks and the procedural knowledge needed to perform tasks [6], but not on other components we needed for our analysis. Analysis methods such as these could, in fact, be used in conjunction with the process-space model to determine procedural information.

Other analysis methods focus on analyzing work context. The speech acts model [8] is used in workflow analysis. However, the model's emphasis on work as conversation and negotiation between parties in the process was not suited for our work in analyzing the science inquiry process. Activity theory is similar to the process space model. However, even proponents of activity theory state that it can be difficult to use for design (e.g., [9]). We found that the process-space model gave us a rich vocabulary for our design and was straightforward to incorporate in our design process.

In the end, we feel that this case study contributes the following:

• A framework for performing a learner-centered needs analysis. By refining a method for identifying a more detailed set of learner needs, we can develop a stronger set of scaffolding strategies to support the learner.

• An initial set of process scaffolding strategies to support learners engaging in complex work processes such as science inquiry.

• A software implementation to test our framework for identifying leaner needs.

At this writing, we are currently conducting more extensive user testing, with a set of ninth grade students using Symphony daily in class to investigate air quality problems of increasing complexity. Our early results are encouraging, as we are seeing the students working effectively with Symphony on their science questions. As we continue with this project, we want to explore further refinements of both our LCD methodology and the process-space model, seeing the strengths and weaknesses of the model. We are also looking at how our design process extends towards developing collaborative tools for science inquiry, exploring the effects multiple roles in the process space analysis on the design of our tools.

ACKNOWLEDGMENTS

The authors would like to thank the programmers, artists, teachers, students, and faculty involved with the Symphony project. This work is funded by grants from the National Science Foundation and the National Physical Science Consortium.

REFERENCES

1. Buchanan, R. *Wicked Problems in Design Thinking.* In V. Margolin and R. Buchanan (Eds.) *The Idea of Design.* MIT Press, 1995.

2. Collins, A., Brown, J.S., and Newman, S.E. Cognitive Apprenticeship: Teaching the Crafts of Reading, Writing, and Mathematics. In L.B. Resnick (Ed.) *Knowing, Learning, and Instruction: Essays in Honor of Robert Glaser*, Lawrence Erlbaum Associates, Hillsdale NJ, 1989.

3. Conklin, E.J. and Weil, W. Wicked Problems: Naming the Pain in Organizations. http://www.3mco.fi/meetingnetwork/readingroom/gds s_wicked.html.

4. Fitzpatrick, G., and Welsh, J. Process Support: Inflexible Imposition or Chaotic Composition. *Interacting with Computers* 7, 2, 1995.

5. Jackson, S.L., Krajcik, J., and Soloway, E. The Design of Guided Learner-Adaptable Scaffolding in Interactive Learning Environments. *Proceedings of CHI '98* (Los Angeles CA, May 1998), ACM Press, 187-194.

6. John, B.E. and Kieras, D.E. The GOMS Family of Analysis Techniques: Tools for Design and Evaluation. *Technical Report CMU-CS-94-181*, School of Computer Science, Carnegie-Mellon University.

7. Linn, M.C. Key to the Information Highway. *Communications of the ACM*, 39, 4, 1996, 34-35.

8. Medina-Mora, R., Winograd, T., Flores, R., and Flores, F. The Action Workflow Approach To Workflow Management Technology. *Proceedings of CSCW '92* (Toronto, Canada), ACM Press. 281-288.

9. Nardi, B.A. Studying Context: A Comparison of Activity Theory, Situated Action Models, and Distributed Cognition. *Proceedings of the EWHCI '92*, 352-359.

10. National Research Council. *National Science Education Standards*. National Academy Press, Washington DC, 1996.

11. Sandoval, W.A. and Reiser, B.J. Evolving Explanations in High School Biology. Presented at the Annual Meeting of the American Education Research Association. Chicago, March 24-28, 1997, http://www.ls.sesp.nwu.edu/bguile/papers.html.

12. Soloway, E, Jackson, S.L, Klein, J., et. al. Learning Theory in Practice: Case Studies of Learner-Centered Design. *Proceedings of CHI '96* (Vancouver, Canada, April 1996) ACM Press.

13. Springmeyer, R. R., Blattner, M. M., and Max, N. L. A Characterization of the Scientific Data Analysis Process. *Proceedings of IEEE Visualization '92*, IEEE Press, 235-242.

14. Suthers, D., Toth, E.E., and Weiner, A. An Integrated Approach to Implementing Collaborative Inquiry in the Classroom. *Proceedings of CSCL '97* (Toronto, Canada, 1997), 10-14.

15. Wallace, R., Soloway, E., Krajcik, J., et.al. ARTEMIS: Learner-Centered Design of an Information Seeking Environment for K-12 Education. *Proceedings of CHI '98* (Los Angeles CA, May 1998), ACM Press, 195-202.

The Reader's Helper:
A Personalized Document Reading Environment

Jamey Graham

California Research Center

Ricoh Silicon Valley, Inc.

2882 Sand Hill Road, Suite 115

Menlo Park, CA 94025, USA

jamey@rsv.ricoh.com

ABSTRACT

Over the last two centuries, reading styles have shifted away from the reading of documents from beginning to end and toward the skimming of documents in search of relevant information. This trend continues today where readers, often confronted with an insurmountable amount of text, seek more efficient methods of extracting relevant information from documents. In this paper, a new document reading environment is introduced called the Reader's Helper™, which supports the reading of electronic and paper documents. The Reader's Helper analyzes documents and produces a relevance score for each of the reader's topics of interest, thereby helping the reader decide whether the document is actually worth skimming or reading. Moreover, during the analysis process, topic of interest phrases are automatically annotated to help the reader quickly locate relevant information. A new information visualization tool, called the Thumbar™, is used in conjunction with relevancy scoring and automatic annotation to portray a continuous, dynamic thumb-nail representation of the document. This further supports rapid navigation of the text.

Keywords

document annotation, information visualization, content recognition, intelligent agents, digital libraries, probabilistic reasoning, user interface design, reading online

INTRODUCTION

Around 1750AD there was a dramatic change in the way people read documents [8]. Before this time, readers consumed documents *intensively*, reading the document from start to finish, sometimes several times or even out loud to a group. By the early 1800's, however, readers tended to read *extensively*, reading documents only once or skimming the documents in search of relevant information to determine whether the document was worth reading in its entirety. Today, with the advent of the World Wide Web (WWW) and the growing collection of electronic documents, this style is likely to continue: there are simply too many potentially use-

ful documents and not enough time to read them all [14]. Office workers, in particular, are forced to optimize their daily reading by sifting through the vast amount of information, establishing a balance between in-depth understanding and expediency. Reading intensively versus extensively can be thought of as *vertical versus horizontal* reading [6]. That is, in the past, readers read the document from beginning to end (vertical); now, they scan and browse the text (horizontal).

Few applications available today fully support the reading process. There are, however, several applications which condense or locate documents for the user. Applications such as [13, 15] provide a synopsis of the text which can sometimes be used to determine the document's relevance. Other systems search for and retrieve documents relevant to an evolving user profile [3, 16]. The learning of user profiles over time provides an evolutionary process which enables the system to improve the quality of documents retrieved for the user. Another system supports users as they search digital libraries by showing query keywords in the context of the sentences they appear in a document [17]. Thus, users can quickly access the database based on the presence or absence of a particular context they are seeking. Another application inserts supplemental information in the form of an annotation into a news story if the story contains key phrases from the subject database [9]. This offers the reader additional information not necessarily provided by the author of the original text. The work by [7] supports the skimming of documents by representing the topics of a text as *content capsules*. Using a special visualization tool portraying the document as a thumb-nail image, topics are presented to the reader at the location in the text where they occur. This allows the reader to quickly view the highlights of the document in the context of the surrounding text structure.

Despite the growing number of applications used to locate and evaluate documents, there are few, if any, applications that focus on the actual *text reading* process. I believe that readers require a personalized environment that supports the skimming of documents and the extraction of information. I have created a new document reading environment called the Reader's Helper, to act as both the reader's document browser and personal agent, advising the reader of relevant documents and of the relevant text within each document. The Reader's Helper is not a search engine; it does not search for or deliver documents to the user. Instead, it *helps readers help themselves* to be more productive in reading by evaluating documents the reader views and by providing visual tools for showing the locations of the relevant portions of the text. In the following sections the Reader's Helper system is describe, both in terms of the user interface and the underlying content recognition subsystem. Future issues and potential research directions are also discussed.

THE READER'S HELPER

The Reader's Helper (RH) application integrates existing technology—a WWW browser, highlighting key words, and probabilistic reasoning—with a unique information visualization tool in support of readers who read both online and paper documents. The RH uses information about each reader in evaluating the content of a document. It calculates a *relevance* value to determine if a document is applicable to a reader. The current prototype is composed of a specialized WWW browser and an annotation agent responsible for recognizing the reader's *topics of interest* in a document. The way the annotation agent understands what is important to the reader is through a *reader profile* which contains personal information about the reader. In the following sections the electronic document browsing environment is described in terms of the user interface and followed by a description of the *paper-based* version of the RH.

The User Interface

One of the most important aspects of an electronic document reading environment is the user interface. The difficulty of reading electronic documents is well known [18]. Readers therefore often rely on the printed document because of the high resolution and flexibility offered by paper. A design goal for the RH was to provide the reader with an easy to use interface that emphasizes the relevant content of the document, and, as a consequence, *personalizes* the document. This should not only increase the appeal of reading electronic documents but also the efficiency with which they can be consumed. There are three main methods that work in concert to improve the readability of an electronic document. First, a relevance score is computed for each topic that is important to the reader with respect to a document. Each topic score is an estimation of the relevancy of the document to the reader, offering a *first appraisal* of the document. This is directly associated with the horizontal reading trend mentioned earlier: most readers do not have time to completely analyze all of the documents they must process and so it is desirable to have a quantitative measure of each document's relevancy. Second, a new information visualization tool, called the Thumbar, shows an overview of both the document and the results of annotating the document. Hence, the reader can quickly navigate to the more relevant parts of a document based on the

visual information present in a thumb-nail. Thirdly, after the RH has completed the analysis of a document, it is automatically annotated to depict the most relevant portions of the document. As the reader reads the document, key phrases are pointed out by way of highlighting to help guide the reader through the text.

The Thumbar

Figure 1 shows the RH document browser displaying a HTML source document (from the CHI '97 Online Proceedings [19]). On the left hand side of the display is the Thumbar (**1.1** and **1.2**). The Thumbar is a unique information visualization tool whose name is derived from the concept of a thumb-nail image combined with the functionality of a scrollbar. The reader may drag a lens **1.2** up and down to reposition the view of the document in the document area **1.3** in the manner of a scrollbar. The Thumbar allows readers to *look ahead* in the text to see more of the document's structure and content. By using a Thumbar, a reader can quickly scan the document for a desired image, chart or even text structure and scroll accordingly. The work by [22] supports the notion that humans are very good at recognizing small images. Recent work by [20] further exploits this concept in a system where icons of documents are used as the retrieval cues to a large document database. It was found that users could recognize the thumb-nail images of documents (based on the text structure and the images in the text) to retrieve several documents which "looked" like the document they were seeking.

The Thumbar is a dynamic representation of the document contained in the browser. Its contents and shape change as the document itself is personalized. For instance, after annotating a document, the Thumbar presents relevant keyword phrases as red lines (instead of the typical gray or black lines). This clearly indicates to the reader where the relevant information is located in the document, similar to the way attribute-mapped scroll-bars [24], TileBars [10] and the Mural [12] depict relevant information in a document. This visual information, however, can be changed. For example, by "turning off" a concept that has scored well in the document, the red lines in the Thumbar change back to the normal gray or black lines as if there were no annotation at that location at all. Thus, the reader can create a representation of the document based on a combination of concepts **1.4** either turned on or off. Another way of altering the annotation is by using the *sensitivity threshold meter* **1.5** which can be used to manipulate the concepts that are active in the document. This is done by setting a threshold and only allowing concepts whose similarity scores equal or surpass this threshold to be visible as annotations.

As with any HTML document, there is no formal pagination as long as the document is contained in the browser (the pagination is set when the document is sent to the printer). Instead, there is simply the concept of "a screenful" of the document which can change if the user resizes their browser

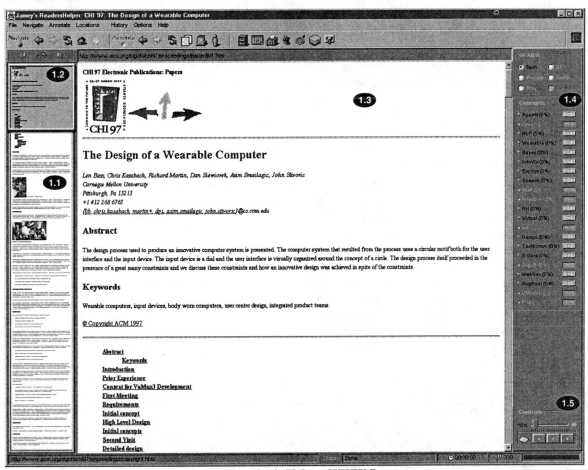

Figure 1 - The Reader's Helper WWW Browser

window. The Thumbar 🔵 represents a reduced version of the original document based on a user defined reduction ratio (e.g. in figure 1, the reduction ratio is 6 which means that the Thumbar is 1/6th the size of the document area 🔵). The entire representation of text in the Thumbar is presented using a proportionally reduced line for each word. This method of portraying a navigable thumb-nail of text is similar to [4], used for software visualization.

If the document is resized, the Thumbar is resized to represent the same screenful depicted in the document area. The use of a thumb-nail icon to represent a page in a document is of course not a new idea. Adobe Systems, for instance, uses a similar method of displaying icons for the individual pages in a document [1]. The Adobe method, however, portrays a static representation of the document (i.e., the thumb-nail image does not automatically change when the document is edited) and does not support using a lens for navigation throughout the document. The Adobe method is also based on a formally paginated document with distinct thumb-nails for each page. In the Thumbar, there is no pagination and therefore, the document is viewed as a continuous stream of text and images by which one can navigate to any location in the document.

If the document cannot be fully contained in the Thumbar

(because the document is too long), a green line is drawn across the bottom of the Thumbar. Dragging the lens down to the green line causes the entire thumb-nail image to scroll upwards, thereby revealing more of the document. Once the document has been scrolled in this way, a green line will also appear at the top of the Thumbar indicating that more of the document is available above. To go back to the beginning of the document, the reader may again drag the lens upward to the green line which, thereby causing the thumb-nail image to scroll back down. Alternatively, there are buttons at the top of the Thumbar for repositioning the lens at either the top 🔳 or the bottom 🔳 of the document. The user may also choose to view the entire document in the Thumbar. This has the disadvantage, however, of reducing the clarity of thumb-nail information.

With the help of a Thumbar attached to the document browser, the reader can look ahead in the document to evaluate its content and structure. This is not possible in most document browsing systems available today where readers are restricted to one page or screenful at a time. This ability to look ahead in a document is quite useful for reading documents as it leverages off of the design principle of providing a global (macro) and local (micro) representation of information [23]. The global representation portrays coarse information while the local representation portrays fine grained information. In this instance, the Thumbar presents an overview (macro) of the document and the document area presents the detailed (micro) information. This particular innovation adds value to the document reading and browsing experience.

Document Annotation

Figure 2 shows the HTML document from figure 1 after it has been annotated by the annotation agent. The locations of relevant phrases in the document are shown in red in the Thumbar. Also, the pattern of bolded words **2.2** in figure 2 matches the highlighting pattern in the Thumbar lens **2.1**. Using the lens the reader can quickly reposition the document to areas containing relevant phrases. Notice also that there are four concepts with non-zero scores in this document **2.3**. Each concept has a score in the label and a grid meter that is populated according to the value of the score. By simply looking at the collection of concepts the reader can quickly see that this document is indeed similar to several topics of interest based on which grid meters have color and to what extent. This is a important but subtle part of the interface design. This is based on the belief that readers will quickly learn the location of concepts in the concept area **2.3**

and as a consequence of highlighting in the grid meter, quickly know if the document discusses the desired topics of interest and which topics are covered. Note that each concept is also a button which can be turned on or off. For instance, the user may choose to only view the annotations for Wearable, turning off all other scoring concepts. Concepts may also be turned off prior to analyzing a document.

Highlighting Styles

Three highlighting styles are provided for use while reading a document **2.4**. These styles currently include 1) highlighting only the phrase, 2) bolding the phrase and highlighting the sentence in which it appears, and 3) underlining the phrase. The reader may select the highlighting style at anytime, and personalize the color schemes and styles in the reader profile.

Sensitivity Meter

Also represented in figure 2 is the *sensitivity threshold meter* **2.5**. This meter can be used to set the threshold for the document area and Thumbar, restricting the annotation to concepts scoring above the specified threshold. For instance, the concept Design currently has a score of 76%. The reader could use the sensitivity meter to increase the

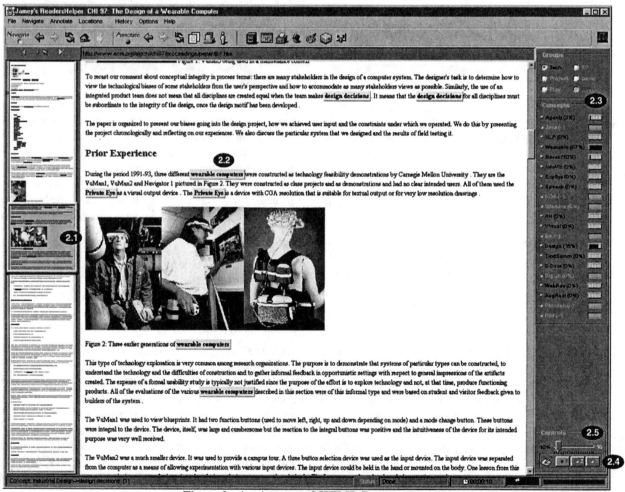

Figure 2 - An Annotated HTML Document

threshold to a value greater than 76% and all annotations associated with the Design concept would disappear from the display. This gives the user control of showing only the higher scoring concepts when reading a document, further supporting the concept of personalizing the document.

Summaries

The annotation agent automatically generates a summary of the document based on the concept hits found in the text. For instance, given the annotated document in figure 2, a user might want to read only the sentences that have hits in them for the concept Design. This document is generated automatically by the RH after it is done analyzing the document. Figure 3 shows a summary of the document annotated in figure 2. The toolbar button **3.1** invokes the summary function to present the reader with a list of available summaries. In figure 3 each sentence containing a keyword phrase for the concept Design is listed in the order of appearance in the document **3.2**. This interface provides a way for the reader to view all relevant sentences at once. Associated with each sentence is a hypertext link **3.3** back into the same sentence in the annotated document. Another summary generated by the RH lists all key phrases for each concept and the number of hits each phrase has in the document. Each hit is represented as a hypertext link which points back to the location of the hit in the annotated document. The value of this summary is to show how broad the coverage is with respect to the concept's key phrases.

The use of RH outside the target document

The RH also provides access to an archive of previously annotated documents. Each time a document is annotated in the RH, a local copy of the document is stored in the reader's private document archive so that it can be accessed again.

Calendar Interface

Readers can use a calendar interface to the archive for retrieving documents based on their date of annotation. The calendar keeps track of all documents annotated by record-

ing the date, time and the most relevant concept on the day the annotation occurred. There are two ways to view the calendar: as a standard calendar month (days listed in columns from left to right, etc.) with entries on each day an annotation occurred, or as a *timeline* so that more information about the document can be presented to the user.

Similar Documents Interface

Another way to access the document archive is by viewing documents that are similar in content. This is possible using the *similar documents* interface. Each time a document is annotated, the RH annotation agent records how each concept in the reader's profile performed (i.e. the concept score is logged with respect to the document's unique ID). When a reader requests to see all documents which are similar to the current document in the browser, the system uses the concept information for the current document to generate a list of documents from the archive that have scored similarly. For instance, in figure 4 we see the current state of the concepts after annotating a document (**4.1** & **4.2**). The ExpSys **4.1** concept (Expert Systems) has a score of 80% and the NLP **4.2** concept (Natural Language Processing) has a score of 63%. Now the system must generate a collection of documents which have scored similarly to the way this document scored. In other words, *what documents in my collection or the group's collection have an emphasis on both expert systems and natural language understanding?* Because the RH annotation agent records all concept scores for each document annotation, the answer can be easily generated and presented to the reader.

Figure 4 shows the title of the document **4.3** previously annotated which generated the scores in the concept area: Adding Intelligence to the Interface. The similar document subsystem creates a list for each concept **4.4** of the documents which have scored above a user defined threshold (e.g. 50%). The list is composed of the title of the document which is a hypertext link to the document in the archive. From this list we can see that one document scored

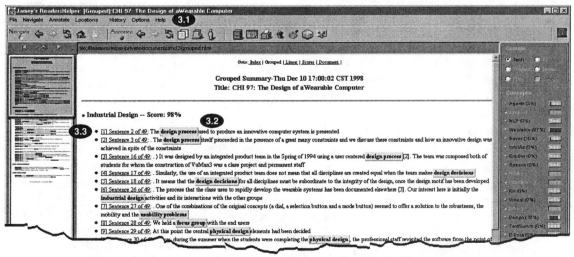

Figure 3 - Summary of sentences relating to the "Design" concept

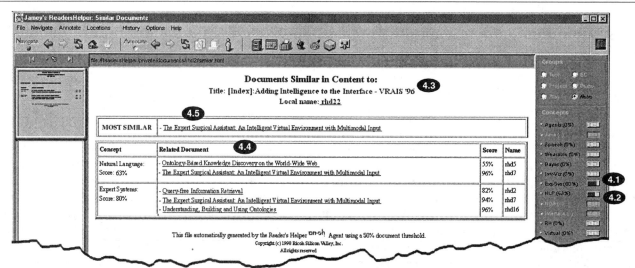

Figure 4 - Documents similar in content to the document "Adding Intelligence to the Interface"

as well as the original document did with both concepts: The Expert Surgical Assistant: An Intelligent Virtual Environment with Multimodal Input. This document is emphasized in the ❹❺ area as MOST SIMILAR since it is most like the document we have currently been viewing.

Paper-based Reader's Helper

As mentioned above, many people prefer paper documents for reading since paper is higher resolution, higher contrast, more portable and readily supports reader note taking and highlighting. To provide for this, a *paper-based* RH has been created that again adds content to the original document by printing the document in a special way. Figure 5 shows a portion of a document printed by the RH. This figure shows a cover sheet (on the right) and the first page of the document (on the left). The cover sheet contains a complete thumb-nail representation of the document ❺❶ with annotations portrayed as red text. Unlike the electronic version of the Thumbar, the paper version portrays the thumb-nail text using a very small typeface so that word presentation and text structure are enhanced. This version of the thumb-nail is also paginated and laid out in columns with pages starting from top to bottom, left to right, each numbered in a small margin to the right of each image. The reader may use the cover sheet to quickly scan the document for relevant areas. At the top of the coversheet is the title and document information ❺❷. The list of the top three topics of interest found to be relevant in this document are printed below the title ❺❸. This information is also displayed at the bottom of every page in the document ❺❻.

Each page in the document contains six thumb-nail images of the surrounding five pages along with the current page in the left-hand margin ❺❹. This allows the reader to look ahead in the paper document to view the surrounding pages and their relevance with respect to the topics of interest. The annotations in the document are presented as yellow boxes surrounding the key phrases ❺❺. The page number

margin to the right of each thumb-nail image is shaded when the reader is viewing that page. The shaded area moves downward as the reader turns the pages (moves forward in the document) to indicate the page location in the thumb-nail image. On documents longer than 7 pages, the shaded area does not shift downward once the reader turns to page 3. Instead, the thumb-nail image is shifted upward, similarly to the online version of the Thumbar. The shaded area stays in the third cell to show the surrounding context for the current page being viewed in terms of past and future pages in the document. When the document gets closer to the end and the last page of the document is visible in the thumb-nail, the shaded area is again shifted downward until the end of the document is reached.

UNDERLYING TECHNOLOGY

The underlying technology used in the RH is described below. This includes reader profiles and the content recognition method.

Reader Profiles

The RH uses reader *profiles* to define the topics of interest for each reader. The topics of interest are called *concepts* since they tend to represent a meaning which the reader would like the system to recognize when analyzing documents. Concepts are defined by a collection of keyword phrases which represent the overall topic of interest. For instance, if a reader is interested in the concept of Intelligent Agents, several keyword phrases can be used to define this topic: adaptive agents, personal assistants, Patti Maes, cooperative information agents. When a document is processed by the RH, a probability is generated for each concept representing the likelihood the document is about that concept. This likelihood is called the *concept similarity measure*. At present, concept definitions are hand-coded by the reader in the profile. The process is actually quite simple and only involves defining a name for a concept and populating it with the keyword phrases.

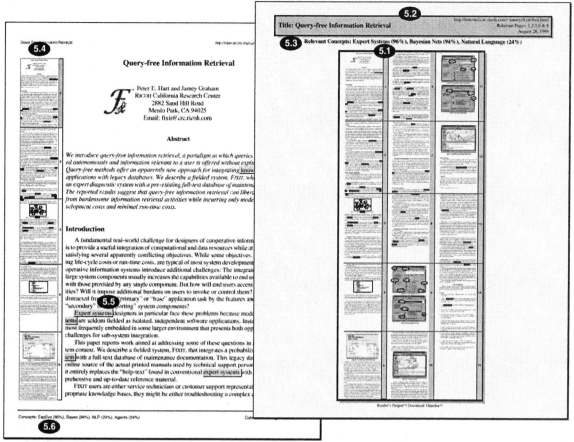

Figure 5 - The Paper-based RH showing the cover sheet and the first page from the document.

Probability-Based Content Recognition

The concept similarity measure is computed in a Bayesian belief network [11] based on keyword phrase frequency and the location and proximity of keywords in the document (figure 6). Most text summarization systems exploit the location of a sentence in a document [13], and for this reason the location of the keyword phrase similarly influences the probability of the concept it supports. The phrase proximity feature rewards hits occurring in close proximity to each other. This supposition is based on rewarding hits in areas of the document that might be emphasizing one of the reader's topics of interest. Even though the current three-feature concept belief network represents a somewhat simplified expression of content evaluation in a document, it has provided adequate results in our initial prototype. In the future we plan to experiment with more sophisticated content analysis methods by taking into consideration document structure and semantics and potentially the reader's browsing and reading history. The pattern matching is performed by an annotation agent using the key word phrases which define the reader's topics of interest. It

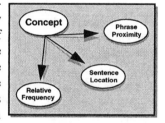

Figure 6 - A sample belief network.

is conducted before the document is parsed, as the stream of characters is received from the site hosting the document so that special tags can be added to the document to denote relevance and location in the text. The result is a version of the document automatically annotated to point out relevant areas of the document. A concept similarity value is computed at the end of this analysis and is immediately used to update the user interface so that the reader can see the concept scores while the document is being parsed and laid out in the browser.

IMPLEMENTATION

The RH system was implemented in Java on a PC running Windows NT 4.0. It also runs under the Solaris and Linux operating systems as well. It is HTML 3.2 compatible and can be used for regular browsing of the WWW.

CONCLUSION

With the emergence of the WWW, it is now quite clear that sophisticated online reading environments are not only useful but required for keeping pace with the increasing volume of text available in electronic form. The goal of this project was to design a system that makes reading electronic documents more efficient. Based on our experience using the RH, we feel that automatic document annotation, used in conjunction with the Thumbar, provides many benefits over the current state of the art. There is, of course, a lot of work yet to be done. As discussed in [2,21], active reading not only requires identification of relevant text but writing on the text, i.e. manually annotating the document. Future RH systems will support manual annotations. The definition and automatic maintenance of reader profiles will most certainly provide challenges for researchers [3,16]. This of course is directly tied to the content recognition methods which also presents a challenge because of the complexity of understanding natural language and presenting a quantitative measure of relevancy.

ACKNOWLEDGEMENTS

I would like to thank my colleague Dr. David Stork for first proposing the Reader's Helper concept and for his continued brain storming support, especially in the areas of learning based methods for profile maintenance. I would also like to thank Dr. Ziming Liu for his assistance in discovering and distilling information regarding how people read documents. Finally, I'd like to thank Dr. Jonathan Hull and Dr. Peter Hart for their leadership and guidance during the course of this project.

REFERENCES

1. Adobe Acrobat, Adobe Acrobat 3.0 Technology: A Mini-White Paper for Developers. Available at http://www.adobe.com/prodindex/acrobat/devwhitepaper.html.

2. Andler, A., Gujar, A., Harrison, B., O'Hara, K. and Sellen, A. A Diary Study of Work-related Reading: Design Implications for Digital Reading Devices. *Proceedings of CHI '98* (Los Angeles, CA, April 1998), ACM Press, 241-248.

3. Balabanovic, M. and Shoham, Y. Learning Information Retrieval Agents: Experiments with Automated Web Browsing. *AAAI-95 Spring Symposium on Information Gathering from Heterogeneous, Distributed Environments*, 1995.

4. Ball, T. and Eick, S.G. Software Visualization in the Large. IEEE Computer, Vol. 29, No. 4, April 1996, pp. 33-43.

5. Bass, L., Kasabach, C., Martin, R., Siewiorek, D., Smailagic, A., and Stivoric, J. The Design of a Wearable Computer. *Online Proceedings of CHI '97* (Atlanta, GA, March 1997), http://www.acm.org/sigchi/chi97/proceedings/paper/ljb1.htm.

6. Birkerts, S., The Gutenberg Elegies: The Fate of Reading in an Electronic Age. *Fawcett Books*, November, 1995.

7. Boguraev, B., Kennedy, C. Bellamy, R., Brawer, S. Wong, Y.Y., Swartz, J. Dynamic Presentation of Document Content for Rapid On-Line Skimming., *AAAI Spring 1998 Symposium on Intelligent Text Summarization*, Stanford University, 23-25 March, 1998.

8. Darnton, R. Toward a history of reading. *Wilson Quarterly* 13(4): 87-102, 1989.

9. Elo, S. PLUM: Contextualizing News for Communities Through Augmentation. Master's Thesis, *MIT Media Laboratory*, (1995) http://mu.www.media.mit.edu/people/elo/www/thesis-doc.html.

10. Hearst, M. TileBars: Visualization of Term Distribution Information in Full Text Information Access. *Online Proceedings of CHI'95* (Denver, CO, May 1995), http://www.acm.org/sigchi/chi95/Electronic/documnts/papers/mah_bdy.htm.

11. Heckerman, D. and Wellman, M.P. Bayesian Networks, *Comm. ACM*, Vol. 38, No. 3, March, 1995, pgs. 27-30.

12. Spring, M. B., Morse, E. and Heo, M. Multi-level Navigation of a Document Space. *Leveraging Cyberspace Conference* (Xerox PARC, Palo Alto, CA, October 1996), http://www.lis.pitt.edu/~spring/mlnds/mlnds/mlnds.html.

13. Kupiec, J., Pedersen, J., and Chen, F. A trainable document summarizer. *Proceedings of the 18th ACM-SIGIR Conference*, 1995.

14. Levy, D. I Read the News Today, Oh Boy: Reading and Attention, *ACM Digital Libraries*. Philadelphia, PA, USA, pgs. 202-211, 1997.

15. Mahesh, K. Hypertext Summary Extraction for Fast Document Browsing. *AAAI-97 Symposium on Natural Language Processing for the World Wide Web*, Stanford University, March 24-26, 1997.

16. Moukas, A., and Maes, P. Amalthaea: An Evolving Multiagent Information Filtering and Discovery System for the WWW. *First issue of the Journal of Autonomous Agents and Multi-Agent Systems*, 1998.

17. Nevill-Manning C.G., Witten I.H. and Paynter G.W. Browsing in digital libraries: a phrase-based approach. *Proc. Digital Libraries '97*, Philadelphia (1997), 230-236.

18. O'Hara, K. and Sellen, A.J. A Comparison of Reading Paper and On-line Documents. *Online Proceedings of CHI '97*, (Atlanta, GA, March 1997), http://www.acm.org/sigchi/chi97/proceedings/paper/koh.htm.

19. *Online Proceedings of CHI '97*, available at http://www.acm.org/sigchi/chi97.

20. Peairs, M. Iconic Paper. *Proceedings of the Third International Conference on Document Analysis and Recognition*, Montreal, Canada, August 14-16, 1995, 1174-1179.

21. Schilit, B. Golovchinsky, G. and Price, M. Beyond Paper: Supporting Active Reading with Free Form Digital Ink Annotations. *Proceedings of CHI '98* (Los Angeles, CA, April 1998), 249-256.

22. Standing, L., Conezio, J. and Haber, R.N. Perception and memory for pictures: S*ingle-trial learning of 2500 visual stimuli, Psychon. Sci.*, 1970 Vol. 19 (2).

23. Tufte, E.R. Envisioning Information. *Graphics Press*, Cheshire, Connecticut, 1990.

24. Wroblewski, D. and Hill, W.C. Attribute-mapped Scroll Bars. U.S. Patent Number 5,479,600, December 26, 1995.

VR's Frames of Reference: A Visualization Technique for Mastering Abstract Multidimensional Information

Marilyn C. Salzman
Human Factors & Applied
Cognitive Psychology
George Mason University
Fairfax VA 22030 USA
+1 303 541 6454
mcsalzm@advtech.uswest.com

Chris Dede
Graduate School of Education
George Mason University
Fairfax VA 22030 USA
+1 703 993 2019
cdede@gmu.edu

R. Bowen Loftin
Virtual Environment
Technologies Lab
University of Houston
Houston TX 77023 USA
+1 713 743 1006
bowen@uh.edu

ABSTRACT

This paper describes a research study that investigated how designers can use frames of reference (egocentric, exocentric, and a combination of the two) to support the mastery of abstract multidimensional information. The primary focus of this study was the relationship between FORs and mastery; the secondary focus was on other factors (individual characteristics and interaction experience) that were likely to influence the relationship between FORs and mastery. This study's outcomes (1) clarify how FORs work in conjunction with other factors in shaping mastery, (2) highlight strengths and weaknesses of different FORs, (3) demonstrate the benefits of providing multiple FORs, and (4) provide the basis for our recommendations to HCI researchers and designers.

Keywords

Virtual reality, visualization, interaction design, visual design, education applications

INTRODUCTION

In today's knowledge-based society, the ability to visualize and manipulate abstract and multidimensional information is crucial for communicating and understanding ideas [5, 14]. Whether working in scientific, environmental, political, or even social domains, people frequently find themselves trying to visualize complex information. They use visualization techniques such as graphically representing information, adopting different frames of reference, imagining how information changes over time, etc. to help with this task [9, 10].

A testament to the power of visualization lays in the history of scientific discovery. Many of our great scientists (e.g., Albert Einstein, August Kekulé, and James Watson) made conceptual leaps by visualizing abstract phenomena [14]. For example, Einstein's ability to imagine what it would be like to ride on a beam of light gave him insights into his

theory of relativity. Unfortunately, the visualization abilities of these scientists are extraordinary - visualization is difficult for most people [5, 18]. Thus, techniques that can help people recognize patterns, reason qualitatively about physical processes, translate among frames of reference, and envision dynamic models are important.

In the area of graphic design and HCI, considerable attention has been given to the development of visualization techniques to support these processes [e.g., 6, 17]. The goal in using visualization techniques is to enable people to rely on their perceptual abilities when looking for patterns and relationships in information. McCormick, DeFanti, and Brown [10] provide an elegant description of what designers are trying to achieve through visualization:

> "Visualization … transforms the symbolic into the geometric, enabling researchers to observe their simulations and computations. Visualization offers a method for seeing the unseen. It enriches the process of scientific discovery and fosters profound and unexpected insights."

Although visualization techniques can be powerful, they can also be confusing or misleading. Our everyday experiences demonstrate this. Take graphical interaction plots (the kind of graph used in the *Results & Discussion* section) as an example. Most likely you can remember instances in which such graphs clarified a complex set of interactions and other instances in which the graphs were either too complex to comprehend or very misleading (e.g., because the scale of the graph exaggerated minor differences). As this simple example illustrates, the visualization techniques that designers employ can be powerfully enlightening or they can be seriously deceptive. Therefore, investigating major types of visualization techniques to identify their strengths and weaknesses is essential to the HCI research agenda. Through careful research, we help designers understand how to use these techniques to support communication and mastery.

One common visualization technique - frames of reference (FORs) - warrants such investigation. Designers of visualization environments often use FORs, or different perspectives, in an attempt to highlight patterns and important relationships. Although there are numerous FORs, many can be classified as exocentric or egocentric. The *exocentric FOR* provides a view of an environment or phenomena from the outside, while the *egocentric FOR* provides a view from within. In this paper, we are concerned with these two FORs, as well as with a third FOR that we call the *bicentric FOR*. The bicentric FOR is a visualization technique in which users alternate between the egocentric and exocentric FORs.

Lessons from Previous Research on FORs

A review of the literature indicates that more research on FORs can be used for visualization is needed. It also underscores the importance of examining FORs within the context of factors such as individual characteristics and interaction experiences.

Studies to date have not examined how FORs can be used to support the mastery of complex and abstract information. These studies have focused primarily on navigational performance and spatial learning. Nevertheless, this body of research provides insights into important issues to consider. First, it is important to examine performance during the learning process as well as mastery outcomes. Prior research shows that FORs can affect how people perform in an environment as well as what they learn from their experiences [13, 16]. Second, we need to explore how well different FORs support the learning of different kinds of information. Specifically, prior research suggests that the exocentric view might help people notice global information (general trends in the data) and that the egocentric view can help people notice local information (or details about that information) [e.g., 2, 11, 19]. Third, we need to consider the environment in which people are asked to apply their knowledge. Prior research indicates that translating between FORs can be difficult, making it easier for someone to answer questions from the FOR in which they learned than from an alternative FOR [1].

Finally, we need to consider the role external factors such as individual characteristics and interaction experiences play in shaping the relationship between FORs and mastery. Individual differences research suggests that characteristics such as gender, spatial ability and domain experience can affect how adept people are with visualization tools [12] and their aptitudes for mastering abstract information [7]. Additionally, dimensions of the interaction experience (e.g., usability, simulator sickness, motivation, and presence) can facilitate or hinder the task, in this case to master abstract information.

Research Goals & Hypotheses

We designed this study to address the following research questions: (1) how do FORs influence mastery?, and (2) how do other factors (i.e., individual characteristics and interaction experience) influence the relationship between FORs and mastery?

Figure 1 summarizes how we expected the FORs of a visualization environment to work with the other factors to shape the learning process and mastery outcomes. Frames of reference influence mastery. The effectiveness of FORs depends on the concept being learned and the environment in which people have to apply their knowledge. Individual characteristics (e.g., gender, spatial ability, domain experience, etc.) influence mastery and potentially moderate the relationship between FORs and mastery. Dimensions of the interaction experience (e.g., usability, motivation, simulator sickness, etc.) mediate the relationship between FORs and mastery (to be affected by FORs and, in turn, to influence mastery).

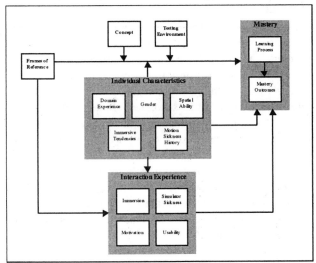

Figure 1. A hypothetical model describing how FORs and other factors work together to influence mastery outcomes.

METHODS

Participants

Forty-eight students, 30 males and 18 females, completed the study. Participants were juniors and seniors in advanced physics classes at a local high school. None were familiar with the concepts covered in this study.

Design

The general design of this study was a mixed 3 (FOR group, between) x 2 (force-motion or FM concept, within) x 2 (descriptive-causal or DC concept, within) factorial design. The three FOR groups were egocentric, exocentric, and bicentric (alternating between egocentric and exocentric FORs). Participants were assigned randomly to a FOR group such that groups were proportionally balanced on gender.

After providing background information, students learned about electric fields via a visualization environment that supported the FOR to which they were assigned. They were asked to master *descriptive* (definitions and representations) and *causal* (rules explaining relationships) information concerning *force* (the distribution of force in electric fields) and *motion* (how test charges are propelled by forces in electric fields). Approximately 3 days after completing the lessons, students participated in a testing session, during which their mastery of the concepts was assessed.

Independent measures & materials

Visualization environment

The environment used in this study was MaxwellWorld (MW), an immersive VR visualization environment that was developed by Project ScienceSpace [3]. MW was designed to help students master a complex and abstract domain of science - electric fields. In very simple terms, an electric field represents the distribution of force that a standard charged particle (a test charge) would have at any point throughout a space surrounding charged particles.

MW allowed students to build electric fields by placing charged particles (source charges) in a three-dimensional space. Students could then manipulate abstract and multidimensional representations of the electric field. These representations (e.g., test charge traces, and field lines, and moving test charges with path markers) provided information about the distribution of force in the electric field and how a charged particle would move if it were released in the electric field. Figure 2 illustrates MW's interface and representations.

MW's physical interface was typical of current high-end virtual reality. Hardware included a Silicon Graphics Onyx Reality Engine2 graphics workstation, a Silicon Graphics Indy workstation, Virtual Research's VR4 headmounted display (HMD), a 3Ball, menu device, and Polhemus magnetic tracking system. The workstations were used to create the sounds and graphics used in MW. The remaining equipment enabled the user to interact with MW. On his or her head, the user wore the HMD. In one hand, the user held the 3-ball, which was represented in MW as a virtual hand. In the other hand, he or she held menu device, which was represented in MW as a hand holding a menu system (Figure 3). The Polhemus tracking system monitored the location of the HMD, the 3Ball, and the menu device. This enabled the user to control where he or she was looking and to use the virtual hand, menus, and direct manipulation to perform tasks in MW.

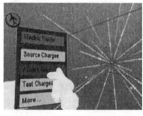

Figure 2. The virtual hand and menus with an electric field in the background.

Figure 3. A person interacting with MW.

FOR group

Students interacted with MW from one of three FORs: egocentric, exocentric, and bicentric. In the exocentric FOR, students explored electric fields from a distance. In the egocentric FOR, students explored electric fields as a test charge immersed within the fields. In the bicentric FOR, students alternated between the egocentric and exocentric FORs for successive learning activities.

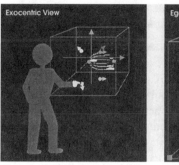
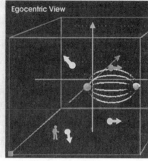

Figure 4. Egocentric and exocentric FORs in MW.

Lessons

Scripted lessons served to guide participants through the learning process and to structure their inquiries about force and motion while using MW. Lessons were administered verbally to one student at a time. They consisted of a series of learning activities; each learning activity consisted of a cycle of predictions and observations. Thus, participants began each activity by making a verbal prediction about the outcomes of that activity; they then tested their predictions; finally, they discussed their observations.

Lessons focused on electric field concepts. Note that the electric field domain was deemed appropriate for investigating how FORs influence mastery of abstract multidimensional information for several reasons. First, the principles underlying the phenomena are abstract and multidimensional. Thus, mastery of electric fields requires students to perform typical visualization tasks: to work with abstract concepts, imagine how changes to source charges change the field, and to recognize and understand patterns in electric field representations. Second, prior research with students studying electric fields demonstrated that they have trouble mastering electric field concepts [3]. Third, some electric field concepts rely primarily on global relationships and others depend more on local relationships.

Concepts being learned – FM concept & DC concept

Students studied two electric field concepts (FM concept): (1) the distribution of force in electric fields, and (2) the motion of test charges through electric fields. Their lessons covered two types of information (DC concept): descriptive (symbolic, or *what*, information = definitions, representations) and causal (conceptual, or *why*, information = how concepts are organized, rules to explain relationships) [15]. To learn about *force*, students studied how forces were distributed in simple and complex electric fields, observed how changes to the electric field affected the distribution of force, and tried to apply rules of superposition (the addition of forces) to explain the distribution of force. To learn about *motion*, students explored how test charges (imaginary charged particles) were propelled by the forces in electric fields (the speed and path they would follow). The concepts of force and motion were selected because an analysis of these concepts suggested understanding force depends more heavily on global than local judgments and that understanding motion requires more local than global judgments.

Dependent measures & materials

Learning process
Participant comments (predictions and observations) provided the basis for monitoring the learning process. Comments for each learning activity were logged during the lessons. Six activities (two at the beginning, middle, and end of the lesson) for force and for motion had synthesis questions asking students to try to summarize key concepts.

Mastery
The mastery test was a transfer test, administered outside of the VR environment. It was developed and refined based on the outcomes of several pilot tests and the expertise of two physics teachers. The test consisted of several kinds of questions: concepts, sketches, and demonstrations. Further, each question had two parts: a *descriptive* component, requiring the student to describe a phenomena; and *causal* component, asking students to explain their responses.

Concepts and sketches were administered via a paper and pencil test. Concepts required students to imagine a force or motion scenario, determine whether it could be true, and explain why; sketches had students use the information presented in a sketch to answer questions about the distribution of force or the motion of a test charge within it. The demonstrations were administered verbally using three-dimensional manipulatives and required students to explore electric fields and demonstrate the distribution of force or the motion of a test charge within them.

Test environment
The test environment was manipulated during the mastery test's demonstrations. All students completed both ego-referenced and exo-referenced demonstrations. For exo-referenced demonstrations, the electric fields were built on a desktop using small manipulatives. For ego-referenced demonstrations, the electric fields were built around the student using larger manipulatives. Thus, students were outside the electric fields for the exo-referenced demonstrations of the test and immersed within the electric fields for the ego-referenced demonstrations, mimicking the exocentric and egocentric FORs in MW.

Individual Characteristics
Individual characteristics included gender, domain experience (science and computers), spatial ability (spatial patterns and spatial visualization), immersive tendencies, and motion sickness history. ETS's CS-2 and VZ-2 [4] were used to measure the two dimensions of spatial ability. Singer & Witmer's [20] Immersive Tendencies Questionnaire and Kennedy et al's [8] Motion Sickness History were used to assess each participant's propensity towards immersion and sickness.

Interaction Experience
Immersion, simulator sickness, usability, and motivation were measured. Singer & Witmer's [20] Presence Questionnaire and Kennedy et al's [8] Simulator Sickness Questionnaire were used to assess how immersed participants were and how they felt physically when using MW. Performance-based usability was assessed via task time and problem rates. Subjective usability and motivation were assessed via 7 point anchored rating scales.

RESULTS & DISCUSSION

How do FORs influence mastery?
Mean mastery scores for each group are shown in Table 1. To determine whether FORs influenced mastery and whether the effectiveness of a FOR depended on the concept being learned or test environment, we conducted two mixed 3 x 2 x 2 analyses of variance (ANOVAs). We also examined learning process data.

Mastery score	FOR group		
	Egocentric	Exocentric	Bicentric
Force	**.636 (.139)**	**.636 (.134)**	**.733 (.109)**
Descriptive	.742 (.113)	.745 (.137)	.811 (.093)
Causal	.525 (.176)	.528 (.149)	.643 (.129)
Ego-referenced*	.632 (.173)	.583 (.216)	.739 (.164)
Exo-referenced*	.587 (.178)	.666 (.157)	.744 (.154)
Motion	**.556 (.160)**	**.494 (.142)**	**.651 (.112)**
Descriptive	.644 (.148)	.601 (.135)	.733 (.084)
Causal	.469 (.179)	.387 (.156)	.568 (.174)
Ego-referenced*	.582 (.193)	.440 (.179)	.708 (.175)
Exo-referenced*	.571 (.178)	.496 (.193)	.623 (.142)

Table 1. Mean mastery scores across FOR groups. * Means are based on the demonstrations only.

The first ANOVA (FOR group by FM concept by DC concept) enabled us (1) to compare overall performance across the groups and (2) to determine whether the groups differed in the extent to which they mastered different kinds of information (FM concept = force vs. motion; DC concept = descriptive vs. causal).

As illustrated in Figure 5, there were significant main effects for FOR group (F_{grp} (2, 45) = 4.64, p = .01), FM concept (F_{fm} (1, 45) = 32.33, p = .0001) and DC concept (F_{dc} (1, 45) = 420.36, p = .0001). There were no significant interactions. Of central interest to us were the main effect for FOR group and the lack of interactions. These two outcomes suggested that the FOR students used in MW influenced mastery outcomes but that the FORs did not differentially affect how well students mastered force and motion or descriptive (what) and causal (why) information.

Two planned comparisons helped to clarify how the groups performed relative to one another. The first contrasted the egocentric and exocentric groups to determine whether students learned more from the egocentric or exocentric FOR. It showed that overall mastery scores for these two FOR groups were not statistically different ($F_{ego-vs-exo}$ (1, 45) = .53, p = .47). The second compared the mastery scores for the egocentric and exocentric groups to the mastery scores for the bicentric group. Students benefited more by learning via a combination of FORs than via one of the single FORs ($F_{\text{single-vs-bi}}$ (1, 45) = 9.20, p = .004).

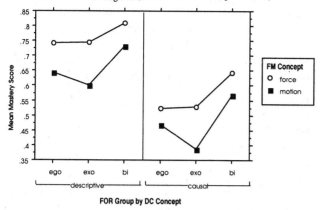

Figure 5. Mastery scores for different concepts.

Learning process data yielded further insights into the FORs. The accuracy and content of predictions, observations, and synthesis questions provided evidence that students in different groups noticed different kinds of information. For example, students in the exocentric group appeared to be more focused on global aspects of the field than on local ones. Accuracy on synthesis questions demonstrated that the superior performance of the bicentric group evolved over time and that this group was slightly more successful in remediating their misconceptions about force and motion than other groups. Finally, mean accuracy during the lessons was highly and positively correlated with mastery outcomes (r (48) = .71, p = .0001).

The second ANOVA (FOR group by FM concept by test environment) focused on demonstration outcomes. It enabled us examine whether the FOR groups differed in the extent to which they were able to adopt different FORs when problem solving (test environment = ego-referenced vs. exo-referenced). Thus, our focus concerned test environment effects. There was not a main effect for test environment. Overall performance (collapsed across FOR groups) on the ego-referenced and exo-referenced portions of the test were roughly equivalent. However, there was a significant FOR group by test environment interaction ($F_{\text{grp*tstenv}}$ (2, 45) = 22.91, p = .0001). Relative performance of the groups varied as a function of the test environment.

An examination of simple effects within each group (comparing ego- and exo-referenced performance) helped to clarify the FOR group by test environment interaction. The exocentric group's ego-referenced scores were significantly lower (-.070) than their exo-referenced scores ($F_{\text{testenv@ego}}$ (1, 15) = 9.53, p = .01). The reverse was true of egocentric and bicentric groups (+.028 and +.039 respectively), although this difference was significant only for the bicentric group ($F_{\text{tstenv@bi}}$ (1, 15) = 5.96, p = .03). To summarize, the exocentric group had trouble working in the ego-referenced environment while the other groups did not and the other groups did not have trouble translating to

the exo-referenced environment, always doing at least as well as or better than the exocentric group.

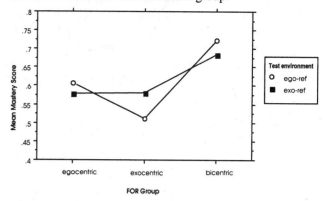

Figure 6. Mastery scores in different testing environments.

How do other factors influence the FOR-mastery relationship?

Both individual characteristics and interaction experiences played important roles in shaping mastery. Individual characteristics explained 23.4% of the variability in mastery scores (R^2 = .234, F (4, 44) = 3.28, p = .02). Gender played the largest role in predicting mastery, with males outperforming females (β_{gender} = .44, t = 3.05, p = .004). Spatial ability (a linear composite of the CS-2 and VZ-2 test scores was used here) was marginally predictive of mastery (β_{spat} = .26, t = 1.85, p = .07). Finally, one aspect of domain experience, total science classes, was predictive of mastery (β_{sci} = -.30, t = -2.03, p = .05); while the other, hours per week using computers, was not. Somewhat counterintuitive, people with domain experience (i.e., more science classes) tended to do more poorly on the mastery test.

To determine whether the effects of FORs varied as a function of individual characteristics, we examined the interaction between individual characteristics and FOR group. Via hierarchical regression, we found none of the interactions to be significant. Thus, the effect of FORs on mastery did not vary as a function of gender, spatial ability, or domain experience.

Interaction experiences explained 30.1% of the variance in mastery scores (R^2 = .301, F (6, 41) = 2.382, p = .017). Task time and simulator sickness were the strongest predictors (β_{time} = -.369, t = -2.645, p = .012; β_{sick} = -.333, t = -2.174, p = .036). As expected, higher simulator sickness resulted in lower mastery; longer task times were also associated with poorer performance on the mastery test. Other measures of usability, immersion, and motivation were not significant predictors of mastery.

In this study, there was high variability in the interaction experiences that could not be attributed to the FORs. In fact a MANOVA showed that FOR group did not significantly predict usability, simulator sickness, immersion and motivation (Wilks Λ = .742, F(12, 80) = 1.17, p = .32). Instead, some aspects of the interaction experience

493

appeared to differ as a function of individual characteristics. For example, spatial ability and domain experience were significant predictors of one aspect of usability - task time ($R^2 = .234$, F (3, 44) = 4.60, $p = .004$). Higher domain experience and spatial ability enabled users to complete the lessons more efficiently. Spatial ability was also predictive of simulator sickness; students with higher spatial ability scores experienced fewer simulator sickness symptoms.

Looking at the big picture

Figure 7 illustrates key relationships in this study:

- The bicentric group did better during the learning process and on the mastery test than the other groups.

- The role of concept deserves further investigation. During the lessons, the FORs seemed to highlight different information, but these differences did not result in differential mastery of the concepts.

- People who had been exposed to the egocentric FOR (the egocentric and bicentric groups) performed well in the ego-referenced and exo-referenced testing environments. In contrast, people who had only the exocentric FOR had difficulty problem solving in the exo-referenced testing environment.

- Gender, simulator sickness, and usability were important predictors of mastery outcomes.

- Individual characteristics such as spatial ability and domain experience helped explain variability in the interaction experience.

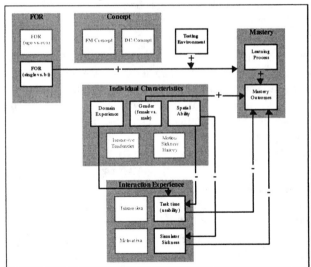

Figure 7. A model illustrating the web of relationships found in this study. Gray boxes represent factors that did not play a substantial role in this study.

CONCLUSIONS

Investigating the relationship between FORs and mastery in the context of other potentially important factors provided insights into both of our research questions.

How do FORs influence mastery? This study highlighted some important considerations when using FORs to support mastery of abstract information. First, people benefited from multiple FORs. Second, during the lessons, FORs seemed to highlight different information. However, at least in this study, these differences did not result in differential mastery of the concepts. Additionally, providing an egocentric FOR in a visualization tool seems to help people adopt that perspective when problem solving.

How do other factors influence the relationship between FORs and mastery? First, gender is an important issue to consider because it played a substantial role in influencing mastery. Second, at least in this study, the benefits of the FORs were not moderated by individual characteristics. Third, particularly important aspects of the interaction experience were usability (time on task) and simulator sickness because they influenced mastery. Finally, study outcomes suggested that we should consider both individual characteristics and interface characteristics (e.g., FORs) when trying to understand the interaction experience.

Recommendations for HCI research & design

This study's outcomes provide the basis for a number of recommendations for researchers and designers interested in understanding the strengths and weaknesses of FORs for visualization and mastery. HCI researchers, we recommend:

- Consider studying not only how single FORs affect performance but also how they work in combination. This study indicated that multiple FORs have benefits.

- Carefully construct test environments to avoid bias yet provide ecological validity. The test environment can bias how FOR groups performed relative to one another. The strategy used in this study worked well: to create a mastery test that (1) assessed people's abilities to transfer what they learned to typical problems outside of the visualization environment and (2) provided a mechanism for checking the extent to which translating between FORs was an issue.

- Study the relationship between FORs and performance in a broader context. This study indicated that this relationship occurs within a complex web of relationships among individual characteristics and facets of the interaction experience.

- Capture and analyze what people notice and how they behave as they interact with FORs. In this study, the learning process was useful for assessing why mastery differed among the FORs.

- Address some of this study's limitations by investigating FORs in other visualization environments with different kinds of users and tasks.

We offer the following advice to designers of visualization environments.

- When the goal is to help people understand abstract information consider providing multiple FORs. In this study, the bicentric FOR facilitated mastery.

- When selecting one FOR over another, carefully consider the type of information the visualization environment needs to convey. The exocentric FOR can help draw user's attention to global aspects of the information; the egocentric FOR can be used to draw the user's attention to local information.

- It is important to think about the characteristics of the problem-solving environment to which users will be transferring their knowledge. For example, if the ability to adopt an egocentric perspective is important for learning or problem solving, enable users to do so in the visualization interface. This study showed that the people learning in the exocentric perspective had trouble adopting an egocentric perspective during problem solving.

- Consider how individual differences might affect how people respond to and learn from the visualization environment. Additionally, examine how visualization techniques affect interaction experiences and how those experiences impact task performance. In this study, gender, usability, and simulator sickness all had substantial impacts on mastery.

- Explore using FORs in combination with other visualization techniques. Assessing the potential of a variety of techniques can help us achieve McCormick, DeFanti, and Brown's vision for visualization tools [8].

ACKNOWLEDGMENTS

This work is supported by NSF's AAT (RED-9353320) and by NASA (NAG 9-713). We gratefully acknowledge Katy Ash, Deborah Boehm-Davis, Chris Chuter, Sheldon Fu, Billy Lyons, Dane Toler, & Joe Redish.

REFERENCES

1. Arthur, E., Hancock, P., & Chrysler, S. (1994) Spatial orientation in virtual worlds. In *Proceedings of HFES '94* (pp. 328-332). Santa Monica, CA: HFES.

2. Barfield, W., Rosenberg, C., & Furness T. A. (1995). Situational awareness as a function of frame of reference, virtual eyepoint elevation, and geometric field of view. *International Journal of Aviation Psychology, 5(3)*, 233-256.

3. Dede, C., Salzman, M., Loftin, B., & Sprague, D. (in press). Multisensory immersion as a modeling environment for learning complex scientific concepts. To be published in Roberts, N., Feurzeig, W., & Hunter, B. (Eds.) *Computer Modeling and Simulation in Science Education.* New York: Springer-Verlag.

4. Ekerstrom, R. B., French, J. W., Harman, H. H., & Derman, D. (1994). *Manual for Kit of Factor-Referenced Cognitive Tests.* Princeton, NJ: Educational Testing Service.

5. Gordin, D. N. & Pea, R. D. (1995). Prospects for scientific visualization as an educational technology. *The Journal of the Learning Sciences, 4(3)*, 249-279.

6. Grinstein, G. & Levkowitz, H. (Eds.). (1995). *Perceptual Issues in Visualization.* New York: Springer-Verlag.

7. Halpern, D. (1992). *Sex Differences in Cognitive Abilities.* Hillsdale, NJ: Lawrence Erlbaum Associates, Publishers.

8. Kennedy, R., Norman, E., Berbaum, K., and Lilienthal, M. (1993). Simulator sickness questionnaire: An enhanced method for quantifying simulator sickness. *The Int. Journal of Aviation Psych., 3(3)*, 203-220.

9. Lohse, G. L., Biolsi, K. Walker, N. & Rueter, H. H. (1994). A classification of visual representations. *Communications of the ACM, 37(12)*, 36-39.

10. McCormick, B., DeFanti, T., & Brown, R. (1987). Visualization in scientific computing and computer graphics. *ACM SIGRAPH*, 21(6), 1-87.

11. McCormick, E. P. (1995). *Virtual Reality Features of Frames of Reference and Display Dimensionality with Stereopsis: Their Effects on Scientific Visualization.* Unpublished master's thesis, University of Illinois at Urbana-Champaign, Urbana, Illinois.

12. Norman, K. (1995). *Interface Apparency and Manipulatability: Cognitive Gateways through the Spatial Visualization Barrier in CBTs.* Available: http://www.lap.umd.edu/LAPFolder/NSFIA/proposal.html.

13. Presson, C., DeLange, N., & Hazelrigg, M. (1989). Orientation specificity in spatial memory: What makes a path different from a map of the path? *Journal of Experimental Psychology: Learning, Memory, and Cognition, 15*, 887-897.

14. Rieber, L. P. (1994). Visualization as an aid to problem-solving: Examples from history. In *Proceedings of AECT '94* (pp. 1018-1023).

15. Shute, V. (1995). SMART: Student modeling approach for responsive tutoring. *User Modeling and user-adapted interaction, 5*, 1-44.

16. Thorndike, P. W., & Hayes-Roth, B. (1982). Differences in spatial knowledge acquired from maps and navigation. *Cognitive Psychology, 14*, 560-589.

17. Tufte, E. R. (1997). *Visual Explanations.* Cheshire, CT: Graphics Press.

18. West, T. G. (1991). *In the Mind's Eye: Visual Thinkers, Gifted People with Learning Difficulties, Computer Images, and the Ironies of Creativity.* Buffalo, NY: Prometheus Books.

19. Wickens, C. D. & Prevett, T. T. (1995). Exploring the dimensions of egocentricity in aircraft navigation displays. *Journal of Experimental Psychology: Applied, 1(2)*, 110-135.

20. Witmer, B., & Singer, M. (in press). Measuring presence in virtual environments. A presence questionnaire. *Presence.*

FotoFile: A Consumer Multimedia Organization and Retrieval System

Allan Kuchinsky, Celine Pering, Michael L. Creech, Dennis Freeze, Bill Serra, Jacek Gwizdka*

Hewlett Packard Laboratories

1501 Page Mill Road

Palo Alto, CA 94304 USA

+1 650 857 1501

{kuchinsk, celine, dff, creech, bills} @ hpl.hp.com

(* Current address: jacek@ie.utoronto.ca , Interactive Media Laboratory: Department of Mechanical and Industrial Engineering, University of Toronto, 4 Taddle Creek Rd, Toronto, Ontario, Canada M5S 1A4)

ABSTRACT

FotoFile is an experimental system for multimedia organization and retrieval, based upon the design goal of making multimedia content accessible to non-expert users. Search and retrieval are done in terms that are natural to the task. The system blends human and automatic annotation methods. It extends textual search, browsing, and retrieval technologies to support multimedia data types.

Keywords

Multimedia computing, information organization, retrieval, browsing, visualization, content-based indexing and retrieval, digital photography, digital video, metadata, media objects

INTRODUCTION

Technologies and applications for consumer digital media are evolving rapidly. Examples of these technologies are digital still and video cameras, multimedia personal computers, broadband multimedia networks, and recordable CD/DVD. These technologies enable consumers to create and access ever-increasing amounts of content, from a wide variety of sources [1] and formats. As a result, there are significant challenges to be overcome to effectively organize and access this media information.

Consumer research conducted by Hewlett Packard has found that organization and retrieval of digital images is a source of great frustration to customers. Consumers were found to be particularly resistant to the notion of organizing and managing home media, seeing these

activities as tedious and error prone. They described photos thrown in shoeboxes and home videos sitting on shelves unviewed.

We derived our approach to making multimedia content accessible to non-experts by

- analyzing the strengths and weaknesses of current commercial products and experimental systems, and

- conducting user research to understand the consumer's perspective on the problem and to gauge customers' reactions to the different approaches.

CURRENT APPROACHES

Technologies for multimedia organization and retrieval have been applied with some success to problems in the business/professional domain. It is not clear, however, that these approaches and technologies are well-suited for consumer-oriented applications. Consumers, in general, have less time, patience, and motivation to learn new technologies.

Traditional keyword-based search technologies are very powerful and flexible. There are a number of commercial image management products that enable a user to search and retrieve visual information based upon indices formed from the user's annotations. Image database products from Extensis (Fetch) [2], Imscape (Kudo Image Browser) [3], Canto (Cumulus) [4], and Digital Now (Showcase) [5] allow a user to browse through files as galleries of thumbnails or as textual lists. The user can typically sort media objects by name, file type, folder, or volume.

The strength of the keyword-based approach is that information about media objects can be expressed in terms that are personally meaningful to the user (i.e., in terms of attributes like creation date, location, subject, and identities of people). Such semantic information about media objects, frequently referred to as *metadata*, provides a rich structure for effective searching. The disadvantage is that making such metadata available usually means that keywords and textual annotations must be entered manually. This works for business applications, where there is an economic incentive for time and effort being devoted to indexing activities. Lacking these same economic incentives, consumers are more resistant to the task of data entry.

An alternative approach, content-based indexing and retrieval, provides some degree of automation for this process by automatically extracting features, such as color or texture, directly from visual data [6]. Products from Virage [7] and IBM (QBIC) [8] implement mechanisms for content-based retrieval of images. By using the intrinsic visual attributes of images, such as color, structure, texture, and composition, to perform queries; users can search collections by instructing the system to retrieve images that are visually similar to the sample image. Images returned by the query are ordered by the degree of similarity to the base image.

The content-based indexing and retrieval approach frees the user from the task of data entry, and it utilizes people's perceptual abilities. These technologies work well in situations where a user wants to locate a visual image that is similar to a sample image. The disadvantage is that these systems only extract low-level syntactic features (measures of color and texture), which are not as personally meaningful to consumers as keyword-based attributes.

An additional concern we had with current technological approaches was whether they correctly map to consumers' likely information-seeking behaviors. Much attention has been paid to the task of direct search, in which a user knows the target. Relatively little attention has been paid to the activities of browsing through collections of materials, where the user doesn't have a very specific goal in mind, and serendipitous discovery is important [9]. It is likely that browsing will be a preferred information seeking behavior for consumers, and it should, accordingly, receive more systematic support from search/discovery technologies.

USER RESEARCH

To understand the consumer's perspective on the multimedia organization and retrieval problem and to gauge customers' reactions to the different approaches, we conducted a set of focus group sessions in the Denver and San Francisco areas. We were looking to more fully understand how people inherently organize visual materials and, in particular, to gather information on the perceived tradeoffs between

- manual vs. automated annotation, and

- direct search vs. browsing.

In order to understand the differences between business and consumer usage, we held different focus groups for business and home participants, respectively.

The sessions began with a discussion of how the participants currently organize, find, and share photos. This was followed by a group exercise in organizing a set of travel photos. We then presented participants with mockups of concepts for keyword-based indexing and search, visually-based search (content-based indexing and retrieval), and visual overview (browsing).

Our key findings from these sessions were that:

- Keyword-based search was the easiest concept for home participants to grasp. However, they saw drawbacks, both in the time-intensive nature of entering keywords for photos and in the possibilities for many false "hits" while searching.

- Participants readily grasped the benefits of automated indexing. However, the home participants thought that they would use keyword-based search more frequently.

- Home participants reacted very favorably to the notion of browsing, much more favorably than did business participants.

We drew two conclusions from these findings; first, that consumers would desire the benefits of both keyword-based search and automated indexing; second, that there may be a considerable role for browsing techniques in supporting consumers' multimedia information seeking activities.

THE *FOTOFILE* SYSTEM

Based upon our analysis of current approaches and our findings from user research, we developed a hybrid approach to address the problems of multimedia organization and retrieval for consumers. We prototyped a number of techniques which make it easier for consumers to manually annotate content and to fit the annotation task more naturally into the flow of activities that consumers find enjoyable. We also utilized a number of automated content-based indexing techniques in order to both substitute for manual annotation where appropriate and to provide novel capabilities for content creation and organization. Finally, we augmented direct search tools with techniques for browsing and visualization of large digital media collections.

FotoFile, shown in Figure 1, is an application for organizing and managing consumer digital media, such as photos and audio/video recordings. It illustrates a number of aspects of our hybrid approach.

FotoFile displays multimedia in a photo-centric way by displaying *media objects* that consist of a photo with related sound and video attached. For video content,

FotoFile generates photos by extracting keyframes from the video. The leftmost pane is a *Content Index*, which enables the user to annotate and search for materials. An *a priori* set of pre-defined metadata attributes is used to represent common properties of media objects, such as *creation date*, *location*, *subject*, *people*, *title*, and *description*. Users can assign arbitrary values within the defined *metadata* types, e.g. annotating the *location* of a photo as "Grand Canyon". Another pre-defined metadata attribute, called *favorite*, can be used to tag certain images as the "best" images in a collection, e.g. my favorite photos from the Grand Canyon vacation.

The central pane is an *Image Palette*, which provides functionality analogous to a light table. The user can arrange, delete, and display media objects at different resolutions in the *Image Palette*. The palette is also used to display search results and newly imported materials, and it also serves as a temporary storage area for creating albums.

The rightmost pane is an *Album Editor* that provides tools for composition of digital albums, which can then be "played back" or sent electronically to others.

In order to match the user's expectations for how pictures are arranged, *FotoFile* uses a photo album as the primary organizational metaphor. A photo album is a metaphor with which people can quickly relate when thinking about organizing photos, and therefore the mental model relies on user intuition rather than explicit instruction. In *FotoFile*, an *Album* is a persistent collection of media objects, which are arranged on "pages". Each image is also accompanied by annotations, which can be in the form of text, audio, or video. Furthermore, in order to simplify album retrieval, the user can assign a representative image for the album cover to aid in selection from a list. Having a cover image that is representative of the album in the user's mind enables fast visual recognition, rather than relying on information recall.

Techniques to Ease the Task of Manual Annotation

Bulk Annotation

We provide mechanisms for bulk annotation, which enable the user to quickly annotate large numbers of items with a minimal number of gestures. For example, the user can select multiple media objects in the *Image Palette*, select several values within the *Content Index*, and then press the Annotate button. This results in the assignment of all selected values to all of the selected media objects.

Symmetry between Annotation and Search

Since we were designing *FotoFile* for home usage, we designed the annotation and search interfaces to use the same basic mechanism. There is a visual and gestural symmetry between the actions for annotation and search. Users only need to learn one tool for both activities.

To annotate content, the user selects one or more metadata attribute/value pairs, and presses the Annotate button. At that time, the selected attributes are applied to all selected media objects. To retrieve content, the user again selects one or more attribute/value pairs, and presses the Search button. At that time, all media objects that have the selected attributes are immediately displayed in the *Image Palette*. There are several search modes, including Boolean operations and a similarity-based search built upon automated feature extraction [18].

Since there is no default mode, the user is free to intermix the annotation and search activities, which we believe will result in a better-annotated corpus of material than would occur if the user only had a dedicated authoring mode available.

Use of Narrative Structure to Help Organize Content

Annotating content manually is time consuming, and it transforms the process of creating photo albums from an enjoyable activity into a very tedious one. On the other hand, people like to tell stories with photos [10] and the organization of photos into stories can provide us with a significant amount of information that can serve as metadata. That is, we can use narrative structure underlying the events captured in photos as a source of their organization and annotation. This effectively turns the organization process into a storytelling activity, an activity that is more enjoyable than the task of organization, which carries with it the connotation of "work".

Whereas with conventional photography, storytelling is typically done using prepared albums and collages, whose structures are fixed, digital photography allows the user to employ more dynamic collections of photos in storytelling. The user can arrange small groups of photos into segments that correspond to single narrative episodes. These segments can be reused in different situations and combined in different ways, depending upon the interaction between storyteller and audience. The model of usage is of two or more people sitting together by a computer, much in the same way that people sit together and go through photo albums. An alternative model of usage is one wherein the storyteller shares groupings of photos and annotations over the Internet.

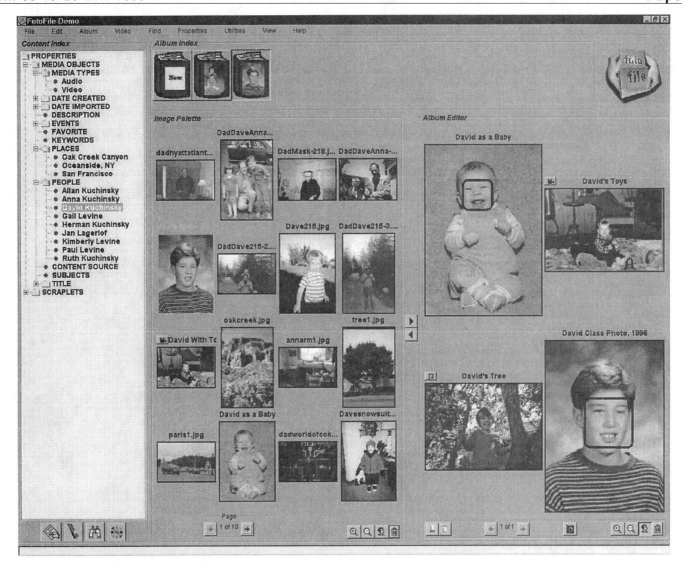

Figure 1. Building a Multimedia *Album* in *FotoFile*.

Building on the metaphor of a scrapbook, we call these small groupings of photos *scraplets* (shown in Figure 2). A scraplet can be assigned a name and other properties, thus providing annotation for a grouping that can be useful in retrieving the grouping at a later time. We believe that such grouping and lightweight annotating will fit naturally within the activity of preparing a story, thus providing a more enjoyable mechanism for eliciting metadata from consumers. Moreover, use of voice annotation may bring additional emotional power to stories that are shared over the Internet.

The selection of photos for grouping into scraplets is based upon two assumptions. *First*, the user should have a personal memory of the events depicted in the photos. *Second*, chronological ordering of events is a dominant organization principle of human episodic memory [11]. Using the same photos in multiple scraplets links them implicitly. The links are displayed during album playback to indicate to the user multiple possible story lines.

Benefits of Automated Feature Extraction

The use of automated feature extraction tools enables *FotoFile* to generate some of the annotation that would otherwise have to be manually entered. It also provides novel capabilities for content creation and organization.

Face Recognition

The black rectangular highlights on the pictures of David in Figure 1 denote faces that have been recognized by a face detection and recognition system [12] [13]. Information about recognized faces appears in the *Content Index* in an identical manner to metadata gathered by human annotation. This is one example of the integration of automated and human annotation in our approach, and it results in a hybrid system where the user guides the mechanisms.

When given photos that contain faces of new people, the face recognition system attempts to match the identity of the face (see Figure 3). The user either corrects or confirms the choice; the system then can more accurately match faces to their correct identities in subsequent photos. Once a face is matched to a name, that name will be assigned as an annotation to all subsequently seen photos that contain faces that match the original. To handle the false positives and false negatives of the face recognition system, a user must confirm face matches (see

Figure 4) before the annotations associated with these faces are validated (i.e., added to the *Content Index*). Users view the matched identities of faces through tooltips displayed when the mouse sprite enters the rectangular highlight surrounding a face.

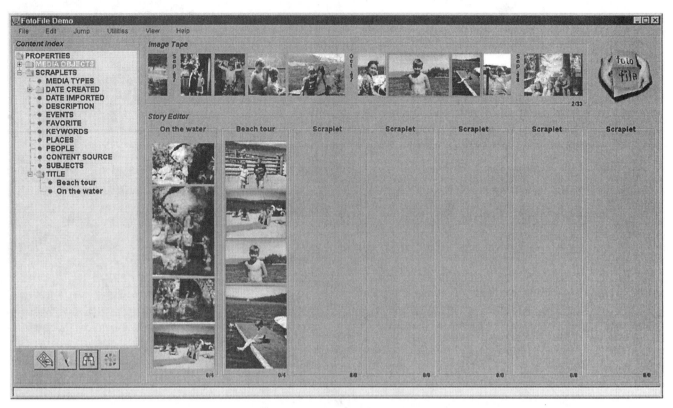

Figure 2. *Scraplets* created in the Story-Editing Environment. Organizing photos via multimedia "scraplets" reduces the tedious effort of manual annotation.

Figure 3. First photo of Merrick is not matched to any other faces by the recognizer; user enters name *Merrick*.

Figure 4. Subsequent photo of Merrick is matched by the recognizer.

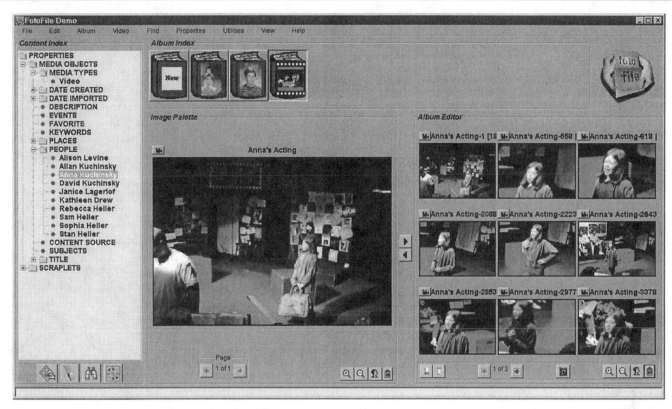

Figure 5. An Automatically Generated *Video Album.*

Video Shot Detection

The *FotoFile* user can automatically generate "albums" of video clips extracted from longer video sequences using the video shot detection and keyframe extraction algorithms [14][15]. Video shot detection is the process of detecting boundaries between consecutive shots so that sequences of interrelated video frames can be grouped together. Examples of shot boundaries include abrupt shot changes caused by turning the camera off, as well as more sophisticated shot transitions like fades, dissolves, and wipes. A user can easily create an album that contains a series of video clips that comprise a video (see Figure 5). Each clip represents a playable segment of video. Since each video segment is itself a media object, it can be rearranged, or placed in different albums—just like any *FotoFile* media object.

Video Keyframe Extraction

During the shot detection process, a keyframe extraction algorithm [15] is used to generate a set of video frames (still images) which best represent the content of each shot. These keyframes attempt to represent abrupt changes in video content as well as slower, ordered changes like pans and zooms. Each resulting keyframe is associated with a video clip that starts with that frame and continues to the end of the shot. The set of these keyframes imposes an extra

structure on shots which help users fine-tune their selection and manipulation of video clips and shots.

Keyframe extraction is also used to derive a representative picture for each video imported into *FotoFile*.

Browsing and Visualization of the Content Space

We believe that consumers' information-seeking activities differ from those of information retrieval professionals, and that this is particularly true when the information involves home media such as photos or videos.

In these settings, directed search may be less frequent, whereas riffling and browsing through collections of materials becomes the norm (and serendipity is expected).

We provide support for these activities by integrating visualization and browsing tools into *FotoFile*, such as the *Hyperbolic Tree* package from Inxight Software [16][17]. Figure 6 shows a hyperbolic tree built from the attributes and values in the *Content Index*.

One problem observed in usability studies of the *Hyperbolic Tree* [21] was that items on the outside rim of the display tended to group strongly, with users often assuming that they belonged in the same category. It was suggested that careful use of alternative perceptual coding for semantic categories could alleviate this problem. We have achieved this by providing additional views based on

Figure 6. Viewing the *Content Index* via the *Hyperbolic Tree.*

the use of automated image feature-extraction software [18]. Image content is analyzed to extract measures for color distribution and texture, and a clustering algorithm [19] recursively partitions the collection of media objects to form the tree model displayed by the *Hyperbolic Tree.* In this way, media objects that are visually similar to each other will appear closer to each other in the visualization space. This adds structure to the browsing activity, enabling the user to visualize related clusters of materials in an intuitive manner.

DISCUSSION

With *FotoFile,* we have attempted to balance tradeoffs across two dimensions of information-seeking behaviors:

- Combining the strengths of both human annotation and automated feature extraction.

- Accommodating both directed search and exploratory browsing and visualization.

Based upon our findings from user research, we have attempted to integrate these capabilities in a way that is suited to the needs of the consumer environment. In order to provide an integration that is easily understandable and usable, we need to emphasize certain capabilities more than others. To determine the appropriate balance points, additional user research is needed. In particular, we need to determine:

- The degree to which consumers will perform annotation if the benefits are significant and meaningful.

- The usability and usefulness to consumers of browsing and visualization environments.

One challenge in designing credible studies of this nature is in defining the right metrics for data analysis. Consumer information-seeking behavior is different from that of specialists performing directed searches in textual databases, where large numbers of people are searching over large information spaces for materials indexed by some unknown person. The characteristics of an information-seeking environment for consumers involve relatively few people searching (e.g., immediate family members) over a small amount of information (less than several thousand items in a collection) that they have personally indexed, or that was indexed by someone they know. In many cases, serendipitous discovery is a significant (but often unstated) goal. The traditional metrics of *recall* and *precision* may not be as applicable. Alternative measures might include the level of goal attainment, the efficiency (number of actions) to reach a goal, the utility of the information found, which annotations and features are used for later retrieval by both novices and experts, and subjective measures of user satisfaction [20].

CONCLUSION

We have built an experimental multimedia organization and retrieval system that attempts to balance tradeoffs between (1) human annotation versus automated feature extraction, and (2) directed search versus exploratory browsing and visualization. The ultimate goal is to make multimedia content accessible to non-expert users.

Photography and home movies are activities that address deep human needs; the need for creative expression, the need to preserve memories, the need to build personal relationships with others. Digital photography and digital video can provide powerful and novel ways for people to express, preserve, and connect. However, new technologies often raise new problems; the problem of multimedia organization and retrieval is brought about by the very technology that makes it possible for people to create and access ever-increasing amounts of content, from a widening diversity of sources.

By helping consumers to better manage content, we hope to enable people to take full advantage of the benefits provided by digital media technologies.

ACKNOWLEDGMENTS

We owe a great debt to HongJiang Zhang, John Wang, and Wei-Ying Ma for their excellent work in content-based indexing and retrieval, which has been incorporated into our prototypes. Thanks and praise to Rick Steffens, Mike Krause, and others at HP's Colorado Memory Systems Division for their support, encouragement, and inspiration. Ella Tallyn made substantial contributions to both the visual design of *FotoFile* and the conceptual design of our use of narrative structures in *FotoFile*.

REFERENCES

1. Kuchinsky, A., Bit Velocity is Not Enough: Content and Service Issues for Broadband Residential Information Services, *IEEE 3rd International Workshop on Community Networking*, Antwerp, Belgium, May, 1996.

2. Extensis Corporation, http://www.extensis.com/.

3. Imspace Systems Corporation, http://imspace.com/.

4. Canto Software, http://www.canto-software.com/.

5. Digital Now, http://www.digitalnow.com/.

6. Furht, B. Smoliar, S., Zhang, H., and Furht, B. *Video and Image Processing in Multimedia Systems*, Kluwer Academic Publishers, 1995. Conger., S., and Loch, K.D. (eds.).

7. Virage Incorporated, http://www.virage.com/.

8. IBM, http://www-i.almaden.ibm.com/cs/showtell/qbic/.

9. Chang, S.J., and Rice, R.E., Browsing: a Multidimensional Framework, in Williams, M.E. (ed), *Annual Review of Information Science and Technology*, Vol. 28, pp. 231-276, Medford, NJ, 1993..

10. Chalfen, R. *Snapshot Versions of Life*. Bowling Green State University Press, Bowling Green, Ohio, 1987.

11. Tulving, E. *Elements of Episodic Memory*. Oxford, UK: Oxford University Press, 1983.

12. Turk, M., and Pentland, A. Eigenfaces for Recognition. *Journal of Cognitive Neuroscience*, Vol. 3, No. 1, pp. 71-86, 1991.

13. H.A. Rowley, S. Baluja and T. Kanade. Neural network-based face detection. *IEEE Trans. on Pattern Analysis and Machine Intelligence*, vol. 20, no. 1, pp. 23-38, Jan. 1998.

14. H.J. Zhang, C. Y. Low and S. W. Smoliar. Video parsing and browsing using compressed data. *Multimedia Tools and Applications*, vol. 1, pp. 89-111, 1995.

15. H.J. Zhang, et al. An integrated system for content-based video retrieval and browsing. *Pattern Recognition*, Pergomon Press/Pattern Recognition Society, May 1997.

16. John Lamping, Ramana Rao, and Peter Pirolli. A focus+context technique based on hyperbolic geometry for visualizing large hierarchies. In *Proceedings of the ACM SIGCHI Conference on Human Factors in Computing Systems* (May 1995), ACM.

17. Inxight Software, Inc., http://www.inxight.com.

18. W.Y. Ma and H.J. Zhang. Content-based image indexing and retrieval. Chapter 13, *The Handbook of Multimedia Computing*, edited by Borko Furht, CRC Press LLC, 1998.

19. R. Duda and P. Hart. *Pattern Classification and Scene Analysis*. Wiley Publications: NY, 1973.

20. Wilson, K. Evaluating Information Exploration Interfaces, position paper for Workshop on Innovation in Information Exploration Environments, *CHI'98 Conference on Human Factors in Computing Systems*, http://www.fxpal.com/CHI98IE/.

21. Czerwinski, M. and Larson, K., Trends in Future Web Designs: What's Next for the HCI Professional?, *ACM Interactions*, November-December, 1998, pp. 9-14.

Hyper Mochi Sheet: A Predictive Focusing Interface for Navigating and Editing Nested Networks through a Multi-focus Distortion-Oriented View

Masashi Toyoda and Etsuya Shibayama
Department of Mathematical and Computing Sciences
Tokyo Institute of Technology
2-12-1 Oookayama, Meguro-ku,
Tokyo 152–8552 JAPAN
+81-3-5734-3870
{toyoda,etsuya}@is.titech.ac.jp

ABSTRACT

Multi-focus distortion-oriented views are useful in viewing large information on a small screen, but still have problems in managing multiple foci during editing. The user may have to navigate information space by focusing and defocusing multiple parts to obtain multi-focus layouts that change according to various editing situations. As a result, it becomes haphazard to navigate and edit large nested networks such as hypertexts. We propose a user interface for quickly obtaining desirable layouts. The interface uses two techniques: focus size prediction and predictive focus selection. These techniques are based on a user test and experiences in applications. We also describe two example applications.

Keywords

distortion-oriented view, multi-focus, editing, navigation

INTRODUCTION

Multi-focus distortion-oriented views [14, 10, 1, 4] are useful in viewing large information on a small screen. These views provide more flexible layouts of focused parts while preserving the overall context compared to single-focus distortion-oriented views[8, 13, 12, 7, 5]. As such they seemingly have the potential for scalable *editing* of large networks such as visual programs and hypertexts. In reality, however, they have not yet supported efficient editing interfaces of large networks due to problems in managing multiple foci. More flexibility and freedom of multi-focus layouts often require more work by the user than in single-focus views, in which a change of layout involves only focus movement and change in magnification factor. Rather, in multi-focus views, the user may have to perform boring focusing and defocusing operations on multiple parts of the screen to obtain a layout

suitable for a particular editing situation, which changes frequently during editing.

Before discussing the problems in detail, we show our objective applications, which are editors that handle hierarchically nested networks with hyperlinks such as visual programs, hypertexts, and file systems. In Figures 1 and 2, we show two concrete applications.

Figure 1 shows the KLIEG visual programming environment [15], which addresses the scalability problem. KLIEG allows the programmer to edit multiple modules in one view and to construct nested data-flow networks for programming in the large. In Figure 1, there are four modules at the top level (**nqueens**, **combiners**, **master_worker_nqueens**, and **dispatchers**). In this case, to edit **master_worker_nqueens** referring **combiners** and **dispatchers**, the user magnifies these modules and shrinks **nqueens**. In addition, a program includes invisible hyperlinks from components to their definitions and documents, and a document is also a hypertext. When the user follows a hyperlink, KLIEG automatically focuses its destination and defocuses unnecessary foci. Using KLIEG, the user can easily drag-and-drop components between modules and can navigate a program with hyperlinks.

Figure 2 shows a novel presentation tool, which can handle hierarchically structured slides with hyperlinks. In effect, it can be used as a 2D visual outline processor for hypertexts. It allows the creator to edit a presentation through multi-focus views. It can also simultaneously show multiple slides and their overview during presentation. Each picture in Figure 2 is a different view of the same presentation. The top view is an overview, and the bottom view is a focus+context view in which a slide titled "Structure of Diagrams" is being focused. With a single mouse operation, the presenter can follow a hyperlink from a slide to the next one, and the system automatically moves the focus to the next slide and adjusts slide sizes. The creator of the presentation does not have to explicitly designate these sizes during editing, rather, the system predicts the sizes from a history of editing operations.

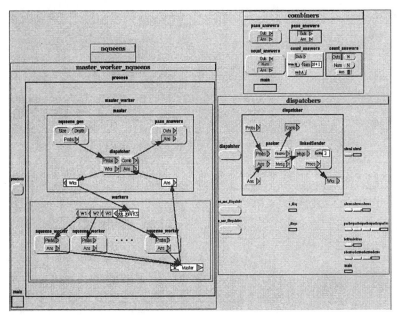

Figure 1: A visual programming environment KLIEG

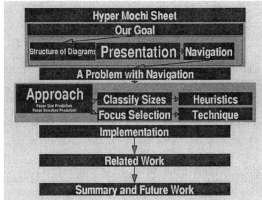

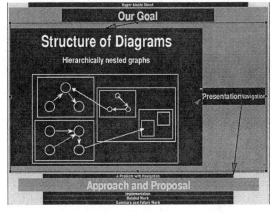

Figure 2: A presentation tool

To be more specific, our algorithm is intended to address the following problems:

- The user can resize a node to arbitrary sizes during editing, but it is tedious to resize the node for focusing and defocusing every time on editing its contents. It might be useful if the system allows the user to focus and defocus a node in simple operations. However, since a set of appropriate node sizes for focusing and defocusing is different from each node, it is a tedious task to explicitly designate these sizes for each node.
- A desirable layout after following a link may vary according to the current editing situation. When the user follows a hyperlink, it is always necessary to focus the destination of the link, but the source and other foci may or may not be necessary. On one hand, if the user still wants to edit the source, both the source and the destination should be focused. On the other hand, after the user finished editing the source, it is not necessary to retain the focus on the source.

To address these problems, we propose a user interface that allows the user to obtain easily desirable layouts for various editing situations. We implemented this interface as a library; Hyper Mochi Sheet. The interface uses the following predictive techniques.

- *Focus size prediction* automatically determines a pair of node size, one being used when the node is focused and the other being used when the node is defocused. It is not necessary for the user to explicitly set these sizes, rather, our technique predicts appropriate sizes of nodes using a history of editing commands.
- *Predictive focus selection* automatically selects necessary

foci and discards unnecessary foci during navigation with hyperlinks. When the interface focuses and defocuses nodes, it uses sizes predicted by the focus size prediction. Since necessities of foci may depend on application semantics, Hyper Mochi Sheet provides a default focusing behavior that can be customized by the application programmer.

The next section discusses related work. Then we describe the basic interface of Hyper Mochi Sheet. This is followed by explanations of prediction techniques, and an evaluation. Finally, we conclude.

RELATED WORK

There have been various user interfaces that handle hierarchical networks with multi-focus distortion-oriented views [10, 14, 1, 4]. There have been, however, little research supporting automatic multi-focus management and hyperlink navigation. Our approach is a new attempt to support them using predictive techniques that are mainly used in PBD (programming-by-demonstration) systems such as [9, 6].

Layout-independent Fisheye View[10] shows an algorithm that can be used for navigating nested networks. However, it describes merely an algorithm and there are few discussions about the way to construct the user interface.

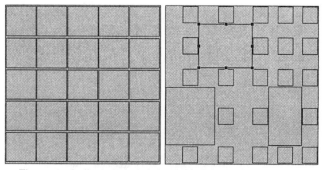

Figure 3: A distortion view in Hyper Mochi Sheet

The Continuous Zoom (CZ)[1] uses smooth animation during zooming, and supports efficient navigation through the hierarchy of a nested network. However, it neither supports navigation with hyperlinks nor editing graphs. The Intelligent Zoom[2] combines the CZ with intelligent supports in network supervisory control systems. It suggests opening (magnifying) a node in an alarm condition, and when the node is opened it automatically selects an appropriate representation from several aspects of the node such as a bar chart and a trend diagram. However, since it merely suggests opening and closing nodes, it does not reduce explicit focusing and defocusing.

The rubber sheet approach[14] and 3-dimensional pliable surface[4] put emphasis on interfaces that support flexible selection of a shape as a focal region. It is, however, difficult to access nodes deep in a hierarchy. The user must specify focal regions and stretch them repeatedly for accessing deep information. It is a tedious and boring task.

Pad++[3] is a single focus and pan/zoom based interface. It supports multiple foci by multiple windows called portals. Since it does not perform automatic portal management, the user has to create, delete, and arrange multiple portals manually. Pad++ also supports hyperlink navigation in a single focus view, but it does not address multi-focus issues in hyperlink navigation.

PBD systems, such as Metamouse[9] and Eager[6], predict operations that the user will perform next. These systems automatically extract patterns of recurring operations from a history, and create macros by generalizing these patterns. However, in our approach, the purpose is to reduce explicit designation of sizes and necessary foci. Therefore it is often necessary to predict operations that have never been performed.

BASIC INTERFACE OF HYPER MOCHI SHEET

To make distortion views, we use an approach similar to the Continuous Zoom[1]. Figure 3 displays an application of our approach to a 2D grid graph. When some nodes are magnified in the left view, it becomes impossible to display all nodes in their desirable sizes on the screen. In this case, all nodes are compressed uniformly in the horizontal and verti-

cal directions keeping relative positions of nodes as the right view.

In addition to the continuous zoom algorithm, our algorithm avoids overlapping of nodes by simply aligning nodes in the horizontal and vertical directions during moving and resizing nodes. To use screen space more efficiently, it also meshes adjoining rows or columns together. For example, in the right view of Figure 3, two columns in the left are meshed together.

The user can focus and defocus nodes by stretching and shrinking them with handles that are shown as small black rectangles in Figure 3. The width and height of a node can be stretched independently to each direction. In addition the user can move nodes by dragging.

We also use semantic zooming [11], which changes an amount of information of a node according to its size. For example, in Figure 2, when a slide is small, we can see only its title. When a slide is large enough, we can see details of the slide.

FOCUS SIZE PREDICTION

Focus size prediction automatically determines a pair of node size[1] in the following.

- *Small size* is used when the node is defocused. The node area of this size is smaller than the large size. It is possible to edit inside roughly in this size.
- *Large size* is used when the node is focused. The user can edit inside details of the node. The node area of this size is larger than the small size.

The system predicts these sizes from a history of editing commands. It is not necessary for the user to explicitly set these sizes during editing. Once the small and large sizes of a node are determined, the user can easily select one of these sizes by clicking a mouse button or by using a popup-menu. Changes to the large size and the small size perform instant focusing and defocusing, respectively. These commands are useful when the user edits one node repeatedly and when the user navigates edited networks.

We do not provide any other intermediate sizes for the prediction, although they are useful in some situations. This decision simplifies size changing commands and makes the prediction easy but useful. Note that the determination of sizes is not trivial, because the user can resize nodes to arbitrary sizes in arbitrary orders during editing. For example, when the user stretches a node from its small size, it is difficult to distinguish whether the user want to modify its small size or its large size.

Preliminary User Test

We performed a preliminary user test to investigate when the user determines small and large sizes during editing. We use the editor in which the user must set these sizes of each node explicitly. By tracing command histories, we tried to find out typical sequences of commands around size setting.

---

[1] In the following, a size stands for a pair of width and height of a node.

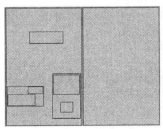 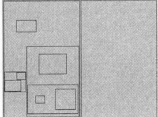

Figure 4: The diagram used in the user test: all rectangle sizes are set to small

Figure 5: The diagram that shows the detailed view of the bottom-right rectangles

Table 1: Command Sequences around SetSmall

Initial size	Command Sequences around SetSmall	Subjects 1	2	3	4	5	6	7	8
small	Shrink+.**SetSmall**.except Shrink	5	6	5	5	3	5	9	2
	–	2	2	2	1	1	1		
small	Expand.**SetSmall**.Expand or Large	2	1	1	1	1	2	2	2
	Small	1	1	1					
	–						1	1	1
large	Shrink+.**SetSmall**.Small							2	
	Large	1							
small	Expand.Shrink.**SetSmall**.Any				2				
	Others							3	3

Shrink: resize to a smaller size, Expand: resize to a larger size
Small: change to the small size, Large: change to the large size
+: one or more execution of the command
–: the node was left

Table 2: Command Sequences around SetLarge

Initial size	Command Sequences around SetLarge	Subjects 1	2	3	4	5	6	7	8
small	*.Expand.**SetLarge**.Small	6	7	3	5	2	2	2	3
	Shrink					3			
large	Expand+.**SetLarge**.Small				1	1	6		
	Shrink+.**SetLarge**.Small					1		1	1
	Others	1		3		1		3	2

*: alternative sequence of commands that may be empty

Method

- *System*: We used a simple editor for drawing nested nodes. The editor provides typical editing commands such as adding, removing, resizing, and moving nodes. For node size setting, it provides SetSmall and SetLarge commands that store the current node size as the small size and the large size, respectively. The editor also provides Small and Large commands for changing a node to the corresponding size.
- *Subjects*: Seven student volunteers and an instructor of computer science served as subjects in the user test. All subjects were familiar with typical window-based GUIs.
- *Task*: Subjects were required to draw a diagram, which is shown in the left hand side of Figure 4, on the right blank area, and to set small and large sizes of all nodes. This diagram consists of 13 nested rectangles[2], and sizes of each node have been set. The default size of each node is its small size. Figure 5 shows the diagram in which bottom-right rectangles are changed to its large size. Each subject was instructed to set sizes immediately when he decided sizes, and to edit without hurry. In addition, we did not limit the time for the task.
- *Procedure*: Before performing the task, subjects were given an explanation of the system and a practice trial on a part of the diagram. We spent about 10 minutes on this session.

Result and Observations　Tables 1 and 2 show patterns of command sequences around SetSmall and SetLarge respectively, and the number of times each pattern was used by each subject. A pattern begins when the node was in its small or large size after its creation[3] or changing its size. This is the initial size in the pattern and is followed by a command sequence performed on the node before the execution of set command. The pattern also includes a command performed after the set command.

We considered only resize related commands such as resizes (Shrink and Expand) and size changes (Small and Large), because we could not find distinctive regularity from other commands. Note that we treated consecutive resizes on a sin-

---

[2]Some nodes are not displayed in Figure 4, because their parent nodes are too small

[3]A node is in small size at the creation time

gle node as a single resize command, since such a sequence stands for a fine tuning of the size.

We show observations of the result in the following.

1. SetSmall occurs after repeated Shrink from the small size in most cases (See the first pattern in Table 1).

2. SetSmall also occurs after a single Expand from the small size, and is mostly followed by Expand or Large (See the second pattern in Table 1). In some cases, SetSmall is followed by Small, but SetLarge occurs more frequently between Expand and Small (See the first pattern in Table 2).

3. SetLarge mostly occurs after Expand and before Small (See Table 2). Both SetSmall and SetLarge may occur after Shrink from large size and before Small (See the third pattern in Table 1).

4. Among six SetLarge commands performed by the subject 5, three of them occur before Shrink. The subject first set the large size then shrunk and set the small size, though most subjects set the small size first. In the fourth pattern in Table 1, we can see this sequence before SetSmall.

Prediction Algorithm

Based on the above observations, we designed and implemented a size prediction algorithm. Our design policies are (1) to give a higher priority to patterns used by most subjects, (2) to satisfy subjects as fairly as possible, and (3) to keep the algorithm simple.

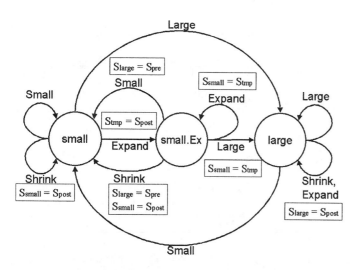

Figure 6: A state transition chart for predicting size

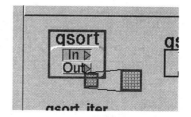

Figure 7: Size correction interface

The algorithm is based on state transitions on each node that are shown in Figure 6. The state is changed when the user performs a command on the node, and a label on an arrow represents the command. There are three states: small, small.Ex, and large. The small and large states represent that the node is in the corresponding sizes, and small.Ex represents that the node has been expanded repeatedly from the small size. The small.Ex state is necessary, since the size is uncertain when the node is expanded from the small size (See the observation 2).

When a transition occurs, the small and large sizes (S_{small} and S_{large}) may be changed. In Figure 6, rectangles include actions performed after the transition. S_{pre} and S_{post} represent the sizes before and after the transition, respectively, and S_{tmp} represents the temporal store of a size. We describe the reason for each action in the following.

- *Shrink from small*: According to the observation 1, S_{small} is changed to S_{post}.
- *Expand from small*: Since S_{post} may be either size, S_{post} is stored temporary into S_{tmp}.
- *Expand or Large from small.Ex*: According to the observation 2, S_{small} is changed to S_{tmp}.
- *Small from small.Ex*: According to the observation 3, S_{large} is changed to S_{pre}.
- *Shrink from small.Ex*: We don't ignore the observation 4 to satisfy subjects fairly (This is policy 2). In fact, there are few conflicts with other observation. In this case, S_{large} and S_{small} are changed to S_{pre} and S_{post}, respectively.
- *Shrink or Expand from large*: According to the observation 3, S_{post} may be the small size in the case after Shrink from large. In this algorithm, S_{large} is changed to S_{post}, because there are three subjects who used SetLarge and is only one who used SetSmall. This decision follows the design policies 1 and 3.

Size Correction Interface

Since prediction may be error-prone, manual correction is necessary. We provide an interface to correct a size by choosing a size from the size history of the node. When the user performs a size changing command on a node, two buttons appear near the node (Figure 7). The smaller button changes the size to the next smaller size in the history and the larger button the next larger size. If the predicted size is acceptable, the user can ignore these buttons. This interface allows the user to correct size precisely to a past size rather than using handle interface.

PREDICTIVE FOCUS SELECTION

During navigation with hyperlinks, the system predicts foci that will be unnecessary, and automatically discards these foci. Focus selection enables the user to obtain almost desirable layout only by following hyperlinks.

Hyperlink Navigation Examples

As an example, we show a simple navigation using a presentation tool in Figure 8. In case of viewing slides one after another, the focus on the current slide will become unnecessary when the user follows a hyperlink. In Figure 8 (b), the system automatically shrinks the title slide when the user follows the hyperlink to the slide "Our Goal." In Figure 8 (c), the slide "Our Goal" is shrunken in the same way.

Figure 9 shows another navigation example in a visual programming environment. In case of editing visual programs, it is necessary to retain foci on nodes that are in the middle of editing. In Figure 9 (a), the user is editing a data-flow diagram **master** at the center of the bottom-left module, and intends to check the behavior of the **pass_answers** component by following the hyperlink to its definition part. In this case, the system can predict that **master** is still necessary because there are unconnected components in the network. Therefore, the system retains the focus on **master** when the user follows the hyperlink (Figure 9 (b)).

Prediction Method

To realize such automatic focus management, Hyper Mochi Sheet library provides each node with a boolean function $f(F)$, which returns true if the focused (large size) node F is still necessary. Programmers can reflect application semantics in their applications by defining customized $f(F)$ for each node. For example, in visual programming editor,

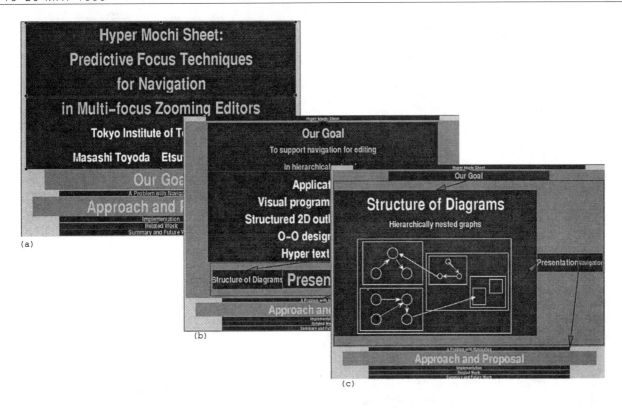

Figure 8: A hyperlink navigation in our presentation tool

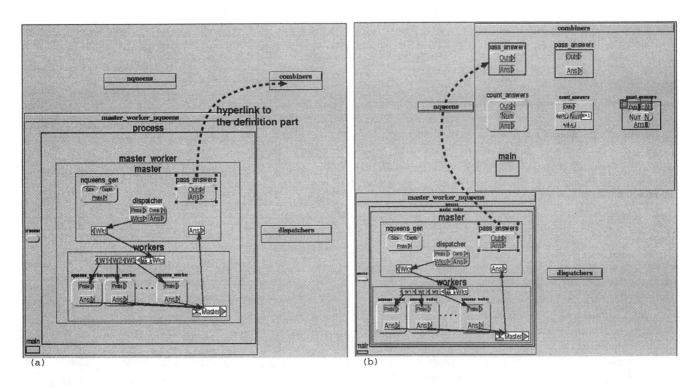

Figure 9: A hyperlink navigation in a visual programming environment

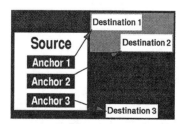

Figure 10: Hyperlink structure

$f(F)$ returns true if there exist unconnected ports in the node F. The default implementation of $f(F)$ returns false if all child nodes in the F are in the small size.

When the user follows a hyperlink from an *anchor* (See Figure 10), the system changes the size of the *destination* to its large size, and stores the *source* and the destination in the *focus list*. Simultaneously, the system changes the sizes of all the ancestor nodes of the destination to their large size in parent-to-child order, so that the destination will be visible. After magnifying the destination, the system checks whether each node except the destination in the focus list satisfies f. If f returns false with a node in the list, the node size is changed to its small size. Then the system changes the sizes of ancestors in child-to-parent order. Before changing the size of an ancestor A, the system checks $f(A)$. If $f(A)$ returns false, A is changed to its small size, and if not, the system stops changing sizes of upper ancestors.

In addition, the system animates transition from one layout to another, so that the user is not confused even if the layout drastically changes during navigation.

EVALUATION

In this section, we describe an experiment to evaluate the feasibility of the focus size prediction technique. We leave evaluations of the predictive focus selection and integration of two techniques for future work because of difficulties that are caused by their application dependent characteristics. The number of implemented applications is not enough to formally evaluate all techniques, even though we consider that they seem fine so far.

Method

- *System*: We used a simple presentation editor with the focus size prediction function. Differences from the editor in the preliminary user test are that a node has one line editable text inside, and that the editor does not provide size setting commands (SetSmall and SetLarge). A text in a node is not displayed when the node has child nodes and the node is large enough[4] to display its children.
- *Subjects*: Ten student volunteers served as subjects. Four of them were also ones of the preliminary user test. All

---

[4] A node is large enough if the width and height of the node are larger than 70 pixels.

Figure 11: The table of contents used in the experiment

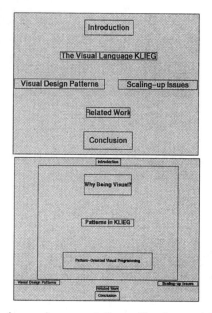

Figure 12: A sample presentation written by a subject

subjects were familiar with typical window-based GUIs.

- *Task*: Subjects were required to edit a simple presentation based on the table of contents shown in Figure 11. Each subject was instructed (1) to represent the presentation hierarchy as nested nodes like Figure 12, (2) to put some empty text boxes as contents of each leaf section such as "1 Introduction" and "2.2.1 Basic Usage," (3) to arrange nodes as you like, and (4) to edit without hurry and we did not limit the time for the task. In addition, we did not force for subjects to check node sizes during editing.
- *Procedure*: Before performing the task, subjects were given an explanation of the system and a practice trial on a part of the presentation. We spent about 10 minutes on this session. After each subject performed task, we checked whether sizes of each section are along to the subject's intention. In this session, we asked subjects about correctness of sizes using Large and Small commands.

Table 3: The number of use of the size correction interface and the number of prediction errors checked after the task

		Subjects									
		1	2	3	4	5	6	7	8	9	10
# of size corrections on 17 sections	Small	1	4	1	0	3	1	0	3	4	3
	Large	1	0	1	0	2	1	0	4	0	0
# of errors in 17 sections	Small	2	0	0	0	1	0	0	0	0	0
	Large	2	0	3	0	0	3	3	0	3	3
total	Small	3	4	1	0	4	1	0	3	4	3
	Large	3	0	4	0	2	4	3	4	3	3

Result and Discussion

Table 3 shows the number of the use of the size correction interface, and the number of prediction errors. The use of the size correction interface means that a subject found and corrected a wrong node size, which was not along to the subject's intention, during editing. An error was counted when a wrong node size was found during the check session after the task. Each number was counted for each size. Subjects 1 to 4 were also ones of the preliminary user test, but there were no significant differences in the result from other subjects.

In spite of the fixed algorithm, error rates are significantly small. The average error ratio after the task is 6% (the best is 0% and the worst is 11%). Even in total error ratio, the average is only 14% and the worst is 20%.

Note that the prediction algorithm almost suits all subjects, though they edited the presentation in various manners. Some subjects resized nodes without using Small and Large command, and some subjects used Small and Large command on about half of the nodes. In addition, some subjects first decided a large size of a node, and other subjects decided a small size first.

CONCLUSION

We have proposed two prediction techniques for managing multiple foci of distortion-oriented views during navigation and editing nested networks. The focus size prediction automatically determines appropriate sizes of nodes. We showed reasonable accuracy of this technique with an experiment. The predictive focus selection automatically defocuses unnecessary foci during navigation with hyperlinks. Application programmers can reduce the error rate of this technique by customizing prediction methods for their applications.

It is shown that our techniques are useful for a visual programming editor and a presentation tool. We believe that the techniques can be applied to other applications, such as hypertexts, file systems, and object-oriented software designs, with appropriate heuristics. We plan to implement these applications and to construct a framework that allows the programmer to introduce more application semantics as prediction keys.

ACKNOWLEDGEMENTS

We would like to thank Satoshi Matsuoka, Shin Takahashi, and the TRIP meeting members for their helpful advice. We also thank our test users for their participation.

REFERENCES

1. L. Bartram, A. Ho, J. Dill, and F. Henigman. The Continuous Zoom: A Constrained Fisheye Technique for Viewing and Navigating Large Information Space. In *Proceedings of UIST '95*, pages 207–215, November 1995.

2. L. Bartram, R. Ovans, J. Dill, M. Dyck, A. Ho, and W. S. Havens. Contextual Assistance in User Interfaces to Complex, Time Critical Systems: The Intelligent Zoom. In *Graphics Interface '94*, pages 216–224, 1994.

3. B. B. Bederson and J. D. Hollan. Pad++: A Zooming Graphical Interface for Exploring Alternate Interface Physics. In *Proceedings of UIST '94*, pages 17–26, November 1994.

4. M. S. T. Carpendale, D. J. Cowperthwaite, and F. D. Fracchia. 3-Dimensional Pliable Surfaces: For the Effective Presentation of Visual Information. In *Proceedings of UIST '95*, pages 217–226, November 1995.

5. W. Citrin and C. Santiago. Incorporating Fisheying into a Visual Programming Environment. In *Proc. 1996 IEEE Symposium on Visual Languages*, pages 20–27, 1996.

6. A. Cypher. EAGER: Programming Repetitive Tasks by Example. In *Proceedings of ACM CHI'91*, pages 33–39, April 1991.

7. J. Lamping and R. Rao. Laying out and Visualizing Large Trees Using a Hyperbolic Space. In *Proceedings of UIST '94*, pages 13–14, November 1994.

8. J. D. Mackinlay, G. G. Robertson, and S. K. Card. The Perspective Wall: Detail and Context Smoothly Integrated. In *Proceedings of ACM CHI'91*, pages 173–179, 1991.

9. D. L. Maulsby, I. H. Witten, and K. A. Kittlitz. Metamouse: Specifying Graphical Procedures by Example. In *Proceedings of SIGGRAPH '89*, volume 23, pages 127–136, July 1989.

10. E. G. Noik. Exploring Large Hyperdocuments: Fisheye Views of Nested Networks. In *ACM Conference on Hypertext and Hypermedia*, pages 14–18, 1993.

11. K. Perlin and D. Fox. Pad: An Alternative Approach to the Computer Interface. In *SIGGRAPH 93 Conference Proceedings*, pages 57–64, 1993.

12. G. G. Robertson and J. D. Mackinlay. The Document Lens. In *Proceedings of UIST '93*, pages 101–108, November 1993.

13. M. Sarkar and M. H. Brown. Graphical Fisheye Views of Graphs. In *Proceedings of ACM CHI'92*, pages 83–91, 1992.

14. M. Sarkar, S. S. Snibbe, O. J. Tversky, and S. P. Reiss. Streching the Rubber Sheet: A Metaphor for Viewing Large Layouts on Small Screens. In *Proceedings of UIST '93*, pages 81–91, November 1993.

15. M. Toyoda, B. Shizuki, S. Takahashi, S. Matsuoka, and E. Shibayama. Supporting Design Patterns in a Visual Parallel Data-flow Programming Environment. In *Proc. 1997 IEEE Symposium on Visual Languages*, pages 76–83, September 1997.

Excentric Labeling:

Dynamic Neighborhood Labeling for Data Visualization

Jean-Daniel Fekete

Ecole des Mines de Nantes

4, rue Alfred Kastler, La Chantrerie

44307 Nantes, France

Jean-Daniel.Fekete@emn.fr

www.emn.fr/fekete

Catherine Plaisant

Human-Computer Interaction Laboratory

UMIACS, University of Maryland

College Park, MD 20742, USA

plaisant@cs.umd.edu

www.cs.umd.edu/hcil

ABSTRACT

The widespread use of information visualization is hampered by the lack of effective labeling techniques. An informal taxonomy of labeling methods is proposed. We then describe "excentric labeling", a new dynamic technique to label a neighborhood of objects located around the cursor. This technique does not intrude into the existing interaction, it is not computationally intensive, and was easily applied to several visualization applications. A pilot study with eight subjects indicates a strong speed benefit over a zoom interface for tasks that involve the exploration of large numbers of objects. Observations and comments from users are presented.

Keywords

Visualization, Label, Dynamic labeling, Evaluation

INTRODUCTION

A major limiting factor to the widespread use of information visualization is the difficulty of labeling information abundant displays. Information visualization uses the powerful human visual abilities to extract meaning from graphical information [1-2]. Color, size, shape position or orientation are mapped to data attributes. This visualization helps users find trends, and spot exceptions or relationships between elements on the display. Experimental studies have been able to show significant task completion time reduction and recall rate improvements when using graphical displays instead of tabular text displays (e.g., [3]) However textual information in the form of labels remains critical in identifying elements of the display. Unfortunately, information visualization systems often lack adequate labeling strategies. Often labels are entirely missing and users have to peck at graphical objects one at a time. Sometimes labels overlap each other to the point of obscuring the data and being less usable; or they are spread out in such a way that the relation between objects and labels becomes ambiguous. The problem becomes acute when the data density increases and the labels are very long.

To address this problem we propose "excentric labeling" as a new dynamic technique to label a neighborhood of objects (Figures 1-3). Because it does not interfere with normal interaction and has a low computational overhead, it can easily be applied to a variety of visualization applications.

The labeling problem is not new. It has been extensively studied for cartographic purposes [4] where printing or report generation is the main purpose of the application. Very few solutions have been proposed to automate the labeling process of interactive applications. In this paper, we propose an informal taxonomy of labeling methods, then describe our excentric labeling technique in detail, discuss its benefits and limitations, and illustrate how it can benefit a variety of applications.

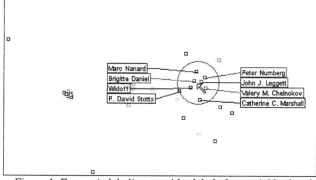

Figure 1: Excentric labeling provides labels for a neighborhood of objects. The focus of the labeling is centered on the cursor position. Labels are updated smoothly as the cursor moves over the display, allowing hundreds of labels to be reviewed in a few seconds. The color of the label border matches the object color.

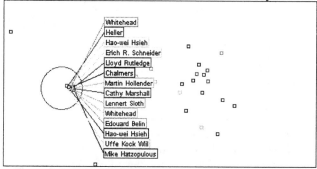

Figure 2: Labels are spread to avoid overlapping, possibly revealing objects clumped together on the display.

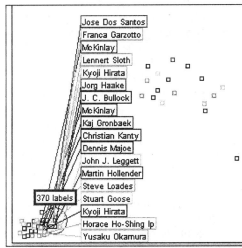

Figure 3: Special algorithms handle border effects (e.g., corners) When objects are too numerous, the total number of objects in the focus area is shown, along with a subset of the labels.

TAXONOMY OF LABELING TECHNIQUES

The labeling challenge can be stated as follows: given a set of graphical objects, find a layout to position all names so that each name (label) is:

1. Readable.
2. Non-ambiguously related to its graphical object.
3. Does not hide any other pertinent information.

Completeness (the labeling of all objects) is desired but not always possible.

Labeling techniques can be classified into two categories: static and dynamic. The goal of static labeling is to visually associate labels with a maximum of (all if possible) graphic objects in the best possible manner. But good static techniques are usually associated with delays not suitable for interactive exploration. Dynamic labeling began with interactive computer graphics and visualization. Two attributes account for the "dynamic" adjective: the set of objects to be labeled can change dynamically, and the number and layout of displayed labels can also change in real time, according to user actions.

Static Techniques

Static techniques have been used for a long time in cartography. Christensen et al., [4] wrote a recent summary of label placement algorithms. Cartography also needs to deal with path labeling and zone labeling, which is less widespread in visualization. We do not address those two issues in this article. But the same algorithms can be used for both cartography and general visualization. Since static techniques have to find "the" best labeling possible, the set of objects has to be carefully chosen to avoid a too high density in objects or labels. In cartography, this is achieved by aggregating some information and forgetting (sampling) others (this process is called "generalization"). This technique could be nicknamed the "label-at-all-cost"

technique since one of the constraints is to label all objects of the display.

For data visualization, a similar process of aggregation can be applied to achieve a reasonable result with static techniques (e.g., aggregation is used in the semantic zooming of Pad++ [5] or LifeLines [6,7]), but the logic of aggregation and sampling is mainly application dependent. Label sampling has been used occasionally [8].

The most common techniques (see Table 1) remain the "No Label" technique, and the "Rapid Label-all" technique which leads to overlaps and data occlusion (e.g., in the hyperbolic browser [9]). Also common is the "Label-What-You-Can" technique in which only labels that fit are displayed; other labels that would overlap or occlude data objects are not shown (e.g., in LifeLines),

Some visualizations avoid the problem completely by making the labels the primary objects. For example WebTOC [10] uses a textual table of contents and places color and size coded bars next to each label.

Dynamic techniques

Dynamic labeling techniques are more varied. The classic infotip or "cursor sensitive balloon label" consists of showing the label of an object right next to the object when the cursor passes over it. The label can also be shown on the side in a fixed window, which is appropriate when labels are very long and structured.

In the "All or Nothing" technique, labels appear when the number of objects on the screen falls below a fixed limit (e.g., 25 for the dynamic query and starfield display of the FilmFinder [11]). This is acceptable when the data can be easily and meaningfully filtered to such a small subset, which is not always the case. Another common strategy is to require zooming until enough space is available to reveal the labels; this requires extensive navigation to see all the labels. This technique can be combined elegantly with the static aggregation technique to progressively reveal more and more details - and refined labels - as the zoom ratio increases.

The overview and detail view combination is an alternative zooming solution [12]. The detail view can also be deformed to spread objects until all labels fit (i.e., in the way of a labeling magic lens [13]). Those last two techniques require either a tool selection or dedicated screen space.

Chalmers et al., proposed dynamic sampling where only one to three labels are displayed, depending on the user's activity. Cleveland [2] describes temporal brushing: labels appear as the cursor passes over the objects (similarly to the infotip), but those labels remain on the screen while new labels are displayed, possibly overlapping older ones.

Type	Technique	Comments/Problems
STATIC	No label	No labels!
	Label-only-when-you-can (i.e. after filtering objects)	Need effective filters. Labels are rarely visible.
	Rapid Label-All	High risk of overlaps or ambiguous linking to objects
	Optimized Label-All	Often slow - may not be possible
	Optimized Label-All with aggregation and sampling	Effective but application dependant- may not be possible
DYNAMIC		
One at a time	Cursor sensitive balloon label	Requires series of precise selection to explore space (slow), cannot reach overlapped objects.
	Cursor Sensitive label in side-window	Same as above. Constant eye movement can be a problem, but avoids occlusion of other objects.
	Temporal brushing (Cleveland)	More labels visible at a time, but overlapping problem.
Global display change	Zoom until labels appear	May require extensive navigation to see many labels (can be effectively combined with semantic zooming, e.g., Pad++)
	Filter until labels appear	May require several filtering to see labels (can be effectively combined with Zooming, e.g., starfields)
Sampling	Dynamic sampling (Chalmers et al.)	Few labels are visible.
Focus + context	Overview and detail view without deformation	Effective when objects are separated enough in the detail view to allow labels to fit (not guaranteed)
	Overview and detail with deformation/transformation (i.e.fisheye or magic lenses)	Deformation might allow enough room for labels to fit. (not guaranteed). May require tool or mode to be selected.
	Global deformation of space (e.g., Hyperbolic Browser)	Requires intensive navigation and dexterity to rapidly deform the space and reveal all labels (e.g., by fanning the space).
	Labeling of objects in focus area (excentric labeling)	Spreads overlapping labels, and align them. Can be disorienting at first. Need to learn to stop cursor to better read labels.

Table 1: Taxonomy of labeling techniques

EXCENTRIC LABELING

Excentric labeling is a dynamic technique of neighborhood labeling for data visualization (Figures 1-3). When the cursor stays more than one second over an area where objects are available, all labels in the neighborhood of the cursor are shown without overlap, and aligned to facilitate reading. A circle centered on the position of the cursor defines the neighborhood or focus region. A line connects each label to the corresponding object. The style of the lines matches the object attributes (e.g., color). The text of the label always appears in black on a white background for better readability. Once the excentric labels are displayed, users can move the cursor around the window and the excentric labels are updated dynamically. Excentric labeling stops either when an interaction is started (e.g., a mouse click) or the user moves the cursor quickly to leave the focus region. This labeling technique does not require the use of a special interface tool. Labels are readable (non-overlapping and aligned), they are non-ambiguously related to their graphical objects and they don't hide any information inside the user's focus region.

Algorithm and Variations

To compute the layout of labels, we experimented with several variants of the following algorithm:

1. Extract each label and position for interesting graphic objects in the focus region.
2. Compute an initial position.
3. Compute an ordering.
4. Assign the labels to either a right or left set.
5. Stack the left and right labels according to their order.
6. Minimize the vertical distance of each set from the computed initial position.
7. Add lines to connect the labels to their related graphic object.

So far, we have used three main variations of this algorithm: non-crossing lines labeling, vertically coherent labeling and horizontally coherent labeling (the last two can be combined). Each uses a different method to compute the initial position, the ordering, to assign the labels to the stacks and to join the labels to their related graphic objects.

Non-Crossing Lines Labeling – Radial Labeling

The non-crossing lines labeling layout (Figure 4) avoids line crossings but does not maintain the vertical or horizontal ordering of labels. This technique facilitates the task of tracing the label back to the corresponding object. It can be used in cartography-like applications where ordering is unimportant. The initial position on the circle (step 2 of previous section) is computed with a radial projecting onto the circumference of the focus circle[1]. It is always possible to join the object to the circumference

---

[1] The name « excentric » comes from this technique which was the first implemented. The name is meant to evoke the center origin of the lines and the unconventional look of the widget. It is an accepted old spelling of eccentric, and close to the French spelling « excentrique ».

without crossing another radial spoke (but two radii - or spokes- may overlap). Then, we order spokes in counter-clockwise order starting at the top (step 3). The left set is filled with labels from the top to the bottom and the right set is filled with the rest.

Labels are left justified and regularly spaced vertically. We maintain a constant margin between the left and right label blocks and the focus circle to draw the connecting lines. For the left part, three lines are used to connect objects to their label: from the object to the position on the circumference, then to the left margin, and to the right side of the label box. This third segment is kept as small as possible for compactness, therefore barely visible in Figure 4, except for the bottom-left label. For the right labels, only two lines are used from the object to the initial position to the left of the label. The margins contain the lines between the circumference and the labels.

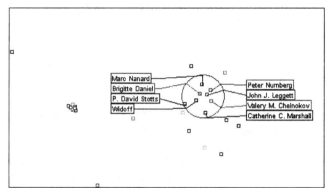

Figure 4: This figure shows the same data as in Figure 1 but using the non-crossing - or radial - algorithm.

Vertically Coherent Labeling

When the vertical ordering of graphic objects has a important meaning we use a variant algorithm that does not avoid line crossing but maintains the relative vertical order of labels. This will be appropriate for most data visualization, for example in the starfield application FilmFinder [11], films can be sorted by attributes like popularity or length, therefore labels should probably be ordered by the same attribute. Instead of computing the initial position in step 2 by projecting the labels radially to the circumference, we start at the actual Y position of the object. The rest of the algorithm is exactly the same. Figure 1 and 2 shows examples using the vertically coherent algorithm. We believe that the vertically coherent algorithm is the best default. Crossing can occur but we found that moving slightly the cursor position animates the label connecting lines and helps find the correspondence between objects and their labels.

Horizontally Coherent Labeling

When the horizontal ordering of graphic objects has a special meaning, we further modify the algorithm in step 5. Instead of left justifying the labels, we move them horizontally so that they follow the same ordering as the graphic objects, as in Figure 5. This algorithm should be

used with caution as it was found confusing by several of our reviewers.

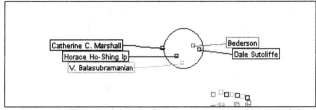

Figure 5: Here the labels order respect the Y ordering and the indentation of the labels reflects the X ordering of the objects, for example Catherine Marshall is the furthest left object in the focus circle so the label is also the furthest left.

Dealing with window boundaries

When the focus region is near the window boundaries, chances are that the label positions computed by the previous algorithms will fall outside of the window and the labels appear truncated (e.g., the first characters of the left stack labels would not be visible when the cursor is on the left side of the window).

To deal with window boundaries the following rules are applied. If some labels are cut on the left stack, then move them to the right stack (symmetric for the right side.) When labels become hidden on the upper part of the stack (i.e., near the upper boundary), move them down (symmetric for the bottom). Combining those rules takes care of the corners of the window (Figure 6).

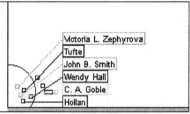

Figure 6: When the focus is close to the window boundaries, labels are moved so that they always fall inside the window.

DISCUSSION

Excentric labeling seem to fill a gap in information visualization techniques by allowing the exploration of hundreds of object labels in dense visualization screens in a matter of seconds. Many labels can be shown at once (probably around 20 at a time is optimum.) They are quite readable and can be ordered in a meaningful way. Links between objects and labels remain apparent, especially when matching color is used. The technique is simple and computationally inexpensive enough to allow for rapid exploration. Of course, these algorithms don't solve all the problems that may occur when labeling, and excentric labeling is most likely to be used in conjunction with other techniques (e.g., zooming).

Dealing with too many labels

We estimate that about 20-30 excentric labels are best displayed at a time, depending on the screen size. When more objects fall in the focus region, the screen becomes filled by labels and there is often no way to avoid that some labels fall outside the window. We implemented two "fallback" strategies: (1) showing the number of items in the focus region, and (2) showing a subset of those labels in addition to the number of objects (see Figure 3). The sample could be chosen randomly or by using the closest objects to the focus point. Although not entirely satisfactory, this method is a major improvement over the usual method of showing no labels at all, a pile of overlapping labels, or a subset of labels without mention of the missing ones.

The dynamic update of this object counts allow a rapid exploration of the data density on the screen. Of course, (this is data visualization after all) the number of objects should also been be represented graphically by changing the font or box size to reflect the magnitude of the number of objects. Showing the density and clustering of objects can also be shown using a glowing colored halo [14].

Dealing with long labels

Labels can be so long that they just don't fit on either side of the focus point. There is no generic way to deal with this problem but truncation is likely to be the most useful method. Depending on the application, labels may be truncated on the right, or on the left (e.g., when the labels are web addresses), or they may be truncated following special algorithms. Some applications may provide a long and a short label to use as a substitute when needed (e.g., Acronyms). Using smaller fonts for long labels might help in some cases. If long lines occur infrequently, breaking long labels in multiple lines is also possible.

Limiting discontinuities

One of the drawback of the dymamic aspect of excentric labeling is that the placement of an object's label will vary while the cursor is moving around the object. This is needed to allow new labels to be added when the focus area covers more objects, but leads to discontinuities in the placement of labels. For example, when the cursor moves from the left side of an object to its right side, the label will move from the right to the left stack. This effect is actually useful to confirm the exact position of a label but might be found confusing by first time users. We found that discontinuties were more common with the non-crossing algorithm than the Y coherent algorithm, which we therefore favor, despite the risk of lines crossing.

The evaluation section shows how users quickly learned to avoid this problem by hopping from place to place instead of continuously move the cursor.

Faciliting selection of objects

Excentric labeling does not interfere with the normal selection of objects but since it can reveal labels of objects that are hidden, it makes sense to use excentric labels as selection menus. Pressing a control key – or the right mouse "menu" button if it is not used in the application, can temporarily "freeze" the excentric labeling, free the cursor, and allow users to select any of the labels instead.

Furthermore, if objects are so numerous that only a subset is shown with the excentric labels, the temporary menu can become a scrolling list, guarantying access to all objects in the focus area.

OTHER OPTIONS TO CONSIDER

Depending on the application, several options might be considered:

- Changing the size and shape of the focus area can be allowed, either at the user's initiative, or dynamically as a function of the label density (with the condition that the automatic size change would be very noticeable);

- When too many items are in the focus area, excentric labels can show not only the number of objects but also a glyph or bar chart summarizing the contents of the area (e.g., showing the color distribution of the points in the focus).

- Labels can inherit more graphic attributes from the objects they reference, as is often done in cartography. We show examples where the color of the label border matches the object's color. But text font size, style or color can also be used if clear coding conventions exist and if adequate readability is preserved.

USE WITHIN EXISTING VISUALIZATION APPLICATIONS

We have implemented excentric labels within three different applications: a Java version of starfield display/dynamic query visualization [11] (Figure 7), a Java implementation of LifeLines [6-7] (Figure 9), and a map applet to be used for searching people in a building. The addition of excentric labeling to the first two applications was done in a few hours. The last program was built from scratch as an evaluation tool.

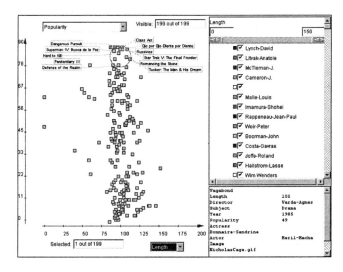

Figure 7: Excentric labeling seemed effective in a Java implementation of a starfield/dynamic query environment similar to the FilmFinder [11], or the Spotfire commercial product derived from it (www.spotfire.com). Excentric labeling provides a rapid way to review the names of the data objects and to fathom the density of the overlapping areas.

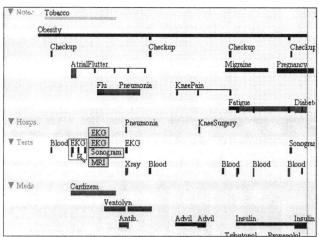

Figure 8: In LifeLines,[6-7] excentric labeling can be useful as it guarantees that all events in the focus area are labeled, even if events overlap. Chronological order is best for ordering labels, reinforced by color coding. In this example, the focus area is a small rectangle (i.e. a time range), only one column is used and there are no connecting lines. The label background is yellow to make them more visible.

EVALUATION

Excentric labeling is not meant to replace other labeling techniques but to complement them. Depending on the task, users may chose to use one or another technique. For example, to see the label of a single object, the infotip works well. To review in detail an area of the screen, zooming will be best to increase the resolution of the objects and also reveal more labels. But to quickly gain an understanding or the composition of one or several areas of interest, the infotip become tedious, the zoom may never reveal overlapping objects and the deformations are potentially disorienting as all objects have to move. In those conditions the excentric labels might become a useful addition. On the other hand it is a new feature that requires time to learn and may be found distractive.

Comparing labeling techniques is a challenge because of the many parameters involved. Screen size, zooming ratio, zooming speed, size of the excentric focus area, deformation rate, etc. would have a strong influence on the usefulness of the techniques. Making them all variables of a giant experiment would not be practical. Therefore we chose to focus our evaluation on a series of usability observations linked to an informal experiment in which we compare excentric labeling with a "virtual" instantaneous zoom. We choose to compare with a zoom because it is a very commonly used general technique.

We used the application shown in Figure 9. The map of a building is displayed with names assigned randomly to offices. Subjects have to determine if a given name appears next to one of three red dots shown on the map. This task simulates a situation where users have already identified areas of interest (e.g., areas close to both vending machines and printers, or close to the secretaries offices) and they are now looking for an empty space or someone

they know close to those points. A similar situation might be users looking at the names of objects in clusters revealed on visualization.

The questions asked were of the form: "is <the name> in the neighborhood of one of the red dots?" Subjects reply by selecting "yes" or "no". Subjects were told that the names either didn't exist at all, or were within one or two offices from the dots. The technique was quickly demo-ed, users could practice with four tasks and ask questions before the timed part of the experiment started. The time to perform each task and the number of errors were recorded. The total test lasted about 30 minutes per subject.

Subjects using excentric labels (Figure 9) had to move the cursor over and around each highlighted point and read the labels. Subjects using the zooming interface had to move the cursor over each highlighted point, left click to zoom until they can read the labels (2 or 3 zoom operations), right click to zoom back out and/or pan to the next point. The zoom was reset before the next task started.

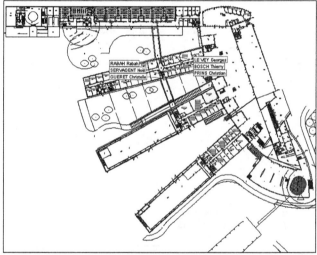

Figure 9: Map with a section of the building dynamically labeled. This application is being used to compare excentric labeling with a plain zooming interface when performing tasks that require the review of many labels.

In the Java application a zoom or pan takes about 3/4 seconds to redraw, this lead to a four time speed advantage for the excentric labels over the zoom in our first pilot test, and was dependant on the speed of the CPU. Our redraw time is representative of many zooming interfaces, but in order to avoid any obvious bias in favor of the excentric labeling, we chose to run the final test ignoring all redraw time, i.e. the clock was stopped during all redraws in the zooming interface version. We could have made the excentric labeling technique better for the task by making the focus area larger to "fit" the region users needed to search but we deliberately made it smaller, so that we could observe users browsing by having to move the cursor around the area. Overall we tried to simulate a fair and interesting situation to observe and verify the existence of speed improvements.

Eight subjects performed eight tasks for each interface. Task sets and order was counterbalanced. For six of the eight tasks the name could be found near the dots, while for the two other tasks, the name didn't exist.

Results

For the six "bounded" tasks where the name could be found there was about a 60% speed advantage for the excentric labels over the "virtual instantaneous zoom". The average time to complete the six tasks was significantly faster ($p<0,005$) with excentric labeling than with the virtual instantaneous zoom [Figure 10]. Of course the advantage would have been even much larger if we had counted the delays of the zooms and pans (an average of 10 per task, so 30 to 60 sec. additional time).

For the tasks where the searched name did not exist, there was so much variation among the eight subjects that a conclusion could not be made in this small study. Some users gave up rapidly while other searched for a long time. Both interfaces had a small number of errors (2 for zoom, 3 for excentric).

	Excentric Labels	Virtual Instantaneous Zoom	*Zoom with delays (estimated)*
Mean time to complete the six tasks (in sec.)	69.7	113.3	*140-170 function of CPU speed & application*
Standard Deviation	7.9	21.1	
Total # errors	3	2	

Figure 10a: Comparison of mean time for eight users to complete the tasks (see Figure 10b)

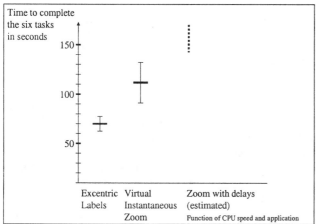

Figure 10b: Comparison of mean time for eight users to complete the 6 tasks where the names were found, for excentric labels, and for a virtual instantaneous zoom with all redraw delays removed. Any delay in zooming and panning would further increase the effect in favor of excentric labeling.

In addition to this measured effect, more was learned about the benefits and drawbacks of the interfaces by observing the eight users performing the hundred tasks of the entire test, as well as other users who helped polish the procedure by running earlier tests.

- We observed that all users quickly learned to use the excentric labels. Users would at first move the cursor a lot and seem annoyed by the continuous updates of the labels while they moved. By the end of the practice most had already stabilized their cursor, hopping in discrete steps around the red dots (we did not give specific instructions about this in the demo, letting users finds the best way to use the interface). A careful user could cover the search area around a dot in 2 or 3 steps, others would review more sets of labels by stopping in more places. Several users said that they realized they were looking at the same labels several times.

- Unsurprisingly, we observed that with the zoom interface users (who were all computer users) were already comfortable with the zoom technique. Many complained about the number of operations required to complete the tasks. Most users got lost at least once while panning and had to zoom out to find the red dots they had lost. They often over-zoomed and had to back up. On the other hand, when correctly zoomed and centered there were no problems.

Users were encouraged to "think-aloud" but generated comments only during the training phase and following the test. Comments tell the stories:

- Zoom: "I feel comfortable doing that, it's like yahoo's maps", "Where is that dot? I thought I would find it by panning there." "Oops, wrong way", "Once I am zoomed I feel confident I am looking at the right offices", "All that zooming is tiring".

- Excentric: "Ho, I like that", "It's hard to know what changed when I move the cursor". "It's better to stop moving". "I probably look at too many labels". "It would be nice if the neighborhood I am searching fit entirely in the circle". "I like the way it shows me that there are so many people here while I could not tell by just looking at the map".

- One user nicely compared the techniques by saying: "With the zoom I am confident that I read only the names in the right offices, but with the excentric label I can more easily go re-check the previous dots. We did observe that, in the tasks where the searched name did not exist, users went back to check the dots with excentric labels, while fewer did it with the zoom, or it took them a very long time.

CONCLUSION

Despite the numerous techniques found in visualization systems to label the graphical objects of the display, labeling remains a challenging problem for information visualization. We believe that excentric labeling provides a novel way for users to rapidly explore objects descriptions once patterns have been found in the display and effectively extract meaning from information visualization. Early evaluation results are promising. Users rapidly learn to use the excentric labels and stop the cursor to read the labels. A significant speed improvement was measured over a zoom interface for tasks requiring the rapid review of large numbers of labels. Finally we have demonstrated that the technique can easily be combined with a variety of applications, making excentric labels a promising new feature for information visualization environments.

ACKNOWLEDGEMENT

This work was started while Jean-Daniel Fekete visited the University of Maryland during the summer 1998. We thank all members of the HCIL lab for their constructive feedback, especially Julia Li for her initial research of the labeling problem and implementation in LifeLines, and Ben Shneiderman for suggesting the main-axis projection. David Doermann nicely allowed us to use his Java implementation of the starfield/dynamic query environment. This work was supported in part by IBM through the Shared University Research (SUR) program.

DEMONSTRATION

Excentric labeling is implemented in Java. A demo program can be found at **http://www.cs.umd.edu/hcil/excentric**

REFERENCES

1. Card, S, Mackinlay, J., and Shneiderman, Ben, *Readings in Information Visualization: Using Vision to Think*, Morgan Kaufmann Publishers, San Francisco, 1999

2. Cleveland, William, *Visualizing Data,* Hobart Press, Summit, NJ (1993).

3. Lindwarm-Alonso D., Rose, A., Plaisant, C., and Norman, K., Viewing personal history records: A comparison of tabular format and graphical presentation using LifeLines, *Behaviour & Information Technology*, *17*, 5, (1998) 249-262.

4. Christensen J., Marks J., Shieber S. Labeling point features on map and diagrams, to appear in ACM *Transactions on Graphics*.

5. Bederson, Ben B. and Hollan, James D., PAD++: A zooming graphical user interface for exploring alternate interface physics, *Proceedings of UIST '94* (1994), 17-27.

6. Plaisant, Catherine, Rose, Anne, Milash, Brett, Widoff, Seth, and Shneiderman, Ben, LifeLines: Visualizing personal histories, *Proc. of ACM CHI96 Conference: Human Factors in Computing Systems*, ACM, New York, NY (1996), 221-227, 518.

7. Plaisant, C., Mushlin, R., Snyder, A., Li, J., Heller, D., and Shneiderman, B.(1998), LifeLines: Using visualization to enhance navigation and analysis of patient records, *Proc. of 1998 American Medical Informatics Association Annual Fall Symposium* (1998), 76-80, AMIA, Bethesda, MD.

8. Chalmers M., Ingram R. & Pfranger C., Adding imageability features to information displays, *Proc. UIST'96*, 33-39, ACM.

9. Lamping, John, Rao, Ramana, and Pirolli, Peter, A focus + context technique based on hyperbolic geometry for visualizing large hierarchies, *Proc. of ACM CHI'95 Conference: Human Factors in Computing Systems*, ACM, New York, NY (1995), 401-408.

10. Nation, D. A., Plaisant, C., Marchionini, G., Komlodi, A., Visualizing websites using a hierarchical table of contents browser: WebTOC, *Proc. 3rd Conference on Human Factors and the Web*, Denver, CO (June 1997).

11. Ahlberg, Christopher and Shneiderman, Ben, Visual information seeking: Tight coupling of dynamic query filters with starfield displays, *Proc. CHI'94 Conference: Human Factors in Computing Systems*, ACM, New York, NY (1994), 313-321 + color plates.

12. Plaisant, C., Carr, D., and Shneiderman, B., Image-browser taxonomy and guidelines for designers, *IEEE Software 12*, 2 (March 1995), 21-32.

13. Stone, M., Fishkin, K., Bier, E., The moveable filter as a user interface, Proc. CHI'94, 306-312 (1994) ACM New York.

14. Hoffmann, C, Kim, Y, Winkler, R., Walrath, J, Emmerman, P., Visualization for situation awareness. Proc. of the Workshop on New Paradigms in Information Visualization and Manipulation (NPIV'98 in conjunction with ACM CIKM'98) also at http://www.cs.umbc.edu/cikm/npiv

Embodiment in Conversational Interfaces: Rea

J. Cassell, T. Bickmore, M. Billinghurst, L. Campbell, K. Chang, H. Vilhjálmsson, H. Yan

Gesture and Narrative Language Group

MIT Media Laboratory

E15-315

20 Ames St, Cambridge, Massachusetts

+1 617 253 4899

{justine, bickmore, markb, elwin, tetrion, hannes, yanhao}@media.mit.edu

ABSTRACT

In this paper, we argue for *embodied conversational characters* as the logical extension of the metaphor of human – computer interaction as a conversation. We argue that the only way to fully model the richness of human face-to-face communication is to rely on conversational analysis that describes sets of conversational behaviors as fulfilling conversational functions, both interactional and propositional. We demonstrate how to implement this approach in Rea, an embodied conversational agent that is capable of both multimodal input understanding and output generation in a limited application domain. Rea supports both social and task-oriented dialogue. We discuss issues that need to be addressed in creating embodied conversational agents, and describe the architecture of the Rea interface.

Keywords

Conversational Characters, Multimodal Input, Intelligent Agents, Multimodal Output

INTRODUCTION

The metaphor of face-to-face conversation has been successfully applied to human-interface design for quite some time. One of the early descriptions of this metaphor gave a list of features of face-to-face conversation that could be fruitfully applied to HCI, including mixed initiative, non-verbal communication, sense of presence, rules for transfer of control, and so forth [1]. However, although these features have gained widespread recognition, human – computer conversation has never become more than a metaphor. That is, designers have not taken the metaphor seriously in such a way as to design a computer that could hold up its end of the conversation.

In the current paper we argue that while this metaphor has been useful to HCI, its use to date has been just that; a metaphor. We believe that interfaces that are truly conversational have the promise of being more intuitive to learn, more resistant to communication breakdown, and more functional in high *noise* environments. Therefore, we propose to leverage the full breadth and power of human conversational competency by imbuing the computer with all of the conversational skills that humans have; to whit, the ability to use the face, hands, and melody of the voice to regulate the process of conversation, as well as the ability to use verbal and nonverbal means to contribute content to the ongoing conversation.

In addition, we argue that the only way to accomplish such a goal of *embodying* the interface is to implement a model of *conversational function*. This means that particular conversational behaviors (such as head nods and expressions of agreement) are generated and understood in terms of the functions that they fulfill in the ongoing conversation (such as 'take turn', 'contribute new information').

To provide a practical example of this approach, we present Rea, an embodied conversational agent whose verbal and nonverbal behaviors are designed in terms of conversational functions. Rea is not designed with the metaphor of the interface as a conversation, but actually implements the social, linguistic, and psychological conventions of conversation. Rea differs from other dialogue systems, and other conversational agents in three ways:

- Rea has a human-like body, and uses her body in human-like ways during the conversation. That is, she uses eye gaze, body posture, hand gestures, and facial displays to organize and regulate the conversation.

- The underlying approach to conversational understanding and generation in Rea is based on discourse functions. Thus, each of the users' inputs are interpreted in terms of their conversational function and responses are generated according to the desired function to be fulfilled. Such models have been described for other conversational systems: for example Brennan and Hulteen describe a general framework for applying conversational theory to speech interfaces [7]. Our work extends this by developing a conversational model that that relies on the function of non-verbal behaviors as well as speech, and that makes explicit the interactional and propositional contribution of these conversational behaviors.

- Rea is being designed to respond to visual, audio and speech cues normally used in face to face conversation, such as speech, shifts in gaze, gesture, and non-speech audio (feedback sounds). She is being designed to generate these cues, ensuring a full symmetry between input and output modalities. This is a step towards enabling Rea to participate on more of an equal footing with the user in a human-computer conversation.

Developing an embodied conversational agent is a complex endeavor that draws on many fields. We begin this paper by describing several motivations for building embodied conversational agents. We then review past work in relevant HCI areas, and in several theories of conversation. Examination of these theories leads us to believe that a conversational function approach may be the most appropriate for a conversational agent. We then present Rea, and describe how we have begun to implement conversational function in an embodied interface agent.

Motivation

Embodied conversational agents may be defined as those that have the same properties as humans in face-to-face conversation, including:

- The ability to recognize and respond to verbal and non-verbal input
- The ability to generate verbal and non-verbal output.
- The use of conversational functions such as turn taking, feedback, and repair mechanisms.
- A performance model that allows contributions whose role is to negotiate conversational process, as well as contributions whose role is to contribute new propositions to the discourse.

There are a number of motivations for developing interfaces with these attributes, including:

Intuitiveness. Conversation is an intrinsically human skill that is learned over years of development and is practiced daily. Conversational interfaces provide an intuitive paradigm for interaction, since the user is not required to learn new skills.

Redundancy and Modality Switching: Embodied conversational interfaces support redundancy and complementarity between input modes. This allows the user and system to increase reliability by conveying information in more than one modality, and to increase expressiveness by using each modality for the type of expression it is most suited to.

The Social Nature of the Interaction. Whether or not computers look human, people attribute to them human-like properties such as friendliness, or cooperativeness [22]. An embodied conversational interface can take advantage of this and prompt the user to naturally engage the computer in human-like conversation. If the interface is well-designed to reply to such conversation, the interaction may be improved

As we shall show in the next section, there has been significant research in the areas of conversational analysis and multimodal interfaces. However there has been little work in the recognition and use of conversational cues for conversational interfaces, or the development of computational conversational models that support non-speech input and output. A prime motivation for our work is the belief that effective embodied conversational interfaces cannot be built without an understanding of verbal and non-verbal conversational cues, and their function in conversation.

RELATED WORK

There are many challenges that must be overcome before embodied conversational interfaces reach their full potential. These range from low-level issues such as capturing user input to high level problems such as agent planning and dialogue generation. In this section we review related work in three areas; multimodal interfaces, models of conversation, and conversational agent interfaces.

Multimodal Interfaces

Embodied conversational agents are similar to *multimodal* systems in that information from several modalities must be integrated into one representation of speaker intention. One of the first multimodal systems was *Put-That-There*, developed by Bolt, Schmandt and their colleagues [5]. *Put That There* used speech recognition and a six-degree-of-freedom space sensing device to gather input from a user's speech and the location of a cursor on a wall-sized display, allowing for simple deictic reference to visible entities. More recently, several systems have built on this early work. Koons allowed users to maneuver around a two-dimensional map using spoken commands, deictic hand gestures, and eye gaze [16]. In this system, nested frames were employed to gather and combine information from the different modalities. As in Put-that-There, speech drove the analysis of the gesture: if information is *missing* from speech, then the system will search for the missing information in the gestures and/or gaze. Time stamps unite the actions in the different modalities into a coherent picture. Wahlster used a similar method, also depending on the linguistic input to guide the interpretation of the other modalities [27]. Bolt and Herranz described a system that allows a user to manipulate graphics with two-handed semi-iconic gesture [6]. Using a cutoff point and time stamping, motions can be selected that relate to the intended movement mentioned in speech. Sparrell used a scheme based on stop-motion analysis: whenever there is a significant stop or slowdown in the motion of the user's hand, then the preceding motion segment is grouped and analyzed for features such as finger posture and hand position [23]. In all of these systems interpretation is not carried out until the user has finished the utterance.

Johnston describes an approach to understanding of user input based on unification across grammars that can express input from multiple modalities[14]. While the system does treat modalities equally (vs. filling in utterance-based forms) it is still based on a mapping between combinations of specific gestures and utterances on the one hand, and user intentions (commands) on the other hand. In addition, all behaviors are treated as propositional -- none of them control the envelope of the user-computer interaction.

Although these works are primarily command-based rather than conversational, there are some lessons we can learn from them, such as the importance of modeling the user and developing interfaces which use existing deeply ingrained conversational behaviors [21]. They also highlight areas of potential difficulty, such as the fact that humans do not naturally use gesture according to a grammar with standards of form or function, and the problem of recognition errors in speech and gesture.

Missing from these systems is a concept of non-verbal function with respect to conversational function. That is, in the systems reviewed thus far, there is no discourse structure over the sentence (no notion of "speaking turn" or "information structure" [24]). Therefore the role of gesture and facial expression cannot be analyzed at more than a sentence-constituent-replacement level. Gestures are only analyzed as support for referring expressions (gestures provide the referent for demonstratives such as "that"). What is needed is a discourse structure that can take into account why one uses a verbal or nonverbal device in a particular situation, and a conversational structure that can account for how non-verbal behaviors function in conversation regulation – such as turn-taking – as well as conversational content.

Conversational Models

Even though conversation is considered an orderly event, governed by rules, no two conversations look exactly the same and the set of behaviors exhibited differs from person to person and from conversation to conversation. Therefore to successfully build a model of how conversation works, one can not refer to surface features, or *conversational behaviors* alone. Instead, the emphasis has to be on identifying the fundamental phases and high level structural elements that make up a conversation. These elements are then described in terms of their role or *function* in the exchange. Typical discourse functions include *conversation invitation, turn taking, providing feedback, contrast and emphasis*, and *breaking away* [10][15].

It is important to realize that each of these functions can be realized in several different manners. The form we give to a particular discourse function depends on, among other things, current availability of modalities, type of conversation, cultural patterns and personal style. For example to emphasize a point one can strike a fist into the table, nod the head, raise the eyebrows, apply rising intonation or construct some combination of these. In a different context these behaviors may carry a different meaning, for example a head nod can indicate back-channel feedback or a salutation rather than emphasis.

Despite the fact that different behaviors may fulfill the same function, it is striking the extent to which such non-verbal behaviors coordinate and regulate conversation. It is clear that through gaze, eyebrow raises and head nods both speakers and listeners collaborate in the construction of synchronized turns, and efficient conversation. In this way, these non-verbal behaviors participate in *grounding* the conversation [11], and fill the functions that Brennan &

Hulteen (1995) suggest are needed for more robust speech interfaces [7].

An important aspect of the grounding of a conversation is evidence of understanding [11]. This includes means such as paraverbals ("huh?", "Uh-huh!") and other back channel feedback. A conversational model that uses both positive and negative feedback enables an agent to recognize a misunderstanding and initiate the appropriate repair mechanisms.

To further clarify these types of roles fulfilled by discourse behaviors, the contribution to the conversation can be divided into *propositional information* and *interactional information*. Propositional information corresponds to the content of the conversation. This includes meaningful speech as well as hand gestures and intonation used to complement or elaborate upon the speech content (gestures that indicate size in the sentence "it was *this* big" or rising intonation that indicates a question with the sentence "you went to the store"). Interactional information consists of cues that regulate the conversational process and includes a range of nonverbal behaviors (quick head nods to indicate that one is following) as well as regulatory speech ("huh?", "do go on").

In short, the interactional discourse functions are responsible for creating and maintaining an open channel of communication between the participants, while propositional functions shape the actual content.

Although the way in which conversation incorporates speech and other movements of the body has been studied for some time, there have been few attempts by the engineering community to develop embodied computer interfaces based on this understanding. On the contrary, embodied conversational characters have, for the most part been built with hardwired associations between verbal and non-verbal conversational behaviors, without a clear flexible notion of conversational function underlying those behaviors. In interfaces of this sort, there is no possibility for one modality to take over for another, or the two modalities to autonomously generate complementary information. Thus, a primary goal of our work is to map multiple modalities onto discourse functions, both for input and output. Input events in different modalities may be mapped onto the same discourse function, while in different conversational states the same function may lead to different conversational behaviors, based on state, as well as the availability of input and output modalities.

Embodied Conversational Interfaces

Other researchers have built embodied conversational agents, with varying degrees of conversational ability. Ball et al. are building an embodied conversational interface that will eventually integrate spoken language input, a conversational dialogue manager, reactive 3D animation, and recorded speech output [3]. Each successive iteration of their computer character has made significant strides in the use of these different aspects of an embodied dialogue system. Although their current system uses a tightly constrained grammar for NLP and a small set of pre-recorded utterances that their character can utter, it is expected that their system will become more generative in the near future. Their embodiment takes the form of a parrot. This has allowed them to simulate gross "wing gestures" (such as cupping a wing to one ear when the parrot has not understood a user's request) and facial displays (scrunched brows as the parrot finds an answer to a question). The parrot's output, however, is represented as a set of conversational behaviors, rather than a set of conversational functions. Therefore, modalities cannot share the expressive load, or pick up the slack for one another in case of noise, or in the case of one modality not being available. Nor can any of the modalities regulate a conversation with the user, since user interactional behaviors cannot be perceived or responded to.

Loyall and Bates build engaging characters that allow the viewer to suspend disbelief long enough to interact in interesting ways with the character, or to be engaged by the character's interactions with another computer character [17]. Associating natural language with non-verbal behaviors is one way of giving their characters believability. In our work, the causality is somewhat the opposite: we build characters that are believable enough to allow the use of language to be human-like. That is, we believe that the use of gesture and facial displays does make the characters life-like and therefore believable, but these communicative behaviors also play integral roles in enriching the dialogue, and regulating the process of the conversation. It is these latter functions that are most important to us. In addition, like Ball et al., the Oz group has chosen a very non-human computer character—Woggles, which look like marbles with eyes. Researchers such as Ball and Bates argue that humanoid characters raise users' expectations beyond what can be sustained by interactive systems and therefore should be avoided. We argue the opposite, that humanoid interface agents do indeed raise users' expectations . . . up to what they expect from humans, and therefore lower their difficulty in interacting with the computer, which is otherwise for them an unfamiliar interlocutor (as is a marble, as well).

Noma & Badler have created a virtual human weatherman, based on the *Jack* human figure animation system [20]. In order to allow the weatherman to gesture, they assembled a library of presentation gestures culled from books on public speaking, and allowed authors to embed those gestures as commands in text that will be sent to a speech-to text system. This is a useful step toward the creation of presentation agents of all sorts, but does not deal with the autonomous generation of non-verbal behaviors in conjunction with speech. Other efforts along these lines include André et al. [1] and Beskow and McGlashan [4].

The work of Thórisson provides a good first example of how discourse and non-verbal function might be paired in a conversational multimodal interface [26]. In this work the main emphasis was the development of a multi-layer multimodal architecture that could support fluid face-to-face dialogue between a human and graphical agent. The agent, Gandalf, was capable of discussing a graphical model of the solar system in an educational application. Gandalf recognized and displayed interactional information such as

head orientation, simple pointing and beat gestures and canned speech events. In this way it was able to perceive and generate turn-taking and back channel behaviors that lead to a more natural conversational interaction.

However, Gandalf had limited ability to recognize and generate propositional information, such as providing correct intonation for speech emphasis on speech output, or a content-carrying gesture with speech. "Animated Conversation" [8] was a system that automatically generated context-appropriate gestures, facial movements and intonational patterns. In this case the challenge was to generate conversation between two artificial agents and the emphasis was on the production of non-verbal propositional behaviors that emphasized and reinforced the content of speech. Since there was no interaction with a real user, the interactional information was very limited, and not reactive (although some interactional types of face and head movements, such as nods, were generated).

Rea is an attempt to develop an agent with both propositional and interactional understanding and generation, which can interact with the user in real time. As such it combines elements of the Gandalf and Animated Agents projects into a single interface and moves towards overcoming the limitations of each. In the next section we describe interaction with the Rea agent and its implementation.

REA: AN EMBODIED CONVERSATIONAL AGENT

The Rea Interface

Rea ("Real Estate Agent") is a computer generated humanoid that has an articulated graphical body, can sense the user passively through cameras and audio input, and is capable of speech with intonation, facial display, and gestural output (Figure 1). The system currently consists of a large projection screen on which Rea is displayed and in front of which the user stands. Two cameras mounted on top of the projection screen track the user's head and hand positions in space. Users wear a microphone for capturing speech input. A single SGI Octane computer runs the graphics and conversation engine of Rea, while several other computers manage the speech recognition and generation and image processing.

Figure 1. User Interacting with Rea

A Sample Interaction

Rea's domain of expertise is real estate and she acts as a real estate agent showing users the features of various models of houses that appear on-screen behind her. The following is a excerpt from a sample interaction:

Lee approaches the projection screen. Rea is currently turned side on and is idly gazing about. As the user moves within range of the cameras, Rea turns to face him and says "Hello, my name is Rea, what's your name?"

"Lee"

"Hello Lee would you like to see a house?" Rea says with rising intonation at the end of the question.

"That would be great"

A picture of a house appears on-screen behind Rea.

"This is a nice Victorian on a large lot" Rea says gesturing towards the house. "It has two bedrooms and a large kitchen with.."

"Wait, tell me about the bedrooms" Lee says interrupting Rea by looking at her and gesturing with his hands while speaking.

"The master bedroom is furnished with a four poster bed, while the smaller room could be used for a children's bedroom or guest room. Do you want to see the master bedroom?".

"Sure, show me the master bedroom". Lee says, overlapping with Rea.

"I'm sorry, I didn't quite catch that, can you please repeat what you said", Rea say.

And the house tour continues...

Rea is designed to conduct a mixed initiative conversation, pursuing the goal of describing the features of a house that fits the user's requirements while also responding to the users' verbal and non-verbal input that may lead in new directions. When the user makes cues typically associated with turn taking behavior such as gesturing, Rea allows herself to be interrupted, and then takes the turn again when she is able. She is able to initiate conversational repair when she misunderstands what the user says, and can generate combined voice and gestural output. For the moment, Rea's responses are generated from an Eliza-like engine that mirrors features of the user's last utterance [28], but efforts are currently underway to implement an incremental natural language and gesture generation engine, along the lines of [8].

In order to carry on natural conversation of this sort, Rea uses a conversational model that supports multimodal input and output as constituents of conversational functions. That is, input and output is interpreted and generated based on the discourse functions it serves. The multimodal conversational model and the underlying Rea architecture are discussed in the next sections.

Implementation

While Rea is capable of understanding speech, and making reasonable contributions to an ongoing conversation about realty, to date our primary effort has been in the interactional component of the conversational model. This component manages several discourse functions. The functions currently being managed are:

- Acknowledgment of user's presence - by posture, turning to face the user;

- Feedback function - Rea gives feedback in several modalities: she may nod her head or emit a paraverbal (e.g. "mmhmm") or a short statement such as "I see" in response to short pauses in the user's speech; she raises her eyebrows to indicate partial understanding of a phrase or sentence.

- Turntaking function – Rea tracks who has the speaking turn, and only speaks when she holds the turn. Currently Rea always allows verbal interruption, and yields the turn as soon as the user begins to speak . If the user gestures she will interpret this as expression of a desire to speak [15], and therefore halt her remarks at the nearest sentence boundary. Finally, at the end of her speaking turn she turns to face the user to indicate the end of her turn.

Other functions have both interactional and propositional content. For example:

- Greeting and Farewell functions - Rea speaks and gestures when greeting and saying goodbye.

- Emphasis function - people may emphasize particular linguistic items by prosodic means (pitch accents) or by accompanying the word with a beat gesture (short formless wave of the hand). Recognizing emphasis is important for determining which part of the utterance is key to the discourse. For example, the user may say "I'd like granite floor tiles," to which Rea can reply "granite is a good choice here;" or the user might say "I'd like granite floor tiles," where Rea can reply "tile would go well here." We are developing a gesture classification system to detect the 'beat' gestures that often indicate emphasis. On the output side, we plan to allow Rea to generate emphasis using either modality.

These conversational functions are realized as conversational behaviors. For turn taking, for example, the specifics are as follows:

If Rea has the turn and is speaking and the user begins to gesture, this is interpreted as the user *wanting turn* function. If Rea has the turn and is speaking and the user begins to speak, this is interpreted as the user *taking turn* function. If the user is speaking and s/he pauses for less than 500 msec., this is interpreted as the *wanting feedback* function. If the user is speaking and issues a declarative sentence and stops speaking and gesturing, or says an imperative or interrogative phrase, their input is interpreted as a *giving turn* function. Finally, if the user has the turn and continues gesturing after having finished uttering a declarative sentence, or if s/he begins another phrase after having uttered a declarative sentence, with a pause of less than 500 msec, this is interpreted as a *holding turn* function. This approach is summarized in Table 1.

State	User Input	Input Function
Rea speaking	Gesture	Wanting turn
	Speech	Taking turn
User speaking	Pause of <500 msec.	Wanting feedback
	Imperative phrase	Giving turn
	Interrogative phrase	Giving turn
	Declarative phrase & pause >500 msec. & no gesture	Giving turn
	Declarative phrase & long gesture or pause	Holding turn

Table 1. Functional interpretation of turn taking input

Thus, speech may convey different interactional information; it may be interpreted as taking turn, giving turn, or holding turn depending on the conversational state and what is conveyed by the other modalities.

A similar approach is taken for generation of conversational behaviors. Rea generates speech, gesture and facial expressions based on the current conversational state and the conversational function she is trying to convey. For example, when the user first approaches Rea ("User

State	Output Function	Behaviors
User Present	Open interaction	Look at user. Smile. Headtoss.
	Attend	Face user.
	End of interaction	Turn away.
	Greet	Wave, "hello" .
Rea Speaking	Give turn	Relax hands. Look at user. Raise eyebrows
	Signoff	Wave. "bye"
User Speaking	Give feedback	Nod head Paraverbal
	Want turn.	Look at user. Raise hands. Paraverbal("umm").
	Take turn.	Look at user. Raise hands to begin gesturing. Speak.

Table 2. Output Functions

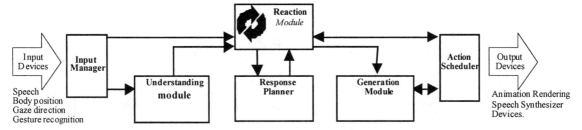

Figure 2: The Rea Software Architecture

Present" state), she signals her openness to engage in conversation by looking at the user, smiling, and/or tossing her head. When conversational turn-taking begins, she orients her body to face the user at a 45 degree angle. When the user is speaking and Rea wants the turn she looks at the user and utters a paraverbal ("umm"). When Rea is finished speaking and ready to give the turn back to the user she looks at the user, drops her hands out of gesture space and raises her eyebrows in expectation. Table 2 summarizes Rea's current interactional output behaviors.

By modeling behavioral categories as discourse functions we have developed a natural and principled way of combining multiple modalities, in both input and output. Thus when REA decides to give feedback, for example, she can choose any of several modalities based on what is appropriate at the moment.

Architecture

Figure 2 shows the modules of the Rea architecture. The three points that differentiate Rea from other embodied conversational agents are mirrored in the organization of the system architecture.

- Input is accepted from as many modalities as there are input devices. However the different modalities are integrated into a single semantic representation that is passed from module to module. This representation is a KQML frame [13].

- The KQML frame has slots for interactional and propositional information so that the regulatory and content-oriented contribution of every conversational act can be maintained throughout the system.

- The categorization of behaviors in terms of their conversational functions is mirrored by the organization of the architecture which centralizes decisions made in terms of functions (the understanding, response planner, and generation modules), and moves to the periphery decisions made in terms of behaviors (the input manager and action scheduler).

In addition, a distinction is drawn between *reactive* and *deliberative* communicative actions [26]. The Input Manager and Action Scheduler interact with external devices and together with the Reaction Module respond immediately (under 500 msec.) to user input or system commands. Performing head nods when the user pauses briefly is an example of a reactive conversational behavior. The other modules are more "deliberative" in nature and perform non-trivial inferencing actions that can take multiple real-time cycles to complete. These modules are written in C++ and CLIPS, a rule-based expert system language [12].

Input Manager

The input manager currently supports three types of input:

- *Gesture Input:* STIVE vision software produces 3D position and orientation of the head and hands[2].

- *Audio Input:* A simple audio processing routine detects the onset and cessation of speech.

- *Grammar Based Speech Recognition:* IBM ViaVoice returns text from a set of phrases defined by a grammar.

In all cases the features sent to the Input Manager are time stamped with start and end times in milliseconds. The various computers are synchronized to within a few milliseconds of each other. This synchronization is key for associating verbal and nonverbal behaviors. Latency in input devices can have a significant impact on the functioning of the system, since delays of milliseconds can have significant meaning in conversation. For example, if Rea delays before giving a "yes" response it can be interpreted by the user as indecision. Thus, our goal is to minimize input device and processing latencies wherever possible.

Low level gesture and audio detection events are sent to the reaction module straight away. These events are also stored in a buffer so that when recognized speech arrives a high-level multimodal KQML frame can be created containing mixed speech, audio and gesture events. This is sent to the understanding module for interpretation.

Understanding Module

The Understanding Module fuses all input modalities into a coherent understanding of what the user might be doing based on the current conversational state.

Reaction Module

The Reaction Module is responsible for the "action selection" component of the architecture, which determines at each moment in time what the character should be doing.

Response Planner Module

The Response Planner formulates sequences of actions, some or all of which will need to be executed during future execution cycles, to carry out desired communicative or task goals.

Generation Module

The Generation Module realizes a complex action request from the Reasoning Module by producing one or more coordinated primitive actions (such as speech or gesture generation, or facial expression), sending them to the Action Scheduler, and monitoring their execution.

Action Scheduling Module

The Action Scheduling Module is the "Motor controller" for the character, responsible for coordinating action at the lowest level. It takes multiple action requests from multiple requestors (i.e. the Reaction and Generation Modules) and attempts to carry them out.

Conclusion

User-testing of Gandalf, capable of some of the conversational functions also described here, showed that users relied on the interactional competency of the system to negotiate turn-taking, and that they preferred such a system to another embodied character capable of only emotional expression. However, Gandalf did not handle repairs gracefully, and users were comparatively more disfluent when using the system [9]. Our next step is to test Rea to see whether the current mixture of interactional and propositional conversational functions, including turn-taking and repair, allow users to engage in more efficient and fluent interaction with the system.

The functional approach provides abstraction that not only serves theoretical goals but also gives important leverage for multi-cultural scalability. The inner workings of the system deal with a set of universal conversational functions while the outer modules, both on the input and output side, are responsible for mapping them onto largely culture-specific surface behaviors. The architecture allows us to treat the mappings as an easily exchangeable part in the form of a specification file.

In this paper we have argued that embodied conversational agents are a logical and needed extension to the conversational metaphor of human – computer interaction. We argue, however, that embodiment needs to be based on an understanding of conversational function, rather than a additive – and ad hoc -- model of the relationship between nonverbal modalities and verbal conversational behaviors.

We demonstrated our approach with the Rea system. Increasingly capable of making an intelligent content-oriented – or *propositional* – contribution to the conversation, Rea is also sensitive to the regulatory – or *interactional* -- function of verbal and non-verbal conversational behaviors, and is capable of producing regulatory behaviors to improve the interaction by helping the user remain aware of the state of the conversation. Rea is an embodied conversational agent who can hold up her end of the conversation.

REFERENCES

1. Andre, E., Rist, T., Mueller, J. Integrating Reactive and Scripted Behaviors in a Life-Like Presentation Agent. In Proceedings of Autonomous Agents 98, (Minneapolis/St. Paul, May 1998), ACM Press,

2. Azarbayejani, A., Wren, C. and Pentland A. Real-time 3-D tracking of the human body. In *Proceedings of IMAGE'COM 96*, (Bordeaux, France, May 1996).

3. Ball, G., Ling, D., Kurlander, D., Miller, D., Pugh, D., Skelly, T., Stankosky, A., Thiel, D., Van Dantzich, M. and T. Wax. Lifelike computer characters: the persona project at Microsoft Research. In *Software Agents*, J. M. Bradshaw (ed.), MIT Press, Cambridge, MA, 1997.

4. Beskow, J. and McGlashan, S. Olga - A Conversational Agent with Gestures, In *Proceedings of the IJCAI'97 workshop on Animated Interface Agents - Making them Intelligent*, (Nagoya, Japan, August 1997), Morgan-Kaufmann Publishers, San Francisco.

5. Bolt, R.A. Put-that-there: voice and gesture at the graphics interface. *Computer Graphics*, 14(3), 1980, 262-270.

6. Bolt, R.A. and Herranz, E. Two-handed gesture in multi-modal natural dialog. In *Proceedings of UIST `92, Fifth Annual Symposium on User Interface Software and Technology*, (Monterey, CA, November 1992). ACM Press, 7-14.

7. Brennan, S.E. and Hulteen, E.A. Interaction and Feedback in a Spoken Language System. *Knowledge-Based Systems*, 8,2 (April-June 1995), 143-151.

8. Cassell, J., Pelachaud, C., Badler, N.I., Steedman, M., Achorn, B., Beckett, T., Douville, B., Prevost, S. and Stone, M. Animated conversation: rule-based generation of facial display, gesture and spoken intonation for multiple conversational agents. *Computer Graphics (SIGGRAPH '94 Proceedings)*, 28(4): 413-420.

9. Cassell, J. and Thórisson, K. The Power of a Nod and a Glance: Envelope vs. Emotional Feedback in Animated Conversational Agents. *Journal of Applied Artificial Intelligence*, in press.

10. Cassell, J., Torres, O. and Prevost, S. Turn taking vs. Discourse Structure: how best to model multimodal conversation. In Wilks (ed.) *Machine Conversations*. Kluwer, The Hague, 1998.

11. Clark, H.H. and Brennan, S.E. Grounding in Communication. In *Shared Cognition: Thinking as Social Practice*, J. Levine, L.B. Resnick and S.D. Behrend, (eds.). APA Books, Washington, D.C, 1991.

12. CLIPS Reference Manual Version 6.0. *Technical Report*, Number JSC-25012, Software Technology Branch, Lyndon B. Johnson Space Center, Houston, TX, 1994.

13. Finin, T., Fritzson, R. KQML as an Agent Communication Language. In *The Proceedings of the Third International Conference on Information and Knowledge Management* (CIKM'94), ACM Press, November 1994.

14. Johnston, M., Cohen, P. R., McGee, D., Oviatt, S. L., Pittman, J. A. and Smith, I. Unification-based multimodal integration. In *Proceedings of the 35th Annual Meeting of the Association for Computational Linguistics*, (Madrid, Spain, 1997).

15. Kendon, A. The negotiation of context in face-to-face interaction. In A. Duranti and C. Goodwin (eds.), *Rethinking context: language as interactive phenomenon*. Cambridge University Press. NY, 1990.

16. Koons, D.B. Sparrell, C.J. and Thorisson, K.R. Integrating simultaneous input from speech, gaze and hand gestures. In *Intelligent Multi-Media Interfaces* M.T. Maybury (Ed.), AAAI Press/MIT Press, 1993.

17. Loyall, A. and Bates, J. Personality-rich believable agents that use language. In Proceedings of Agents '97 (Marina del Rey, CA, February 1997), ACM Press,

18. Nagao, K. and Takeuchi, A. Social interaction: multimodal conversation with social agents. *Proceedings of the 12th National Conference on Artificial Intelligence (AAAI-94)*, (Seattle, WA, August 1994), AAAI Press/MIT Press, vol. 1, 22-28.

19. Nickerson, R.S. On Conversational Interaction with Computers. In *User Oriented Design of Interactive Graphics Systems: Proceedings of the ACM SIGGRAPH Workshop* (1976), ACM Press, 681-683.

20. Noma, T. and Badler, N. (1997). A virtual human presenter. In *Proceedings of the IJCAI'97 workshop on Animated Interface Agents - Making them Intelligent*, (Nagoya, Japan, August, 1997), Morgan-Kaufmann Publishers, San Francisco.

21. Oviatt, S.L. User-Centered Modeling for Spoken Language and Multimodal Interfaces, *IEEE Multimedia*, 3, 4, (Winter 1996), 26-35.

22. Reeves, B. and Nass, C. *The Media Equation: How People Treat Computers, Television, and New Media Like Real People and Places*. Cambridge University Press, 1996.

23. Sparrell, C. J. *Coverbal Iconic Gestures in Human-Computer Interaction*. S.M. Thesis, MIT Media Arts and Sciences Section, 1993.

24. Steedman, M. Structure and intonation. *Language*, 1991, 67(2), 190-296.

25. Takeuchi, A. and Nagao, K. Communicative facial displays as a new conversational modality. In *Proceedings of InterCHI 93*, (Amsterdam, Netherlands April 1993), 187-193.

26. Thórisson, K. R. *Communicative Humanoids: A Computational Model of Psychosocial Dialogue Skills*. PhD Thesis, MIT Media Laboratory, 1996.

27. Wahlster, W., André, E., Graf, W. and Rist, T. Designing illustrated texts. In *Proceedings of the 5th EACL* (Berlin, Germany, April 1991), 8-14

28. Weizenbaum, J. Eliza. A computer program for the study of natural language communication between man and machine. *Communications of the ACM*, 1966, 9, 26-45.

Emotional Interfaces for Interactive Aardvarks: Designing Affect into Social Interfaces for Children

Erik Strommen
Microsoft Corporation
One Microsoft Way
Redmond, WA 98052 USA
+1 425 882 8080
erikstr@microsoft.com

Kristin Alexander
Knowledge Kids Enterprises
1250 45th. St., Suite 150
Emeryville, CA 94608 USA
+1 510 595 2470
kristina@leapfrogtoys.com

ABSTRACT
Character-based social interfaces present a unique opportunity to integrate emotion into technology interactions. The present paper reports on the use of three emotional interactions (humor, praise, and affection) in the audio interfaces for two character-based interactive learning toys. The reasons for selecting the emotions used, the design rationale for their application, and findings from usability testing are reviewed. It is suggested that as a form of pretend play-acting akin to puppetry, social interfaces can engage the emotions of users in a variety of beneficial ways.

KEYWORDS: Learning, audio interface, children, social interface, emotion

INTRODUCTION
Social interfaces and affect
The past few years have witnessed a growing interest in interfaces that engage users not just cognitively, but emotionally as well. Most of these efforts are driven by a practical desire for better interfaces. Social interfaces, for example, are thought to make technology use more enjoyable and natural by mimicking familiar social conventions [20,21]. Building interfaces that engage user emotions has a far stronger rationale when the users are children, however. Most interactive products for children have an explicitly educational aim. And there is a clear consensus in the psychological and educational fields that a variety of positive emotions play critical roles in fostering learning and mental growth in children [2,8,23]. Emotions in educational interfaces for children therefore can do more than just improve the interface's quality. They can play an important role in achieving the learning goals of the product itself.

Previous research on emotion in children's interfaces has tended to emphasize task-related considerations, such as motivation for persistence [22], rather than social engagement with the interface itself. This focus is perfectly appropriate when the human-computer relationship is viewed as that of a user to a tool. Under the "technology as tool" model, task motivation, the satisfaction of a job well done, and the intrinsic pleasure of feeling in control of the interaction are the only emotions that matter [31]. Just as designers of screwdrivers or drills do not consider issues of warmth or playfulness when making a tool effective and easy to use, interface designers have not concerned themselves with such issues when building interactive tools such as spreadsheets or phone menus.

Emotional engagement at the interface has assumed more importance in recent years, as interactive technologies have become part of aspects of human activity other than work and have been taken up by users other than adults. A "social" model of interaction, in which interfaces are deliberately designed to mimic familiar human social interactions, has appeared as a complementary alternative to the tool model. The social model sees the human-computer relationship as not just a user-tool engagement, but also as a partnership or collaboration between the user and the computer [13,21]. The merits of the social approach have been the subject of some debate [9,12,20]. Whatever one's opinion, though, there is empirical support for one key element of the social approach: computers do seem to elicit behavioral and affective responses in users that mimic their social responses to other people.

Social mimicry as an interface model
A growing body of literature has documented that adult users respond to a variety of computer interface elements, such as voices or faces, as if they were being produced by human agents [26,29,36]. In addition, there are studies demonstrating that adult users respond to specific emotions in the interface as if they were being produced by human agents [11,25]. Such systematic research data on children's reactions to social elements in interfaces is lacking. However, two previous studies of speech output for

children have reported that the emotional tone of the speech had a strong influence on children's reception of the spoken message [16,33]. And more concretely, Microsoft's ActiMates Barney interactive character appears to successfully use a social interface to elicit playful pleasure from children. Such evidence suggests that children most likely respond to social interfaces in a manner similar to adults [34].

Because of their ability to invoke emotional responses in users, social interfaces, particular those embodying specific characters and personalities, provide a unique opportunity to integrate affect into interactive learning. But in what manner? Computers As Social Actors (CASA) is a model of HCI that suggests that principles of human social interaction can also be applied to human-computer interaction [11,27]. The CASA approach theoretically encompasses all elements of HCI design, from pop-up menus to error messages. However, it has particular relevance for character-based interfaces, where the user engages the interface in an explicitly social manner. The present paper describes the successful application of the CASA concept to the design of emotional interactions in the audio interface of a character-based interactive learning toy.

Meet Arthur and D.W.

It is obviously an advantage if the characters in the interface are already familiar and appealing to intended users. Arthur and D.W. are fictional siblings, the creations of children's author Marc Brown. They have been familiar to American children for more than 15 years. They are the central characters in more than 30 children's books, a popular television series, and several educational CD-ROM titles, all aimed at the four- to eight-year-old population. Arthur and D.W. are anthropomorphized aardvarks who live in a suburban neighborhood with other animal families. Their animal-like appearance notwithstanding, Arthur and D.W's behavior is completely human, as are their personalities. They are highly individual, with their own specific traits and preferences, while sharing the same interests and concerns as their audience. Arthur and D.W. also have appealing social styles. In all their fictional adventures, they are loyal and devoted friends, playful and fun-loving. They show strong personal integrity, as well as empathy toward others. It is not surprising that children find Arthur and D.W. to be very sympathetic characters. Relying on this affection to elicit social and emotional responses from children was the starting point for the interfaces for two new ActiMates characters: ActiMates Arthur and ActiMates D.W.

ACTIMATES CHARACTERS AS SOCIAL INTERFACES

ActiMates characters are animated, interactive plush dolls. ActiMates Arthur and D.W. (hereafter A/Arthur and A/D.W.) are both approximately 13 inches in height. Motors provide simple arm and head movement, and a small loudspeaker provides audible speech, allowing the

Figure 1. ActiMates D.W. and ActiMates Arthur. Children respond to the character's speech and gestures by squeezing sensors located in the hands, feet, ears, and watch (visible on right arm).

character to gesture and speak. Children interact with A/Arthur and A/D.W. by actuating seven sensors located inspecific parts of the character's body: One in a watch on the character's right arm, and one in each hand, foot, and ear. (See Figure 1.) A ROM chip hidden in each character's body allows the characters to respond to children's inputs. The characters move using programmed motion, and speak using a pre-recorded, digitized speech vocabulary of more than 4,000 phrases.

A/Arthur and A/D.W.'s sensor interfaces are organized by the sensor's location on the character's body. Separate functions are associated with the ears, watch, and feet sensors.

Ears are to hear what A/Arthur and A/D.W. are thinking

Squeezing the ears allows children to "eavesdrop" on A/Arthur or A/D.W.'s thoughts. Each ear squeeze plays one of dozens of unique phrases that ask questions, offer opinions, share jokes, and give compliments. The content of these phrases is scripted to reflect the individual thoughts and feelings of the fictional characters Arthur or D.W. Phrases with emotional content fell into several categories:

Jokes. A/Arthur and A/D.W. share silly ideas or comical events with the child. Arthur, for example, says "You know what's gross?" and then proceeds to name something silly, such as "sweaty gym socks," that elicits humorous reactions of disgust from the child.

Secrets. A/Arthur and A/D.W. say, "Come closer, I want to tell you a secret!" and then confide an embarrassing fact or a private opinion to the child.

Playful Teasing. A/Arthur and A/D.W. make mock requests or gently tease the child with information they know, such as the child's birthday.

Compliments. A/Arthur and A/D.W. both express affection for the child, through such comments as "I'm lucky to have a friend like you!"

The watch is for telling time

When the watch is squeezed, the character says the current time, date, and day of the week. If the date is a holiday, the character announces that fact along with the date. The character can be programmed to know a specific birthday, and will treat that date as a holiday.

Feet are for games

When a foot is squeezed, the characters play games. Both A/Arthur and A/D.W. play the same games. The games include:

Rhyme Time. The character says two words and the child must squeeze a hand sensor if they rhyme (e.g. parrot, carrot) or a foot sensor if they do not (parrot, dolphin).

How Long Is That? The character challenges the child to estimate a specific length of time (5, 10, 15, or 20 seconds) and squeeze a hand sensor when the duration is passed.

The Stopwatch Game. In this game, children perform actions, such as standing on one foot, while the character times the duration. Children squeeze a hand sensor to stop the clock and hear the character report how long the activity lasted.

The Memory Game. In this game, children memorize, then execute, progressively longer lists of sensor squeezes ("Hand, foot, ear, foot..."). Each time the list is correctly input using the character sensors, a new element is added to the list on the next round.

Silly Sentences. The character combines randomly selected adjectives, nouns, and verbs to create nonsense sentences such as "The jiggling wombat does the cha-cha with the stinky antelope!"

Countdown. In this game, the character says, "Let's count down backward and then say {phrase}," where the phrases are randomly selected lines such as "Surprise!" or "Blast off!"

Unlike the ears, feet, and watch, the hand sensors do not have a dedicated function. Instead, they are integrated with the ear and foot functions and serve different purposes in each context. They are part of game interfaces when games are active. In the ear phrase menu, they serve to repeat the last phrase spoken, so children can repeat a given phrase on demand.

Personality and the audio interface

The foundation of the A/Arthur and A/D.W. social interface is the personality of the individual characters. Personality plays a crucial role in human social interaction. The consistency of an individual's preferences, attitudes, and

actions over time creates a consistent set of expectations in others that makes the behavior of familiar individuals predictable. Even very young children have been shown to make predictions based on knowledge of personality and personal attributes [10,14,29]. Consistency of personality creates consistency in the social interface, by making the character's interactions predictable.

As plush dolls, A/Arthur and A/D.W. have fixed facial features, and thus must rely exclusively on speech and gesture as an interface. Fortunately, speech is a rich medium for conveying affect. Speech patterns convey critical information about personality and emotion. When applied to the audio interface, they can provide authenticity and a feeling of realism [37]. While it is possible to simulate different emotional elements using synthesized speech [17], a special requirement for interfaces based on familiar characters from television is that their voices must be recognizable in order to be accepted as authentic. To meet this constraint, speech for the interfaces was created from recordings made by voice actors, rather than synthesized.

The familiarity of the voice is only the most basic element requirement of character speech, however. The degrees to which the character's speech is both natural sounding and true to the character in content and style also establish character authenticity and realism. Specific features in the ActiMates audio interface addressed each of these aspects of speech.

Spontaneous variation and conversational speech

Two strategies were used to make the characters' spoken comments seen natural, rather than "canned" or programmed. The goal of both strategies was to avoid the highly repetitive and unnaturally rigid language so common to interactive systems. The existing literature on audio interface design tends to emphasize issues of consistency and brevity of comments as key interface features that promote efficiency of navigation [28]. The cost of the efficiency gained by such standardization, however, is robotic and unnatural-sounding speech. Human speakers are very inconsistent, spontaneously varying their utterances even when saying the very same thing over again at different times. In a character-based interface, including such natural variations makes the interface speech seem more the speech of another person than of a machine.

The first way variability was added to the interface was by varying the syntactic constructions of specific interface instructions. Instead of consistently using a fixed "action-input" sequence to give interface instructions (e.g. "To play a game, squeeze my toe!"), A/Arthur and A/D.W. randomly alternate action-input and input-action versions of the same information, using a "Squeeze my toe to play a game!" construction as well. The second way variability was added to the character's speech was by randomly varying the order of phrases in the ear menu and the order in which games are presented when the foot is squeezed. This randomization creates a sense of unpredictability that contributes to the impression that the characters are making spontaneous, rather than programmed, responses to the child.

Characteristic speech and authenticity
Spontaneous variation makes character speech more natural sounding. A second issue in a personality-based interface is the familiarity and authenticity of the character, established through idiosyncratic language and comments. Two personality-specific speech elements were used in the design to establish the character's identity. The first is the inclusion of random interjections when games are initiated. Starting a game, A/Arthur and A/D.W. say, for example, "Let's play a memory game!" or "I know! Let's play a memory game! Or "Hey! Let's play a memory game!" The use of "Hey!" and "I know!" as interjections is not only consistent with the speech patterns of the Arthur and D.W. fictional characters, but with the colloquial speech in the four- to eight-year-old target user age group as well. The other personality-specific language in the interface is the use of "signature" phrases from each fictional character, such as Arthur's exasperated "Oh, brother!" and comments from D.W. that reflect her self-confidence, such as "You know what? I know everything!" Such phrases reinforce the character's identity for the child, and add to the overall authenticity of the character as a familiar social actor.

A voice that matches the character's voice on television and CD-ROMs, naturalistic variation in speech, and the use of characteristic speech patterns serve a specific purpose in the interface. They encourage children to respond emotionally to A/Arthur and A/D.W. in the same manner as they do to the Arthur and D.W. they see on television or on CD-ROM. This emotional engagement is a prerequisite for engaging the specific emotions targeted by the design during play with the ActiMates characters.

THREE VALUABLE EMOTIONS
Three specific emotional interactions were selected for inclusion in the A/Arthur and A/D.W. interfaces. Each emotion met three criteria. First, the emotion was consistent with the personalities of the individual characters; second, there was clear empirical support for the benefits of the emotions to children's learning and development; and third, the emotion could be integrated into the interface in an appropriate manner. The emotional interactions that met these criteria are: praise and encouragement, laughter and humor, and warmth and affection. A summary of the specific places they are used in the interface is shown in Table 1.

Praise and encouragement
In the Arthur television program and books, encouragement and praise account for a large amount of the content of the interactions among Arthur, D.W., their friends, and family. Praise plays a valuable role in learning. Task-sensitive

Table 1. Content associated with specific emotions

Praise and encouragement	Laughter and humor	Warmth and affection
Rhyme Time	Silly Sentences	Secrets
Stopwatch Game	Action prompts	Playful Teasing
Memory Game	Playful Teasing	Compliments
How Long Is That	Action prompts	
Count-Down	Jokes	

praise is a form of social reinforcement that has repeatedly been shown to affect both task performance and motivation [5,8]. It is also implicated in task persistence when children are mastering new material [24]. Five of A/Arthur and A/D.W.'s games use praise from the character to encourage play: Rhyme Time, The Stopwatch Game, The Memory Game, How Long Is That, and Countdown. In each of these games, correct responses are cheered and praised by the characters. In The Memory Game, where the list to be memorized gets longer with each successful round, praise is even more performance-specific: with each round, as longer lists are correctly recalled, praise becomes more energetic and enthusiastic in tone to match the challenge in each round.

Testing demonstrated that praise motivated children's performance during games. They smiled or nodded in response to character praise, and several even responded verbally (e.g. A/Arthur: "You're good at this!" Child: "I know!"). User testing of the games during product development also identified an additional role for praise beyond reinforcement for success: praise was found to lessen the aversive feelings that accompany failure. Failure was an issue for two games: The Memory game (TMG) and How long is that? (HLIT). Unlike Rhyme Time and Countdown, which are simple, single-trial games that are easy to play, TMG and HLIT are more challenging. Both require sustained effort and repeated trials for success, meaning that failures are frequent.

In the initial designs for both games, when children failed a round by making an error, a new round of the game started immediately after the error was confirmed by the character, with the character simply saying, "Let's try again!" Children's reactions to this transition from failure to a new round were striking: They often looked down or looked away from the character, and interacted less frequently with the character for several minutes afterward. Adding praise for the effort ("That was hard!" or "That was a tough one!") prior to starting the new round seemed to soften the blow, by acknowledging the difficulty of the task. In subsequent testing with the new phrase added, the decline in positive affect and interaction that had accompanied failures without the comment did not recur.

The second place that praise and encouragement was used in the interface was during periods of user inactivity. After a fixed amount of time has passed during which the child has not actuated a sensor, A/Arthur and A/D.W. either make a suggestion ("Squeeze my toe to play a game!") or randomly give a spontaneous statement of admiration or praise ("You know what? You RULE!" "You're so cool!" "Don't stop now! You're doing great!" etc.) These phrases serve two purposes. First, they make the characters seem less task-driven, by diluting interface directives about the sensors with personal statements directed to the child. (See [34] for the use of this same strategy, for the same effect, in a different social interface). The second is to motivate the child to continue interacting with the character. Results from user testing suggested these phrases achieved the desired effect: children's responses to spontaneous praise after a period of inactivity were to smile and touch the character, an action often followed spontaneously by sensor inputs and renewed play.

Laughter and humor

Laughter, silliness, and comedy play a role in all of Arthur and D.W.'s adventures in the Arthur books and television show. Humor has clear value for the developing child. Generating humorous behavior, sharing humorous experiences, and responding to humorous situations with amusement are behaviors that all correlate with a variety of positive social and cognitive measures [23]. Humor is effective in learning situations as well [7,40]. And perhaps most critically, humor and laughter are powerful social behaviors. Laughter and smiling are far more likely in social situations than in solitary situations, suggesting their fundamentally social nature [1]. Humor also has benefits for social interaction. It reduces social distance, and humorous peers are rated as better liked [32,38]. Social humor and laughter are so pervasive that facilitating them is not difficult. One of the most robust findings in social psychology is the "contagious" nature of laughter and smiling. When another person is present, children respond more readily and freely to humorous material – especially if the other person is laughing or reacting with pleasure to the same humorous stimuli [6].

Laughter is used in two content areas in the ActiMates interface: in the Silly Sentence (SS) game and as part of phrases that are said when the ear is squeezed. In SS, the character says a nonsense sentence, then laughs in reaction to the content, occasionally commenting "That's funny!" or "That's silly!" In testing, children tended to smile when the character laughed, and visually attended to the character. Several actually responded verbally when the character said "That's funny!" by agreeing ("It sure is, Arthur!") or disagreeing ("No, it's not.")

Laughter was also used after practical jokes that A/Arthur and A/D.W. played on the user, and after they made humorous comments. For example, A/D.W. (whose hair is made of yarn) has an ear phrase "Does my hair look stringy to you? (giggle)". Most girls tested in A/D.W.'s formative research reacted with smiles and giggles. They remarked on the comment to others, laughing or grinning, as well. In many cases, they spontaneously began grooming the character's hair after hearing this phrase. Both characters also joke about their own interface, saying for example, "I'd squeeze your foot if I could reach it! (giggle)." A majority of children smiled or laughed in response to hearing this line, and several four-year olds (the youngest age tested) jokingly held their feet up to the character.

Humor without explicit laughter is used in the interface in many more of the characters' ear phrases. A/D.W., for example, says "I'm not afraid of anything! Except maybe..." and then randomly adds a ludicrous exception, such as "...bugs that are bigger than my head!" These comments were designed to convey that even someone with D.W.'s courageous nature can still have fears. Similarly, A/Arthur asks "Are my glasses on straight? I don't want to look goofy!" This phrase gently communicates Arthur's concern with looking foolish to others, an anxiety the fictional character shares with his target users.

Warmth and Affection

Empirical studies have long linked warm and affectionate interactions with positive outcomes and adjustment in children on a variety of measures. The affection and warmth of peers and authority figures has been shown to influence mental growth in children, increase motivation, enhance feelings of self-esteem and positive-self regard, and more [2,3,19,30]. Affection among friends and family is a significant emotional theme in Arthur and D.W.'s television and book adventures, as well. In both the television program and the books, characters explicitly comment on how much they value their friendships ("Arthur, you're the best friend a guy could have!"), and on how much they enjoy each other's company ("How can I have my first sleepover without you? You're my best friend!").

A/Arthur and A/D.W. utilize warmth and affection in the interface in a variety of ear phrases. Each character has several distinct ear phrases that express affection and admiration for the child user. For example, A/D.W. confides "I'm lucky to have a friend like you!" A/Arthur says "I wish you were in class with me!" The two characters also have ear phrases to build affection through two indirect strategies: sharing Secrets and Playful Teasing. Both characters confide in the child user, saying "Come closer, I want to tell you a secret!" and then divulge a personal preference or opinion. Playful Teasing builds intimacy by using personal knowledge of the child in a playful manner. Once they are programmed to know the child's birthday, the characters randomly announce their knowledge, saying in a playful tone, "I know YOUR birthday! Your birthday is {month/date}!"

Testing of these different ear phrases with children revealed that the phrases were received positively by children of both sexes. The typical reaction to affectionate language was for children to smile, comment, and interact with the character. Girls often had another striking reaction: they would pull the character physically closer to them. When secrets were presented, children actually leaned closer to the characters to hear the confidential information. The divulging of secrets had a particularly striking effect for girls using A/D.W.: several girls turned to the researcher and giggled as they confided the secret they had just learned.

PUPPETS, PRETEND, AND HCI
The strategy behind the use of character-based social interfaces is to build on the social responses of users in order to support technology interaction. A/Arthur and A/D.W. use this strategy to achieve an additional goal: fostering beneficial emotions in young users during their playful learning efforts. Character-appropriate emotional interactions that are beneficial to development were included in the interface where they supported the content most effectively. User testing indicated that these interactions achieved their intended goal of eliciting the appropriate emotional responses in children. The result is an interface that promotes mental growth through the systematic use of social responses to positive affect, and one that children find highly engaging and appealing, as well.

Social interfaces for children have broader goals than helping a user complete a task efficiently. Their mimicry of human interaction makes such interfaces more like a form of puppetry than strictly a form of tool. Puppetry invites children to pretend that inanimate objects are sentient, and to respond to their speech and actions as if they are being produced by social agents. Such pretend or "as if" engagement is a sophisticated form of dual representation in which children interact with an object, such as a doll, by endowing it with imaginary properties (making it talk, for example), while simultaneously understanding that the doll is just a toy. Pretend play fosters intellectual growth in children precisely because it engages them in two levels of thinking simultaneously: in the physical world of the toy and in the imaginary world where the toys are used as props for acting out imagined events [4,15,18]. Putting these intellectually rich processes to work in technology interfaces makes the interface itself a prop for pretend engagement, a design philosophy very different from the traditional, tool-based notion that interfaces should be "transparent" or invisible to the user [31].

If social interfaces are a form of pretend, it is worth noting that the CASA model itself is in fact based on a premise strikingly similar to pretend play. "The CASA paradigm maintains that individuals can be induced to behave *as if* computers warranted human considerations, even though users *know* that the machines do not actually warrant this treatment...[11, p.552, italics in original]." The A/Arthur and A/D.W. social interfaces induce pleasant emotions in users in a manner consistent with human interaction, even though children know that Actimates characters are toys and not peers. The effectiveness of such interfaces suggests that the interpersonal CASA approach appears to have much to offer as a conceptual model for character-based interface designs. Children treat character-based social interfaces as if they are pretend playmates: friendly guides, assistants, or partners who have a specific, user-assigned social role to play in any given interaction. A straightforward way to have character interfaces "behave" as users expect them to in such situations is to make them mimic social interactions as closely as possible in their responses and actions to user inputs.

Pretend playmate social interfaces enrich technology interaction by adding playful elements such as humor, warmth, spontaneity, and personality to the interface. Such interfaces are certainly not suitable for all technology applications. There are sound theoretical reasons, for example, why play-based interactions are inappropriate for productivity tools [35]. But in situations where learning and mental growth are goals of the interaction, and where children are the intended users, pretend playmate interfaces have a valuable role. That they can facilitate children's emotional as well as cognitive development says as much about the power of the playful imagination as it does about social interfaces. That they can engage user emotions as dramatically as they do suggests that we have only begun to understand all the different ways that technology, applied in a developmentally appropriate manner, can be used to support mental growth.

REFERENCES
1. Bainum, C., Lounsbury, K., and Pollio, H. The development of laughing and smiling in nursery school children. *Child Development*, 55, 5 (1984), 1946-1957.

2. Bornstein, M. H. *Maternal responsiveness: Characteristics and consequences.* Jossey-Bass, San Francisco CA, 1989.

3. Bornstein, M. H., Haynes, O. M., O'Reilly, A. W., and Painter, K. M. Solitary and collaborative pretense play in early childhood: Sources of individual variation in the development of representational competence. *Child Development*, 67, 6 (1996), 2910-2929.

4. Bretherton, I. and Beeghly, M. Pretence: Acting 'as if.' In J.J. Lockman and N.L. Hazen (Eds.) *Action in Social Context: Perspectives on Early Development.* Plenum Press, NY, 1989, pp. 239-271.

5. Cameron, J. and Pierce, W. Reinforcement, Reward, and Intrinsic Motivation: A Meta-Analysis *Review of Educational Research*, 64, 3 (Fall 1994), 363-423.

6. Chapman, A. and Wright, D. Social enhancement of laughter: An experimental analysis of some companion variables. *Journal of Experimental Child Psychology*, 21, 2 (1976), 201-218.

7. Coleman, J. All seriousness aside: The laughing-learning connection. *International Journal of Instructional Media*, 19, 3 (1992), 269-276

8. Delin, C. R. and Baumeister, R. F. Praise: More than just social reinforcement. *Journal for the Theory of Social Behaviour*, 24, 3 (September 1994), 219-241.

9. Don, A., Brennan, S., Laurel, B., and Shneiderman, B. Anthropomorphism: From ELIZA to Terminator 2. In *Proceedings of CHI'92 (May 3-7, 1992, Monterey, CA)*, pp. 67 –70.

10. Dozier, M. Functional measurement assessment of young children's ability to predict future behavior. *Child Development*, 62 (1991), 1091- 1099

11. Fogg, B. J. and Nass, C. Silicon sycophants: The effects of computers that flatter. *International Journal of Human-Computer Studies*, 46, 5 (May 1997), 551-561.

12. Friedman, B. and Kahn, P. Human agency and responsible computing: Implications for computer system design. *Journal of Systems Software*, 17 (1992), 7-14

13. Frohlich, D. Direct Manipulation and other lessons. In M. Helander, T. Landauer, and P. Prabhu (eds.), *Handbook of human-computer interaction*. North Holland, NY, 1997, 463-488.

14. Frye, D. and Moore, C. (eds.) *Children's theories of mind: Mental states and social understanding.* Lawrence Erlbaum Associates, Hillsdale NJ, 1991.

15. Garvey, C. *Play.* Harvard University Press. Cambridge MA, 1990.

16. Grover, S. A field study in the use of cognitive-developmental principles in microcomputer design for young children. *Journal of Educational Research*, 79 (1996), 325-332.

17. Henton, C. and Edelman, B. Generating and manipulating emotional synthetic speech on a personal computer. *Multimedia Tools and Applications*, 3 (1996), 105-125.

18. Herron, R. E. and Sutton-Smith, B. (eds.) *Child's play.* Robert E. Kreiger Publishing Company, Malabar FL, 1982.

19. Jennings, K. and Connors, R. Mothers' interactional style and children's competence at 3 years. *International Journal of Behavioral Development*, 12 (1989), 155-175.

20. Laurel, B. Interface agents: Metaphors with character. In B.Laurel (ed.) *The Art of Human-Computer Interface Design*, Addison-Wesley, Reading MA., 1990, 355-365

21. Maes, P. Intelligent software. In J. Moore, E. Edmonds, and A Puerta (eds.), *Proceedings of IUI'97: International Conference on Intelligent User Interfaces.* (ACM, NY, 1997), 41-43.

22. Malone, T. and Lepper, M. 1987. Making learning fun: A taxonomy of intrinsic motivations for learning. In (R. Snow and M. Farr (eds.). *Aptitude, Learning, and Instruction, Volume 3: Conative and Affective Processes Analyses.* Lawrence Erlbaum Associates, Hillsdale NJ, 1987, 223-253.

23. McGhee, P. The contribution of humor to children's social development. *Journal of Children in Contemporary Society*, 20, 1-2 (1988), 119-134.

24. Meddock, T, Parsons, J., and Hill, K. Effects of an Adult's Presence and Praise on Young Children's Performance *Journal of Experimental Child Psychology*; 12, 2 (October 1971), 197-211.

25. Morkes, J., Kernal, H.K., and Nass, C. Humor in task-oriented computer-mediated communication and human-computer interaction. In *CHI'98 Summary* (Los Angeles CA 1998), ACM Press, 215-216.

26. Nass, C. and Steuer, J. Voices, Boxes, and Sources of Messages: Computers and Social Actors. *Human Communication Research*, 19, 4 (June 1993), 504-527.

27. Nass, C., Steuer, J. and Tauber, E.R. Computers are social actors. *Proceedings of CHI'94* (Boston MA, April 1994). ACM Press, 72-77.

28. Resnick, P. and Virzi, R. A. Relief from the Audio Interface Blues: Expanding the Spectrum of Menu, List, and Form Styles, *ACM Transactions on Computer-Human Interaction*, 2, 2 (1995), 145-176.

29. Resnik, P. and Lammers, H. The influence of self-esteem on cognitive responses to machine-like vs. human-like computer feedback. *Journal of Social Psychology*, 125, 6 (1986), 761-769.

30. Rueter, M. A. and Conger, R. D. Interaction style, problem- solving behavior, and family problem-solving effectiveness. *Child Development*, 66 (1995), 98-115.

31. Schneiderman, B. Direct manipulation for comprehensible, predictable, and controllable user interfaces. *Proceedings of The International Conference on Intelligent User Interfaces* (Orlando FL, January 1997), ACM Press, 33-39.

32. Sletta, O, Sobstad, F., and Valas, H. Humour, peer acceptance, and perceived social competence in preschool and school-aged children. *British Journal of Educational Psychology*, 65 (1995), 179-195.

33. Strommen, E. F. "What did he say?": Speech output in preschool software. In S. Gayle (ed.), *Proceedings of NECC '91* (Phoenix AR, June 1991). International Society for Technology in Education, Eugene OR, 149-151.

34. Strommen, E. F. (1998). When the interface is a talking dinosaur: Learning across media with ActiMates Barney, in *Proceedings of ACM CHI'98* (Los Angeles CA, April 1998), ACM Press, 288-295.

35. Thomas, P. and Macredie, R. Games and the design of human-computer interfaces. *Educational and Training Technology International,* 31 (1994), 134-142.

36. Walker J. H., Sproull, L., and Subramani, R. 1994. Using a human face in an interface. *Proceedings of CHI'94* (Boston, MA April 1994), ACM Press, 85-91.

37. Walker, M., Cahn, J., and Whittaker, S. 1997. Improvising linguistic style: Social and affective bases for agent personality. *Proceedings of Autonomous Agents'97* (Marina Del Rey CA), ACM Press, 96-105

38. Warners-Kleverlann, N., Oppenheimer, L., and Sherman, L. To be or not to be humorous: Does it make a differences? *Humor* 9, 2 (1996), 117-141.

39. Yuill, N. and Pearson, A. The development of bases for trait attribution: Children's understanding of traits as causal mechanisms based on desire. *Developmental Psychology*, 34 (1998), 574-586.

40. Zillmann, D. and Bryant, J. Guidelines for the effective use of humor in children's educational television programs. *Journal of Children in Contemporary Society*, 20 (1998), 201-221.

Bridging Strategies for VR-Based Learning

Tom Moher
Andrew Johnson
Electronic Visualization Laboratory
EECS Department
University of Illinois at Chicago
Chicago, IL 60607 USA
{moher, ajohnson}@eecs.uic.edu

Stellan Ohlsson[1]
Mark Gillingham[2]
[1]Department of Psychology
[2]College of Education
University of Illinois at Chicago
Chicago, IL 60607 USA
{Stellan, MarkGill}@uic.edu

ABSTRACT

A distributed immersive virtual environment was deployed as a component of a pedagogical strategy for teaching third grade children that the Earth is round. The displacement strategy is based on the theory that fundamental conceptual change requires an alternative cognitive starting point which doesn't invoke the features of pre-existing models. While the VR apparatus helped to establish that alternative framework, conceptual change was strongly influenced by the bridging activities which related that experience to the target domain. Simple declarations of relevance proved ineffective. A more articulated bridging process involving physical models was effective for some children, but the multiple representations employed required too much model-matching for others.

Keywords

Learning environments, conceptual change, virtual reality, user models

INTRODUCTION

The expense and concomitant inaccessibility of immersive virtual reality (VR) technologies has invited skepticism over their value as instructional media, particularly for school-age children. Nonetheless, a growing number of researchers [11, 31] have begun to explore methods of effective deployment of these technologies in support of learning.

We believe that VR offers potential benefits for some kinds of learning goals. However, the high costs of investigation in this domain imposes special responsibilities on researchers. At the least, we believe that research in VR and learning should be directed toward learning problems which are:

1. important (represented in recognized curricula standards),
2. hard (demonstrably difficult, or resistant to traditional methods),
3. a priori arguably enhanced by VR technologies, and
4. informed by contemporary theory and practice in education, psychology, and cognitive science.

In this paper, we describe an ongoing research project in which immersive VR is deployed as a component of a

pedagogical strategy for teaching third grade children that the Earth is round. This goal is well represented in the AAAS Project 2061 *Science for all Americans* report, and is a standard component of elementary school science curricula.

Perhaps less well known is that this fact, and, more importantly, the implications surrounding it, are not easily accommodated by young learners. A rich body of literature demonstrates that children often react to the assertion that the Earth is round by forming blended mental models conditioned by their prior experience, or even distinct multiple models, in an attempt to incorporate the new information.

In the remaining sections, we argue that the "Round Earth" case is an exemplar of an important problem in learning that involves fundamental conceptual change. We propose a novel strategy—*displacement learning*—to address that problem, and discuss how VR technologies may be well suited to support that strategy. Finally, we describe an ongoing research project that employs that strategy to address the Round Earth problem, and present empirical evidence of both the potential effectiveness and fragility of its implementation.

A LEARNING PARADOX

The acquisition of deep ideas might well follow laws other than the learning of either propositions or skills [22]. Briefly put, the acquisition of deep ideas moves from the specific to the abstract, while skill acquisition moves from general methods to increasingly domain-specific expertise. The vehicle for skill acquisition is deliberate practice [14]; the vehicle of deep learning is reflective exploration.

Fundamental conceptual change encounters a peculiar paradox. The ideas that underpin advanced understanding in different fields are typically more fundamental than the ideas a novice learner might bring into the field from prior experience [10, 20]. This fact helps explain the puzzling observation that although many deep ideas can be stated in less than a page of text, systematic attempts to teach them nevertheless fail with alarming frequency [6]. Educational researchers, particularly in the fields of science and mathematics, have found over and over again that seemingly thoughtful programs for teaching deep ideas can be unsuccessful (e.g., [25]).

This outcome can be understood in terms of one of the central principles of the learning sciences: *Existing knowledge is the main tool for understanding new experience or new discourse.* In other words, both direct experience and discourse (oral or written) is understood by being analyzed in terms of, or assimilated to, existing knowledge structures. For example, a fairy tale is understood by being subsumed under the reader's existing schema or story grammar for fairy tales. This subsumption process operates without difficulty when experience or discourse is congruent with existing organizing ideas. A narrative of a baseball game, for example, is completely comprehensible to someone who already knows the nature, structure and character of the game. Learning from instructional discourse with a similarly constrained goal is also relatively unproblematic.

However, when either experience or discourse (instructional or otherwise) attempts to communicate a concept that is both different from, and more fundamental than, the learner's existing ideas, a paradox occurs. Although the intent behind the discourse is to replace the learner's existing ideas, those existing ideas are the learner's only tools by which to acquire the new idea [13, 14]. Research in the cognitive sciences has documented that the typical outcome of this fact is distortion: the novel idea is misunderstood in the process of—and as a byproduct of—being assimilated to prior knowledge.

A simple and compelling example of this effect has been documented by Nussbaum [21] and by Vosniadou [29] and Vosniadou and Brewer [30]: Young children tend to believe that the Earth is flat. One's concept of the shape of the Earth has profound consequences for one's interpretation of both experience and discourse, so the shift from a flat Earth to a spherical Earth view counts, at an elementary level, as deep learning in our framework. Empirical studies have demonstrated that if children are told that the Earth is round, they often react to the novel information by constructing a mental model of the Earth as a pancake, flat yet round. The intended message is distorted in the process of assimilation to mean that the Earth is circular (rather than spherical).

Although simple (to adults), we suggest that the flat Earth/round Earth case is prototypical of deep conceptual learning that exemplifies the essential features of the learning paradox at any age level: both experience and discourse that attempt to communicate ideas that are deeper or more fundamental than the ideas the learner already has tends to be distorted in the comprehension process, because those prior ideas are the main tools for understanding. This is the learning paradox [4]. Support for deep learning must overcome this paradox.

CIRCUMVENTING THE LEARNING PARADOX

If the learning paradox is real, how is anything new ever learned? A *transformational* account assumes that new knowledge is created via operations on prior knowledge. Prior knowledge serves as raw material, and new knowledge is the result of generalization, specialization or some other type of cognitive operation, applied to that raw material.

One example of a transformational approach is the classical induction hypothesis: knowledge is created by extracting commonalities across a set of exemplars or instances. Inductive approaches to learning (sometimes referred to as

similarity-based approaches) encounter several unsolved problems, including how to handle exceptions and disjunctions [3]. Another example of a transformational view is the attempt to conceptualize science learning as a form of belief revision, an approach that provides students with evidence to the effect that their intuitive beliefs (sometimes called misconceptions) are false, and that they need to replace them with more accurate beliefs (e.g., [17]). Researchers from Piaget [23] to Karmiloff-Smith [19] have tried to explain cognitive development in terms of so-called transition mechanisms [28]. However, there is as yet no widely accepted description of a developmental transition mechanism. In general, any transformational account of cognitive change assumes the existence of powerful transformations that can traverse the space of possible conceptualizations without search.

In contrast, a *displacement* account of cognitive change assumes that a new understanding of a domain or phenomenon begins by establishing an *alternative cognitive starting point*, an idea or concept that is established outside the learner's existing system of domain knowledge. Initially, such an alternative representation of the domain might be rudimentary, lack detail and have few concrete examples, justifications or arguments associated with it, and hence be completely dominated by the prior, well-established representation. However, over time, all available representations of a domain compete for attentional resources and a representation that is useful in dealing with certain types of situations or problems gradually gains strength and might eventually displace the previous representation. The existence of a compete/evaluate phase allows displacement theories to postulate weaker and hence more plausible operations on prior knowledge than those required by a transformational account. Displacement theories of cognitive change also have support in biology and neuroscience [7].

The displacement framework suggests a particular instructional strategy for supporting deep conceptual learning: fundamental ideas which contrast with the learner's current ideas need to be established on their own terms, so to speak, before they are brought into contact with the learner's prior ideas. In other words, a new idea should not be taught by directly confronting or transforming the learner's current idea, but by establishing an alternative knowledge structure or representation, a cognitive seed out of which a deeper understanding of the relevant domain can grow. After reviewing the evidence related to the learning of so-called ontological categories, Chi [8] reached a similar conclusion: " ... instruction about a new ontological category must proceed by teaching this new ontological category of concepts independently of the old or existing conceptions." (p. 179) We claim that this conclusion holds not just for ontological categories, but for fundamental concepts in general.

The strategy described so far provides us with considerable power to help learners construct alternative mental representations of particular facets of reality. Although crucial, this is not enough. Our overall strategy dictates a second step: eventually, the alternative representation must be brought into contact with the learner's prior knowledge of the domain and absorb or subsume it. Unless learners eventually bring their experience in the displaced domain into contact with everyday experience in the target domain, the learning objective is not reached. The last tactic in our educational strategy is therefore to help the learner interface their new ideas with their prior knowledge. We call activities that aim to do this *bridging activities*. Cognitive research on analogy [9, 15, 18] provide a rich theoretical basis for the design of bridging activities.

THE ASTEROID WORLD

In an attempt to apply these principles to the round earth problem, we constructed a distributed, immersive VR environment that allowed children to explore a small-diameter asteroid. Two distinct interfaces were provided: at any given time, one child was in a CAVE (a three meter cube with rear-projected head-tracked stereo video on three walls and a floor) and the other seated at an ImmersaDesk (a single rear-projected stereo video display approximately the size of a drafting table).

The child in the CAVE (the *astronaut*) was situated on the virtual asteroid surface (Figure 1), and navigated using three buttons on a hand-held wand to move left, right, or forward. (Usability tests employing an isometric thumb joystick were disastrous!) Astronauts were charged with collecting fuel cells (through a proximity trigger) scattered about the surface of the asteroid in order to enable the marooned space ship to return to Earth.

Figure 1. The astronaut/CAVE view of the asteroid. The space ship sits at the North Pole.

The child at the ImmersaDesk (the *mission controller*) was afforded a view of the asteroid from somewhere out in space, along with a direct video feed of the astronaut's view (Figure 2). Mission control used an isometric thumb joystick to rotate and tilt the view of the asteroid, and was charged with directing the astronaut (represented by an avatar on the asteroid) toward available fuel cells. An audio link connects the two users, and additional audio cues are provided when fuel cells are acquired, and when time limits are approaching.

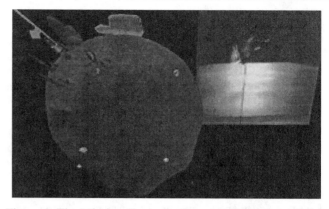

Figure 2. The Mission Controller/ImmersaDesk view of the asteroid. The mission controller simultaneously sees the avatar of the astronaut moving around the spherical asteroid and the view from the astronaut's perspective of the slightly rounded surface of the asteroid.

PILOT STUDY 1

A great deal of component knowledge is subsumed under the rubric of "knowing that the Earth is round." We prepared a 16-item questionnaire (inspired by the items used in [29, 30]) designed to probe for understanding of the following concepts (see Appendix):

1. that the Earth is (roughly) spherical in shape,
2. that there is no absolute "up" or "down" associated with a particular portion of the Earth,
3. that the Earth is continuous and circumnavigable, and
4. that the horizon is a curved edge which may partially or totally occlude objects on the other side (or in space).

Subjects were drawn from a local Chicago public elementary school. The children were third grade students who were required to attend summer school because they had scored below the minimum requirement on the Iowa Test of Basic Skills for promotion to the fourth grade.

Individual oral pre-test interviews based on the questionnaire and lasting 15-20 minutes were conducted at a Chicago public school a day or two prior to their VR experience. Subjects responded to the items with verbal answers, drawings (sometime annotated), gestures, and the construction of PlayDoh models; each assessment was recorded on audio tape.

The children were brought in pairs to a university campus, given a cover story describing the "rescue" scenario, and were given brief training by and adult guide in the use of the VR apparatus. The two distinct interfaces allowed us to employ a tightly coupled "jigsaw" collaboration scheme [2], alternating each child between the two (positively interdependent) roles of astronaut and mission controller. Upon completion of the task, the subjects were brought together in front of the ImmersaDesk for a bridging activity, and an adult interviewer led them through a brief recounting of their experience using the mission controller view as a referent. Each of the four identified knowledge components was reviewed and reinforced in the context of the asteroid, and in each case, the students were told that the same facts applied to the Earth as well, citing similarities and differences (size) between the two celestial bodies. Immediately following the bridging activity, the children were brought to a different room, and interviewed separately (post-test) using the same questionnaire. Following completion of the assessment, they were transported back to their school.

Ten children completed the entire protocol. For each subject, the audio tapes and written documents were reviewed for evidence of learning in each of the four component knowledge areas.

The results were disheartening. Where we had hoped that conversation between the children might focus on apparent contradictions to their daily experience (e.g., "hey, you're upside down," "no, I'm not!"), the discourse focused almost exclusively on the mechanics of the apparatus and the nominal goal of collecting fuel cells. Among the ten subjects, four began with highly immature models of the Earth's shape (typically, pancake shapes); of those four subjects, all continued to hold to their naive models in the post-test interviews. The remaining six subjects had indicated a belief in the sphericality of Earth in the pre-tests, but all fell short on one or more of the remaining knowledge components. Among those six, there was limited improvement in the relativity of up and down questions, and in the circumnavigability questions. Still, the robust outcome we had hoped for was obviously missing.

We called a halt to the first pilot study, and considered the factors that may have led to our limited success. While we were able to identify numerous potential sources (including the design of the application interfaces, novelty effects, learning and attention deficit disorders among our subject pool, social and communications difficulties among subject pairs, and more), we focused on what we believed were the two most important issues: overengagement in the task at the expense of learning, and the failure to bridge learning about the asteroid to the subjects' mental models of Earth.

PILOT STUDY 2

To address these issues, a second pilot study was conducted, with two important protocol changes. First, the initial "training" period with the VR apparatus was modified so that the adult guide spent several minutes drawing the subjects' attention to salient features of the asteroid which reflected the target knowledge components prior to establishing the nominal task goal. We hoped that this would help to overcome the subjects' overwhelming focus on the mechanics of collecting the fuel cells while at the same time serving as an advance organizer for the target knowledge goals.

Second, we made a significant change in the bridging activity following the VR experience. We built a feature-faithful Styrofoam scale model of the asteroid, and purchased a larger commercial Earth globe. In place of the joint ImmersaDesk debriefing, we substituted individual bridging sessions lasting about 15 minutes for each participant. During those sessions, we systematically reviewed each of the knowledge components, using a

discussion to relate the subjects' experience in the VR environment first to the Styrofoam model of the asteroid, then to the Earth globe, citing the analogies between the two physical models. In each case, movable stick-on props and figurines were used to represent VR objects and the participants themselves. Out of concern that the immediacy and nature of the revised bridging activity might lead to surface similarity in the post-test, we delayed the follow-up assessments until the next day, back at the children's school. As it turned out, the discovery nature of the bridging activity itself proved useful in comparing the persistence of apparent learning.

Ten children participated in the second pilot study, drawn from the same subject pool as in the first pilot. There was little direct evidence that the change in the initial training protocol had much effect; the children's dialogues continued to be almost exclusively operational. However, unlike the first pilot, there were some success stories. Among the eight children, seven reflected immature initial (pancake) models; among this group, two appeared to have adopted a spherical model of Earth by the time of the post-test, and a third subject moved to a dual model of Earth in which one component was spherical. In the following, we contrast the experience of an apparently successful learner with one whose post-test interview did not appear to reflect conceptual change.

A Case of Learning Failure

Ebony is a nine-year old third grader. During her pre-test, Ebony drew a circle to represent the Earth, with land masses scattered around the interior of the circle. Her PlayDoh model of the Earth was shaped like a pancake. When asked what was in the area around the Earth on her drawing, Ebony indicated that there was water "underneath" her circle, and a moon "above" the circle. She indicated that there was an end to the earth, and that an animal could accidentally fall off the end "onto the ground." Ebony responded to the "baskets" question (Appendix, question 15) by insisting that the girls would put balls in each other's baskets. She indicated that the balls would fall through the "shafts" (Appendix, question 16).

Following her VR experience, Ebony was quite animated in her discussion, and operational descriptions of the event dominated her spontaneous discourse. When asked what she did, she responded "I was going around a moon, and it was like a big ball." The interviewer asked again, "Was it more like a pancake, or more like a ball?" Ebony reiterated that it was "like a ball." The interviewer told Ebony that "the Earth is like a ball, too, only larger," with which she appeared to concur, elaborating with "and heavier, too." The interviewer asked Ebony what would happen if you were on the asteroid and you kept walking, to which she responded "You would fall off but she [her VR partner] didn't fall" because "she was kinda like stuck." After the interviewer had indicated that the same phenomenon would hold on the Earth, he asked why people in Australia didn't fall off. She answered that "They don't walk on the globe."

In her post-test the following day, Ebony was still quite excited about the VR experience, and continued to discuss the operational characteristics of the controls. She noted that (at the ImmersaDesk) "you move the ball around" to the operational characteristics of the controls. She noted that (at the ImmersaDesk) "you move the ball around" to help direct her friend. She answered the decontextualized up/down questions correctly (Appendix, questions 1, 2), but when asked to build a PlayDoh model of the Earth, she produced a pancake shape, indicating that the "bottom" of the pancake was where oceans, lakes, rivers, and the beach were located. When asked directly whether her shape was more like a pancake or a ball, Ebony replied "a pancake." The interviewer asked her whether she remembered talking about the shape of the Earth the day before ("Yes") and asked what he had told her, to which she replied "The Earth is round, almost like a ball. And the green stuff is like Earth, and the blue stuff is like the sea." Ebony continued to believe that there was an end of the Earth (Appendix, questions 9, 10), and that if you walked past, you would fall "into the mountains or something, or the hills, or far away." Asked why she didn't fall off when she was on the asteroid, she replied "Cause I was an astronaut and it was like I was glued on." Ebony's drawing of Earth continue to have a strict orientation (moon on top, circular Earth in the middle, lakes and oceans on the bottom). Her response to the horizontal shaft question, unlike on the pre-test, had the ball falling toward the bottom of the page.

A Case of Conceptual Change

Celandra is also a nine-year-old third grade student. During her pre-test, Celandra held that up and down were absolute for all people on the Earth, and made a circular drawing to reflect the Earth's shape, with people living "all over" the interior of the circle. Her PlayDoh model was pancake-shaped, with people living "only on the top." Celandra reported that people couldn't see things far away "because it's too far and it might be cloudy." She answered the airplane question (Appendix, question 7) by saying that the airplane would go to the end of the Earth, where it was "very cold and it would be like different people." An animal could accidentally fall off the Earth, into a "big open space...under the ground." The sun and moon were sometimes not visible because they "went to another planet" or were "behind some clouds." Celandra's basket (Figure 3) and shafts pictures reflected an absolute notion of up and down.

When asked what she had done in the VR experience, Celandra gave a strictly operational response, describing the number of fuel cells collected and the interaction with her partner. When asked the shape of the asteroid, she said it was "like a ball" rather than a pancake, and expressed strong agreement that the Styrofoam model was like the asteroid. Celandra said that the space surrounding the Styrofoam model was filled with stars. She indicated that if you continued to walk around the asteroid, "you'd end up back to the space ship again, but on a different side [of the ship]." When asked the same question regarding the Earth, she believed that she would return to Chicago, where she started. Celandra felt that during her VR experience it felt like she might fall off the asteroid, but she didn't, because "it's a round ball," and that people on the south pole of Earth wouldn't fall off, either.

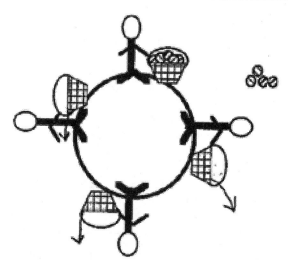

Figure 3. Celandra's balls falling out of the baskets during her pre-test; down is always toward the bottom of the page.

During her post-test, Celandra believed that up and down were relative to where you were on Earth, and that "up" in China was not the same as "up" in Chicago "because the earth is like a ball and people who are down up under the earth then they won't fall off." She pointed over her head when asked where "down" was for people in China. In contrast to her pre-test, Celandra created a sphere for her PlayDoh Earth model, and indicated that people live "up here and down here," pointing to both northern and southern hemispheres. She couldn't see where a cannon ball lands on the other side of the Earth, she said, because "it's blocked. Cuz the earth is just round and it's like a ball and it's blocked by the ball."

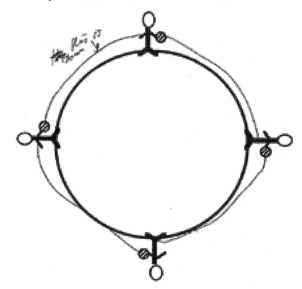

Figure 4. Celandra's balls falling "down" during her post-tests; down is clockwise in the figure.

Flying straight for a long time in an airplane would take her back to Chicago, she stated, and she would never get to the end of the Earth because "it's a round ball." People couldn't fall off the Earth because "people live up and down, and [pointing to the South Pole of her PlayDoh model] down is up for them." She continued to believe that the moon and the sun became invisible because of clouds or their movement to other planets. The space surrounding her PlayDoh model was filled with "stars," but the space surrounding her (circular) drawing of Earth was filled with "oceans." Celandra's shaft models were correct in both orientations; the released balls picture (Figure 4) at first appeared incorrect, but she explained that the labeled arc was "down" to the person on the left side of the circle.

Analysis

To Ebony, the VR experience was engaging, but appeared to have little effect on her model of the Earth. Her observation that her friend should have fallen of the asteroid, but didn't, along with her feeling of being "glued on," indicated that she believed the VR representation to be unrealistic. She readily accepted that the shape of the VR and Styrofoam asteroids were spherical ("like a ball"), and concurred that the shape of the Earth globe was also spherical. Ebony's response that Australians didn't fall off the Earth because "they don't walk on the globe" indicated to us that she viewed the Earth globe and the Earth as distinct (unrelated) objects. This was reinforced during her post-test, when she created a pancake PlayDoh model of Earth, then replied to the interviewer's question about the prior day's experience by describing the Earth as a blue and green ball—a clear reference to the globe.

Celandra, in contrast, appeared to undergo a fundamental conceptual change, from a flat pancake with an ominous "end" to a spherical body where up and down were relative to position. Her model was not perfect—there were still oceans outside her drawing of Earth, and while she understood occlusion for Earth-bound objects, she didn't use the same reasoning for other celestial bodies. Nonetheless, she appeared to understand that what she had learned about the asteroid also now applied to *her* Earth as well.

DISCUSSION

While immersive VR is sometimes derided as a technology in search of application, it provides visualization and interaction features which appear to hold promise for learning applications. Salzman, et. al. [26] cite three promising features of VR with respect to learning: three-dimensional immersion, multiple frames of reference, and multisensory cues. Our asteroid environment utilizes all three of these VR features.

Was the VR experience an integral part of the learning for our subjects? For those subjects who appeared to undergo conceptual change, we believe that it was effective in helping to establish an "alternative cognitive starting point," as required by the displacement learning model. Unlike Ebony, who continued to hold a "separate reality," these subjects found the asteroid a plausible reality, and were able to use their experience to subsequently reason about how things might be on Earth.

But accepting the VR asteroid as plausible was not enough. Subjects in both pilot studies who appeared to find the asteroid believable did not successfully bridge their knowledge to the target domain. For subjects in pilot study

1, we believe that the fault lay in the abruptness of the intended bridging activity, and that simply telling them that their new knowledge applied to Earth left them too tools with which to bridge between two apparently dissimilar representations.

The pilot study 2 subjects who succeeded in changing their concept of Earth did so, we believe, because the revised bridging procedures afforded them an articulated chain of representations from source to target domain, with each new representation being sufficiently similar to its predecessor to be accepted.

The "long path back" didn't work for everyone in pilot study 2; we still had more failures than successes. Here, a reasonable interpretation might be that revising the bridging procedure introduced too many intermediate representations, and that the cognitive demands were simply too great for the subjects to handle [1]. (After all, these children had to deal with six distinct external representations: two versions of the VR asteroid, the Styrofoam asteroid model, the Earth globe, their 2-D drawings, and their PlayDoh models.)

It is not new news that transfer of learning does not always occur, and the issue as to when, and under which circumstances, it does occur, remains an unresolved (and perpetually engaging) problem [16, 24, 27]. In the context of programming systems, there has been a great deal of evidence demonstrating the difficulty of transfer (e.g., [5]) between representations.

VR is good at delivering multiple, even believable, representations, and in so doing, seems an attractive medium for displacement learning strategies. If the representations used are too far from the target domain, however, they run the risk of being viewed as a separate reality. If they are too numerous, they run the risk of overwhelming the learner in feature matching.

At a time when even the phrase *virtual reality* has no consensus definition, it is implausible that decontextualized results demonstrating its generalized efficacy as a learning medium are even achievable. The important job for researchers interested in VR-based learning environments is to find workable balances among available technologies, learning goal, users' developmental stage, interaction designs, social settings, and a host of other factors, which demonstrate promise—not proofs—of concept.

Our discussion has avoided altogether the most decontextualized aspect of the work reported: its locus. We used real school children, but we did it (for the most part) in an unreal setting—a one-shot experience in a university laboratory. We are currently working with teachers at a local public elementary school in planning a multi-year deployment of VR technologies within an established curriculum structure. We hope to be able to report more evidence concerning the use of VR and displacement learning, including a revisiting of the Round Earth problem, based on that experience.

ACKNOWLEDGMENTS

We wish to thank Shirley Woodard, Program Director of South Loop Elementary School in Chicago, IL, and her third grade students, for their enthusiastic participation in the Round Earth project. Joe Alexander, Carlos Orrego, Maria Roussos, Mike Tolio, Jospephine Anstey, Jim Costigan, Tom Frisch, Jason Leigh, Dave Pape, and Tom DeFanti were instrumental to the application design, development, and support. Jyoti Jain, Mark Orr, Josh Hemmerich, and Elaine Ohlsson assisted in the development and application of the assessment interviews.

This research was supported by funding from the National Science Foundation award EIA 9720351, supported by NSF awards CDA-9303433, CDA-9512272, NCR-9712283, CDA-9720351, and the NSF ASC Parnerships for Advance Computational Infrastructure program. The CAVE and ImmersaDesk are trademakrs of the Board of Trustees of the University of Illinois.

REFERENCES

1. Ainsworth, S., Bibby, P.A., & Wood, D.J. (1997). Information technology and multiple representations: New opportunities—new problems. *Journal of Information Technology for Teacher Education*, 6, 93-104.

2. Aronson, E., Blaney, N., Stephan, C., Sikes, J., & Snapp, M. (1978). *The Jigsaw Classroom*. Beverly Hills, CA: Sage.

3. Angluin, D., & Smith, C. H. (1983). Inductive inference: Theory and methods. *Computing Surveys, 15*, 237-269.

4. Bereiter, C., (1985). Toward a solution of the learning paradox. *Review of Educational Research, 55*, 201-226.

5. Bonar, J. & Cunningham, R. (1988). Bridge: Tutoring the programming process. In J. Psotka, L. Massey, and S. Mutter (Eds.), *Intelligent tutoring systems: Lessons learned* (pp. 409-434). Hillsdale, NJ: Lawrence Erlbaum.

6. Bruer, J. T. (1994). *Schools for thought: A science of learning in the classroom*. Cambridge, MA: MIT Press.

7. Calvin, W. H. (1996). *The cerebral code*. Cambridge, MA: MIT Press.

8. Chi, M. T. H. (1992). Conceptual change within and across ontological categories: Examples from learning and discovery in science. In R. N. Giere, (Ed.), *Cognitive models of science* (pp. 129-186). Minneapolis, Minnesota: University of Minnesota Press.

9. Clement, J. (1988). Observed methods for generating analogies in scientific problem solving. *Cognitive Science, 12*, 563-586.

10. Confrey, J. (1990). A review of research on student conceptions in mathematics, science, and programming. In C. B. Cazdan, (Ed.), *Review of research in education* (Vol. 16, pp. 3-56). Washington, DC: American Educational Research Association.

11. Dede, C., Salzman, M., & Loftin, R. (1996) ScienceSpace: Virtual Realities for Learning Complex and Abstract Scientific Concepts. In *Proceedings VRAIS '96* (pp.246-253).

12. DiSessa, A. A. (1988). Knowledge in pieces. In G. Forman & P. Pufall, (Eds.), Constructivism in the computer age (pp. 49-70). Hillsdale, NJ: Erlbaum.

13. DiSessa, A. A. (1993). Toward an epistemology of physics. *Cognition and Instruction, 10*, 105-225.

14. Ericsson, K. A., Krampe, R. Th., & Tesch-Romer, C. (1993). The role of deliberate practice in the acquisition of expert performance. *Psychological Review, 100*, 363-406.

15. Gentner, D., Rattermann, M., Forbus, K. (1993). The role of similarity in transfer. *Cognitive Psychology, 25*, 524-575.

16. Gick, M., & Holyoak, J. (1987). The cognitive basis for knowledge transfer. In S. Cormier and J.Hagman (Eds.), Transfer of learning (pp. 9-46). San Diego, CA: Academic Press.

17. Hewson, P. W., & Hewson, M. G. A. (1984). The role of conceptual conflict in conceptual change and the design of science instruction. *Instructional Science, 13*, 1-13.

18. Holyoak, K. J., & Thagard, P. (1995). *Mental leaps*. Cambridge, MA: Cambridge University Press.

19. Karmiloff-Smith, A. (1992). *Beyond modularity: A developmental perspective on cognitive science*. Cambridge, MA: MIT Press.

20. McCloseky, (1983). Intuitive theories of motion. In D. Gentner & A. L. Stevens, (Eds.), *Mental models* (pp. 299-323). Hillsdale, NJ: Erlbaum.

21. Nussbaum, J. (1985). The Earth as a cosmic body. In R. Driver, E. Guesne, & A. Tiberghien (Eds.), *Children's ideas in science* (pp.170-192). Milton Keynes, UK: Open University Press.

22. Ohlsson, S. (1995a). Learning to do and learning to understand: A lesson and a challenge for cognitive modeling. In P. Reimann and H. Spada, (Eds.), *Learning in humans and machines: Towards an interdisciplinary learning science*. Oxford, UK: Elsevier.

23. Piaget, J. (1985). *The equilibration of cognitive structures*. Chicago, IL: The University of Chicago Press.

24. Reber, A. (1993). *Implicit learning and tacit knowledge*. New York: Oxford University Press.

25. Resnick, L. B., & Omanson, S. (1987). Learning to understand arithmetic. In R. Glaser, (Ed.), *Advances in instructional psychology* (Vol. 3, pp. 41-95). Hillsdale, NJ: Erlbaum.

26. Salzman, M., Dede, C., Loftin, R., & Chen, J. A. (1998)A model for understanding how virtual reality aids complex conceptual learning. *Presence* (in press).

27. Singley, M., & Anderson, J. R. (1989). *The transfer of cognitive skill*. Cambridge, MA: Harvard University Press.

28. Sternberg, R. J., (Ed.), (1984). *Mechanisms of cognitive development*. New York: W. H. Freeman.

29. Vosniadou, S. (1994). Capturing and modeling the process of conceptual change. *Learning and Instruction, 4*, 45-69.

30. Vosniadou. S., & Brewer, W. F. (1994). Mental models of the day/night cycle. *Cognitive Science, 18,* 123-183.

31. Youngblut, C. (1998) Educational uses of virtual reality technology. Technical Report IDA Document D-2128, Institute for Defense Analyses, Alexandria, VA.

APPENDIX: INTERVIEW QUESTIONS

1. Which way is "up" (for you)? Which way is "down" (for you)? Is up and down always that way?

2. Which way is "down" for people in China? If you were pointing up and someone in China were pointing up, would you be pointing in the same direction?

3. Draw a picture of the Earth.

4. Show where people live (on your drawing).

5. Can people see things that are very far away?

6. If we shoot a cannon ball from here to <u>Australia</u>/<u>China</u>, can we see where it lands? If now, why not? (Draw a picture.)

7. If you jump into an airplane and fly in the same direction (at the same height) for a very long time, how far could you go? Where would you end up if you just kept going and going?

8. Would you ever come back to where you started? (If yes, please draw a picture.)

9. Would you ever get to the end of the Earth? If yes, what does the end look like? If no, why does the Earth have no end?

10. Could you/an animal accidentally fall off the Earth? If yes, how would that happen? To where would you fall? If no, why not?

11. *With regard to the child's drawing of the Earth, ask:* "What is here?" while pointing to the region on the side of the drawing. If yes, what is here?

12. Show where the moon is (on the Earth drawing). Can the moon be anywhere else?

13. Where is the moon during the day when we cannot see it?

14. Draw a sunset. Why is the sun disappearing? Why can't we see it during the night? Where does it go?

15. With regard to the following drawing: What happens if you put the balls in the "other" <u>baskets</u>/<u>let go of the balls</u>?

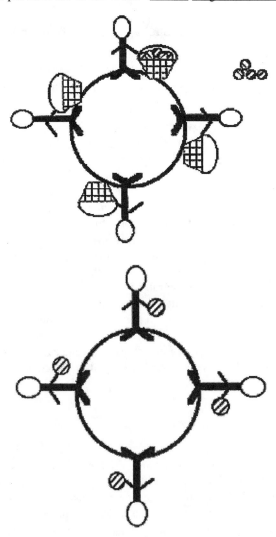

16. In these pictures of the Earth, a <u>shaft</u> has been drilled all the way through. What happens when the persons lets go of the ball?

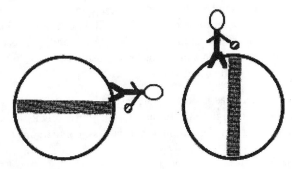

The Tangled Web We Wove: A Taskonomy of WWW Use

Michael D. Byrne[1], **Bonnie E. John**[2], **Neil S. Wehrle**[3], **David C. Crow**[4]

[1]Department of Psychology
[2]Human-Computer Interaction Institute
[3]School of Design
Carnegie Mellon University
Pittsburgh, PA 15213

[4]Trilogy Development Group
6034 West Courtyard Dr.
Austin, TX 78730

byrne@acm.org, bej@cs.cmu.edu, nsw+@andrew.cmu.edu, david.crow@acm.org

ABSTRACT

A prerequisite to the effective design of user interfaces is an understanding of the tasks for which that interface will actually be used. Surprisingly little task analysis has appeared for one of the most discussed and fastest-growing computer applications, browsing the World-Wide Web (WWW). Based on naturally-collected verbal protocol data, we present a taxonomy of tasks undertaken on the WWW. The data reveal that several previous claims about browsing behavior are questionable, and suggests that that widget-centered approaches to interface design and evaluation may be incomplete with respect to good user interfaces for the Web.

Keywords

World-Wide Web, task analysis, video protocols

INTRODUCTION

A great deal of public and research interest has been devoted to the World-Wide Web (or WWW) in recent years. Most of this research effort has focused on the technical aspects of the Web and the application of new Web-based technologies. Our concern, however, is with the usability of the Web, in particular the use of browsers. In order to perform any kind of sensible usability evaluation, be it empirical, analytical, or heuristic, it is necessary to first understand the tasks users engage in while browsing. That is, in order to determine which HCI techniques and/or approaches are most likely to aid in Web usability, it is first necessary to understand what is that users actually do with their time while using the Web.

While there has been valuable research on patterns of Web use (e.g. navigation patterns [1, 7]), these "click-studies" provide little information about the task contexts in which the users' actions occurred. For example, a click study can provide information about how often pages are visited and links are traversed, but not the tasks in which users were engaged while doing so. The focus of the present research is to gain a clearer understanding of the tasks users engage in while browsing the Web and the time spent doing those tasks. This will enable rating the relative importance of various interface analysis methods—there is little to be gained by analyzing tasks which users rarely perform, or which cost users very little time.

Further, we wanted to observe the tasks users normally perform in their daily Web use, rather than giving them artificial tasks. While observing users doing specific tasks can be useful, it is possible that the task or tasks used in the study might not reflect the tasks that users do when left to make their own decisions about how their time is allocated. Other naturalistic studies of user behavior [e.g. 2] have found that undirected user behavior is much more complex and interleaved than directed behavior.

THE STUDY

Participants were asked to browse the WWW as they would on a normal work day and provide verbal protocols describing what they were doing as they browsed. A video camera was set up to record both the protocol and the user's screen as they browsed, for one day of browsing. The participants were eight volunteers from the university community, all of whom were experienced Web users. We attempted to collect a reasonable cross-section of users and had faculty, students, secretarial staff, and research staff included in the sample. In order to encourage the participants to engage in the kind of browsing they would do normally, they were videotaped in their offices (or home in the case of one student participant) using their normal workstation. While it is possible that participants altered their browsing patterns due to the presence of the video camera, we explicitly discouraged this. A variety of platforms and browsers were used, with Netscape Navigator running on a Power Macintosh being the most frequent choice. Approximately 5.75 hours of videotape was

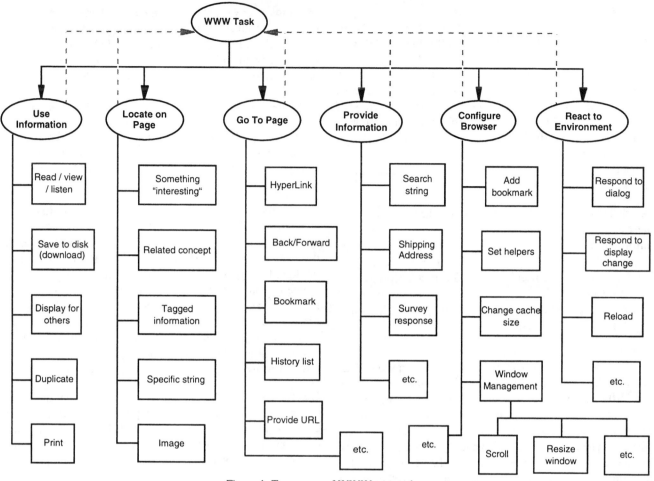

Figure 1. Taxonomy of WWW user tasks

collected and analyzed, of which 5 hours was WWW browsing. The amount of data generated and analyzed for each participant ranged from approximately 15 minutes to over 74 minutes. One of two analysts coded each videotape.

TASKONOMY

We constructed a taxonomy of tasks (a "taskonomy", shown in Figure 1) through a combination of our prior research into information-finding, analysis of the the capabilities of the Web and Web browsers, personal introspection, and observing our first three users. We observed six general classes of Web tasks: Use Information, Locate on Page, Go To Page, Provide Information, Configure Browser, and React to Environment.

As an example of how we constructed this taskonomy, consider the task Locate on Page. Our prior research in the use of a textual on-line help system [6] indicated that when attempting to locate information, users could search for a specific string or a related concept. Since web pages also include images, we included a category for locating an image. Introspecting, we added a category for locating something "interesting." Finally, we observed one of our

first three users searching for information that would be tagged with a specific string (explained below).

While we had to add one subcategory to fully cover the five additional protocols (Go To Page using the history list that pops up when the Back button is depressed in newer versions of Netscape), the six main categories remained unchanged. That is, the taskonomy was virtually unchanged after analyzing the first three users, and then successfully covered the remaining five protocols (only two events out of 892 new events fell outside the original taskonomy, both of which were the unforeseen type of Goto). More details about the coding scheme can be found at: <http://act.psy.cmu.edu/ACT/people/ byrne/webtask/guide.html>.

We chose to code the protocols at this level because we believed this to be a useful first pass at understanding how users allocated their time in terms of tasks and behaviors. Other levels of abstraction are both possible and potentially useful and should be pursued in follow-up research.

Use Information

Use Information describes any activity (or series of activities) in which the user was attempting to use a piece of information from the WWW. The Use Information subcategories were based on our observations of what the first three users did with the information they obtained from the Web. Information on the Web can serve a variety of purposes: it can be read, listened to, viewed or watched (e.g. images, animations, layouts), duplicated (e.g. copy and paste), downloaded to a local disk, displayed for others, printed. Most activities done while browsing the Web are in service of a Use Information task.

A Use Information task began whenever the user initiated a new activity with the goal of making use of some piece of information. The task was considered complete whenever the desired use had been made or the user explicitly gave up. For example, if a user had a Use Information(print) task, it would be considered started as soon as the user did anything to find that piece of information and ended when the Print dialog had finished.

Locate

Frequently, using a piece of information or going to a URL requires finding that information or link on a Web page, which typically requires some visual search. We called these activities Locate tasks. Users could search for a specific word, which we called Locate String search. Users also searched for particular images (e.g. graphic links), coded as Locate Image. They could be looking for something not necessarily a particular word or image but anything related to a concept (e.g. "I'm looking for 'photography' or 'cameras' or something like that"), which we termed Locate Related. Another class of searches can be best described as Locate Interesting, in which a user is seeking no specific word or concept, but is simply looking for something that might catch their interest. The most difficult kind of search to explain, but one which was observed, was what we called Locate Tagged. When a user was looking for a particular piece of information and did not know what it was that they were looking for, but knew some tag that would identify it as the piece of information they wanted, it was coded as Locate Tagged. For example, one user wanted to know the resolution of a printer he was considering purchasing. He did not know the number of dots per inch for the printer, but knew that the number he wanted would be tagged with something like "resolution" or "DPI" or the like. This is distinct from Locate Related in that it is not the concept that the user is searching for, but a value pointed to by some tag matching a concept or word.

Locate tasks were coded as beginning either as soon as the relevant page was visually available to be searched (usually after loading) or the user's protocol gave evidence they were searching. Locates were typically considered complete when the user explicitly indicated they had found the item or when a mouse movement was made to the target item. Alternately, a Locate task could be coded as finished when the user gave up, either explicitly or by navigating to a page not linked to the current one (e.g. clicking "back").

Note that our use of Locate does not mean "Locate a page on the Web" but is more like "Locate an item on a page." Locating a particular page on the WWW can require one simple GoTo (e.g. if the page is bookmarked) or a series of Locates and GoTos (e.g. following a series of hyperlinks).

Go To

Any activity which caused the browser to display a particular URL we considered a Go To. Most browsers support a wide array of ways in which a browser can be directed to a URL, including the back/forward button, bookmarks, hyperlinks, typing in a URL, history menus, a Home button, and others. Our subcategories of GoTo were based on an analysis of the methods supported by the browsers used. Go To tasks are typically fairly rapid, but they can be time-consuming, such as when typing a long URL is involved, the network response is slow, or the browser takes a long time to render the page.

GoTos were coded as starting as soon as the command that caused the browser to change pages was initiated (for example, as soon as users pointed at the URL field in the toolbar) and were coded as complete as soon as the destination page was displayed with enough content that it was possible for the user to interact with it.

Provide Information

Users not only use the Web to get information, but to send it as well. They provide product selections, authentication information, shipping addresses, search criteria, and so on. These activities were all classified as Provide Info tasks. Provide info tasks were coded as beginning as soon as the user began the mouse move or typing that supplied the information (usually in a form) and ended as soon as there was confirmation that the information had been received (typically by the display of the response page). There are a potentially infinite number of kinds of information users could be providing, so we made no strong commitments to particular subcategorization.

Configure

There is a wide variety of browser state information that is user-configurable, and changing the state of the browser (other than which URL to view) we termed Configure tasks. The kinds of Configure tasks available to the user depended on the number of user-configurable options provided by the browsing software. The most obvious aspect of a browser that users can (and frequently do) change is the state of the window or windows. Users can change the size, location, order, scroll position, and number of browser windows (among other things). There are other things about the browser that users can change, however, such as bookmarks and assorted other preferences like cache size.

Configure tasks were coded as beginning as soon as a mouse move or keystroke involved in changing whatever aspect of the browser state change began, and ended whenever the final state at the end of the task had been reached.

React

While most browsing activities are user-driven rather than browser-driven, there are times when the browser demands something of the user. We classified these situations as React tasks. These are typically in the form of a responding to a dialog box (e.g. where to save a file, can't find a DNS entry, etc.), but can take other forms. One common other form is the use of the Reload button—the user is reacting to some problem with a page display. Many React tasks have Configure tasks as subgoals. For example, when a page is loaded that has a fixed-width table in it that is wider than the current window, this often causes the user to react with a Configure task to change the window width.

React tasks were coded as beginning whenever a dialog or extraneous window appeared, or whenever the mouse movement to the control (e.g. the "Reload" button) required to react to the situation started. React tasks were considered complete when the dialog or window had been dismissed or when the action initiated by the React task completed (e.g. the page had reloaded).

Subtask Sequencing

In general, these tasks cascaded a great deal and had subtasks. For example, one user wanted to download a paper written by a colleague. Thus, the top-level goal was to Use Information (download). The user decided to use a search engine to find the colleague's page, which generated a Go To Page (bookmark) task to get to the engine. Once there, the user engaged in a Provide Information task to tell the search engine what to look for, followed by a Locate on Page task to find the appropriate link. This was followed by another Go To Page (hyperlink) task to the relevant page, then another Locate on Page to find a link to the paper itself. The entire episode counts as a single Use Information task, with several subtasks performed in sequence:

UseInfo(download)
    GoTo(bookmark)
    ProvideInfo(search criterion)
    Locate (related)
    GoTo(hyperLink)
    Locate(related)

This episode generated six task instances. Note that the

duration of the top-level Use Information task would include the time taken for all the subtasks—the task covers the time beginning when the user begins their attempt to download the file until the download is complete.

Use Information tasks are not the only kinds of tasks that can have subtasks. In fact, all of the task types can (and did) have subtasks. Locate tasks often have Configure subtasks, such as scrolling the window. Provide Information tasks can generate Use Information tasks (often Duplicate) to provide form fill-in values. Configure tasks rarely have subtasks, but do occasionally (such as a Use Information subtask to determine what it is that a particular preference does). React tasks, as previously mentioned, often have Configure subtasks. Furthermore, tasks at *any* level could generate subtasks—this did not occur only at the top level. Since each task type can generate one or more of the other types as a subtask at any level, there is very little *a priori* hierarchy that can be imposed on the taxonomy.

RESULTS

We originally expected the tasks to form a hierarchy, but we discovered that any one of these general classes of tasks can generate any other type of task as a subgoal, thus, the "hierarchy" is tangled and nearly flat—not so much a strict hierarchy.

Top-level Categories

We found that our six top-level tasks (Use Information, Go To, Locate, Provide Information, Configure, and React) did an excellent job of capturing the types of behavior engaged in by our users. All episodes in the protocols fit into these six categories. Not surprisingly, some tasks were more frequent than other and some took both more total time and more time per task. Results for the top-level tasks are presented in Figures 2 and 3.

Note that the most common (in terms of raw number) class of events are actually Configure events. Users often needed to scroll the page in the window, and each time a user scrolled, this created a Configure task (frequently as a subtask of Locate). This finding conflicts with other reports that users are reluctant to scroll [4].

However, in terms of total time it is clear that the tasks that dominated our users' browsing was Use Information. This is hardly surprising since the widespread dissemination of information cheaply and quickly was the original purpose of the WWW. The next most time-consuming activity was Locate. Locate often had Configure as a subtask, because users often needed to scroll to locate the item for which they were looking.

The GoTo class of tasks occupied our users for a fair amount of time as well. What is striking about this number is that most of the time taken to perform a GoTo is time

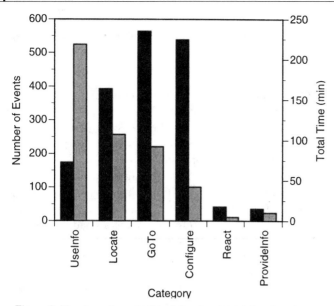

Figure 2. Number of events (black bars) and total time in minutes (gray bars) for each type of top-level task

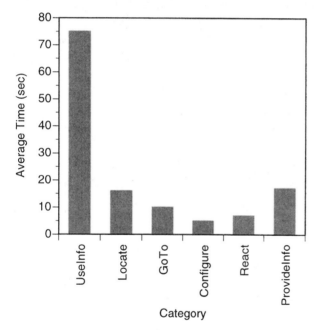

Figure 3. Average time (in seconds) spent on each top-level task category

waiting for the page to load. Over 50% of that GoTo time is, in fact, simply users waiting for page loads.

Note also that the time spent sums to more total time than we had videotape. This is because tasks nest within one another, as previously discussed.

Average times are revealing as well. The average Use Information task took our users over a minute. There are two reasons these tasks are so much longer than the other

task types. First, these tasks include reading. Despite claims to the contrary [5], some users actually do spend time reading, rather than merely scanning, Web pages. Second, Use Information tasks typically had more subtasks. The information to be used often had to be found using a series of Locates and Gotos.

Provide Info tasks were the next longest on average. These tasks typically involve at least some typing, and can sometimes require a large number of clicks and keystrokes. Provide Info tasks also have system response time included, as a Provide Info task was not scored as being completed until the response page was displayed.

Several of the task categories have interesting divisions. In particular, Use Information, Locate, and GoTo have useful subcategories. Provide Informations and Reacts were neither especially frequent or particularly time-consuming, so those will not be considered in greater detail. Configure tasks were frequent, but the bulk of them (477 out of 538, taking up 33 minutes total time) were scrolling.

Use Information

Use Information was the dominant category in terms of both total and average time. While this is hardly surprising, this does raise the question of what is it that users want to do with the information they get from the Web—why are they browsing in the first place.

The breakdown of Use Information tasks by subcategories is presented in Figures 4 and 5, again by total number, of tasks observed, total time spent, and average time per task. These data are clearly dominated by Read tasks in terms of

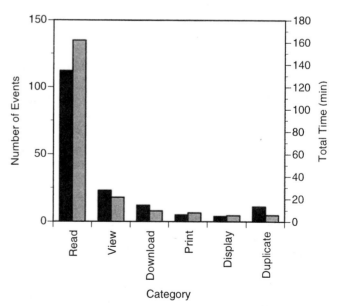

Figure 4. Number of events (black bars) and total time in minutes (gray bars) for each type of Use Information task

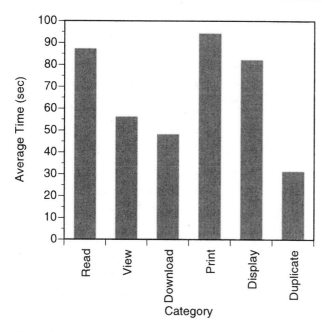

Figure 5. Average time spent on each type of Use Information task (in seconds)

number and total time. With respect to average time, only the Read subcategory has sufficient number of events to provide a stable estimate.

Locate

When looking for an item on a page, there are various levels of specificity users have in mind. These were categorized into one of four types: String (or Image), Interesting, Related, and Tagged. Breakdowns by type for number of observations, total time, and average time are presented in Figures 6 and 7.

It is noteworthy that the Tagged search was the least common in terms of both frequency and total time. Tagged searches tended to occur only at the leaf nodes of multi-page searches, which were guided primarily by other types of search.

String searches, which are the most specific type of search, were the most rapid on average. Searching for specific strings was not as common as the more general types of searches and tended to be a result of users looking for a specific text-based anchor which they knew was already present on a page. Thus, these searches were probably aided both by the users' spatial memory for the page and the fact that revisitation of links is common. Revisitation often meant the sought-after link had been visited recently, and most browsers display recently-visited text in a different color than non-anchor, non-visited text. (Visual search for a distinct color is typically very rapid. [8])

The relative frequency of searches for something Interesting

is also noteworthy. In typical laboratory studies of WWW use [e.g. 3], users are given specific search goals. However, we intentionally did not give users such targets, which likely resulted in a greater number of less-directed searches for things that just appeared "interesting" to the user.

GoTo

While most Web browsers support a wide array of methods for changing the URL being viewed, actual usage patterns suggest that users tend to rely mostly on a small number of methods. Figures 8 and 9 present the number, total time, and average time of the GoTo tasks performed by our users. GoTo task times also include time that most users would rather not spend, time waiting for pages to load. (The GoTo operation is not considered complete until the new URL is

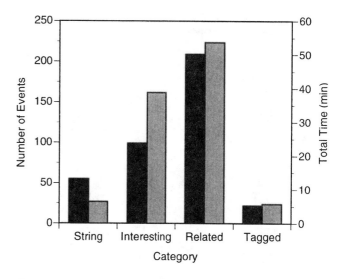

Figure 6. Number of events (black bars) and total time in minutes (gray bars) for each type of Locate task

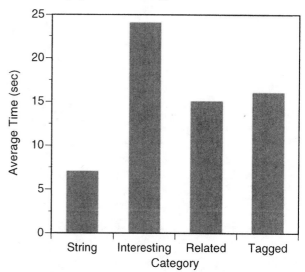

Figure 7. Average time (in seconds) spent on each type of Locate task

displayed.) Overall, our users spent over 47 minutes waiting (of the 5 hours total time spent browsing), and nearly all of this waiting was time spent waiting for pages to load. This number is probably a significant underestimation of the proportion of time average users spend waiting, as all but one of our participants had high-speed ethernet-based network connections (the Carnegie Mellon campus is served by a T3). Furthermore, one of the most experienced users—also an experienced programmer—had an aggressive multi-window browsing strategy clearly motivated by the desire to get something else done while waiting for slow pages to load. Thus, this is likely a very conservative estimate of the amount of time wasted by waiting.

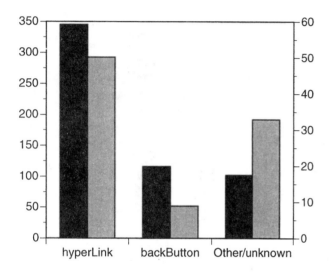

Figure 8. Number of events (black bars) and total time in minutes (gray bars) for each type of Goto task

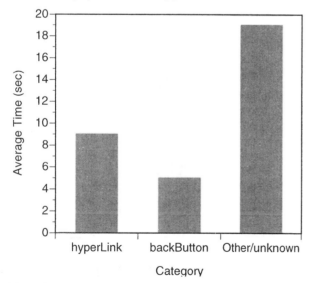

Figure 9. Average time (in seconds) spent on each type of Goto task

Following hyperlinks was the most common way to change the URL being viewed, with the next most common method being the "back" button. Notice that, on average, the "back" button is much faster than following hyperlinks. This is almost certainly due to the fact that the page accessed by the "back" button is usually cached by the browser. This suggests that the gains that could by had by better caching algorithms and higher network bandwidth may be considerable.

Most of the "other" GoTo's involve typing in a URL, and thus these types of GoTo's require a great deal more time. URLs appear to be particularly difficult for users to type because of the unusual punctuation and preponderance of nonwords. Other types of navigation, such as the use of history menus, were quite infrequent. This may be because the user interfaces of most history systems are less than optimally matched to the way users think about Web navigation [7]. Alternatively, it may simply be that users rarely back up more than a page or two at a time.

DISCUSSION
Implications for WWW Browser Design
What these data suggest is that time spent worrying about things like button layouts and history menus may not have much impact on normal Web browsing. Users do not spend a great deal of time interacting with the GUI widgets of their browsers relative to the amount of time they spend engaged in things like reading, visual search, and waiting. On the other hand, this may well be because the functionality or interface provided to users to support their tasks are poor. It is not clear whether users would spend more time interacting with GUI widgets if they were better designed. For example, we observed little use of the history system. This may be because the history system is poorly designed, as suggested by [7]. However, it might also be the case that users would make little use of history systems no matter how implemented.

An obvious case where widget design could make a difference is scrolling. Users spend a great deal of time scrolling (approximately 40 minutes in our 5-hour sample was spent scrolling), and advances which reduce the latency of scroll operations (such as wheeled mice like the Microsoft IntelliMouse) have the potential to save users considerable time. Whether such devices actually do save users time is still an open question, but the potential is clearly there.

Because users spend so much time waiting, improving the performance of the caching and rendering algorithms in browsers should clearly be a high priority as it could potentially save users considerable time. Improving system performance to reduce waiting time is hardly a new suggestion in HCI; however, this appears particularly salient in the case of the Web. Even pages that clearly should have been cached (e.g. those loaded by the "back" button) took an average of approximately five seconds to be fully loaded and rendered.

Implications for Page Design

Users are willing to scroll through and read long passages, despite claims to the contrary [5] based on "classic directed tasks." In undirected situations, if users find essays or articles that are of interest to them, they do read them. This suggests that long, textual Web pages are not necessarily a bad idea but should be designed for readability. On the other hand, users do spend a great deal of time searching pages for items related to a target concept, and there may be tradeoffs between readability and "scanability" of a page. These data suggest that the tradeoffs should be carefully evaluated. For some pages it may indeed be worthwhile to sacrifice readability for searchability—but for other pages this may only distract and annoy users.

Some of the initial decisions made in designing browsers defaults were excellent. For example, most Web browsers underline and color links, which can be a tremendous aid to the visual search process—visual search for a target that can be discriminated on the basis of color alone are typically very rapid [8]. However, HTML now allows designers to override this and make link colors different than the defaults. Most page design guidelines advise against this, and our data is in agreement with this guideline—anything that slows visual search is likely to cost users time.

Overall, the clearest point that these data make is that WWW browsing is a complex mixture of a variety of behaviors, and any attempt to improve the interface to the Web needs to be sensitive to this variety.

FUTURE WORK

Although the summary data presented here give a high-level view of what people are doing when they browse the Web, the verbal protocols hold a wealth of detail. The current analyses are clearly limited. Future analyses can and should include analyses at higher levels of abstraction (e.g. strategies and patterns of behaviors), and analysis of the contents of the tasks in which users engage rather than just the behaviors. For example, the current analyses did not consider whether or not a given Locate was successful or not, or what it was that was being Located, but merely that the user was trying to locate something on a page. Integration with click studies, which can provide more detailed information about the exact contents of the Web pages being browsed (e.g. "what percentage of the links on a given page are visited?"), is also likely to provide further insight into browsing behavior.

Furthermore, the sample of users and environments is also clearly limited. A wider sampling of users, browsers, and network environments would not only improve the generality of the results, but allow for more careful consideration of individual differences. We expect that more detailed analysis of naturalistic studies such as this one will provide considerable design guidance.

ACKNOWLEDGEMENTS

This research was sponsored by the National Science Foundation (NSF), Award #IRI-9457628 and by and by the National Institute for Mental Health (NIMH), fellowship #2732-MH19102. It was also supported by generous contributions from the Xerox corporation. The views and conclusions contained herein are those of the authors and should not be interpreted as necessarily representing the official policies or endorsements, either expressed or implied, of Xerox, the NSF, the NIMH, the U.S. Government, or any other organization.

REFERENCES

1. Catledge, L. D., & Pitkow, J. E. (1995). Characterizing browsing strategies in the World-Wide Web. In Proceedings of the Third International World Wide Web Conference, http://www.igd.fhg.de/www/www95/papers/, Darmstadt, Germany.

2. Cypher, A. (1986) The structure of users' activities. In Norman, D.A. and Draper, S.W., (eds.) *User Centered System Design*, pp. 243-263.

3. Morkes, J., & Nielsen, J. (1997). Concise, SCANNABLE, and Objective: How to Write for the Web. http://www.useit.com/papers/webwriting/writing.html

4. Nielsen, J. (1996). Top Ten Mistakes in Web Design. http://www.sun.com/columns/alertbox/9605.html

5. Nielsen, J. (1997). How Users Read on the Web. http://www.useit.com/alertbox/9710a.html

6. Peck, V. A. & John, B. E. (1992) Browser-Soar: A cognitive model of a highly interactive task. In Human Factors in Computing Systems: Proceedings of CHI 92 (pp. 165-172). New York: ACM Press.

7. Tauscher, L., & Greenberg, S. (1997). Revisitation patterns in World Wide Web navigation. In *Human Factors in Computing Systems: Proceedings of CHI 97* (pp. 399–406). New York: ACM Press.

8. Triesman, A., & Gelade, G. (1980). A feature-integration theory of attention. *Cognitive Psychology, 12*, 97–136.

An Empirical Evaluation of User Interfaces for Topic Management of Web Sites

Brian Amento[1,2], Will Hill[1], Loren Terveen[1], Deborah Hix[2], and Peter Ju[1]

[1]AT&T Labs - Research
180 Park Avenue, P.O. Box 971
Florham Park, NJ 07932 USA
{pju, willhill, terveen}@research.att.com

[2]Department of Computer Science
Virginia Tech
Blacksburg, VA 24061 USA
{brian, hix}@cs.vt.edu

ABSTRACT

Topic management is the task of gathering, evaluating, organizing, and sharing a set of web sites for a specific topic. Current web tools do not provide adequate support for this task. We created the *TopicShop* system to address this need. TopicShop includes (1) a webcrawler that discovers relevant web sites and builds site profiles, and (2) user interfaces for exploring and organizing sites. We conducted an empirical study comparing user performance with TopicShop vs. Yahoo™. TopicShop subjects found over 80% more high-quality sites (where quality was determined by independent expert judgements) while browsing only 81% as many sites and completing their task in 89% of the time. The site profile data that TopicShop provides – in particular, the number of pages on a site and the number of other sites that link to it – was the key to these results, as users exploited it to identify the most promising sites quickly and easily.

KEYWORDS

information access, information retrieval, information visualization, human-computer interaction, computer supported cooperative work, social filtering

INTRODUCTION: THE TOPIC MANAGEMENT TASK

An important task that many web users perform is gathering, evaluating, and organizing relevant information resources for a given topic; we call this *topic management*. Sometimes users investigate topics of professional interest, at other times topics of personal interest. Users may create collections of web information resources for their own use or for sharing with coworkers or friends. For example, someone might gather a collection of web sites on wireless telephony as part of a report they're preparing for their boss and a collection on the X-Files as a service to their fellow fans. Librarians might prepare topical collections for their clients, and teachers for their students [1].

Topic management is a difficult task that is not supported well by current web tools. A common way to find an initial set of (potentially) relevant resources is to use a search engine like AltaVista or a directory like Yahoo. At this point, however, a user's work has just begun: the initial set usually is quite large, consisting of dozens to hundreds of sites of varying quality and relevance, covering assorted aspects of the topic. Users typically want to select a manageable number – say 10 to 20 – of high-quality sites that cover the topic. With existing tools, users simply have to browse and view resources one after another until they are satisfied they have a good set, or, more likely, they get tired and give up. Browsing a web site is an expensive operation, both in time and cognitive effort. And bookmarks, probably the most common form of keeping track of web sites, are a fairly primitive organizational technique.

We have designed a system called *TopicShop* to support the topic management task directly. TopicShop includes three main components:

- a webcrawler, which discovers web sites relevant to a user-specified set of seed sites and creates site profiles which can be used to inform user evaluation of sites;

- a Java applet, which serves as a front end to the webcrawler; it lets users specify seed sites for a topic, track the progress of the webcrawler, and explore sites as they are discovered and profiled; and

- the TopicShop Explorer, an interface that lets users view thumbnail images of sites and site profiles, sort sites by their properties, organize sites into categories, both spatially and by using folders, and easily share results by exchanging files via email, disks, etc.

This paper reports on an empirical evaluation of the TopicShop Explorer. Since Yahoo is a state of the art, widely used tool for exploring collections of web resources on specific topics, we chose to investigate how subjects performed on topic management tasks using either TopicShop or Yahoo.

In the remainder of the paper, we discuss related work, describe the features of TopicShop, and discuss the design and results of the study in detail.

RELATED WORK

Our work aims to create algorithms for extracting useful information from the web and interfaces to aid users in comprehending and organizing web sites. We have written previously [13] about information structures and analysis algorithms we developed. We also performed studies showing that links between web sites carry useful information, in particular, that connectivity correlates with expert quality judgements [14]. The work reported here builds on this previous work, but focuses on user interfaces. In particular, it investigates two major issues:

- what useful information can we provide to users to inform their evaluation of web resources, enabling them to browse fewer and higher quality sites?

- how can we design interfaces that help users easily and effectively explore collections of resources and organize resources for later use by themselves and others?

Others have looked at these questions. For example, Abrams, Baecker, and Chignell [1] carried out a study of how several hundred web users used bookmarks. Bookmarks were a very popular way to create personal information spaces of web resources. They observed a number of strategies for organizing bookmarks, including a flat ordered list, a single level of folders, and hierarchical folders. They also made four design recommendations to help users manage their bookmarks more effectively. First, bookmarks must be easy to organize, e.g., via automatic sorting techniques. Second, visualization techniques are necessary to provide comprehensive overviews of large sets of bookmarks. Third, rich representations of sites are required; many users noted that site titles are not accurate descriptors of site content. Finally, tools for managing bookmarks must be well integrated with web browsers.

Our focus is different than Abrams et al. Bookmarks typically are gathered opportunistically, even casually, as users happen to encounter interesting sites, and bookmark files usually span many different topics. In contrast, we are interested in situations where users are explicitly engaged in gathering and organizing a collection of related resources for a specific topic. Nonetheless, many of Abrams et al.'s specific observations and recommendations are relevant to our work. In particular, as we illustrate later, TopicShop supports all the user organizational strategies they observed and follows their design recommendations.

A number of researchers have created interfaces to support users in managing collections of information resources. SenseMaker [2] focuses on supporting users in the contextual evolution of their interest in a topic. They

attempt to make it easy to evolve a collection, e.g., expanding it by query-by-example operations or limiting it by applying a filter. Scatter/Gather [11] supports the browsing of large collections of text, allowing users to iteratively reveal topic structure and locate desirable documents. Card, Robertson, and York [3] describe the WebBook, which uses a book metaphor to group a collection of related web pages for viewing and interaction, and the WebForager, an interface that lets users view and manage multiple WebBooks. Mackinlay, Rao, and Card [8] developed a novel user interface for accessing articles from a citation database. The central UI object is a "Butterfly", which represents one article, its references, and its citers. The interface makes it easy for users to browse from one article to a related one, group articles, and generate queries to retrieve articles that stand in a particular relationship to the current article.

Other researchers have investigated techniques for determining information about web sites to aid user comprehension of the sites. For example, Kleinberg [7] defines algorithms that identify *authoritative* and *hub* pages within a hypertext document. Authorities and hubs are mutually dependent: a good authority is a page that is linked to by many hubs, and a good hub is one that links to many authorities. Several systems, including WebQuery [4] and twURL [15], group or sort pages by their degree (the number of other pages in the collection they are connected with). Pirolli, Pitkow, and Rao [10] developed a categorization algorithm that used hyperlink structure, text similarity, and user access data to categorize web pages into various functional roles, such as "head", "index", and "content". Later Pitkow and Pirolli [12] experimented with clustering algorithms based on co-citation analysis [5], in which pairs of documents were clustered based on the number of times they were both cited by a third document.

While our work shares many goals of previous work, it differs in several respects. First, as discussed elsewhere [13], we designed novel information structures and algorithms for building collections of resources. Second, we seek to provide exploration and organization techniques that are both powerful and very easy to use; we attempt to achieve this goal with a user interface that is an enhanced version of the Microsoft Windows™ file explorer that users already are familiar with. Finally, and most important, we performed an empirical study that has yielded both quantitative results that show the utility of TopicShop and qualitative results that help us better understand the topic management task and how to support it more effectively.

THE TOPICSHOP SYSTEM

The Webcrawler and Java Applet

Topic management obviously begins with the identification of a collection of relevant resources. We have developed an algorithm [13] that takes as input a user-specified set of web sites (the "seeds") and follows links from the seeds to construct a graph of the seed sites and closely connected sites. Sites reached by following links from the seeds are likely to be on the same topic.

For purposes of this paper, however, the discovery of new sites is not relevant; what is relevant is that our webcrawler heuristically groups web pages into web sites and builds profiles of the sites it fetches.

Pages are grouped into sites using heuristics that look at the directory structure of URLs. For example, if the crawler encounters a link to the URL http://a/b/page1.html, and http://a/b/index.html is a site known to the crawler, it records this URL as part of the site. Further, if the link was encountered while the crawler was analyzing the site http://x/y/, a link is recorded from the site http://x/y/ to the site http://a/b/index.html.

Site profiles are built by fetching a fairly large number of pages from each site. Profiles contain the following data:

- title (of the site's root page),
- a thumbnail image (of the site's root page),
- links to and from other sites,

- internal html pages, images, audio files, and movie files.

Users build a TopicShop collection by identifying a set of seed sites on a topic of interest (e.g., by finding a topic-specific index page or using a search engine) and then running a Java applet that sends the seed pages to the webcrawler running on our server. As the crawler runs, it continually sends its results to the applet; thus, the user can begin viewing and exploring sites immediately. When a crawl is completed, the server creates a special type of Microsoft Windows™ file for each site that contains the site profile data. The server then compresses all the files into one archive file which is downloaded to the user's computer.

The TopicShop Explorer: Evaluating, Managing, and Sharing Collections of Resources

Once users save and uncompress the downloaded file, they view and manage their collections using the TopicShop Explorer, a customized version of the normal Windows file explorer. The TopicShop Explorer is a small Windows executable that interprets and processes site profile files.

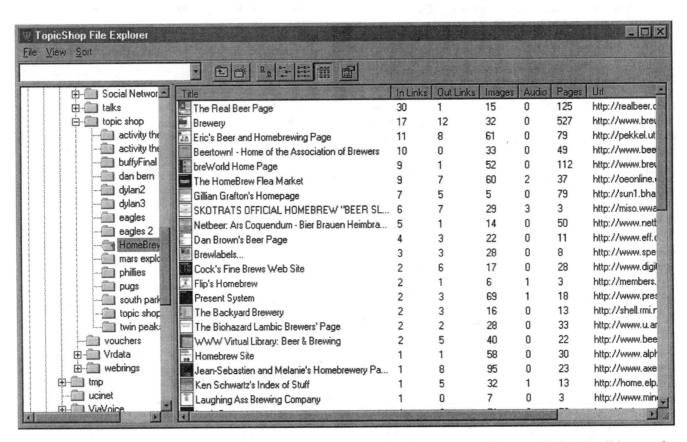

Figure 1: TopicShop Explorer, details view. Each web resource (site) is represented by a small thumbnail image, the site title, properties of the site itself – number of internal pages, images, and audio files – and the site's relations to other sites – number of in links and out links. By clicking on a column, users can sort by the appropriate property.

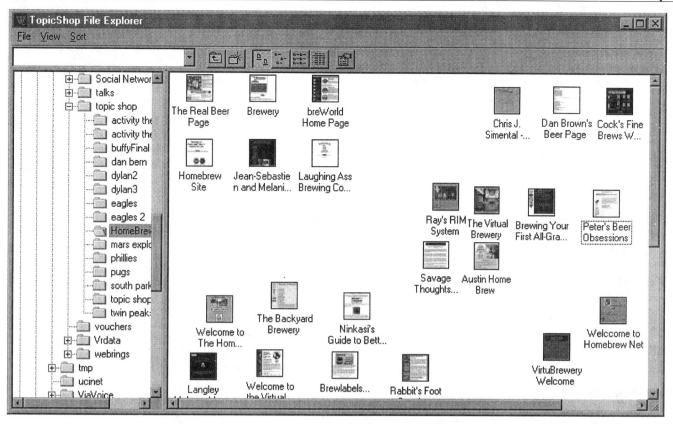

Figure 2: TopicShop Explorer, icons view. Each site is represented by a large thumbnail image and the site title. Users can organize sites by arranging them spatially, a technique especially useful in the early stages of exploration.

Users can view their collections in two different ways: details (Figure 1) or icons (Figure 2). The main feature of the details view is that it shows site profile information, and the main feature of the icons view is that users can arrange icons spatially. We will explain the user interface properties further as we consider the three main design goals of the TopicShop Explorer.

Design Goals

1. *Make relevant but invisible information visible.* We hypothesize that making site profile information visible will significantly inform users in evaluating a collection of sites. No longer must they decide to visit sites — a time-consuming process — based solely on titles and (sometimes) brief textual annotations. (A chief complaint of subjects in the Abrams et al [1] study was that titles were inadequate descriptors of site content — and that was for sites that users already had browsed and decided to bookmark.) Instead, users can choose to visit only sites that have been endorsed (linked to) by many other sites or sites that are rich in a particular type of content (e.g., images or audio files). In addition to site profile data, the thumbnail images also are quite useful; most notably, they are effective visual identifier for sites users already have visited.

2. *Make it simple for users to explore and organize resources.* In the details view, users can sort resources

by any property (e.g. number of in-links, out-links, images, etc.) simply by clicking on the label at the top of the column that displays that property. In either view, right-clicking on a site brings up a window that shows the profile data from which the numbers in the columns are derived, e.g., lists of all sites that link to the selected site and all internal pages of the site. Double-clicking on a site will send the user's default web browser to that site.

Users can organize resources both spatially (in the icons view) and by creating subfolders and moving resources into the subfolders. Nardi & Barreau [9] found that users of graphical file systems preferred spatial location as a technique for organizing their files. We believe spatial organization is particularly useful early in the exploration process while users are still discovering important distinctions among resources and user-defined categories have not yet explicitly emerged. As categories do become explicit, users can create folders to contain sites in each of the categories.

3. *Integrate topic management into a user's normal computing and communications environment.* The TopicShop Explorer may not look like a novel interface at all; interestingly enough, this was an explicit goal. We wanted it to be as similar to the

normal Windows Explorer as possible so Windows users could apply all their existing knowledge, thus minimizing learning time and maximizing ease of use. Further, this decision makes it very easy for collections of resources to be shared. Since a collection is just a normal Windows folder containing files (of the special type that we designed), they can be shared in all the normal ways. As we already have explained, a collection can be compressed and downloaded. It can also be emailed. And if users share a common network, collections simply can be read directly from any machine on the network.

EMPIRICAL STUDY

We wanted a suitable baseline topic management tool for comparison to TopicShop. Yahoo is the most popular tool for locating collections of web sites (according to the Media Metrix PC metering company, results available at http://searchwnginewatch.com/reports/mediametrix.html).

Bookmark lists are a common means of organizing collections of web resources. Therefore, we decided that subjects would use either TopicShop or Yahoo/bookmarks.

We chose two topics for the study: home brewing (of beer) and the TV program "Buffy the Vampire Slayer" – each contained about 60 sites in their corresponding Yahoo category. Our choice of these topics was influenced by the fact that pursuing special interests, including hobbies and media fandom, is one of the main ways people use the web. To quantify this, we studied a set of approximately 770K queries issued to the Magellan search engine between March 1997 and August 1998. We determined that 42% of the queries had to do with entertainment topics, including media fandom (categorization was done on the 515 most popular query strings, which cumulatively accounted for 96K query instances; categorization was done by two independent raters, inter-rater reliability of 87%.)

Design

The experiment was a 2x2, between subjects design, with topic (home brewing or Buffy) and user interface (TopicShop or Yahoo) as factors. Sixteen members of our lab volunteered to participate, giving four subjects per each of four conditions. None of the subjects had seen TopicShop before, although some were familiar with the general concepts.

The two main metrics we wanted to measure were the quality of resources users gathered and the amount of effort (time and total number of sites browsed) required. To give a quality baseline, four experts for each topic were presented a list of the sites (in random order) on that topic; only titles were presented, no Yahoo annotations or TopicShop profile data. This meant that the experts had to browse each site and evaluate it based on its content and layout. Each expert collected the 20 "best" sites. For this study, we defined "best" as a set of sites that collectively

provided a useful and comprehensive overview for someone wanting to learn about the topic. During analysis, we used the "expert intersection", the set of resources that all experts for a given topic selected, as the yardstick for measuring the quality of resources selected by the subjects.

Subjects for a given topic, whether they used TopicShop or Yahoo, were presented with the same set of approximately 60 sites (obtained from the Yahoo category) to evaluate. Yahoo subjects saw (as usual) site titles and, for about half the sites, a brief textual annotation. For the TopicShop condition, we applied our webcrawler to the Yahoo sites to produce site profiles; TopicShop subjects thus had access to site tiles, thumbnail images, and profile data, as shown in Figures 1 and 2.

Methodology

Subjects were assigned randomly to one of the four conditions. To begin the experiment, subjects received 15 minutes of instruction and training in the task and user interface. TopicShop subjects were shown the basic interface features and taught how to collect sites by dragging and dropping icons into folders. Yahoo subjects were shown a sample list of sites and taught how to collect sites by bookmarking. After training, subjects performed a short task to ensure that they were comfortable with collecting and organizing sites.

For the main task, subjects investigated the sites for their assigned topic by using the interface (TopicShop or Yahoo) and browsing to sites. Subjects within a single topic were presented with the same collection of sites in both interface conditions. They were asked to choose the 15 "best" (as defined previously) sites and rank them by quality. Subjects were asked to complete the task in 45 minutes and were kept informed of the elapsed time. Clearly, there is a relationship between time on task and quality of results: the more time spent, the better results one can expect. By limiting the amount of time, we hoped to focus on any differences in the quality of results (i.e., the sites users selected) between the two interfaces. And people don't spend unlimited amounts of time browsing, so we wanted to see whether users could find high-quality sites in a limited amount of time.

The task ended when subjects were satisfied with their collections of sites. Subjects then completed a short questionnaire. Finally, an informal interview was conducted to reveal strategies subjects used to perform the task, their reactions to the interface, and what could help them to complete the task more effectively.

Results

We first compared the set of resources chosen by each subject to the expert intersection. For each topic, the expert intersection contained 12 resources. For the Buffy topic, Yahoo subjects selected an average of 5.0 sites that were in the expert intersection, while TopicShop subjects selected

7.5 expert-endorsed sites. For home brewing, Yahoo subjects matched 4.3 sites and TopicShop subjects matched 9.3. Overall, Yahoo subjects selected 4.6 sites from the expert intersection, while TopicShop subjects selected over 80% more, or 8.4 ($p < 0.05$). These results are summarized in Table 1. Notice that choosing sites at random would result in obtaining 3 sites in the expert intersection. (Users selected 15 out of 60 sites, or 25%; 25% of the 12 sites in the expert intersection is 3 sites.) The Yahoo score of 4.6 is not that much better than random selection. This probably is due to task time limit of 45 minutes. If Yahoo subjects had had unlimited time, undoubtedly they would have been able to find more high quality sites. To sum up, we see that TopicShop users found significantly better resources in the time given to complete the task.

Mean Number of High-Quality sites Identified

Topic	Interface Type	
	Yahoo	TopicShop
Buffy	5.0	7.5
Home brewing	4.3	9.3
Average over Topic	4.6	8.4

Table 1: Expert intersection analysis

It also is revealing to examine the amount of work subjects performed to complete their tasks. A study of data from the search engine Excite (51,473 queries, 18,113 users) showed that 86% of all users looked at no more than 30 pages returned in response to their query [6]. In our study, Yahoo users browsed an average of 44 sites, while TopicShop subjects visited about 36, or about 19% less. Further, the task of constructing a high-quality collection of resources is more difficult than doing a simple search; the task is global, since one is trying to develop a comprehensive overview of a topic, so more sites must be considered. By providing additional dynamic data up front, TopicShop enables users to make better decisions about which sites to immediately rule out and which to investigate further. Yahoo users can rely only on textual annotations, which are provided by site maintainers. While these annotations are sometimes helpful, they can be out-of-date or self-promotional, so are not necessarily good indications of the perceived quality of a site.

We also analyzed time on task. We did not expect a large difference since we gave users a (soft) limit of 45 minutes to complete the task and kept them aware of elapsed time during the experiment. Still, TopicShop subjects took about 11% less time (41.5 minutes vs. 46.6 minutes for Yahoo).

While the differences in time and effort were not statistically significant (although we hope they will be in a larger study we are preparing to conduct), they do show

that TopicShop subjects did not obtain better quality results at the cost of more work.

The questionnaire gave us data on what information subjects found most useful in evaluating a site. TopicShop subjects were asked to rank the utility of the site profile attributes, including the title and the number of in-links, out-links, images, audio files, and pages on the site. Subjects ranked these properties on a scale of 1 (most useful) to 7 (least useful). Three of these properties — in-links (2.00), title (2.75), and number of pages (3.00) — were ranked most highly. The other four properties had an average score greater than 5. Even though many subjects noted that title is not a very good indication of quality, it still was perceived as one of the most useful site properties. In interviews, subjects explained that titles were useful mainly as memory aids for sites. Thus, subjects considered the number of endorsements (in links) and the size of a site (in pages) to be the most useful indicators of quality.

The questionnaire also asked subjects what additional information would have helped them in evaluating sites. Six of the eight Yahoo subjects said that the number of links between sites would be very useful. One subject even made it a point to go to the links page of every site visited to see not only what sites were linked to, but also to read any annotations or recommendations made by the site author. Thus, link information was rated as highly useful by those subjects who saw it and as desirable by those subjects who did not.

User Exploration Strategies

Most Yahoo subjects, lacking any better options, simply looked through the initial 60 sites in alphabetical order, reverse alphabetical order, or sometimes a combination of the two. A few users tried reading all the titles and annotations to make some judgements about the sites before browsing them; however, many times the initial judgement of a site proved inaccurate once it was browsed, so even these users often reverted to exhaustive alphabetical search. Of course, users still read annotations as they proceeded methodically through the list of sites, but did not rely on the annotations to decide which sites to browse. Users also often browsed a few sites at random to try to cover a good sample of the available sites.

TopicShop subjects used different strategies, ones that were informed by the data in the TopicShop Explorer. They spent more time prior to browsing sites on exploration within the TopicShop interface, sorting the columns and watching how the arrangement of sites changed. They were mainly looking for sites that appeared near the top in multiple sorts. Many also attempted to get a rough idea of how sites were distributed in each column. Eventually, subjects tended to proceed by selecting a property they thought was useful and evaluating the first few sites in that column. After they exhausted the quality sites in the column, they would move on to another column and continue. Some subjects would also visit some sites at the low end of the data columns to convince themselves that the profile data could be trusted.

As evidence of the influence of the TopicShop explorer on user strategies, let us consider the overlap in sites selected by subjects. TopicShop subjects arrived at a much larger common set of sites. The intersection for the eight TopicShop subjects across both topics was 9.5 sites, while the eight Yahoo subjects averaged an intersection of only 2.5 sites. It makes sense that TopicShop users would agree with each other quite a bit, even more than they agreed with the experts, since they relied on the same data and tended to pursue the same strategies for selecting resources.

To better evaluate the utility of the TopicShop data, we created purely automated versions using the "gather from the top of the column" strategy. We defined six sets of sites mechanically: five of the sets consisted simply of the top 15 sites for each numeric site profile attribute, and the sixth consisted of the top three sites on each attribute.

Recall that the Yahoo subjects had an overall average expert intersection of 4.6 (out of 12). All the automated TopicShop strategies performed better, with an average expert intersection of 5.6. We found it surprising and noteworthy that a purely mechanical strategy using only the TopicShop site profile data could outperform human subjects who had to rely only on Yahoo's site titles and annotations. (Again, we assume that the task time limit was a factor; with enough time to browse and evaluate site content, we expect that people would outperform these mechanical strategies. Of course, who has enough time?)

We also observed a common, but unproductive strategy: nearly all subjects initially assumed that personal home pages (as determined by the title and site location) would be of low quality. They supposed that they could immediately eliminate these sites and select only from the resulting, smaller subset. However, subjects quickly realized that this was not true – after visiting a few personal pages, they found that some were of quite high quality, so subjects abandoned this strategy.

Design Implications

Observations, interviews, and questionnaires suggested four significant design improvements to the TopicShop user interface.

The first design improvement is to add additional site profile data about the front page of a site. We observed that most subjects made their judgement of a site by viewing only the front page of the site. It makes sense that the "front door" page of a site should be both attractive and representative of the site as a whole – after all, the site author designs it to be the initial impression a visitor to the site experiences. The front page usually gives a good idea of the amount and type of content available on the site as well as the production quality.

Users navigated to a total of 639 web sites, and looked at only the front page of over half the sites. And of the 240 sites that users selected for their collection of the best resources, users browsed only the front page of 91. Among the 399 sites that users rejected, 285 sites were rejected after browsing the front page. Overall, users viewed an average of 2.39 pages per site. Thus, we see that a user's initial impression of a site is extremely important. Therefore, we will analyze site front door pages and present the results as additional site profile data in a future design.

The second design change we will incorporate into TopicShop is better methods for creating subcategories of a topic. A key need that subjects in both interface conditions discussed was support for lightweight, flexible categorization. As users explore sites, they create rough mental groupings, using site similarity, site type (general information sites, specific subtopic sites, personal sites, etc.), or even site layout.

While TopicShop lets users create folders and group subcategories of sites within folders, our observations of subjects showed that this seems to be too much overhead for users when they are starting out. Their mental groupings remain indistinct until they have encountered a sufficient number and variety of sites to enable them to articulate the organizing principle of their categories. Further, categories may be split or combined several times in early stages of exploration. And while the icons view of TopicShop does support this flexible, lightweight categorization (and several subjects used and liked it), this view hides the important site profile data from immediate view. We have two potential design solutions that could be added to TopicShop to better support categorization.

Linked views are one solution to this problem. One window would show the icons view, another would show the details view, with user selections mirrored in both windows. Users then could spatially arrange sites as they form opinions about the types of sites within a topic, while simultaneously sorting sites based on profile data. As users develop firm categories, they could create folders to hold sites within each category.

Another potential design solution is a coloring scheme. Users could assign a color to a group of sites at any time, then add other sites as they continue to browse. Then, whenever sites are sorted, they would be sorted first by color (i.e., group), then whatever other property the user specified. This would let users quickly create groups and still keep all sites in a single window. Again, when users are satisfied that a group really is a category, a folder can be created to contain it.

A third improvement to the design of TopicShop is to add two levels of annotations. One of the TopicShop design goals was to make it easy to reuse and share topical collections. Subjects affirmed that this was important. In support of this desire, all 16 subjects mentioned that they wanted to record comments about sites as they visited and collected them. Comments can be recorded for individual sites as well as user defined categories. These comments would be useful both to the original users when they returned to their collections in the future and to people with whom they shared the collections. The comments would explain why sites were selected, why they were considered high quality, and what they were good for.

The final design change involves sorting techniques within TopicShop. Currently, sorting in TopicShop is limited to a single column, but subjects expressed a desire for several more powerful sorting techniques. First, they wanted to combine several columns, e.g., sorting by the sum of in-links and out-links. Second, they wanted to be able to do a multi-level sort. For example, one might want to sort sites primarily by number of pages, then break ties by using another property, e.g., the number of in-links.

CONCLUSIONS

As the amount of information on the web continues to grow, tools that support users in finding and managing collections of topical resources will become increasingly significant. The focus must move from compiling collections to helping users comprehend and manage them. Our goal is to reduce the time users must spend sifting through "relevant" – but poor quality – sites and increase the amount of time they can devote to exploring high-quality information.

We showed that TopicShop users can find nearly twice as many high-quality web sites while considering fewer sites and taking less time than Yahoo users. By mining the rich data that already exist in the structure of web sites and content of their pages, TopicShop helps users quickly identify small and manageable subsets of web resources. Finally, the user exploration strategies and additional user needs that our study revealed will lead to significant improvements in the design of TopicShop and similar tools.

ACKNOWLEDGMENTS

We thank all the subjects who participated in our studies. We also appreciate design suggestions and many other useful comments from Julia Hirschberg, Lynn Cherny, Erik Ostrom, Steve Whittaker, and Bonnie Nardi.

REFERENCES

1. Abrams, D., Baecker, R., and Chignell, M. Information Archiving with Bookmarks: Personal Web Space Construction and Organization, in *Proceedings of CHI'98* (Los Angeles CA, April 1998), ACM Press, 41-48.

2. Baldonado, M.Q.W., and Winograd, T. An Information-Exploration Interface Supporting the Contextual Evolution of a User's Interests, in *Proceedings of CHI'97* (Atlanta GA, March 1997), ACM Press, 11-18.

3. Card, S.K., Robertson, G.C., and York, W. The WebBook and the Web Forager: An Information Workspace for the World-Wide Web, in *Proceedings of CHI'96* (Vancouver BC, April 1996), ACM Press, 111-117.

4. Carrière, J., and Kazman R. WebQuery: Searching and Visualizing the Web through Connectivity, in *Proceedings of WWW6* (Santa Clara CA, April 1997).

5. Garfield, E. *Citation Indexing*. ISI Press, Philadelphia, PA, 1979.

6. Jansen, B. J., Spink, A., Bateman, J., and Saracevic, T. Searchers, the Subjects They Search, and Sufficiency: A Study of a Large Sample of EXCITE Searches, submitted to *WebNet'98*.

7. Kleinberg, J.M. Authoritative Sources in a Hyperlinked Environment, in *Proceedings of 1998 ACM-SIAM Symposium on Discrete Algorithms*.

8. Mackinlay, J.D., Rao, R., and Card, S.K. An Organic User Interface for Searching Citation Links, in *Proceedings of CHI'95* (Denver CO, May 1995), ACM Press, 67-73.

9. Nardi, B. and Barreau D. Finding and Reminding: File Organization from the Desktop. *ACM SIGCHI Bulletin, 27, 3,* July 1995.

10. Pirolli, P., Pitkow, J., and Rao, R. Silk from a Sow's Ear: Extracting Usable Structures from the Web, in *Proceedings of CHI'96* (Vancouver BC, April 1996), ACM Press, 118-125.

11. Pirolli, P., Schank, P., Hearst, M., and Diehl, Scatter/Gather Browsing Communicates the Topic Structure of a Very Large Text Collection, in *Proceedings of CHI'96* (Vancouver BC, April 1996), ACM Press, 213-220.

12. Pitkow, J., and Pirolli, P. Life, Death, and Lawfulness on the Electronic Frontier, in *Proceedings of CHI'97* (Atlanta GA, March 1997), ACM Press, 383-390.

13. Terveen, L.G., and Hill, W.C. Finding and Visualizing Inter-site Clan Graphs, in *Proceedings of CHI'98* (Los Angeles CA, April 1998), ACM Press, 448-455.

14. Terveen, L.G., and Hill, W.C. Evaluating Emergent Collaboration on the Web, in *Proceedings of CSCW'98* (Seattle WA, November 1998), ACM Press.

15. *What is twURL?* http://www.roir.com/whatis.html

Visualizing Implicit Queries
For Information Management and Retrieval

Mary Czerwinski, Susan Dumais, George Robertson,
Susan Dziadosz, Scott Tiernan and Maarten van Dantzich
Microsoft Research
One Microsoft Way
Redmond, WA 98052 USA
+1 425-703-4882
marycz@microsoft.com

ABSTRACT

In this paper, we describe the use of similarity metrics in a novel visual environment for storing and retrieving favorite web pages. The similarity metrics, called *Implicit Queries*, are used to automatically highlight stored web pages that are related to the currently selected web page. Two experiments explored how users manage their personal web information space with and without the Implicit Query highlighting and later retrieve their stored web pages. When storing and organizing web pages, users with Implicit Query highlighting generated slightly more categories. Implicit Queries also led to significant performance improvements in web page retrieval. Specifically, when asked to find previously stored web pages, users with Implicit Query highlighting were reliably faster at locating target web pages.

Keywords

Information management, information retrieval, 3D, similarity, categorization, information visualization, classification

INTRODUCTION

The digital revolution has brought with it the problem of information overload. Even the simplest user query for information is accompanied by a results list that can be overwhelming. In addition, very little support is provided to help users in collecting, organizing and determining relevancy of retrieved items [3, 8, 16]. A careful examination of the graphical user interface and of similarity analysis methods is needed in order to address these sensemaking hurdles.

Usually query results are presented textually, as lists of e-mail, Internet documents or news reports. However, today nearly all web pages include some form of distinguishable

Figure 1. Data Mountain with Implicit Query results shown (highlighted pages to left of selected page).

graphics (e.g., a company logo) that users might associate in memory with that page. To take advantage of this, we present a visualization that allows users to manually create a spatial layout of the thumbnails of their documents in a 3D environment.

As an organizational aid to the user, we use document similarity metrics and visual highlighting cues to indicate that web pages are semantically related in this personal information space. This paper will compare two such metrics, one user-driven and one content-driven, used to determine web page similarity relations during sensemaking tasks.

Current web browsers try to alleviate the sensemaking problems raised above through the use of bookmarks or favorites mechanisms, wherein users store the URLs of interesting web pages in order to build a personalized information space. Despite these user interface mechanisms, a 1998 survey of over 10,000 web users revealed that one of the most common problems users have with the web is organizing the information that they gather there [7]. In related research, Abrams, et al. [1] studied the bookmark archives and personal Web habits of users and made recommendations for improving the design of existing favorites management systems. Abrams surveyed 322 Web users, and analyzed the bookmarks of 50 Web users in detail. He found that bookmarks were used to reduce the cognitive load of managing URL addresses (by aiding memory and keeping history), to facilitate access, and to create information spaces for personal and group use. Bookmarks were often added sporadically—perhaps not surprisingly when too many favorite pages were piling up in a user's list. Almost 40% of those studied used no organization and simply left web pages in the order they were added to the favorites list; 50% used a hierarchy of one (30%) or more (20%) levels. Most users organized at the time they created a bookmark and cleaned up only occasionally. The initial use of folders began after a user had about 35 bookmarks. Abrams also found that 50% of the bookmarks had been visited in the last 3 months; 67% in the last 6 months; and 97% in the last year. Some ease of use recommendations provided by Abrams included providing aids in the browser for semi-automatic filing, time- or usage-based orderings, and much better tools for helping users in their organizing task. These findings provided the primary motivation for the research described in this paper.

We describe a new interaction that helps users quickly recognize and use the categorical structure they need to organize their favorite web pages. The interaction technique includes the Data Mountain [13], a novel visual environment for laying out personal web pages in a 3D space (described below), and an Implicit Query technique which shows the user which items are related to their current interest. Our Implicit Query algorithms determine similarities among web pages, and present the results in a visual format that has been observed to be useful and usable. This approach allows users to focus on relevant items instead of searching through large numbers of pages in the space. We have initially applied this idea to interaction with documents on the Web, although the interaction technique could be applied to any electronic document management task.

DATA MOUNTAIN WITH IMPLICIT QUERY

The Data Mountain is a (3D) document management system (see Figure 2). The design and implementation of the Data Mountain is described in [13], so only a short overview of the environment will be provided here. Currently the Data Mountain is being used as an alternative to a web browser's favorites or bookmark mechanism. It should be understood that other forms of documents should work equally well in the new environment.

The Data Mountain uses a planar surface (tilted at 65 degrees; see Figure 2), on which documents are dragged. A document being dragged remains visible so that the user is always aware of the surrounding pages. The user can place

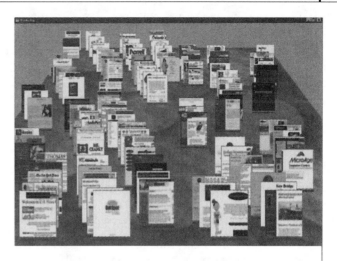

Figure 2: Data Mountain with 100 web pages.

her web pages (or documents) anywhere on the surface. In practice, the user creates meaning by organizing the space in which she lays out these documents. In our study, each user was allowed to freely choose an organizational method and adjust it at any point throughout the study.

When the user clicks on a page stored on the Data Mountain, the page is animated forward to a preferred viewing position, as shown in Figure 1. When in the preferred viewing position, another click will put the page back on the Data Mountain in its last known location. In practice, a click on a URL would allow the user to follow that link. Also, a stored page can be moved at any time by dragging it with the mouse. Since the page is visible during the move, the user knows where the page will be when the drag is terminated. The movement is continuous and constrained to the surface of the Data Mountain.

When a user moves a page around on the Data Mountain, it is likely to "bump" into other pages. Objects are not allowed to intersect, and the user's dragging action is not constrained. Instead, we handle collisions by displacing previously placed pages, thus continually maintaining a minimum distance between all pages, and transitively propagating displacement to neighbors as necessary. The user dragging the page continually sees what state will result when the drag is terminated (i.e., there is no animated settling time). This displacement technique also ensures that pages never get fully obscured.

There are a number of cues designed to facilitate spatial cognition. The most obvious are the 3D depth cues of perspective view, accompanying size differences, and occlusion, particularly when pages are being moved. Simple, circular landmarks on the surface of the Data Mountain also offer spatial cues, which may or may not be utilized during page placement or retrieval. Less obvious, but also quite important, are the shadows cast by web pages.

Subtle but pervasive spatial audio cues accompany all animations and user actions to reinforce the visual cues. The sound effects are highly dynamic. For example while dragging a page, the user hears a humming sound that changes pitch based on the speed at which the page is moved. With careful use of the timbre, stereo and attenuation of the humming sound, users are thus provided an additional spatial location indicator. Finally, as the user moves a page, other pages that move out of the way as needed are accompanied by yet another distinctive sound.

For identification purposes, we provided a pop-up labels similar to tool-tips to display web page titles. The title appears as soon as the mouse moves over a page.

In order to support users' information management and retrieval tasks on the World Wide Web (WWW), we use what we call *Implicit Queries*. Implicit Queries are generated automatically, based on the current focus of the user's attention. In our system, the web page that the user has currently selected is the basis for queries launched implicitly in the background. Much richer models of users' interests are easy to incorporate as well [6], but were not needed for this experiment. Web pages that are similar to the currently selected page are then highlighted to aid users' organization and use of their web information space. Figure 1 shows an example where the selected page has something to do with entertainment. For this particular user, most of the entertainment-related pages are on the left side of the layout and are highlighted so that the pattern is easily seen, yet not distracting. In color, this highlighting is very obvious—it is much less obvious in a black and white reproduction, so Figure 1 has been retouched to make clear where the highlighting is.

Prior work on similarity metrics in the user interface

A number of previous systems (for example, Spire [18] and Galaxy of News [11]) have used document similarity metrics as a way to organize (or lay out) documents, bringing similar documents closer together. Information access in these systems is achieved primarily by navigation. The Data Mountain differs fundamentally by allowing the user to determine the layout of the documents, and the Implicit Query mechanism highlights related documents in the context of the user-defined organization. By maintaining spatial consistency with the user's organization, our system is able to more effectively leverage human spatial memory [13].

Many systems show the results of *explicit* queries from users, usually as ranked lists. Some systems post the results of an explicit search against a known structure [4]. These structures may be expert-generated hierarchies or automatically derived (e.g., from the link structure of a Web site or by a statistical analysis of inter-item similarities). The resulting structures are shown using a variety of representations -- clusters, 2D and 3D spaces, tree-maps.

All of these systems take a known structure and show how search results fit into that organization. While these approaches are similar to ours in that respect, it is important to note that the organizing structures used by these systems are generated by domain experts or statistical methods and not by the user.

In contrast to these systems that use explicit queries, we have developed an interaction technique which relieves the user from having to generate an explicit query and so reduces the amount of cognitive processing required to retrieve related information. Much less work has been done on Implicit Queries and interfaces to them. The Rembrance Agent by Rhodes and Starner from MIT [12] described an approach similar to our general Implicit Query idea. They implemented a continuously running process which monitored what a user was reading and automatically sent this information to a backend server which indexed personal information such as email, notes and papers. The query consisted of whatever information was being read or typed into the current emacs buffer. The results were presented as a ranked list of titles in a separate window, and were thus very limited compared to our Data Mountain.

Schilit et al. [15] developed the XLibris system to support what they call "active reading". Reading was enhanced by computation using a kind of Implicit Query mechanism. Highlights made by the user via pen markings were used to issue an automated query for related materials. It is not clear that the use of highlighting to drive search is optimal, since people highlight and annotate for many different reasons [9]. The results are shown as thumbnails in the margin, which provides a local context, but no global inter-item similarities are shown as in the Data Mountain.

Our work on visualizing the results of Implicit Queries combines two ideas in a novel and a powerful way. We use a rich visual representation of objects and their inter-relations on the user-determined spatial layout of the Data Mountain along with Implicit Queries for information management. In addition, we empirically evaluate the usefulness of our system to support users in information organization and retrieval tasks.

Previous research on highlighting techniques

Much research has been performed on the usefulness of highlighting in attracting attention to relevant information in a display [17]. For instance, it is well known that the techniques of reverse video, color, boldness (or brightness), underlining, and flashing are all effective highlighting techniques, although some of them can actually be disruptive if applied inappropriately. For our Implicit Query highlighting, we examined over 20 highlighting techniques, some inspired by previously reported research [5, 10]. Based on our informal observations of which techniques were more most effective without causing undue disruption, we chose to implement a simple green outline to display which web pages were related to the currently selected web page.

Finally, it should be noted that we have chosen a binary approach to highlighting similarities in the web pages stored on the Data Mountain, as opposed to the continuous approaches we considered. We chose a binary approach purposefully, as we were concerned about the possibly distracting effect that Implicit Query highlighting would have on the user's primary task. We also assumed that a binary approach would lessen the decision-making burden on users. However, we have prototyped many designs that show the relevance score along a continuum in the visualization.

USER STUDIES OF DATA MOUNTAIN IMPLICIT QUERY

We tested our visualization and Implicit Query user interface ideas in two studies. The first study examined how users managed and stored 100 favorite web pages with and without Implicit Queries during their web page interactions. It was our hypothesis that the Implicit Query algorithms and highlighting would provide a useful guide to users during their web page organization. Although users were not required to follow the query recommendations in any way, we further hypothesized that users would indeed group together the highlighted pages. In addition, it was hypothesized that Implicit Query highlighting would improve memory of where pages were stored spatially on the data mountain, due to subjects' having spent more time attending to related pages and considering the suggestions proffered by the system. This hypothesis was based on the theoretical notion of "levels of processing" [2]. According to this theory, information can be processed more or less deeply, ranging from a shallow analysis (attention to surface features) to a deeper, semantic analysis. Information that is processed more deeply has been shown to be more likely to be remembered over time.

In these studies, we also explored two similarity metrics to drive the Implicit Queries. Looking at the content (word) overlap of pages generated one metric, while the other was derived from a group of subjects' previous organizations of the same web pages. We expected that the Implicit Query suggestions coming from subjects' previous organizational strategies might be the "best case" for a similarity metric, and so hypothesized a performance advantage for this algorithm.

In the second study, we examined whether or not this system guidance during web page organization would actually benefit subsequent retrieval of those previously stored favorite web pages. Any retrieval time advantages will be realized over and over again as subjects repeatedly revisit the page later.

EXPERIMENT 1

Methods

Subjects

Thirty-five subjects of intermediate web ability and who were experienced Microsoft Internet Explorer™ 4.0 (IE4) users at work or home participated in the experiment. All users were required to successfully answer a series of screening questions pertaining to web browser and Internet knowledge in order to qualify for participation. The number of females and males was balanced. 15 subjects organized their web pages with no Implicit Query mechanism. 20 subjects were aided by one of two Implicit Query algorithms (9 subjects used algorithm 1 or IQ1; 11 used algorithm 2 or IQ2). The experimental sessions involved two studies, an organizational phase and a retrieval phase. For clarity, methods and results of the two phases will be described separately as Experiment 1 and Experiment 2. The Methods for Experiment 1, the organizational phase, are described below.

Material

One hundred web pages were used in this study; 50 of the pages came from PC Magazine's list of top web sites (and so were likely to have been seen by at least some of the participants) and 50 pages were selected randomly from the Yahoo!™ database. The web pages were downloaded onto a web server located on the computer the subject worked at.

We used two algorithms to generate a set of matching pages for each web page in the study, a co-occurrence algorithm and a content-based algorithm. *IQ1 – co-occurrence similarity.* The first similarity measure was derived from a page-page co-occurrence matrix based on seven previous subjects' categorizations. Only subjects whose categorizations were relatively clear and discrete spatially were used for this algorithm's derivation. We counted the number of times that a pair of pages co-occurred in the same cluster – this number varied between 0 and 7. This algorithm essentially tells the user, "Other people thought these pages were related." *IQ2 – content-based similarity.* For the content-based similarity computations, the popular vector space model from information retrieval was used [14]. Documents were pre-processed to remove the HTML markup. Words on a standard stop list of common words along with 10 web-specific words were omitted, and white space or punctuation was used to delimit words. Each document was represented as a vector of words with entries representing the frequency of occurrence of a word in that document. The similarity between documents was measured by taking the dot product of the document vectors divided by the lengths of the vectors.

Once we generated these two measures of similarity, we set a threshold for each algorithm. Only web pages that matched the target web page at a level of similarity above the threshold were recommended as "related" to the user. We wanted the two algorithms to recommend roughly the same average number of matches per page. The thresholds we chose generated, on average, 4.2 and 4.3 matches per page respectively. In the co-occurrence algorithm (IQ1), this threshold produced 39 pages that had no match above the threshold. There were 28 pages that had no match above the threshold for the content-based algorithm (IQ2).

To indicate which pages were identified as matching the page being viewed, we highlight the related pages with a bright green frame as shown in Figure 1. Highlighting automatically occurs when subjects are presented with a new page for storage during the first phase of the study. Selecting any page on the Data Mountain causes its related pages to be highlighted.

Procedure

Subjects were shown 100 web pages sequentially (order was randomized for each subject) and asked to store them on the Data Mountain. They were allowed to create any organization they wanted and were encouraged to create a personally meaningful structure that mimicked how they stored favorite web pages at home. Subjects were told that they would have to use their organization for a retrieval task in the second half of the test.

For the subjects who were in the Implicit Query conditions, related pages were highlighted according to the IQ1 or IQ2 algorithms. We briefly interrupted each subject in the Implicit Query conditions to discuss the green highlighting after 10 minutes of their organization phase had elapsed. We asked them if they had noticed the highlighting, and what they thought it was for. We then explained its purpose and informed participants that they were free to use or ignore the suggestions. Some subjects noticed the highlighting, figured out its purpose and requested validation of their assumption before 10 minutes had passed, which motivated an early intervention. When this occurred, we discussed it with the subjects at the time of their request. The discussion time, on average, took less than 1 minute.

After all 100 pages had been saved on the Data Mountain, the subjects were given time to fine-tune their organization until they were personally satisfied with it.

The main independent variable of interest in Experiment 1 was the between subjects variable of which Implicit Query matching algorithm was used (no Implicit Query, IQ1, or IQ2). The number and type of categories, organization time, and subjective satisfaction ratings were the dependent measures of interest.

Results

Influences on information management behavior

Most subjects adopted an organization based on semantic categories. A few users stored files alphabetically and one used no apparent organization. Table 1 shows the number of subjects following each of the observed organizational strategies. For subjects who categorized semantically we asked them to circle and label their categories. For the discussion of the number and overlap of the categories in the data, we only used subjects who actually constructed semantic categories.

Number of categories

On average, subjects in the Implicit Query conditions created more categories than did subjects without the Implicit Query highlighting during the organization phase of the study, $F(2,26)=4.24$, $p=.025$. Post hoc tests showed that IQ0 had reliably fewer categories than IQ1 ($p<.01$), and the difference with IQ2 was borderline significant ($p=.1$). The average number of categories for each group is shown in Table 2.

Implicit Query Condition	Semantic	Alphabetic	No Org.
IQ0: No Implicit Query	11	3	1
IQ1-: Co-occurrence based	8	1	0
IQ2: Content based	10	1	0

Table 1. Number of participants that used a particular organizational strategy while storing web pages.

Implicit Query Condition	Avg. # of Categories (Standard Deviations in parentheses)
IQ0: No Implicit Query	9.3 (3.6)
IQ1: Co-occurrence based	15.6 (5.8)
IQ2: Content based	12.8 (4.9)

Table 2. Averages and standard deviations for the number of categories observed in each Implicit Query condition.

Overlap of category concepts

Subjects' organizations were analyzed for their amount of overlap with each other. In order to do this, we used the layouts that subjects had circled and labeled for us. We identified 20 categories that subjects used very frequently, and reduced their category structures into these 20 categories. In order to check our data reduction procedure, we compared two authors' classification efforts on the same layouts for inter-rater reliability. On average, we obtained 90% agreement across Implicit Query conditions for two independent observers. One subject was primarily responsible for the inter-rater disagreement, and for this subject the 2 raters only agreed 50% of the time.

Once it was determined that the categorization scheme was a reliable one, subjects' clusters were analyzed for consistency. We found no reliable differences in how often subjects agreed with each other in terms of categories maintained during the storage phase of the study $F(2,26)=.164$, $p=.85$. In other words, having an Implicit Query mechanism did not result in more or less agreement between subjects and their organizational schemes.

Organizing Time

Although subjects were not encouraged to be efficient during the organize phase of the experiment, we did record organization times across Implicit Query conditions for most subjects. Unfortunately, this data was not available for five of the Implicit Query subjects due to experimenter error. Therefore, we pooled all Implicit Query subjects together and ran a t-test between the organization times with and without Implicit Query. On average, Implicit Query groups took significantly longer organizing their web pages on the Data Mountain (79 minutes) than users without Implicit Query (51 minutes), $t(29)=-3.6$, $p=.001$, two-tailed. This is not surprising, given that Implicit Query users created somewhat more categories than those participants without Implicit Query. Implicit Query users also often determined whether or not to follow the system recommendation for where to store a web page, which could have taken extra time as well.

Satisfaction measures

Participants provided satisfaction ratings at the end of the study session. One subject is not included in the analysis of the Implicit Query condition 2 due to her not filling out any answers on the questionnaire. A multivariate ANOVA (using Implicit Query condition as a between subjects factor and each questionnaire item as a multivariate response) revealed a reliable interaction between Implicit Query condition and one questionnaire item, $F(2,31)=7.09$, $p=0.003$. The questionnaire item that drove this effect, "I was satisfied with my organizational scheme; 1=Disagree, 5=Agree", accounted for over 31% of the variance in the data. Scheffe post-hoc analyses showed that subjects in the no Implicit Query (IQ0) and the co-occurrence-based algorithm (IQ1) groups were not different from each other on this questionnaire item (average ratings = 3.6, SD=0.22 and 4.0, SD=0.28, respectively). Subjects in the content-based algorithm (IQ2) condition, however, were less satisfied than the other two groups (average rating = 2.6, SD=0.25).

A few satisfaction items pertained only to the Implicit Query visualization, and so only groups IQ1 and IQ2 responded to these questions. Analyses of these results revealed that the co-occurrence algorithm built from previous subjects' organizations of the 100 web pages (IQ1), was rated as significantly less distracting than the content-based algorithm (IQ2), $t(18)=-2.04$, $p=.01$, two-tailed. Subjects' ratings of the IQ1 highlighting as more useful than IQ2 reached borderline significance, $t(18)=1.8$, $p=.09$, two-tailed. No other significant effects emerged from analysis of the satisfaction data.

Discussion

The results of the organization phase of this study were mixed, and suggest that good Implicit Queries in the user interface in the storage of information during web

interaction might lead to slightly more detailed categorization at the cost of significantly longer storage times. Satisfaction data suggests that subjects are equally satisfied with their organizations with no Implicit Query or with co-occurrence based Implicit Query, but are significantly less satisfied with content-based Implicit Query. Results further indicated that users spent more time organizing their web pages when Implicit Query highlighting was provided, and built a slightly more detailed organization of their personal web space based on that highlighting. According to Levels of Processing Theory [2], this increased time spent in information management could result in a deeper encoding of subjects' web page locations on the Data Mountain and might therefore facilitate subsequent web page retrieval in both speed and accuracy. This assumes that because subjects were spending more time organizing their web pages with Implicit Query highlighting, they were thinking more carefully about their organization.

EXPERIMENT 2

In Experiment 2, we assessed whether or not the presence of the Implicit Query highlighting during web page storage improved web page retrieval performance. We compared the IQ0, IQ1 and IQ2 groups on average retrieval times, the number of incorrect pages retrieved, and the number of failed retrieval attempts for the 100 web pages. It is extremely important to note here that the Implicit Query highlighting was disabled for this phase of the experiment. In other words, a subject's target web page did not highlight during its retrieval trial, nor were web pages that might be related to the target highlighted. While such highlighting would be desirable in practice, we felt it would be too beneficial for experimental purposes.

Methods

Subjects, Materials and Procedure

The same thirty-five subjects participated in the second study. After a short break following the organizational study, the subjects started retrieval. For the second study, participants were shown a retrieval cue consisting of the textual title of the web page, and asked to find the corresponding page on the Data Mountain. The retrieval cue was presented in a small, rectangular window below the display window of the Data Mountain. The cues were presented in a random order for each subject. If a subject could not find the target page within two minutes, the subject was instructed to proceed to the next retrieval trial. Since the Implicit Query highlighting was not enabled during this phase of the experiment, there are no visible differences in the user interface among the experimental conditions in this phase.

The three primary dependent measures used in Experiment 2 were web page retrieval time, the number of incorrect pages selected, and the number of failed attempts to retrieve a web page. Retrieval time (or reaction time) was defined as the time to select the correct item. Incorrect selections referred to the total number of pages selected that were not the target page, not including failed retrieval trials. Failed retrievals occurred when the subject either took longer than two minutes for retrieval or chose to stop searching for an item.

Results

Retrieval Time

Only trials in which subjects found the correct web page within the allotted two-minute timeframe are included in the reaction time analysis for both sessions. Figure 3 shows the retrieval time results. The average retrieval time was 14.25 seconds (SD=9.35) for the subjects with no Implicit Query algorithm, 6.5 seconds (SD=1.9) for the co-occurrence algorithm, and 7.3 (SD=2.0) seconds for the content-based algorithm. The difference between the three conditions was significant, $F(2,32)=5.4$, $p=.009$. Post-hoc analyses showed that the no Implicit Query group was significantly slower than both Implicit Query conditions, which were not different from each other. (The standard deviation for the no Implicit Query group was very high due primarily to one subject. We did reanalyze the results without her data, and no change in the pattern of significant findings was observed).

Incorrect Selections

On average there were very few visits to incorrect pages. The average number of incorrect retrievals in the no Implicit Query algorithm condition = 3.5 (SD=3.6), the IQ1 average = 3.0 (SD=1.6) and for the IQ2 algorithm the average number of incorrect retrievals = 4.7 (SD=3.6). There were no significant differences in the average number of incorrect pages retrieved across the 3 conditions, $F(2,32)=.78$, $p=.47$.

Failed Retrievals

There were an average of 4.8 (SD=3.1) trial failures in the no Implicit Query condition, compared to an average of 2.0 (SD=2.4), on average, in the IQ1 algorithm and 5.0 (SD=6.1) in the IQ2 algorithm, and this difference was once again not statistically significant, $F(2,32)=1.6$, $p=.2$.

Discussion

Experiment 2 supported our hypothesis that Implicit Queries benefited users by allowing them to more quickly retrieve stored web pages, with no speed/accuracy tradeoff. A likely reason for this benefit in retrieval performance is that subjects worked longer and were somewhat more detailed in their categorization of their web pages. In other words, when Implicit Query highlighting was used during the organization of favorites, storage time increased but retrieval time was subsequently greatly reduced. We believe that typical uses of any one piece of information will have one storage incident and many subsequent retrievals. So, by reducing retrieval time at the expense of storage time, we have significantly shifted and reduced overall cognitive load for the user when finding previously viewed

information for the task at hand. Although subjects were somewhat more satisfied with their organizations using IQ1, no retrieval differences were observed.

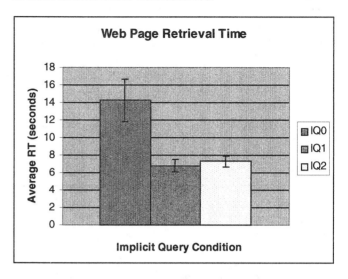

Figure 3. Average web page retrieval time, including standard error of the mean, for each Implicit Query condition.

A concern about the generality of these results is that we tested subjects' retrievals on the same day that they stored the web pages, an unlikely scenario in everyday web page access. In subsequent studies in our laboratory, we brought subjects back 6 weeks and 6 months after they stored their web pages on the Data Mountain. There was no decrement in performance when subjects returned and were asked to retrieve their web pages after either a 6-week period or a 6-month period of disuse. Details of these further studies are forthcoming. We suspect retrieval time would be reduced even further if highlighting were used during retrieval.

CONCLUSION

This paper reported two studies that examined users' web page organizations and later retrievals using a combination of two interaction techniques, the Data Mountain and Implicit Queries. Previous research [13] had already demonstrated enhanced performance for web page retrieval in the Data Mountain, when compared to current browser favorites mechanisms (one-dimensional visual text lists). The addition of Implicit Query highlighting has improved performance further still. It is interesting that a passive technique, such as highlighting similar web pages during organization, resulted in significantly improved retrieval performance. Future work will focus on user interface visualizations for queries in much larger scale information spaces. We will also continue to investigate the influence that Implicit Queries have on individual users' organizational styles. For instance, there was some indication that users without Implicit Queries tended to use an alphabetic organizational strategy more often. We will examine the use of alternative highlighting mechanisms, and explore the use of Implicit Queries at the time of retrieval as well as storage. Much of this future work will be carried out using alternative 3D visual metaphors.

ACKNOWLEDGMENTS

We thank the User Interface Research Group at Microsoft and Kevin Larson for their help and valuable comments on this paper.

REFERENCES

1. Abrams, D., Baecker, R.& Chignell, M. (1998). Information archiving with bookmarks: Personal web space construction and organization, in *Proceedings of CHI '98* (Los Angeles CA, May, 1998), ACM Press, 41-48.

2. Craik, F.I.M. & Lockhart, R.S. (1972). Levels of processing: A framework for memory research. *Journal of Verbal Learning and Verbal Behaviour,* 11, 671-684.

3. Dumais, S.T. (1988). Textual information retrieval. In M. Helander (Ed.) Handbook of Human-Computer Interaction. Elsevier Science Publishers (North Holland). .

4. Hearst, M. and Karadi, C. Cat-a-cone: An interactive interface for specifying searches and viewing retrieval results using a large category hierarchy. In *Proceedings of the 20th Annual International ACM SIGIR Conference on Research and Development in Information Retrieval*, July 1997, 246-255.

5. Hirtle, S., Sorrows, M.E. & Cai, G. (1998). Clusters on the World Wide Web: Creating neighborhoods of make-believe, in *Proceedings of Hypertext and Hypermedia '98* (Pittsburgh PA, 1998), ACM Press, 289-290.

6. Horvitz, E., Breese, J., Heckerman, D., Hovel. D. & Rommelse, K. (1998). The Lumiere project: Bayesian user modeling for inferring the goals and needs of software users. *Proceedings of the Fourteenth Conference on Uncertainty in Artificial Intelligence.*

7. Kehoe, C., Pitkow, J. & Rogers, J. (1998). GVU's 9th WWW User Survey, http://www.gvu.gatech.edu/user_surveys

8. Marchionini, Gary (1995). *Information Seeking in Electronic Environments.* Cambridge University Press.

9. Marshall, C.C. (1998). Toward an ecology of hypertext annotation, in *Proceedings of Hypertext and Hypermedia '98* (Pittsburgh PA, June, 1998), ACM Press, 40-49.

10. Olsen, D.R. Jr., Boyarski, D., Verratti, T., Phelps, M., Moffett, J.L. & Lo, E.L. (1998). Generalized pointing: Enabling multiagent interaction, in *Proceedings of CHI '98* (Los Angeles CA, May, 1998), ACM Press, 526-533.

11. Rennison, E. (1994). Galaxy of news: An approach to visualizing and understanding expansive news landscapes. In *Proceedings of ACM UIST '94 Symposium on User Interface Software & Technology*, Marina del Ray, CA: ACM, 3-12.

12. Rhodes, B. and Starner, T. A continuously running automated information retrieval system. In *Proceedings of The First International Conference on The Practical Application of Intelligent Agents and Multi Agent Technology (PAAM '96)*, London, UK, April 1996, pp. 487-495.

13. Robertson, G., Czerwinski, M., Larson, K., Robbins, D., Thiel, D. & van Dantzich, M. (1998). Data Mountain: Using Spatial Memory for Document Management, Paper to appear in *Proceedings of ACM UIST '98 Symposium on User Interface Software & Technology*, November, San Francisco, CA.

14. Salton, G.McGill, M. (1983*). Introduction to Modern Information Retrieval.* McGraw Hill.

15. Schilit, B.N., Golovchinsky, G. & Price, M.N. (1998). Beyond paper: Supporting active reading with free form digital ink annotations, in *Proceedings of CHI '98* (Los Angeles CA, May, 1998), ACM Press, 249-256.

16. Shneiderman, B., Byrd, D. & Croft, B. (1998). Sorting out searching: A user-interface framework for text searches*. Communications of the ACM, 41(4),* 1998, 95-98.

17. Tullis, T.S. (1997). Screen Design. In (Eds.) Helander, M., Landauer, T.K. & Prabhu, P.'s*, Handbook of human-computer interaction*, 2nd Edition, Elsevier Science, B.V., 503-531.

18. Wise, J.A., Thomas, J.J., Pennock, K., Lantrip, D., Pottier, M., Shur, A., and Crow, V. (1995). Visualizing the Non-Visual: Spatial analysis and interaction with information from text documents. In *Proceedings of Information Visualization 1995*, IEEE Computer Society Press, 51-58.

Patterns of Entry and Correction in Large Vocabulary Continuous Speech Recognition Systems

Clare-Marie Karat, Christine Halverson, Daniel Horn*, and John Karat

IBM T.J. Watson Research Center
30 Saw Mill River Road
Hawthorne, NY 10532 USA
+1 914 784 7612
ckarat, halve, jkarat@us.ibm.com

*University of Michigan
Collaboratory for Research on Electronic Work
701 Tappan Street, Room C2420
Ann Arbor, MI 48109-1234
danhorn@umich.edu

ABSTRACT

A study was conducted to evaluate user performance and satisfaction in completion of a set of text creation tasks using three commercially available continuous speech recognition systems. The study also compared user performance on similar tasks using keyboard input. One part of the study (Initial Use) involved 24 users who enrolled, received training and carried out practice tasks, and then completed a set of transcription and composition tasks in a single session. In a parallel effort (Extended Use), four researchers used speech recognition to carry out real work tasks over 10 sessions with each of the three speech recognition software products. This paper presents results from the Initial Use phase of the study along with some preliminary results from the Extended Use phase. We present details of the kinds of usability and system design problems likely in current systems and several common patterns of error correction that we found.

Keywords

Speech recognition, input techniques, speech user interfaces, analysis methods

INTRODUCTION

Automatic speech recognition (ASR) technology has been under development for over 25 years, with considerable resources devoted to developing systems which can translate speech input into character strings or commands. We are just beginning to see fairly wide application of the technology. Though the technology may not have gained wide acceptance at this time, industry and research seem committed to improving the technology to the point that it becomes acceptable. While speech may not replace other input modalities, it may prove to be a very powerful means of human-computer communication.

However, there are some fundamental factors to keep in

mind when considering the value of ASR and how rapidly and widely it will spread. First, speech recognition technology involves errors that are fundamentally different from user errors with other input techniques [2]. When users press keys on a keyboard, they can feel quite certain of the result. When users say words to an ASR system, they may experience system errors – errors in which the system output does not match their input – that they do not experience with other devices. Imagine how user behavior might be different if keyboards occasionally entered a random letter whenever you typed the "a" key. While there is ongoing development of speech recognition technology aimed at lowering error rates, we cannot expect the sort of error free system behavior we experience with keyboards in the near future. How we go from an acoustic signal to some useful translation of the signal remains technically challenging, and error rates in the 1-5% range are the best anyone should hope for.

Second, while we like to think that speech is a natural form of communication [1,9] it is misleading to think that this means that it is easy to build interfaces that will provide a natural interaction with a non-human machine [10]. While having no difference between human-human and human-computer communication might be a laudable goal, it is not one likely to be attainable in the near future. Context aids human understanding in ways that are not possible with machines (though there are ongoing efforts to provide machines with broad contextual and social knowledge) [7]. A great deal of the ease we take for granted in verbal communication goes away when the listener doesn't understand the meaning of what we say.

Finally we argue that it takes time and practice to develop a new form of interaction [4,6]. Speech user interfaces (SUIs) will evolve as we learn about problems users face with current designs and work to remedy them. The systems described in this paper represent the state-of-the-art in large vocabulary speech recognition systems. They provide for continuous speech recognition (as opposed to isolated word recognition), require speaker training for acceptable performance, and have techniques for distinguishing commands from dictation.

Text Creation and Error Correction

We are particularly interested in text creation by knowledge workers – individuals who "solve problems and generate outputs largely by resort to structures internal to themselves rather than by resort to external rules or procedures [5]." Text – in the form of reports or communication with others – is an important part of this output. While formal business communications used to pass through a handwritten stage before being committed to a typed document, this seems to be becoming less frequent. Knowledge workers who used to rely on secretarial help are now more likely to produce their own text by directly entering it into a word processor. We do not have a clear picture of how changes in the processes of text creation have impacted the quality of the resulting text, even though it seems that much of the text produced by knowledge workers – from newspaper articles to academic papers – is now created in an electronic form.

Efforts to develop new input technologies continue. ASR is clearly one of the promising technologies. We do not know how a change in modality of entry might impact the way in which people create text. For example, does voice entry affect the composition process? There is some suggestion that it does not impact composition quality [3,8]. Have people learned to view keyboards as "more natural" forms of communication with systems? While people can certainly dictate text faster than they can type, throughput with ASR systems is generally slower. Measures which include the time to make corrections favor keyboard-mouse input over speech – partially because error correction takes longer with speech. Some attempts have been made to address this in current systems, but the jury is still out on how successful such efforts have been.

Error detection and correction is an important arena in which to examine modality differences. For keyboard-mouse entry there are at least two ways in which someone might be viewed as making an error. One can mistype something – actually pressing one sequence of keys when one intended to enter another. Such user errors can be detected and corrected either immediately after they were made, within a few words of entry, during a proofreading of the text, or not at all. Another error is one of intent, requiring editing the text. In both cases, correction can be made by backspacing and retyping, by selecting the incorrect text and retyping, or by dialog techniques generally available in word processing systems such as Find/Replace or Spell Checking. While we do not have a clear picture of the proportion of use of the various techniques available, our observations suggest that all are used to some extent by experienced computer users.

There are some parallels for error correction in ASR systems. By monitoring the recognized text, users can correct misrecognitions with a speech command equivalent of "backspacing" (current systems generally have several variations of a command that remove the most recently recognized text – such as SCRATCH or UNDO. There are ways of selecting text (generally by saying the command SELECT and the string to be located), after which redictating will replace the selected text with newly recognized text. Additionally, correction dialogs provide users with a means of selecting a different choice from a list of possible alternatives or entering a correction by spelling it. These different correction mechanisms provide a range of techniques that map well to keyboard-mouse techniques. However, we do not have evidence of how efficient or effective they are. This study was designed to answer these questions. We were interested in several comparisons – keyboard and speech for text entry, modality effects on transcription and composition tasks, and error correction in different modalities.

SYSTEMS

Three commercially available large vocabulary continuous speech recognition systems were used in this study. All were shipped as products in 1998. These systems were IBM ViaVoice 98 Executive, Dragon Naturally Speaking Preferred 2.0, and L&H Voice Xpress Plus (referred to as IBM, Dragon and L&H below). While the products are all different in significant ways, they share a number of important features that distinguish them from earlier ASR products. First, they all recognize continuous speech. Earlier versions required users to dictate using pauses between words. Second, all have integrated command recognition into the dictation so that the user does not need to explicitly identify an utterance as text or command. In general, the systems provide the user with a command grammar (a list of specific command phrases), along with some mechanism for entering the commands as text. Commands can be entered as text by having the user alter the rate at which the phrase is dictated – pausing between words causes a phrase to be recognized as text rather than as a command.

While all of the systems function without specific training of a user's voice, we found the speaker independent recognition performance insufficiently accurate for the purposes of our study. To improve recognition performance, we had all users carry out speaker enrollment – the process of reading a body of text to the system and then having the system develop a speaker-specific speech model. All products require a 133-166MHz Pentium processor machine with 32MB RAM – we ran our study using 200MHz machines with 64MB RAM.

METHOD

There were different procedures used for the Initial Use and the Extended Use subjects in the study. Although the design of the Initial Use study was constructed to allow for statistical comparisons between the three systems, we report on general patterns observed across the systems as they are of more general interest to the design of successful ASR systems.

Initial Use

Subjects in the Initial Use study were 24 employees of IBM in the New York metropolitan area who were knowledge workers. All were native English speakers and experienced computer users with good typing skills. Half of the subjects were male and half were female, with gender balanced across the conditions in the study. The age range of the subjects was from 20 to 55 years old. An effort was made to balance the ages of the subjects in the various conditions. Each subject was assigned to one of three speech recognition products, IBM, Dragon, or L&H. Half of the subjects completed the text creation tasks using speech first and then did a similar set using keyboard-mouse, and half did keyboard-mouse followed by speech. Subjects received a $75 award for their participation in the three hour long session. All sessions were videotaped.

On arrival at the lab, the experimenter introduced the subject to the purpose, approximate length of time, and content of the usability session. The stages of the experimental session were:

1. Provide session overview and introduction.
2. Enroll user in assigned system.
3. Complete text tasks using first modality.
4. Complete text tasks using second modality.
5. Debrief the user.

The experimenter told the subject to try and complete the tasks using the product materials and to think aloud during the session. (While this could cause interference with the primary task, our subjects switched between think aloud and task modes fairly easily.) The experimenter explained that assistance would be provided if the subject got stuck. The experimenter then left the subject and moved to the Control Room. The subject's first task was to enroll in the ASR system (the systems were pre-installed on the machines). Enrollment took from 30 minutes to 1.5 hours for the subject to complete, depending on the system and the subject's speed in reading the enrollment text. After enrollment was completed, the subject was given a break while the system developed a speech model for the subject by completing an analysis of the speech data. After the break, the subject attempted to complete a series of text creation tasks. All text was created in each product's dictation application that provided basic editing functions (similar to Windows 95 WordPad), and did not include advanced functions such as spelling or grammar checkers.

Before engaging in the speech tasks, all participants underwent a training session with the experimenter present to provide instruction. This session was standardized across the three systems. Basic areas such as text entry and correction were covered. Each subject dictated a body of text supplied by the experimenter, composed a brief document, learned how to correct mistakes, and was given free time to explore the functions of the system. During the training session, each subject was shown how to make corrections as they went along as well as making

corrections by completing dictation and going back and proofreading. Sample tasks in both transcription and composition were completed in this phase. Each subject was allowed approximately 40 minutes for the speech training scenario. Subjects were given no training for keyboard-mouse text creation tasks.

In the text creation phase for each modality, each subject attempted to complete four tasks - two composition and two transcription tasks. The order of the tasks (transcription or composition) was varied across subjects with half doing composition tasks followed by transcription tasks, and half doing transcription followed by composition. In all, each subject attempted to complete eight tasks – four composition and four transcription, with two of each task type in each modality.

For each composition task, subjects were asked to compose a response to a message (provided on paper) in the simple text entry window of the dictation application. Each of the responses were to contain three points for the reply to be considered complete and accurate. For example, in one of the composition tasks, the subject was asked to compose a message providing a detailed meeting agenda, meeting room location, and arrangements for food. Composition tasks included social and work related responses, and subjects were asked to compose "short replies." The quality of each response was later evaluated based on whether the composed messages contained a complete (included consideration of the three points) and clear (was judged as well written by evaluators) response. All subjects used the same four composition tasks, with an equal number of subjects using speech and keyboard-mouse to complete each task.

For transcription tasks, subjects attempted to complete the entry of two texts in each modality. There were four texts that ranged from 71 to 86 words in length. These texts were drawn from an old western novel. The subjects entered the text in the appropriate modality and were asked to make all corrections necessary to match the content of the original text. The resulting texts were later evaluated for accuracy and completeness by comparing them to the original materials. Evaluators counted uncorrected entry errors and omissions.

In the keyboard-mouse modality tasks, subjects completed composition and transcription tasks using standard keyboard and mouse interaction techniques in a simple edit window provided with each system. Subjects were given 20 minutes to complete the four keyboard-mouse tasks. All subjects completed all tasks within the time limit.

In the speech modality tasks, subjects completed the composition and transcription tasks using voice, but were free to use keyboard and mouse for cursor movements or to make corrections they felt they could not make using speech commands. We intentionally did not restrict subjects to the use of speech to carry out the speech modality tasks, and all subjects made some use of the keyboard and mouse. Subjects were given 40 minutes to complete the four speech tasks.

After each of the tasks (enrollment and eight text tasks), subjects filled out a brief questionnaire on their experience completing the task. After completing the four tasks for each modality, subjects filled out a questionnaire addressing their experience with that modality. After completing all tasks, the experimenter joined the subject for a debriefing session in which the subject was asked a series of questions about their reactions to the ASR technology.

Extended Use

Subjects in the Extended Use study were the four co-authors of this paper. In this study, the subjects used each of the three speech recognition products for 10 sessions of approximately one hour duration; a total of 30 sessions across the products. During the session the subjects would use speech recognition software to carry out actual work related correspondence. After completing at least 20 sessions, subjects completed the set of transcription tasks used in the Initial Use study. We limit the presentation of the results of the Extended Use phase of the study to some general comparisons with the Initial Use data.

RESULTS

For the analysis of the Initial Use sessions, we carried out a detailed analysis of the videotapes of the experimental sessions. This included a coding of all of the pertinent actions carried out by subjects in the study. Misrecognitions of text and commands and attempts to recover from them were coded, along with a range of usability and system problems. Particular attention was paid to the interplay of text entry and correction segments during a task, as well as strategies used to make corrections. Because of the extensive time required to do this, we completed the detailed analysis for 12 of the 24 subjects in the Initial Use phase of the study (four randomly selected subjects from each of the three systems, maintaining gender balance). Thus we report performance data from 12 subjects, but include all 24 subjects in reporting results where possible. Additionally, we report selected data from the four subjects in the Extended Use phase. The data reported from the three speech recognition systems are collapsed into a single group here.

Typing versus Dictating – Overall Efficiency

Our initial comparison of interest is the efficiency of text entry using speech and keyboard-mouse for transcription and composition tasks. We measure efficiency by time to complete the tasks and by entry rate. The entry rate that we present is corrected words per minute (cwpm), and is the number of words in the final document divided by the time the subject took to enter the text and make corrections. The average length of the composed texts was not significantly different between the speech and keyboard-mouse tasks and was similar to the average length of the transcriptions (71.5

and 73.1 words for speech and keyboard-mouse compositions respectively and 77.8 words for transcriptions). Table 1 below summarizes the results for task completion rates for the various tasks.

	Speech	Keyboard-mouse
Transcription	13.6 cwpm 7.52 min	32.5 cwpm 2.64 min
Composition	7.8 cwpm 9.96 min	19.0 cwpm 4.64 min
Average	8.74 min	3.64 min

Table 1. Mean corrected words per minute and time per task by entry modality and task type (N=12).

Creating text was significantly slower for the speech modality than for keyboard-mouse (F=29.2, p<0.01). By comparison, subjects in the Extended Use study completed the same transcription using ASR in an average 3.10 minutes (25.1 cwpm). The main effect for modality held for both the transcription tasks and the composition tasks. Composition tasks took longer than transcription tasks (F=18.6, p<0.01). This is to be expected given the inherent difference between simple text entry and crafting a message. There was no significant interaction between the task type and modality, suggesting that the modality effect was persistent across task type.

Given this clear difference in the overall time to complete the tasks, we were interested in looking for quantitative and qualitative differences in the performance. There are several areas in which we were interested in comparing text entry through typing to entry with ASR. These included: 1) number of errors detected and corrected in the two modalities, 2) differences in inline correction and proofreading as a means of correction, and 3) differences in overall quality of the resulting document. We consider evidence for each of these comparisons in turn.

Errors detected and corrected

A great deal of effort is put into lowering the error rates in ASR systems, in an attempt to approach the accuracy assumed for users' typing. For text entry into word processing systems, users commonly make errors (typing mistakes, misspellings and such) as they enter. Many of these errors are corrected as they go along – something that is supported by current word processing programs that highlight misspellings or grammatical errors. We were interested in data on the comparison of entry errors in the two modalities, and their detection and correction.

Table 2 presents data summarizing the average number of correction episodes for the different task types and input modalities. A correction episode is an effort to correct one or more words through actions that (1) identified the error, and (2) corrected it. Thus if a subject selected one or more words using a single select action and retyped or redictated a correction, we scored this as a correction episode. A major question is how the number of error correction episodes compares for ASR systems and keyboard-mouse entry.

	Speech	Keyboard-mouse
Transcription	11.3 (7.3)	8.4 (2.2)
Composition	13.5 (6.2)	12.7 (2.4)

Table 2. Mean number of correction episodes per task by entry modality (N=12). Length in steps is in parentheses.

While the average number of corrections made is slightly higher for the speech tasks than for the keyboard-mouse tasks, the length of the correction episodes is much longer. Interestingly, the improved performance for Extended Use subjects on transcription tasks cannot be accounted for entirely by reduced correction episodes – subjects averaged 8.8 per task. The average number of steps per correction episode is much shorter for the Extended Use subjects – averaging 3.5 steps compared to 7.3 for Initial Use subjects.

In general, the keyboard corrections simply involved backspacing or moving the cursor to the point at which the error occurred, and then retyping (we coded these as a move step followed by a retype step). In a few instances, the user would mistype during correction, resulting in a second retype step. About 80% of the keyboard-mouse corrections were simple position/retype episodes.

For speech corrections there was much more variability. In most cases a misrecognized word could be corrected using a simple locate/redictate command pair comparable to the keyboard-mouse pattern. Such a correction was coded as a voice move, followed by a voice redictate, that was marked to indicate success or failure. Variations include command substitutions such as the sequence voice select, voice delete, and voice redictate. More often the average number of commands required was much greater - generally due to problems with the speech commands themselves that then needed to be corrected, although the overall patterns can still be seen in terms of move to the error, select it and operate on it. Typical patterns included:

1. Simple redictation failures in which the user selected the misrecognized word or phrase (usually using a voice select command), followed by a redictation of the misrecognized word which also was misrecognized. Users would continue to try to redictate, would use correction dialogs that allow for alternative selection or spelling, or would abandon speech as a correction mechanism and complete the correction using keyboard-mouse

2. Cascading failures in which a command used to attempt a correction was misrecognized and had to be corrected itself as a part of the correction episode. Such episodes proved very frustrating for subjects and took considerable time to recover from.

3. Difficulties using correction dialogs in which the user abandoned a correction attempt for a variety of reasons. This included difficulties brought on by mode differences in the correction dialog (e.g., commonly used correction commands such as UNDO would not work in correction dialogs) or difficulties with the spelling mechanism.

High Level Correction Strategies – Inline versus Proofreading Corrections

Another question is whether users employ different correction strategies for the two input modalities. This could be demonstrated in either high-level strategies (such as "correct as you go along" versus "enter and then correct") or in lower-level differences such as the use of specific correction techniques. In Table 3 we present data for the transcription and composition tasks combined, comparing the average number of errors corrected in a task before completion of text entry (Inline) and after reaching the end of the text (Proofreading).

	Speech	Keyboard-mouse
Inline	8.6	8.8
Proofreading	4.2	1.6

Table 3. Average errors corrected per task by phase of entry (N=12).

There are two things to point out in these data. First, there are significantly more correction episodes in inline than in proofreading for both modalities (t=7.18, p<.006 for speech and t=8.64, p<.001 for keyboard-mouse). Performance on the keyboard-mouse tasks demonstrated that subjects are quite used to correcting as they go along, and try to avoid separate proofreading passes. For the speech modality however, subjects still had significant errors to correct in proofreading. In comparison, subjects in the Extended Use study rarely made inline corrections in transcription tasks (less than once per task on average).

Subjects gave us reasons for an increased reliance on proofreading. They commented that they felt aware of when they might have made a typing error, but felt less aware of when misrecognitions might have occurred. Note that in keyboard-mouse tasks, errors generally are user errors, while in speech tasks errors generally are system errors. By this we mean that for keyboard-mouse, systems reliably produce output consistent with user input. A typist can often "feel" or sense without looking at the display when an error might have occurred. For speech input, the user quickly learns that output is highly correlated with speech input, but that it is not perfect. Users do not seem to have a very reliable model of when an error might have occurred, and must either constantly monitor the display for errors or rely more heavily on a proofreading pass to detect them.

Second, the number of inline correction episodes is nearly equal for the two conditions. This suggests a transfer of cognitive skill from the more familiar keyboard and mouse interaction. As in typing, subjects were willing to switch from input mode to correction mode fairly easily and did not try to rely completely on proofreading for error correction.

Lower-level strategies for error correction

Almost all keyboard-mouse corrections were made inline and simply involved using the backspace key or mouse to point and select followed by typing. In comparison, the voice corrections were much more varied. This is undoubtedly due to the wide range of possible errors in the ASR systems compared to keyboard-mouse entry. The major classes of possible errors in ASR include:

- **Simple misrecognitions** in which a single spoken word intended as text is recognized as a different text word.

- **Multi-word misrecognitions** in which a series of words are recognized as a different series of words.

- **Command misrecognitions** in which an utterance intended as a command is inserted in the text.

- **Dictation as command misrecognitions** in which an utterance intended as dictation is taken as a command.

All of these occurred in all of the systems in the study. In addition, subjects did some editing of content in their documents. Because errors in ASR are correctly spelled words it is difficult to separate edits from errors in all cases. In what follows these are treated the same since both use the same techniques for correction.

Methods of making corrections in the two modalities can be compared. For example, keyboard-mouse corrections could be made by making a selection with the mouse and then retyping, by positioning the insertion point with cursor keys and then deleting errors and retyping, or by simply backspacing and retyping. These segment into two categories: deleting first then entering text or selecting text and entering over the selection. In speech, these kinds of corrections are possible in a variety of ways using redictation after positioning (with voice, keyboard or mouse). In addition, there is use of a correction dialog which allows spelling (all systems) or selection of an alternative word (in two of the three systems). Table 4 summarizes the techniques used by subjects to make corrections in the texts.[1]

The dominant technique for keyboard entry is to erase text back to the error and retype. This includes the erasure of text that was correct, and reentering it. For speech, the dominant technique was to select the text in error, and to redictate. In only a minority of the corrections (8%) did the

---

[1] Only one of the 12 subjects used an explicitly multi-modal strategy for correction. That subject relied on the keyboard to move to the error and switched to speech to select and redictate the text.

subjects utilize the systems' correction dialog box. Almost a third of the corrections were to correct problems created during the original correction attempt. For example, while correcting the word "kiss" to "keep" in "kiss the dog", the command "SELECT kiss" is misrecognized as the dictated text "selected kiss", which must be deleted in addition to correcting the original error.

	Speech	Keyboard-mouse
Select text then reenter	38%	27%
Delete then reenter	23%	73%
Correction box	8%	NA
Correcting problems caused during correction	32%	NA

Table 4. Patterns of Error Correction based on overall corrections (N=12).

Low use of the correction dialogs may be explained by two phenomena. First, correction dialogs were generally used after other methods had failed (62% of all correction dialogs). Second, 38% of the time a problem occurred during the interaction inside the correction dialog with 38% of these resulting in canceling out of the dialog. Understanding more fully why the features of the correction dialogs are not better utilized is an area for future study.

Overall Quality of Typed and Dictated Texts

There are two areas in which we tried to evaluate the relative quality of the results of text entry in the two modalities. For transcription tasks, we evaluated the overall accuracy of the transcriptions – that is, we asked how many mismatches there were between the target document and the produced document. For composition tasks we asked three peers, not part of the study, to evaluate several aspects of the messages produced by subjects. These judges independently counted the number of points that the message covered (there were three target points for each message). We also asked for a count of errors in the final message and for an evaluation of the overall clarity. Finally, for each of the four composition tasks, we asked the judges to rank order the 24 messages in terms of quality from best to worst.

In Table 5 we summarize the overall quality measures for the texts produced. These measures include average number of errors in the final products for both the transcription and composition tasks, and the average quality rank for texts scored by three judges for the composition tasks.

There were many more errors in the final transcription documents for the speech tasks than for the keyboard-mouse tasks. The errors remaining in the final documents were broken into three categories: wrong words (including misspellings), format errors (including capitalization and punctuation errors), and missing words. The average number of wrong words (F=25.4, p<.001) and format errors (F=12.6, p<.001) were significantly lower for keyboard-mouse compared with speech tasks. There was no difference in the number of missing words.

	Speech	Keyboard-mouse
Transcription errors	3.8 errors	1.0 errors
Composition errors	1.8 errors	1.1 errors
Composition (rank)	13.2	11.4

Table 5. Mean quality measures by modality (N=24).

Composition quality showed a similar pattern. Errors in composition included obviously wrong words (e.g., grammar errors) or misspellings. There were fewer errors in the keyboard-mouse texts than in the speech texts (F=7.9, p<0.01). Judges were asked to rank order the texts for each of the four composition tasks from best (given a score of 1) to worst (given a score of 24). While the mean score was lower (better) for keyboard-mouse texts than for speech texts, the difference was not statistically significant.

Transcription versus Composition

For both the keyboard-mouse modality and the speech modality, composition tasks take longer than transcription tasks. We did not find significant differences in the length or readability of texts composed in the two modalities. Additionally, topics such as correction techniques or error frequencies did not seem to vary between modalities and task types.

Subjective Results – Questionnaire Data

Subjects (N=24) in the Initial Use study consistently report being dissatisfied with the ASR software for performing the experimental tasks. When asked to compare their productivity using the two modalities in the debriefing session, subjects gave a modal response of "much less productive" for speech on a 7-point scale ranging from "much more productive" to "much less productive", and 21 of 24 subjects responded "less" or "much less productive". Subjects' top reasons for their ratings, (frequency of response in parentheses summed across several questions) were:

- Speech recognition is unreliable, error prone (34).
- Error correction in speech is much too hard – and correction can just lead to more errors (20).
- Not knowing how to integrate the use of speech and keyboard-mouse efficiently (19).
- Keyboard is much faster (14).
- Command language problems (13).
- It is harder to talk and think than to type and think (7).

Additionally, when asked if the software was good enough to purchase, 21 of 24 subjects responded "No" to a binary

Yes/No choice. The three subjects that reported a willingness to purchase the software all gave considerable qualifications to their responses. When asked for the improvements that would be necessary for ASR technology to be useful, subjects' top responses included:

- Corrections need to be much easier to make (27).
- Speech recognition needs to be more accurate (25).
- Need feedback to know when there is a mistake (8).
- Command language confusion between command and dictation needs to be fixed (8).

DISCUSSION

There are many interesting patterns in the data presented above. Early speech recognition products varied in the strategies of error correction that they encouraged for users. For example, IBM's VoiceType system encouraged users (in documentation and online help) to dictate first and then switch to correction mode, while Dragon Dictate encouraged users to make corrections immediately after an error was dictated. To a large extent these strategies were encouraged to have user behavior correspond to system designs, and not because of a user driven reason. The systems in the current study all accommodate inline correction and post-entry correction equally well. One thing that the results of the Initial Use study point to is the general tendency for subjects to make corrections as they go along, rather than in a proofreading pass. Table 2 shows that subjects made many more corrections inline than they did after completion of entry in both the speech and keyboard-mouse conditions.

When subjects made errors in keyboard-mouse text entry, they tended to correct the error within a few words of having made it. In contrast, some subjects made specific mention of not being as aware of when a misrecognition had occurred and needing to "go back to" a proofreading stage for the speech tasks. Taken together with the tendency toward inline correction, this suggests supporting users in knowing when a misrecognition has occurred.

Misrecognition Corrections

The most common command used in any of the systems is the command to reverse the immediately preceding action. While each of the systems has multiple variant commands for doing this (some mixture of UNDO, SCRATCH, and DELETE), users generally rely on a single form that they use consistently. However, the command variants have subtle distinctions that were frequently lost on the subjects in this study. Many of the usability problems with respect to these commands appear related to the users strategy of relying on a single form for a command, even if it was not appropriate for the tasks at hand. Developing more complex strategies for selecting between command forms seems to require additional expertise. We do not observe these confusions at this level in the Extended Use study.

Quality Measures

Attempts to compare the composition quality of texts produced by speech input and more traditional input generally predate the existence of real systems for ASR [e.g., 3,8]. The current study shows no statistical difference between the quality of the texts composed using speech recognition as compared to keyboard and mouse.

Subjective Results

The majority of subjects felt that they would be less or much less productive with speech recognition than with keyboard and mouse using the current products. They provided some clear insights into where efforts need to be made to improve these systems in order for them to be useful and usable. Top concerns include the performance of the systems and several key user interface issues. There is a critical need to learn about people's performance and satisfaction with multi-modal patterns. The field needs to better understand the use of commands and people's ability and satisfaction with natural language commands. Also, there are intriguing issues to be researched regarding cognitive load issues in speech recognition and how to provide feedback to users. The subjects said that they were excited about the future possibility of using speech to complete their work. They were pleased with the feeling of freedom that speaking allowed them, and the ease and naturalness of it.

CONCLUSIONS

It is interesting to note that several of the Initial Use subjects commented that keyboard entry seemed "much more natural" than speech for entering text. While this seems like an odd comment at some level, it reflects the degree to which some people have become accustomed to using keyboards. This relates both to the comfort with which people compose text at a keyboard and to well learned methods for inline error detection and correction. Speech is also a well learned skill, though as this study shows, the ways to use it in communicating with computers are not well established for most users. There is potential for ASR to be an efficient text creation technique – the Extended Use subjects entered transcription text at an average rate of 107 uncorrected words per minute – however correction took them over three times as long as entry time on average.

When desktop ASR systems first began appearing about 5 years ago, it was assumed that their wide-scale acceptance would have to await solutions to "mode problems" (the need to explicitly indicate dictation or command modes), and the development of continuous speech recognition algorithms which were sufficiently accurate. While all of the commercial systems evaluated in this study have these features, our results indicate that our technically sophisticated subject pool is far from satisfied with the current systems as an alternative to keyboard for general text creation. They have given a clear prioritization of changes needed in the design of these systems. These changes merit significant attention.

It is possible – though we do not think it is very likely – that less skilled computer users would react to the software more positively. The methods for error correction, and the complexity that compound errors can produce, leads us to believe that decreased rather than increased performance would have to be tolerated by any users – even those with limited typing skills. While this might be acceptable for some populations (RSI sufferers or technology adopters), wide scale acceptance awaits design improvements beyond this current generation of products.

REFERENCES

1. Clark, H. H. & Brennan, S. E. (1991). Grounding in communication. In J. Levine, L. B. Resnick, and S. D. Behrand (Eds.), Shared Cognition: Thinking as Social Practice. APA Books, Washington.

2. Danis, C. & Karat, J. (1995). Technology-driven design of speech recognition systems. In G. Olson and S. Schuon (eds.) Symposium on designing interactive systems. ACM: New York, 17-24.

3. Gould, J. D., Conti, J., & Hovanyecz, T. (1983). Composing letters with a simulated listening typewriter. Communications of the ACM, 26, 4, 295-308.

4. Karat, J. (1995). Scenario use in the design of a speech recognition system. In J. Carroll (ed.) Scenario-based design. New York: Wiley.

5. Kidd, A. (1994). The marks are on the knowledge worker, in *Proceedings of CHI '94* (Boston MA, April 1994), ACM Press, 186-191.

6. Lai, J. & Vergo, J. (1997). MedSpeak: Report Creation with Continuous Speech Recognition, in *Proceedings of CHI '97* (Atlanta GA, March 1997), ACM Press, 431 - 438.

7. Laurel, B. (1993). Computers as Theatre. Adison Wesley, New York.

8. Ogozalek, V.Z., & Praag, J.V. (1986). Comparison of elderly and younger users on keyboard and voice input computer-based composition tasks, in *Proceedings of CHI '86*, ACM Press, 205-211.

9. Oviatt, S. (1995). Predicting spoken disfluencies during human-computer interaction. Computer Speech and Language, 9, 19-35.

10. Yankelovich, N., Levow, G. A., & Marx, M. (1995). Designing SpeechActs: Issues in speech user interfaces, in *Proceedings of CHI '95* (Denver CO, May 1995), ACM Press, 369-376.

Mutual Disambiguation of Recognition Errors in a Multimodal Architecture*

Sharon Oviatt**

Center for Human-Computer Communication

Oregon Graduate Institute of Science and Technology

oviatt@cse.ogi.edu; http://www.cse.ogi.edu/~oviatt/

ABSTRACT

As a new generation of multimodal/media systems begins to define itself, researchers are attempting to learn how to combine different modes into strategically integrated whole systems. In theory, well designed multimodal systems should be able to integrate complementary modalities in a manner that supports mutual disambiguation (MD) of errors and leads to more robust performance. In this study, over 2,000 multimodal utterances by both native and accented speakers of English were processed by a multimodal system, and then logged and analyzed. The results confirmed that multimodal systems can indeed support significant levels of MD, and also higher levels of MD for the more challenging accented users. As a result, although speech recognition as a stand-alone performed far more poorly for accented speakers, their multimodal recognition rates did not differ from those of native speakers. Implications are discussed for the development of future multimodal architectures that can perform in a more robust and stable manner than individual recognition technologies. Also discussed is the design of interfaces that support diversity in tangible ways, and that function well under challenging real-world usage conditions.

Keywords

multimodal architecture, speech and pen input, recognition errors, mutual disambiguation, robust performance, diverse users

INTRODUCTION

Multimodal systems process combined natural input modes— such as speech, pen, touch, manual gestures, gaze, and head and body movements— in a coordinated manner with multimedia system output. These systems represent a new direction for computing that draws from novel input and output technologies currently becoming available. They also represent a research-level paradigm shift away from conventional WIMP interfaces toward providing users with greater expressive power, naturalness, flexibility and portability.

Since the appearance of Bolt's [1] "Put That There" demonstration system, which processed speech in parallel with manual pointing, a variety of multimodal systems has emerged. Some rudimentary ones process speech combined with mouse pointing, such as the early CUBRICON system

[8]. Others recognize speech while determining the location of pointing from users' manual gestures or gaze [7]. Recent multimodal systems now recognize a broader range of signal integrations, which no longer are limited to the simple point-and-speak combinations handled by earlier systems. For example, the Quickset system integrates speech with pen input that includes drawn graphics, symbols, gestures and pointing [5]. It uses a semantic unification process to combine the meaningful multimodal information carried by two input signals, both of which are rich and multidimensional.

Complementarity of Modalities

One major challenge for the design of multimodal systems involves learning how to combine different modes into a strategically integrated whole system. In theory, well designed multimodal systems should be able to integrate complementary modalities to yield a highly synergistic blend in which the strengths of each mode are capitalized upon and used to overcome weaknesses in the other [4, 11]. This approach promotes the philosophy of using component technologies to their natural advantage, and of combining them in a manner that permits mutual compensation. One implication is that the resulting multimodal interface may be capable of functioning more robustly than individual recognition-based technologies, which are inherently error-prone [9]. However, empirical research is needed to examine the possibility of a performance advantage in error handling, to assess its specific nature, and to explore the usage contexts in which it may occur.

Error Handling in Multimodal Interfaces

There are several reasons why a multimodal interface potentially can support better error handling than a unimodal recognition-based one, such as a spoken language interface. The following factors all are capable of leading to better error avoidance and more rapid recovery:

First, *users will select the input mode that they judge to be less error prone for particular lexical content, which leads to error avoidance.* That is, when free to interact multimodally, they exercise good intuitions about the accuracy of a modality for conveying particular content. For example, they are more likely to write rather than speak a foreign

---

*This research was supported in part by Grant No. IRI-9530666 from the National Science Foundation, Contract No. DABT63-95-C-007 from DARPA, and donations from Intel and Microsoft.
**Author: Center for Human-Computer Communication, Department of Computer Science, Oregon Graduate Institute of Science & Technology, P.O. Box 91000, Portland, OR, 97291.

surname when addressing a computer [16]. In this respect, a well-designed multimodal interface that gives users flexibility can leverage from their natural ability to use modes accurately and efficiently. Furthermore, the degree of error avoidance possible when using a flexible multimodal interface can be substantial.

Secondly, *users' language is simplified when interacting multimodally, which reduces the complexity of natural language processing and avoids errors.* For example, when users are interacting multimodally they speak fewer words, briefer utterances, fewer referring expressions, less anaphora and linguistic indirection, fewer complex spatial descriptions, and fewer disfluencies than when interacting with unimodal spoken language [10, 15]. In short, there is evidence that multimodal language can be simpler and less ambiguous than unimodal speech, and these altered linguistic features generally would be associated with a reduction in system recognition errors.

Thirdly, *users tend to switch modes after system errors, which facilitates error recovery.* That is, people's natural predilection during multimodal interaction is to switch input modes when they encounter a system recognition error. In fact, their likelihood of mode switching following a system error is 3-fold higher than during baseline periods when recognition is error-free [12]. Since the confusion matrices differ for the same lexical content when delivered via different modes, a mode shift could effectively shortcut a string of repeated system failures (i.e., *spiral errors*), thereby facilitating error recovery.

The fourth reason why multimodal systems support more graceful error handling is that *users report less subjective frustration with errors when interacting multimodally, even when errors are as frequent as in a unimodal interface* [12]. This reduction in users' level of frustration may result from a greater sense of control when they can switch actively between modes. All of the factors outlined above essentially are user-centered reasons why multimodal systems support improved error avoidance, recovery, and user satisfaction with error handling.

Goals and Predictions of the Study
The present study aimed to investigate a fifth possible basis for superior error handling in multimodal systems, but in this case a by-product of the multimodal architecture's design. This study explored whether a multimodal architecture can support *mutual disambiguation* (MD) of input signals. Mutual disambiguation involves recovery from unimodal recognition errors within a multimodal architecture, which leads to more stable and robust performance [9]. For example, a speech recognizer might misrecognize "ditches" and instead rank the singular "ditch" as first choice on its n-best list, although parallel recognition of several ink lines could result in recovery of the correct plural during multimodal interpretation.

A second goal was to explore whether the relative advantage of multimodal over unimodal processing would be more pronounced in some usage contexts than others. The study investigated whether input from users defined as "challenging" (i.e., accented speakers) could be processed more successfully by a multimodal system than a traditional unimodal one, such as a spoken language system. In particular, it assessed whether the MD rates supported by the architecture would be higher for accented speakers of English, in comparison with native ones. It was expected that speech recognition would be degraded for accented speakers and, as a result, that a higher percentage of their utterances with MD would involve retrieval of incorrect speech interpretations rather than gestural ones. That is, with respect to mutual disambiguation of input modes within a multimodal architecture, it was predicted that gestural input would disambiguate error-prone speech more often for accented speakers, whereas speech input would disambiguate faulty gesture recognition more often for native speakers. To pursue these goals, the Quickset pen/voice multimodal system was adapted for testing. In addition, a novel metric of mutual disambiguation was developed, and an automated tool was created for logging and analyzing MD during multimodal system processing.

Apart from analyzing MD, recognition rates also were assessed for the two component input signals, speech and gesture, and for multimodal processing after these signals were integrated. If MD is supported by multimodal processing, then it was predicted that spoken language recognition rates would be higher when processing occurs within a multimodal architecture than when conducted as a stand-alone recognition process. Finally, although it was anticipated that speech recognition rates would be poorer for accented speakers than native ones, if the system indeed supports higher MD rates for this group, then their multimodal recognition rates should more closely resemble those of native speakers— yielding a closing of the performance gap between the two groups.

METHOD
Subjects, Tasks & Procedure
Sixteen people participated as paid volunteers, eight native speakers of English and eight accented non-native speakers. The non-native speakers represented a range of different languages from the Asian, Indian, European, and African continents— including Mandarin, Cantonese, Tamil, Hindi, Spanish, Turkish, and Yoruba. All of the non-native speakers of English still were active speakers of their native language part of the day. In terms of duration of experience speaking English while resident in the U.S., the non-native speakers varied widely from 1.5 weeks to 23 years, with the strength of their accents varying from mild to strong.

Within the native and non-native speaker groups, half were male and half female. Participants' ages ranged from mid-20s through mid-50s. Their professional backgrounds were broad-spectrum white collar, ranging from scientists and business personnel to facilities support staff.

During the study, volunteers were given an orientation to the Quickset system, including its map-based interface and capabilities. Using the system, they were shown how to set up simulations involving community fire and flood control activities. After this orientation, they also practiced using all of the system's basic capabilities.

While engaged in simulation activities, users could issue commands to the system to: (1) Scroll, zoom, or otherwise control the system's map display (e.g., "Scroll here" [draws arrow upward]; "Zoom in" [circles school]), (2) Automatically locate objects on the map (e.g., "Show me the hospital" [points to map]), (3) Add objects to the map as individual entities or subsets (e.g., "Backburn zone" [draws irregular rectangular area]; "Volunteers... here" [marks point], "here" [marks point], "here" [marks point]), (4) Orient or otherwise define objects on the map (e.g., "Wind-speed 40 miles an hour" [draws arrow toward northeast]; "Airstrips... facing this way" [draws arrow toward north-east], "facing this way" [draws arrow north], (5) Specify the movement of entities (e.g., "Remove residents" [delete mark over municipal building]; "Helicopter follow this route" [draws line], (6) Ask questions about map objects (e.g., "Show number of gallons" [places question mark over water tower]), and (7) Regulate general map capabilities (e.g., "Print map" [check mark]). Figure 1 illustrates the Quickset interface during a simulated fire control scenario. In this example, the user said "pan" and drew an arrow down to indicate the area they wanted to see.

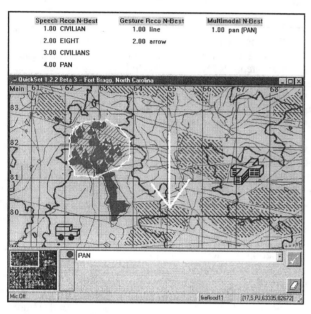

Figure 1: Quickset user interface during a multimodal command to "pan" the map, which illustrates MD occurring such that speech and gesture choices were pulled up on their n-best lists to produce a correct multimodal interpretation by the system

During testing, participants sat in a quiet office environment in front of a Wacom flat-panel LCD display with digitizer that presented the color Quickset map. They communicated multimodally[1] with the system using pen input and by speaking their information. They spoke to the Quickset system with an Andrea noise-canceling microphone head-set. A separate audio recording of the users' speech was captured using a table-top Crown microphone, and fed into the STAMP multimodal data logger (described below). In addition, a record of all pen input and system responding on the map interface was videorecorded for use in conjunction with the STAMP data logger.

---

[1] Although the Quickset system can process either unimodal or multimodal utterances, users only were asked to deliver multimo-dal commands. This generated maximum data on the occurrence of MD during multimodal processing.

Each volunteer entered approximately 100 multimodal commands to Quickset, 50 involving a fire control task and another 50 on a flood control task. The order of completing tasks was counterbalanced. All commands were processed by the Quickset system. After each multimodal command was received, Quickset confirmed its semantic interpreta-tion. For example, if an airstrip was recognized, then an air-strip icon would be added in the correct map location and the system's verbatim recognition confirmed in the text field beneath the map. Participants were told that if the system was correct, they could simply enter their next command. If for any reason the system did not correctly recognize their command after three attempts, they were told to skip over it to the next one. They also were shown how to correct any system errors that occurred by erasing and reentering their input. After each session, volunteers were interviewed briefly about the system, its performance, and its features.

Research Design

The research design was a completely-crossed factorial with two between-subject factors: (1) Native speaker status— unaccented native vs. accented non-native speech, and (2) Gender— male vs. female. The order of presenta-tion of each subtask, fire and flood control, was counterbal-anced within each condition. In total, data were available for analysis from 16 users and over 2,000 multimodal commands.[2]

Quickset Multimodal System

As described earlier, Quickset is a multimodal pen/voice system that supports map-based interactions, especially simulation scenarios. It is a distributed system that runs on a hand-held PC, and uses a multi-agent architecture for par-allel processing of spoken and pen-based input. Different versions of the Quickset system and its interface have been developed for use with different application domains. The sections that follow specify system features relevant to the fire and flood manage-ment tasks developed for this study, with a fo-cus on describing the system's signal and lan-guage processing. The system's architectural flow for processing these components is il-lustrated in Figure 2. For a detailed description of the Quickset system's functionality, interface design, natural language processing, multi-agent architecture, and hard-ware and software char-acteristics, see [5].

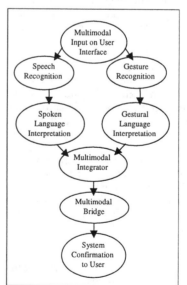

Figure 2: Multimodal architecture for handling signal and language processing of parallel speech and gesture input

---

[2] This total includes approximately 1600 original commands and over 400 repair attempts.

Vocabulary and Grammar
A total vocabulary of over 400 spoken words and 9 types of gestures[3] were used in conjunction with the fire and flood management tasks in this study. In addition, given the grammatical combinations possible between the speech and gesture vocabulary, a total of over 200 unique multimodal utterances were available within these tasks. The gesture recognition for Quickset was developed at OGI, and the speech recognition was Microsoft's Whisper 3.0. Both recognizers provided n-best lists with probability estimates. The vocabulary and grammar used in this study for speech, gestures, and multimodal constructions were selected to sample broadly from those available within the Quickset system. According to task analysis, Quickset multimodal constructions often were spatial location commands [see 14 for details].

Signal Processing & N-best Recognition
In Quickset, pen-based and spoken input each are time-stamped to mark their beginning and end. For pen-based input, time-stamping occurs for the beginning and end of each stroke, which is an internal data structure that represents all tracking of the pen's x,y coordinates, and this data structure then is sent to the gesture recognizer for signal-level processing. Gestures can be quite ambiguous, and the same stroke can have different legitimate interpretations in different contexts. During processing, the gesture recognizer produces an n-best list of possible meaningful interpretations, each of which is associated with a probability estimate. These signal-level stroke interpretations then are passed on for processing by the natural language agent to create a gestural parse n-best list before being integrated with the parallel speech interpretation.

For spoken input, time-stamping begins and the speech recognition engine is engaged when an acoustic signal exceeding a minimum energy threshold is picked up. Time-stamping ends when the signal's energy falls below this threshold for a given duration, after which speech processing is completed. Since the interface is a tap-to-speak one,[4] a pen-down event indicating that the user's input was intentional also is a prerequisite for time-stamping and processing. Like gesture processing, the speech recognizer generates an n-best list of lexical interpretations, each associated with a probability estimate that represents the likelihood that the incoming speech signal matches a particular string of phonemes in the speech recognizer's model. These signal-level interpretations then are filtered by the natural language agent's parser, which forms a spoken language n-best list.

To interpret a whole multimodal command, the time-stamps for speech and gestural input are compared by the integrator agent. Based on results of empirical analysis of the synchronization patterns typical of speech and pen input in a similar domain [14], an integration rule is applied to these time-stamped signals. The integrator will combine speech and pen signals and attempt to process their multimodal

meaning: (1) in all cases for which there is temporal overlap between signals, and (2) in cases involving sequential signals if the speech signal begins within four seconds of the end of gesture. When the architecture's synchronization rules permit joint processing, and one or more successful unifications (see details below) yield candidates for inclusion on the final multimodal n-best list, then these lexical items also are ranked on that list according to their probability estimates. The top-ranked multimodal integration then is sent to the architecture's application bridge agent, at which point this system interpretation is confirmed as the user's intended command.

Semantic Unification
In addition to temporal rules, the multimodal architecture imposes constraints based on authentication and semantic unification before joint processing of signals is permitted for a multimodal command. With respect to semantic unification, typed feature structures are employed to provide a common meaning representation for speech and gesture [2]. Unification is an operation that compares two partial specifications of information and combines them into a single complete semantic interpretation, if they are compatible. Multimodal integration is mediated by a unification operation over feature structures that represent the semantic interpretations of the spoken and gestural components of a multimodal utterance. Each candidate string in the n-best lists for both speech and gesture recognition is parsed by a unification-based parser, and then is assigned a feature structure representation of its semantic interpretation. Each of these representations is underspecified or partial until the modes are integrated during the unification process by the multimodal integration agent, at which point full interpretations are generated. The multimodal integration agent examines the cross-product of the spoken and gestural interpretations, filtering out combined interpretations that do not unify [6]. The remaining "legal" unifications then comprise the final multimodal n-best list, which is rank-ordered by probability estimates that are derived by combining probability estimates from the spoken and gestural components. For further details on Quickset's unification and multimodal integration capabilities, see [6].

STAMP Multimodal Analysis Tool
To support this research, a new multimodal data analysis tool was designed to analyze overall multimodal system performance, including the unimodal pieces of the architecture and their capacity for mutual disambiguation. The videotaped record of each user's multimodal commands during human-computer interaction with the map interface, as well as the system's processing results for each command, was routed to the STAMP multimodal data logger. STAMP was designed to permit researchers to analyze multimodal system performance. It: (1) records data on users' multimodal input and system processing as these events are captured during user testing, (2) organizes this information into a database that supports coordinated replay of the users' multimodal commands and the system's processing results (i.e., in the form of n-best recognition lists for individual modalities and their combined interpretation), and (3) supports the flexible and automated analysis of different indices of multimodal system performance. The STAMP suite of multimodal analysis tools consists of four separate pieces: a data logger, a loader, a marking/analysis tool, and a video controller.

---

[3] Gesture types also could have subtypes (e.g., different map orientations for arrows, such as N, NE, E).

[4] Quickset is typically used with a tap-to-speak interface, because speech during tap-to-speak interaction is known to be substantially more intelligible than that during open-microphone interaction [13].

For each user utterance directed to the system, STAMP uses side-by-side display screens to permit flexible replay of the user's multimodal command on the map along with the system's synchronized recognition results for each of its components. System processing is summarized as a collection of four to five n-best lists, as illustrated in Figure 3, for: (1) speech signal recognition, (2) gesture signal recognition, (3) interpretation of parsed spoken language, (4) interpretation of parsed gestural language, and (5) final semantic interpretation of the multimodal language. Based on a comparison of user input and system processing, STAMP then generates automatic summaries of the multimodal system's recognition and mutual disambiguation rates averaged over subjects, conditions, or a whole corpus. Details of the multimodal data logger tool, its output, and the dependent measures and analyses that it supports have been described elsewhere [3].

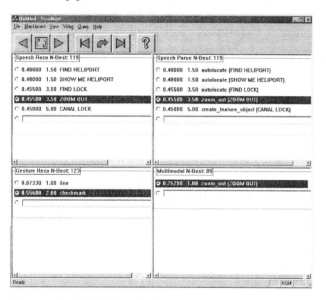

Figure 3: STAMP's display of system processing for a multimodal command, summarized as a set of n-best lists

Dependent Measures

Users' multimodal commands were scored for the measures outlined below except when: (1) a human performance error occurred (e.g., user gestured off screen), (2) a technical problem occurred (e.g., ink skipped), or (3) the command was extraneous or repeated too many times.

Mutual disambiguation

The rate of mutual disambiguation per subject (MD_j) was calculated as the percentage of all their scorable integrated commands (N_j) in which the rank of the correct lexical choice on the multimodal n-best list (R_i^{MM}) was lower than the average rank of the correct lexical choice on the speech and gesture n-best lists (R_i^s and R_i^g), minus the number of commands in which the rank of the correct choice was higher on the multimodal n-best list than its average rank on the speech and gesture n-best lists, or:

$$MD_j = \frac{1}{N_j} \sum_{i=1}^{N_j} Sign\left(\frac{R_i^s + R_i^G}{2} - R_i^{MM} \right)$$

MD was calculated both at the signal processing level (i.e., based on rankings in the speech and gesture signal n-best

lists), and at the parse level after natural language processing (i.e., based on the spoken and gestural parse n-best lists). Scorable commands included all those that the system integrated successfully, and that contained the correct lexical information somewhere in the speech, gesture and multimodal n-best lists.

Multimodal Pull-ups of Speech & Gesture

During MD, either the correct lexical choice for speech, for gesture, or for both were retrieved from a worse-ranked position than first choice on their respective n-best lists. When MD was present, the ratio of all such *architectural pull-ups* that involved speech versus gesture being retrieved and moved up in rank by the system also was calculated.

Speech Recognition

The total percentage of multimodal commands for which the speech input was correct was computed for each subject, and then averaged for each condition. Speech recognition was correct whenever the correct lexical choice was ranked first on the speech signal n-best list. Errors were scored at the utterance level, and any departure in verbatim lexical content was considered an error and therefore an incorrect utterance. This strict percent correct speech recognition rate was computed for all first attempts at a command, and also for all commands up to a maximum three tries apiece.

Gesture Recognition

The total percentage of multimodal commands for which the gesture input was correct was computed for each subject, and then averaged for each condition. Gesture recognition was correct whenever the correct gesture choice was ranked first on the gesture signal n-best list. Since the gesture set only contained individual gestures (i.e., not compound ones), this percent correct gesture recognition rate effectively was the inverse of a gesture word error rate. This rate was computed for both first attempts at each command, and up to three tries apiece.

Multimodal Recognition

The total percentage of multimodal commands that were correct was computed for each subject, and then averaged for each condition. A multimodal command was correct whenever the correct lexical choice was ranked first on the final multimodal n-best list. Errors were scored at the verbatim utterance rather than word level, so any error within a multimodal utterance was considered an incorrect command. For example, if "here" was recognized as "and here," then the command was not scored as correct even though an appropriate system response might have occurred. This percent correct multimodal recognition rate was computed for first attempts at a given command, as well as up to three attempts apiece.

Comparative Spoken Language Processing

To compare the performance of traditional spoken language processing with that occurring within a multimodal architectural framework, an estimate was made of the percent correct recognition rate for the spoken language processing component as a stand-alone (i.e., speech signal & natural language processing modules), as opposed to the percent correct recognition rate for comparable spoken language processing within the multimodal architectural framework (i.e., speech signal, natural language, and unification processing modules with architectural constraints). The latter estimate was based on the same calculation as the multimodal recognition rate, after removing all commands known to have failed exclusively due to gesture recognition.

RESULTS

Mutual Disambiguation

One out of eight commands processed by the multimodal system produced the correct response because of mutual disambiguation that occurred between the input signals. More specifically, an average of 7.4% of multimodal utterances contained signal-level MD for native male speakers, and 9.6% for native females. These percentages increased to 14.8% for non-native male speakers, and 15.1% for non-native females. Analysis of variance confirmed that these MD levels were significantly different as a function of native speech status, $F = 8.04$ (df = 1, 12), $p < .015$. However, no significant difference was present as a function of gender, $F < 1$, or the interaction between native speech and gender, $F < 1$. A planned independent t-test confirmed that signal-level MD was significantly elevated for non-native speakers compared with native ones (i.e., 15.0% of utterances versus 8.5%, respectively), $t = 3.01$ (df = 14), $p < .005$, one-tailed. In short, signal MD values were 76% higher for non-native than native speakers.

This pattern of results was replicated with analyses based on parse-level MD values.[5] On average, 25.2% of multimodal utterances contained parse-level MD for native male speakers and 25.8% for native females, increasing to 30.4% for non-native male speakers and 33.0% for non-native females. Analysis of variance also confirmed that these MD levels were significantly different for non-native than native speakers, $F = 5.24$ (df = 1, 12), $p < .045$. However, no significant difference was evident as a function of gender, $F < 1$, nor the interaction between native speech and gender, $F < 1$. A planned independent t-test again confirmed that parse-level MD was significantly elevated for non-native speakers compared with native ones (31.7% of utterances versus 25.5%, respectively), $t = 2.42$ (df = 14), $p < .015$, one-tailed.

Table 1. Relation between spoken command length, speech recognition errors, and cases of mutual disambiguation (MD) in which speech was pulled-up.

	% TOTAL COMMANDS IN CORPUS	% SPEECH RECOGNITION ERRORS	% MD WITH SPEECH PULL-UPS
1-SYLLABLE	40%	58.2%	84.6%
2-7 SYLLABLES	60%	41.8%	15.4%

Table 1 shows the relation between the length in syllables of spoken commands in the multimodal corpus, the percent of speech recognition errors accounted for, and the percent of multimodal commands in which the system pulled up the speech signal during MD. Table 1 basically reveals that although single-syllable words represented just 40% of all commands, they nonetheless accounted for 58.2% of speech

---

[5] Since the same gestured or spoken lexical item could have different meanings in different multimodal command contexts (e.g., circle to create an area, or to select), this naturally generated ambiguity increased the baseline values for parse-level MD above those of signal-level MD.

recognition errors, which was significantly greater than chance according to Wilcoxon signed-ranks test, $z = 2.79$ (df = 16), $p < .003$, one-tailed. In addition, single-syllable words accounted for 84.6% of cases in which the speech signal was pulled up during MD, which again was significantly greater than chance according to Wilcoxon signed-ranks test, $z = 3.54$ (df = 16), $p < .001$, one-tailed.

Users' MD rates did not change significantly as a function of presentation order between the first and second tasks, $t < 1$. That is, the MD rates appeared stable over the 1-hour test session, with no enhancement due to practice.

Multimodal Pull-ups of Speech & Gesture

The percentage of speech signal pull-ups during MD averaged just 3.7% of multimodal commands for native speakers, but increased to 11.2% for non-native speakers. An independent t-test confirmed that the percent of cases in which *speech* was pulled up was higher for *non-native* speakers than native ones, $t = 4.99$ (df = 14), $p < .001$, one-tailed. In contrast, the percentage of gesture signal pull-ups during MD averaged 7.1% of multimodal commands for native speakers and 5.2% for non-native ones. An independent t-test confirmed that the percent of cases in which *gesture* was pulled up was higher for *native* speakers than non-native ones, $t = 1.77$ (df = 14), $p < .05$, one-tailed. Overall, the average ratio of speech to total signal pull-ups was .35 for native speakers, but increased to .65 for non-native speakers. An independent t-test confirmed that the ratio of speech to total signal pull-ups also was significantly higher for non-native speakers, $t = 4.59$ (df = 14), $p < .001$, one-tailed.

Speech Recognition

Analysis of variance confirmed that the speech recognition rate was significantly different as a function of native speech status, $F = 8.65$ (df = 1, 12), $p < .015$. However, no significant difference was present due to gender, $F < 1$, or the interaction between native speech and gender, $F < 1$. As expected, the verbatim utterance-level speech recognition rate was 72.6%[6] for native speakers, dropping to 63.1% for accented non-native ones— or a 9.5% degradation overall for non-native speakers. A planned independent t-test confirmed that this decrease in performance was a significant one, $t = 3.12$ (df = 14), $p < .004$, one-tailed.[7]

Gesture Recognition

Contrary to expectations, an analysis of variance also revealed that the gesture recognition rate was significantly different as a function of native speech status, $F = 4.90$ (df

---

[6] The verbatim recognition rates reported in this study for speech, gesture, and multimodal recognition were adopted for making precise comparisons, but they are underestimates of the system's ability to respond correctly since close paraphrases were counted as errors (e.g., "zoom" and "zoom in"). The utterance-level rates reported here also result in lower estimates than a word-level rate, since multimodal commands averaged three words. As a result, the absolute recognition rates per se should not be interpreted literally as performance estimates.

[7] Results reported for this and other system recognition rates were for first attempts at a given command, although all significant findings reported in this paper also were replicated with analyses based on users' first three command attempts.

= 1, 12), p < .05. However, no significant difference was present as a function of gender, F < 1, or the interaction between native speech status and gender, F < 1. The gesture recognition rate was 83.2% for native speakers, but increased to 86.5% for non-native ones— or 3.4% higher overall. This change represented a small but significant increase in performance for non-native speakers, t = 2.32 (df = 14), p < .036, two-tailed.

Multimodal Recognition

The multimodal recognition rate was predicted to remain lower for accented speakers than native ones, although the difference between groups was expected to be less divergent than their speech recognition rates. Instead, the verbatim utterance-level multimodal recognition rate was 77.2% for native speakers and 71.7% for non-native ones, a 5.5% departure that no longer represented a statistically reliable difference between groups, based on a planned independent t-test, t = 1.31 (df = 14), N.S., one-tailed. There also was no difference in multimodal recognition due to gender, t < 1.

Comparative Spoken Language Processing

As predicted, spoken language processing conducted within a multimodal architecture yielded significantly higher recognition rates for both user groups than spoken language processing as a stand-alone, paired t = 14.48 (df = 15), p < .001, one-tailed. The absolute change in the utterance-level recognition rate for speech processed within a multimodal architecture was +13.3%— which represented a 41.3% reduction in the total error rate for spoken language processing as a stand-alone. This advantage for speech processed within a multimodal architecture was equally evident in the native and non-native speaker groups.

Table 2. Overview of mutual disambiguation levels and recognition rate differentials for native and accented speakers.

	NATIVE SPEAKERS	ACCENTED SPEAKERS
MD LEVELS:		
Signal MD level	8.5%	15.0%*
Parse MD level	25.5%	31.7%*
Ratio of speech signal pull-ups	.35	.65*
RECOGNITION RATE DIFFERENTIAL: †		
Speech	+9.5%*	—
Gesture	—	+3.4%*
Multimodal	—	—

*Rates representing a significant elevation between groups.
†Recognition rate differentials show the percentage of advantage for a user group when a significant difference was present.

DISCUSSION

This research has demonstrated that multimodal systems can be designed that are capable of functioning in a more robust and stable manner than individual recognition technologies, which are inherently error-prone. In fact, a 41% reduction in the total error rate was revealed for spoken language processing within a multimodal architecture, compared with spoken language processing as a standalone.

One by-product of designing a multimodal architecture clearly is the superior error handling that is possible due to mutual disambiguation of the system's input modes. In the multimodal system analyzed in this study, one in eight commands that were recognized correctly by the multimodal system succeeded because of mutual disambiguation, even though one or both component recognizers had failed to identify the user's intended meaning. This disambiguation occurred because architectural constraints imposed by semantic unification ruled out incompatible speech and gesture integrations, which effectively pruned recognition errors from the n-best lists of the component input modes. As a result, it frequently was possible to retrieve a correct lexical item ranked lower on an n-best list in a manner that basically yielded an architectural pull-up.

The example shown in Figure 1 illustrates double MD during an error-prone monosyllabic command by an accented speaker. In this case, the fourth-ranked speech choice "pan" was the only alternative that could integrate with the second-ranked arrow gesture, and none of the other speech alternatives integrated with the line on the gesture n-best list. During this integration process, each input mode provides a context for interpreting the other, thereby helping to disambiguate its meaning. In the design of future multimodal architectures, research should explore natural language and dialogue processing techniques other than unification which also may be effective in supporting or optimizing mutual disambiguation of errors.

The rate of mutual disambiguation also was higher for accented non-native speakers than native speakers of English— by a substantial 76%. Although speech recognition rates were much poorer for accented speakers, as would be predicted— their multimodal recognition rates actually did not differ significantly from those of native speakers. The factor mainly responsible for closing this gap in multimodal performance was their higher MD levels. A second factor appears to have been their slightly but significantly elevated gesture recognition rates. It is possible that accented speakers' self-awareness about the vulnerability of their speech recognition may have resulted in efforts to compensate via their gestural input.

There often may be asymmetries in a multimodal interface as to which mode is the more fragile in terms of reliability of recognition. When one mode is expected to be less reliable, the most strategic approach will be to select an alternate mode that can act as a complement and stabilizer in promoting overall mutual disambiguation. In this study, speech recognition was the more fragile mode for accented speakers, with two-thirds of all architectural pull-ups retrieving poorly ranked speech input. However, the reverse was true for native speakers, with two-thirds of pull-ups retrieving lower ranked gestures. Future research could be helpful in defining how different user groups and usage contexts may influence overall MD rates, or asymmetries in the reliability of modes that require compensation in a multimodal interface.

When a spoken language system must process a diverse array of accented speech patterns, as from speakers in the present study, one problem is that the recognizer's substitution errors will be extremely heterogeneous. In contrast, for native English speakers the pattern of lexical confusions typically is relatively predictable, such that a speech vocabulary can be crafted for an application that minimizes highly-confusable errors. Unfortunately, when a realistic array of accented speech must be processed, the strategy of minimizing errors by tailoring vocabulary selection becomes infeasible. Given this more challenging real-world usage context, a multimodal architecture that supports mutual disambiguation may provide a more viable and flexible long-term alternative for reducing system errors. In general, the present results suggest that multimodal interfaces can be developed that support diverse user groups in tangible ways, and that function more reliably than unimodal recognition technologies during challenging real-world usage conditions.

ACKNOWLEDGMENTS

Thanks to J. Clow and C. Slattery for assistance with data collection and analysis, and to J. Clow for implementing the STAMP multimodal analysis tool. Thanks also to D. McGee for adapting the Quickset interface for the fire and flood management scenarios, and to M. Johnston and J. Pittman for extending the speech and gesture vocabulary and grammar. Finally, thanks to P. Cohen for numerous discussions about multimodal architectures, and to our research volunteers for their enthusiasm and generous commitment of time.

REFERENCES

1. Bolt, R.A. Put that there: Voice and gesture at the graphics interface. *Computer Graphics,* 1980, 14 (3): 262-270.

2. Carpenter, R. The logic of typed feature structures. Cambridge, MA.: Cambridge University Press, 1992.

3. Clow, J. & Oviatt, S. L. STAMP: A suite of tools for analyzing multimodal system processing, *Proceedings of the International Conference on Spoken Language Processing,* in press.

4. Cohen, P., Dalrymple, M., Moran, D., Pereira, F. Synergistic use of direct manipulation and natural language, *CHI '89 Conference Proceedings,* ACM/ Addison Wesley: New York, NY, 1989, 227-234.

5. Cohen, P., Johnston, M., McGee, D., Oviatt, S., Pittman, J., Smith, I., Chen, L. and Clow, J. Quickset: Multimodal interaction for distributed applications. *Proceedings of the Fifth ACM International Multimedia Conference,* New York, NY: ACM Press, 1997, 31-40.

6. Johnston, M., Cohen, P.R., McGee, D., Oviatt, S.L., Pittman, J.A. & Smith, I. Unification-based multimodal integration. *Proceedings of the 35th Annual Meeting of the Association for Computational Linguistics,* San Francisco, CA.: Morgan Kaufmann, 1997, 281-288.

7. Koons, D.B., Sparrell, C.J. & Thorisson, K.R. Integrating simultaneous input from speech, gaze, and hand gestures. In *Intelligent Multimedia Interfaces,* M. Maybury, Ed. MIT Press: Menlo Park, CA, 1993, 257-276.

8. Neal, J.G. & Shapiro, S.C. Intelligent multi-media interface technology. In *Intelligent User Interfaces,* J. Sullivan & S. Tyler, Eds. ACM: New York, 1991, 11-43.

9. Oviatt, S.L. Ten myths of multimodal interaction, Communications of the ACM, in press.

10. Oviatt, S.L. Multimodal interactive maps: Designing for human performance, *Human-Computer Interaction,* 1997, 12 (1 & 2) 93-129.

11. Oviatt, S.L. Pen/voice: Complementary multimodal communication, *Proceedings of Speech Tech '92,* New York, NY.

12. Oviatt, S.L., Bernard, J. & Levow, G. Linguistic adaptations during spoken and multimodal error resolution, *Language and Speech,* in press.

13. Oviatt, S.L., Cohen, P. & Wang, M. Toward interface design for human language technology: Modality and structure as determinants of linguistic complexity, *Speech Communication,* 1994, 15 (3-4), 283-300.

14. Oviatt, S. L., DeAngeli, A. & Kuhn, K. Integration and synchronization of input modes during multimodal human-computer interaction, *Proceedings of the CHI '97 Conference,* New York, NY: ACM Press, 415-422.

15. Oviatt, S. L. & Kuhn, K. Referential features and linguistic indirection in multimodal language, *Proceedings of the International Conference on Spoken Language Processing,* in press.

16. Oviatt, S. L. & Olsen, E. Integration themes in multimodal human-computer interaction, *Proceedings of the International Conference on Spoken Language Processing,* (ed. by Shirai, Furui & Kakehi), Acoustical Society of Japan, 1994, vol. 2, 551-554.

Model-based and Empirical Evaluation of Multimodal Interactive Error Correction

Bernhard Suhm
Interactive Systems Laboratories
Carnegie Mellon University/
Universität Karlsruhe
bsuhm@ira.uka.de

Brad Myers
*Human Computer Interaction
Institute*
Carnegie Mellon University
bam@cs.cmu.edu

Alex Waibel
Interactive Systems Laboratories
Carnegie Mellon University /
Universität Karlsruhe
ahw@cs.cmu.edu

ABSTRACT

Our research addresses the problem of error correction in speech user interfaces. Previous work hypothesized that switching modality could speed up interactive correction of recognition errors (so-called *multimodal* error correction). We present a user study that compares, on a dictation task, multimodal error correction with conventional interactive correction, such as speaking again, choosing from a list, and keyboard input. Results show that multimodal correction is faster than conventional correction without keyboard input, but slower than correction by typing for users with good typing skills. Furthermore, while users initially prefer speech, they learn to avoid ineffective correction modalities with experience. To extrapolate results from this user study we developed a performance model of multimodal interaction that predicts input speed including time needed for error correction. We apply the model to estimate the impact of recognition technology improvements on correction speeds and the influence of recognition accuracy and correction method on the productivity of dictation systems. Our model is a first step towards formalizing multimodal (recognition-based) interaction.

Keywords

multimodal interaction, interactive error correction, quantitative performance model, speech and pen input, speech user interfaces.

INTRODUCTION

As speech recognition technology matures, speech user interfaces have begun to replace traditional interfaces. For example, speech systems replace live human operators in automated call centers, and voice input is available as an alternative to keyboard input in automatic dictation systems. Speech recognition technology, however, comes with inherent limitations. Our research addresses the problem of recognition errors due to imperfect recognition. Assuming that recognition remains imperfect despite continued progress in recognition algorithms

(even human recognition is imperfect), we investigate *interactive* error correction methods. Efficient and graceful error correction is crucial in the design of speech user interfaces (as noted, for example, in [2]).

We conducted an informal survey of interactive correction methods used in current speech recognition applications. These applications used the following four correction methods: repeating using continuous speech (from here on *respeaking*), typing, choosing from a list of alternative words, and clarification dialogues. (Clarification dialogues allow the user to make corrections within the context of a spoken dialogue.) What are the drawbacks of these methods? Previous research shows that both correction by respeaking and by choosing from a list can be ineffective in continuous speech applications [17]. Correction by typing assumes keyboard input. Keyboard input is not available in some applications, and it is effective only for users with good typing skills. Clarification dialogues are appropriate mostly for one category of speech user interfaces, so-called conversational speech applications [3]. Our work currently focuses on non-conversational applications.

Previous work hypothesized that error correction could benefit from switching multimodal [12, 13]. It is commonly believed that redundant use of several modalities contributes to the ease of human-to-human communication. Multimodal human-computer interfaces aim to benefit from redundant use of modalities in human-computer interaction in similar ways. Our research explores the benefits of multimodal interaction in the context of error correction. Since words that are confused by automatic recognition systems tend to be different across modalities, switching between modalities for correction should eliminate repeated recognition errors; but to-date, no empirical study with real recognition systems has confirmed this hypothesis.

To test this hypothesis, we have implemented multimodal interactive correction methods [10, 17]. We integrated multimodal correction in an automatic dictation system to build a prototype *multimodal* dictation system. Recognition output is displayed on the screen, and the user locates recognition errors by selecting misrecognized words. The user corrects by deleting, inserting, or replacing misrecognized words. In multimodal correction, there is a choice of different correction modalities:

repeating input using continuous speech, (verbal) spelling, handwriting, and editing using gestures drawn on a touch-sensitive display (e.g., deleting words with an X or scratching gesture, or changing the position of the cursor with a caret gesture). This paper describes a user study of interactive multimodal error correction and presents a predictive performance model of multimodal, recognition-based interaction. *Recognition-based* means that user input must be interpreted using an automatic recognition system [13].

We begin by describing our empirical evaluation of interactive error correction on a dictation application. The main goal of the user study was to provide empirical evidence for the hypothesis that multimodal correction expedites error correction in speech user interfaces. The study shows that unimodal correction (using the same modality for input and correction) is ineffective, and that multimodal correction is effective. Furthermore, the study compares current interactive correction methods (with and without keyboard input) with multimodal correction methods. Finally, the study investigates which modalities users prefer by analyzing usage frequencies of different modalities. To test whether accuracy influences modality choice, we correlated usage frequency with modality accuracy. Our longitudinal analysis of usage frequencies shows that learning effects do occur.

We then describe a simple performance model of multimodal interaction that we apply to error correction in order to extrapolate the results of the user study. Predictive models are particularly useful in multimodal interfaces, since they abstract from current recognition performance. Previous work proposed a quantitative performance model for speech-only interfaces [11]. This model predicted task completion time using critical path analysis. The model accounts for imperfect recognition by modeling error correction as repetition of input. The authors reported a good match between model predictions and empirical data. To our knowledge, the model was never applied to multimodal interaction.

The performance model presented in this paper predicts the interaction throughput of multimodal, recognition-based interaction. Throughput includes the time necessary for error correction. We apply the model to predict what correction accuracies are necessary to achieve certain correction speeds. For example, we predict what accuracy is necessary to beat speed of correction by typing for people with poor, average, and good typing skills. Using this model, we extrapolate the results of our user study to the performance of commercially available dictation recognizers. The model is validated using data from the user study. In conclusion, we discuss implications of this work for document creation using speech recognition, error correction in speech user interfaces, and future multimodal applications.

EMPIRICAL EVALUATION OF A MULTIMODAL DICTATION SYSTEM

This section describes our empirical evaluation of interactive multimodal error correction in the context of a prototype multimodal dictation system. The user study pursued three research goals: providing empirical evidence for the effectiveness of multimodal correction, comparing multimodal with current interactive correction methods, and investigating user preferences between modalities.

Experiment Conditions and Method

We used a prototype multimodal dictation system that enhances JANUS, a state-of-the-art large vocabulary speech recognizer [14], with multimodal interactive error correction. For handwriting and spelling recognition, we used specialized recognizers: Npen++ [9] and Nspell [6]. All recognizers were constrained to the same 20,000 word vocabulary. For gesture recognition, we enhanced a template matcher [15] with heuristics. More details are described in [17].

Participants read aloud either one or more sentences, which were chosen from newspaper text. After reading a sentence, the recognition result was displayed on the screen. Then, participants visually located recognition errors, selected them by tapping on the screen, and corrected them using one of the available correction methods. Which methods are available depended on the experimental condition. Participants were instructed to correct all errors, as quickly as possible (within the constraints of the condition).

Experimental conditions compared multimodal correction to conventional correction with and without keyboard input ("Keyboard&List" and "Respeak&List" condition, respectively). We considered correction by keyboard and mouse input separately in the "Keyboard&List" condition, differentiating participants based on their typing skill. Table 1 shows the experimental conditions by indicating for each experiment condition which of the different correction methods (shown in the first column) are available. We decided on a within-subject, repeated measures design to minimize the impact of the known high variation of recognition accuracy across users.

Experimental Condition	Respeak & List	Multi-modal	Keyboard & List
Choose from List of Alternatives	X	X	X
Respeaking	X	X	
Spelling		X	
Handwriting		X	
Pen Gestures	X	X	
Keyboard / Mouse			X

Table 1: Experimental conditions, with the available correction methods shown as rows.

Fifteen participants were recruited from the local campus community, five in each of the categories of typing skill (slow, average, and fast typist). Participants included students and administrative staff, they were balanced in gender, and most participants did not have any prior experience with speech-recognition software.

Before the study, participants learned to use the different correction modalities in a 45-60 minute long tutorial and practice session. After this session, all participants showed sufficient familiarity with the different correction methods on trial tasks. The participants then proceeded to the three experimental sessions, one for each condition. Three different sets of sentences were randomly assigned to the experimental sessions using a 3x3 Latin Square, to avoid order effects. After completing the experimental sessions, participants filled out a post-experimental questionnaire. The participants were asked which modality they perceived to be most efficient, and which modality they would prefer if all modalities had equal accuracy.

Data Collection and Evaluation Measures

During experimental sessions, we collected data in two ways. First, the prototype multimodal dictation system created a time-stamped record of all spoken, written, and typed user interaction. This record was later manually annotated with the correct system response for each interaction, to assess recognition accuracies. For analysis of modality choice patterns, the record also contains for each recognition error the sequence of modalities used, until successful correction. All sessions were videotaped – the second method of data collection.

We measured performance at the level of a single input modality using the following three measures: input rate (i.e., how many words can a user enter per minute), system response time (i.e., how much time does automatic recognition require), and recognition accuracies (i.e., the probability of recognizing a word correctly). To distinguish between initial input and input occuring during correction of recognition errors, we use the term *correction accuracy* whenever we discuss recognition accuracy on correction input. In other words, the correction accuracy is the probability of success for the current correction attempt.

To assess performance at the task-level, we defined two measures. *Correction speed* is the average number of errors that can be successfully corrected per minute, including multiple correction attempts when necessary. For example, a correction speed of 6 cpm (corrections per minute) means that a user spends on the average 10 seconds to correct each misrecognized word. *System throughput* is the average number of words that can be sucessfully entered per minute, including the time necessary for the correction of recognition errors.

Results

Research Question 1: Why is multimodal correction more effective than unimodal correction?

Answer: To confirm the hypothesis that unimodal correction (by repeating input in the same modality) is less accurate than multimodal correction, we calculated the correction accuracy for consecutive correction attempts *in the same modality*. Note that the counter for the correction attempt is reset after each switch of modality, even if the same recognition error is being corrected. For example, if a user corrected a recognition error in three attempts, using speech for the first two attempts, and handwriting for the final attempt, this final attempt is assigned to attempt category "1", being the first attempt after a switch of modality.

Figure 1 shows correction accuracies assuming that the original input was in speech. If users repeat input in speech, correction accuracy is much lower than if users switch to a different modality (40% for speech, 75% and 80% for handwriting and spelling). If multiple correction attempts are necessary, correction accuracy in successive attempts remains high if the user switches modality after each attempt. In terms of Figure 1, this means staying within category "1". An analysis of variance confirms that corrections in the same modality are significantly more difficult to recognize ($F(2,6)=36.2$, $p<0.01$).

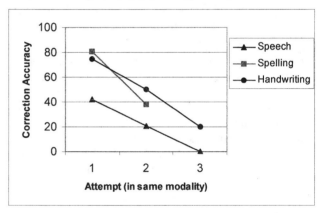

Figure 1: Deterioration of accuracy of repeated correction attempts in the same modality

Research Question 2: How does multimodal correction compare with current interactive correction methods?

Answer: Table 2 shows the correction speed in corrections per minute (in short *cpm*) for conventional keyboard-free correction ("Respeak&List"), correction by keyboard and mouse ("Keyboard&List"), and multimodal correction. Multimodal correction is faster than conventional keyboard-less correction by respeaking and choosing from alternatives (confirmed by post-hoc comparisons). The comparison to correction by keyboard and mouse input depends on the user's typing skill. We measured a range of correction speeds in the "Keyboard&List" condition, which corresponds to different typing skills. (The average typing rates of our participants on plain text were 23, 35, and 40 wpm for the slow, average, and fast typists, respectively). While multimodal correction is about as fast as correction by typing for users with average typing skills, it is slower for users with good typing skills.

Table 2 also shows a range of speeds for multimodal correction, which corresponds to different variations of multimodal correction. For experienced users, we measured 6.8 cpm, which is almost as fast as correction by typing for users with good typing skills. Speed of multimodal correction increases with experience because users learn to avoid ineffective correction methods.

Correction Method	Correction Speed [cpm]
Respeak & List	2.3
Keyboard & List	5.9 – 7.3
Multimodal	4.5 – 6.8

Table 2: Speed of conventional and multimodal correction

Research Question 3: Which modality do users prefer?

Answer: We analyzed the development of user preferences in the course of the experiment by estimating modality usage frequencies every forty correction interactions (which corresponds to one time unit in Figure 2 below) and by determining the correlation between usage frequency and correction accuracy. A positive correlation indicates that users prefer more accurate modalities.

Figure 2 shows how modality choice changed in the course of the experiment for one typical user. Corrections by handwriting were the most accurate modality for this user. This user clearly learns to prefer handwriting over the less accurate modalities of speech and choice from a list. In general, across all users, the correlation between usage frequency and correction accuracy becomes significantly more positive with experience ($F(2,4)=7.25$, $p<0.05$), i.e., users learn to prefer more accurate modalities.

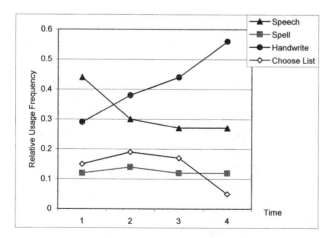

Figure 2: Usage frequencies of different modalities for a typical user. The time axis represents the duration of the experiment (~1 hour)

The initial bias towards speech is consistent with data from the post-experimental questionnaire, in which participants indicated that they would prefer speech if it had the same accuracy as other modalities.

PERFORMANCE MODEL OF MULTIMODAL RECOGNITION-BASED INTERACTION

In speech-based, and more generally in multimodal interfaces, the performance of the recognition systems has a huge impact on overall interface performance. To extrapolate the results of our user study of interactive error correction to future recognition performance, we developed a simple performance model of multimodal interaction that predicts interaction throughput as a function of recognition performance. We estimated the basic model parameters based on data from our user study and applied the model to multimodal error correction.

The Performance Model

Our performance model of recognition-based multimodal human-computer interaction predicts interaction throughput. We chose interaction throughput as the performance variable because a rational user can be expected to prefer methods that minimize effort, and time is the most important factor determining user effort. Since our definition of throughput includes the time necessary to correct any recognition errors, this measure combines time factors and recognition accuracy into a single performance measure. The following paragraphs describe the model in the context of error correction in dictation applications to derive predictions for the correction speed; but it can be generalized to other situations as well.

The model uses four basic parameters: recognition accuracy, input rate, recognition speed, and overhead time. The recognition accuracy $WA(m)$ is defined as the probability of recognizing a word (or more generally, an input item) correctly using modality m. (In the context of error correction, we use the term correction accuracy $CA(m)$.) The input time $T_{input}(m)$ is the average time to input a word in modality m and is measured in seconds per word. We denote its inverse, the input rate (or speed), as $V_{input}(m)$ (e.g., speaking and handwriting rate). The speed of recognition is captured in the real-time factor $R(m)$. It indicates how many times longer than real-time automatic recognition in modality m takes. For example, R=1 means recognition finishes at the same time as user input, without any delay. Lastly, all other times necessary to complete an interaction in modality m are summarized in the overhead time $T_{Overhead}(m)$, which is measured in seconds per correction attempt. The overhead includes the time to plan or select an appropriate interaction method and the time to initiate an interaction, such as moving the hand to the screen to write or gesture on it. Hence, the overhead time depends both on modality and interface implementation.

We model a recognition-based multimodal interaction by the following steps: the user plans the interaction, chooses a modality, provides the necessary input, waits for the system to interpret the input, and finally decides whether correction is necessary.

How much time does such a multimodal interaction require? The steps of planning, choosing the modality, and the preparation of the actual input correspond to the overhead time. Then, user input in modality m and its automatic interpretation takes $R(m)$ times $T_{input}(m)$ seconds. We therefore model a single interaction with the following simple linear additive relationship:

$$T_{Attempt}(m){=}T_{Overhead}(m){+}R(m)T_{Input}(m)$$

Equation 1: Basic Decomposition of Time per Interaction into Overhead, Input, and System Response Time

Based on this estimate for the time for one correction attempt, the correction speed is the quotient of 60 seconds and the total time to correct an error. Since error correction attempts occur sequentially, the average total time is the product of the number of attempts and the time per attempt. Denoting the average number of corrections attempts until success in modality m as $N(m)$, the correction speed can therefore be estimated as:

$$V_{Correct}(m){=}\frac{60sec}{N(m)T_{Attempt}(m)}$$

Equation 2: Factorization of Correction Speed into Time per Interaction and Interaction Attempts

Assuming a constant recognition accuracy across repeated correction attempts (a simplifying assumption, as Figure 1 showed), the average number of interaction attempts until success can be developed into a geometric series, and the expected average number of correction attempts can be calculated as $N(m){=}1/CA(m)$.

To apply the model, some of its parameters are replaced by standard estimates, while other parameters correspond to the independent variables of the problem under question. For example, to predict the correction speed as a function of correction accuracy, we replace input rates by standard estimates, set the overhead times and real-time factors to certain values, and use correction accuracy as independent variable.

	Speech	Spelling	Handwriting
Input Rate V_{input} [wpm]	47 (5)	26 (6)	18 (4)
CA [%]	36 (23)	80 (17)	86 (6)
Realtime Factor R	2.6	1.5	1.3
$T_{Overhead}$ [sec./correction]	5.4 (2.1)	4.3 (0.7)	3.5 (1.1)

Table 3: Model parameters for multimodal error correction. The widths of 95% confidence intervals are shown in parentheses.

How can the model parameters be estimated? Recognition accuracy and speed are standard performance parameters for any recognition system and easily measured. Modality input rates have to be measured once; for standard input modalities (such as handwriting or typing), they can be found in the literature. Finally, overhead times depend on interface implementation and modality.

We divided the data from our fifteen participants into a training set (to estimate model parameters, cf. Table 3) consisting of nine participants and a test set consisting of six participants, two in each category of typing skill. Table 3 shows estimates measured on the training set for input rate (in words per minute), correction accuracies CA (in %), realtime factors, and overhead times (in seconds per correction). Some of these estimates will be used for predictions in following subsections.

Some readers may know that current spelling and handwriting recognizers report accuracies of 90% and more on standard benchmark tasks, raising the question why we measured much lower speeds for multimodal correction in our study? The performance of current recognizers is lower on correction input than on standard benchmarks because corrections are more difficult to recognize. More details can be found in [17].

Application to Interactive Multimodal Error Correction

This section applies our model to the following three questions about interactive error correction in a multimodal dictation system:

1) How does correction speed depend on recognition accuracy and modalities, and how does this affect the speed of multimodal versus unimodal correction?

2) What recognition accuracy is necessary to beat typing in correction speed?

3) What is the total system throughput of a multimodal dictation system as a function of dictation accuracy and error correction?

Correction Speed with Imperfect Recognition

Correction speed depends on the performance of available recognizers and on the modality. To predict correction speed as a function of recognition performance and modality m, $T_{Attempt}(m)$ in Equation 2 is replaced by Equation 1, and we used estimates for input rates as shown in Table 3. We then assumed recognition in real-time for all modalities (R=1) in anticipation of faster computers. Finally, to normalize for implementation specific differences in the overhead time across modalities (as shown in Table 3), we set $T_{Overhead}{=}3.0$ seconds for all modalities, which is more optimistic than the measured values.

Figure 3 shows that at best, with 100% recognition accuracy, correction by respeaking achieves 24 corrections per minute (cpm), and correction by handwriting 15 cpm. This compares favorably to correction by typing for users with good typing skills (>12 cpm).

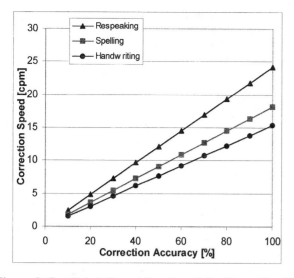

Figure 3: Predicted Correction Speed for Repeating in Continuous Speech, Spelling, and Handwriting

Furthermore, we can use Figure 3 to predict under what conditions unimodal correction by speech could be as efficient as multimodal correction. Since speech is the fastest modality for text input, speech would also be the most effective correction modality in a dictation system, if recognition was accurate enough. For example, multimodal corrections by spelling are 80% accurate with current recognizers (cf. Table 3). Figure 3 predicts that corrections by speech would be faster if they were more than 60% accurate, across repeated correction attempts. While our recognizer achieved only 36% accuracy on speech corrections (cf. Table 3), adapting the speech recognizer on correction input can significantly increase correction accuracy [16].

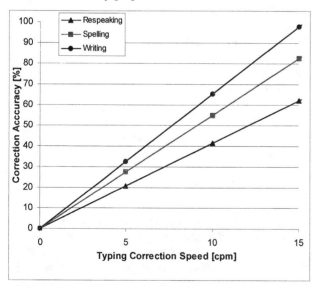

Figure 4: Repair accuracy to beat typing in correction speed

Comparing Multimodal with Typing Correction
To compare multimodal correction and correction by typing, we answer the following question: Which

correction accuracy is necessary to beat typing in correction speed, across different typing skills?

This question can be easily answered using our model by comparing the speed of multimodal correction as a function of correction accuracy with the speed of correction by typing, as shown in Figure 4.

For example, fast non-secretarial typists can correct up to 15 errors per minute using keyboard and choice from the N-best list (as measured in our study). To reach this correction speed, accuracy for corrections by repeating in continuous speech would have to be recognized at more than 65% accuracy. Corrections by spelling would have to be 85% accurate, and corrections by handwriting almost 100% accurate. Hence multimodal correction would beat correction by typing even for users with good typing skills if correction accuracy could be further improved.

Throughput of Dictation Systems
Moving beyond the issue of error correction, this section discusses implications on the overall text production process. To assess the potential productivity gain of multimodal input methods, we first apply the model to predict system throughput as a function of dictation accuracy and error correction, and then compare the system throughput of three text production methods: a *multimodal dictation system* (i.e., first dictate text, then correct multimodally without any keyboard input), a *conventional dictation system* (i.e., first dictate, then correct using keyboard and choosing from alternatives) and a *standard text editor* (i.e., type the whole text). Note that our usage of the term throughput is different from some commercial vendors of dictation systems who exclude the time necessary for correction.

Our performance model can be applied to predict the throughput of dictation systems as follows. Text production with a dictation system consists of three steps: dictation, automatic interpretation of spoken input, and correction of recognition errors. How much time do these steps require? A user with speaking rate $V_{Input}(dictate)$ (in wpm) dictates $wordN = V_{Input}(dictate) * 1\ minute$ words in one minute. Then, the speech recognizer needs $T_1 = R(m)*1min$ to interpret the dictation input. During automatic interpretation of the dictation input at accuracy $WA(dictate)$, on the average $errorN = wordN*(1-WA(dictate))$ recognition errors occur. The correction of these recognition errors using correction method m requires $T_2 = errorN*T_{Correct}(m)$ seconds, where $T_{Correct}(m)$ is the inverse of the correction speed $V_{Correct}(m)$ (as derived in Equation 2). The total time to input $wordN$ words including correction time is thus $T = T_1 + T_2$, leading to a simple formula for the throughput as function of correction method and dictation accuracy.

Figure 5 shows the system throughput for different text production methods. We extrapolate results from our user study, which were achieved with a dictation accuracy of 75%, to current commercial dictation recognizers that achieve 90% accuracy in real-time. Commercial recognizers achieve higher accuracies by adapting the speech recognizer to the user's voice. We decided not to adapt our recognizer to each participant to keep the length of experimental sessions within acceptable limits.

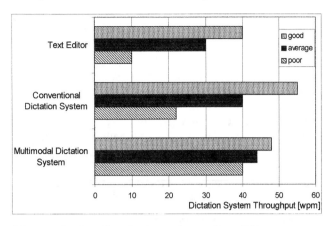

Figure 5: Predicted throughput for different text production methods, across typing skills, for 90% dictation accuracy.

Since typing speed obviously has a large impact on this comparison, the results are tabulated across different typing skills. For the multimodal dictation system, "poor" refers to novice users and "good" refers to experienced users. Since the experiment did not cover very slow typists, results for the slow category are based upon predictions from the performance model. As can be seen, a multimodal dictation system compares favorably to fast (non-secretarial) typing of 40 wpm - without requiring any keyboard input. For users with good typing skills, a conventional dictation system is still the most efficient text production method.

Performance Model Validation

We validated our performance model by comparing model predictions with results of our empirical evaluation. As measure of the goodness of fit for our model, we use the average absolute error of model predictions, as suggested elsewhere [7].

Correction Method	$V_{Correct}$ measured	$V_{Correct}$ predicted	Signed Error
Multimodal	4.5	3.7	-18%
Keyboard & List ("slow" typists)	5.9	6.2	5%
Keyboard & List (average typists)	6.2	7.0	13%
Keyboard & List ("fast" typists)	7.3	7.2	-1%

Table 4: Validation correction speed predictions

Table 4 compares the correction speed predictions with the measured values, averaged across the appropriate subsets of the test set. The average absolute error is 17% for multimodal correction (N=12) and 12% for correction using keyboard and list (N=6, two test participants in each

of the three categories of typing skill). These absolute errors are within reasonable range for such empirical models – despite the simplifying assumptions of the model as presented here. Predictions of dictation system throughput (input speed including error correction) match empirical data equally well (cf. [17]).

4. DISCUSSION

We first raise several concerns about the external validity of our study and show how model predictions alleviate them. We then discuss implications of this research on dictation and other (multimodal) speech recognition applications.

Validity of Results

As key result of the user study we found that accuracy decreases in repeated correction attempts unless modality is switched. This observation appears to generalize across modalities, and across state-of-the-art recognition systems [17]. The magnitude of this effect, and thus whether multimodal correction is faster than unimodal correction, depends on the recognition system used. For current recognition systems, our study showed that there is a gain in using multimodal correction. But if accuracy was significantly improved (by using different recognition algorithms on correction input, cf. [16]), unimodal correction by respeaking could outperform multimodal correction. Model predictions help to decide whether multimodal correction is beneficial.

A second external validity concern is the influence of implementation details. We argue that they do not change our main results. Furthermore, effects of implementation modifications can be estimated using our performance model. For example, halving the overhead time (i.e., the time spent on locating errors in recognition output and on starting a correction) for each modality would increase the speed of multimodal correction to the level of fast unskilled typing – without any further improvement in recognition accuracy! Overhead time could be significantly reduced, for instance, by automatically highlighting recognition errors.

Finally, our study did not control for how users switch between dictation and error correction in the overall process of text production. While this may have a significant impact on the absolute text production speeds, it does not affect the comparison of different correction methods – the focus of our study.

Implications for Dictation Systems

Related work suggested that automatic speech recognition technology could significantly increase productivity on dictation tasks [4, 5]. However, formal evaluations of dictation systems reported either only small productivity increases [1], or lack of user acceptance despite significant productivity increases [8].

Our results suggest that not only high recognition accuracy, but also adequate error correction is crucial to ensure high text production speeds in dictation systems. Furthermore, the productivity gain of dictation systems may be smaller than widely assumed. First, most potential users of dictation systems have good typing skills, and our results showed that for skilled typists, the productivity gain of dictation systems is rather modest. Second, studies suggest that for creation of documents, not input speed, but the skill required to compose text is the main limiting factor [4].

Implications for other Speech Recognition Applications

Our study explored the trade-off between speed and accuracy of different modalities only for text input. The most efficient input modality depends not only on input speed and accuracy, but also on the task. For example, for entry of numerical data, handwriting digits is about as fast as speech. We believe that the flexibility to change modality depending on the task is a great advantage of future multimodal input technologies.

Furthermore, applications other than dictation may limit which alternative modalities are available. However, error correction even benefits from just one alternative modality. If speech is the only modality available (e.g., in telephone applications), the speech user interface designer should consider switching between different speech modalities, such as continuous, discrete, and spelled speech.

CONCLUSIONS

This paper provides useful insights for designers of speech (and multimodal) user interfaces. Our study showed that multimodal correction is faster than conventional correction without keyboard input. Furthermore, we showed that recognition accuracy has a significant influence on user choice between modalities: with practice, users learn to avoid ineffective modalities in favor of more effective modalities. Our research suggests that multimodal input methods are particularly attractive for applications that do not allow fast keyboard input (e.g., small mobile devices), and for users with poor typing skills.

The performance model of multimodal human-computer interaction presented in this paper is a first step towards formalizing multimodal interaction. We showed how predictions from such a model help answer important design decisions in speech user interfaces, effectively complementing results from empirical evaluations. Future work may generalize the model to provide a general framework for multimodal interaction.

ACKNOWLEDGMENTS

This research was sponsored by the DARPA under the Department of Navy, Office of Naval Research under grant number N00014-93-1-0806. The views and conclusions in this document are those of the authors and should not be interpreted as necessarily representing the official policies or endorsements, either expressed or implied, of the U.S. Government.

Thanks to my colleagues of the Interactive Systems Laboratories at Universität Karlsruhe and Carnegie Mellon University who developed the continuous speech, spelling and cursive handwriting recognizers used in our prototype. Sincere thanks also to David Novick, Chloe Meadows, and to all participants of the user studies.

REFERENCES:

1. Alto, P., et al. "Experimenting Natual-Language Dictation with a 20000-Word Speech Recognizer," in VLSI and Computer Peripherals. 1989. IEEE Computer Society Press. 2: pp. 78-81.

2. Baber, C., Stammers, R.B., and Usher, D.M., "Error correction requirements in automatic speech recognition," in Contemporary Ergonomics, E.J. Levesey, Editor 1990, Taylor and Francis. London.

3. Gibbon, D., Moore, R., and Winski, R., eds. Handbook of Standards and Resources for Spoken Language Systems. 1997, Mouton de Gruyter: Berlin, New York.

4. Gould, J.D., "How Experts Dictate." Journal of Experimental Psychology: Human Perception and Performance, 1978. 4(4): pp. 648-661.

5. Gould, J.D., Conti, J., and Hovanyecz, T., "Composing Letters with a Simulated Listening Typewriter." Communications of the ACM, 1983. 26(4): pp. 295-308.

6. Hild, H., Buchstabiererkennung mit neuronalen Netzen in Auskunftssystemen. Fakultät für Informatik Fredericiana, 1997, Karlsruhe. 216 pages.

7. Kieras, D.E., Wood, S., D., and Meyer, D.E., "Predictive Engineering Models Based on the EPIC Architecture for a Multimodal High-Performance Human-Computer Interaction Task." ACM Transactions on Computer-Human Interaction, 1997. 4(3): pp. 230-275.

8. Lai, J. and Vergo, J. "MedSpeak: Report Creation with Continuous Speech Recognition," in International Conference on Computer-Human Interaction CHI. 1997. Atlanta (USA). 1: pp. 431-438.

9. Manke, S., Finke, M., and Waibel, A. "NPen++: A Writer Independent, Large Vocabulary On-Line Cursive Handwriting Recognition System," in International Conference on Document Analysis and Recognition. 1995. Montreal.

10. McNair, A.E. and Waibel, A. "Improving Recognizer Acceptance through Robust, Natural Speech Repair," in International Conference on Spoken Language Processing. 1994. Yokohama (Japan). 3: pp. 1299-1302.

11. Mellor, B. and Baber, C. "Modelling of Speech-based User Interfaces," in European Conference on Speech Communication and Technology. 1997. Rhodes (Greece): ESCA. 4: pp. 2263-2266.

12. Oviatt, S. and VanGent, R. "Error Resolution During Multimodal Human-Computer Interaction," in International Conference on Spoken Language Processing. 1996. Philadelphia (PA). 2: pp. 204-207.

13. Rhyne, J.R. and Wolf, C.G., "Recognition-Based User Interfaces," in Advances in Human-Computer Interaction, H.R. Hartson and D. Hix, Editors. 1993, Ablex Publishing. Norwood (NJ). pp. 191-212.

14. Rogina, I. and Waibel, A. "The JANUS Speech Recognizer," in ARPA Workshop on Spoken Language Technology. 1995. Austin (TX). Morgan Kaufmann. pp. 166-169.

15. Rubine, D., "Specifying Gestures by Example." ACM Journal on Computer Graphics, 1991. 25(4): pp. 329-337.

16. Soltau, H., 1998. Personal Communication.

17. Suhm, B., Multimodal Interactive Error Recovery for Non-Conversational Speech User Interfaces. PhD, Computer Science Department, Fredericiana University, 1998, Karlsruhe.

Cooperative Inquiry:
Developing New Technologies for Children with Children

Allison Druin

Human-Computer Interaction Lab

University of Maryland

College Park, MD 20742

+1 301 405 7406

allisond@umiacs.umd.edu

ABSTRACT

In today's homes and schools, children are emerging as frequent and experienced users of technology [3, 14]. As this trend continues, it becomes increasingly important to ask if we are fulfilling the technology needs of our children. To answer this question, I have developed a research approach that enables young children to have a voice throughout the technology development process. In this paper, the techniques of *cooperative inquiry* will be described along with a theoretical framework that situates this work in the HCI literature. Two examples of technology resulting from this approach will be presented, along with a brief discussion on the *design-centered learning* of team researchers using cooperative inquiry.

Keywords

Children, design techniques, educational applications, cooperative design, participatory design, cooperative inquiry, intergenerational design team, KidPad, PETS.

CHILDREN AS OUR RESEARCH PARTNERS

Today's technologies are becoming a critical part of our children's daily lives [3, 9, 14]. From school learning experiences to after-school play, technology is changing the way children live and learn. In fact, children have been found to be an important new consumer group that must be satisfied as technology users [17].

In recent years, numerous methodologies have been developed that bring technology users into the development process. Users have been described as active partners [6, 16, 29], inspectors or testers [24, 25], or research participants to be observed and/or interviewed [5, 13, 18]. Thanks to user input, technology can be shaped and changed in ways that may be meaningful and useful for future technology users. While user involvement is well understood as important to the technology research and development process, users that are children are less

commonly involved than adults [9, 10]. When children's input is sought out, it is typically done so over short periods of time (e.g., a day, a few weeks, perhaps a few months). Children are most frequently asked to be technology testers in workshops or school settings [e.g., 20, 26]. However, researchers have begun to see the limitations of what children can contribute in these situations [10, 27].

During the past four years, my research has involved children as active research partners. Some people question whether children are capable of contributing throughout the research and development process [27, 28]. I believe that children can and should be partners throughout a team research experience. Just as computer scientists or educators may be limited in their range of experience, so too are children. But each has their own expertise to contribute depending on what the team needs are during the research and development process. The intergenerational teams I have led have included members with diverse ages, disciplines, and experience [10, 11]. Children have been an essential part of these teams, along with educators, computer scientists, and artists.

Initially, the activities of our teams were structured to reflect methodologies that call for bringing *adult* users into the design process (e.g., cooperative design, participatory design, contextual inquiry). While these methodologies offered an excellent starting point for us, we quickly found that they needed to be adapted and changed to suit our teams that included children. Over the years, our interview procedures, note-taking practices, data analysis, and day-to-day team interactions evolved to become more inclusive of our child partners. This has lead to the development of *cooperative inquiry*, an approach to creating new technologies for children, with children.

This paper will present a theoretical framework that situates cooperative inquiry in the HCI literature. In addition, the research techniques of cooperative inquiry will be discussed, and two examples will be given to demonstrate this approach. This paper will conclude by describing another critical outcome of the cooperative inquiry process: *design-centered learning*. Self-reported learning in areas such as team collaboration and communication skills will be discussed.

A THEORETICAL FRAMEWORK

While cooperative inquiry is unique in many aspects due to child involvement, it is also grounded in HCI research and theories of cooperative design [16], participatory design [29], contextual inquiry [5], activity theory [23], and situated action [32]. Cooperative inquiry is an approach to research that includes three crucial aspects which reflect the HCI literature above: (1) a multidisciplinary partnership with children; (2) field research that emphasizes understanding context, activities, and artifacts; (3) iterative low-tech and high-tech prototyping. These three aspects form a framework for research and design with children. In the sections that follow, this framework will be discussed as it relates to other HCI research and theories.

Multidisciplinary Research Partnership with Users

Cooperative inquiry is based upon the belief that partnering with users is an important way to understand what is needed in developing new technologies. This belief can be seen in work done over the last 20 or more years in the cooperative design of Scandinavia [6, 16], the participatory design of the United States [15, 21, 29], and the consensus participation of England [22]. As Greenbum and Kyng have explained [16], "We see the need for users to become full partners in the cooperative system development process….Full participation of (users) requires training and active cooperation, not just token representation" [pp. ix-1].

This partnership between users and researchers from different disciplines was exemplified in the Scandinavia cooperative design work beginning in the 1970s. It was during this time that employee influence through trade unions grew, and collaborations between workers, management, and researchers influenced how new technologies could be created for and used in the workplace. Cooperative design methods supported the development of new technologies for carpenters, typographers, bankers, manufacturers, and more [6, 16, 29].

This approach to design attempted to capture the complexity and somewhat "messy" real-life world of the workplace. It was found that many times there were not sequential tasks accomplished by one person, but many tasks done in parallel and in collaboration with others. Interestingly enough, this description could also easily refer to the complexity and "messiness" of a child's world. In any case, this workplace design approach was not confined to the Scandinavian countries for long. Today researchers from around the world are applying these ideas and practices in their own work [1, 2].

Field Research: context, activities, and artifacts

Cooperative inquiry is also grounded in the traditions of field research. A great deal of information can quickly be understood about the needs of users from the activities and artifacts that are a part of a user's context. Contextual

design [5, 18], activity theory [23] and situated action [7, 32] all discuss the importance of these crucial elements in researching and developing new technology. It is the methodology of contextual inquiry (now a part of the contextual design process) that our intergenerational design teams found most useful with children.

With contextual inquiry, a team of researchers observe and analyze the users' environment for patterns of activity, communication, artifacts, and cultural relationships. Diagrams and models are developed from field experiences that eventually may lead to the design of storyboards, prototypes and new technology [5]. It is from this type of research inquiry that the method "cooperative inquiry" gets its name. I have found that this process of capturing field data, is extremely important in working with children as research partners. Young children, particularly from ages 3-7 have a difficult time abstractly describing what their technology needs and wants may be. When discussions take place in the context of a child's home, school, or public play space, it is much easier for the child to express his/her ideas [10]. Later in this paper this modified form of contextual inquiry with children will be described.

Iterative Low-tech and High-tech Prototyping

The third aspect of cooperative inquiry calls for intergenerational design teams to visualize their ideas through prototyping techniques. Again, since children may have a difficult time communicating to adults exactly what they are imagining, prototyping offers a concrete way to discuss ideas. The "low-tech prototyping" or "mock-ups" found in the cooperative design and participatory design literature [12, 21] have been an inspiration for my work with children.

By using paper, crayons, clay, string and more, low-tech prototyping gives equal footing to child and adult [10, 21]. There is never a need to teach people how to prototype, since using basic art supplies comes naturally to the youngest and oldest design partners. This form of prototyping is inexpensive, yet quite effective in quickly brainstorming new ideas or directions [10]. It is from these low-tech prototypes that high-tech prototypes emerge. As team ideas evolve, continued iterations of prototypes are developed. In the section that follows further description of prototyping with children is described.

COOPERATIVE INQUIRY: THE RESEARCH METHODS

Based upon the previous theoretical framework, the cooperative inquiry approach to partnering with children has become a reality. The goal in developing cooperative inquiry was to find techniques that can support intergenerational design teams in understanding what children as technology users do now; what they might do tomorrow; and what they envision for their future. It is not easy for an adult to step into a child's world, and likewise it is not easy for a child to step into an adult's world. I have found no single technique that can give teams all the answers they are looking for, so a combination of techniques has been adapted or developed that form the methodology of cooperative inquiry. These techniques do not necessarily offer a magic formula for working with children, but rather a philosophy and approach to research that can be used to gather data, developing prototypes, and forging new research directions.

At the University of Maryland, we use cooperative inquiry with an on-going intergenerational design team. I chose to establish this on-going partnership rather than work with many different children over short periods of time. In this way, children are not subjects for testing, but research partners who I have come to know and respect. Children and adults alike gather field data, initiate ideas, test, and develop new prototypes. Team members do what they are capable of, and learn from each other throughout the process.

The current team includes two faculty members, two graduate students, two staff members and six children (ages 7-11 years old). The disciplines of computer science, education, robotics, and art are represented. Members of the team meet two afternoons a week in our lab or out in the field. Over the summer we met for two intensive weeks, eight hours a day. At the time of this writing, the team has been together for almost a year and is expected to be together for almost two years.

In the sections that follow, the three techniques that comprise cooperative inquiry will be explained.

Contextual Inquiry

The first technique adapted for use with children is *contextual inquiry*. This is based upon the work of Beyer and Holtzblatt [5]. What their work tells us is that researchers should collect data in the users own environment. However, in our case at the University of Maryland, the researchers are not just adults who gather data from a child's world. Both adults and children observe, take notes, and interact with child users. Children are expected to be researchers along with their adult partners. This differentiates this form of contextual inquiry from that of others who work with users as informants but not necessarily as researchers [5].

At first, we attempted to have all team members take notes in the same way. This was too difficult for both children and adults. The adults in our team saw the need to gather data by writing detailed text descriptions. But the child researchers could just not accomplish this in a way that yielded meaningful results. On the other hand, the children wanted to combine drawings with small amounts of text to create cartoon-like flow charts (see Figure 1). The adult team members using this method felt too self-conscious about their drawings and were concerned that they would miss the details needed. Therefore, the team compromised and adults developed their own note-taking forms and the children developed theirs.

For adults, note-taking occurred most effectively in pairs. One note-taker recorded the activities of the child(ren) being observed and the other note-taker recorded quotes of what was said. Both note-takers recorded the time so that the quotes and activities could be synchronized in later data analysis.

Our team does not find video cameras to be successful in capturing data for contextual inquiry purposes. In my previous work at the University of New Mexico we also did not find video useful [10]. We found that when children saw a video camera in the room, they tended to "perform" or to "freeze". In addition, even with small unobtrusive cameras, we found it difficult to capture data in small bedrooms and large public spaces. The sound captured in public spaces was difficult to understand. In addition, we found that the video images were incomplete in private spaces. It was difficult to know where to place cameras when it was unknown where children would sit, stand, or move in their own environment.

During the note-taking experience, there were at least two note-takers and always one researcher who was an *interactor*. The interactor did not take notes but instead, was the person who initiated discussion and asked questions concerning the activity. We found that if there were no interactor, the children being observed would feel uncomfortable—as if they were "on stage." We also found that if the interactor took notes, the children being observed clearly felt uncomfortable and distracted. Instead, we found that the interactor should become a participant observer, talking naturally to children, free from note-pads, and becoming a part of the active experience. This is very different from contextual inquiry experiences with adults where note-taking is less of an issue.

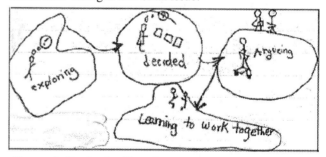

Figure 1: Contextual inquiry notes by a 7-year old child

Interestingly enough, we found that child researchers had a difficult time being interactors. Children would tend to get involved in what was going on and forget that they were there to do research and should let the other child lead the action. On the other hand, adult researchers also had a difficult time being interactors. Traditional "power structures" or relationships between adults and children could easily emerge, where adults could tend to steer the child(ren) being observed as a parent or teacher might. One way we found that helps change these traditional power structures is to have adults wear informal clothing so that they look less like an authority figure, and more like a peer.

The interactor should not to be confused with an interviewer. The interactor is not there to ask hours of questions that might force the child(ren) being observed to stop what is naturally being done. Instead, the interactor is there to ask questions that are directed to what is going on at the moment (e.g., How come you're doing that? Why do you like that? What's this?). In this way, the interactor is annotating the activities with information for the note-takers to capture.

After the field research experience, the team typically meets back at the lab to analyze the captured data. Our technique of visualizing the data gathered, again diverges from the techniques of Beyer and Holtzblatt [5]. We have found that children's activities are often more exploratory than task-directed, especially when children are not told what to do by an adult parent or teacher [10]. We are most interested in capturing these exploratory experiences, for they tell us what children want to do as opposed to what adults expect of them. In our experience, the diagrams or models suggested by Beyer and Holtzblatt became extremely complex and difficult to understand when trying to capture the exploratory experiences of children. Therefore, we found it more effective to diagram these experiences based on *Patterns of Activity* and *Roles the Child Played* [10]. In Table 1, a portion of the information gathered by an adult researcher is shown. This information is broken up into six columns: *Time, Quotes, Activities, Activity Pattern, Roles,* and *Design Ideas*.

The *Time* column is used to synchronize quotes with activities. The *Quotes* column contains phrases and sentences said by the child(ren) during a session. The *Activities* column contains the observed actions of the child(ren) during a session. While the first three columns contain raw data from observations, the *Activity Pattern* column is developed by the researchers during data analysis and is based on repetitive patterns that emerge in the *Quotes* and *Activities* columns. The *Roles* column is also

developed by the researchers, from the data in the *Quotes* and *Activities* columns. The *Roles* column describes "the who" children are when they are interacting with technology (e.g., searcher, storyteller, researcher, learner, etc.). Finally, the last column contains the *Design Ideas*. It is a culmination of all the information gathered or generated. This column is also the start of the brainstorming process. It offers new ideas for the development of technology that can be related directly to the observed data. When someone asks, "Where did that idea come from?" it is easy to refer back to the related data.

Once these adult notes have been compiled for a session, the adult diagrams are compared with the child notes. The adult diagrams are highlighted in the places that the child researchers have recorded in their notes. In this way, child and adult perspectives are captured. It is interesting to note, that many times child researchers offered summaries of the data that enabled adult partners to see something they had originally missed.

Participatory Design
The second technique that comprises cooperative inquiry was adapted from *participatory design*. This is not to say that participatory design techniques must follow contextual inquiry. However, we did find that contextual inquiry enabled us to first explore numerous ideas through observation. Then, during our data visualization, we could focus on an area of interest to pursue in more depth with participatory design prototyping. For example, our contextual inquiry observations led to an understanding that children wanted to be storytellers with technology. This insight was taken into a participatory design session where low-tech materials were used to prototype storytelling technologies for the future. Later in this paper examples of the storytelling technologies that were ultimately developed will be discussed.

In general, I have found that children ages 7-10 years old make the most effective prototyping partners [10]. These children are verbal and self-reflective enough to discuss what they are thinking. They can understand the abstract

RAW DATA:			DATA ANALYSIS:		
Time	Quotes	Activities	Activity Patterns	Roles	Design Ideas
39:20	"I want the playing one."	Child clicks on the scared cat and tries to take out another one. It doesn't work.	Difficulty with mouse dragging.		Look for alternative input devices or don't use dragging with a mouse.
39:50	"Awww. The kitten was afraid."	Child clicks on another basket with a cat.	Tells stories about actions on screen.	Storyteller	Offer children storytelling opportunities with technology.
40:20	"Which one's the playful one?"	Child looks for a playful cat.	Child knows what she likes.	Searcher	
41:00	"I don't want to name my kitty."	Child doesn't name her cat when prompted to by the computer.	Child knows what she likes.		
41:30	"That's to give milk."	Child clicks on different icons to see what they do.	Tests out what can be done.	Explorer	Make technology easy to explore.

Table 1: Portion of a contextual inquiry diagram created by adults

idea of designing something with low-tech protoyping tools that will be turned into future technologies. Children at this age, however, don't seem to be too heavily burdened with pre-conceived notions of the way things "are supposed to be", something we typically see in children older than 10 years [10].

It is interesting to note that low-tech prototyping is deceivingly simple. It seems that all that is needed are some art supplies, a few children and some adults. But what makes it a difficult process for many adults is relating to children as design partners. Many adults are not quite sure how much they should allow a child to lead and how much they should lead. For example, some adults prefer to sit back and let the children do all the work—they assume that since the art supplies are child-like then the design process is only for children. This is not true. Children and adults must work together. No partner should make all the design decisions, child or adult. In addition, the selection of low-tech protoyping tools is critical. Some researchers feel that it matters very little what materials are given, and that the ideas will emerge whatever the resources. Others feel that a standardized box of materials can be developed for all occasions [Personal Communication, April 1998]. I disagree with both approaches. We have found that the materials need to be purchased with some care to reflect the area of research the team is exploring [10]. For example, the materials I had purchased for a particular session ended up being limited and frustrating to the design team. However the week before, when prototyping a different idea, these same materials (e.g., clay, string, paper, crayons) were just fine.

Whatever the case, the low-tech prototyping materials matter and the team dynamics are critical. This process takes time to understand and facilitate well. Low-tech prototyping is a much more effective design tool when done in concert with contextual inquiry. Based on design ideas that have emerged from contextual inquiry notes, protoyping can focus discussion and be a bridge for collaborative brainstorming activities.

Technology Immersion

Finally, the third technique of cooperative inquiry is what I have come to call *technology immersion* [8]. This process grew out of a need to see how children use large amounts of technology over a concentrated period of time. If children are only observed with the technology resources they currently have, then what children might do in the future with better circumstances could be missed [10]. Many children still have minimal access to technology in their homes or school. If time is not a limiting factor then access to the newest technologies can be. However, in the future we see these limitations changing. Therefore, by establishing today a technology-rich, time-intensive environment for children, the observation techniques of contextual inquiry can be used to capture many activity patterns that might otherwise be over-looked.

With technology immersion, it is critical that children not only have access to technology in a concentrated way, but are also decision-makers about what they do in that environment. Children must be asked to make their own choices when using different kinds of technology. There must be enough technology options so that no child ever has to share a computer if he or she does not choose. There must also be enough time so that children can accomplish a task that is meaningful. Without these ingredients, it is difficult to understand children's technology wants or needs. If adults are fully in control, then the activity patterns seen are those of adults, not children.

I have initiated such technology immersion experiences in my own labs. In addition, I also had the opportunity to establish a technology immersion experience at ACM's CHI 96 conference. This particular experience has come to be called CHIkids and is now an on-going part of the annual CHI conferences [8]. At CHIkids, children explore technology over five days, 10 hours a day, by being multimedia storytellers, software testers, newsroom reporters, and more. This technology immersion experience has come to be more than just another way to understand what children want in technology. It has come to be a way to bring children into the CHI conference as active participants and partners. In a sense, CHIkids can be said to be a very large intergenerational design team (at CHI 98 we had over 65 child and 25 adult participants).

But not every technology immersion experience needs to be on the scale of CHIkids. Our design team recently shared an experience between six children and six adults over 10 days, 8 hours a day. In those 10 days we came to understand more about children's activity patterns and roles than in the last six months of our research combined. This is not to say that a technology immersion experience isn't exhausting. It is. It may be the most difficult of the cooperative inquiry techniques, since it is so intense. In addition, during such an experience, tempers can flare, energy wears thin; the space never seems to be big enough; but all in all, it is an exciting experience to see what children can do with technology [8]. Technology immersion in combination with contextual inquiry and low-tech prototyping can be extremely effective in highlighting patterns and roles that are not obvious in short contextual inquiry sessions. We have found technology immersion experiences most useful after initial contextual inquiry and participatory design sessions have been done.

COOPERATIVE INQUIRY IN PRACTICE

Two projects over the past three years demonstrate our use of the cooperative inquiry process. When we began these projects, our methodology was still being developed, and what we did wasn't even given a name. Over time, the common research practices became more obvious, and cooperative inquiry took form. In a sense, cooperative inquiry was as much a part of what our design teams developed, as the technology that was created.

KidPad

KidPad was our first example of using cooperative inquiry [10, 11]. This technology, based upon Pad++ [4], was first developed at the University of New Mexico and continues to be developed at the University of Maryland. KidPad is a zooming storytelling tool that enables children to collaboratively create stories (see Figure 2).

The act of zooming from one story object to the next, makes visually explicit where children are going and where they have been. In traditional applications that don't use zooming to navigate, different objects that are semantically related are linked visually by jumping from one object to the next (e.g., links on the web). Children have explained this as "...closing your eyes and when you open them you're in a new place. Zooming lets you keep your eyes open" [10].

Figure 2: "The Eye", a story made in KidPad

In one example shown above (see Figure 2), a group of three Native American children (age 8) from New Mexico created a zooming story. It was about an eye "that could see what you looked like on the outside and on the inside, and even more on the inside. It could see your questions." In their story, the eye had special powers and could zoom in to see that the boy felt like a girl inside. The eye could zoom in even more and see the boy was asking why this was so. The story ended with the eye explaining to the boy, "You are both inside and outside. There is no reason to ask why" [Research notes, October 1996].

To develop KidPad, a team of educators and computer scientists worked with over 40 children (ages 8-10) in the New Mexico public schools. While we had not yet established an on-going intergenerational design team, the techniques of cooperative inquiry were used in formative studies. A version of contextual inquiry was used where only adults were observers, but the diagramming techniques previously described were used. Low-tech prototyping also contributed to our ideas, but was done only on special occasions for conference tutorials and industry workshops. At both CHI 96 and CHI 97, KidPad was tested during the technology immersion experience of CHIkids. All of these early cooperative inquiry techniques led to the development of KidPad. Children told us in many ways that they wanted to be collaborative storytellers using technology.

Our work continues today on a collaborative version of KidPad where two mice can be used simultaneously to create zooming stories [31]. For more details on the KidPad environment see [11].

PETS

Another research project we have developed using cooperative inquiry techniques is PETS: a Personal Electronic Teller of Stories (see Figure 3). While this is also a storytelling technology, it is quite different from KidPad. The PETS environment makes use of physical robotic animal parts to enable children to build fanciful animals that can act out the stories they write. This project is being developed at the University of Maryland with our intergenerational team of researchers. We began our work on this project by conducting field research in the university's robotics labs, using the contextual inquiry techniques previously described. Participatory design sessions with low-tech prototyping followed. From this, high-tech prototypes were begun. Over the summer, we had a technology immersion experience where we solidified our ideas and developed new directions for the future. For more details on the PETS research, see the CHI 99 video paper, in these conference proceedings.

Figure 3: PETS robotic storytelling animal

DESIGN-CENTERED LEARNING

Typically when people consider the outcome of a design process, it is the technology that is discussed. To me, this is important, but is not the only result of my work. I find what the team members can learn as a result of the research and development experience to be critical. There are many references to this learning as an outcome of the cooperative or participatory design process [12, 15, 22]. In addition, there are also educational researchers that refer to this kind of learning as a *community of practice* [19]. They describe this to be a community of people with different skills that learn as they work toward shared goals. This leaning experience has also been described by Shneiderman as *Relate—Create—Donate*, where students can have a meaningful learning experience with technology by using it to perform a service to the community [30].

I give the name *design-centered learning* to learning outcomes that can be related to the cooperative inquiry process. Design-centered learning occurs in both children and adults, novices and technology experts, technical and non-technical professionals. When diverse people partner together in the research and design process, design-centered learning can emerge. By surveying an intergenerational team over time, I have seen five areas of self-reported design-centered learning [Research notes, August 1998]:

---

(1) I learned about the design process
All team members discussed understanding the technology design process in new ways.

(2) I learned respect for my design partners
Both adults and children discussed their mutual appreciation for the work that the other could accomplish.

(3) I learned to communicate and collaborate in a team
Children and adults discussed the difficulties and the rewards of learning team communication and collaboration skills.

(4) I learned new technology skills and knowledge
All team members mentioned technical skills they had come to learn (e.g., building robots, designing software).

(5) I learned new content knowledge
In the case of the team working on the PETS project, children and adults discussed learning more about animals.

Table 2: Self-reported design-centered learning

These design-centered learning outcomes were summarized after children and adult team members were asked to write on Post-It Notes what they thought they might have learned from their team research experience. Each participant voluntarily wrote ideas. When all were done, the notes were stuck on a whiteboard to analyze by the team. This summary was completed after working together for six months (Phase I of our research). A second study on Phase II will be performed using a variety of data collection methods after a year of team work. It is expected that this study will describe intergenerational team changes in communication, collaboration, and design-centered learning.

SUMMARY

In summary, cooperative inquiry has been developed to support intergenerational design teams in developing new technologies for children, with children. While this approach requires time, resources, and the desire to work with children, I have found it a thought-provoking and rewarding experience. Cooperative inquiry can lead to exciting results in the development of new technologies and design-centered learning. The cooperative inquiry methodology continues to evolve as we use the techniques over time. In addition, a new intergenerational team will be established shortly at the University of Maryland that will be compared to the existing team.

ACKNOWLEDGMENTS

Over the years, this work could not have taken shape without the support, talents, and inspiration of numerous partners. Child partners in New Mexico include students at the Lowell and Hawthorne elementary schools. Child partners at the University of Maryland include Alex, Hanne, Isabella, Lauren, Rebecca and Thomas. Adult collaborators at the University of Maryland and New Mexico include Ben Bederson, Jim Hendler, Jaime Montemayor, Jason Stewart, Angela Boltman, Britt McAlister, Eric Fiterman, Aurelie Plaisant, Debbie Knotts, and Adrian Miura. And on-going inspiration and intellectual discussion had come by way of Ben Shneiderman, Catherine Plaisant, Anne Rose, Joseph JaJa, and Stan Bennett. Financial support has come from the Sony Corporation, the Intel Research Council, and DARPA's H-CI Initiative (#N66001-94-C-6039). To all of you, my deepest thanks.

REFERENCES

1. *Proceedings of PDC'90: Participatory Design Conference* (1990). Palo Alto, CA: Computer Professionals for Social Responsibility.

2. *Proceedings of PDC'96: Participatory Design Conference* (1996). Cambridge, MA: Computer Professionals for Social Responsibility.

3. *Report to the President on the use of technology to strengthen K-12 education in the United States* (1997). President's Committee of Advisors on Science and Technology, Executive Office of the President of the United States, Washington, DC.

4. Bederson, B., Hollan, J., Perlin, K., Meyer, J., Bacon, D., & Furnas, G. (1996). Pad++: A zoomable graphical sketchpad for exploring alternate interface physics. *Journal of Visual Languages and Computing, 7*, 3-31.

5. Beyer, H., & Holtzblatt, K. (1998). *Contextual design: defining customer-centered systems*. San Francisco, CA: Morgan Kaufmann.

6. Bjerknes, G., Ehn, P., & Kyng, M. (Eds.), (1987). *Computers and democracy: A Scandinavian challenge*. Aldershot, UK: Alebury.

7. Bødker, S. (1991). *Through the interface: A human activity approach to user interface design*. Hillsdale, NJ: Lawrence Erlbaum.

8. Boltman, A., Druin, A., & Miura, A. (1998). What children can tell us about technology: The CHIkids model of technology immersion. *CHI 98 Tutorial*, ACM Press.

9. Druin, A. (1996). A place called childhood. *Interactions, 3*(1), 17-22.

10. Druin, A., Bederson, B., Boltman, A., Miura, A., Knotts-Callahan, D., & Platt, M. (1999). Children as our technology design partners. A. Druin (Ed.), *The design of children's technology* (pp. 51-72). San Francisco, CA: Morgan Kaufmann.

11. Druin, A., Stewart, J., Proft, D., Bederson, B., & Hollan, J. (1997). KidPad: A design collaboration between children, technologists, and educators. *In Proceedings of Human Factors in Computing Systems (CHI 97)* ACM Press, pp. 463-470.

12. Ehn, P. (1993). Scandinavian design: On participation and skill. D. Schuler, & A. Namioka (Eds.), *Participatory design: Principles and practices* (pp. 41-77). Hillsdale, NJ: Lawrence Erlbaum.

13. Erickson, K., & Stull, D. (1998). *Doing team ethnography: Warnings and advise.* Thousand Oaks, CA: Sage.

14. Fulton, K. (1997). *Learning in the digital age: Insights into the issues.* Santa Monica, CA: Milken Exchange on Education Technology .

15. Greenbaum, J. (1993). A design of one's own: Toward participatory design in the United States. D. Schuler, & A. Namioka (Eds.), *Participatory design: Principles and practices* (pp. 27-37). Hillsdale, NJ: Lawrence Erlbaum.

16. Greenbaum, J., & Kyng, M. (Eds.), (1991). *Design at work: Cooperative design of computer systems.* Hillsdale, NJ: Lawrence Erlbaum.

17. Heller, S. (1998, August). The meaning of children in culture becomes a focal point for scholars. *The Chronicle of Higher Education*, pp. A14-A16.

18. Holtzblatt, K., & Jones, S. (1995). R. M. Baecker, J. Grudin, W. A. S. Buxton, & S. Greenberg (Eds.), *Readings in Human-Computer Interaction: Toward the year 2000 (2nd ed.).* San Francisco, CA: Morgan Kaufmann.

19. Lave, J. (1992). *Cognition in practice.* Cambridge: Cambridge University Press.

20. Loh, B., Radinsky, J., Rusell, E., Gomez, L. M., Reiser, B. J., & Edelson, D. C. (1998). The progress portfolio: Designing reflective tools for a classroom context. *In Proceedings of Human Factors in Computing Systems (CHI 98)* ACM Press, pp. 627-634.

21. Muller, M. J., Wildman, D. M., & White, E. A. (1994). Participatory design through games and other techniques. *CHI 94 Tutorial*, ACM Press.

22. Mumford, E., & Henshall, D. (1979/1983). *Designing participatively: A participative approach to computer systems design.* UK: Manchester Business School.

23. Nardi, B. (Ed.), (1996). *Context and consciousness: Activity theory and Human-Computer Interaction.* Cambridge, MA: MIT Press.

24. Nielsen, J. (1995). Scenarios in discount usability engineering. J. Carroll (Ed.), *Scenario-based design: Envisioning work and technology in system development* (pp. 151-167). New York: Wiley.

25. Nielsen, J., & Mack, R. L. (1994). *Usability inspection methods.* New York: Wiley.

26. Oosterholt, R., Kusano, M., & de Vries, G. (1996). Interaction design and human factors support in the development of a personal communicator for children. *In Proceedings of Human Factors in Computing Systems (CHI 96)* ACM Press, pp. 450-457.

27. Scaife, M., & Rogers, Y. (1999). Kids as informants: Telling us what we didn't know or confirming what we knew already. A. Druin (Ed.), *The design of children's technology* (pp. 27-50). San Francisco, CA: Morgan Kaufmann.

28. Scaife, M., Rogers, Y., Aldrich, F., & Davies, M. (1997). Designing for or designing with? Informant design for interactive learning environments. *In Proceedings of Human Factors in Computing Systems (CHI 97)* ACM Press, pp. 343-350.

29. Schuler, D., & Namioka, A. (Eds.), (1993). *Participatory design: Principles and practices.* Hillsdale, NJ: Lawrence Erlbaum.

30. Shneiderman, B. (1998). Relate--Create--Donate: A teaching/learning philosophy for cyber-generation. *Computers and Education*, pp. 1-15.

31. Stewart, J., Raybourn, E., Bederson, B. B., & Druin, A. (1998). When two hands are better than one: Enhancing collaboration using single display groupware. *In Proceedings of Extended Abstracts of Human Factors in Computing Systems (CHI 98)* ACM Press, pp. 287-288.

32. Suchman, L. (1987). *Plans and situated actions.* Cambridge: Cambridge University Press.

Projected Realities
Conceptual Design for Cultural Effect

William Gaver   **Anthony Dunne**
Royal College of Art, London
w.gaver / a.dunne @rca.ac.uk

ABSTRACT

As a part of a European Union sponsored project, we have proposed a system which aggregates people's expressions over a widening network of public electronic displays in a massive Dutch housing development. Reflecting ideas from contemporary arts as well as from research on media spaces, this is an example of a conceptual design intended to produce meaningful effects on a local culture. In this paper, we describe the methods and ideas that led to this proposal, as an example of research on technologies from the traditions of artist-designers.

Keywords: design research, conceptual art, collaborative systems, awareness

INTRODUCTION

As a part of the two-year, European Union funded Presence project, we are working to find innovative interaction techniques that can help increase the presence of the elderly within their local communities.

One of the communities we are working with is the Bijlmer: a large planned housing development just outside Amsterdam in the Netherlands [see 2]. Built in the early 70's, it is made up of dozens of buildings, each 10 stories tall and averaging 1.5 km long, set in green parkland with canals, ponds, fields and forests. The Bijlmer has an extremely poor reputation in the Netherlands—only partially deserved, we now believe—with widespread unemployment, drug abuse, and crime.

Projected Realities

After a year of work, we eventually arrived at a proposal for the Projected Realities system, a network of electronic displays with which the elders would facilitate people in expressing their opinions and images of the Bijlmer over increasingly larger areas.

The system would involve four main components. Commercial *scanners* would be reconfigured into furniture, for transport on trolleys, or to hang on walls. Elders could use the scanner devices to mediate the collection of digital images from local inhabitants. These images—perhaps of photographs, objects, or faces—would be stored in a central database, along with a numerical representation of their emotional content.

Mains radio devices would be small displays used at home by elders and other citizens to access images and slogans transmitted from the central database via the existing power lines. The attitudes expressed by their choices would be registered implicitly, or they might also register them more explicitly.

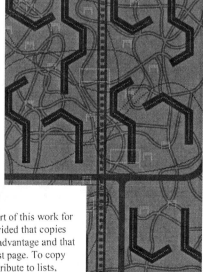

Bijlmer overview

Location of the Bijlmer

Slogan furniture, mainly in the outdoor areas of the Bijlmer, would use text displays to show a selection of provocative statements compiled by the elders. Pedestrians could choose their own slogan to display among 30 or so options, or watch as slogans change automatically, reflecting local attitudes aggregated from nearby mains radio devices.

The images scanned by the elders would be displayed on large electronic *image boards* set along the roads and rail lines that ring the Bijlmer. The selection would depend on the values displayed by groups of slogan furniture linked to a particular image board. Commuters and travellers would thus be afforded new views into the area, beyond the sights of the foreboding housing blocks themselves.

This network of electronic displays would project an increasingly coherent expression of the Bijlmer, encouraging inhabitants to reflect on their own values, those of the diverse cultural groups sharing the district, and those of the surrounding culture. A nervous system for the Bijlmer, it would help to provoke awareness of the existing community both to inhabitants and to the surrounding culture.

Design Research

The Projected Realities proposal may sound unusual to the CHI community. In this paper, we hope to explain how we developed the design, and the rationale behind it.

The proposal is an example of our approach to research on technologies from the traditions of artist-designers [see 7, 12]. Our intention—and our brief—in this project was not to tackle the Bijlmer's apparent problems directly, nor to produce a public art work that merely comments on the situation. Instead, our primary concern has been to find new ways that technology can enter and affect everyday culture. Thus the Projected Realities proposal resembles a media space in its emphasis on peripheral awareness and commu-

nication, but uses unusual devices, images and statements to encourage new forms of engagement for the local elders. This emphasis on offering new opportunities through design rather than solving problems underlies much of what we do and how we do it.

This paper is organised around three aspects of our work that we would particularly like to illustrate. First, in our version of user studies, we were interested in opening a dialog about possibilities with the elders, rather than diagnosing their problems, and so used techniques from the conceptual arts to provoke their reactions, instead of more scientific methods to study their needs.

Second, the ways we developed and communicated ideas also reflected an arts-design tradition. In this tradition, the designer's subjective stance is an important part of the design process. Our methods were intended to acknowlededg this and encourage both our own creativity and that of the elders. In generating ideas for the Bijlmer, we used brainstorming over time and visual problem-solving to develop design ideas synthesising our views of the area. In presenting them to the groups, we used impressionistic images and narratives to sketch out the cultural effects we intended to make. We hope to show that, while unconventional for most HCI practitioners, techniques like these are appropriate and effective methods for generating innovative designs—thus our decision to devote 1/3 of this paper to a stream of images parallelling the text.

Finally, the resulting designs themselves are positioned in an intellectual context of design and art, rather than science or engineering. This project, for example, takes insights from media space research [e.g., 4], but uses conceptual art strategies [e.g., 9] to situate them in an urban environment. In discussing our work, we would like to illustrate how the arts can serve as basic research for this kind of design.

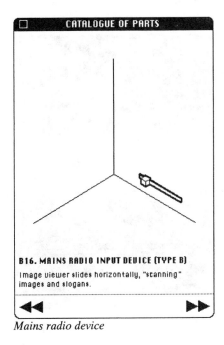

Mains radio device

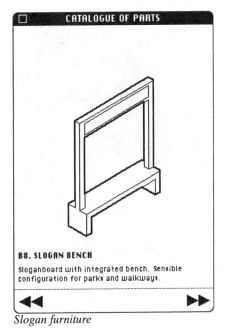

Slogan furniture

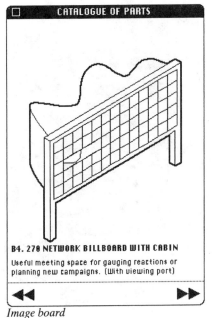

Image board

UNDERSTANDING THE USERS: CULTURAL PROBES

To start the project, we gave cultural probes to the 10 members of the elder group: packets of maps, postcards, photo albums and other items to which they could respond and post back to us.

We designed the probes in response to a number of converging concerns. The brief of the Presence Project, to increase the presence of elders in their local communities, allows us wide latitude in our choice of interpretation, technologies, and approaches. With the ability to pursue an experimental approach to our designs, we didn't need *information* about the elders, so much as *inspiration*—clues about their attitudes, their aesthetics, and their desires.

The strategy we took in designing the probes borrows from a tradition of cultural provocation in the arts stemming from Dada or the Surrealists [10], in which tactics of ambiguity, absurdity, or opacity are used to strip away habitual interpretations and open new possibilities. For instance, the probes are reminiscent of the Fluxus yearboxes [9], in which whimsical and humourous objects, often readymades, were presented in package form.

The Cultural Probes were particularly influenced by the Situationists [1,11]. A radical group centred in Paris from the late '50's to the 70's, they used a variety of strategies to counter the all-encompassing, media-fuelled "Spectacle" created by commercial culture. For instance, the maps included in the probes echo their psychogeographic maps, which showed the varying emotional neighbourhoods of urban areas in ways that official maps do not represent. More generally, we tried to emulate their tactics of pleasure and intrigue as a means of discovery, taking them to more traditional concerns of user centred design.

The Probe Materials

The probe materials addressed people's emotional, aesthetic, and experiential reactions to their environments, but in open-ended, provocative, and oblique ways. For instance, one of the half dozen maps we included—each in the form of an unfolded envelope to be mailed back to us—asked "if the Bijlmer were a body..." and included precut stickers showing images of limbs, ears, eyes, and internal organs to identify corresponding parts of the area. Postcards asked questions such as "tell us a piece of advice," or "why do we have politicians?" A disposable camera, repackaged to remove it from its commercial origins, included a list of requests for photographs such as "what you will wear today," "something beautiful," or "something ugly," while leaving 10-15 shots to be chosen freely. Finally, a small photo album was included, with the request to send us "6 - 10 pictures that tell us your story."

Giving and Receiving

The probes succeeded not only in eliciting materials that inspired our designs, but also in provoking the elders to respond to our experimental approach. When presented to the group, they sparked intense discussions with the elders about our intentions, their lives, and the community. In the weeks following our return we received large amounts of material in the post—about half the items in all, though some only included notes about why they weren't completed, which we had encouraged in case of difficulty. The hundreds of pictures, maps and postcards offered a surprising and intimate view of the area which was crucial for our designs.

Several features of the probes seemed to play a role in their success. First, we tried to avoid stereotypes of elders as needy or feeble, instead focusing both on their rich experiences, and their opportunities for life free from the need to work. Adopting this attitude meant, in part, that we felt

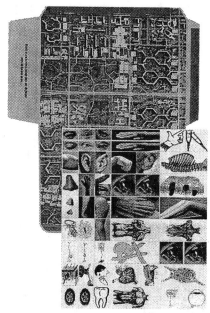

Map

Postcard

Camera

able to challenge or provoke them with the probes. Second, the probe materials were preaddressed and stamped to be returned to us separately. This emphasised their flexibility and our lives in another country, undermining the typical unapproachability of scientific experts. Finally, the probe materials were crafted to be pleasurable and intriguing, yet not professionally finished. They reflected the energy we had put into them, and revealed our tastes and interests to the group. At the same time, they used a slightly clinical aesthetics to encourage detachment and curiosity.

The materials were not designed for a summary analysis. Instead, most of what we learned from the Cultural Probes was articulated through our designs, rather than in explicit reports. We thought of the proposals as our turn in a conversation that had started with the probes and continued with the elders' responses. Presenting the proposals to the group implied our perceptions of themselves and their community, as well as suggesting possibilities for change.

METHODS: EXPLORATIONS AND SKETCHES

As returns from the Cultural Probes gathered, we started to generate ideas about designs for the Bijlmer. This was done in two phases. In the first phase, we generated a loose collection of proposals and presented them to the group and our colleagues for discussion. In the second phase, we used their reactions to focus and integrate the concepts into the current proposal. In this section, we discuss our method for developing and presenting the two rounds of proposals. In the next section, we describe the proposals themselves and their conceptual underpinnings.

Brainstorming in Slow Motion

In developing our proposal for the Bijlmer, we started by exploring a wide space of ideas, knowing that we would narrow them progressively later in the project. This initial exploration was analogous to the traditional brainstorming sessions familiar to designers, in which people toss out as many ideas as possible, with none being criticised and all recorded. Exploring seemingly impractical ideas is useful in this process, often allowing the discovery of new spaces for design.

In practice, learning from improbable ideas takes time, but traditional brainstorming sessions tend to be relatively brief. Although ideas are not supposed to be evaluated in brainstorms, groups often reject ideas that seem too conservative or too frivolous. With little time to explore ideas deeply, it is difficult to go beyond obvious or familiar possibilities. We found that intermittent, ongoing conversations about ideas worked better for our group than focused brainstorming sessions, allowing our ideas to be filtered naturally over time.

For example, security was an overriding issue as we started to generate ideas, in part due to returns from the probes stressing the "junkies and thieves" in the area. Sparked off by a chance photograph of the area, we started thinking about cages for the elders, in which they could sit or walk safely outside.

The idea of cages for elders is clearly an insulting idea, one we would never propose seriously. From a conceptual perspective, however, developing the notion was a useful (if crude) way to highlight the problems of designing purely to combat fear. The images and stories we explored reminded us throughout our later designs that if we overemphasised security, the systems we produced might themselves become electronic cages.

Having adopted an extreme view of the area as a dangerous no-man's land made contradictory evidence of the everyday social life in the area more noticeable. We started to attend to images that revealed this more homely side of the

"Thieves and junkies hanging around..."

Cages for the elderly

Everyday Bijlmer life

Bijlmer: people gardening or picnicking in the parkland surrounding the housing blocks, or enjoying parties within. Eventually, these two perspectives became integrated in our view of the Bijlmer as enjoying a rich cultural life in a harsh environment, and made us aware that its undesirable reputation is neither wholly deserved, nor an accurate reflection of the inhabitants' feelings.

Brainstorming over time allowed these ideas to grow or be discarded naturally, without undue need for explicit justification or criticism. Instead of analysing fundamental needs to guide design, we clarified our understanding of the Bijlmer through designs that synthesised our responses to the many sources of evidence we had.

Impressionistic Scenarios

In our designs, we focused on the kinds of social or cultural interventions that might be meaningful, rather than specific instantiations. Insofar as we discussed particular artifacts, they were *placeholders*, embodying the kinds of possibilities we wanted from our designs, but not necessarily the particular technologies or forms. Sketches of devices or system were a way of thinking through issues and possibilities for us, were always understood to be provisional.

Communicating ideas at this level was a challenge when we presented them to the elders for feedback: if the ideas were presented too abstractly, people could not imagine living with the systems; if they were presented too concretely, the elders would focus on the details rather than the overall intentions. In both phases, then, we sought to present our ideas in a way that would encourage people to consider the cultural effects the systems might make, rather than the specific devices implementing them.

For the first phase of design we approached this by compiling an impressionistic book of images and text to sketch our ideas. To convey the openness of the proposals, we mixed a wide range of graphical styles in the presentation, from diagrams overlaid on photographs, to collages, to relabeled mail-order catalogs. Text was used as a kind of background to the collection, separating categories and explaining the intentions of our ideas. Using this plethora of styles, we tried to create a kind of filmic feeling to the presentation, allowing people to explore the space of possibilities as if glimpsing fictional worlds in which they already existed.

For the second phase, we produced a series of interactive simulations to be used onscreen in order to capture the experience of using the systems and seeing them change over time. The core of the presentation was an overview of the system, and simple, more specific pieces showing each element. In addition to the specific proposals, we also included a "catalog of parts," which allowed people to scroll through and see different elements that might appear in the system. This worked well in allowing us to become more specific about the kinds of artifacts we had in mind, while still exploring a space of possibilities.

Both the storybook and interactive simulations encouraged the elders—and us—to imagine the world implied by our designs, rather than deciding whether or not the specific examples made sense. We wanted them to enter this world for a while, to tell us what their everyday lives might be like, and about the successes and failures they might anticipate. For them to envision it this way helped us develop the ideas in realistic directions, a more precise and useful process than merely accepting or rejecting ideas wholesale.

RESULTS: DESIGN FOR CULTURAL EFFECTS

The proposals developed through this process responded to our perceptions of the elders' lives in the Bijlmer, and the possibilities we saw for increasing communication and awareness in the area. They capture the results of the

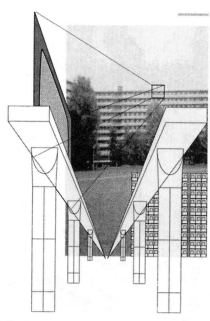

Early image board sketch

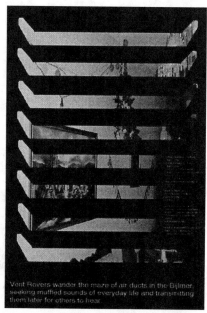

Vent rovers

Psychogeographic pager

Probes, and our brainstorming over time. In addition, they reflect the influence of the arts as well as more traditional issues from HCI and CSCW.

Three Clusters

Our initial design stage resulted in three clusters of ideas for possible interventions in the Bijlmer. One that appears relatively unchanged in the current proposal is for image boards to be placed along the highways and railtracks ringing the area, showing images scanned by the elderly or perhaps snapshots being developed in photographic shops. This proposal reflects our perception that the Bijlmer's notoriety is misleading: people are proud of living in this culturally varied community, and would like to challenge its poor reputation.

Another set of ideas explored new ways that people might inhabit the huge housing blocks. This started with the suggestion that security cameras in different parts of the buildings might be linked, with the output of one showing on a monitor near its partner. Like the cages, this responded to a focus on security. But the possibilities of new social patterns offered by this kind of corridor media space moved beyond a neighbourhood watch scheme to one amplifying the area's real community.

The idea of linking security cameras also responded to people's alienation from the physical fabric of the buildings themselves. Several of our proposals suggested ways to colonise this infrastructure. Inspired by National Geographic articles about telematic devices used to explore volcanoes, reefs, and gopher burrows, we thought of robots that would travel the ventilation system, recording and broadcasting domestic sounds to allow glimpses of other lives. Ultimately, this led us to mains radio technology, which we thought might form the basis of internal intercoms or radio stations.

A final set of ideas updated the Situationists' psychogeographical maps, already reflected by the cultural probes. The elders could carry psychogeographic pagers, allowing them to signal where they felt afraid, safe, bored, or intrigued. The combined output might appear as maps or public displays, control public lighting, or be read by handheld meters. These ideas again respond to security worries in the Bijlmer, but also to its hidden attractions: markets, underground churches, solitary flower beds and ponds.

The group reacted positively to the ideas, apparently recognising themselves in our suggestions. Image boards were received enthusiastically as a way to counter the area's bad reputation. Linked security cameras intrigued them, as did the ventrovers, and they agreed with our impression that the friendly mingling of different cultures is a strength of the area. Finally, they clearly understood the idea that psychogeographical pagers could help capture everyday knowledge about good and bad areas within the Bijlmer.

As we discussed living with the systems, however, they raised many issues we hadn't imagined. For instance, they were afraid that the ventrovers would let thieves know when they weren't home, and thought linked security cameras might compromise privacy. More fundamentally, they weren't sure the psychogeographical pagers would be useful because the emotional topology of the area is already a familiar background to their everyday activities. Instead, they suggested the idea was more useful to reassure their friends about visiting them in the Bijlmer and to guide them once they arrived.

Focusing and Integrating

Informed by the reactions of the elder group in the Bijlmer, we refined and focused our ideas into the more definite proposal for the area outlined at the beginning of this paper. Many of the placeholders were discarded, as some ideas no

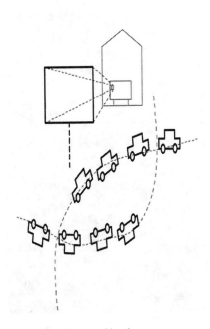

Images from the workbook

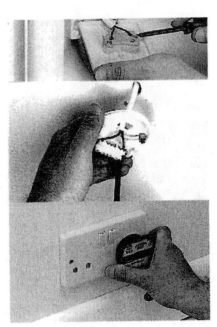

Mains radio study

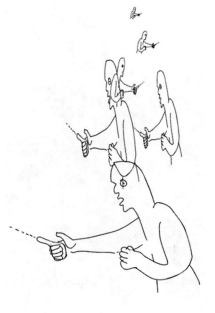

"muggers creating zones of fear..."

longer seemed meaningful or practical given the reactions of the group. We didn't abandon the concepts behind the proposals, however, but instead found new ways to express them within an overall system.

In this process, for instance, the psychogeographical pagers were transformed into the current slogan furniture concept. Rather than try to reveal the good and bad areas of the Bijlmer, it became possible to make explicit people's existing understandings as a vehicle to promote greater cultural understanding. Slogan furniture became interesting as a way of expressing attitudes about the local environment, and encouraging reflection and communication about different perceptions of the Bijlmer.

Similarly, though literally inhabiting the infrastructure using robots proved undesirable, the idea of using the infrastructure as a link between individual inhabitants and the surrounding community seemed strong. Realising that both the image boards and slogan furniture were allowing expression in public areas, we changed the direction of the mains radio devices to allow individual inhabitants to have access to the community's culture within their own homes.

An important innovation of the current proposal was in combining the elements into an integrated system. If each were separate, their display would reflect only the individuals or groups who last controlled them. Linked together, however, and their display allows a more organic expression of the culture to emerge. People might display an image at home, and then see local slogan furniture indicating that their neighbours feel the same way. They might see a particular slogan reflecting local attitudes, and change it to send the neighbourhood a different message. Or they might dislike what the local imageboard is showing, and scan new images that better reflect their perceptions. Taken separately, the devices act as means for expression—at

home, in the neighbourhood, or to the outside. Together, they take on aspects of a communications medium as well.

APPLYING CONTEMPORARY ART

In this paper, we have tried to illustrate our approach to working as artist-designers doing research. The effects of working within this conceptual and cultural context can be seen throughout the project, from our strategy for getting to know the users, to our methods of developing and communicating ideas, to the aims and techniques of the proposed system itself.

The Projected Realities proposal needs to be developed further before elements of the system can be put in place in the Bijlmer. We believe the role of design research at this stage is to suggest technologies that are plausible, concentrating on the effects they should achieve rather than details of their implementation. From this point of view, the proposal itself is a finished piece of work, opening new perspectives on the design of technologies for elders in urban communities. It may function like architectural proposals which, even if never built, are influential in the field [e.g., 9].

The Projected Realities system responds to the theme of presence in complex ways. In the home, mains radio devices might allow elders to become more aware of their neighbours, their lives and values. The slogan furniture allow attitudes and values to be more publicly shared or even confronted within the community, while imageboards expand this to the surrounding society. These devices give new ways for the elders to make their presence felt, and to feel the presence of others—but in fact, they amplify, and thus draw attention to, ways that are already present.

Our proposals involve issues familiar to HCI, particularly from work on media spaces [4] demonstrating how technologies used on the periphery of attention can allow new

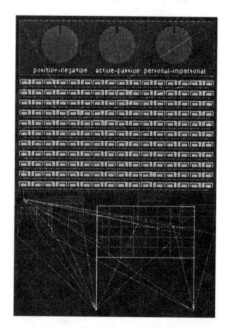

forms of sociality to emerge [6, 8].

The approach we took to these technologies, however, were more directly influenced by the work of a number of contemporary artists [see 9]. For instance, Jenny Holtzer has displayed "truisms" in public spaces (e.g.: "children are the hope of the future," "children are the most cruel of all"). In provoking people to agree or disagree, these works—clearly referred to by the slogan furniture—ultimately raise questions about the status of such statements. Gillian Wearing photographed people holding signs on which they had written down what they were thinking; we hope the image boards and slogan furniture might elicit insights into people's attitudes as striking as those she attained. Krzysztof Wodiczko [5] has projected images onto buildings and designed portable shelters for the homeless; our designs are similarly aimed at making local issues apparent. Finally, Atelier Van Lieshout [3] design urban shelters which take a poetic approach to issues of urban survivalism; we are also interested in public furniture hinting at new forms of social inhabitation.

In applying to design the tactics of artists such as these, we are extending the notion of awareness [see 4] from a concern with peoples' presence and activities to one including the attitudes and emotions of diverse cultural groups. This kind of *provocative awareness* relies on strangeness and amplification to draw attention to issues of concern in the community. In this way, the Projected Realities system is intended not only to support ongoing relationships, but to act as a sociocultural intervention at personal, community, or political levels.

The Projected Reality proposal is for a system intended to exist over time in the Bijlmer, growing in value and meaning with use. While drawing on the arts, it is neither intended to be judged in a gallery context, nor as a personal statement about our perceptions of the Bijlmer. Instead, like any good collaborative technology, it is intended to form a new channel of expression and communication that people in the Bijlmer can appropriate for themselves. In suggesting that the Projected Reality system might raise awareness, communication and presence, we are also hopeful that it might be used for subversion, local obsessions, or play.

ACKNOWLEDGMENTS

The Presence project is supported by a European Union grant under the I3 initiative. Elena Pacenti of the Domus Academy collaborated closely on the Cultural Probes, and Ben Hooker, Shona Kitchen, and Brendon Walker made innumerable contributions as design assistants. We thank the members of the Bijlmer user group, and particularly Danielle van Diemen, the local coordinator, for their enthusiastic participation in the project. We are also grateful to our partners from the Domus Academy, Netherlands Design Institute, Telenor, Human Factors Solutions, Scuola Superiore de Santa Ana, and IDEA. Finally, we thank Anne Schlottmann, Fiona Raby, and Colin Burns for useful comments.

REFERENCES

1. Andreotti, L. and Costa, X. (eds.) *Theory of the dérive and other Situationist writings on the city.* Museo d'Art Contemporani de Barcelona, 1996.

2. Special issue on the Bijlmer, *Archis.* Rotterdam, 1997(3).

3. Atelier van Lieshout, *A manual.* Cologne, Kölnischer Kunstverein and Museum Boijmans van Beuningen, 1997.

4. Bly, S., Harrison, S., and Irwin, S. Media spaces: Bringing people together in a video, audio, and computing environment. *Communications of the ACM 36*, 1 (1993), 28 - 47.

5. Borja-Villel, M. (ed.) *Krzysztof Wodiczko: Instruments, projeccions, vehicles.* Fundació Antoni Tàpies, Barcelona, 1992.

6. Dourish, P., Adler, A., Bellotti, V., and Henderson, A. Your place or mine? Learning from long-term use of audio-video communication. *Computer-Supported Cooperative Work, 5*, 1 (1996), 33-62.

7. Dunne, A., and Gaver, W. The Pillow: Artist-Designers in the digital age, in the *CHI'97 Conference Companion.* (1997) ACM Press.

8. Gaver, W. Affordances for interaction: The social is material for design. Ecological Psychology 8, 2 (1996), 111-130.

9. Godfrey, T. *Conceptual art.* Phaidon Press, London, 1998.

10. Levy, J. *Surrealism.* First printed by Black Sun Press in 1936; reprinted by Da Capo Press, 1995.

11. Plant, S. *The most radical gesture: The Situationist International in a postmodern age*, London, Routledge, 1992.

12. Winograd, T. (ed.) *Bringing design to software.* New York, ACM Press, 1996.

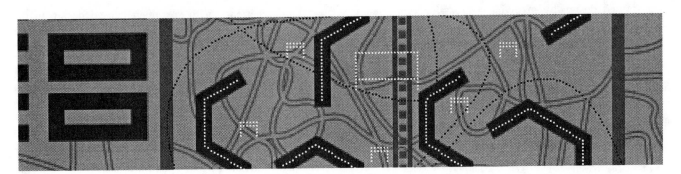

Customer-Focused Design Data in a Large, Multi-Site Organization

Paula Curtis
Tammy Heiserman
David Jobusch
Mark Notess
Hewlett-Packard Company
3404 E. Harmony Road
Fort Collins, CO 80528 USA
+1 970 898 4331
{ paula | tammy | djob | mhn }@fc.hp.com

Jayson Webb
R&R Research, Inc.
1373 Grandview Ave, Suite 210
Columbus, OH 43212 USA
+1 614 486 7517
jaysonw@r-r-research.com

ABSTRACT

Qualitative user-centered design processes such as contextual inquiry can generate huge amounts of data to be organized, analyzed, and represented. When you add the goal of spreading the resultant understanding to the far reaches of a large, multi-site organization, many practical barriers emerge.

In this paper we describe experience creating and communicating representations of contextually derived user data in a large, multi-site product development organization. We describe how we involved a distributed team in data collection and analysis and how we made the data representations portable. We then describe how we have engaged over 200 people from five sites in thinking through the user data and its implications on product design.

Keywords

contextual design, contextual inquiry, affinity, user data, customer-focused design, organizational change, distributed teams

INTRODUCTION

Over the past decade, many product development organizations have gained experience doing requirements analysis and design by involving a cross-functional team with end-user work contexts [14]. The value of first-hand observation in real use contexts has been well established; processes for gathering and analyzing data have been developed and communicated throughout the SIGCHI community through conference tutorials, workshops [11], a special interest group devoted to contextual design, as well as through books and articles [1,2,4,10]. Consultants

specializing in contextual processes have emerged [5,8]. Independent of the CHI community, contextual data is receiving increased attention. [7, p.200ff; 3, p. 188].

In our own organization—the Hewlett-Packard Enterprise Systems Group—we have been investigating and applying contextual methods for nearly five years. Our initial efforts focused on product strategy within the single development lab we have all been associated with, at one site. Out of these efforts, our lab eventually shipped a very successful product, Ignite-UX, a tool for rapidly deploying multiple systems with pre-defined configurations [9]. The enthusiasm for Ignite-UX gave us the credibility within our larger organization to propose use of customer-focused design teams on a broader scale.

In August 1997 we took a proposal to division management to sponsor a project cutting across multiple development labs and sites. In making this proposal, we considered whether we should propose a pilot project in order to gain experience doing customer-focused design across sites. We rejected this idea for several reasons:

- Pilot projects are often targeted at work that is peripheral to the business—to minimize the cost of failure. But this also minimizes the benefit of success.

- Our experience with customer-focused design in one lab had been compelling—we were eager to apply it to something much bigger.

- Our management had been talking about making our development process more customer-focused. We claimed that to achieve this across a large organization, we needed a success that everyone would value—we needed to aim at a project whose success our future depended upon.

We went to division management proposing that we form a customer-focused design team to target the operating system design of our next major server product. (Since this product has not been announced yet, we refer to it in this paper as NBB—"next big box.") Our proposal was accepted, so we began the formation of the NCFT (the NBB Customer Focus Team). This paper describes the project as well as the process we used for collecting, analyzing, and sharing the data.

PROJECT DESCRIPTION

The NCFT was staffed with software developers and project managers. A senior human factors engineer (Paula) joined the team as the process consultant. In preparation for leading this team, Paula took a two-week Contextual Design Leadership class from InContext.

Forming the NCFT took about four months. During this time there was a large reorganization and delivery of a major software release. Once the leaders were identified, we were able to recruit team members from four of the five sites, representing five different software labs, covering the different levels in the software stack. We stipulated that team members would have to devote at least 50% of their time to this effort. We also looked for influential designers who would ultimately be responsible for the development of this product.

We initiated the team with a three-day workshop. The first two days were spent in a contextual inquiry training class. The third day was a planning day to roll out responsibilities, schedule, and next steps. Regular communication was important for this geographically dispersed team so we held weekly phone conferences, and initially met face-to-face on a monthly basis. We also set up a web site containing process information and tracking our customer contacts.

Product marketing gave us an initial set of customer names. With their help, we developed a set of criteria for selecting customers to visit on our first round of data collection. We divided up the list of about 20 names among the team members and immediately set up phone conferences with the field contact for each customer account.

DATA COLLECTION AND ANALYSIS

Over 1500 individual notes about customer work were generated by 7 customer visits conducted in under 3 months. This section describes the process for collecting the work data and organizing the resulting large amount of qualitative data about customer work practices.

Collecting the Data

The structure of each customer visit varied depending on the wishes of the customer and the type of work done by the customer. This section describes a typical visit—how the data were gathered and recorded.

The visit teams varied in size from two to eight people. Typically we had four people, with a representative from each site. Initially, the visits were conducted by NCFT members, who had been trained in contextual inquiry (CI). Later on, we included one or two people with no CI training in order to give them firsthand experience with the customer.

The visit agenda varied, but had these common elements:

- Initial meeting with the HP account team. They briefed us on customer "hot buttons" and issues to watch out for during the visit. We also used this time to work out visit logistics.

- Presentation of NBB overview to customer interviewees and key decision makers. Both the field team and customer sponsors expected this type of presentation. It provided an opportunity for us to elicit high level issues and questions.

- Contextual Interviews. The heart of our visit, the interviews, lasted two hours and were conducted by pairs of interviewers. One person led the interview and the other person took notes. We learned early on that HP support engineers handled the majority of the hardware configuration, so we conducted CIs with them, in addition to the customer system administrators.

- Interpretation session. Because our visit team typically contained people from across the country, we debriefed the visit at the field office near the customer site. These were often late night sessions as we walked through the presentation meeting and each interview, collecting work notes and developing models. The notes were collected on a laptop computer, and displayed on a PC projector during the interpretation session. The physical, sequence, and flow models were hand drawn on poster paper. We skipped the context model because of time constraints. After debriefing each interview, we also brainstormed a list of key insights. These formed the basis of the executive summaries that we mailed out after each visit. Before dashing off to catch our planes, we also brainstormed "what went well" and "what could be improved" for the visit.

Once visit team members returned from the visit, they hosted sharing sessions at their site. The sharing sessions, which typically lasted two hours, covered work models, key insights, and customer stories. To facilitate these sessions, we mailed a copy of the models to each site. New insights, design ideas, and data holes that were identified during the sharing sessions were e-mailed to the entire NCFT, and added to our data.

Format of the Qualitative Data

In contextual inquiry interpretation sessions, much of the qualitative data is captured in work models [2]. Those work models are then consolidated across customers into a set of consolidated models. We created a consolidated flow model and put it on-line in Microsoft PowerPoint™, and we used a large-format copier to reproduce multiple physical models. We were short on sequence models and so did not consolidate them. The consolidated models are fairly straightforward to reproduce on paper or online. The less tractable problem was how to manage the 1500 work notes before and after affinitizing them.

Notes from the interpretation and sharing sessions were captured in a file that allowed three tab-delimited fields to be typed. An example note is shown below.

```
WN   U1     Note about the work.  This is
typically 1 to 3 sentences.
```

The first field is a note code. The note codes used were: WN=work note, BD=breakdown, H=data hole, I=insight, DI=design idea [2]. The second field is a user identifier (the code for the user who was observed in the contextual inquiry). The third field is the note itself.

Notes from all of the interpretation and sharing sessions were gathered into one large file so that they could be organized using an affinity diagram process [2]. The notes were then numbered to provide a unique identifier to be used by data manipulation programs (described later) to access individual notes. We randomized the notes so that during the affinity process, one person wouldn't be posting notes all from one interview. The numbered notes looked like:

```
WN32 U1    Note about the work.  This is
typically 1 to 3 sentences.
```

To prepare the notes for the affinity diagram process (described next), each note was printed on a 3M Post-it™ To do this, a mail merge was done in Microsoft Word™ using the file containing all of the tab-delimited notes. The resulting merge document was created as mailing labels such that each note would fit on one Post-it on an 8-1/2x11 inch page 3M makes containing six Post-its (2 across and 3 down).

Organizing the Qualitative Data – the Affinity Diagram

Eighteen people spent about a day and a half creating the affinity diagram. The affinity team consisted of NCFT technical and marketing team members, people from teams whose products needed to interact with NCFT, and process leaders for the NCFT project.

Participants pulled individual notes from the sheets of Post-its described in the previous section. Each of the individual notes was placed on "butcher paper" (a long sheet of paper, 3-4 feet wide) that was hung around the walls of a room. During the affinitization process, three levels of organizing headings were placed above groups of notes. The yellow work notes were organized in groups of 4-8 under blue notes. These blue headings were in turn organized beneath pink notes, which were organized under green notes at the highest level of the affinity. After creating the initial affinity grouping in this way, people later added more hand written notes (data holes and design ideas) to the affinity diagram.

In the end, about 1800 notes were stuck to about 25 yards of butcher paper. We called this collection of paper "the wall". Managing "the wall" was a daunting task.

MAKING THE DATA SHARABLE

Before building the affinity, we had committed to making it available on our internal web and to providing paper copies to each of the participating HP sites. It wasn't until the affinity had been created and we saw the volume of paper that had been generated that we fully realized the data management problem we had to address.

Given the time, effort, and expense that went into creating the initial affinity, and the pressure to get the results out quickly, our first step was to record the new data and affinity hierarchy online. We began by adding new notes created during the building of the affinity to the original file using the encoding described earlier.

To capture the affinity hierarchy, a second file was created that contained a numbered list of the hierarchy levels and the codes (just the work note codes, not the text) of the customer data associated with those levels. The codes could be used to index the first file to recreate the original affinity. A snippet of the second file is shown below.

```
1 Life of the Admin
1.1 Experience required to do the job
1.1.1 I rely on my experience to do
WN106
WN934
WN223
1.1.2 "Real Admins" use command line
interfaces
...
```

Once the new data and the affinity hierarchy had been recorded, we rolled up the paper version of the affinity and put it away, determined to find something less cumbersome.

Putting the Data Online

We wanted to provide an online version of the affinity that would permit viewers to access the entire affinity but not require them to wade through numerous web pages.

Through Perl script programming and cgi-bin setup on our web server, we created what we called our "affinity explorer." The program read the two files describing the affinity and produced a two-column table viewable through a web browser (Figure 1). The left column of the table shows the levels of the affinity as a hierarchical list, expanded to the currently selected level of the affinity. The right column shows the contents of the selected item. All entries in the table are hyperlinks that re-run the script with a new level to explore, letting the viewer easily move around the many levels of the affinity hierarchy.

As subsequent design ideas and other notes were captured, we recorded them in a third file along with the affinity level or code number of the customer data that inspired it. A simple modification to the script was made to use this file to lookup available design ideas for affinity items as they were viewed.

- 1 Life of the Admin
  - 1.1 I am not empowered to do the work
  - 1.2 I don't get what I need from the vendor so I do it myself
  - 1.3 Experience is required to do the job
    - *1.3.1 I rely on my experience to do the job*
    - 1.3.2 I can't avoid interaction with the OS because my tools fall short
    - 1.3.3 "Real admins" use command line interface
  - 1.4 Lack of experience is a problem
  - 1.5 How I manage systems
  - 1.6 How I handle hardware problems
  - 1.7 How I handle software problems
  - 1.8 My work environment
  - 1.9 Group Dynamics
- 2 Structuring the System the Way I Want

1 Life of the Admin 💡

1.3 Experience is required to do the job 💡

1.3.1 I rely on my experience to do the job 💡

System admin tasks are not very formalized: Stuff isn't written down; Rely on experience; People don't leave the company very often. (I140 U62)

They've lost some of their binders. (BD24 G51)

They have no rules to filter daily email reports or determine when email reports need attention. (BD52 U62)

They are unaware of the System Recovery facility in HP–UX. (BD71 U65)

The things they look for in ps, iostat, vmstat, sar, etc. are all rules of thumb based on instinct/experience. (I148 G63)

I use experience to validate end–user problems (WN583 G63)

Figure 1. The web-based affinity explorer is easily navigable by clicking on any of the numbered headings. The right-hand side is color-coded to match the original note colors (indicating hierarchy).

This approach let us quickly get the affinity on the web, publish design ideas as soon as they were submitted, and minimize maintenance—one Perl script and two data files rather than a potentially huge number of web pages.

Putting "the Wall" on Paper

Another goal was to create an electronic version of the affinity diagram that could be distributed to other sites, where it could be printed as needed. We expected to use PC presentation software to produce diagrams reflecting our original affinity.

Unfortunately, the presentation software with which we were familiar required manual drawing of the diagram boxes and/or reentering all of the text we already had online—something we hadn't anticipated and wanted to avoid.

We ended up using Inspiration Pro® [6], a PC-based diagramming package that could import the data we had already transcribed and automatically convert it into diagrams. With it we were able to reproduce our original affinity, right down to the green, blue, pink, and yellow colors of the original Post-its.

Printing Inspiration's diagram output on large format paper using an HP DesignJet plotter resulted in the paper version of the affinity we wanted. Figure 2 shows what a piece of the printed affinity looks like (but without color).

With the right software, we were able to generate both web and paper versions of our affinity from a single set of data. The original affinity diagram, with its many sheets of butcher paper and 1800 Post-its has been in storage ever since. Anyone who has spent much time taking down, rolling up, unrolling, and putting up dozens of large sheets of paper covered with hundreds of Post-its will appreciate how much quicker and simpler it is to deal with a printed diagram on just a few sheets of paper.

COMMUNICATING THE DATA

Once we had "the wall" complete, online, and printable, we

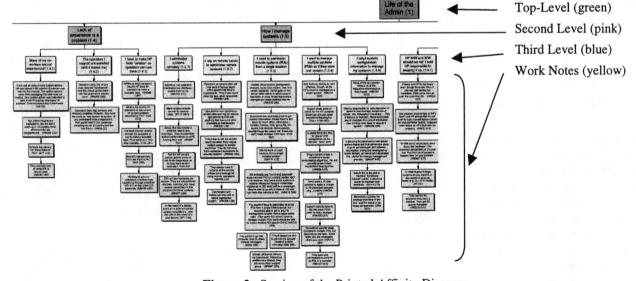

Top-Level (green)
Second Level (pink)
Third Level (blue)
Work Notes (yellow)

Figure 2. Section of the Printed Affinity Diagram

set out to share our customer understanding with the larger organization. In particular, we wanted to make sure key designers and decision-makers, including hardware and software R&D, marketing, manufacturing—and especially our sponsors—were able to grasp and apply what we'd learned.

Taking the Show on the Road

The road show team consisted of three people from three of the five sites we visited. This team created an e-mail invitation and an agenda. We discovered that setting up a road show works best when you have a local champion to clear the way. This person can find the right room (large!), identify the attendees, and handle other logistics. The local champion was also able to talk with invitees and encourage attendance. We always required an RSVP so we could get a headcount and attendance list. This helped us know a little bit about our audience ahead of time.

We ran a dozen sessions at five sites in four states across the country in five weeks. We arrived in town the night before a session so that we could prepare the room. To facilitate discussion, we arranged the chairs in a "U"-shape and removed the tables from the room. We then wallpapered the room with our printed affinity. We had to be creative to get the entire wall in the room, often covering up pictures, windows, and even the back of the door to the room. Sometimes we hung two rows worth of data on a wall. Once we wallpapered the hallway leading to the room. We also prepared our flip charts and tested the overhead projector.

A road show day had two components: getting people into the data, and getting them to synthesize with the data (visioning). The sections below describe the typical day.

1. Introduce participants (who you are, what you do, what you hope to get out of the day)

During the introduction, we listened for people's key issues. Often we could point out interesting data on the wall that addressed someone's area of interest. We also listened for questions about the process we used to collect the data so we could anticipate questions they might have about the validity of our data. We always pointed out people in the room or local to the site who helped us collect the data. This helped establish credibility with the participants.

2. Introduce the data and the procedure for "walking the wall"

This procedure is described elsewhere [2, pp. 201-202], but it includes "interacting" with the wall—adding design ideas or other notes to the affinity as they come to mind. Initially people were slow to put up their comments. We found if we walked the wall with them and put up our own notes, they would eventually follow suit. We usually allowed a little over an hour for walking the wall, and we kept the room quiet so folks could reflect on what they were reading. We found that people would think more about what they were reading if they were identifying ways to address the customer problem (design ideas) or more information that they needed (data holes). As they added their notes to the affinity, we asked them to code them with the affinity note or section they pertained to (so we could add their notes to our data files in the right places) and to put their name on the note (so we could get back to them with clarifications or questions).

3. Everyone walks the wall of customer data

People responded variously to the wall walk. Some breezed through it in 30-40 minutes. Others lingered over portions of it and had to be pried away at the end. Some followed our advice and walked the entire wall once, looking at the hierarchy, before going deep into a particular area. Others searched for the portion that dealt with their favorite topic. Others pointed out to us where our notes were misplaced in the hierarchy. Overall, everyone seemed engaged during the wall walk.

4. Share other work models

After the wall walk we shared our physical and task flow diagrams with the group. We told numerous stories of the customer visits, often selecting the stories based on participants' responsibilities and interests. This portion of the agenda was quite lively, with lots of clarifying questions being asked. Participants were surprised at the issues raised by the customer environment.

5. Group discussion of key learnings from the customer data

After lunch, we brainstormed key learnings from the customer data. Rarely did we have to seed this discussion! Usually we filled several flip chart pages with people's insights. Once we had a good list, we introduced the visioning portion of our agenda.

6. Brainstorm visioning topics

We then brainstormed visioning topics, broke the group into three teams, assigning one of the road show leaders to each team to be the scribe.

7. Visioning

The visioning exercise is described elsewhere [2, pp. 277-282]. The exercise ended with each team sharing their vision with the larger group.

Steps 6 and 7 were crucial to firmly engaging the participants in the data. The visioning exercise required them to take a customer point-of-view: they had to internalize the data, and synthesize new solutions based on that understanding. This is very different from traditional technology-centric design. Even though we did not use all of the visioning results, each participant had a chance to experience customer-focused design and feel the power of contextual data.

8. NCFT next steps

At the end of the day, we told the participants what the NCFT would be doing next. People were eager to hear what would happen to their ideas. We told them we would affinitize their wall annotations and put them online so the larger organization could access their ideas. We also said we would use the gaps they identified in our data to help us ask the right questions on future customer visits.

9. Retrospective of the day

The last agenda topic encouraged participants to tell us what they thought of the day. We wanted to know how we could improve our presentation of customer data. We heard several similar questions repeatedly, so we added the answers to our introduction:

- *How do I get quantitative data from the wall? For example, I want to know what percentage of customers wants feature XYZ?* Our response: The contextual design process obtains qualitative data, not quantitative. Use surveys and other techniques to obtain quantitative data.

- *Can't you give me the top five customer requirements we should address?* Our response: We don't know your products as well as you do. We believe it's better to give you all of the customer data and let you decide what is the most important feature to work on. Also, feature lists tend to lose the work practice or the intention behind the request. We often design the wrong product if we don't understand why the customer wants the feature.

- *How is our organization going to use this data to prioritize the work we do?* Our response: That's why we are here! We want you aware of the customer requirements as you plan your work for the next year

- *Will this wall of customer data live on? Who's going to preserve it?* Our response: We need to know how useful this was to you. Let us know how you use it and how it changes your products. If we determine this was of great value to the organization, we will keep our wall alive as we do more customer visits.

- *Can you organize the wall based on different criteria? I'm only interested in customers in the XYZ industry.* Our response: All of the data is online. If you are interested in doing that work, let us know and we'll help you gather what you need to do it yourself. We believe work practice doesn't change much across this customer base. There just weren't fundamental differences in how our diverse customers did their work to keep their computer systems up and running.

RESULTS AND DISCUSSION

The manager responsible for bringing NBB to market has already said he considers the NCFT an "unqualified success." Doing anything with a large, multi-site organization is a significant challenge. When we began the NCFT effort, no participants beyond the ones from our own lab in Colorado had any experience with contextual methods. In 2.5 months, we visited seven customers,

conducted 40 contextual interviews, collected and affinitized over 1800 notes. In the several months that followed, while continuing to design, we shared the data with over 200 people in five locations, spanning seven levels of organizational hierarchy. As a result of the road show, nearly 1000 ideas were added to the data.

One road show participant commented some months later that the NCFT work "was and continues to be some of the most valuable work I've seen within HP."

The customer data gave us a good understanding of how NBB would be deployed in customer environments. This enabled us to develop a prioritized set of usage models (ways NBB would be used based upon the needs of the applications customers deploy in their environments). We were then able to determine the operating system features and tools needed to support the top usage models. The customer understanding helped us protect key features and decide which features weren't essential. Prior to this activity, many labs involved in NBB development were operating with differing or only vague assumptions on how customers would use the machine. The NCFT work provided the impetus to select just a few uses and then focus development on supporting those well.

The NCFT is not without its costs—or critics. From January to June, 1998, 50 engineer months were spent gathering and analyzing data. The cost of the program so far (in addition to people's time) has been $65,000, chiefly for travel and consultants. However, it is important to note that much of this money would have been spent by individual organizations doing similar (but disjoint) activities even if the NCFT had never been formed. Although it is too early to draw firm conclusions, we (and our sponsors) believe the money was well spent.

The most common criticism of the process is that it doesn't produce a prioritized list of customer issues. People get overwhelmed in their initial encounter with the data and wonder, "What do I do as a result?" The contextual design process requires deeper engagement with customer data than many developers (and managers) are familiar with, or, sometimes, interested in. Despite this criticism, we have resisted the urge to provide a quick list of official design implications—we're holding out for the bigger payoff we expect from requiring a thorough understanding of our customers' work.

Lessons Learned in Data Management

At the outset, we had not thought through our data management needs in detail, so we invented much of our process as needs arose. Our key learnings from this experience were:

- Thus far, the online affinity web page has been visited over 400 times. While it is difficult to assess how the online data has been used throughout the organization, people have told us it is a useful reference once they have been exposed to the data more proactively (through the road show).

- Being able to have more than one paper copy of the affinity was very valuable because it allowed us to leave the affinity on display at each site.

- With better planning we wouldn't have had to change data formats so many times (MS Word→HTML→MS Word→ASCII→Inspiration Pro→HTML). Next time, we would probably use Inspiration Pro as our primary storage format and generate the other formats as needed for mail merge or online display.

- The Inspiration Pro software allowed us to scale the affinity diagram to the optimal size (large enough to read from a few feet away but otherwise as compact as possible).

- Printing the notes on the 3M Post-it note sheets provided a big usability and productivity benefit over either handwritten notes or notes printed on paper that had to be cut into strips and taped up. However, the Post-it note sheets are expensive.

- Even more expensive was printing multiple copies of the affinity on a color large-format plotter—several thousand dollars at the local copy center! Smaller projects will find it hard to justify the expense.

Lessons Learned on the Road

The work we put into the road show was well-spent. Without the broad sharing of data at an early stage, most of the organization would either be unaware of our efforts or unimpressed with our accomplishments. Simply putting the data online and sending out an announcement would not have been sufficient. Without the shared experience provided by the road shows, most people wouldn't have invested the time required to understand and use the wealth of data that was available.

Key to the success of the road show were

- creating portable, printable data representations

- spending half the time on visioning

- targeting key designers and decision-makers from multiple functions

Getting the right people invited became easier over time as higher-level managers, after experiencing the data themselves, gave us lists of key people they wanted to be sure participated. Some of the key lessons we learned from doing the road show were:

- It worked! The presentation effectively introduced a broad audience to a large amount of customer data, as well as to a new design method, in a relatively short period of time.

- Data hunger. An unanticipated result was that all the sites wanted to keep "the wall" up. Sometimes they moved it to a major aisle way, and we heard reports of numerous people standing in those aisles, studying the data.

- Vision convergence. Our large, diverse organization came up with very similar visions across the dozen or so sessions we conducted. All had common elements, and toward the end of the road show, we could predict what the visions would look like. This result has been a major help with organizational alignment— something that's often a problem in large, distributed organizations.

- Individual differences. There were multiple reactions to our wall of customer data. Some people felt overwhelmed and wanted us to just give them the highlights. Engineers were thrilled to get access to so much data. Still others were only interested in the data pertaining to their own area.

- Getting to know ourselves better. We often acted as a liaison between groups that needed to talk to each other. We learned a lot about what various teams do, and we found many overlapping efforts going on. We were able to put these teams in touch with each other.

We did not execute the contextual design process completely or perfectly—we cut some corners to speed ourselves along. In particular, we lacked a strong set of sequence models. Nevertheless, the data and models we presented were more than enough to significantly impact product direction, provide a strong taste of the value of contextual data.

Future Directions

Other projects within the Enterprise Systems Group using contextual design methods have already been able to directly leverage data collected by the NCFT. A team working on developing new solutions around software patching was able to take notes from the affinity diagram related to software patches and incorporate those into a patching-focused affinity process. Also, the patching team is currently sharing its data and early design concepts with part of the NCFT working on system management to help understand how new patching solutions might fit in the NCFT framework. We will watch these cross-project interactions with interest to see what we can learn about making qualitative design data more easily leverageable.

The visibility of the NCFT data has affected organizations outside of the Enterprise Systems Group also. Other divisions have begun their own contextual design efforts after seeing the NCFT data.

One challenge we faced with NCFT is that the NBB hardware design was nearly complete when the team formed. Despite our being directed to focus on software issues, the contextual design process makes it difficult to ignore issues that keep showing up even if those issues are outside the focus area. The NCFT was able to have some late impact on the hardware design, but we would like to explore extending our process to include hardware design at the appropriate point in their design life cycle.

The process we followed with the NCFT left us with a couple of challenges we have not yet figured out how to address:

- *How do we deal with the many good design ideas the affinity provokes?* Many of these ideas fall outside the scope of the immediate project. Currently, we have no process in place to ensure such ideas find appropriate homes elsewhere in our organization. We log all the design ideas and make them available online, but as yet we have no process for ensuring these ideas are given appropriate consideration.

- *How do we document the impact the data has had on products?* Because we shared our data so broadly, we haven't be able to track all the impacts it has had on different products. Yet these impacts are key to justifying the cost of our project and promoting future projects.

CONCLUSIONS

The NCFT has been able to make a significant contribution to a large organization's customer understanding. We are currently getting requests for "round two" of the road show—people want to see what we've done as a result of gathering the data. As we write, we are busy iterating designs with customers, and we will share these more broadly in the months ahead. The customer impacts will not be felt until after this is published. But the enthusiasm and engagement we've seen from our large, multi-site organization justify the sharing of these intermediate results.

ACKNOWLEDGMENTS

We thank the entire "NCFT" for their hard work and enthusiasm, especially Matthew Diaz and Patrick MacRoberts, who helped with the road show. Karen Holtzblatt and Hugh Beyer, as well as Chris Rockwell, have been our long-time expert consultants and encouragers. In carrying this work forward, we honor the memory of Marcel Meier, who sponsored our foray into contextual design five years ago.

REFERENCES

1. Beyer, H., and Holtzblatt, K. Apprenticing with the Customer. *Commun. ACM* 38, 5 (May 1995), 45-52.

2. Beyer, H., and Holtzblatt, K. *Contextual Design: Defining Customer-Centered Systems.* Morgan Kaufmann Publishers, Inc., San Francisco, CA, 1998.

3. Christensen, C. *The Innovator's Dilemma: When New Technologies Cause Great Firms to Fail.* Harvard Business School Press, Boston, 1997.

4. Holtzblatt, K. If We're a Team Why Don't We Act Like One? *interactions 1*,3 (July 1994), 17-20.

5. InContext Enterprises URL: http://www.incent.com.

6. Inspiration Software, Inc. URL: http://www.inspiration.com

7. Leonard-Barton, D. *Wellsprings of Knowledge: Building and Sustaining the Sources of Innovation.* Harvard Business School Press, Boston, 1995.

8. R&R Research URL: http://www.r-r-research.com.

9. Rockwell, C. Customer Connection Creates a Winning Product: Building Success with Contextual Techniques. In press in *interactions*.

10. Wixon, D., and Ramey, J. *Field Methods Casebook for Software Design.* John Wiley and Sons, Inc. New York, 1996.

11. Wixon, D., and Ramey, J. Field Oriented Design Techniques: Case Studies and Organizing Dimensions. *SIGCHI Bulletin 28*,3 (July 1996), 21-26.

Video Figures

The following papers of the CHI 99 Conference Proceedings have video figures which can be found at the end of the CHI 99 Video Program:

Towards Usable VR: An Empirical Study of User Interfaces for Immersive Virtual Environments
　　Robert W. Lindeman, *George Washington University*
　　John L. Sibert, *George Washington University*
　　James K. Hahn, *George Washington University*

Hyper Mochi Sheet: A Predictive Focusing Interface for Navigating and Editing Nested Networks through a Multifocus Distortion-Oriented View
　　Masashi Toyoda, *Tokyo Institute of Technology*
　　Etsuya Shibayama, *Tokyo Institute of Technology*

Touch-Sensing Input Devices
　　Ken Hinckley, *Microsoft Research*
　　Mike Sinclair, *Microsoft Research*

Bridging Physical and Virtual Worlds with Electronic Tags
　　Roy Want, *Xerox PARC*
　　Kenneth P. Fishkin, *Xerox PARC*
　　Anuj Gujar, *Xerox PARC*
　　Beverly L. Harrison, *Xerox PARC*

Flatland: New Dimensions in Office Whiteboards
　　Elizabeth D. Mynatt, *Georgia Institute of Technology*
　　Takeo Igarashi, *University of Tokyo*
　　W. Keith Edwards, *Xerox Palo Alto Research Center*
　　Anthony LaMarca, *Xerox Palo Alto Research Center*

Urp: A Luminous-Tangible Workbench for Urban Planning and Design
　　John Underkoffler, *MIT Media Laboratory, Tangible Media Group*
　　Hiroshi Ishii, *MIT Media Laboratory, Tangible Media Group*

PingPongPlus: Design of Athletic-Tangible Interface for Computer-Supported Cooperative Play
　　Hiroshi Ishii, *MIT Media Laboratory*
　　Craig Wisneski, *MIT Media Laboratory*
　　Julian Orbanes, *MIT Media Laboratory*
　　Ben Chun, *MIT Media Laboratory*
　　Joe Paradiso, *MIT Media Laboratory*

Sympathetic Interfaces: Using a Plush Toy to Direct Synthetic Characters
　　Michael Patrick Johnson, *MIT Media Laboratory*
　　Andrew Wilson, *MIT Media Laboratory*
　　Christopher Kline, *MIT Media Laboratory*
　　Bruce Blumberg, *MIT Media Laboratory*
　　Aaron Bobick, *MIT Media Laboratory*

Embodiment in Conversational Interfaces: Rea
　　J. Cassell, *MIT Media Laboratory*
　　T. Bickmore, *MIT Media Laboratory*
　　M. Billinghurst, *MIT Media Laboratory*
　　L. Campbell, *MIT Media Laboratory*
　　K. Chang, *MIT Media Laboratory*
　　H. Vilhjalmsson, *MIT Media Laboratory*
　　H. Yan, *MIT Media Laboratory*

i-Land: An Interactive Landscape for Creativity and Innovation
　　Norbert A. Streitz, *German National Research Center for Information Technology*
　　JF6rg GeiDFler, *German National Research Center for Information Technology*
　　Torsten Holmer, *German National Research Center for Information Technology*
　　Shin'ichi Konomi, *German National Research Center for Information Technology*
　　Christian MFCller-Tomfelde, *German National Research Center for Information Technology*
　　Wolfgang Reischl, *German National Research Center for Information Technology and Darmstadt School of Design*
　　Petra Rexroth, *German National Research Center for Information Technology*
　　Peter Seitz, *German National Research Center for Information Technology*
　　Ralf Steinmetz, *German National Research Center for Information Technology and Darmstadt School of Design*

Copies of the *CHI 99 Video Proceedings* are available in VHS (PAL or NTSC) and may be ordered prepaid from:

ACM Member Services
1515 Broadway
New York, NY 10036, USA
Telephone: +1 212 626 0500
Fax: +1 212 944 1318
Email: acmorder@acm.org

NTSC Video
ACM Order Number: 608994
ISBN Number: 1-58113-160-7

Pal Video
ACM Order Number: 608993
ISBN Number: 1-58113-159-3

Tangible Progress: Less is More in Somewire Audio Spaces (Page 104)
Andrew Singer, Debby Hindus, Lisa Stifelman, and Sean White

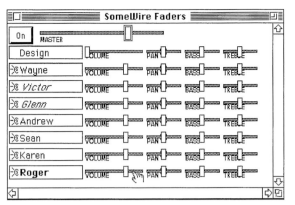

Figure 2. A Faders display. The local user, Roger, is listening to all users except 'Design', the name denoting a group meeting room

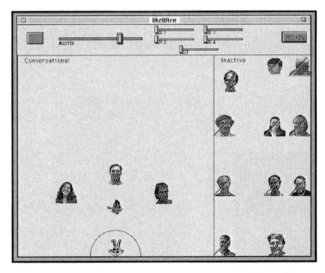

. Figure 3. A Vizwire display. The local user, the Rabbit, is talking to four remote users

Left pan		S	O	F	T	E	S	T		Right pan	
Left pan					Center Pan					Right pan	
Left pan					Center Pan					Right pan	Info Zone
Left pan		L	O	U	D	E	S	T		Right pan	Assign Zone

Figure 4. ToonTown prototype (top) and the meaning of each position on the board (bottom)

Sympathetic Interfaces: Using a Plush Toy to Direct Synthetic Characters (Page 152)

Michael Patrick Johnson, Andew Wilson, Bruce Blumberg, Christopher Kline, and
Aaron Bobick

Color Plate 1: The user's view of the scene. The chicken, raccoon and henhouse with eggs is visible.

Color Plate 2: The installation setup. Here, one of the project members controls the chicken as the raccoon makes a diving leap for him. Photo: ©Webb Chappell

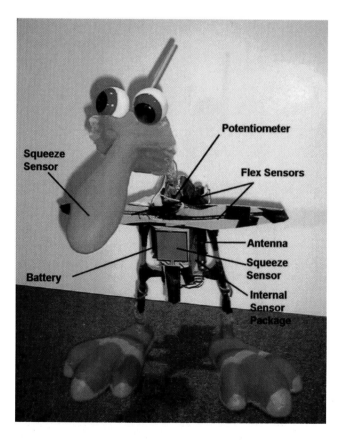

Color Plate 3: The external view of the doll.

Color Plate 4: The chicken armature with attached sensors.

Implementing Interface Attachments Based on Surface Representations (Page 191)

Dan R. Olsen, Jr., Scott E. Hudson, Thom Verratti, Jeremy M. Heiner, and Matt Phelps

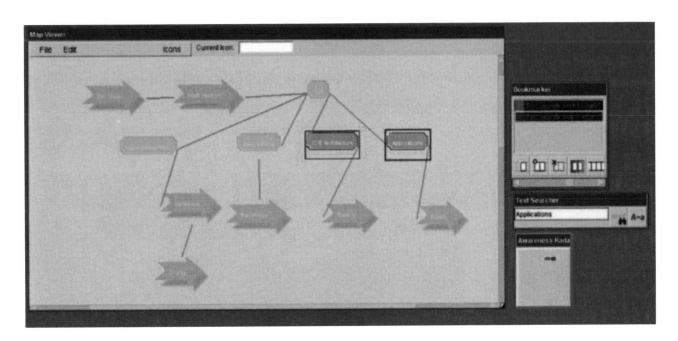

Figure 1 – Application with Attachments

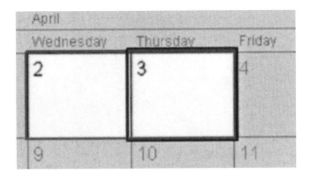

Figure 4 – Bookmark Highlighting

The Reader's Helper: A Personalized Document Reading Environment (Page 481)

Jamey Graham

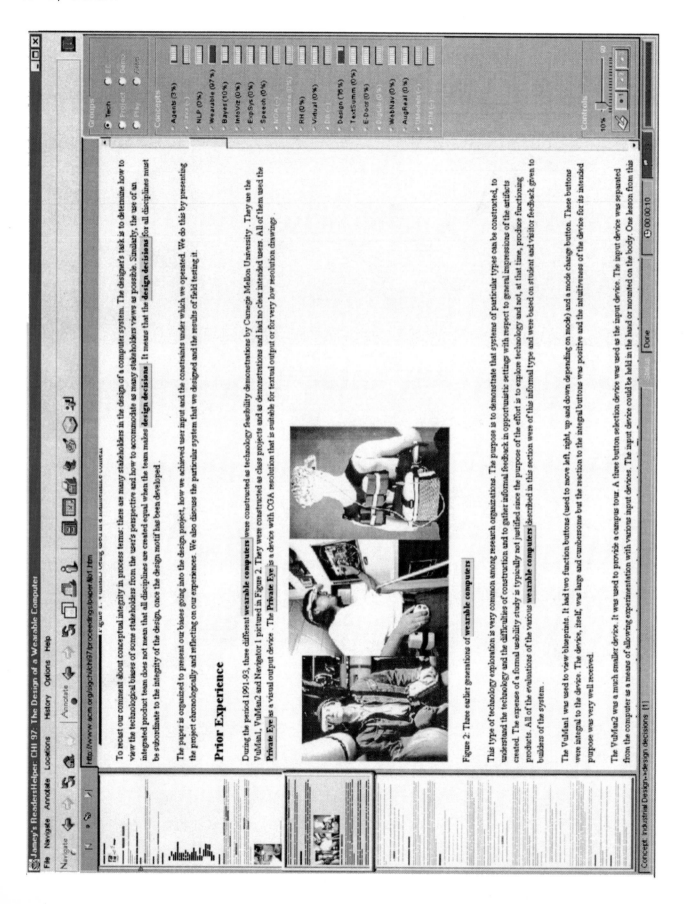

Figure 2 - An Annotated HTML Document

An Empirical Evaluation of User Interfaces for Topic Management of Web Sites (Page 552)

Brian Amento, Will Hill, Loren Terveen, Deborah Hix, and Peter Ju

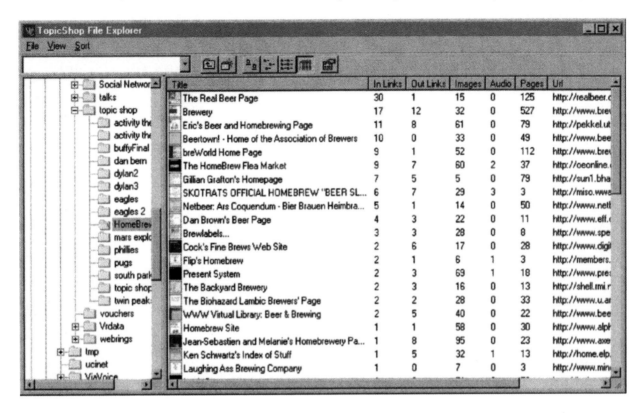

Figure 1: TopicShop Explorer, details view. Each web resource (site) is represented by a small thumbnail image, the site title, properties of the site itself – number of internal pages, images, and audio files – and the site's relations to other sites – number of in links and out links. By clicking on a column, users can sort by the appropriate property.

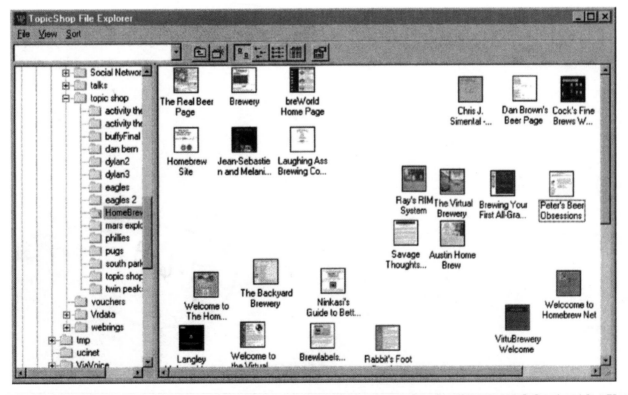

Figure 2: TopicShop Explorer, icons view. Each site is represented by a large thumbnail image and the site title. Users can organize sites by arranging them spatially, a technique especially useful in the early stages of exploration

Software for Use

A Practical Guide to the Models and Methods of Usage-Centered

Authored by
Larry L. Constantine, Constantine & Lockwood, Ltd
Lucy A. D. Lockwood, Constantine & Lockwood, Ltd

Order Number: 704971
ISBN: 0-201-92478-1
Binding: Paperback
Publication Year: 1998
Total Pages: 600
Nonmember: $32.95
Member: $29.65
Student Member: $29.65
SIG - only
Member: $32.95

"The clearest, most thorough, and most practical explanations I have seen of use cases, scenarios, and their use in analysis and design. I am already applying some of what I have learned, and I expect to use more soon."

In the quest for quality, software developers have long focused on improving the internal architecture of their products. Larry L. Constantine--who originally created structured design to effect such improvement--now joins with well-known consultant Lucy A. D. Lockwood to turn the focus of software development to the external architecture. In this book, they present the models and methods of a revolutionary approach to software that will help programmers deliver more usable software--software that will enable users to accomplish their tasks with greater ease and efficiency.

Recognizing usability as the key to successful software, Constantine and Lockwood provide concrete tools and techniques that programmers can employ to meet that end. Much more than just another set of rules for good user-interface design, this book guides readers through a systematic software-development process. This process, called usage-centered design, weaves together two major threads in software-development methods: use cases (also used with UML) and essential modeling. With numerous examples and case studies of both conventional and specialized software applications, the authors illustrate what has been shown in practice to work and what has proved to be of greatest practical value.

AD99